# VICTORIAN PROSE AND POETRY

# THE OXFORD ANTHOLOGY OF ENGLISH LITERATURE

General Editors: Frank Kermode and John Hollander

## Medieval English Literature
J. B. TRAPP, Librarian, Warburg Institute, London

## The Literature of Renaissance England
JOHN HOLLANDER, Hunter College;
and FRANK KERMODE, University College London

## The Restoration and the Eighteenth Century
MARTIN PRICE, Yale University

## Romantic Poetry and Prose
HAROLD BLOOM, Yale University;
and LIONEL TRILLING, Columbia University

## Victorian Prose and Poetry
LIONEL TRILLING and HAROLD BLOOM

## Modern British Literature
FRANK KERMODE and JOHN HOLLANDER

# Victorian Prose and Poetry

LIONEL TRILLING
Columbia University

HAROLD BLOOM
Yale University

New York  OXFORD UNIVERSITY PRESS
London  Toronto

Copyright © 1973 by Oxford University Press, Inc.
Library of Congress Catalogue Card Number: 72–92353
printing, last digit: 29 28 27 26 25 24 23

Selections from works by the following authors were made possible by the kind permission of their respective publishers and representatives:

Gerard Manley Hopkins: *The Poems of Gerard Manley Hopkins*, fourth edition, edited by W. H. Gardner and N. H. MacKenzie, reprinted by permission of Oxford University Press.
Edward Lear: *Teapots and Quails and Other New Nonsenses*, edited by Davison and Hofer, reprinted by permission of John Murray Ltd.

Printed in the United States of America

# General Editors' Preface

The purpose of the Oxford Anthology is to provide students with a selective canon of the entire range of English Literature from the beginnings to recent times, with introductory matter and authoritative annotation. Its method is historical, in the broadest sense, and its arrangement, commentary, and notes, both analytic and contextual, have benefited not only from the teaching experience of the several editors, but from a study of the virtues and shortcomings of comparable works. A primary aim has been to avoid the insulation of any one section from the influence of others, and more positively, to allow both student and instructor to come to terms with the manner in which English literature has generated its own history. This aim has been accomplished in several ways.

First, a reorganization of chronological phases has allowed the Tudor and Stuart periods to be unified under the broad heading of the English Renaissance, with two editors collaborating over the whole extended period. Similarly, the nineteenth century has two editors, one for the poetry of the whole period, and one for the prose. This arrangement seemed appropriate in every way, especially since neither of these scholars could be called a narrow specialist in "Romantic" or "Victorian," as these terms are used in semester- or course-labels.

Every contributing editor has worked and taught in at least one period or field outside the one for which he is, in this anthology, principally responsible, and none has ever allowed specialization to reduce his broader commitment to humane studies more largely considered. Thus we were able to plan a work which called for an unusual degree of cross reference and collaboration. During a crucial phase in the preparation of the text, the editors held daily discussions of their work for a period of months. By selection, allusion, comparison, by direction and indirection, we contrived to preserve continuity between epochs, and to illuminate its character. At the same time, the close co-operation of the various editors has precluded the possibility of common surrender to any single dominating literary theory; and the teacher need have no fear that he must prepare to do battle with some critical Hydra showing a head on every page.

The method of selecting text was consistent with these principles. In the eighteenth- and nineteenth-century sections it was our general policy to exclude the novel, for obvious reasons of length; but in the twentieth, where short fiction becomes more prominent and more central, we have included entire works of fiction, or clearly defined parts of them—for example, Heart of Darkness, "The Dead," the "Nausicaa" episode of Ulysses, and St. Mawr. On the other hand we were persuaded, after much reflection, that a different principle must apply in the cases of Spenser and Milton, where we waived the requirement of completeness. To have given the whole of one book—say, the First of The Faerie Queene—would have been a solution as easy as it is, no doubt, defensible; but it is asking a great deal of students to see that portion of the poem as an epitome of the rest, which is often so delightfully different; and we decided that we must provide selections from the whole poem, with linking commentary. We did the same for Paradise Lost though without abandoning the practice of providing complete texts when this was both possible and desirable; for example, Comus is reprinted entire, and so is a lesser-known but still very important masque, Jonson's Pleasure Reconciled to Virtue, which is interesting not only in relation to Comus but as an illustration of the part poetry can play in political spectacle and—more generally—in the focusing of the moral vision. Minor texts have been chosen for their exemplary force and their beauty, as well as to embody thematic concerns. If the teacher wishes, he or she may work, both within and across periods, with recurrent patterns as large as the conception of the Earthly Paradise, or with sub-genres as small but as fascinating as the Mad Song. It will also be evident from certain patterns of selection—The Tempest as the Shakesperean play, the very large amount of Blake, the emphasis given to D. H. Lawrence's poems as well as his fiction—that a genuinely modern taste, rather than an eager modishness, has helped to shape our presentation of the historical canon. It is also hoped that the unusually generous sampling of material in certain sections—notably the Renaissance, eighteenth century, and the Romantics—will allow the teacher to use secondary or minor works, if he so chooses, to highlight these newer concerns or to fill in contextual background.

As for the annotations, the editors have never been afraid to be lively or even speculative. They have consistently tried to avoid usurping the teacher's role, as providing standard or definitive readings might do. On the other hand, the commentary goes beyond merely providing a lowest common denominator of information by suggesting interpretive directions and levels along which the teacher is free to move or not; and of course he always has the freedom to disagree. The editors have been neither prudish nor portentous in their tone, nor have they sought—in the interests of some superficial consistency, but with leaden effect—to efface their personal styles.

Texts have all been based on the best modern editions, which happen quite often to be published by the Oxford University Press. Spelling and punctuation have been modernized throughout, save in three instances: portions of the medieval period, and the texts of Spenser and Blake, two poets whose spelling and punctuation are so far from idiosyncrasies to be silently normalized that they constitute attempts to refashion poetic language. In the medieval section, modern verse translations of Beowulf (by C. W. Kennedy) and of Gawain (by Brian Stone) have been adopted. Glossaries of literary and historical terms in all periods have been provided, sometimes keyed to the annotations, sometimes supplementing the larger headnotes. These, it will be noticed, seek to illuminate the immediate contexts of the literature of a period rather than to provide a dense précis of its social, political, and economic history. Similarly, the reading lists at the end of each volume are not exhaustive bibliographies; in the happy instance where a teacher finds an extensive bibliography advisable, he or she will want to supply one.

A word about the pictures. They are not to be thought of simply as illustrations, and certainly not as mere decorations, but rather as part of the anthologized material, like the musical examples and the special sections (such as the one on Ovidian mythology in the Renaissance and on the Urban Scene in the eighteenth century). Throughout, the reader is introduced to the relations between poem as speaking picture, and picture as mute poem. Aside from contextual and anecdotal illustration, of which there is indeed a good deal, the pictorial examples allow teachers, or students on their own, to explore some of the interrelations of texts and the visual arts in all periods, whether exemplified in Renaissance emblems or in contemporary illustrations of Victorian poems.

Finally, an inevitable inadequate word of acknowledgment. To the English Department of Dartmouth College the editors are deeply indebted for having so generously and hospitably provided a place in which to work together for a sustained period. The staff of the Dartmouth College Library was extraordinarily helpful and attentive.

All of the editors would like to extend a note of gratitude to the many academics throughout the United States who willingly made suggestions as to what should be included as well as excluded. A special note of thanks to Jim Cox of Dartmouth College and Paul Dolan of the State University of New York at Stony Brook for their challenging and always helpful comments.

And finally to the entire staff of the New York branch of the Oxford University Press who have done more than could be humanly expected in connection with the planning and execution of this book. We would especially like to thank our editor John Wright, as well as Leona Capeless and her staff, Mary Ellen Evans, Patricia Cristol, Joyce Berry, Deborah Zwecher, and Jean Shapiro. An unusual but very deserved note of thanks to the Production people, especially Gerard S. Case and Leslie Phillips and to the designer, Frederick Schneider, whose excellent work speaks for itself.

New York                                                              Frank Kermode
September 1972                                                        John Hollander

# Contents

* An asterisk is used to indicate that a work does not appear in its entirety.

# The Pre-Raphaelite Poets, 615

# VICTORIAN PROSE AND POETRY

# Victorian Prose

It has become common practice, almost the rule, to begin a summary account of the Victorian Age by noting the dramatic improvement in its reputation over relatively recent years. In the early decades of the twentieth century the word Victorian was not likely to be used except pejoratively, in condescension or contempt—perhaps never to such an extent had a new epoch defined itself by its explicit and passionate rejection of its predecessor. Victorianism was understood to be the sum of all that stood in the way of what the new age regarded as its own best characteristics, such freedom as is implied by mobility, such truth as follows from candor. No past age had ever been so precisely conceived as an entity with a personality and a conscious will which it sought to impose upon the human spirit and which had to be resisted. The essence of this gross historical monster was known to be an insensate devotion to respectability, with all that this suggests of compromise and conformity, of conceal-ment and dissembling. The classic statement of the view was Lytton Strachey's *Eminent Victorians*, published in 1918 to great acclaim, which undertook to "shoot a sudden revealing searchlight into obscure recesses, hitherto undivined," the implica-tion being that the Victorian Age was a vast hypocrisy, from whose face the mask was now at last to be torn.

Doubtless the change in this view was largely spontaneous, the result of the natural tendency of any cultural and historical animus to diminish in intensity and, in the process of time, to yield to curiosity about its object, then to a patronizing affection, and, at last, to serious interest and admiration. In the case of Victorian culture this development was reinforced by the uncertainties that began to overtake the spirit of the new age, leading it to perceive in the past age what it was beginning to confront in itself, the anomalies and contradictions which mark any cultural epoch and which, while they constitute its failure, are also the measure of its accomplishment. Viewed thus soberly and with the sympathy which arises from shared defeats, the Victorian Age came to seem very close to our own and to be, in some part of its achievement, exemplary and enviable.

But one element of the earlier conception of the Victorian Age which has remained unaltered is the impression it makes of being an entity. And, indeed, this is how the age thought of itself. As we make acquaintance with its literature, we cannot but feel that no national epoch was ever so aware of its existence as this one, so filled with the sense of having a particular destiny, even of being charged with a unique mission. This national and cultural self-consciousness, which presents itself as a principle of integration overriding all social and political differences, even those that were extreme, is in large part to be accounted for by the pre-eminent power of England through the latter two-thirds of the nineteenth century. The English navy dominated the seas, gave England a decisive role in world affairs, and made possible the rule of the farthest-flung empire known to history, a hegemony which was dramatized in 1897 when Victoria, the queen of this relatively small island nation, at the Jubilee which celebrated the sixtieth year of her reign and made the occasion for an outpouring of the loyalty and devotion of her subjects, took the title of Empress of India.

The power of British arms, made fully manifest earlier in the century at the battles of Trafalgar and Waterloo, was sustained by British wealth. It was in England that the Industrial Revolution was furthest advanced; the English superiority in manufacture and trade was not effectually challenged until the end of the century. The new economic dispensation brought its characteristic problems, and in the degree that industrial growth was rapid these were distressing, yet the necessity of confronting them had the effect of enhancing Victorian England's consciousness of a peculiar destiny and mission, of confirming the epoch's sense of being different from all periods that had gone before it and being perhaps not really continuous with them. Nothing so much shaped the identity of the Victorian Age as its consciousness of being *modern*.

In this, of course, the Victorian period was continuing a defining trait of the preceding cultural epoch of the nineteenth century, which also was marked by a lively awareness of what Hazlitt called, using the phrase as the title of one of his books, The Spirit of the Age. The difference between the self-consciousness of the Romantic period and that of the Victorian period is chiefly quantitative—in the later period there were more people whose sense of life was decisively conditioned by their perception that the age was an entity about which quite precise predications could be made, as Carlyle made them in two memorable essays, one of which is called *Signs of the Times*, the other *Characteristics*. A simple index of the increase in the number of persons who shared in this consciousness of modernity is the proliferation through the Victorian epoch of the kind of periodical which took this set of mind for granted and served its interests. The Romantic Age had seen the establishment of great organs of opinion—*The Edinburgh Review, The Quarterly Review, Blackwood's Magazine*—which undertook to deal with problems, issues, and tendencies, doing so in a partisan spirit, to be sure, but with a show, by no means always false, of learning and serious thought. In the Victorian period such journals became far more numerous—*The Westminster Review, Fraser's Magazine, The Cornhill Magazine, Macmillan's Magazine, The Fortnightly Review, The Saturday Review, The Athenaeum, The Pall Mall Gazette* are especially memorable—and the size of their audiences grew. Nothing quite comparable to them now exists in either England or the United States. They were not directed to what later came to be called an "intellectual" or "highbrow" audience, although much of what they published would nowadays be thought appropriate to such an audience, but to a category of readers which their editors would have characterized simply as "thoughtful."

To read the files of these journals, or, what is a more likely experience, to read the best-remembered work of the great prose writers of the age, much of which made its first appearance in their pages, is to recognize not only the self-consciousness of the

Victorian period but also how strong a sense of community in his audience and with his audience a writer of the time could count upon. Such judgments are of course relative and this one must not be understood as intending to minimize the extent of the divisions of opinion that did of course exist. Yet we have only to listen to the voices of the great Victorian writers as they addressed their audience to appreciate the assumption they were able to make—that they were speaking to people who, in the face of all differences, knew that they had much in common, who were there to be spoken to. The intonations of direct address, of men speaking to men, is perhaps most explicit in the novelists of the day; in one degree or another, Dickens, Thackeray, Trollope, and George Eliot thought of themselves as directly confronting the reader, telling their stories with a due concern for his interest, comfort, and moral welfare. This show of companionly regard waned with the century and came eventually to be thought old-fashioned; it was replaced by an attitude which pretends to deny the actual presence of the reader or makes it but an inessential part of the act of narration—it is as though the reader is being permitted to overhear the speaker if he has a mind to. But for the Victorian novelist the reader was a personal presence, as the novelist was a personal presence for the reader.

This trust in the reciprocal relationship of reader and writer is characteristic of all the great prose of the Victorian period; it is a *speaking* prose. Its voices are various in their intonations, some being reminiscent of the pulpit, some of the floor of the House of Commons, some of an Oxford lecture hall or senior common room, but all are charged with the confidence that they will be listened to and that what they are talking about lies within every hearer's experience and comprehension. They talk much about here and now, about England and English life, and they count on their readers to believe that there really is an English nation, with particular problems to confront and decisions to make, and with a definable destiny to pursue. There has never been an American writer who could make a similar assumption—from the beginning America has been too vast to permit it. And although even at the present time the sense of community is probably greater in England than in America, no English writer can any longer make such an assumption.

To us today the rapport that existed between the writer and his audience seems one of the most remarkable and engaging aspects of the Victorian epoch. In an age of commanding public figures, none were more established in esteem and affection than writers. Dickens was admired and loved as no writer had been before or has been since. Carlyle and Ruskin sometimes taxed the patience of their readers but they came to be held almost in awe, as sacred repositories of truth. Newman was sourly regarded for many years after his conversion to Catholicism, but upon the publication of his autobiography, *Apologia Pro Vita Sua,* the tide of English feeling turned and he became the object of an almost tender regard. The instances can be multiplied to include virtually every important literary figure of the age.

If this responsiveness to literary and intellectual genius is indeed a salient characteristic of Victorian England, what conclusions may be drawn from it about the English people and national life? That the people were of an unusual sensitivity and profoundly committed to spiritual values? That the national life was being shaped by the powers of imagination and reason? At such proposals the admired writers of the age would have gaped in amazement. The audience to which they addressed themselves were members of the middle class, that great and growing middle class of nineteenth-century England whose dominant position in the nation was the wonder of Europe. This was the class which had made England the "workshop of Europe," an achievement which scarcely argued the likelihood that a spiritual ideal would have dominion over it, and the writers never wearied in their denunciation of its benighted condition and of the gross materialism of its interests. It was the class of which Matthew Arnold said that it was "drugged with business" and to which he gave the name of Philistines, the enemies of the Chosen People, of those who lived by the light of thought and beauty. Carlyle held it chiefly to blame for the social chaos of England and for the injustice and misery which so widely prevailed. Ruskin and William Morris scolded it for the moral obtuseness of which its style of life was an expression—it was the middle class, they said, that had made the cities of England dirty and ugly and their own homes ugly and vulgar. Dickens was remorseless in his mockery of its complacency and self-righteousness and in his reprobation of the unfeeling hardness of its self-concern.

If the middle class is properly to be described in this harsh fashion, surely it is a paradox or an anomaly that the national culture which this class dominated should have given so hearty a response to writers for whom the indictment of the failings of the middle class was a chief part of their enterprise. The contradiction can be quite easily resolved: a first step in that direction is to realize the sheer size of the middle class and the consequent variety of its component elements. Defined in its middling position by the working class below it and the aristocracy above it, the middle class ranged from shopkeepers and small businessmen through the owners of factories of one size or another to entrepreneurs and bankers, and it included members of the professions, whose increasing number was an important feature of Victorian life. The class was so little homogeneous in point of economic establishment that it commonly was, and might well continue to be, referred to in the plural—the middle *classes,* among which are to be distinguished a lower-middle, a middle-middle, and an upper-middle class, each marked by its own mode of life, social ambitions, and cultural standards. There was no discernible difference between the life style of the upper-middle class and the aristocracy, and association between the two was much freer than on the Continent. William Morris was the son of a successful stockbroker, yet his nineteenth-century biographer frequently refers to him as an "aristocrat." What made for this easy interfusion of classes was the English social category of "gentleman," which the great French social theorist Tocqueville found so remarkable and to which he ascribed the stability of English society in contrast to the periodic revolutions of the French; membership in the loose but significant order of gentlemen did not depend upon a man's birth and blood but upon his manners and mode of life. As compared with the affluent freedom of the upper-middle class, the existence of the lower-middle class was exiguous and precarious, yet by contrast with that of the working class it was privileged, and as such was a status which was cherished.

Given this much diversity within the middle class itself, it is not surprising that many of its individual members should themselves turn a questioning eye upon its ethos and seek to repudiate or meliorate those unamiable traits that were commonly ascribed to it. It is, after all, only within certain limits that the characteristics of his class determine the character of an individual. Thus, a certain James Ruskin rose from respectable but humble origins to become a prosperous wine merchant; he lived according to a religious creed of the rigorous simplistic kind which was often said to limit the intellectual and emotional range of the middle-class man but which in his case was tempered by a taste for books, paintings, and landscape, and this he indulged as he became more affluent. His son John was reared in all the strictness of the Protestant ethic, but he was not discouraged from indulging in his passion for the things for which his father had a taste and from them he derived the principles upon which he was to base his assault on English life as the middle class had shaped it. Those who read what John Ruskin wrote and, in one way or another, responded to what he said and held him in honor for having said it, were, like him, members of the middle class who had attained to a degree of freedom from this class ethos.

In the development of critical self-awareness in the middle class, an element of its historical tradition played a decisive part. The Victorian middle class was often said to be impervious to ideas at a time when ideas were coming to rule the world. Matthew Arnold made this a chief article of his indictment of the Philistine mentality and explained it as a legacy of the middle-class Puritanism of the seventeenth century, which he characterized as having been indifferent to ideas and preoccupied with right-doing according to an unexamined code of conduct. In point of fact, however, Puritanism, although certainly moralistic, was also, in its great day, highly intellectual; it brought to bear a current of ideas upon the established conceptions of society and the polity. Such intellectual activity was natural in an energetic class bent on power. And if in the years after the Puritan revolution it had abated, at least in that part of the middle class which was in the Puritan line of descent, now that the middle class was in a new stage of its progress toward power there was reason for it to be revived.

But however mistaken Arnold may have been in his understanding of the Puritan tradition, clearly he was right in the emphasis he put upon the predominantly Protestant character of the English middle class in its middle and lower reaches— upon, that is, its attitude of nonconformism or dissent vis-à-vis the established Church of England. Arnold will nevertheless have misled us if he is understood to be saying that the dissenting form of Christian faith was the sole, or even the most forceful, religious influence upon the culture of the age. The passionate intensity of the dissenting sects, of which he makes much, argues the continuing, even if diminishing, strength of the Church of England and its centrality in the cultural life of the nation.

Nothing is more difficult than to represent the religious situation of England in the nineteenth century. It is charged with contradiction. Any account of it must begin with the great religious revival of the eighteenth century which is associated with the name of John Wesley. This resulted not only in the foundation of the Methodist Movement as a powerful new dissenting sect, but also in the formation within the Church of England of the influential party of Evangelicism, which laid stress on personal conversion and on a pious rectitude of life and did much to overcome the worldliness and negligence of the clergy and the indifference of the laity. The effect of the revival upon the tone of English life in the nineteenth century was decisive; to it may be traced the high value set upon sobriety and respectability as the appropriate mien of a god-fearing people. Yet Emerson in his *English Traits*, which was published in 1856 and based on two extended visits in 1833 and 1847–48, says explicitly and without qualification that the English do not believe in God. In the course of the book he recurs again and again to what is for him the most admirable of all the traits of the English nation, its sincerity. These are people, he says, who insist that the truth be told whatever its consequences may be; for themselves and for others this is their first requirement, the thing they most respect. In only one department of life do they abrogate sincerity—they have no actual religious belief, and therefore, Emerson says, nothing is "so odious as the polite bows to God" which they are always making in their books and newspapers.

A judgment of the accuracy of Emerson's observation must be a divided one. It is both true and not true. As we look backward, it is plain to see that even before the second half of the nineteenth century the English were on the way to their present indifference to religion. The working class had for a considerable time been alienated from the Church of England and was becoming increasingly disaffected from the dissenters. Among the educated class an actual and conscious personal faith was becoming ever rarer. Yet though this was so, there was abundant reason to conclude that England was a religious nation. Nothing engaged public attention more readily than religious questions. The Oxford Movement was the effort on the part of a few learned and pious men to strengthen Christian faith and the Church of England by reviving doctrines and modes of observance which had fallen into disuse; no undertaking could have been more recondite, yet it came to have the status of a scandal, so eagerly was it followed and talked about, so conscious were people of its implications for the national life. The attempt of the church to discipline Bishop Colenso for questioning the plausibility of certain statements of the Bible—most notoriously the dimensions of Noah's ark, which, if it was of the stated size, could not have housed all that many animals—made a *cause célèbre*, one of several of similar kind.

It is true that every educated person understood the force of the intellectual tendencies that were putting religious faith at issue. Personal crises of faith were common. But the suffering they were presumed to entail was the measure of the high store still accorded a settled and assured belief: it was the more precious because it might at any time be called upon to undergo the ordeal of doubt or because it had done so and survived. As late as 1888 the reading public could be shocked, or at least titillated, because the saintly young clergyman who was the hero of Mrs. Humphry Ward's popular novel, *Robert Elsmere*, felt constrained by intellectual honesty to repudiate every supernatural element of his faith and to formulate on his deathbed a creed which could scarcely be considered religious at all, consisting as it did of nothing more than the imperative of social and moral effort. The great Gladstone himself took time from his parliamentary duties to review the book at enormous length.

Yet Emerson was of course right in his judgment of the state of English religion. Much of what passed for belief was mere habit of imagination. And this was becoming ever more difficult to maintain—less and less did it seem possible for the imagination to be at ease with the ancient picture of the universe that was essential to the literal plausibility of the Christian story. The traditional iconography of religion, whether it figured over the altar or in the mind, inevitably came to seem anachronistic, made so by the remorseless progress of science in establishing the scarcely imaginable vastness of the universe and the immutability of its laws. The universe depicted by science could not accommodate, except perhaps in some abstract and therefore not immediate and compelling form, a conception of man's destiny such as was described by Creation, the Fall, the giving of the Law, Judgment, and Redemption.

Sigmund Freud has said that the belief that the universe is purposive "stands or falls with the religious system." This is true, and nothing in the loss of religious belief was more painful than to be required to regard the universe as being without purpose, which is to say, without coherence, without meaning. When that happened, it might seem that the very foundation of the mind had been shaken, that reason was threatened with overthrow. It was thus that Carlyle experienced his discovery of the purposelessness of the universe—his despair brought him to the verge of insanity, as did Tennyson's in a like situation. The dark night of nihilism was a common event in the lives of thoughtful men of the nineteenth century.

Yet the Victorians did not easily surrender their hope of shoring up their faith in the purposiveness of the universe after the religious system had fallen. Carlyle, by an impassioned exercise of will, discovered the "open secret" that the universe, despite all appearances to the contrary, was a spiritual entity, by which he meant that it was capable of having an intention in which man was implicated. Tennyson, in In Memoriam, struggled through the bleakness of nihilism into which his perception of the manifest fortuitousness of life had cast him and reached a faith in an inherent universal purpose. All that Matthew Arnold permitted to be postulated of God was a certain—alas, not very decisive—tendency toward the establishment of moral good: God, he said, is "the power not ourselves that makes for righteousness." And although science seemed ever more strictly to deny that the attributes of spirit were to be found in the universe, there was one scientific development which might be thought ambiguous in this respect. The idea of evolution—which was current and influential long before the publication of Darwin's Origin of Species in 1859 dramatized and popularized it—did of course contribute to the doubt that man had his origins in, and his nature from, the special purpose of a divine creator, but at the same time it licensed the speculation that the universe was not wholly accidental, that in the development of forms of life from simplicity to complexity, from lower to higher, there was manifested an inherent end in view, presumably beneficent. In the late years of the nineteenth century this speculation was formulated (notably by the French philosopher Henri Bergson) in the idea of a goal-directed "life force." It gained a certain currency among the educated classes, and in the early years of the twentieth century it was popularized by the writings of H. G. Wells and Bernard Shaw. The implication was that the "life force" had the attributes of spirit and that it might even be thought of as Divine. It was an idea too abstract to win authority over either the heart or the mind.

Yet if the Victorians failed in their effort to sustain the hegemony of spirit in the cosmos, they achieved a quite impressive degree of success in another venture on behalf of spirit—their formulation of the possibility of its being established in and realized through society. Hegel, in his Philosophy of History, characterized the modern age, the epoch beginning with the Renaissance, by its accelerating commitment to what he called "secular spirituality." He meant by this that the Christian idea that the actual, quotidian world is antithetical to spirit and to the hope of spiritual perfection was giving way to the idea that it is exactly in the world and through the activities required by the world that the spiritual destiny of mankind is fulfilled. The energies of aspiration which were once directed to the supernal goal proposed by Christianity were transferred to the temporal scene, to the development of the human spirit in history. That development was conceived in terms of the defining attribute of spirit, which is freedom—the ability to transcend the limiting conditions of material existence and to achieve autonomy and self-determination.

The central issue of Victorian culture was whether society was to be regarded as a spiritual entity or as a material and mechanical entity. This question, it may be said, was prompted by the existence and condition of the working class.

In recent years a number of social historians have undertaken to show that the life of the working class in England in the nineteenth century was in fact not so terrible as it was represented to be, not only by Friedrich Engels in his famous *Condition of the Working Class in England in 1844* (1845) but also by academic scholars who did not share Engels's radical political bias. However cogent such revisionist arguments may be, they must obviously pertain only to the historical "long view" of the question; they can have little bearing upon what sensitive observers at the time responded to as the immediate social actuality. Doubtless we can uncover circumstances which in some degree qualify the many appalling accounts of working-class distress; and there are indeed tendencies to be discerned which, as they developed through the century, resulted in a notable melioration of working-class life. But these considerations can in no substantial way alter our understanding of the momentous situation which the Victorians confronted, especially in the early years of their epoch. Whatever in point of statistical precision was happening to real wages over this or that decade, or whatever the extent to which the diet of workers was becoming more varied, what inevitably comes home to us in indication of the condition of the working class are such gross and bulking facts as that in a particular month of a particular year, March of 1842, in consequence of an extended crisis in the economy, the official count of paupers in England and Wales stood at 1,429,089.

It was to this disaster that Carlyle responded by writing *Past and Present*, dashing it off in a white heat in two months of 1843. Expectably enough, among the emotions which inform the book compassion plays a large part, as well as bitterness over the deficiency of compassion which permitted so much distress to go without substantial relief. But the ruling emotion of *Past and Present* is neither of these but indignation at the way in which the social organization was viewed by those who held power in England. Carlyle has his quarrel with the aristocratic class but the chief objects of his anger and contempt are the middle class and the social theory that rationalized its practice—its absolute belief in the immutable operation of the given economic system, its never-to-be-questioned assumption that the economy is continuous with nature itself and that its processes are governed by "laws" which are as sternly indifferent to human preference and will as are the scientifically verifiable laws of nature. Although the human consequences of the operation of the laws of economics might be deplored by persons of good will, they were regarded by the middle class as so fixed that any attempt to interfere with them could only invite catastrophe. The doctrine of laissez-faire, of letting the processes of economics work themselves out, was sacrosanct. The law of supply and demand, by which prices and wages are governed, was as intractable as the law of gravity.

It needed a quite extreme degree of deprivation and suffering in the population to persuade even large-minded men to question such a view of the social organization. And perhaps it ought to be remarked that even these people directed their criticism not against the established form of society, with its extremes of privilege and deprivation, but only against the opinion that society, as established, was ineluctably bound by economic law and that it could not implement such intentions as it might have to prevent the suffering of multitudes of its members. Their judgment did not impute blame to the established and traditional form of English society, which is to say, to its class structure. Far from being concerned with social equality, Carlyle was committed to a firm class system. And this in general was the tendency of Victorian criticism of the existing society. Matthew Arnold did indeed speak eloquently of a time when class differences would no longer exist; he was nevertheless content to accept them in the present. In his later years William Morris became a Marxist and envisaged a perfect equality among men, but up to that point he took class for granted as an inexpugnable condition of social life. As for Ruskin, who incurred the imputation of madness—of literal insanity—for having attacked the economic doctrine of laissez-faire, he was wholly conservative in the matter of differences of class status. The relation of master and servant, of higher and lower, these had been confirmed as a natural propriety by ancient traditions, including that of religion, and despite the fact that English society might permit considerably more social mobility than societies on the Continent, the idea of class, defined by differences in mode of life, manner, and personal temperament, was deep in the English grain (and still is) to an extent which it is often difficult for an American to understand.

Actually, in fact, the traditional relation of master and servant, of superior and inferior, which under feudalism had made the pattern of a whole society, was often taken as the criterion by which the relations that had come to prevail under the industrial dispensation were to be judged. What distressed Carlyle, and Ruskin after him, was that the social theory of the nineteenth century no longer considered the relation between higher and lower as a human and personal one, involving reciprocal obligations. By the factory owner the worker was regarded and dealt with not as if he were a fellow being, even though of a different social order, but as an abstract unit of the work force; between him and his employer the only tie was what Carlyle called the "cash-nexus": he was paid his wages, whose amount was determined by the iron law which applied to that transaction, often so little as to make his existence marginal, even problematical, and if the operation of cognate laws brought it about that there was no work, then there were no wages; the cash-nexus was broken without ado. Granted that in human terms this was to be regretted, the overriding logic of the prevailing conception of society, which had nothing to do with human terms, argued that it was necessary and inevitable, that society could no longer function in any other way. The machine had not only brought about a new method of production which had changed the nature of work and the traditional modes of life; it had also imposed itself as the model of what society is and must be, precluding from the social arrangement all possibility of mind, intention, and will.

On nothing so much do the Victorian writers agree as that the machine principle, the manifest antithesis to spirit, was corrupting the life of England. Its grossest, most readily observable effect was the dehumanization of the worker, who had become a mere element of the process of production, an object, raw material to be used at need, his cost as a source of energy reckoned in no different way than that of coal. But the dehumanizing influence of the machine principle extended well beyond this one class, and how far it went is suggested by Emerson in *English Traits*. Speaking of the admirable freedom of English life and the permission it gives to the expression of individuality, suddenly, without transition or any awareness that he is contradicting himself, Emerson says:

> Machinery has been applied to all work and carried to such perfection that little is left for the men but to mind the engines and feed the furnaces. But the machines require punctual service, and as they never tire they prove too much for their tenders. Mines, forges, mills, breweries, railroads, steam-pump, steam-plow, drill of regiments, drill of police, rule of court and shop-rule are

operated to give a mechanical regularity to all the habit and action of men. A terrible machine has possessed itself of the ground, the air, the men and women, and hardly even thought is free.

Emerson wrote in 1856, when life was far less mechanized than now, yet his sense of the—at least implicit—threat of the machine, even in a society which he characterized by the large measure of individual liberty it granted, was this drastic. His view was in accord with that of the Victorian writers. Between the condition of the working class and that of the privileged or even relatively privileged classes the difference was so great and so apparent as to lead Disraeli to make his often-quoted statement that England was not one nation but two. Yet the Victorian social critics make it their constant theme that the privileged classes, most especially the middle class, are equally in thrall to machinery—they too, although in subtler and less manifest ways than the working class, have suffered a disastrous curtailment of freedom and a diminution of spirit. Among Dickens's many representations of the deteriorated humanity of the commercial middle class, the character of Mr. Podsnap in *Our Mutual Friend* is doubtless the most memorable. From the name of this person Dickens derived the word (which came into common use) to denote the sum of typical middle-class attitudes, Podsnappery. Here is part of the famous first account of Mr. Podsnap:

> Mr. Podsnap's world was not a very large world, morally; no, nor even geographically: seeing that although his business was sustained upon commerce with other countries, he considered other countries, with that important reservation, a mistake, and of their manners and customs would conclusively observe, "Not English!" when, PRESTO! with a flourish of the arm, and a flush of the face, they were swept away. Elsewise, the world got up at eight, shaved close at a quarter-past, breakfasted at nine, went to the City at ten, came home at half-past five, and dined at seven. Mr. Podsnap's notions of the Arts in their integrity might have been stated thus. Literature; large print, respectively descriptive of getting up at eight, shaving close at a quarter-past, breakfasting at nine, going to the City at ten, coming home at half-past five, and dining at seven. Painting and Sculpture; models and portraits representing Professors of getting up at eight, shaving close at a quarter-past, breakfasting at nine, going to the City at ten, coming home at half-past five, and dining at seven. Music; a respectable performance (without variations) on stringed and wind instruments, sedately expressive of getting up at eight, shaving close at a quarter-past, breakfasting at nine, going to the City at ten, coming home at half-past five, and dining at seven. Nothing else to be permitted to those same vagrants the Arts, on pain of excommunication. Nothing else To Be—anywhere!

The connection that Dickens makes between the mechanical regularity of Mr. Podsnap's daily routine and his small-minded, egotistical view of art exemplifies a salient tendency of the Victorians' criticism of their society. In the resistance offered to the de-spiritualization of which the machine was both the agent and the metaphor, art played a decisive part. It may be said, indeed, that never before had art been assigned so large a function. This was nothing less than to supply the place of religion as the guide to life and as the guarantor and evidence of man's spiritual nature.

The view of art and its function which was held by the great Victorian critics descends in its essential characteristics from the Romantics. Coleridge had represented poetry as being the mediator between man and the universe, by which he meant that the imagination, the chief faculty of poetry, served to transform the "inanimate cold world" of ordinary, quotidian perception into a living entity which, as it were in grateful reciprocation of this gift of life, sustains and enhances man's spiritual powers. Shelley had said that it was not the prescriptions of moralizing religion that made the true basis of the ethical life but, rather, the exercise of the imagination as it was brought into activity by poetry. In the succeeding period Matthew Arnold expressed strong reservations about the English Romantic Movement as a whole and was far from being in sympathy with the intellectual temperament of either Coleridge or Shelley, yet in effect he echoed their view of the power and function of art when, in his essay *The Study of Poetry* (see below), he said that "the future of poetry is immense" and gave as his ground for his prediction the failure of the religion of his time to engage the imagination as religion had done in the past. The purport of his essay is that poetry, in what he represents to be its highest development, can generate the large emotions, the confidence in a spiritual destiny, and the sense of the cosmic significance of human existence which were once exclusively associated with religion. In the intellectual generations after Arnold's there was less emphasis upon those qualities of art which might make it seem cognate with religion, but for Walter Pater and Oscar Wilde the experience of art and what followed from it in the way of heightened perception and emotion were in effect the justification of human existence.

Another, less transcendent, function which the Victorian writers assigned to art is summarized in a famous phrase of Arnold's. "Poetry," Arnold said, "is the criticism of life," by which he meant that poetry, which may be taken to stand for art in general, is the paradigm or model of what life ideally should be and is not. The intention and ability of art to impose order upon multiplicity, to achieve the beauty and significance of coherence, proposes the right conduct of public life. And the power of sympathy and compassion that characterizes art, its responsiveness to nature and man, proposes the right development of the personal life. Increasingly, under the influence of Ruskin and the most notable of his disciples, William Morris, the enterprise of art came to be one of the most readily available criteria in the judgment of Victorian life. The motives of the artist, his dedication to his work for its own sake, were set in opposition to the Mr. Podsnaps of the world, which were those of pecuniary gain and what that brought in the way of power and social advancement. The nature of his work, the gratification he found in its autonomous, self-sufficing purpose, stood in striking antithesis both to the alienated labor forced upon the working classes and the alienated occupations of the more advantaged. We in our time are more circumspect than the great Victorian critics of society in the credence we give to the idea that art has a redemptive and liberating power, yet some vestigial faith in it does remain with us and we still, if a little wryly, shape our conception of the good life according to the paradigm of art.

# THOMAS CARLYLE
1795–1881

The career of Thomas Carlyle, at least up to its climax of achievement, may be thought of as a paradigm of English intellectual culture in the Victorian Age. The gifted peasant boy was bred up in the rigor of the Calvinist creed and destined by his family to become a minister of a church which was legendary for the piety and steadfastness of its members. In his university days he experienced an attenuation of his personal faith and found it ever more uncertain that he had a religious calling and, before many years had passed, his developing skepticism brought him to the point of entire unbelief. Yet the whole tendency of his thought in his characteristically best work was directed toward realizing for himself and enforcing upon the world a new form of belief which, by an act of inspired translation, he derived from the one he had repudiated—a secular spirituality which, in its demands upon faith and conduct and in the positive significance it assigned to life, was to be no less imperative than the religion in which he had been reared.

Carlyle was born in 1795 in the little town of Ecclefechan in Dumfrieshire, in the south of Scotland, the eldest of the nine children of a small farmer and stone-mason. It was from the "bold, glowing," and strikingly metaphorical speech of his father that he derived the outrageous boldness of his own style. From both parents in their confrontation of a necessitous life he learned the lesson of duty performed not as an imposed routine but as an expression of reverence for the divine Taskmaster of the stern but sustaining Calvinist creed. When he was eleven, the opportunities for schooling being limited in Ecclefechan, he was sent to the more populous town of Annan, where he lodged with an aunt and attended the local academy. There he was well grounded in mathematics and French and acquired some Latin and a very little Greek. In 1809 he went to Edinburgh to enter the university, making the hundred-mile journey from Ecclefechan on foot; he was fourteen, which at the time was the usual age of beginning students. His life at Edinburgh was penurious, largely solitary, and intellectually not gratifying, but he gave himself to mathematics and distinguished himself in that discipline and took advantage of the libraries of the city to read enormously and in every direction.

When he was nineteen, he returned to his old school at Annan as mathematical tutor, and two years later, in 1816, was appointed to a tutorship at a new school in the larger town of Kirkcaldy. It was while Carlyle was in Kirkcaldy that he read Hume and Gibbon and came to understand that he no longer believed as a Christian. A career in divinity being now at last out of the question and teaching being a hated blind alley, he went to Edinburgh in 1819 with a view to settling upon a profession. He thought of becoming a scientist or an engineer and for a short time undertook the study of law, but the *métier* upon which he finally settled was the precarious one of literary journalism. In one field of literature he became uniquely expert: his reading of Madame de Staël's *Germany* (1813) aroused his interest in German thought; he mastered the language and found in this different and brilliant culture the basis of the affirmation he was eventually to make against the desperate state of mind which had been induced by his skepticism.

The Edinburgh years were a black time for Carlyle. As a consequence of his loss of belief in its divine governance, the universe presented itself to him as a mere mechanism, and human life as devoid of all value and meaning. The despair in which the experience of nothingness issued threatened his sanity and even his life. This distress came to crisis in 1822, presumably in the way that Carlyle has described in the most memorable passage in all his work, the chapter of *Sartor Resartus* called "The Everlasting No" (see below), and it was fully transcended in the affirmation set forth in the chapter called "The Everlasting Yea" (see below), in which, by an act of the imaginative will, he conceived the universe to be not a mere mechanical construct but a spiritual entity, with its own intentions which, although they are but implicit, are yet discernible and give interpretable signs of their being at one with man's best hopes.

In 1822 Carlyle became a tutor in the wealthy Buller family, a post which gave him the opportunity to see something of the great world, including London, which he visited for the first time at the age of twenty-nine, and sufficient leisure to pursue his own work, which was becoming ever surer of its direction. In 1823–24 he published (anonymously in the London Magazine) his life of Schiller and in 1824 his translation of Goethe's novel of personal growth and development, Wilhelm Meister's Apprenticeship. Most of his writing at this time dealt with the achievements of German authors, by all of whom secular spirituality—the phrase is Hegel's—was taken for granted; without reference to the Christian God and giving no credence to the Christian cosmology, they understood man's life to be a spiritual undertaking which was no less exigent and no less momentous than it had been thought to be under the religious dispensation.

In 1827 Carlyle made his famous marriage with Jane Baillie Welsh, a young woman who was his superior in social position and his equal not, certainly, in genius but in intellectual vivacity and independence. The year following, the couple took up residence in a farmhouse at Craigenputtock, a property of Jane Carlyle's parents. The locality was not only isolated but dreary, and the six years spent there put a strain on the marriage, for Jane loved the pleasures of society; yet it was at this time that Carlyle began to make his name with the essays he contributed to the English journals and it was to Craigenputtock that Emerson journeyed to pay his respects in 1833 on his first visit to England.

In that year Carlyle decided to try his fortunes in London. He brought with him the manuscript of Sartor Resartus (written in 1830–31), for which he had hitherto failed to find a publisher. Its acceptance by Fraser's Magazine gave him the hope of an auspicious start, which, however, was dashed by the vehement dislike with which the difficult and eccentric work was met on all sides upon its publication in 1833–34. (It was, however, a resounding success in America when Emerson arranged for its publication in 1836.) In the two years following, Carlyle devoted himself to the research for and the composition of the work that was to establish him as one of the leading literary personages of his time and place, The French Revolution. Its success was delayed by the appalling accident that befell the manuscript of the first volume—Carlyle gave it to his friend John Stuart Mill to read and criticize, and Mill's housemaid, thinking it waste paper, burned it; Carlyle, after a night of anguish, dauntlessly resolved to rewrite the volume. When the work was completed in 1837 Carlyle said to his wife that he was ready to tell the world: "You have not had for a hundred years any book that comes more direct and flamingly from the heart of man." Many of the best minds of England thought this to be so and gave their assent to the passionate lesson it imparted with an unparalleled dramatic force, that a modern society characterized by falsehood, conventionality, and indifference will incur the terrible justice of a bloody end.

Over the next four years Carlyle's literary output took chiefly the form of lectures, of which he gave four series, the most notable being Heroes and Hero-Worship, and the Heroic in History of 1841, in which, against the rising tendency to interpret the development of nations and of civilization itself in terms of general and abstract causes, he set his intensely held view that the decisive element in all cultural achievement is the individual person of genius.

In 1843, being at the time at work on his life of Cromwell, he interrupted that project at the behest of his ever-growing concern with the "Condition of England Question" to write—in two months—the brilliant anatomy of English social and political life *Past and Present*. None of Carlyle's works touching upon the nature of man's life in community is more stirring in its representation of the anomalies and injustices of English society in its commitment to the principles of materialism and laissez-faire. Yet it is in this remarkable book that, while seeking to press upon the complacent classes the realization of the truth that we are all members of each other, he crystallizes his doubt that all men in their membership of each other can get done what needs to be done for the common good and reinforces his belief that authority and power must be invested in the hands of only a few.

From this point on, Carlyle's speculative powers coarsened. His dismay at disorder became a hatred of process—what needed to be done had to be done at once, by fiat, at command. He thought more and more in terms of salvation by absolute monarchs like Frederick the Great whose biography he wrote (published in 1865) and whom he did not think he had belittled when he said that this sovereign's appropriate surrogate was the army drill-sergeant. In 1867, as the Second Reform Bill was about to be passed, he published his intemperate essay *Shooting Niagara, and After?* in which he proclaimed that the extension of the franchise would inevitably bring chaos and ruin to England.

Thereafter, although he was to live for thirteen years longer, he was silent, partly in disgust and despair, partly by reason of a physical infirmity which made the act of writing difficult and eventually impossible. His wife died in 1866 and his grief was the heavier because of his guilt over the sorrow he had caused her by his curiously flagrant neglect of her in her last years. He lived chiefly in lonely seclusion although held in the highest honor—those who did not acknowledge him to be a seer still did not fail to understand that he was a genius. At his death in 1881, the Dean of Westminster offered burial in the Abbey, but Carlyle had left instructions that he be buried beside his parents in the Ecclefechan churchyard, without religious rites of any kind.

# Sartor Resartus

When *Sartor Resartus* had gone through a few numbers of *Fraser's Magazine* (1833–34), one of the old subscribers expressed the judgment passed upon the work by most of its early readers when he wrote to the editor threatening cancellation if there was "any more of that damned stuff." We must not be too quick to scorn this blunt gentleman. If he was bewildered, there was reason for him to be, he was meant to be; if he had difficulty in comprehension, that was according to plan; if he thought the language outlandish, not even really English, so he was meant to think. *Sartor Resartus* is an outrageous book and if one is to get on with it, one must consent to be outraged. It is a work in the mode of the grotesque; it is willful,

eccentric, intentionally putting stumbling blocks in the way of the reader's understanding. By turns it is mock-solemn and truly solemn, comic and sentimental, ironic
and passionate. It levies on many genres and is by turns a treatise on sociology, a
discourse on philosophy, a sentimental novel, a series of sermons, a satire on pedantic
scholarship, a biography, a cryptic autobiography. Its very language confounds expectation, only reluctantly consents to be English, and proclaims itself as never comfortable unless it is in close touch with German. In its teasing arbitrariness *Sartor
Resartus* is in the line of descent from Rabelais's *Gargantua and Pantagruel* and Sterne's
*Tristram Shandy;* it draws on the elaborate ironic humor of Jean Paul Richter's tales.
And it was not for nothing that in his university days Carlyle was nicknamed
"Jonathan" and "the Dean"—there is much of Swift in the book and the famous
garment of *The Tale of a Tub* had a decisive part in its first conception.

The Latin phrase that is its title means "the tailor retailored" or "the tailor
reclothed." The metaphor of clothing has two distinct references. One is to the material world, which is the garment of indwelling spirit. The other is to human institutions which clothe the spirit of man in its communal existence. In the former use of
the metaphor, both the spirit and the garment are essentially immutable. In the latter
use, the spirit is variable and the garments which invest it may become outgrown or
go out of fashion and must from time to time be discarded for new ones.

The work purports to be an account of a treatise on the Philosophy of Clothes
by a scholar who once held the professorial chair of Things-in-General at the German
University of Weissnichtwo, which is to say Know-not-where. The account is given
by an English writer, who refers to himself as the Editor; in his youth he visited
Weissnichtwo and here made the acquaintance of the Professor. In his enterprise
he receives the assistance of the Professor's closest friend and associate, a worthy
man named Heuschrecke (Scarecrow), who sends him masses of manuscripts found
among the Professor's effects, some of them autobiographical.

This material became available not through the Professor's death but through his
mysterious disappearance; it is suggested that some day he will return as mysteriously
as he vanished. The name of the Professor is Diogenes Teufelsdröckh: Diogenes
means "born of God," Teufelsdröckh is "devil's dung." The conjunction of the two
names proposes the dual nature of man.

Book I consists of the Editor's paraphrase of Teufelsdröckh's extrapolation of the
clothes metaphor and this is resumed in the third and last book, which ends with
the news of the mysterious disappearance. Book II is devoted to the biography of
Teufelsdröckh, beginning with a mysterious and reverend stranger bringing him, a
new-born infant in a basket, to an aged and worthy couple in the little town of
Entefuhl (Duck Puddle) and putting him in their charge. In the basket are gold
coins and other indications of the exalted—by which is implied the divine—lineage
of the child. It cannot fail to be seen that the legendary account of the child's
developing sense of himself and the world is based upon Carlyle's own experience.
After his university days the young Teufelsdröckh becomes a tutor in a noble family
and falls in love with the daughter of the house, Blumine. His hope of ever winning
his beloved is frustrated by the difference in their social positions and also by
Blumine's having fallen in love with his English friend, Towgood. After a period of
wandering over the world, seeking surcease from his sorrow over his loss, Teufelsdröckh undergoes, as Carlyle did, the metaphysical crisis which is the climax of the
book.

In written German all nouns are capitalized, and it is one of the idiosyncrasies of Carlyle's style that he approximates this practice.

## From Sartor Resartus

### The Everlasting No [1]

Under the strange nebulous envelopment, wherein our Professor has now shrouded himself, no doubt but his spiritual nature is nevertheless progressive, and growing: for how can the 'Son of Time,' in any case, stand still? We behold him, through those dim years, in a state of crisis, of transition: his mad Pilgrimings, and general solution into aimless Discontinuity, what is all this but a mad Fermentation; wherefrom, the fiercer it is, the clearer product will one day evolve itself?

Such transitions are ever full of pain: thus the Eagle when he moults is sickly; and, to attain his new beak, must harshly dash-off the old one upon rocks. What Stoicism soever our Wanderer, in his individual acts and motions, may affect, it is clear that there is a hot fever of anarchy and misery raging within; coruscations of which flash out: as, indeed, how could there be other? Have we not seen him disappointed, bemocked of Destiny, through long years? All that the young heart might desire and pray for has been denied; nay, as in the last worst instance, offered and then snatched away. Ever an 'excellent Passivity'; but of useful, reasonable Activity, essential to the former as Food to Hunger, nothing granted: till at length, in this wild Pilgrimage, he must forcibly seize for himself an Activity, though useless, unreasonable. Alas, his cup of bitterness, which had been filling drop by drop, ever since that first 'ruddy morning' in the Hinterschlag Gymnasium,[2] was at the very lip; and then with that poison-drop, of the Towgood-and-Blumine[3] business, it runs-over, and even hisses-over in a deluge of foam.

He himself says once, with more justice than originality: 'Man is, properly speaking, based upon Hope, he has no other possession but Hope; this world of his is emphatically the Place of Hope.' What, then, was our Professor's possession? We see him, for the present, quite shut-out from Hope; looking not into the golden orient, but vaguely all round into a dim copper firmament, pregnant with earthquake and tornado.

Alas, shut-out from Hope, in a deeper sense than we yet dream of! For, as he wanders wearisomely through this world, he has now lost all tidings of another and higher.[4] Full of religion, or at least of religiosity,[5] as our Friend has since exhibited himself, he hides not that, in those days, he was wholly

---

1. This selection is from Bk. II, Chap. VII.
2. A Gymnasium is a German classical secondary school. The name of this one is Behind-beat.
3. The immediate cause of Teufelsdröckh's despair is the loss of Blumine, the girl he loved, to his English friend Towgood.
4. Presumably under the influence of rationalism he has lost his religious faith.
5. Carlyle probably intends this word to mean a disposition to be religious. It now has the pejorative meaning of an excessive or affected piety.

irreligious: 'Doubt had darkened into Unbelief,' says he; 'shade after shade goes grimly over your soul, till you have the fixed, starless, Tartarean[6] black.' To such readers as have reflected, what can be called reflecting, on man's life, and happily discovered, in contradiction to much Profit-and-loss Philosophy,[7] speculative and practical, that Soul is *not* synonymous with Stomach; who understand, therefore, in our Friend's words, 'that, for man's well-being, Faith is properly the one thing needful; how, with it, Martyrs, otherwise weak, can cheerfully endure the shame and the cross; and without it, worldlings puke-up their sick existence, by suicide, in the midst of luxury': to such it will be clear that, for a pure moral nature, the loss of his religious Belief was the loss of everything. Unhappy young man! All wounds, the crush of long-continued Destitution, the stab of false Friendship and of false Love, all wounds in thy so genial heart, would have healed again, had not its life-warmth been withdrawn. Well might he exclaim, in his wild way: 'Is there no God, then; but at best an absentee God, sitting idle, ever since the first Sabbath, at the outside of his Universe, and *seeing* it go?[8] Has the word Duty no meaning;[9] is what we call Duty no divine Messenger and Guide, but a false earthly Fantasm, made-up of Desire and Fear, of emanations from the Gallows and from Dr. Graham's Celestial-Bed?[10] Happiness of an approving Conscience! Did not Paul of Tarsus, whom admiring men have since named Saint, feel that *he* was "the chief of sinners";[11] and Nero of Rome, jocund in spirit (*wohlgemuth*), spend much of his time in fiddling? Foolish Word-monger and Motive-grinder, who in thy Logic-mill hast an earthly mechanism for the Godlike itself, and wouldst fain grind me out Virtue from the husks of Pleasure,—I tell thee, Nay! To the unregenerate Prometheus Vinctus[12] of a man, it is ever the bitterest aggravation of his wretchedness that he is conscious of Virtue, that he feels himself the victim not of suffering only, but of injustice. What then? Is the heroic inspiration we name Virtue but some Passion; some bubble of the blood, bubbling in the direction others *profit* by? I know not: only this I know, If what thou namest Happiness be our true aim, then are we all astray. With Stupidity and sound Digestion man may front much. But what, in these dull unimaginative days, are the terrors of Conscience to the diseases of the Liver! Not on Morality, but on Cookery, let us build our stronghold: there brandishing our frying-pan, as censer, let us offer sweet incense to the Devil, and live at ease on the fat things *he* has provided for his Elect!'

Thus has the bewildered Wanderer to stand, as so many have done, shouting

6. Tartarus was the innermost region of Hades in the *Iliad*.
7. A reference to the ethical theory of Utilitarianism, which proposed that the desirability of an action could be determined by a calculation of the degree of pleasure or of pain it would give rise to.
8. A summary of the Deist conception of the relation of God to the universe—once the universe had been brought into being and set in motion, God had no involvement with it.
9. In the mechanical universe of the Deists there is no inherent moral law—the God of that universe makes no demands upon mankind.
10. James Graham (1745–94), a famous quack doctor, invented a bed which he claimed cured sterility.
11. I Timothy 1:15.
12. Prometheus Bound; the title of Aeschylus' play in which the rebellious Titan, chained to a rock by command of Zeus, defies his tormentor.

question after question into the Sibyl-cave of Destiny, and receive no Answer but an Echo. It is all a grim Desert, this once-fair world of his; wherein is heard only the howling of wild-beasts, or the shrieks of despairing, hate-filled men; and no Pillar of Cloud by day, and no Pillar of Fire by night, any longer guides the Pilgrim. To such length has the spirit of Inquiry carried him. 'But what boots it (*was thut's*)?' cries he: 'it is but the common lot in this era. Not having come to spiritual majority prior to the *Siècle de Louis Quinze*,[13] and not being born purely a Loghead (*Dummkopf*), thou hadst no other outlook. The whole world is, like thee, sold to Unbelief; their old Temples of the Godhead, which for long have not been rainproof, crumble down; and men ask now. Where is the Godhead; our eyes never saw him?'

Pitiful enough were it, for all these wild utterances, to call our Diogenes wicked. Unprofitable servants as we all are, perhaps at no era of his life was he more decisively the Servant of Goodness, the Servant of God, than even now when doubting God's existence. 'One circumstance I note,' says he: 'after all the nameless woe that Inquiry, which for me, what it is not always, was genuine Love of Truth, had wrought me, I nevertheless still loved Truth, and would bate no jot of my allegiance to her. "Truth!" I cried, "though the Heavens crush me for following her: no Falsehood! though a whole celestial Lubberland[14] were the price of Apostasy." In conduct it was the same. Had a divine Messenger from the clouds, or miraculous Handwriting on the wall, convincingly proclaimed to me *This thou shalt do*, with what passionate readiness, as I often thought, would I have done it, had it been leaping into the infernal Fire. Thus, in spite of all Motive-grinders, and Mechanical Profit-and-Loss Philosophies, with the sick ophthalmia and hallucination they had brought on, was the Infinite nature of Duty[15] still dimly present to me: living without God in the world, of God's light I was not utterly bereft; if my as yet sealed eyes, with their unspeakable longing, could nowhere see Him, nevertheless in my heart He was present, and His heaven-written Law still stood legible and sacred there.'

Meanwhile, under all these tribulations, and temporal and spiritual destitutions, what must the Wanderer, in his silent soul, have endured! 'The painfullest feeling,' writes he, 'is that of your own Feebleness (*Unkraft*); ever, as the English Milton says, to be weak is the true misery.[16] And yet of your Strength there is and can be no clear feeling, save by what you have prospered in, by what you have done. Between vague wavering Capability and fixed indubitable Performance, what a difference! A certain inarticulate Self-consciousness dwells dimly in us; which only our Works can render articulate and decisively discernible. Our Works are the mirror wherein the spirit first sees its natural lineaments. Hence, too, the folly of that impossible Precept, *Know thyself;*[17] till it be translated into this partially possible one, *Know what thou canst work-at.*

13. "The century of Louis XV"; Carlyle has in mind Voltaire's historical work of that name, which gives an account of the development of the Age of Reason, which Carlyle detested.
14. An imaginary land of plenty and laziness.
15. Infinite in the sense of being absolute, by implication divine.
16. *Paradise Lost* I.157: "To be weak is miserable."
17. This maxim was inscribed on the temple of Apollo at Delphi.

'But for me, so strangely unprosperous had I been, the net-result of my Workings amounted as yet simply to—Nothing. How then could I believe in my Strength, when there was as yet no mirror to see it in? Ever did this agitating, yet, as I now perceive, quite frivolous question, remain to me insoluble: Hast thou a certain Faculty, a certain Worth, such even as the most have not; or art thou the completest Dullard of these modern times? Alas! the fearful Unbelief is unbelief in yourself; and how could I believe? Had not my first, last Faith in myself, when even to me the Heavens seemed laid open, and I dared to love, been all-too cruelly belied? The speculative Mystery of Life grew ever more mysterious to me: neither in the practical Mystery [18] had I made the slightest progress, but been everywhere buffeted, foiled, and con-temptuously cast-out. A feeble unit in the middle of a threatening Infinitude, I seemed to have nothing given me but eyes, whereby to discern my own wretchedness. Invisible yet impenetrable walls, as of Enchantment, divided me from all living: was there, in the wide world, any true bosom I could press trustfully to mine? O Heaven, No, there was none! I kept a lock upon my lips: why should I speak much with that shifting variety of so-called Friends, in whose withered, vain and too-hungry souls Friendship was but an incredible tradition? In such cases, your resource is to talk little, and that little mostly from the Newspapers. Now when I look back, it was a strange isolation I then lived in. Then men and women around me, even speaking with me, were but Figures; I had, practically, forgotten that they were alive, that they were not merely automatic. In midst of their crowded streets and assemblages, I walked solitary; and (except as it was my own heart, not another's, that I kept devour-ing) savage also, as the tiger in his jungle. Some comfort it would have been, could I, like a Faust, have fancied myself tempted and tormented of the Devil; for a Hell, as I imagine, without Life, though only diabolic Life, were more frightful: but in our age of Down-pulling and Disbelief, the very Devil has been pulled down, you cannot so much as believe in a Devil.[19] To me the Universe was all void of Life, of Purpose, of Volition, even of Hostility: it was one huge, dead, immeasurable Steam-engine, rolling on, in its dead indifference, to grind me limb from limb. O, the vast, gloomy, solitary Gol-gotha,[20] and Mill of Death! Why was the Living banished thither companion-less, conscious? Why, if there is no Devil; nay, unless the Devil is your God?'

A prey incessantly to such corrosions, might not, moreover, as the worst aggravation to them, the iron constitution even of a Teufelsdröckh threaten to fail? We conjecture that he has known sickness; and, in spite of his loco-motive habits, perhaps sickness of the chronic sort. Hear this, for example: 'How beautiful to die of broken-heart, on Paper![21] Quite another thing in practice; every window of your Feeling, even of your Intellect, as it were, begrimed and mud-bespattered, so that no pure ray can enter; a whole Drug-

18. Carlyle is playing with two meanings of "mystery"—in his second use of the word it signifies a trade or a craft.
19. That is, even positive evil is preferred by Teufelsdröckh to a mechanical universe.
20. Calvary, where Christ was crucified; literally, "Place of Skulls."
21. A satiric allusion to the emulation of the emotions of the despairing heroes of novels of the late 18th and early 19th centuries, of whom Goethe's Werther was the first.

shop in your inwards; the fordone soul drowning slowly in quagmires of Disgust!'

Putting all which external and internal miseries together, may we not find in the following sentences, quite in our Professor's still vein, significance enough? 'From Suicide a certain aftershine (*Nachschein*) of Christianity withheld me: perhaps also a certain indolence of character; for, was not that a remedy I had at any time within reach? Often, however, was there a question present to me: Should some one now, at the turning of that corner, blow thee suddenly out of Space, into the other World, or other No-World, by pistol-shot,—how were it? On which ground, too, I have often, in sea-storms and sieged cities and other death-scenes, exhibited an imperturbability, which passed, falsely enough, for courage.'

'So had it lasted,' concludes the Wanderer, 'so had it lasted, as in bitter protracted Death-agony, through long years. The heart within me, unvisited by any heavenly dewdrop, was smouldering in sulphurous, slow-consuming fire. Almost since earliest memory I had shed no tear; or once only when I, murmuring half-audibly, recited Faust's Deathsong, that wild *Selig der den er im Siegesglanze findet* (Happy whom *he* finds in Battle's splendour),[22] and thought that of this last Friend even I was not forsaken, that Destiny itself could not doom me not to die. Having no hope, neither had I any definite fear, were it of Man or of Devil: nay, I often felt as if it might be solacing, could the Arch-Devil himself, though in Tartarean terrors, but rise to me, that I might tell him a little of my mind. And yet, strangely enough, I lived in a continual, indefinite, pining fear, tremulous, pusillanimous, apprehensive of I knew not what: it seemed as if all things in the Heavens above and the Earth beneath would hurt me; as if the Heavens and the Earth were but boundless jaws of a devouring monster, wherein I, palpitating, waited to be devoured.

'Full of such humour, and perhaps the miserablest man in the whole French Capital or Suburbs, was I, one sultry Dog-day,[23] after much perambulation, toiling along the dirty little *Rue Saint-Thomas de l'Enfer*,[24] among civic rubbish enough, in a close atmosphere, and over pavements hot as Nebuchadnezzar's Furnace;[25] whereby doubtless my spirits were little cheered; when, all at once, there rose a Thought in me, and I asked myself: "What *art* thou afraid of? Wherefore, like a coward, dost thou forever pip and whimper, and go cowering and trembling? Despicable biped! what is the sum-total of the worst that lies before thee? Death? Well, Death; and say the pangs of Tophet[26] too, and all that the Devil and Man may, will or can do against thee! Hast thou not a heart; canst thou not suffer whatsoever it be; and, as a Child of Freedom, though outcast, trample Tophet itself under thy feet, while it consumes thee? Let it come, then; I will meet it and defy it!" And as I so thought, there rushed like a stream of fire over my whole soul; and I shook base Fear

22. Adapted from Goethe's *Faust* I. iv. 1573–76.
23. The dog-days are the hot, sultry period between mid-July and September, so called because the "dog-star" Sirius rises and sets with the sun. They are thought to be unwholesome for body and mind.
24. The street's name is St. Thomas-in-Hell. By this use of his own Christian name, Carlyle invites us to guess that Teufelsdröckh's experience was his own.
25. Daniel 3:19.
26. Hell.

away from me forever. I was strong, of unknown strength; a spirit, almost a god. Ever from that time, the temper of my misery was changed: not Fear or whining Sorrow was it, but Indignation and grim fire-eyed Defiance. 'Thus had the EVERLASTING NO[27] (*das ewige Nein*) pealed authoritatively through all the recesses of my Being, of my ME; and then was it that my whole ME stood up, in native God-created majesty, and with emphasis recorded its Protest. Such a Protest, the most important transaction in Life, may that same Indignation and Defiance, in a psychological point of view, be fitly called. The Everlasting No had said: "Behold, thou art fatherless, outcast, and the Universe is mine (the Devil's)"; to which my whole Me now made answer: "*I am not thine, but Free, and forever hate thee!*"

'It is from this hour that I incline to date my Spiritual New-birth, or Baphometic[28] Fire-baptism; perhaps I directly thereupon began to be a Man.'

[The chapter following "The Everlasting No" is called "The Centre of Indifference." It recounts how Teufelsdröckh, after having passed his crisis, investigates the world in an objective way, looking for some sign of spirituality in human institutions. His bitter, life-denying state of feeling has been overcome, but nothing of a positive kind has come to take its place. He lives in a condition of neutral feeling, enduring life rather than living it.]

### The Everlasting Yea[1]

'Temptations in the Wilderness!'[2] exclaims Teufelsdröckh: 'Have we not all to be tried with such? Not so easily can the old Adam,[3] lodged in us by birth, be dispossessed. Our Life is compassed round with Necessity; yet is the meaning of Life itself no other than Freedom, than Voluntary Force: thus have we a warfare; in the beginning, especially, a hard-fought battle. For the God-given mandate, *Work thou in Welldoing*, lies mysteriously written, in Promethean Prophetic Characters, in our hearts; and leaves us no rest, night or day, till it be deciphered and obeyed; till it burn forth, in our conduct, a visible, acted Gospel of Freedom. And as the clay-given[4] mandate, *Eat thou and be filled*, at the same time persuasively proclaims itself through every nerve,—must not there be a confusion, a contest, before the better Influence can become the upper?

'To me nothing seems more natural than that the Son of Man, when such God-given mandate first prophetically stirs within him, and the Clay must

27. There is the chance of at least momentary misunderstanding here—the Everlasting No is spoken *to* Teufelsdröckh, not *by* him. His great moment is his defiance and negation of it. That it is called Everlasting suggests Carlyle's awareness that it is inherent in the nature of life, that it cannot be overcome by reason but only by will.
28. Devilish. Baphomet was the idol or symbolic figure which the Knights Templars were said to worship when they were accused of being infidels. The name may be a corruption of Mahomet.

1. From Bk. II, Chap. IX.
2. The allusion is to the temptation of Christ by Satan, Matthew 4:1.
3. Colossians 3:9. The "old Adam" is man unregenerate. Adam is the Hebrew word for man.
4. In the second of the two versions of the creation of man in Genesis, Adam is moulded by God of clay.

now be vanquished, or vanquish,—should be carried of the spirit into grim Solitudes, and there fronting the Tempter do grimmest battle with him; defiantly setting him at naught, till he yield and fly. Name it as we choose: with or without visible Devil, whether in the natural Desert of rocks and sands, or in the populous Desert of selfishness and baseness,—to such Temptation are we all called. Unhappy if we are not! Unhappy if we are but Half-men, in whom that divine handwriting has never blazed forth, all-subduing, in true sun-splendour; but quivers dubiously amid meaner lights: or smoulders, in dull pain, in darkness, under earthly vapours!—Our Wilderness is the wide World in an Atheistic Century; our Forty Days are long years of suffering and fasting: nevertheless, to these also comes an end. Yes, to me also was given, if not Victory, yet the consciousness of Battle, and the resolve to persevere therein while life or faculty is left. To me also, entangled in the enchanted forests, demon-peopled, doleful of sight and of sound, it was given, after weariest wanderings, to work out my way into the higher sunlit slopes— of that Mountain which has no summit, or whose summit is in Heaven only!'

He says elsewhere, under a less ambitious figure; as figures are, once for all, natural to him: 'Has not thy Life been that of most sufficient men (tüchtigen Männer) thou hast known in this generation? An outflush of foolish young Enthusiasm, like the first fallow-crop, wherein are as many weeds as valuable herbs: this all parched away, under the Droughts of practical and spiritual Unbelief, as Disappointment, in thought and act, often-repeated gave rise to Doubt, and Doubt gradually settled into Denial! If I have had a second-crop, and now see the perennial green-sward, and sit under umbrageous cedars, which defy all Drought (and Doubt); herein too, be the Heavens praised, I am not without examples, and even exemplars.'

So that, for Teufelsdröckh also, there has been a 'glorious revolution': [5] these mad shadow-hunting and shadow-hunted Pilgrimings of his were but some purifying 'Temptation in the Wilderness,' before his Apostolic work (such as it was) could begin; which Temptation is now happily over, and the Devil once more worsted! Was 'that high moment in the Rue de l'Enfer,' then, properly the turning-point of the battle; when the Fiend said, Worship me or be torn in shreds; and was answered valiantly with an Apage, Satana? [6]— Singular Teufelsdröckh, would thou hadst told thy singular story in plain words! But it is fruitless to look there, in those Paper-bags,[7] for such. Nothing but innuendoes, figurative crotchets: a typical Shadow, fitfully wavering, prophetico-satiric; no clear logical Picture. 'How paint to the sensual eye,' asks he once, 'what passes in the Holy-of-Holies of Man's Soul; in what words, known to these profane times, speak even afar-off of the unspeakable?' We ask in turn: Why perplex these times, profane as they are, with needless obscurity, by omission and by commission? Not mystical only is our Professor, but whimsical; and involves himself, now more than ever, in eye-bewildering chiaroscuro.[8] Successive glimpses, here faithfully imparted, our more gifted readers must endeavour to combine for their own behoof.

5. The phrase commonly used to describe the deposition of King James II in 1688.
6. "Get thee hence, Satan," Matthew 4:8–10.
7. Teufelsdröckh kept his autobiographical manuscripts in six paper bags.
8. Light and shade (in painting).

He says: 'The hot Harmattan-wind [9] had raged itself out; its howl went silent within me; and the long-deafened soul could now hear. I paused in my wild wanderings; and sat me down to wait, and consider; for it was as if the hour of change drew nigh. I seemed to surrender, to renounce utterly, and say: Fly, then, false shadows of Hope; I will chase you no more, I will believe you no more. And ye too, haggard spectres of Fear, I care not for you; ye too are all shadows and a lie. Let me rest here: for I am way-weary and life-weary; I will rest here, were it but to die: to die or to live is alike to me; alike insignificant.'—And again: 'Here, then, as I lay in that CENTRE OF INDIFFERENCE; cast, doubtless by benignant upper Influence, into a healing sleep, the heavy dreams rolled gradually away, and I awoke to a new Heaven and a new Earth.[10] The first preliminary moral Act, Annihilation of Self (*Selbsttödtung*), had been happily accomplished; and my mind's eyes were now unsealed, and its hands ungyved.' [11]

Might we not also conjecture that the following passage refers to his Locality, during this same 'healing sleep'; that his Pilgrim-staff lies cast aside here, on 'the high table-land'; and indeed that the repose is already taking wholesome effect on him? If it were not that the tone, in some parts, has more of riancy, even of levity, than we could have expected! However, in Teufelsdröckh, there is always the strangest Dualism: light dancing, with guitar-music, will be going on in the fore-court, while by fits from within comes the faint whimpering of woe and wail. We transcribe the piece entire:

'Beautiful it was to sit there, as in my skyey Tent, musing and meditating; on the high table-land, in front of the Mountains; over me, as roof, the azure Dome, and around me, for walls, four azure-flowing curtains,—namely, of the Four azure winds, on whose bottom-fringes also I have seen gilding. And then to fancy the fair Castles that stood sheltered in these Mountain hollows; with their green flower-lawns, and white dames and damosels, lovely enough: or better still, the straw-roofed Cottages, wherein stood many a Mother baking bread, with her children round her;— all hidden and protectingly folded-up in the valley-folds; yet there and alive, as sure as if I beheld them. Or to see, as well as fancy, the nine Towns and Villages, that lay round my mountain-seat, which, in still weather, were wont to speak to me (by their steeple-bells) with metal tongue; and, in almost all weather, proclaimed their vitality by repeated Smoke-clouds; whereon, as on a culinary horologe,[12] I might read the hour of the day. For it was the smoke of cookery, as kind housewives at morning, mid-day, eventide, were boiling their husbands' kettles; and ever a blue pillar rose up into the air, successively or simultaneously, from each of the nine, saying, as plainly as smoke could say: Such and such a meal is getting ready here. Not uninteresting! For you have the whole Borough, with all its love-makings and scandal-mongeries, contentions and contentments, as in miniature, and could cover it all with your hat.—If, in my wide Wayfarings, I had learned to look into the business of the World in its details, here perhaps

9. A hot, dry, dusty wind that blows from the Sahara.
10. Revelation 21:1.
11. Unshackled.
12. Clock.

was the place for combining it into general propositions, and deducing inferences therefrom.

'Often also could I see the black Tempest marching in anger through the Distance: round some Schreckhorn,[13] as yet grim-blue, would the eddying vapour gather, and there tumultuously eddy, and flow down like a mad witch's hair; till, after a space, it vanished, and, in the clear sunbeam, your Schreckhorn stood smiling grim-white, for the vapour had held snow. How thou fermentest and elaboratest, in thy great fermenting-vat and laboratory of an Atmosphere, of a World, O Nature!—Or what is Nature? Ha! why do I not name thee GOD? Art not thou the "Living Garment of God"?[14] O Heavens, is it, in very deed, HE, then, that ever speaks through thee; that lives and loves in thee, that lives and loves in me?

'Fore-shadows, call them rather fore-splendours, of that Truth, and Beginning of Truths, fell mysteriously over my soul. Sweeter than Dayspring to the Shipwrecked in Nova Zembla; ah, like the mother's voice to her little child that strays bewildered, weeping, in unknown tumults; like soft streamings of celestial music to my too-exasperated heart, came that Evangel. The Universe is not dead and demoniacal, a charnel-house with spectres; but godlike, and my Father's!

'With other eyes, too, could I now look upon my fellow man; with an infinite Love, an infinite Pity. Poor, wandering, wayward man! Art thou not tried, and beaten with stripes, even as I am? Ever, whether thou bear the royal mantle or the beggar's gabardine, art thou not so weary, so heavy-laden; and thy Bed of Rest is but a Grave. O my Brother, my Brother, why cannot I shelter thee in my bosom, and wipe away all tears from thy eyes![15] Truly, the din of many-voiced Life, which, in this solitude, with the mind's organ, I could hear, was no longer a maddening discord, but a melting one; like inarticulate cries, and sobbings of a dumb creature, which in the ear of Heaven are prayers. The poor Earth, with her poor joys, was now my needy Mother, not my cruel Stepdame; Man, with his so mad Wants and so mean Endeavours, had become the dearer to me; and even for his sufferings and his sins, I now first named him Brother. Thus was I standing in the porch of that "Sanctuary of Sorrow";[16] by strange, steep ways had I too been guided thither; and ere long its sacred gates would open, and the "Divine Depth of Sorrow" lie disclosed to me.'

The Professor says, he here first got eye on the Knot that had been strangling him, and straightway could unfasten it, and was free. 'A vain interminable controversy,' writes he, 'touching what is at present called Origin of Evil, or some such thing, arises in every soul, since the beginning of the world; and in every soul, that would pass from idle Suffering into actual Endeavouring, must first be put an end to. The most, in our time, have to go content with a simple, incomplete enough Suppression of this controversy; to a few some Solution of it is indispensable. In every new era, too, such

13. "Peak of Terror," in the Bernese Alps, Switzerland.
14. But if so, surely not identical with the being that wears it!
15. See Revelation 21:4.
16. The phrase is derived from Goethe's novel *Wilhelm Meister's Apprenticeship*, which Carlyle translated.

Solution comes-out in different terms; and ever the Solution of the last era has become obsolete, and is found unserviceable. For it is man's nature to change his Dialect from century to century; he cannot help it though he would. The authentic *Church-Catechism* of our present century has not yet fallen into my hands: meanwhile, for my own private behoof, I attempt to elucidate the matter so. Man's Unhappiness, as I construe, comes of his Greatness; it is because there is an Infinite in him, which with all his cunning he cannot quite bury under the Finite.[17] Will the whole Finance Ministers and Uphol-sterers and Confectioners of modern Europe undertake, in joint-stock company, to make one Shoeblack HAPPY? They cannot accomplish it, above an hour or two; for the Shoeblack also has a Soul quite other than his Stomach; and would require, if you consider it, for his permanent satisfaction and saturation, simply this allotment, no more, and no less: *God's infinite Universe altogether to him-self*, therein to enjoy infinitely, and fill every wish as fast as it rose. Oceans of Hochheimer,[18] a Throat like that of Ophiuchus:[19] speak not of them; to the infinite Shoeblack they are as nothing. No sooner is your ocean filled, than he grumbles that it might have been of better vintage. Try him with half of a Universe, of an Omnipotence, he sets to quarrelling with the proprietor of the other half, and declares himself the most maltreated of men.—Always there is a black spot in our sunshine: it is even as I said, the *Shadow of Ourselves*.

'But the whim we have of Happiness is somewhat thus. By certain valuations, and averages, of our own striking, we come upon some sort of average terrestrial lot; this we fancy belongs to us by nature, and of indefeasible right. It is simple payment of our wages, of our deserts; requires neither thanks nor complaint; only such *overplus* as there may be do we account Happiness; any *deficit* again is Misery. Now consider that we have the valuation of our own deserts ourselves, and what a fund of Self-conceit there is in each of us,—do you wonder that the balance should so often dip the wrong way, and many a Blockhead cry: See there, what a payment; was ever worthy gentleman so used!—I tell thee, Blockhead, it all comes of thy Vanity; of what thou *fanciest* those same deserts of thine to be. Fancy that thou deservest to be hanged (as is most likely), thou wilt feel it happiness to be only shot: fancy that thou deservest to be hanged in a hair-halter, it will be a luxury to die in hemp.

'So true is it, what I then say, that *the Fraction of Life can be increased in value not so much by increasing your Numerator as by lessening your Denom-inator*. Nay, unless my Algebra deceive me, *Unity* itself divided by *Zero* will give *Infinity*. Make thy claim of wages of zero, then; thou hast the world under thy feet. Well did the Wisest of our time write: "It is only with Renuncia-tion (*Entsagen*) that Life, properly speaking, can be said to begin." [20]

'I asked myself: What is this that, ever since earliest years, thou hast been fretting and fuming, and lamenting and self-tormenting, on account of? Say it in a word: is it not because thou art not HAPPY? Because the THOU (sweet gentleman) is not sufficiently honoured, nourished, soft-bedded, and lov-ingly cared for? Foolish soul! What Act of Legislature was there that *thou*

---

17. This idea was central to the thought of the great *Pensées* of Pascal.
18. A Rhine wine from the district of Hochheim.
19. The serpent which is held by a man in the constellation Serpentarius.
20. Goethe in *Wilhelm Meister's Apprenticeship*.

shouldst be Happy? A little while ago thou hadst no right to *be* at all. What if thou wert born and predestined not to be Happy, but to be Unhappy! Art thou nothing other than a Vulture, then, that fliest through the Universe seeking after somewhat to *eat;* and shrieking dolefully because carrion enough is not given thee? Close thy *Byron;* open thy *Goethe.*' [21]

'*Es leuchtet mir ein,* I see a glimpse of it!' [22] cries he elsewhere: 'there is in man a HIGHER than Love of Happiness: he can do without Happiness, and instead thereof find Blessedness! Was it not to preach-forth this same HIGHER than sages and martyrs, the Poet and the Priest, in all times, have spoken and suffered; bearing testimony, through life and through death, of the Godlike that is in Man, and how in the Godlike only has he Strength and Freedom? Which God-inspired Doctrine art thou also honoured to be taught; O Heavens! and broken with manifold merciful Afflictions, even till thou become contrite, and learn it! O, thank thy Destiny for these; thankfully bear what yet remain: thou hadst need of them; the Self in thee needed to be annihilated. By benignant fever-paroxysms is Life rooting out the deep-seated chronic Disease, and triumphs over Death. On the roaring billows of Time, thou art not engulfed, but borne aloft into the azure of Eternity. Love not Pleasure; love God.[23] This is the EVERLASTING YEA, wherein all contradiction is solved: wherein whoso walks and works, it is well with him.'

And again: 'Small is it that thou canst trample the Earth with its injuries under thy feet, as old Greek Zeno [24] trained thee: thou canst love the Earth while it injures thee, and even because it injures thee; for this a Greater than Zeno was needed, and he too was sent.[25] Knowest thou that *"Worship of Sorrow"?* The Temple thereof, founded some eighteen centuries ago, now lies in ruins, overgrown with jungle, the habitation of doleful creatures: nevertheless, venture forward; in a low crypt, arched out of falling fragments, thou findest the Altar still there, and its sacred Lamp perennially burning.'

Without pretending to comment on which strange utterances, the Editor will only remark, that there lies beside them much of a still more questionable character; unsuited to the general apprehension; nay wherein he himself does not see his way. Nebulous disquisitions on Religion, yet not without bursts of splendour; on the 'perennial continuance of Inspiration';  on Prophecy; that there are 'true Priests, as well as Baal-Priests,[26] in our own day': with more of the like sort. We select some fractions, by way of finish to this farrago.[27]

21. By this famous and often-quoted injunction Carlyle means that one should turn from the egoistic mode of apprehending the world which emphasizes the limitations that are put upon man's powers and pleasures and turn to a more objective, less egoistic view which leads to the acceptance of life's conditions and the practical dealing with them.
22. Said by Wilhelm Meister.
23. II Timothy 3:4: "Traitors, needy, high-minded, lovers of pleasure more than lovers of God."
24. Stoic philosopher, 3rd century B.C. Zeno lived to be 98. One day, coming from his school, he fell and broke a finger, whereupon he struck the earth, exclaiming, "I am coming, why do you call me?" and immediately went home and committed suicide.
25. Christ. "The Worship of Sorrow"—the phrase is derived from Goethe—is Christianity, which in its established form ("the Temple") is now ruined, although its essence is to be cherished.
26. Baal is a generic name for false gods.
27. Conglomeration; random mixture.

'Cease, my much-respected Herr von Voltaire,'[28] thus apostrophises the Professor: 'shut thy sweet voice; for the task appointed thee seems finished. Sufficiently hast thou demonstrated this proposition, considerable or otherwise: That the Mythus[29] of the Christian Religion looks not in the eighteenth century as it did in the eighth. Alas, were thy six-and-thirty quartos, and the six-and-thirty thousand other quartos and folios, and flying sheets or reams, printed before and since on the same subject, all needed to convince us of so little! But what next? Wilt thou help us to embody the divine Spirit of that Religion in a new Mythus, in a new vehicle and vesture, that our Souls, otherwise too like perishing, may live? What! thou hast no faculty in that kind? Only a torch for burning, no hammer for building? Take our thanks, then, and——thyself away.

'Meanwhile what are antiquated Mythuses to me? Or is the God present, felt in my own heart, a thing which Herr von Voltaire will dispute out of me; or dispute into me? To the "Worship of Sorrow" ascribe what origin and genesis thou pleasest, has not that Worship originated, and been generated; is it not here? Feel it in thy heart, and then say whether it is of God! This is Belief; all else is Opinion,—for which latter whoso will let him worry and be worried.'

'Neither,' observes he elsewhere, 'shall ye tear-out one another's eyes, struggling over "Plenary Inspiration,"[30] and suchlike: try rather to get a little even Partial Inspiration, each of you for himself. One BIBLE I know, of whose Plenary Inspiration doubt is not so much as possible; nay with my own eyes I saw the God's-Hand writing it: thereof all other Bibles are but leaves,—say, in Picture-Writing to assist the weaker faculty.'[31]

Or, to give the wearied reader relief, and bring it to an end, let him take the following perhaps more intelligible passage:

'To me, in this our life,' says the Professor, 'which is an internecine warfare with the Time-spirit, other warfare seems questionable. Hast thou in any way a Contention with thy brother, I advise thee, think well what the meaning thereof is. If thou gauge it to the bottom, it is simply this: "Fellow, see! thou art taking more than thy share of Happiness in the world, something from my share: which, by the Heavens, thou shalt not; nay I will fight thee rather."— Alas, and the whole lot to be divided is such a beggarly matter, truly a "feast of shells,"[32] for the substance has been spilled out: not enough to quench one Appetite; and the collective human species clutching at them!—Can we not, in all such cases, rather say: "Take it, thou too-ravenous individual; take that pitiful additional fraction of a share, which I reckoned mine, but which thou so wantest; take it with a blessing: would to Heaven I had enough for thee!"— If Fichte's *Wissenschaftslehre*[33] be, "to a certain extent, Applied Christianity,"

28. For Carlyle, Voltaire (1694–1778) often figures as the leader of the movement of skeptical rationalism and therefore as the chief enemy of the spiritual life.
29. Myth, in the sense of a story that explains. The old mythus of Christianity, Carlyle is saying, is doubtless, as Voltaire undertook to show, no longer acceptable, but the essence of Christianity is still precious and can be arrayed in the "clothes" of a new mythus.
30. The doctrine that the Bible is divinely inspired and is literally true in all its statements.
31. Carlyle probably means that the universe is the truly inspired Bible.
32. Empty egg shells; the allusion is obscure.
33. Johann Gottlieb Fichte (1762–1814) published *The Doctrine of Knowledge* in 1794. The quoted description of it was made by Novalis (1772–1801), the German mystical poet.

surely to a still greater extent, so is this. We have here not a Whole Duty of Man,[34] yet a Half Duty, namely the Passive half: could we but do it, as we can demonstrate it!

'But indeed Conviction, were it never so excellent, is worthless till it convert itself into Conduct. Nay properly Conviction is not possible till then; inasmuch as all Speculation is by nature endless, formless, a vortex amid vortices: only by a felt indubitable certainty of Experience does it find any centre to revolve round, and so fashion itself into a system. Most true is it, as a wise man teaches us, that "Doubt of any sort cannot be removed except by Action." [35] On which ground, too, let him who gropes painfully in darkness or uncertain light, and prays vehemently that the dawn may ripen into day, lay this other precept well to heart, which to me was of invaluable service: "*Do the Duty which lies nearest thee,*" [36] which thou knowest to be a Duty! Thy second Duty will already have become clearer.

'May we not say, however, that the hour of Spiritual Enfranchisement is even this: When your Ideal World, wherein the whole man has been dimly struggling and inexpressibly languishing to work, becomes revealed, and thrown open; and you discover, with amazement enough, like the Lothario in *Wilhelm Meister,* that your "America is here or nowhere"? [37] The Situation that has not its Duty, its Ideal, was never yet occupied by man. Yes here, in this poor, miserable, hampered, despicable Actual, wherein thou even now standest, here or nowhere is thy Ideal: work it out therefrom; and working, believe, live, be free. Fool! the Ideal is in thyself, the impediment too is in thyself: thy Condition is but the stuff thou art to shape that same Ideal out of: what matters whether such stuff of this sort or that, so the Form thou give it be heroic, be poetic? O thou that pinest in the imprisonment of the Actual, and criest bitterly to the gods for a kingdom wherein to rule and create, know this of a truth: the thing thou seekest is already with thee, "here or nowhere," couldst thou only see!

'But it is with man's Soul as it was with Nature: the beginning of Creation is—Light.[38] Till the eye have vision, the whole members are in bonds.[39] Divine moment, when over the tempest-tost Soul, as once over the wild-weltering Chaos, it is spoken: Let there be Light! Ever to the greatest that has felt such moment, is it not miraculous and God-announcing; even as, under simpler figures, to the simplest and least. The mad primeval Discord is hushed; the rudely-jumbled conflicting elements bind themselves in to separate Firmaments: deep silent rock-foundations are built beneath; and the skyey vault with its everlasting Luminaries above: instead of a dark wasteful Chaos, we have a blooming, fertile, heaven-encompassed World.

'I too could now say to myself: Be no longer a Chaos, but a World, or even Worldkin. Produce! Produce! Were it but the pitifullest infinitesimal fraction

34. *The Whole Duty of Man* was an enormously popular devotional book of unknown authorship published in 1658.
35. Goethe, in *Wilhelm Meister's Apprenticeship.*
36. *Ibid.*
37. America figures in this statement as the land of promise, where the ideal may be realized.
38. See Genesis 1:3.
39. Derived from Matthew 6:22–23.

of a Product, produce it, in God's name! 'Tis the utmost thou hast in thee: out with it, then. Up, up! Whatsoever thy hand findeth to do, do it with thy whole might. Work while it is called To-day; for the Night cometh, wherein no man can work.'[40]

### Natural Supernaturalism [1]

It is in his stupendous Section, headed Natural Supernaturalism, that the Professor first becomes a Seer; and, after long effort, such as we have witnessed, finally subdues under his feet this refractory Clothes-Philosophy, and takes victorious possession thereof. Phantasms enough he has had to struggle with; 'Cloth-webs and Cobwebs,' of Imperial Mantles, Superannuated Symbols, and what not: yet still did he courageously pierce through. Nay, worst of all, two quite mysterious, world-embracing Phantasms, TIME and SPACE, have ever hovered round him, perplexing and bewildering: but with these also he now resolutely grapples, these also he victoriously rends asunder. In a word, he has looked fixedly on Existence, till, one after the other, its earthly hulls and garnitures have all melted away; and now, to his rapt vision, the interior celestial Holy of Holies lies disclosed.

Here, therefore, properly it is that the Philosophy of Clothes attains to Transcendentalism; this last leap, can we but clear it, takes us safe into the promised land, where Palingenesia,[2] in all senses, may be considered as beginning. 'Courage, then!' may our Diogenes exclaim, with better right than Diogenes the First [3] once did. This stupendous Section we, after long painful meditation, have found not to be unintelligible; but, on the contrary, to grow clear, nay radiant, and all-illuminating. Let the reader, turning on it what utmost force of speculative intellect is in him, do his part; as we, by judicious selection and adjustment, shall study to do ours:

'Deep has been, and is, the significance of Miracles,' thus quietly begins the Professor; 'far deeper perhaps than we imagine. Meanwhile, the question of questions were: What specially is a Miracle? To that Dutch King of Siam, an icicle had been a miracle; [4] whoso had carried with him an air-pump, and vial of vitriolic ether, might have worked a miracle.[5] To my Horse, again, who unhappily is still more unscientific, do not I work a miracle, and magical "Open

---

40. See Ecclesiastes 9:10 and John 9:4.

1. From Bk. III, Chap. VIII. The paradox of the title of this chapter may be said to summarize the doctrine of Sartor Resartus, that the universe is not to be defined by its merely material existence, that its processes are not mechanical. Rather is it a living thing, by implication endowed with purpose and will, which, though they are higher than man's, and inscrutable, are yet cognate with man's own purpose and will. Thus conceived, the universe is a perpetual wonder, which is to say a "miracle." It is not, as Deism taught, a universe contrived by God, who thereafter stands apart from his creation; God is present in the universe, whose "natural" laws are therefore "supernatural."

2. Rebirth.

3. The Cynic philosopher whose legend is that he lived in a tub and went about in daylight with a lantern seeking an honest man. The story is told of him that, as a boring lecture was nearing its end, he cried to his neighbors in the audience, "Courage! I see land."

4. He is referred to in the section on miracles in Hume's Inquiry Concerning Human Understanding (1751).

5. I.e., making ice.

*sesame!"* [6] every time I please to pay twopence, and open for him an impassable *Schlagbaum,* or shut Turnpike?

' "But is not a real Miracle simply a violation of the Laws of Nature?" ask several. Whom I answer by this new question: What are the Laws of Nature? To me perhaps the rising of one from the dead were no violation of these Laws, but a confirmation; were some far deeper Law, now first penetrated into, and by Spiritual Force, even as the rest have all been, brought to bear on us with its Material Force.

'Here too may some inquire, not without astonishment: On what ground shall one, that can make Iron swim,[7] come and declare that therefore he can teach Religion? To us, truly, of the Nineteenth Century, such declaration were inept enough; which nevertheless to our fathers, of the First Century, was full of meaning.

' "But is it not the deepest Law of Nature that she be constant?" cries an illuminated class: "Is not the Machine of the Universe fixed to move by unalterable rules?" Probable enough, good friends: nay I, too, must believe that the God, whom ancient inspired men assert to be "without variableness or shadow of turning," [8] does indeed never change; that Nature, that the Universe, which no one whom it so pleases can be prevented from calling a Machine, does move by the most unalterable rules. And now of you, too, I make the old inquiry: What those same unalterable rules, forming the complete Statute-Book of Nature, may possibly be?

'They stand written in our Works of Science, say you; in the accumulated records of Man's Experience?—Was Man with his Experience present at the Creation, then, to see how it all went on? Have any deepest scientific individuals yet dived-down to the foundations of the Universe, and gauged everything there? Did the Maker take them into His counsel; that they read His ground-plan of the incomprehensible All; and can say, This stands marked therein, and no more than this? Alas, not in anywise! These scientific individuals have been nowhere but where we also are; have seen some hand-breadths deeper than we see into the Deep that is infinite, without bottom as without shore.

'Laplace's [9] Book on the Stars, wherein he exhibits that certain Planets, with their Satellites, gyrate round our worthy Sun, at a rate and in a course, which, by greatest good fortune, he and the like of him have succeeded in detecting,— is to me as precious as to another. But is this what thou namest "Mechanism of the Heavens," and "System of the World"; this, wherein Sirius and the Pleiades, and all Herschel's [10] Fifteen-thousand Suns per minute, being left out, some paltry handful of Moons, and inert Balls, had been—looked at, nicknamed, and

---

6. The magical formula for opening the door of the cave in the story of Ali Baba and the Forty Thieves in *The Arabian Nights.* Sesame is a seed commonly used in the Near East for food and oil.

7. See II Kings 6:6, where Elisha makes an axe-head swim.

8. See James 1:17.

9. The Marquis Pierre Simon de Laplace (1749–1827), the great French astronomer and mathematician, author of *Exposition du système du monde* (1796), the famous conclusion to which is the "Book on the Stars" to which Carlyle refers, and of *Mécanique céleste* (1799–1825), called by Carlyle "Mechanism of the Heavens."

10. Sir William Herschel (1738–1822), English astronomer of German birth who discovered a large number of celestial bodies.

marked in the Zodiacal Way-bill; so that we can now prate of their Whereabout; their How, their Why, their What, being hid from us, as in the signless Inane? 'System of Nature! To the wisest man, wide as is his vision, Nature remains of quite *infinite* depth, of quite infinite expansion; and all Experience thereof limits itself to some few computed centuries and measured square-miles. The course of Nature's phases, on this our little fraction of a Planet, is partially known to us: but who knows what deeper courses these depend on; what infinitely larger Cycle (of causes) our little Epicycle [11] revolves on? To the Minnow every cranny and pebble, and quality and accident, of its little native Creek may have become familiar: but does the Minnow understand the Ocean Tides and periodic Currents, the Trade-winds, and Monsoons, and Moon's Eclipses; by all which the condition of its little Creek is regulated, and may, from time to time (*unmiraculously* enough), be quite overset and reversed? Such a Minnow is Man; his Creek this Planet Earth; his Ocean the immeasurable All; his Monsoons and periodic Currents the mysterious Course of Providence through Æons of Æons.

'We speak of the Volume of Nature: and truly a Volume it is,—whose Author and Writer is God. To read it! Dost thou, does man, so much as well know the Alphabet thereof? With its Words, Sentences, and grand descriptive Pages, poetical and philosophical, spread out through Solar Systems, and Thousands of Years, we shall not try thee. It is a Volume written in celestial hieroglyphs, in the true Sacred-writing; of which even Prophets are happy that they can read here a line and there a line. As for your Institutes, and Academies of Science, they strive bravely; and, from amid the thick-crowded, inextricably intertwisted hieroglyphic writing, pick-out, by dextrous combination, some Letters in the vulgar Character, and therefrom put together this and the other economic Recipe, of high avail in Practice. That Nature is more than some boundless Volume of such Recipes, or huge, well-nigh inexhaustible Domestic-Cookery Book, of which the whole secret will in this manner one day evolve itself, the fewest dream.

'Custom,' continues the Professor, 'doth make dotards of us all.[12] Consider well, thou wilt find that Custom is the greatest of Weavers; and weaves air-raiment for all the Spirits of the Universe; whereby indeed these dwell with us visibly, as ministering servants, in our houses and workshops; but their spiritual nature becomes, to the most, forever hidden. Philosophy complains that Custom has hoodwinked us, from the first; that we do everything by Custom, even Believe by it; that our very Axioms, let us boast of Free-thinking as we may, are oftenest simply such Beliefs as we have never heard questioned. Nay, what is Philosophy throughout but a continual battle against Custom; an ever-renewed effort to *transcend* the sphere of blind Custom, and so become Transcendental?

'Innumerable are the illusions and legerdemain-tricks of Custom: but of all these, perhaps the cleverest is her knack of persuading us that the Miraculous, by simple repetition, ceases to be Miraculous. True, it is by this means we

---

11. In the Ptolemaic system of astronomy a small circle whose center moves on the circumference of a larger circle at whose center is the earth.
12. See *Hamlet* III.i.83: "Thus conscience doth make cowards of us all."

live; for man must work as well as wonder: and herein is Custom so far a kind nurse, guiding him to his true benefit. But she is a fond foolish nurse, or rather we are false foolish nurslings, when, in our resting and reflecting hours, we prolong the same deception. Am I to view the Stupendous with stupid indifference, because I have seen it twice, or two-hundred, or two-million times? There is no reason in Nature or in Art why I should: unless, indeed, I am a mere Work-Machine, for whom the divine gift of Thought were no other than the terrestrial gift of Steam is to the Steam-engine; a power whereby Cotton might be spun, and money and money's worth realised.

'Notable enough too, here as elsewhere, wilt thou find the potency of Names; [13] which indeed are but one kind of such custom-woven, wonder-hiding Garments. Witchcraft, and all manner of Spectre-work, and Demonology, we have now named Madness and Diseases of the Nerves. Seldom reflecting that still the new question comes upon us: What is Madness, what are Nerves? Ever, as before, does Madness remain a mysterious-terrific, altogether *infernal* boiling-up of the Nether Chaotic Deep, through this fair-painted Vision of Creation, which swims thereon, which we name the Real.[14] Was Luther's Picture of the Devil [15] less a Reality, whether it were formed within the bodily eye, or without it? In every the wisest Soul lies a whole world of internal Madness, an authentic Demon Empire; out of which, indeed, his world of Wisdom has been creatively built together; and now rests there, as on its dark foundations does a habitable flowery Earth-rind.

'But deepest of all illusory Appearances, for hiding Wonder, as for many other ends, are your two grand fundamental world-enveloping Appearances, SPACE and TIME.[16] These, as spun and woven for us from before Birth itself, to clothe our celestial ME for dwelling here, and yet to blind it,—lie all-embracing, as the universal canvas, or warp and woof, whereby all minor Illusions, in this Phantasm Existence, weave and paint themselves. In vain, while here on Earth, shall you endeavour to strip them off; you can, at best, but rend them asunder for moments, and look through.

'Fortunatus [17] had a wishing Hat, which when he put on, and wished himself Anywhere, behold he was There. By this means had Fortunatus triumphed over Space, he had annihilated Space; for him there was no Where, but all was Here. Were a Hatter to establish himself, in the Wahngasse of Weissnich-two,[18] and make felts of this sort for all mankind, what a world we should have of it! Still stranger, should, on the opposite side of the street, another Hatter establish himself; and as his fellow-craftsman made Space-annihilating Hats, make Time-annihilating! Of both would I purchase, were it with my last

13. Carlyle refers to the primitive belief that if one knows the name of a person or deity, one can exercise a degree of power over him.

14. This view of the *significance* of madness, although in accord with an established poetic belief, was at odds with the prevailing psychiatry.

15. When the Devil appeared to him as he was translating the Bible, Luther hurled his leaden inkstand at the Tempter.

16. Carlyle writes here under the influence of Immanuel Kant (1724–1804), who, in his *Critique of Pure Reason* (1781), advanced the idea that space and time are forms of perception characteristic of the human mind, not in themselves "realities."

17. The hero of a medieval legend. The magic hat was stolen from the Sultan of Cairo.

18. Folly Alley of the University of Know-not-where.

groschen; [19] but chiefly of this latter. To clap-on your felt, and, simply by wishing that you were Any*where*, straightway to be *There!* Next to clap-on your other felt, and, simply by wishing that you were Any*when*, straightway to be *Then!* This were indeed the grander: shooting at will from the Fire-Creation of the World to its Fire-Consummation; here historically present in the First Century, conversing face to face with Paul and Seneca; [20] there prophetically in the Thirty-first, conversing also face to face with other Pauls and Senecas, who as yet stand hidden in the depth of that late Time!

'Or thinkest thou it were impossible, unimaginable? Is the Past annihilated, then, or only past; is the Future non-extant, or only future? Those mystic faculties of thine, Memory and Hope, already answer: already through those mystic avenues, thou the Earth-blinded summonest both Past and Future, and communest with them, though as yet darkly, and with mute beckonings. The curtains of Yesterday drop down, the curtains of To-morrow roll up; but Yesterday and To-morrow both *are*. Pierce through the Time-element, glance into the Eternal. Believe what thou findest written in the sanctuaries of Man's Soul, even as all Thinkers, in all ages, have devoutly read it there: that Time and Space are not God, but creations of God; that with God as it is a universal HERE, so is it an everlasting NOW.

'And seest thou therein any glimpse of IMMORTALITY?—O Heaven! Is the white Tomb of our Loved One, who died from our arms, and had to be left behind us there, which rises in the distance, like a pale, mournfully receding Milestone, to tell how many toilsome uncheered miles we have journeyed on alone,—but a pale spectral Illusion! [21] Is the lost Friend still mysteriously Here, even as we are Here mysteriously, with God!—Know of a truth that only the Time-shadows have perished, or are perishable; that the real Being of whatever was, and whatever is, and whatever will be, *is* even now and forever. This, should it unhappily seem new, thou mayest ponder at thy leisure; for the next twenty years, or the next twenty centuries: believe it thou must; understand it thou canst not.

'That the Thought-forms, Space and Time, wherein, once for all, we are sent into this Earth to live, should condition and determine our whole Practical reasonings, conceptions, and imagings or imaginings,—seems altogether fit, just, and unavoidable. But that they should, furthermore, usurp such sway over pure spiritual Meditation, and blind us to the wonder everywhere lying close on us, seems nowise so. Admit Space and Time to their due rank as Forms of Thought; nay even, if thou wilt, to their quite undue rank of Realities: and consider, then, with thyself how their thin disguises hide from us the brightest God-effulgences! Thus, were it not miraculous, could I stretch forth my hand and clutch the Sun? Yet thou seest me daily stretch forth my hand and therewith clutch many a thing, and swing it hither and thither. Art thou a grown baby, then, to fancy that the Miracle lies in miles of distance, or in pounds

19. A very small German coin.
20. There was once an unfounded belief that Seneca, the Roman poet and Stoic philosopher, met or corresponded with St. Paul.
21. In the loss of faith in the supernatural elements of Christianity nothing was harder for the Victorians to bear than the negation of personal immortality, the thought that after death they would not be reunited with their loved ones. See Tennyson's *In Memoriam*.

avoirdupois of weight; and not to see that the true inexplicable God-revealing Miracle lies in this, that I can stretch forth my hand at all; that I have free Force to clutch aught therewith? Innumerable other of this sort are the deceptions, and wonder-hiding stupefactions, which Space practises on us.

'Still worse is it with regard to Time. Your grand anti-magician, and universal wonder-hider, is this same lying Time. Had we but the Time-annihilating Hat, to put on for once only, we should see ourselves in a World of Miracles, wherein all fabled or authentic Thaumaturgy, and feats of Magic, were outdone. But unhappily we have not such a Hat; and man, poor fool that he is, can seldom and scantily help himself without one.

'Were it not wonderful, for instance, had Orpheus, or Amphion,[22] built the walls of Thebes by the mere sound of his Lyre? Yet tell me, Who built these walls of Weissnichtwo; summoning-out all the sandstone rocks, to dance along from the Steinbruch [23] (now a huge Troglodyte [24] Chasm, with frightful green-mantled pools); and shape themselves into Doric and Ionic pillars, squared ashlar houses and noble streets? Was it not the still higher Orpheus, or Orpheuses, who, in past centuries, by the divine Music of Wisdom, succeeded in civilising Man? Our highest Orpheus [25] walked in Judea, eighteen hundred years ago: his sphere-melody, flowing in wild native tones, took captive the ravished souls of men; and, being of a truth sphere-melody, still flows and sounds, though now with thousandfold Accompaniments, and rich symphonies, through all our hearts; and modulates, and divinely leads them. Is that a wonder, which happens in two hours; and does it cease to be wonderful if happening in two-million? Not only was Thebes built by the music of an Orpheus; but without the music of some inspired Orpheus was no city ever built, no work that man glories-in ever done.

'Sweep away the Illusion of Time; glance, if thou hast eyes, from the near moving-cause to its far-distant Mover: The stroke that came transmitted through a whole galaxy of elastic balls, was it less a stroke than if the last ball only had been struck, and sent flying? O, could I (with the Time-annihilating Hat) transport thee direct from the Beginnings to the Endings, how were thy eye-sight unsealed, and thy heart set flaming in the Light-sea of celestial wonder! Then sawest thou that this fair Universe, were it in the meanest province thereof, is in very deed the star-domed City of God; [26] that through every star, through every grass-blade, and most through every Living Soul, the glory of a present God still beams. But Nature, which is the Time-vesture of God, and reveals Him to the wise, hides Him from the foolish.

'Again, could anything be more miraculous than an actual authentic Ghost? The English Johnson longed, all his life, to see one; but could not, though he went to Cock Lane,[27] and thence to the church-vaults, and tapped-on coffins.

22. Orpheus was a son of Apollo whose music tamed wild beasts. Amphion was a son of Zeus; his lyre was given to him by Hermes and with its magic he could move stones.
23. Quarry.
24. A prehistoric cave-dweller.
25. Christ.
26. The name of St. Augustine's long treatise.
27. The Cock Lane ghost was very famous in its day, 1762. It made noises at 33 Cock Lane, Smithfield. Upon investigation, in which Dr. Johnson took part, it was discovered to be an imposition practiced by the family who tenanted the house.

Foolish Doctor! Did he never, with the mind's eye as well as with the body's, look round him into that full tide of human Life he so loved; did he never so much as look into Himself? The good Doctor was a Ghost, as actual and authentic as heart could wish; well-nigh a million of Ghosts were travelling the streets by his side. Once more I say, sweep away the illusion of Time; compress the threescore years into three minutes: what else was he, what else are we? Are we not Spirits, that are shaped into a body, into an Appearance; and that fade-away again into air and Invisibility? This is no metaphor, it is a simple scientific *fact:* we start out of Nothingness, take figure, and are Apparitions; round us, as round the veriest spectre, is Eternity; and to Eternity minutes are as years and æons. Come there not tones of Love and Faith, as from celestial harp-strings, like the Song of beatified Souls? And again, do not we squeak and jibber [28] (in our discordant, screech-owlish debatings and recriminatings); and glide bodeful, and feeble, and fearful; or uproar (*poltern*), and revel in our mad Dance of the Dead,—till the scent of the morning air summons us to our still Home; and dreamy Night becomes awake and Day? Where now is Alexander of Macedon: does the steel Host, that yelled in fierce battle-shouts at Issus and Arbela,[29] remain behind him; or have they all vanished utterly, even as perturbed Goblins must? Napoleon too, and his Moscow Retreats and Austerlitz Campaigns! [30] Was it all other than the veriest Spectre-hunt; which has now, with its howling tumult that made Night hideous, flitted away?— Ghosts! There are nigh a thousand-million walking the Earth openly at noontide; some half-hundred have vanished from it, some half-hundred have arisen in it, ere thy watch ticks once.

'O Heaven, it is mysterious, it is awful to consider that we not only carry each a future Ghost within him; but are, in very deed, Ghosts! These Limbs, whence had we them; this stormy Force; this life-blood with its burning Passion? They are dust and shadow; [31] a Shadow-system gathered round our ME; wherein, through some moments or years, the Divine Essence is to be revealed in the Flesh. That warrior on his strong war-horse, fire flashes through his eyes; force dwells in his arm and heart: but warrior and war-horse are a vision; a revealed Force, nothing more. Stately they tread the Earth, as if it were a firm substance: fool! the earth is but a film; it cracks in twain, and warrior and war-horse sink beyond plummet's sounding.[32] Plummet's? Fantasy herself will not follow them. A little while ago, they were not; a little while, and they are not, their very ashes are not.

'So has it been from the beginning, so will it be to the end. Generation after generation takes to itself the Form of a Body; and forth-issuing from Cimmerian [33] Night, on Heaven's mission APPEARS. What Force and Fire is in

28. *Hamlet* I.i.116. The subject of ghosts raises further echoes of the first act of *Hamlet* as the chapter moves to its conclusion.
29. Towns where Alexander defeated Darius and brought about the downfall of the Persian empire.
30. At Austerlitz (1805) Napoleon defeated the combined armies of Austria and Russia.
31. Carlyle translates Horace's phrase "Pulvis et umbra sumus," *Odes* IV.vii.16.
32. A reference to *The Tempest* V.i.56. A plummet is the weight on the end of a line to measure the depth of water.
33. The Cimmerians were a legendary tribe who lived in a land of endless gloom near Hades.

each he expends: one grinding in the mill of Industry; one hunter-like climbing the giddy Alpine heights of Science; one madly dashed in pieces on the rocks of Strife, in war with his fellow:—and then the Heaven-sent is recalled; his earthly Vesture falls away, and soon even to Sense becomes a vanished Shadow. Thus, like some wild-flaming, wild-thundering train of Heaven's Artillery, does this mysterious MANKIND thunder and flame, in long-drawn, quick-succeeding grandeur, through the unknown Deep. Thus, like a God-created, fire-breathing Spirit-host, we emerge from the Inane; haste stormfully across the astonished Earth; then plunge again into the Inane. Earth's mountains are levelled, and her seas filled up, in our passage: can the Earth, which is but dead and a vision, resist Spirits which have reality and are alive? On the hardest adamant some footprint of us is stamped-in; the last Rear of the host will read traces of the earliest Van. But whence?—O Heaven, whither? Sense knows not; Faith knows not; only that it is through Mystery to Mystery, from God and to God.

> We are such stuff
> As Dreams are made of, and our little Life
> Is rounded with a sleep! [34]

1833–34                                                                    1838


# On Heroes, Hero-Worship, and the Heroic in History

### From *The Hero as Poet. Dante; Shakespeare* [1]

The Hero as Divinity, the Hero as Prophet, are productions of old ages; not to be repeated in the new. They presuppose a certain rudeness of conception, which the progress of mere scientific knowledge puts an end to. There needs to be, as it were, a world vacant, or almost vacant of scientific forms, if men in their loving wonder are to fancy their fellow-man either a god or one speaking with the voice of a god. Divinity and Prophet are past. We are now to see our Hero in the less ambitious, but also less questionable, character of Poet; a character which does not pass. The Poet is a heroic figure belonging to all ages; whom all ages possess, when once he is produced, whom the newest age as the oldest may produce;—and will produce, always when Nature pleases. Let Nature send a Hero-soul; in no age is it other than possible that he may be shaped into a Poet.

Hero, Prophet, Poet,—many different names, in different times and places, do we give to Great Men; according to varieties we note in them, according to the sphere in which they have displayed themselves! We might give many more names, on this same principle. I will remark again, however, as a fact not unimportant to be understood, that the different *sphere* constitutes the grand origin of such distinction; that the Hero can be Poet, Prophet, King, Priest or what you will, according to the kind of world he finds himself born

---

34. *The Tempest* IV.i.156–58. Shakespeare says "Dreams are made *on.*"

1. This excerpt is from Lecture III given May 12, 1840; the part of the lecture that deals at length with Dante has been omitted.

into. I confess, I have no notion of a truly great man that could not be *all* sorts of men. The Poet who could merely sit on a chair, and compose stanzas, would never make a stanza worth much. He could not sing the Heroic warrior, unless he himself were at least a Heroic warrior too. I fancy there is in him the Politician, the Thinker, Legislator, Philosopher;—in one or the other degree, he could have been, he is all these. So too I cannot understand how a Mirabeau,[2] with that great glowing heart, with the fire that was in it, with the bursting tears that were in it, could not have written verses, tragedies, poems, touched all hearts in that way, had his course of life and education led him thitherward. The grand fundamental character is that of Great Man; that the man be great. Napoleon has words in him which are like Austerlitz Battles.[3] Louis Fourteenth's Marshals are a kind of poetical men withal; the things Turenne [4] says are full of sagacity and geniality, like sayings of Samuel Johnson. The great heart, the clear deep-seeing eye: there it lies; no man whatever, in what province soever, can prosper at all without these. Petrarch and Boccaccio [5] did diplomatic messages, it seems, quite well: one can easily believe it; they had done things a little harder than these! Burns, a gifted song-writer, might have made a still better Mirabeau. Shakespeare,—one knows not what *he* could not have made, in the supreme degree.

True, there are aptitudes of Nature too. Nature does not make all great men, more than all other men, in the self-same mould. Varieties of aptitude doubtless; but infinitely more of circumstance; and far oftenest it is the *latter* only that are looked to. But it is as with common men in the learning of trades. You take any man, as yet a vague capability of a man, who could be any kind of craftsman; and make him into a smith, a carpenter, a mason: he is then and thenceforth that and nothing else. And if, as Addison complains,[6] you sometimes see a street-porter staggering under his load on spindle-shanks, and near at hand a tailor with the frame of a Samson handling a bit of cloth and small Whitechapel [7] needle,—it cannot be considered that aptitude of Nature alone has been consulted here either!—The Great Man also, to what shall he be bound apprentice? Given your Hero, is he to become Conqueror, King, Philosopher, Poet? It is an inexplicably complex controversial-calculation between the world and him! He will read the world and its laws; the world with its laws will be there to be read. What the world, on *this* matter, shall permit and bid is, as we said, the most important fact about the world.—

Poet and Prophet differ greatly in our loose modern notions of them. In some old languages, again, the titles are synonymous; *Vates* [8] means both Prophet and

2. The brilliant French statesman and orator (1749–91). Of all the leaders of the French Revolution he was the one whom Carlyle most admired.
3. At the battle of Austerlitz (1805), Napoleon defeated the combined armies of Austria and Russia. Napoleon's utterances on mankind, statecraft, and even literature are often memorable.
4. One of the sage and genial things said by this great general (1611–75) was, "God is always on the side of the strongest battalions."
5. Petrarch (1304–74), the great Italian poet and humanist, and Boccaccio (1313–75), the Italian scholar and writer of tales.
6. Joseph Addison (1672–1719), English essayist. He makes the complaint Carlyle refers to in the *Spectator*, No. 307 (February 1712).
7. A poor district of London.
8. The Latin *vates* originally meant soothsayer or seer and came later to mean also poet.

Poet: and indeed at all times, Prophet and Poet, well understood, have much kindred of meaning. Fundamentally indeed they are still the same; in this most important respect especially, That they have penetrated both of them into the sacred mystery of the Universe; what Goethe calls 'the open secret.' [9] 'Which is the great secret?' asks one.—'The *open* secret,'—open to all, seen by almost none! That divine mystery, which lies everywhere in all Beings, 'the Divine Idea of the World, that which lies at the bottom of Appearance,' as Fichte styles it; [10] of which all Appearance, from the starry sky to the grass of the field, but especially the Appearance of Man and his work, is but the *vesture*, the embodiment that renders it visible. This divine mystery *is* in all times and in all places; veritably is. In most times and places it is greatly overlooked; and the Universe, definable always in one or the other dialect, as the realised Thought of God, is considered a trivial, inert, commonplace matter,—as if, says the Satirist,[11] it were a dead thing, which some upholsterer had put together! It could do no good, at present, to *speak* much about this; but it is a pity for every one of us if we do not know it, live ever in the knowledge of it. Really a most mournful pity;—a failure to live at all, if we live otherwise!

But now, I say, whoever may forget this divine mystery, the *Vates*, whether Prophet or Poet, has penetrated into it; is a man sent hither to make it more impressively known to us. That always is his message; he is to reveal that to us,— that sacred mystery which he more than others lives ever present with. While others forget it, he knows it;—I might say, he has been driven to know it; without consent asked of *him*, he finds himself living in it, bound to live in it. Once more, here is no Hearsay, but a direct Insight and Belief; this man too could not help being a sincere man! Whosoever may live in the shows of things, it is for him a necessity of nature to live in the very fact of things. A man, once more, in earnest with the Universe, though all others were but toying with it. He is a *Vates*, first of all, in virtue of being sincere.[12] So far Poet and Prophet, participators in the 'open secret,' are one.

With respect to their distinction again: The *Vates* Prophet, we might say, has seized that sacred mystery rather on the moral side, as Good and Evil, Duty and Prohibition; the *Vates* Poet on what the Germans call the æsthetic side, as Beautiful, and the like. The one we may call a revealer of what we are to do, the other of what we are to love. But indeed these two provinces run into one another, and cannot be disjoined. The Prophet too has his eye on what we are to love: how else shall he know what it is we are to do? The highest Voice ever heard on this earth said withal, 'Consider the lilies of the field; they toil not, neither do they spin: yet Solomon in all his glory was not arrayed like one of these.' [13] A glance, that, into the deepest deep of

9. Carlyle often recurred to this statement of Goethe's, made in his *Maxims and Reflections*. An open secret is a matter that is ostensibly secret but actualy known to all. This open secret is that the universe is informed by spirit.
10. Johann Gottlieb Fichte (1762–1814), German philosopher and political thinker. The passage quoted is from *The Nature of the Scholar* (1805).
11. Carlyle himself. See "Natural Supernaturalism" in *Sartor Resartus*, above.
12. As Emerson remarked in his *English Traits*, the Victorians set great conscious store by the quality of sincerity (which is doubtless why the French said the English were hypocrites). On the value of sincerity Carlyle was the most articulate of the Victorians.
13. Matthew 6:28–29.

Beauty. 'The lilies of the field,'—dressed finer than earthly princes, springing-up there in the humble furrow-field; a beautiful *eye* looking-out on you, from the great inner Sea of Beauty! How could the rude Earth make these, if her Essence, rugged as she looks and is, were not inwardly Beauty? In this point of view, too, a saying of Goethe's, which has staggered several, may have meaning: 'The Beautiful,' he intimates, 'is higher than the Good: the Beautiful includes in it the Good.' The *true* Beautiful; which however, I have said some-where,[14] 'differs from the *false* as Heaven does from Vauxhall!' [15] So much for the distinction and identity of Poet and Prophet.—

In ancient and also in modern periods we find a few Poets who are accounted perfect; whom it were a kind of treason to find fault with. This is noteworthy; this is right: yet in strictness it is only an illusion. At bottom, clearly enough, there is no perfect Poet! A vein of Poetry exists in the hearts of all men; no man is made altogether of Poetry. We are all poets when we *read* a poem well. The 'imagination that shudders at the Hell of Dante,' [16] is not that the same faculty, weaker in degree, as Dante's own? No one but Shakespeare can embody, out of *Saxo Gammaticus,* [17] the story of Hamlet as Shakespeare did: but every one models some kind of story out of it; every one embodies it better or worse. We need not spend time in defining. Where there is no specific difference, as between round and square, all definition must be more or less arbitrary. A man that has *so* much more of the poetic element developed in him as to have become noticeable, will be called Poet by his neighbours. World-Poets too, those whom we are to take for perfect Poets, are settled by critics in the same way. One who rises *so* far above the general level of Poets will, to such and such critics, seem a Universal Poet; as he ought to do. And yet it is, and must be, an arbitrary distinction. All Poets, all men, have some touches of the Universal; no man is wholly made of that. Most Poets are very soon for-gotten: but not the noblest Shakespeare or Homer of them can be remembered *forever;*—a day comes when he too is not!

Nevertheless, you will say, there must be a difference between true Poetry and true Speech not poetical: what is the difference? On this point many things have been written, especially by late German Critics, some of which are not very intelligible at first. They say, for example, that the Poet has an *infinitude* in him; communicates an *Unendlichkeit,* a certain character of 'infinitude,' to whatsoever he delineates. This, though not very precise, yet on so vague a matter is worth remembering: if well meditated, some meaning will gradually be found in it. For my own part, I find considerable meaning in the old vulgar distinction of Poetry being *metrical,*[18] having music in it, being a Song. Truly, if pressed to give a definition, one might say this as soon as anything else: If your delineation be authentically *musical,* musical, not in word only, but in heart and substance, in all the thoughts and utterances

14. In his essay on Diderot.
15. A public garden on the Thames in London, in which evening entertainment of various kinds was provided. It was opened in 1661 and closed in 1859.
16. Carlyle quotes from his own essay on Burns.
17. The Danish historian of the 13th century whose *Gesta Danorum* tells the story of Hamlet.
18. On the relation of meter to the essential nature of poetry, see Wordsworth, Preface to *Lyrical Ballads,* and Coleridge, *Biographia Literaria,* Chap. XIV.

of it, in the whole conception of it, then it will be poetical; if not, not.—
Musical: how much lies in that! A *musical* thought is one spoken by a mind
that has penetrated into the inmost heart of the thing; detected the inmost
mystery of it, namely the *melody* that lies hidden in it; the inward harmony
of coherence which is its soul, whereby it exists, and has a right to be, here
in this world. All inmost things, we may say, are melodious; naturally utter
themselves in Song. The meaning of Song goes deep. Who is there that, in
logical words, can express the effect music has on us? A kind of inarticulate
unfathomable speech, which leads us to the edge of the Infinite, and lets us
for moments gaze into that!

Nay all speech, even the commonest speech, has something of song in it:
not a parish in the world but has its parish-accent;—the rhythm or *tune* to
which the people there *sing* what they have to say! Accent is a kind of
chanting; all men have accent of their own,—though they only *notice* that of
others. Observe too how all passionate language does of itself become musical,
—with a finer music than the mere accent; the speech of a man even in
zealous anger becomes a chant, a song. All deep things are Song. It seems
somehow the very central essence of us, Song; as if all the rest were but
wrappages and hulls! The primal element of us; of us, and of all things. The
Greeks fabled of Sphere-Harmonies; it was the feeling they had of the inner
structure of Nature; that the soul of all her voices and utterances was perfect
music. Poetry, therefore, we will call *musical Thought*. The Poet is he who
*thinks* in that manner. At bottom, it turns still on power of intellect; it is a
man's sincerity and depth of vision that makes him a Poet. See deep enough,
and you see musically; the heart of Nature *being* everywhere music, if you
can only reach it.

The *Vates* Poet, with his melodious Apocalypse of Nature, seems to hold a
poor rank among us, in comparison with the *Vates* Prophet; his function, and
our esteem of him for his function, alike slight. The Hero taken as Divinity;
the Hero taken as Prophet; then next the Hero taken only as Poet: does it
not look as if our estimate of the Great Man, epoch after epoch, were continually diminishing? We take him first for a god, then for one god-inspired;
and now, in the next stage of it, his most miraculous word gains from us only
the recognition that he is a Poet, beautiful verse-maker, man of genius, or
suchlike!—It looks so; but I persuade myself that intrinsically it is not so.
If we consider well, it will perhaps appear that in man still there is the *same*
altogether peculiar admiration for the Heroic Gift, by what name soever
called, that there at any time was.

I should say, if we do not now reckon a Great Man literally divine, it is
that our notions of God, of the supreme unattainable Fountain of Splendour,
Wisdom and Heroism, are ever rising *higher;* not altogether that our reverence
for these qualities, as manifested in our like, is getting lower. This is worth
taking thought of. Sceptical Dilettantism,[19] the curse of these ages, a curse
which will not last forever, does indeed in this the highest province of human

19. A dilettante is a dabbler in the arts. By dilettantism Carlyle means a general lack of
intellectual and moral seriousness.

things, as in all provinces, make sad work; and our reverence for great men, all crippled, blinded, paralytic as it is, comes out in poor plight, hardly recognisable. Men worship the shows of great men; the most disbelieve that there is any reality of great men to worship. The dreariest, fatallest faith; believing which, one would literally despair of human things. Nevertheless look, for example, at Napoleon! A Corsican lieutenant of artillery; that is the show of *him:* yet is he not obeyed, *worshipped* after his sort, as all the Tiaraed and Diademed [20] of the world put together could not be? High Duchesses, and ostlers [21] of inns, gather round the Scottish rustic, Burns;—a strange feeling dwelling in each that they had never heard a man like this; that, on the whole, this is the man! In the secret heart of these people it still dimly reveals itself, though there is no accredited way of uttering it at present, that this rustic, with his black brows and flashing sun-eyes, and strange words moving laughter and tears, is of a dignity far beyond all others, incommensurable with all others. Do not we feel it so? But now, were Dilettantism, Scepticism, Triviality, and all that sorrowful brood, cast-out of us,—as, by God's blessing, they shall one day be; were faith in the shows of things entirely swept-out, replaced by clear faith in the *things,* so that a man acted on the impulse of that only, and counted the other non-extant; what a new livelier feeling towards this Burns were it!

Nay here in these pages, such as they are, have we not two mere Poets, if not deified, yet we may say beatified? Shakespeare and Dante are Saints of Poetry; really, if we will think of it, *canonised,* so that it is impiety to meddle with them. The unguided instinct of the world, working across all these perverse impediments, has arrived at such result. Dante and Shakespeare are a peculiar Two. They dwell apart, in a kind of royal solitude; none equal, none second to them: in the general feeling of the world, a certain transcendentalism, a glory as of complete perfection, invests these two. They *are* canonised, though no Pope or Cardinals took hand in doing it! Such, in spite of every perverting influence, in the most unheroic times, is still our indestructible reverence for heroism.—We will look a little at these Two, the Poet Dante and the Poet Shakespeare: what little it is permitted us to say here of the Hero as Poet will most fitly arrange itself in that fashion. . . .

As Dante, the Italian man, was sent into our world to embody musically the Religion of the Middle Ages, the Religion of our Modern Europe, its Inner Life; so Shakespeare, we may say, embodies for us the Outer Life of our Europe as developed then, its chivalries, courtesies, humours, ambitions, what practical way of thinking, acting, looking at the world, men then had. As in Homer we may still construe Old Greece; so in Shakespeare and Dante, after thousands of years, what our modern Europe was, in Faith and in Practice, will still be legible. Dante has given us the Faith or soul; Shakespeare, in a not less noble way, has given us the Practice or body. This latter also we were

20. That is, the elite and powerful. A tiara is a jewelled headdress worn by women on formal occasions; a diadem is a royal headdress.
21. An ostler (or hostler) was the man who took charge of horses at an inn.

to have: a man was sent for it, the man Shakespeare. Just when that chivalry way of life had reached its last finish, and was on the point of breaking down into slow or swift dissolution, as we now see it everywhere, this other sovereign Poet, with his seeing eye, with his perennial singing voice, was sent to take note of it, to give long-enduring record of it. Two fit men: Dante, deep, fierce as the central fire of the world; Shakespeare, wide, placid, far-seeing, as the Sun, the upper light of the world. Italy produced the one world-voice; we English had the honour of producing the other.

Curious enough how, as it were by mere accident, this man came to us. I think always, so great, quiet, complete and self-sufficing is this Shakespeare, had the Warwickshire Squire [22] not prosecuted him for deer-stealing, we had perhaps never heard of him as a Poet! The woods and skies, the rustic Life of Man in Stratford there, had been enough for this man! But indeed that strange outbudding of our whole English Existence, which we call the Elizabethan Era, did not it too come as of its own accord? The 'Tree Igdrasil' [23] buds and withers by its own laws,—too deep for our scanning. Yet it does bud and wither, and every bough and leaf of it is there, by fixed eternal laws; not a Sir Thomas Lucy but comes at the hour fit for him. Curious, I say, and not sufficiently considered: how everything does coöperate with all; not a leaf rotting on the highway but is indissoluble portion of solar and stellar systems; no thought, word or act of man but has sprung withal out of all men, and works sooner or later, recognisably or irrecognisably, on all men! It is all a Tree: circulation of sap and influences, mutual communication of every minutest leaf with the lowest talon of a root, with every other greatest and minutest portion of the whole. The Tree Igdrasil, that has its roots down in the Kingdoms of Hela [24] and Death, and whose boughs overspread the highest Heaven!—

In some sense it may be said that this glorious Elizabethan Era with its Shakespeare, as the outcome and flowerage of all which had preceded it, is itself attributable to the Catholicism of the Middle Ages. The Christian Faith, which was the theme of Dante's Song, had produced this Practical Life which Shakespeare was to sing. For Religion then, as it now and always is, was the soul of Practice; the primary vital fact in men's life. And remark here, as rather curious, that Middle-Age Catholicism was abolished, so far as Acts of Parliament could abolish it, before Shakespeare, the noblest product of it, made his appearance.[25] He did make his appearance nevertheless. Nature at her own time, with Catholicism or what else might be necessary, sent him forth; taking small thought of Acts of Parliament. King-Henrys, Queen-Elizabeths [26] go their way; and Nature too goes hers. Acts of Parliament, on

---

22. He is named below—the Sir Thomas Lucy who is said to have prosecuted Shakespeare for deer-stealing and to be the original of the Justice Shallow of II *Henry IV* and *The Merry Wives of Windsor.*

23. In Northern mythology Igdrasil (or Yggdrasil) is the "world tree" which represents all living nature; it supports heaven and connects heaven, earth, and hell.

24. Hela (or Hel) was the daughter of the malevolent god Loki. She was the queen of the dead and the lower regions and lived under the roots of the tree Igdrasil.

25. In 1534.

26. The Tudor monarchs instrumental in suppressing Catholicism in England.

the whole, are small, notwithstanding the noise they make. What Act of Parliament, debate at St. Stephen's,[27] on the hustings [28] or elsewhere, was it that brought this Shakespeare into being? No dining at Freemasons' Tavern, opening subscription-lists, selling of shares, and infinite other jangling and true or false endeavouring! This Elizabethan Era, and all its nobleness and blessedness, came without proclamation, preparation of ours. Priceless Shakespeare was the free gift of Nature; given altogether silently;—received altogether silently, as if it had been a thing of little account. And yet, very literally, it is a priceless thing. One should look at that side of matters too.

Of this Shakespeare of ours, perhaps the opinion one sometimes hears a little idolatrously expressed is, in fact, the right one; I think the best judgment not of this country only, but of Europe at large, is slowly pointing to the conclusion, That Shakespeare is the chief of all Poets hitherto; the greatest intellect who, in our recorded world, has left record of himself in the way of Literature. On the whole, I know not such a power of vision, such a faculty of thought, if we take all the characters of it, in any other man. Such a calmness of depth; placid joyous strength; all things imaged in that great soul of his so true and clear, as in a tranquil unfathomable sea! It has been said, that in the constructing of Shakespeare's Dramas there is, apart from all other 'faculties' as they are called, an understanding manifested, equal to that in Bacon's *Novum Organum*.[29] That is true; and it is not a truth that strikes every one. It would become more apparent if we tried, any of us for himself, how, out of Shakespeare's dramatic materials, *we* could fashion such a result! The built house seems all so fit,—everyway as it should be, as if it came there by its own law and the nature of things,—we forget the rude disorderly quarry it was shaped from. The very perfection of the house, as if Nature herself had made it, hides the builder's merit. Perfect, more perfect than any other man, we may call Shakespeare in this: he discerns, knows as by instinct, what condition he works under, what his materials are, what his own force and its relation to them is. It is not a transitory glance of insight that will suffice; it is deliberate illumination of the whole matter; it is a calmly *seeing* eye; a great intellect, in short. How a man, of some wide thing that he has witnessed, will construct a narrative, what kind of picture and delineation he will give of it,—is the best measure you could get of what intellect is in the man. Which circumstance is vital and shall stand prominent; which unessential, fit to be suppressed; where is the true *beginning*, the true sequence and ending? To find out this, you task the whole force of insight that is in the man. He must *understand* the thing; according to the depth of his understanding, will the fitness of his answers be. You will try him so. Does like join itself to like; does the spirit of method stir in that confusion, so that its embroilment becomes order? Can the man say, *Fiat lux*, Let there be

27. In the reign of Edward VI, St. Stephen's Chapel, Westminster, was assigned to the use of Parliament. The House of Commons continued to sit here until 1834, when the chapel was destroyed by fire.
28. A platform from which political candidates address the voters; political campaigning in general. The word is not in use in America.
29. The treatise (1620) in which Francis Bacon undertook to describe the intellectual method by which man could extend his dominion over nature.

light; [30] and out of chaos make a world? Precisely as there is *light* in himself, will he accomplish this.

Or indeed we may say again, it is in what I called Portrait-painting, delineating of men and things, especially of men, that Shakespeare is great. All the greatness of the man comes out decisively here. It is unexampled, I think, that calm creative perspicacity of Shakespeare. The thing he looks at reveals not this or that face of it, but its inmost heart, and generic secret: it dissolves itself as in light before him, so that he discerns the perfect structure of it. Creative, we said: poetic creation, what is this too but *seeing* the thing sufficiently? The *word* that will describe the thing, follows of itself from such clear intense sight of the thing. And is not Shakespeare's *morality*, his valour, candour, tolerance, truthfulness; his whole victorious strength and greatness, which can triumph over such obstructions, visible there too? Great as the world! No *twisted*, poor convex-concave mirror, reflecting all objects with its own convexities and concavities; a perfectly *level* mirror;—that is to say withal, if we will understand it, a man justly related to all things and men, a good man. It is truly a lordly spectacle how this great soul takes-in all kinds of men and objects, a Falstaff, an Othello, a Juliet, a Coriolanus; sets them all forth to us in their round completeness; loving, just, the equal brother of all. *Novum Organum*, and all the intellect you will find in Bacon, is of a quite secondary order; earthly, material, poor in comparison with this. Among modern men, one finds, in strictness, almost nothing of the same rank. Goethe alone, since the days of Shakespeare, reminds me of it. Of him too you say that he *saw* the object; you may say what he himself says of Shakespeare: 'His characters are like watches with dial-plates of transparent crystal; they show you the hour like others, and the inward mechanism also is all visible.'

The seeing eye! It is this that discloses the inner harmony of things; what Nature meant, what musical idea Nature has wrapped-up in these often rough embodiments. Something she did mean. To the seeing eye that something were discernible. Are they base, miserable things? You can laugh over them, you can weep over them; you can in some way or other genially relate yourself to them;—you can, at lowest, hold your peace about them, turn away your own and others' face from them, till the hour come for practically exterminating and extinguishing them! At bottom, it is the Poet's first gift, as it is all men's, that he have intellect enough. He will be a Poet if he have: a Poet in word; or failing that, perhaps still better, a Poet in act. Whether he write at all; and if so, whether in prose or in verse, will depend on accidents: who knows on what extremely trivial accidents,—perhaps on his having had a singing-master, on his being taught to sing in his boyhood! But the faculty which enables him to discern the inner heart of things, and the harmony that dwells there (for whatsoever exists has a harmony in the heart of it, or it would not hold together and exist), is not the result of habits or accidents, but the gift of Nature herself; the primary outfit for a Heroic Man in what sort soever. To the Poet, as to every other, we say first of all, *See.* If you cannot do that, it is of no use to keep stringing rhymes together, jingling sensibilities against each other, and *name* yourself a Poet; there is no hope for you. If you can,

30. Genesis 1:3.

there is, in prose or verse, in action or speculation, all manner of hope. The crabbed old Schoolmaster used to ask, when they brought him a new pupil, 'But are ye sure he's *not a dunce?*'[31] Why, really one might ask the same thing, in regard to every man proposed for whatsoever function; and consider it as the one inquiry needful: Are ye sure he's not a dunce? There is, in this world, no other entirely fatal person.

For, in fact, I say the degree of vision that dwells in a man is a correct measure of the man. If called to define Shakespeare's faculty, I should say superiority of Intellect, and think I had included all under that. What indeed are faculties? We talk of faculties as if they were distinct, things separable; as if a man had intellect, imagination, fancy, &c., as he has hands, feet and arms. That is a capital error. Then again, we hear of a man's 'intellectual nature,' and of his 'moral nature,' as if these again were divisible, and existed apart. Necessities of language do perhaps prescribe such forms of utterance; we must speak, I am aware, in that way, if we are to speak at all. But words ought not to harden into things for us. It seems to me, our apprehension of this matter is, for the most part, radically falsified thereby. We ought to know withal, and to keep for ever in mind, that these divisions are at bottom but *names;* that man's spiritual nature, the vital Force which dwells in him, is essentially one and indivisible; that what we call imagination, fancy, understanding, and so forth, are but different figures of the same Power of Insight, all indissolubly connected with each other, physiognomically related; that if we knew one of them, we might know all of them. Morality itself, what we call the moral quality of a man, what is this but another *side* of the one vital Force whereby he is and works? All that a man does is physiognomical of him. You may see how a man would fight, by the way in which he sings; his courage, or want of courage, is visible in the word he utters, in the opinion he has formed, no less than in the stroke he strikes. He is *one;* and preaches the same Self abroad in all these ways.

Without hands a man might have feet, and could still walk: but, consider it, without morality, intellect were impossible for him; a thoroughly immoral *man* could not know anything at all! To know a thing, what we can call knowing, a man must first *love* the thing, sympathise with it: that is, be *virtuously* related to it. If he have not the justice to put down his own selfishness at every turn, the courage to stand by the dangerous-true at every turn, how shall he know? His virtues, all of them, will lie recorded in his knowledge. Nature, with her truth, remains to the bad, to the selfish and the pusillanimous forever a sealed book: what such can know of Nature is mean, superficial, small; for the uses of the day merely.—But does not the very Fox know something of Nature? Exactly so: it knows where the geese lodge! The human Reynard,[32] very frequent everywhere in the world, what more does he know but this and the like of this? Nay, it should be considered, too, that if the Fox had not a certain vulpine [33] *morality,* he could not even know where the geese were, or get at the geese! If he spent his time in splenetic atrabiliar [34]

---

31. This schoolmaster was known to Carlyle in his boyhood.
32. The name under which a fox figures in several satirical beast-fables of the Middle Ages.
33. Of or pertaining to a fox (from *vulpes,* Latin for fox).
34. Splenetic: ill-humored, peevish; atrabiliar: inclined to melancholy, surly.

reflections on his own misery, his ill usage by Nature, Fortune and other Foxes, and so forth; and had not courage, promptitude, practicality, and other suitable vulpine gifts and graces, he would catch no geese. We may say of the Fox too, that his morality and insight are of the same dimensions; different faces of the same internal unity of vulpine life!—These things are worth stating; for the contrary of them acts with manifold very baleful perversion, in this time: what limitations, modifications they require, your own candour will supply.

If I say, therefore, that Shakespeare is the greatest of Intellects, I have said all concerning him. But there is more in Shakespeare's intellect than we have yet seen. It is what I call an unconscious intellect; there is more virtue in it than he himself is aware of. Novalis beautifully remarks of him, that those Dramas of his are Products of Nature too, deep as Nature herself. I find a great truth in this saying. Shakespeare's Art is not Artifice; the noblest worth of it is not there by plan or precontrivance.[35] It grows-up from the deeps of Nature, through this noble sincere soul, who is a voice of Nature. The latest generations of men will find new meanings in Shakespeare, new elucidations of their own human being; 'new harmonies with the infinite structure of the Universe; concurrences with later ideas, affinities with the higher powers and senses of man.' This well deserves meditating. It is Nature's highest reward to a true simple great soul, that he get thus to be *a part of herself.* Such a man's works, whatsoever he with utmost conscious exertion and forethought shall accomplish, grow up withal *un*consciously,[36] from the unknown deeps in him;—as the oak-tree grows from the Earth's bosom, as the mountains and waters shape themselves; with a symmetry grounded on Nature's own laws, conformable to all Truth whatsoever. How much in Shakespeare lies hid; his sorrows, his silent struggles known to himself; much that was not known at all, not speakable at all; like *roots,* like sap and forces working underground! Speech is great; but Silence is greater.[37]

Withal the joyful tranquillity of this man is notable. I will not blame Dante for his misery: it is as battle without victory; but true battle,—the first, indispensable thing. Yet I call Shakespeare greater than Dante, in that he fought truly, and did conquer. Doubt it not, he had his own sorrows: those *Sonnets* of his will even testify expressly in what deep waters he had waded, and swum struggling for his life;—as what man like him ever failed to have to do? It seems to me a heedless notion, our common one, that he sat like a bird on the bough; and sang forth, free and offhand, never knowing the troubles of other men. Not so; with no man is it so. How could a man travel forward from rustic deer-poaching to such tragedy-writing, and not fall-in with sorrows by the way? Or, still better, how could a man delineate a Hamlet, a Coriolanus, a Macbeth, so many suffering heroic hearts, if his own heroic heart had never suffered?—And now, in contrast with all this, observe his

---

35. See Coleridge on Shakespeare and the organic nature of his art.
36. For the unconsciousness of artistic creation, see Shelley, *A Defence of Poetry.* Carlyle set great store by the idea that the mind was at its best and most likely to approach truth when it was not aware of its processes.
37. It is a common joke about Carlyle that no one has uttered so many words about silence as he.

mirthfulness, his genuine overflowing love of laughter! You would say, in no point does he *exaggerate* but only in laughter. Fiery objurgations, words that pierce and burn, are to be found in Shakespeare; yet he is always in measure here; never what Johnson would remark as a specially 'good hater.' [38] But his laughter seems to pour from him in floods; he heaps all manner of ridiculous nicknames on the butt he is bantering, tumbles and tosses him in all sorts of horse-play; you would say, with his whole heart laughs. And then, if not always the finest, it is always a genial laughter. Not at mere weakness, at misery or poverty; never. No man who *can* laugh, what we call laughing, will laugh at these things. It is some poor character only *desiring* to laugh, and have the credit of wit, that does so. Laughter means sympathy; good laughter is not 'the crackling of thorns under the pot.' [39] Even at stupidity and pretension this Shakespeare does not laugh otherwise than genially. Dogberry and Verges [40] tickle our very hearts; and we dismiss them covered with explosions of laughter: but we like the poor fellows only the better for our laughing; and hope they will get on well there, and continue Presidents of the City-watch. [41] Such laughter, like sunshine on the deep sea, is very beautiful to me.

.  .  .

. . . His [Shakespeare's] works are so many windows, through which we see a glimpse of the world that was in him. All his works seem, comparatively speaking, cursory, imperfect, written under cramping circumstances; giving only here and there a note of the full utterance of the man. Passages there are that come upon you like splendour out of Heaven; bursts of radiance, illuminating the very heart of the thing: you say, 'That is *true*, spoken once and forever; wheresoever and whensoever there is an open human soul, that will be recognised as true!' Such bursts, however, make us feel that the surrounding matter is not radiant; that it is, in part, temporary, conventional. Alas, Shakespeare had to write for the Globe Play-house: his great soul had to crush itself, as it could, into that and no other mould. It was with him, then, as it is with us all. No man works save under conditions. The sculptor cannot set his own free Thought before us; but his Thought as he could translate it into the stone that was given, with the tools that were given. *Disjecta membra* [42] are all that we find of any Poet, or of any man.

Whoever looks intelligently at this Shakespeare may recognise that he too was a *Prophet*, in his way; of an insight analogous to the Prophetic, though he took it up in another strain. Nature seemed to this man also divine; *unspeakable*, deep as Tophet, [43] high as Heaven: 'We are such stuff as Dreams

---

38. The remark, made by Johnson about his friend Richard Bathurst, was recorded by Mrs. Thrale in her *Anecdotes of the Late Samuel Johnson* (1786).
39. Ecclesiastes 6:6.
40. Comic characters in *Much Ado About Nothing*.
41. Dogberry and Verges are both members of the watch, or police force, of the city of Messina.
42. "Scattered parts."
43. Hebrew word for hell.

are made of!' [44] That scroll in Westminster Abbey,[45] which few read with understanding, is of the depth of any seer. But the man sang; did not preach, except musically. We called Dante the melodious Priest of Middle-Age Catholicism. May we not call Shakespeare the still more melodious Priest of a *true* Catholicism, the 'Universal Church' of the Future and of all times? No narrow superstition, harsh asceticism, intolerance, fanatical fierceness or perversion: a Revelation, so far as it goes, that such a thousandfold hidden beauty and divineness dwells in all Nature; which let all men worship as they can! We may say without offence, that there rises a kind of universal Psalm out of this Shakespeare too; not unfit to make itself heard among the still more sacred Psalms. Not in disharmony with these, if we understood them, but in harmony! —I cannot call this Shakespeare a 'Sceptic,' as some do; his indifference to the creeds and theological quarrels of his time misleading them. No: neither unpatriotic, though he says little about his Patriotism; nor sceptic, though he says little about his Faith. Such 'indifference' was the fruit of his greatness withal: his whole heart was in his own grand sphere of worship (we may call it such): these other controversies, vitally important to other men, were not vital to him.

But call it worship, call it what you will, is it not a right glorious thing, and set of things, this that Shakespeare has brought us? For myself, I feel that there is actually a kind of sacredness in the fact of such a man being sent into this Earth. Is he not an eye to us all; a blessed heaven-sent Bringer of Light? —And, at bottom, was it not perhaps far better that this Shakespeare, everyway an unconscious man, was *conscious* of no Heavenly message? He did not feel, like Mahomet, because he saw into those internal Splendours, that he specially was the 'Prophet of God': and was he not greater than Mahomet in that? Greater; and also, if we compute strictly, as we did in Dante's case, more successful. It was intrinsically an error that notion of Mahomet's, of his supreme Prophethood: and has come down to us inextricably involved in error to this day; dragging along with it such a coil of fables, impurities, intolerances, as makes it a questionable step for me here and now to say, as I have done, that Mahomet was a true Speaker at all, and not rather an ambitious charlatan, perversity and simulacrum; no Speaker, but a Babbler! Even in Arabia, as I compute, Mahomet will have exhausted himself and become obsolete, while this Shakespeare, this Dante may still be young;—while this Shakespeare may still pretend to be a Priest of Mankind, of Arabia as of other places, for unlimited periods to come!

Compared with any speaker or singer one knows, even with Æschylus or Homer, why should he not, for veracity and universality, last like them? He is *sincere* as they; reaches deep down like them, to the universal and perennial. But as for Mahomet, I think it had been better for him *not* to be so conscious! Alas, poor Mahomet; all that he was *conscious* of was a mere error; a futility

---

44. *The Tempest* IV.i.157. Here, as in his quotation of the passage at the end of the "Natural Supernaturalism" chapter of *Sartor Resartus,* Carlyle substitutes "made of" for Shakespeare's "made on."

45. Carlyle refers to the statue, designed by William Kent, which is part of the memorial to Shakespeare set up in the Poets' Corner of Westminster Abbey in 1741. The line just quoted is inscribed on the scroll that Shakespeare holds.

and triviality,—as indeed such ever is. The truly great in him too was the unconscious: that he was a wild Arab lion of the desert, and did speak-out with that great thunder-voice of his, not by words which he *thought* to be great, but by actions, by feelings, by a history which *were* great! His Koran [46] has become a stupid piece of prolix absurdity; we do not believe, like him, that God wrote that! The Great Man here too, as always, is a Force of Nature: whatsoever is truly great in him springs-up from the *in*articulate deeps.

Well: this is our poor Warwickshire Peasant, who rose to be Manager of a Playhouse, so that he could live without begging; whom the Earl of Southampton [47] cast some kind glances on; whom Sir Thomas Lucy, many thanks to him, was for sending to the Treadmill! [48] We did not account him a god, like Odin, while he dwelt with us;—on which point there were much to be said. But I will say rather, or repeat: In spite of the sad state Hero-worship now lies in, consider what this Shakespeare has actually become among us. Which Englishman we ever made, in this land of ours, which million of Englishmen, would we not give-up rather than the Stratford Peasant? There is no regiment of highest Dignitaries that we would sell him for. He is the grandest thing we have yet done. For our honour among foreign nations, as an ornament to our English Household, what item is there that we would not surrender rather than him? Consider now, if they asked us, Will you give-up your Indian Empire or your Shakespeare, you English; never have had any Indian Empire, or never have had any Shakespeare? Really it were a grave question. Official persons would answer doubtless in official language; but we, for our part too, should not we be forced to answer: Indian Empire, or no Indian Empire; we cannot do without Shakespeare! Indian Empire will go, at any rate, some day; but this Shakespeare does not go, he lasts forever with us; we cannot give-up our Shakespeare!

Nay, apart from spiritualities; and considering him merely as a real, marketable, tangibly-useful possession. England, before long, this Island of ours, will hold but a small fraction of the English: in America, in New Holland, east and west to the very Antipodes, there will be a Saxondom covering great spaces of the Globe. And now, what is it that can keep all these together into virtually one Nation, so that they do not fall-out and fight, but live at peace, in brotherlike intercourse, helping one another? This is justly regarded as the greatest practical problem, the thing all manner of sovereignties and governments are here to accomplish: what is it that will accomplish this? Acts of Parliament, administrative prime-ministers cannot. America is parted from us, so far as Parliament could part it. Call it not fantastic, for there is much reality in it: Here, I say, is an English King, whom no time or chance, Parliament or combination of Parliaments, can dethrone! This King Shakespeare, does not he shine, in crowned sovereignty, over us all, as the noblest, gentlest, yet strongest of rallying-signs; *in*destructible; really more valuable in that point of view than any other means or appliance whatsoever? We can fancy

46. The Bible of Mohammedans. It is considered to be the Word of God communicated directly to Mohammed.
47. Henry Wriothesley, 3rd Earl of Southampton (1573–1624), was Shakespeare's patron.
48. A mill worked by persons who tread on steps on the periphery of a large wheel having a horizontal axis. It was once used in prisons, but not in Shakespeare's day.

him as radiant aloft over all the Nations of Englishmen, a thousand years hence. From Paramatta, from New York, wheresoever, under what sort of Parish-Constable soever, English men and women are, they will say to one another: 'Yes, this Shakespeare is ours; we produced him, we speak and think by him; we are of one blood and kind with him.' The most common-sense politician, too, if he pleases, may think of that.

Yes, truly, it is a great thing for a Nation that it get an articulate voice; that it produce a man who will speak-forth melodiously what the heart of it means! Italy, for example, poor Italy lies dismembered, scattered asunder, not appearing in any protocol or treaty as a unity at all; yet the noble Italy is actually *one:* Italy produced its Dante; Italy can speak! The Czar of all the Russias, he is strong, with so many bayonets, Cossacks [49] and cannons; and does a great feat in keeping such a tract of Earth politically together; but he cannot yet speak. Something great in him, but it is a dumb greatness. He has had no voice of genius, to be heard of all men and times. He must learn to speak. He is a great dumb monster hitherto. His cannons and Cossacks will all have rusted into nonentity, while that Dante's voice is still audible. The Nation that has a Dante is bound together as no dumb Russia can be.—We must here end what we had to say of the *Hero-Poet.*

1840                                                                                                    1841

## Past and Present

In 1837 English industry entered a period of depression which was to continue for some years to come. Unemployment was general and the wages of those who did still have work were often inadequate to meet the costs of the barest necessities. The gravity of the crisis is made plain by the official count of paupers in England and Wales for March 1842—1,429,089, or one out of every eleven persons in the population. Carlyle, in the intensity of his distress over the suffering of the working class, found it impossible to continue work on his life of Cromwell, and in December of 1842 he laid it aside to write *Past and Present,* which he did at incredible speed, finishing it in two months. It was published in April 1843. Perhaps no book of the Victorian Age had so direct, immediate, and proliferating an influence. Its effect is to be seen in—to choose but a few examples—Disraeli's *Sybil* (1845), one of the first novels to represent the actualities of factory life; in Kingsley's *Alton Locke* (1850), which depicts the dreadful conditions of London sweatshops; in Mrs. Gaskell's two remarkable novels of working-class life, *Mary Barton* (1848) and *North and South* (1855); in Ruskin's concern with the iniquitous effects of laissez-faire economics— it is not too much to say that it changed the nature of English upper-class sensibility, and ultimately the course of English social and political policy.

*Past and Present* is divided into four books, of which the first, third, and fourth deal with the present, the second with the past. Book I is devoted to a description of the condition of England and to an account of the ignoble state of thought and feeling to which it may be ascribed. Book II presents a brilliant paradigm of how

49. A people of the southern part of Russia, notable for their skill as horsemen; they served as cavalrymen and were used against rebellious elements of the population.

social heedlessness and disorganization are to be dealt with. It is based on the chronicle of a monk, Jocelin by name, a member of the monastery of St. Edmundsbury at the end of the twelfth century. This work, which had been published by the Camden Society in 1840, tells of the disarray into which the affairs of the monastery had fallen through the incompetence of its old abbot, of how the monks choose as their new abbot one of their number, Brother Samson, and of how he labors to restore the community to order and prosperity, succeeding in this purpose through his firmness of faith, his unremitting effort, and his clear-sighted practicality, not least through his readiness to impose his will upon the captious and self-seeking members of his little polity. Books III and IV draw out for the contemporary crisis the lessons of this moving achievement of seven centuries before.


# From Past and Present

## Labour [1]

For there is a perennial nobleness, and even sacredness, in Work.[2] Were he never so benighted, forgetful of his high calling, there is always hope in a man that actually and earnestly works: in Idleness alone is there perpetual despair. Work, never so Mammonish,[3] mean, *is* in communication with Nature; the real desire to get Work done will itself lead one more and more to truth, to Nature's appointments and regulations, which are truth.

The latest Gospel in this world is, Know thy work and do it. 'Know thyself': [4] long enough has that poor 'self' of thine tormented thee; thou wilt never get to

1. The selections from *Past and Present* are Chaps. XI, XII, and XIII from Bk. III.
2. One of the notable cultural phenomena of the 19th century was the revision of certain traditional attitudes toward work. In Judaeo-Christian thought work was one of the punitive consequences of the sin of Adam—"In the sweat of thy face shalt thou eat bread." Among the upper classes the view long prevailed that work was inappropriate to a fully developed man, a gentleman. It was in the order of things for him to bear arms and serve the state; physical labor and the routines of work were degrading to him. This aspect of the aristocratic ethos was rationalized in the Renaissance, sometimes with reference to the philosophic support provided by the views of Plato. (See, below, the opening paragraphs of Matthew Arnold's *Literature and Science*.) Yet it was in the Renaissance that the feeling about work began to change, partly by reason of the growing prestige of art and science, partly by reason of the opposition offered to the aristocratic ethos by that of the middle class. Yet even so late as the early years of the 19th century, Carlyle could think it necessary to press upon the English upper classes the practical necessity as well as the spiritual value of work. To understand why this should be so we must not only recognize the continuing force of the old aristocratic ethos, the credence still given to the idea that there were many things a gentleman could not do and still be a gentleman, but also the paucity of the occupations available to young men at the time. Apart from the army and navy and the church, the only really honorable profession was the law; politics needed a solid income; medicine was not yet a calling for the well-born; architecture was suspect; engineering was likely to be thought only for the Scotch; journalism was distinctly low; the academic posts were few in number; the so-called "helping professions" had not yet been invented. In these circumstances it is not surprising that although work would of course be a necessity, it was, as an ideal, in a quite ambiguous state.
3. The god of riches and worldliness. See Luke 16:13: "Ye cannot serve God and Mammon."
4. See, above, *Sartor Resartus*, "The Everlasting No," note 17.

'know' it, I believe! Think it not thy business, this of knowing thyself; thou art an unknowable individual: know what thou canst work at; and work at it, like a Hercules! [5] That will be thy better plan.

It has been written, 'an endless significance lies in Work'; [6] a man perfects himself by working. Foul jungles are cleared away, fair seedfields rise instead, and stately cities; and withal the man himself first ceases to be a jungle and foul unwholesome desert thereby. Consider how, even in the meanest sorts of Labour, the whole soul of a man is composed into a kind of real harmony, the instant he sets himself to work! [7] Doubt, Desire, Sorrow, Remorse, Indignation, Despair itself, all these like helldogs lie beleaguering the soul of the poor day-worker, as of every man: but he bends himself with free valour against his task, and all these are stilled, all these shrink murmuring far off into their caves. The man is now a man. The blessed glow of Labour in him, is it not as purifying fire, wherein all poison is burnt up, and of sour smoke itself there is made bright blessed flame!

Destiny, on the whole, has no other way of cultivating us. A formless Chaos, once set it *revolving*, grows round and ever rounder; ranges itself, by mere force of gravity, into strata, spherical courses; is no longer a Chaos, but a round compacted World. What would become of the Earth, did she cease to revolve? In the poor old Earth, so long as she revolves, all inequalities, irregularities disperse themselves; all irregularities are incessantly becoming regular. Hast thou looked on the Potter's wheel,—one of the venerablest objects; old as the Prophet Ezekiel and far older? [8] Rude lumps of clay, how they spin themselves up, by mere quick whirling, into beautiful circular dishes. And fancy the most assiduous Potter, but without his wheel; reduced to make dishes, or rather amorphous botches, by mere kneading and baking! Even such a Potter were Destiny, with a human soul that would rest and lie at ease, that would not work and spin! Of an idle unrevolving man the kindest Destiny, like the most assiduous Potter without wheel, can bake and knead nothing other than a botch; let her spend on him what expensive colouring, what gilding and enamelling she will, he is but a botch. Not a dish; no, a bulging, kneaded, crooked, shambling, squint-cornered, amorphous botch,—a mere enamelled vessel of dishonour! Let the idle think of this.

Blessed is he who has found his work; let him ask no other blessedness. He

5. Like Hercules, that is, not in strength but in the execution of the tasks—the Twelve Labors—that were imposed upon him.
6. Carlyle is doubtless referring to one of Goethe's many statements about the psychic and spiritual value of work. Even his Werther, the type of brooding subjectivism which Carlyle seeks to discredit, speaks in praise of work.
7. One may readily agree with Carlyle on the salutary emotional effects of work and yet feel that he is heedless in the way he develops this idea. It is surely to be doubted that the "meanest kind" of work induces a "real harmony" in the soul of the worker, that a man becomes "a man" when he is required, as he is by many kinds of work, to function like a machine. On Carlyle's behalf, however, it is to be said that he had before his eyes the consequences of unemployment, of many men suffering the disintegrating effects of having no occupation at all.
8. It is a little difficult to understand why Carlyle conceives of work as essentially a *circular* activity, which gives form to the soul as, by their circular movement, the primeval gases were shaped into the heavenly bodies and as the pot is given its form on the potter's wheel.

has a work, a life-purpose; he has found it, and will follow it! How, as a free-flowing channel, dug and torn by noble force through the sour mud-swamp of one's existence, like an ever-deepening river there, it runs and flows;—draining-off the sour festering water, gradually from the root of the remotest grass-blade; making, instead of pestilential swamp, a green fruitful meadow with its clear-flowing stream. How blessed for the meadow itself, let the stream and *its* value be great or small! Labour is Life: from the inmost heart of the Worker rises his god-given Force, the sacred celestial Life-essence breathed into him by Almighty God, from his inmost heart awakens him to all nobleness,—to all knowledge, 'self-knowledge' and much else, so soon as Work fitly begins. Knowledge? The knowledge that will hold good in working, cleave thou to that; for Nature herself accredits that, says Yea to that. Properly thou hast no other knowledge but what thou hast got by working: the rest is yet all a hypothesis of knowledge; a thing to be argued of in schools, a thing floating in the clouds, in endless logic-vortices, till we try it and fix it. 'Doubt, of whatever kind, can be ended by Action alone.'

And again, hast thou valued Patience, Courage, Perseverance, Openness to light; readiness to own thyself mistaken, to do better next time? All these, all virtues, in wrestling with the dim brute Powers of Fact, in ordering of thy fellows in such wrestle, there and elsewhere not at all, thou wilt continually learn. Set down a brave Sir Christopher [9] in the middle of black ruined Stone-heaps, of foolish unarchitectural Bishops, redtape Officials, idle Nell-Gwyn Defenders of the Faith; [10] and see whether he will ever raise a Paul's Cathedral out of all that, yea or no! Rough, rude, contradictory are all things and persons, from the mutinous masons and Irish hodmen, up to the idle Nell-Gwyn De-fenders, to blustering redtape Officials, foolish unarchitectural Bishops. All these things and persons are there not for Christopher's sake and his Cathedral's; they are there for their own sake mainly! Christopher will have to conquer and constrain all these,—if he be able. All these are against him. Equitable Nature herself, who carries her mathematics and architectonics not on the face of her, but deep in the hidden heart of her,—Nature herself is but partially for him; will be wholly against him, if he constrain her not! His very money, where is it to come from? The pious munificence of England lies far-scattered, distant, unable to speak, and say, 'I am here';—must be spoken to before it can speak. Pious munificence, and all help, is so silent, invisible like the gods; impediment, contradictions manifold are so loud and near! O brave Sir Christopher, trust thou in those notwithstanding, and front all these; understand all these; by valiant patience, noble effort, insight, by man's strength, vanquish and compel all these,—and, on the whole, strike down victoriously the last topstone of

9. Sir Christopher Wren (1632–1723), the best known of English architects, who, after the great Fire of London in 1666 was put in charge of the reconstruction of innumerable churches and public buildings. His most famous work is St. Paul's Cathedral, where he is buried; the tablet marking his grave is inscribed *Si monumentam requiris, circumpice* (If you seek his monument, look around you).

10. A reference to Charles II, one of whose mistresses was the actress Nell Gwynn. The title "Defender of the Faith" was first given to Henry VIII by the pope in 1521; it con-tinued to be used by English monarchs despite the break with Rome.

that Paul's Edifice; thy monument for certain centuries, the stamp 'Great Man' impressed very legibly on Portland-stone [11] there!—

Yes, all manner of help, and pious response from Men or Nature, is always what we call silent; cannot speak or come to light, till it be seen, till it be spoken to. Every noble work is at first 'impossible.' In very truth, for every noble work the possibilities will lie diffused through Immensity; inarticulate, undiscoverable except to faith. Like Gideon [12] thou shalt spread out thy fleece at the door of thy tent; see whether under the wide arch of Heaven there be any bounteous moisture, or none. Thy heart and life-purpose shall be as a miraculous Gideon's fleece, spread out in silent appeal to Heaven: and from the kind Immensities, what from the poor unkind Localities and town and country Parishes there never could, blessed dew-moisture to suffice thee shall have fallen!

Work is of a religious nature:—work is of a *brave* nature; which it is the aim of all religion to be. All work of man is as the swimmer's: a waste ocean threatens to devour him; if he front it not bravely, it will keep its word. By incessant wise defiance of it, lusty rebuke and buffet of it, behold how it loyally supports him, bears him as its conqueror along. 'It is so,' says Goethe, 'with all things that man undertakes in this world.' [13]

Brave Sea-captain, Norse Sea-King—Columbus, my hero, royalest Sea-king of all! it is no friendly environment this of thine, in the waste deep waters; around thee mutinous discouraged souls, behind thee disgrace and ruin, before thee the unpenetrated veil of Night. Brother, these wild water-mountains, bounding from their deep bases (ten miles deep, I am told), are not entirely there on thy behalf! Meseems *they* have other work than floating thee forward: —and the huge Winds, that sweep from Ursa Major [14] to the Tropics and Equators, dancing their giant-waltz through the kingdoms of Chaos and Immensity, they care little about filling rightly or filling wrongly the small shoulder-of-mutton sails in this cockle-skiff of thine! Thou art not among articulate-speaking friends, my brother; thou art among immeasurable dumb monsters, tumbling, howling wide as the world here. Secret, far off, invisible to all hearts but thine, there lies a help in them: see how thou wilt get at that. Patiently thou wilt wait till the mad Southwester spend itself, saving thyself by dextrous science of defence, the while: valiantly, with swift decision, wilt thou strike in, when the favouring East, the Possible, springs up. Mutiny of men thou wilt sternly repress; weakness, despondency, thou wilt cheerily encourage: thou wilt swallow down complaint, unreason, weariness, weakness of others and thyself; —how much wilt thou swallow down! There shall be a depth of Silence in thee, deeper than this Sea, which is but ten miles deep: a Silence unsoundable; known to God only. Thou shalt be a Great man. Yes, my World-Soldier, thou of

---

11. Limestone from the Isle of Portland off the coast of Dorsetshire.
12. Judges 6:37. Gideon asks God for a sign of his favorable intentions toward the Israelites: "Behold, I will put a fleece of wool in the floor; and if the dew be on the fleece only, and it is dry upon all the earth beside then I shall know that thou wilt save Israel by mine hand, as thou hast said."
13. A summary of a passage in *Wilhelm Meister's Apprenticeship*.
14. The constellation of the Great Bear.

the World Marine-service,—thou wilt have to be *greater* than this tumultuous unmeasured World here round thee is: thou, in thy strong soul, as with wrestler's arms, shalt embrace it, harness it down; and make it bear thee on,—to new Americas, or whither God wills!

### Reward

'Religion,' I said; for, properly speaking, all true Work is Religion: and what-soever Religion is not Work may go and dwell among the Brahmins, Antino-mians, Spinning Dervishes,[1] or where it will; with me it shall have no harbour. Admirable was that of the old Monks, '*Laborare est Orare,* Work is Worship.'

Older than all preached Gospels was this unpreached, inarticulate, but in-eradicable, forever-enduring Gospel: Work, and therein have wellbeing. Man, Son of Earth and of Heaven, lies there not, in the innermost heart of thee, a Spirit of active Method, a Force for Work;—and burns like a painfully-smouldering fire, giving thee no rest till thou unfold it, till thou write it down in beneficent Facts around thee! What is immethodic, waste, thou shalt make methodic, regulated, arable; obedient and productive to thee. Wheresoever thou findest Disorder, there is thy eternal enemy; attack him swiftly, subdue him; make Order of him, the subject not of Chaos, but of Intelligence, Divinity and Thee! The thistle that grows in thy path, dig it out, that a blade of useful grass, a drop of nourishing milk, may grow there instead. The waste cotton-shrub, gather its waste white down, spin it, weave it; that, in place of idle litter, there may be folded webs, and the naked skin of man be covered.

But above all, where thou findest Ignorance, Stupidity, Brute-mindedness,—yes, there, with or without Church-tithes[2] and Shovel-hat,[3] with or without Talfourd-Mahon Copyrights,[4] or were it with mere dungeons and gibbets and crosses, attack it, I say; smite it wisely, unweariedly, and rest not while thou livest and it lives; but smite, smite, in the name of God! The Highest God, as I understand it, does audibly so command thee; still audibly, if thou have ears to hear. He, even He, with his *unspoken* voice, awfuler than any Sinai thunders or syllabled speech of Whirlwinds; for the SILENCE of deep Eternities, of Worlds from beyond the morning-stars, does it not speak to thee? The unborn Ages; the old Graves, with their long-mouldering dust, the very tears that wetted it now all dry,—do not these speak to thee, what ear hath not heard? The deep Death-kingdoms, the Stars in their never-resting courses, all Space and all Time, proclaim it to thee in continual silent admonition. Thou too, if ever man should,

1. Brahmins: members of the highest caste of Hindus. Antinomians: members of a Christian sect that holds that faith alone, as against good works, is necessary to salvation. Spinning (or whirling) Dervishes: members of one of several Moslem sects that achieve ecstasy by chanting religious formulas and doing whirling dances.
2. Taxes paid for the support of the established church.
3. A stiff, broad-brimmed, low-crowned hat, turned up at the sides, formerly worn by English clergymen.
4. The Copyright Act of 1842 was passed largely through the efforts of Sir Thomas Noon Talfourd and Lord Philip Stanhope. Carlyle's reference to the new law would seem to intend the (not quite cogent) suggestion that the copyright doesn't exempt stupid books from attack.

shalt work while it is called Today. For the Night cometh, wherein no man can work.[5]

All true Work is sacred; in all true Work, were it but true hand-labour, there is something of divineness. Labour, wide as the Earth, has its summit in Heaven. Sweat of the brow; and up from that to sweat of the brain, sweat of the heart; which includes all Kepler calculations, Newton meditations,[6] all Sciences, all spoken Epics, all acted Heroisms, Martyrdoms,—up to that 'Agony of bloody sweat,'[7] which all men have called divine! O brother, if this is not 'worship,' then I say, the more pity for worship; for this is the noblest thing yet discovered under God's sky. Who art thou that complainest of thy life of toil? Complain not. Look up, my wearied brother; see thy fellow Workmen there, in God's Eternity; surviving there, they alone surviving: sacred Band of the Immortals, celestial Bodyguard of the Empire of Mankind. Even in the weak Human Memory they survive so long, as saints, as heroes, as gods; they alone surviving; peopling, they alone, the unmeasured solitudes of Time! To thee Heaven, though severe, is *not* unkind; Heaven is kind,—as a noble Mother; as that Spartan Mother, saying while she gave her son his shield, 'With it, my son, or upon it!'[8] Thou too shalt return *home* in honour; to thy far-distant Home, in honour; doubt it not,—if in the battle thou keep thy shield! Thou, in the Eternities and deepest Death-kingdoms, art not an alien; thou everywhere art a denizen! Complain not; the very Spartans did not *complain*.

And who art thou that braggest of thy life of Idleness; complacently showest thy bright gilt equipages; sumptuous cushions; appliances for folding of the hands to mere sleep? Looking up, looking down, around, behind or before, discernest thou, if it be not in Mayfair[9] alone, any *idle* hero, saint, god, or even devil? Not a vestige of one. In the Heavens, in the Earth, in the Waters under the Earth, is none like unto thee. Thou art an original figure in this Creation; a denizen in Mayfair alone, in this extraordinary Century or Half-Century alone! One monster there is in the world: the idle man. What is his 'Religion'? That Nature is a Phantasm, where cunning beggary or thievery may sometimes find good victual. That God is a lie; and that Man and his Life are a lie.—Alas, alas, who of us *is* there that can say, I have worked? The faithfulest of us are unprofitable servants;[10] the faithfulest of us know that best. The faithfulest of us may say, with sad and true old Samuel,[11] 'Much of my life has been trifled away!' But he that has, and except 'on public occasions' professes to have, no function but that of going idle in a graceful or graceless manner; and of begetting sons to go idle; and to address Chief Spinners and Diggers, who at

---

5. See, above, *Sartor Resartus,* "The Everlasting Yea," note 40.
6. Johann Kepler (1571–1630), German astronomer; Sir Isaac Newton (1642–1727), English astronomer.
7. Luke 22:44.
8. For the Spartans, to lose one's shield in battle was the ultimate disgrace.
9. In the 19th century the most fashionable part of London. The name became synonymous with fashionable society. See, below, Oscar Wilde, *The Importance of Being Earnest.*
10. See Luke 17:10.
11. Dr. Samuel Johnson, who often reproached himself for bad habits of work. Boswell mentions this in referring to one of Johnson's *Meditations,* written on his 55th birthday: "I have done nothing. The need of doing, therefore, is pressing since the time of doing is short."

least *are* spinning and digging, 'Ye scandalous persons who produce too much' —My Corn-Law friends,[12] on what imaginary still richer Eldorados, and true iron-spikes with law of gravitation, are ye rushing!

As to the Wages of Work there might innumerable things be said; there will and must yet innumerable things be said and spoken, in St. Stephen's and out of St. Stephen's; [13] and gradually not a few things be ascertained and written, on Law-parchment, concerning this very matter:—'Fair day's-wages for a fair day's-work' is the most unrefusable demand! Money-wages 'to the extent of keeping your worker alive that he may work more'; these, unless you mean to dismiss him straightway out of this world, are indispensable alike to the noblest Worker and to the least noble!

One thing only I will say here, in special reference to the former class, the noble and noblest; but throwing light on all the other classes and their arrangements of this difficult matter: The 'wages' of every noble Work do yet lie in Heaven or else Nowhere. Not in Bank-of-England bills, in Owen's Labour-bank,[14] or any the most improved establishment of banking and money-changing, needest thou, heroic soul, present thy account of earnings. Human banks and labour-banks know thee not; or know thee after generations and centuries have passed away, and thou art clean gone from 'rewarding,'—all manner of bank-drafts, shop-tills, and Downing-street Exchequers [15] lying very invisible, so far from thee! Nay, at bottom, dost thou need any reward? Was it thy aim and life-purpose to be filled with good things for thy heroism; to have a life of pomp and ease, and be what men call 'happy,' in this world, or in any other world? I answer for thee deliberately, No. The whole spiritual secret of the new epoch lies in this, that thou canst answer for thyself, with thy whole clearness of head and heart, deliberately, No!

My brother, the brave man has to give his Life away. Give it, I advise thee;— thou dost not expect to *sell* thy Life in an adequate manner? What price, for example, would content thee? The just price of thy LIFE to thee,—why, God's entire Creation to thyself, the whole Universe of Space, the whole Eternity of Time, and what they hold: that is the price which would content thee; that, and if thou wilt be candid, nothing short of that! It is thy all; and for it thou wouldst have all. Thou art an unreasonable mortal;—or rather thou art a poor *infinite* mortal, who, in thy narrow clay-prison here, *seemest* so unreasonable! Thou wilt never sell thy Life, or any part of thy Life, in a satisfactory manner. Give it, like a royal heart; let the price be Nothing: thou *hast* then, in a certain sense, got All for it! The heroic man,—and is not every man, God be thanked, a

12. The Corn Laws, restricting the importation of breadstuffs in order to maintain the price of domestic wheat, were the subject of fierce controversy in the early 19th century. They were repealed in 1846 in consequence of the wide distress in England and the Irish famine of 1845.

13. Until it burned down in 1834 St. Stephen's Chapel in Westminster was where the House of Commons met.

14. In 1832 the socialist reformer Robert Owen (1771–1858) formed the Equitable Labour Exchange. In transactions with the Exchange "Labour notes" were used as currency, prices being calculated on the basis of the cost of raw material and the time expended on the manufacture of the article.

15. The official residence of the chancellor of the exchequer, like that of the prime minister, is in Downing Street.

potential hero?—has to do so, in all times and circumstances. In the most heroic age, as in the most unheroic, he will have to say, as Burns said proudly and humbly of his little Scottish Songs, little dewdrops of Celestial Melody in an age when so much was unmelodious: 'By Heaven, they shall either be invaluable or of no value; I do not need your guineas for them!'[16] It is an element which should, and must, enter deeply into all settlements of wages here below. They never will be 'satisfactory' otherwise; they cannot, O Mammon Gospel, they never can! Money for my little piece of work 'to the extent that will allow me to keep working'; yes, this,—unless you mean that I shall go my ways *before* the work is all taken out of me: but as to 'wages'—!—

On the whole, we do entirely agree with those old Monks, *Laborare est Orare*. In a thousand senses, from one end of it to the other, true Work *is* Worship. He that works, whatsoever be his work, he bodies forth the form of Things Unseen; a small Poet every Worker is. The idea, were it but of his poor Delf Platter, how much more of his Epic Poem, is as yet 'seen,' half-seen, only by himself; to all others it is a thing unseen, impossible; to Nature herself it is a thing unseen, a thing which never hitherto was;—very 'impossible,' for it is as yet a No-thing! The Unseen Powers had need to watch over such a man; he works in and for the Unseen. Alas, if he look to the Seen Powers only, he may as well quit the business; his No-thing will never rightly issue as a Thing, but as a Deceptivity, a Sham-thing,—which it had better not do!

Thy No-thing of an Intended Poem, O Poet who hast looked merely to reviewers, copyrights, booksellers, popularities, behold it has not yet become a Thing; for the truth is not in it! Though printed, hotpressed,[17] reviewed, celebrated, sold to the twentieth edition: what is all that? The Thing, in philosophical uncommercial language, is still a No-thing, mostly semblance and deception of the sight;—benign Oblivion incessantly gnawing at it, impatient till Chaos, to which it belongs, do reabsorb it!—

He who takes not counsel of the Unseen and Silent, from him will never come real visibility and speech. Thou must descend to the *Mothers*,[18] to the *Manes*,[19] and Hercules-like [20] long suffer and labour there, wouldst thou emerge with victory into the sunlight. As in battle and the shock of war,—for is not this a battle?—thou too shalt fear no pain or death, shalt love no ease or life; the voice of festive Lubberlands,[21] the noise of greedy Acheron [22] shall alike lie silent under thy victorious feet. Thy work, like Dante's, shall 'make thee lean for many years.'[23] The world and its wages, its criticisms, counsels, helps, impediments, shall be as a waste ocean-flood; the chaos through which thou art to swim and sail. Not the waste waves and their weedy gulf-streams, shalt thou

---

16. Burns wrote to this effect in a letter of September 16, 1792.
17. Hotpressing was a process to make paper glossy.
18. The Mothers are mysterious figures in Part II of Goethe's *Faust* inhabiting a shadowy realm which Faust visits. They seem to have a connection with the Platonic conception of Ideas—they have in charge the forms that existence may take.
19. The spirits of the dead (Latin).
20. See note 5.
21. Lubberland is a mythical place of plenty and laziness.
22. The river of Hades, the infernal region; also Hades itself.
23. Opening lines of Dante's *Paradise* XXV.

take for guidance: thy star alone,—'*Se tu segui tua stella!*' [24] Thy star alone, now clear-beaming over Chaos, nay now by fits gone out, disastrously eclipsed: this only shalt thou strive to follow. O, it is a business, as I fancy, that of weltering your way through Chaos and the murk of Hell! Green-eyed dragons watching you, three-headed Cerberuses,[25]—not without sympathy of *their* sort! '*Eccovi l' uom ch' è stato all' Inferno.*' [26] For in fine, as Poet Dryden says, you do walk hand in hand with sheer Madness, all the way,[27]—who is by no means pleasant company! You look fixedly into Madness, and *her* undiscovered, boundless, bottomless Night ompiic, that you may extort new Wisdom out of it, as an Eurydice from Tartarus.[28] The higher the Wisdom, the closer was its neighbourhood and kindred with mere Insanity; literally so;—and thou wilt, with a speechless feeling, observe how highest Wisdom, struggling up into this world, has oftentimes carried such tinctures and adhesions of Insanity still cleaving to it hither!

All Works, each in their degree, are a making of Madness sane;—truly enough a religious operation; which cannot be carried on without religion. You have not work otherwise; you have eye-service, greedy grasping of wages, swift and ever swifter manufacture of semblances to get hold of wages. Instead of better felt-hats to cover your head, you have bigger lath-and-plaster hats set travelling the streets on wheels. Instead of heavenly and earthly Guidance for the souls of men, you have 'Black or White Surplice' Controversies,[29] stuffed hair-and-leather Popes; [30]—terrestrial *Law-wards,*[31] Lords and Law-bringers, 'organising Labour' in these years, by passing Corn-Laws. With all which, alas, this distracted Earth is now full, nigh to bursting. Semblances most smooth to the touch and eye; most accursed, nevertheless, to body and soul. Semblances, be they of Sham-woven Cloth or of Dilettante Legislation, which are *not* real wool or substance, but Devil's-dust, accursed of God and man! No man has

24. Dante, *Inferno* VI. Said by Ulysses to Dante when Ulysses explains why he undertook his last fatal voyage.
25. The monstrous dog guarding the gates of Hades. One of the tasks of Hercules was to bring him to earth and take him back again.
26. "Behold the man who has been in Hell." According to Boccaccio, this was said of Dante by the people of Florence.
27. A reference to Dryden's line "Great wits are sure to madness near allied," *Absolom and Achitophel,* l. 163.
28. When his wife Eurydice died and descended to Hades (Tartarus), the great musician Orpheus, by means of the magic of his song, was able to follow her and prevail upon Pluto, the king of the underworld, to permit her to return to life.
29. A reference to the revived interest in ecclesiastical ceremony, including the use by clergymen of a variety of vestments in church services. The Oxford Movement (1833–45) was itself not much concerned with this question, but its emphasis upon tradition and the continuity of the Anglican Church with the Roman Catholic did much to stimulate the ceremonial tendency among the members of the so-called High Church party.
30. An earlier chapter of *Past and Present* (Bk. III, Chap. I, "Phenomena") relates an incident in which the pope, being afflicted with rheumatism, cannot happily follow the custom of kneeling as he rides through the streets blessing the people on the feast day of Corpus Christi; his cardinals consult and order the construction of a kneeling figure within which the pope can sit comfortably, only his face and hands being visible.
31. The etymology is Old English: *hlaf,* bread, loaf + *weard,* keeper, ward. See, below, the etymology of "lady."

worked, or can work, except religiously; not even the poor day-labourer, the weaver of your coat, the sewer of your shoes. All men, if they work not as in a Great Taskmaster's eye,[32] will work wrong, work unhappily for themselves and you.

Industrial work, still under bondage to Mammon, the rational soul of it not yet awakened, is a tragic spectacle. Men in the rapidest motion and self-motion; restless, with convulsive energy, as if driven by Galvanism,[33] as if possessed by a Devil; tearing asunder mountains,—to no purpose, for Mammonism is always Midas-eared![34] This is sad, on the face of it. Yet courage: the beneficent Destinies, kind in their sternness, are apprising us that this cannot continue. Labour is not a devil, even while encased in Mammonism; Labour is ever an imprisoned god, writhing unconsciously or consciously to escape out of Mammonism! Plugson of Undershot,[35] like Taillefer of Normandy,[36] wants victory; how much happier will even Plugson be to have a Chivalrous victory than a Chactaw[37] one! The unredeemed ugliness is that of a slothful People. Show me a People energetically busy; heaving, struggling, all shoulders at the wheel; their heart pulsing, every muscle swelling, with man's energy and will;—I show you a People of whom great good is already predicable; to whom all manner of good is yet certain, if their energy endure. By very working, they will learn; they have, Antæus-like,[38] their foot on Mother Fact: how can they but learn?

The vulgarest Plugson of a Master-Worker, who can command Workers, and get work out of them, is already a considerable man. Blessed and thrice-blessed symptoms I discern of Master-Workers who are not vulgar men; who are Nobles, and begin to feel that they must act as such: all speed to these, they are England's hope at present! But in this Plugson himself, conscious of almost no nobleness whatever, how much is there! Not without man's faculty, insight, courage, hard energy, is this rugged figure. His words none of the wisest; but his actings cannot be altogether foolish. Think, how were it, stoodst thou suddenly in his shoes! He has to command a thousand men. And not imaginary commanding; no, it is real, incessantly practical. The evil passions of so many men (with the Devil in them, as in all of us) he has to vanquish; by manifold force of speech and of silence, to repress or evade. What a force of silence, to

32. A phrase from Milton's sonnet "How Soon Hath Time."
33. That is, electricity. Luigi Galvani (1737–98) was the discoverer of electricity produced by chemical action.
34. The unfortunate King Midas, when asked to judge a musical contest between Apollo and Pan, preferred Pan, whereupon Apollo gave him ass's ears.
35. Plugson is the generic name which, earlier in Past and Present, Carlyle has given to manufacturers. The place name "of Undershot" is mockingly assigned to him for two reasons: because his factory is powered by undershot water-wheels, that is, wheels moved by water passing under them; and because he has the unthinking tenacity of the English bulldog, which has "undershot" jaws.
36. Taillefer was the minstrel who sang the Song of Roland to the army of William the Conqueror before the Battle of Hastings. The point of the comparison is to suggest that the archaic mode of military heroism and the modern mode of industrial enterprise have something in common.
37. Choctaw—generically, "wild Indian," savage.
38. In Greek mythology, a gigantic wrestler, son of Earth, who, whenever he was thrown, gained renewed strength from contact with his mother. Hercules conquered him by lifting him in the air and squeezing him to death.

say nothing of the others, is in Plugson! For these his thousand men he has to provide raw-material, machinery, arrangement, houseroom; and ever at the week's end, wages by due sale. No Civil-List,[39] or Goulburn-Baring Budget [40] has he to fall back upon, for paying of his regiment; he has to pick his supplies from the confused face of the whole Earth and Contemporaneous History, by his dexterity alone. There will be dry eyes if he fail to do it!—He exclaims, at present, 'black in the face,' near strangled with Dilettante Legislation; 'Let me have elbow-room, throat-room, and I will not fail! No, I will spin yet, and conquer like a giant: what "sinews of war" lie in me, untold resources towards the Conquest of this Planet, if instead of hanging me, you husband them, and help me!'—My indomitable friend, it is *true; and* thou shalt and must be helped.

This is not a man I would kill and strangle by Corn-Laws, even if I could! No, I would fling my Corn-Laws and Shot-belts[41] to the Devil; and try to help this man. I would teach him, by noble precept and low-precept, by noble example most of all, that Mammonism was not the essence of his or of my station in God's Universe; but the adscititious excrescence of it; the gross, terrene, godless embodiment of it; which would have to become, more or less, a godlike one. By noble *real* legislation, by true *noble's*-work, by unwearied, valiant, and were it wageless effort, in my Parliament and in my Parish, I would aid, constrain, encourage him to effect more or less this blessed change. I should know that it would have to be effected; that unless it were in some measure effected, he and I and all of us, I first and soonest of all, were doomed to perdition! [42]—Effected it will be; unless it were a Demon that made this Universe; which I, for my own part, do at no moment, under no form, in the least believe.

May it please your Serene Highnesses, your Majesties, Lordships and Lawwardships, the proper Epic of this world is not now 'Arms and the Man'; [43] how much less, 'Shirt-frills and the Man': no, it is now 'Tools and the Man': that, henceforth to all time, is now our Epic;—and you, first of all others, I think, were wise to take note of that!

### Democracy

If the Serene Highnesses and Majesties do not take note of that, then, as I perceive, *that* will take note of itself! The time for levity, insincerity, and idle babble and play-acting, in all kinds, is gone by; it is a serious, grave time. Old long-vexed questions, not yet solved in logical words or parliamentary laws, are fast solving themselves in facts, somewhat unblessed to behold! This largest of questions, this question of Work and Wages, which ought, had we heeded

39. The account of the appropriation made by Parliament for the support of the royal family. Until 1901 this included the pensions to individuals that were in the royal bounty.
40. Sir Francis Thornhill Baring was chancellor of the exchequer from 1839 to 1841; he was succeeded in the office by Henry Goulburn, 1841–46.
41. The belt that transmits power from the undershot wheel to the machine.
42. Carlyle proceeds to give this instruction to Plugson in Bk. IV, Chap. IV, of *Past and Present*. The chapter is entitled "Captains of Industry"; its theme is that the members of the manufacturing class must conceive of themselves as leaders of an industrial army, having the sense of responsibility appropriate to such a function and an authority deriving from this responsibility.
43. The opening line of the *Aeneid:* "Arma virumque cano" (Arms and the man I sing).

Heaven's voice, to have begun two generations ago or more, cannot be delayed longer without hearing Earth's voice. 'Labour' will verily need to be somewhat 'organised,' as they say,—God knows with what difficulty. Man will actually need to have his debts and earnings a little better paid by man; which, let Parliaments speak of them or be silent of them, are eternally his due from man, and cannot, without penalty and at length not without death-penalty, be withheld. How much ought to cease among us straightway; how much ought to begin straightway, while the hours yet are!

Truly they are strange results to which this of leaving all to 'Cash'; of quietly shutting-up the God's Temple, and gradually opening wide-open the Mammon's Temple, with 'Laissez-faire, and Every man for himself,'—have led us in these days! We have Upper, speaking Classes, who indeed do 'speak' as never man spake before; the withered flimsiness, the godless baseness and barrenness of whose Speech might of itself indicate what kind of Doing and practical Governing went on under it! For speech is the gaseous element out of which most kinds of Practice and Performance, especially all kinds of moral Performance, condense themselves, and take shape; as the one is, so will the other be. Descending, accordingly, into the Dumb Class in its Stockport Cellars and Poor-Law Bastilles,[1] have we not to announce that they also are hitherto unexampled in the History of Adam's Posterity?

Life was never a May-game for men: in all times the lot of the dumb millions born to toil was defaced with manifold sufferings, injustices, heavy burdens, avoidable and unavoidable; not play at all, but hard work that made the sinews sore and the heart sore. As bond-slaves, *villani, bordarii, sochemanni*,[2] nay indeed as dukes, earls and kings, men were oftentimes made weary of their life; and had to say, in the sweat of their brow and of their soul, Behold, it is not sport, it is grim earnest, and our back can bear no more! Who knows not what massacrings and harryings there have been; grinding, long-continuing, unbearable injustices,—till the heart had to rise in madness. . . .

And yet I will venture to believe that in no time, since the beginnings of Society, was the lot of those same dumb millions of toilers so entirely unbearable as it is even in the days now passing over us. It is not to die, or even to die of hunger, that makes a man wretched; many men have died; all men must die,—the last exit of us all is in a Fire-Chariot of Pain. But it is to live miserable we know not why; to work sore and yet gain nothing; to be heart-worn, weary, yet isolated, unrelated, girt-in with a cold universal Laissez-faire: it is to die slowly all our life long, imprisoned in a deaf, dead, Infinite Injustice, as in the accursed iron belly of a Phalaris' Bull![3] This is and remains forever intolerable to all men whom God has made. Do we wonder at French Revolutions, Chartisms, Revolts of Three Days? The times, if we will consider them, are really unexampled.

---

1. The homes for the indigent established by the Poor Laws were called Bastilles after the famous prison in Paris whose destruction by the mob in 1789 was the symbolic beginning of the French Revolution.
2. Names for the lowest classes in the feudal system.
3. Phalaris, an ancient tyrant, punished criminals by putting them into a brazen bull which was heated by fire.

Never before did I hear of an Irish Widow reduced to 'prove her sisterhood by dying of typhus-fever and infecting seventeen persons,'—saying in such undeniable way, 'You *see* I was your sister!' [4] Sisterhood, brotherhood, was often forgotten; but not till the rise of these ultimate Mammon and Shotbelt Gospels did I ever see it so expressly denied. If no pious Lord or *Law-ward* would remember it, always some pious Lady ('*Hlaf-dig*,' Benefactress, '*Loaf-giveress*,' they say she is,—blessings on her beautiful heart!) was there, with mild mother-voice and hand, to remember it; some pious thoughtful *Elder*, what we now call 'Prester,' *Presbyter* or 'Priest,' was there to put all men in mind of it, in the name of the God who had made all.

Not even in Black Dahomey [5] was it ever, I think, forgotten to the typhus-fever length. Mungo Park,[6] resourceless, had sunk down to die under the Negro Village-Tree, a horrible White object in the eyes of all. But in the poor Black Woman, and her daughter who stood aghast at him, whose earthly wealth and funded capital consisted of one small calabash [7] of rice, there lived a heart richer than *Laissez-faire:* they, with a royal munificence, boiled their rice for him; they sang all night to him, spinning assiduous on their cotton distaffs, as he lay to sleep: 'Let us pity the poor white man; no mother has he to fetch him milk, no sister to grind him corn!' Thou poor black Noble One,—thou *Lady* too: did not a God make thee too; was there not in thee too something of a God!—

Gurth, born thrall of Cedric the Saxon,[8] has been greatly pitied by Dryas-dust [9] and others. Gurth, with the brass collar round his neck, tending Cedric's pigs in the glades of the wood, is not what I call an exemplar of human felicity: but Gurth, with the sky above him, with the free air and tinted boscage and umbrage [10] round him, and in him at least the certainty of supper and social lodging when he came home; Gurth to me seems happy, in comparison with many a Lancashire and Buckinghamshire [11] man of these days, not born thrall of anybody! Gurth's brass collar did not gall him: Cedric *deserved* to be his master. The pigs were Cedric's, but Gurth too would get his parings of them. Gurth had the inexpressible satisfaction of feeling himself related indissolubly, though in a rude brass-collar way, to his fellow-mortals in this Earth. He had

---

4. In the chapter of *Past and Present* called "Mammonism," Carlyle relates the case of an Irish widow whom no one would help in her destitution; she died of typhus, having infected seventeen persons in her vicinity, all of whom died. In refusing to help her, her neighbors had said in effect " 'No; impossible; thou art no sister of ours.' But she proves her sisterhood; her typhus-fever kills *them;* they actually were her brothers, though denying it. Had human creature ever to go lower for a proof?"
5. Nation of West Africa; its inhabitants at one time practiced human sacrifice and cannibalism.
6. Mungo Park (1771–1806), Scottish surgeon and famous African explorer. He died in a conflict with the natives.
7. A hollow gourd used as a dish.
8. In Scott's *Ivanhoe* Cedric the Saxon is a well-to-do farmer and Gurth is his thrall or serf.
9. Dryasdust is the fictitious stuffy antiquarian whom Sir Walter Scott addresses in the prefaces to some of his novels. Carlyle frequently uses the name to refer to pedantic scholars generally.
10. Thickets and shade.
11. Industrial counties of England.

superiors, inferiors, equals.—Gurth is now 'emancipated' long since; has what we call 'Liberty.' Liberty, I am told, is a divine thing. Liberty when it becomes the 'Liberty to die by starvation' is not so divine!

Liberty? The true liberty of a man, you would say, consisted in his finding out, or being forced to find out the right path, and to walk thereon. To learn, or to be taught, what work he actually was able for; and then by permission, persuasion, and even compulsion, to set about doing of the same! That is his true blessedness, honour, 'liberty' and maximum of wellbeing: if liberty be not that, I for one have small care about liberty. You do not allow a palpable madman to leap over precipices; you violate his liberty, you that are wise; and keep him, were it in strait-waistcoats, away from the precipices! Every stupid, every cowardly and foolish man is but a less palpable madman: his true liberty were that a wiser man, that any and every wiser man, could, by brass collars, or in whatever milder or sharper way, lay hold of him when he was going wrong, and order and compel him to go a little righter. O, if thou really art my *Senior,* Seigneur, my *Elder,* Presbyter or Priest,—if thou art in very deed my *Wiser,* may a beneficent instinct lead and impel thee to 'conquer' me, to command me! If thou do know better than I what is good and right, I conjure thee in the name of God, force me to do it; were it by never such brass collars, whips and handcuffs, leave me not to walk over precipices! That I have been called, by all the Newspapers, a 'free man' will avail me little, if my pilgrimage have ended in death and wreck. O that the Newspapers had called me slave, coward, fool, or what it pleased their sweet voices to name me, and I had attained not death, but life!—Liberty requires new definitions.

A conscious abhorrence and intolerance of Folly, of Baseness, Stupidity, Poltroonery and all that brood of things, dwells deep in some men: still deeper in others an *un*conscious abhorrence and intolerance, clothed moreover by the beneficent Supreme Powers in what stout appetites, energies, egoisms so-called, are suitable to it;—these latter are your Conquerors, Romans, Normans, Russians, Indo-English; Founders of what we call Aristocracies. Which indeed have they not the most 'divine right' to found;—being themselves very truly "Αριστοι,[12] BRAVEST, BEST; and conquering generally a confused rabble of WORST, or at lowest, clearly enough, of WORSE? I think their divine right, tried, with affirmatory verdict, in the greatest Law-Court [13] known to me, was good! A class of men who are dreadfully exclaimed against by Dryasdust; of whom nevertheless beneficent Nature has oftentimes had need; and may, alas, again have need.

When, across the hundredfold poor scepticisms, trivialisms and constitutional cobwebberies of Dryasdust, you catch any glimpse of a William the Conqueror, a Tancred of Hauteville [14] or suchlike,—do you not discern veritably some rude outline of a true God-made King; whom not the Champion of England cased in tin, but all Nature and the Universe were calling to the throne? It is absolutely necessary that he get thither. Nature does not mean her poor Saxon children to perish, of obesity, stupor or other malady, as yet: a stern Ruler and Line of Rulers therefore is called in,—a stern but most beneficent *perpetual*

12. Aristoi.
13. That is, the law court of history.
14. A Norman hero of the First Crusade.

*House-Surgeon* is by Nature herself called in, and even the appropriate *fees* are provided for him! Dryasdust talks lamentably about Hereward [15] and the Fen Counties; [16] fate of Earl Waltheof; [17] Yorkshire and the North reduced to ashes: all which is undoubtedly lamentable. But even Dryasdust apprises me of one fact: 'A child, in this William's reign, might have carried a purse of gold from end to end of England.' My erudite friend, it is a fact which outweighs a thousand! Sweep away thy constitutional, sentimental and other cobwebberies; look eye to eye, if thou still have any eye, in the face of this big burly William Bastard [18] thou wilt see a fellow of most flashing discernment, of most strong lion-heart;—in whom, as it were, within a frame of oak and iron, the gods have planted the soul of 'a man of genius'! Dost thou call that nothing? I call it an immense thing!—Rage enough was in this Willelmus Conquæstor, [19] rage enough for his occasions;—and yet the essential element of him, as of all such men, is not scorching *fire*, but shining illuminative *light*. Fire and light are strangely interchangeable; nay, at bottom, I have found them different forms of the same most godlike 'elementary substance' in our world: a thing worth stating in these days. The essential element of this Conquæstor is, first of all, the most sun-eyed perception of what *is* really what on this God's-Earth;—which, thou wilt find, does mean at bottom 'Justice,' and 'Virtues' not a few: *Conformity* to what the Maker has seen good to make; that, I suppose, will mean Justice and a Virtue or two?—

Dost thou think Willelmus Conquæstor would have tolerated ten years' jargon, one hour's jargon, on the propriety of killing Cotton-manufacturers by partridge Corn-Laws? [20] I fancy, this was not the man to knock out of his night's-rest with nothing but a noisy bedlamism in your mouth! 'Assist us still better to bush the partridges; strangle Plugson who spins the shirts?'—*Par la Splendeur de Dieu!* [21]—Dost thou think Willelmus Conquæstor, in this new time, with Steamengine Captains of Industry [22] on one hand of him, and Joe-Manton Captains of Idleness [23] on the other, would have doubted which *was* really the Best; which did deserve strangling, and which not?

I have a certain indestructible regard for Willelmus Conquæstor. A resident House-Surgeon, provided by Nature for her beloved English People, and even furnished with the requisite fees, as I said; for he by no means felt himself doing Nature's work, this Willelmus, but his own work exclusively! And his own work withal it was; informed *'par la Splendeur de Dieu.'*—I say, it is necessary to get the work out of such a man, however harsh that be! When a

15. Hereward the Wake was a Saxon of the 11th century who resisted the Normans.
16. Lincolnshire and adjacent counties, so called because of their marshy districts; it was here that Hereward's uprisings took place.
17. Earl of Northumberland (d. 1076), suspected by William the Conqueror of having sought the aid of the Danish fleet; he was executed and came later to be regarded as an English martyr.
18. William the Conqueror was of illegitimate birth.
19. Carlyle's Latin for William the Conqueror.
20. "Partridge Corn-Laws" because they are supported by the aristocracy, whose addiction to sports, including the shooting of game birds, Carlyle often mocked.
21. By the glory of God!
22. See note 42 to the section captioned "Reward" (above).
23. Joe Manton was the celebrated maker of fine shotguns. Carlyle had earlier characterized the idle aristocracy by its admiration of his products.

world, not yet doomed for death, is rushing down to ever-deeper Baseness and Confusion, it is a dire necessity of Nature's to bring in her ARISTOCRACIES, her BEST, even by forcible methods. When their descendants or representatives cease entirely to *be* the Best, Nature's poor world will very soon rush down again to Baseness; and it becomes a dire necessity of Nature's to cast them out. Hence French Revolutions, Five-point Charters,[24] Democracies, and a mournful list of *Etceteras*, in these our afflicted times.

To what extent Democracy has now reached, how it advances irresistible with ominous, ever-increasing speed, he that will open his eyes on any province of human affairs may discern. Democracy is everywhere the inexorable demand of these ages, swiftly fulfilling itself. From the thunder of Napoleon battles, to the jabbering of Open-vestry in St. Mary Axe,[25] all things announce Democracy. A distinguished man, whom some of my readers will hear again with pleasure, thus writes to me what in these days he notes from the Wahngasse of Weissnichtwo, where our London fashions seem to be in full vogue. Let us hear the Herr Teufelsdröckh again,[26] were it but the smallest word!

'Democracy, which means despair of finding any Heroes to govern you, and contented putting-up with the want of them,—alas, thou too, *mein Lieber*,[27] seest well how close it is of kin to *Atheism*, and other sad *Isms:* he who discovers no God whatever, how shall he discover Heroes, the visible Temples of God?—Strange enough meanwhile it is, to observe with what thoughtlessness, here in our rigidly Conservative Country, men rush into Democracy with full cry. Beyond doubt, his Excellenz the Titular-Herr Ritter Kauderwälsch von Pferdefuss-Quacksalber,[28] he our distinguished Conservative Premier himself, and all but the thicker-headed of his Party, discern Democracy to be inevitable as death, and are even desperate of delaying it much!

'You cannot walk the streets without beholding Democracy announce itself: the very Tailor has become, if not properly Sansculottic,[29] which to him would be ruinous, yet a Tailor unconsciously symbolising, and prophesying with his scissors, the reign of Equality. What now is our fashionable coat? A thing of superfinest texture, of deeply meditated cut; with Malines-lace [30] cuffs; quilted

24. The "People's Charter" from which the Chartist Movement derived its name had actually six points, all having to do with the rationalizing and equalizing of the suffrage. The movement came into prominence in 1838 and disappeared by 1850. With the exception of the one about annual parliaments, all its "points" are now in force.

25. A reference to the tendency in the administration of the temporal affairs of the Church of England to allow the parishioners who paid rates to express their opinions.

26. Carlyle is not quoting from *Sartor Resartus*. These are presumably newly discovered utterances of Teufelsdröckh.

27. My dear friend.

28. Translated: Mr. Knight Gibberish Horsefoot-Quackdoctor. Sir Robert Peel was the Conservative prime minister who had repealed the Corn Laws and, despite his party affiliation, did much to advance the cause of democracy in England.

29. "Sans culottes" (without breeches) was the name given by the aristocrats to the members of the extreme republican party in the days just before the French Revolution; these radicals had refused to wear the short breeches and silk stockings characteristic of aristocratic dress and adopted instead the loose trousers of the working class. Carlyle in this paragraph and the next is taking account of the change that was taking place in men's fashions, in which the upper classes were giving up their relatively bright and elaborate clothes for the dark suits that tend to make all men seem equal and alike.

30. Lace made in the Belgian town of Malines.

with gold; so that a man can carry, without difficulty, an estate of land on his back? *Keineswegs,* By no manner of means! The Sumptuary Laws [31] have fallen into such a state of desuetude as was never before seen. Our fashionable coat is an amphibium between barn-sack and drayman's doublet. The cloth of it is studiously coarse; the colour a speckled soot-black or rust-brown gray; the nearest approach to a Peasant's. And for shape,—thou shouldst see it! The last consummation of the year now passing over us is definable as Three Bags; a big bag for the body, two small bags for the arms, and by way of collar a hem! The first Antique Cheruscan [32] who, of felt-cloth or bear's-hide, with bone or metal needle, set about making himself a coat, before Tailors had yet awakened out of Nothing,—did not he make it even so? A loose wide poke for body, with two holes to let out the arms; this was his original coat: to which holes it was soon visible that two small loose pokes, or sleeves, easily appended, would be an improvement.

'Thus has the Tailor-art, so to speak, overset itself, like most other things; changed its centre-of-gravity; whirled suddenly over from zenith to nadir. Your Stulz, [33] with huge somerset, [34] vaults from his high shopboard down to the depths of primal savagery,—carrying much along with him! For I will invite thee to reflect that the Tailor, as topmost ultimate froth of Human Society, is indeed swift-passing, evanescent, slippery to decipher; yet significant of much, nay of all. Topmost evanescent froth, he is churned-up from the very lees, and from all intermediate regions of the liquor. The general outcome he, visible to the eye, of what men aimed to do, and were obliged and enabled to do, in this one public department of symbolising themselves to each other by covering of their skins. A smack of all Human Life lies in the Tailor: its wild struggles towards beauty, dignity, freedom, victory; and how, hemmed-in by Sedan and Huddersfield [35] by Nescience, Dulness, Prurience, [36] and other sad necessities and laws of Nature, it has attained just to this: Gray savagery of Three Sacks with a hem!

'When the very Tailor verges towards Sansculottism, is it not ominous? The last Divinity of poor mankind dethroning himself; sinking *his* taper too, flame downmost, like the Genius of Sleep or of Death; admonitory that Tailor time shall be no more!—For, little as one could advise Sumptuary Laws at the present epoch, yet nothing is clearer than that where ranks do actually exist, strict division of costumes will also be enforced; that if we ever have a new Hierarchy and Aristocracy, acknowledged veritably as such, for which I daily pray Heaven, the Tailor will reawaken; and be, by volunteering and appointment, consciously and unconsciously, a safeguard of that same.'—Certain farther observations, from the same invaluable pen, on our never-ending changes of mode, our 'perpetual nomadic and even ape-like appetite for change and mere change' in all the equipments of our existence, and the 'fatal

31. Laws regulating dress, diet, etc.
32. An ancient German tribe.
33. A fashionable tailor.
34. Somersault.
35. Towns, one French, one English, devoted to the weaving of woolen goods.
36. Carlyle is not using this word in its present-day sexual sense, but in its quite literal original sense of *itching*—the result of wearing wool!

revolutionary character' thereby manifested, we suppress for the present. It may be admitted that Democracy, in all meanings of the word, is in full career; irresistible by any Ritter Kauderwälsch or other Son of Adam, as times go. 'Liberty' is a thing men are determined to have.

But truly, as I had to remark in the mean while, 'the liberty of not being oppressed by your fellow man' is an indispensable, yet one of the most insignificant fractional parts of Human Liberty. No man oppresses thee, can bid thee fetch or carry, come or go, without reason shown. True; from all men thou art emancipated: but from Thyself and from the Devil—? No man, wiser, unwiser, can make thee come or go: but thy own futilities, bewilderments, thy false appetites for Money, Windsor Georges [37] and suchlike? No man oppresses thee, O free and independent Franchiser: but does not this stupid Porter-pot [38] oppress thee? No Son of Adam can bid thee come or go; but this absurd Pot of Heavy-wet,[39] this can and does! Thou art the thrall not of Cedric the Saxon, but of thy own brutal appetites and this scoured dish of liquor. And thou pratest of thy 'liberty'? Thou entire blockhead!

Heavy-wet and gin: alas, these are not the only kinds of thraldom. Thou who walkest in a vain show, looking out with ornamental dilettante sniff and serene supremacy at all Life and all Death; and amblest jauntily; perking up thy poor talk into crotchets, thy poor conduct into fatuous somnambulisms;— and *art* as an 'enchanted Ape' under God's sky, where thou mightest have been a man, had proper Schoolmasters and Conquerors, and Constables with cat-o'-nine tails, been vouchsafed thee; dost thou call that 'liberty'? Or your unreposing Mammon-worshipper again, driven, as if by Galvanisms, by Devils and Fixed-Ideas, who rises early and sits late, chasing the impossible; straining every faculty to 'fill himself with the east wind,'—how merciful were it, could you, by mild persuasion, or by the severest tyranny so-called, check him in his mad path, and turn him into a wiser one! All painful tyranny, in that case again, were but mild 'surgery'; the pain of it cheap, as health and life, instead of galvanism and fixed-idea, are cheap at any price.

Sure enough, of all paths a man could strike into, there *is*, at any given moment, a *best path* for every man; a thing which, here and now, it were of all things *wisest* for him to do;—which could he be but led or driven to do, he were then doing 'like a man,' as we phrase it; all men and gods agreeing with him, the whole Universe virtually exclaiming Well-done to him! His success, in such case, were complete; his felicity a maximum. This path, to find this path and walk in it, is the one thing needful for him. Whatsoever forwards him in that, let it come to him even in the shape of blows and spurnings, is liberty: whatsoever hinders him, were it ward-motes,[40] open-vestries, pollbooths, tremendous cheers, rivers of heavy-wet, is slavery.

The notion that a man's liberty consists in giving his vote at election-hustings, and saying, 'Behold, now I too have my twenty-thousandth part of a Talker in our National Palaver; will not all the gods be good to me?'—is one of the pleasantest! Nature nevertheless is kind at present; and puts it into the heads

37. A reference to royalty and its pomp.
38. Porter is a dark strong beer.
39. Slang term for strong beer.
40. Meeting of the citizens of a ward, a section of the city.

PAST AND PRESENT 71

of many, almost of all. The liberty especially which has to purchase itself by social isolation, and each man standing separate from the other, having 'no business with him' but a cash-account: this is such a liberty as the Earth seldom saw;—as the Earth will not long put up with, recommend it how you may. This liberty turns out, before it have long continued in action, with all men flinging up their caps round it, to be, for the Working Millions a liberty to die by want of food; for the Idle Thousands and Units, alas, a still more fatal liberty to live in want of work; to have no earnest duty to do in this God's-World any more. What becomes of a man in such predicament? Earth's Laws are silent; and Heaven's speak in a voice which is not heard. No work, and the ineradicable need of work, give rise to new very wondrous life-philosophies, new very wondrous life-practices! Dilettantism, Pococurantism,[41] Beau-Brummelism,[42] with perhaps an occasional half-mad, protesting burst of Byronism, establish themselves. . . .

. . . England will either learn to reverence its Heroes, and discriminate them from its Sham-Heroes and Valets and gaslighted Histrios;[43] and to prize them as the audible God's-voice, amid all inane jargons and temporary market-cries, and say to them with heart-loyalty, 'Be ye King and Priest, and Gospel and Guidance for us': or else England will continue to worship new and ever-new forms of Quackhood,—and so, with what resiliences and reboundings matters little, go down to the Father of Quacks! Can I dread such things of England? Wretched, thick-eyed, gross-hearted mortals, why will ye worship lies, and 'Stuffed Clothes-suits created by the ninth-parts of men'! It is not your purses that suffer; your farm-rents, your commerces, your mill-revenues, loud as ye lament over these; no, it is not these alone, but a far deeper than these: it is your souls that lie dead, crushed down under despicable Night-mares, Atheisms, Brain-fumes; and are not souls at all, but mere succedanea[44] for *salt* to keep your bodies and their appetites from putrefying! Your cotton-spinning and thrice-miraculous mechanism, what is this too, by itself, but a larger kind of Animalism? Spiders can spin, Beavers can build and show con-trivance; the Ant lays-up accumulation of capital, and has, for aught I know, a Bank of Antland. If there is no soul in man higher than all that, did it reach to sailing on the cloud-rack, and spinning sea-sand; then I say, man is but an animal, a more cunning kind of brute: he has no soul, but only a succeda-neum for salt. Whereupon, seeing himself to be truly of the beasts that perish, he ought to admit it, I think;—and also straightway universally to kill himself; and so, in a manlike manner at least *end*, and wave these brute-worlds *his* dignified farewell!—

1843                                                                                           1843

41. *Pococurante* is an Italian expression for a person who is indifferent or unconcerned.
42. George Bryan Brummel (1778–1840), generally called Beau Brummel, was the famous dandy and leader of London fashion.
43. Stage actors.
44. Substitutes.

# JOHN STUART MILL
1806–1873

The boyhood of John Stuart Mill makes one of the great legends of the nineteenth century. We read it sometimes as a fairy story, a tale of wonder which is about wonder itself and how the young hero achieved the ability to experience it, and sometimes as a myth, an explanation of one of the mysteries of human existence. Inevitably we read it in the light of another great nineteenth-century story of boyhood, Wordsworth's *Prelude*. The account of his rearing that Mill gives in his *Autobiography* (1873) is, we might say, a sort of *Anti-Prelude*, and it is a commonplace of the comparison to recall that Wordsworth, in the course of celebrating the fortunate lack of supervision and constraint which characterized his own upbringing, contrasts it with a newfangled systematic education, designed to produce a model boy, which closely approximates the one which Mill in fact received.

Mill was born in 1806, the eldest child of James Mill, who, far more than fathers commonly are, was his son's fate. The elder Mill was the son of a poor Scotch shoemaker and of a mother who, having resolved that he was to distinguish himself, subordinated the life of the family to that end. Trained for the ministry at the University of Edinburgh, James Mill seems to have alienated the rural congregations by his intense intellectuality, and, failing to secure a pulpit, went to London to try his fortune as a journalist. He achieved some success as an editor of and a contributor to Conservative journals, although his actual opinions were radical. At the age of thirty-five he formed a close association with Jeremy Bentham, the father of the Utilitarian philosophy, the ethical doctrine, still of wide influence, which holds that actions are good in proportion to their "utility," by which is meant the extent of the happiness they promote, the criterion of public acts being "the greatest happiness of the greatest number." Bentham was then sixty, a man of considerable means and famous throughout the world for his works on jurisprudence. Under the protection of Bentham's position and financial benevolence, James Mill felt free to express his radicalism, while Bentham, for his part, was led by Mill to understand that his hopes for reform could be realized only through political agitation. But the two men did not anticipate anything like a rapid realization of their projects for the revision of society, and as they thought of the future they felt some anxiety over how their ideas would be carried forward after their deaths. Young disciples were needed who would be properly trained in the Benthamite doctrine. As the first of these they chose James Mill's son, John Stuart. He was then three years old.

In the education devised by the two friends and administered by the father of the pupil, there was no intention of making a prodigy, only of going about the pedagogical job in the most efficient way possible. The pupil himself was later to say that he had brought no special aptitude to the project, that the result that had been achieved with him could have been achieved with any child. This is surely not true—his natural endowment was unquestionably of a superior kind, like that of the younger Pitt, an accomplished classical scholar before he was ten, or that of Macaulay, who compiled a universal history before he was eight. But these examples of precocious mental power will suggest that Mill's was neither unique nor out of the course of nature. At any rate, at the age of three he was introduced to Greek by a rational and humane method which excluded grammatical rules. He read *Aesop's Fables*, moved on to Xenophon, thence to Herodotus; at the age of seven he was reading Plato's dialogues, which he later said was not a wise choice since he was not yet up to comprehending them. He began Latin at eight and almost at once was reading Cicero. His father carried him through arithmetic, geometry, and algebra, but not being himself grounded in mathematics beyond that point, turned him loose to master trigonometry, conic sections, calculus, and the higher mathematics on his own.

He read widely in history for pleasure and out of natural curiosity; at the age of six and a half he wrote a fifteen-hundred word summary of the history of Rome. He was instructed in logic, both ancient and modern, and a considerable amount of speculative philosophy. He was introduced to economics at twelve, receiving instruction from his father and having as one of his set tasks making a summary of the treatise of his father's friend David Ricardo. In addition to pursuing his own studies, he was required to be responsible for the instruction of his younger sisters and brothers. Outside the family circle, in which, actually, there was for him no intimacy, he knew no one of his own age. His sole form of exercise was going on walks with his father.

When he was fourteen, his father's tuition ceased. Mill judged that it had brought him to the point of knowledge and intellectual competence which young men educated in the conventional way reached at twenty-one; he meant, of course, those who were gifted and earnest in their studies, but even so, he surely underestimated how far he had gone.

The sequel was disastrous. But when Mill relates what he calls "the crisis in his mental history" to the education he had received, he is at pains to discriminate among those elements of the system which were harmful and those which were not. He does not deplore the rigorousness of the pedagogy, or the substance of most of what he had learned. Such blame as he imputes—he does not do so eagerly: he is what the education made him and he gives no indication of not being essentially content with himself—falls only upon the quality or tone of the instruction, upon its excess of abstractness, ultimately upon the temperament of the teacher. For James Mill was a harsh, sharp-tongued man, much given to irony, a mode of expression by which children are peculiarly hurt and confused; nor was his acerbity tempered by moments of affection. What is more, as Mill made explicit in a passage deleted from the published version of the Autobiography, he received no affection from his mother and gave her none; in the Autobiography she is never mentioned. Mrs. Mill had no pretensions to intellect and was not educated; she was the harassed mother of nine, and doubtless she was the less able to respond warmly to her children, especially her eldest son, because she had come to be held in contempt by her husband. It was a household of gloom and lovelessness and its effect on Mill was for a while extreme. That he transcended the deprivation of his childhood, that he discovered and asserted the importance of the affections and became a large-minded, generous-spirited, and, in his own way, affectionate man, makes the engaging point of his story.

The trouble that was in store for him was not quick to manifest itself. When his studies with his father were at an end in 1820, Mill spent a happy year in France, half of it in the family of Sir Samuel Bentham, Jeremy's brother. Lady Bentham especially had a worldly, humanizing influence upon him; he was a personally propossessing youth, actually quite handsome, and his hostess undertook to put him on the way to being a gentleman, seeing to it that he had clothes that fitted, and lessons in fencing, singing, and the piano, and that he learned to bear the interruption of his compulsive routine of study for the sake of frivolous pleasures. Upon his return to England he undertook the study of psychology and read Roman law with the eminent jurist John Austin, and considered and rejected a career at the bar. In 1818 his father had published his monumental *History of India,* which led in the following year to his appointment to the staff of India House, which had in charge the administration of India. In 1823 John followed him into that office as a clerk. The post permitted him sufficient leisure to pursue his intellectual interests. He became an adherent and exponent of Bentham's ideas. He studied the history of the French Revolution with a view to writing about it, contributed to the *Westminster Review,* the new organ of the growing Benthamite or "philosophical radical" group, and met with the most gifted young men of his day in one or another debating or discussion society.

His life, as he says at the beginning of the chapter of the *Autobiography* in which he describes the famous crisis, was, at the age of twenty-one, as fulfilled and happy as he could wish. How the darkness fell and the manner in which the day broke again may be read in his own words. He emerged from the crisis with a changed view of man and of the nature of human existence, to which he later gave classic expression in the pair of essays he published in the *Westminster Review,* one on Bentham in 1838, the other on Coleridge in 1840. He represents these antithetical figures as exemplary of the two dominant intellectual tendencies of the age, the one rational, practical, and radical, the other imaginative, spiritual, and conservative; intending to keep them in balance as constituting the two elements of a valuable dialectic, he cannot keep it from being discerned that it is to Coleridge that his greater sympathy goes.

In 1830 Mill made the acquaintance of Harriet Taylor, an attractive, spirited, and intellectually energetic young woman who was the wife of a wealthy London merchant, a good man whom she had once seemed to love and still regarded with affection and respect. Mill and Harriet Taylor fell in love, avowed their love, and could do nothing decisive about it. Mrs. Taylor was the mother of three children to whom she was devoted, and in any case divorce in those days was virtually impossible. The husband, though grieved, behaved with uncommon magnanimity. Until his death Mrs. Taylor and Mill were in intimate relation with each other, although not sexually, out of regard for Mr. Taylor. The arrangement made enough scandal to cause pain to all the parties to it and to lead to Mill's rather bitter withdrawal from society. Mr. Taylor died in 1849 and Mill and his widow married in 1851. Despite the tendency of writers about Mill to conclude that his estimate of Mrs. Taylor's intellectual powers was extravagant, there can be no doubt that they were of a high order, and although Mill may have credited her with a greater part in the conception and execution of his own work than the facts warrant, she unquestionably exercised a very considerable influence upon his thought. She was, for example, the effectual author of one chapter, on the development of the working-class character, in *Principles of Political Economy,* and it was at her insistence that Mill deleted from that work his arguments against the feasibility of socialism, an act which was the portent of his later increasingly favorable view of socialism.

The range of Mill's intellectual activities was exceptional and in two major disciplines his authority was pre-eminent for many decades. His *System of Logic,* begun when he was twenty-four, was published in 1843 and was at once adopted as the official textbook of the subject at Oxford and subsequently at Cambridge, and sold widely to the general public. Its chapters on the logic of the moral sciences owes something to the French thinker Auguste Comte, although the developed political theory of Comte's positive philosophy was to horrify Mill by its authoritatianism. *The Principles of Political Economy* was equally successful when it appeared in 1848. Dickens hated it and Ruskin wrote *Unto This Last* against it, but the public exhausted thirty-two editions of the work in fifty years.

In 1858 the East India Company was dissolved by act of Parliament and Mill retired on a handsome pension. His wife died in that same year and he was inconsolable, although he stoically sought what surcease could be found in work. In 1859 he published *On Liberty*, generally regarded as the classic statement of the rights of the individual in relation both to constituted government and to public opinion. *Representative Government*, which advocated proportional representation as essential to the maintenance of true democracy, appeared in 1861. In 1865 he was elected to parliament for Westminster despite his refusal to canvass or to commit himself to making the interests of his constituency his first concern; he took an active part in the debates including those on the Reform Bill of 1867 and made the first proposal ever offered to a legislative body on behalf of the rights of women; despite some buffoonery it was listened to with general respect and won a surprising number of votes. He was defeated in the general election of 1868 and retired to Avignon, where his wife was buried. His last work published in his lifetime was *The Subjection of Women* (1869), written eight years earlier, which was received in most quarters with a quite extraordinary antagonism, although it delighted and heartened a small minority. The constant companion of Mill's last years was his stepdaughter Helen Taylor, who was with him when he died in Avignon in 1873.

# What Is Poetry?

Poetry was not wholly neglected in Mill's famous education. His father set him to reading the English poets because, as he explained, through some quirk of the human intellect, ideas expressed in verse commanded a readier credence than those in prose. This view seems to us a fantastic one, yet it was in accord with the received Utilitarian conception of poetry as formulated by Bentham himself, who held that the poet practiced one of the arts of persuasion, undertaking to stimulate the passions and excite the prejudices of his readers to the end of making the worse appear appear the better reason. Perhaps nothing in John Stuart Mill's life was as momentous as the discovery, which he so movingly describes in his account of his mental crisis, that poetry spoke to the innermost part of his being. He may have been what he says he was an "unpoetical nature," but he became one of the best readers of poetry of his time; it was he who, of all English critics, was quickest to perceive the genius of Tennyson and to respond to the stern pathos of Alfred de Vigny. In this brief essay he undertakes to refute the idea upon which the Utilitarian denigration of poetry is based, that, like oratory, it is directed to a public audience with a view to forming opinion through the subversion of rational judgment.

# What Is Poetry?

It has often been asked, What is Poetry? And many and various are the answers which have been returned. The vulgarest of all—one with which no person possessed of the faculties to which Poetry addresses itself can ever have been satisfied—is that which confounds poetry with metrical composition: [1] yet to this wretched mockery of a definition, many have been led back, by the failure of all their attempts to find any other that would distinguish what they have been accustomed to call poetry, from much which they have known only under other names.

That, however, the word 'poetry' imports something quite peculiar in its nature, something which may exist in what is called prose as well as in verse, something which does not even require the instrument of words, but can speak through the other audible symbols called musical sounds, and even through the visible ones which are the language of sculpture, painting, and architecture; all this, we believe, is and must be felt, though perhaps indistinctly, by all upon whom poetry in any of its shapes produces any impression beyond that of tickling the ear. The distinction between poetry and what is not poetry, whether explained or not, is felt to be fundamental: and where every one feels a difference, a difference there must be. All other appearances may be fallacious, but the appearance of a difference is a real difference. Appearances too, like other things, must have a cause, and that which can cause anything, even an illusion, must be a reality. And hence, while a half-philosophy disdains the classifications and distinctions indicated by popular language, philosophy carried to its highest point frames new ones, but rarely sets aside the old, content with correcting and regularizing them. It cuts fresh channels for thought, but does not fill up such as it finds ready-made; it traces, on the contrary, more deeply, broadly, and distinctly, those into which the current has spontaneously flowed.

Let us then attempt, in the way of modest inquiry, not to coerce and confine nature within the bounds of an arbitrary definition, but rather to find the boundaries which she herself has set, and erect a barrier round them; not calling mankind to account for having misapplied the word 'poetry,' but attempting to clear up the conception which they already attach to it, and to bring forward as a distinct principle that which, as a vague feeling, has really guided them in their employment of the term.

The object of poetry is confessedly to act upon the emotions; and therein is poetry sufficiently distinguished from what Wordsworth affirms to be its logical opposite, namely, not prose, but matter of fact or science.[2] The one addresses itself to the belief, the other to the feelings. The one does its work by convincing or persuading, the other by moving. The one acts by presenting a proposition to the understanding, the other by offering interesting objects of contemplation to the sensibilities.

This, however, leaves us very far from a definition of poetry. This distinguishes it from one thing, but we are bound to distinguish it from everything. To bring thoughts or images before the mind for the purpose of acting upon

1. On this erroneous conception see Wordsworth, Preface to *Lyrical Ballads*.
2. *Ibid.*

the emotions, does not belong to poetry alone. It is equally the province (for example) of the novelist: and yet the faculty of the poet and that of the novelist are as distinct as any other two faculties; as the faculties of the novelist and of the orator, or of the poet and the metaphysician. The two characters may be united, as characters the most disparate may; but they have no natural connexion.

Many of the greatest poems are in the form of fictitious narratives, and in almost all good serious fictions there is true poetry. But there is a radical distinction between the interest felt in a story as such, and the interest excited by poetry; for the one is derived from incident, the other from the representation of feeling. In one, the source of the emotion excited is the exhibition of a state or states of human sensibility; in the other, of a series of states of mere outward circumstances. Now, all minds are capable of being affected more or less by representations of the latter kind, and all, or almost all, by those of the former; yet the two sources of interest correspond to two distinct, and (as respects their greatest development) mutually exclusive, characters of mind.

At what age is the passion for a story, for almost any kind of story, merely as a story, the most intense? In childhood. But that also is the age at which poetry, even of the simplest description, is least relished and least understood; [3] because the feelings with which it is especially conversant are yet undeveloped, and not having been even in the slightest degree experienced, cannot be sympathized with. In what stage of the progress of society, again, is storytelling most valued, and the story-teller in greatest request and honour?—In a rude state like that of the Tartars and Arabs at this day, and of almost all nations in the earliest ages. But in this state of society there is little poetry except ballads, which are mostly narrative, that is, essentially stories, and derive their principal interest from the incidents. Considered as poetry, they are of the lowest and most elementary kind: the feelings depicted, or rather indicated, are the simplest our nature has; such joys and griefs as the immediate pressure of some outward event excites in rude minds, which live wholly immersed in outward things, and have never, either from choice or a force they could not resist, turned themselves to the contemplation of the world within. Passing now from childhood, and from the childhood of society, to the grown-up men and women of this most grown-up and unchildlike age—the minds and hearts of greatest depth and elevation are commonly those which take greatest delight in poetry; the shallowest and emptiest, on the contrary, are, at all events, not those least addicted to novel-reading.[4] This accords, too, with all analogous experience of human nature. The sort of persons whom not merely in books, but in their lives, we find perpetually engaged in hunting for excitement from without, are invariably those who do not possess, either in the vigour of their intellectual powers or in the depth of their sensibilities, that which would

3. There are theorists of pedagogy who would refuse to accept this statement.
4. For a considerable part of the 19th century, the novel, despite its great exemplars of the 18th century, was still likely to be regarded with a certain condescension and even disdain. Matthew Arnold, for example, pays it no heed, and it is not until Pater—see his *Romanticism*—that it is dealt with as the coeval of poetry. Mill, of course, here has chiefly in mind novels that have no pretensions to literary excellence.

enable them to find ample excitement nearer home. The most idle and frivolous persons take a natural delight in fictitious narrative; the excitement it affords is of the kind which comes from without. Such persons are rarely lovers of poetry, though they may fancy themselves so, because they relish novels in verse. But poetry, which is the delineation of the deeper and more secret workings of human emotion, is interesting only to those to whom it recalls what they have felt, or whose imagination it stirs up to conceive what they could feel, or what they might have been able to feel, had their outward circumstances been different.

Poetry, when it is really such, is truth; and fiction also, if it is good for anything, is truth: but they are different truths. The truth of poetry is to paint the human soul truly: the truth of fiction is to give a true picture of life. The two kinds of knowledge are different, and come by different ways, come mostly to different persons. Great poets are often proverbially ignorant of life. What they know has come by observation of themselves; they have found within them one highly delicate and sensitive specimen of human nature, on which the laws of emotion are written in large characters, such as can be read off without much study. Other knowledge of mankind, such as comes to men of the world by outward experience, is not indispensable to them as poets: but to the novelist such knowledge is all in all; he has to describe outward things, not the inward man; actions and events, not feelings; [5] and it will not do for him to be numbered among those who, as Madame Roland said of Brissot,[6] know man but not *men*.

All this is no bar to the possibility of combining both elements, poetry and narrative or incident, in the same work, and calling it either a novel or a poem; but so may red and white combine on the same human features, or on the same canvas. There is one order of composition which requires the union of poetry and incident, each in its highest kind—the dramatic. Even there the two elements are perfectly distinguishable, and may exist of unequal quality, and in the most various proportion. The incidents of a dramatic poem may be scanty and ineffective, though the delineation of passion and character may be of the highest order; as in Goethe's admirable *Torquato Tasso;* [7] or again, the story as a mere story may be well got up for effect, as is the case with some of the most trashy productions of the Minerva press: [8] It may even be, what those are not, a coherent and probable series of events, though there be scarcely a feeling exhibited which is not represented falsely, or in a manner absolutely commonplace. The combination of the two excellencies is what renders Shakespeare so generally acceptable, each sort of readers finding in him what is suitable to their faculties. To the many he is great as a story-teller, to the few as a poet.

5. The statement must be thought a curious one in the light of the chief concern of two great novels of the 18th century, Richardson's *Clarissa* and Rousseau's *La Nouvelle Héloïse.*
6. Jean-Pierre Brissot was a journalist and a figure of note in the Girondin party of the French Revolution. He was the friend of Madame Roland, one of the most brilliant personalities of the time. She made the comment on him in her *Mémoires.*
7. Written in 1790 and based on the life of the 16th-century Italian poet.
8. Established at the end of the 18th century and notorious for the extravagantly sentimental and improbable novels it issued.

In limiting poetry to the delineation of states of feeling, and denying the name where nothing is delineated but outward objects, we may be thought to have done what we promised to avoid—to have not found, but made a definition, in opposition to the usage of language, since it is established by common consent that there is a poetry called descriptive. We deny the charge. Description is not poetry because there is descriptive poetry, no more than science is poetry because there is such a thing as a didactic poem.[9] But an object which admits of being described, or a truth which may fill a place in a scientific treatise, may also furnish an occasion for the generation of poetry, which we thereupon choose to call descriptive or didactic. The poetry is not in the object itself, nor in the scientific truth itself, but in the state of mind in which the one and the other may be contemplated. The mere delineation of the dimensions and colours of external objects is not poetry, no more than a geometrical ground-plan of St. Peter's or Westminster Abbey is painting. Descriptive poetry consists, no doubt, in description, but in description of things as they appear, not as they are; and it paints them not in their bare and natural lineaments, but seen through the medium and arrayed in the colours of the imagination set in action by the feelings. If a poet describes a lion, he does not describe him as a naturalist would, nor even as a traveller would, who was intent upon stating the truth, the whole truth, and nothing but the truth. He describes him by imagery, that is, by suggesting the most striking likenesses and contrasts which might occur to a mind contemplating the lion, in the state of awe, wonder, or terror, which the spectacle naturally excites, or is, on the occasion, supposed to excite. Now this is describing the lion professedly, but the state of excitement of the spectator really. The lion may be described falsely or with exaggeration, and the poetry be all the better; but if the human emotion be not painted with scrupulous truth, the poetry is bad poetry, *i.e.* is not poetry at all, but a failure.

Thus far our progress towards a clear view of the essentials of poetry has brought us very close to the last two attempts at a definition of poetry which we happen to have seen in print, both of them by poets and men of genius. The one is by Ebenezer Elliott, the author of *Corn-Law Rhymes*,[10] and other poems of still greater merit. 'Poetry,' says he, 'is impassioned truth.' The other is by a writer in *Blackwood's Magazine,* and comes, we think, still nearer the mark. He defines poetry, 'man's thoughts tinged by his feelings.' There is in either definition a near approximation to what we are in search of. Every truth which a human being can enunciate, every thought, even every outward impression, which can enter into his consciousness, may become poetry when shown through any impassioned medium, when invested with the colouring of joy, or grief, or pity, or affection, or admiration, or reverence, or awe, or even hatred or terror: and, unless so coloured, nothing, be it as interesting as it may, is poetry. But both these definitions fail to discriminate between poetry

9. In its literal sense "didactic" means simply "intended to instruct." The pejorative connotation it has acquired is in large part due to the reversal of taste which led to the rejection of the poetry of the 18th century written with a view to instruction. Pope's *Essay on Criticism* is a didactic poem of a high order.

10. In the Preface to this volume of poems (1831) which had as their theme the iniquity of the high import duty on wheat.

and eloquence. Eloquence, as well as poetry, is impassioned truth; eloquence, as well as poetry, is thoughts coloured by the feelings. Yet common apprehension and philosophic criticism alike recognise a distinction between the two: there is much that every one would call eloquence, which no one would think of classing as poetry. A question will sometimes arise, whether some particular author is a poet; and those who maintain the negative commonly allow, that though not a poet, he is a highly eloquent writer. The distinction between poetry and eloquence appears to us to be equally fundamental with the distinction between poetry and narrative, or between poetry and description, while it is still farther from having been satisfactorily cleared up than either of the others.

Poetry and eloquence are both alike the expression or utterance of feeling. But if we may be excused the antithesis, we should say that eloquence is *heard,* poetry is *over*heard. Eloquence supposes an audience; the peculiarity of poetry appears to us to lie in the poet's utter unconsciousness of a listener.[11] Poetry is feeling confessing itself to itself, in moments of solitude, and embodying itself in symbols which are the nearest possible representations of the feeling in the exact shape in which it exists in the poet's mind. Eloquence is feeling pouring itself out to other minds, courting their sympathy, or endeavouring to influence their belief or move them to passion or to action.

All poetry is of the nature of soliloquy. It may be said that poetry which is printed on hot-pressed paper [12] and sold at a bookseller's shop, is a soliloquy in full dress, and on the stage. It is so; but there is nothing absurd in the idea of such a mode of soliloquizing. What we have said to ourselves, we may tell to others afterwards; what we have said or done in solitude, we may voluntarily reproduce when we know that other eyes are upon us. But no trace of consciousness that any eyes are upon us must be visible in the work itself. The actor knows that there is an audience present; but if he act as though he knew it, he acts ill. A poet may write poetry not only with the intention of printing it, but for the express purpose of being paid for it; that it should *be* poetry, being written under such influences, is less probable; not, however, impossible; but no otherwise possible than if he can succeed in excluding from his work every vestige of such lookings-forth into the outward and every-day world, and can express his emotions exactly as he has felt them in solitude, or as he is conscious that he should feel them though they were to remain for ever unuttered, or (at the lowest) as he knows that others feel them in similar circumstances of solitude. But when he turns round and addresses himself to another person; when the act of utterance is not itself the end, but a means to an end,—viz. by the feelings he himself expresses, to work upon the feelings, or upon the belief, or the will, of another,—when the expression of his emotions, or of his thoughts tinged by his emotions, is tinged also by that purpose, by that desire of making an impression upon another mind, then it ceases to be poetry, and becomes eloquence.

Poetry, accordingly, is the natural fruit of solitude and meditation; elo-

11. But see the statement with which Wordsworth begins his definition of the poet in the Preface to *Lyrical Ballads*: "To whom does he address himself? . . . He is a man speaking to men." Farther on in the essay Mill qualifies the formulation he makes here.
12. Paper processed to be glossy.

quence, of intercourse with the world. The persons who have most feeling of their own, if intellectual culture has given them a language in which to express it, have the highest faculty of poetry; those who best understand the feelings of others, are the most eloquent. The persons, and the nations, who commonly excel in poetry, are those whose character and tastes render them least dependent upon the applause, or sympathy, or concurrence of the world in general. Those to whom that applause, that sympathy, that concurrence are most necessary, generally excel most in eloquence. And hence, perhaps, the French, who are the least poetical of all great and intellectual nations,[13] are among the most eloquent: the French, also, being the most sociable, the vainest, and the least self-dependent.

If the above be, as we believe, the true theory of the distinction commonly admitted between eloquence and poetry; or even though it be not so, yet if, as we cannot doubt, the distinction above stated be a real *bonâ fide* [14] distinction, it will be found to hold, not merely in the language of words, but in all other language, and to intersect the whole domain of art.

Take, for example, music: we shall find in that art, so peculiarly the expression of passion, two perfectly distinct styles; one of which may be called the poetry, the other the oratory of music. This difference, being seized, would put an end to much musical sectarianism. There has been much contention whether the music of the modern Italian school, that of Rossini [15] and his successors, be impassioned or not. Without doubt, the passion it expresses is not the musing, meditative tenderness, or pathos, or grief of Mozart or Beethoven. Yet it is passion, but garrulous passion—the passion which pours itself into other ears; and therein the better calculated for dramatic effect, having a natural adaptation for dialogue. Mozart also is great in musical oratory; but his most touching compositions are in the opposite style—that of soliloquy. Who can imagine 'Dove sono' [16] *heard?* We imagine it *over*heard.

Purely pathetic music commonly partakes of soliloquy. The soul is absorbed in its distress, and though there may be bystanders, it is not thinking of them. When the mind is looking within, and not without, its state does not often or rapidly vary; and hence the even, uninterrupted flow, approaching almost to monotony, which a good reader, or a good singer, will give to words or music of a pensive or melancholy cast. But grief taking the form of a prayer, or of a complaint, becomes oratorical; no longer low, and even, and subdued, it assumes a more emphatic rhythm, a more rapidly returning accent; instead of a few slow equal notes, following one after another at regular intervals, it crowds note upon note, and often assumes a hurry and bustle like joy. Those who are familiar with some of the best of Rossini's serious compositions,[17] such as the air 'Tu che i miseri conforti,' in the opera of *Tancredi*,[18] or the duet 'Ebben per

13. This settled opinion of the English through the 19th century has been largely overcome.
14. "In good faith."
15. Gioachino Antonio Rossini (1792–1868), Italian operatic composer of enormous popularity.
16. "Where are fled?"—the aria in Act III of Mozart's *The Marriage of Figaro*, in which the Countess sings of her vanished moments of happiness.
17. "Serious" as against his brilliant comic operas, which include *The Barber of Seville.*
18. "You who comfort the miserable." *Tancredi*, produced in 1813, was Rossini's first opera.

mia memoria,' in *La Gazza Ladra*,[19] will at once understand and feel our meaning. Both are highly tragic and passionate; the passion of both is that of oratory, not poetry. The like may be said of that most moving invocation in Beethoven's *Fidelio*—

> Komm, Hoffnung, lass das letzete Stern
> Der Müde nicht erbleichen;[20]

in which Madame Schröder-Devrient[21] exhibited such consummate powers of pathetic expression. How different from Winter's beautiful 'Paga fui,'[22] the very soul of melancholy exhaling itself in solitude; fuller of meaning, and, therefore, more profoundly poetical than the words for which it was composed —for it seems to express not simple melancholy, but the melancholy of remorse.

If, from vocal music, we now pass to instrumental, we may have a specimen of musical oratory in any fine military symphony or march: while the poetry of music seems to have attained its consummation in Beethoven's Overture to *Egmont*,[23] so wonderful in its mixed expression of grandeur and melancholy.

In the arts which speak to the eye, the same distinctions will be found to hold, not only between poetry and oratory, but between poetry, oratory, narrative, and simple imitation or description.

Pure description is exemplified in a mere portrait or a mere landscape—productions of art, it is true, but of the mechanical rather than of the fine arts, being works of simple imitation, not creation. We say, a mere portrait, or a mere landscape, because it is possible for a portrait or a landscape, without ceasing to be such, to be also a picture; like Turner's[24] landscapes, and the great portraits by Titian or Vandyke.[25]

Whatever in painting or sculpture expresses human feeling—or character, which is only a certain state of feeling grown habitual—may be called, according to circumstances, the poetry, or the eloquence, of the painter's or the sculptor's art: the poetry, if the feeling declares itself by such signs as escape from us when we are unconscious of being seen; the oratory, if the signs are those we use for the purpose of voluntary communication.

The narrative style answers to what is called historical painting, which it is the fashion among connoisseurs to treat as the climax of the pictorial art.[26] That it is the most difficult branch of the art we do not doubt, because, in its perfection, it includes the perfection of all the other branches: as in like manner an epic poem, though in so far as it is epic (*i.e.* narrative) it is not poetry at

19. "So I do remember." *La Gazza Landra* (The Thieving Magpie) was produced in 1817.
20. "Come, Hope, let not the weary one's last star go out." *Fidelio* was produced in 1805.
21. A highly gifted German soprano, especially admired for her singing of the role of Leonore in *Fidelio*, for which Beethoven himself praised her. Mill would have heard her when she sang the part in the London production of the opera in 1832, the year before he wrote this essay.
22. "I have been contented," in *Il Ratto di Proserpina* (The Rape of Proserpine) by Peter von Winter, produced in London in 1804.
23. It was composed in 1811, as part of a suite of incidental music for Goethe's play.
24. J. M. W. Turner (1775–1851), the great English landscape painter.
25. Tiziano Vecelli (*c.* 1477–1576), the greatest master of the Venetian school of painting; his portraits are superb. Sir Anthony Vandyke (1599–1641), Flemish painter, influenced by Titian; he settled in England in 1632.
26. Historical painting continued to be an important genre through the 19th century.

all, is yet esteemed the greatest effort of poetic genius, because there is no kind whatever of poetry which may not appropriately find a place in it. But an historical picture as such, that is, as the representation of an incident, must necessarily, as it seems to us, be poor and ineffective. The narrative powers of painting are extremely limited. Scarcely any picture, scarcely even any series of pictures, tells its own story without the aid of an interpreter. But it is the single figures which, to us, are the great charm even of an historical picture. It is in these that the power of the art is really seen. In the attempt to narrate, visible and permanent signs are too far behind the fugitive audible ones, which follow so fast one after another, while the faces and figures in a narrative picture, even though they be Titian's, stand still. Who would not prefer one Virgin and Child of Raphael, to all the pictures which Rubens,[27] with his fat, frouzy Dutch Venuses, ever painted?[28] Though Rubens, besides excelling almost every one in his mastery over the mechanical parts of his art, often shows real genius in *grouping* his figures, the peculiar problem of historical painting. But then, who, except a mere student of drawing and colouring, ever cared to look twice at any of the figures themselves? The power of painting lies in poetry, of which Rubens had not the slightest tincture—not in narrative, wherein he might have excelled.

The single figures, however, in an historical picture, are rather the eloquence of painting than the poetry: they mostly (unless they are quite out of place in the picture) express the feelings of one person as modified by the presence of others. Accordingly the minds whose bent leads them rather to eloquence than to poetry, rush to historical painting. The French painters, for instance, seldom attempt, because they could make nothing of, single heads, like those glorious ones of the Italian masters, with which they might feed themselves day after day in their own Louvre. They must all be historical; and they are, almost to a man, attitudinizers. If we wished to give any young artist the most impressive warning our imagination could devise against that kind of vice in the pictorial, which corresponds to rant in the histrionic art, we would advise him to walk once up and once down the gallery of the Luxembourg.[29] Every figure in French painting or statuary seems to be showing itself off before spectators: they are not poetical, but in the worst style of corrupted eloquence.

1833                                                              1833, 1859

## From On Liberty

*Of Individuality, as One of the Elements of Well-being*[1]

Such being the reasons which make it imperative that human beings should be free to form opinions and to express their opinions without reserve; and such

27. Peter Paul Rubens (1577–1640), Flemish painter, generally accounted the greatest exponent of baroque art in northern Europe.
28. Many!
29. A palace in Paris. The interior is sumptuously decorated with statues and historical and allegorical paintings of little merit.
1. This is Chap. III.

the baneful consequences to the intellectual, and through that to the moral nature of man, unless this liberty is either conceded or asserted in spite of prohibition; let us next examine whether the same reasons do not require that men should be free to act upon their opinions—to carry these out in their lives without hindrance, either physical or moral, from their fellow men, so long as it is at their own risk and peril. This last proviso is of course indispensable. No one pretends that actions should be as free as opinions. On the contrary, even opinions lose their immunity when the circumstances in which they are expressed are such as to constitute their expression a positive instigation to some mischievous act. An opinion that corn dealers are starvers of the poor, or that private property is robbery, ought to be unmolested when simply circulated through the press, but may justly incur punishment when delivered orally to an excited mob assembled before the house of a corn dealer, or when handed about among the same mob in the form of a placard. Acts, of whatever kind, which without justifiable cause do harm to others may be, and in the more important cases absolutely require to be, controlled by the unfavorable sentiments, and, when needful, by the active interference of mankind. The liberty of the individual must be thus far limited; he must not make himself a nuisance to other people. But if he refrains from molesting others in what concerns them, and merely acts according to his own inclination and judgment in things which concern himself, the same reasons which show that opinion should be free prove also that he should be allowed, without molestation, to carry his opinions into practice at his own cost. That mankind are not infallible; that their truths, for the most part, are only half-truths; that unity of opinion, unless resulting from the fullest and freest comparison of opposite opinions, is not desirable, and diversity not an evil, but a good, until mankind are much more capable than at present of recognizing all sides of the truth, are principles applicable to men's modes of action not less than to their opinions. As it is useful that while mankind are imperfect there should be different opinions, so it is that there should be different experiments of living; that free scope should be given to varieties of character, short of injury to others; and that the worth of different modes of life should be proved practically, when anyone thinks fit to try them. It is desirable, in short, that in things which do not primarily concern others individuality should assert itself. Where not the person's own character but the traditions of customs of other people are the rule of conduct, there is wanting one of the principal ingredients of human happiness, and quite the chief ingredient of individual and social progress.

In maintaining this principle, the greatest difficulty to be encountered does not lie in the appreciation of means toward an acknowledged end, but in the indifference of persons in general to the end itself. If it were felt that the free development of individuality is one of the leading essentials of well-being; that it is not only a co-ordinate element with all that is designated by the terms civilization, instruction, education, culture, but is itself a necessary part and condition of all those things, there would be no danger that liberty should be undervalued, and the adjustment of the boundaries between it and social control would present no extraordinary difficulty. But the evil is that individual spontaneity is hardly recognized by the common modes of thinking as having any intrinsic worth, or deserving any regard on its own account. The majority, being satisfied with the ways of mankind as they now are (for it is they who make them what they are), cannot comprehend why those ways should not be good enough for everybody; and what is more, spontaneity forms no part of the ideal of the majority of moral and social reformers, but is rather looked on with jealousy, as a troublesome and perhaps rebellious obstruction to the general acceptance of what these reformers, in their own judgment, think would be best for mankind. Few persons, out of Germany, even comprehend the meaning of the doctrine which Wilhelm von Humboldt,[2] so eminent both as a *savant* and as a politician, made the text of a treatise—that 'the end of man, or that which is prescribed by the eternal or immutable dictates of reason, and not suggested by vague and transient desires, is the highest and most harmonious development of his powers to a complete and consistent whole'; that, therefore, the object 'toward which every human being must ceaselessly direct his efforts, and on which especially those who design to influence their fellow men must ever keep their eyes, is the individuality of power and development'; that for this there are two requisites, 'freedom, and variety of situations'; and that from the union of these arise 'individual vigour and manifold diversity,' which combine themselves in 'originality.'

Little, however, as people are accustomed to a doctrine like that of von Humboldt, and surprising as it may be to them to find so high a value attached to individuality, the question, one must nevertheless think, can only be one of degree. No one's idea of excellence in conduct is that people should do absolutely nothing but copy one another. No one would assert that people ought not to put into their mode of life, and into the conduct of their concerns, any impress whatever of their own judgment or of their own individual character. On the other hand, it would be absurd to pretend that people ought to live as if nothing whatever had been known in the world before they came into it; as if experience had as yet done nothing toward showing that one mode of existence, or of conduct, is preferable to another. Nobody denies that people should be so taught and trained in youth as to know and benefit by the ascertained results of human experience. But it is the privilege and proper condition of a human being, arrived at the maturity of his faculties, to use and interpret experience in his own way. It is for him to find out what part of recorded experience is properly applicable to his own circumstances and character. The traditions and customs of other people are, to a certain extent, evidence of what their experience has taught *them*—presumptive evidence, and as such, have a claim to his deference: but, in the first place, their experience may be too narrow, or they may have not interpreted it rightly. Secondly, their interpretation of experience may be correct, but unsuitable to him. Customs are made for customary circumstances and customary characters; and his circumstances or his character may be uncustomary. Thirdly, though the customs be both good as customs and suitable to him, yet to conform to custom merely *as* custom does not educate or develop in him any of the qualities which are the distinctive endowment of a human being. The human faculties of perception,

---

2. Karl Wilhelm von Humboldt (1767–1835), German statesman and philologist, friend of Schiller and Goethe. The work to which Mill refers was written in 1792, published posthumously (1851), and translated into English in 1854 as *The Sphere and Duties of Government*.

judgment, discriminative feeling, mental activity, and even moral preference are exercised only in making a choice. He who does anything because it is the custom makes no choice. He gains no practice either in discerning or in desiring what is best. The mental and moral, like the muscular, powers are improved only by being used. The faculties are called into no exercise by doing a thing merely because others do it, no more than by believing a thing only because others believe it. If the grounds of an opinion are not conclusive to the person's own reason, his reason cannot be strengthened, but is likely to be weakened, by his adopting it: and if the inducements to an act are not such as are consentaneous to his own feelings and character (where affection, or the rights of others, are not concerned), it is so much done toward rendering his feelings and character inert and torpid instead of active and energetic.

He who lets the world, or his own portion of it, choose his plan of life for him has no need of any other faculty than the ape-like one of imitation. He who chooses his plan for himself employs all his faculties. He must use observation to see, reasoning and judgment to foresee, activity to gather materials for decision, discrimination to decide, and when he has decided, firmness and self-control to hold to his deliberate decision. And these qualities he requires and exercises exactly in proportion as the part of his conduct which he determines according to his own judgment and feelings is a large one. It is possible that he might be guided in some good path, and kept out of harm's way, without any of these things. But what will be his comparative worth as a human being? It really is of importance, not only what men do, but also what manner of men they are that do it. Among the works of man which human life is rightly employed in perfecting and beautifying, the first in importance surely is man himself. Supposing it were possible to get houses built, corn grown, battles fought, causes tried, and even churches erected and prayers said by machinery —by automatons in human form—it would be a considerable loss to exchange for these automatons even the men and women who at present inhabit the more civilized parts of the world, and who assuredly are but starved specimens of what nature can and will produce. Human nature is not a machine to be built after a model, and set to do exactly the work prescribed for it, but a tree, which requires to grow and develop itself on all sides, according to the tendency of the inward forces which make it a living thing.

It will probably be conceded that it is desirable people should exercise their understandings, and that of intelligent following of custom, or even occasionally an intelligent deviation from custom, is better than a blind and simply mechanical adhesion to it. To a certain extent it is admitted that our understanding should be our own; but there is not the same willingness to admit that our desires and impulses should be our own likewise, or that to possess impulses of our own, and of any strength, is anything but a peril and a snare. Yet desires and impulses are as much a part of a perfect human being as beliefs and restraints; and strong impulses are only perilous when not properly balanced, when one set of aims and inclinations is developed into strength, while others, which ought to coexist with them, remain weak and inactive. It is not because men's desires are strong that they act ill; it is because their consciences are weak. There is no natural connection between strong impulses and a weak conscience. The natural connection is the other way. To say that one person's desires and feelings are stronger and more various than those of another is merely to say that he has more of the raw material of human nature and is therefore capable, perhaps of more evil, but certainly of more good. Strong impulses are but another name for energy. Energy may be turned to bad uses; but more good may always be made of an energetic nature than of an indolent and impassive one. Those who have most natural feeling are always those whose cultivated feelings may be made the strongest. The same strong susceptibilities which make the personal impulses vivid and powerful are also the source from whence are generated the most passionate love of virtue and the sternest self-control. It is through the cultivation of these that society both does its duty and protects its interests, not by rejecting the stuff of which heroes are made, because it knows not how to make them. A person whose desires and impulses are his own—are the expression of his own nature, as it has been developed and modified by his own culture—is said to have a character. One whose desires and impulses are not his own has no character, no more than a steam engine has a character. If, in addition to being his own, his impulses are strong and are under the government of a strong will, he has an energetic character. Whoever thinks that individuality of desires and impulses should not be encouraged to unfold itself must maintain that society has no need of strong natures—is not the better for containing many persons who have much character—and that a high general average of energy is not desirable.

In some early states of society, these forces might be, and were, too much ahead of the power which society then possessed of disciplining and controlling them. There has been a time when the element of spontaneity and individuality was in excess, and the social principle had a hard struggle with it. The difficulty then was to induce men of strong bodies or minds to pay obedience to any rules which required them to control their impulses. To overcome this difficulty, law and discipline, like the Popes struggling against the Emperors, asserted a power over the whole man, claiming to control all his life in order to control his character—which society had not found any other sufficient means of binding. But society has now fairly got the better of individuality; and the danger which threatens human nature is not the excess, but the deficiency, of personal impulses and preferences. Things are vastly changed since the passions of those who were strong by station or by personal endowment were in a state of habitual rebellion against laws and ordinances, and required to be rigorously chained up to enable the persons within their reach to enjoy any particle of security. In our times, from the highest class of society down to the lowest, everyone lives as under the eye of a hostile and dreaded censorship. Not only in what concerns others, but in what concerns only themselves, the individual or the family do not ask themselves, what do I prefer? or, what would suit my character and disposition? or, what would allow the best and highest in me to have fair play and enable it to grow and thrive? They ask themselves, what is suitable to my position? what is usually done by persons of my station and pecuniary circumstances? or (worse still) what is usually done by persons of a station and circumstances superior to mine? I do not mean that they choose what is customary in preference to what suits their own inclination. It does not occur to them to have any inclination except for what is customary. Thus the mind itself is bowed to the yoke: even in what people do for pleasure, conformity is the first thing thought of; they like in crowds; they exercise choice only among things commonly done; peculiarity of taste, eccentricity of conduct are shunned equally with crimes, until by dint of not following their own nature they have no nature to follow: their human capacities are withered and starved; they become incapable of any strong wishes or native pleasures, and are generally without either opinions or feelings of home growth, or properly their own. Now is this, or is it not, the desirable condition of human nature?

It is so, on the Calvinistic theory. According to that, the one great offense of man is self-will. All the good of which humanity is capable is comprised in obedience. You have no choice; thus you must do, and no otherwise: 'Whatever is not a duty is a sin.' Human nature being radically corrupt, there is no redemption for anyone until human nature is killed within him. To one holding this theory of life, crushing out any of the human faculties, capacities, and susceptibilities is no evil: man needs no capacity but that of surrendering himself to the will of God; and if he uses any of his faculties for any other purpose but to do that supposed will more effectually, he is better without them. This is the theory of Calvinism; and it is held, in a mitigated form, by many who do not consider themselves Calvinists; the mitigation consisting in giving a less ascetic interpretation to the alleged will of God, asserting it to be his will that mankind should gratify some of their inclinations, of course not in the manner they themselves prefer, but in the way of obedience, that is, in a way prescribed to them by authority, and, therefore, by the necessary condition of the case, the same for all.

In some such insidious form there is at present a strong tendency to this narrow theory of life, and to the pinched and hidebound type of human character which it patronizes. Many persons, no doubt, sincerely think that human beings thus cramped and dwarfed are as their Maker designed them to be, just as many have thought that trees are a much finer thing when clipped into pollards,[3] or cut out into figures of animals,[4] than as nature made them. But if it be any part of religion to believe that man was made by a good Being, it is more consistent with that faith to believe that this Being gave all human faculties that they might be cultivated and unfolded, not rooted out and consumed, and that he takes delight in every nearer approach made by his creatures to the ideal conception embodied in them, every increase in any of their capabilities of comprehension, of action, or of enjoyment. There is a different type of human excellence from the Calvinistic: a conception of humanity as having its nature bestowed on it for other purposes than merely to be abnegated. 'Pagan self-assertion' is one of the elements of human worth, as well as 'Christian self-denial.'[5] There is a Greek ideal of self-development, which the Platonic and Christian ideal of self-government blends with, but does not supersede.

3. A tree whose top branches are cut back to the trunk so that it will produce a thick growth of new shoots.
4. Frequently done in elaborate gardens of the 18th and 19th centuries.
5. "Sterling's *Essays.*" (Mill). John Sterling (1806–44) was a friend of Mill and Carlyle; the latter wrote his biography.

It may be better to be a John Knox [6] than an Alcibiades,[7] but it is better to be a Pericles [8] than either; nor would a Pericles, if we had one in these days, be without anything good which belonged to John Knox.

It is not by wearing down into uniformity all that is individual in themselves, but by cultivating it and calling it forth, within the limits imposed by the rights and interests of others, that human beings become a noble and beautiful object of contemplation; and as the works partake the character of those who do them, by the same process human life also becomes rich, diversified, and animating, furnishing more abundant aliment to high thoughts and elevating feelings, and strengthening the tie which binds every individual to the race, by making the race infinitely better worth belonging to. In proportion to the development of his individuality, each person becomes more valuable to himself, and is, therefore, capable of being more valuable to others. There is a greater fullness of life about his own existence, and when there is more life in the units there is more in the mass which is composed of them. As much compression as is necessary to prevent the stronger specimens of human nature from encroaching on the rights of others cannot be dispensed with; but for this there is ample compensation even in the point of view of human development. The means of development which the individual loses by being prevented from gratifying his inclinations to the injury of others are chiefly obtained at the expense of the development of other people. And even to himself there is a full equivalent in the better development of the social part of his nature, rendered possible by the restraint put upon the selfish part. To be held to rigid rules of justice for the sake of others develops the feelings and capacities which have the good of others for their object. But to be restrained in things not affecting their good, by their mere displeasure, develops nothing valuable except such force of character as may unfold itself in resisting the restraint. If acquiesced in, it dulls and blunts the whole nature. To give any fair play to the nature of each, it is essential that different persons should be allowed to lead different lives. In proportion as this latitude has been exercised in any age has that age been noteworthy to posterity. Even despotism does not produce its worst effects so long as individuality exists under it; and whatever crushes individuality is despotism, by whatever name it may be called and whether it professes to be enforcing the will of God or the injunctions of men.

Having said that the individuality is the same thing with development, and that it is only the cultivation of individuality which produces, or can produce, well-developed human beings, I might here close the argument; for what more or better can be said of any condition of human affairs than that it brings human beings themselves nearer to the best thing they can be? Or what worse can be said of any obstruction to good than that it prevents this? Doubtless, however, these considerations will not suffice to convince those who most need convincing; and it is necessary further to show that these developed human beings are

6. John Knox (1505–72), Scottish religious reformer, associate of Calvin. He often serves as the prototype of rigorous Puritan morality.
7. Alcibiades (c. 450–404 B.C.), the brilliant and profligate Athenian politician and general.
8. Pericles (c. 500–429 B.C.), the chief and best-remembered Athenian statesman of his day, often cited as the prototype of enlightened civic virtue.

of some use to the undeveloped—to point out to those who do not desire liberty, and would not avail themselves of it, that they may be in some intelligible manner rewarded for allowing other people to make use of it without hindrance.

In the first place, then, I would suggest that they might possibly learn something from them. It will not be denied by anybody that originality is a valuable element in human affairs. There is always need of persons not only to discover new truths and point out when what were once truths are true no longer, but also to commence new practices and set the example of more enlightened conduct and better taste and sense in human life. This cannot well be gainsaid by anybody who does not believe that the world has already attained perfection in all its ways and practices. It is true that this benefit is not capable of being rendered by everybody alike; there are but few persons, in comparison with the whole of mankind, whose experiments, if adopted by others, would be likely to be any improvement on established practice. But these few are the salt of the earth; without them, human life would become a stagnant pool. Not only is it they who introduce good things which did not before exist; it is they who keep the life in those which already exist. If there were nothing new to be done, would human intellect cease to be necessary? Would it be a reason why those who do the old things should forget why they are done, and do them like cattle, not like human beings? There is only too great a tendency in the best beliefs and practices to degenerate into the mechanical; and unless there were a succession of persons whose ever-recurring originality prevents the grounds of those beliefs and practices from becoming merely traditional, such dead matter would not resist the smallest shock from anything really alive, and there would be no reason why civilization should not die out, as in the Byzantine Empire. Persons of genius, it is true, are, and are always likely to be, a small minority; but in order to have them, it is necessary to preserve the soil in which they grow. Genius can only breathe freely in an *atmosphere* of freedom. Persons of genius are, *ex vi termini*,[9] more individual than any other people—less capable, consequently, of fitting themselves, without hurtful compression, into any of the small number of moulds which society provides in order to save its members the trouble of forming their own character. If from timidity they consent to be forced into one of these moulds, and to let all that part of themselves which cannot expand under the pressure remain unexpanded, society will be little the better for their genius. If they are of a strong character and break their fetters, they become a mark for the society which has not succeeded in reducing them to commonplace, to point out with solemn warning as 'wild,' 'erratic,' and the like—much as if one should complain of the Niagara river for not flowing smoothly between its banks like a Dutch canal.

I insist thus emphatically on the importance of genius and the necessity of allowing it to unfold itself freely both in thought and in practice, being well aware that no one will deny the position in theory, but knowing also that almost everyone, in reality, is totally indifferent to it. People think genius a fine thing if it enables a man to write an exciting poem or paint a picture. But in its true sense, that of originality in thought and action, though no one says that it is not a thing to be admired, nearly all, at heart, think that they can do very

9. By definition; literally "by the force of the term."

well without it. Unhappily this is too natural to be wondered at. Originality is the one thing which unoriginal minds cannot feel the use of. They cannot see what it is to do for them: how should they? If they could see what it would do for them, it would not be originality. The first service which originality has to render them is that of opening their eyes: which being once fully done, they would have a chance of being themselves original. Meanwhile, recollecting that nothing was ever done which someone was not the first to do, and that all good things which exist are the fruits of originality, let them be modest enough to believe that there is something still left for it to accomplish, and assure themselves that they are more in need of originality, the less they are conscious of the want.

In sober truth, whatever homage may be professed, or even paid, to real or supposed mental superiority, the general tendency of things throughout the world is to render mediocrity the ascendant power among mankind. In ancient history, in the Middle Ages, and in a diminishing degree through the long transition from feudality to the present time, the individual was a power in himself; and if he had either great talents or a high social position, he was a considerable power. At present individuals are lost in the crowd. In politics it is almost a triviality to say that public opinion now rules the world. The only power deserving the name is that of masses, and of governments while they make themselves the organ of the tendencies and instincts of masses. This is as true in the moral and social relations of private life as in public transactions. Those whose opinions go by the name of public opinion are not always the same sort of public: in America, they are the whole white population; in England, chiefly the middle class. But they are always a mass, that is to say, collective mediocrity. And what is a still greater novelty, the mass do not now take their opinions from dignitaries in Church or State, from ostensible leaders, or from books. Their thinking is done for them by men much like themselves, addressing them or speaking in their name, on the spur of the moment, through the newspapers. I am not complaining of all this. I do not assert that anything better is compatible, as a general rule, with the present low state of the human mind. But that does not hinder the government of mediocrity from being mediocre government. No government by a democracy or a numerous aristocracy, either in its political acts or in the opinions, qualities, and tone of mind which it fosters, ever did or could rise above mediocrity except in so far as the sovereign Many have let themselves be guided (which in their best times they always have done) by the counsels and influence of a more highly gifted and instructed *one* or *few*. The initiation of all wise or noble things comes and must come from individuals; generally at first from some one individual. The honour and glory of the average man is that he is capable of following that initiative; that he can respond internally to wise and noble things, and be led to them with his eyes open. I am not countenancing the sort of 'hero-worship'[10] which applauds the strong man of genius for forcibly seizing on the government of the world and making it do his bidding in spite of itself. All he can claim is freedom to point out the way. The power of compelling others into it

10. A reference to Carlyle's *On Heroes, Hero-Worship, and the Heroic in History* (1841). See above.

is not only inconsistent with the freedom and development of all the rest, but corrupting to the strong man himself. It does seem, however, that when the opinions of masses of merely average men are everywhere become or becoming the dominant power, the counterpoise and corrective to that tendency would be the more and more pronounced individuality of those who stand on the higher eminences of thought. It is in these circumstances most especially that exceptional individuals, instead of being deterred, should be encouraged in acting differently from the mass. In other times there was no advantage in their doing so, unless they acted not only differently but better. In this age, the mere example of nonconformity, the mere refusal to bend the knee to custom, is itself a service. Precisely because the tyranny of opinion is such as to make eccentricity a reproach, it is desirable, in order to break through that tyranny, that people should be eccentric. Eccentricity has always abounded when and where strength of character has abounded; and the amount of eccentricity in a society has generally been proportional the amount of genius, mental vigour, and moral courage it contained. That so few now dare to be eccentric marks the chief danger of the time.

I have said that it is important to give the freest scope possible to uncustomary things, in order that it may in time appear which of these are fit to be converted into customs. But independence of action and disregard of custom are not solely deserving of encouragement for the chance they afford that better modes of action, and customs more worthy of general adoption, may be struck out; nor is it only persons of decided mental superiority who have a just claim to carry on their lives in their own way. There is no reason that all human existence should be constructed on some one or some small number of patterns. If a person possesses any tolerable amount of common sense and experience, his own mode of laying out his existence is the best, not because it is the best in itself, but because it is his own mode. Human beings are not like sheep; and even sheep are not undistinguishably alike. A man cannot get a coat or a pair of boots to fit him unless they are either made to his measure or he has a whole warehouseful to choose from; and is it easier to fit him with a life than with a coat, or are human beings more like one another in their whole physical and spiritual conformation than in the shape of their feet? If it were only that people have diversities of taste, that is reason enough for not attempting to shape them all after one model. But different persons also require different conditions for their spiritual development; and can no more exist healthily in the same moral than all the variety of plants can in the same physical, atmosphere and climate. The same things which are helps to one person toward the cultivation of his higher nature are hindrances to another. The same mode of life is a healthy excitement to one, keeping all his faculties of action and enjoyment in their best order, while to another it is a distracting burden which suspends or crushes all internal life. Such are the differences among human beings in their sources of pleasure, their susceptibilities of pain, and the operation on them of different physical and moral agencies that, unless there is a corresponding diversity in their modes of life, they neither obtain their fair share of happiness, nor grow up to the mental, moral, and aesthetic stature of which their nature is capable. . . .

There is one characteristic of the present direction of public opinion peculiarly calculated to make it intolerant of any marked demonstration of individuality. The general average of mankind are not only moderate in intellect, but also moderate in inclinations; they have no tastes or wishes strong enough to incline them to do anything unusual, and they consequently do not understand those who have, and class all such with the wild and intemperate whom they are accustomed to look down upon. Now, in addition to this fact which is general, we have only to suppose that a strong movement has set in toward the improvement of morals, and it is evident what we have to expect. In those days such a movement has set in; much has actually been effected in the way of increased regularity of conduct and discouragement of excesses; and there is a philanthropic spirit abroad for the exercise of which there is no more inviting field than the moral and prudential improvement of our fellow creatures. These tendencies of the times cause the public to be more disposed than at most former periods to prescribe general rules of conduct and endeavour to make everyone conform to the approved standard. And that standard, express or tacit, is to desire nothing strongly. Its ideal of character is to be without any marked character—to maim by compression, like a Chinese lady's foot,[11] every part of human nature which stands out prominently and tends to make the person markedly dissimilar in outline to commonplace humanity.

As is usually the case with ideals which exclude one-half of what is desirable, the present standard of approbation produces only an inferior imitation of the other half. Instead of great energies guided by vigourous reason and strong feelings strongly controlled by a conscientious will, its result is weak feelings and weak energies, which therefore can be kept in outward conformity to rule without any strength either of will or of reason. Already energetic characters on any large scale are becoming merely traditional.[12] There is now scarcely any outlet for energy in this country except business. The energy expended in this may still be regarded as considerable. What little is left from that employment is expended on some hobby, which may be a useful, even a philanthropic, hobby, but is always some one thing, and generally a thing of small dimensions. The greatness of England is now all collective; individually small, we only appear capable of anything great by our habit of combining; and with this our moral and religious philanthropists are perfectly contented. But it was men of another stamp than this that made England what it has been; and men of another stamp will be needed to prevent its decline.

The despotism of custom is everywhere the standing hindrance to human advancement, being in unceasing antagonism to that disposition to aim at something better than customary, which is called, according to circumstances, the spirit of liberty, or that of progress or improvement. The spirit of improvement is not always a spirit of liberty, for it may aim at forcing improvements on an unwilling people; and the spirit of liberty, in so far as it resists such attempts, may ally itself locally and temporarily with the opponents of improvement; but the only unfailing and permanent source of improvement is liberty, since by it there are as many possible independent centers of improve-

11. It was once the custom to bind the feet of Chinese girl children of the aristocratic class to keep them small; this resulted in deformity and in difficulty in walking.
12. The fear that personal and national energy would be lost is characteristic of the Victorian Age.

ment as there are individuals. The progressive principle, however, in either shape, whether as the love of liberty or of improvement, is antagonistic to the sway of custom, involving at least emancipation from that yoke; and the contest between the two constitutes the chief interest of the history of mankind. The greater part of the world has, properly speaking, no history, because the despotism of Custom is complete. This is the case over the whole East. Custom is there, in all things, the final appeal; justice and right mean conformity to custom; the argument of custom no one, unless some tyrant intoxicated with power, thinks of resisting. And we see the result. Those nations must once have had originality; they did not start out of the ground populous, lettered, and versed in many of the arts of life; they made themselves all this, and were then the greatest and most powerful nations of the world. What are they now? The subjects or dependents of tribes whose forefathers wandered in the forests when theirs had magnificent palaces and gorgeous temples, but over whom custom exercised only a divided rule with liberty and progress. A people, it appears, may be progressive for a certain length of time, and then stop: when does it stop? When it ceases to possess individuality. If a similar change should befall the nations of Europe, it will not be in exactly the same shape: the despotism of custom with which these nations are threatened is not precisely stationariness. It proscribes singularity, but it does not preclude change, provided all change together. We have discarded the fixed costumes of our forefathers; everyone must still dress like other people, but the fashion may change once or twice a year. We thus take care that when there is a change, it shall be for change's sake, and not from any idea of beauty or convenience; for the same idea of beauty or convenience would not strike all the world at the same moment, and be simultaneously thrown aside by all at another moment. But we are progressive as well as changeable: we continually make new inventions in mechanical things, and keep them until they are again superseded by better; we are eager for improvement in politics, in education, even in morals, though in this last our idea of improvement chiefly consists in persuading or forcing other people to be as good as ourselves. It is not progress that we object to; on the contrary, we flatter ourselves that we are the most progressive people who ever lived. It is individuality that we war against: we should think we had done wonders if we had made ourselves all alike, forgetting that the unlikeness of one person to another is generally the first thing which draws the attention of either to the imperfection of his own type and the superiority of another, or the possibility, by combining the advantages of both, of producing something better than either. We have a warning example in China—a nation of much talent and, in some respects, even wisdom, owing to the rare good fortune of having been provided at an early period with a particularly good set of customs, the work, in some measure, of men to whom even the most enlightened European must accord, under certain limitations, the title of sages and philosophers. They are remarkable, too, in the excellence of their apparatus for impressing, as far as possible, the best wisdom they possess upon every mind in the community, and securing that those who have appropriated most of it shall occupy the posts of honour and power. Surely the people who did this have discovered the secret of human progressiveness and must have kept themselves steadily at the head of the movement of the world.

On the contrary, they have become stationary—have remained so for thousands of years; and if they are ever to be further improved, it must be by foreigners. They have succeeded beyond all hope in what English philanthropists are so industriously working at—in making a people all alike, all governing their thoughts and conduct by the same maxims and rules; and these are the fruits. The modern *régime* of public opinion is, in an unorganized form, what the Chinese educational and political systems are in an organized; and unless individuality shall be able successfully to assert itself against this yoke, Europe, notwithstanding its noble antecedents and its professed Christianity, will tend to become another China.

What is it that has hitherto preserved Europe from this lot? What has made the European family of nations an improving, instead of a stationary, portion of mankind? Not any superior excellence in them, which, when it exists, exists as the effect, not as the cause, but their remarkable diversity of character and culture. Individuals, classes, nations have been extremely unlike one another: they have struck out a great variety of paths, each leading to something valuable; and although at every period those who travelled in different paths have been intolerant of one another, and each would have thought it an excellent thing if all the rest could have been compelled to travel his road, their attempts to thwart each other's development have rarely had any permanent success, and each has in time endured to receive the good which the others have offered. Europe is, in my judgment, wholly indebted to this plurality of paths for its progressive and many-sided development. But it already begins to possess this benefit in a considerably less degree. It is decidely advancing toward the Chinese ideal of making all people alike. M. de Tocqueville,[13] in his last important work, remarks how much more the Frenchmen of the present day resemble one another than did those even of the last generation. The same remark might be made of Englishmen in a far greater degree. In a passage already quoted from Wilhelm von Humboldt, he points out two things as necessary conditions of human development—because necessary to render people unlike one another—namely, freedom and variety of situations. The second of these two conditions is in this country every day diminishing. The circumstances which surround different classes and individuals, and shape their characters, are daily becoming more assimilated. Formerly, different ranks, different neighbourhoods, different trades and professions lived in what might be called different worlds; at present, to a great degree in the same. Comparatively speaking, they now read the same things, listen to the same things, see the same things, go to the same places, have their hopes and fears directed to the same objects, have the same rights and liberties, and the same means of asserting them. Great as are the differences of position which remain, they are nothing to those which have ceased. And the assimilation is still proceeding. All the political changes of the age promote it, since they all tend

13. Alexis de Tocqueville (1805–59), the great historian and social theorist, published the first volume of his brilliant *Democracy in America* in 1835, the second in 1840. He predicted the eventual triumph of democratic principles throughout the world, a development which he regarded with ambivalence. His views had great influence on Mill. The work to which Mill refers is *L'Ancien Régime*, an investigation into the causes of the French Revolution.

to raise the low and to lower the high. Every extension of education promotes it, because education brings people under common influences and gives them access to the general stock of facts and sentiments. Improvement in the means of communication promotes it, by bringing the inhabitants of distant places into personal contact, and keeping up a rapid flow of changes of residence between one place and another. The increase of commerce and manufactures promotes it, by diffusing more widely the advantages of easy circumstances and opening all objects of ambition, even the highest, to general competition, whereby the desire of rising becomes no longer the character of a particular class, but of all classes. A more powerful agency than even all these, in bringing about a general similarity among mankind, is the complete establishment, in this and other free countries, of the ascendancy of public opinion in the State. As the various social eminences which enabled persons entrenched on them to disregard the opinion of the multitude gradually become levelled; as the very idea of resisting the will of the public, when it is positively known that they have a will, disappears more and more from the minds of practical politicians, there ceases to be any social support for nonconformity—any substantive power in society which, itself opposed to the ascendancy of numbers, is interested in taking under its protection opinions and tendencies at variance with those of the public.

The combination of all these causes forms so great a mass of influences hostile to individuality that it is not easy to see how it can stand its ground. It will do so with increasing difficulty unless the intelligent part of the public can be made to feel its value—to see that it is good there should be differences, even though not for the better, even though, as it may appear to them, some should be for the worse. If the claims of individuality are ever to be asserted, the time is now while much is still wanting to complete the enforced assimilation. It is only in the earlier stages that any stand can be successfully made against the encroachment. The demand that all other people shall resemble ourselves grows by what it feeds on. If resistance waits till life is reduced *nearly* to one uniform type, all deviations from that type will come to be considered impious, immoral, even monstrous and contrary to nature. Mankind speedily become unable to conceive diversity when they have been for some time unaccustomed to see it.

1854                                                                           1859


## *From* On the Subjection of Women

### [On the Equality of the Sexes]

. . . If it be said that the doctrine of the equality of the sexes rests only on theory, it must be remembered that the contrary doctrine also has only theory to rest upon. All that is proved in its favour by direct experience, is that mankind have been able to exist under it, and to attain the degree of improvement and prosperity which we now see; but whether that prosperity has been attained sooner, or is now greater, than it would have been under the other system, experience does not say. On the other hand, experience does say, that every step in improvement has been so invariably accompanied by a step made in raising the social position of women, that historians and philosophers have been led to adopt their elevation or debasement as on the whole the surest test and most correct measure of the civilization of a people or an age. Through all the progressive period of human history, the condition of women has been approaching nearer to equality with men. This does not of itself prove that the assimilation must go on to complete equality; but it assuredly affords some presumption that such is the case.

Neither does it avail anything to say that the *nature* of the two sexes adapts them to their present functions and position, and renders these appropriate to them. Standing on the ground of common sense and the constitution of the human mind, I deny that any one knows, or can know, the nature of the two sexes, as long as they have only been seen in their present relation to one another. If men had ever been found in society without women, or women without men, or if there had been a society of men and women in which the women were not under the control of the men, something might have been positively known about the mental and moral differences which may be inherent in the nature of each. What is now called the nature of women is an eminently artificial thing—the result of forced repression in some directions, unnatural stimulation in others. It may be asserted without scruple, that no other class of dependents have had their character so entirely distorted from its natural proportions by their relation with their masters; for, if conquered and slave races have been, in some respects, more forcibly repressed, whatever in them has not been crushed down by an iron heel has generally been let alone, and if left with any liberty of development, it has developed itself according to its own laws; but in the case of women, a hot-house and stove cultivation has always been carried on of some of the capabilities of their nature, for the benefit and pleasure of their masters. . . .

Hence, in regard to that most difficult question, what are the natural differences between the two sexes—a subject on which it is impossible in the present state of society to obtain complete and correct knowledge—while almost everybody dogmatizes upon it, almost all neglect and make light of the only means by which any partial insight can be obtained into it. This is an analytic study of the most important department of psychology, the laws of the influence of circumstances on character. For, however great and apparently ineradicable the moral and intellectual differences between men and women might be, the evidence of their being natural differences could only be negative. Those only could be inferred to be natural which could not possibly be artificial—the residuum, after deducting every characteristic of either sex which can admit of being explained from education or external circumstances. The profoundest knowledge of the laws of the formation of character is indispensable to entitle any one to affirm even that there is any difference, much more what the difference is, between the two sexes considered as moral and rational beings; and since no one, as yet, has that knowledge (for there is hardly any subject which, in proportion to its importance, has been so little studied), no one is thus far entitled to any positive opinion on the subject. Conjectures are all that can at present be made; conjectures more or less probable, according as more or less authorized by such knowledge as we yet have of the laws of psychology, as applied to the formation of character.

Even the preliminary knowledge, what the differences between the sexes now are, apart from all question as to how they are made what they are, is still in the crudest and most incomplete state. Medical practitioners and physiologists have ascertained, to some extent, the differences in bodily constitution; and this is an important element to the psychologist: but hardly any medical practitioner is a psychologist. Respecting the mental characteristics of women; their observations are of no more worth than those of common men. It is a subject on which nothing final can be known, so long as those who alone can really know it, women themselves, have given but little testimony, and that little, mostly suborned. It is easy to know stupid women. Stupidity is much the same all the world over. A stupid person's notions and feelings may confidently be inferred from those which prevail in the circle by which the person is surrounded. Not so with those whose opinions and feelings are an emanation from their own nature and faculties. It is only a man here and there who has any tolerable knowledge of the character even of the women of his own family. I do not mean, of their capabilities; these nobody knows, not even themselves, because most of them have never been called out. I mean their actually existing thoughts and feelings. . . .

. . . It is but of yesterday that women have either been qualified by literary accomplishments, or permitted by society, to tell anything to the general public. As yet very few of them dare tell anything, which men, on whom their literary success depends, are unwilling to hear. Let us remember in what manner, up to a very recent time, the expression, even by a male author, of uncustomary opinions, or what are deemed eccentric feelings, usually was, and in some degree still is, received; and we may form some faint conception under what impediments a woman, who is brought up to think custom and opinion her sovereign rule, attempts to express in books anything drawn from the depths of her own nature. The greatest woman who has left writings behind her sufficient to give her an eminent rank in the literature of her country, thought it necessary to prefix as a motto to her boldest work, "Un homme peut braver l'opinion; une femme doit s'y soumettre." [1] The greater part of what women write about women is mere sycophancy to men. In the case of unmarried women, much of it seems only intended to increase their chance of a husband. Many, both married and unmarried, overstep the mark, and inculcate a servility beyond what is desired or relished by any man, except the very vulgarest. But this not so often the case as, even at a quite late period, it still was. Literary women are becoming more freespoken, and more willing to express their real sentiments. Unfortunately, in this country especially, they

1. A man is able to defy opinion, a woman should submit herself to it. "Title page of Mme de Staël's *Delphine*" (Mill). Mme de Staël, the daughter of Jacques Necker, the great Swiss financier who became Louis XVI's chief minister, was a gifted and vivacious intellectual and liberal hated and persecuted by Napoleon. In 1800 she published a study of the relation of literature to social institutions; in 1810 she published her account of the artistic and philosophical culture of Germany; both are still of great interest. *Delphine* (1802) is a novel in letters; its heroine has been called the first "modern woman" in French fiction.

are themselves such artificial products, that their sentiments are compounded of a small element of individual observation and consciousness, and a very large one of acquired associations. This will be less and less the case, but it will remain true to a great extent, as long as social institutions do not admit the same free development of originality in women which is possible to men. When that time comes, and not before, we shall see, and not merely hear, as much as it is necessary to know of the nature of women, and the adaptation of other things to it. . . .

1861                                                                       1869


# Autobiography

### From *A Crisis in My Mental History. One Stage Onward*[1]

For some years after this time I wrote very little, and nothing regularly, for publication: and great were the advantages which I derived from the inter- mission. It was of no common importance to me, at this period, to be able to digest and mature my thoughts for my own mind only, without any immediate call for giving them out in print. Had I gone on writing, it would have much disturbed the important transformation in my opinions and char- acter, which took place during those years. The origin of this transformation, or at least the process by which I was prepared for it, can only be explained by turning some distance back.

From the winter of 1821, when I first read Bentham, and especially from the commencement of the *Westminster Review*, I had what might truly be called an object in life; to be a reformer of the world. My conception of my own happiness was entirely identified with this object. The personal sym- pathies I wished for were those of fellow labourers in this enterprise. I endeavoured to pick up as many flowers as I could by the way; but as a serious and permanent personal satisfaction to rest upon, my whole reliance was placed on this: and I was accustomed to felicitate myself on the certainty of a happy life which I enjoyed, through placing my happiness in something durable and distant, in which some progress might be always making, while it could never be exhausted by complete attainment. This did very well for several years, during which the general improvement going on in the world and the idea of myself as engaged with others in struggling to promote it, seemed enough to fill up an interesting and animated existence. But the time came when I awakened from this as from a dream. It was in the autumn of 1826. I was in a dull state of nerves, such as everybody is occasionally liable to; unsusceptible to enjoyment or pleasurable excitement; one of those moods when what is pleasure at other times, becomes insipid or indifferent; the state, I should think, in which converts to Methodism usually are, when smitten by their first 'conviction of sin.' In this frame of mind it occurred to me to put the question directly to myself, 'Suppose that all your objects in life were realized; that all the changes in institutions and opinions which you are looking

1. From Chap. V.

forward to, could be completely effected at this very instant: would this be a great joy and happiness to you?' And an irrepressible self-consciousness distinctly answered, 'No!' At this my heart sank within me: the whole foundation on which my life was constructed fell down. All my happiness was to have been found in the continual pursuit of this end. The end had ceased to charm, and how could there ever again be any interest in the means? I seemed to have nothing left to live for.

At first I hoped that the cloud would pass away of itself; but it did not. A night's sleep, the sovereign remedy for the smaller vexations of life, had no effect on it. I awoke to a renewed consciousness of the woful fact. I carried it with me into all companies, into all occupations. Hardly anything had power to cause me even a few minutes oblivion of it. For some months the cloud seemed to grow thicker and thicker. The lines in Coleridge's 'Dejection'—I was not then acquainted with them—exactly describe my case:

> A grief without a pang, void, dark and drear,
> A drowsy, stifled, unimpassioned grief,
> Which finds no natural outlet or relief
> In word, or sigh, or tear.[2]

In vain I sought relief from my favourite books; those memorials of past nobleness and greatness, from which I had always hitherto drawn strength and animation. I read them now without feeling, or with the accustomed feeling *minus* all its charm; and I became persuaded, that my love of mankind, and of excellence for its own sake, had worn itself out. I sought no comfort by speaking to others of what I felt. If I had loved any one sufficiently to make confiding my griefs a necessity, I should not have been in the condition I was. I felt, too, that mine was not an interesting, or in any way respectable distress. There was nothing in it to attract sympathy. Advice, if I had known where to seek it, would have been most precious. The words of Macbeth to the physician often occurred to my thoughts.[3] But there was no one on whom I could build the faintest hope of such assistance. My father, to whom it would have been natural to me to have recourse in any practical difficulties, was the last person to whom, in such a case as this, I looked for help. Everything convinced me that he had no knowledge of any such mental state as I was suffering from, and that even if he could be made to understand it, he was not the physician who could heal it. My education, which was wholly his work, had been conducted without any regard to the possibility of its ending in this result; and I saw no use in giving him the pain of thinking that his plans had failed, when the failure was probably irremediable, and at all events, beyond the power of *his* remedies. Of other friends, I had at that time none to whom I had any hope of making my condition intelligible. It was however abundantly intelligible to myself; and the more I dwelt upon it, the more hopeless it appeared.

My course of study had led me to believe, that all mental and moral feelings

---

2. "Dejection: An Ode," ll. 21–24.
3. "Canst thou not minister to a mind diseas'd . . . ?" V.iii.40–45.

and qualities, whether of a good or of a bad kind, were the results of association; [4] that we love one thing and hate another, take pleasure in one sort of
action or contemplation, and pain in another sort, through the clinging of
pleasurable or painful ideas to those things, from the effect of education or of
experience. As a corollary from this, I had always heard it maintained by
my father, and was myself convinced, that the object of education should be
to form the strongest possible associations of the salutary class; associations
of pleasure with all things beneficial to the great whole, and of pain with all
things hurtful to it. This doctrine appeared inexpugnable; but it now seemed
to me on retrospect, that my teachers [5] had occupied themselves but super-
ficially with the means of forming and keeping up these salutary associations.
They seemed to have trusted altogether to the old familiar instruments, praise
and blame, reward and punishment. Now I did not doubt that by these means,
begun early and applied unremittingly, intense associations of pain and
pleasure, especially of pain, might be created, and might produce desires and
aversions capable of lasting undiminished to the end of life. But there must
always be something artificial and casual in associations thus produced. The
pains and pleasures thus forcibly associated with things, are not connected
with them by any natural tie; and it is therefore, I thought, essential to the
durability of these associations, that they should have become so intense and
inveterate as to be practically indissoluble, before the habitual exercise of the
power of analysis had commenced. For I now saw, or thought I saw, what
I had always before received with incredulity—that the habit of analysis has
a tendency to wear away the feelings: as indeed it has when no other mental
habit is cultivated, and the analysing spirit remains without its natural com-
plements and correctives. The very excellence of analysis (I argued) is that
it tends to weaken and undermine whatever is the result of prejudice; that it
enables us mentally to separate ideas which have only casually clung together:
and no associations whatever could ultimately resist this dissolving force, were
it not that we owe to analysis our clearest knowledge of the permanent
sequences in nature; the real connexions between Things, not dependent on
our will and feelings; natural laws, by virtue of which, in many cases, one
thing is inseparable from another in fact; which laws, in proportion as they
are clearly perceived and imaginatively realized, cause our ideas of things
which are always joined together in Nature, to cohere more and more closely
in our thoughts. Analytic habits may thus even strengthen the associations
between causes and effects, means and ends, but tend altogether to weaken

4. The doctrine of the Association of Ideas, which dominated English psychology in the
later 18th and early 19th century and played an important part in the thought of Coleridge
and Wordsworth, has an ancient provenance, going back to Plato and Aristotle. But it was
David Hume who developed it in the form in which it was received and carried forward by
David Hartley and James Mill. It proposes that mental experiences which occur together
or in close connection with each other tend to cohere in such a way that when any one
of them is subsequently presented to the mind, the others will accompany it. Behaviorism,
with its idea of the susceptibility of the mind to "conditioning" and its implication that the
mind is essentially a complex of such imposed experiences, is a modern version of the
Associationist School.
5. Mill may have put the word in the plural because he included Bentham among his
teachers. But he probably means to refer to the authors of books on psychology.

those which are, to speak familiarly, a *mere* matter of feeling. They are therefore (I thought) favourable to prudence and clearsightedness, but a perpetual
worm at the root both of the passions and of the virtues; and above all, fearfully undermine all desires, and all pleasures, which are the effects of association, that is, according to the theory I held, all except the purely physical and
organic; of the entire insufficiency of which to make life desirable, no one
had a stronger conviction than I had. These were the laws of human nature
by which, as it seemed to me, I had been brought to my present state. All
those to whom I looked up, were of opinion that the pleasure of sympathy
with human beings, and the feelings which made the good of others, and especially of mankind on a large scale, the object of existence, were the greatest
and surest sources of happiness. Of the truth of this I was convinced, but to
know that a feeling would make me happy if I had it, did not give me the
feeling. My education, I thought, had failed to create these feelings in sufficient
strength to resist the dissolving influence of analysis, while the whole course
of my intellectual cultivation had made precocious and premature analysis the
inveterate habit of my mind. I was thus, as I said to myself, left stranded at
the commencement of my voyage, with a well equipped ship and a rudder,
but no sail; without any real desire for the ends which I had been so carefully
fitted out to work for: no delight in virtue or the general good, but also just
as little in anything else. The fountains of vanity and ambition seemed to have
dried up within me, as completely as those of benevolence. I had had (as I
reflected) some gratification of vanity at too early an age: I had obtained
some distinction, and felt myself of some importance, before the desire of
distinction and of importance had grown into a passion: and little as it was
which I had attained, yet having been attained too early, like all pleasures
enjoyed too soon, it had made me *blasé* and indifferent to the pursuit. Thus
neither selfish nor unselfish pleasures were pleasures to me. And there seemed
no power in nature sufficient to begin the formation of my character anew,
and create in a mind now irretrievably analytic, fresh associations of pleasure
with any of the objects of human desire.

These were the thoughts which mingled with the dry heavy dejection of
the melancholy winter of 1826–7. During this time I was not incapable of my
usual occupations. I went on with them mechanically, by the mere force of
habit. I had been so drilled in a certain sort of mental exercise, that I could
still carry it on when all the spirit had gone out of it. I even composed and
spoke several speeches at the debating society,[6] how, or with what degree
of success I know not. Of four years continual speaking at that society, this is
the only year of which I remember next to nothing. Two lines of Coleridge,
in whom alone of all writers I have found a true description of what I felt,
were often in my thoughts, not at this time (for I had never read them), but
in a later period of the same mental malady:

> Work without hope draws nectar in a sieve,
> And hope without an object cannot live.[7]

6. This was the Speculative Society which Mill and a group of brilliant young men from
Oxford and Cambridge founded in 1825.
7. Coleridge, "Work Without Hope," ll. 13–14.

In all probability my case was by no means so peculiar as I fancied it, and I doubt not that many others have passed through a similar state; but the idiosyncrasies of my education had given to the general phenomenon a special character, which made it seem the natural effect of causes that it was hardly possible for time to remove. I frequently asked myself, if I could, or if I was bound to go on living, when life must be passed in this manner. I generally answered to myself, that I did not think I could possibly bear it beyond a year. When, however, not more than half that duration of time had elapsed, a small ray of light broke in upon my gloom. I was reading, accidentally, Marmontel's Memoirs,[8] and came to the passage which relates his father's death, the distressed position of the family, and the sudden inspiration by which he, then a mere boy, felt and made them feel that he would be everything to them—would supply the place of all that they had lost. A vivid conception of the scene and its feelings came over me, and I was moved to tears. From this moment my burthen grew lighter. The oppression of the thought that all feeling was dead within me, was gone. I was no longer hopeless: I was not a stock or a stone. I had still, it seemed, some of the material out of which all worth of character, and all capacity for happiness, are made. Relieved from my ever present sense of irremediable wretchedness, I gradually found that the ordinary incidents of life could again give me some pleasure; that I could again find enjoyment, not intense, but sufficient for cheerfulness, in sunshine and sky, in books, in conversation, in public affairs; and that there was, once more, excitement, though of a moderate kind, in exerting myself for my opinions, and for the public good. Thus the cloud gradually drew off, and I again enjoyed life: and though I had several relapses, some of which lasted many months, I never again was as miserable as I had been.

The experiences of this period had two very marked effects on my opinions and character. In the first place, they led me to adopt a theory of life, very unlike that on which I had before acted, and having much in common with what at that time I certainly had never heard of, the anti-self-consciousness theory of Carlyle.[9] I never, indeed, wavered in the conviction that happiness is the test of all rules of conduct, and the end of life. But I now thought that this end was only to be attained by not making it the direct end. Those only are happy (I thought) who have their minds fixed on some object other than their own happiness; on the happiness of others, on the improvement of mankind, even on some art or pursuit, followed not as a means, but as itself an ideal end. Aiming thus at something else, they find happiness by the way. The enjoyments of life (such was now my theory) are sufficient to make it a pleasant thing, when they are taken *en passant*,[10] without being made a prin-

---

8. Jean-François Marmontel (1723–99), French man of letters and contributor to the *Encyclopédie*. His *Mémoires d'un père* appeared in 1804. In view both of Mill's ambivalent relation to his father and of his sense of separation from the rest of the family—his relations with his brothers and sisters were never warm and later became hostile, and in the *Autobiography* he makes not a single reference to his mother—the episode that made the occasion of his tears is significant indeed.

9. In his essay *Characteristics* and in *Sartor Resartus*, especially the chapter "The Everlasting Yea."

10. "In passing."

cipal object. Once make them so, and they are immediately felt to be insufficient. They will not bear a scrutinizing examination. Ask yourself whether you are happy, and you cease to be so. The only chance is to treat, not happiness, but some end external to it, as the purpose of life. Let your self-consciousness, your scrutiny, your self-interrogation, exhaust themselves on that; and if otherwise fortunately circumstanced you will inhale happiness with the air you breathe, without dwelling on it or thinking about it, without either forestalling it in imagination, or putting it to flight by fatal questioning. This theory now became the basis of my philosophy of life. And I still hold to it as the best theory for all those who have but a moderate degree of sensibility and of capacity for enjoyment, that is, for the great majority of mankind.[11]

The other important change which my opinions at this time underwent, was that I, for the first time, gave its proper place, among the prime necessities of human well-being, to the internal culture of the individual. I ceased to attach almost exclusive importance to the ordering of outward circumstances, and the training of the human being for speculation and for action. I had now learnt by experience that the passive susceptibilities needed to be cultivated as well as the active capacities, and required to be nourished and enriched as well as guided. I did not, for an instant, lose sight of, or undervalue, that part of the truth which I had seen before; I never turned recreant to intellectual culture, or ceased to consider the power and practice of analysis as an essential condition both of individual and of social improvement. But I thought that it had consequences which required to be corrected, by joining other kinds of cultivation with it. The maintenance of a due balance among the faculties, now seemed to me of primary importance. The cultivation of the feelings became one of the cardinal points in my ethical and philosophical creed. And my thoughts and inclinations turned in an increasing degree towards whatever seemed capable of being instrumental to that object.

I now began to find meaning in the things which I had read or heard about the importance of poetry and art as instruments of human culture. But it was some time longer before I began to know this by personal experience. The only one of the imaginative arts in which I had from childhood taken great pleasure, was music; the best effect of which (and in this it surpasses perhaps every other art) consists in exciting enthusiasm; in winding up to a high pitch those feelings of an elevated kind which are already in the character, but to which this excitement gives a glow and a fervour, which though transitory at its utmost height, is precious for sustaining them at other times. This effect of music I had often experienced; but, like all my pleasurable susceptibilities, it was suspended during the gloomy period. I had sought relief again and again from this quarter, but found none. After the tide had turned, and I was in process of recovery, I had been helped forward by music, but in a much less elevated manner. I at this time first became acquainted with Weber's *Oberon*,[12] and the extreme pleasure which I drew from its delicious melodies

11. Compare the counsel given in this paragraph with that of "The Everlasting Yea."
12. The last opera of Carl Maria Friedrich Ernst von Weber (1786–1826) was written for production in London, its libretto based on Wieland's *Oberon*. Its production in 1826 was a great success.

did me good, by showing me a source of pleasure to which I was as susceptible as ever. The good however was much impaired by the thought, that the pleasure of music (as is quite true of such pleasure as this was, that of mere tune) fades with familiarity, and requires either to be revived by intermittence, or fed by continual novelty. And it is very characteristic both of my then state, and of the general tone of my mind at this period of my life, that I was seriously tormented by the thought of the exhaustibility of musical combinations. The octave consists only of five tones and two semitones, which can be put together in only a limited number of ways, of which but a small proportion are beautiful: most of these, it seemed to me, must have been already discovered, and there could not be room for a long succession of Mozarts and Webers, to strike out as these had done, entirely new and surpassingly rich veins of musical beauty. This source of anxiety may perhaps be thought to resemble that of the philosophers of Laputa, who feared lest the sun should be burnt out.[13] It was, however, connected with the best feature in my character, and the only good point to be found in my very unromantic and in no way honourable distress. For though my dejection, honestly looked at, could not be called other than egotistical, produced by the ruin, as I thought, of my fabric of happiness, yet the destiny of mankind in general was ever in my thoughts, and could not be separated from my own. I felt that the flaw in my life, must be a flaw in life itself; that the question was, whether, if the reformers of society and government could succeed in their objects, and every person in the community were free and in a state of physical comfort, the pleasures of life, being no longer kept up by struggle and privation, would cease to be pleasures. And I felt that unless I could see my way to some better hope than this for human happiness in general, my dejection must continue; but that if I could see such an outlet, I should then look on the world with pleasure; content as far as I was myself concerned, with any fair share of the general lot.

This state of my thoughts and feelings made the fact of my reading Words worth for the first time (in the autumn of 1828) an important event in my life. I took up the collection of his poems from curiosity, with no expectation of mental relief from it, though I had before resorted to poetry with that hope. In the worst period of my depression I had read through the whole of Byron (then new to me) to try whether a poet, whose peculiar department was supposed to be that of the intenser feelings, could rouse any feeling in me. As might be expected, I got no good from this reading, but the reverse. The poet's state of mind was too like my own. His was the lament of a man who had worn out all pleasures, and who seemed to think that life, to all who possess the good things of it, must necessarily be the vapid uninteresting thing which I found it. His Harold and Manfred[14] had the same burthen on them which I had; and I was not in a frame of mind to derive any comfort from the vehement sensual passion of his Giaours, or the sullenness of his Laras.[15] But while Byron was exactly what did not suit my condition, Wordsworth was exactly what did. I had looked into The Excursion two or three years before,

---

13. Swift's Gulliver's Travels III.ii.
14. The heroes of Byron's Childe Harold's Pilgrimage (1812, 1816, 1818) and Manfred (1817).
15. The Giaour was published in 1813, Lara, its sequel, in 1814.

and found little in it; and should probably have found as little, had I read it at this time. But the miscellaneous poems, in the two-volume edition of 1815 [16] (to which little of value was added in the latter part of the author's life), proved to be the precise thing for my mental wants at that particular juncture.

In the first place, these poems addressed themselves powerfully to one of the strongest of my pleasurable susceptibilities, the love of rural objects and natural scenery; to which I had been indebted not only for much of the pleasure of my life, but quite recently for relief from one of my longest relapses into depression. In this power of rural beauty over me, there was a foundation laid for taking pleasure in Wordsworth's poetry; the more so, as his scenery lies mostly among mountains, which, owing to my early Pyrenean excursion, were my ideal of natural beauty.[17] But Wordsworth would never have had any great effect on me, if he had merely placed before me beautiful pictures of natural scenery. Scott does this still better than Wordsworth, and a very second-rate landscape does it more effectually than any poet. What made Words-worth's poems a medicine for my state of mind, was that they expressed, not mere outward beauty, but states of feeling, and of thought coloured by feeling, under the excitement of beauty.[18] They seemed to be the very culture of the feelings, which I was in quest of.[19] In them I seemed to draw from a source of inward joy, of sympathetic and imaginative pleasure, which could be shared in by all human beings; which had no connexion with struggle or imperfec-tion, but would be made richer by every improvement in the physical or social condition of mankind. From them I seemed to learn what would be the peren-nial sources of happiness, when all the greater evils of life shall have been removed. And I felt myself at once better and happier as I came under their influence. There have certainly been, even in our own age, greater poets than Wordsworth; but poetry of deeper and loftier feeling could not have done for me at that time what his did. I needed to be made to feel that there was real, permanent happiness in tranquil contemplation. Wordsworth taught me this, not only without turning away from, but with a greatly increased interest in, the common feelings and common destiny of human beings. And the delight which these poems gave me, proved that with culture of this sort, there was nothing to dread from the most confirmed habit of analysis. At the conclusion of the Poems came the famous Ode, falsely called Platonic,[20] 'Intimations of Immortality': in which, along with more than his usual sweetness of melody and rhythm, and along with the two passages of grand imagery but bad philosophy so often quoted, I found that he too had had similar experience to mine; that he also had felt that the first freshness of youthful enjoyment of life was not lasting; but that he had sought for compensation, and found it, in the way in which he was now teaching me to find it. The result was that I

16. The first collected edition of Wordsworth's poems.
17. In 1820–21 Mill lived in France in the home of Samuel Bentham, brother of Jeremy, and, with Sir Samuel and his wife, visited the Pyrenees.
18. This is Wordsworth's own doctrine, expressed in the Preface to Lyrical Ballads.
19. See Matthew Arnold, Memorial Verses, for a comparison of Byron and Wordsworth. Arnold characterizes Wordsworth, as Mill does, by his power to "make us feel."
20. Wordsworth in a note to the Ode denied that its informing idea derives from Plato's doctrine of pre-natal existence and consciousness.

gradually, but completely, emerged from my habitual depression, and was never again subject to it. I long continued to value Wordsworth less according to his intrinsic merits, than by the measure of what he had done for me. Compared with the greatest poets, he may be said to be the poet of unpoetical natures, possessed of quiet and contemplative tastes. But unpoetical natures are precisely those which require poetic cultivation. This cultivation Wordsworth is much more fitted to give, than poets who are intrinsically far more poets than he.

It so fell out that the merits of Wordsworth were the occasion of my first public declaration of my new way of thinking, and separation from those of my habitual companions who had not undergone a similar change. The person with whom at that time I was most in the habit of comparing notes on such subjects was Roebuck,[21] and I induced him to read Wordsworth, in whom he also at first seemed to find much to admire: but I, like most Wordsworthians, threw myself into strong antagonism to Byron, both as a poet and as to his influence on the character. Roebuck, all whose instincts were those of action and struggle, had, on the contrary, a strong relish and great admiration of Byron, whose writings he regarded as the poetry of human life, while Wordsworth's, according to him, was that of flowers and butterflies. We agreed to have the fight out at our Debating Society, where we accordingly discussed for two evenings the comparative merits of Byron and Wordsworth, propounding and illustrating by long recitations our respective theories of poetry: Sterling[22] also, in a brilliant speech, putting forward his particular theory. This was the first debate on any weighty subject in which Roebuck and I had been on opposite sides. The schism between us widened from this time more and more, though we continued for some years longer to be companions. In the beginning, our chief divergence related to the cultivation of the feelings. Roebuck was in many respects very different from the vulgar notion of a Benthamite or Utilitarian. He was a lover of poetry and of most of the fine arts. He took great pleasure in music, in dramatic performances, especially in painting, and himself drew and designed landscapes with great facility and beauty. But he never could be made to see that these things have any value as aids in the formation of character. Personally, instead of being, as Benthamites are supposed to be, void of feeling, he had very quick and strong sensibilities. But, like most Englishmen who have feelings, he found his feelings stand very much in his way. He was much more susceptible to the painful sympathies than to the pleasurable, and looking for his happiness elsewhere, he wished that his feelings should be deadened rather than quickened. And in truth the English character, and English social circumstances, make it so seldom possible to derive happiness from the exercise of the sympathies, that it is not wonderful if they count for little in an Englishman's scheme of life. In most other countries the paramount importance of the sympathies as a constituent of individual happiness is an axiom, taken for granted rather than needing any

21. John Arthur Roebuck (1801–79) became a politician of radical views, although in later life he often took reactionary positions. Mill viewed his career with dismay and in an early draft of the *Autobiography* expressed his disapproval at length.
22. John Sterling (1806–44) was a friend and disciple of Coleridge and Mill. Carlyle wrote his biography.

formal statement; but most English thinkers almost seem to regard them as necessary evils, required for keeping men's actions benevolent and compassionate. Roebuck was, or appeared to be, this kind of Englishman. He saw little good in any cultivation of the feelings, and none at all in cultivating them through the imagination, which he thought was only cultivating illusions. It was in vain I urged on him that the imaginative emotion which an idea when vividly conceived excites in us, is not an illusion but a fact, as real as any of the other qualities of objects; and far from implying anything erroneous and delusive in our mental apprehension of the object, is quite consistent with the most accurate knowledge and most perfect practical recognition of all its physical and intellectual laws and relations. The intensest feeling of the beauty of a cloud lighted by the setting sun, is no hindrance to my knowing that the cloud is vapour of water, subject to all the laws of vapours in a state of suspension; and I am just as likely to allow for, and act on, these physical laws whenever there is occasion to do so, as if I had been incapable of perceiving any distinction between beauty and ugliness. . . .

1861, 1871                                                                      1873


# JOHN HENRY CARDINAL NEWMAN
1801–1890

With the exception of John Stuart Mill, all the great prose writers of the Victorian Age whose work is represented in this volume were reared in one or another form of Christian belief. All set store by the cardinal Christian virtues of faith, hope, and charity. All were dedicated to what they would have agreed to call the life of the spirit. Yet only one man among them, John Henry Newman, lived and died an actual believer, giving assent not alone with his heart to Christian sentiment but also with his mind to Christian doctrine, making faith as it was confirmed by reason the very substance of his life.

It must be said at once that, except by reason of his genius, Newman was not singular among his fellow-countrymen at large. Throughout his lifetime religion was of vital importance to the English, not only as a public issue capable of arousing intense feelings but also as a power, although doubtless an ever less manifested one, in the lives of individuals. But for members of the intellectual class, although they might hold religion in elegiac esteem and be tenacious of its "values," it was not a living, imperative presence. It still touched but it did not shape their lives. It did not command their observance in acts of devotion nor their intellectual assent to its formularies of belief. Among the class of intellectuals, Newman stood pre-eminent for his intellectual abilities; none surpassed him in mental power; none equaled him in subtlety of thought. Yet to doctrines that his notable contemporaries could not suppose to come within the range of credibility he not only gave his eager assent but based upon that assent his hope of salvation.

Newman's life in religion began early in his temporal life. He was born in London in 1801, the eldest son of a banker. He was a quiet, meditative boy, even more responsive than children usually are to stories of wonder; reading the *Arabian Nights*, he wished their marvels were true. He records that his mind ran on unknown influences, magical powers, and talismans. He thought that life might be a dream and he an angel "and all this world a deception." The "mistrust of the reality of material phenomena"—Wordsworth in *Ode: Intimations of Immortality* and in his note on that poem speaks eloquently of the part that such a dubiety played in his childhood, and indeed it is not an uncommon experience of children—stayed with him all his life and was a decisive element of his thought. At the age of fifteen, when he was a pupil at a private school in Ealing, near London, through the influence of one of the masters he read certain books of Calvinist tendency which led him to conceive of the existence of God as equal in self-evidence with his own. Such actually Calvinist doctrine as established itself in his mind he later repudiated, but the clear knowledge of God's existence never left him. It was at this time, he tells us, that he understood it to be the will of God that he live a cellbate life.

He entered Trinity College, Oxford, in 1817, a reserved, shy, and solitary youth. Although he was an earnest student, he did not take his degree with high honors. Yet his actual abilities were patent enough to win for him in 1822 the prized election to a fellowship at Oriel, at that time the most distinguished intellectually of the Oxford colleges. It was at Oriel that the course of his religious life was to be set, although not immediately. The college had among its Fellows a group of churchmen of formidable dialectical skill with whom Newman was in closest association. This group, which came to be known as the "Noetics"—the word derives from the Greek word that means "pertaining to the intellect"—was relatively liberal in the views it held on the relation of church and state, and, without being in any sense heterodox, inclined to criticize traditional orthodoxies. From its members Newman learned to be precise in his reasoning and, as he says, to "prefer intellectual excellence to moral." In time, however, the rationalism of the Noetics lost its hold upon him and he began to move toward friends, also members of Oriel, whose religious thought was of an opposite tendency; among these Hurrell Froude, Edward Pusey, and John Keble are the most eminent. It was Froude who first led him to question the idea that the Anglican Church was, in its ideal conception, essentially and necessarily Protestant rather than Catholic.

In 1824 Newman took holy orders; he was appointed public tutor at Oriel in 1826 and vicar of the University Church of St. Mary's in 1828. In 1832 he resigned the Oriel tutorship, for he insisted, against the views of the provost of the college, that it was a post of "substantially religious nature" which required that he seek to affect the moral and spiritual lives of his pupils. This will suggest the growing intensity and intransigence of his religious character. His account of the Mediterranean tour he made with Froude in 1832 is charged with the impassioned consciousness that England was on the point of religious crisis. A serious and prolonged illness on the tour strengthened his feeling that he was called to do battle for the faith, and he returned home in 1833 with the sense of mission burning within him.

At this time, it must be clear, Newman felt no attraction to Catholicism. When he had been in Rome, what he saw of Catholicism had only repelled him. His concern was solely with the fortunes of the Church of England, which did indeed seem to be at a low ebb. A Whig parliament had already abolished several unneeded bishoprics of the English Church in Ireland and now seemed on the point of proceeding to the disestablishment of the Church of England. In 1833, a few days after Newman's return from the Continent, John Keble preached on "National Apostasy" in St. Mary's before the judges of assize and denounced the interference of Parliament with the church. According to orthodox Anglican doctrine, the bishops were in direct line of succession from the Apostles, and the basis of Keble's charge of apostasy was that the temporal power had presumed to negate the spiritual authority thus derived. The famous sermon is commonly regarded as the inauguration of the Oxford Movement, which undertook to combat the rationalistic and liberal tendencies manifesting themselves in religious thought, of which the Noetic group was but a special instance, and to establish as a ground of renewed faith that part of the Anglican tradition which might be identified as antedating its Protestantism.

It was not a project likely to win wide support in the nation. The immediate occasion to which the Oxford Movement responded was the political expression of a state of thought and feeling to which the Protestant tradition of individual judgment and sectarianism contributed equally with the liberal rationalism which verged upon indifference or even hostility to religion. This state of the national mind the members of the Oxford Movement sought to reverse. They repelled the imputation of any wish to bring the Church of England to Roman Catholicism, insisting that they wished to take the *via media*, the middle way, between the Protestant and the Catholic views of tradition and authority, as a new basis of piety. The long-standing antipathy of the English to Catholicism was still strong and the *via media* proposed much too close an approximation to the ancient church they had been taught to fear. The prospect of a renewed piety could not engage the interest of nonconformists, who were quite content with their own state of religious feeling; nor that of conservative churchmen, who set piety below propriety; nor that of liberals of rationalistic bent, the less so because the basis of piety was to be a recognition of ancient tradition and the intellectual authority of the church.

The adherents of the Movement carried on their campaign for the renovation of the conception of the church in a series of *Tracts for the Times*—whence their name of Tractarians—which, despite their often formidable erudition, were widely bought. Religious dispute was of the very essence of English history; the Oxford Movement revived old and interesting feelings, and even had the charm of a scandal. Yet the Movement, however far its echoes may have reached, was in the end limited in its effect to an ecclesiastical and predominantly academic group, chiefly centered in Oxford. Here the emotions and ideas which had their rise in 1833 continued in force for some decades, playing an important and often decisive part in the lives of many members of the university, undergraduates as well as dons.

The Newman of the Oxford Movement was not the Newman of the early Oxford days; the shy young man had become a leader of great charismatic power. Even before 1833 he was generally regarded as one of the most influential teachers in the university; his spiritual dedication and the assiduity with which he carried out his duties as a tutor evoked from his pupils a profound admiration and loyalty. His Sunday afternoon sermons at St. Mary's became famous and formed the rationale of the new religious mode. He was in charge of the publication of *Tracts for the Times*. He drew men to him and exercised great influence upon them. Many of his personal adherents, he was distressed to see, found it impossible to stay in the *via media* and moved toward Rome, and he was greatly troubled about what his own direction must be when he discovered that there was reason to believe that the Anglican position was analogous to that of certain groups condemned as heretical by the ancient church, whose authority Anglicanism was presumed to acknowledge.

In 1841, in the famous Tract 90, he ventured upon the direct controversion of the conventional Anglican position on the Thirty-Nine Articles, which formulate the doctrine of the Church of England. The Articles, Newman said, had been intended as safeguards not against the doctrines of the Catholic Church but against the possible errors of communicants of the Church of England. The view was a tenable one but it provoked a scandalized outcry. At the request of his bishop, Newman broke off the publication of the Tracts, but he knew that his days as an Anglican were numbered. In the next year he retired to Littlemore, a hamlet near Oxford which was part of St. Mary's parish, and here he and a few friends lived in quasi-monastic retirement. It was at this time that he wrote The Development of Christian Doctrine in which he argued that because the church is a living organism, its doctrine is perpetually in growth and has as much authority in its later phases as Protestants concede it to have had in its primitive days. In 1845 his long travail of spirit was ended when he was received into the Roman Catholic Church.

The nature of the intellectual process which led to Newman's decision and which ruled his religious life from beginning to end is likely to be remote from the sympathetic comprehension of most people in our day. This is not to say that religious belief, even though its attenuation is taken for granted throughout the West, is beyond ready understanding. Faith in the existence of a deity and conformity to a mode of conduct and of sensibility that follows from that faith are recognized forms of experience and on the whole they are treated with respect even by those who reject them. What is nowadays difficult to comprehend is the elaborate and rigorous system of predications by which Newman set such store, predications not about the existence of the deity—that was for Newman a fact of experience—but about the nature of the universe created by the deity, about the mysteries through which his nature and his will were to be apprehended, about his true ecclesiastical surrogate on earth, about the authority of the Catholic Church, its creeds, doctrines, dogmas. It is with the last of these, the precise formulations of particular beliefs, that the contemporary difficulty is greatest. If we give credence to the validity of religious faith, we can go on to understand a preference for one religious communion as against another, a choice of forms of belief, of which one more than another gratifies personal temperament or intellectual or moral predilection. But to direct, as Newman did, a natively powerful and highly trained intellect and a vast historical scholarship to the demonstration that, for a multitude of irrefutable reasons, one church rather than another is the sole guardian of truth and the single gateway to salvation—of this enterprise the modern mind (and increasingly, we may say, even the modern Catholic mind) is pretty sure to be impatient.

Yet thus it was that men once thought about their faith and it is a common discovery that if one lends oneself to Newman's process of religious reasoning with the natural sympathy of the historic imagination, one finds that it speaks with a startling immediacy and cogency. As one critic has described the experience of reading Newman, "the challenge that he offers to one's assumptions is so lively and so real, his sense of the world is so subtle and coherent, and his psychological perception is so complex and shrewd that any reader who takes pleasure in endangering his own fixed ideas must be grateful for the exhilaration that Newman can give."

In 1846 Newman went to Rome and was ordained in the Catholic Church. He was given the degree of Doctor of Divinity, but not much more than this in the way of welcome, for the Italian hierarchy regarded this Englishman's theological writings with suspicion, and long continued to do so. He joined the semi-monastic, chiefly pedagogical Congregation of the Oratory, founded in Florence in the sixteenth century by Saint Philip Neri, and returned to England as head of the Oratory at Egbaston, near Birmingham. His life in most of its outward aspects was not a happy one. By his conversion he sacrificed all his Oxford friendships; many Anglicans regarded him as a traitor not only to the English Church but virtually to England itself. The converts from Anglicanism with whom he was associated—their number was quite considerable—were inclined to extreme views as to the authority of the church and the pope and tended to regard his moderation in this matter, especially his belief that the laity should have a part in the intellectual life of the church and that questions of belief should be openly dealt with, as evidence of tepidity. In 1852 he was made rector-elect of the proposed Catholic University in Dublin, for which he had the high hopes expressed in his famous lectures on *The Idea of a University* (1852). Although these discourses put themselves in opposition to the view that theology is not a science and therefore should not be part of a university curriculum, they are generally held to constitute a peculiarly cogent and eloquent defense of liberal education. During his years in Dublin he made good progress toward his goal, but his admirable plans were brought to naught by indifference and small-minded jealousies and in 1856 he resigned the post, in which in fact he had never been confirmed. In 1857 Cardinal Wiseman informed him of the desire of the Catholic bishops of England that he undertake a new translation of the Bible, but when Newman eagerly got the project under way at the Oratory, Wiseman withdrew his support from it. He was made editor of a liberal Catholic magazine, *The Rambler,* but he had scarcely begun the work when his bishop required him to resign. His unpopularity with his co-religionists became almost proverbial.

In 1863 Charles Kingsley, an Anglican divine widely known as a novelist and historian of extreme anti-Catholic views, made a public statement which impugned Newman's integrity as a priest and his honor as an English gentleman. How Newman responded to this slur by writing his most widely read book, *Apologia Pro Vita Sua,* and how warmly the English public responded to it are related below in the Headnote to Chapter V of the *Apologia.* It was in the new atmosphere created by the *Apologia* that he wrote and published what may well be the most brilliant of his works, *An Essay in Aid of a Grammar of Assent* (1870), and republished his early Anglican works (1877). In 1878 he was greatly touched when Protestant Oxford made its peace with him and he was elected to an honorary fellowship in his old college, Trinity. In 1879 he was made a cardinal of his church. He died in 1890.

# *From* The Tamworth Reading Room [1]

### Secular Knowledge Not a Principle of Action

People say to me, that it is but a dream to suppose that Christianity should regain the organic power in human society which once it possessed. I cannot help that; I never said it could. I am not a politician; I am proposing no

1. In 1840, Sir Robert Peel (1788–1850), "the most liberal of conservatives and the most conservative of liberals," soon to be prime minister for a second time, made a gift of a library and reading room to the town of Tamworth, which he represented in Parliament.

measures, but exposing a fallacy, and resisting a pretence. Let Benthamism [2] reign, if men have no aspirations; but do not tell them to be romantic, and then solace them with glory; do not attempt by philosophy what once was done by religion. The ascendency of Faith may be impracticable, but the reign of Knowledge is incomprehensible. The problem for statesmen of this age is how to educate the masses, and literature and science cannot give the solution.

Not so deems Sir Robert Peel; his firm belief and hope is, 'that an increased sagacity will administer to an exalted faith; that it will make men not merely believe in the cold doctrines of Natural Religion, but that it will so prepare and temper the spirit and understanding, that they will be better qualified to comprehend the great scheme of human redemption.' He certainly thinks that scientific pursuits have some considerable power of impressing religion upon the mind of the multitude. I think not, and will now say why.

Science gives us the grounds or premises from which religious truths are to be inferred; but it does not set about inferring them, much less does it reach the inference;—that is not its province. It brings before us phenomena, and it leaves us, if we will, to call them works of design, wisdom, or benevolence; and further still, if we will, to proceed to confess an Intelligent Creator. We have to take its facts, and to give them a meaning, and to draw our own conclusions from them. First comes Knowledge, then a view, then reasoning, and then belief. This is why Science has so little of a religious tendency; deductions have no power of persuasion. The heart is commonly reached, not through the reason, but through the imagination, by means of direct impressions, by the testimony of facts and events, by history, by description. Persons influence us, voices melt us, looks subdue us, deeds inflame us. Many a man will live and die upon a dogma: no man will be a martyr for a conclusion.[3] A conclusion is but an opinion; it is not a thing which *is*, but which *we are* '*certain about*'; and it has often been observed, that we never say we are certain without implying that we doubt. To say that a thing *must* be, is to admit that it *may not* be. No one, I say, will die for his own calculations; he dies for realities. This is why a literary religion is so little to be depended upon; it looks well in fair weather, but its doctrines are opinions, and, when called to suffer for them, it slips them between its folios, or burns them at its hearth. And this again is the secret of the distrust and raillery with which moralists have been so commonly visited. They say and do not. Why? Because they are contemplating the fitness of things, and they live by the square, when they should be realizing their high maxims in the concrete. Now Sir Robert thinks better of natural history, chemistry, and astronomy, than of such ethics; but they too, what are they more than

His address at the opening of the institution expressed the current optimistic view of the good effects of secular education upon the working classes. Newman made the address the occasion for a series of seven letters or discourses, published in 1841 in the *Times* and signed "Catholicus," in which he examined the claims put forward for secular education as a decisive force for social good.

2. The philosophical position deriving from the writings of Jeremy Bentham (1748–1832); Utilitarianism, the ethical doctrine which holds that actions are to be judged by their "utility," that is to say, by the extent to which they promote the happiness of mankind.

3. This sentence and the third following, which reiterates the sense of this one, are perhaps more frequently quoted than anything Newman wrote. As well as brief utterances can, they propose what Newman meant by "faith."

divinity *in posse?*[4] He protests against 'controversial divinity': [5] is *inferential* much better?

I have no confidence, then, in philosophers who cannot help being religious, and are Christians by implication. They sit at home, and reach forward to distances which astonish us; but they hit without grasping, and are sometimes as confident about shadows as about realities. They have worked out by a calculation the lie of a country which they never saw, and mapped it by means of a gazetteer; and like blind men, though they can put a stranger on his way, they cannot walk straight themselves, and do not feel it quite their business to walk at all.

Logic makes but a sorry rhetoric with the multitude; first shoot round corners, and you may not despair of converting by a syllogism. Tell men to gain notions of a Creator from His works, and, if they were to set about it (which nobody does), they would be jaded and wearied by the labyrinth they were tracing. Their minds would be gorged and surfeited by the logical operation. Logicians are more set upon concluding rightly, than on right conclusions. They cannot see the end for the process. Few men have that power of mind which may hold fast and firmly a variety of thoughts. We ridicule 'men of one idea'; but a great many of us are born to be such, and we should be happier if we knew it. To most men argument makes the point in hand only more doubtful, and considerably less impressive. After all, man is *not* a reasoning animal; he is a seeing, feeling, contemplating, acting animal. He is influenced by what is direct and precise. It is very well to freshen our impressions and convictions from physics, but to create them we must go elsewhere. Sir Robert Peel 'never can think it possible that a mind can be so constituted, that, after being familiarized with the wonderful discoveries which have been made in every part of experimental science, it can retire from such contemplations without more enlarged conceptions of God's providence, and a higher reverence for His name.' If he speaks of religious minds, he perpetrates a truism; if of irreligious, he insinuates a paradox.

Life is not long enough for a religion of inferences; we shall never have done beginning, if we determine to begin with proof. We shall ever be laying our foundations; we shall turn theology into evidences, and divines into textuaries. We shall never get at our first principles. Resolve to believe nothing, and you must prove your proofs and analyze your elements, sinking further and further, and finding 'in the lowest depth a lower deep,' till you come to the broad bosom of scepticism. I would rather be bound to defend the reasonableness of assuming that Christianity is true, than to demonstrate a moral governance from the physical world. Life is for action. If we insist on proofs for everything, we shall never come to action: to act you must assume, and that assumption is faith.

4. Potentially.
5. In his fifth letter, "Secular Knowledge Not a Principle of Social Unity," Newman had said that there was nothing wrong with religious views' being expressed controversially. "Christianity," he said, "is a faith, faith implies a doctrine, a doctrine proposition, propositions yes or no, yes or no differences. Differences, then, are the natural attendants on Christianity, and you cannot have Christianity and not have differences." He would not have admitted that there was any contradiction between this state of affairs and the sentences commented on in note 3 above.

Let no one suppose that in saying this I am maintaining that all proofs are equally difficult, and all propositions equally debatable. Some assumptions are greater than others, and some doctrines involve postulates larger than others, and more numerous. I only say that impressions lead to action, and that reasonings lead from it. Knowledge of premisses, and inferences upon them,—this is not to *live*. It is very well as a matter of liberal curiosity and of philosophy to analyze our modes of thought; but let this come second, and when there is leisure for it, and then our examinations will in many ways even be subservient to action. But if we commence with scientific knowledge and argumentative proof, or lay any great stress upon it as the basis of personal Christianity, or attempt to make man moral and religious by Libraries and Museums, let us in consistency take chemists for our cooks, and mineralogists for our masons.

Now I wish to state all this as matter of fact, to be judged by the candid testimony of any persons whatever. Why we are so constituted that Faith, not Knowledge or Argument, is our principle of action, is a question with which I have nothing to do; but I think it is a fact, and if it be such, we must resign ourselves to it as best we may, unless we take refuge in the intolerable paradox, that the mass of men are created for nothing, and are meant to leave life as they entered it. So well has this practically been understood in all ages of the world, that no Religion has yet been a Religion of physics or of philosophy. It has ever been synonymous with Revelation. It never has been a deduction from what we know: it has ever been an assertion of what we are to believe. It has never lived in a conclusion; it has never been a message, or a history, or a vision. No legislator or priest ever dreamed of educating our moral nature by science or by argument. There is no difference here between true Religions and pretended. Moses was instructed, not to reason from the creation, but to work miracles. Christianity is a history supernatural, and almost scenic: it tells us what its Author is, by telling us what He has done. I have no wish at all to speak otherwise than respectfully of conscientious Dissenters, but I have heard it said by those who were not their enemies, and who had known much of their preaching, that they had often heard narrow-minded and bigoted clergymen, and often Dissenting ministers of a far more intellectual cast; but that Dissenting teaching came to nothing,—that it was dissipated in thoughts which had no point, and inquiries which converged to no centre, that it ended as it began, and sent away its hearers as it found them;—whereas the instruction in the Church, with all its defects and mistakes, comes to some end, for it started from some beginning. Such is the difference between the dogmatism of faith and the speculations of logic.

Lord Brougham himself, as we have already seen, has recognized the force of this principle. He has not left his philosophical religion to argument; he has committed it to the keeping of the imagination. Why should he depict a great republic of letters, and an intellectual Pantheon, but that he feels that instances and patterns, not logical reasonings, are the living conclusions which alone have a hold over the affections, or can form the character?

1841                                                                      1841

# *From* Discourses to Mixed Congregations [1]

## Faith and Private Judgment

When we consider the beauty, the majesty, the completeness, the resources, the consolations, of the Catholic Religion, it may strike us with wonder, my brethren, that it does not convert the multitude of those who come in its way. Perhaps you have felt this surprise yourselves; especially those of you who have been recently converted, and can compare it, from experience, with those religions which the millions of this country choose instead of it. You know from experience how barren, unmeaning, and baseless those religions are; what poor attractions they have, and how little they have to say for themselves. Multitudes, indeed, are of no religion at all; and you may not be surprised that those who cannot even bear the thought of God, should not feel drawn to His Church; numbers, too, hear very little about Catholicism, or a great deal of abuse and calumny against it, and you may not be surprised that they do not all at once become Catholics; but what may fairly surprise those who enjoy the fulness of Catholic blessings is, that those who see the Church ever so distantly, who see even gleams or the faint lustre of her majesty, nevertheless should not be so far attracted by what they see as to seek to see more,—should not at least put themselves in the way to be led on to the Truth, which of course is not ordinarily recognised in its Divine authority except by degrees. Moses, when he saw the burning bush, turned aside to see 'that great sight'; [2] Nathaniel, though he thought no good could come out of Nazareth, at least followed Philip to Christ, when Philip said to him, 'Come and see'; [3] but the multitudes about us see and hear, in some measure, surely,—many in ample measure,—and yet are not persuaded thereby to see and hear more, are not moved to act upon their knowledge. Seeing they see not, and hearing they hear not; they are contented to remain as they are; they are not drawn to inquire, or at least not drawn on to embrace.

Many explanations may be given of this difficulty; I will proceed to suggest to you one, which will sound like a truism, but yet has a meaning in it. Men do not become Catholics, because they have not faith. Now you may ask me, how this is saying more than that men do not believe the Catholic Church *because* they do not believe it; which is saying nothing at all. Our Lord, for instance, says, 'He who cometh to Me shall not hunger, and he who believeth in Me shall never thirst'; [4]—to believe then and to come are the same thing. If they had faith, of course they would join the Church, for the very meaning, the very exercise of faith, is joining the Church. But I mean something more than this: faith is a state of mind, it is a particular mode of thinking and acting, which is exercised, always indeed towards God, but in very various ways. Now I mean

---

1. In 1846, Newman went to Rome, where he was ordained a priest of the Catholic Church. In 1847 he returned to England and in Birmingham he established the Oratory (see Headnote) where the rest of his life was spent. It was at this time that he delivered *Discourses to Mixed Congregations,* his first sermons as a Catholic. This selection is Discourse X.
2. Exodus 3:3.
3. John 1:45–46.
4. John 4:14. Like many of Newman's quotations from the Bible, this does not conform exactly to the text of the King James version. Newman often quoted from memory and sometimes he had in mind the (Catholic) Douay-Rheims version.

to say, that the multitude of men in this country have not this habit or character
of mind. We could conceive, for instance, their believing in their own religions,
even if they did not believe in the Church; this would be faith, though a faith
improperly directed; but they do not believe even their own religions; they do
not believe in anything at all. It is a definite defect in their minds: as we might
say that a person had not the virtue of meekness, or of liberality, or of prudence,
quite independently of this or that exercise of the virtue, so there is such a
religious virtue as faith, and there is such a defect as the absence of it. Now
I mean to say that the great mass of men in this country have not this particular
virtue called faith, have not this virtue at all. As a man might be without eyes
or without hands, so they are without faith; it is a distinct want or fault in their
soul; and what I say is, that since they have not this faculty of religious belief,
no wonder they do not embrace that, which cannot really be embraced without
it. They do not believe any teaching at all in any true sense; and therefore they
do not believe the Church in particular.

Now, in the first place, what is faith? it is assenting to a doctrine as true,
which we do not see, which we cannot prove, because God says it is true, who
cannot lie. And further than this, since God says it is true, not with His own
voice, but by the voice of His messengers, it is assenting to what man says, not
simply viewed as a man, but to what he is commissioned to declare, as a
messenger, prophet, or ambassador from God. In the ordinary course of this
world we account things true either because we see them, or because we can
perceive that they follow and are deducible from what we do see; that is, we
gain truth by sight or by reason, not by faith. You will say indeed, that we
accept a number of things which we cannot prove or see, on the word of others;
certainly, but then we accept what they say only as the word of man; and we
have not commonly that absolute and unreserved confidence in them, which
nothing can shake. We know that man is open to mistake, and we are always
glad to find some confirmation of what he says, from other quarters, in any
important matter; or we receive his information with negligence and uncon-
cern, as something of little consequence, as a matter of opinion; or, if we act
upon it, it is as a matter of prudence, thinking it best and safest to do so. We take
his word for what it is worth, and we use it either according to our necessity,
or its probability. We keep the decision in our own hands, and reserve to ourselves the right of re-opening the question whenever we please. This is very different from Divine faith; he who believes that God is true, and that this is
His word, which He has committed to man, has no doubt at all. He is as
certain that the doctrine taught is true, as that God is true; and he is certain,
*because* God is true, *because* God has spoken, not because he sees its truth or
can prove its truth. That is, faith has two peculiarities;—it is most certain,
decided, positive, immovable in its assent, and it gives this assent not because
it sees with eye, or sees with the reason, but because it receives the tidings from
one who comes from God.

This is what faith was in the time of the Apostles, as no one can deny; and
what it was then, it must be now, else it ceases to be the same thing. I say, it
certainly was this in the Apostles' time, for you know they preached to the
world that Christ was the Son of God, that He was born of a Virgin, that He
had ascended on high, that He would come again to judge all, the living and

the dead. Could the world see all this? could it prove it? how then were men to receive it? why did so many embrace it? on the word of the Apostles, who were, as their powers showed, messengers from God. Men were told to submit their reason to a living authority. Moreover, whatever an Apostle said, his converts were bound to believe; when they entered the Church, they entered it in order to learn. The Church was their teacher; they did not come to argue, to examine, to pick and choose, but to accept whatever was put before them. No one doubts, no one can doubt this, of those primitive times. A Christian was bound to take without doubting all that the Apostles declared to be revealed; if the Apostles spoke, he had to yield an internal assent of his mind; it would not be enough to keep silence, it would not be enough not to oppose: it was not allowable to credit in a measure; it was not allowable to doubt. No; if a convert had his own private thoughts of what was said, and only kept them to himself, if he made some secret opposition to the teaching, if he waited for further proof before he believed it, this would be a proof that he did not think the Apostles were sent from God to reveal His will; it would be a proof that he did not in any true sense believe at all. Immediate, implicit submission of the mind was, in the lifetime of the Apostles, the only, the necessary token of faith; then there was no room whatever for what is now called private judgment. No one could say: 'I will choose my religion for myself, I will believe this, I will not believe that; I will pledge myself to nothing; I will believe just as long as I please, and no longer; what I believe to-day I will reject to-morrow, if I choose. I will believe what the Apostles have as yet said, but I will not believe what they shall say in time to come.' No; either the Apostles were from God, or they were not; if they were, everything that they preached was to be believed by their hearers; if they were not, there was nothing for their hearers to believe. To believe a little, to believe more or less, was impossible; it contradicted the very notion of believing: if one part was to be believed, every part was to be believed; it was an absurdity to believe one thing and not another; for the word of the Apostles, which made the one true, made the other true too; they were nothing in themselves, they were all things, they were an infallible authority, as coming from God. The world had either to become Christian, or to let it alone; there was no room for private tastes and fancies, no room for private judgment.

Now surely this is quite clear from the nature of the case; but is also clear from the words of Scripture. 'We give thanks to God,' says St. Paul, 'without ceasing, because when ye had received from us the word of hearing, which is of God, ye received it, not as the word of men, but (as it is indeed) the Word of God.' [5] Here you see St. Paul expresses what I have said above; that the Word comes from God, that it is spoken by men, that it must be received, not as man's word, but as God's word. So in another place he says: 'He who despiseth these things, despiseth not man, but God, who hath also given in us His Holy Spirit.' [6] Our Saviour had made a like declaration already: 'He that heareth you, heareth Me; and he that despiseth you, despiseth Me; and he that despiseth Me, despiseth Him that sent Me.' [7] Accordingly, St. Peter on the day

5. I Thessalonians 2:13.
6. I Thessalonians 4:8.
7. Luke 10:16.

of Pentecost said: 'Men of Israel, *hear* these words, God hath raised up this Jesus, whereof *we* are *witnesses*. Let all the house of Israel *know most certainly* that God hath made this Jesus, whom you have crucified, both Lord and Christ.' [8] At another time he said: 'We ought to obey God, rather than man; we are *witnesses* of these things, and so *is the Holy Ghost*, whom God has given to all who obey Him.' [9] And again: 'He commanded us to preach to the people, and to testify that it is He (Jesus) who hath been appointed by God to be the Judge of the living and of the dead.' [10] And you know that the persistent declaration of the first preachers was: 'Believe and thou shalt be saved': they do not say, 'prove our doctrine by your own reason,' nor 'wait till you see before you believe'; but, 'believe without seeing and without proving, because our word is not our own, but God's word.' Men might indeed use their reason in inquiring into the pretensions of the Apostles; they might inquire whether or not they did miracles; they might inquire whether they were predicted in the Old Testament as coming from God; but when they had ascertained this fairly in whatever way, they were to take all the Apostles said for granted without proof; they were to exercise their faith, they were to be saved by hearing. Hence, as you perhaps observed, St. Paul significantly calls the revealed doctrine 'the word of hearing,' in the passage I quoted; men came to hear, to accept, to obey, not to criticise what was said; and in accordance with this he asks elsewhere: 'How shall they believe Him, whom they have not heard? and how shall they hear without a preacher? Faith cometh by hearing, and hearing by the word of Christ.' [11]

Now, my dear brethren, consider, are not these two states or acts of mind quite distinct from each other;—to believe simply what a living authority tells you, and to take a book, such as Scripture, and to use it as you please, to master it, that is, to make yourself the master of it, to interpret it for yourself, and to admit just what you choose to see in it, and nothing more? Are not these two procedures distinct in this, that in the former you submit, in the latter you judge? At this moment I am not asking you which is the better, I am not asking whether this or that is practicable now, but are they not two ways of taking up a doctrine, and not one? is not submission quite contrary to judging? Now, is it not certain that faith in the time of the Apostles consisted in submitting? and is it not certain that it did not consist in judging for one's self. It is in vain to say that the man who judges from the Apostles' writings, does submit to those writings in the first instance, and therefore has faith in them; else why should he refer to them at all? There is, I repeat, an essential difference between the act of submitting to a living oracle, and to his written words; in the former case there is no appeal from the speaker, in the latter the final decision remains with the reader. Consider how different is the confidence with which you report another's words in his presence and in his absence. If he be absent, you boldly say that he holds so and so, or said so and so; but let him come into the room in the midst of the conversation, and your tone is immediately changed. It is then, 'I *think* I have heard you say something *like* this,

8. Acts 10:34–43.
9. Acts 5:32.
10. Acts 10:42.
11. Romans 10:14–17.

or what I *took* to be this'; or you modify considerably the statement or the fact to which you originally pledged him, dropping one-half of it for safety sake, or retrenching the most startling portions of it; and then after all you wait with some anxiety to see whether he will accept any portion of it at all. The same sort of process takes place in the case of the written document of a person now dead. I can fancy a man magisterially expounding St. Paul's Epistle to the Galatians or to the Ephesians, who would be better content with the writer's absence than his sudden re-appearance among us; lest the Apostle should take his own meaning out of his commentator's hands and explain it for himself. In a word, though he says he has faith in St. Paul's writings, he confessedly has no faith in St. Paul; and though he may speak much about truth as found in Scripture, he has no wish at all to be like one of these Christians whose names and deeds occur in it.

I think I may assume that this virtue, which was exercised by the first Christians, is not known at all among Protestants now; or at least if there are instances of it, it is exercised towards those, I mean their own teachers and divines, who expressly disclaim that they are fit objects of it, and who exhort their people to judge for themselves. Protestants, generally speaking, have not faith, in the primitive meaning of that word; this is clear from what I have been saying, and here is a confirmation of it. If men believed now as they did in the times of the Apostles, they could not doubt nor change. No one can doubt whether a word spoken by God is to be believed; of course it is; whereas any one, who is modest and humble, may easily be brought to doubt of his own inferences and deductions. Since men now-a-days deduce from Scripture, instead of believing a teacher, you may expect to see them waver about; they will feel the force of their own deductions more strongly at one time than at another, they will change their minds about them, or perhaps deny them altogether; whereas this cannot be, while a man has faith, that is, belief that what a preacher says to him comes from God. This is what St. Paul especially insists on, telling us that Apostles, prophets, evangelists, pastors, and teachers, are given us that 'we may all attain to unity of faith,' and, on the contrary, in order 'that we be *not* as children tossed to and fro, and carried about by every gale of doctrine.' [12] Now, in matter of fact, do not men in this day change about in their religious opinions without any limit? Is not this, then, a proof that they have not that faith which the Apostles demanded of their converts? If they had faith, they would not change. Once believe that God has spoken, and you are sure He cannot unsay what He has already said; He cannot deceive; He cannot change; you have received it once for all; you will believe it ever.

Such is the only rational, consistent account of faith; but so far are Protestants from professing it, that they laugh at the very notion of it. They laugh at the notion itself of men pinning their faith (as they express themselves) upon Pope or Council; they think it simply superstitious and narrow-minded, to profess to believe just what the Church believes, and to assent to whatever she will say in time to come on matters of doctrine. That is, they laugh at the bare notion of doing what Christians undeniably did in the time of the Apostles. Observe, they do not merely ask whether the Catholic Church has a claim to teach, has

12. Ephesians 4:14.

authority, has the gifts;—this is a reasonable question;—no, they think that
the very state of mind which such a claim involves in those who admit it,
namely, the disposition to accept without reserve or question, that *this* is
slavish. They call it priestcraft to insist on this surrender of the reason, and
superstition to make it. That is, they quarrel with the very state of mind which
all Christians had in the age of the Apostles; nor is there any doubt (who will
deny it?) that those who thus boast of not being led blindfold, of judging for
themselves, of believing just as much and just as little as they please, of hating
dictation, and so forth, would have found it an extreme difficulty to hang on the
lips of the Apostles, had they lived at their date, or rather would have simply
resisted the sacrifice of their own liberty of thought, would have thought life
eternal too dearly purchased at such a price, and would have died in their
unbelief. And they would have defended themselves on the plea that it was
absurd and childish to ask them to believe without proof, to bid them give up
their education, and their intelligence, and their science, and in spite of all
those difficulties which reason and sense find in the Christian doctrine, in spite
of its mysteriousness, its obscurity, its strangeness, its unacceptableness, its
severity, to require them to surrender themselves to the teaching of a few
unlettered Galilæans, or a learned indeed but fanatical Pharisee. This is what
they would have said then; and if so, is it wonderful they do not become
Catholics now? The simple account of their remaining as they are, is, that they
lack one thing,—they have not faith; it is a state of mind, it is a virtue, which
they do not recognise to be praiseworthy, which they do not aim at possessing.

What they feel now, my brethren, is just what both Jew and Greek felt before
them in the time of the Apostles, and what the natural man has felt ever since.
The great and wise men of the day looked down upon faith, then as now, as if
it were unworthy the dignity of human nature: 'See your vocation, brethern,
that there are not,' among you, 'many wise according to the flesh, not many
mighty, not many noble; but the foolish things of the world hath God chosen
to confound the strong, and the mean things of the world, and the things that
are contemptible, hath God chosen, and things that are not, that He might
destroy the things that are, that no flesh might glory in His sight.' [13] Hence the
same Apostle speaks of 'the foolishness of preaching.' Similar to this is what
our Lord had said in His prayer to the Father: 'I thank Thee, Father, Lord of
heaven and earth, because thou hast hid these things from the wise and
prudent, and hast revealed them unto little ones.' [14] Now, is it not plain that
men of this day have just inherited the feelings and traditions of these falsely
wise and fatally prudent persons in our Lord's day? They have the same obstruction in their hearts to entering the Catholic Church, which Pharisees and
Sophists had before them; it goes against them to believe her doctrine, not so
much for want of evidence that she is from God, as because, if so, they shall
have to submit their minds to living men, who have not their own cultivation
or depth of intellect, and because they must receive a number of doctrines,
whether they will or no, which are strange to their imagination and difficult to
their reason. The very characteristic of the Catholic teaching and of the Catholic

13. I Corinthians 1:26–29.
14. Matthew 11:25.

teacher is to them a preliminary objection to their becoming Catholics, so great, as to throw into the shade any argument however strong, which is producible in behalf of the mission of those teachers and the origin of that teaching. In short, they have not faith.

They have not in them the principle of faith; and I repeat, it is nothing to the purpose to urge that at least they firmly believe Scripture to be the Word of God. In truth, it is much to be feared that their acceptance of Scripture itself is nothing better than a prejudice or inveterate feeling impressed on them when they were children. A proof of it is this; that, while they profess to be so shocked at Catholic miracles, and are not slow to call them 'lying wonders,' they have no difficulty at all about Scripture narratives, which are quite as difficult to the reason as any miracles recorded in the history of the Saints. I have heard on the contrary of Catholics who have been startled at first reading in Scripture the narratives of the ark in the deluge, of the tower of Babel, of Balaam and Balac, of the Israelites' flight from Egypt and entrance into the promised land, and of Esau's and Saul's rejection; which the bulk of Protestants receive without any effort of mind. How, then, do these Catholics accept them? by faith. They say, 'God is true, and every man a liar.' How come Protestants so easily to receive them? by faith? Nay, I conceive that in most cases there is no submission of the reason at all; simply they are so familiar with the passages in question, that the narrative presents no difficulties to their imagination; they have nothing to overcome. If, however, they *are* led to contemplate these passages in themselves, and to try them in the balance of probability, and to begin to question about them, as will happen when their intellect is cultivated, then there is nothing to bring them back to their former habitual or mechanical belief; they know nothing of submitting to authority, that is, they know nothing of faith; for they have no authority to submit to. They either remain in a state of doubt without any great trouble of mind, or they go on to ripen into utter disbelief on the subjects in question, though they may say nothing about it. Neither before they doubt, nor when they doubt, is there any token of the presence in them of a power subjecting reason to the Word of God. No; what looks like faith, is a mere hereditary persuasion, not a personal principle; it is a habit which they have learned in the nursery, which has never changed into anything higher, and which is scattered and disappears, like a mist, before the light, such as it is, of reason. If, however, there are Protestants, who are not in one or other of these two states, either of credulity or of doubt, but who firmly believe in spite of all difficulties, they certainly have some claim to be considered under the influence of faith; but there is nothing to show that such persons, where they are found, are not in the way to become Catholics, and perhaps they are already called so by their friends, showing in their own examples the logical, indisputable connexion which exists between possessing faith and joining the Church.

If, then, faith be now the same faculty of mind, the same sort of habit or act, which it was in the days of the Apostles, I have made good what I set about showing. But it must be the same; it cannot mean two things; the Word cannot have changed its meaning. Either say that faith is not necessary now at all, or take it to be what the Apostles meant by it, but do not say that you have it, and then show me something quite different, which you have put in the place of it.

In the Apostles' days the peculiarity of faith was submission to a living authority; this is what made it so distinctive; this is what made it an act of submission at all; this is what destroyed private judgment in matters of religion. If you will not look out for a living authority, and will bargain for private judgment, then say at once that you have not Apostolic faith. And in fact you have it not; the bulk of this nation has it not; confess you have it not; and then confess that this is the reason why you are not Catholics. You are not Catholics because you have not faith. Why do not blind men see the sun? because they have no eyes. In like manner it is vain to discourse upon the beauty, the sanctity, the sublimity of the Catholic doctrine and worship, where men have no faith to accept it as Divine. They may confess its beauty, sublimity, and sanctity, without believing it; they may acknowledge that the Catholic religion is noble and majestic; they may be struck with its wisdom, they may admire its adaptation to human nature, they may be penetrated by its tender and winning bearing, they may be awed by its consistency. But to commit themselves to it, that is another matter; to choose it for their portion, to say with the favoured Moabitess, 'Whithersoever thou shalt go, I will go! and where thou shalt dwell, I will dwell; thy people shall be my people, and thy God my God,' [15] this is the language of faith. A man may revere, a man may extol, who has no tendency whatever to obey, no notion whatever of professing. And this often happens in fact: men are respectful to the Catholic religion; they acknowledge its services to mankind, they encourage it and its professors; they like to know them, they are interested in hearing of their movements, but they are not, and never will be Catholics. They will die as they have lived, out of the Church, because they have not possessed themselves of that faculty by which the Church is to be approached. Catholics who have not studied them or human nature, will wonder they remain where they are; nay, they themselves, alas for them! will sometimes lament they cannot become Catholics. They will feel so intimately the blessedness of being a Catholic, that they will cry out, 'Oh, what would I give to be a Catholic! Oh, that I could believe what I admire! but I do not, and I can no more believe merely because I wish to do so, than I can leap over a mountain. I should be much happier were I a Catholic; but I am not; it is no use deceiving myself; I am what I am; I revere, I cannot accept.'

Oh, deplorable state! deplorable because it is utterly and absolutely their own fault, and because such great stress is laid in Scripture, as they know, on the necessity of faith for salvation. Faith is there made the foundation and commencement of all acceptable obedience. It is described as the 'argument' or 'proof of things not seen'; by faith men have understood that God is, that He made the world, that He is a rewarder of those who seek Him, that the flood was coming, that their Saviour was to be born. 'Without faith it is impossible to please God'; 'by faith we stand'; 'by faith we walk'; 'by faith we overcome the world.' When our Lord gave to the Apostles their commission to preach all over the world, He continued, 'He that believeth and is baptised, shall be saved; but he that believeth not, shall be condemned.' [16] And He declared to

15. Ruth 1:16–17.
16. Mark 16:16.

Nicodemus, 'He that believeth in the Son, is not judged; but he that doth not believe is already judged, because he believeth not in the Name of the Only-begotten Son of God.' [17] He said to the Pharisees, 'If you believe not that I am He, ye shall die in your sins.' [18] To the Jews, 'Ye believe not, because ye are not of My sheep.' [19] And you may recollect that before His miracles, He commonly demands faith of the supplicant: 'All things are possible,' He says, 'to him that believeth'; [20] and we find in one place, 'He could not do any miracle,' on account of the unbelief of the inhabitants.

Has faith changed its meaning, or is it less necessary now? Is it not still what it was in the Apostles' day, the very characteristic of Christianity, the special instrument of renovation, the first disposition for justification, one out of the three theological virtues? God might have renewed us by other means, by sight, by reason, by love, but He has chosen to 'purify our hearts by faith'; it has been His will to select an instrument which the world despises, but which is of immense power. He preferred it, in His infinite wisdom, to every other; and if men have it not, they have not the very element and rudiment, out of which are formed, on which are built, the Saints and Servants of God. And they have it not; they are living, they are dying, without the hopes, without the aids of the Gospel, because, in spite of so much that is good in them, in spite of their sense of duty, their tenderness of conscience on many points, their benevolence, their uprightness, their generosity, they are under the dominion (I must say it) of a proud fiend; they have this stout spirit within them, they determine to be their own masters in matters of thought, about which they know so little; they consider their own reason better than any one's else; they will not admit that any one comes from God who contradicts their own view of truth. What! is none their equal in wisdom anywhere? is there none other whose word is to be taken on religion? is there none to wrest from them their ultimate appeal to themselves? Have they in no possible way the occasion or opportunity of faith? Is it a virtue, which, in consequence of their transcendent sagacity, their prerogative of omniscience, they must give up hope of exercising? If the pretensions of the Catholic Church do not satisfy them, let them go somewhere else, if they can. If they are so fastidious that they cannot trust her as the oracle of God, let them find another more certainly from Him than the House of His own institution, which has ever been called by His name, has ever maintained the same claims, has ever taught one substance of doctrine, and has triumphed over those who preached any other. Since Apostolic faith was in the beginning reliance on man's word, as being God's word, since what faith was then such it is now, since faith is necessary for salvation, let them attempt to exercise it towards another, if they will not accept the Bride of the Lamb. Let them, if they can, put faith in some of those religions which have lasted a whole two or three centuries in a corner of the earth. Let them stake their eternal prospects on kings and nobles and parliaments and soldiery, let them take some mere fiction of the law, or abortion of the schools, or idol of a populace, or upstart of a crisis, or oracle of lecture-rooms, as the prophet of God. Alas! they are

17. John 3:18.
18. John 8:21, 24.
19. John 10:26.
20. Mark 9:23.

hardly bestead if they must possess a virtue, which they have no means of exercising,—if they must make an act of faith, they know not on whom, and know not why!

What thanks ought we to render to Almighty God, my dear brethren, that He has made us what we are! It is a matter of grace. There are, to be sure, many cogent arguments to lead one to join the Catholic Church, but they do not force the will. We may know them, and not be moved to act upon them. We may be convinced without being persuaded. The two things are quite distinct from each other, seeing you ought to believe, and believing; reason, if left to itself, will bring you to the conclusion that you have sufficient grounds for believing, but belief is the gift of grace. You are then what you are, not from any excellence or merit of your own, but by the grace of God who has chosen you to believe. You might have been as the barbarian of Africa, or the freethinker of Europe, with grace sufficient to condemn you, because it had not furthered your salvation. You might have had strong inspirations of grace and have resisted them, and then additional grace might not have been given to overcome your resistance. God gives not the same measure of grace to all. Has He not visited you with over-abundant grace? and was it not necessary for your hard hearts to receive more than other people? Praise and bless Him continually for the benefit; do not forget, as time goes on, that it is of grace; do not pride yourselves upon it; pray ever not to lose it; and do your best to make others partakers of it.

And you, my brethren, also, if such be present, who are not as yet Catholics, but who by your coming hither seem to show your interest in our teaching, and you wish to know more about it, you too remember, that though you may not yet have faith in the Church, still God has brought you into the way of obtaining it. You are under the influence of His grace; He has brought you a step on your journey; He wishes to bring you further, He wishes to bestow on you the fulness of His blessings, and to make you Catholics. You are still in your sins; probably you are laden with the guilt of many years, the accumulated guilt of many a deep, mortal offence, which no contrition has washed away, and to which no Sacrament has been applied. You at present are troubled with an uneasy conscience, a dissatisfied reason, an unclean heart, and a divided will; you need to be converted. Yet now the first suggestions of grace are working in your souls, and are to issue in pardon for the past and sanctity for the future. God is moving you to acts of faith, hope, love, hatred of sin, repentance; do not disappoint Him, do not thwart Him, concur with Him, obey Him. You look up, and you see, as it were, a great mountain to be scaled; you say, 'How can I possibly find a path over these giant obstacles, which I find in the way of my becoming Catholic? I do not comprehend this doctrine, and I am pained at that; a third seems impossible; I never can be familiar with one practice, I am afraid of another; it is one maze and discomfort to me, and I am led to sink down in despair.' Say not so, my dear brethren, look up in hope, trust in Him who calls you forward. 'Who art thou, O great mountain, before Zorobabel? but a plain.' [21] He will lead you forward step by step, as He has led forward many a one before you. He will make the crooked straight and the

21. Zechariah 4:7.

rough plain. He will turn the streams, and dry up the rivers, which lie in your path. 'He shall strengthen your feet like harts' feet, and set you up on high places. He shall widen your steps under you, and your tread shall not be weakened.' [22] 'There is no God like the God of the righteous; He that mounts the heaven is thy Helper; by His mighty working the clouds disperse; His dwelling is above, and underneath are the everlasting arms; He shall cast out the enemy from before thee, and shall say, Crumble away.' [23] 'The young shall faint, and youths shall fall; but they that hope in the Lord shall be new-fledged in strength, they shall take feathers like eagles, they shall run and not labour, they shall walk and not faint.' [24]

1849                                                                              1849


# The Idea of a University [1]

### From *Knowledge Viewed in Relation to Professional Skill*

I

I have been insisting, in my two preceding Discourses, first, on the cultivation of the intellect, as an end which may reasonably be pursued for its own sake; and next, on the nature of that cultivation, or what that cultivation consists in. Truth of whatever kind is the proper object of the intellect; its cultivation then lies in fitting it to apprehend and contemplate truth. Now the intellect in its present state, with exceptions which need not here be specified, does not discern truth intuitively, or as a whole. We know, not by a direct and simple vision, not at a glance, but, as it were, by piecemeal and accumulation, by a mental process, by going round an object, by the comparison, the combination, the mutual correction, the continual adaptation, of many partial notions, by the employment, concentration, and joint action of many faculties and exercises of mind. Such a union and concert of the intellectual powers, such an enlargement and development, such a comprehensiveness, is necessarily a matter of training. And again, such a training is a matter of rule; it is not mere application, however exemplary, which introduces the mind to truth, nor the reading many books, nor the getting up many subjects, nor the witnessing many experiments, nor the attending many lectures. All this is short of enough; a man may have done it all, yet be lingering in the vestibule of knowledge:—he may not realize what his mouth utters; he may not see with his mental eye what confronts him; he may have no grasp of things as they are; or at least he may have no power at all of advancing one step forward of himself, in consequence of what he has already acquired, no power of discriminating between truth and false-

22. Psalms 18:33.
23. Deuteronomy 33:26–27.
24. Isaiah 11:30–31.

1. The nine discourses which comprise *The Idea of a University* were delivered in Dublin in 1852. (The one presented here is from Discourse VII.) Their purpose was to define for the Irish clergy and laity the principles by which a projected Catholic university in Ireland should be shaped. In 1854 Newman, at the invitation of the Irish bishops, went to Dublin as rector of the new institution. For a variety of reasons, the enterprise failed, and after four unhappy years Newman returned to Birmingham.

hood, of sifting out the grains of truth from the mass, of arranging things according to their real value, and, if I may use the phrase, of building up ideas. Such a power is the result of a scientific formation of mind; it is an acquired faculty of judgment, of clear-sightedness, of sagacity, of wisdom, of philosophical reach of mind, and of intellectual self-possession and repose,— qualities which do not come of mere acquirement. The bodily eye, the organ for apprehending material objects, is provided by nature; the eye of the mind, of which the object is truth, is the work of discipline and habit.

This process of training, by which the intellect, instead of being formed or sacrificed to some particular or accidental purpose, some specific trade or profession, or study or science, is disciplined for its own sake, for the perception of its own proper object, and for its own highest culture, is called Liberal Education; and though there is no one in whom it is carried as far as is conceivable, or whose intellect would be a pattern of what intellects should be made, yet there is scarcely any one but may gain an idea of what real training is, and at least look towards it, and make its true scope and result, not something else, his standard of excellence; and numbers there are who may submit themselves to it, and secure it to themselves in good measure. And to set forth the right standard, and to train according to it, and to help forward all students towards it according to their various capacities, this I conceive to be the business of a University.

II

Now this is what some great men are very slow to allow; they insist that Education should be confined to some particular and narrow end, and should issue in some definite work, which can be weighed and measured. They argue as if every thing, as well as every person, had its price; and that where there has been a great outlay, they have a right to expect a return in kind. This they call making Education and Instruction 'useful,' and 'Utility' becomes their watchword. With a fundamental principle of this nature, they very naturally go on to ask, what there is to show for the expense of a University; what is the real worth in the market of the article called 'a Liberal Education,' on the supposition that it does not teach us definitely how to advance our manufactures, or to improve our lands, or to better our civil economy; or again, if it does not at once make this man a lawyer, that an engineer, and that a surgeon; or at least if it does not lead to discoveries in chemistry, astronomy, geology, magnetism, and science of every kind.

.   .   .

V

. . . Let us take 'useful,' as Locke [2] takes it, in its proper and popular sense, and then we enter upon a large field of thought, to which I cannot do justice in one discourse, though today's is all the space that I can give to it. I say, let

2. John Locke (1632–1704), the English philosopher; his *On Education* urged that emphasis be put on practical subjects. Newman has been dealing with an attack on Oxford education, particularly on classical studies, which had been made a generation before by a group of writers in the *Edinburgh Review*. He identifies Locke as the originator of the ideas advanced by the Edinburgh group and undertakes to deal with the great man rather than with his followers.

us take 'useful' to mean, not what is simply good, but what *tends* to good, or is the *instrument* of good; and in this sense also, Gentlemen, I will show you how a liberal education is truly and fully a useful, though it be not a professional, education. 'Good' indeed means one thing, and 'useful' means another; but I lay it down as a principle, which will save us a great deal of anxiety, that, though the useful is not always good, the good is always useful. Good is not only good, but reproductive of good; this is one of its attributes; nothing is excellent, beautiful, perfect, desirable for its own sake, but it overflows, and spreads the likeness of itself all around it. Good is prolific; it is not only good to the eye, but to the taste; it not only attracts us, but it communicates itself; it excites first our admiration and love, then our desire and our gratitude, and that, in proportion to its intenseness and fulness in particular instances. A great good will impart great good. If then the intellect is so excellent a portion of us, and its cultivation so excellent, it is not only beautiful, perfect, admirable, and noble in itself, but in a true and high sense it must be useful to the possessor and to all around him; not useful in any low, mechanical, mercantile sense, but as diffusing good, or as a blessing, or a gift, or power, or a treasure, first to the owner, then through him to the world, I say then, if a liberal education be good, it must necessarily be useful too.

VI

You will see what I mean by the parallel of bodily health. Health is a good in itself, though nothing came of it, and is especially worth seeking and cherishing; yet, after all, the blessings which attend its presence are so great, while they are so close to it and so redound back upon it and encircle it, that we never think of it except as useful as well as good, and praise and prize it for what it does, as well as for what it is, though at the same time we cannot point out any definite and distinct work or production which it can be said to effect. And so as regards intellectual culture, I am far from denying utility in this large sense as the end of education, when I lay it down that the culture of the intellect is a good in itself and its own end; I do not exclude from the idea of intellectual culture what it cannot but be, from the very nature of things; I only deny that we must be able to point out, before we have any right to call it useful, some art, or business, or profession, or trade, or work, as resulting from it, and as its real and complete end. The parallel is exact: as the body may be sacrificed to some manual or other toil, whether moderate or oppressive, so may the intellect be devoted to some specific profession; and I do not call *this* the culture of the intellect. Again, as some member or organ of the body may be inordinately used and developed, so may memory, or imagination, or the reasoning faculty; and *this* again is not intellectual culture. On the other hand, as the body may be tended, cherished, and exercised with a simple view to its general health, so may the intellect also be generally exercised in order to its perfect state; and this *is* its cultivation.

Again, as health ought to precede labour of the body, and as a man in health can do what an unhealthy man cannot do, and as of this health the properties are strength, energy, agility, graceful carriage and action, manual dexterity, and endurance of fatigue, so in like manner general culture of mind is the best aid to professional and scientific study, and educated men can do what illiterate cannot; and the man who has learned to think and to reason and to compare and to discriminate and to analyze, who has refined his taste, and formed his judgment, and sharpened his mental vision, will not indeed at once be a lawyer, or a pleader, or an orator, or a statesman, or a physician, or a good landlord, or a man of business, or a soldier, or an engineer, or a chemist, or a geologist, or an antiquarian, but he will be placed in that state of intellect in which he can take up any one of the sciences or callings I have referred to, or any other for which he has a taste or special talent, with an ease, a grace, a versatility, and a success, to which another is a stranger. In this sense then, and as yet I have said but a very few words on a large subject, mental culture is emphatically *useful*.

If then I am arguing, and shall argue, against professional or scientific knowledge as the sufficient end of a university education, let me not be supposed, Gentlemen, to be disrespectful towards particular studies, or arts, or vocations, and those who are engaged in them. In saying that law or medicine is not the end of a university course, I do not mean to imply that the university does not teach law or medicine. What indeed can it teach at all, if it does not teach something particular? It teaches *all* knowledge by teaching all *branches* of knowledge, and in no other way. I do but say that there will be this distinction as regards a professor of law, or of medicine, or of geology, or of political economy, in a university and out of it, that out of a university he is in danger of being absorbed and narrowed by his pursuit, and of giving lectures which are the lectures of nothing more than a lawyer, physician, geologist, or political economist; whereas in a university he will just know where he and his science stand, he has come to it, as it were, from a height, he has taken a survey of all knowledge, he is kept from extravagance by the very rivalry of other studies, he has gained from them a special illumination and largeness of mind and freedom and self-possession, and he treats his own in consequence with a philosophy and a resource, which belongs not to the study itself, but to his liberal education.

This then is how I should solve the fallacy, for so I must call it, by which Locke and his disciples would frighten us from cultivating the intellect, under the notion that no education is useful which does not teach us some temporal calling, or some mechanical art, or some physical secret. I say that a cultivated intellect, because it is a good in itself, brings with it a power and a grace to every work and occupation which it undertakes, and enables us to be more useful, and to a greater number. There is a duty we owe to human society as such, to the state to which we belong, to the sphere in which we move, to the individuals towards whom we are variously related, and whom we successively encounter in life; and that philosophical or liberal education, as I have called it, which is the proper function of a University, if it refuses the foremost place to professional interests, does but postpone them to the formation of the citizen, and, while it subserves the larger interests of philanthropy, prepares also for the successful prosecution of those merely personal objects, which at first sight it seems to disparage.

.   .   .

X

But I must bring these extracts to an end.[3] To-day I have confined myself to saying that that training of the intellect, which is best for the individual himself, best enables him to discharge his duties to society. The Philosopher, indeed, and the man of the world differ in their very notion, but the methods, by which they are respectively formed, are pretty much the same. The Philosopher has the same command of matters of thought, which the true citizen and gentleman has of matters of business and conduct. If then a practical end must be assigned to a University course, I say it is that of training good members of society. Its art is the art of social life, and its end is fitness for the world. It neither confines its views to particular professions on the one hand, nor creates heroes or inspires genius on the other. Works indeed of genius fall under no art; heroic minds come under no rule; a University is not a birthplace of poets or of immortal authors, of founders of schools, leaders of colonies, or conquerors of nations. It does not promise a generation of Aristotles or Newtons, of Napoleons or Washingtons, of Raphaels or Shakespeares, though such miracles of nature it has before now contained within its precincts. Nor is it content on the other hand with forming the critic or the experimentalist, the economist or the engineer, though such too it includes within its scope. But a University training is the great ordinary means to a great but ordinary end; it aims at raising the intellectual tone of society, at cultivating the public mind, at purifying the national taste, at supplying true principles to popular enthusiasm and fixed aims to popular aspiration, at giving enlargement and sobriety to the ideas of the age, at facilitating the exercise of political power, and refining the intercourse of private life. It is the education which gives a man a clear conscious view of his own opinions and judgments, a truth in developing them, an eloquence in expressing them and a force in urging them. It teaches him to see things as they are, to go right to the point, to disentangle a skein of thought, to detect what is sophistical, and to discard what is irrelevant. It prepares him to fill any post with credit, and to master any subject with facility. It shows him how to accommodate himself to others, how to throw himself into their state of mind, how to bring before them his own, how to influence them, how to come to an understanding with them, how to bear with them. He is at home in any society, he has common ground with every class; he knows when to speak and when to be silent; he is able to converse, he is able to listen; he can ask a question pertinently, and gain a lesson seasonably, when he has nothing to impart himself; he is ever ready, yet never in the way; he is a pleasant companion, and a comrade you can depend upon; he knows when to be serious and when to trifle, and he has a sure tact which enables him to trifle with gracefulness and to be serious with effect. He has the repose of a mind which lives in itself, while it lives in the world, and which has resources for its happiness at home when it cannot go abroad. He has a gift which serves him in public, and supports him in retirement, without which good fortune is but vulgar, and with which failure and disappointment have a charm. The art

3. Sections 8 and 9 consist largely of quotations from the article in the *Quarterly Review* (1810) in which John Davison defended Oxford from the Edinburgh writers.

which tends to make a man all this, is in the object which it pursues as useful as the art of wealth or the art of health, though it is less susceptible of method, and less tangible, less certain, less complete in its result.

1852                                                                1852, 1859, 1873

# Apologia Pro Vita Sua

Newman's autobiography, *Apologia Pro Vita Sua* (Defense [or explanation, not "apology"] of His Life), was composed under circumstances whose drama is of the essence of the work itself. In the January 1864 issue of *Macmillan's Magazine* Charles Kingsley published a long review of J. A. Froude's intensely Protestant *History of England*, in the course of which he attacked several aspects of Catholicism, including the church's attitude toward truth. "Truth for its own sake," Kingsley said, "had never been a virtue with the Roman clergy." And he went on: "Father Newman informs us that it need not, and on the whole ought not be; that cunning is the weapon which Heaven has given to the Saints. . . ."

Kingsley is an engaging figure and in his day he was both popular and influential. An Anglican clergyman, he had taken an active part in movements to secure justice for the working classes; he was Professor of History at Cambridge and the author of novels, poems, and popular works of science which were widely read and which are still of no small charm. His intellect has been characterized as "rough but manly" and he would not have disliked the description; in matters of religion his views were simple, directed more to conduct than to faith, and strongly opposed to Catholicism, which he thought of as un-English.

To the slur on his personal probity and on that of his church, Newman responded with spirit. He called for a retraction and an apology. These Kingsley offered, but in a form that Newman could not possibly consider adequate. Newman replied to the accusation of untruthfulness in a pamphlet which included the letters that had passed between the two men. Although Newman was at the time far from popular, it was generally thought that he was in the right of the matter. Had the affair ended here, the *Apologia* might never have been written, but Kingsley rejoined to Newman's pamphlet with one of his own, an illogical and intensely bitter attack. Within a matter of days, Newman began the *Apologia*, which, by unremitting labor, he completed in three months. It was first issued in an unusual fashion, in weekly parts as it came from his pen. Its reception was all that he might have hoped for. The English intellectual public was almost completely won over to Newman's side and took this isolated, virtually exiled, man to its heart as a great *English* figure, which was what Kingsley had tried to show he was not. It was just this effect that Newman had hoped for—not that he personally should be vindicated in his Englishness, of which truth-telling was an element, but that it should be freely granted that there was nothing in the belief of Catholics that made inappropriate their full participation in the national life.

For many years the crucial chapter of the *Apologia* was felt to be Chapter IV, "History of My Religious Opinions from 1841 to 1845," in which Newman relates the agonized steps by which he came to the realization that he could no longer continue his commitment to the Anglican Church but had to turn to Catholicism. That chapter is indeed of great importance in the understanding of Newman (and the religious life of England at the time), yet for the contemporary reader its detailed account of the particularities of doctrine will seem less immediate than the passionate account which Newman gives in Chapter V of the nature of the faith in which he came to rest.

## Apologia Pro Vita Sua

### From *Position of My Mind Since 1845* [1]

From the time that I became a Catholic, of course I have no further history of my religious opinions to narrate. In saying this, I do not mean to say that my mind has been idle, or that I have given up thinking on theological subjects; but that I have had no variations to record, and have had no anxiety of heart whatever. I have been in perfect peace and contentment; I never have had one doubt. I was not conscious to myself, on my conversion, of any change, intellectual or moral, wrought in my mind. I was not conscious of firmer faith in the fundamental truths of Revelation, or of more self-command; I had not more fervour; but it was like coming into port after a rough sea; and my happiness on that score remains to this day without interruption.

Nor had I any trouble about receiving those additional articles,[2] which are not found in the Anglican Creed. Some of them I believed already, but not any one of them was a trial to me. I made a profession of them upon my reception with the greatest ease, and I have the same ease in believing them now. I am far of course from denying that every article of the Christian Creed, whether as held by Catholics or by Protestants, is beset with intellectual difficulties; and it is simple fact, that, for myself, I cannot answer those difficulties. Many persons are very sensitive of the difficulties of Religion; I am as sensitive of them as any one; but I have never been able to see a connexion between apprehending those difficulties, however keenly, and multiplying them to any extent, and on the other hand doubting the doctrines to which they are attached. Ten thousand difficulties do not make one doubt, as I understand the subject; difficulty and doubt are incommensurate. There of course may be difficulties in the evidence; but I am speaking of difficulties intrinsic to the doctrines themselves, or to their relations with each other. A man may be annoyed that he cannot work out a mathematical problem, of which the answer is or is not given to him, without doubting that it admits of an answer, or that a certain particular answer is the true one. Of all points of faith, the being of a God is, to my own apprehension, encompassed with most difficulty, and yet borne in upon our minds with most power.

People say that the doctrine of Transubstantiation [3] is difficult to believe;

1. This is from Chap. V.
2. Doctrinal statements issued by a church.
3. The doctrine holds that at the consecration of the elements of the Eucharist, i.e. the bread and wine of the Holy Communion, the whole substance of the bread and of the wine is changed into the body and blood of Christ. This is also known as the doctrine of the Real Presence.

I did not believe the doctrine till I was a Catholic. I had no difficulty in believing it, as soon as I believed that the Catholic Roman Church was the oracle of God, and that she had declared this doctrine to be part of the original revelation. It is difficult, impossible, to imagine, I grant;—but how is it difficult to believe? Yet Macaulay thought it so difficult to believe,[4] that he had need of a believer in it of talents as eminent as Sir Thomas More,[5] before he could bring himself to conceive that the Catholics of an enlightened age could resist 'the overwhelming force of the argument against it.' 'Sir Thomas More,' he says, 'is one of the choice specimens of wisdom and virtue; and the doctrine of transubstantiation is a kind of proof charge. A faith which stands that test, will stand any test.' But for myself, I cannot indeed prove it, I cannot tell *how* it is; but I say, 'Why should it not be? What's to hinder it? What do I know of substance or matter? just as much as the greatest philosophers, and that is nothing at all';—so much is this the case, that there is a rising school of philosophy now, which considers phenomena to constitute the whole of our knowledge in physics.[6] The Catholic doctrine leaves phenomena alone. It does not say that the phenomena go; on the contrary, it says that they remain; nor does it say that the same phenomena are in several places at once. It deals with what no one on earth knows any thing about, the material substances themselves. And, in like manner, of that majestic Article of the Anglican as well as of the Catholic Creed,—the doctrine of the Trinity in Unity.[7] What do I know of the Essence [8] of the Divine Being? I know that my abstract idea of three is simply incompatible with my idea of one; but when I come to the question of concrete fact, I have no means of proving that there is not a sense in which one and three can equally be predicated of the Incommunicable God.

But I am going to take upon myself the responsibility of more than the mere Creed of the Church; as the parties accusing me are determined I shall do. They say, that now, in that I am a Catholic, though I may not have offences of my own against honesty [9] to answer for, yet, at least, I am answerable for the offences of others, of my co-religionists, of my brother priests, of the Church herself. I am quite willing to accept the responsibility; and, as I have been able, as I trust, by means of a few words, to dissipate, in the minds of all those who do not begin with disbelieving me, the suspicion with which so many Protestants start, in forming their judgment of Catholics, viz. that our Creed is actually set up in inevitable superstition and hypocrisy, as the original sin of Catholicism; so now I will proceed, as before, identifying myself with the Church and vindicating it,—not of course denying the enormous mass of sin and error which exists of necessity in that world-wide multiform Communion,—

4. Thomas Babington Macaulay (1800–1859), famous historian and essayist, expressed this view in his essay on von Ranke's *History of the Popes*.
5. Sir Thomas More (1478–1535), the great humanist, author of *Utopia*, was Lord Chancellor to Henry VIII. He was executed for his religious beliefs. In 1935 he was canonized by Pope Pius XI.
6. Perhaps a reference to the empiricism of J. S. Mill.
7. The triune nature of God—the Father, the Son, and the Holy Spirit—considered as coequal, coeternal, and indivisible.
8. Essence comprises the permanent phases of being, those which define the nature of an entity. The doctrine of the Trinity is held by the church to be a mystery.
9. See the Headnote to this work.

but going to the proof of this one point, that its system is in no sense dishonest, and that therefore the upholders and teachers of that system, as such, have a claim to be acquitted in their own persons of that odious imputation.

Starting then with the being of a God, (which, as I have said, is as certain to me as the certainty of my own existence, though when I try to put the grounds of that certainty into logical shape I find a difficulty in doing so in mood and figure to my satisfaction,) I look out of myself into the world of men, and there I see a sight which fills me with unspeakable distress. The world seems simply to give the lie to that great truth, of which my whole being is so full; and the effect upon me is, in consequence, as a matter of necessity, as confusing as if it denied that I am in existence myself. If I looked into a mirror, and did not see my face, I should have the sort of feeling which actually comes upon me, when I look into this living busy world, and see no reflexion of its Creator. This is, to me, one of those great difficulties of this absolute primary truth, to which I referred just now. Were it not for this voice, speaking so clearly in my conscience and my heart, I should be an atheist, or a pantheist, or a polytheist when I looked into the world. I am speaking for myself only; and I am far from denying the real force of the arguments in proof of a God, drawn from the general facts of human society and the course of history, but these do not warm me or enlighten me; they do not take away the winter of my desolation, or make the buds unfold and the leaves grow within me, and my moral being rejoice. The sight of the world is nothing else than the prophet's scroll, full of 'lamentations, and mourning, and woe.' [10]

To consider the world in its length and breadth, its various history, the many races of man, their starts, their fortunes, their mutual alienation, their conflicts; and then their ways, habits, governments, forms of worship; their enterprises, their aimless courses, their random achievements and acquirements, the impotent conclusion of long-standing facts, the tokens so faint and broken of a superintending design, the blind evolution of what turn out to be great powers or truths, the progress of things, as if from unreasoning elements, not towards final causes, the greatness and littleness of man, his far-reaching aims, his short duration, the curtain hung over his futurity, the disappointments of life, the defeat of good, the success of evil, physical pain, mental anguish, the prevalence and intensity of sin, the pervading idolatries, the corruptions, the dreary hopeless irreligion, that condition of the whole race, so fearfully yet exactly described in the Apostle's words, 'having no hope and without God in the world,' [11]—all this is a vision to dizzy and appal; and inflicts upon the mind the sense of a profound mystery, which is absolutely beyond human solution.

What shall be said to this heart-piercing, reason-bewildering fact? I can only answer, that either there is no Creator, or this living society of men is in a true sense discarded from His presence. Did I see a boy of good make and mind, with the tokens on him of a refined nature, cast upon the world without provision, unable to say whence he came, his birth-place or his family connexions, I should conclude that there was some mystery connected with his history, and that he was one, of whom, from one cause or other, his parents were ashamed.

10. Ezekiel 2:9–10.
11. Ephesians 2:12.

Thus only should I be able to account for the contrast between the promise and the condition of his being. And so I argue about the world;—*if* there be a God, *since* there is a God, the human race is implicated in some terrible aboriginal calamity. It is out of joint with the purposes of its Creator. This is a fact as true as the fact of its existence; and thus the doctrine of what is theologically called original sin becomes to me almost as certain as that the world exists, and as the existence of God.

And now, supposing it were the blessed and loving will of the Creator to interfere in this anarchical condition of things, what are we to suppose would be the methods which might be necessarily or naturally involved in His purpose of mercy? Since the world is in so abnormal a state, surely it would be no surprise to me, if the interposition were of necessity equally extraordinary—or what is called miraculous. But that subject does not directly come into the scope of my present remarks. Miracles as evidence, involve a process of reason, or an argument; and of course I am thinking of some mode of interference which does not immediately run into argument. I am rather asking what must be the face-to-face antagonist, by which to withstand and baffle the fierce energy of passion and the all-corroding, all-dissolving scepticism of the intellect in religious inquiries? I have no intention at all of denying, that truth is the real object of our reason, and that, if it does not attain to truth, either the premiss or the process is in fault; but I am not speaking here of right reason,[12] but of reason as it acts in fact and concretely in fallen man. I know that even the unaided reason, when correctly exercised, leads to a belief in God, in the immortality of the soul, and in a future retribution; but I am considering the faculty of reason actually and historically; and in this point of view, I do not think I am wrong in saying that its tendency is towards a simple unbelief in matters of religion. No truth, however sacred, can stand against it, in the long run; [13] and hence it is that in the pagan world, when our Lord came, the last traces of the religious knowledge of former times were all but disappearing from those portions of the world in which the intellect had been active and had had a career.

And in these latter days, in like manner, outside the Catholic Church things are tending,—with far greater rapidity than in that old time from the circumstance of the age,—to atheism in one shape or other. What a scene, what a prospect, does the whole of Europe present at this day! and not only Europe, but every government and every civilization through the world, which is under the influence of the European mind! Especially, for it most concerns us, how sorrowful, in the view of religion, even taken in its most elementary, most attenuated form, is the spectacle presented to us by the educated intellect of England, France, and Germany! Lovers of their country and of their race, religious men, external to the Catholic Church, have attempted various expedients to arrest fierce wilful human nature in its onward course, and to bring it into subjection. The necessity of some form of religion for the interests of humanity, has been generally acknowledged: but where was the concrete representative of things invisible, which would have the force and the toughness necessary to

12. That is, reason in its ideal exercise.
13. Here Newman states with an audacious simplicity the natural antagonism of reason to faith and its power to destroy faith—if faith submits to the destruction.

be a breakwater against the deluge? Three centuries ago the establishment of religion, material, legal, and social, was generally adopted as the best expedient for the purpose, in those countries which separated from the Catholic Church; and for a long time it was successful; but now the crevices of those establishments are admitting the enemy. Thirty years ago, education was relied upon:[14] ten years ago there was a hope that wars would cease for ever, under the influence of commercial enterprise and the reign of the useful and fine arts;[15] but will any one venture to say there is any thing any where on this earth, which will afford a fulcrum for us, whereby to keep the earth from moving onwards?

The judgment, which experience passes whether on establishments[16] or on education, as a means of maintaining religious truth in this anarchical world, must be extended even to Scripture, though Scripture be divine.[17] Experience proves surely that the Bible does not answer a purpose for which it was never intended. It may be accidentally the means of the conversion of individuals; but a book, after all, cannot make a stand against the wild living intellect of man,[18] and in this day it begins to testify, as regards its own structure and contents, to the power of that universal solvent, which is so successfully acting upon religious establishments.

Supposing then it to be the Will of the Creator to interfere in human affairs, and to make provisions for retaining in the world a knowledge of Himself, so definite and distinct as to be proof against the energy of human scepticism, in such a case,—I am far from saying that there was no other way,—but there is nothing to surprise the mind, if He should think fit to introduce a power into the world, invested with the prerogative of infallibility in religious matters. Such a provision would be a direct, immediate, active, and prompt means of withstanding the difficulty; it would be an instrument suited to the need; and, when I find that this is the very claim of the Catholic Church, not only do I feel no difficulty in admitting the idea, but there is a fitness in it, which recommends it to my mind. And thus I am brought to speak of the Church's infallibility, as a provision, adapted by the mercy of the Creator, to preserve religion in the world, and to restrain that freedom of thought, which of course in itself is one of the greatest of our natural gifts, and to rescue it from its own suicidal excesses. And let it be observed that, neither here nor in what follows, shall I have occasion to speak directly of Revelation in its subject-matter, but in reference to the sanction which it gives to truths which may be known independently of it,—as it bears upon the defence of natural religion.[19] I

14. See, above, the selection from *The Tamworth Reading Room*, the series of articles Newman published in 1841 dealing with the optimism over the spread of popular education.

15. Perhaps a reference to the expectations aroused by the international representation of manufactured goods at the Great Exhibition of 1851.

16. That is, religious organizations.

17. Newman affirms the Catholic view that the Bible, literally read and interpreted only according to the reader's own lights, cannot be a reliable guide to belief.

18. One of Newman's most memorable phrases and a decisive clue to the ground of his ecclesiastical views.

19. Religion derived from human reason and experience apart from revelation and supernatural evidence.

say, that a power, possessed of infallibility in religious teaching, is happily adapted to be a working instrument, in the course of human affairs, for smiting hard and throwing back the immense energy of the aggressive, capricious, untrustworthy intellect:—and in saying this, as in the other things that I have to say, it must still be recollected that I am all along bearing in mind my main purpose, which is a defence of myself.

I am defending myself here from a plausible charge brought against Catholics, as will be seen better as I proceed. The charge is this: that I, as a Catholic, not only make profession to hold doctrines which I cannot possibly believe in my heart, but that I also believe in the existence of a power on earth, which at its own will imposes upon men any new set of *credenda*,[20] when it pleases, by a claim to infallibility; in consequence, that my own thoughts are not my own property; that I cannot tell that to-morrow I may not have to give up what I hold to-day, and that the necessary effect of such a condition of mind must be a degrading bondage, or a bitter inward rebellion relieving itself in secret infidelity, or the necessity of ignoring the whole subject of religion in a sort of disgust, and of mechanically saying every thing that the Church says, and leaving to others the defence of it. As then I have above spoken of the relation of my mind towards the Catholic Creed, so now 1 shall speak of the attitude which it takes up in the view of the Church's infallibility.

And first, the initial doctrine of the infallible teacher must be an emphatic protest against the existing state of mankind. Man had rebelled against his Maker. It was this that caused the divine interposition: and to proclaim it must be the first act of the divinely-accredited messenger. The Church must denounce rebellion as of all possible evils the greatest. She must have no terms with it; if she would be true to her Master, she must ban and anathematize it. This is the meaning of a statement of mine which has furnished matter for one of those special accusations to which I am at present replying: I have, however, no fault at all to confess in regard to it; I have nothing to withdraw, and in consequence I here deliberately repeat it. I said, "The Catholic Church holds it better for the sun and moon to drop from heaven, for the earth to fail, and for all the many millions on it to die of starvation in extremest agony, as far as temporal affliction goes, than that one soul, I will not say, should be lost, but should commit one single venial sin, should tell one wilful untruth, or should steal one poor farthing without excuse.'[21] I think the principle here enunciated to be the mere preamble in the formal credentials of the Catholic Church, as an Act of Parliament might begin with a 'Whereas.' It is because of the intensity of the evil which has possession of mankind, that a suitable antagonist has been provided against it; and the initial act of that divinely-commissioned power is of course to deliver her challenge and to defy the enemy. Such a preamble then gives a meaning to her position in the world, and an interpretation to her whole course of teaching and action.

In like manner she has ever put forth, with most energetic distinctness, those other great elementary truths, which either are an explanation of her mission

---

20. "Things that are to be believed."
21. The statement had been made in Newman's *On Certain Difficulties of Anglicans* (1851) and cited against him by Kingsley.

or give a character to her work. She does not teach that human nature is irreclaimable, else wherefore should she be sent? not, that it is to be shattered and reversed, but to be extricated, purified, and restored; not, that it is a mere mass of hopeless evil, but that it has the promise upon it of great things, and even now, in its present state of disorder and excess, has a virtue and a praise proper to itself. But in the next place she knows and she preaches that such a restoration, as she aims at effecting in it, must be brought about, not simply through certain outward provisions of preaching and teaching, even though they be her own, but from an inward spiritual power or grace imparted directly from above, and of which she is the channel. She has it in charge to rescue human nature from its misery, but not simply by restoring it on its own level, but by lifting it up to a higher level than its own. She recognizes in it real moral excellence though degraded, but she cannot set it free from earth except by exalting it towards heaven. It was for this end that a renovating grace was put into her hands; and therefore from the nature of the gift, as well as from the reasonableness of the case, she goes on, as a further point, to insist, that all true conversion must begin with the first springs of thought, and to teach that each individual man must be in his own person one whole and perfect temple of God, while he is also one of the living stones which build up a visible religious community. And thus the distinctions between nature and grace,[22] and between outward and inward religion, become two further articles in what I have called the preamble of her divine commission.

Such truths as these she vigorously reiterates, and pertinaciously inflicts upon mankind; as to such she observes no half-measures, no economical reserve, no delicacy or prudence. 'Ye must be born again,' [23] is the simple, direct form of words which she uses after her Divine Master: 'your whole nature must be re-born; your passions, and your affections, and your aims, and your conscience, and your will,- must all be bathed in a new element, and reconsecrated to your Maker,—and, the last not the least, your intellect.' It was for repeating these points of her teaching in my own way, that certain passages of one of my Volumes have been brought into the general accusation which has been made against my religious opinions. The writer [24] has said that I was demented if I believed, and unprincipled if I did not believe, in my own statement, that a lazy, ragged, filthy, story-telling beggar-woman, if chaste, sober, cheerful, and religious, had a prospect of heaven, such as was absolutely closed to an accomplished statesman, or lawyer, or noble, be he ever so just, upright, generous, honourable, and conscientious, unless he had also some portion of the divine Christian graces;—yet I should have thought myself defended from criticism by the words which our Lord used to the chief priests, 'The publicans and harlots go into the kingdom of God before you.' And I was subjected again to the same alternative of imputations, for having ventured to say that consent to an unchaste wish was indefinitely more henious than any lie viewed apart from its causes, its motives, and its consequences: though a lie, viewed under the limitation of these conditions, is a random utterance, an almost outward act,

22. One of the *Discourses Addressed to Mixed Congregations* (1849) deals with these distinctions.
23. John 3:7.
24. He was Samuel Wilberforce (1805–73), Bishop of Oxford, later of Winchester.

not directly from the heart, however disgraceful and despicable it may be, however prejudicial to the social contract, however deserving of public reprobation; whereas we have the express words of our Lord to the doctrine that 'whoso looketh on a woman to lust after her, hath committed adultery with her already in his heart.' [25] On the strength of these texts, I have surely as much right to believe in these doctrines which have caused so much surprise, as to believe in original sin, or that there is a supernatural revelation, or that a Divine Person suffered, or that punishment is eternal.

Passing now from what I have called the preamble of that grant of power, which is made to the Church, to that power itself, Infallibility,[26] I premise two brief remarks:—1. on the one hand, I am not here determining any thing about the essential seat of that power, because that is a question doctrinal, not historical and practical; 2. nor, on the other hand, am I extending the direct subject-matter, over which that power of Infallibility has jurisdiction, beyond religious opinion:—and now as to the power itself.

This power, viewed in its fulness, is as tremendous as the giant evil which has called for it. It claims, when brought into exercise but in the legitimate manner, for otherwise of course it is but quiescent, to know for certain the very meaning of every portion of that Divine Message in detail, which was committed by our Lord to His Apostles. It claims to know its own limits, and to decide what it can determine absolutely and what it cannot. It claims, moreover, to have a hold upon statements not directly religious, so far as this,—to determine whether they indirectly relate to religion, and, according to its own definitive judgment, to pronounce whether or not, in a particular case, they are simply consistent with revealed truth. It claims to decide magisterially, whether as within its own province or not, that such and such statements are or are not prejudicial to the *Depositum* [27] of faith, in their spirit or in their consequences, and to allow them, or condemn and forbid them, accordingly. It claims to impose silence at will on any matters, or controversies, of doctrine, which on its own *ipso dixit*,[28] it pronounces to be dangerous, or inexpedient, or inopportune. It claims that, whatever may be the judgment of Catholics upon such acts, these acts should be received by them with those outward marks of reverence, submission, and loyalty, which Englishmen, for instance, pay to the presence of their sovereign, without expressing any criticism on them on the ground that in their matter they are inexpedient, or in their manner violent or harsh. And lastly, it claims to have the right of inflicting spiritual punishment, of cutting off from the ordinary channels of the divine life, and of simply excommunicating, those who refuse to submit themselves to its formal declarations. Such is the infallibility lodged in the Catholic Church, viewed in the concrete, as clothed and surrounded by the appendages of its high sov-

25. Matthew 5:27.
26. The doctrine of the infallibility of the church—that it cannot err in teaching revealed truth—is of great antiquity. The doctrine of the infallibility of the pope was promulgated at the Vatican Council of 1870 after much, and often bitter, debate within the Catholic fold. It holds that when the pope speaks *ex cathedra*—that is, in his character of head of the church and in virtue of his apostolic authority—what he lays down concerning faith and morals—these matters alone—is binding to all communicants.
27. "That which is laid down."
28. "He himself said it."

ereignty: it is, to repeat what I said above, a supereminent prodigious power sent upon earth to encounter and master a giant evil.

And now, having thus described it, I profess my own absolute submission to its claim. I believe the whole revealed dogma as taught by the Apostles, as committed by the Apostles to the Church, and as declared by the Church to me. I receive it, as it is infallibly interpreted by the authority to whom it is thus committed, and (implicitly) as it shall be, in like manner, further interpreted by that same authority till the end of time. I submit, moreover, to the universally received traditions of the Church, in which lies the matter of those new dogmatic definitions which are from time to time made, and which in all times are the clothing and the illustration of the Catholic dogma as already defined. And I submit myself to those other decisions of the Holy See, theological or not, through the organs which it has itself appointed, which, waiving the question of their infallibility, on the lowest ground come to me with a claim to be accepted and obeyed. Also, I consider that, gradually and in the course of ages, Catholic inquiry has taken certain definite shapes, and has thrown itself into the form of a science, with a method and a phraseology of its own, under the intellectual handling of great minds, such as St. Athanasius, St. Augustine, and St. Thomas; and I feel no temptation at all to break in pieces the great legacy of thought thus committed to us for these latter days.

All this being considered as the profession which I make *ex animo*,[29] as for myself, so also on the part of the Catholic body, as far as I know it, it will at first sight be said that the restless intellect of our common humanity is utterly weighed down, to the repression of all independent effort and action whatever, so that, if this is to be the mode of bringing it into order, it is brought into order only to be destroyed. But this is far from the result, far from what I conceive to be the intention of that high Providence who has provided a great remedy for a great evil,—far from borne out by the history of the conflict between Infallibility and Reason in the past, and the prospect of it in the future. The energy of the human intellect 'does from opposition grow'; it thrives and is joyous, with a tough elastic strength, under the terrible blows of the divinely-fashioned weapon, and is never so much itself as when it has lately been overthrown. It is the custom with Protestant writers to consider that, whereas there are two great principles in action in the history of religion, Authority and Private Judgment, they have all the Private Judgment to themselves, and we have the full inheritance and the superincumbent oppression of Authority. But this is not so; it is the vast Catholic body itself, and it only, which affords an arena for both combatants in that awful, never-dying duel. It is necessary for the very life of religion, viewed in its large operations and its history, that the warfare should be incessantly carried on. Every exercise of Infallibility is brought out into act by an intense and varied operation of the Reason, both as its ally and as its opponent, and provokes again, when it has done its work, a re-action of Reason against it; and, as in a civil polity the State exists and endures by means of the rivalry and collision, the encroachments and defeats of its constituent parts, so in like manner Catholic Christendom is no simple exhibition of religious absolutism, but presents a continuous picture of Authority

29. "From my own soul."

and Private Judgment alternately advancing and retreating as the ebb and flow of the tide;—it is a vast assemblage of human beings with wilful intellects and wild passions, brought together into one by the beauty and the Majesty of a Superhuman Power,—into what may be called a large reformatory or training-school, not as if into a hospital or into a prison, not in order to be sent to bed, not to be buried alive, but (if I may change my metaphor) brought together as if into some moral factory,[30] for the melting, refining, and moulding, by an incessant, noisy process, of the raw material of human nature, so excellent, so dangerous, so capable of divine purposes.

St. Paul says in one place that his Apostolical power is given him to edification, and not to destruction. There can be no better account of the Infallibility of the Church. It is a supply for a need, and it does not go beyond that need. Its object is, and its effect also, not to enfeeble the freedom or vigour of human thought in religious speculation, but to resist and control its extravagance. What have been its great works? All of them in the distinct province of theology:—to put down Arianism, Eutychianism, Pelagianism, Manichæism, Lutheranism, Jansenism.[31] Such is the broad result of its action in the past;—and now as to the securities which are given us that so it ever will act in time to come.

First, Infallibility cannot act outside of a definite circle of thought, and it must in all its decisions, or *definitions*, as they are called, profess to be keeping within it. The great truths of the moral law, of natural religion, and of Apostolical faith, are both its boundary and its foundation. It must not go beyond them, and it must ever appeal to them. Both its subject-matter, and its articles in that subject-matter, are fixed. And it must ever profess to be guided by Scripture and by tradition. It must refer to the particular Apostolic truth which it is enforcing, or (what is called) *defining*. Nothing, then, can be presented to me, in time to come, as part of the faith, but what I ought already to have received, and hitherto have been kept from receiving (if so) merely because it has not been brought home to me. Nothing can be imposed upon me different in kind from what I hold already,—much less contrary to it. The new truth which is promulgated, if it is to be called new, must be at least homogeneous, cognate, implicit, viewed relatively to the old truth. It must be what I may even have guessed, or wished, to be included in the Apostolic revelation; and at least it will be of such a character, that my thoughts readily concur in it or coalesce with it, as soon as I hear it. Perhaps I and others actually have always believed it, and the only question which is now decided in my behalf, is, that I have henceforth the satisfaction of having to believe, that I have only been holding all along what the Apostles held before me.

Let me take the doctrine which Protestants consider our greatest difficulty, that of the Immaculate Conception.[32] Here I entreat the reader to recollect my

30. Newman's exquisite literary tact surely fails him here in these images of the world as a "large reformatory or training school" and as a "moral factory." The image of the world as a hospital, originated by Newman, is used to great effect by T. S. Eliot in the lyric in "East Coker" which begins "The wounded surgeon plies the steel. . . ."
31. Heresies from the 5th century to the 17th.
32. The doctrine that the soul of the Virgin Mary was, from its first existence, free of the stain of original sin. It is often confused with the doctrine of the Virgin birth.

main drift, which is this. I have no difficulty in receiving the doctrine; and that, because it so intimately harmonizes with that circle of recognized dogmatic truths, into which it has been recently received;—but if *I* have no difficulty, why may not another have no difficulty also? why may not a hundred? a thousand? Now I am sure that Catholics in general have not any intellectual difficulty at all on the subject of the Immaculate Conception; and that there is no reason why they should. Priests have no difficulty. You tell me that they *ought* to have a difficulty;—but they have not. Be large-minded enough to believe, that men may reason and feel very differently from yourselves; how is it that men, when left to themselves, fall into such various forms of religion, except that there are various types of mind among them, very distinct from each other? From my testimony then about myself, if you believe it, judge of others also who are Catholics: we do not find the difficulties which you do in the doctrines which we hold; we have no intellectual difficulty in that doctrine in particular, which you call a novelty of this day. We priests need not be hypocrites, though we be called upon to believe in the Immaculate Conception. To that large class of minds, who believe in Christianity after our manner,—in the particular temper, spirit, and light, (whatever word is used,) in which Catholics believe it,—there is no burden at all in holding that the Blessed Virgin was conceived without original sin; indeed, it is a simple fact to say, that Catholics have not come to believe it because it is defined, but that it was defined because they believed it.

So far from the definition in 1854 [33] being a tyrannical infliction on the Catholic world, it was received every where on its promulgation with the greatest enthusiasm. It was in consequence of the unanimous petition, presented from all parts of the Church to the Holy See, in behalf of an *ex cathedra* declaration that the doctrine was Apostolic, that it was declared so to be. I never heard of one Catholic having difficulties in receiving the doctrine, whose faith on other grounds was not already suspicious. Of course there were grave and good men, who were made anxious by the doubt whether it could be formally proved to be Apostolical either by Scripture or tradition, and who accordingly, though believing it themselves, did not see how it could be defined by authority and imposed upon all Catholics as a matter of faith; but this is another matter. The point in question is, whether the doctrine is a burden. I believe it to be none. So far from it being so, I sincerely think that St. Bernard and St. Thomas, who scrupled at it in their day,[34] had they lived into this, would have rejoiced to accept it for its own sake. Their difficulty, as I view it, consisted in matters of words, ideas, and arguments. They thought the doctrine inconsistent with other doctrines; and those who defended it in that age had not that precision in their view of it, which has been attained by means of the long disputes of the centuries which followed. And in this want of precision lay the difference of opinion, and the controversy.

Now the instance which I have been taking suggests another remark; the

33. In this year Pope Pius IX defined the doctrine of the Immaculate Conception.
34. St. Bernard of Clairvaux (1090–1153) and St. Thomas Aquinas (1225–74) both opposed the doctrine of the Immaculate Conception. They were more or less at one in holding the view that the Virgin was not conceived without the stain of original sin but was purified before birth.

number of those (so called) new doctrines will not oppress us, if it takes eight centuries to promulgate even one of them. Such is about the length of time through which the preparation has been carried on for the definition of the Immaculate Conception. This of course is an extraordinary case; but it is difficult to say what is ordinary, considering how few are the formal occasions on which the voice of Infallibility has been solemnly lifted up. It is to the Pope in Ecumenical Council that we look, as to the normal seat of Infallibility: now there have been only eighteen such Councils since Christianity was,—an average of one to a century,—and of these Councils some passed no doctrinal decree at all, others were employed on only one, and many of them were concerned with only elementary points of the Creed. . . .

Now I will go on in fairness to say what I think *is* the great trial to the Reason, when confronted with that august prerogative of the Catholic Church, of which I have been speaking. I enlarged just now upon the concrete shape and circumstances, under which pure infallible authority presents itself to the Catholic. That authority has the prerogative of an indirect jurisdiction on subject-matters which lie beyond its own proper limits, and it most reasonably has such a jurisdiction. It could not act in its own province, unless it had a right to act out of it. It could not properly defend religious truth, without claiming for that truth what may be called its *pomœria;* [35] or, to take another illustration, without acting as we act, as a nation, in claiming as our own, not only the land on which we live, but what are called British waters. The Catholic Church claims, not only to judge infallibly on religious questions, but to animadvert on opinions in secular matters which bear upon religion, on matters of philosophy, of science, of literature, of history, and it demands our submission to her claim. It claims to censure books, to silence authors, and to forbid discussions. In this province, taken as a whole, it does not so much speak doctrinally, as enforce measures of discipline. It must of course be obeyed without a word, and perhaps in process of time it will tacitly recede from its own injunctions. In such cases the question of faith does not come in at all; for what is matter of faith is true for all times, and never can be unsaid. Nor does it at all follow, because there is a gift of infallibility in the Catholic Church, that therefore the parties who are in possession of it are in all their proceedings infallible. 'O, it is excellent,' says the poet, 'to have a giant's strength, but tyrannous, to use it like a giant.' [36] I think history supplies us with instances in the Church, where legitimate power has been harshly used. To make such admission is no more than saying that the divine treasure, in the words of the Apostle, is 'in earthen vessels'; [37] nor does it follow that the substance of the acts of the ruling power is not right and expedient, because its manner may have been faulty. Such high authorities act by means of instruments; we know how such instruments claim for themselves the name of their principals, who thus get the credit of faults which really are not theirs. But granting all this to an extent greater than can with any show of reason be imputed to the ruling power in the Church, what difficulty is there in the fact of this want of prudence or moderation more than can be urged, with far

---

35. Limits or boundaries.
36. *Measure for Measure* II.ii.107–9.
37. II Corinthians 4:7.

greater justice, against Protestant communities and institutions? What is there in it to make us hypocrites, if it has not that effect upon Protestants? We are called upon, not to profess any thing, but to submit and be silent, as Protestant Churchmen have before now obeyed the royal command to abstain from certain theological questions. Such injunctions as I have been contemplaing are laid merely upon our actions, not upon our thoughts. How, for instance, does it tend to make a man a hypocrite, to be forbidden to publish a libel? his thoughts are as free as before: authoritative prohibitions may tease and irritate, but they have no bearing whatever upon the exercise of reason.

So much at first sight; but I will go on to say further, that, in spite of all that the most hostile critic may urge about the encroachments or severities of high ecclesiastics, in times past, in the use of their power, I think that the event has shown after all, that they were mainly in the right, and that those whom they were hard upon were mainly in the wrong. . . . In reading ecclesiastical history, when I was an Anglican, it used to be forcibly brought home to me, how the initial error of what afterwards became heresy was the urging forward some truth against the prohibition of authority at an unseasonable time. There is a time for every thing, and many a man desires a reformation of an abuse, or the fuller development of a doctrine, or the adoption of a particular policy, but forgets to ask himself whether the right time for it is come: and, knowing that there is no one who will be doing any thing towards its accomplishment in his own lifetime unless he does it himself, he will not listen to the voice of authority, and he spoils a good work in his own century, in order that another man, as yet unborn, may not have the opportunity of bringing it happily to perfection in the next. He may seem to the world to be nothing else than a bold champion for the truth and a martyr to free opinion, when he is just one of those persons whom the competent authority ought to silence; and, though the case may not fall within that subject-matter in which that authority is infallible, or the formal conditions of the exercise of that gift may be wanting, it is clearly the duty of authority to act vigorously in the case. Yet its act will go down to posterity as an instance of a tyrannical interference with private judgment, and of the silencing of a reformer, and of a base love of corruption or error; and it will show still less to advantage, if the ruling power happens in its proceedings to evince any defect of prudence or consideration. And all those who take the part of that ruling authority will be considered as time-servers, or indifferent to the cause of uprightness and truth; while, on the other hand, the said authority may be accidentally supported by a violent ultra party, which exalts opinions into dogmas, and has it principally at heart to destroy every school of thought but its own.

Such a state of things may be provoking and discouraging at the time, in the case of two classes of persons; of moderate men who wish to make differences in religious opinion as little as they fairly can be made; and of such as keenly perceive, and are honestly eager to remedy, existing evils,—evils, of which divines in this or that foreign country know nothing at all, and which even at home, where they exist, it is not every one who has the means of estimating. This is a state of things both of past time and of the present. We live in a wonderful age; the enlargement of the circle of secular knowledge just now is simply a bewilderment, and the more so, because it has the promise of continuing, and that with greater rapidity, and more signal results. Now these discoveries, certain or probable, have in matter of fact an indirect bearing upon religious opinions, and the question arises how are the respective claims of revelation and of natural science to be adjusted. Few minds in earnest can remain at ease without some sort of rational grounds for their religious belief; to reconcile theory and fact is almost an instinct of the mind. When then a flood of facts, ascertained or suspected, comes pouring in upon us, with a multitude of others in prospect, all believers in Revelation, be they Catholic or not, are roused to consider their bearing upon themselves, both for the honour of God, and from tenderness for those many souls who, in consequence of the confident tone of the schools of secular knowledge, are in danger of being led away into a bottomless liberalism of thought.

I am not going to criticize here that vast body of men, in the mass, who at this time would profess to be liberals in religion; and who look towards the discoveries of the age, certain or in progress, as their informants, direct or indirect, as to what they shall think about the unseen and the future. The Liberalism [38] which gives a colour to society now, is very different from that character of thought which bore the name thirty or forty years ago. Now it is scarcely a party; it is the educated lay world. When I was young, I knew the word first as giving name to a periodical, set up by Lord Byron and others.[39] Now, as then, I have no sympathy with the philosophy of Byron. Afterwards, Liberalism was the badge of a theological school, of a dry and repulsive character,[40] not very dangerous in itself, though dangerous as opening the door to evils which it did not itself either anticipate or comprehend. At present it is nothing else than that deep, plausible scepticism, of which I spoke above, as being the development of human reason, as practically exercised by the natural man.

The Liberal religionsts of this day are a very mixed body, and therefore I am not intending to speak against them. There may be, and doubtless is, in the hearts of some or many of them a real antipathy or anger against revealed truth, which it is distressing to think of. Again; in many men of science or literature there may be an animosity arising from almost a personal feeling; it being a matter of party, a point of honour, the excitement of a game, or a satisfaction to the soreness or annoyance occasioned by the acrimony or narrowness of apologists for religion, to prove that Christianity or that Scripture is untrustworthy. Many scientific and literary men, on the other hand, go on, I am confident, in a straightforward impartial way, in their own province and on their own line of thought, without any disturbance from religious difficulties in themselves, or any wish at all to give pain to others by the result of their investigations. It would ill become me, as if I were afraid of truth of any kind, to blame those who pursue secular facts, by means of the reason which God has given them, to their logical conclusions: or to be angry with science, because religion is bound in duty to take cognizance of its teaching. But putting these particular classes of men aside, as having no special call on the sympathy of

38. See *Liberalism*, below.
39. *The Liberal* was founded in 1822 by Byron, Shelley, and Leigh Hunt. Four numbers appeared.
40. A reference to the rationalistic theology of the Anglican prelate Richard Whately (1787–1863) and his followers, called Noetics (see the Headnote to Newman).

the Catholic, of course he does most deeply enter into the feelings of a fourth and large class of men, in the educated portions of society, of religious and sincere minds, who are simply perplexed,—frightened or rendered desperate, as the case may be,—by the utter confusion into which late discoveries or speculations have thrown their most elementary ideas of religion. Who does not feel for such men? who can have one unkind thought of them? I take up in their behalf St. Augustine's beautiful words, 'Illi in vos sæviant,' &c.[41] 'Let them be fierce with you who have no experience of the difficulty with which error is discriminated from truth, and the way of life is found amid the illusions of the world.' How many a Catholic has in his thoughts followed such men, many of them so good, so true, so noble! how often has the wish risen in his heart that some one from among his own people should come forward as the champion of revealed truth against its opponents! Various persons, Catholic and Protestant, have asked me to do so myself; but I had several strong difficulties in the way. One of the greatest is this, that at the moment it is so difficult to say precisely what it is that is to be encountered and overthrown. I am far from denying that scientific knowledge is really growing, but it is by fits and starts; hypotheses rise and fall; it is difficult to anticipate which of them will keep their ground, and what the state of knowledge in relation to them will be from year to year. In this condition of things, it has seemed to me to be very undignified for a Catholic to commit himself to the work of chasing what might turn out to be phantoms, and, in behalf of some special objections, to be ingenious in devising a theory, which, before it was completed, might have to give place to some theory newer still, from the fact that those former objections had already come to nought under the uprising of others. It seemed to be specially a time, in which Christians had a call to be patient, in which they had no other way of helping those who were alarmed, than that of exhorting them to have a little faith and fortitude, and to 'beware,' as the poet says, 'of dangerous steps.' [42] This seemed so clear to me, the more I thought of the matter, as to make me surmise, that, if I attempted what had so little promise in it, I should find that the highest Catholic Authority was against the attempt, and that I should have spent my time and my thought, in doing what either it would be imprudent to bring before the public at all, or what, did I do so, would only complicate matters further which were already complicated, without my interference, more than enough. And I interpret recent acts of that authority as fulfilling my expectation; I interpret them as tying the hands of a controversialist, such as I should be, and teaching us that true wisdom, which Moses inculcated on his people, when the Egyptians were pursuing them, 'Fear ye not, stand still; the Lord shall fight for you, and ye shall hold your peace.' [43] And so far from finding a difficulty in obeying in this case, I have cause to be thankful and to rejoice to have so clear a direction in a matter of difficulty.

But if we would ascertain with correctness the real course of a principle, we must look at it at a certain distance, and as history represents it to us. Nothing carried on by human instruments, but has its irregularities, and affords ground for criticism, when minutely scrutinized in matters of detail. I have been speak-

41. Newman's translation follows.
42. William Cowper (1731–1800), *The Needless Alarm*, ll. 132–33.
43. Exodus 14:13–14.

ing of that aspect of the action of an infallible authority, which is most open to invidious criticism from those who view it from without; I have tried to be fair, in estimating what can be said to its disadvantage, as witnessed at a particular time in the Catholic Church, and now I wish its adversaries to be equally fair in their judgment upon its historical character. Can, then, the infallible authority, with any show of reason, be said in fact to have destroyed the energy of the Catholic intellect? Let it be observed, I have not here to speak of any conflict which ecclesiastical authority has had with science, for this simple reason, that conflict there has been none; and that, because the secular sciences, as they now exist, are a novelty in the world, and there has been no time yet for a history of relations between theology and these new methods of knowledge, and indeed the Church may be said to have kept clear of them, as is proved by the constantly cited case of Galileo.[44] Here 'exceptio probat regulam': [45] for it is the one stock argument. Again, I have not to speak of any relations of the Church to the new sciences, because my simple question all along has been whether the assumption of infallibility by the proper authority is adapted to make me a hypocrite, and till that authority passes decrees on pure physical subjects and calls on me to subscribe them, (which it never will do, because it has not the power,) it has no tendency to interfere by any of its acts with my private judgment on those points. The simple question is, whether authority has so acted upon the reason of individuals, that they can have no opinion of their own, and have but an alternative of slavish superstition or secret rebellion of heart; and I think the whole history of theology puts an absolute negative upon such a supposition. . . .

There is only one other subject, which I think it necessary to introduce here, as bearing upon the vague suspicions which are attached in this country to the Catholic Priesthood. It is one of which my accusers have before now said much,—the charge of reserve and economy.[46] They found it in no slight degree

44. Galileo Galilei (1564–1642), the great physicist and astronomer, was a strong proponent of the Copernican theory, which his researches had done much to confirm and develop. In 1616 the church condemned the Copernican theory as being against Scripture and heretical, and affirmed the Ptolemaic theory. When Galileo continued to teach the Copernican theory despite his having promised not to do so, he was threatened with torture and abjured his doctrine. Although Newman had once defended the principle on which the church had acted in this instance, he here admits that the church had been mistaken, although exceptionally.

45. "The exception proves the rule."

46. The idea of "reserve or economy" was central to the occasion of the Apologia, Kingsley having said in effect that this idea, recognized and approved by the Catholic Church, put Newman, as a Catholic priest, in an ambiguous relation to truth-telling. It was perhaps inevitable that the idea should be misunderstood, as the Oxford English Dictionary makes clear in its exceptionally full definition of and comment on the theological sense of "economy": "a. The judicious handling of doctrine, i.e. the preservation of it in such a manner as to suit the needs or to conciliate the prejudices of the persons addressed. b. This sense has been (by misapprehension or word-play) often treated as an application of [the sense of the word which denotes careful management of resources so as to make them go as far as possible]. Hence the phrase economy (as if 'cautious or sparing use') of truth." The OED goes on to comment on the polemical use of the word, doing so with particular reference to Newman: "Newman's history of the Arians (1833) contained a section on the use of 'the Economy' by the [Church] Fathers. The word was eagerly caught up by popular writers and used contemptuously, as if it were a euphemistic name for dishonest evasion; in this sense it is still frequently met with. . . ."

on what I have said on the subject in my History of the Arians, and in a note upon one of my Sermons in which I refer to it. The principle of Reserve is also advocated by an admirable writer in two numbers of the Tracts for the Times,[47] and of these I was the Editor.

Now, as to the Economy itself, it is founded upon the words of our Lord, 'Cast not your pearls before swine'; and it was observed by the early Christians more or less, in their intercourse with the heathen populations among whom they lived. In the midst of the abominable idolatries and impurities of that fearful time, the Rule of the Economy was an imperative duty. But that rule, at least as I have explained and recommended it, in anything that I have written, did not go beyond (1) the concealing the truth when we could do so without deceit, (2) stating it only partially, and (3) representing it under the nearest form possible to a learner or inquirer, when he could not possibly understand it exactly. I conceive that to draw Angels with wings is an instance of the third of these economical modes; and to avoid the question, 'Do Christians believe in a Trinity?' by answering, 'They believe in only one God,' would be an instance of the second. As to the first, it is hardly an Economy, but comes under what is called the 'Disciplina Arcani.'[48] The second and third economical modes Clement calls *lying;* meaning that a partial truth is in some sense a lie, as is also a representative truth. And this, I think, is about the long and the short of the ground of the accusation which has been so violently urged against me, as being a patron of the Economy.

Of late years I have come to think, as I believe most writers do, that Clement meant more than I have said. I used to think he used the word 'lie' as an hyperbole, but I now believe that he, as other early Fathers, thought that, under certain circumstances, it was lawful to tell a lie. This doctrine I never maintained, though I used to think, as I do now, that the theory of the subject is surrounded with considerable difficulty; and it is not strange that I should say so, considering that great English writers declare without hesitation that in certain extreme cases, as to save life, honour, or even property, a lie is allowable. And thus I am brought to the direct question of truth, and of the truthfulness of Catholic priests generally in their dealings with the world, as bearing on the general question of their honesty, and of their internal belief in their religious professions.

It would answer no purpose, and it would be departing from the line of writing which I have been observing all along, if I entered into any formal discussion on this question; what I shall do here, as I have done in the foregoing pages, is to give my own testimony on the matter in question, and there to leave it. Now first I will say, that, when I became a Catholic, nothing struck me more at once than the English out-spoken manner of the Priests. It was the same at Oscott, at Old Hall Green, at Ushaw;[49] there was nothing of that smoothness, or mannerism, which is commonly imputed to them, and they

---

47. *Tracts for the Times* were published from 1833 to 1841 by the members of the Oxford Movement. The two Tracts referred to are 80 and 87 by Isaac Williams.
48. *Arcanum,* Latin, a mystery or secret. The phrase refers to concealing the doctrines of the church in time of persecution.
49. Catholic seminaries.

were more natural and unaffected than many an Anglican clergyman. The many years, which have passed since, have only confirmed my first impression. I have ever found it in the priests of this Diocese; did I wish to point out a straightforward Englishman, I should instance the Bishop, who has, to our great benefit, for so many years presided over it.

And next, I was struck, when I had more opportunity of judging of the Priests, by the simple faith in the Catholic Creed and system, of which they always gave evidence, and which they never seemed to feel, in any sense at all, to be a burden. And now that I have been in the Church nineteen years, I cannot recollect hearing of a single instance in England of an infidel priest. Of course there are men from time to time, who leave the Catholic Church for another religion, but I am speaking of cases, when a man keeps a fair outside to the world and is a hollow hypocrite in his heart.

I wonder that the self-devotion of our priests does not strike a Protestant in this point of view. What do they gain by professing a Creed, in which, if their enemies are to be credited, they really do not believe? What is their reward for committing themselves to a life of self-restraint and toil, and perhaps to a premature and miserable death? The Irish fever cut off between Liverpool and Leeds thirty priests and more, young men in the flower of their days, old men who seemed entitled to some quiet time after their long toil. There was a bishop cut off in the North; but what had a man of his ecclesiastical rank to do with the drudgery and danger of sick calls, except that Christian faith and charity constrained him? Priests volunteered for the dangerous service. It was the same with them on the first coming of the cholera, that mysterious awe-inspiring infliction. If they did not heartily believe in the Creed of the Church, then I will say that the remark of the Apostle had its fullest illustration:—'If in this life only we have hope in Christ, we are of all men most miserable.' What could support a set of hypocrites in the presence of a deadly disorder, one of them following another in long order up the forlorn hope, and one after another perishing? And such, I may say, in its substance, is every Mission-Priest's life. He is ever ready to sacrifice himself for his people. Night and day, sick or well himself, in all weathers, off he is, on the news of a sick call. The fact of a parishioner dying without the Sacraments through his fault is terrible to him; why terrible, if he has not a deep absolute faith, which he acts upon with a free service? Protestants admire this, when they see it; but they do not seem to see as clearly, that it excludes the very notion of hypocrisy.

Sometimes, when they reflect upon it, it leads them to remark on the wonderful discipline of the Catholic priesthood; they say that no Church has so well ordered a clergy, and that in that respect it surpasses their own; they wish they could have such exact discipline among themselves. But is it an excellence which can be purchased? is it a phenomenon which depends on nothing else than itself, or is it an effect which has a cause? You cannot buy devotion at a price. 'It hath never been heard of in the land of Chanaan, neither hath it been seen in Theman. The children of Agar, the merchants of Meran, none of these have known its way." [50] What then is that wonderful charm,

50. Baruch 3:22–23.

which makes a thousand men act all in one way, and infuses a prompt obedience to rule, as if they were under some stern military compulsion? How difficult to find an answer, unless you will allow the obvious one, that they believe intensely what they profess!

[Newman continues his exposition of "reserve and economy" by adducing cognate ideas drawn from the writings of admired English Protestants—Jeremy Taylor, Milton, Paley, Johnson.]

And now, if Protestants wish to know what our real teaching is, as on other subjects, so on that of lying, let them look, not at our books of casuistry, but at our catechisms. Works on pathology do not give the best insight into the form and the harmony of the human frame; and, as it is with the body, so is it with the mind. The Catechism of the Council of Trent was drawn up for the express purpose of providing preachers with subjects for their Sermons; and, as my whole work has been a defence of myself, I may here say that I rarely preach a Sermon, but I go to this beautiful and complete Catechism to get both my matter and my doctrine. There we find the following notices about the duty of Veracity:—

[Newman cites eleven paragraphs from The Catechism by Decree of the Holy Council of Trent.]

To one other authority I appeal on this subject, which commands from me attention of a special kind, for it is the teaching of a Father. It will serve to bring my work to a conclusion.

'St. Philip,' says the Roman Oratorian who wrote his Life, 'had a particular dislike of affectation both in himself and others, in speaking, in dressing, or in any thing else.

'He avoided all ceremony which savoured of worldly compliment, and always showed himself a great stickler for Christian simplicity in every thing; so that, when he had to deal with men of worldly prudence, he did not very readily accommodate himself to them.

'And he avoided, as much as possible, having anything to do with *two-faced persons*, who did not go simply and straightforwardly to work in their transactions.

'*As for liars, he could not endure them*, and he was *continually reminding* his spiritual children, *to avoid them as they would a pestilence.*'

These are the principles on which I have acted before I was a Catholic; these are the principles which, I trust, will be my stay and guidance to the end.

I have closed this history of myself with St. Philip's name upon St. Philip's feast-day; and, having done so, to whom can I more suitably offer it, as a memorial of affection and gratitude, than to St. Philip's sons, my dearest brothers of this House, the Priests of the Birmingham Oratory, Ambrose St. John, Henry Austin Mills, Henry Bittleston, Edward Caswall, William Paine Neville, and Henry Ignatius Dudley Ryder? who have been so faithful to me; who have been so sensitive of my needs; who have been so indulgent to my failings; who have carried me through so many trials; who have grudged no sacrifice, if I asked for it; who have been so cheerful under discouragements of my causing; who have done so many good works, and let me have the credit of them;—with whom I have lived so long, with whom I hope to die.

And to you especially, dear Ambrose St. John; [51] whom God gave me, when He took every one else away; who are the link between my old life and my new; who have now for twenty-one years been so devoted to me, so patient, so zealous, so tender; who have let me lean so hard upon you; who have watched me so narrowly; who have never thought of yourself, if I was in question.

And in you I gather up and bear in memory those familiar affectionate companions and counsellors, who in Oxford were given to me, one after another, to be my daily solace and relief; and all those others, of great name and high example, who were my thorough friends, and showed me true attachment in times long past; and also those many younger men, whether I knew them or not, who have never been disloyal to me by word or deed; and of all these, thus various in their relations to me, those more especially who have since joined the Catholic Church.

And I earnestly pray for this whole company, with a hope against hope, that all of us, who once were so united, and so happy in our union, may even now be brought at length, by the Power of the Divine Will, into One Fold and under One Shepherd.

1864                                                                      1864, 1865


### Liberalism [1]

I have been asked to explain more fully what it is I mean by 'Liberalism,' because merely to call it the Anti-dogmatic Principle is to tell very little about it. . . .

Whenever men are able to act at all, there is the chance of extreme and intemperate action; and therefore, when there is exercise of mind, there is the chance of wayward or mistaken exercise. Liberty of thought is in itself a good; but it gives an opening to false liberty. Now by Liberalism I mean false liberty of thought, or the exercise of thought upon matters, in which, from the constitution of the human mind, thought cannot be brought to any successful issue, and therefore is out of place. Among such matters are first principles of whatever kind; and of these the most sacred and momentous are especially to be reckoned the truths of Revelation. Liberalism then is the mistake of subjecting to human judgment those revealed doctrines which are in their nature beyond and independent of it, and of claiming to determine on intrinsic grounds the truth and value of propositions which rest for their reception simply on the external authority of the Divine Word.

·  ·  ·

51. Ambrose St. John (1815–75) had been attached to Newman since 1843. He was a considerable scholar, a student of German biblical criticism. Newman, according to directions left by him, was buried in the same grave with St. John.

1. When Newman published the *Apologia* as a volume in 1865, he added several "Notes," amounting to brief essays, in which he dealt at fuller length with matters touched on in the text. Of these the note on Liberalism is the first. In its entirety, it gives an account of the development of the Liberal tendency in the thought of Newman's Anglican opponents at Oxford. Nothing could better suggest the distance at which Newman stood from the dominant tendency of English life in his time.

I conclude this notice of Liberalism in Oxford, and the party which was antagonistic to it,[2] with some propositions in detail, which, as a member of the latter, and together with the High Church, I earnestly denounced and abjured.

1. No religious tenet is important, unless reason shows it to be so.

Therefore, e.g. the doctrine of the Athanasian Creed [3] is not to be insisted on, unless it tends to convert the soul; and the doctrine of the Atonement [4] is to be insisted on, if it does convert the soul,

2. No one can believe what he does not understand.

Therefore, e.g. there are no mysteries in true religion.

3. No theological doctrine is any thing more than an opinion which happens to be held by bodies of men.

Therefore, e.g. no creed, as such, is necessary for salvation.

4. It is dishonest in a man to make an act of faith in what he has not had brought home to him by actual proof.

Therefore, e.g. the mass of men ought not absolutely to believe in the divine authority of the Bible.

5. It is immoral in a man to believe more than he can spontaneously receive as being congenial to his moral and mental nature.

Therefore, e.g. a given individual is not bound to believe in eternal punishment.

6. No revealed doctrines or precepts may reasonably stand in the way of scientific conclusions.

Therefore, e.g. Political Economy may reverse our Lord's declarations about poverty and riches, or a system of Ethics may teach that the highest condition of body is ordinarily essential to the highest state of mind.

7. Christianity is necessarily modified by the growth of civilization, and the exigencies of times.

Therefore, e.g. the Catholic priesthood, though necessary in the Middle Ages, may be superseded now.

8. There is a system of religion more simply true than Christianity as it has ever been received.

2. Newman's own party, that of the Tractarians.
3. The Anglican coolness to the Athanasian Creed is a response to its statement that the doctrines it affirms—among them that of the Trinity—must be believed at the risk of damnation.
4. That is, "at-one-ment"—man's reconciliation with God through the sacrificial death of Christ.

Therefore, e.g. we may advance that Christianity is the 'corn of wheat' which has been dead for 1800 years, but at length will bear fruit; and that Mahometanism is the manly religion, and existing Christianity the womanish.

9. There is a right of Private Judgment: that is, there is no existing authority on earth competent to interfere with the liberty of individuals in reasoning and judging for themselves about the Bible and its contents, as they severally please.

Therefore, e.g. religious establishments requiring subscriptions are Anti-christian.

10. There are rights of conscience such, that every one may lawfully advance a claim to profess and teach what is false and wrong in matters, religious, social, and moral, provided that to his private conscience it seems absolutely true and right.

Therefore, e.g. individuals have a right to preach and practise fornication and polygamy.

11. There is no such thing as a national or state conscience.

Therefore, e.g. no judgments can fall upon a sinful or infidel nation.

12. The civil power has no positive duty, in a normal state of things, to maintain religious truth.

Therefore, e.g. blasphemy and sabbath-breaking are not rightly punishable by law.

13. Utility and expedience are the measure of political duty.

Therefore, e.g. no punishment may be enacted, on the ground that God commands it: e.g. on the text, 'Whoso sheddeth man's blood, by man shall his blood be shed.' [5]

14. The Civil Power may dispose of Church property without sacrilege.

Therefore, e.g. Henry VIII committed no sin in his spoliations. [6]

15. The Civil Power has the right of ecclesiastical jurisdiction and administration.

Therefore, e.g. Parliament may impose articles of faith on the Church or suppress Dioceses. [7]

16. It is lawful to rise in arms against legitimate princes.

Therefore, e.g. the Puritans in the 17th century, and the French in the 18th, were justifiable in their Rebellion and Revolution respectively.

5. Genesis 9:6.
6. In abolishing the monasteries.
7. In 1833, Parliament, on Liberal principles, disestablished 10 bishoprics of the Anglican Church in Ireland. This act outraged the proponents of the autonomy of the church and led to their organizing an intellectual opposition to the Liberal conception of the church which came to be known as the Oxford Movement.

17. The people are the legitimate source of power.

Therefore, e.g. Universal Suffrage is among the natural rights of man.

18. Virtue is the child of knowledge, and vice of ignorance.

Therefore, e.g. education, periodical literature, railroad travelling, ventilation, drainage, and the arts of life, when fully carried out, serve to make a population moral and happy.

All of these propositions, and many others too, were familiar to me thirty years ago, as in the number of the tenets of Liberalism, and, while I gave into none of them except No. 12, and perhaps No. 11, and partly No. 1, before I began to publish, so afterwards I wrote against most of them in some part or other of my Anglican works. . . .

I need hardly say that the above Note is mainly historical. How far the Liberal party of 1830–40 really held the above eighteen Theses, which I attributed to them, and how far and in what sense I should oppose those Theses now, could scarcely be explained without a separate Dissertation.

1864                                                              1864, 1865

# JOHN RUSKIN
1819–1900

In 1909 the Italian poet Emilio Marinetti issued his famous *Futurist Manifesto*. This flamboyant document, which totally repudiated the past and peremptorily demanded that art dedicate itself to an authentically modern sensibility based on recognition of the beauty and vitality of the machine, is generally regarded as the charter of Aesthetic Modernism, even of those movements of art upon which the Futurist principles had no direct influence. Some three years after the publication of the *Manifesto,* Marinetti gave a lecture in London on the Futurist program and in the course of it put a question to his audience which, he made plain, was crucial to any hope they might have of aesthetic salvation: "When, then," he asked in impatient disdain, "When, then, will you disencumber yourselves of the lymphatic ideology of your deplorable Ruskin?"

The question was shocking in its impiousness and it was doubtless heard with an appalled relief. By 1912 the educated English public was fatigued with Ruskin—he had said so much and had said it for so long, ever since 1843. By the pertinacity, passion, and brilliance of his teaching he had shaped the minds of three intellectual generations in their relation to art. No one had ever made art so momentous; in every sentence he wrote about it was the urgently communicated belief that created objects had a decisive bearing upon the moral and spiritual life and that one's preferences in pictures or buildings, or even household utensils, were indicative of one's relation to oneself, one's fellow men, and the universe. The theorists and practitioners of the new movements certainly held art to be no less momentous than Ruskin said it was, but, however diverse their aesthetic principles might be, they were at one in saying that such moral considerations as Ruskin adduced were irrelevant to the aesthetic experience, and, indeed, qualified art's chief claim to momentousness, its autonomy. Marinetti's English audience may not have been ready to accept the full challenge of the new art, but they had been prepared by their fellow countrymen Walter Pater and Oscar Wilde to acknowledge a growing impatience with Ruskin's overtly moralizing tone and with his insistence upon the necessity of maintaining a sensibility which was consonant with religious faith even while admitting that religion as a system of belief was not tenable. It was just this sensibility that they found burdensome and in the assault that Marinotti made upon "their" Ruskin, which went to extremes of irreverence in its explanation of just why he was "deplorable," they heard the promise of liberation from it.

Given the extent and authority of Ruskin's influence, the revolt against it was inevitable. But with the passing decades it becomes ever more apparent by how much Ruskin transcends the conception of his work which made it a piously received doctrine in the Victorian Age and a burden in the early twentieth century. An evangelical anxiety over the moral and spiritual effect of art is indeed an essential part of Ruskin's thought, to be dealt with by each cultural generation after its own fashion. (One might venture the guess that at the present time it will enlist rather more sympathy than it did a quarter-century ago.) There is this much reason to deplore it, that for some readers—both those too easily reassured and those too easily distressed by moral discourse—it has the effect of obscuring those aspects of Ruskin's criticism that are not specifically moral, for example, his investigations into the formal or purely aesthetic elements of art which, so far from being in opposition to such ideas of modern theory as are vital and liberating, actually formulated them before they were given polemical expression in the articles of modernist faith. It is hard to point to any other body of criticism which is equal to Ruskin's in the range of its interests, in the multitudinousness and precision of its perceptions, in the cogency of the questions it raises, in the courage with which it tests and contradicts its own conclusions.

But if one can, so to speak, provisionally deplore Ruskin's moral impulse as it operates in his art criticism, one recognizes it as definitive of the imagination which informs his great work in social criticism. Taking together what he achieved in the two genres, one may well recognize in Ruskin the pre-eminent intellectual genius of Victorian England.

He was born in London in 1819, the only child of a middle-aged Scottish couple of strict evangelical principles and increasing affluence; his father was a wine merchant, specializing in sherry. The boy's natural precocity was emphasized and developed by the rigorously supervised solitude in which he was reared. He was a destined child, intended for the evangelical clergy, eventually for a bishopric. He was instructed early in reading, in music, in drawing. He was required to learn by heart long chapters of the Bible as well as to read it through aloud from beginning to end about once every year. His father, despite the strictness of his religious views, had a quite considerable feeling for artistic culture; he collected pictures and it was his custom to read aloud every evening from Walter Scott's novels. When John was four, his father began the practice of taking his wife and son with him on the annual tours he made to visit the great country houses whose cellars he supplied; Ruskin was thus early given his first experiences of architecture and landscape, as well as of the collections of paintings which many of the great houses could boast. When he was fourteen he was given a copy of the illustrated edition of Samuel Rogers's *Italy*. The poem itself had but little significance for him; the illustrations of J. M. W. Turner were decisive in his life. For one thing, his pleasure in the pictures, shared by his father, was so great that, at his mother's suggestion, it was resolved that the family should go to see for themselves the scenes depicted; thus began the long series of Continental tours—made in considerable style, in a traveling carriage and with servants in attendance—that Ruskin went on with his parents; it was thus that he acquired his extensive knowledge of the works of art of many cities. An equally important effect of the gift was that it inaugurated the passionate devotion to the work of Turner which was to be at the center of Ruskin's intellectual life for many years.

After a desultory but adequate schooling, largely under private tuition, Ruskin entered Christ Church, Oxford, in 1837. His experience of Oxford was pleasant but cool and remote—doubtless in part because his mother, anxious over his health, had taken up residence in the town and because Ruskin spent every evening with her—and it was interrupted by frequent tours with his parents and once by what seemed the serious threat of tuberculosis. He won the Newdigate Poetry Prize in 1839 but the degree he took in 1841 was undistinguished.

In his engaging autobiography, *Praeterita* (Foreshadowings), Ruskin comments wryly on the snobbery that had led his father to choose for him the most socially elite college of the university. "His ideal for my future," Ruskin says, ". . . was that I should enter at college into the best society, take all the prizes every year, and a double first to finish with; marry Lady Clara Vere de Vere; write poetry as good as Byron's, only pious; preach sermons as good as Bossuet's, only Protestant; be made at forty Bishop of Winchester, and at fifty Primate of England." These expectations the son proceeded to disappoint, but it must be said for the elder Ruskin that, although he long grieved over the unachieved bishopric, he took a measure of satisfaction in the enterprise to which his son then addressed himself and may even be said to have advanced it. Ruskin undertook to write a book in which Turner would be defended and canonized; his father had his own degree of admiration for the painter and was a cautious collector of his minor work. In 1843, when Ruskin published *Modern Painters* (by "A Graduate of Oxford"), Turner was seventy and had long been famous and honored. But Turner's bold later style distressed conventional taste and in response to an attack upon him Ruskin proposed to lay down the principles by which Turner was properly to be judged. The full title of the work will suggest its ambitious range and its uncompromising didacticism: *Modern Painters: Their Superiority in the Art of Landscape Painting to All the Ancient Masters Proved by Examples of the True, the Beautiful, and the Intellectual from the Works of Modern Artists, Especially from Those of J. M. W. Turner, Esq., R.A.* The book was not warmly received by painters, not even by Turner, a transcendent genius but a curmudgeonly man. The public, however, was delighted by the lucidity and eloquence of the prose in which its vigorous judgments were expressed.

In 1845, when he was twenty-six, Ruskin made his first tour alone, which is to say with his valet and a courier but without his parents. It was on this journey, undertaken to forward Volume II of *Modern Painters* (1846), that he became aware of the insufficiency of his knowledge of Italian painting and undertook to revise for a second edition of Volume I (1846) the judgments he had passed upon it. In 1848 he married a distant cousin, Euphemia Gray. The marriage was in every way disastrous. It had been arranged by the parents of the bride and groom; it was never consummated, and in 1854 it was annulled when Effie fell in love with Ruskin's friend, the Pre-Raphaelite painter John Everett Millais.

Suspending work on *Modern Painters,* Ruskin began the study of the cathedrals of Normandy and in 1849 brought out *The Seven Lamps of Architecture,* of which Kenneth Clark has said that, in the history of taste, it is perhaps the most influential book ever published. The work is equally charged with exquisite aesthetic sensibility and stern moral prescription; its peculiar achievement is that it succeeds in bringing its two energies into accord with each other. The thesis of the work is that greatness in art is dependent upon and is the index of the cognate quality in the life of the community that produces it; this quality in its ideality is defined by the "lamps" of Sacrifice, Truth, Power, Beauty, Life, Memory, and Obedience.

*The Stones of Venice* (1851, 1853) further developed and refined Ruskin's character-istic interpretation of particular works of art in terms of the moral assumptions, social forms, and technology out of which they had come. One chapter of this work, "The Nature of Gothic" (see below) had from the first an exceptional appeal and an incalculable influence on both the aesthetic and social thought of the age.

After 1854, art criticism began to take a second place in Ruskin's painfully intense intellectual life. Questions of social justice pressed ever more urgently upon him and in 1860 his distressed concern led him to make an assault upon the economic basis of English society through an attempt to discredit the method and assumptions of political economy. In four essays published in the *Cornhill Magazine,* collected as *Unto This Last* (see below), Ruskin undertook to controvert the virtually universal belief that the economic arrangements of a nation come into being in the course of nature, that they are to be viewed with the detached objectivity which science brings to bear upon the physical processes of nature, and that no more than the physical proc-esses of nature are they susceptible to moral judgment or interference. He cogently argued the inefficiency as well as the inhumanity of the system which was taken for granted by the political economists, of whom John Stuart Mill was at the time the most authoritative, and proposed a substitute derived from the ethics of three traditional institutions, the household, the learned professions (medicine and law), and the army, none of which sanctioned unchecked competition and the exclusive motive of economic self-interest. Such was the outcry against this view, which is now given ready assent and even a degree of implementation, that Thackeray, who edited the *Cornhill,* was obliged to discontinue the series. The same response was given to the essays of 1862–63 in *Fraser's Magazine* later collected as *Munera Pulveris* (Money of the Dust).

Ruskin's father died in 1864; his mother lived until 1870 and supervised much of her son's life until her death. In 1863 Ruskin showed the initial signs of mental illness and these appeared with increasing intensity during the thirty-five years of life still before him. They were exacerbated over the course of the next few years by his unhappy love for a young girl whom he wished to marry, by the deaths of dear friends, and by acute distress over the realization that his Christian faith had left him. His work from that time on is likely to be touched by eccentricity, but for the most part it shows but little falling off in essential cogency; the beautiful *Praeterita,* composed between 1885 and 1889, is the last work of his genius. His illness was of an intermittent kind and in his periods of health he worked with his characteristic energy. Such was the regard in which he eventually came to be held after the opprobrium that met his economic writings had abated that, although for reasons of health he had resigned the Slade Professorship of Art at Oxford to which he had been elected in 1869, he was called to the chair again in 1883. By the time of his death the considerable fortune left him by his father had been dispersed in his philanthropic enterprises; he founded the Guild of St. George to encourage the return to agricultural life, began several enlightened industrial enterprises, and undertook to instruct the young gentlemen of Oxford in the dignity of labor by supervising their construction of a road—one of the young gentlemen was Oscar Wilde.

Ruskin died in 1900 at Brantwood, his home on Lake Coniston in the Lake District. It may well be that the person for whom his death had most meaning was a young Frenchman to be known to fame as Marcel Proust. Proust had first heard about Ruskin in his student days and when he was in his mid-twenties he developed a passion for this English author whose language he could read only with difficulty. He was to translate into French two of Ruskin's books, *The Bible of Amiens* and *Sesame and Lilies* (1904, 1906), and through Ruskin he was to find, as his biographer G. D. Painter puts it, his salvation—after a period of desiccated feeling, his reading of Ruskin had reaffirmed for him the value of life and shown him his mission as an artist. On the news of Ruskin's death he said to a friend, "My grief is healthy and full of consolations, for I realize what a trivial thing death is, when I see how intensely this dead man lives, and how I admire and listen to his words, and seek to understand and obey him. . . ." And at the end of his essay on Ruskin (1900) he used of his master the words that Ruskin had used of Turner: "It is through these eyes, now closed for ever in the grave, that unborn generations will look upon nature."

# From Modern Painters

### Of the Real Nature of Greatness of Style [1]

I doubt not that the reader was ill-satisfied with the conclusion arrived at in the last chapter.[2] That 'great art' is art which represents what is beautiful and good, may not seem a very profound discovery; and the main question may be thought to have been all the time lost sight of, namely, 'What is beautiful, and what is good?' No; those are not the main, at least not the first questions; on the contrary, our subject becomes at once opened and simplified as soon as we have left those the *only* questions. For observe, our present task, accord-

1. This selection is Chap. 3 of Vol. II, Part IV.
2. The chapter is entitled "Of Realization." It follows the chapter "Of the Received Opinions Touching the 'Grand Style,'" in which Ruskin undertakes to refute the canons of taste formulated by the famous painter Sir Joshua Reynolds in the presidential discourses which he delivered at the Royal Academy of Art between 1769 and 1790. (They had aroused the scorn which William Blake expresses in the marginal comments to the collected *Discourses*.) The conclusion arrived at in "Of Realization" is that "true criticism of art never can consist in the mere application of rules; it can be just only when it is founded on quick sympathy with the innumerable instincts and changeful efforts of human nature, chastened and guided by unchanging love of all things that God has created to be beautiful and pronounced good."

ing to our old plan, is merely to investigate the relative degrees of the *beautiful* in the art of different masters; and it is an encouragement to be convinced, first of all, that what is lovely will also be great, and what is pleasing, noble. Nor is the conclusion so much a matter of course as it at first appears, for, surprising as the statement may seem, all the confusion into which Reynolds has plunged both himself and his readers, in the essay we have been examining, results primarily from a doubt in his own mind *as to the existence of beauty at all.* In the next paper I alluded to, No. 82 (which needs not, however, to be examined at so great length), he calmly attributes the whole influence of beauty to custom, saying, that 'he has no doubt, if we were more used to deformity than to beauty, deformity would then lose the idea now annexed to it, and take that of beauty; as if the whole world should agree that Yes and No should change their meanings; Yes would then deny, and No would affirm!'

The world does, indeed, succeed—oftener than is, perhaps, altogether well for the world—in making Yes mean No, and No mean Yes. But the world has never succeeded, nor ever will, in making itself delight in black clouds more than in blue sky, or love the dark earth better than the rose that grows from it. Happily for mankind, beauty and ugliness are as positive in their nature as physical pain and pleasure, as light and darkness, or as life and death; and though they may be denied or misunderstood in many fantastic ways, the most subtle reasoner will at last find that colour and sweetness are still attractive to him, and that no logic will enable him to think the rainbow sombre, or the violet scentless. But the theory that beauty was merely a result of custom was very common in Johnson's time. Goldsmith has, I think, expressed it with more force and wit than any other writer, in various passages of the *Citizen of the World*.[3] And it was, indeed, a curious retribution of the folly of the world of art, which for some three centuries had given itself recklessly to the pursuit of beauty, that at last it should be led to deny the very existence of what it had so morbidly and passionately sought. It was as if a child should leave its home to pursue the rainbow, and then, breathless and hopeless, declare that it did not exist. Nor is the lesson less useful which may be gained in observing the adoption of such a theory by Reynolds himself. It shows how completely an artist may be unconscious of the principles of his own work, and how he may be led by instinct to *do* all that is right, while he is misled by false logic to *say* all that is wrong. For nearly every word that Reynolds wrote was contrary to his own practice; he seems to have been born to teach all error by his precept, and all excellence by his example; he enforced with his lips generalization and idealism, while with his pencil he was tracing the patterns of the dresses of the belles of his day;[4] he exhorted his pupils to attend only to the invariable,

3. Oliver Goldsmith (1730–74) published a series of *Chinese Letters* in a London periodical in the course of 1760 which were collected as *The Citizen of the World* in 1762. They purport to be written by a philosophical Chinese living in London. In one of his letters he says that the women of England are unendurably ugly judged by the standards of China—they have feet ten inches long "and teeth of a most odious whiteness."
4. The chief theme of Reynolds's lectures was the "grand style" as it was to be achieved in what was said to be the highest genre of art, historical painting. Reynolds's own great achievement was not in this genre but in his entrancing portraits, chiefly of women.

while he himself was occupied in distinguishing every variation of womanly temper; and he denied the existence of the beautiful, at the same instant that he arrested it as it passed, and perpetuated it for ever.

But we must not quit the subject here. However inconsistently or dimly expressed, there is, indeed, some truth in that commonly accepted distinction between high and low art. That a thing should be beautiful is not enough; there is, as we said in the outset, a higher and lower range of beauty, and some ground for separating into various and unequal ranks painters who have, nevertheless, each in his several way, represented something that was beautiful or good.

Nor, if we would, can we get rid of this conviction. We have at all times some instinctive sense that the function of one painter is greater than that of another, even supposing each equally successful in his own way; and we feel that, if it were possible to conquer prejudice, and do away with the iniquities of personal feeling, and the insufficiencies of limited knowledge, we should all agree in this estimate, and be able to place each painter in his right rank, measuring them by a true scale of nobleness. We feel that the men in the higher classes of the scale would be, in the full sense of the word, Great,—men whom one would give much to see the faces of but for an instant; and that those in the lower classes of the scale (though none were admitted but who had true merit of some kind) would be very small men, not greatly exciting either reverence or curiosity. And with this fixed instinct in our minds, we permit our teachers daily to exhort their pupils to the cultivation of 'great art,'—neither they nor we having any very clear notion as to what the greatness consists in: but sometimes inclining to think it must depend on the space of the canvas, and that art on a scale of six feet by ten is something spiritually separated from that on a scale of three feet by five;—sometimes holding it to consist in painting the nude body, rather than the body decently clothed;—sometimes being convinced that it is connected with the study of past history, and that the art is only great which represents what the painter never saw, and about which he knows nothing;—and sometimes being firmly persuaded that it consists in generally finding fault with, and endeavouring to mend, whatsoever the Divine wisdom has made. All which various errors, having yet some notes and atoms of truth in the make of each of them, deserve some attentive analysis, for they come under that general law,—that 'the corruption of the best is the worst.' [5] There are not worse errors going than these four; and yet the truth they contain, and the instinct which urges many to preach them, are at the root of all healthy growth in art. We ruin one young painter after another by telling him to follow great art, without knowing ourselves what greatness is; and yet the feeling that it verily is something, and that there are depths and breadths, shallows and narrows, in the matter, is all that we have to look to, if we would ever make our art serviceable to ourselves or others. To follow art for the sake of being a great man, and therefore to cast about continually for some means of achieving position or attracting admiration, is the surest way of ending in total extinction. And yet it is only by honest reverence for art itself, and by great self-respect in the practice of it, that it can be rescued from dilettantism,

---

5. An English proverb, derived from the Latin "Corruptio optimi pessima."

raised to approved honourableness, and brought to the proper work it has to accomplish in the service of man.

Let us therefore look into the facts of the thing, not with any metaphysical, or otherwise vain and troublesome effort at acuteness, but in a plain way; for the facts themselves are plain enough, and may be plainly stated, only the difficulty is, that out of these facts, right and left, the different forms of misapprehension branch into grievous complexity, and branch so far and wide, that if once we try to follow them, they will lead us quite from our mark into other separate, though not less interesting discussions. The best way will be, therefore, I think, to sketch out at once in this chapter, the different characters which really constitute 'greatness' of style, and to indicate the principal directions of the outbranching misapprehensions of them; then, in the succeeding chapters, to take up in succession those which need more talk about them, and follow out at leisure whatever inquiries they may suggest.

I. *Choice of Noble Subject.*—Greatness of style consists, then: first, in the habitual choice of subjects of thought which involve wide interests and profound passions, as opposed to those which involve narrow interests and slight passions. The style is greater or less in exact proportion to the nobleness of the interests and passions involved in the subject. The habitual choice of sacred subjects, such as the Nativity, Transfiguration, Crucifixion (if the choice be sincere), implies that the painter has a natural disposition to dwell on the highest thoughts of which humanity is capable; it constitutes him so far forth a painter of the highest order, as, for instance, Leonardo, in his painting of the Last Supper: he who delights in representing the acts or meditations of great men, as, for instance, Raphael painting the School of Athens,[6] is, so far forth, a painter of the second order: he who represents the passions and events of ordinary life, of the third. And in this ordinary life, he who represents deep thoughts and sorrows, as, for instance, Hunt, in his Claudio and Isabella,[7] and such other works, is of the highest rank in his sphere; and he who represents the slight malignities and passions of the drawing-room, as, for instance, Leslie,[8] of the second rank; he who represents the sports of boys, or simplicities of clowns, as Webster or Teniers,[9] of the third rank; and he who represents brutalities and vices (for delight in them, and not for rebuke of them), of no rank at all, or rather of a negative rank, holding a certain order in the abyss.

The reader will, I hope, understand how much importance is to be attached

6. Raffaello Santi (1483–1520), the Italian painter who stands with Michelangelo and Leonardo as pre-eminent in his age. His most popular paintings are his Madonnas, but he also worked on a grander scale in his historical paintings. The *School of Athens* is one of four frescoes in the Vatican.

7. William Holman Hunt (1827–1910) was, with John Everett Millais and Dante Gabriel Rossetti, one of the initiators of the Pre-Raphaelite Movement (see note 14). The painting Ruskin refers to represents the scene in Shakespeare's *Measure for Measure* in which the chaste Isabella is urged by her brother Claudio to accept the bargain Angelo has offered her, that she give herself to him in exchange for his sparing Claudio's life.

8. Charles Robert Leslie (1794–1859), English painter, American by birth, very popular in his day. His pictures usually represent scenes, mostly humorous, from famous novels and plays.

9. Thomas Webster (1800–1886) specialized in scenes of school life. David Teniers, the younger (1610–90), the Flemish painter known for his realistic portrayal of daily life, including low life.

to the sentence in the first parenthesis, 'if the choice be sincere'; for choice of subject is, of course, only available as a criterion of the rank of the painter, when it is made from the heart. Indeed, in the lower orders of painting, the choice is always made from such a heart as the painter has; for his selection of the brawls of peasants or sports of children can, of course, proceed only from the fact that he has more sympathy with such brawls or pastimes than with nobler subjects. But the choice of the higher kind of subjects is often insincere; and may, therefore, afford no real criterion of the painter's rank. The greater number of men who have lately painted religious or heroic subjects have done so in mere ambition, because they had been taught that it was a good thing to be a 'high art' painter; and the fact is that in nine cases out of ten, the so-called historical or 'high art' painter is a person infinitely inferior to the painter of flowers or still life. He is, in modern times, nearly always a man who has great vanity without pictorial capacity, and differs from the landscape or fruit painter merely in misunderstanding and over-estimating his own powers. He mistakes his vanity for inspiration, his ambition for greatness of soul, and takes pleasure in what he calls 'the ideal,' merely because he has neither humility nor capacity enough to comprehend the real.

But also observe, it is not enough even that the choice be sincere. It must also be wise. It happens very often that a man of weak intellect, sincerely desiring to do what is good and useful, will devote himself to high art subjects because he thinks them the only ones on which time and toil can be usefully spent, or, sometimes, because they are really the only ones he has pleasure in contemplating. But not having intellect enough to enter into the minds of truly great men, or to imagine great events as they really happened, he cannot become a great painter; he degrades the subjects he intended to honour, and his work is more utterly thrown away, and his rank as an artist in reality lower, than if he had devoted himself to the imitation of the simplest objects of natural history. The works of Overbeck [10] are a most notable instance of this form of error.

It must also be remembered, that in nearly all the great periods of art the choice of subject has not been left to the painter. His employer,—abbot, baron, or monarch,—determined for him whether he should earn his bread by making cloisters bright with choirs of saints, painting coats of arms on leaves of romances, or decorating presence chambers with complimentary mythology; and his own personal feelings are ascertainable only by watching, in the themes assigned to him, what are the points in which he seems to take most pleasure. Thus, in the prolonged ranges of varied subjects with which Benozzo Gozzoli [11] decorated the cloisters of Pisa, it is easy to see that love of simple domestic incident, sweet landscape, and glittering ornament, prevails slightly over the solemn elements of religious feeling, which, nevertheless, the spirit of the age

10. Johann Friedrich Overbeck (1789–1869), the painter who undertook to revive Christian art in his native Germany. He turned for his inspiration to Raphael and established a small brotherhood of like-minded artists, the so-called "Nazarenes," dedicated to an ascetic, pious, and laborious life of producing "noble" paintings of sacred subjects. They were precursors of the English Pre-Raphaelites (see note 14). Overbeck's own work is not greatly esteemed by reason of its dryness and pedantry.
11. Italian painter (1420–97).

instilled into him in such measure as to form a very lovely and noble mind, though still one of the second order. In the work of Orcagna,[12] an intense solemnity and energy in the sublimest groups of his figures, fading away as he touches inferior subjects, indicates that his home was among the archangels, and his rank among the first of the sons of men; while Correggio,[13] in the side-long grace, artificial smiles, and purple languors of his saints, indicates the inferior instinct which would have guided his choice in quite other directions, had it not been for the fashion of the age, and the need of the day.

It will follow, of course, from the above considerations, that the choice which characterizes the school of high art is seen as much in the treatment of a subject as in its selection, and that the expression of the thoughts of the persons represented will always be the first thing considered by the painter who worthily enters that highest school. For the artist who sincerely chooses the noblest subject will also choose chiefly to represent what makes that subject noble, namely, the various heroism or other noble emotions of the persons represented. If, instead of this, the artist seeks only to make his picture agreeable by the composition of its masses and colours, or by any other merely pictorial merit, as fine drawing of limbs, it is evident, not only that any other subject would have answered his purpose as well, but that he is unfit to approach the subject he has chosen, because he cannot enter into its deepest meaning, and therefore cannot in reality have chosen it for that meaning. Nevertheless, while the expression is always to be the first thing considered, all other merits must be added to the utmost of the painter's power; for until he can both colour and draw beautifully he has no business to consider himself a painter at all, far less to attempt the noblest subjects of painting; and, when he has once possessed himself of these powers, he will naturally and fitly employ them to deepen and perfect the impression made by the sentiment of his subject.

The perfect unison of expression, as the painter's main purpose, with the full and natural exertion of his pictorial power in the details of the work, is found only in the old Pre-Raphaelite periods, and in the modern Pre-Raphaelite school.[14] In the works of Giotto,[15] Angelico.[16] Orcagna, John

12. Andrea di Cione, Italian painter, sculptor, worker in mosaic, architect (c. 1308–c. 1368).
13. Antonio Allegri da Correggio, Italian painter (1494–1534), famous for the brilliance and gusto of his execution and for the uniqueness of his style and vision. Ruskin's adverse opinion of his work does not generally prevail.
14. The Pre-Raphaelite Movement in England was but a single instance, though the most famous one, of a desire on the part of European painters to escape from what they had come to think of as the commonplace of virtuosity, of the highly developed techniques of representation that descended from the High Renaissance (see note 10). The members of the Pre-Raphaelite Brotherhood—the P.R.B., as it was called—sought for a directness and simplicity of representation which, as they thought, put them in the line of the painters before Raphael, before, that is, the achievements of Renaissance knowledge and technique made the elemental piety of a painting of less account than its powers of complex representation. Much of the early Pre-Raphaelite work undertook to be hard and dry, but with the passage of time it began to show a degree of sumptuousness; this is especially true of Rossetti, Millais, and Burne-Jones.
15. Giotto (c. 1266–1337), a Florentine, is the most admired painter of the period before the Renaissance. He was also an architect of great attainments.
16. Fra Angelico (1387–1455), Italian painter, a friar of the Dominican order. He is

Bellini,[17] and one or two more, these two conditions of high art are entirely fulfilled, so far as the knowledge of those days enabled them to be fulfilled; and in the modern Pre-Raphaelite school they are fulfilled nearly to the uttermost. Hunt's *Light of the World*,[18] is, I believe, the most perfect instance of expressional purpose with technical power, which the world has yet produced.

Now in the Post-Raphaelite period of ancient art, and in the spurious high art of modern times, two broad forms of error divide the schools; the one consisting in (A) the superseding of expression by technical excellence, and the other in (B) the superseding of technical excellence by expression.

A. Superseding expression by technical excellence.—This takes place most frankly, and therefore most innocently, in the work of the Venetians. They very nearly ignore expression altogether, directing their aim exclusively to the rendering of external truths of colour and form. Paul Veronese [19] will make the Magdalene wash the feet of Christ with a countenance as absolutely unmoved as that of any ordinary servant bringing a ewer to her master, and will introduce the supper at Emmaus [20] as a background to the portraits of two children playing with a dog. Of the wrongness or rightness of such a proceeding we shall reason in another place; at present we have to note it merely as displacing the Venetian work from the highest or expressional rank of art. But the error is generally made in a more subtle and dangerous way. The artist deceives himself into the idea that he is doing all he can to elevate his subject by treating it under rules of art, introducing into it accurate science, and collecting for it the beauties of (so-called) ideal form; whereas he may, in reality, be all the while sacrificing his subject to his own vanity or pleasure, and losing truth, nobleness, and impressiveness for the sake of delightful lines or creditable pedantries.

B. Superseding technical excellence by expression.—This is usually done under the influence of another kind of vanity. The artist desires that men should think he has an elevated soul, affects to despise the ordinary excellence of art, contemplates with separated egotism the course of his own imaginations or sensations, and refuses to look at the real facts round about him, in order that he may adore at leisure the shadow of himself. He lives in an element of what he calls tender emotions and lofty aspirations; which are, in fact,

---

celebrated for the lyric grace and delicacy of his work. He was admired by the Pre-Raphaelites because he did not respond to the scientific naturalism which was influential in his day.

17. Giovanni Bellini (*c.* 1430–1516), Venetian painter, the son of Iacopo Bellini and brother of Gentile Bellini. To his two great pupils, Giorgione and Titian, he passed on his concern with light and color which was to be characteristic of the Venetian school of painting in contrast to the Florentine emphasis upon form.

18. In 1854 Hunt, who was a man of intense religious feeling, painted this picture, which is an allegorical representation of Christ knocking on the door of the human soul. Ruskin's admiration of it was shared by many and it may well have been, through reproductions, the best known picture in England in the later 19th century. It is now a byword for sentimentality and dull execution.

19. Paolo Veronese (1528–88), Venetian painter. His indifference to the religious content of his ostensibly religious paintings once got him into trouble with the Inquisition, which charged that he had left the Magdalene out of a Scriptural scene to which her presence was essential and had introduced dogs, buffoons, dwarfs, and German soldiers.

20. Luke 24:13.

nothing more than very ordinary weaknesses or instincts, contemplated through a mist of pride. A large range of modern German art comes under this head.

A more interesting and respectable form of this error is fallen into by some truly earnest men, who, finding their powers not adequate to the attainment of great artistical excellence, but adequate to rendering, up to a certain point, the expression of the human countenance, devote themselves to that object alone, abandoning effort in other directions, and executing the accessories of their pictures feebly or carelessly. With these are associated another group of philosophical painters, who suppose the artistical merits of other parts *adverse* to the expression, as drawing the spectator's attention away from it, and who paint in grey colour, and imperfect light and shade, by way of enforcing the purity of their conceptions. Both these classes of conscientious but narrow-minded artists labour under the same grievous mistake of imagining that wilful fallacy can ever be either pardonable or helpful. They forget that colour, if used at all, must be either true or false, and that what *they* call chastity, dignity, and reserve is, to the eye of any person accustomed to nature, pure, bold, and impertinent falsehood. It does not in the eyes of any soundly minded man, exalt the expression of a female face that the cheeks should be painted of the colour of clay, nor does it in the least enhance his reverence for a saint to find the scenery around him deprived, by his presence, of sunshine. It is an important consolation, however, to reflect that no artist ever fell into any of these last three errors (under head B) who had really the capacity of becoming a great painter. No man ever despised colour who could produce it; and the error of these sentimentalists and philosophers is not so much in the choice of their manner of painting, as in supposing themselves capable of painting at all. Some of them might have made efficient sculptors, but the greater number had their mission in some other sphere than that of art, and would have found, in works of practical charity, better employment for their gentleness and sentimentalism, than in denying to human beauty its colour, and to natural scenery its light; in depriving heaven of its blue, and earth of its bloom, valour of its glow, and modesty of its blush.

II. *Love of Beauty.*—The second characteristic of the great school of art is, that it introduces in the conception of its subject as much beauty as is possible, consistently with truth.[21]

---

21. "As here, for the first time, I am obliged to use the terms Truth and Beauty in a kind of opposition, I must therefore stop for a moment to state clearly the relation of these two qualities of art; and to protest against the vulgar and foolish habit of confusing truth and beauty with each other. People with shallow powers of thought, desiring to flatter themselves with the sensation of having attained profundity, are continually doing the most serious mischief by introducing confusion into plain matters, and then valuing themselves on being confounded. Nothing is more common than to hear people who desire to be thought philosophical, declare that 'beauty is truth,' and 'truth is beauty.' I would most earnestly beg every sensible person who hears such an assertion made, to nip the germinating philosopher in his ambiguous bud; and beg him, if he really believes his own assertion, never henceforward to use two words for the same thing. The fact is, truth and beauty are entirely distinct, though often related, things. One is a property of statements, the other of objects. The statement that two and two make four is true, but it is neither beautiful nor ugly, for it is invisible; a rose is lovely, but it is neither true nor false, for it is silent. That which shows nothing cannot be fair, and that which asserts nothing cannot be false. Even

For instance, in any subject consisting of a number of figures, it will make as many of those figures beautiful as the faithful representation of humanity will admit. It will not deny the facts of ugliness or decrepitude, or relative inferiority and superiority of feature as necessarily manifested in a crowd, but it will, so far as it is in its power, seek for and dwell upon the fairest forms, and in all things insist on the beauty that is in them, not on the ugliness. In this respect, schools of art become higher in exact proportion to the degree in which they apprehend and love the beautiful. Thus, Angelico, intensely loving all spiritual beauty, will be of the highest rank; and Paul Veronese and Correggio, intensely loving physical and corporeal beauty, of the second rank; and Albert Dürer,[22] Rubens,[23] and in general the Northern artists, apparently insensible to beauty, and caring only for truth, whether shapely or not, of the third rank; [24] and Teniers and Salvator, Caravaggio,[25] and other such wor-

the ordinary use of the words false and true, as applied to artificial and real things, is inaccurate. An artificial rose is not a 'false' rose, it is not a rose at all. The falseness is in the person who states, or induces the belief, that it *is* a rose.

"Now, therefore, in things concerning art, the words true and false are only to be rightly used while the picture is considered as a statement of facts. The painter asserts that this which he has painted is the form of a dog, a man, or a tree. If it be *not* the form of a dog, a man, or a tree, the painter's statement is false; and, therefore, we justly speak of a false line, or false colour; not that any lines or colours can in themselves be false, but they become so when they convey a statement that they resemble something which they do *not* resemble. But the beauty of the lines or colours is wholly independent of any such statement. They may be beautiful lines, though quite inaccurate, and ugly lines though quite faithful. A picture may be frightfully ugly, which represents with fidelity some base circumstance of daily life; and a painted window may be exquisitely beautiful, which represents men with eagles' faces, and dogs with blue heads and crimson tails (though, by the way, this is not in the strict sense *false* art, as we shall see hereafter, inasmuch as it means no assertion that men ever *had* eagles' faces). If this were not so, it would be impossible to sacrifice truth to beauty; for to attain the one would always be to attain the other. But, unfortunately, this sacrifice is exceedingly possible, and it is chiefly this which characterizes the false schools of high art, so far as high art consists in the pursuit of beauty. For although truth and beauty are independent of each other, it does not follow that we are at liberty to pursue whichever we please. They are indeed separable, but it is wrong to separate them; they are to be sought together in the order of their worthiness; that is to say, truth first, and beauty afterwards. High art differs from low art in possessing an excess of beauty in addition to its truth, not in possessing excess of beauty inconsistent with truth." (Ruskin)

Ruskin, in dealing with the idea of the equivalence of truth and beauty, does not refer to Keats's famous statement of it at the end of "Ode on a Grecian Urn," perhaps because he perceived that Keats had in mind something more complex than the common formulation he is here dealing with.

22. Albrecht Dürer (1471–1528), the great German painter and engraver. In his last years he wrote theoretical works on geometry and perspective and anatomy.
23. Peter Paul Rubens (1577–1640), Flemish painter, generally accounted the greatest exemplar in northern Europe of the dramatic, exuberant style known as baroque.
24. An art critic of today of whatever school of thought could receive this judgment of Dürer and Rubens only in wide-eyed amazement.
25. Salvator Rosa (1615–73), Neapolitan painter, is celebrated for his wild, often savage, scenes which are peopled with shepherds, sailors, and soldiers; he has not a touch of "nobility." Caravaggio (1569–1609) took a principled stand against idealism and painted biblical scenes in a harshly realistic manner, using crude peasant faces as his models and dramatizing them with extreme contrasts of light and shadow. Ruskin goes so far in his condemnation of these men as to assign them, in the last phrase of the paragraph, to the forces of Hell.

shippers of the depraved, of no rank, or as we said before, of a certain order in the abyss.

The corruption of the schools of high art, so far as this particular quality is concerned, consists in the sacrifice of truth to beauty. Great art dwells on all that is beautiful; but false art omits or changes all that is ugly. Great art accepts Nature as she is, but directs the eyes and thoughts to what is most perfect in her; false art saves itself the trouble of direction by removing or altering whatever it thinks objectionable. The evil results of which proceeding are twofold.

First. That beauty deprived of its proper foils and adjuncts ceases to be *Evil first, that* enjoyed as beauty, just as light deprived of all shadow ceases *we lose the true* to be enjoyed as light. A white canvas cannot produce an *force of beauty.* effect of sunshine; the painter must darken it in some places before he can make it look luminous in others; nor can an uninterrupted succession of beauty produce the true effect of beauty; it must be foiled by inferiority before its own power can be developed. Nature has for the most part mingled her inferior and noble elements as she mingles sunshine with shade, giving due use and influence to both, and the painter who chooses to remove the shadow, perishes in the burning desert he has created. The truly high and beautiful art of Angelico is continually refreshed and strengthened by his frank portraiture of the most ordinary features of his brother monks and of the recorded peculiarities of ungainly sanctity; but the modern German and Raphaelesque schools lose all honour and nobleness in barber-like admiration of handsome faces, and have, in fact, no real faith except in straight noses, and curled hair. Paul Veronese opposes the dwarf to the soldier, and the negress to the queen; Shakespeare places Caliban beside Miranda, and Autolycus beside Perdita; [26] but the vulgar idealist withdraws his beauty to the safety of the saloon,[27] and his innocence to the seclusion of the cloister; he pretends that he does this in delicacy of choice and purity of sentiment, while in truth he has neither courage to front the monster, nor wit enough to furnish the knave.

It is only by the habit of representing faithfully all things, that we can truly *Evil second,—* learn what is beautiful, and what is not. The ugliest objects *we lose the true* contain some element of beauty; and in all it is an element *quantity of* peculiar to themselves, which cannot be separated from their *beauty.* ugliness, but must either be enjoyed together with it or not at all. The more a painter accepts nature as he finds it, the more unexpected beauty he discovers in what he at first despised; but once let him arrogate the right of rejection, and he will gradually contract his circle of enjoyment, until what he supposed to be nobleness of selection ends in narrowness of perception. Dwelling perpetually upon one class of ideas, his art becomes at once monstrous and morbid; until at last he cannot faithfully represent even what he

26. Caliban is the misshapen savage slave to Prospero in *The Tempest;* Miranda is Prospero's lovely daughter; in *The Winter's Tale* Autolycus is a ragged, pilfering peddler, Perdita the exquisite shepherdess, actually a princess.
27. Saloon: a large room for receiving people or displaying pictures. Its use to mean a drinking place has led to the substitution of the original French *salon* for its anglicized form. "Vulgar idealist" is a striking phrase for an important idea; it might be turned on many of the Pre-Raphaelite works that Ruskin admired, most especially *The Light of the World.*

chooses to retain; his discrimination contracts into darkness, and his fastidious-ness fades into fatuity.

High art, therefore, consists neither in altering, nor in improving nature; but in seeking throughout nature for 'whatsoever things are lovely, and whatso-ever things are pure'; [28] in loving these, in displaying to the utmost of the painter's power such loveliness as is in them, and directing the thoughts of others to them by winning art or gentle emphasis. Of the degree in which this can be done, and in which it may be permitted to gather together, without falsifying, the finest forms or thoughts, so as to create a sort of perfect vision, we shall have to speak hereafter: at present, it is enough to remember that art (*cæteris paribus*) [29] is great in exact proportion to the love of beauty shown by the painter, provided that love of beauty forfeit no atom of truth.

III. *Sincerity.*—The next [30] characteristic of great art is that it includes the largest possible quantity of Truth in the most perfect possible harmony. If it were possible for art to give all the truths of nature it ought to do it. But this is not possible. Choice must always be made of some facts which *can* be repre-sented, from among others which must be passed by in silence, or even, in some respects, misrepresented. The inferior artist chooses unimportant and scattered truths; the great artist chooses the most necessary first, and afterwards the most consistent with these, so as to obtain the greatest possible and-most harmonious *sum*. For instance, Rembrandt [31] always chooses to represent the exact force with which the light on the most illumined part of an object is opposed to its obscurer portions. In order to obtain this, in most cases, not very important truth, he sacrifices the light and colour of five-sixths of his picture, and the expression of every character of objects which depends on tenderness of shape or tint. But he obtains his single truth, and what picturesque and forcible expression is dependent upon it, with magnificent skill and subtlety. Veronese, on the contrary, chooses to represent the great relations of visible things to each other, to the heaven above, and to the earth beneath [32] them. He holds it more important to show how a figure stands relieved from delicate air, or marble wall; how as a red, or purple, or white figure, it separates itself, in clear discernibility, from things not red, nor purple, nor white; how infinite daylight shines round it; how innumerable veils of faint shadow invest it; how its blackness and darkness are, in the excess of their nature, just as limited and local as its intensity of light; all this, I say, he feels to be more important than showing merely the exact *measure* of the spark of sunshine that gleams on a dagger-hilt, or glows on a jewel. All this, moreover, he feels to be harmonious,— capable of being joined in one great system of spacious truth. And with in-evitable watchfulness, inestimable subtlety, he unites all this in tenderest balance, noting in each hair's-breadth of colour, not merely what its rightness or wrongness is in itself, but what its relation is to every other on his canvas; restraining, for truth's sake, his exhaustless energy, reining back, for truth's

28. Philippians 4:8.
29. "Other things being equal."
30. "I name them in order of *in*creasing, not decreasing importance." (Ruskin)
31. Rembrandt van Rijn (1606–69), the greatest of Dutch painters.
32. Exodus 20:4.

sake, his fiery strength; veiling, before truth, the vanity of brightness; penetrating, for truth, the discouragement of gloom; ruling his restless invention
with a rod of iron; pardoning no error, no thoughtlessness, no forgetfulness;
and subduing all his powers, impulses, and imaginations, to the arbitrament of
a merciless justice, and the obedience of an incorruptible verity.

I give this instance with respect to colour and shade: but, in the whole field
of art, the difference between the great and inferior artists is of the same kind,
and may be determined at once by the question, which of them conveys the
largest sum of truth?

It follows from this principle, that in general all *great* drawing is *distinct*
*Corollary 1st:* drawing; for truths which are rendered indistinctly might, for
*Great art is* the most part, as well not be rendered at all. There are, indeed,
*generally dis-* certain facts of mystery, and facts of indistinctness, in all ob-
*tinct.* jects, which must have their proper place in the general harmony, and the reader will presently find me, when we come to that part of our
investigation, telling him that all good drawing must in some sort be *indistinct.*
We may, however, understand this apparent contradiction, by reflecting that
the highest knowledge always involves a more advanced perception of the fields
of the unknown; and, therefore, it may most truly be said, that to know anything well involves a profound sensation of ignorance, while yet it is equally
true that good and noble knowledge is distinguished from vain and useless
knowledge chiefly by its clearness and distinctness, and by the vigorous consciousness of what is known and what is not.

So in art. The best drawing involves a wonderful perception and expression
of indistinctness; and yet all noble drawing is separated from the ignoble by
its distinctness, by its fine expression and firm assertion of *Something;* whereas
the bad drawing, without either firmness or fineness, expresses and asserts
*Nothing.* The first thing, therefore, to be looked for as a sign of noble art, is a
clear consciousness of what is drawn and what is not; the bold statement, and
frank confession—'This I know,' 'that I know not'; and, generally speaking, all
haste, slurring, obscurity, indecision, are signs of low art, and all calmness,
distinctness, luminousness, and positiveness, of high art.

It follows, secondly, from this principle, that as the great painter is always
*Corollary 2nd:* attending to the sum and harmony of his truths rather than
*Great art is* to one or the other of any group, a quality of Grasp is visible
*generally* in his work, like the power of a great reasoner over his sub-
*large in masses* 
*and in scale.* ject, or a great poet over his conception, manifesting itself
very often in missing out certain details or less truths (which, though good in
themselves, he finds are in the way of others), and in a sweeping manner of
getting the beginnings and ends of things shown at once, and the squares and
depths rather than the surfaces: hence, on the whole, a habit of looking at
large masses rather than small ones; and even a physical largeness of handling,
and love of working, if possible, on a large scale; and various other qualities,
more or less imperfectly expressed by such technical terms as breadth, massing,
unity, boldness, etc., all of which are, indeed, great qualities, when they mean
breadth of truth, weight of truth, unity of truth, and courageous assertion of
truth; but which have all their correlative errors and mockeries, almost uni-

versally mistaken for them,—the breadth which has no contents, the weight which has no value, the unity which plots deception, and the boldness which faces out fallacy.

And it is to be noted especially respecting largeness of scale, that though for the most part it is characteristic of the more powerful masters, they have both more invention wherewith to fill space (as Ghirlandajo wished that he might paint all the walls of Florence) [33] and, often, an impetuosity of mind which makes them like free play for hand and arm (besides that they usually desire to paint everything in the foreground of their picture of the natural size), yet, as this largeness of scale involves the placing of the picture at a considerable distance from the eye, and this distance involves the loss of many delicate details, and especially of the subtle lines of expression in features, it follows that the masters of refined detail and human expression are apt to prefer a small scale to work upon; so that the chief masterpieces of expression which the world possesses are small pictures by Angelico, in which the figures are rarely more than six or seven inches high; in the best works of Raphael and Leonardo the figures are almost always less than life, and the best works of Turner do not exceed the size of 18 inches by 12.

As its greatness depends on the sum of truth, and this sum of truth can *Corollary 3rd: Great art is always delicate.* always be increased by delicacy of handling, it follows that all great art must have this delicacy to the utmost possible degree. This rule is infallible and inflexible. All coarse work is the sign of low art. Only, it is to be remembered, that coarseness must be estimated by the distance from the eye; it being necessary to consult this distance, when great, by laying on touches which appear coarse when seen near; but which, so far from being coarse, are, in reality, more delicate in a master's work than the finest close handling, for they involve a calculation of result, and are laid on with a subtlety of sense precisely correspondent to that with which a good archer draws his bow; the spectator seeing in the action nothing but the strain of the strong arm, while there is in reality, in the finger and eye, an ineffably delicate estimate of distance, and touch on the arrow plume. And, indeed, this delicacy is generally quite perceptible to those who know what the truth is, for strokes by Tintoret [34] or Paul Veronese, which were done in an instant, and look to an ignorant spectator merely like a violent dash of loaded colour (and are, as such, imitated by blundering artists), are, in fact, modulated by the brush and finger to that degree of delicacy that no single grain of the colour could be taken from the touch without injury; and little golden particles of it, not the size of a gnat's head, have important share and function in the balances of light in a picture perhaps fifty feet long. Nearly *every* other rule applicable to art has some exception but this. This has absolutely none. All great art is delicate art, and all coarse art is bad art. Nay, even, to a certain extent, all *bold* art is bad art; for boldness is not the proper word to apply to the courage and swiftness of a great master, based on knowledge, and coupled with fear and love. There is as much difference between the

---

33. Vasari, in his *Lives of the Painters* (1550), records the expression of this wish by Ghirlandaio, the Florentine painter (1483–1561).
34. The brilliant Venetian painter, generally called Tintoretto (1518–94). Ruskin alludes to the rapidity with which he executed his work; it led to his being nicknamed *Il Furioso*.

boldness of the true and the false masters, as there is between the courage of a sure woman and the shamelessness of a lost one.[35]

IV. *Invention.*—The last characteristic of great art is that it must be inventive, that is, be produced by the imagination. In this respect, it must precisely fulfil the definition already given of poetry; and not only present grounds for noble emotion, but furnish these grounds by *imaginative power.* Hence there is at once a great bar fixed between the two schools of Lower and Higher art. The lower merely copies what is set before it, whether in portrait, landscape, or still-life; the higher either entirely imagines its subject, or arranges the materials presented to it, so as to manifest the imaginative power in all the three phases which have been already explained in the second volume.

And this was the truth which was confusedly present in Reynolds's mind when he spoke, as above quoted,[36] of the difference between Historical and Poetical Painting. *Every relation of the plain facts which the painter saw is proper historical* painting. If those facts are unimportant (as that he saw a gambler quarrel with another gambler, or a sot [37] enjoying himself with another sot), then the history is trivial; if the facts are important (as that he saw such and such a great man look thus, or act thus, at such a time), then the history is noble: in each case perfect truth of narrative being supposed, otherwise the whole thing is worthless, being neither history nor poetry, but plain falsehood. And farther, as greater or less elegance and precision are manifested in the relation or painting of the incidents, the merit of the work varies; so that, what with difference of subject, and what with difference of treatment, historical painting falls or rises in changeful eminence, from Dutch trivialities [38] to a Velasquez [39] portrait, just as historical talking or writing varies in eminence, from an old woman's story-telling up to Herodotus.[40] Besides which, certain operations of the imagination come into play inevitably, here and there, so as to touch the history with some light of poetry, that is, with some light shot forth of the narrator's mind, or brought out by the way he has put the accidents together: and wherever the imagination has thus had anything to do with the matter at all (and it must be somewhat cold work where it has not), then, the confines of the lower and higher schools touching each other, the work is coloured by both; but there is no reason why, therefore, we should in the least confuse the historical and poetical characters, any more than that we should confuse blue with crimson, because they may overlap each other, and produce purple.

Now, historical or simply narrative art is very precious in its proper place

35. Ruskin uses an established Victorian phrase for a woman who has committed a sexual transgression. That he should have instituted this comparison between two kinds of artists and two kinds of women is indicative of the nature of the Victorian sexual ethos.
36. In the chapter on the "grand style," Ruskin quotes Reynolds to the effect that in the grand—or historical—style, minute attention to detail should be avoided. "To mingle the Dutch [i.e. detailed] with the Italian school is to join contraries, which cannot subsist together, and which destroy the efficacy of each other." (Reynolds)
37. Drunkard.
38. Dutch painting characteristically represented the details of daily life, often naturalistically but sometimes in a heightened and "poetic" way.
39. Velasquez (1599–1660), the great Spanish painter.
40. Herodotus, Greek historian of the 4th century B.C., called the Father of History.

and way, but it is never *great* art until the poetical or imaginative power touches it; and in proportion to the stronger manifestation of this power, it becomes greater and greater, while the highest art is purely imaginative, all its materials being wrought into their form by invention; and it differs, therefore, from the simple historical painting, exactly as Wordsworth's stanza, above quoted, differs from Saussure's plain narrative of the parallel fact; [41] and the imaginative painter differs from the historical painter in the manner that Wordsworth differs from Saussure.

Farther, imaginative art always *includes* historical art; so that, strictly speaking, according to the analogy above used, we meet with the pure blue, and with the crimson ruling the blue and changing it into kingly purple, but not with the pure crimson: for all imagination must deal with the knowledge it has before accumulated; it never produces anything but by combination or contemplation. Creation, in the full sense, is impossible to it. And the mode in which the historical faculties are included by it is often quite simple, and easily seen. Thus, in Hunt's great poetical picture of *The Light of the World*, the whole thought and arrangement of the picture being imaginative, the several details of it are wrought out with simple portraiture; the ivy, the jewels, the creeping plants, and the moonlight being calmly studied or remembered from the things themselves. But of all these special ways in which the invention works with plain facts, we shall have to treat farther afterwards.

And now, finally, since this poetical power includes the historical, if we glance back to the other qualities required in great art, and put all together, we find that the sum of them is simply the sum of all the powers of man. For as (1) the choice of the high subject involves all conditions of right moral choice, and as (2) the love of beauty involves all conditions of right admiration, and as (3) the grasp of truth involves all strength of sense, evenness of judgment, and honesty of purpose, and as (4) the poetical power involves all swiftness of invention, and accuracy of historical memory, the sum of all these powers is the sum of the human soul. Hence we see why the word "Great" is used of this art. It is literally great. It compasses and calls forth the entire human spirit, whereas any other kind of art, being more or less small or narrow, compasses and calls forth only *part* of the human spirit. Hence the idea of its magnitude is a literal and just one, the art being simply less or greater in proportion to the number of faculties it exercises and addresses. And this is the ultimate meaning of the definition I gave of it long ago, as containing the 'greatest number of the greatest ideas.' [42]

Such, then, being the characters required in order to constitute high art, if the reader will think over them a little, and over the various ways in which they may be falsely assumed, he will easily perceive how spacious and dangerous a field of discussion they open to the ambitious critic, and of error to

---

41. In a footnote to a passage in the chapter on the "grand style" Ruskin quotes a passage from Wordsworth's "The Affliction of Margaret" and a passage of similar import from Saussure's prose narrative of his actual travels *Voyages dans les Alpes*. (Horace Bénédict de Saussure (1740–99), known for his scientific studies of the plants and weather of the Alps.) The first, he says, is poetry because it is invented or made by the writer; the second is not poetry, however affecting it is, but true utterance.

42. In Vol. II of *Modern Painters*.

the ambitious artist; he will see how difficult it must be, either to distinguish what is truly great art from the mockeries of it, or to rank the real artists in anything like a progressive system of greater and less. For it will have been observed that the various qualities which form greatness are partly inconsistent with each other (as some virtues are, docility and firmness for instance), and partly independent of each other; and the fact is, that artists differ not more by mere capacity, than by the component *elements* of their capacity, each possessing in very different proportions the several attributes of greatness; so that, classed by one kind of merit, as, for instance, purity of expression, Angelico will stand highest; classed by another, sincerity of manner, Veronese will stand highest; classed by another, love of beauty, Leonardo will stand highest; and so on: hence arise continual disputes and misunderstandings among those who think that high art must always be one and the same, and that great artists ought to unite all great attributes in an equal degree.

In one of the exquisitely finished tales of Marmontel,[43] a company of critics are received at dinner by the hero of the story, an old gentleman, somewhat vain of his *acquired* taste, and his niece, by whose incorrigible *natural* taste he is seriously disturbed and tormented. During the entertainment, 'On parcourut tous les genres de littérature, et pour donner plus d'essor à l'érudition et à la critique, on mit sur le tapis cette question toute neuve, sçavoir, lequel méritoit la préférence de Corneille ou de Racine. L'on disoit même là-dessus les plus belles choses du monde, lorsque la petite nièce, qui n'avoit pas dit un mot, s'avisa de demander naïvement lequel des deux fruits, de l'orange ou de la pêche, avoit le goût le plus exquis et méritoit le plus d'éloges. Son oncle rougit de sa simplicité, et les convives baissèrent tous les yeux sans daigner répondre à cette bêtise. Ma nièce, dit Fintac, à votre âge, il faut sçavoir écouter, et se taire.' [44]

I cannot close this chapter with shorter or better advice to the reader, than merely, whenever he hears discussions about the relative merits of great masters, to remember the young lady's question. It is, indeed, true that there *is* a relative merit, that a peach is nobler than a hawthorn berry, and still more a hawthorn berry than a bead of the nightshade; but in each rank of fruits, as in each rank of masters, one is endowed with one virtue, and another with another; their glory is their dissimilarity, and they who propose to themselves in the training of an artist that he should unite the colouring of Tintoret, the finish of Albert Dürer, and the tenderness of Correggio, are no wiser than a horticulturist would be, who made it the object of his labour to produce a fruit

---

43. Jean-François Marmontel (1723–99), French man of letters and contributor to the *Encyclopédie*. It was a passage in his *Memoirs of a Father* that so greatly helped John Stuart Mill in his great emotional crisis.
44. Ruskin quotes from "The Connoisseur," one of the *Moral Tales*, published in book form in 1761 and in 1789–92. "They ran through all the literary genres and to give more play to erudition and criticism they raised what was an entirely new question, namely, who deserved the preference, Corneille or Racine. On this subject they said the finest things in the world, when the little niece who had not yet said a word, took it into her head to ask simply which of two fruits, the orange or the peach, had the more exquisite taste and deserved the greater praise. Her uncle blushed at her naïveté and the guests all dropped their eyes at this lapse from good sense. 'Niece,' said Fintac, 'at your age, one should listen and be silent.' "

which should unite in itself the lusciousness of the grape, the crispness of the nut, and the fragrance of the pine.

And from these considerations one most important practical corollary is to be deduced, with the good help of Mademoiselle Agathe's simile, namely, that the greatness or smallness of a man is, in the most conclusive sense, determined for him at his birth, as strictly as it is determined for a fruit whether it is to be a currant or an apricot. Education, favourable circumstances, resolution, and industry can do much; in a certain sense they do *everything;* that is to say, they determine whether the poor apricot shall fall in the form of a green bead, blighted by the east wind, and be trodden under foot, or whether it shall expand into tender pride, and sweet brightness of golden velvet. But apricot out of currant,—great man out of small,—did never yet art or effort make; and, in a general way, men have their excellence nearly fixed for them when they are born; a little cramped and frost-bitten on one side, a little sun-burnt and fortune-spotted on the other, they reach, between good and evil chances, such size and taste as generally belong to the men of their calibre, and, the small in their serviceable bunches, the great in their golden isolation, have, these no cause for regret, nor those for disdain.

Therefore it is, that every system of teaching is false which holds forth 'great art' as in any wise to be taught to students, or even to be aimed at by them. Great art is precisely that which never was, nor will be taught, it is pre-eminently and finally the expression of the spirits of great men; so that the only wholesome teaching is that which simply endeavours to fix those characters of nobleness in the pupils' mind, of which it seems easily susceptible; and without holding out to him, as a possible or even probable result, that he should ever paint like Titian, or carve like Michael Angelo, enforces upon him the manifest possibility, and assured duty, of endeavouring to draw in a manner at least honest and intelligible; and cultivates in him those general charities of heart, sincerities of thought, and graces of habit which are likely to lead him, throughout life, to prefer openness to affectation, realities to shadows, and beauty to corruption.

1856                                                                     1856

# The Stones of Venice

### From *The Nature of Gothic* [1]

. . . I shall endeavour . . . to give the reader in this chapter an idea, at once broad and definite, of the true nature of *Gothic* architecture, properly so called; not of that of Venice only, but of universal Gothic: for it will be one of the most interesting parts of our subsequent inquiry, to find out how far Venetian architecture reached the universal or perfect type of Gothic, and how far it either fell short of it, or assumed foreign and independent forms.

The principal difficulty in doing this arises from the fact that every building of the Gothic period differs in some important respect from every other; and

1. From Chap. 6 of Vol. II.

many include features which, if they occurred in other buildings, would not be considered Gothic at all; so that all we have to reason upon is merely, if I may be allowed so to express it, a greater or less degree of *Gothicness* in each building we examine. And it is this *Gothicness*,—the character which, according as it is found more or less in a building, makes it more or less Gothic,—of which I want to define the nature; and I feel the same kind of difficulty in doing so which would be encountered by any one who undertook to explain, for instance, the nature of Redness, without any actually red thing to point to, but only orange and purple things. Suppose he had only a piece of heather and a dead oak-leaf to do it with. He might say, the colour which is mixed with the yellow in this oak-leaf, and with the blue in this heather, would be red, if you had it separate; but it would be difficult, nevertheless, to make the abstraction perfectly intelligible: and it is so in a far greater degree to make the abstraction of the Gothic character intelligible, because that character itself is made up of many mingled ideas, and can consist only in their union. That is to say, pointed arches do not constitute Gothic, nor vaulted roofs, nor flying buttresses, nor grotesque sculptures; but all or some of these things, and many other things with them, when they come together so as to have life. . . .

. . . We shall find that Gothic architecture has external forms, and internal elements. Its elements are certain mental tendencies of the builders, legibly expressed in it; as fancifulness, love of variety, love of richness, and such others. Its external forms are pointed arches, vaulted roofs, &c. And unless both the elements and the forms are there, we have no right to call the style Gothic. It is not enough that it has the Form, if it have not also the power and life. It is not enough that it has the Power, if it have not the form. We must therefore inquire into each of these characters successively; and determine first, what is the Mental Expression, and secondly, what the Material Form, of Gothic architecture, properly so called. . . .

I believe, then, that the characteristic or moral elements of Gothic are the following, placed in the order of their importance:

1. Savageness.            4. Grotesqueness.
2. Changefulness.         5. Rigidity.
3. Naturalism.            6. Redundance.

These characters are here expressed as belonging to the building; as belonging to the builder, they would be expressed thus:—1. Savageness, or Rudeness. 2. Love of Change. 3. Love of Nature. 4. Disturbed Imagination. 5. Obstinacy. 6. Generosity. And I repeat, that the withdrawal of any one, or any two, will not at once destroy the Gothic character of a building, but the removal of a majority of them will. I shall proceed to examine them in their order.

1. *Savageness.* I am not sure when the word 'Gothic' was first generically applied to the architecture of the North; [2] but I presume that, whatever the

2. The first use of the word in description of architecture was probably by Giorgio Vasari, a pupil of Michelangelo. Writing in the 16th century, he spoke of the architectural monuments of the Middle Ages as having been built by the Goths, meaning the German barbarians hostile to Rome, and described the buildings as being a clutter of spires and grotesque ornament, lacking all sense of form and beauty. The word "Gothic" came to be applied to all "rude" art. "All that has nothing of the Ancient gust [i.e. the classic taste]," said Dryden in 1695, "is called a barbarous or Gothique manner."

date of its original usage, it was intended to imply reproach, and express the barbaric character of the nations among whom that architecture arose. It never implied that they were literally of Gothic lineage, far less that their architecture had been originally invented by the Goths themselves; but it did imply that they and their buildings together exhibited a degree of sternness and rudeness, which, in contradistinction to the character of Southern and Eastern nations, appeared like a perpetual reflection of the contrast between the Goth and the Roman in their first encounter. And when that fallen Roman, in the utmost impotence of his luxury, and insolence of his guilt, became the model for the imitation of civilised Europe, at the close of the so-called Dark ages,[3] the word Gothic became a term of unmitigated contempt, not unmixed with aversion. From that contempt, by the exertion of the antiquaries and architects of this century, Gothic architecture has been sufficiently vindicated; [4] and perhaps some among us, in our admiration of the magnificent science of its structure, and sacredness of its expression, might desire that the term of ancient reproach should be withdrawn, and some other, of more apparent honourableness, adopted in its place. There is no chance, as there is no need, of such a substitution. As far as the epithet was used scornfully, it was used falsely; but there is no reproach in the word, rightly understood; on the contrary, there is a profound truth, which the instinct of mankind almost unconsciously recognises. It is true, greatly and deeply true, that the architecture of the North is rude and wild; but it is not true, that, for this reason, we are to condemn it, or despise. Far otherwise: I believe it is in this very character that it deserves our profoundest reverence. . . .

If, however, the savageness of Gothic architecture, merely as an expression of its origin among Northern nations, may be considered, in some sort, a noble character, it possesses a high nobility still, when considered as an index, not of climate, but of religious principle.

In the 13th and 14th paragraphs of Chapter XXI of the first volume of this work, it was noticed that the systems of architectural ornament, properly so called, might be divided into three:—1. Servile ornament, in which the execution or power of the inferior workman is entirely subjected to the intellect of the higher;—2. Constitutional ornament, in which the executive inferior power is, to a certain point, emancipated and independent, having a will of its own, yet confessing its inferiority and rendering obedience to higher powers;—and 3. Revolutionary ornament, in which no executive inferiority is admitted at all. I must here explain the nature of these divisions at somewhat greater length.

3. The "Dark ages" was once a common way of referring to the medieval period. It has long gone out of use, even for the earliest centuries of the epoch.
4. Gothic architecture began to be admired in the 18th century; the most famous example of the new taste is the house which Horace Walpole built at Strawberry Hill in 1747, which was designed as "a little Gothic castle." In the early 19th century the so-called Gothic Revival gathered momentum; the new Houses of Parliament, begun in 1840, were in the Gothic style, which became, indeed, one of the accepted modes of Victorian architecture —to Ruskin's dismay, because he judged it to be used conventionally, without feeling, and commonly with machine-made elements. Within recent years his judgment has been questioned and Victorian Gothic has many admirers among architects and historians of architecture.

Of Servile ornament, the principal schools are the Greek, Ninevite,[5] and Egyptian; but their servility is of different kinds. The Greek master-workman was far advanced in knowledge and power above the Assyrian or Egyptian. Neither he nor those for whom he worked could endure the appearance of imperfection in anything; and, therefore, what ornament he appointed to be done by those beneath him was composed of mere geometrical forms,—balls, ridges, and perfectly symmetrical foliage,—which could be executed with absolute precision by line and rule, and were as perfect in their way, when completed, as his own figure sculpture. The Assyrian and Egyptian, on the contrary, less cognisant of accurate form in anything, were content to allow their figure sculpture to be executed by inferior workmen, but lowered the method of its treatment to a standard which every workman could reach, and then trained him by discipline so rigid, that there was no chance of his falling beneath the standard appointed. The Greek gave to the lower workman no subject which he could not perfectly execute. The Assyrian gave him subjects which he could only execute imperfectly, but fixed a legal standard for his imperfection. The workman was, in both systems, a slave.[6]

But in the mediæval, or especially Christian, system of ornament, this slavery is done away with altogether; Christianity having recognised, in small things as well as great, the individual value of every soul. But it not only recognises its value; it confesses its imperfection, in only bestowing dignity upon the acknowledgment of unworthiness. That admission of lost power and fallen nature, which the Greek or Ninevite felt to be intensely painful, and, as far as might be, altogether refused, the Christian makes daily and hourly, contemplating the fact of it without fear, as tending, in the end, to God's greater glory. Therefore, to every spirit which Christianity summons to her service, her exhortation is: Do what you can, and confess frankly what you are unable to do; neither let your effort be shortened for fear of failure, nor your confession silenced for fear of shame. And it is, perhaps, the principal admirableness of the Gothic schools of architecture, that they thus receive the results of the labour of inferior minds; and out of fragments full of imperfection, and betraying that imperfection in every touch, indulgently raise up a stately and unaccusable whole.

But the modern English mind has this much in common with that of the Greek, that it intensely desires, in all things, the utmost completion or perfection compatible with their nature. This is a noble character in the abstract, but becomes ignoble when it causes us to forget the relative dignities of that nature itself, and to prefer the perfectness of the lower nature to the imperfection of the higher; not considering that as, judged by such a rule, all the brute animals would be preferable to man, because more perfect in their functions and kind,

---

5. Nineveh was the capital city of the Assyrian empire.
6. "The third kind of ornament, the Renaissance, is that in which the inferior detail becomes principal, the executor of every minor portion being required to exhibit skill and possess knowledge as great as that which is possessed by the master of the design; and in the endeavour to endow him with this skill and knowledge, his own original power is overwhelmed, and the whole building becomes a wearisome exhibition of well-educated imbecility. . . ." (Ruskin)

and yet are always held inferior to him, so also in the works of man, those which·are more perfect in their kind are always inferior to those which are, in their nature, liable to more faults and shortcomings. For the finer the nature, the more flaws it will show through the clearness of it; and it is a law of this universe, that the best things shall be seldomest seen in their best form. The wild grass grows well and strongly, one year with another; but the wheat is, according to the greater nobleness of its nature, liable to the bitterer blight. And therefore, while in all things that we see, or do, we are to desire perfection, and strive for it, we are nevertheless not to set the meaner thing, in its narrow accomplishment, above the nobler thing, in its mighty progress; not to esteem smooth minuteness above shattered majesty; not to prefer mean victory to honourable defeat; not to lower the level of our aim, that we may, the more surely enjoy the complacency of success. . . . Now, in the make and nature of every man, however rude or simple, whom we employ in manual labour, there are some powers for better things: some tardy imagination, torpid capacity of emotion, tottering steps of thought, there are, even at the worst; and in most cases it is all our own fault that they *are* tardy or torpid. But they cannot be strengthened, unless we are content to take them in their feebleness, and unless we prize and honour them in their imperfection above the best and most perfect manual skill. And this is what we have to do with all our labourers; to look for the *thoughtful* part of them, and get that out of them, whatever we lose for it, whatever faults and errors we are obliged to take with it. For the best that is in them cannot manifest itself, but in company with much error. Understand this clearly: You can teach a man to draw a straight line, and to cut one; to strike a curved line, and to carve it; and to copy and carve any number of given lines or forms, with admirable speed and perfect precision; and you find his work perfect of its kind: but if you ask him to think about any of those forms, to consider if he cannot find any better in his own head, he stops; his execution becomes hesitating; he thinks, and ten to one he thinks wrong; ten to one he makes a mistake in the first touch he gives to his work as a thinking being. But you have made a man of him for all that. He was only a machine before, an animated tool.

And observe, you are put to stern choice in this matter. You must either make a tool of the creature, or a man of him. You cannot make both. Men were not intended to work with the accuracy of tools, to be precise and perfect in all their actions. If you will have that precision out of them, and make their fingers measure degrees like cog-wheels, and their arms strike curves like compasses, you must unhumanise them. All the energy of their spirits must be given to make cogs and compasses of themselves. All their attention and strength must go to the accomplishment of the mean act. The eye of the soul must be bent upon the finger-point, and the soul's force must fill all the invisible nerves that guide it, ten hours a day, that it may not err from its steely precision, and so soul and sight be worn away, and the whole human being be lost at last—a heap of sawdust, so far as its intellectual work in this world is concerned; saved only by its Heart, which cannot go into the form of cogs and compasses, but expands, after the ten hours are over, into fireside humanity. On the other hand, if you will make a man of the working creature, you cannot make a tool. Let him but begin to imagine, to think, to try to do anything worth doing; and the engine-turned precision is lost at once. Out come all his roughness, all his dulness, all his incapability; shame upon shame, failure upon failure, pause after pause: but out comes the whole majesty of him also; and we know the height of it only, when we see the clouds settling upon him. And, whether the clouds be bright or dark, there will be transfiguration behind and within them.

And now, reader, look round this English room of yours, about which you have been proud so often, because the work of it was so good and strong, and the ornaments of it so finished. Examine again all those accurate mouldings, and perfect polishings, and unerring adjustments of the seasoned wood and tempered steel. Many a time you have exulted over them, and thought how great England was, because her slightest work was done so thoroughly. Alas! if read rightly, these perfectnesses are signs of a slavery in our England a thousand times more bitter and more degrading than that of the scourged African, or helot [7] Greek. Men may be beaten, chained, tormented, yoked like cattle, slaughtered like summer flies, and yet remain in one sense, and the best sense, free. But to smother their souls within them, to blight and hew into rotting pollards [8] the suckling branches of their human intelligence, to make the flesh and skin which, after the worm's work on it, is to see God,[9] into leathern thongs to yoke machinery with,—this it is to be slave-masters indeed; and there might be more freedom in England, though her feudal lords' lightest words were worth men's lives, and though the blood of the vexed husbandman dropped in the furrows of her fields, than there is while the animation of her multitudes is sent like fuel to feed the factory smoke, and the strength of them is given daily to be wasted into the fineness of a web, or racked into the exactness of a line.

And, on the other hand, go forth again to gaze upon the old cathedral front, where you have smiled so often at the fantastic ignorance of the old sculptors: examine once more those ugly goblins, and formless monsters, and stern statues, anatomiless and rigid; but do not mock at them, for they are signs of the life and liberty of every workman who struck the stone; a freedom of thought, and rank in scale of being, such as no laws, no charters, no charities can secure; but which it must be the first aim of all Europe at this day to regain for her children.

Let me not be thought to speak wildly or extravagantly. It is verily this degradation of the operative into a machine, which, more than any other evil of the times, is leading the mass of the nations everywhere into vain, incoherent, destructive struggling for a freedom of which they cannot explain the nature to themselves. Their universal outcry against wealth, and against nobility, is not forced from them either by the pressure of famine, or the sting of mortified pride. These do much, and have done much in all ages; but the foundations of society were never yet shaken as they are at this day. It is not that men are ill fed, but that they have no pleasure in the work by which they make their bread, and therefore look to wealth as the only means of pleasure. It is

7. A serf in ancient Sparta.
8. A tree whose top branches have been cut back to the trunk so that it will produce a thick growth of new shoots. The practice of pollarding, common in France, is usually spoken of with dislike in England. It is not clear why these pollards should rot.
9. Ruskin's rhetoric has got out of hand here—it can scarcely be "flesh and skin" that will "see God," not even after the grave worms have finished with them.

not that men are pained by the scorn of the upper classes, but they cannot endure their own; for they feel that the kind of labour to which they are condemned is verily a degrading one, and makes them less than men. . . .

We have much studied and much perfected, of late, the great civilised invention of the division of labour; only we give it a false name. It is not, truly speaking, the labour that is divided; but the men:—Divided into mere segments of men—broken into small fragments and crumbs of life; so that all the little piece of intelligence that is left in a man is not enough to make a pin, or a nail, but exhausts itself in making the point of a pin, or the head of a nail. Now it is a good and desirable thing, truly, to make many pins in a day; but if we could only see with what crystal sand their points were polished,—sand of human soul, much to be magnified before it can be discerned for what it is, —we should think there might be some loss in it also. And the great cry that rises from all our manufacturing cities, louder than their furnace blast, is all in very deed for this,—that we manufacture everything there except men; we blanch cotton, and strengthen steel, and refine sugar, and shape pottery; but to brighten, to strengthen, to refine, or to form a single living spirit, never enters into our estimate of advantages. And all the evil to which that cry is urging our myriads can be met only in one way: not by teaching nor preaching, for to teach them is but to show them their misery, and to preach to them, if we do nothing more than preach, is to mock at it. It can be met only by a right understanding, on the part of all classes, of what kinds of labour are good for men, raising them, and making them happy; by a determined sacrifice of such convenience, or beauty, or cheapness as is to be got only by the degradation of the workman; and by equally determined demand for the products and results of healthy and ennobling labour.

And how, it will be asked, are these products to be recognised, and this demand to be regulated? Easily: by the observance of three broad and simple rules:

1. Never encourage the manufacture of any article not absolutely necessary, in the production of which *Invention* has no share.

2. Never demand an exact finish for its own sake, but only for some practical or noble end.

3. Never encourage imitation or copying of any kind, except for the sake of preserving record of great works.

The second of these principles is the only one which directly rises out of the consideration of our immediate subject; but I shall briefly explain the meaning and extent of the first also, reserving the enforcement of the third for another place.

1. Never encourage the manufacture of anything not necessary, in the production of which invention has no share.

For instance. Glass beads are utterly unnecessary, and there is no design or thought employed in their manufacture. They are formed by first drawing out the glass into rods; these rods are chopped up into fragments of the size of beads by the human hand, and the fragments are then rounded in the furnace. The men who chop up the rods sit at their work all day, their hands vibrating with a perpetual and exquisitely timed palsy, and the beads dropping beneath their vibration like hail. Neither they, nor the men who draw out the rods or fuse the fragments, have the smallest occasion for the use of any single human faculty; and every young lady, therefore, who buys glass beads is engaged in the slave-trade, and in a much more cruel one than that which we have so long been endeavouring to put down.

But glass cups and vessels may become the subjects of exquisite invention; and if in buying these we pay for the invention, that is to say for the beautiful form, or colour, or engraving, and not for mere finish of execution, we are doing good to humanity. . . .

. . . Our modern glass is exquisitely clear in its substance, true in its form, accurate in its cutting. We are proud of this. We ought to be ashamed of it. The old Venice glass was muddy, inaccurate in all its forms, and clumsily cut, if at all. And the old Venetian was justly proud of it. For there is this difference between the English and Venetian workman, that the former thinks only of accurately matching his patterns, and getting his curves perfectly true and his edges perfectly sharp, and becomes a mere machine for rounding curves and sharpening edges, while the old Venetian cared not a whit whether his edges were sharp or not, but he invented a new design for every glass that he made, and never moulded a handle or a lip without a new fancy in it. And therefore, though some Venetian glass is ugly and clumsy enough, when made by clumsy and uninventive workmen, other Venetian glass is so lovely in its forms that no price is too great for it; and we never see the same form in it twice. Now you cannot have the finish and the varied form too. If the workman is thinking about his edges, he cannot be thinking of his design; if of his design, he cannot think of his edges. Choose whether you will pay for the lovely form or the perfect finish, and choose at the same moment whether you will make the worker a man or a grindstone.

Nay, but the reader interrupts me,—'If the workman can design beautifully, I would not have him kept at the furnace. Let him be taken away and made a gentleman, and have a studio, and design his glass there, and I will have it blown and cut for him by common workmen, and so I will have my design and my finish too.' . . .

. . . How wide the separation is between original and second-hand execution, I shall endeavour to show elsewhere; it is not so much to our purpose here as to mark the other and more fatal error of despising manual labour when governed by intellect; for it is no less fatal an error to despise it when thus regulated by intellect, than to value it for its own sake. We are always in these days endeavouring to separate the two; we want one man to be always thinking, and another to be always working, and we call one a gentleman, and the other an operative; whereas the workman ought often to be thinking, and the thinker often to be working, and both should be gentlemen, in the best sense. As it is, we make both ungentle, the one envying, the other despising, his brother; and the mass of society is made up of morbid thinkers, and miserable workers. Now it is only by labour that thought can be made healthy, and only by thought that labour can be made happy; and the two cannot be separated with impunity. It would be well if all of us were good handicraftsmen in some kind, and the dishonour of manual labour done away with altogether; so that though there should still be a trenchant distinction of race between nobles and commoners, there should not, among the latter, be a trenchant distinction of employment, as between idle and working men, or between men of liberal and illiberal professions. All professions should be liberal, and there should be less pride felt in peculiarity of employment, and more in excellence of achievement. . . .

. . . Hitherto I have used the words imperfect and perfect merely to distinguish between work grossly unskilful, and work executed with average precision and science; and I have been pleading that any degree of unskillfulness should be admitted, so only that the labourer's mind had room for expression. But, accurately speaking, no good work whatever can be perfect, and *the demand for perfection is always a sign of a misunderstanding of the ends of art.*

. . . Imperfection is in some sort essential to all that we know of life. It is the sign of life in a mortal body, that is to say, of a state of progress and change. Nothing that lives is, or can be, rigidly perfect; part of it is decaying, part nascent. The foxglove blossom,—a third part bud, a third part past, a third part in full bloom,—is a type of the life of this world. And in all things that live there are certain irregularities and deficiencies which are not only signs of life, but sources of beauty. No human face is exactly the same in its lines on each side, no leaf perfect in its lobes, no branch in its symmetry. All admit irregularity as they imply change; and to banish imperfection is to destroy expression, to check exertion, to paralyse vitality. All things are literally better, lovelier, and more beloved for the imperfections which have been divinely appointed, that the law of human life may be Effort, and the law of human judgment, Mercy.

Accept this then for a universal law, that neither architecture nor any other noble work of man can be good unless it be imperfect; and let us be prepared for the otherwise strange fact, which we shall discern clearly as we approach the period of the Renaissance, that the first cause of the fall of the arts of Europe was a relentless requirement of perfection, incapable alike either of being silenced by veneration for greatness, or softened into forgiveness of simplicity.

Thus far then of the Rudeness or Savageness, which is the first mental element of Gothic architecture. It is an element in many other healthy architectures also, as in Byzantine and Romanesque; but true Gothic cannot exist without it.

The second mental element above named was CHANGEFULNESS, or Variety.

I have already enforced the allowing independent operation to the inferior workman, simply as a duty *to him,* and as ennobling the architecture by rendering it more Christian. We have now to consider what reward we obtain for the performance of this duty, namely, the perpetual variety of every feature of the building.

Wherever the workman is utterly enslaved, the parts of the building must of course be absolutely like each other; for the perfection of his execution can only be reached by exercising him in doing one thing, and giving him nothing else to do. . . .

How much the beholder gains from the liberty of the labourer may perhaps be questioned in England, where one of the strongest instincts in nearly every mind is that Love of Order which makes us desire that our house windows should pair like our carriage horses, and allows us to yield our faith unhesitatingly to architectural theories which fix a form for everything, and forbid variation from it. I would not impeach love of order: it is one of the most useful elements of the English mind; it helps us in our commerce and in all purely practical matters; and it is in many cases one of the foundation stones of morality. Only do not let us suppose that love of order is love of art. It is true that order, in its highest sense, is one of the necessities of art, just as time is a necessity of music; but love of order has no more to do with our right enjoyment of architecture or painting, than love of punctuality with the appreciation of an opera. . . .

Let us then understand at once, that change or variety is as much a necessity to the human heart and brain in buildings as in books; that there is no merit, though there is some occasional use, in monotony; and that we must no more expect to derive either pleasure or profit from an architecture whose ornaments are of one pattern, and whose pillars are of one proportion, than we should out of a universe in which the clouds were all of one shape, and the trees all of one size.

And this we confess in deeds, though not in words. All the pleasure which the people of the nineteenth century take in art, is in pictures, sculpture, minor objects of virtù,[10] or mediæval architecture, which we enjoy under the term picturesque: no pleasure is taken anywhere in modern buildings, and we find all men of true feeling delighting to escape out of modern cities into natural scenery: hence, as I shall hereafter show, that peculiar love of landscape which is characteristic of the age. . . .

I must now refer for a moment, before we quit the consideration of this, the second mental element of Gothic, to the opening of the third chapter of the 'Seven Lamps of Architecture,' in which the distinction was drawn between man gathering and man governing; between his acceptance of the sources of delight from nature, and his development of authoritative or imaginative power in their arrangement: for the two mental elements, not only of Gothic, but of all good architecture, which we have just been examining, belong to it, and are admirable in it, chiefly as it is, more than any other subject of art, the work of man, and the expression of the average power of man. A picture or poem is often little more than a feeble utterance of man's admiration of something out of himself; but architecture approaches more to a creation of his own, born of his necessities, and expressive of his nature. It is also, in some sort, the work of the whole race, while the picture or statue are the work of one only, in most cases more highly gifted than his fellows. And therefore we may expect that the first two elements of good architecture should be expressive of some great truths commonly belonging to the whole race, and necessary to be understood or felt by them in all their work that they do under the sun. And observe what they are: the confession of Imperfection, and the confession of Desire of Change. The building of the bird and the bee need not express anything like this. It is perfect and unchanging. But just because we are something better than birds or bees, or building must confess that we have not reached the perfection we can imagine, and cannot rest in the condition we have attained. If we pretend to have reached either perfection or satisfaction, we have de-

10. Objects of beauty or interest such as a collector would wish to possess.

graded ourselves and our work. God's work only may express that; but ours may never have that sentence written upon it,—'And behold, it was very good.' And, observe again, it is not merely as it renders the edifice a book of various knowledge, or a mine of precious thought, that variety is essential to its nobleness. The vital principle is not the love of *Knowledge*, but the love of *Change*. It is that strange *disquietude* of the Gothic spirit that is its greatness; that restlessness of the dreaming mind, that wanders hither and thither among the niches, and flickers feverishly around the pinnacles, and frets and fades in labyrinthine knots and shadows along wall and roof, and yet is not satisfied, nor shall be satisfied. The Greek could stay in his triglyph furrow, and be at peace; but the work of the Gothic heart is fretwork still, and it can neither rest in, nor from, its labour, but must pass on, sleeplessly, until its love of change shall be pacified for ever in the change that must come alike on them that wake and them that sleep.

The third constituent element of the Gothic mind was stated to be NATURALISM; that is to say, the love of natural objects for their own sake, and the effort to represent them frankly, unconstrained by artistical laws. . . .

We are to remember, in the first place, that the arrangement of colours and lines is an art analogous to the composition of music, and entirely independent of the representation of facts. Good colouring does not necessarily convey the image of anything but itself. It consists in certain proportions and arrangements of rays of light, but not in likenesses to anything. A few touches of certain greys and purples laid by a master's hand on white paper, will be good colouring; as more touches are added beside them, we may find out that they were intended to represent a dove's neck, and we may praise, as the drawing advances, the perfect imitation of the dove's neck. But the good colouring does not consist in that imitation, but in the abstract qualities and relations of the grey and purple.

In like manner, as soon as a great sculptor begins to shape his work out of the block, we shall see that its lines are nobly arranged, and of noble character. We may not have the slightest idea for what the forms are intended, whether they are of man or beast, of vegetation or drapery. Their likeness to anything does not affect their nobleness. They are magnificent forms, and that is all we need care to know of them, in order to say whether the workman is a good or bad sculptor.

Now the noblest art is an exact unison of the abstract value, with the imitative power, of forms, and colours. It is the noblest composition, used to express the noblest facts. But the human mind cannot in general unite the two perfections: it either pursues the fact to the neglect of the composition, or pursues the composition to the neglect of the fact.

And it is intended by the Deity that it *should* do this; the best art is not always wanted. Facts are often wanted without art, as in a geological diagram; and art often without facts, as in a Turkey carpet. And most men have been made capable of giving either one or the other, but not both; only one or two, the very highest, can give both.

Observe then. Men are universally divided, as respects their artistical qualifications, into three great classes; a right, a left, and a centre. On the right side are the men of facts, on the left the men of design,[11] in the centre the men of both.

The three classes of course pass into each other by imperceptible gradations. The men of facts are hardly ever altogether without powers of design; the men of design are always in some measure cognisant of facts; and as each class possesses more or less of the powers of the opposite one, it approaches to the character of the central class. Few men, even in that central rank, are so exactly throned on the summit of the crest that they cannot be perceived to incline in the least one way or the other, embracing both horizons with their glance. Now each of these classes has, as I above said, a healthy function in the world, and correlative diseases or unhealthy functions; and, when the work of either of them is seen in its morbid condition, we are apt to find fault with the class of workmen, instead of finding fault only with the particular abuse which has perverted their action. . . .

. . . The Gothic builders were of that central class which unites fact with design; but . . . the part of the work which was more especially their own was the truthfulness. Their power of artistical invention or arrangement was not greater than that of Romanesque and Byzantine workmen: by those workmen they were taught the principles, and from them received their models, of design; but to the ornamental feeling and rich fancy of the Byzantine the Gothic builder added a love of *fact* which is never found in the South. Both Greek and Roman used conventional foliage in their ornament, passing into something that was not foliage at all, knotting itself into strange cup-like buds or clusters, and growing out of lifeless rods instead of stems; the Gothic sculptor received these types, at first, as things that ought to be, just as we have a second time received them; but he could not rest in them. He saw there was no veracity in them, no knowledge, no vitality. Do what he would, he could not help liking the true leaves better; and cautiously, a little at a time, he put more of nature into his work, until at last it was all true, retaining, nevertheless, every valuable character of the original well-disciplined and designed arrangement.

There is, however, one direction in which the Naturalism of the Gothic workmen is peculiarly manifested; and this direction is even more characteristic of the school than the Naturalism itself; I mean their peculiar fondness for the forms of Vegetation. In rendering the various circumstances of daily life, Egyptian and Ninevite sculpture is as frank and as diffuse as the Gothic. From the highest pomps of state or triumphs of battle, to the most trivial domestic arts and amusements, all is taken advantage of to fill the field of granite with the perpetual interest of a crowded drama; and the early Lombardic and Romanesque sculpture is equally copious in its description of the familiar circumstances of war and the chase. But in all the scenes portrayed by the workmen of these nations, vegetation occurs only as an explanatory accessary; the reed is introduced to mark the course of the river, or the tree to mark the covert of the wild beast, or the ambush of the enemy, but there is no especial interest

11. "Design is used in this place as expressive of the power to arrange lines and colours nobly. By facts I mean facts perceived by the eye and the mind, not facts accumulated by knowledge. . . ." (Ruskin)

in the forms of the vegetation strong enough to induce them to make it a subject of separate and accurate study. Again, among the nations who followed the arts of design exclusively, the forms of foliage introduced were meagre and general, and their real intricacy and life were neither admired nor expressed. But to the Gothic workman the living foliage became a subject of intense affection, and he struggled to render all its characters with as much accuracy as was compatible with the laws of his design and the nature of his material, not unfrequently tempted in his enthusiasm to transgress the one and disguise the other.

. . . In that careful distinction of species, and richness of delicate and undisturbed organisation, which characterise the Gothic design, there is the history of rural and thoughtful life, influenced by habitual tenderness, and devoted to subtle inquiry; and every discriminating and delicate touch of the chisel, as it rounds the petal or guides the branch, is a prophecy of the development of the entire body of the natural sciences, beginning with that of medicine, of the recovery of literature, and the establishment of the most necessary principles of domestic wisdom and national peace.

I have before alluded to the strange and vain supposition, that the original conception of Gothic architecture had been derived from vegetation,—from the symmetry of avenues, and the interlacing of branches. It is a supposition which never could have existed for a moment in the mind of any person acquainted with early Gothic; but, however idle as a theory, it is most valuable as a testimony to the character of the perfected style. It is precisely because the reverse of this theory is the fact, because the Gothic did not arise out of, but developed itself into, a resemblance to vegetation, that this resemblance is so instructive as an indication of the temper of the builders. It was no chance suggestion of the form of an arch from the bending of a bough, but a gradual and continual discovery of a beauty in natural forms which could be more and more perfectly transferred into those of stone, that influenced at once the heart of the people, and the form of the edifice. The Gothic architecture arose in massy and mountainous strength, axe-hewn, and iron-bound, block heaved upon block by the monk's enthusiasm and the soldier's force; and cramped and stanchioned into such weight of grisly wall, as might bury the anchoret in darkness, and beat back the utmost storm of battle, suffering but by the same narrow crosslet the passing of the sunbeam, or of the arrow. Gradually, as that monkish enthusiasm became more thoughtful, and as the sound of war became more and more intermittent beyond the gates of the convent or the keep, the stony pillar grew slender and the vaulted roof grew light, till they had wreathed themselves into the semblance of the summer woods at their fairest, and of the dead field-flowers, long trodden down in blood, sweet monumental statues were set to bloom for ever, beneath the porch of the temple, or the canopy of the tomb.

The fourth essential element of the Gothic mind was above stated to be the sense of the GROTESQUE; but I shall defer the endeavour to define this most curious and subtle character until we have occasion to examine one of the divisions of the Renaissance schools, which was morbidly influenced by it (Vol. III, Chap. III). It is the less necessary to insist upon it here, because every reader familiar with Gothic architecture must understand what I mean, and will, I believe, have no hesitation in admitting that the tendency to delight in fantastic and ludicrous, as well as in sublime, images, is a universal instinct of the Gothic imagination.

The fifth element above named was RIGIDITY; and this character I must endeavour carefully to define, for neither the word I have used, nor any other that I can think of, will express it accurately. For I mean, not merely stable, but *active* rigidity; the peculiar energy which gives tension to movement, and stiffness to resistance, which makes the fiercest lightning forked rather than curved, and the stoutest oak-branch angular rather than bending, and is as much seen in the quivering of the lance as in the glittering of the icicle.

I have before had occasion (Vol. I, Chapter XIII, § vii) to note some manifestations of this energy or fixedness; but it must be still more attentively considered here, as it shows itself throughout the whole structure and decoration of Gothic work. Egyptian and Greek buildings stand, for the most part, by their own weight and mass, one stone passively incumbent on another: but in the Gothic vaults and traceries there is a stiffness analogous to that of the bones of a limb, or fibres of a tree; an elastic tension and communication of force from part to part, and also a studious expression of this throughout every visible line of the building. And, in like manner, the Greek and Egyptian ornament is either mere surface engraving, as if the face of the wall had been stamped with a seal, or its lines are flowing, lithe, and luxuriant; in either case, there is no expression of energy in the framework of the ornament itself. But the Gothic ornament stands out in prickly independence, and frosty fortitude, jutting into crockets, and freezing into pinnacles; here starting up into a monster, there germinating into a blossom; anon knitting itself into a branch, alternately thorny, bossy, and bristly, or writhed into every form of nervous entanglement; but, even when most graceful, never for an instant languid, always quickset; erring, if at all, ever on the side of brusquerie.

The feelings or habits in the workman which give rise to this character in the work, are more complicated and various than those indicated by any other sculptural expression hitherto named. There is, first, the habit of hard and rapid working; the industry of the tribes of the North, quickened by the coldness of the climate, and giving an expression of sharp energy to all they do (as above noted, Vol. I, Chap. XIII, § vii), as opposed to the languor of the Southern tribes, however much of fire there may be in the heart of that languor, for lava itself may flow languidly. There is also the habit of finding enjoyment in the signs of cold, which is never found, I believe, in the inhabitants of countries south of the Alps. Cold is to them an unredeemed evil, to be suffered, and forgotten as soon as may be; but the long winter of the North forces the Goth (I mean the Englishman, Frenchman, Dane, or German), if he would lead a happy life at all, to find sources of happiness in foul weather as well as fair, and to rejoice in the leafless as well as in the shady forest. And this we do with all our hearts; finding perhaps nearly as much contentment by the Christmas fire as in the summer sunshine, and gaining health and strength on the ice-fields of winter, as well as among the meadows of spring. So that there is nothing adverse or painful to our feelings in the cramped and stiffened structure of vegetation checked by cold. . . .

There are many subtle sympathies and affections which join to confirm the Gothic mind in this peculiar choice of subject; and when we add to the influence of these, the necessities consequent upon the employment of a rougher material, compelling the workman to seek for vigour of effect, rather than refinement of texture or accuracy of form, we have direct and manifest causes for much of the difference between the Northern and Southern cast of conception: but there are indirect causes holding a far more important place in the Gothic heart, though less immediate in their influence on design. Strength of will, independence of character, resoluteness of purpose, impatience of undue control, and that general tendency to set the individual reason against authority, and the individual deed against destiny, which, in the Northern tribes, has opposed itself throughout all ages to the languid submission, in the Southern, of thought to tradition, and purpose to fatality, are all more or less traceable in the rigid lines, vigorous and various masses, and daringly projecting and independent structure of the Northern Gothic ornament: while the opposite feelings are in like manner legible in the graceful and softly guided waves and wreathed bands, in which Southern decoration is constantly disposed; in its tendency to lose its independence, and fuse itself into the surface of the masses upon which it is traced; and in the expression seen so often, in the arrangement of those masses themselves, of an abandonment of their strength to an inevitable necessity, or a listless repose.

There is virtue in the measure, and error in the excess, of both these characters of mind, and in both of the styles which they have created; the best architecture, and the best temper, are those which unite them both; and this fifth impulse of the Gothic heart is therefore that which needs most caution in its indulgence. It is more definitely Gothic than any other, but the best Gothic building is not that which is *most* Gothic: it can hardly be too frank in its confession of rudeness, hardly too rich in its changefulness, hardly too faithful in its naturalism; but it may go too far in its rigidity, and, like the great Puritan spirit in its extreme, lose itself either in frivolity of division, or perversity of purpose. It actually did so in its later times; but it is gladdening to remember that in its utmost nobleness, the very temper which has been thought most adverse to it, the Protestant spirit of self-dependence and inquiry, was expressed in its every line. Faith and aspiration there were, in every Christian ecclesiastical building, from the first century to the fifteenth; but the moral habits to which England in this age owes the kind of greatness that she has,—the habits of philosophical investigation, of accurate thought, of domestic seclusion and independence, of stern self-reliance, and sincere upright searching into religious truth,—were only traceable in the features which were the distinctive creation of the Gothic schools, in the veined foliage, and thorny fretwork, and shadowy niche, and buttressed pier, and fearless height of subtle pinnacle and crested tower, sent like an 'unperplexed question up to Heaven.' [12]

Last, because the least essential, of the constituent elements of this noble school, was placed that of REDUNDANCE,—the uncalculating bestowal of the wealth of its labour. There is, indeed, much Gothic, and that of the best period, in which this element is hardly traceable, and which depends for its

12. "See the beautiful description of Florence in Elizabeth Browning's *Casa Guidi Windows,* which is not only a noble poem, but the only book I have seen which, favouring the Liberal cause in Italy, gives a just account of the incapacities of the modern Italian." (Ruskin)

effect almost exclusively on loveliness of simple design and grace of uninvolved proportion: still, in the most characteristic buildings, a certain portion of their effect depends upon accumulation of ornament; and many of those which have most influence on the minds of men, have attained it by means of this attribute alone. And although, by careful study of the school, it is possible to arrive at a condition of taste which shall be better contented by a few perfect lines than by a whole façade covered with fretwork, the building which only satisfies such a taste is not to be considered the best. For the very first requirement of Gothic architecture being, as we saw above, that it shall both admit the aid, and appeal to the admiration, of the rudest as well as the most refined minds, the richness of the work is, paradoxical as the statement may appear, a part of its humility. No architecture is so haughty as that which is simple; which refuses to address the eye, except in a few clear and forceful lines; which implies, in offering so little to our regards, that all it has offered is perfect; and disdains, either by the complexity of the attractiveness of its features, to embarrass our investigation, or betray us into delight. That humility, which is the very life of the Gothic school, is shown not only in the imperfection, but in the accumulation, of ornament. The inferior rank of the workman is often shown as much in the richness, as the roughness, of his work; and if the co-operation of every hand, and the sympathy of every heart, are to be received, we must be content to allow the redundance which disguises the failure of the feeble, and wins the regard of the inattentive. There are, however, far nobler interests mingling, in the Gothic heart, with the rude love of decorative accumulation: a magnificent enthusiasm, which feels as if it never could do enough to reach the fulness of its ideal; an unselfishness of sacrifice, which would rather cast fruitless labour before the altar than stand idle in the market; [13] and, finally, a profound sympathy with the fulness and wealth of the material universe, rising out of that Naturalism whose operation we have already endeavoured to define. . . .

We have now, I believe, obtained a view approaching to completeness of the various moral or imaginative elements which composed the inner spirit of Gothic architecture. . . .

1852                                                                                        1853


# From Unto This Last [1]

## The Roots of Honour

Among the delusions which at different periods have possessed themselves of the minds of large masses of the human race, perhaps the most curious— certainly the least creditable—is the modern *soi-disant* [2] science of political

---

13. Matthew 20:3.

1. The title derives from Jesus' parable of the vineyard, in which the workers who had been hired earliest, and had therefore worked most, protest because they are paid no more than those who had been hired latest and worked least. To them the master of the vineyard said: "Take that thine is, and go thy way: I will give unto this last, even as unto thee." Matthew 20:4.

2. Self-styled, so-called.

economy, based on the idea that an advantageous code of social action may be determined irrespectively of the influence of social affection.

Of course, as in the instances of alchemy, astrology, witchcraft, and other such popular creeds, political economy has a plausible idea at the root of it. 'The social affections,' says the economist, 'are accidental and disturbing elements in human nature; but avarice and the desire of progress are constant elements. Let us eliminate the inconstants, and, considering the human being merely as a covetous machine, examine by what laws of labour, purchase, and sale, the greatest accumulative result in wealth is attainable. Those laws once determined, it will be for each individual afterwards to introduce as much of the disturbing affectionate element as he chooses, and to determine for himself the result on the new conditions supposed.'

This would be a perfectly logical and successful method of analysis, if the accidentals afterwards to be introduced were of the same nature as the powers first examined. Supposing a body in motion to be influenced by constant and inconstant forces, it is usually the simplest way of examining its course to trace it first under the persistent conditions, and afterwards introduce the causes of variation. But the disturbing elements in the social problem are not of the same nature as the constant ones; they alter the essence of the creature under examination the moment they are added; they operate, not mathematically, but chemically. introducing conditions which render all our previous knowledge unavailable. We made learned experiments upon pure nitrogen, and have convinced ourselves that it is a very manageable gas: but behold! the thing which we have practically to deal with is its chloride; and this, the moment we touch it on our established principles, sends us and our apparatus through the ceiling.

Observe, I neither impugn nor doubt the conclusions of the science, if its terms are accepted. I am simply uninterested in them, as I should be in those of a science of gymnastics which assumed that men had no skeletons. It might be shown, on that supposition, that it would be advantageous to roll the students up into pellets, flatten them into cakes, or stretch them into cables; and that when these results were effected, the re-insertion of the skeleton would be attended with various inconveniences to their constitution. The reasoning might be admirable, the conclusions true, and the science deficient only in applicability. Modern political economy stands on a precisely similar basis. Assuming, not that the human being has no skeleton, but that it is all skeleton, it founds an ossifiant theory of progress on this negation of a soul; and having shown the utmost that may be made of bones, and constructed a number of interesting geometrical figures with death's-heads and humeri, successfully proves the inconvenience of the reappearance of a soul among these corpuscular structures. I do not deny the truth of this theory: I simply deny its applicability to the present phase of the world.

This inapplicability has been curiously manifested during the embarrassment caused by the late strikes of our workmen. Here occurs one of the simplest cases, in a pertinent and positive form, of the first vital problem which political economy has to deal with (the relation between employer and employed); and at a severe crisis, when lives in multitudes, and wealth in masses, are at stake, the political economists are helpless—practically mute; no demonstrable solution of the difficulty can be given by them, such as may convince or calm the opposing parties. Obstinately the masters take one view of the matter; obstinately the operatives another; and no political science can set them at one.

It would be strange if it could, it being not by 'science' of any kind that men were ever intended to be set at one. Disputant after disputant vainly strives to show that the interests of the masters are, or are not, antagonistic to those of the men: none of the pleaders ever seeming to remember that it does not absolutely or always follow that the persons must be antagonistic because their interests are. If there is only a crust of bread in the house, and mother and children are starving, their interests are not the same. If the mother eats it, the children want it; if the children eat it, the mother must go hungry to her work. Yet it does not necessarily follow that there will be 'antagonism' between them, that they will fight for the crust, and that the mother, being strongest, will get it, and eat it. Neither, in any other case, whatever the relations of the persons may be, can it be assumed for certain that, because their interests are diverse, they must necessarily regard each other with hostility, and use violence or cunning to obtain the advantage.

Even if this were so, and it were as just as it is convenient to consider men as actuated by no other moral influences than those which affect rats or swine, the logical conditions of the question are still indeterminable. It can never be shown generally either that the interests of master and labourer are alike, or that they are opposed; for, according to circumstances, they may be either. It is, indeed, always the interest of both that the work should be rightly done, and a just price obtained for it; but, in the division of profits, the gain of the one may or may not be the loss of the other. It is not the master's interest to pay wages so low as to leave the men sickly and depressed, nor the workman's interest to be paid high wages if the smallness of the master's profit hinders him from enlarging his business, or conducting it in a safe and liberal way. A stoker ought not to desire high pay if the company is too poor to keep the engine-wheels in repair.

And the varieties of circumstance which influence these reciprocal interests are so endless, that all endeavour to deduce rules of action from balance of expediency is in vain. And it is meant to be in vain. For no human actions ever were intended by the Maker of men to be guided by balances of expediency, but by balances of justice. He has therefore rendered all endeavours to determine expediency futile for evermore. No man ever knew, or can know, what will be the ultimate result to himself, or to others, of any given line of conduct. But every man may know, and most of us do know, what is a just and unjust act. And all of us may know also, that the consequences of justice will be ultimately the best possible, both to others and ourselves, though we can neither say what is best, nor how it is likely to come to pass.

I have said balances of justice, meaning, in the term justice, to include affection,—such affection as one man owes to another. All right relations between master and operative,[3] and all their best interests, ultimately depend on these.

We shall find the best and simplest illustration of the relations of master and operative in the position of domestic servants.[4]

3. An industrial worker.
4. It should be realized that virtually all of Ruskin's middle-class readers, even those of

We will suppose that the master of a household desires only to get as much work out of his servants as he can, at the rate of wages he gives. He never allows them to be idle; feeds them as poorly and lodges them as ill as they will endure, and in all things pushes his requirements to the exact point beyond which he cannot go without forcing the servant to leave him. In doing this, there is no violation on his part of what is commonly called 'justice.' He agrees with the domestic for his whole time and service, and takes them;—the limits of hardship in treatment being fixed by the practice of other masters in his neighbourhood; that is to say, by the current rate of wages for domestic labour. If the servant can get a better place, he is free to take one, and the master can only tell what is the real market value of his labour, by requiring as much as he will give.

This is the politico-economical view of the case, according to the doctors of that science; who assert that by this procedure the greatest average of work will be obtained from the servant, and therefore, the greatest benefit to the community, and through the community, by reversion, to the servant himself.

That, however, is not so. It would be so if the servant were an engine of which the motive power was steam, magnetism, gravitation, or any other agent of calculable force. But he being, on the contrary, an engine whose motive power is a Soul, the force of this very peculiar agent, as an unknown quantity, enters into all the political economist's equations, without his knowledge, and falsifies every one of their results. The largest quality of work will not be done by this curious engine for pay, or under pressure, or by help of any kind of fuel which may be supplied by the chaldron. It will be done only when the motive force, that is to say, the will or spirit of the creature, is brought to its greatest strength by its own proper fuel; namely, by the affections.

It may indeed happen, and does happen often, that if the master is a man of sense and energy, a large quantity of material work may be done under mechanical pressure, enforced by strong will and guided by wise method; also it may happen, and does happen often, that if the master is indolent and weak (however good-natured), a very small quantity of work, and that bad, may be produced by the servant's undirected strength, and contemptuous gratitude. But the universal law of the matter is that, assuming any given quantity of energy and sense in master and servant, the greatest material result obtainable by them will be, not through antagonism to each other, but through affection for each other; and that if the master, instead of endeavouring to get as much work as possible from the servant, seeks rather to render his appointed and necessary work beneficial to him, and to forward his interests in all just and wholesome ways, the real amount of work ultimately done, or good rendered, by the person so cared for, will indeed be the greatest possible.

Observe, I say, 'of good rendered,' for a servant's work is not necessarily or always the best thing he can give his master. But good of all kinds, whether in material service, in protective watchfulness of his master's interest and credit, or in joyful readiness to seize unexpected and irregular occasions of help.

---

quite modest means, would have had at least one domestic servant; a fairly affluent family might have three or four. The servants invariably lived in the house, generally in cramped quarters. The relations of servants to their employers—known always as "master" and "mistress"—was a matter of lively interest for humorists.

Nor is this one whit less generally true because indulgence will be frequently abused, and kindness met with ingratitude. For the servant who, gently treated, is ungrateful, treated ungently, will be revengeful; and the man who is dishonest to a liberal master will be injurious to an unjust one.

In any case, and with any person, this unselfish treatment will produce the most effective return. Observe, I am here considering the affections wholly as a motive power; not at all as things in themselves desirable or noble, or in any other way abstractedly good. I look at them simply as an anomalous force, rendering every one of the ordinary political economist's calculations nugatory; while, even if he desired to introduce this new element into his estimates, he has no power of dealing with it; for the affections only become a true motive power when they ignore every other motive and condition of political economy. Treat the servant kindly, with the idea of turning his gratitude to account, and you will get, as you deserve, no gratitude, nor any value for your kindness; but treat him kindly without any economical purpose, and all economical purposes will be answered; in this, as in all other matters, whosoever will save his life shall lose it, whoso loses it shall find it.[5]

The next clearest and simplest example of relation between master and operative is that which exists between the commander of a regiment and his men.

Supposing the officer only desires to apply the rules of discipline so as, with least trouble to himself, to make the regiment most effective, he will not be able, by any rules, or administration of rules, on this selfish principle, to develop the full strength of his subordinates. If a man of sense and firmness, he may, as in the former instance, produce a better result than would be obtained by the irregular kindness of a weak officer; but let the sense and firmness be the same in both cases, and assuredly the officer who has the most direct personal relations with his men, the most care for their interests, and the most value for their lives, will develop their effective strength, through their affection for

5. "The difference between the two modes of treatment, and between their effective material results, may be seen very accurately by a comparison of the relations of Esther and Charlie in *Bleak House*, with those of Miss Brass and the Marchioness in *Master Humphrey's Clock*.

"The essential value and truth of Dickens's writings have been unwisely lost sight of by many thoughtful persons, merely because he presents his truth with some colour of caricature. Unwisely, because Dickens's caricature, though often gross, is never mistaken. Allowing for his manner of telling them, the things he tells us are always true. I wish that he could think it right to limit his brilliant exaggeration to works written only for public amusement: and when he takes up a subject of high national importance, such as that which he handled in *Hard Times*, that he would use severer and more accurate analysis. The usefulness of that work (to my mind, in several respects, the greatest he has written) is with many persons seriously diminished because Mr. Bounderby is a dramatic monster, instead of a characteristic example of a worldly master; and Stephen Blackpool a dramatic perfection, instead of a characteristic example of an honest workman. But let us not lose the use of Dickens's wit and insight, because he chooses to speak in a circle of stage fire. He is entirely right in his main drift and purpose in every book he has written; and all of them, but especially *Hard Times*, should be studied with close and earnest care by persons interested in social questions. They will find much that is partial, and, because partial, apparently unjust; but if they examine all the evidence on the other side, which Dickens seems to overlook, it will appear, after all their trouble, that his view was the finally right one, grossly and sharply told." (Ruskin)

his own person, and trust in his character, to a degree wholly unattainable by other means. The law applies still more stringently as the numbers concerned are larger; a charge may often be successful, though the men dislike their officers; a battle has rarely been won, unless they loved their general.

Passing from these simple examples to the more complicated relations existing between a manufacturer and his workmen, we are met first by certain curious difficulties, resulting, apparently, from a harder and colder state of moral elements. It is easy to imagine an enthusiastic affection existing among soldiers for the colonel. Not so easy to imagine an enthusiastic affection among cotton-spinners for the proprietor of the mill. A body of men associated for purposes of robbery (as a Highland clan in ancient times) shall be animated by perfect affection, and every member of it be ready to lay down his life for the life of his chief.[6] But a band of men associated for purposes of legal production and accumulation is usually animated, it appears, by no such emotions, and none of them are in anywise willing to give his life for the life of his chief. Not only are we met by this apparent anomaly, in moral matters, but by others connected with it, in administration of system. For a servant or a soldier is engaged at a definite rate of wages, for a definite period; but a workman at a rate of wages variable according to the demand for labour, and with the risk of being at any time thrown out of his situation by chances of trade. Now, as, under these contingencies, no action of the affections can take place, but only an explosive action of *dis*affections, two points offer themselves for consideration in the matter.

The first—How far the rate of wages may be so regulated as not to vary with the demand for labour.

The second—How far it is possible that bodies of workmen may be engaged and maintained at such fixed rate of wages (whatever the state of trade may be), without enlarging or diminishing their number, so as to give them permanent interest in the establishment with which they are connected, like that of the domestic servants in an old family, or an *esprit de corps*, like that of the soldiers in a crack regiment.

The first question is, I say, how far it may be possible to fix the rate of wages irrespectively of the demand for labour.

Perhaps one of the most curious facts in the history of human error is the denial by the common political economist of the possibility of thus regulating wages; while, for all the important, and much of the unimportant, labour on the earth, wages are already so regulated.

We do not sell our prime-ministership by Dutch auction;[7] nor, on the decease of a bishop, whatever may be the general advantages of simony[8] do we (yet) offer his diocese to the clergyman who will take the episcopacy at the lowest contract. We (with exquisite sagacity of political economy!) do indeed

6. Ruskin could count on his audience's familiarity with an affecting instance of such loyalty in Sir Walter Scott's widely read first novel, *Waverley* (1814).
7. An auction in which the property is offered at a high price, then at gradually lowered prices until someone buys it.
8. The buying or selling of ecclesiastical offices.

sell commissions, but not openly, generalships:[9] sic, we do not inquire for a physician who takes less than a guinea; litigious,[10] we never think of reducing six-and-eightpence to four-and-sixpence; caught in a shower, we do not canvass the cabmen, to find one who values his driving at less than sixpence a mile.

It is true that in all these cases there is, and in every conceivable case there must be, ultimate reference to the presumed difficulty of the work, or number of candidates for the office. If it were thought that the labour necessary to make a good physician would be gone through by a sufficient number of students with the prospect of only half-guinea fees, public consent would soon withdraw the unnecessary half-guinea. In this ultimate sense, the price of labour is indeed always regulated by the demand for it; but so far as the practical and immediate administration of the matter is regarded, the best labour always has been, and is, as all labour ought to be, paid by an invariable standard.

'What!' the reader, perhaps, answers amazedly: 'pay good and bad workmen alike?'

Certainly. The difference between one prelate's sermons and his successor's,— or between one physician's opinion and another's,—is far greater, as respects the qualities of mind involved, and far more important in result to you personally, than the difference between good and bad laying of bricks (though that is greater than most people suppose). Yet you pay with equal fee, contentedly, the good and bad workmen upon your soul, and the good and bad workmen upon your body; much more may you pay, contentedly, with equal fees, the good and bad workmen upon your house.

'Nay, but I choose my physician and (?) my clergyman, thus indicating my sense of the quality of their work.' By all means, also, choose your brick-layer; that is the proper reward of the good workman, to be 'chosen.' The natural and right system respecting all labour is, that it should be paid at a fixed rate, but the good workman employed, and the bad workman unemployed. The false, unnatural, and destructive system is when the bad workman is allowed to offer his work at half-price, and either take the place of the good, or force him by his competition to work for an inadequate sum.

This equality of wages, then, being the first object towards which we have to discover the directest available road; the second is, as above stated, that of maintaining constant numbers of workmen in employment, whatever may be the accidental demand for the article they produce.

I believe the sudden and extensive inequalities of demand which necessarily arise in the mercantile operations of an active nation, constitute the only essential difficulty which has to be overcome in a just organization of labour. The subject opens into too many branches to admit of being investigated in a paper of this kind; but the following general facts bearing on it may be noted.

The wages which enable any workman to live are necessarily higher, if his work is liable to intermission, than if it is assured and continuous; and however severe the struggle for work may become, the general law will always hold,

9. It was not until 1871 that the old (and entirely legal) practice of buying and selling army commissions was abolished; however, generalships, as Ruskin indicates, could be secured only by promotion.
10. When we have it in mind to go to law against someone.

that men must get more daily pay if, on the average, they can only calculate on work three days a week, than they would require if they were sure of work six days a week. Supposing that a man cannot live on less than a shilling a day, his seven shillings he must get, either for three days' violent work, or six days' deliberate work. The tendency of all modern mercantile operations is to throw both wages and trade into the form of a lottery, and to make the workman's pay depend on intermittent exertion, and the principal's profit on dexterously used chance.

In what partial degree, I repeat, this may be necessary, in consequence of the activities of modern trade, I do not here investigate; contenting myself with the fact, that in its fatallest aspects it is assuredly unnecessary, and results merely from love of gambling on the part of the masters, and from ignorance and sensuality in the men. The masters cannot bear to let any opportunity of gain escape them, and frantically rush at every gap and breach in the walls of Fortune, raging to be rich, and affronting, with impatient covetousness, every risk of ruin; while the men prefer three days of violent labour, and three days of drunkenness, to six days of moderate work and wise rest. There is no way in which a principal, who really desires to help his workmen, may do it more effectually than by checking these disorderly habits both in himself and them; keeping his own business operations on a scale which will enable him to pursue them securely, not yielding to temptations of precarious gain; and, at the same time, leading his workmen into regular habits of labour and life, either by inducing them rather to take low wages in the form of a fixed salary, than high wages, subject to the chance of their being thrown out of work; or, if this be impossible, by discouraging the system of violent exertion for nominally high day wages, and leading the men to take lower pay for more regular labour.

In effecting any radical changes of this kind, doubtless there would be great inconvenience and loss incurred by all the originators of movement. That which can be done with perfect convenience and without loss, is not always the thing that most needs to be done, or which we are most imperatively required to do.

I have already alluded to the difference hitherto existing between regiments of men associated for purposes of violence, and for purposes of manufacture; in that the former appear capable of self-sacrifice—the latter, not; which singular fact is the real reason of the general lowness of estimate in which the profession of commerce is held, as compared with that of arms. Philosophically, it does not, at first sight, appear reasonable (many writers have endeavoured to prove it unreasonable) that a peaceable and rational person, whose trade is buying and selling, should be held in less honour than an unpeaceable and often irrational person, whose trade is slaying. Nevertheless, the consent of mankind has always, in spite of the philosophers, given precedence to the soldier.

And this is right.

For the soldier's trade, verily and essentially, is not slaying, but being slain. This, without well knowing its own meaning, the world honours it for. A bravo's trade is slaying; but the world has never respected bravos more than merchants: the reason it honours the soldier is, because he holds his life at the service of the State. Reckless he may be—fond of pleasure or of adventure—

all kinds of bye-motives and mean impulses may have determined the choice of his profession, and may affect (to all appearance exclusively) his daily conduct in it; but our estimate of him is based on this ultimate fact—of which we are well assured—that, put him in a fortress breach, with all the pleasures of the world behind him, and only death and his duty in front of him, he will keep his face to the front; and he knows that this choice may be put to him at any moment, and has beforehand taken his part—virtually takes such part continually—does, in reality, die daily.

Not less is the respect we pay to the lawyer and physician, founded ultimately on their self-sacrifice. Whatever the learning or acuteness of a great lawyer, our chief respect for him depends on our belief that, set in a judge's seat, he will strive to judge justly, come of it what may. Could we suppose that he would take bribes, and use his acuteness and legal knowledge to give plausibility to iniquitous decisions, no degree of intellect would win for him our respect. Nothing will win it, short of our tacit conviction, that in all important acts of his life justice is first with him; his own interest, second.

In the case of a physician, the ground of the honour we render him is clearer still. Whatever his science, we should shrink from him in horror if we found him regard his patients merely as subjects to experiment upon; much more, if we found that, receiving bribes from persons interested in their deaths, he was using his best skill to give poison in the mask of medicine.

Finally, the principle holds with utmost clearness as it respects clergymen. No goodness of disposition will excuse want of science in a physician or of shrewdness in an advocate; but a clergyman, even though his power of intellect be small, is respected on the presumed ground of his unselfishness and serviceableness.

Now there can be no question but that the tact, foresight, decision, and other mental powers, required for the successful management of a large mercantile concern, if not such as could be compared with those of a great lawyer, general, or divine, would at least match the general conditions of mind required in the subordinate officers of a ship, or of a regiment, or in the curate of a country parish. If, therefore, all the efficient members of the so-called liberal professions are still, somehow, in public estimate of honour, preferred before the head of a commercial firm, the reason must lie deeper than in the measurement of their several powers of mind.

And the essential reason for such preference will be found to lie in the fact that the merchant is presumed to act always selfishly. His work may be very necessary to the community; but the motive of it is understood to be wholly personal. The merchant's first object in all his dealings must be (the public believe) to get as much for himself, and leave as little to his neighbour (or customer) as possible. Enforcing this upon him, by political statute, as the necessary principle of his action; recommending it to him on all occasions, and themselves reciprocally adopting it; proclaiming vociferously, for law of the universe, that a buyer's function is to cheapen, and a seller's to cheat,—the public, nevertheless, involuntarily condemn the man of commerce for his compliance wtih their own statement, and stamp him for ever as belonging to an inferior grade of human personality.

This they will find, eventually, they must give up doing. They must not

cease to condemn selfishness; but they will have to discover a kind of commerce which is not exclusively selfish. Or, rather, they will have to discover
that there never was, or can be, any other kind of commerce; that this which
they have called commerce was not commerce at all, but cozening; and that
a true merchant differs as much from a merchant according to laws of modern
political economy, as the hero of the *Excursion* from Autolycus.[11] They will
find that commerce is an occupation which gentlemen will every day see more
need to engage in, rather than in the businesses of talking to men, or slaying
them: that, in true commerce, as in true preaching, or true fighting, it is
necessary to admit the idea of occasional voluntary loss;—that sixpences have
to be lost, as well as lives, under a sense of duty; that the market may have
its martyrdoms as well as the pulpit; and trade its heroisms, as well as war.

May have—in the final issue, must have—and only has not had yet, because
men of heroic temper have always been misguided in their youth into other
fields, not recognizing what is in our days, perhaps, the most important of all
fields; so that, while many a zealous person loses his life in trying to teach
the form of a gospel, very few will lose a hundred pounds in showing the
practice of one.

The fact is, that people never have had clearly explained to them the true
functions of a merchant with respect to other people. I should like the reader
to be very clear about this.

Five great intellectual professions, relating to daily necessities of life, have
hitherto existed—three exist necessarily, in every civilized nation:

The Soldier's profession is to *defend* it.

The Pastor's, to *teach* it.

The Physician's, to *keep it in health*.

The Lawyer's, to *enforce justice* in it.

The Merchant's, to *provide* for it.

And the duty of all these men is, on due occasion, to *die* for it.

'On due occasion,' namely:—

The Soldier, rather than leave his post in battle.

The Physician, rather than leave his post in plague.

The Pastor, rather than teach Falsehood.

The Lawyer, rather than countenance Injustice.

The Merchant—What is *his* 'due occasion' of death?

It is the main question for the merchant, as for all of us. For, truly, the
man who does not know when to die, does not know how to live.

Observe, the merchant's function (or manufacturer's, for in the broad sense
in which it is here used the word must be understood to include both) is to
provide for the nation. It is no more his function to get profit for himself out
of that provision than it is a clergyman's function to get his stipend. The stipend
is a due and necessary adjunct, but not the object, of his life, if he be a true
clergyman, any more than his fee (or *honorarium*) is the object of life to a
true physician. Neither is his fee the object of life to a true merchant. All three,
if true men, have a work to be done irrespective of fee—to be done even at

11. The former, in Wordsworth's poem, is a peddler of the highest probity and benevolence; the latter, in Shakespeare's *The Winter's Tale*, is a peddler who prefers pilfering
to selling.

any cost, or for quite the contrary of fee; the pastor's function being to teach, the physician's to heal, and the merchant's, as I have said, to provide. That is to say, he has to understand to their very root the qualities of the thing he deals in, and the means of obtaining or producing it; and he has to apply all his sagacity and energy to the producing or obtaining it in perfect state, and distributing it at the cheapest possible price where it is most needed.

And because the production or obtaining of any commodity involves necessarily the agency of many lives and hands, the merchant becomes in the course of his business the master and governor of large masses of men in a more direct, though less confessed way, than a military officer or pastor; so that on him falls, in great part, the responsibility for the kind of life they lead: and it becomes his duty, not only to be always considering how to produce what he sells in the purest and cheapest forms, but how to make the various employments involved in the production, or transference of it, most beneficial to the men employed.

And as into these two functions, requiring for their right exercise the highest intelligence, as well as patience, kindness, and tact, the merchant is bound to put all his energy, so for their just discharge he is bound, as soldier or physician is bound, to give up, if need be, his life, in such way as it may be demanded of him. Two main points he has in his providing function to maintain: first, his engagements (faithfulness to engagements being the real root of all possibilities in commerce); and, secondly, the perfectness and purity of the thing provided; so that, rather than fail in any engagement, or consent to any deterioration, adulteration, or unjust and exorbitant price of that which he provides, he is bound to meet fearlessly any form of distress, poverty, or labour, which may, through maintenance of these points, come upon him.

Again: in his office as governor of the men employed by him, the merchant or manufacturer is invested with a distinctly paternal authority and responsibility. In most cases, a youth entering a commercial establishment is withdrawn altogether from home influence; his master must become his father, else he has, for practical and constant help, no father at hand: in all cases the master's authority, together with the general tone and atmosphere of his business, and the character of the men with whom the youth is compelled in the course of it to associate, have more immediate and pressing weight than the home influence, and will usually neutralize it either for good or evil; so that the only means which the master has of doing justice to the men employed by him is to ask himself sternly whether he is dealing with such subordinate as he would with his own son, if compelled by circumstances to take such a position.

Supposing the captain of a frigate saw it right, or were by any chance obliged, to place his own son in the position of a common sailor; as he would then treat his son, he is bound always to treat every one of the men under him. So, also, supposing the master of a manufactory saw it right, or were by any chance obliged, to place his own son in the position of an ordinary workman; as he would then treat his son, he is bound always to treat every one of his men. This is the only effective, true, or practical RULE which can be given on this point of political economy.

And as the captain of a ship is bound to be the last man to leave his ship in case of wreck, and to share his last crust with the sailors in case of famine, so the manufacturer, in any commercial crisis or distress, is bound to take the suffering of it with his men, and even to take more of it for himself than he allows his men to feel; as a father would in a famine, shipwreck, or battle, sacrifice himself for his son.

All which sounds very strange: the only real strangeness in the matter being, nevertheless, that it should so sound. For all this is true, and that not partially nor theoretically, but everlastingly and practically: all other doctrine than this respecting matters political being false in premises, absurd in deduction, and impossible in practice, consistently with any progressive state of national life; all the life which we now possess as a nation showing itself in the resolute denial and scorn, by a few strong minds and faithful hearts, of the economic principles taught to our multitudes, which principles, so far as accepted, lead straight to national destruction. Respecting the modes and forms of destruction to which they lead, and, on the other hand, respecting the farther practical working of true polity, I hope to reason further in a following paper.

1860                                                                                          1860

# MATTHEW ARNOLD
1822–1888

Matthew Arnold's life in literature falls into two parts, the division being marked by the Preface to the *Poems* of 1853 (see below). It cannot quite be said that this striking essay signalizes the end of Arnold's career as a poet; some of the poems he was still to write are among his most memorable. But after 1853 it is as a critic rather than as a poet that Arnold stands before the world.

It may be thought an open question whether, if Arnold had written nothing but poetry, he would be as well established a poet as in fact he is, at least in literary history, if not in the highest esteem of strict criticism. He was never accounted a great poet, yet his poems had in his own day, and for a considerable time thereafter, an appeal which was disproportionate to their aesthetic success. They spoke with a personal immediacy to a small, influential class of persons who were conscious of the peculiar pathos of modern existence, and perhaps they seemed the more immediate because they were less fully achieved as works of art than they might have been. In a later day, when cultural melancholy has come to seem an archaic emotion and when aesthetic judgment has become more exigent, the claims that can be made for Arnold's poetry probably cannot be large, and sometimes—not always—it seems fair to say that Arnold is not essentially a poet at all, not *naturally* a poet, as, say, Keats and Shelley and Tennyson are naturally poets even when they are at their least impressive. Yet his poems are never less than memorable; they command attention and respect—and, often, affection—as the record of what was felt about the modern world by the man who became Matthew Arnold the critic, who, putting aside the pathos of nostalgia and self-pity which make the essence of his poems, addressed himself to the modern world with an energy that still communicates itself.

The Preface to the *Poems* of 1853 is, we might say, a manifesto against nostalgia and self-pity. It is commonly characterized as anti-Romantic, a belated rearguard skirmish in defense of classicism. The description is accurate but academic. Despite appearances to the contrary, Arnold is really as little interested in a theory of literature called classicism as was Aristotle, to whose *Poetics* he resorted for the informing idea of the Preface. Like Aristotle, his interest in what literature should be is controlled by his conception of what a man should be, not only in himself, for the sake of his own well-being as an individual, but also in relation to the polity, in order to function properly as a citizen. Aristotle's theory of tragedy proposes the idea that tragedy, if it is successful, has a salutary, even a therapeutic, effect: it rids the mind of two oppressive and incapacitating emotions, pity and terror, and establishes the condition in which the mind may perceive and decide as it ideally should. It is not pity and terror that Arnold identifies as the impediments to the health and right conduct of the mind but, rather, doubt—the mind's sense of being divided within itself and of engaging in a dialogue with itself that comes to no resolution in decision and action. The Preface undertakes to explain why Arnold, in collecting into one volume the poems of his two earlier volumes, *The Strayed Reveller, and Other Poems* (1849) and *Empedocles on Etna, and Other Poems* (1852), was omitting the long title poem of the second. The poem had as its protagonist the ancient Greek philosopher who, according to legend, ended his life by flinging himself into the crater of the volcano. The greater part of the poem consists of Empedocles' rehearsal of the reasons, both metaphysical and political, why his life has come to seem of no worth to him and best brought to its end. Such a poem, Arnold says, does not give the reader the kind of joy which it is the function of art to give and which tragedy—it is one of the riddles of the human heart that this is so—does pre-eminently give. The poem fails to give joy not because it represents a sad or painful situation but because it represents a situation in which "a continuous state of mental distress is prolonged, unrelieved by incident, hope, or resistance; in which there is everything to be endured, nothing to be done." It can serve only to enervate, immobilize, and depress the spirits of the reader. At a later time Arnold restored *Empedocles on Etna* to the canon of his work, but at this time it was his belief that it should be sacrificed for, we may say, the good of the polity.

Arnold's commitment to a career in criticism was confirmed by his election to the Professorship of Poetry at Oxford in 1857. He was the first layman to occupy the chair and the first to lecture in English rather than in Latin. At the end of the five-year term he was re-elected. This was a considerable honor but it did not bring Arnold into the quiet and presumed detachment of university life. Although the Oxford Professor of Poetry is obliged to give public lectures, he does not instruct or supervise students and is not required to be in residence except intermittently; during his incumbency of the professorship Arnold continued in his duties as an inspector of elementary schools. This post, to which he had been appointed in 1849, was an onerous one, entailing much travel in uncomfortable trains, sojourns in gloomy hotels, interviewing principals and teachers, examining pupils, reading their papers far into the night, dealing with committees, thinking about the purposes of that strange new enterprise, the education of the population at large, and the means by which this was best to be achieved. Among the great writers of the Victorian Age, Arnold's experience of the modern world was unique in its immediacy and abrasiveness. We may suppose that it had a decisive part in shaping the chief preoccupation of his criticism, which was the definition of the quality of mind best able to take action to cope with the difficulties of modern life.

It was to this concern that Arnold addressed himself in his inaugural lecture at

Oxford, *On the Modern Element in Literature* (published in 1869). As in the 1853 Preface, his emphasis falls on the *effect* that literature produces. To be called great, he says, a work of literature must be both "adequate" and "fortifying." The adequacy of a work is its intellectual wholeness and cogency, its power of making the world accessible to comprehension; the fortifying quality of a work is its power of giving to the reader the energy and courage needed to confront the asperities and confusions of the modern world. In his lectures *On Translating Homer* (1861) he identifies the defining traits of Homer's style as being *rapidity, plainness,* and *directness*—of diction and syntax and also of thought—and *nobility,* and it is manifest that in thus characterizing Homer's style he is adumbrating the qualities he wished to see established in English life. This exposition of the "grand style" Homer exemplifies proposes implicitly the possibility that the national character might come to be marked by the "grand style"—Homer serves as a criterion by which Arnold makes his judgment of the class that increasingly determined the quality of the English rational life, the middle class; it was a class he was later to characterize as being "drugged with business," small in its aims, petty in its conception of the world.

In 1859 Arnold began to be involved with popular education at a higher level than formerly; he was charged with the investigation of the schools of France, and later of Germany, Switzerland, and Italy, and he set forth his findings in reports and essays which had considerable influence on the shaping of national policy, although his views of what constitutes a truly democratic system of education went well beyond what the government was prepared to put into effect. In 1865 he published his epoch-making volume *Essays in Criticism.*

No sooner has the epithet been used than it seems a strange one—*Essays in Criticism* does not have the look and feel of an epoch-making book. The essays that make up the volume had all appeared previously in periodicals and several had been lectures given by Arnold at Oxford. Their subjects are not related to each other in any obvious sense, and at least some of them must seem of only marginal inherent importance. And the tone of the essays, though certainly serious, is not momentous; as compared with the tone of Carlyle's or Ruskin's, it is curiously modest. It manifestly does not seek to dominate the reader but, rather, to put him at ease so that he may the more readily perceive for himself the ideational object that is being presented to him. The title of the volume is in accord with its time; it now seems commonplace enough but Arnold chose it with care: these are *essays,* "in the old sense of the word *Essay,*" that is to say, they are attempts, specimens; they are essays *in* criticism, by which Arnold meant to put emphasis on the idea of criticism as a procedure rather than as what the etymology of the word proposes, the passing of judgment. It is the process which makes right judgment possible—criticism is the effort "to see the object as in itself it really is."

If we seek the explanation of the pre-eminence of Arnold's criticism and why he is often described as virtually the founding father of modern criticism in the English-speaking world, one decisive factor is the tone of his critical writing, its representation of criticism as a procedure by which accurate perception is to be gained and in which the reader is invited to take part, on, as it were, equal terms with the critic. Coleridge may be thought a greater critic than Arnold in the sense of being more intellectually ambitious and more complex, comprehensive, and systematic, and the perceptivity of two of Arnold's contemporaries, Carlyle and Ruskin, especially the latter, is of the highest order, yet it is Arnold who naturalized criticism as a modern intellectual mode and institutionalized it by defining its function and thus, by implication, its ideal operation as well.

Another reason for Arnold's special eminence in criticism is the extent to which his conception of the critical enterprise goes beyond specifically literary criticism. On a first reading of The Function of Criticism at the Present Time the question might well arise whether Arnold has any concern at all with literary criticism, for everything he says about criticism has reference to the part it might play in the practical world. But it is exactly through his conception of the possible range of the critical enterprise that Arnold brought literary criticism to its present high status in the intellectual life.

If Arnold's conception of criticism puts its first emphasis upon the procedure through which accuracy of perception is achieved, it by no means suggests that judgment is not of its essence. In another defining statement Arnold says that criticism is "a disinterested endeavour to learn and propagate the best that is known and thought in the world."

The word "disinterested" requires comment. One of the misfortunes that has overtaken the English language in our time is that this word is commonly interchanged with "uninterested." Traditionally the words have very different meanings. To be "uninterested" means that one's attention is not engaged by the matter at hand, that one is indifferent, unconcerned. To be "disinterested" means that one has nothing personally to gain from the matter at hand, that one deals with it in an impartial, unbiased, and unselfish way. Careful writers still distinguish between the two words. If they say of a judge that he is uninterested in the case before him, they mean to impute blame; if they say that he has ruled in the case in a disinterested way, they intend praise.

At a time when the latent conflict of class interests had become manifest and threatened to grow in intensity, Arnold entertained the hope, perhaps doomed to be a forlorn one, that from the critical spirit, of which disinterestedness is an essential quality, there might derive not only an ideal of disinterestedness in political life but also a principle by which that ideal could be made practicable. The last of his Oxford lectures was to be the first chapter of Culture and Anarchy, the work in which he sought to discover this principle. (When it was given as a lecture in June 1867, it was called Culture and Its Enemies and this was its title as a chapter in the first edition of the book [1869]; in the second edition [1875] it was called Sweetness and Light.)

The "anarchy" which Arnold had in mind was of no extreme kind. In the agitation that preceded the passing of the Reform Bill of 1867, which gave the suffrage to the urban working class, there had indeed been public disorders, and Arnold remarks upon them at length. But he did not envisage anything like the breakdown of all political authority in England; by anarchy he meant the absence of any cohering principle of political life by which not merely social peace but grace of life might be attained. The principle by which anarchy is to be overcome he calls "culture."

The sense in which Arnold uses this word is peculiar to him. He does not use it, as anthropologists and sociologists later came to do, to refer to the totality of a society's institutions, beliefs, arts, and modes of behavior. Nor does he use it in the more restricted sense in which it signifies the general intellectual and artistic activity of a society. Arnold's "culture" is to be understood as an elaboration of his conception of criticism—it is the ideal response to the fact that the world in modern times is moved by ideas to an extent never known before and that the welfare of humanity and of any particular nation depends upon bringing the power of intelligence, of imaginative reason, to bear upon social and political life.

In his exploration of how this is to be done and of what stands in the way of its being done, Arnold identifies two opposing dispositions of the human mind, to which he gives the names "Hebraism" and "Hellenism." Hebraism is the disposition to religious faith and to strictness of conscience, to the single-minded conception of what is true and righteous, and to the determination to make it prevail. Hellenism is the disposition to intelligence, to setting store by ideas, to the flexibility of mind that permits the testing of ideas and the withdrawal from them should they not meet the test. In themselves, Arnold says, the two dispositions are equally necessary to human development. What at any given historical moment make the predominance of one preferable to that of the other are the circumstances which at that time prevail. For the present situation of England, Arnold feels that it is not Hebraism that is needed—of Hebraism there is more than enough: the sincere but narrow religious and moral feeling of the middle class, in direct line of descent from the Puritan revolution of the seventeenth century, is the dominant tone of English life. What is needed is the free play of mind which is characteristic of Hellenism. The activity of imaginative reason, based upon "the best that has been known and thought in the world," and having its own kind of religious and moral intention, that of making "reason and the will of God prevail," is what Arnold means by culture.

It is to the Hellenic openness and flexibility of mind which culture fosters that Arnold looks for the acceptance of the idea of the state, which alone, he believes, can hold out to English political life the hope of coherence and peace. To this idea, Arnold says, the middle class is sure to respond with the antagonism of an old and settled conviction, understandably so, because in its rise to its present power it had to overcome the restrictions put upon both its economic enterprise and its liberty of conscience by the state as it was constituted in former times. But culture envisages a state which of its nature cannot oppress or discriminate against any class; while representing all the classes, the newly enfranchised working class as well as the middle class and the aristocracy, it will be above all classes and thus able to deal with each in a disinterested way. Nothing could be easier, surely, than to object that in a society in which classes are defined by their relative economic advantages the state will not be—cannot be—disinterested in an absolute way. Yet in this century the English state has of course become substantially what Arnold wished it would be. Even when all the still existing class antagonisms and acrimonies have been taken into account, it must be said that England has achieved a far firmer national unity than might ever have been thought possible from an inspection of its class structure.

Arnold's poetry still makes its appeal. His criticism is still central in the tradition, its position there attested to if only by the frequency with which its particular judgments are disputed a century after they were made. His political writings still are pertinent. But the religious writings to which he chiefly gave himself between 1870 and 1877 no longer command attention. The issue to which they address themselves has ceased to be a vital one. These works—they include *St. Paul and Protestantism* (1870), *Literature and Dogma* (1873), and *God and the Bible* (1875)—were written out of Arnold's residual but still positive feeling for religion. When Arnold said of culture that it had for its function the task of making "reason and the will of God prevail," he was not lightly using a pious phrase. He did believe in God, although not in a way that an average religious countryman of his would have understood. The purpose of his writings about religion was to purge religious belief of its traditional supernaturalism and the intellectual constructs that were based upon it, which must eventually distress a modern mind and alienate it from religion itself. In Arnold's view, the essence of religion was simply a faith in the moral order of the universe; about that order no specific predications could be made. Religion was to be defined as "morality touched with emotion"; God was to be no more precisely conceived than as "the power not ourselves that makes for righteousness"; the Bible was to be read as "literature" rather than as "dogma"—literature of the most moving kind, still communicating, in concepts and language not ours but nevertheless to be readily understood and deeply felt if properly read, the truths of the moral life. In their own day Arnold's religious writings were widely popular among educated people who rejected much in traditional religion but who yet were reluctant to abandon all faith; with the disappearance of the situation that brought them into being, their interest is to be found only in the often brilliant imaginative sympathy with which Arnold speaks of the religious modes of the past.

Arnold's mature life was a quiet one and perhaps it is to be called happy, although it was touched by the deep sadness of the death of three of his sons. One of the engaging aspects of his temperament is that, although he felt and spoke of the tragic seriousness of life and the necessity of meeting it with fortitude and dutifulness, he loved gaiety and indeed believed that there was no surer sign of the health both of persons and societies. In 1883 he went on an extended lecture tour of America and made a second visit in 1886; in the same year he resigned his post as Inspector of schools. He died suddenly of heart failure in 1888.

# From First Edition of *Poems*

### Preface

In two small volumes of Poems, published anonymously, one in 1849, the other in 1852,[1] many of the poems which compose the present volume have already appeared. The rest are now published for the first time.

I have, in the present collection, omitted the poem from which the volume published in 1852 took its title.[2] I have done so, not because the subject of it was a Sicilian Greek born between two and three thousand years ago, although many persons would think this a sufficient reason. Neither have I done so because I had, in my own opinion, failed in the delineation which I intended to effect. I intended to delineate the feelings of one of the last of the Greek religious philosophers, one of the family of Orpheus and Musæus,[3] having

---

1. *The Strayed Reveller, and Other Poems* and *Empedocles on Etna, and Other Poems.* On their title pages the only indication of authorship was "By A."
2. Empedocles (*c.*493–*c.*433 B.C.), Sicilian philosopher, scientist, poet, orator, statesman, and miracle worker.
3. Mythic singers, whose music had supernatural power. Of the two, Orpheus is the more clearly defined in legend; the poems attributed to him were the basis of the religious cult of Orphism.

survived his fellows, living on into a time when the habits of Greek thought and feeling had begun fast to change, character to dwindle, the influence of the Sophists [4] to prevail. Into the feelings of a man so situated there entered much that we are accustomed to consider as exclusively modern; how much, the fragments of Empedocles himself which remain to us are sufficient at least to indicate. What those who are familiar only with the great monuments of early Greek genius suppose to be its exclusive characteristics, have disappeared: the calm, the cheerfulness, the disinterested objectivity have disappeared; the dialogue of the mind with itself has commenced; modern problems have presented themselves; we hear already the doubts, we witness the discouragement, of Hamlet and of Faust.

The representation of such a man's feelings must be interesting, if consistently drawn. We all naturally take pleasure, says Aristotle, in any imitation or representation whatever: [5] this is the basis of our love of poetry; and we take pleasure in them, he adds, because all knowledge is naturally agreeable to us; not to the philosopher only, but to mankind at large. Every representation, therefore, which is consistently drawn may be supposed to be interesting, inasmuch as it gratifies this natural interest in knowledge of all kinds. What is *not* interesting, is that which does not add to our knowledge of any kind; that which is vaguely conceived and loosely drawn; a representation which is general, indeterminate, and faint, instead of being particular, precise, and firm.

Any accurate representation may therefore be expected to be interesting; but, if the representation be a poetical one, more than this is demanded. It is demanded, not only that it shall interest, but also that it shall inspirit and rejoice the reader; that it shall convey a charm, and infuse delight. For the Muses, as Hesiod [6] says, were born that they might be 'a forgetfulness of evils, and a truce from cares': and it is not enough that the poet should add to the knowledge of men, it is required of him also that he should add to their happiness. 'All art,' says Schiller, 'is dedicated to Joy, and there is no higher and no more serious problem, than how to make men happy. The right art is that alone, which creates the highest enjoyment.' [7]

A poetical work, therefore, is not yet justified when it has been shown to be an accurate, and therefore interesting representation; it has to be shown also that it is a representation from which men can derive enjoyment. In presence of the most tragic circumstances, represented in a work of art, the feeling of enjoyment, as is well known, may still subsist; the representation of the most utter calamity, of the liveliest anguish, is not sufficient to destroy it; the more tragic the situation, the deeper becomes the enjoyment; and the situation is more tragic in proportion as it becomes more terrible.

What then are the situations, from the representation of which, though accurate, no poetical enjoyment can be derived? They are those in which the

4. Literally "wise men," but the term came to be used pejoratively of professional teachers who instructed in one or another intellectual discipline not for its own sake but as a means of getting on in life.
5. In the *Poetics* I, II, IV, VII, XIV.
6. *Theogony* (Genealogy of the Gods) 52–56. Hesiod lived in the 8th century B.C.
7. Friedrich Schiller (1759–1805) in his preface to *The Bride of Messina* (1803), which discusses the use of the chorus in tragedy.

suffering finds no vent in action; in which a continuous state of mental distress is prolonged, unrelieved by incident, hope, or resistance; in which there is everything to be endured, nothing to be done. In such situations there is inevitably something morbid, in the description of them something monotonous. When they occur in actual life, they are painful, not tragic; the representation of them in poetry is painful also.

To this class of situations, poetically faulty as it appears to me, that of Empedocles, as I have endeavoured to represent him, belongs; and I have therefore excluded the poem from the present collection.

And why, it may be asked, have I entered into this explanation respecting a matter so unimportant as the admission or exclusion of the poem in question? I have done so, because I was anxious to avow that the sole reason for its exclusion was that which has been stated above; and that it has not been excluded in deference to the opinion which many critics of the present day appear to entertain against subjects chosen from distant times and countries: against the choice, in short, of any subjects but modern ones.

'The poet,' it is said,[8] and by an intelligent critic, 'the poet who would really fix the public attention must leave the exhausted past, and draw his subjects from matters of present import, and *therefore* both of interest and novelty.'

Now this view I believe to be completely false. It is worth examining, inasmuch as it is a fair sample of a class of critical dicta everywhere current at the present day, having a philosophical form and air, but no real basis in fact; and which are calculated to vitiate the judgment of readers of poetry, while they exert, so far as they are adopted, a misleading influence on the practice of those who make it.

What are the eternal objects of poetry, among all nations, and at all times? They are actions; human actions;[9] possessing an inherent interest in themselves, and which are to be communicated in an interesting manner by the art of the poet. Vainly will the latter imagine that he has everything in his own power; that he can make an intrinsically inferior action equally delightful with a more excellent one by his treatment of it. He may indeed compel us to admire his skill, but his work will possess, within itself, an incurable defect.

The poet, then, has in the first place to select an excellent action; and what actions are the most excellent? Those, certainly, which most powerfully appeal to the great primary human affections: to those elementary feelings which subsist permanently in the race, and which are independent of time. These feelings are permanent and the same; that which interests them is permanent and the same also. The modernness or antiquity of an action, therefore, has nothing to do with its fitness for poetical representation; this depends upon its inherent qualities. To the elementary part of our nature, to our passions, that which is great and passionate is eternally interesting; and interesting solely in proportion to its greatness and to its passion. A great human action of a thousand years ago is more interesting to it than a smaller human action

8. "In the *Spectator* of April 2, 1853. The words quoted were not used with reference to poems of mine." (Arnold) The emphasis of "therefore" was supplied by Arnold. The "intelligent critic" was R. S. Rintoul, the editor of *The Spectator*.
9. Aristotle says so in *Poetics* VI, IX, X.

of to-day, even though upon the representation of this last the most consummate skill may have been expended, and though it has the advantage of appealing by its modern language, familiar manners, and contemporary allusions, to all our transient feelings and interests. These, however, have no right to demand of a poetical work that it shall satisfy them; their claims are to be directed elsewhere. Poetical works belong to the domain of our permanent passions; let them interest these, and the voice of all subordinate claims upon them is at once silenced.

Achilles, Prometheus, Clytemnestra, Dido,—what modern poem presents personages as interesting, even to us moderns, as these personages of an 'exhausted past'? We have the domestic epic dealing with the details of modern life which pass daily under our eyes; [10] we have poems representing modern personages in contact with the problems of modern life, moral, intellectual, and social; these works have been produced by poets the most distinguished of their nation and time; yet I fearlessly assert that *Hermann and Dorothea, Childe Harold, Jocelyn, The Excursion,*[11] leave the reader cold in comparison with the effect produced upon him by the latter books of the *Iliad,* by the *Oresteia,* or by the episode of Dido. And why is this? Simply because in the three last-named cases the action is greater, the personages nobler, the situations more intense: and this is the true basis of the interest in a poetical work, and this alone.

It may be urged, however, that past actions may be interesting in themselves, but that they are not to be adopted by the modern poet, because it is impossible for him to have them clearly present to his own mind, and he cannot therefore feel them deeply, nor represent them forcibly. But this is not necessarily the case. The externals of a past action, indeed, he cannot know with the precision of a contemporary; but his business is with its essentials. The outward man of Oedipus or of Macbeth, the houses in which they lived, the ceremonies of their courts, he cannot accurately figure to himself; but neither do they essentially concern him. His business is with their inward man; with their feelings and behaviour in certain tragic situations, which engage their passions as men; these have in them nothing local and casual; they are as accessible to the modern poet as to a contemporary.

The date of an action, then, signifies nothing: the action itself, its selection and construction, this is what is all-important. This the Greeks understood far more clearly than we do. The radical difference between their poetical theory and ours consists, as it appears to me, in this: that, with them, the poetical character of the action in itself, and the conduct of it, was the first consideration; with us, attention is fixed mainly on the value of the separate thoughts and images which occur in the treatment of an action. They regarded the whole; we regard the parts. With them, the action predominated over the expression of it; with us, the expression predominates over the action. Not that they failed in expression, or were inattentive to it; on the contrary, they are the highest models of expression, the unapproached masters of the *grand*

10. Arnold may have had in mind *The Bothie of Taber-na-Fuosich* (1848), by his close friend Arthur Hugh Clough, which tells in hexameters, the epic meter, the love story of a young Oxford radical; or Alexander Smith's *A Life Drama* (1853).
11. Long poems by Goethe, Byron, Lamartine, and Wordsworth.

*style.*[12] But their expression is so excellent because it is so admirably kept in its right degree of prominence; because it is so simple and so well subordinated; because it draws its force directly from the pregnancy of the matter which it conveys. For what reason was the Greek tragic poet confined to so limited a range of subjects? Because there are so few actions which unite in themselves, in the highest degree, the conditions of excellence: and it was not thought that on any but an excellent subject could an excellent poem be constructed. A few actions, therefore, eminently adapted for tragedy, maintained almost exclusive possession of the Greek tragic stage. Their significance appeared inexhaustible; they were as permanent problems, perpetually offered to the genius of every fresh poet. This too is the reason of what appears to us moderns a certain baldness of expression in Greek tragedy; of the triviality with which we often reproach the remarks of the chorus, where it takes part in the dialogue: that the action itself, the situation of Orestes, or Merope, or Alc-mæon,[13] was to stand the central point of interest, unforgotten, absorbing, principal; that no accessories were for a moment to distract the spectator's attention from this; that the tone of the parts was to be perpetually kept down, in order not to impair the grandiose effect of the whole. The terrible old mythic story on which the drama was founded stood, before he entered the theatre, traced in its bare outlines upon the spectator's mind; it stood in his memory, as a group of statuary, faintly seen, at the end of a long and dark vista: then came the poet, embodying outlines, developing situations, not a word wasted, not a sentiment capriciously thrown in: stroke upon stroke, the drama proceeded: the light deepened upon the group; more and more it revealed itself to the riveted gaze of the spectator: until at last, when the final words were spoken, it stood before him in broad sunlight, a model of immortal beauty.

This was what a Greek critic demanded; this was what a Greek poet endeavoured to effect. It signified nothing to what time an action belonged. We do not find that the *Persæ*[14] occupied a particularly high rank among the dramas of Æschylus, because it represented a matter of contemporary interest; this was not what a cultivated Athenian required. He required that the permanent elements of his nature should be moved; and dramas of which the action, though taken from a long-distant mythic time, yet was calculated to accomplish this in a higher degree than that of the *Persæ*, stood higher in his estimation accordingly. The Greeks felt, no doubt, with their exquisite sagacity of taste, that an action of present times was too near them, too much mixed up

12. In 1861 Arnold gave his series of lectures *On Translating Homer*, in the course of which he discusses the conception of the "grand style" in art and implies that its cultivation has certain good intellectual and social consequences. The grand style arises, he says, "when a noble nature, poetically gifted, treats with simplicity or with severity a serious subject."

13. Orestes took vengeance on his mother, Clytemnestra, for the murder of his father, Agamemnon; he figures in tragedies by Aeschylus, Sophocles, and Euripides. Merope, the widow of a murdered king, is married by force to the murderer; her story is the subject of plays by Euripides, Voltaire, and others, including Arnold himself, whose *Merope* appeared in 1858. Alcmaeon was the subject of several lost Greek tragedies; like Orestes, he avenged his father by slaying his mother.

14. *The Persians*, produced in 472 B.C., dealt with events of the recent invasion of Greece by the Persians.

with what was accidental and passing, to form a sufficiently grand, detached, and self-subsistent object for a tragic poem. Such objects belonged to the domain of the comic poet, and of the lighter kinds of poetry. For the more serious kinds, for *pragmatic* poetry, to use an excellent expression of Polybius,[15] they were more difficult and severe in the range of subjects which they permitted. Their theory and practice alike, the admirable treatise of Aristotle, and the unrivalled works of their poets, exclaim with a thousand tongues—'All depends upon the subject; choose a fitting action, penetrate yourself with the feeling of its situations; this done, everything else will follow.'

But for all kinds of poetry alike there was one point on which they were rigidly exacting: the adaptability of the subject to the kind of poetry selected, and the careful construction of the poem.

How different a way of thinking from this is ours! We can hardly at the present day understand what Menander [16] meant, when he told a man who enquired as to the progress of his comedy that he had finished it, not having yet written a single line, because he had constructed the action of it in his mind. A modern critic would have assured him that the merit of his piece depended on the brilliant things which arose under his pen as he went along. We have poems which seem to exist merely for the sake of single lines and passages; not for the sake of producing any total impression. We have critics who seem to direct their attention merely to detached expressions, to the language about the action, not to the action itself. I verily think that the majority of them do not in their hearts believe that there is such a thing as a total impression to be derived from a poem at all, or to be demanded from a poet; they think the term a commonplace of metaphysical criticism. They will permit the poet to select any action he pleases, and to suffer that action to go as it will, provided he gratifies them with occasional bursts of fine writing, and with a shower of isolated thoughts and images. That is, they permit him to leave their poetical sense ungratified, provided that he gratifies their rhetorical sense and their curiosity. Of his neglecting to gratify these, there is little danger. He needs rather to be warned against the danger of attempting to gratify these alone; he needs rather to be perpetually reminded to prefer his action to everything else; so to treat this, as to permit its inherent excellences to develop themselves, without interruption from the intrusion of his personal peculiarities; most fortunate, when he most entirely succeeds in effacing himself, and in enabling a noble action to subsist as it did in nature.

But the modern critic not only permits a false practice; he absolutely prescribes false aims.—'A true allegory of the state of one's own mind in a representative history,' the poet is told, 'is perhaps the highest thing that one can attempt in the way of poetry.' [17] And accordingly he attempts it. An allegory of the state of one's own mind, the highest problem of an art which imitates actions! No assuredly, it is not, it never can be so: no great poetical work has ever been produced with such an aim. *Faust* itself, in which something of the

15. Greek historian of Rome (202?–125 B.C.). "Pragmatic" would seem to mean "serious," in the sense of being committed to establishing the relation of cause and effect in human affairs.
16. Greek comic dramatist (342–292 B.C.).
17. Arnold quotes from an article in the *North British Review*, XIX (August 1853), p. 180.

kind is attempted, wonderful passages as it contains, and in spite of the unsurpassed beauty of the scenes which relate to Margaret, *Faust* itself, judged as a whole, and judged strictly as a poetical work, is defective: its illustrious author, the greatest poet of modern times, the greatest critic of all times, would have been the first to acknowledge it; he only defended his work, indeed, by asserting it to be 'something incommensurable.' [18]

The confusion of the present times is great, the multitude of voices counselling different things bewildering, the number of existing works capable of attracting a young writer's attention and of becoming his models, immense. What he wants is a hand to guide him through the confusion, a voice to prescribe to him the aim which he should keep in view, and to explain to him that the value of the literary works which offer themselves to his attention is relative to their power of helping him forward on his road towards this aim. Such a guide the English writer at the present day will nowhere find. Failing this, all that can be looked for, all indeed that can be desired, is, that his attention should be fixed on excellent models; that he may reproduce, at any rate, something of their excellence, by penetrating himself with their works and by catching their spirit, if he cannot be taught to produce what is excellent independently.

Foremost among these models for the English writer stands Shakespeare: a name the greatest perhaps of all poetical names; a name never to be mentioned without reverence. I will venture, however, to express a doubt, whether the influence of his works, excellent and fruitful for the readers of poetry, for the great majority, has been of unmixed advantage to the writers of it. [19] Shakespeare indeed chose excellent subjects; the world could afford no better than Macbeth, or Romeo and Juliet, or Othello; he had no theory respecting the necessity of choosing subjects of present import, or the paramount interest attaching to allegories of the state of one's own mind; like all great poets, he knew well what constituted a poetical action; like them, wherever he found such an action, he took it; like them, too, he found his best in past times. But to these general characteristics of all great poets he added a special one of his own; a gift, namely, of happy, abundant, and ingenious expression, eminent and unrivalled: so eminent as irresistibly to strike the attention first in him, and even to throw into comparative shade his other excellences as a poet. Here has been the mischief. These other excellences were his fundamental excellences *as a poet;* what distinguishes the artist from the mere amateur, says Goethe, is *Architectonicè* in the highest sense; [20] that power of execution, which creates, forms, and constitutes: not the profoundness of single thoughts, not the richness of imagery, not the abundance of illustration. But these attractive accessories of a poetical work being more easily seized than the spirit of the whole,

18. J. Eckermann, *Conversations with Goethe,* January 3, 1830.
19. By this date Shakespeare had become virtually sacrosanct in England, in large part through the expressed adoration of the Romantic writers, and for Arnold to suggest that anything but good could follow from emulating him in any way was an act of some courage—see what he says about Hallam's comment on Shakespeare farther on—and likely to be thought a perversity. Arnold's letters to his friend Clough continually express his sense of the danger of modern English poets' basing themselves on the "multitudinousness" of the Elizabethans, "those d_____d Elizabethan poets."
20. Goethe, *Concerning the So-called Dilettantism* (1799).

and these accessories being possessed by Shakespeare in an unequalled degree, a young writer having recourse to Shakespeare as his model runs great risk of being vanquished and absorbed by them, and, in consequence, of reproducing, according to the measure of his power, these, and these alone. Of this preponderating quality of Shakespeare's genius, accordingly, almost the whole of modern English poetry has, it appears to me, felt the influence. To the exclusive attention on the part of his imitators to this it is in a great degree owing, that of the majority of modern poetical works the details alone are valuable, the composition worthless. In reading them one is perpetually reminded of that terrible sentence on a modern French poet:—*Il dit tout ce qu'il veut, mais malheureusement il n'a rien à dire.*[21]

Let me give an instance of what I mean. I will take it from the works of the very chief among those who seem to have been formed in the school of Shakespeare: of one whose exquisite genius and pathetic death render him for ever interesting. I will take the poem of *Isabella, or the Pot of Basil,* by Keats. I choose this rather than the *Endymion,* because the latter work (which a modern critic has classed with the *Fairy Queen!*),[22] although undoubtedly there blows through it the breath of genius, is yet as a whole so utterly incoherent, as not strictly to merit the name of a poem at all. The poem of *Isabella,* then, is a perfect treasure-house of graceful and felicitous words and images: almost in every stanza there occurs one of those vivid and picturesque turns of expression, by which the object is made to flash upon the eye of the mind, and which thrill the reader with a sudden delight. This one short poem contains, perhaps, a greater number of happy single expressions which one could quote than all the extant tragedies of Sophocles. But the action, the story? The action in itself is an excellent one; but so feebly is it conceived by the poet, so loosely constructed, that the effect produced by it, in and for itself, is absolutely null. Let the reader, after he has finished the poem of Keats, turn to the same story in the *Decameron:* [23] he will then feel how pregnant and interesting the same action has become in the hands of a great artist, who above all things delineates his object; who subordinates expression to that which it is designed to express.

I have said that the imitators of Shakespeare, fixing their attention on his wonderful gift of expression, have directed their imitation to this, neglecting his other excellences. These excellences, the fundamental excellences of poetical art, Shakespeare no doubt possessed them,—possessed many of them in a splendid degree; but it may perhaps be doubted whether even he himself did not sometimes give scope to his faculty of expression to the prejudice of a higher poetical duty. For we must never forget that Shakespeare is the great poet he is from his skill in discerning and firmly conceiving an excellent action, from his power of intensely feeling a situation, of intimately associating himself with a character; not from his gift of expression, which rather even leads him astray, degenerating sometimes into a fondness for curiosity of expression, into an irritability of fancy, which seems to make it impossible for him to say a

---

21. "He says all that he wishes to, but unhappily he has nothing to say." This is thought to have been said of Théophile Gautier (1811–72).
22. In the same issue of the *North British Review* in which Arnold had come on the sentence about "a true allegory of the state of one's own mind."
23. Of Boccaccio, 4th day, 5th tale.

thing plainly, even when the press of the action demands the very directest language, or its level character the very simplest. Mr. Hallam,[24] than whom it is impossible to find a saner and more judicious critic, has had the courage (for at the present day it needs courage) to remark, how extremely and faultily difficult Shakespeare's language often is. It is so: you may find main scenes in some of his greatest tragedies, *King Lear* for instance, where the language is so artificial, so curiously tortured, and so difficult, that every speech has to be read two or three times before its meaning can be comprehended. This over-curiousness of expression is indeed but the excessive employment of a wonderful gift,—of the power of saying a thing in a happier way than any other man; nevertheless, it is carried so far that one understands what M. Guizot [25] meant, when he said that Shakespeare appears in his language to have tried all styles except that of simplicity. He has not the severe and scrupulous self-restraint of the ancients, partly, no doubt, because he had a far less cultivated and exacting audience. He has indeed a far wider range than they had, a far richer fertility of thought; in this respect he rises above them. In his strong conception of his subject, in the genuine way in which he is penetrated with it, he resembles them, and is unlike the moderns. But in the accurate limitation of it, the conscientious rejection of superfluities, the simple and rigorous development of it from the first line of his work to the last, he falls below them, and comes nearer to the moderns. In his chief works, besides what he has of his own, he has the elementary soundness of the ancients; he has their important action and their large and broad manner; but he has not their purity of method. He is therefore a less safe model; for what he has of his own is personal, and inseparable from his own rich nature; it may be imitated and exaggerated, it cannot be learned or applied as an art. He is above all suggestive; more valuable, therefore, to young writers as men than as artists. But clearness of arrangement, rigour of development, simplicity of style,—these may to a certain extent be learned; and these may, I am convinced, be learned best from the ancients, who, although infinitely less suggestive than Shakespeare, are thus, to the artist, more instructive.

What then, it will be asked, are the ancients to be our sole models? the ancients with their comparatively narrow range of experience, and their widely different circumstances? Not, certainly, that which is narrow in the ancients, nor that in which we can no longer sympathise. An action like the action of the *Antigone* of Sophocles, which turns upon the conflict between the heroine's duty to her brother's corpse and that to the laws of her country, is no longer one in which it is possible that we should feel a deep interest.[26] I am speaking too, it will be remembered, not of the best sources of intellectual stimulus for the general reader, but of the best models of instruction for the individual writer. This last may certainly learn of the ancients, better than

---

24. Henry Hallam (1777–1859), historian, father of Arthur Hallam, Tennyson's dear friend; the remark is made in his *Introduction to the Literature of Europe* (1838–39) III.91–92.
25. F. P. G. Guizot (1787–1874), French statesman and historian. He discusses Shakespeare's sonnets in *Shakespeare et son temps* (1852), p. 114.
26. Arnold is surely mistaken about this. The interest of *Antigone* transcends the archaic particularities of situation and proves to be quite compelling to the modern reader.

anywhere else, three things which it is vitally important for him to know:—the all-importance of the choice of a subject; the necessity of accurate construction; and the subordinate character of expression. He will learn from them how unspeakably superior is the effect of the one moral impression left by a great action treated as a whole, to the effect produced by the most striking single thought or by the happiest image. As he penetrates into the spirit of the great classical works, as he becomes gradually aware of their intense significance, their noble simplicity, and their calm pathos, he will be convinced that it is this effect, unity and profoundness of moral impression, at which the ancient poets aimed; that it is this which constitutes the grandeur of their works, and which makes them immortal. He will desire to direct his own efforts towards producing the same effect. Above all, he will deliver himself from the jargon of modern criticism, and escape the danger of producing poetical works conceived in the spirit of the passing time, and which partake of its transitoriness.

The present age makes great claims upon us: we owe it service, it will not be satisfied without our admiration. I know not how it is, but their commerce with the ancients appears to me to produce, in those who constantly practise it, a steadying and composing effect upon their judgment, not of literary works only, but of men and events in general. They are like persons who have had a very weighty and impressive experience: they are more truly than others under the empire of facts, and more independent of the language current among those with whom they live. They wish neither to applaud nor to revile their age; they wish to know what it is, what it can give them, and whether this is what they want. What they want, they know very well; they want to educe and cultivate what is best and noblest in themselves; they know, too, that this is no easy task—χαλεπόν, as Pittacus said, χαλεπὸν ἐσθλὸν ἔμμεναι[27]— and they ask themselves sincerely whether their age and its literature can assist them in the attempt. If they are endeavouring to practise any art, they remember the plain and simple proceedings of the old artists, who attained their grand results by penetrating themselves with some noble and significant action, not by inflating themselves with a belief in the pre-eminent importance and greatness of their own times. They do not talk of their mission, nor of interpreting their age, nor of the coming poet; all this, they know, is the mere delirium of vanity; their business is not to praise their age, but to afford to the men who live in it the highest pleasure which they are capable of feeling. If asked to afford this by means of subjects drawn from the age itself, they ask what special fitness the present age has for supplying them. They are told that it is an era of progress, an age commissioned to carry out the great ideas of industrial development and social amelioration. They reply that with all this they can do nothing; that the elements they need for the exercise of their art are great actions, calculated powerfully and delightfully to affect what is permanent in the human soul; that so far as the present age can supply such actions, they will gladly make use of them; but that an age wanting in moral grandeur can with difficulty supply such, and an age of spiritual discomfort with difficulty be powerfully and delightfully affected by them.

27. "It is hard to achieve excellence." Pittacus (c.650–510 B.C.), a statesman and one of the so-called Seven Sages of Greece. He seems to have been much admired for his "favorite sayings," all of which are crashing platitudes.

A host of voices will indignantly rejoin that the present age is inferior to the past neither in moral grandeur nor in spiritual health. He who possesses the discipline I speak of will content himself with remembering the judgments passed upon the present age, in this respect, by the men of strongest head and widest culture whom it has produced; by Goethe and by Niebuhr.[28] It will be sufficient for him that he knows the opinions held by these two great men respecting the present age and its literature; and that he feels assured in his own mind that their aims and demands upon life were such as he would wish, at any rate, his own to be; and their judgment as to what is impeding and disabling such as he may safely follow. He will not, however, maintain a hostile attitude towards the false pretensions of his age: he will content himself with not being overwhelmed by them. He will esteem himself fortunate if he can succeed in banishing from his mind all feelings of contradiction, and irritation, and impatience; in order to delight himself with the contemplation of some noble action of a heroic time, and to enable others, through his representation of it, to delight in it also.

I am far indeed from making any claim, for myself, that I possess this discipline; or for the following poems, that they breathe its spirit. But I say, that in the sincere endeavour to learn and practise, amid the bewildering confusion of our times, what is sound and true in poetical art, I seemed to myself to find the only sure guidance, the only solid footing, among the ancients. They, at any rate, knew what they wanted in art, and we do not. It is this uncertainty which is disheartening, and not hostile criticism. How often have I felt this when reading words of disparagement or of cavil: that it is the uncertainty as to what is really to be aimed at which makes our difficulty, not the dissatisfaction of the critic, who himself suffers from the same uncertainty! *Non me tua fervida terrent Dicta; . . . Dii me terrent, et Jupiter hostis.*[29]

Two kinds of *dilettanti*,[30] says Goethe, there are in poetry: he who neglects the indispensable mechanical part, and thinks he has done enough if he shows spirituality and feeling; and he who seeks to arrive at poetry merely by mechanism, in which he can acquire an artisan's readiness, and is without soul and matter. And he adds, that the first does most harm to art, and the last to himself. If we must be *dilettanti*: if it is impossible for us, under the circumstances amidst which we live, to think clearly, to feel nobly, and to delineate firmly: if we cannot attain to the mastery of the great artists;—let us, at least, have so much respect for our art as to prefer it to ourselves. Let us not bewilder our successors; let us transmit to them the practice of poetry, with its boundaries and wholesome regulative laws, under which excellent works may again, perhaps, at some future time, be produced, not yet fallen into oblivion through our neglect, not yet condemned and cancelled by the influence of their eternal enemy, caprice.

1853                                                                          1853

28. Barthold Georg Niebuhr (1776–1831), a gifted German historian of Rome, influential in England.
29. Virgil, *Aeneid* XII.894–95. "Your hot words do not frighten me; . . . What frightens me is the gods and the enmity of Jupiter."
30. See note 20 above.

# From The Function of Criticism at the Present Time

Many objections have been made to a proposition which, in some remarks of mine on translating Homer,[1] I ventured to put forth; a proposition about criticism, and its importance at the present day. I said: 'Of the literature of France and Germany, as of the intellect of Europe in general, the main effort, for now many years, has been a critical effort; the endeavour, in all branches of knowledge, theology, philosophy, history, art, science, to see the object as in itself it really is.' I added, that owing to the operation in English literature of certain causes, 'almost the last thing for which one would come to English literature is just that very thing which now Europe most desires,—criticism'; and that the power and value of English literature was thereby impaired. More than one rejoinder declared that the importance I here assigned to criticism was excessive, and asserted the inherent superiority of the creative effort of the human spirit over its critical effort. And the other day, having been led by Mr. Shairp's excellent notice of Wordsworth [2] to turn again to his biography, I found, in the words of this great man, whom I, for one, must always listen to with the profoundest respect,[3] a sentence passed on the critic's business, which seems to justify every possible disparagement of it. Wordsworth says in one of his letters:—

'The writers in these publications' (the Reviews), 'while they prosecute their inglorious employment, can not be supposed to be in a state of mind very favourable for being affected by the finer influences of a thing so pure as genuine poetry.'

And a trustworthy reporter of his conversation quotes a more elaborate judgment to the same effect:—

'Wordsworth holds the critical power very low, infinitely lower than the inventive; and he said to-day that if the quantity of time consumed in writing critiques on the works of others were given to original composition, of whatever kind it might be, it would be much better employed; it would make a man find out sooner his own level, and it would do infinitely less mischief. A false or malicious criticism may do much injury to the minds of others; a stupid invention, either in prose or verse, is quite harmless.'

It is almost too much to expect of poor human nature, that a man capable of producing some effect in one line of literature, should, for the greater good of society, voluntarily doom himself to impotence and obscurity in another. Still less is this to be expected from men addicted to the composition of the 'false or malicious criticism' of which Wordsworth speaks. However, everybody would admit that a false or malicious criticism had better never have been written. Everybody, too, would be willing to admit, as a general proposition, that the critical faculty is lower than the inventive. But is it true that criticism is really, in itself, a baneful and injurious employment; is it true that all time given to

1. The conclusion of Lecture II of *On Translating Homer* (1861).
2. John Campbell Shairp (1819–85), a Scottish academic and man of letters, was a college-mate of Arnold's. His essay on Wordsworth appeared in the *North British Review*, XLI (August 1864).
3. A personal piety and affection played its part in Arnold's feeling for Wordsworth; the Arnold and Wordsworth families were neighbors in the Lake District, where the Arnolds had their summer home, and Wordsworth took an interest in Matthew as a boy and a young man.

writing critiques on the works of others would be much better employed if it were given to original composition, of whatever kind this may be? Is it true that Johnson had better have gone on producing more *Irenes* instead of writing his *Lives of the Poets;* [4] nay, is it certain that Wordsworth himself was better employed in making his Ecclesiastical Sonnets [5] than when he made his celebrated Preface, [6] so full of criticism, and criticism of the works of others? Wordsworth was himself a great critic, and it is to be sincerely regretted that he has not left us more criticism; Goethe was one of the greatest of critics, [7] and we may sincerely congratulate ourselves that he has left us so much criticism. Without wasting time over the exaggeration which Wordsworth's judgment on criticism clearly contains, or over an attempt to trace the causes,—not difficult, I think, to be traced, [8]—which may have led Wordsworth to this exaggeration, a critic may with advantage seize an occasion for trying his own conscience, and for asking himself of what real service at any given moment the practice of criticism either is or may be made to his own mind and spirit, and to the minds and spirits of others.

The critical power is of lower rank than the creative. True; but in assenting to this proposition, one or two things are to be kept in mind. It is undeniable that the exercise of a creative power, that a free creative activity, is the highest function of man; it is proved to be so by man's finding in it his true happiness. But it is undeniable, also, that men may have the sense of exercising this free creative activity in other ways than in producing great works of literature or art; if it were not so, all but a very few men would be shut out from the true happiness of all men. They may have it in well-doing, they may have it in learning, they may have it even in criticising. This is one thing to be kept in mind. Another is, that the exercise of the creative power in the production of great works of literature or art, however high this exercise of it may rank, is not at all epochs and under all conditions possible; and that therefore labour may be vainly spent in attempting it, which might with more fruit be used in preparing for it, in rendering it possible. This creative power works with elements, with materials; what if it has not those materials, those elements, ready for its use? In that case it must surely wait till they are ready. Now, in literature, —I will limit myself to literature, for it is about literature that the question arises,—the elements with which the creative power works are ideas; the best ideas, on every matter which literature touches, current at the time. At any rate we may lay it down as certain that in modern literature no manifestation of the creative power not working with these can be very important or fruitful. And I say *current* at the time, not merely accessible at the time; for creative literary genius does not principally show itself in discovering new ideas, that is rather the business of the philosopher. The grand work of literary genius is a work of synthesis and exposition, not of analysis and discovery; its gift lies in

---

4. Dr. Johnson's tragedy *Irene* (1749) is a dull work; his *Lives of the Poets* (1779–81) a continuing delight.
5. This sonnet sequence on the history of the Church of England (1821–22) is among the least rewarding of Wordsworth's works.
6. To the 1800 edition of *Lyrical Ballads,* expanded in 1802.
7. In the Preface to the *Poems* of 1853, Arnold rates him the very greatest of critics.
8. That is, to resentment of the harsh treatment he received from critics.

the faculty of being happily inspired by a certain intellectual and spiritual atmosphere, by a certain order of ideas, when it finds itself in them; of dealing divinely with these ideas, presenting them in the most effective and attractive combinations,—making beautiful works with them, in short. But it must have the atmosphere, it must find itself amidst the order of ideas, in order to work freely; and these it is not so easy to command. This is why great creative epochs in literature are so rare, this is why there is so much that is unsatisfactory in the productions of many men of real genius; because for the creation of a master-work of literature two powers must concur, the power of the man and the power of the moment, and the man is not enough without the moment; [9] the creative power has, for its happy exercise, appointed elements, and those elements are not in its own control.

Nay, they are more within the control of the critical power. It is the business of the critical power, as I said in the words already quoted, 'in all branches of knowledge, theology, philosophy, history, art, science, to see the object as in itself it really is.' Thus it tends, at last, to make an intellectual situation of which the creative power can profitably avail itself. It tends to establish an order of ideas, if not absolutely true, yet true by comparison with that which it displaces; to make the best ideas prevail. Presently these new ideas reach society, the touch of truth is the touch of life, and there is a stir and growth everywhere; out of this stir and growth come the creative epochs of literature.

Or, to narrow our range, and quit these considerations of the general march of genius and of society,—considerations which are apt to become too abstract and impalpable,—every one can see that a poet, for instance, ought to know life and the world before dealing with them in poetry; and life and the world being in modern times very complex things, the creation of a modern poet, to be worth much, implies a great critical effort behind it; else it must be a comparatively poor, barren, and short-lived affair. This is why Byron's poetry had so little endurance in it,[10] and Goethe's so much; both Byron and Goethe had a great productive power, but Goethe's was nourished by a great critical effort providing the true materials for it, and Byron's was not; Goethe knew life and the world, the poet's necessary subjects, much more comprehensively and thoroughly than Byron. He knew a great deal more of them, and he knew them much more as they really are.

It has long seemed to me that the burst of creative activity in our literature, through the first quarter of this century, had about it in fact something premature; and that from this cause its productions are doomed, most of them, in spite of the sanguine hopes which accompanied and do still accompany them, to prove hardly more lasting than the productions of far less splendid epochs. And this prematureness comes from its having proceeded without having its proper data, without sufficient materials to work with. In other words, the English poetry of the first quarter of this century, with plenty of energy, plenty of creative force, did not know enough. This makes Byron so empty a matter,

---

9. Arnold here shows the influence of Hippolyte Taine (1828–23), whose *Histoire de la littérature anglaise* had appeared in 1863. Taine was concerned to formulate a sort of natural history of culture; in it the idea of "the moment" at which a historical or cultural figure emerges plays an important part.

10. Still and all, it manages to keep going!

Shelley so incoherent, Wordsworth even, profound as he is, yet so wanting in completeness and variety. Wordsworth cared little for books, and disparaged Goethe. I admire Wordsworth, as he is, so much that I cannot wish him different; and it is vain, no doubt, to imagine such a man different from what he is, to suppose that he *could* have been different. But surely the one thing wanting to make Wordsworth an even greater poet than he is,—his thought richer, and his influence of wider application,—was that he should have read more books, among them, no doubt, those of that Goethe whom he disparaged without reading him.

But to speak of books and reading may easily lead to a misunderstanding here. It was not really books and reading that lacked to our poetry at this epoch; Shelley had plenty of reading, Coleridge had immense reading. Pindar[11] and Sophocles—as we all say so glibly, and often with so little discernment of the real import of what we are saying—had not many books; Shakespeare was no deep reader. True; but in the Greece of Pindar and Sophocles, in the England of Shakespeare, the poet lived in a current of ideas in the highest degree animating and nourishing to the creative power; society was, in the fullest measure, permeated by fresh thought, intelligent and alive. And this state of things is the true basis for the creative power's exercise, in this it finds its data, its materials, truly ready for its hand; all the books and reading in the world are only valuable as they are helps to this. Even when this does not actually exist, books and reading may enable a man to construct a kind of semblance of it in his own mind, a world of knowledge and intelligence in which he may live and work. This is by no means an equivalent to the artist for the nationally diffused life and thought of the epochs of Sophocles or Shakespeare; but, besides that it may be a means of preparation for such epochs, it does really constitute, if many share in it, a quickening and sustaining atmosphere of great value. Such an atmosphere the many-sided learning and the long and widely-combined critical effort of Germany formed for Goethe, when he lived and worked. There was no national glow of life and thought there as in the Athens of Pericles or the England of Elizabeth. That was the poet's weakness. But there was a sort of equivalent for it in the complete culture and unfettered thinking of a large body of Germans. That was his strength. In the England of the first quarter of this century there was neither a national glow of life and thought, such as we had in the age of Elizabeth, nor yet a culture and a force of learning and criticism such as were to be found in Germany. Therefore the creative power of poetry wanted, for success in the highest sense, materials and a basis; a thorough interpretation of the world was necessarily denied to it.

At first sight it seems strange that out of the immense stir of the French Revolution and its age should not have come a crop of works of genius equal to that which came out of the stir of the great productive time of Greece, or out of that of the Renascence, with its powerful episode the Reformation. But the truth is that the stir of the French Revolution took a character which essentially distinguished it from such movements as these. These were, in the main, disinterestedly[12] intellectual and spiritual movements; movements in

---

11. Pindar (518–438 B.C.), Greek lyric poet of great genius.
12. The word "disinterested" is of crucial importance in this essay. See the comment on it in the Headnote to Arnold above.

which the human spirit looked for its satisfaction in itself and in the increased play of its own activity. The French Revolution took a political, practical character. The movement which went on in France under the old *régime*, from 1700 to 1789, was far more really akin than that of the Revolution itself to the movement of the Renascence; the France of Voltaire and Rousseau told far more powerfully upon the mind of Europe than the France of the Revolution. Goethe reproached this last expressly with having 'thrown quiet culture back.' Nay, and the true key to how much in our Byron, even in our Wordsworth, is this!—that they had their source in a great movement of feeling, not in a great movement of mind. The French Revolution, however,—that object of so much blind love and so much blind hatred,—found undoubtedly its motive-power in the intelligence of men, and not in their practical sense; this is what distinguishes it from the English Revolution of Charles the First's time. This is what makes it a more spiritual event than our Revolution, an event of much more powerful and world-wide interest, though practically less successful; it appeals to an order of ideas which are universal, certain, permanent. 1789 asked of a thing, Is it rational? 1642 asked of a thing, Is it legal? or, when it went furthest, Is it according to conscience? This is the English fashion, a fashion to be treated, within its own sphere, with the highest respect; for its success, within its own sphere, has been prodigious. But what is law in one place is not law in another; what is law here to-day is not law even here tomorrow; and as for conscience, what is binding on one man's conscience is not binding on another's. The old woman who threw her stool at the head of the surpliced minister in St. Giles's Church at Edinburgh obeyed an impulse to which millions of the human race may be permitted to remain strangers.[13] But the prescriptions of reason are absolute, unchanging, of universal validity; *to count by tens is the easiest way of counting*—that is a proposition of which every one, from here to the Antipodes, feels the force; at least I should say so if we did not live in a country where it is not impossible that any morning we may find a letter in the *Times* declaring that a decimal coinage is an absurdity.[14] That a whole nation should have been penetrated with an enthusiasm for pure reason and with an ardent zeal for making its prescriptions triumph, is a very remarkable thing, when we consider how little of mind, or anything so worthy and quickening as mind, comes into the motives which alone, in general, impel great masses of men. In spite of the extravagant direction given to this enthusiasm, in spite of the crimes and follies in which it lost itself, the French Revolution derives from the force, truth, and universality of the ideas which it took for its law, and from the passion with which it could inspire a multitude for these ideas, a unique and still living power; it is—it will probably long remain—the greatest, the most animating event in history. And as no sincere passion for the things of the mind, even though it turn out in many respects an unfortunate passion, is ever quite thrown away and quite barren of good,

13. When Charles I prescribed a new church service for Scotland in 1637, riots broke out; according to tradition, they began with the incident Arnold refers to.

14. A decimal coinage went into effect in Britain in 1971 after having been discussed for more than a century. In 1863 a bill proposing a decimal system was introduced into Parliament and defeated. One of Trollope's novels, *The Prime Minister* (1875), teases the idea as a harmless eccentricity.

France has reaped from hers one fruit—the natural and legitimate fruit, though not precisely the grand fruit she expected: she is the country in Europe where *the people* is most alive.

But the mania for giving an immediate political and practical application to all these fine ideas of the reason was fatal. Here an Englishman is in his element: on this theme we can all go on for hours. And all we are in the habit of saying on it has undoubtedly a great deal of truth. Ideas cannot be too much prized in and for themselves, cannot be too much lived with; but to transport them abruptly into the world of politics and practice, violently to revolutionise this world to their bidding,—that is quite another thing. There is the world of ideas and there is the world of practice; the French are often for suppressing the one and the English the other; but neither is to be suppressed. A member of the House of Commons said to me the other day: 'That a thing is an anomaly, I consider to be no objection to it whatever.' I venture to think he was wrong; that a thing is an anomaly *is* an objection to it, but absolutely and in the sphere of ideas: it is not necessarily, under such and such circumstances, or at such and such a moment, an objection to it in the sphere of politics and practice. Joubert [15] has said beautifully: 'C'est la force et le droit qui règlent toutes choses dans le monde; la force en attendant le droit.' (Force and right are the governors of this world; force till right is ready.) *Force till right is ready;* and till right is ready, force,[16] the existing order of things, is justified, is the legitimate ruler. But right is something moral, and implies inward recognition, free assent of the will; we are not ready for right,—*right,* so far as we are concerned, *is not ready,*—until we have attained this sense of seeing it and willing it. The way in which for us it may change and transform force, the existing order of things, and become, in its turn, the legitimate ruler of the world, should depend on the way in which, when our time comes, we see it and will it. Therefore for other people enamoured of their own newly discerned right, to attempt to impose it upon us as ours, and violently to substitute their right for our force, is an act of tyranny, and to be resisted. It sets at nought the second great half of our maximum, *force till right is ready.* This was the grand error of the French Revolution; and its movement of ideas, by quitting the intellectual sphere and rushing furiously into the political sphere, ran, indeed, a prodigious and memorable course, but produced no such intellectual fruit as the movement of ideas of the Renascence, and created, in opposition to itself, what I may call an *epoch of concentration.* The great force of that epoch of concentration was England; and the great voice of that epoch of concentration was Burke.[17] It is the fashion to treat Burke's writings on the French Revolution as superannuated and conquered by the event; as the eloquent but unphilosophical tirades of bigotry and prejudice. I will not deny that they are often disfigured by the violence and passion of the moment, and that in some directions Burke's view

15. Joseph Joubert (1754–1824), French essayist to whom Arnold devotes one of the *Essays in Criticism.*
16. Arnold here boldly confronts the fact that the element of force is implicit in what we call government.
17. Edmund Burke (1729–97), one of England's most notable statesmen and political philosophers, opposed the French Revolution in his brilliant and eloquent *Reflections on the French Revolution* (1790).

was bounded, and his observation therefore at fault. But on the whole, and for those who can make the needful corrections, what distinguishes these writings is their profound, permanent, fruitful, philosophical truth. They contain the true philosophy of an epoch of concentration, dissipate the heavy atmosphere which its own nature is apt to engender round it, and make its resistance rational instead of mechanical.

But Burke is so great because, almost alone in England, he brings thought to bear upon politics, he saturates politics with thought. It is his accident that his ideas were at the service of an epoch of concentration, not of an epoch of expansion; it is his characteristic that he so lived by ideas, and had such a source of them welling up within him, that he could float even an epoch of concentration and English Tory politics with them. It does not hurt him that Dr. Price [18] and the Liberals were enraged with him; it does not even hurt him that George the Third and the Tories were enchanted with him. His greatness is that he lived in a world which neither English Liberalism nor English Toryism is apt to enter;—the world of ideas, not the world of catchwords and party habits. So far is it from being really true of him that he 'to party gave up what was meant for mankind,' [19] that at the very end of his fierce struggle with the French Revolution, after all his invectives against its false pretensions, hollowness, and madness, with his sincere conviction of its mischievousness, he can close a memorandum on the best means of combating it, some of the last pages he ever wrote,[20]—the *Thoughts on French Affairs,* in December 1791,—with these striking words:—

'The evil is stated, in my opinion, as it exists. The remedy must be where power, wisdom, and information, I hope, are more united with good intentions than they can be with me. I have done with this subject, I believe, for ever. It has given me many anxious moments for the last two years. *If a great change is to be made in human affairs, the minds of men will be fitted to it; the general opinions and feelings will draw that way. Every fear, every hope will forward it; and then they who persist in opposing this mighty current in human affairs, will appear rather to resist the decrees of Providence itself, than the mere designs of men. They will not be resolute and firm, but perverse and obstinate.'*

That return of Burke upon himself has always seemed to me one of the finest things in English literature, or indeed in any literature. That is what I call living by ideas: when one side of a question has long had your earnest support, when all your feelings are engaged, when you hear all round you no language but one, when your party talks this language like a steam-engine and can imagine no other,—still to be able to think, still to be irresistibly carried, if so it be, by the current of thought to the opposite side of the question, and, like Balaam, to be unable to speak anything *but what the Lord has put in your mouth.*[21] I

18. Richard Price, D.D. (1723–91), was a nonconformist minister, a writer on moral philosophy, and a vocal partisan of the French Revolution. Burke singles him out for attack in the *Reflections.*
19. Said by Oliver Goldsmith of his friend Burke in his poem *Retaliation* (1774).
20. Arnold is in error here—the pages are not the last Burke ever wrote; in 1796 he published *Letter to a Noble Lord* and *Letters on a Regicide Peace,* in which he voiced his relentless condemnation of the Revolution.
21. Numbers 22, 23. The point of the story is that Balaam blessed the Israelites although he had been sent by his king to curse them.

know nothing more striking, and I must add that I know nothing more un-English.

For the Englishman in general is like my friend the Member of Parliament, and believes, point-blank, that for a thing to be an anomaly is absolutely no objection to it whatever. He is like the Lord Auckland [22] of Burke's day, who, in a memorandum on the French Revolution, talks of 'certain miscreants, assuming the name of philosophers, who have presumed themselves capable of establishing a new system of society.' The Englishman has been called a political animal, and he values what is political and practical so much that ideas easily become objects of dislike in his eyes, and thinkers 'miscreants,' because ideas and thinkers have rashly meddled with politics and practice. This would be all very well if the dislike and neglect confined themselves to ideas transported out of their own sphere, and meddling rashly with practice; but they are inevitably extended to ideas as such, and to the whole life of intelligence; practice is everything, a free play of the mind is nothing. The notion of the free play of the mind upon all subjects being a pleasure in itself, being an object of desire, being an essential provider of elements without which a nation's spirit, whatever compensations it may have for them, must, in the long run, die of inanition, hardly enters into an Englishman's thoughts. It is noticeable that the word *curiosity*, which in other languages is used in a good sense, to mean, as a high and fine quality of man's nature, just this disinterested love of a free play of the mind on all subjects, for its own sake,— it is noticeable, I say, that this word has in our language no sense of the kind, no sense but a rather bad and disparaging one.[23] But criticism, real criticism, is essentially the exercise of this very quality. It obeys an instinct prompting it to try to know the best that is known and thought in the world, irrespectively of practice, politics, and everything of the kind; and to value knowledge and thought as they approach this best, without the intrusion of any other considerations whatever. This is an instinct for which there is, I think, little original sympathy in the practical English nature, and what there was of it has undergone a long benumbing period of blight and suppression in the epoch of concentration which followed the French Revolution.

But epochs of concentration cannot well endure for ever; epochs of expansion, in the due course of things, follow them. Such an epoch of expansion seems to be opening in this country. In the first place all danger of a hostile forcible pressure of foreign ideas upon our practice has long disappeared; like the traveller in the fable, therefore, we begin to wear our cloak a little more loosely.[24] Then, with a long peace, the ideas of Europe steal gradually and amicably in, and mingle, though in infinitesimally small quantities at a time, with our own notions. Then, too, in spite of all that is said about the absorbing and brutalising influence of our passionate material progress, it

22. William Eden, first Baron Auckland (1744–1814), was ambassador to The Hague during the French Revolution.
23. That is, personal inquisitiveness, intrusiveness into the affairs of others. Arnold speaks at fuller length of the English attitude toward the word in *Culture and Anarchy*. Pater in his essay *Romanticism* (see below) makes curiosity one of the elements of good modern literature.
24. Referring to Aesop's fable of the contest between the wind and the sun to see which could first make a traveler take off his cloak.

seems to me indisputable that this progress is likely, though not certain, to lead in the end to an apparition of intellectual life; and that man, after he has made himself perfectly comfortable and has now to determine what to do with himself next, may begin to remember that he has a mind, and that the mind may be made the source of great pleasure. I grant it is mainly the privilege of faith, at present, to discern this end to our railways, our business, and our fortune-making; but we shall see if, here as elsewhere, faith is not in the end the true prophet. Our ease, our travelling, and our unbounded liberty to hold just as hard and securely as we please to the practice to which our notions have given birth, all tend to beget an inclination to deal a little more freely with these notions themselves, to canvass them a little, to penetrate a little into their real nature. Flutterings of curiosity, in the foreign sense of the word, appear amongst us, and it is in these that criticism must look to find its account. Criticism first; a time of true creative activity, perhaps,—which, as I have said, must inevitably be preceded amongst us by a time of criticism,— hereafter, when criticism has done its work.

It is of the last importance that English criticism should clearly discern what rule for its course, in order to avail itself of the field now opening to it, and to produce fruit for the future, it ought to take. The rule may be summed up in one word,—*disinterestedness*. And how is criticism to show disinterestedness? By keeping aloof from what is called 'the practical view of things'; by resolutely following the law of its own nature, which is to be a free play of the mind on all subjects which it touches. By steadily refusing to lend itself to any of those ulterior, political, practical considerations about ideas, which plenty of people will be sure to attach to them, which perhaps ought often to be attached to them, which in this country at any rate are certain to be attached to them quite sufficiently, but which criticism has really nothing to do with. Its business is, as I have said, simply to know the best that is known and thought in the world, and by in its turn making this known, to create a current of true and fresh ideas. Its business is to do this with inflexible honesty, with due ability; but its business is to do no more, and to leave alone all questions of practical consequences and applications, questions which will never fail to have due prominence given to them. Else criticism, besides being really false to its own nature, merely continues in the old rut which it has hitherto followed in this country, and will certainly miss the chance now given to it. For what is at present the bane of criticism in this country? It is that practical considerations cling to it and stifle it. It subserves interests not its own. Our organs of criticism are organs of men and parties having practical ends to serve, and with them those practical ends are the first thing and the play of mind the second; so much play of mind as is compatible with the prosecution of those practical ends is all that is wanted. An organ like the *Revue des Deux Mondes*,[25] having for its main function to understand and utter the best that is known and thought in the world, existing, it may be said, as just an organ for a free play of the mind, we have not. But we have the *Edinburgh Review*, existing as an organ of the old Whigs, and for as much

25. Founded in 1829; it was especially notable for its literary and philosophical contributions. It ceased publication in 1944.

play of the mind as may suit its being that; we have the *Quarterly Review*, existing as an organ of the Tories, and for as much play of mind as may suit its
being that; we have the *British Quarterly Review*, existing as an organ of the
political Dissenters,[26] and for as much play of mind as may suit its being that;
we have the *Times*, existing as an organ of the common, satisfied, well-to-do
Englishman, and for as much play of mind as may suit its being that. And
so on through all the various fractions, political and religious, of our society;
every fraction has, as such, its organ of criticism, but the notion of combining
all fractions in the common pleasure of a free disinterested play of mind meets
with no favour. Directly this play of mind wants to have more scope, and to
forget the pressure of practical considerations a little, it is checked, it is made
to feel the chain. We saw this the other day in the extinction, so much to
be regretted, of the *Home and Foreign Review*.[27] Perhaps in no organ of
criticism in this country was there so much knowledge, so much play of mind;
but these could not save it. The *Dublin Review* subordinates play of mind to
the practical business of English and Irish Catholicism, and lives. It must
needs be that men should act in sects and parties, that each of these
sects and parties should have its organ, and should make this organ subserve
the interests of its action; but it would be well, too, that there should be a
criticism, not the minister of these interests, not their enemy, but absolutely
and entirely independent of them. No other criticism will ever attain any
real authority or make any real way towards its end,—the creating a current
of true and fresh ideas.

It is because criticism has so little kept in the pure intellectual sphere,
has so little detached itself from practice, has been so directly polemical and
controversial, that it has so ill accomplished, in this country, its best spiritual
work; which is to keep man from a self-satisfaction which is retarding and
vulgarising, to lead him towards perfection, by making his mind dwell upon
what is excellent in itself, and the absolute beauty and fitness of things. A
polemical practical criticism makes men blind even to the ideal imperfection
of their practice, makes them willingly assert its ideal perfection, in order the
better to secure it against attack; and clearly this is narrowing and baneful
for them. If they were reassured on the practical side, speculative considerations of ideal perfection they might be brought to entertain, and their spiritual
horizon would thus gradually widen. Sir Charles Adderley [28] says to the Warwickshire farmers:—

'Talk of the improvement of breed! Why, the race we ourselves represent,
the men and women, the old Anglo-Saxon race, are the best breed in the
whole world. . . . The absence of a too enervating climate, too unclouded
skies, and a too luxurious nature, has produced so vigorous a race of people,
and has rendered us so superior to all the world.'

Mr. Roebuck [29] says to the Sheffield cutlers:—

26. Members of religious sects opposed to the Church of England and expressing their
opposition politically.
27. Published in London 1862–64.
28. A Conservative politician (1814–1905) who inherited a great estate in Warwickshire.
29. John Arthur Roebuck (1801–79) was an aggressively radical politician who sometimes took anomalous reactionary positions.

'I look around me and ask what is the state of England? Is not property safe? Is not every man able to say what he likes? Can you not walk from one end of England to the other in perfect security? I ask you whether, the world over or in past history, there is anything like it? Nothing. I pray that our unrivalled happiness may last.'

Now obviously there is a peril for poor human nature in words and thoughts of such exuberant self-satisfaction, until we find ourselves safe in the streets of the Celestial City.

> Das wenige verschwindet leicht dem Blicke
> Der vorwärts sieht, wie viel noch übrig bleibt—

says Goethe; [30] 'the little that is done seems nothing when we look forward and see how much we have yet to do.' Clearly this is a better line of reflection for weak humanity, so long as it remains on this earthly field of labour and trial.

But neither Sir Charles Adderley nor Mr. Roebuck is by nature inaccessible to considerations of this sort. They only lose sight of them owing to the controversial life we all lead, and the practical form which all speculation takes with us. They have in view opponents whose aim is not ideal, but practical; and in their zeal to uphold their own practice against these innovators, they go so far as even to attribute to this practice an ideal perfection. Somebody has been wanting to introduce a six-pound franchise,[31] or to abolish church-rates,[32] or to collect agricultural statistics by force, or to diminish local self-government. How natural, in reply to such proposals, very likely improper or ill-timed, to go a little beyond the mark, and to say stoutly, 'Such a race of people as we stand, so superior to all the world! The old Anglo-Saxon race, the best breed in the whole world! I pray that our unrivalled happiness may last! I ask you whether, the world over or in past history, there is anything like it?' And so long as criticism answers this dithyramb by insisting that the old Anglo-Saxon race would be still more superior to all others if it had no church-rates, or that our unrivalled happiness would last yet longer with a six-pound franchise, so long will the strain, 'The best breed in the whole world!' swell louder and louder, everything ideal and refining will be lost out of sight, and both the assailed and their critics will remain in a sphere, to say the truth, perfectly unvital, a sphere in which spiritual progression is impossible. But let criticism leave church-rates and the franchise alone, and in the most candid spirit, without a single lurking thought of practical innovation, confront with our dithyramb this paragraph on which I stumbled in a newspaper immediately after reading Mr. Roebuck:—

'A shocking child murder has just been committed at Nottingham. A girl named Wragg left the workhouse there on Saturday morning with her young illegitimate child. The child was soon afterwards found dead on Mapperly Hills, having been strangled. Wragg is in custody.'

Nothing but that; but, in juxtaposition with the absolute eulogies of Sir

30. In *Iphigenie auf Tauris* I.ii.91–92.
31. A proposal to liberalize suffrage by giving the vote to anyone who owned land or buildings worth a rent of £6 a year.
32. Taxes imposed on behalf of the Church of England.

Charles Adderley and Mr. Roebuck, how eloquent, how suggestive are those few lines! 'Our old Anglo-Saxon breed, the best in the whole world!'—how much that is harsh and ill-favoured there is in this best! *Wragg!* If we are to talk of ideal perfection, of 'the best in the whole world,' has any one reflected what a touch of grossness in our race, what an original shortcoming in the more delicate spiritual perceptions, is shown by the natural growth amongst us of such hideous names,—Higginbottom, Stiggins, Bugg! In Ionia and Attica [33] they were luckier in this respect than 'the best race in the world'; by the Ilissus [34] there was no Wragg, poor thing! And 'our unrivalled happiness';—what an element of grimness, bareness, and hideousness mixes with it and blurs it; the workhouse, the dismal Mapperly Hills,[35]—how dismal those who have seen them will remember; the gloom, the smoke, the cold, the strangled illegitimate child! 'I ask you whether, the world over or in past history, there is anything like it?' Perhaps not, one is inclined to answer; but at any rate, in that case, the world is [not] very much to be pitied. And the final touch,—short, bleak, and inhuman: *Wragg is in custody.* The sex lost in the confusion of our unrivalled happiness; or (shall I say?) the superfluous Christian name lopped off by the straightforward vigour of our old Anglo-Saxon breed! There is profit for the spirit in such contrasts as this; criticism serves the cause of perfection by establishing them. By eluding sterile conflict, by refusing to remain in the sphere where alone narrow and relative conceptions have any worth and validity, criticism may diminish its momentary importance, but only in this way has it a chance of gaining admittance for those wider and more perfect conceptions to which all its duty is really owed. Mr. Roebuck will have a poor opinion of an adversary who replies to his defiant songs of triumph only by murmuring under his breath, *Wragg is in custody;* but in no other way will these songs of triumph be induced gradually to moderate themselves, to get rid of what in them is excessive and offensive, and to fall into a softer and truer key.

It will be said that it is a very subtle and indirect action which I am thus prescribing for criticism, and that, by embracing in this manner the Indian virtue of detachment [36] and abandoning the sphere of practical life, it condemns itself to a slow and obscure work. Slow and obscure it may be, but it is the only proper work of criticism. The mass of mankind will never have any ardent zeal for seeing things as they are; very inadequate ideas will always satisfy them. On these inadequate ideas reposes, and must repose, the general practice of the world. That is as much as saying that whoever sets himself to see things as they are will find himself one of a very small circle; but it is only by this small circle resolutely doing its own work that adequate ideas will ever get current at all. The rush and roar of practical life will always have a dizzying and attracting effect upon the most collected spectator, and tend to draw him into its vortex; most of all will this be the case where that life is so powerful as it is in England. But it is only by remaining collected, and refusing to lend himself to the point of view of the practical man, that the critic can do the

33. Districts of Greece.
34. A river near Athens.
35. The coal-mining environs of Nottingham.
36. Reference to the Buddhist ideal of disengagement from worldly activity.

practical man any service; and it is only by the greatest sincerity in pursuing his own course, and by at last convincing even the practical man of his sincerity, that he can escape misunderstandings which perpetually threaten him.

For the practical man is not apt for fine distinctions, and yet in these distinctions truth and the highest culture greatly find their account. But it is not easy to lead a practical man,—unless you reassure him as to your practical intentions, you have no chance of leading him,—to see that a thing which he has always been used to look at from one side only, which he greatly values, and which, looked at from that side, quite deserves, perhaps, all the prizing and admiring which he bestows upon it,—that this thing, looked at from another side, may appear much less beneficent and beautiful, and yet retain all its claims to our practical allegiance. Where shall we find language innocent enough, how shall we make the spotless purity of our intentions evident enough, to enable us to say to the political Englishman that the British Constitution itself, which, seen from the practical side, looks such a magnificent organ of progress and virtue, seen from the speculative side,—with its compromises, its love of facts, its horror of theory, its studied avoidance of clear thoughts,— that, seen from this side, our august Constitution sometimes looks,—forgive me, shade of Lord Somers! [37]—a colossal machine for the manufacture of Philistines? [38] How is Cobbett [39] to say this and not be misunderstood, blackened as he is with the smoke of a lifelong conflict in the field of political practice? how is Mr. Carlyle to say it and not be misunderstood, after his furious raid into this field with his *Latter-day Pamphlets?* how is Mr. Ruskin, after his pugnacious political economy? [40] I say, the critic must keep out of the region of immediate practice in the political, social, humanitarian sphere, if he wants to make a beginning for that more free speculative treatment of things, which may perhaps one day make its benefits felt even in this sphere, but in a natural and thence irresistible manner.

Do what he will, however, the critic will still remain exposed to frequent misunderstandings, and nowhere so much as in this country. For here people are particularly indisposed even to comprehend that without this free disinterested treatment of things, truth and the highest culture are out of the question. So immersed are they in practical life, so accustomed to take all their notions from this life and its processes, that they are apt to think that truth and culture themselves can be reached by the processes of this life, and that it is an impertinent singularity to think of reaching them in any other. 'We are all *terræ filii,*'[41] cries their eloquent advocate; 'all Philistines together.

37. John Somers, Baron Somers (1651–1716), eminent constitutional lawyer who, after the abdication of James II, presided over the commission that drafted the Bill of Rights.
38. Arnold's name for the middle classes in their resistance to reason and culture. The Philistines were neighbors and enemies of the people of Israel, the "children of light"; for their deplorable conduct, see Judges and Milton's *Samson Agonistes.* Arnold, in his essay on Heinrich Heine, refers to Heine's use of the word in the sense he himself was to establish in the language by his frequent iteration of it.
39. William Cobbett (1762–1835), the famous political journalist and pamphleteer, a passionate fighter for reform and democracy.
40. In *Unto This Last* (1860–62). With these essays, Ruskin turned from art criticism to economics. The first essays appeared in *Cornhill Magazine* and made such a scandal by the heterodoxy of their views that the series was discontinued.
41. "Sons of the earth."

Away with the notion of proceeding by any other course than the course dear to the Philistines; let us have a social movement, let us organise and combine a party to pursue truth and new thought, let us call it *the liberal party*, and let us all stick to each other, and back each other up. Let us have no nonsense about independent criticism, and intellectual delicacy, and the few and the many. Don't let us trouble ourselves about foreign thought; we shall invent the whole thing for ourselves as we go along. If one of us speaks well, applaud him; if one of us speaks ill, applaud him too; we are all in the same move-ment, we are all liberals, we are all in pursuit of truth.' In this way the pursuit of truth becomes really a social, practical, pleasurable affair, almost requiring a chairman, a secretary, and advertisements; with the excitement of an occasional scandal, with a little resistance to give the happy sense of difficulty overcome; but, in general, plenty of bustle and very little thought. To act is so easy, as Goethe says; to think is so hard! It is true that the critic has many temptations to go with the stream, to make one of the party movement, one of these *terræ filii;* it seems ungracious to refuse to be a *terræ filius,* when so many excellent people are; but the critic's duty is to refuse, or, if resistance is vain, at least to cry with Obermann: *Périssons en résistant.*[42]

[At this point Arnold digresses from the main line of his argument to cite examples of "bustle and very little thought" in the religious life of England. This excursion of three long paragraphs, crowded with topical allusions, has lost interest with the passage of time and has been omitted.]

For criticism, these are elementary laws; but they never can be popular, and in this country they have been very little followed, and one meets with immense obstacles in following them. That is a reason for asserting them again and again. Criticism must maintain its independence of the practical spirit and its aims. Even with well-meant efforts of the practical spirit it must express dissatisfaction, if in the sphere of the ideal they seem impoverishing and limiting. It must not hurry on to the goal because of its practical im-portance. It must be patient, and know how to wait; and flexible, and know how to attach itself to things and how to withdraw from them. It must be apt to study and praise elements that for the fulness of spiritual perfection are wanted, even though they belong to a power which in the practical sphere may be maleficent. It must be apt to discern the spiritual shortcomings or illusions of powers that in the practical sphere may be beneficent. And this without any notion of favouring or injuring, in the practical sphere, one power or the other; without any notion of playing off, in this sphere, one power against the other. When one looks, for instance, at the English Divorce Court,—an institution which perhaps has its practical conveniences, but which in the ideal sphere is so hideous; an institution which neither makes divorce impossible

42. "Let us die resisting." Obermann is the writer of the letters which make up the novel—if that is what it is to be called—to which he gives his name. It was published in 1804, the work of Etienne Pivert de Senancour (1770–1846), and in its day was famous and influential. Over many years, Obermann, who lives in isolation in a Swiss Alpine valley, writes to a friend describing his melancholy sense of the emptiness of life, his inability to engage in any purposeful activity. Arnold was among the many young men who found in the book the confirmation of their own feeling of alienation from the modern world; he celebrates it in an early poem, *Stanzas in Memory of the Author of "Obermann,"* and in a late one, *Obermann Once More.*

nor makes it decent, which allows a man to get rid of his wife, or a wife of her husband, but makes them drag one another first, for the public edification, through a mire of unutterable infamy,—when one looks at this charming institution, I say, with its crowded trials, its newspaper reports, and its money compensations, this institution in which the gross unregenerate British Philistine has indeed stamped an image of himself,—one may be permitted to find the marriage theory of Catholicism refreshing and elevating. Or when Protestantism, in virtue of its supposed rational and intellectual origin, gives the law to criticism too magisterially, criticism may and must remind it that its pretensions, in this respect, are illusive and do it harm; that the Reformation was a moral rather than an intellectual event; that Luther's theory of grace no more exactly reflects the mind of the spirit than Bossuet's philosophy of history reflects it; [43] and that there is no more antecedent probability of the Bishop of Durham's stock of ideas being agreeable to perfect reason than of Pope Pius the Ninth's.[44] But criticism will not on that account forget the achievements of Protestantism in the practical and moral sphere; nor that, even in the intellectual sphere, Protestantism, though in a blind and stumbling manner, carried forward the Renascence, while Catholicism threw itself violently across its path.

I lately heard a man of thought and energy contrasting the want of ardour and movement which he now found amongst young men in this country with what he remembered in his own youth, twenty years ago. 'What reformers we were then!' he exclaimed; 'what a zeal we had! how we canvassed every institution in Church and State, and were prepared to remodel them all on first principles!' He was inclined to regret, as a spiritual flagging, the lull which he saw. I am disposed rather to regard it as a pause in which the turn to a new mode of spiritual progress is being accomplished. Everything was long seen, by the young and ardent amongst us, in inseparable connection with politics and practical life. We have pretty well exhausted the benefits of seeing things in this connection, we have got all that can be got by so seeing them. Let us try a more disinterested mode of seeing them; let us betake ourselves more to the serener life of the mind and spirit. This life, too, may have its excesses and dangers; but they are not for us at present. Let us think of quietly enlarging our stock of true and fresh ideas, and not, as soon as we get an idea or half an idea, be running out with it into the street, and trying to make it rule there. Our ideas will, in the end, shape the world all the better for maturing a little. Perhaps in fifty years' time it will in the English House of Commons be an objection to an institution that it is an anomaly, and my friend the Member of Parliament will shudder in his grave. But let us in the meanwhile rather endeavour that in twenty years' time it may, in English literature, be an objection to a proposition that it is absurd. That will be a

43. Jacques Bénigne Bossuet (1627–1704), French bishop famous as a preacher, moralist, and religious polemicist, advanced the view that historical events were providential, designed for the establishment of Christianity and particularly of the Roman Catholic Church.
44. He was pope from 1846 to 1878; his "stock of ideas" is set over against those of the Bishop of the Church of England.

change so vast, that the imagination almost fails to grasp it. *Ab integro sæclo-rum nascitur ordo.*[45]

If I have insisted so much on the course which criticism must take where politics and religion are concerned, it is because, where these burning matters are in question, it is most likely to go astray. I have wished, above all, to insist on the attitude which criticism should adopt towards things in general; on its right tone and temper of mind. But then comes another question as to the subject-matter which literary criticism should most seek. Here, in general, its course is determined for it by the idea which is the law of its being; the idea of a disinterested endeavour to learn and propagate the best that is known and thought in the world, and thus to establish a current of fresh and true ideas. By the very nature of things, as England is not all the world, much of the best that is known and thought in the world cannot be of English growth, must be foreign; by the nature of things, again, it is just this that we are least likely to know, while English thought is streaming in upon us from all sides, and takes excellent care that we shall not be ignorant of its existence. The English critic of literature, therefore, must dwell much on foreign thought, and with particular heed on any part of it, which, while significant and fruitful in itself, is for any reason specially likely to escape him. Again, judging is often spoken of as the critic's one business, and so in some sense it is; but the judgment which almost insensibly forms itself in a fair and clear mind, along with fresh knowledge, is the valuable one; and thus knowledge, and ever fresh knowledge, must be the critic's great concern for himself. And it is by com-municating fresh knowledge, and letting his own judgment pass along with it,—but insensibly, and in the second place, not the first, as a sort of companion and clue, not as an abstract law-giver,—that the critic will generally do most good to his readers. Sometimes, no doubt, for the sake of establishing an author's place in literature, and his relation to a central standard (and if this is not done, how are we to get at our *best in the world?*) criticism may have to deal with a subject-matter so familiar that fresh knowledge is out of the question, and then it must be all judgment; an enunciation and detailed appli-cation of principles. Here the great safeguard is never to let oneself become abstract, always to retain an intimate and lively consciousness of the truth of what one is saying, and, the moment this fails us, to be sure that something is wrong. Still, under all circumstances, this mere judgment and application of principles is, in itself, not the most satisfactory work to the critics; like mathe-matics, it is tautological, and cannot well give us, like fresh learning, the sense of creative activity.

But stop, some one will say; all this talk is of no practical use to us what-ever; this criticism of yours is not what we have in our minds when we speak of criticism; when we speak of critics and criticism, we mean critics and criti-cism of the current English literature of the day; when you offer to tell criticism its function, it is to this criticism that we expect you to address yourself. I am sorry for it, for I am afraid I must disappoint these expectations. I am bound by my own definition of criticism: *a disinterested endeavour to learn and*

45. "From the renewal of the ages is order born." Virgil, *Eclogues* IV.5.

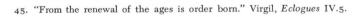

*propagate the best that is known and thought in the world.* How much of current English literature comes into this 'best that is known and thought in the world'? Not very much, I fear; certainly less, at this moment, than of the current literature of France or Germany. Well, then, am I to alter my definition of criticism, in order to meet the requirements of a number of practising English critics, who, after all, are free in their choice of a business? That would be making criticism lend itself just to one of those alien practical considerations, which, I have said, are so fatal to it. One may say, indeed, to those who have to deal with the mass—so much better disregarded—of current English literature, that they may at all events endeavour, in dealing with this, to try it, so far as they can, by the standard of the best that is known and thought in the world; one may say, that to get anywhere near this standard, every critic should try and possess one great literature, at least, besides his own; and the more unlike his own, the better. But, after all, the criticism I am really concerned with,—the criticism which alone can much help us for the future, the criticism which, throughout Europe, is at the present day meant, when so much stress is laid on the importance of criticism and the critical spirit,—is a criticism which regards Europe as being, for intellectual and spiritual purposes, one great confederation, bound to a joint action and working to a common result; and whose members have, for their proper outfit, a knowledge of Greek, Roman, and Eastern antiquity, and of one another. Special, local, and temporary advantages being put out of account, that modern nation will in the intellectual and spiritual sphere make most progress, which most thoroughly carries out this programme. And what is that but saying that we too, all of us, as individuals, the more thoroughly we carry it out, shall make the more progress?

There is so much inviting us!—what are we to take? what will nourish us in growth towards perfection? That is the question which, with the immense field of life and of literature lying before him, the critic has to answer; for himself first, and afterwards for others. In this idea of the critic's business the essays brought together in the following pages [46] have had their origin; in this idea, widely different as are their subjects, they have, perhaps, their unity.

I conclude with what I said at the beginning: to have the sense of creative activity is the great happiness and the great proof of being alive, and it is not denied to criticism to have it; but then criticism must be sincere, simple, flexible, ardent, ever widening its knowledge. Then it may have, in no contemptible measure, a joyful sense of creative activity; a sense which a man of insight and conscience will prefer to what he might derive from a poor, starved, fragmentary, inadequate creation. And at some epochs no other creation is possible.

Still, in full measure, the sense of creative activity belongs only to genuine creation; in literature we must never forget that. But what true man of letters ever can forget it? It is no such common matter for a gifted nature to come into possession of a current of true and living ideas, and to produce amidst the inspiration of them, that we are likely to underrate it. The epochs of Æschylus and Shakespeare make us feel their pre-eminence. In an epoch like

46. The essay served as the introduction to *Essays in Criticism.*

those is, no doubt, the true life of literature; there is the promised land, towards which criticism can only beckon. That promised land it will not be ours to enter, and we shall die in the wilderness: but to have desired to enter it, to have saluted it from afar, is already, perhaps, the best distinction among contemporaries; it will certainly be the best title to esteem with posterity.
1864                                                                                    1864, 1865


# The Study of Poetry

Of *The Study of Poetry*, the most ambitious and famous of Arnold's late critical essays, T. S. Eliot said that it is "a classic in English criticism; so much is said in so little space, with such economy and with such authority." The praise has the more force, and an especial interest, as coming from a writer who, both as critic and as poet, put himself in opposition to every canon of taste the essay proposes. In this opposition Eliot is not alone—in our time *The Study of Poetry* exists in the aura of the controversy it provokes. It is challenged in its first premise, that poetry has a "future" which is "immense," that it confronts "high destinies" of which it must be worthy.

Whatever store contemporary critics and poets set upon poetry—and they are intransigent in affirming its everlasting importance—they do not envision its existence to be thus grandiose. They are not likely to accept the condition that Arnold makes for the realization of its potentialities, in effect that it speaks with that largeness of utterance, chiefly about the tragic aspects of life, which will make its voice cognate with that of religion in its emotive aspects. It is this that constitutes Arnold's criterion of greatness in poetry. But the taste and theory of our time are much less concerned with greatness than Arnold was, or at least they are less certain than he was that the word should imply chiefly largeness or grandness of spirit. Our age is drawn rather to such qualities as suggest the personal authenticity of the poetic voice and these, it feels, do not readily consort with the solemnity of greatness. Arnold's roster of English poets is judged strangely incomplete in its silent omissions—it takes no heed, for example, of Donne, Marvell, Herbert, and Vaughan—and culpable in its explicit exclusion of Dryden and Pope, who are held not to be poets at all. But when all possible objections to the essay have been made, it stands as what Eliot says it is, a classic of English criticism. It is that, many will feel, exactly in the degree that we are led to dispute it. The value of a work of literary criticism is not to be measured by the readiness or warmth of assent we give to its judgments but by its ability to induce us to think directly and immediately about literature. Of *The Study of Poetry* it can be said that, Dr. Johnson on *Lycidas* alone excepted, no work of criticism so well instructs us by the disagreement it arouses.


## *From* The Study of Poetry

'The future of poetry is immense, because in poetry, where it is worthy of its high destinies, our race, as time goes on, will find an ever surer and surer stay. There is not a creed which is not shaken, not an accredited dogma which is not shown to be questionable, not a received tradition which does not threaten to dissolve. Our religion has materialised itself in the fact, in the supposed fact; it has attached its emotion to the fact, and now the fact is failing it. But for poetry the idea is everything; the rest is a world of illusion, of divine illusion. Poetry attaches its emotion to the idea; the idea *is* the fact. The strongest part of our religion to-day is its unconscious poetry.'[1]

Let me be permitted to quote these words of my own, as uttering the thought which should, in my opinion, go with us and govern us in all our study of poetry. In the present work[2] it is the course of one great contributory stream to the world-river of poetry that we are invited to follow. We are here invited to trace the stream of English poetry. But whether we set ourselves, as here, to follow only one of the several streams that make the mighty river of poetry, or whether we seek to know them all, our governing thought should be the same. We should conceive of poetry worthily, and more highly than it has been the custom to conceive of it. We should conceive of it as capable of higher uses, and called to higher destinies, than those which in general men have assigned to it hitherto. More and more mankind will discover that we have to turn to poetry to interpret life for us, to console us, to sustain us. Without poetry, our science will appear incomplete; and most of what now passes with us for religion and philosophy will be replaced by poetry. Science, I say, will appear incomplete without it. For finely and truly does Wordsworth call poetry 'the impassioned expression which is in the countenance of all science'; and what is a countenance without its expression? Again, Wordsworth finely and truly calls poetry 'the breath and finer spirit of all knowledge': our religion, parading evidences such as those on which the popular mind relies now;[3] our philosophy, pluming itself on its reasonings about causation and finite and infinite being; what are they but the shadows and dreams and false shows of knowledge? The day will come when we shall wonder at ourselves for having trusted to them, for having taken them seriously; and the more we perceive their hollowness, the more we shall prize 'the breath and finer spirit of knowledge' offered to us by poetry.

But if we conceive thus highly of the destinies of poetry, we must also set our standard for poetry high, since poetry, to be capable of fulfilling such high destinies, must be poetry of a high order of excellence. We must accustom ourselves to a high standard and to a strict judgment. Sainte-Beuve[4] relates that

1. Arnold quotes a slightly abbreviated version of the paragraph which concludes the introduction he had written for an ephemeral book called *The Hundred Greatest Men* (1879).
2. Arnold refers to the comprehensive anthology *The English Poets,* to which his essay serves as the introduction.
3. Arnold here recurs to the idea, already touched on in the opening paragraph, which was at the center of the criticism of English religious life he had been making over the previous decade—that the basis of popular faith was the literal interpretation of the Bible, specifically the credence given to miracles; this, he held, could not possibly maintain itself in the face of developing science, and unless English Protestantism found a more spiritual ground for belief, it would have none at all.
4. Charles-Augustin Sainte-Beuve (1804–69), the French critic for whom Arnold often expressed high respect.

Napoleon one day said, when somebody was spoken of in his presence as a charlatan: 'Charlatan as much as you please; but where is there *not* charlatanism?'—'Yes,' answers Sainte-Beuve, 'in politics, in the art of governing mankind, that is perhaps true. But in the order of thought, in art, the glory, the eternal honour is that charlatanism shall find no entrance; herein lies the inviolableness of that noble portion of man's being.' It is admirably said, and let us hold fast to it. In poetry, which is thought and art in one, it is the glory, the eternal honour, that charlatanism shall find no entrance; that this noble sphere be kept inviolate and inviolable. Charlatanism is for confusing or obliterating the distinctions between excellent and inferior, sound and unsound or only half-sound, true and untrue or only half-true. It is charlatanism, conscious or unconscious, whenever we confuse or obliterate these. And in poetry, more than anywhere else, it is unpermissible to confuse or obliterate them. For in poetry the distinction between excellent and inferior, sound and unsound or only half-sound, true and untrue or only half-true, is of paramount importance. It is of paramount importance because of the high destinies of poetry. In poetry, as a criticism of life[5] under the conditions fixed for such a criticism by the laws of poetic truth and poetic beauty, the spirit of our race will find, we have said, as time goes on and as other helps fail, its consolation and stay. But the consolation and stay will be of power in proportion to the power of the criticism of life. And the criticism of life will be of power in proportion as the poetry conveying it is excellent rather than inferior, sound rather than unsound or half-sound, true rather than untrue or half-true.

The best poetry is what we want; the best poetry will be found to have a power of forming, sustaining, and delighting us, as nothing else can. A clearer, deeper sense of the best in poetry, and of the strength and joy to be drawn from it, is the most precious benefit which we can gather from a poetical collection such as the present. And yet in the very nature and conduct of such a collection there is inevitably something which tends to obscure in us the consciousness of what our benefit should be, and to distract us from the pursuit of it. We should therefore steadily set it before our minds at the outset, and should compel ourselves to revert constantly to the thought of it as we proceed.

Yes; constantly, in reading poetry, a sense for the best, the really excellent, and of the strength and joy to be drawn from it, should be present in our minds and should govern our estimate of what we read. But this real estimate, the only true one, is liable to be superseded, if we are not watchful, by two other kinds of estimate, the historic estimate and the personal estimate, both of which are fallacious. A poet or a poem may count to us historically, they may count to us on grounds personal to ourselves, and they may count to us really. They may count to us historically. The course of development of a

---

5. No phrase of Arnold's is more often quoted or more often objected to than this one. Among the objections that of T. S. Eliot is probably the best known—Eliot said that as a definition of poetry the phrase must seem "frigid to anyone who has felt the full surprise and elevation of a new experience of poetry." To which the reply might be made that Arnold meant—at least in part—that it is exactly the full surprise and elevation of a new experience of poetry that constitutes a criticism of life, of life as it is all too habitually lived.

nation's language, thought, and poetry, is profoundly interesting; and by regarding a poet's work as a stage in this course of development we may easily bring ourselves to make it of more importance as poetry than in itself it really is, we may come to use a language of quite exaggerated praise in criticising it; in short, to overrate it. So arises in our poetic judgments the fallacy caused by the estimate which we may call historic. Then, again, a poet or a poem may count to us on grounds personal to ourselves. Our personal affinities, likings, and circumstances have great power to sway our estimate of this or that poet's work, and to make us attach more importance to it as poetry than in itself it really possesses, because to us it is, or has been, of high importance. Here also we overrate the object of our interest, and apply to it a language of praise which is quite exaggerated. And thus we get the source of a second fallacy in our poetic judgments—the fallacy caused by an estimate which we may call personal.

Both fallacies are natural. It is evident how naturally the study of the history and development of a poetry may incline a man to pause over reputations and works once conspicuous but now obscure, and to quarrel with a careless public for skipping, in obedience to mere tradition and habit, from one famous name or work in its national poetry to another, ignorant of what it misses, and of the reason for keeping what it keeps, and of the whole process of growth in its poetry. The French have become diligent students of their own early poetry, which they long neglected; the study makes many of them dissatisfied with their so-called classical poetry, the court-tragedy of the seventeenth century, a poetry which Pellisson [6] long ago reproached with its want of the true poetic stamp, with its *politesse stérile et rampante*,[7] but which nevertheless has reigned in France as absolutely as if it had been the perfection of classical poetry indeed. The dissatisfaction is natural; yet a lively and accomplished critic, M. Charles d'Héricault, the editor of Clément Marot,[8] goes too far when he says that 'the cloud of glory playing round a classic is a mist as dangerous to the future of a literature as it is intolerable for the purposes of history.' 'It hinders,' he goes on, 'it hinders us from seeing more than one single point, the culminating and exceptional point; the summary, fictitious and arbitrary, of a thought and of a work. It substitutes a halo for a physiognomy, it puts a statue where there was once a man, and, hiding from us all trace of the labour, the attempts, the weaknesses, the failures, it claims not study but veneration; it does not show us how the thing is done, it imposes upon us a model. Above all, for the historian this creation of classic personages is inadmissible; for it withdraws the poet from his time, from his proper life, it breaks historical relationships, it blinds criticism by conventional admiration, and renders the investigation of literary origins unacceptable. It gives us a human personage no longer, but a God seated immovable amidst His perfect

6. Paul Pellisson (1624–93), French man of letters. His history of the French Academy was praised by Sainte-Beuve.
7. "Sterile and truckling urbanity." (In French the word "rampant" means just the opposite of what it means in English.)
8. A witty and graceful poet (1496–1544), whose work had some influence on English poets of the 16th century, including Spenser. Héricault's edition of Marot's poems appeared from 1868 to 1872.

work, like Jupiter on Olympus; and hardly will it be possible for the young student, to whom such work is exhibited at such a distance from him, to believe that it did not issue ready made from that divine head.'

All this is brilliantly and tellingly said, but we must plead for a distinction. Everything depends on the reality of a poet's classic character. If he is a dubious classic, let us sift him; if he is a false classic, let us explode him. But if he is a real classic, if his work belongs to the class of the very best (for this is the true and right meaning of the word *classic, classical*), then the great thing for us is to feel and enjoy his work as deeply as ever we can, and to appreciate the wide difference between it and all work which has not the same high character. This is what is salutary, this is what is formative; this is the great benefit to be got from the study of poetry. Everything which interferes with it, which hinders it, is injurious. True, we must read our classic with open eyes, and not with eyes blinded with superstition; we must perceive when his work comes short, when it drops out of the class of the very best, and we must rate it, in such cases, at its proper value. But the use of this negative criticism is not in itself, it is entirely in its enabling us to have a clearer sense and a deeper enjoyment of what is truly excellent. To trace the labour, the attempts, the weaknesses, the failures of a genuine classic, to acquaint oneself with his time and his life and his historical relationships, is mere literary dilettantism unless it has that clear sense and deeper enjoyment for its end. It may be said that the more we know about a classic the better we shall enjoy him; and, if we lived as long as Methuselah [9] and had all of us heads of perfect clearness and wills of perfect steadfastness, this might be true in fact as it is plausible in theory. But the case here is much the same as the case with the Greek and Latin studies of our schoolboys. The elaborate philological groundwork which we require them to lay is in theory an admirable preparation for appreciating the Greek and Latin authors worthily. The more thoroughly we lay the groundwork, the better we shall be able, it may be said, to enjoy the authors. True, if time were not so short, and schoolboys' wits not so soon tired and their power of attention exhausted; only, as it is, the elaborate philological preparation goes on, but the authors are little known and less enjoyed. So with the investigator of 'historic origins' in poetry. He ought to enjoy the true classic all the better for his investigations; he often is distracted from the enjoyment of the best, and with the less good he over-busies himself, and is prone to overrate it in proportion to the trouble which it has cost him.

The idea of tracing historic origins and historical relationships cannot be absent from a compilation like the present. And naturally the poets to be exhibited in it will be assigned to those persons for exhibition who are known to prize them highly, rather than to those who have no special inclination towards them. Moreover, the very occupation with an author, and the business of exhibiting him, disposes us to affirm and amplify his importance. In the present work, therefore, we are sure of frequent temptation to adopt the historic estimate, or the personal estimate, and to forget the real estimate; which latter, nevertheless, we must employ if we are to make poetry yield us

9. Genesis 5:27 says 969 years.

its full benefit. So high is that benefit, the benefit of clearly feeling and of deeply enjoying the really excellent, the truly classic in poetry, that we do well, I say, to set it fixedly before our minds as our object in studying poets and poetry, and to make the desire of attaining it the one principle to which, as the *Imitation* [10] says, whatever we may read or come to know, we always return. *Cum multa legeris et cognoveris, ad unum semper oportet redire principium.*[11]

The historic estimate is likely in especial to affect our judgment and our language when we are dealing with ancient poets; the personal estimate when we are dealing with poets our contemporaries, or at any rate modern. The exaggerations due to the historic estimate are not in themselves, perhaps, of very much gravity. Their report hardly enters the general ear; probably they do not always impose even on the literary men who adopt them. But they lead to a dangerous abuse of language. So we hear Caedmon,[12] amongst our own poets, compared to Milton. I have already noticed the enthusiasm of one accomplished French critic for 'historic origins.' Another eminent French critic, M. Vitet,[13] comments upon that famous document of the early poetry of his nation, the *Chanson de Roland*.[14] It is indeed a most interesting document. The *joculator* or *jongleur* [15] Taillefer, who was with William the Conqueror's army at Hastings, marched before the Norman troops, so said the tradition, singing 'of Charlemagne and of Roland and of Oliver, and of the vassals who died at Roncevaux'; and it is suggested that in the *Chanson de Roland* by one Turoldus or Théroulde,[16] a poem preserved in a manuscript of the twelfth century in the Bodleian Library at Oxford, we have certainly the matter, perhaps even some of the words, of the chant which Taillefer sang. The poem has vigour and freshness; it is not without pathos. But M. Vitet is not satisfied with seeing in it a document of some poetic value, and of very high historic and linguistic value; he sees in it a grand and beautiful work, a monument of epic genius. In its general design he finds the grandiose conception, in its details he finds the constant union of simplicity with greatness, which are the marks, he truly says, of the genuine epic, and distinguish it from the artificial epic of literary ages. One thinks of Homer; this is the sort of praise which is given to Homer, and justly given. Higher praise there cannot well be, and it is the praise due to epic poetry of the highest order only, and to no other. Let us try, then, the *Chanson de Roland* at its best. Roland, mortally wounded, lay himself down under a pine-tree, with his face turned towards Spain and the enemy:—

10. *The Imitation of Christ* by Thomas à Kempis (1380–1471), a devotional work once of great influence.
11. "When you have read and learned many things, you ought always return to the one principle." III.xliii.2.
12. Cædmon, who lived in the 7th century, wrote an Old English poem on the events of Genesis which Milton treated in *Paradise Lost;* hence the comparison.
13. Ludovic Vitet (1802–73), French politician and man of letters.
14. An epic poem of the 11th century. Its climactic episode is the courageous effort of Roland and Oliver, the two leaders of the rearguard of Charlemagne's army, to hold the pass of Roncevaux (Roncevalles) against the Saracens.
15. Minstrel.
16. It is not known exactly who this person is; he may have been the author of the poem, or the author of its source, or merely its scribe.

De plusurs choses à remembrer li prist,
De tantes teres cume li bers cunquist,
De dulce France, des humes de sun lign,
De Carlemagne sun seignor ki l'nurrit.[17]

That is primitive work, I repeat, with an undeniable poetic quality of its own. It deserves such praise, and such praise is sufficient for it. But now turn to Homer:—

"Ὡς φάτο· τοὺς δ' ἤδη κατέχεν φυσίζοος αἶα
ἐν Λακεδαίμονι αὖθι, φίλῃ ἐν πατρίδι γαίῃ.[18]

We are here in another world, another order of poetry altogether; here is rightly due such supreme praise as that which M. Vitet gives to the *Chanson de Roland*. If our words are to have any meaning, if our judgments are to have any solidity, we must not heap that supreme praise upon poetry of an order immeasurably inferior.

Indeed there can be no more useful help for discovering what poetry belongs to the class of the truly excellent, and can therefore do us most good, than to have always in one's mind lines and expressions of the great masters, and to apply them as a touchstone to other poetry. Of course we are not to require this other poetry to resemble them; it may be very dissimilar. But if we have any tact we shall find them, when we have lodged them well in our minds, an infallible touchstone [19] for detecting the presence or absence of high poetic quality, and also the degree of this quality, in all other poetry which we may place beside them. Short passages, even single lines, will serve our turn quite sufficiently. Take the two lines which I have just quoted from Homer, the poet's comment on Helen's mention of her brothers;—or take his

῏Α δειλώ, τί σφῶϊ δόμεν Πηλῆϊ ἄνακτι
θνητῷ; ὑμεῖς δ' ἐστὸν ἀγήρω τ' ἀθανάτω τε.
ἦ ἵνα δυστήνοισι μετ' ἀνδράσιν ἄλγε' ἔχητον; [20]

the address of Zeus to the horses of Peleus;—or take finally this

Καὶ σέ, γέρον, τὸ πρὶν μὲν ἀκούομεν ὄλβιον εἶναι·[21]

the words of Achilles to Priam, a suppliant before him. Take that incomparable line and a half of Dante, Ugolino's tremendous words:—

17. " 'Then began he to call many things to remembrance,—all the lands which his valour conquered, and pleasant France, and the men of his lineage, and Charlemagne his liege lord who nourished him.'—*Chanson de Roland* iii.939–42." (Arnold)
18. " 'So said she; they long since in Earth's soft arms were reposing, / There, in their own dear land, their fatherland, Lacedaemon.'—*Iliad* iii.243–44. (translated by Dr. Hawtrey)." (Arnold)
19. A touchstone is a hard black stone formerly used to test the quality of gold or silver by comparing the streak which is left on the stone by the metal being tested with that left by the standard alloy.
20. " 'Ah, unhappy pair, why gave we you to King Peleus, to a mortal? but ye are without old age, and immortal. Was it that with men born to misery ye might have sorrow?' *Iliad* xvii.443–45." (Arnold) Peleus was the father of Achilles.
21. " 'Nay, and thou too, old man, in former days wast, as we hear, happy.'—*Iliad* xxiv.543." (Arnold) Priam has come to Achilles to beg the return of the corpse of his son Hector, whom Achilles has slain.

Io no piangeva; sì dentro impietrai.
Piangevan elli . . .[22]

take the lovely words of Beatrice to Virgil—

Io son fatta da Dio, sua mercè, tale,
Che la vostra miseria non mi tange,
Nè fiamma d' esto incendio non m' assale . . .[23]

take the simple, but perfect, single line—

In la sua volontade è nostra pace.[24]

Take of Shakespeare a line or two of Henry the Fourth's expostulation with sleep—

Wilt thou upon the high and giddy mast
Seal up the ship-boy's eyes, and rock his brains
In cradle of the rude imperious surge . . .[25]

and take, as well, Hamlet's dying request to Horatio—

If thou didst ever hold me in thy heart,
Absent thee from felicity awhile,
And in this harsh world draw thy breath in pain
To tell my story . . .[26]

Take of Milton that Miltonic passage—

Darken'd so, yet shone
Above them all the archangel; but his face
Deep scars of thunder had intrench'd, and care
Sat on his faded cheek . . .[27]

add two such lines as—

And courage never to submit or yield
And what is else not to be overcome . . .[28]

and finish with the exquisite close to the loss of Proserpine, the loss

. . . which cost Ceres all that pain
To seek her through the world.[29]

These few lines, if we have tact and can use them, are enough even of themselves to keep clear and sound our judgments about poetry, to save us from fallacious estimates of it, to conduct us to a real estimate.

22. " 'I wailed not, so of stone grew I within;—*they* wailed.' *Inferno* xxxiii.39–40." (Arnold)
23. " 'Of such sort hath God, thanked be His mercy, made me, that your misery toucheth me not, neither doth the flame of His fire strike me.'—*Inferno* ii.91–93." (Arnold)
24. " 'In His will is our peace.'—*Paradiso* iii.85." (Arnold)
25. II *Henry IV* III.i.18–20.
26. *Hamlet* V.ii.357–60.
27. *Paradise Lost* I.599–602.
28. *Ibid.* IV.108–9.
29. *Ibid.* IV.271–72.

The specimens I have quoted differ widely from one another, but they have in common this: the possession of the very highest poetical quality. If we are thoroughly penetrated by their power, we shall find that we have acquired a sense enabling us, whatever poetry may be laid before us, to feel the degree in which a high poetical quality is present or wanting there. Critics give themselves great labour to draw out what in the abstract constitutes the characters of a high quality of poetry. It is much better simply to have recourse to concrete examples;—to take specimens of poetry of the high, the very highest, quality, and to say: The characters of a high quality of poetry are what is expressed *there*. They are far better recognised by being felt in the verse of the master, than by being perused in the prose of the critic. Nevertheless if we are urgently pressed to give some critical account of them, we may safely, perhaps, venture on laying down, not indeed how and why the characters arise, but where and in what they arise. They are in the matter and substance of the poetry, and they are in its manner and style. Both of these, the substance and matter on the one hand, the style and manner on the other, have a mark, an accent, of high beauty, worth, and power. But if we are asked to define this mark and accent in the abstract, our answer must be: No, for we should thereby be darkening the question, not clearing it. The mark and accent are as given by the substance and matter of that poetry, by the style and manner of that poetry, and of all other poetry which is akin to it in quality.

Only one thing we may add as to the substance and matter of poetry, guiding ourselves by Aristotle's profound observation that the superiority of poetry over history consists in its possessing a higher truth and a higher seriousness ( φιλοσοφώτερον καὶ σπουδαιότερον ).[30] Let us add, therefore, to what we have said, this: that the substance and matter of the best poetry acquire their special character from possessing, in an eminent degree, truth and seriousness. We may add yet further what is in itself evident, that to the style and manner of the best poetry their special character, their accent, is given by their diction, and, even yet more, by their movement. And though we distinguish between the two characters, the two accents, of superiority, yet they are nevertheless vitally connected one with the other. The superior character of truth and seriousness, in the matter and substance of the best poetry, is inseparable from the superiority of diction and movement marking its style and manner. The two superiorities are closely related, and are in steadfast proportion one to the other. So far as high poetic truth and seriousness are wanting to a poet's matter and substance, so far also, we may be sure, will a high poetic stamp of diction and movement be wanting to his style and manner. In proportion as this high stamp of diction and movement, again, is absent from a poet's style and manner, we shall find, also, that high poetic truth and seriousness are absent from his substance and matter.

So stated, these are but dry generalities; their whole force lies in their application. And I could wish every student of poetry to make the application of them for himself. Made by himself, the application would impress itself upon his mind far more deeply than made by me. Neither will my limits allow me

---

30. *Poetics* IX. Poetry is more philosophical and serious than history because history relates what has been, but poetry relates what might be: the generality of poetry makes it superior to the particularity of history.

to make any full application of the generalities above propounded; but in the hope of bringing out, at any rate, some significance in them, and of establishing an important principle more firmly by their means, I will, in the space which remains to me, follow rapidly from the commencement the course of our English poetry with them in my view.

Once more I return to the early poetry of France, with which our own poetry, in its origins,[31] is indissolubly connected. In the twelfth and thirteenth centuries, that seed-time of all modern language and literature, the poetry of France had a clear predominance in Europe. Of the two divisions of that poetry, its productions in the *langue d'oil* and its productions in the *langue d'oc*,[32] the poetry of the *langue d'oc*, of southern France, of the troubadours, is of importance because of its effect on Italian literature;—the first literature of modern Europe to strike the true and grand note, and to bring forth, as in Dante and Petrarch it brought forth, classics. But the predominance of French poetry in Europe, during the twelfth and thirteenth centuries, is due to its poetry of the *langue d'oil*, the poetry of northern France and of the tongue which is now the French language. In the twelfth century the bloom of this romance-poetry was earlier and stronger in England, at the court of our Anglo-Norman kings, than in France itself. But it was a bloom of French poetry; and as our native poetry formed itself, it formed itself out of this. The romance-poems which took possession of the heart and imagination of Europe in the twelfth and thirteenth centuries are French; 'they are,' as Southey [33] justly says, 'the pride of French literature, nor have we anything which can be placed in competition with them.' Themes were supplied from all quarters; but the romance-setting which was common to them all, and which gained the ear of Europe, was French. This constituted for the French poetry, literature, and language, at the height of the Middle Age, an unchallenged predominance. The Italian Brunetto Latini,[34] the master of Dante, wrote his *Treasure* in French because, he says, 'la parleure en est plus délitable et plus commune à toutes gens.'[35] In the same century, the thirteenth, the French romance-writer, Christian of Troyes,[36] formulates the claims, in chivalry and letters, of France, his native country, as follows:—

> Or vous ert par ce livre apris,
> Que Gresse ot de chevalerie
> Le premier los et de clergie;
> Puis vint chevalerie à Rome,
> Et de la clergie la some,
> Qui ore est en France venue.

31. Arnold takes no account of the long tradition of Old English poetry.
32. *Oil* (*oui*) and *oc* both mean "yes," the former in the northern dialect of French, the latter in the southern dialect. It is from the *langue d'oil* that modern French descends.
33. Robert Southey (1774–1843), appointed Poet Laureate in 1813, the butt of Byron's "The Vision of Judgment."
34. 13th-century Italian scholar and philosopher.
35. "French speech is pleasanter and more in use among all peoples."
36. Actually Chrétien de Troyes flourished in the second half of the 12th century. He was one of the great literary figures of his age. The quotation that follows is from the opening of his *Cligès*.

Diex doinst qu'ele i soit retenue,
Et que li lius li abelisse
Tant que de France n'isse
L'onor qui s'i est arestée!

'Now by this book you will learn that first Greece had the renown for chivalry and letters: then chivalry and the primacy in letters passed to Rome, and now it is come to France. God grant it may be kept there; and that the place may please it so well, that the honour which has come to make stay in France may never depart thence!'

Yet it is now all gone, this French romance-poetry, of which the weight of substance and the power of style are not unfairly represented by this extract from Christian of Troyes. Only by means of the historic estimate can we persuade ourselves now to think that any of it is of poetical importance.

But in the fourteenth century there comes an Englishman nourished on this poetry, taught his trade by this poetry, getting words, rhyme, metre from this poetry; for even of that stanza which the Italians used, and which Chaucer derived immediately from the Italians, the basis and suggestion was probably given in France. Chaucer (I have already named him) fascinated his contemporaries, but so too did Christian of Troyes and Wolfram of Eschenbach.[37] Chaucer's power of fascination, however, is enduring; his poetical importance does not need the assistance of the historic estimate; it is real. He is a genuine source of joy and strength, which is flowing still for us and will flow always. He will be read, as time goes on, far more generally than he is read now. His language is a cause of difficulty for us; but so also, and I think in quite as great a degree, is the language of Burns. In Chaucer's case, as in that of Burns, it is a difficulty to be unhesitatingly accepted and overcome.

If we ask ourselves wherein consists the immense superiority of Chaucer's poetry over the romance-poetry—why it is that in passing from this to Chaucer we suddenly feel ourselves to be in another world, we shall find that his superiority is both in the substance of his poetry and in the style of his poetry. His superiority in substance is given by his large, free, simple, clear yet kindly view of human life,—so unlike the total want, in the romance-poets, of all intelligent command of it. Chaucer has not their helplessness; he has gained the power to survey the world from a central, a truly human point of view. We have only to call to mind the Prologue to *The Canterbury Tales*. The right comment upon it is Dryden's: 'It is sufficient to say, according to the proverb, that *here is God's plenty*.' And again: 'He is a perpetual fountain of good sense.'[38] It is by a large, free, sound representation of things, that poetry, this high criticism of life, has truth of substance; and Chaucer's poetry has truth of substance.

Of his style and manner, if we think first of the romance-poetry and then of Chaucer's divine liquidness of diction, his divine fluidity of movement, it is difficult to speak temperately. They are irresistible, and justify all the rapture with which his successors speak of his 'gold dew-drops of speech.'[39] Johnson

---

37. A German poet of the 12th century, perhaps best known for his *Parzival*. He is a major character in Wagner's opera *Tannhäuser*.
38. Both sentences are from Dryden's Preface to his *Fables* (1700).
39. John Lydgate (c.1370–c.1451) says this in his poem *The Life of Our Lady*.

misses the point entirely when he finds fault with Dryden for ascribing to Chaucer the first refinement of our numbers, and says that Gower also can show smooth numbers and easy rhymes.[40] The refinement of our numbers means something far more than this. A nation may have versifiers with smooth numbers and easy rhymes, and yet may have no real poetry at all. Chaucer is the father of our splendid English poetry; he is our 'well of English undefiled,'[41] because by the lovely charm of his diction, the lovely charm of his movement, he makes an epoch and founds a tradition. In Spenser, Shakespeare, Milton, Keats, we can follow the tradition of the liquid diction, the fluid movement, of Chaucer; at one time it is his liquid diction of which in these poets we feel the virtue, and at another time it is his fluid movement. And the virtue is irresistible.

Bounded as is my space, I must yet find room for an example of Chaucer's virtue, as I have given examples to show the virtue of the great classics. I feel disposed to say that a single line is enough to show the charm of Chaucer's verse; that merely one line like this—

O martyr souded in virginitee![42]

has a virtue of manner and movement such as we shall not find in all the verse of romance-poetry;—but this is saying nothing. The virtue is such as we shall not find, perhaps, in all English poetry, outside the poets whom I have named as the special inheritors of Chaucer's tradition. A single line, however, is too little if we have not the strain of Chaucer's verse well in our memory; let us take a stanza. It is from *The Prioress's Tale*, the story of the Christian child murdered in a Jewery—

My throte is cut unto my nekke-bone
Saidè this child, and as by way of kinde
I should have deyd, yea, longè time agone;
But Jesu Christ, as ye in bookès finde,
Will that his glory last and be in minde,
And for the worship of his mother dere
Yet may I sing O Alma [43] loud and clere.

Wordsworth has modernised this Tale, and to feel how delicate and evanescent is the charm of verse, we have only to read Wordsworth's first three lines of this stanza after Chaucer's—

My throat is cut unto the bone, I trow,
Said this young child, and by the law of kind
I should have died, yea, many hours ago.

The charm is departed. It is often said that the power of liquidness and fluidity in Chaucer's verse was dependent upon a free, a licentious dealing with lan-

40. John Gower (c.1325–1408), poet and friend of Chaucer; Johnson makes the claim for Gower's refinement in *Idler*, No. 72.
41. Spenser thus praised Chaucer in *The Faerie Queene* IV.ii.32.
42. *The Prioress's Tale*, l. 127. "The French *soudé*: soldered, fixed fast." (Arnold) Actually Chaucer wrote "souded to."
43. The hymn *Alma Redemptoris Mater* (O Gracious Mother of the Redeemer).

guage, such as is now impossible; upon a liberty, such as Burns too enjoyed, of making words like *neck, bird,* into a dissyllable by adding to them, and words like *cause, rhyme,* into a dissyllable by sounding the *e* mute. It is true that Chaucer's fluidity is conjoined with this liberty, and is admirably served by it; but we ought not to say that it was dependent upon it. It was dependent upon his talent. Other poets with a like liberty do not attain to the fluidity of Chaucer; Burns himself does not attain to it. Poets, again, who have a talent akin to Chaucer's, such as Shakespeare or Keats, have known how to attain to his fluidity without the like liberty.

And yet Chaucer is not one of the great classics. His poetry transcends and effaces, easily and without effort, all the romance-poetry of Catholic Christendom; it transcends and effaces all the English poetry contemporary with it; it transcends and effaces all the English poetry subsequent to it down to the age of Elizabeth. Of such avail is poetic truth of substance, in its natural and necessary union with poetic truth of style. And yet, I say, Chaucer is not one of the great classics. He has not their accent. What is wanting to him is suggested by the mere mention of the name of the first great classic of Christendom, the immortal poet who died eighty years before Chaucer,—Dante. The accent of such verse as

> In la sua volontade è nostra pace . . .[44]

is altogether beyond Chaucer's reach; we praise him, but we feel that this accent is out of the question for him. It may be said that it was necessarily out of the reach of any poet in the England of that stage of growth. Possibly; but we are to adopt a real, not a historic, estimate of poetry. However we may account for its absence, something is wanting, then, to the poetry of Chaucer, which poetry must have before it can be placed in the glorious class of the best. And there is no doubt what that something is. It is the σπουδαιότης,[45] the high and excellent seriousness, which Aristotle assigns as one of the grand virtues of poetry. The substance of Chaucer's poetry, his view of things and his criticism of life, has largeness, freedom, shrewdness, benignity; but it has not this high seriousness. Homer's criticism of life has it, Dante's has it, Shakespeare's has it. It is this chiefly which gives to our spirits what they can rest upon; and with the increasing demands of our modern ages upon poetry, this virtue of giving us what we can rest upon will be more and more highly esteemed. A voice from the slums of Paris, fifty or sixty years after Chaucer, the voice of poor Villon [46] out of his life of riot and crime, has at its happy moments (as, for instance, in the last stanza of *La Belle Heaulmière* [47]) more of this

44. "In His will is our peace."
45. The word may be transliterated as "spoudaiotes."
46. François Villon ( 1431–? ), French poet and brawler, who, after long neglect, came to be admired in the 19th century. Swinburne translated the poem of which Arnold speaks.
47. "The name *Heaulmière* is said to be derived from a headdress ( helm ) worn as a mark by courtesans. In Villon's ballad, a poor old creature of this class laments her days of youth and beauty. The last stanza of the ballad runs thus—Ainsi le bon temps regretons / Entre nous, pauvres vieilles sottes. / Assises bas, à croppetons, / Tout en ung tas comme pelottes; / A petit feu de chenevottes / Tost allumées, tost estainctes. / Et jadis fusmes si mognottes! / Ainsi en prend à maintz et maintes.—Thus amongst ourselves we regret the good time, poor silly old things, low-seated on our heels, all in a heap like so many balls,

important poetic virtue of seriousness than all the productions of Chaucer. But its apparition in Villon, and in men like Villon is fitful; the greatness of the great poets, the power of their criticism of life, is that their virtue is sustained.

To our praise, therefore, of Chaucer as a poet there must be this limitation; he lacks the high seriousness of the great classics, and therewith an important part of their virtue. Still, the main fact for us to bear in mind about Chaucer is his sterling value according to that real estimate which we firmly adopted for all poets. He has poetic truth of substance, though he has not high poetic serious-ness, and corresponding to his truth of substance he has an exquisite virtue of style and manner. With him is born our real poetry.

For my present purpose I need not dwell on our Elizabethan poetry, or on the continuation and close of this poetry in Milton. We all of us profess to be agreed in the estimate of this poetry; we all of us recognise it as great poetry, our greatest, and Shakespeare and Milton as our poetical classics. The real esti-mate,[48] here, has universal currency. With the next age of our poetry divergency and difficulty begin. An historic estimate of that poetry has established itself; and the question is, whether it will be found to coincide with the real estimate.

The age of Dryden, together with our whole eighteenth century which followed it, sincerely believed itself to have produced poetical classics of its own, and even to have made advance, in poetry, beyond all its predecessors. Dryden regards as not seriously disputable the opinion 'that the sweetness of English verse was never understood or practised by our fathers.'[49] Cowley could see nothing at all in Chaucer's poetry.[50] Dryden heartily admired, and, as we have seen, praised its matter admirably; but of its exquisite manner and movement all he can find to say is that 'there is the rude sweetness of a Scotch tune in it, which is natural and pleasing, though not perfect.'[51] Addison, wish-ing to praise Chaucer's numbers, compares them with Dryden's own.[52] And all through the eighteenth century, and down even into our own times, the stereotyped phrase of approbation for good verse found in our early poetry has been, that it even approached the verse of Dryden, Addison, Pope, and Johnson.

Are Dryden and Pope poetical classics? Is the historic estimate, which repre-sents them as such, and which has been so long established that it cannot easily give way, the real estimate? Wordsworth and Coleridge, as is well known, denied it; but the authority of Wordsworth and Coleridge does not weigh much with the young generation, and there are many signs to show that the eighteenth century and its judgments are coming into favour again. Are the favourite poets of the eighteenth century classics?

It is impossible within my present limits to discuss the question fully. And what man of letters would not shrink from seeming to dispose dictatorially of

---

by a little fire of hemp-stalks, soon lighted, soon spent. And once we were such darlings! So fares it with many and many a one." (Arnold)

48. By "real estimate" Arnold means the estimate which is made of the intrinsic quality of the work, without reference to the personal or historical considerations he has spoken of earlier.

49. Preface to the *Fables.*

50. Dryden cites this opinion, *ibid.*

51. *Ibid.*

52. In *An Account of the Greatest English Poets.*

the claims of two men who are, at any rate, such masters in letters as Dryden and Pope; two men of such admirable talent, both of them, and one of them, Dryden, a man, on all sides, of such energetic and genial power? And yet, if we are to gain the full benefit from poetry, we must have the real estimate of it. I cast about for some mode of arriving, in the present case, at such an estimate without offence. And perhaps the best way is to begin, as it is easy to begin, with cordial praise.

When we find Chapman,[53] the Elizabethan translator of Homer, expressing himself in his preface thus: 'Though truth in her very nakedness sits in so deep a pit, that from Gades to Aurora and Ganges few eyes can sound her, I hope yet those few here will so discover and confirm that, the date being out of her darkness in this morning of our poet, he shall now gird his temples with the sun,'—we pronounce that such a prose is intolerable. When we find Milton writing: 'And long it was not after, when I was confirmed in this opinion, that he, who would not be frustrate of his hope to write well hereafter in laudable things, ought himself to be a true poem,' [54]—we pronounce that such a prose has its own grandeur, but that it is obsolete and inconvenient. But when we find Dryden telling us: 'What Virgil wrote in the vigour of his age, in plenty and at ease, I have undertaken to translate in my declining years; struggling with wants, oppressed with sickness, curbed in my genius, liable to be misconstrued in all I write,' [55]—then we exclaim that here at last we have the true English prose, a prose such as we would all gladly use if we only knew how. Yet Dryden was Milton's contemporary.

But after the Restoration the time had come when our nation felt the imperious need of a fit prose. So, too, the time had likewise come when our nation felt the imperious need of freeing itself from the absorbing preoccupation which religion in the Puritan age had exercised. It was impossible that this freedom should be brought about without some negative excess, without some neglect and impairment of the religious life of the soul; and the spiritual history of the eighteenth century shows us that the freedom was not achieved without them. Still, the freedom was achieved; the preoccupation, an undoubtedly baneful and retarding one if it had continued, was got rid of. And as with religion amongst us at that period, so it was also with letters. A fit prose was a necessity; but it was impossible that a fit prose should establish itself amongst us without some touch of frost to the imaginative life of the soul. The needful qualities for a fit prose are regularity, uniformity, precision, balance. The men of letters, whose destiny it may be to bring their nation to the attainment of a fit prose, must of necessity, whether they work in prose or in verse, give a predominating, and almost exclusive attention to the qualities of regularity, uniformity, precision, balance. But an almost exclusive attention to these qualities involves some repression and silencing of poetry.

We are to regard Dryden as the puissant and glorious founder, Pope as the splendid high priest, of our age of prose and reason, of our excellent and

53. George Chapman (1559?–1634?), playwright and translator; Arnold quotes from the commentary after his translation of Book I of the *Iliad*.
54. From *An Apology for Smectymnuus*.
55. From "Postcript to the Reader"—Dryden's translation of Virgil (1697).

indispensable eighteenth century. For the purposes of their mission and destiny their poetry, like their prose, is admirable. Do you ask me whether Dryden's verse, take it almost where you will, is not good?

> A milk-white Hind, immortal and unchanged,
> Fed on the lawns and in the forest ranged.[56]

I answer: Admirable for the purposes of the inaugurator of an age of prose and reason. Do you ask me whether Pope's verse, take it almost where you will, is not good?

> To Hounslow Heath I point, and Banstead Down;
> Thence comes your mutton, and these chicks my own.[57]

I answer: Admirable for the purposes of the high priest of an age of prose and reason. But do you ask me whether such verse proceeds from men with an adequate poetic criticism of life, from men whose criticism of life has a high seriousness, or even, without that high seriousness, has poetic largeness, freedom, insight, benignity? Do you ask me whether the application of ideas to life in the verse of these men, often a powerful application, no doubt, is a powerful *poetic* application? Do you ask me whether the poetry of these men has either the matter or the inseparable manner of such an adequate poetic criticism; whether it has the accent of

> Absent thee from felicity awhile . . .

or of

> And what is else not to be overcome . . .

or of

> O martyr souded in virginitee!

I answer: It has not and cannot have them; it is the poetry of the builders of an age of prose and reason. Though they may write in verse, though they may in a certain sense be masters of the art of versification, Dryden and Pope are not classics of our poetry, they are classics of our prose.

Gray is our poetical classic of that literature and age; the position of Gray is singular, and demands a word of notice here. He has not the volume or the power of poets who, coming in times more favourable, have attained to an independent criticism of life. But he lived with the great poets, he lived, above all, with the Greeks, through perpetually studying and enjoying them; and he caught their poetic point of view for regarding life, caught their poetic manner. The point of view and the manner are not self-sprung in him, he caught them of others; and he had not the free and abundant use of them. But whereas Addison and Pope never had the use of them, Gray had the use of them at times. He is the scantiest and frailest of classics in our poetry, but he is a classic.

And now, after Gray, we are met, as we draw towards the end of the eighteenth century, we are met by the great name of Burns. We enter now on

---

56. The opening lines of *The Hind and the Panther.*
57. *Imitations of Horace* II.2.143–44. Certainly Arnold has not done justice to Pope's powers by his choice of this couplet!

times where the personal estimate of poets begins to be rife, and where the real estimate of them is not reached without difficulty. But in spite of the disturbing pressures of personal partiality, of national partiality, let us try to reach a real estimate of the poetry of Burns.

By his English poetry Burns in general belongs to the eighteenth century, and has little importance for us.

> Mark ruffian Violence, distain'd with crimes,
> Rousing elate in these degenerate times;
> View unsuspecting Innocence a prey,
> As guileful Fraud points out the erring way;
> While subtle Litigation's pliant tongue
> The life-blood equal sucks of Right and Wrong! [58]

Evidently this is not the real Burns, or his name and fame would have disappeared long ago. Nor is Clarinda's love-poet, Sylvander,[59] the real Burns either. But he tells us himself: 'These English songs gravel me to death. I have not the command of the language that I have of my native tongue. In fact, I think that my ideas are more barren in English than in Scotch. I have been at *Duncan Gray* to dress it in English, but all I can do is desperately stupid.' [60] We English turn naturally, in Burns, to the poems in our own language, because we can read them easily; but in those poems we have not the real Burns.

The real Burns is of course in his Scotch poems. Let us boldly say that of this poetry, a poetry dealing perpetually with Scotch drink, Scotch religion, and Scotch manners, a Scotchman's estimate is apt to be personal. A Scotchman is used to this world of Scotch drink, Scotch religion, and Scotch manners; he has a tenderness for it; he meets its poet half way. In this tender mood he reads pieces like the *Holy Fair* or *Halloween*. But this world of Scotch drink, Scotch religion, and Scotch manners is against a poet, not for him, when it is not a partial countryman who reads him; for in itself it is not a beautiful world, and no one can deny that it is of advantage to a poet to deal with a beautiful world. Burns's world of Scotch drink, Scotch religion, and Scotch manners, is often a harsh, a sordid, a repulsive world; even the world of his *Cottar's Saturday Night* is not a beautiful world. No doubt a poet's criticism of life may have such truth and power that it triumphs over its world and delights us. Burns may triumph over this world, often he does triumph over his world, but let us observe how and where. Burns is the first case we have had where the bias of the personal estimate tends to mislead; let us look at him closely—he can bear it.

Many of his admirers will tell us that we have Burns, convivial, genuine, delightful, here—

> Leeze me on drink! it gies us mair
> Than either school or college;
> It kindles wit, it waukens lair,
> It pangs us fou o' knowledge.

58. "On the Death of Lord Dundas," ll. 25–30.
59. Under this affected pastoral name Burns carried on a correspondence with a Mrs. Maclehose, whom he styled Clarinda.
60. In a letter of October 19, 1794.

>Be't whisky gill or penny wheep
>    Or ony stronger potion,
>It never fails, on drinking deep,
>    To kittle up our notion
>            By night or day.[61]

There is a great deal of that sort of thing in Burns, and it is unsatisfactory, not because it is bacchanalian poetry, but because it has not that accent of sincerity which bacchanalian poetry, to do it justice, very often has. There is something in it of bravado, something which makes us feel that we have not the man speaking to us with his real voice; something, therefore, poetically unsound.

With still more confidence, will his admirers tell us that we have the genuine Burns, the great poet, when his strain asserts the independence, equality, dignity, of men, as in the famous song *For a' that and a' that*—

>A prince can mak' a belted knight,
>    A marquis, duke, and a' that;
>But an honest man's aboon his might,
>    Guid faith he mauna fa' that!
>        For a' that, and a' that,
>            Their dignities, and a' that,
>        The pith o' sense, and pride o' worth,
>            Are higher rank than a' that.

Here they find his grand, genuine touches; and still more, when this puissant genius, who so often set morality at defiance, falls moralising—

>The sacred lowe o' weel-placed love
>    Luxuriantly indulge it;
>But never tempt th' illicit rove,
>    Tho' naething should divulge it:
>I waive the quantum o' the sin,
>    The hazard o' concealing,
>But och! it hardens a' within,
>    And petrifies the feeling.[62]

Or in a higher strain—

>Who made the heart, 'tis He alone
>    Decidedly can try us;
>He knows each chord, its various tone;
>    Each spring, its various bias.
>Then at the balance let's be mute,
>    We never can adjust it;
>What's *done* we partly may compute,
>    But know not what's resisted.[63]

61. "The Holy Fair," ll. 163–71.
62. "Epistle to a Young Friend," ll. 41–48.
63. "Address to the Unco Guid," ll. 57–64.

Or in a better strain yet, a strain, his admirers will say, unsurpassable—

> To make a happy fire-side clime
> To weans and wife,
> That's the true pathos and sublime
> Of human life.[64]

There is criticism of life for you, the admirers of Burns will say to us; there is the application of ideas to life! There is, undoubtedly. The doctrine of the last-quoted lines coincides almost exactly with what was the aim and end, Xenophon tells us,[65] of all the teaching of Socrates. And the application is a powerful one; made by a man of vigorous understanding, and (need I say?) a master of language.

But for supreme poetical success more is required than the powerful application of ideas to life; it must be an application under the conditions fixed by the laws of poetic truth and poetic beauty. Those laws fix as an essential condition, in the poet's treatment of such matters as are here in question, high seriousness;—the high seriousness which comes from absolute sincerity. The accent of high seriousness, born of absolute sincerity, is what gives to such verse as

> In la sua volontade è nostra pace  . . .

to such criticism of life as Dante's, its power. Is this accent felt in the passages which I have been quoting from Burns? Surely not; surely, if our sense is quick, we must perceive that we have not in those passages a voice from the very inmost soul of the genuine Burns; he is not speaking to us from these depths, he is more or less preaching. And the compensation for admiring such passages less, from missing the perfect poetic accent in them, will be that we shall admire more the poetry where that accent is found.

No; Burns, like Chaucer, comes short of the high seriousness of the great classics, and the virtue of matter and manner which goes with that high seriousness is wanting to his work. At moments he touches it in a profound and passionate melancholy, as in those four immortal lines taken by Byron as a motto for *The Bride of Abydos*, but which have in them a depth of poetic quality such as resides in no verse of Byron's own—

> Had we never loved sae kindly,
> Had we never loved sae blindly,
> Never met, or never parted,
> We had ne'er been broken-hearted.

But a whole poem of that quality Burns cannot make; the rest, in the *Farewell to Nancy*,[66] is verbiage.

We arrive best at the real estimate of Burns, I think, by conceiving his work as having truth of matter and truth of manner, but not the accent or

---

64. "Epistle to Dr. Blacklock," ll. 51–54.
65. In *Memorabilia* IV.iv. Xenophon (c.427–c.354) was a Greek historian and essayist best known for the *Anabasis*.
66. The poem is also called "Ae Fond Kiss." Arnold quotes ll. 13–16.

the poetic virtue of the highest masters. His genuine criticism of life, when the sheer poet in him speaks, is ironic; it is not—

> Thou Power Supreme, whose mighty scheme
> These woes of mine fulfil,
> Here firm I rest, they must be best
> Because they are Thy will! [67]

It is far rather: *Whistle owre the lave o't!* Yet we may say of him as of Chaucer, that of life and the world, as they come before him, his view is large, free, shrewd, benignant,—truly poetic, therefore; and his manner of rendering what he sees is to match. But we must note, at the same time, his great difference from Chaucer. The freedom of Chaucer is heightened, in Burns, by a fiery, reckless energy; the benignity of Chaucer deepens, in Burns, into an overwhelming sense of the pathos of things;—of the pathos of human nature, the pathos, also, of non-human nature. Instead of the fluidity of Chaucer's manner, the manner of Burns has spring, bounding swiftness. Burns is by far the greater force, though he has perhaps less charm. The world of Chaucer is fairer, richer, more significant than that of Burns; but when the largeness and freedom of Burns get full sweep, as in *Tam o' Shanter*, or still more in that puissant and splendid production, *The Jolly Beggars*, his world may be what it will, his poetic genius triumphs over it. In the world of *The Jolly Beggars* there is more than hideousness and squalor, there is bestiality; yet the piece is a superb poetic success. It has a breadth, truth, and power which make the famous scene in Auerbach's Cellar, of Goethe's *Faust*,[68] seem artificial and tame beside it, and which are only matched by Shakespeare and Aristophanes.

Here, where his largeness and freedom serve him so admirably, and also in those poems and songs where to shrewdness he adds infinite archness and wit, and to benignity infinite pathos, where his manner is flawless, and a perfect poetic whole is the result,—in things like the address to the mouse whose home he had ruined, in things like *Duncan Gray, Tam Glen, Whistle and I'll Come To You My Lad, Auld Lang Syne* (this list might be made much longer)—here we have the genuine Burns, of whom the real estimate must be high indeed. Not a classic, nor with the excellent σπουδαιότης [69] of the great classics, nor with a verse rising to a criticism of life and a virtue like theirs; but a poet with thorough truth of substance and an answering truth of style, giving us a poetry sound to the core. We all of us have a leaning towards the pathetic, and may be inclined perhaps to prize Burns most for his touches of piercing, sometimes almost intolerable, pathos; for verse like—

> We twa hae paidl't i' the burn
> From mornin' sun till dine;
> But seas between us braid hae roar'd
> Sin auld lang syne . . .[70]

67. "Winter: A Dirge," ll. 17–20.
68. As his first act, after his compact with Mephistopheles, Faust visits a wine cellar and engages in riotous horseplay with a group of drunken students.
69. "High seriousness."
70. "Auld Lang Syne," ll. 17–20.

where he is as lovely as he is sound. But perhaps it is by the perfection of soundness of his lighter and archer masterpieces that he is poetically most wholesome for us. For the votary misled by a personal estimate of Shelley, as so many of us have been, are, and will be,—of that beautiful spirit building his many-coloured haze of words and images

> Pinnacled dim in the intense inane— [71]

no contact can be wholesomer than the contact with Burns at his arohoot and soundest. Side by side with the

> On the brink of the night and the morning
>     My coursers are wont to respire,
> But the Earth has just whispered a warning
>     That their flight must be swifter than fire . . .[72]

of *Prometheus Unbound*, how salutary, how very salutary, to place this from *Tam Glen*—

> My minnie does constantly deave me
>     And bids me beware o' young men;
> They flatter, she says, to deceive me;
>     But wha can think sae o' Tam Glen?

But we enter on burning ground as we approach the poetry of times so near to us—poetry like that of Byron, Shelley, and Wordsworth—of which the estimates are so often not only personal, but personal with passion. For my purpose, it is enough to have taken the single case of Burns, the first poet we come to of whose work the estimate formed is evidently apt to be personal, and to have suggested how we may proceed, using the poetry of the great classics as a sort of touchstone, to correct this estimate, as we had previously corrected by the same means the historic estimate where we met with it. A collection like the present, with its succession of celebrated names and celebrated poems, offers a good opportunity to us for resolutely endeavouring to make our estimates of poetry real. I have sought to point out a method which will help us in making them so, and to exhibit it in use so far as to put any one who likes in a way of applying it for himself.

At any rate the end to which the method and the estimate are designed to lead, and from leading to which, if they do lead to it, they get their whole value,—the benefit of being able clearly to feel and deeply to enjoy the best, the truly classic, in poetry,—is an end, let me say it once more at parting, of supreme importance. We are often told that an era is opening in which we are to see multitudes of a common sort of readers, and masses of a common

71. Shelley, *Prometheus Unbound* III.iv.204.
72. *Ibid.* II.v.1–4. In his essay on Shelley, included in *Essays in Criticism, Second Series*, Arnold says of Shelley's poetry, "Let no one suppose that a want of humour and a self-delusion such as Shelley's have no effect upon a man's poetry. The man Shelley, in very truth, is not entirely sane, and Shelley's poetry is not entirely sane either. The Shelley of actual life is a vision of beauty and radiance, indeed, but availing nothing, effecting nothing. And in poetry, no less than in life, he is a beautiful and ineffectual angel beating in the void his luminous wings in vain."

sort of literature; that such readers do not want and could not relish anything better than such literature, and that to provide it is becoming a vast and profitable industry. Even if good literature entirely lost currency with the world, it would still be abundantly worthwhile to continue to enjoy it by oneself. But it never will lose currency with the world, in spite of momentary appearances; it never will lose supremacy. Currency and supremacy are insured to it, not indeed by the world's deliberate and conscious choice, but by something far deeper,—by the instinct of self-preservation in humanity.

1880                                                                  1880, 1888

# Literature and Science

Arnold's reputation in the United States developed slowly, but by the end of the 1870's it was firmly established. In 1883, moved by the financial considerations of his approaching retirement from his post in the Education Office, Arnold agreed to make a lecture tour of America. Like that of Oscar Wilde in the previous year, it was a strenuous experience, not the least because of the ambivalence with which the lecturer was regarded. In the later nineteenth century, Americans were avid for what they had learned from Arnold to call "culture," which they presumed to have its source in Europe, particularly in England. At the same time, they were intent upon making it plain that they would accept no condescension from those who brought the precious commodity from across the ocean. Arnold certainly had no intention of condescending, for he was the most courteous of men, but he was, after all, coming to speak the Word, his English manners were thought odd and "superior," and the opinions he had expressed about American life, while not censorious, had not been exactly flattering; there was in consequence a considerable amount of ragging in the press and a constant chatter of defensive gossip about his manner on the platform, his voice, his whiskers, his ruddy complexion, his eye-glass, the cut of his trousers. Through it all Arnold maintained his good humor and good sense and by the end of his visit he had won almost all hearts. He, for his part, took home a better opinion of American life than the one he had brought with him.

He had prepared for the tour a repertory of three lectures, all being on matters likely to engage American interest. One was on Emerson, the nation's pre-eminent writer, who had died the year before. Another, Numbers; or the Majority and the Remnant, was a consideration of the role of intellect in a democracy. The third was Literature and Science, which he had given as the Rede Lecture at Cambridge University in 1881 and revised with his American audiences in mind. All three lectures were published in Discourses in America (1885).

So far as Literature and Science is controversial, it is a reply to the address Science and Culture, which T. H. Huxley had delivered in 1880 on the occasion of the opening of the Science College at Birmingham. This institution had been endowed by Sir Josiah Mason, a wealthy manufacturer of humble origin, who had stipulated in the trust that no provision be made at the college for "mere literary instruction and education." Had Huxley been consulted on this point, he would almost certainly have urged against it, for he was a man of wide cultivation, responsive to literature, and firmly of the opinion that literature was of value in the education of scientists. But he was, Darwin excepted, the best-known English scientist of his time, the chief proponent of the scientific outlook, and he had ample reason to feel that the neglect of science by the English educational system constituted an intellectual scandal. Whatever his private reservations about Mason's exclusion of literature from the college may have been, he consented to accept and defend it publicly because it redressed the grievance of science at being kept from its proper place in the intellectual life of the nation. He characterized the culpable national attitude to science by reference to the definition of culture that Arnold had put forward. He did not quarrel with Arnold's general conception of culture, of which criticism is the essence; on the contrary, he expressed himself as being in hearty accord with it. But he objected to it in the one respect that it assumes that "the best that has been thought and said in the world" consists chiefly, if not exclusively, of literature. Science is given no part in it. In advancing science to a place in the body of knowledge and thought with which culture works, Huxley is at pains to say that he is concerned only with the enlarging intellectual effect of scientific study, not at all with the utilitarian application of science to industry. And he goes on to suggest that science has potentially as much bearing upon the practical moral life of society as Arnold says literature has: the laws of social existence no less than those of nature are susceptible of being known through the methods of science.

Huxley was wholly justified in his protest of the insensate indifference to science on the part of those who had charge of the educational system of England, and his claims for the critical and cultural importance of the scientific mode of thought are obviously cogent. Yet Arnold was right in perceiving that his lecture, though temperate and rational in itself, was a portent of the modern tendency to belittle the educational value of humane letters; and it is to this threat that his own lecture eloquently responds.


*From* Literature and Science

Practical people talk with a smile of Plato and of his absolute ideas; [1] and it is impossible to deny that Plato's ideas do often seem unpractical and impracticable, and especially when one views them in connection with the life of a great work-a-day world like the United States. The necessary staple of the life of such a world Plato regards with disdain; handicraft and trade and the working professions he regards with disdain; but what becomes of the life of an industrial modern community if you take handicraft and trade and the working professions out of it? The base mechanic arts and handicrafts, says Plato, bring about a natural weakness in the principle of excellence in a man, so that he cannot govern the ignoble growths in him, but nurses them, and cannot understand fostering any other. Those who exercise such arts and trades, as they have their bodies, he says, marred by their vulgar businesses,

1. For Plato ideas are "absolute" in the sense that they are the essential "forms" or archetypes of things—of material objects, of institutions, of virtues—and remain constant through all the changes which take place in those things as they are apparent to man's senses and intellect. He conceived ideas, thus defined, to have their existence not in the mind but in a realm of their own.

so they have their souls, too, bowed and broken by them. And if one of these uncomely people has a mind to seek self-culture and philosophy, Plato compares him to a bald little tinker, who has scraped together money, and has got his release from service, and has had a bath, and bought a new coat, and is rigged out like a bridegroom about to marry the daughter of his master who has fallen into poor and helpless estate.[2]

Nor do the working professions fare any better than trade at the hands of Plato. He draws for us an inimitable picture of the working lawyer, and of his life of bondage; he shows how this bondage from his youth up has stunted and warped him, and made him small and crooked of soul, encompassing him with difficulties which he is not man enough to rely on justice and truth as means to encounter, but has recourse, for help out of them, to falsehood and wrong. And so, says Plato, this poor creature is bent and broken, and grows up from boy to man without a particle of soundness in him, although exceedingly smart and clever in his own esteem.[3]

One cannot refuse to admire the artist who draws these pictures. But we say to ourselves that his ideas show the influence of a primitive and obsolete order of things, when the warrior caste and the priestly caste were alone in honour, and the humble work of the world was done by slaves. We have now changed all that; the modern majesty consists in work, as Emerson declares; [4] and in work, we may add, principally of such plain and dusty kind as the work of cultivators of the ground, handicraftsmen, men of trade and business, men of the working professions. Above all is this true in a great industrious community such as that of the United States.

Now education, many people go on to say, is still mainly governed by the ideas of men like Plato, who lived when the warrior caste and the priestly or philosophical class were alone in honour, and the really useful part of the community were slaves. It is an education fitted for persons of leisure in such a community. This education passed from Greece and Rome to the feudal communities of Europe, where also the warrior caste and the priestly caste were alone held in honour, and where the really useful and working part of the community, though not nominally slaves as in the pagan world, were practically not much better off than slaves, and not more seriously regarded. And how absurd it is, people end by saying, to inflict this education upon an industrious modern community, where very few indeed are persons of leisure, and the mass to be considered has not leisure, but is bound, for its own great good, and for the great good of the world at large, to plain labour and to industrial pursuits, and the education in question tends necessarily to make men dissatisfied with these pursuits and unfitted for them!

That is what is said. So far I must defend Plato, as to plead that his view of education and studies is in the general, as it seems to me, sound enough, and fitted for all sorts and conditions of men, whatever their pursuits may be. 'An intelligent man,' says Plato, 'will prize those studies which result in his soul getting soberness, righteousness, and wisdom, and will less value the

2. *Republic* VI.ix.
3. *Theatatus* 172–73.
4. *Literary Ethics.* "Feudalism and Orientalism had long enough thought it majestic to do nothing: the modern majesty consists in work."

others.'[5] I cannot consider *that* a bad description of the aim of education, and of the motives which should govern us in the choice of studies, whether we are preparing ourselves for a hereditary seat in the English House of Lords or for the pork trade in Chicago.

Still I admit that Plato's world was not ours, that his scorn of trade and handicraft is fantastic, that he had no conception of a great industrial community such as that of the United States, and that such a community must and will shape its education to suit its own needs. If the usual education handed down to it from the past does not suit it, it will certainly before long drop this and try another. The usual education in the past has been mainly literary. The question is whether the studies which were long supposed to be the best for all of us are practically the best now; whether others are not better. The tyranny of the past, many think, weighs on us injuriously in the predominance given to letters in education. The question is raised whether, to meet the needs of our modern life, the predominance ought not now to pass from letters to science; and naturally the question is nowhere raised with more energy than here in the United States. The design of abasing what is called 'mere literary instruction and education,' and of exalting what is called 'sound, extensive, and practical scientific knowledge,' is, in this intensely modern world of the United States, even more perhaps than in Europe, a very popular design, and makes great and rapid progress.

I am going to ask whether the present movement for ousting letters from their old predominance in education, and for transferring the predominance in education to the natural sciences, whether this brisk and flourishing movement ought to prevail, and whether it is likely that in the end it really will prevail. An objection may be raised which I will anticipate. My own studies have been almost wholly in letters, and my visits to the field of the natural sciences have been very slight and inadequate, although those sciences have always strongly moved my curiosity. A man of letters, it will perhaps be said, is not competent to discuss the comparative merits of letters and natural science as means of education. To this objection I reply, first of all, that his incompetence, if he attempts the discussion but is really incompetent for it, will be abundantly visible; nobody will be taken in; he will have plenty of sharp observers and critics to save mankind from that danger. But the line I am going to follow is, as you will soon discover, so extremely simple, that perhaps it may be followed without failure even by one who for a more ambitious line of discussion would be quite incompetent.

Some of you may possibly remember a phrase of mine which has been the object of a good deal of comment; an observation to the effect that in our culture, the aim being *to know ourselves and the world*, we have, as the means to this end, *to know the best which has been thought and said in the world.*[6] A man of science, who is also an excellent writer and the very prince of debaters, Professor Huxley, in a discourse at the opening of Sir Josiah Mason's college at Birmingham,[7] laying hold of this phrase, expanded it by quoting

5. *Republic* IX.xiii.
6. See *The Function of Criticism at the Present Time*, fourth paragraph from the end.
7. Thomas Henry Huxley (1825–95), the famous English biologist, defender of Darwin's theory of evolution, and popularizer of science. The lecture, *Science and Culture*, was

some more words of mine, which are these: 'The civilised world is to be regarded as now being, for intellectual and spiritual purposes, one great confederation, bound to a joint action and working to a common result; and whose members have for their proper outfit a knowledge of Greek, Roman, and Eastern antiquity, and of one another. Special local and temporary advantages being put out of account, that modern nation will in the intellectual and spiritual sphere make most progress, which most thoroughly carries out this programme.'

Now on my phrase, thus enlarged, Professor Huxley remarks that when I speak of the above-mentioned knowledge as enabling us to know ourselves and the world, I assert *literature* to contain the materials which suffice for thus making us know ourselves and the world. But it is not by any means clear, says he, that after having learnt all which ancient and modern literatures have to tell us, we have laid a sufficiently broad and deep foundation for that criticism of life, that knowledge of ourselves and the world, which constitutes culture. On the contrary, Professor Huxley declares that he finds himself 'wholly unable to admit that either nations or individuals will really advance, if their outfit draws nothing from the stores of physical science. An army without weapons of precision, and with no particular base of operations, might more hopefully enter upon a campaign on the Rhine, than a man, devoid of a knowledge of what physical science has done in the last century, upon a criticism of life.'

This shows how needful it is for those who are to discuss any matter together, to have a common understanding as to the sense of the terms they employ,—how needful, and how difficult. What Professor Huxley says, implies just the reproach which is so often brought against the study of *belles lettres*,[8] as they are called: that the study is an elegant one, but slight and ineffectual; a smattering of Greek and Latin and other ornamental things, of little use for any one whose object is to get at truth, and to be a practical man. So, too, M. Renan[9] talks of the 'superficial humanism' of a school-course which treats us as if we were all going to be poets, writers, preachers, orators, and he opposes this humanism to positive science, or the critical search after truth. And there is always a tendency in those who are remonstrating against the predominance of letters in education, to understand by letters *belles lettres*, and by *belles lettres* a superficial humanism, the opposite of science or true knowledge.

But when we talk of knowing Greek and Roman antiquity, for instance, which is the knowledge people have called the humanities, I for my part mean a knowledge which is something more than a superficial humanism, mainly decorative. 'I call all teaching *scientific*,' says Wolf, the critic of

delivered in 1880. Arnold and Huxley were warm friends; Arnold's niece married Huxley's son.

8. This French phrase, in common use in English, originally denoted literature regarded in its aesthetic aspect, in contradistinction to informative or dialectical writings; it was analogous to the still-current English phrase, "fine arts." But with the passage of time it came to have an adverse or at least condescending connotation, suggesting literature without dignity or force, and the English word "belletristic" is distinctly pejorative. Arnold, of course, uses it in its original meaning.

9. Ernest Renan (1823–92), the influential French critic and historian of religion.

Homer,[10] 'which is systematically laid out and followed up to its original sources. For example: a knowledge of classical antiquity is scientific when the remains of classical antiquity are correctly studied in the original languages.' There can be no doubt that Wolf is perfectly right; that all learning is scientific which is systematically laid out and followed up to its original sources, and that a genuine humanism is scientific.

When I speak of knowing Greek and Roman antiquity, therefore, as a help to knowing ourselves and the world, I mean more than a knowledge of so much vocabulary, so much grammar, so many portions of authors in the Greek and Latin languages. I mean knowing the Greeks and Romans, and their life and genius, and what they were and did in the world; what we get from them, and what is its value. That, at least, is the ideal; and when we talk of endeavouring to know Greek and Roman antiquity, as a help to knowing ourselves and the world, we mean endeavouring so to know them as to satisfy this ideal, however much we may still fall short of it.

The same also as to knowing our own and other modern nations, with the like aim of getting to understand ourselves and the world. To know the best that has been thought and said by the modern nations, is to know, says Professor Huxley, 'only what modern *literatures* have to tell us; it is the criticism of life contained in modern literature.' And yet 'the distinctive character of our times,' he urges, 'lies in the vast and constantly increasing part which is played by natural knowledge.' And how, therefore, can a man, devoid of knowledge of what physical science has done in the last century, enter hopefully upon a criticism of modern life?

Let us, I say, be agreed about the meaning of the terms we are using. I talk of knowing the best which has been thought and uttered in the world; Professor Huxley says this means knowing *literature*. Literature is a large word; it may mean everything written with letters or printed in a book. Euclid's *Elements* and Newton's *Principia* are thus literature. All knowledge that reaches us through books is literature. But by literature Professor Huxley means *belles lettres*. He means to make me say, that knowing the best which has been thought and said by the modern nations is knowing their *belles lettres* and no more. And this is no sufficient equipment, he argues, for a criticism of modern life. But as I do not mean, by knowing ancient Rome, knowing merely more or less of Latin *belles lettres*, and taking no account of Rome's military, and political, and legal, and administrative work in the world; and as, by knowing ancient Greece, I understand knowing her as the giver of Greek art, and the guide to a free and right use of reason and to scientific method, and the founder of our mathematics and physics and astronomy and biology,—I understand knowing her as all this, and not merely knowing certain Greek poems, and histories, and treatises, and speeches,—so as to the knowledge of modern nations also. By knowing modern nations, I mean not merely knowing their *belles lettres*, but knowing also what has been done by such men as Copernicus, Galileo, Newton, Darwin. 'Our ancestors learned,' says Professor Huxley, 'that the earth is the centre of the visible universe, and that man is the cynosure of things terrestrial; and more especially

10. Friedrich August Wolf (1759–1824), German philologist and Homeric scholar. It was he who proposed the idea that the Homeric poems were not by a single author.

was it inculcated that the course of nature had no fixed order, but that it could be, and constantly was, altered.' But for us now, continues Professor Huxley, 'the notions of the beginning and the end of the world entertained by our forefathers are no longer credible. It is very certain that the earth is not the chief body in the material universe, and that the world is not subordinated to man's use. It is even more certain that nature is the expression of a definite order, with which nothing interferes.' 'And yet,' he cries, 'the purely classical education advocated by the representatives of the humanists in our day gives no inkling of all this!'

In due place and time I will just touch upon that vexed question of classical education; but at present the question is as to what is meant by knowing the best which modern nations have thought and said. It is not knowing their *belles lettres* merely which is meant. To know Italian *belles lettres* is not to know Italy, and to know English *belles lettres* is not to know England. Into knowing Italy and England there comes a great deal more, Galileo and Newton, amongst it. The reproach of being a superficial humanism, a tincture of *belles lettres*, may attach rightly enough to some other disciplines; but to the particular discipline recommended when I proposed knowing the best that has been thought and said in the world, it does not apply. In that best I certainly include what in modern times has been thought and said by the great observers and knowers of nature.

There is, therefore, really no question between Professor Huxley and me as to whether knowing the great results of the modern scientific study of nature is not required as a part of our culture, as well as knowing the products of literature and art. But to follow the processes by which those results are reached, ought, say the friends of physical science, to be made the staple of education for the bulk of mankind. And here there does arise a question between those whom Professor Huxley calls with playful sarcasm 'the Levites of culture,' and those whom the poor humanist is sometimes apt to regard as its Nebuchadnezzars.[11]

The great results of the scientific investigation of nature we are agreed upon knowing, but how much of our study are we bound to give to the processes by which those results are reached? The results have their visible bearing on human life. But all the processes, too, all the items of fact, by which those results are reached and established, are interesting. All knowledge is interesting to a wise man, and the knowledge of nature is interesting to all men. It is very interesting to know, that, from the albuminous white of the egg, the chick in the egg gets the materials for its flesh, bones, blood, and feathers; while, from the fatty yolk of the egg, it gets the heat and energy which enable it at length to break its shell and begin the world. It is less interesting, perhaps, but still it is interesting, to know that when a taper burns, the wax is converted into carbonic acid and water. Moreover, it is quite true that the habit of dealing with facts, which is given by the study of nature, is, as the friends of physical science praise it for being, an excellent discipline. The appeal, in the study of nature, is constantly to observation and experiment;

11. The Levites were in charge of the ceremonial observances of the Temple in Jerusalem. Nebuchadnezzar was the Babylonian king who captured Jerusalem. The humanists, Arnold understands Huxley to be saying, are bound by ritual tradition and are tyrannical.

not only is it said that the thing is so, but we can be made to see that it is so. Not only does a man tell us that when a taper burns the wax is converted into carbonic acid and water, as a man may tell us, if he likes, that Charon is punting his ferry-boat on the river Styx, or that Victor Hugo is a sublime poet, or Mr. Gladstone the most admirable of statesmen; but we are made to see that the conversion into carbonic acid and water does actually happen. This reality of natural knowledge it is, which makes the friends of physical science contrast it, as a knowledge of things, with the humanist's knowledge, which is, say they, a knowledge of words. And hence Professor Huxley is moved to lay it down that, 'for the purpose of attaining real culture, an exclusively scientific education is at least as effectual as an exclusively literary education.' And a certain President of the Section for Mechanical Science in the British Association is, in Scripture phrase, 'very bold,' and declares that if a man, in his mental training, 'has substituted literature and history for natural science, he has chosen the less useful alternative.' But whether we go these lengths or not, we must all admit that in natural science the habit gained of dealing with facts is a most valuable discipline, and that every one should have some experience of it.

More than this, however, is demanded by the reformers. It is proposed to make the training in natural science the main part of education, for the great majority of mankind at any rate. And here, I confess, I part company with the friends of physical science, with whom up to this point I have been agreeing. In differing from them, however, I wish to proceed with the utmost caution and diffidence. The smallness of my own acquaintance with the disciplines of natural science is ever before my mind, and I am fearful of doing these disciplines an injustice. The ability and pugnacity of the partisans of natural science makes them formidable persons to contradict. The tone of tentative inquiry, which befits a being of dim faculties and bounded knowledge, is the tone I would wish to take and not to depart from. At present it seems to me, that those who are for giving to natural knowledge, as they call it, the chief place in the education of the majority of mankind, leave one important thing out of their account: the constitution of human nature. But I put this forward on the strength of some facts not at all recondite, very far from it; facts capable of being stated in the simplest possible fashion, and to which, if I so state them, the man of science will, I am sure, be willing to allow their due weight.

Deny the facts altogether, I think, he hardly can. He can hardly deny, that when we set ourselves to enumerate the powers which go to the building up of human life, and say that they are the power of conduct, the power of intellect and knowledge, the power of beauty, and the power of social life and manners,—he hardly deny that this scheme, though drawn in rough and plain lines enough, and not pretending to scientific exactness, does yet give a fairly true representation of the matter. Human nature is built up by these powers; we have the need for them all. When we have rightly met and adjusted the claims of them all, we shall then be in a fair way for getting soberness and righteousness, with wisdom. This is evident enough, and the friends of physical science would admit it.

But perhaps they may not have sufficiently observed another thing: namely, that the several powers just mentioned are not isolated, but there is, in the generality of mankind, a perpetual tendency to relate them one to another in divers ways. With one such way of relating them I am particularly concerned now. Following our instinct for intellect and knowledge, we acquire pieces of knowledge; and presently, in the generality of men, there arises the desire to relate these pieces of knowledge to our sense for conduct, to our sense for beauty,—and there is weariness and dissatisfaction if the desire is baulked. Now in this desire lies, I think, the strength of that hold which letters have upon us.

All knowledge is, as I said just now, interesting; and even items of knowledge which from the nature of the case cannot well be related, but must stand isolated in our thoughts, have their interest. Even lists of exceptions have their interest. If we are studying Greek accents, it is interesting to know that *pais* and *pas*, and some other monosyllables of the same form of declension, do not take the circumflex upon the last syllable of the genitive plural, but vary, in this respect, from the common rule. If we are studying physiology, it is interesting to know that the pulmonary artery carries dark blood and the pulmonary vein carries bright blood, departing in this respect from the common rule for the division of labour between the veins and the arteries. But every one knows how we seek naturally to combine the pieces of our knowledge together, to bring them under general rules, to relate them to principles; and how unsatisfactory and tiresome it would be to go on for ever learning lists of exceptions, or accumulating items of fact which must stand isolated.

Well, that same need of relating our knowledge, which operates here within the sphere of our knowledge itself, we shall find operating, also, outside that sphere. We experience, as we go on learning and knowing,—the vast majority of us experience,—the need of relating what we have learnt and known to the sense which we have in us for conduct, to the sense which we have in us for beauty.

A certain Greek prophetess of Mantineia in Arcadia, Diotima by name,[12] once explained to the philosopher Socrates that love, and impulse, and bent of all kinds, is, in fact, nothing else but the desire in men that good should for ever be present to them. This desire for good, Diotima assured Socrates, is our fundamental desire, of which fundamental desire every impulse in us is only some one particular form. And therefore this fundamental desire it is, I suppose,—this desire in men that good should be for ever present to them,— which acts in us when we feel the impulse for relating our knowledge to our sense for conduct and to our sense for beauty. At any rate, with men in general the instinct exists. Such is human nature. And the instinct, it will be admitted, is innocent, and human nature is preserved by our following the lead of its innocent instincts. Therefore, in seeking to gratify this instinct in question, we are following the instinct of self-preservation in humanity.

But, no doubt, some kinds of knowledge cannot be made to directly serve the instinct in question, cannot be directly related to the sense for beauty, to the sense for conduct. These are instrument-knowledges; they lead on to other knowledges, which can. A man who passes his life in instrument-knowledges

12. In Plato's *Symposium* Socrates speaks of this woman as his great teacher.

is a specialist. They may be invaluable as instruments to something beyond, for those who have the gift thus to employ them; and they may be disciplines in themselves wherein it is useful for every one to have some schooling. But it is inconceivable that the generality of men should pass all their mental life with Greek accents or with formal logic. My friend Professor Sylvester,[13] who is one of the first mathematicians in the world, holds transcendental doctrines as to the virtue of mathematics, but those doctrines are not for common men. In the very Senate House and heart of our English Cambridge[14] I once ventured, though not without an apology for my profaneness, to hazard the opinion that for the majority of mankind a little of mathematics, even, goes a long way. Of course this is quite consistent with their being of immense importance as an instrument to something else; but it is the few who have the aptitude for thus using them, not the bulk of mankind.

The natural sciences do not, however, stand on the same footing with these instrument-knowledges. Experience shows us that the generality of men will find more interest in learning that, when a taper burns, the wax is converted into carbonic acid and water, or in learning the explanation of the phenomenon of dew, or in learning how the circulation of the blood is carried on, than they find in learning that the genitive plural of *pais* and *pas* does not take the circumflex on the termination. And one piece of natural knowledge is added to another, and others are added to that, and at last we come to propositions so interesting as Mr. Darwin's famous proposition that 'our ancestor was a hairy quadruped furnished with a tail and pointed ears, probably arboreal in his habits.'[15] Or we come to propositions of such reach and magnitude as those which Professor Huxley delivers, when he says that the notions of our forefathers about the beginning and the end of the world were all wrong, and that nature is the expression of a definite order with which nothing interferes.

Interesting, indeed, these results of science are, important they are, and we should all of us be acquainted with them. But what I now wish you to mark is, that we are still, when they are propounded to us and we receive them, we are still in the sphere of intellect and knowledge. And for the generality of men there will be found, I say, to arise, when they have duly taken in the proposition that their ancestor was 'a hairy quadruped furnished with a tail and pointed ears, probably arboreal in his habits,' there will be found to arise an invincible desire to relate this proposition to the sense in us for conduct, and to the sense in us for beauty. But this the men of science will not do for us, and will hardly even profess to do. They will give us other pieces of knowledge, other facts, about other animals and their ancestors, or about plants, or about stones, or about stars; and they may finally bring us to those great 'general conceptions of the universe, which are forced upon us all,' says Professor Huxley, 'by the progress of physical science.' But still it will be

13. James Joseph Sylvester (1814–97), the great English mathematician, taught at the new Johns Hopkins University in Baltimore from 1876 to 1884, when he accepted a professorship at Oxford. His striking abilities raised mathematics in America to a new level. He was an accomplished classicist and published verse translations of Horace.
14. Mathematics had long been a pre-eminent study at Cambridge University. See *The Prelude* VI.115–41 and X.304–9 for the charm that the discipline had for Wordsworth.
15. Charles Darwin, *The Descent of Man* (1871) II.CL.xxi.

*knowledge* only which they give us; knowledge not put for us into relation with our sense for conduct, our sense for beauty, and touched with emotion by being so put; not thus put for us, and therefore, to the majority of mankind, after a certain while, unsatisfying, wearying.

Not to the born naturalist, I admit. But what do we mean by a born naturalist? We mean a man in whom the zeal for observing nature is so uncommonly strong and eminent, that it marks him off from the bulk of mankind. Such a man will pass his life happily in collecting natural knowledge and reasoning upon it, and will ask for nothing, or hardly anything, more. I have heard it said that the sagacious and admirable naturalist whom we lost not very long ago, Mr. Darwin, once owned to a friend that for his part he did not experience the necessity for two things which most men find so necessary to them,—religion and poetry; science and the domestic affections, he thought, were enough. To a born naturalist, I can well understand that this should seem so. So absorbing is his occupation with nature, so strong his love for his occupation, that he goes on acquiring natural knowledge and reasoning upon it, and has little time or inclination for thinking about getting it related to the desire in man for conduct, the desire in man for beauty. He relates it to them for himself as he goes along, so far as he feels the need; and he draws from the domestic affections all the additional solace necessary. But then Darwins are extremely rare. Another great and admirable master of natural knowledge, Faraday, was a Sandemanian.[16] That is to say, he related his knowledge to his instinct for conduct and to his instinct for beauty, by the aid of that respectable Scottish secretary, Robert Sandeman. And so strong, in general, is the demand of religion and poetry to have their share in a man, to associate themselves with his knowing, and to relieve and rejoice it, that, probably, for one man amongst us with the disposition to do as Darwin did in this respect, there are at least fifty with the disposition to do as Faraday.

Education lays hold upon us, in fact, by satisfying this demand. Professor Huxley holds up to scorn mediaeval education, with its neglect of the knowledge of nature, its poverty even of literary studies, its formal logic devoted to 'showing how and why that which the Church said was true must be true.' But the great mediaeval Universities were not brought into being, we may be sure, by the zeal for giving a jejune and contemptible education. Kings have been their nursing fathers, and queens have been their nursing mothers, but not for this. The mediæval Universities came into being, because the supposed knowledge, delivered by Scripture and the Church, so deeply engaged men's hearts, by so simply, easily, and powerfully relating itself to their desire for conduct, their desire for beauty. All other knowledge was dominated by this supposed knowledge and was subordinated to it, because of the surpassing strength of the hold which it gained upon the affections of men, by allying itself profoundly with their sense for conduct, their sense for beauty.

But now, says Professor Huxley, conceptions of the universe fatal to the notions held by our forefathers have been forced upon us by physical science.

16. Michael Faraday (1791–1867), the great English chemist and physicist. The Sandemanians were a Protestant sect deriving their name from the Robert Sandeman mentioned by Arnold below.

Grant to him that they are thus fatal, that the new conceptions must and will soon become current everywhere, and that every one will finally perceive them to be fatal to the beliefs of our forefathers. The need of humane letters, as they are truly called, because they serve the paramount desire in men that good should be for ever present to them,—the need of humane letters, to establish a relation between the new conceptions, and our instinct for beauty, our instinct for conduct, is only the more visible. The Middle Age could do without humane letters, as it could do without the study of nature, because its supposed knowledge was made to engage its emotions so powerfully. Grant that the supposed knowledge disappears, its power of being made to engage the emotions will of course disappear along with it,—but the emotions themselves, and their claim to be engaged and satisfied, will remain. Now if we find by experience that humane letters have an undeniable power of engaging the emotions, the importance of humane letters in a man's training becomes not less, but greater, in proportion to the success of modern science in extirpating what it calls 'mediaeval thinking.'

Have humane letters, then, have poetry and eloquence, the power here attributed to them of engaging the emotions, and do they exercise it? And if they have it and exercise it, *how* do they exercise it, so as to exert an influence upon man's sense for conduct, his sense for beauty? Finally, even if they both can and do exert an influence upon the senses in question, how are they to relate to them the results,—the modern results,—of natural science? All these questions may be asked. First, have poetry and eloquence the power of calling out the emotions? The appeal is to experience. Experience shows that for the vast majority of men, for mankind in general, they have the power. Next do they exercise it? They do. But then, *how* do they exercise it so as to affect man's sense for conduct, his sense for beauty? And this is perhaps a case for applying the Preacher's words: 'Though a man labour to seek it out, yet he shall not find it; yea, farther, though a wise man think to know it, yet shall he not be able to find it.' [17] Why should it be one thing, in its effect upon the emotions, to say, 'Patience is a virtue,' and quite another thing, in its effect upon the emotions, to say with Homer,

τλητὸν γὰρ Μοῖραι θυμὸν θέσαν ἀνθρώποισιν— [18]

'for an enduring heart have the destinies appointed to the children of men'? Why should it be one thing, in its effect upon the emotions, to say with the philosopher Spinoza, *Felicitas in eo consistit quod homo suum esse conservare potest*—'Man's happiness consists in his being able to preserve his own essence,' [19] and quite another thing, in its effect upon the emotions, to say with the Gospel, 'What is a man advantaged, if he gain the whole world, and lose himself, forfeit himself?' [20] How does this difference of effect arise? I cannot tell, and I am not much concerned to know; the important thing is that it does arise, and that we can profit by it. But how, finally, are poetry and eloquence

17. "Ecclesiastes viii.17." (Arnold)
18. "*Iliad* xxiv.49." (Arnold)
19. Spinoza, *Ethics* IV.xviii.
20. Luke 9:25.

to exercise the power of relating the modern results of natural science to man's instinct for conduct, his instinct for beauty? And here again I answer that I do not know *how* they will exercise it, but that they can and will exercise it I am sure. I do not mean that modern philosophical poets and modern philosophical moralists are to come and relate for us, in express terms, the results of modern scientific research to our instinct for conduct, our instinct for beauty. But I mean that we shall find, as a matter of experience, if we know the best that has been thought and uttered in the world, we shall find that the art and poetry and eloquence of men who lived, perhaps, long ago, who had the most limited natural knowledge, who had the most erroneous conceptions about many important matters, we shall find that this art, and poetry, and eloquence, have in fact not only the power of refreshing and delighting us, they have also the power,—such is the strength and worth, in essentials, of their authors' criticism of life,—they have a fortifying, and elevating, and quickening, and suggestive power, capable of wonderfully helping us to relate the results of modern science to our need for conduct, our need for beauty. Homer's conceptions of the physical universe were, I imagine, grotesque; but really, under the shock of hearing from modern science that 'the world is not subordinated to man's use, and that man is not the cynosure of things terrestrial,' I could, for my own part, desire no better comfort than Homer's line which I quoted just now,

τλητὸν γὰρ Μοῖραι θυμὸν θέσαν ἀνθρώποισιν—

'for an enduring heart have the destinies appointed to the children of men!'

And the more that men's minds are cleared, the more that the results of science are frankly accepted, the more that poetry and eloquence come to be received and studied as what in truth they really are,—the criticism of life by gifted men, alive and active with extraordinary power at an unusual number of points;—so much the more will the value of humane letters, and of art also, which is an utterance having a like kind of power with theirs, be felt and acknowledged, and their place in education be secured.

Let us therefore, all of us, avoid indeed as much as possible any invidious comparison between the merits of humane letters, as means of education, and the merits of the natural sciences. But when some President of a Section for Mechanical Science insists on making the comparison, and tells us that 'he who in his training has substituted literature and history for natural science has chosen the less useful alternative,' let us make answer to him that the student of humane letters only, will, at least, know also the great general conceptions brought in by modern physical science; for science, as Professor Huxley says, forces them upon us all. But the student of the natural sciences only, will, by our very hypothesis, know nothing of humane letters; not to mention that in setting himself to be perpetually accumulating natural knowledge, he sets himself to do what only specialists have in general the gift for doing genially. And so he will probably be unsatisfied, or at any rate incomplete, and even more incomplete than the student of humane letters only.

I once mentioned in a school-report, how a young man in one of our English training colleges having to paraphrase the passage in *Macbeth* beginning,

Can'st thou not minister to a mind diseased? [21]

turned this line into, 'Can you not wait upon the lunatic?' And I remarked what a curious state of things it would be, if every pupil of our national schools knew, let us say, that the moon is two thousand one hundred and sixty miles in diameter, and thought at the same time that a good paraphrase for

Can'st thou not minister to a mind diseased?

was, 'Can you not wait upon the lunatic?' If one is driven to choose, I think I would rather have a young person ignorant about the moon's diameter, but aware that 'Can you not wait upon the lunatic?' is bad, than a young person whose education had been such as to manage things the other way.

Or to go higher than the pupils of our national schools. I have in my mind's eye a member of our British Parliament who comes to travel here in America, who afterwards relates his travels, and who shows a really masterly knowledge of the geology of this great country and of its mining capabilities, but who ends by gravely suggesting that the United States should borrow a prince from our Royal Family, and should make him their king, and should create a House of Lords of great landed proprietors after the pattern of ours; and then America, he thinks, would have her future happily and perfectly secured. Surely, in this case, the President of the Section for Mechanical Science would himself hardly say that our member of Parliament, by concentrating himself upon geology and mineralogy, and so on, and not attending to literature and history, had 'chosen the more useful alternative.'

If then there is to be separation and option between humane letters on the one hand, and the natural sciences on the other, the great majority of mankind, all who have not exceptional and overpowering aptitudes for the study of nature, would do well, I cannot but think, to choose to be educated in humane letters rather than in the natural sciences. Letters will call out their being at more points, will make them live more.

I said that before I ended I would just touch on the question of classical education, and I will keep my word. Even if literature is to retain a large place in our education, yet Latin and Greek, say the friends of progress, will certainly have to go. Greek is the grand offender in the eyes of these gentlemen. The attackers of the established course of study think that against Greek, at any rate, they have irresistible arguments. Literature may perhaps be needed in education, they say; but why on earth should it be Greek literature? Why not French or German? Nay, 'has not an Englishman models in his own literature of every kind of excellence?' [22] As before, it is not on any weak pleadings of my own that I rely for convincing the gainsayers; it is on the constitution of human nature itself, and on the instinct of self-preservation in humanity. The instinct for beauty is set in human nature, as surely as the instinct for knowledge is set there, or the instinct for conduct. If the instinct for beauty is served by Greek literature and art as it is served by no other literature and art, we may trust to the instinct of self-preservation in humanity for keeping Greek as part of our culture. We may trust to it for even making the study of Greek more prevalent than it is now. Greek will come, I hope, some day to be studied more rationally than at present; but it will be increasingly studied as men increasingly feel the need in them for beauty, and how powerfully Greek art and Greek literature can serve this need. Women will again study Greek, as Lady Jane Grey did; [23] I believe that in that chain of forts, with which the fair host of the Amazons are now engirdling our English universities, I find that here in America, in colleges like Smith College in Massachusetts, and Vassar College in the State of New York, and in the happy families of the mixed universities out West, they are studying it already.[24]

*Defuit una mihi symmetria prisca,*—'The antique symmetry was the one thing wanting to me,' said Leonardo da Vinci; and he was an Italian. I will not presume to speak for the Americans, but I am sure that, in the Englishman, the want of this admirable symmetry of the Greeks is a thousand times more great and crying than in any italian. The results of the want show themselves most glaringly, perhaps, in our architecture, but they show themselves, also, in all our art. *Fit details strictly combined, in view of a large general result nobly conceived;* that is just the beautiful *symmetria prisca* of the Greeks, and it is just where we English fail, where all our art fails. Striking ideas we have, and well-executed details we have; but that high symmetry which, with satisfying and delightful effect, combines them, we seldom or never have. The glorious beauty of the Acropolis at Athens did not come from single fine things stuck about on that hill, a statue here, a gateway there;—no, it arose from all things being perfectly combined for a supreme total effect. What must not an Englishman feel about our deficiencies in this respect, as the sense for beauty, whereof this symmetry is an essential element, awakens and strengthens within him! what will not one day be his respect and desire for Greece and its *symmetria prisca*, when the scales drop from his eyes as he walks the London streets, and he sees such a lesson in meanness as the Strand,[25] for instance, in its true deformity! But here we are coming to our friend Mr. Ruskin's province,[26] and I will not intrude upon it, for he is its very sufficient guardian.

And so we at last find, it seems, we find flowing in favour of the humanities the natural and necessary stream of things, which seemed against them when we started. The 'hairy quadruped furnished with a tail and pointed ears, probably arboreal in his habits,' this good fellow carried hidden in his nature, apparently, something destined to develop into a necessity for humane letters. Nay, more; we seem finally to be even led to the further conclusion that our hairy ancestor carried in his nature, also, a necessity for Greek.

And therefore, to say the truth, I cannot really think that humane letters

23. Lady Jane Grey (*c.* 1537–54) was the great-granddaughter of Henry VII. She was proclaimed Queen of England in 1553 but was deposed and beheaded. She was reputed to be an excellent Greek scholar.
24. Higher education for women and coeducation had an earlier start in America than in England.
25. The Strand is one of the busiest and most important streets of London. Its name is derived from the fact that it once skirted the river Thames. Its aspect is considerably better now than it was in Arnold's day.
26. That is, the criticism of architecture.

are in much actual danger of being thrust out from their leading place in education, in spite of the array of authorities against them at this moment. So long as human nature is what it is, their attractions will remain irresistible. As with Greek, so with letters generally: they will some day come, we may hope, to be studied more rationally, but they will not lose their place. What will happen will rather be that there will be crowded into education other matters besides, far too many; there will be, perhaps, a period of unsettlement and confusion and false tendency; but letters will not in the end lose their leading place. If they lose it for a time, they will get it back again. We shall be brought back to them by our wants and aspirations. And a poor humanist may possess his soul in patience, neither strive nor cry, admit the energy and brilliancy of the partisans of physical science, and their present favour with the public, to be far greater than his own, and still have a happy faith that the nature of things works silently on behalf of the studies which he loves, and that, while we shall all have to acquaint ourselves with the great results reached by modern science, and to give ourselves as much training in its disciplines as we can conveniently carry, yet the majority of men will always require humane letters; and so much the more, as they have the more and the greater results of science to relate to the need in man for conduct, and to the need in him for beauty.

1881, 1883                                                          1882, 1885


# T. H. HUXLEY
1825–1895

It may be thought an amusing small curiosity of Victorian intellectual history that when John Henry Newman was a pupil at the private school at Ealing where he had the decisive experience of his life, the self evidence of God's existence, one of his masters—he is known to have held the young Newman in the highest regard—was the father of T. H. Huxley, among whose claims to fame is the fact that he coined the word "agnostic." It was a word that many Victorians found useful to describe their position as to the existence of God: while disclaiming atheism, it signifies that no predication of either the existence or the non-existence of the Deity can be made on the basis of knowledge.

As Newman dedicated his life to the defense and advancement of religion, especially those of its elements which were transcendent and supernatural, and conceived one of its chief enemies to be the animus and error of the modern scientific imagination, so Huxley was committed to the defense and advancement of science, whose leading antagonist he identified as organized religion. A scientist of great ability, Huxley in time turned from research; although his achievement in that line was considerable, he is now remembered chiefly for his effectiveness as an educator of the public, for having been in his day the pre-eminent exponent of the scientific spirit. As he says in the autobiographical essay he wrote in 1889, he subordinated his ambition for scientific fame to other ends: "to the popularisation of science; to the development and organisation of scientific education; to the endless series of battles over evolution; and to untiring opposition to that ecclesiastical spirit, that clericalism, which in England, as everywhere else, and to whatever denomination it may belong, is the deadly enemy of science."

Thomas Henry Huxley was born at Ealing in 1825. He set store by the first of his Christian names, that of the doubting disciple of Christ, as being indicative of his intellectual temper, although he records of his early childhood a strong identification with the aristocratic vicar of the parish, which led to his preaching to his mother's maids one Sunday morning, his pinafore turned wrong side forward to represent a surplice. His time of systematic education was as short as it was unpleasant. The Ealing school, excellent in Newman's day and for a time thereafter, deteriorated on the death of its headmaster. In 1835, when his son was ten, the elder Huxley gave up teaching and returned to his native Coventry to become manager of a bank. After that, Thomas had no formal instruction. But he read widely in every direction, with a special appetite for science and logical and metaphysical speculation. He held the works of Carlyle in especial admiration and under their influence began to teach himself German. He later went on to the study of French and Italian. In 1841, he undertook the study of medicine, became an assistant to a doctor in one of the poor sections of London, then apprenticed himself to one of his brothers-in-law, attended medical lectures at Sydenham College, and won a Free Scholarship to Charing Cross Hospital. (It is worth relating that the elder Huxley applied to his former pupil, Newman, to support his son's candidacy, and although Huxley's biographer does not say so, we may suppose the request was granted.) In 1845 Huxley took his Bachelor of Medicine degree at the University of London. Through his own enterprise he secured an appointment in the medical service of the navy and was posted to a naval hospital and subsequently to the *Rattlesnake,* a frigate which was being prepared for a long cruise of survey and exploration in Australian and East India waters, to the special end of bringing back an account of the geography, geology, and natural history of New Guinea. For four years the young assistant-surgeon of the ship was unremitting in his researches, carried out with inadequate equipment, chiefly into the physiology of marine animals. (His journal of the cruise was published in 1935.) He sent back numerous scientific articles, some of which were published before his return in 1850; in 1851, on the strength of his paper on the structure of the Medusae (jellyfish), he was elected Fellow of the Royal Society, a coveted honor, and in the following year was awarded the Society's Royal Medal. Despite this signal recognition, he had difficulty in finding a salaried position, but he continued his research and began to be known as a lecturer and writer whose lucidity and charm of presentation could make any scientific subject comprehensible to virtually anyone. By 1854 his posts were numerous; he was Lecturer in Natural History in the Royal School of Mines, Naturalist to the Geological Survey, and Lecturer in Comparative Anatomy at St. Thomas's Hospital; the next year he married the young lady to whom he had become engaged on his visit to Australia. His researches at this period dealt with invertebrates, vertebrates, and plants, and during a visit to Switzerland he undertook the study of the action of glaciers. He was instrumental in the establishment of two important scientific journals, the *Natural History Review* and *Nature.*

In 1859 Charles Darwin published his epoch-making *Origin of Species,* which Huxley reviewed for the London *Times.* Evolution was of course not a new idea for the Victorians. In one or another formulation, the theory that the universe had not been brought into being by a special act of creation but that it and its inhabitants, including man himself, had evolved from more primitive forms, had for some time disquieted the religious imagination; the depth of the distress it could cause is classically exemplified by Tennyson's *In Memoriam*, begun in 1833 and published in 1850. But *The Origin of Species* gave a new force to the idea, partly because it specified by its theory of natural selection the means by which biological evolution proceeds, and it was greeted with a vociferous anger which had its roots in the fear that the supernatural basis of religion stood threatened as never before. Huxley, who had rejected the idea of evolution until Darwin's book convinced him of its truth, was drawn into the great national debate that followed—Darwin himself could not be drawn into controversy—and became the pre-eminent polemicist of the evolutionists.

The most famous, and certainly to him most gratifying, moment of Huxley's career as "Darwin's bulldog," came in the exchange between Bishop Wilberforce and him at the meeting of the British Association at Oxford in 1860. The bishop, who had recently attacked Darwin in an elegant but ignorant article, rose to speak in the discussion period and went on for half an hour ridiculing Darwin and Huxley, his line being that there was really no such thing as evolution. "Then, turning to his antagonist with a smiling insolence, he begged to know, was it through his grandfather or grandmother that he claimed his descent from a monkey?" At this, Huxley said to his neighbor, "The Lord hath delivered him into mine hands," rose to answer the bishop, and concluded his statement by saying that "he was not ashamed to have a monkey for his ancestor; but he would be ashamed to be connected with a man who used great gifts to obscure the truth." (There are many different versions of Huxley's precise words, but all agree as to their purport and the effect they produced in the crowded hall, of elation on the part of the pro-Darwinists, of bitterness on the part of the chiefly clerical anti-Darwinists.)

By 1863, although he continued his researches, Huxley's energies, which were inexhaustible despite his frequent ill-health, were increasingly devoted to science as a cultural issue, as the basis of intellectual and even moral virtue. Huxley became, among other things, a leading theorist of education, and one of his later lectures, *Science and Culture* (1880), was the occasion for Matthew Arnold's *Literature and Science* (see above). His insistence that science had to play a larger part in education than it did was based on intellectual rather than utilitarian grounds; the humanistic bent that had led him from Carlyle to Goethe was permanent, and, despite what might be inferred from Arnold's reply, he had no doubt that literature had to be salient in any effectual system of education. This dedicated exponent of the intellectual value of science undertook the study of Greek in his fifties and made it a first requirement in the training of a scientist that he learn to write well.

The honors that came to Huxley in the course of his life were innumerable, and the responsibilities he assumed were equally beyond count. At one time or another he was president of virtually every scientific association of importance; he served on no less than ten Royal Commissions; he was elected to the first London school board. In 1871 he published his *Manual of the Anatomy of Vertebrated Animals*, which remained a standard text at least until the end of the century. His lectures and essays on scientific subjects, which evinced an ever-growing readiness to bring scientific facts and principles to bear upon the problems of ethics and politics, appeared at frequent intervals and were eagerly read. In 1876 he visited America to give an address on university education at the newly founded Johns Hopkins University and stayed on to lecture through the next year. His health had broken down in 1872; it failed again in 1884 and he gave up his salaried posts to retire on a generous government allowance; yet he carried on the activity which he had come to think of as the one to which he had been peculiarly called, that of offering a ceaseless resistance to the ecclesiastical spirit in its continuing, if ever less sanguine, attacks upon science. He died in 1895.

His grandson Aldous Huxley, before undertaking the career as a novelist which brought him fame, intended to be a biologist but was prevented by an eye disease. Sir Julian Huxley, the elder brother of Aldous, is a biologist of great eminence. Andrew Huxley, the half-brother of Aldous and Julian, was awarded the Nobel Prize in 1963 for his work in physiology.

# On the Physical Basis of Life [1]

In order to make the title of this discourse generally intelligible, I have translated the term 'Protoplasm,' which is the scientific name of the substance of which I am about to speak, by the words 'the physical basis of life.' [2] I suppose that, to many, the idea that there is such a thing as a physical basis, or matter, of life may be novel—so widely spread is the conception of life as a something which works through matter, but is independent of it; and even those who are aware that matter and life are inseparably connected, may not be prepared for the conclusion plainly suggested by the phrase, 'the physical basis or matter of life,' that there is some one kind of matter which is common to all living beings, and that their endless diversities are bound together by a physical, as well as an ideal, unity. In fact, when first apprehended, such a doctrine as this appears almost shocking to common sense.

What, truly, can seem to be more obviously different from one another, in faculty, in form, and in substance, than the various kinds of living beings? What community of faculty can there be between the brightly-coloured lichen,[3] which so nearly resembles a mere mineral incrustation of the bare rock on which it grows, and the painter, to whom it is instinct with beauty, or the botanist, whom it feeds with knowledge?

Again, think of the microscopic fungus—a mere infinitesimal ovoid particle, which finds space and duration enough to multiply into countless millions in the body of a living fly; and then of the wealth of foliage, the luxuriance of flower and fruit, which lies between this bald sketch of a plant and the giant pine of California, towering to the dimensions of a cathedral spire, or the Indian fig, which covers acres with its profound shadow, and endures while nations and empires come and go around its vast circumference. Or, turning

1. This lecture was delivered in 1868 to an Edinburgh audience. When Huxley reprinted it in his collected works in 1892, he remarked in an appended note, "I cannot say I have ever had to complain of lack of hostile criticism; but the preceding essay has come in for more than its fair share of that commodity. . . ."
2. The word is compounded of two Greek elements, *proto*, first in time, earliest, primitive, + *plasma*, moulded thing, figure, form. It was introduced into biological terminology in 1846, by the German scientist H. von Mohl.
3. Pronounced *lī-ken*. Any of numerous plants consisting of a fungus in combination with certain green algae. It forms a crust-like growth on rocks or tree trunks.

to the other half of the world of life, picture to yourselves the great Finner whale,[4] hugest of beasts that live, or have lived, disporting his eighty or ninety feet of bone, muscle, and blubber, with easy roll, among waves in which the stoutest ship that ever left dockyard would flounder hopelessly; and contrast him with the invisible animalcules—mere gelatinous specks, multitudes of which could, in fact, dance upon the point of a needle with the same ease as the angels of the Schoolmen could,[5] in imagination. With these images before your minds, you may well ask, what community of form, or structure, is there between the animalcule and the whale; or between the fungus and the fig-tree? And, *a fortiori*,[6] between all four?

Finally, if we regard substance, or material composition, what hidden bond can connect the flower which a girl wears in her hair and the blood which courses through her youthful veins; or, what is there in common between the dense and resisting mass of the oak, or the strong fabric of the tortoise, and those broad disks of glassy jelly which may be seen pulsating through the waters of a calm sea, but which drain away to mere films in the hand which raises them out of their element?

Such objections as these must, I think, arise in the mind of every one who ponders, for the first time, upon the conception of a single physical basis of life underlying all the diversities of vital existence; but I propose to demonstrate to you that, notwithstanding these apparent difficulties, a threefold unity— namely, a unity of power or faculty, a unity of form, and a unity of substantial composition—does pervade the whole living world.

No very abstruse argumentation is needed, in the first place to prove that the powers, or faculties, of all kinds of living matter, diverse as they may be in degree, are substantially similar in kind.

Goethe has condensed a survey of all powers of mankind into the well-known epigram:—

> Warum treibt sich das Volk so und schreit? Es will sich ernähren
> Kinder zeugen, und die nähren so gut es vermag.
> . . .
> Weiter bringt es kein Mensch, stell' er sich wie er auch will.[7]

In physiological language this means that all the multifarious and compli- cated activities of man are comprehensible under three categories. Either they are immediately directed towards the maintenance and development of the body, or they effect transitory changes in the relative positions of parts of the body, or they tend towards the continuance of the species. Even those mani- festations of intellect, of feeling, and of will, which we rightly name the higher faculties, are not excluded from this classification, inasmuch as to every one

---

4. A whale of elongated shape having a small back fin. Some specimens are even larger than Huxley says, running to a length of over 100 feet.
5. The Schoolmen, or Scholastics as they are also called, were the theological philosophers of the Middle Ages. They were subtle and powerful reasoners, but they did often engage in speculations like the famous one Huxley cites, which to us seem fantastic.
6. "For a stronger reason; all the more."
7. "Why do the people push each other and shout? They want to sustain themselves / Beget children, and sustain them as well as possible. / . . . Further than that no man can advance, however hard he may try." Goethe, *Venetian Epigrams* 10.

but the subject of them, they are known only as transitory changes in the relative positions of parts of the body. Speech, gesture, and every other form of human action are, in the long run, resolvable into muscular contraction, and muscular contraction is but a transitory change in the relative positions of the parts of a muscle. But the scheme which is large enough to embrace the activities of the highest form of life, covers all those of the lower creatures. The lowest plant, or animalcule, feeds, grows, and reproduces its kind. In addition, all animals manifest those transitory changes of form which we class under irritability and contractility; and, it is more than probable, that when the vegetable world is thoroughly explored, we shall find all plants in possession of the same powers, at one time or other of their existence.

I am not now alluding to such phenomena, at once rare and conspicuous, as those exhibited by the leaflets of the sensitive plants, or the stamens of the barberry, but to much more widely spread, and at the same time, more subtle and hidden, manifestations of vegetable contractility. You are doubtless aware that the common nettle owes its stinging property to the innumerable stiff and needle-like, though exquisitely delicate, hairs which cover its surface. Each stinging-needle tapers from a broad base to a slender summit, which, though rounded at the end, is of such microscopic fineness that it readily penetrates, and breaks off in, the skin. The whole hair consists of a very delicate outer case of wood, closely applied to the inner surface of which is a layer of semi-fluid matter, full of innumerable granules of extreme minuteness. This semi-fluid lining is protoplasm, which thus constitutes a kind of bag, full of a limpid liquid, and roughly corresponding in form with the interior of the hair which it fills. When viewed with a sufficiently high magnifying power, the protoplasmic layer of the nettle hair is seen to be in a condition of unceasing activity. Local contractions of the whole thickness of its substance pass slowly and gradually from point to point, and give rise to the appearance of progressive waves, just as the bending of successive stalks of corn by a breeze produces the apparent billows of a corn-field.

But, in addition to these movements, and independently of them, the granules are driven, in relatively rapid streams, through channels in the protoplasm which seem to have a considerable amount of persistence. Most commonly, the currents in adjacent parts of the protoplasm take similar directions; and, thus, there is a general stream up one side of the hair and down the other. But this does not prevent the existence of partial currents which take different routes; and sometimes trains of granules may be seen coursing swiftly in opposite directions within a twenty-thousandth of an inch of one another; while, occasionally, opposite streams come into direct collision, and, after a longer or shorter struggle, one predominates. The cause of these currents seems to lie in contractions of the protoplasm which bounds the channels in which they flow, but which are so minute that the best microscopes show only their effects, and not themselves.

The spectacle afforded by the wonderful energies prisoned within the compass of the microscopic hair of a plant, which we commonly regard as a merely passive organism, is not easily forgotten by one who has watched its display, continued hour after hour, without pause or sign of weakening. The possible complexity of many other organic forms, seemingly as simple as the protoplasm of the nettle, dawns upon one; and the comparison of such a protoplasm to a body with an internal circulation, which has been put forward by an eminent physiologist, loses much of its startling character. Currents similar to those of the hairs of the nettle have been observed in a great multitude of very different plants, and weighty authorities have suggested that they probably occur, in more or less perfection, in all young vegetable cells. If such be the case, the wonderful noonday silence of a tropical forest is, after all, due only to the dulness of our hearing; and could our ears catch the murmur of these tiny Maelstroms,[8] as they whirl in the innumerable myriads of living cells which constitute each tree, we should be stunned, as with the roar of a great city.

Among the lower plants, it is the rule rather than the exception, that contractility should be still more openly manifested at some periods of their existence. The protoplasm of *Algae* and *Fungi* becomes, under many circumstances, partially, or completely, freed from its woody case, and exhibits movements of its whole mass, or is propelled by the contractility of one, or more, hair-like prolongations of its body, which are called vibratile cilia. And, so far as the conditions of the manifestation of the phenomena of contractility have yet been studied, they are the same for the plant as for the animal. Heat and electric shocks influence both, and in the same way, though it may be in different degrees. It is by no means my intention to suggest that there is no difference in faculty between the lowest plant and the highest, or between plants and animals. But the difference between the powers of the lowest plant, or animal, and those of the highest, is one of degree, not of kind, and depends, as Milne-Edwards[9] long ago so well pointed out, upon the extent to which the principle of the division of labour is carried out in the living economy. In the lowest organism all parts are competent to perform all functions, and one and the same portion of protoplasm may successfully take on the function of feeding, moving, or reproducing apparatus. In the highest, on the contrary, a great number of parts combine to perform each function, each part doing its allotted share of the work with great accuracy and efficiency, but being useless for any other purpose.

On the other hand, notwithstanding all the fundamental resemblances which exist between the powers of the protoplasm in plants and in animals, they present a striking difference (to which I shall advert more at length presently), in the fact that plants can manufacture fresh protoplasm out of mineral compounds, whereas animals are obliged to procure it ready made, and hence, in the long run, depend upon plants. Upon what condition this difference in the powers of the two great divisions of the world of life depends, nothing is at present known.

With such qualifications as arise out of the last-mentioned fact, it may be truly said that the acts of all living things are fundamentally one. Is any such unity predicable of their forms? Let us seek in easily verified facts for a reply to this question. If a drop of blood be drawn by pricking one's finger, and viewed with proper precautions, and under a sufficiently high microscopic

8. Whirlpools of extraordinary size and violence. Specifically, as a proper noun, a famous whirlpool off the northwest coast of Norway.
9. Henry Milne-Edwards (1800–1885), eminent French zoologist, the son of an Englishman.

power, there will be seen, among the innumerable multitude of little, circular, discoidal bodies, or corpuscles, which float in it and give it its colour, a comparatively small number of colourless corpuscles, of somewhat larger size and very irregular shape. If the drop of blood be kept at the temperature of the body, these colourless corpuscles will be seen to exhibit a marvellous activity, changing their forms with great rapidity, drawing in and thrusting out prolongations of their substance, and creeping about as if they were independent organisms.

The substance which is thus active is a mass of protoplasm, and its activity differs in detail, rather than in principle, from that of the protoplasm of the nettle. Under sundry circumstances the corpuscle dies and becomes distended into a round mass, in the midst of which is seen a smaller spherical body, which existed, but was more or less hidden, in the living corpuscle, and is called its *nucleus*. Corpuscles of essentially similar structure are to be found in the skin, in the lining of the mouth, and scattered through the whole framework of the body. Nay, more; in the earliest condition of the human organism, in that state in which it has but just become distinguishable from the egg in which it arises, it is nothing but an aggregation of such corpuscles, and every organ of the body was, once, no more than such an aggregation.

Thus a nucleated mass of protoplasm turns out to be what may be termed the structural unit of the human body. As a matter of fact, the body, in its earliest state, is a mere multiple of such units; and in its perfect condition, it is a multiple of such units, variously modified.

But does the formula which expresses the essential structural character of the highest animal cover all the rest, as the statement of its powers and faculties covered that of all others? Very nearly. Beast and fowl, reptile and fish, mollusk, worm, and polype, are all composed of structural units of the same character, namely, masses of protoplasm with a nucleus. There are sundry very low animals, each of which, structurally, is a mere colourless blood-corpuscle, leading an independent life. But, at the very bottom of the animal scale, even this simplicity becomes simplified, and all the phenomena of life are manifested by a particle of protoplasm without a nucleus. Nor are such organisms insignificant by reason of their want of complexity. It is a fair question whether the protoplasm of those simplest forms of life, which people an immense extent of the bottom of the sea, would not outweigh that of all the higher living beings which inhabit the land put together. And in ancient times, no less than at the present day, such living beings as these have been the greatest of rock builders.

What has been said of the animal world is no less true of plants. Imbedded in the protoplasm at the broad, or attached, end of the nettle hair, there lies a spheroidal nucleus. Careful examination further proves that the whole substance of the nettle is made up of a repetition of such masses of nucleated protoplasm, each contained in a wooden case, which is modified in form, sometimes into a woody fibre, sometimes, into a duct or spiral vessel, sometimes into a pollen grain, or an ovule. Traced back to its earliest state, the nettle arises as the man does, in a particle of nucleated protoplasm. And in the lowest plants, as in the lowest animals, a single mass of such protoplasm may constitute the whole plant, or the protoplasm may exist without a nucleus.

Under these circumstances it may well be asked, how is one mass of non-nucleated protoplasm to be distinguished from another? why call one 'plant' and the other 'animal'?

The only reply is that, so far as form is concerned, plants and animals are not separable, and that, in many cases, it is a mere matter of convention whether we call a given organism an animal or a plant. There is a living body called *Aethalium septicum*, which appears upon decaying vegetable substances, and, in one of its forms, is common upon the surfaces of tan-pits.[10] In this condition it is, to all intents and purposes, a fungus, and formerly was always regarded as such; but the remarkable investigations of De Bary [11] have shown that, in another condition, the *Aethalium* is an actively locomotive creature, and takes in solid matters, upon which, apparently, it feeds, thus exhibiting the most characteristic feature of animality. Is this a plant; or is it an animal? Is it both; or is it neither? Some decide in favour of the last supposition, and establish an intermediate kingdom, a sort of biological No Man's Land for all these questionable forms. But, as it is admittedly impossible to draw any distinct boundary line between this no man's land and the vegetable world on the one hand, or the animal, on the other, it appears to me that this proceeding merely doubles the difficulty which, before, was single.

Protoplasm, simple or nucleated, is the formal basis of all life. It is the clay of the potter: which, bake it and paint it as he will, remains clay, separated by artifice, and not by nature, from the commonest brick or sun-dried clod.

Thus it becomes clear that all living powers are cognate, and that all living forms are fundamentally of one character. The researches of the chemist have revealed a no less striking uniformity of material composition in living matter.

In perfect strictness, it is true that chemical investigation can tell us little or nothing, directly, of the composition of living matter, inasmuch as such matter must needs die in the act of analysis,—and upon this very obvious ground, objections, which I confess seem to me to be somewhat frivolous, have been raised to the drawing of any conclusions whatever respecting the composition of actually living matter, from that of the dead matter of life, which alone is accessible to us. But objectors of this class do not seem to reflect that it is also, in strictness, true that we know nothing about the composition of any body whatever, as it is. The statement that a crystal of calc-spar [12] consists of corbonate of lime, is quite true, if we only mean that, by appropriate processes, it may be resolved into carbonic acid and quicklime. If you pass the same carbonic acid over the very quicklime thus obtained, you will obtain carbonate of lime again; but it will not be calc-spar, nor anything like it. Can it, therefore, be said that chemical analysis teaches nothing about the chemical composition of calc-spar? Such a statement would be absurd; but it is hardly more so than the talk one occasionally hears about the uselessness of applying the results of chemical analysis to the living bodies which have yielded them.

One fact, at any rate, is out of reach of such refinements, and this is, that all the forms of protoplasm which have yet been examined contain the four elements, carbon, hydrogen, oxygen, and nitrogen, in very complex union, and that they

10. Where hides are converted into leather by the application of tanning.
11. Heinrich Anton de Bary (1831–88), German botanist. He was the founder of modern mycology, the study of fungi.
12. Calc-spar is calcite, the basic constituent of limestone, marble, and chalk.

behave similarly towards several reagents. To this complex combination, the nature of which has never been determined with exactness, the name of Protein [13] has been applied. And if we use this term with such caution as may properly arise out of our comparative ignorance of the things for which it stands, it may be truly said, that all protoplasm is proteinaceous, or, as the white, or albumen, of an egg is one of the commonest examples of a nearly pure protein matter, we may say that all living matter is more or less albuminoid.

Perhaps it would not yet be safe to say that all forms of protoplasm are affected by the direct action of electric shocks; and yet the number of cases in which the contraction of protoplasm is shown to be affected by this agency increases every day.

Nor can it be affirmed with perfect confidence, that all forms of protoplasm are liable to undergo that peculiar coagulation at a temperature of $40°-50°$ centigrade, which has been called 'heat-stiffening,' though Kühne's [14] beautiful researches have proved this occurrence to take place in so many and such diverse living beings, that it is hardly rash to expect that the law holds good for all.

Enough has, perhaps, been said to prove the existence of a general uniformity in the character of the protoplasm, or physical basis, of life, in whatever group of living beings it may be studied. But it will be understood that this general uniformity by no means excludes any amount of special modifications of the fundamental substance. The mineral, carbonate of lime, assumes an immense diversity of characters, though no one doubts that, under all these Protean [15] changes, it is one and the same thing.

And now, what is the ultimate fate, and what the origin, of the matter of life?

Is it, as some of the older naturalists supposed, diffused throughout the universe in molecules, which are indestructible and unchangeable in themselves; but, in endless transmigration, unite in innumerable permutations, into the diversified forms of life we know? Or, is the matter of life composed of ordinary matter, differing from it only in the manner in which its atoms are aggregated? Is it built up of ordinary matter, and again resolved into ordinary matter when its work is done?

Modern science does not hesitate a moment between these alternatives. Physiology writes over the portals of life—

Debemur morti nos nostraque,[16]

with a profounder meaning than the Roman poet attached to that melancholy line. Under whatever disguise it takes refuge, whether fungus or oak, worm or man, the living protoplasm not only ultimately dies and is resolved into its mineral and lifeless constituents, but is always dying, and, strange as the paradox may sound, could not live unless it died.

13. This word was first used in 1838 by the French scientist Mulder. It was intended to denote the primary substance of the body (see note 2, on protoplasm).
14. Willy Kühne (1817–1900), German physiologist who worked on the physiology of muscle and nerve and on the chemistry of digestion.
15. In Greek mythology Proteus was a minor sea god, who had the power to take any shape he chose in order to avoid answering questions.
16. "We owe ourselves and all that is ours to death." Horace, Ars Poetica I.63.

In the wonderful story of the 'Peau de Chagrin,' [17] the hero becomes possessed of a magical wild ass' skin, which yields him the means of gratifying all his wishes. But its surface represents the duration of the proprietor's life; and for every satisfied desire the skin shrinks in proportion to the intensity of fruition, until at length life and the last handbreadth of the *peau de chagrin* disappear with the gratification of a last wish.

Balzac's studies had led him over a wide range of thought and speculation, and his shadowing forth of physiological truth in this strange story may have been intentional. At any rate, the matter of life is a veritable *peau de chagrin*, and for every vital act it is somewhat the smaller. All work implies waste, and the work of life results, directly or indirectly, in the waste of protoplasm.

Every word uttered by a speaker costs him some physical loss; and, in the strictest sense, he burns that others may have light—so much eloquence, so much of his body resolved into carbonic acid, water, and urea. It is clear that this process of expenditure cannot go on for ever. But, happily, the protoplasmic *peau de chagrin* differs from Balzac's in its capacity of being repaired, and brought back to its full size, after every exertion.

For example, this present lecture, whatever its intellectual worth to you, has a certain physical value to me, which is, conceivably, expressible by the number of grains of protoplasm and other bodily substance wasted in maintaining my vital processes during its delivery. My *peau de chagrin* will be distinctly smaller at the end of the discourse than it was at the beginning. By and by, I shall probably have recourse to the substance commonly called mutton, for the purpose of stretching it back to its original size. Now this mutton was once the living protoplasm, more or less modified, of another animal—a sheep. As I shall eat it, it is the same matter altered, not only by death, but by exposure to sundry artificial operations in the process of cooking.

But these changes, whatever be their extent, have not rendered it incompetent to resume its old functions as matter of life. A singular inward laboratory, which I possess, will dissolve a certain portion of the modified protoplasm; the solution so formed will pass into my veins; and the subtle influences to which it will then be subjected will convert the dead protoplasm into living protoplasm, and transubstantiate sheep into man.

Nor is this all. If digestion were a thing to be trifled with, I might sup upon lobster, and the matter of life of the crustacean would undergo the same wonderful metamorphosis into humanity. And were I to return to my own place by sea, and undergo shipwreck, the crustacean might, and probably would, return the compliment and demonstrate our common nature by turning my protoplasm into living lobster. Or, if nothing better were to be had, I might supply my wants with mere bread, and I should find the protoplasm of the wheat-plant to be convertible into man, with no more trouble than that of the sheep, and with far less, I fancy, than that of the lobster.

Hence it appears to be a matter of no great moment what animal, or what plant, I lay under contribution for protoplasm, and the fact speaks volumes for the general identity of that substance in all living beings. I share this

17. "Skin of the Wild Ass." The novel by Honoré de Balzac (1799–1850) was published in 1834.

catholicity of assimilation with other animals, all of which, so far as we know, could thrive equally well on the protoplasm of any of their fellows, or of any plant; but here the assimilative powers of the animal world cease. A solution of smelling-salts in water, with an infinitesimal proportion of some other saline matters, contains all the elementary bodies which enter into the composition of protoplasm; but, as I need hardly say, a hogshead of that fluid would not keep a hungry man from starving, nor would it save any animal whatever from a like fate. An animal cannot make protoplasm, but must take it ready-made from some other animal, or some plant—the animal's highest feat of constructive chemistry being to convert dead protoplasm into that living matter of life which is appropriate to itself.

Therefore, in seeking for the origin of protoplasm, we must eventually turn to the vegetable world. A fluid containing carbonic acid, water, and nitrogenous salts, which offers such a Barmecide feast [18] to the animal, is a table richly spread to multitudes of plants; and, with a due supply of only such materials, many a plant will not only maintain itself in vigour, but grow and multiply until it has increased a million-fold, or a million million-fold, the quantity of protoplasm which it originally possessed; in this way building up the matter of life, to an indefinite extent, from the common matter of the universe.

Thus, the animal can only raise the complex substance of dead protoplasm to the higher power, as one may say, of living protoplasm; while the plant can raise the less complex substances—carbonic acid, water, and nitrogenous salts—to the same stage of living protoplasm, if not to the same level. But the plant also has its limitations. Some of the fungi, for example, appear to need higher compounds to start with; and no known plant can live upon the uncompounded elements of protoplasm. A plant supplied with pure carbon, hydrogen, oxygen, and nitrogen, phosphorus, sulphur, and the like, would as infallibly die as the animal in his bath of smelling-salts, though it would be surrounded by all the constituents of protoplasm. Nor, indeed, need the process of simplification of vegetable food be carried so far as this, in order to arrive at the limit of the plant's thaumaturgy.[19] Let water, carbonic acid, and all the other needful constituents be supplied except nitrogenous salts, and an ordinary plant will still be unable to manufacture protoplasm.

Thus the matter of life, so far as we know it (and we have no right to speculate on any other), breaks up, in consequence of that continual death which is the condition of its manifesting vitality, into carbonic acid, water, and nitrogenous compounds, which certainly possess no properties but those of ordinary matter. And out of these same forms of ordinary matter, and from none which are simpler, the vegetable world builds up all the protoplasm which keeps the animal world a-going. Plants are the accumulators of the power which animals distribute and disperse.

But it will be observed, that the existence of the matter of life depends on the pre-existence of certain compounds; namely, carbonic acid, water, and certain nitrogenous bodies. Withdraw any one of these three from the world,

18. An illusion of abundance; from the name of an 8th-century Persian family, one of whom, in a story in the *Arabian Nights*, served a beggar a feast of empty dishes.
19. Magic.

and all vital phenomena come to an end. They are as necessary to the proto-plasm of the plant, as the protoplasm of the plant is to that of the animal. Carbon, hydrogen, oxygen, and nitrogen are all lifeless bodies. Of these, carbon and oxygen unite in certain proportions and under certain conditions, to give rise to carbonic acid; hydrogen and oxygen produce water; nitrogen and other elements give rise to nitrogenous salts. These new compounds, like the elemen-tary bodies of which they are composed, are lifeless. But when they are brought together, under certain conditions, they give rise to the still more complex body, protoplasm, and this protoplasm exhibits the phenomena of life.

I see no break in this series of steps in molecular complication, and I am unable to understand why the language which is applicable to any one term of the series may not be used to any of the others. We think fit to call different kinds of matter carbon, oxygen, hydrogen, and nitrogen, and to speak of the various powers and activities of these substances as the properties of the matter of which they are composed.

When hydrogen and oxygen are mixed in a certain proportion, and an electric spark is passed through them, they disappear, and a quantity of water, equal in weight to the sum of their weights, appears in their place. There is not the slightest parity between the passive and active powers of the water and those of the oxygen and hydrogen which have given rise to it. At 32° Fahrenheit, and far below that temperature, oxygen and hydrogen are elastic gaseous bodies, whose particles tend to rush away from one another with great force. Water, at the same temperature, is a strong though brittle solid, whose particles tend to cohere into definite geometrical shapes, and sometimes build up frosty imitations of the most complex forms of vegetable foliage.

Nevertheless we call these, and many other strange phenomena, the prop-erties of the water, and we do not hesitate to believe that, in some way or another, they result from the properties of the component elements of the water. We do not assume that a something called 'aquosity' [20] entered into and took possession of the oxidated hydrogen as soon as it was formed, and then guided the aqueous particles to their places in the facets of the crystal, or amongst the leaflets of the hoarfrost. On the contrary, we live in the hope and in the faith that, by the advance of molecular physics, we shall by and by be able to see our way as clearly from the constituents of water to the properties of water, as we are now able to deduce the operations of a watch from the form of its parts and the manner in which they are put together.

Is the case in any way changed when carbonic acid, water, and nitrogenous salts disappear, and in their place, under the influence of pre-existing living protoplasm, an equivalent weight of the matter of life makes its appearance?

It is true that there is no sort of parity between the properties of the com-ponents and the properties of the resultant, but neither was there in the case of the water. It is also true that what I have spoken of as the influence of pre-existing living matter is something quite unintelligible; but does anybody quite comprehend the *modus operandi* [21] of an electric spark, which traverses a mixture of oxygen and hydrogen?

What justification is there, then, for the assumption of the existence in the

20. Huxley makes up this word from the Latin for water, *aqua:* "waterness."
21. "The way in which it works."

living matter of a something which has no representative, or correlative, in the not living matter which gave rise to it? What better philosophical status has 'vitality' than 'aquosity'? And why should 'vitality' hope for a better fate than the other 'itys' which have disappeared since Martinus Scriblerus [22] accounted for the operation of the meat-jack by its inherent 'meat roasting quality,' [23] and scorned the 'materialism' of those who explained the turning of the spit by a certain mechanism worked by the draught of the chimney.

If scientific language is to possess a definite and constant signification whenever it is employed, it seems to me that we are logically bound to apply to the protoplasm, or physical basis of life, the same conceptions as those which are held to be legitimate elsewhere. If the phenomena exhibited by water are its properties, so are those presented by protoplasm, living or dead, its properties.

If the properties of water may be properly said to result from the nature and disposition of its component molecules, I can find no intelligible ground for refusing to say that the properties of protoplasm result from the nature and disposition of its molecules.

But I bid you beware that, in accepting these conclusions, you are placing your feet on the first rung of a ladder which, in most people's estimation, is the reverse of Jacob's,[24] and leads to the antipodes of heaven. It may seem a small thing to admit that the dull vital actions of a fungus, or a foraminifer,[25] are the properties of their protoplasm, and are the direct results of the nature of the matter of which they are composed. But if, as I have endeavoured to prove to you, their protoplasm is essentially identical with, and most readily converted into, that of any animal, I can discover no logical halting-place between the admission that such is the case, and the further concession that all vital action may, with equal propriety, be said to be the result of the molecular forces of the protoplasm which displays it. And if so, it must be true, in the same sense and to the same extent, that the thoughts to which I am now giving utterance, and your thoughts regarding them, are the expression of molecular changes in that matter of life which is the source of our other vital phenomena.

Past experience leads me to be tolerably certain that, when the propositions I have just placed before you are accessible to public comment and criticism, they will be condemned by many zealous persons, and perhaps by some few of the wise and thoughtful. I should not wonder if 'gross and brutal materialism' were the mildest phrase applied to them in certain quarters. And, most undoubtedly, the terms of the propositions are distinctly materialistic. Nevertheless two things are certain; the one, that I hold the statements to be substantially true; the other, that I, individually, am no materialist, but, on the contrary, believe materialism to involve grave philosophical error.

22. Martinus Scriblerus was a pedantic character invented by Arbuthnot, Pope, and Swift who amused themselves by writing his memoirs. A meat-jack is a clockwork device to keep a roast on a spit turning before an open fire.
23. The most famous example of this kind of explanation occurs in Molière's comedy *The Imaginary Invalid,* in which a physician says that opium puts one to sleep because of its "dormitive quality."
24. In Genesis 28:12 Jacob dreams of a ladder ascending to heaven.
25. Unicellular micro-organism.

This union of materialistic terminology with the repudiation of materialistic philosophy I share with some of the most thoughtful men with whom I am acquainted. And, when I first undertook to deliver the present discourse, it appeared to me to be a fitting opportunity to explain how such a union is not only consistent with, but necessitated by, sound logic. I purposed to lead you through the territory of vital phenomena to the materialistic slough in which you find yourselves now plunged, and then to point out to you the sole path by which, in my judgment, extrication is possible.

An occurrence of which I was unaware until my arrival here last night renders this line of argument singularly opportune. I found in your papers the eloquent address 'On the Limits of Philosophical Inquiry,' which a distinguished prelate of the English Church delivered before the members of the Philosophical Institution on the previous day. My argument, also, turns upon this very point of the limits of philosophical inquiry; and I cannot bring out my own views better than by contrasting them with those so plainly and, in the main, fairly stated by the Archbishop of York.

But I may be permitted to make a preliminary comment upon an occurrence that greatly astonished me. Applying the name of the 'New Philosophy' to that estimate of the limits of philosophical inquiry which I, in common with many other men of science, hold to be just, the Archbishop opens his address by identifying this 'New Philosophy' with the Positive Philosophy of M. Comte [26] (of whom he speaks as its 'founder'); and then proceeds to attack that philosopher and his doctrines vigorously.

Now, so far as I am concerned, the most reverend prelate might dialectically hew M. Comte in pieces, as a modern Agag,[27] and I should not attempt to stay his hand. In so far as my study of what specially characterises the Positive Philosophy has led me, I find therein little or nothing of any scientific value, and a great deal which is as thoroughly antagonistic to the very essence of science as anything in ultramontane [28] Catholicism. In fact, M. Comte's philosophy, in practice, might be compendiously described as Catholicism *minus* Christianity.

But what has Comtism to do with the 'New Philosophy,' as the Archbishop defines it in the following passage?

Let me briefly remind you of the leading principles of this new philosophy.

26. Auguste Comte (1798–1857), the French social philosopher. His principal work is his *Cours de philosophie positive* (1830–42) in which he proposed the idea that there are three historical stages of knowledge: the theological; the metaphysical; and the positive, i.e. the form of knowledge which takes account only of positive facts and observable phenomena. He applied to society the methods of observation and reasoning characteristic of the sciences and was in effect the founder of the modern discipline of sociology. Huxley's famous characterization of his philosophy as "Catholicism *minus* Christianity" refers to his later effort to construct a religion in which the worship of Humanity was substituted for the worship of God and to contrive an elaborate system of sacraments and prayers. Comte had considerable influence in England, most notably on John Stuart Mill.

27. I Samuel 15:33. Agag was an Amalekite king whom Samuel commanded Saul to slay. Saul spared his life but Samuel hewed him in pieces.

28. "Beyond the mountain"—that is, supporting the authority of the pope as against the authority of the national church.

All knowledge is experience of facts acquired by the senses. The traditions of older philosophies have obscured our experience by mixing with it much that the senses cannot observe, and until these additions are discarded our knowledge is impure. Thus metaphysics tell us that one fact which we observe is a cause, and another is the effect of that cause; but, upon a rigid analysis, we find that our senses observe nothing of cause or effect: they observe, first, that one fact succeeds another, and, after some opportunity, that this fact has never failed to follow —that for cause and effect we should substitute invariable succession. An older philosophy teaches us to define an object by distinguishing its essential from its accidental qualities: but experience knows nothing of essential and accidental; she sees only that certain marks attach to an object, and, after many observations, that some of them attach invariably whilst others may at times be absent. . . . As all knowledge is relative, the notion of anything being necessary must be banished with other traditions. [29]

There is much here that expresses the spirit of the 'New Philosophy,' if by that term be meant the spirit of modern science; but I cannot but marvel that the assembled wisdom and learning of Edinburgh should have utttered no sign of dissent, when Comte was declared to be the founder of these doctrines. No one will accuse Scotchmen of habitually forgetting their great countrymen; but it was enough to make David Hume [30] turn in his grave, that here, almost within ear-shot of his house, an instructed audience should have listened, without a murmur, while his most characteristic doctrines were attributed to a French writer of fifty years later date, in whose dreary and verbose pages we miss alike the vigour of thought and the exquisite clearness of style of the man whom I make bold to term the most acute thinker of the eighteenth century—even though that century produced Kant.

But I did not come to Scotland to vindicate the honour of one of the greatest men she has ever produced. My business is to point out to you that the only way of escape out of the 'crass materialism' in which we just now landed, is the adoption and strict working-out of the very principles which the Archbishop holds up to reprobation.

Let us suppose that knowledge is absolute, and not relative, and therefore, that our conception of matter represents that which it really is. Let us suppose, further, that we do know more of cause and effect than a certain definite order of succession among facts, and that we have a knowledge of the necessity of that succession—and hence, of necessary laws—and I, for my part, do not see what escape there is from utter materialism and necessarianism. For it is obvious that our knowledge of what we call the material world is, to begin with, at least as certain and definite as that of the spiritual world, and that our acquaintance with law is of as old a date as our knowledge of spontaneity. Further, I take it to be demonstrable that it is utterly impossible to prove that anything whatever may not be the effect of a material and necessary cause,

29. "The Limits of Philosophical Inquiry, pp. 4 and 5." (Huxley)
30. David Hume (1711–76), the great Scottish philosopher. Huxley wrote an admirable brief life of Hume for the English Men of Letters Series (1878).

and that human logic is equally incompetent to prove that any act is really spontaneous. A really spontaneous act is one which, by the assumption, has no cause; and the attempt to prove such a negative as this is, on the face of the matter, absurd. And while it is thus a philosophical impossibility to demonstrate that any given phenomenon is not the effect of a material cause, any one who is acquainted with the history of science will admit, that its progress has, in all ages, meant, and now, more than ever, means, the extension of the province of what we call matter and causation, and the concomitant gradual banishment from all regions of human thought of what we call spirit and spontaneity.

I have endeavoured, in the first part of this discourse, to give you a conception of the direction towards which modern physiology is tending; and I ask you, what is the difference between the conception of life as the product of a certain disposition of material molecules, and the old notion of an Archaeus [31] governing and directing blind matter within each living body, except this—that here, as elsewhere, matter and law have devoured spirit and spontaneity? And as surely as every future grows out of past and present, so will the physiology of the future gradually extend the realm of matter and law until it is co-extensive with knowledge, with feeling, and with action.

The consciousness of this great truth weighs like a nightmare, I believe, upon many of the best minds of these days. They watch what they conceive to be the progress of materialism, in such fear and powerless anger as a savage feels, when, during an eclipse, the great shadow creeps over the face of the sun. The advancing tide of matter threatens to drown their souls; the tightening grasp of law impedes their freedom; they are alarmed lest man's moral nature be debased by the increase of his wisdom.

If the 'New Philosophy' be worthy of the reprobation with which it is visited, I confess their fears seem to me to be well founded. While, on the contrary, could David Hume be consulted, I think he would smile at their perplexities, and chide them for doing even as the heathen, and falling down in terror before the hideous idols their own hands have raised.

For, after all, what do we know of this terrible 'matter,' except as a name for the unknown and hypothetical cause of states of our own consciousness? And what do we know of that 'spirit' over whose threatened extinction by matter a great lamentation is arising, like that which was heard at the death of Pan,[32] except that it is also a name for an unknown and hypothetical cause, or condition, of states of consciousness? In other words, matter and spirit are but names for the imaginary substrata of groups of natural phenomena.

And what is the dire necessity and 'iron' law under which men groan? Truly, most gratuitously invented bugbears. I suppose if there be an 'iron' law, it is that of gravitation; and if there be a physical necessity, it is that a stone, unsupported, must fall to the ground. But what is all we really know, and can know, about the latter phenomena? Simply, that, in all human experience, stones have fallen to the ground under these conditions; that we have not the

---

31. In the chemical and alchemical thought of Paracelsus (1453–1541), the action of every chemical was said to be under the control of a particular spirit, its Archaeus.
32. Plutarch, *Moralia, Why the Oracles Cease to Give Answers.*

smallest reason for believing that any stone so circumstanced will not fall to the ground; and that we have, on the contrary, every reason to believe that it will so fall. It is very convenient to indicate that all the conditions of belief have been fulfilled in this case, by calling the statement that unsupported stones will fall to the ground, 'a law of Nature.' But when, as commonly happens, we change *will* into *must*, we introduce an idea of necessity which most assuredly does not lie in the observed facts, and has no warranty that I can discover elsewhere. For my part, I utterly repudiate and anathematise the intruder. Fact I know; and Law I know; but what is this Necessity, save an empty shadow of my own mind's throwing?

But, if it is certain that we can have no knowledge of the nature of either matter or spirit, and that the notion of necessity is something illegitimately thrust into the perfectly legitimate conception of law, the materialistic position that there is nothing in the world but matter, force, and necessity, is as utterly devoid of justification as the most baseless of theological dogmas. The fundamental doctrines of materialism, like those of spiritualism, and most other 'isms,' lie outside 'the limits of philosophical inquiry,' and David Hume's great service to humanity is his irrefragable demonstration of what these limits are. Hume called himself a sceptic, and therefore others cannot be blamed if they apply the same title to him; but that does not alter the fact that the name, with its existing implications, does him gross injustice.

If a man asks me what the politics of the inhabitants of the moon are, and I reply that I do not know; that neither I, nor any one else, has any means of knowing; and that, under these circumstances, I decline to trouble myself about the subject at all, I do not think he has any right to call me a sceptic. On the contrary, in replying thus, I conceive that I am simply honest and truthful, and show a proper regard for the economy of time. So Hume's strong and subtle intellect takes up a great many problems about which we are naturally curious, and shows us that they are essentially questions of lunar politics, in their essence incapable of being answered, and therefore not worth the attention of men who have work to do in the world. And he thus ends one of his essays:—

> If we take in hand any volume of Divinity, or school metaphysics, for instance, let us ask, *Does it contain any abstract reasoning concerning quantity or number?* No. *Does it contain any experimental reasoning concerning matter of fact and existence?* No. Commit it then to the flames; for it can contain nothing but sophistry and illusion.[33]

Permit me to enforce this most wise advice. Why trouble ourselves about matters of which, however important they may be, we do know nothing, and can know nothing? We live in a world which is full of misery and ignorance, and the plain duty of each and all of us is to try to make the little corner he can influence somewhat less miserable and somewhat less ignorant than it was before he entered it. To do this effectually it is necessary to be fully possessed of only two beliefs: the first, that the order of Nature is ascertainable

---

33. "Hume's Essay 'Of the Academical or Sceptical Philosophy,' in the *Inquiry Concerning the Human Understanding.*—[Many critics of this passage seem to forget that the subject-matter of Ethics and Aesthetics consists of matters of fact and existence.—1892]." (Huxley)

by our faculties to an extent which is practically unlimited; the second, that our volition [34] counts for something as a condition of the course of events.

Each of these beliefs can be verified experimentally, as often as we like to try. Each, therefore, stands upon the strongest foundation upon which any belief can rest, and forms one of our highest truths. If we find that the ascertainment of the order of nature is facilitated by using one terminology, or one set of symbols, rather than another, it is our clear duty to use the former; and no harm can accrue, so long as we bear in mind, that we are dealing merely with terms and symbols.

In itself it is of little moment whether we express the phenomena of matter in terms of spirit; or the phenomena of spirit in terms of matter. Matter may be regarded as a form of thought, thought may be regarded as a property of matter—each statement has a certain relative truth. But with a view to the progress of science, the materialistic terminology is in every way to be preferred. For it connects thought with the other phenomena of the universe, and suggests inquiry into the nature of those physical conditions, or concomitants of thought, which are more or less accessible to us, and a knowledge of which may, in future, help us to exercise the same kind of control over the world of thought, as we already possess in respect of the material world; whereas, the alternative, or spiritualistic, terminology is utterly barren, and leads to nothing but obscurity and confusion of ideas.

Thus there can be little doubt, that the further science advances, the more extensively and consistently will all the phenomena of Nature be represented by materialistic formulae and symbols.

But the man of science, who, forgetting the limits of philosophical inquiry, slides from these formulae and symbols into what is commonly understood by materialism, seems to me to place himself on a level with the mathematician, who should mistake the $x$'s and $y$'s with which he works his problems, for real entities—and with this further disadvantage, as compared with the mathematician, that the blunders of the latter are of no practical consequence, while the errors of systematic materialism may paralyse the energies and destroy the beauty of a life.

1868                                                                  1868, 1892


# WILLIAM MORRIS

1834–1896

The profound admiration and affection in which William Morris was held by two famous men of the generation after his own will suggest the peculiar power and charm of his genius. William Butler Yeats and Bernard Shaw are legendary in their dissimilarity. The former celebrated an archaic class-bound social structure which alone, he believed, made it possible for life to be instinctual, significant, and beautiful; the latter was in his day the exemplary exponent of the rational reorganization of

---

34. "Or, to speak more accurately, the physical state of which volition is the expression.—[1892]." (Huxley)

society. Disparate as they were in their hopes for life and art, both men acknowledged Morris as master. By Morris's vision of the archaic cultures of northern Europe, in which beauty and authenticity were in perfect union, Yeats in his youth was encouraged in his own dream of heroic existence; Morris was, he said, "my chief of men." In the socialism which was the passionate concern of Morris's late years, Shaw found confirmation of his own impulse toward a radical revision of social forms and ideals.

Morris was born in 1834, at Walthamstow, a town near London and adjacent to the beautiful Epping Forest. His father was a stockbroker of considerable and increasing wealth, who, when William was six, moved his family to Woodford Hall, a stately Georgian mansion virtually within the forest. Here William, after a delicate and threatened infancy, lived an outdoor life and developed the feeling for the primeval nature of the ancient world which was to mark his poetry. In the shaping of his imagination Scott's Waverley novels played a decisive part—he had read all of them by the time he was seven—as doubtless did the suit of toy armor in which he rode his pony over his father's acres. In 1847 his father died and William was sent away to school, the newly founded Marlborough College. He took but little pleasure in school life and kept mostly to himself, but he delighted in the pre-Celtic, Roman, and medieval antiquities of the district and became absorbed in the books on archaeology and ecclesiastical architecture with which the school's library happened to be well stocked; he later said that he learned as a schoolboy all that was to be known about English Gothic.

Under the influence of a devout sister, Morris decided upon a career in the church and with this goal in view he entered Exeter College, Oxford, in 1853. It was here that, early in his first year, he formed his intimate and lifelong friendship with Edward Burne-Jones, later to be, with Dante Gabriel Rossetti and John Everett Millais, one of the notable members of the Pre-Raphaelite group of painters; at the time of their meeting, Burne-Jones, like Morris, planned to take holy orders. The year of Morris's coming to Oxford was the year of the publication of Ruskin's *Stones of Venice,* and the famous chapter, "The Nature of Gothic" (see above), offered a new creed which eventually was to set at naught such inclination to the church as Morris had. For a time Newman and the Oxford Movement—or some approximate notion thereof—meant much to Morris and his friends as offering an ideal of dedication and community which would rescue them from the commonplaceness and complacency of English life. Yet if Newman touched the imagination of these young men, Tennyson commanded it, and it was under the spell of Tennyson that Morris tried his hand at poetry. Nothing is more characteristic of him than the remark he made when his first efforts in this line of work were admired by his friends: "Well," he said, "if this is poetry, it is very easy to write." (For comment on his poetry, see above, p. 617f.)

In 1855, on a tour in France, Morris and Burne-Jones came simultaneously to the realization that it was impossible for them to proceed to holy orders and that they must instead dedicate themselves to art, Burne-Jones as a painter, Morris as an architect. So far as can be discerned, once Morris had made his decision, religion was for him a dead issue, and the influence of its idiom is not to be traced in his prose, as it so readily is in the prose of Carlyle, Ruskin, and Arnold. Morris apprenticed himself to an Oxford firm of architects, which later moved to London, where Morris lived with Burne-Jones and studied painting at night. Painting proved to make a stronger claim upon him than the study of the practical aspects of architecture and he withdrew from his apprenticeship at the end of the first year. Yet painting no more than architecture was to be Morris's true métier, which, however, was soon to make itself known to him. He and Burne-Jones were under the necessity of furnishing their quarters and they were repelled by the ugliness and vulgar sham of the domestic goods offered in the shops. Morris met the situation by drafting designs, more or less medieval in feeling, for tables, chairs, and wardrobes, and a carpenter was engaged to execute them. With this enterprise Morris was launched upon his unique career in what he was to call the "lesser arts," those arts with whose products men are in touch every moment of their daily lives and by which —so Morris believed—their sensibilities, ultimately their conceptions of who and what they are, which is to say their very souls, are conditioned and controlled.

Morris married in 1859, and the building of his home, the famous Red House, gave impetus to his work as a designer. He and his friend Philip Webb, the architect of the house, designed the hangings, the wallpapers, the furniture, virtually every appurtenance of the house except the Persian rugs and the china. Two years later Morris set up as a professional decorator. With a group of friends including Webb, Rossetti, and Burne-Jones he organized the firm generally known as Morris and Company. As a business it grew increasingly business-like and in time was successful; when, in 1881, the Throne and Reception rooms of St. James's Palace were to be redecorated, the commission went to Morris and Company. But although Morris kept his eye on the ledgers, and the more closely as his considerable inherited fortune began to diminish, the company was his continuing act of social and moral criticism, his silent ceaseless commentary on the crassness of English taste, ultimately upon the machine civilization which, he believed, had corrupted the English character and made the root and ground of the dullness and ugliness of English lives. His fabrics and his wallpapers—perhaps these especially—were to recall the English to a delight in growing things, in clear true color, in lightness and grace, and in the discernible touch of an actual craftsman's conceiving mind and competent hand.

In 1876, when he was forty-two, Morris's commentary on English life ceased to be a silent one. In letters and conversations he had long been articulate about his social views, and now he became public and political. Moved by the threat of war with Russia over the Turkish question, he joined the Eastern Question Society, served as its treasurer, and, in the following year, on his own account wrote a manifesto, *To the Working-men of England,* in which he denounced the sentiment for war as the expression of the interests of the aristocratic class, which he went on to characterize as being contemptuously antagonistic to every aspiration of the working class.

Many years before, Morris had signalized his alienation from the upper classes by his careless dress, his pipe, his beard, and his tousled hair (from which came the nickname of his Oxford days, Topsy), and his refusal to dine out. Now, although he was ineluctably the gentleman and even, by brevet at least, the imperious aristocrat, his commitment was increasingly to the workers, not only as members of the class that suffered most under a plutocratic system but also as the potential agents of change. It was at this time that he began his public lectures on the decorative arts, the first of which eventually bore the title *The Lesser Arts.* He described art as the type or paradigm of all work that is appropriate to human beings and emphasized the "lesser" quality of the decorative arts, as against the "high" exigent art of the great creative geniuses, in order to put art, or activities cognate with art, within the reach of the generality of mankind. He was far indeed from agreeing with Carlyle's view (see above, the chapter of *Past and Present* called "Labour") that any work at all was in some degree salutary and humanizing; he held with Ruskin that enforced work, exhausting work, trivial work, mechanical work, work of which the worker does not know the meaning, was exactly dehumanizing. The way in which art could increase man's sense of his community and further his happiness was central to his thought, as the titles of his lectures suggest: *Art and Democracy, Art Under Plutocracy, Hopes and Fears for Art.*

With the passage of the years this interest in the quality of human existence was matched by his concern with the practical means by which that quality might be realized. In 1883 Morris joined the Democratic Federation and, when it became the Social Democratic Federation, accepted membership on its executive board. He read Marx's *Capital* (in French), declared himself a socialist, and became an active public lecturer on socialism. His life was now committed to the multifarious activities of radical politics, the acrimonious deliberations of committees, the debates in dingy meeting halls, the editing of agitational journals, and participation in mass protests. Yet he found time for his own work—for his Utopian novels, *The Dream of John Ball* (1886) and the entrancing *News from Nowhere* (1890); for his verse translations of the *Odyssey* (1887) and of *Beowulf* (1895); for the series of prose romances (the first was *The House of the Wolfings* in 1888), of which Yeats said that they were "so great a joy that they were the only books I was ever to read slowly that I might not come quickly to the end"; for his lecture on tapestry weaving and his weaving of the *Adoration of the Magi* tapestry for Exeter College Chapel; and for the setting up of the Kelmscott Press to manufacture beautiful books, and for designing the typefaces, ornaments, and formats. One of the first publications of the Press was Ruskin's "The Nature of Gothic," with a preface by Morris; its most ambitious undertaking was its edition of Chaucer (long one of Morris's best-loved authors), with illustrations by Burne-Jones and decorative designs by Morris (1896). This great labor was his last. This man of inexhaustible energies began to fail, doubtless as a consequence of the severe attack of rheumatic fever he had suffered in 1864, with its sporadic recurrences over the years. But his physician said after his death in 1896 that what he had died of was "simply being William Morris, and having done more work than most ten men."

# The Beauty of Life

This is the text of a lecture which Morris delivered before the Birmingham Society of Arts and School of Design on February 19, 1880. It represents Morris's social thought at the mid-point of its development. It summarizes his passionate dissatisfaction with the look and tone of English life, to the revision of which his efforts as a designer had been directed for a quarter-century. And it points forward to the decision which he made some three years later, after a reading of Marx's *Capital*, to commit himself to socialism. His concern with the condition of the working class was to become more central to his purposes and more specifically political, but at this point in his life it was already intense.

# The Beauty of Life

'—propter vitam vivendi perdcre causas.'

JUVENAL [1]

I stand before you this evening weighted with a disadvantage that I did not feel last year—I have little fresh to tell you; I can somewhat enlarge on what I said then; here and there I may make bold to give you a practical suggestion, or I may put what I have to say in a way which will be clearer to some of you perhaps; but my message is really the same as it was when I first had the pleasure of meeting you.

It is true that if all were going smoothly with art, or at all events so smoothly that thero wcre bul a few malcontents in the world, you might listen with some pleasure, and perhaps advantage, to the talk of an old hand in the craft concerning ways of work, the snares that beset success, and the shortest road to it, to a tale of workshop receipts [2] and the like: that would be a pleasant talk surely between friends and fellow-workmen: but it seems to me as if it were not for us as yet; nay, maybe we may live long and find no time fit for such restful talk as the cheerful histories of the hopes and fears of our workshops: anyhow to-night I cannot do it, but must once again call the faithful of art to a battle wider and more distracting than that kindly struggle with nature, to which all true craftsmen are born; which is both the building-up and the wearing-away of their lives.

As I look round on this assemblage, and think of all that it represents, I cannot choose but be moved to the soul by the troubles of the life of civilized man, and the hope that thrusts itself through them; I cannot refrain from giving you once again the message with which, as it seems, some chanoo hap has charged me: that message is, in short, to call on you to face the latest danger which civilization is threatened with, a danger of her own breeding: that men in struggling towards the complete attainment of all the luxuries of life for the strongest portion of their race should deprive their whole race of all the beauty of life: a danger that the strongest and wisest of mankind, in striving to attain to a complete mastery over Nature, should destroy her simplest and widest-spread gifts, and thereby enslave simple people to them, and themselves to themselves, and so at last drag the world into a second barbarism more ignoble, and a thousandfold more hopeless, than the first.

Now of you who are listening to me, there are some, I feel sure, who have received this message, and taken it to heart, and are day by day fighting the battle that it calls on you to fight: to you I can say nothing but that if any word I speak discourage you, I shall heartily wish I had never spoken at all: but to be shown the enemy, and the castle we have got to storm, is not to be bidden to run from him; nor am I telling you to sit down deedless in the desert because between you and the promised land lies many a trouble, and death itself maybe: the hope before you you know, and nothing that I can say can take it away from you; but friend may with advantage cry out

1. "—and for the sake of life to sacrifice life's only end." This line is preceded by one which says, "Deem it to be the summit of impiety to prefer existence to honor." *Satires* viii. 83.

2. A "receipt" is the same as a "recipe," which is now the preferred word: a formula for preparing a dish in cookery or a pharmacological prescription.

to friend in the battle that a stroke is coming from this side or that: take my hasty words in that sense, I beg of you.

But I think there will be others of you in whom vague discontent is stirring: who are oppressed by the life that surrounds you; confused and troubled by that oppression, and not knowing on which side to seek a remedy, though you are fain to do so: well, we, who have gone further into those troubles, believe that we can help you: true we cannot at once take your trouble from you; nay, we may at first rather add to it; but we can tell you what we think of the way out of it; and then amidst the many things you will have to do to set yourselves and others fairly on that way, you will many days, nay most days, forget your trouble in thinking of the good that lies beyond it, for which you are working.

But, again, there are others amongst you (and to speak plainly, I daresay they are the majority), who are not by any means troubled by doubt of the road the world is going, nor excited by any hope of its bettering that road: to them the cause of civilization is simple and even commonplace: wonder, hope, and fear no longer hang about it; it has become to us like the rising and setting of the sun; it cannot err, and we have no call to meddle with it, either to complain of its course, or to try to direct it.

There is a ground of reason and wisdom in that way of looking at the matter: surely the world will go on its ways, thrust forward by impulses which we cannot understand or sway: but as it grows in strength for the journey, its necessary food is the life and aspirations of *all* of us: and we discontented strugglers with what at times seems the hurrying blindness of civilization, no less than those who see nothing but smooth, unvarying progress in it, are bred of civilization also, and shall be used up to further it in some way or other, I doubt not: and it may be of some service to those who think themselves the only loyal subjects of progress to hear of our existence, since their not hearing of it would not make an end of it: it may set them a-thinking not unprofitably to hear of burdens that they do not help to bear, but which are nevertheless real and weighty enough to some of their fellow-men, who are helping, even as they are, to form the civilization that is to be.

The danger that the present course of civilization will destroy the beauty of life—these are hard words, and I wish I could mend them, but I cannot, while I speak what I believe to be the truth.

That the beauty of life is a thing of no moment, I suppose few people would venture to assert, and yet most civilized people act as if it were of none, and in so doing are wronging both themselves and those that are to come after them; for that beauty, which is what is meant by *art*, using the word in its widest sense, is, I contend, no mere accident to human life, which people can take or leave as they choose, but a positive necessity of life, if we are to live as nature meant us to; that is, unless we are content to be less than men.

Now I ask you, as I have been asking myself this long while, what proportion of the population in civilized countries has any share at all in that necessity of life?

I say that the answer which must be made to that question justifies my fear that modern civilization is on the road to trample out all the beauty of life, and to make us less than men.

Now if there should be any here who will say: It was always so; there always was a mass of rough ignorance that knew and cared nothing about art; I answer first, that if that be the case, then it was always wrong, and we, as soon as we have become conscious of that wrong, are bound to set it right if we can.

But moreover, strange to say, and in spite of all the suffering that the world has wantonly made for itself, and has in all ages so persistently clung to, as if it were a good and holy thing, this wrong of the mass of men being regardless of art was *not* always so.

So much is now known of the periods of art that have left abundant examples of their work behind them, that we can judge of the art of all periods by comparing these with the remains of times of which less has been left us; and we cannot fail to come to the conclusion that down to very recent days everything that the hand of man touched was more or less beautiful: so that in those days all people who made anything shared in art, as well as all people who used the things so made: that is, *all* people shared in art.

But some people may say: And was that to be wished for? would not this universal spreading of art stop progress in other matters, hinder the work of the world? Would it not make us unmanly? [3] or if not that, would it not be intrusive, and push out other things necessary also for men to study?

Well, I have claimed a necessary place for art, a natural place, and it would be in the very essence of it, that it would apply its own rules of order and fitness to the general ways of life: it seems to me, therefore, that people who are over-anxious of the outward expression of beauty becoming too great a force among the other forces of life, would, if they had had the making of the external world, have been afraid of making an ear of wheat beautiful, lest it should not have been good to eat.

But indeed there seems no chance of art becoming universal, unless on the terms that it shall have little self-consciousness, and for the most part be done with little effort; [4] so that the rough work of the world would be as little hindered by it, as the work of external nature is by the beauty of all her forms and moods: this was the case in the times that I have been speaking of: of art which was made by conscious effort, the result of the individual striving towards perfect expression of their thoughts by men very specially gifted, there was perhaps no more than there is now, except in very wonderful and short periods; though I believe that even for such men the struggle to produce beauty was not so bitter as it now is. But if there were not more great thinkers than there are now, there was a countless multitude of happy workers whose work did express, and could not choose but express, some original thought, and was consequently both interesting and beautiful: now there is certainly no chance of the more individual art becoming common, and either wearying

3. The idea that a concern with art might be a graceful characteristic of women but was not appropriate to the masculine temperament was prevalent among the middle and upper classes in the Victorian period.

4. Morris is proposing here a conception of art which goes counter to the one that prevailed in his time. It is not the art of the genius-artist, the product of his "great brains and miraculously gifted hands," controlled by his ambitions and his exigent ideals, and by his urge to dominate the minds of men, but a much more modest art, the art of the craftsman (who once had been called an artist), naturally manifesting itself in the things of everyday life.

us by its over-abundance, or by noisy self-assertion preventing highly cultivated men taking their due part in the other work of the world; it is too difficult to do: it will be always but the blossom of all the half-conscious work below it, the fulfilment of the shortcomings of less complete minds: but it will waste much of its power, and have much less influence on men's minds, unless it be surrounded by abundance of that commoner work, in which all men once shared, and which, I say, will, when art has really awakened, be done so easily and constantly, that it will stand in no man's way to hinder him from doing what he will, good or evil. And as, on the one hand, I believe that art made by the people and for the people as a joy both to the maker and the user would further progress in other matters rather than hinder it, so also I firmly believe that that higher art produced only by great brains and miraculously gifted hands cannot exist without it: I believe that the present state of things in which it does exist, while popular art is, let us say, asleep or sick, is a transitional state, which must end at last either in utter defeat or utter victory for the arts.

For whereas all works of craftsmanship were once beautiful, unwittingly or not, they are now divided into two kinds, works of art and non-works of art: now nothing made by man's hand can be indifferent: it must be either beautiful and elevating, or ugly and degrading; and those things that are without art are so aggressively; [5] they wound it by their existence, and they are now so much in the majority that the works of art we are obliged to set ourselves to seek for, whereas the other things are the ordinary companions of our everyday life; so that if those who cultivate art intellectually were inclined never so much to wrap themselves in their special gifts and their high cultivation, and so live happily, apart from other men, and despising them, they could not do so: they are as it were living in an enemy's country; at every turn there is something lying in wait to offend and vex their nicer sense and educated eyes: they must share in the general discomfort—and I am glad of it.

So the matter stands: from the first dawn of history till quite modern times, Art, which Nature meant to solace all, fulfilled its purpose; all men shared in it: that was what made life romantic, as people call it, in those days—that and not robber-barons and inaccessible kings with their hierarchy of serving-nobles and other such rubbish: but art grew and grew, saw empires sicken and sickened with them; grew hale again, and haler, and grew so great at last that she seemed in good truth to have conquered everything, and laid the material world under foot. Then came a change at a period of the greatest life and hope in many ways that Europe had known till then: a time of so much and such varied hope that people call it the time of the New Birth: [6] as far as the arts are concerned I deny it that title; rather it seems to me that the great men who lived and glorified the practice of art in those days, were the fruit of the old,

---

5. The ugliness of Victorian domestic objects and architecture—all the more striking by comparison with what had been produced in England only a few years before—was to become proverbial among educated English people, largely through Morris's influence. The passage of time has in some degree abated the harshness of the judgment that was made up through the early years of the 20th century, and it is now possible to find charm in the things that Morris condemned, but although they are often valued as quaint or "interesting" or "amusing," no one is likely to find them beautiful.
6. That is, the Renaissance, a period of which Morris took a dim view.

not the seed of the new order of things: but a stirring and hopeful time it was, and many things were newborn then which have since brought forth fruit enough: and it is strange and perplexing that from those days forward the lapse of time, which, through plenteous confusion and failure, has on the whole been steadily destroying privilege and exclusiveness in other matters, has delivered up art to be the exclusive privilege of a few, and has taken from the people their birthright; while both wronged and wrongers have been wholly unconscious of what they were doing.

Wholly unconscious—yes, but we are no longer so: there lies the sting of it, and there also the hope.

When the brightness of the so called Renaissance faded, and it faded very suddenly, a deadly chill fell upon the arts: that New-birth mostly meant looking back to past times, wherein the men of those days thought they saw a perfection of art, which to their minds was different in kind, and not in degree only, from the ruder suggestive art of their own fathers: this perfection they were ambitious to imitate, this alone seemed to be art to them, the rest was childishness: so wonderful was their energy, their success so great, that no doubt to commonplace minds among them, though surely not to the great masters, that perfection seemed to be gained: and, perfection being gained, what are you to do?—you can go no further, you must aim at standing still—which you cannot do.[7]

Art by no means stood still in those latter days of the Renaissance, but took the downward road with terrible swiftness, and tumbled down at the bottom of the hill, where as if bewitched it lay long in great content, believing itself to be the art of Michael Angelo, while it was the art of men whom nobody remembers but those who want to sell their pictures.[8]

Thus it fared with the more individual forms of art. As to the art of the people; in countries and places where the greater art had flourished most, it went step by step on the downward path with that: in more out-of-the-way places, England for instance, it still felt the influence of the life of its earlier and happy days, and in a way lived on a while; but its life was so feeble, and, so to say, illogical, that it could not resist any change in external circumstances, still less could it give birth to anything new; and before this century began, its last flicker had died out. Still, while it was living, in whatever dotage, it did imply something going on in those matters of daily use that we have been thinking of, and doubtless satisfied some cravings for beauty: and when it was dead, for a long time people did not know it, or what had taken its place, crept so to

---

7. Morris describes in an admirably succinct way the rationale of the impulse to classicism. It is not so much the wish to "stand still" that he is condemning as what he suggests is anterior to it, the restless wish for perfection. Ready as Morris surely was to respond to "greatness" in art, he maintained an attitude of suspicion toward the urgency that characterized it, seeing in this, we might say, an analogue with the commercial competitiveness he denounced. His social ideal of the artist was based on what he conceived to be the function and practice of art in primitive, or relatively primitive, societies, in which, to use the formulation of another of his essays, art "is always part of things intended primarily for the service of the body" rather than of the mind.

8. Just which post-Renaissance artists Morris believes to have been rightly assigned to oblivion he does not say, but the chances are that many of them are now considered to be of high interest.

say into its dead body—that pretence of art, to wit, which is done with machines,[9] though sometimes the machines are called men, and doubtless are so out of working hours: nevertheless long before it was quite dead it had fallen so low that the whole subject was usually treated with the utmost contempt by every one who had any pretence of being a sensible man, and in short the whole civilized world had forgotten that there had ever been an art *made by the people for the people as a joy for the maker and the user.*

But now it seems to me that the very suddenness of the change ought to comfort us, to make us look upon this break in the continuity of the golden chain as an accident only, that itself cannot last: for think how many thousand years it may be since that primaeval man graved with a flint splinter on a bone the story of the mammoth he had seen, or told us of the slow uplifting of the heavily-horned heads of the reindeer that he stalked: think I say of the space of time from then till the dimming of the brightness of the Italian Renaissance! Whereas from that time till popular art died unnoticed and despised among ourselves is just but two hundred years.

Strange too, that very death is contemporaneous with new-birth of something at all events; for out of all despair sprang a new time of hope lighted by the torch of the French Revolution: and things that have languished with the languishing of art, rose afresh and surely heralded its new birth: in good earnest poetry was born again, and the English Language, which under the hands of sycophantic verse-makers had been reduced to a miserable jargon, whose meaning, if it have a meaning, cannot be made out without translation,[10] flowed clear, pure, and simple, along with the music of Blake and Coleridge: take those names, the earliest in date among ourselves, as a type of the change that has happened in literature since the time of George II.[11]

With that literature in which romance, that is to say humanity,[12] was re-born, there sprang up also a feeling for the romance of external nature, which is surely strong in us now, joined with a longing to know something real of the lives of those who have gone before us; of these feelings united you will find the broadest expression in the pages of Walter Scott: it is curious as showing how sometimes one art will lag behind another in a revival, that the man who wrote the exquisite and wholly unfettered naturalism of *The Heart of Midlothian,*[13] for instance, thought himself continually bound to seem to feel ashamed

---

9. The Great Exhibition of 1851 put special emphasis on the triumph of invention in the making of decorative domestic objects by machine.
10. Morris is referring to the poetry of the 18th century, which had generally fallen into low repute in the Victorian period under the influence of the Romantic critics (see Wordsworth's Preface to *Lyrical Ballads* ) and poets (see Keats's *Sleep and Poetry*). Matthew Arnold's *Study of Poetry* rates Dryden and Pope as not really poets at all. Morris had but little sympathy for the 18th century in general, not even for its admirable domestic arts.
11. That Morris does not include Wordsworth among the early Romanticists will suggest his dislike of that poet. Blake was not widely known at the time—Arnold does not mention him in *The Study of Poetry*—but William Rossetti, the brother of Morris's friend, Dante Gabriel Rossetti, was a great enthusiast of Blake's and collected his manuscripts.
12. The engaging downright simplicity of this statement is characteristic of Morris.
13. One of the best of Scott's novels, published 1818. Scott's representations of medieval life and of the tribal ethos of the Scottish highlands would naturally win a warm response from Morris. Although Scott might have been "ashamed" of loving Gothic architecture—the name was intended to be a pejorative one, pointing to the "rudeness" and "roughness" of

of, and to excuse himself for, his love of Gothic Architecture: he felt that it was romantic, and he knew that it gave him pleasure, but somehow he had not found out that it was art, having been taught in many ways that nothing could be art that was not done by a named man under academical rules.

I need not perhaps dwell much on what of change has been since: you know well that one of the master-arts, the art of painting, has been revolutionized. I have a genuine difficulty in speaking to you of men who are my own personal friends, nay, my masters: still, since I cannot quite say nothing of them I must say the plain truth, which is this: never in the whole history of art did any set of men come nearer to the feat of making something out of nothing than that little knot of painters who have raised English art from what it was when as a boy I used to go to the Royal Academy Exhibition, to what it is now.[14]

It would be ungracious indeed for me who have been so much taught by him that I cannot help feeling continually as I speak that I am echoing his words, to leave out the name of John Ruskin [15] from an account of what has happened since the tide, as we hope, began to turn in the direction of art. True it is, that his unequalled style of English and his wonderful eloquence would, whatever its subject-matter, have gained him some sort of a hearing in a time that has not lost its relish for literature; but surely the influence that he has exercised over cultivated people must be the result of that style and that eloquence expressing what was already stirring in men's minds; he could not have written what he has done unless people were in some sort ready for it; any more than those painters could have begun their crusade against the dulness and incompetency that was the rule in their art thirty years ago unless they had some hope that they would one day move people to understand them.

Well, we find that the gains since the turning-point of the tide are these: that there are some few artists who have, as it were, caught up the golden chain dropped two hundred years ago, and that there are a few highly cultivated people who can understand them; and that beyond these there is a vague feeling abroad among people of the same degree, of discontent at the ignoble ugliness that surrounds them.

That seems to me to mark the advance that we have made since the last of popular art came to an end amongst us, and I do not say, considering where we then were, that it is not a great advance, for it comes to this, that though the battle is still to win, there are those who are ready for the battle.

Indeed it would be a strange shame for this age if it were not so: for as every age of the world has its own troubles to confuse it, and its own follies to cumber it, so has each its own work to do, pointed out to it by unfailing signs of the times; and it is unmanly and stupid for the children of any age to say: We will not set our hands to the work; we did not make the troubles, we will

---

the style—it should be remembered that the interest in the Gothic goes back to the middle of the 18th century: Horace Walpole's famous Strawberry Hill, "a little Gothic castle," was begun in 1747.

14. Morris has in mind the group of painters known as the Pre-Raphaelite Brotherhood, to whom he was very close. See Ruskin, *Modern Painters*, note 14.

15. Ruskin, whose influence on Morris is of course decisive, was a strong partisan of the Pre-Raphaelites.

not weary ourselves seeking a remedy for them: so heaping up for their sons a heavier load than they can lift without such struggles as will wound and cripple them sorely. Not thus our fathers served us, who, working late and early, left us at last that seething mass of people so terribly alive and energetic, that we call modern Europe; not thus those served us, who have made for us these present days, so fruitful of change and wondering expectation.

The century that is now beginning to draw to an end, if people were to take to nicknaming centuries, would be called the Century of Commerce; and I do not think I undervalue the work that it has done: it has broken down many a prejudice and taught many a lesson that the world has been hitherto slow to learn: it has made it possible for many a man to live free, who would in other times have been a slave, body or soul, or both: if it has not quite spread peace and justice through the world, as at the end of its first half we fondly hoped it would, it has at least stirred up in many fresh cravings for peace and justice: its work has been good and plenteous, but much of it was roughly done, as needs was; recklessness has commonly gone with its energy, blindness too often with its haste: so that perhaps it may be work enough for the next century to repair the blunders of that recklessness, to clear away the rubbish which that hurried work has piled up; nay even we in the second half of its last quarter may do something towards setting its house in order.

You, of this great and famous town, for instance, which has had so much to do with the Century of Commerce,[16] your gains are obvious to all men, but the price you have paid for them is obvious to many—surely to yourselves most of all: I do not say that they are not worth the price; I know that England and the world could very ill afford to exchange the Birmingham of to-day for the Birmingham of the year 1700: but surely if what you have gained be more than a mockery, you cannot stop at those gains, or even go on always piling up similar ones. Nothing can make me believe that the present condition of your Black Country [17] yonder is an unchangeable necessity of your life and position: such miseries as this were begun and carried on in pure thoughtlessness, and a hundredth part of the energy that was spent in creating them would get rid of them: I do think if we were not all of us too prone to acquiesce in the base byword 'after me the deluge,' [18] it would soon be something more than an idle dream to hope that your pleasant midland hills and fields might begin to become pleasant again in some way or other, even without depopulating them; or that those once lovely valleys of Yorkshire in the 'heavy woollen district,' with their sweeping hill-sides and noble rivers, should not need the stroke of ruin to make them once more delightful abodes of men, instead of the dog-holes that the Century of Commerce has made them.

Well, people will not take the trouble or spend the money necessary to begin-ning this sort of reforms, because they do not feel the evils they live amongst,

16. Early in the 19th century Birmingham became one of the two leading manufacturing cities of England, the other being Manchester. It produces metal-work of all kinds.
17. The name by which the Midland districts of South Staffordshire and North Warwick-shire are known because of the grime from the coal and iron mines and industry.
18. Madame de Pompadour (1721–64), the mistress of Louis XV, said this—actually, "After us the deluge"—although it is commonly attributed to the king himself. The deluge she envisaged was political.

because they have degraded themselves into something less than men; they are unmanly because they have ceased to have their due share of art.[19]

For again I say that therein rich people have defrauded themselves as well as the poor: you will see a refined and highly educated man nowadays, who has been to Italy and Egypt and where not, who can talk learnedly enough (and fantastically enough sometimes) about art, and who has at his fingers' ends abundant lore concerning the art and literature of past days, sitting down without signs of discomfort in a house, that with all its surroundings is just brutally vulgar and hideous: all his education has not done more for him than that.

The truth is, that in art, and in other things besides, the laboured education of a few will not raise even those few above the reach of the evils that beset the ignorance of the great mass of the population: the brutality of which such a huge stock has been accumulated lower down will often show without much peeling through the selfish refinement of those who have let it accumulate. The lack of art, or rather the murder of art, that curses our streets from the sordidness of the surroundings of the lower classes, has its exact counterpart in the dulness and vulgarity of those of the middle classes, and the double-distilled dulness, and scarcely less vulgarity of those of the upper classes.

I say this is as it should be; it is just and fair as far as it goes; and moreover the rich with their leisure are the more like to move if they feel the pinch themselves.

But how shall they and we, and all of us, move? What is the remedy?

What remedy can there be for the blunders of civilization but further civilization? You do not by any accident think that we have gone as far in that direction as it is possible to go, do you?—even in England, I mean?

When some changes have come to pass, that perhaps will be speedier than most people think, doubtless education will both grow in quality and in quantity; so that it may be, that as the nineteenth century is to be called the Century of Commerce, the twentieth may be called the Century of Education. But that education does not end when people leave school is now a mere commonplace; and how then can you really educate men who lead the life of machines, who only think for the few hours during which they are not at work, who in short spend almost their whole lives in doing work which is not proper for developing them body and mind in some worthy way? You cannot educate, you cannot civilize men, unless you can give them a share in art.[20]

Yes, and it is hard indeed as things go to give most men that share; for they do not miss it, or ask for it, and it is impossible as things are that they should either miss or ask for it. Nevertheless everything has a beginning, and many great things have had very small ones; and since, as I have said, these ideas are already abroad in more than one form, we must not be too much discouraged at the seemingly boundless weight we have to lift.

After all, we are only bound to play our own parts, and do our own share of the lifting; and as in no case that share can be great, so also in all cases it is called for, it is necessary. Therefore let us work and faint not; remembering

19. Morris here boldly inverts the view that a concern with art is unmanly (see note 3).
20. Morris means an *active* share, the actual making of art, not the passive "consumption" of it.

that though it be natural, and therefore excusable, amidst doubtful times to feel doubts of success oppress us at whiles, yet not to crush those doubts, and work as if we had them not, is simple cowardice, which is unforgivable. No man has any right to say that all has been done for nothing, that all the faithful unwearying strife of those that have gone before us shall lead us nowhither; that mankind will but go round and round in a circle for ever: no man has a right to say that, and then get up morning after morning to eat his victuals and sleep a-nights, all the while making other people toil to keep his worthless life a-going.

Be sure that some way or other will be found out of the tangle, even when things seem most tangled, and be no less sure that some use will then have come of our work, if it has been faithful, and therefore unsparingly careful and thoughtful.

So once more I say, if in any matters civilization has gone astray, the remedy lies not in standing still, but in more complete civilization.

Now whatever discussion there may be about that often used and often misused word, I believe all who hear me will agree with me in believing from their hearts, and not merely in saying in conventional phrase, that the civilization which does not carry the whole people with it is doomed to fall, and give place to one which at least aims at doing so.

We talk of the civilization of the ancient peoples, of the classical times: well, civilized they were no doubt, some of their folk at least: an Athenian citizen for instance led a simple, dignified, almost perfect life; [21] but there were drawbacks to happiness perhaps in the lives of his slaves: and the civilization of the ancients was founded on slavery.

Indeed, that ancient society did give a model to the world, and showed us for ever what blessings are freedom of life and thought, self-restraint and a generous education: all those blessings the ancient free peoples set forth to the world—and kept them to themselves.

Therefore [22] no tyrant was too base, no pretext too hollow, for enslaving the grandsons of the men of Salamis [23] and Thermopylae: [24] therefore did the descendants of those stern and self-restrained Romans, who were ready to give up everything, and life as the least of things, to the glory of their commonweal, produce monsters of license and reckless folly. Therefore did a little knot of Galilean peasants [25] overthrow the Roman Empire.

Ancient civilization was chained to slavery and exclusiveness, and it fell; the barbarism that took its place has delivered us from slavery and grown into

21. The virtual perfection of Athenian life was often adduced in Victorian England as a criterion by which English life was to be judged, but a reading of Thucydides or Aristophanes or Plato will suggest that the city had its measure of deplorable traits.
22. That is, because the Athenians did not induce other nations to adopt their ideals. Morris has in mind the tendency of the Greeks to look down on other peoples as barbarians.
23. It was at Salamis that the Greeks won their decisive naval victory over the invading Persians in 480 B.C.
24. At the mountain pass of Thermopylae the Greeks were defeated, but the rear-guard action of Leonidas with a small Spartan force, holding the pass to the death against the Persian army, had an inspiring effect on morale. The battle of Salamis took place subsequently.
25. That is, Christians. Morris's attribution of causation seems rather captious.

modern civilization; and that in its turn has before it the choice of never-ceasing growth, or destruction by that which has in it the seeds of higher growth.

There is an ugly word for a dreadful fact, which I must make bold to use—the residuum: that word since the time I first saw it used,[26] has had a terrible significance to me, and I have felt from my heart that if this residuum were a necessary part of modern civilization, as some people openly, and many more tacitly, assume that it is, then this civilization carries with it the poison that shall one day destroy it, even as its elder sister did: if civilization is to go no further than this, it had better not have gone so far: if it does not aim at getting rid of this misery and giving some share in the happiness and dignity of life to all the people that it has created, and which it spends such unwearying energy in creating, it is simply an organized injustice, a mere instrument for oppression, so much the worse than that which has gone before it, as its pretensions are higher, its slavery subtler, its mastery harder to overthrow, because supported by such a dense mass of commonplace well-being and comfort.

Surely this cannot be: surely there is a distinct feeling abroad of this injustice: so that if the residuum still clogs all the efforts of modern civilization to rise above mere population-breeding and money-making, the difficulty of dealing with it is the legacy, first of the ages of violence and almost conscious brutal injustice, and next of the ages of thoughtlessness, of hurry and blindness; surely all those who think at all of the future of the world are at work in one way or other in striving to rid it of this shame.

That to my mind is the meaning of what we call National Education, which we have begun, and which is doubtless already bearing its fruits, and will bear greater, when all people are educated, not according to the money which they or their parents possess, but according to the capacity of their minds.[27]

What effect that will have upon the future of the arts I cannot say, but one would surely think a very great effect; for it will enable people to see clearly many things which are now as completely hidden from them as if they were blind in body and idiotic in mind: and this, I say, will act not only upon those who most directly feel the evils of ignorance, but also upon those who feel them indirectly—upon us, the educated: the great wave of rising intelligence, rife with so many natural desires and aspirations, will carry all classes along with it, and force us all to see that many things which we have been used to look upon as necessary and eternal evils are merely the accidental and temporary growths of past stupidity, and can be escaped from by due effort and the exercise of courage, goodwill, and forethought.

And among those evils, I do, and must always, believe will fall that one which last year I told you that I accounted the greatest of all evils, the heaviest of all slaveries; that evil of the greater part of the population being engaged for by far the most part of their lives in work, which at the best cannot interest

26. He first saw it used in *Culture and Anarchy*, in Arnold's discussion of the three English social classes. After describing the aristocracy, to which he gives the name Barbarians, and the middle classes, which he called the Philistines, Arnold speaks of the working class—"to this vast residuum," he says, "we may with great propriety give the name of Populace."
27. Although the matter has been in constant debate in England for over a century, and although many adjustments have been made, the educational opportunities available to the working class are still more strictly limited than in the United States.

them, or develop their best faculties, and at the worst (and that is the commonest, too) is mere unmitigated slavish toil, only to be wrung out of them by the sternest compulsion, a toil which they shirk all they can—small blame to them.[28] And this toil degrades them into less than men: and they will some day come to know it, and cry out to be made men again, and art only can do it, and redeem them from this slavery; and I say once more that this is her highest and most glorious end and aim; and it is in her struggle to attain to it that she will most surely purify herself, and quicken her own aspirations towards perfection.

But we—in the meantime we must not sit waiting for obvious signs of these later and glorious days to show themselves on earth, and in the heavens, but rather turn to the commonplace, and maybe often dull work of fitting ourselves in detail to take part in them if we should live to see one of them; or in doing our best to make the path smooth for their coming, if we are to die before they are here.

What, therefore, can we do, to guard traditions of time past that we may not one day have to begin anew from the beginning with none to teach us? What are we to do, that we may take heed to, and spread the decencies of life, so that at the least we may have a field where it will be possible for art to grow when men begin to long for it: what finally can we do, each of us, to cherish some germ of art, so that it may meet with others, and spread and grow little by little into the thing that we need?

Now I cannot pretend to think that the first of these duties is a matter of indifference to you, after my experience of the enthusiastic meeting that I had the honour of addressing here last autumn on the subject of the (so called) restoration of St. Mark's at Venice; [29] you thought, and most justly thought, it seems to me, that the subject was of such moment to art in general, that it was a simple and obvious thing for men who were anxious on the matter to address themselves to those who had the decision of it in their hands; even though the former were called Englishmen, and the latter Italians; for you felt that the name of lovers of art would cover those differences: if you had any misgivings, you remembered that there was but one such building in the world, and that it was worth while risking a breach of etiquette, if any words of ours could do anything towards saving it; well, the Italians were, some of them, very naturally, though surely unreasonably, irritated, for a time, and in some of their prints they bade us look at home; that was no argument in favour of the wisdom of wantonly rebuilding St. Mark's façade: but certainly those of us who have not yet looked at home in this matter had better do so speedily, late and over late though it be: for though we have no golden-pictured interiors like St. Mark's Church at home, we still have many buildings which are both

28. The idea that work of any kind "degrades" man affronted a piety of the time which had received confirmation from Carlyle, whose doctrine of the value of work made no distinction between kinds of work.

29. The great cathedral. The enterprise of "restoring" the architectural monuments of the past, which often involved not merely the replacement of damaged elements but also the revision of the existing plan of the building, had been frequently denounced by Ruskin and was resented by serious lovers of art. In 1877 Morris founded the Society for the Protection of Ancient Buildings, known as "Anti-Scrape."

works of ancient art and monuments of history: and just think what is happening to them, and note, since we profess to recognize their value, how helpless art is in the Century of Commerce!

In the first place, many and many a beautiful and ancient building is being destroyed all over civilized Europe as well as in England, because it is supposed to interfere with the convenience of the citizens, while a little forethought might save it without trenching on that convenience; but even apart from that, I say that if we are not prepared to put up with a little inconvenience in our lifetimes for the sake of preserving a monument of art which will elevate and educate, not only ourselves, but our sons, and our sons' sons, it is vain and idle of us to talk about art—or education either. Brutality must be bred of such brutality.

The same thing may be said about enlarging, or otherwise altering for convenience's sake, old buildings still in use for something like their original purposes: in almost all such cases it is really nothing more than a question of a little money for a new site: and then a new building can be built exactly fitted for the uses it is needed for, with such art about it as our own days can furnish; while the old monument is left to tell its tale of change and progress, to hold out example and warning to us in the practice of the arts: and thus the convenience of the public, the progress of modern art, and the cause of education, are all furthered at once at the cost of a little money.

Surely if it be worth while troubling ourselves about the works of art of to-day, of which any amount almost can be done, since we are yet alive, it is worth while spending a little care, forethought, and money in preserving the art of bygone ages, of which (woe worth the while!) so little is left, and of which we can never have any more, whatever goodhap the world may attain to.

No man who consents to the destruction or the mutilation of an ancient building has any right to pretend that he cares about art; or has any excuse to plead in defence of his crime against civilization and progress, save sheer brutal ignorance.

But before I leave this subject I must say a word or two about the curious invention of our own days called Restoration, a method of dealing with works of bygone days which, though not so degrading in its spirit as downright destruction, is nevertheless little better in its results on the condition of those works of art; it is obvious that I have no time to argue the question out to-night, so I will only make these assertions:

That ancient buildings, being both works of art and monuments of history, must obviously be treated with great care and delicacy: that the imitative art of to-day is not, and cannot be the same thing as ancient art, and cannot replace it; and that therefore if we superimpose this work on the old, we destroy it both as art and as a record of history: lastly, that the natural weathering of the surface of a building is beautiful, and its loss disastrous.

Now the restorers hold the exact contrary of all this: they think that any clever architect to-day can deal off-hand successfully with the ancient work; that while all things else have changed about us since (say) the thirteenth century, art has not changed, and that our workmen can turn out work identical with that of the thirteenth century; and, lastly, that the weather-beaten surface of an ancient building is worthless, and to be got rid of wherever possible.

You see the question is difficult to argue, because there seem to be no common grounds between the restorers and the anti-restorers: I appeal therefore to the public, and bid them note, that though our opinions may be wrong, the action we advise is not rash: let the question be shelved awhile: if, as we are always pressing on people, due care be taken of these monuments, so that they shall not fall into disrepair, they will be always there to 'restore' whenever people think proper and when we are proved wrong; but if it should turn out that we are right, how can the 'restored' buildings be restored? I beg of you therefore to let the question be shelved, till art has so advanced among us, that we can deal authoritatively with it, till there is no longer any doubt about the matter.

Surely these monuments of our art and history, which, whatever the lawyers may say, belong not to a coterie, or to a rich man here and there, but to the nation at large, are worth this delay: surely the last relics of the life of the 'famous men and our fathers that begat us' [30] may justly claim of us the exercise of a little patience.

It will give us trouble no doubt, all this care of our possessions: but there is more trouble to come; for I must now speak of something else, of possessions which should be common to all of us, of the green grass, and the leaves, and the waters, of the very light and air of heaven, which the Century of Commerce has been too busy to pay any heed to. And first let me remind you that I am supposing every one here present professes to care about art.

Well, there are some rich men among us whom we oddly enough call manufacturers, by which we mean capitalists who pay other men to organize manufacturers; these gentlemen, many of whom buy pictures and profess to care about art, burn a deal of coal: there is an Act in existence which was passed to prevent them sometimes and in some places from pouring a dense cloud of smoke over the world, and, to my thinking, a very lame and partial Act it is: but nothing hinders these lovers of art from being a law to themselves, and making it a point of honour with them to minimize the smoke nuisance as far as their own works are concerned; and if they don't do so, when mere money, and even a very little of that, is what it will cost them, I say that their love of art is a mere pretence: how can you care about the image of a landscape when you show by your deeds that you don't care for the landscape itself? or what right have you to shut yourself up with beautiful form and colour when you make it impossible for other people to have any share in these things?

Well, and as to the Smoke Act itself: I don't know what heed you pay to it in Birmingham,[31] but I have seen myself what heed is paid to it in other places; Bradford for instance: though close by them at Saltaire [32] they have an

30. Ecclesiasticus 44:1.
31. "Since perhaps some people may read these words who are not of Birmingham, I ought to say that it was authoritatively explained at the meeting to which I addressed these words, that in Birmingham the law is strictly enforced." (Morris) The English have had quite striking success with smoke control—London, for example, no longer has its once-famous "pea-soup" fogs which sometimes were so black as to make movement through the streets impossible.
32. The model town founded by Sir Titus Salt on the river Aire, near Bradford in Yorkshire. Salt was an ingenious textile manufacturer of progressive and benevolent views. The enormous factory at Saltaire—opened 1853—was thoughtfully designed with a view to the safety and comfort of the workers.

example which I should have thought might have shamed them; for the huge chimney there which serves the acres of weaving and spinning sheds of Sir Titus Salt and his brothers is as guiltless of smoke as an ordinary kitchen chimney. Or Manchester: a gentleman of that city told me that the Smoke Act was a mere dead letter there: well, they buy pictures in Manchester and profess to wish to further the arts: but you see it must be idle pretence as far as their rich people are concerned: they only want to talk about it, and have themselves talked of.

I don't know what you are doing about this matter here; but you must forgive my saying, that unless you are beginning to think of some way of dealing with it, you are not beginning yet to pave your way to success in the arts.

Well, I have spoken of a huge nuisance, which is a type of the worst nuisances of what an ill-tempered man might be excused for calling the Century of Nuisances, rather than the Century of Commerce. I will now leave it to the consciences of the rich and influential among us, and speak of a minor nuisance which it is in the power of every one of us to abate, and which, small as it is, is so vexatious, that if I can prevail on a score of you to take heed to it by what I am saying, I shall think my evening's work a good one. Sandwich-papers I mean—of course you laugh: but come now, don't you, civilized as you are in Birmingham, leave them all about the Lickey hills [33] and your public gardens and the like? If you don't I really scarcely know with what words to praise you. When we Londoners go to enjoy ourselves at Hampton Court,[34] for instance, we take special good care to let everybody know that we have had something to eat: so that the park just outside the gates (and a beautiful place it is) looks as if it had been snowing dirty paper. I really think you might promise me one and all who are here present to have done with this sluttish habit, which is the type of many another in its way, just as the smoke nuisance is. I mean such things as scrawling one's name on monuments, tearing down tree boughs, and the like.

I suppose 'tis early days in the revival of the arts to express one's disgust at the daily increasing hideousness of the posters with which all our towns are daubed. Still we ought to be disgusted at such horrors, and I think make up our minds never to buy any of the articles so advertised. I can't believe they can be worth much if they need all that shouting to sell them.

Again, I must ask what do you do with the trees on a site that is going to be built over? do you try to save them, to adapt your houses at all to them? do you understand what treasures they are in a town or a suburb? or what a relief they will be to the hideous dog-holes which (forgive me!) you are probably going to build in their places? I ask this anxiously, and with grief in my soul, for in London and its suburbs we always [35] begin by clearing a site till it is as

---

33. Rural area on the outskirts of Birmingham.
34. Formerly a royal residence, on the Thames, some 12 miles from the center of London. When it and the park surrounding it were opened to the public, it became a favorite holiday spot for Londoners.
35. "Not *quite* always: in the little colony at Bedford Park, Chiswick, as many trees have been left as possible, to the boundless advantage of its quaint and pretty architecture." (Morris) Bedford Park was a model village in a London suburb built in the Georgian style by Norman Shaw, an architect who was influential in leading English taste away from Victorian domestic design. Yeats, who lived there in his boyhood, says, "For years Bedford Park was a romantic excitement."

bare as the pavement: I really think that almost anybody would have been shocked, if I could have shown him some of the trees that have been wantonly murdered in the suburb in which I live (Hammersmith to wit [36]), amongst them some of those magnificent cedars, for which we along the river used to be famous once.

But here again see how helpless those are who care about art or nature amidst the hurry of the Century of Commerce.

Pray do not forget, that any one who cuts down a tree wantonly or carelessly, especially in a great town or its suburbs, need make no pretence of caring about art.

What else can we do to help to educate ourselves and others in the path of art, to be on the road to attaining an *Art made by the people and for the people as a joy to the maker and the user?*

Why, having got to understand something of what art was, having got to look upon its ancient monuments as friends that can tell us something of times bygone, and whose faces we do not wish to alter, even though they be worn by time and grief: having got to spend money and trouble upon matters of decency, great and little; having made it clear that we really do care about nature even in the suburbs of a big town—having got so far, we shall begin to think of the houses in which we live.

For I must tell you that unless you are resolved to have good and rational architecture, it is, once again, useless your thinking about art at all.

I have spoken of the popular arts, but they might all be summed up in that one word Architecture; they are all parts of that great whole, and the art of house-building begins it all: if we did not know how to dye or to weave; if we had neither gold, nor silver, nor silk; and no pigments to paint with, but half-a-dozen ochres and umbers,[37] we might yet frame a worthy art that would lead to everything, if we had but timber, stone, and life, and a few cutting tools to make these common things not only shelter us from wind and weather, but also express the thoughts and aspirations that stir in us.

Architecture would lead us to all the arts, as it did with earlier men: but if we despise it and take no note of how we are housed, the other arts will have a hard time of it indeed.

Now I do not think the greatest of optimists would deny that, taking us one and all, we are at present housed in a perfectly shameful way, and since the greatest part of us have to live in houses already built for us, it must be admitted that it is rather hard to know what to do, beyond waiting till they tumble about our ears.

Only we must not lay the fault upon the builders, as some people seem inclined to do: they are our very humble servants, and will build what we ask for; remember, that rich men are not obliged to live in ugly houses, and yet you see they do; which the builders may be well excused for taking as a sign of what is wanted.

Well, the point is, we must do what we can, and make people understand what we want them to do for us, by letting them see what we do for ourselves.

36. In Kelmscott House, named after his country home, Kelmscott Manor.
37. Ochre: orange-yellow, in various intensities. Umber: brown, in various shades.

Hitherto, judging us by that standard, the builders may well say, that we want the pretence of a thing rather than the thing itself; that we want a show of petty luxury if we are unrich, a show of insulting stupidity if we are rich: and they are quite clear that as a rule we want to get something that shall look as if it cost twice as much as it really did.[38]

You cannot have Architecture on those terms: simplicity and solidity are the very first requisites of it: just think if it is not so: How we please ourselves with an old building by thinking of all the generations of men that have passed through it! do we not remember how it has received their joy, and borne their sorrow, and not even their folly has left sourness upon it? it still looks as kind to us as it did to them. And the converse of this we ought to feel when we look at a newly-built house if it were as it should be: we should feel a pleasure in thinking how he who had built it had left a piece of his soul behind him to greet the new-comers one after another long and long after he was gone:— but what sentiment can an ordinary modern house move in us, or what thought—save a hope that we may speedily forget its base ugliness?

But if you ask me how we are to pay for this solidity and extra expense, that seems to me a reasonable question; for you must dismiss at once as a delusion the hope that has been sometimes cherished, that you can have a building which is a work of art, and is therefore above all things properly built, at the same price as a building which only pretends to be this: never forget when people talk about cheap art in general, by the way, that all art costs time, trouble, and thought, and that money is only a counter to represent these things.

However, I must try to answer the question I have supposed put, how are we to pay for decent houses?

It seems to me that, by a great piece of good luck, the way to pay for them is by doing that which alone can produce popular art among us: living a simpler life, I mean. Once more I say that the greatest foe to art is luxury, art cannot live in its atmosphere.[39]

When you hear of the luxuries of the ancients, you must remember that they were not like our luxuries, they were rather indulgence in pieces of extravagant folly than what we to-day call luxury; which perhaps you would rather call comfort: well, I accept the word, and say that a Greek or Roman of the luxurious time would stare astonished could he be brought back again and shown the comforts of a well-to-do middle-class house.

But some, I know, think that the attainment of these very comforts is what makes the difference between civilization and uncivilization, that they are the essence of civilization. Is it so indeed? Farewell my hope then!—I had thought that civilization meant the attainment of peace and order and freedom, of goodwill between man and man, of the love of truth and the hatred of injustice, and by consequence the attainment of the good life which these things breed, a life free from craven fear, but full of incident: that was what I thought it

38. This desire had become especially salient as a condition of taste in the Victorian period and it was the conscious purpose of manufacturers of household goods to make them look *expensive.*

39. When, in the next paragraph, Morris equates luxury with comfort, he means an ostentation of comfort that denied its actuality.

meant, not more stuffed chairs and more cushions, and more carpets and gas, and more dainty meat and drink—and therewithal more and sharper differences between class and class.

If that be what it is, I for my part wish I were well out of it, and living in a tent in the Persian desert, or a turf hut on the Iceland hill-side. But however it be, and I think my view is the true view, I tell you that art abhors that side of civilization, she cannot breathe in the houses that lie under its stuffy slavery.[40]

Believe me, if we want art to begin at home, as it must, we must clear our houses of troublesome superfluities that are for ever in our way: conventional comforts that are no real comforts, and do but make work for servants and doctors: if you want a golden rule that will fit everybody, this is it:

*Have nothing in your houses that you do not know to be useful, or believe to be beautiful.*

And if we apply that rule strictly, we shall in the first place show the builders and such-like servants of the public what we really want, we shall create a demand for real art, as the phrase goes; and in the second place, we shall surely have more money to pay for decent houses.

Perhaps it will not try your patience too much if I lay before you my idea of the fittings necessary to the sitting-room of a healthy person: a room, I mean, which he would not have to cook in much, or sleep in generally, or in which he would not have to do any very litter-making manual work.[41]

First a book-case with a great many books in it: next a table that will keep steady when you write or work at it: then several chairs that you can move, and a bench that you can sit or lie upon: next a cupboard with drawers: next, unless either the book-case or the cupboard be very beautiful with painting or carving, you will want pictures or engravings, such as you can afford, only not stopgaps,[42] but real works of art on the wall; or else the wall itself must be ornamented with some beautiful and restful pattern: we shall also want a vase or two to put flowers in, which latter you must have sometimes, especially if you live in a town. Then there will be the fireplace of course, which in our climate is bound to be the chief object in the room.

That is all we shall want, especially if the floor be good; if it be not, as, by the way, in a modern house it is pretty certain not to be, I admit that a small carpet which can be bundled out of the room in two minutes will be useful, and we must also take care that it is beautiful, or it will annoy us terribly.

Now unless we are musical, and need a piano (in which case, as far as beauty is concerned, we are in a bad way),[43] that is quite all we want: and

40. Yeats recalls an occasion in which Morris spoke in dispraise even of the houses decorated by himself. "Do you suppose I like that kind of house? I would like a house like a big barn, where one ate in one corner, cooked in another corner, slept in the third corner, and in the fourth received one's friends." What Morris is protesting against is the restless *clutter* of the Victorian home.
41. Morris's audience being chiefly students or practitioners of art, such specifications have point; we may be sure that in the sitting room of a businessman no cooking or manual work was done.
42. Presumably reproductions.
43. The 19th-century domestic piano was pretty sure to be heavy-legged, over-decorated, and gloomy-looking.

we can add very little to these necessaries without troubling ourselves and hindering our work, our thought, and our rest.

If these things were done at the least cost for which they could be done well and solidly, they ought not to cost much; and they are so few, that those that could afford to have them at all, could afford to spend some trouble to get them fitting and beautiful: and all those who care about art ought to take great trouble to do so, and to take care that there be no sham art amongst them, nothing that it has degraded a man to make or sell. And I feel sure, that if all who care about art were to take this pains, it would make a great impression upon the public.

This simplicity you may make as costly as you please or can, on the other hand: you may hang your walls with tapestry instead of whitewash or paper; or you may cover them with mosaic, or have them frescoed by a great painter: all this is not luxury, if it be done for beauty's sake, and not for show: it does not break our golden rule: *Have nothing in your houses which you do not know to be useful or believe to be beautiful.*

All art starts from this simplicity; and the higher the art rises, the greater the simplicity. I have been speaking of the fittings of a dwelling-house—a place in which we eat and drink, and pass familiar hours; but when you come to places which people want to make more specially beautiful because of the solemnity or dignity of their uses, they will be simpler still, and have little in them save the bare walls made as beautiful as may be. St. Mark's at Venice has very little furniture in it, much less than most Roman Catholic churches: its lovely and stately mother St. Sophia of Constantinople had less still, even when it was a Christian church: [44] but we need not go either to Venice or Stamboul [45] to take note of that: go into one of our own mighty Gothic naves (do any of you remember the first time you did so?) and note how the huge free space satisfies and elevates you, even now when window and wall are stripped of ornament: then think of the meaning of simplicity and absence of encumbering gow gaws.

Now after all, for us who are learning art, it is not far to seek what is the surest way to further it; that which most breeds art is art; every piece of work that we do which is well done, is so much help to the cause; every piece of pretence and half-heartedness is so much hurt to it. Most of you who take to the practice of art can find out in no very long time whether you have any gifts for it or not: if you have not, throw the thing up, or you will have a wretched time of it yourselves, and will be damaging the cause by laborious pretence: but if you have gifts of any kind, you are happy indeed beyond most men; for your pleasure is always with you, nor can you be intemperate in the enjoyment of it, and as you use it, it does not lessen, but grows: if you are by chance weary of it at night, you get up in the morning eager for it; or if perhaps in the morning it seems folly to you for a while, yet presently, when your hand has been moving a little in its wonted way, fresh hope has sprung up beneath it and you are happy again. While others are getting through the day like plants thrust into the earth, which cannot turn this way

44. It is also known as Hagia Sophia, Greek for "the holy wisdom." It became a mosque when the Turks captured Constantinople in 1453.
45. Constantinople.

or that but as the wind blows them, you know what you want, and your will is on the alert to find it, and you, whatever happens, whether it be joy or grief, are at least alive.

Now when I spoke to you last year, after I had sat down I was half afraid that I had on some point said too much, that I had spoken too bitterly in my eagerness; that a rash word might have discouraged some of you; I was very far from meaning that: what I wanted to do, what I want to do to-night is to put definitely before you a cause for which to strive.

That cause is the Democracy of Art, the ennobling of daily and common work, which will one day put hope and pleasure in the place of fear and pain, as the forces which move men to labour and keep the world a-going. If I have enlisted any one in that cause, rash as my words may have been, or feeble as they may have been, they have done more good than harm; nor do I believe that any words of mine can discourage any who have joined that cause or are ready to do so: their way is too clear before them for that, and every one of us can help the cause whether he be great or little.

I know indeed that men, wearied by the pettiness of the details of the strife, their patience tried by hope deferred, will at whiles, excusably enough, turn back in their hearts to other days, when if the issues were not clearer, the means of trying them were simpler; when, so stirring were the times, one might even have atoned for many a blunder and backsliding by visibly dying for the cause. To have breasted the Spanish pikes at Leyden,[46] to have drawn sword with Oliver: [47] that may well seem to us at times amidst the tangles of to-day a happy fate: for a man to be able to say, I have lived like a fool, but now I will cast away fooling for an hour, and die like a man—there is something in that certainly: and yet 'tis clear that few men can be so lucky as to die for a cause, without having first of all lived for it. And as this is the most that can be asked from the greatest man that follows a cause, so it is the least that can be taken from the smallest.

So to us who have a Cause at heart, our highest ambition and our simplest duty are one and the same thing: for the most part we shall be too busy doing the work that lies ready to our hands, to let impatience for visibly great progress vex us much; but surely since we are servants of a Cause, hope must be ever with us, and sometimes perhaps it will so quicken our vision that it will outrun the slow lapse of time, and show us the victorious days when millions of those who now sit in darkness [48] will be enlightened by an *Art made by the people and for the people, a joy to the maker and the user.*

1880                                                                      1880

46. The inhabitants of the town defended it from the Spaniards in 1574.
47. The friend and comrade-in-arms who died with Roland defending the pass at Ronces-valles (Roncevaux) for Charlemagne.
48. Psalms 108:11.

# WALTER PATER
1839–1894

When Oscar Wilde entered Magdalen College, Oxford, in 1874, one of the books he read in his first term was Walter Pater's *Studies in the History of the Renaissance*, published in the year before. Twenty-three years later he referred to *The Renaissance*—so the work was re-titled in its second edition—as "that book which had such a strange influence over my life." The reference was made in the remarkable document which goes under the name of *De Profundis* (Out of the Depths), the immensely long auto-biographical letter which Wilde wrote to Lord Alfred Douglas shortly before the end of the prison term to which he had been sentenced after having been tried and found guilty of homosexual practices. Wilde does not further characterize *The Renaissance*; he does not say specifically what its influence was nor why it was "strange." But a famous circumstance of the publication of Pater's volume might tempt us to suppose that Wilde meant to implicate the book in his tragic fate: in its second edition Pater omitted the Conclusion because, as he explained when he restored it in the third edition, he "conceived it might possibly mislead some of the young men into whose hands it might fall. On the whole, I have thought it best to reprint it here, with some slight changes which bring it closer to my original meaning. . . ." (Included here is the 1888 version of the Conclusion.) He had in mind the explicit denial which the Conclusion makes that there is any meaning or any imperative of duty inherent in the universe.

Pater really had not overestimated the subversive potential of the essay. When it speaks of the uncertainty and the tragic brevity of human life, its silence as to religion is absolute—and eloquent: the implication is clear that for men of intelligence and sensibility religion is no longer a possible option. And when it does offer a way of confronting the darkness and cold that encompasses man's short day, it is not a high moral commitment that it proposes, not a noble altruism, or duty, or work, but a complex and urgent hedonism, the "getting of as many pulsations as possible into the given time." The young men into whose hands the book fell, may not have been "misled" by the Conclusion, but it confirmed the natural hedonism of their youth, and Pater, who had no inclination to moral radicalism, feared that his essay, in urging them to cultivate the "ecstasy" of art, might rationalize and license their seeking "success in life" through other forms of ecstasy as well. In later essays Pater considerably qualified the definition of the function of art, which he makes in the Conclusion.

This view had been advanced by Pater not as a philosophic position to be argued but as a self-evident truth which was the basis of his claim that art is of ultimate importance if the emptiness of the universe is to be filled and we are not to live in blank despair. And what he feared, of course, was that this doctrine might mislead young men into moral nihilism. But Wilde did not think that he had fallen into moral nihilism, nor had he. We may count on it that he regarded *The Renaissance* as having exerted its "strange influence" not upon his personal conduct but, rather, upon his cultural situation. Pater's book had effectually set at naught the authority of the theory of art which hitherto had the highest sanction among the enlightened —Ruskin's, in which all aesthetic considerations were directed toward a principle of morality which the universe, deprived of an imaginable and definable divinity, still somehow required and professed. Without engaging Ruskin directly, *The Renais-*

*sance* swept this doctrine aside, and in doing so brought to an end the once-powerful moral mystique of Victorian high culture and opened the way into the uncharted freedom of a new cultural epoch, which is to say a new way—a strange way—of being human.

It must seem an anomaly that a cultural act so drastic should be laid at the door of the man who was the author of *The Renaissance*. No mode of existence could be more demure, more retired from the world and remote from the controversies and debates by which culture proceeds than that of Walter Horatio Pater, Fellow of Brasenose College, Oxford. He was born in 1839, in a district of East London, the son of a physician, a lapsed Catholic probably of Dutch descent, who, shortly after Walter's birth, moved his family to Enfield, in Middlesex. Not much is known of the particulars of Pater's childhood beyond his pleasure in a game of ecclesiastical ceremonial in improvised vestments, but we doubtless derive an accurate sense of his inner life from certain quasi-autobiographical writings in which, in a manner that we would now call Proustian and that may indeed have had some influence on Proust's own manner, he describes the extreme intensity and subtlety with which he perceived and imagined the world. The quality of the sensibility described in these hushed, elaborate evocations of the past is suggested by the passage in the best of them, *The Child in the House,* in which he speaks of his preoccupation with the interfusion of death and beauty, a theme which may be thought to lie at the heart of his aesthetic doctrine: "With this desire of physical beauty mingled itself early the fear of death—the fear of death intensified by the desire of beauty."

At the age of fourteen Pater entered King's School in Canterbury and, expectably enough, was at odds with school life. His attraction to the idea of religion—the idea rather than the actuality—would seem to have been enhanced by his delight in the great cathedral which overshadowed his school and by an acquaintance he formed with the famous Oxford religious figure John Keble. His dubious involvement with religion continued through his second year at Oxford where, although he had lost his faith, he would have proceeded to take holy orders had not some of his serious-minded friends informed the bishop of the postulant's deficient state of belief.

He entered Queen's College in 1858 and found congenial friends there. He read widely in modern literature and traveled several times to Germany; he was an assiduous student and, although he took his degree with only second-class honors, he was an excellent classical scholar. In 1864 he was made a Probationary Fellow of Brasenose College on the basis of his knowledge of German philosophy and in the following year an Actual Fellow.

A tour of Italy in 1865–66 confirmed him in his growing admiration of the Renaissance. The new enthusiasm was coincident with his responsiveness to the Aesthetic Movement, which sought to take art out of its traditional relation to morality and to find its justification only in the fulfillment of its purely aesthetic intentions. In 1873 he collected the essays on Renaissance figures which he had published in periodicals in the intervening years, adding a few new pieces and the Preface and Conclusion (the last had in fact been composed before any of the essays), and brought out *Studies in the History of the Renaissance*. The work established his reputation in the great world, especially among young men, but it had the effect of separating him from most of Oxford. The very name of the book was capable of arousing suspicion and resistance in some quarters, for although henceforward the Renaissance was to gain an ever greater hold on the English imagination, it was not at that time in good odor. Ruskin had long taken every opportunity to denounce it as the epoch which had departed from the faith, sincerity, and organicism of the medieval period in order to cultivate technique, technology, and an egoistic individualism, and William Morris was to carry on this judgment. Benjamin Jowett, Pater's admired teacher of his undergraduate days and by now Master of Balliol College and an influential figure in university councils, was displeased by the tendency of *The Renaissance* and when, in 1874, Pater had reason to expect that the Proctorship, a university post at the disposal of his own college, would be given to him, Jowett effectually opposed the appointment.

Form this point on until his death in Oxford in 1894 Pater's biography is chiefly a record of his publications. He lived with his sisters at Oxford and, in their company, traveled abroad in the long vacations. In 1880 he gave up his teaching at Brasenose so that he might have more time for writing, but he retained his fellowship. From 1885 to 1893 he resided in London for part of each year and took pleasure in the social life of the city. The range of his interests was wide; in addition to the Renaissance, the periods from which he chose the subjects of his essays were ancient Greece, seventeenth-century England, English and French romanticism, and, remarkable in a critic whose roots were deep in academic life, the literature of his own day. Most of his books are, like *The Renaissance*, collections of essays published in periodicals—*Imaginary Portraits* (1887), *Appreciations* (1889), *Plato and Platonism* (1894), and the posthumous *Miscellaneous Studies* (1895), and *Essays from the "Guardian"* (1901). An important exception is his novel, or, as it is sometimes called, philosophical romance, *Marius the Epicurean* (1885), the story of the life of a young Roman in the time of the Antonine emperors, who experiences a variety of philosophical and spiritual influences, is drawn to the personal and moral qualities of the early Christian community, and sacrifices his own life to preserve that of a Christian friend.

Pater's prose is the subject of frequent comment, usually censorious of its tendency toward elaborateness and self-consciousness, even toward a hieratic solemnity. But although it doubtless deserves to be sometimes faulted on these grounds, it must also be admired for its latent and frequently manifest energy and for its superb precision of statement.

## *From* The Renaissance

### *Preface*

Many attempts have been made by writers on art and poetry to define beauty in the abstract, to express it in the most general terms, to find a universal formula for it.[1] The value of these attempts has most often been in the suggestive and penetrating things said by the way. Such discussions help us very

1. Pater refers here to what is called "aesthetics," or the philosophy, or theory, of art, which in the 18th century was especially concerned with the concept of beauty. His point is that he is not concerned with such large abstractions, but, rather, with particular works of art. He calls his enterprise "aesthetic criticism," by which he means no more than "criticism," the purposes of which he specifies. The word "aesthetic" derives from the Greek word that means simply sense-perception. It came into vogue after Pater's use of it and was often intended pejoratively: an "aesthete" was a young man who set too much store by art, to the detriment of his masculinity.

little to enjoy what has been well done in art or poetry, to discriminate between what is more and what is less excellent in them, or to use words like beauty, excellence, art, poetry, with a more precise meaning than they would otherwise have. Beauty, like all other qualities presented to human experience, is relative; and the definition of it becomes unmeaning and useless in proportion to its abstractness. To define beauty, not in the most abstract, but in the most concrete terms possible, to find, not a universal formula for it, but the formula which expresses most adequately this or that special manifestation of it, is the aim of the true student of aesthetics.

'To see the object as in itself it really is,' [2] has been justly said to be the aim of all true criticism whatever; and in aesthetic criticism the first step towards seeing one's object as it really is, is to know one's own impression as it really is, to discriminate it, to realise it distinctly. The objects with which aesthetic criticism deals—music, poetry, artistic and accomplished forms of human life—are indeed receptacles of so many powers or forces: they possess, like the products of nature, so many virtues or qualities. What is this song or picture, this engaging personality presented in life or in a book, to *me*? [3] What effect does it really produce on me? Does it give me pleasure? and if so, what sort or degree of pleasure? How is my nature modified by its presence, and under its influence? The answers to these questions are the original facts with which the aesthetic critic has to do; and, as in the study of light, of morals, of number, one must realise such primary data for oneself, or not at all. And he who experiences these impressions strongly, and drives directly at the discrimination and analysis of them, has no need to trouble himself with the abstract question what beauty is in itself, or what its exact relation to truth or experience—metaphysical questions, as unprofitable as metaphysical questions elsewhere. He may pass them all by as being, answerable or not, of no interest to him.

The aesthetic critic, then, regards all the objects with which he has to do, all works of art, and the fairer forms of nature and human life, as powers or forces producing pleasurable sensations, each of a more or less peculiar or unique kind. This influence he feels, and wishes to explain, analysing it, and reducing it to its elements. To him, the picture, the landscape, the engaging personality in life or in a book, *La Gioconda*,[4] the hills of Carrara,[5] Pico of Mirandola,[6] are valuable for their virtues,[7] as we say, in speaking of a herb, a wine, a gem; for the property each has of affecting one with a special, a

2. See Matthew Arnold, the first paragraph of *The Function of Criticism at the Present Time.*
3. Pater is echoing Arnold, who, in his essay *Heinrich Heine* says of Goethe that his "profound, imperturbable naturalism is absolutely fatal to all routine thinking; he puts the standard, once and for all, inside every man, instead of outside him; when he is told, such a thing must be so . . . he answers with Olympian politeness, 'But *is* it so? is it so to *me?*' "
4. Known also as *Mona Lisa*, the famous portrait by Leonardo da Vinci. Pater's description of it in his essay on Leonardo in *The Renaissance* is often quoted.
5. A town in Tuscany, Italy, famous for its quarries of white marble.
6. Giovanni Pico, Count of Mirandola (1463–94), Italian philosopher of vast learning. He is the subject of one of the essays of *The Renaissance.*
7. Efficacious quality.

unique, impression of pleasure. Our education becomes complete in proportion as our susceptibility to these impressions increases in depth and variety. And the function of the aesthetic critic is to distinguish, analyse, and separate from its adjuncts, the virtue by which a picture, a landscape, a fair personality in life or in a book, produces this special impression of beauty or pleasure, to indicate what the source of that impression is, and under what conditions it is experienced. His end is reached when he has disengaged that virtue, and noted it, as a chemist notes some natural element, for himself and others; and the rule for those who would reach this end is stated with great exactness in the words of a recent critic of Sainte-Beuve:—*De se borner à connaître de près les belles choses, et à s'en nourrir en exquis amateurs, en humanistes accomplis.*[8]

What is important, then, is not that the critic should possess a correct abstract definition of beauty for the intellect, but a certain kind of temperament, the power of being deeply moved by the presence of beautiful objects. He will remember always that beauty exists in many forms. To him all periods, types, schools of taste, are in themselves equal. In all ages there have been some excellent workmen, and some excellent work done. The question he asks is always:—In whom did the stir, the genius, the sentiment of the period find itself? where was the receptacle of its refinement, its elevation, its taste? 'The ages are all equal,' says William Blake, 'but genius is always above its age.'[9]

Often it will require great nicety to disengage this virtue from the commoner elements with which it may be found in combination. Few artists, not Goethe or Byron even, work quite cleanly, casting off all *débris*, and leaving us only what the heat of their imagination has wholly fused and transformed. Take, for instance, the writings of Wordsworth. The heat of his genius, entering into the substance of his work, has crystallised a part, but only a part, of it; and in that great mass of verse there is much which might well be forgotten.[10] But scattered up and down it, sometimes fusing and transforming entire compositions, like the Stanzas on *Resolution and Independence*, and the Ode on the *Recollections of Childhood*,[11] sometimes, as if at random, depositing a fine crystal here or there, in a matter it does not wholly search through and transform, we trace the action of his unique, incommunicable faculty, that strange, mystical sense of a life in natural things, and of man's life as a part of nature, drawing strength and colour and character from local influences, from the hills and streams, and from natural sights and sounds. Well! that is the *virtue*, the active principle in Wordsworth's poetry; and then the function of the critic of Wordsworth is to follow up that active principle, to disengage it, to mark the degree in which it penetrates his verse.

---

8. "To limit themselves to knowing beautiful things at first hand, and to develop themselves as sensitive lovers of art, as accomplished humanists."
9. From Blake's *Annotations to the Works of Sir Joshua Reynolds*, Discourse III, p. 71: "Ages are All Equal. But Genius is Always Above The Age."
10. Pater is in accord with Arnold who, in the introduction to his volume of selections of Wordsworth's poems, said that the best had to be "disengaged from the quantity of inferior work which now obscures them."
11. *Ode: Intimations of Immortality from Recollections of Early Childhood.*

The subjects of the following studies are taken from the history of the *Renaissance*,[12] and touch what I think the chief points in that complex, many-sided movement. I have explained in the first of them what I understand by the word, giving it a much wider scope than was intended by those who originally used it to denote only that revival of classical antiquity in the fifteenth century which was but one of many results of a general excitement and enlightening of the human mind, of which the great aim and achievements of what, as Christian art, is often falsely opposed to the Renaissance, were another result. This outbreak of the human spirit may be traced far into the Middle Age [13] itself, with its qualities already clearly pronounced, the care for physical beauty, the worship of the body, the breaking down of those limits which the religious system of the Middle Age imposed on the heart and the imagination. I have taken as an example of this movement, this earlier Renaissance within the Middle Age itself, and as an expression of its qualities, two little compositions in early French; not because they constitute the best possible expression of them, but because they help the unity of my series, inasmuch as the Renaissance ends also in France, in French poetry, in a phase of which the writings of Joachim du Bellay [14] are in many ways the most perfect illustration; the Renaissance thus putting forth in France an aftermath, a wonderful later growth, the products of which have to the full that subtle and delicate sweetness which belongs to a refined and comely decadence; just as its earliest phases have the freshness which belongs to all periods of growth in art, the charm of *ascêsis*,[15] of the austere and serious girding of the loins in youth.

But it is in Italy, in the fifteenth century, that the interest of the Renaissance mainly lies,—in that solemn fifteenth century which can hardly be studied too much, not merely for its positive results in the things of the intellect and the imagination, its concrete works of art, its special and prominent personalities, with their profound aesthetic charm, but for its general spirit and character, for the ethical qualities of which it is a consummate type.

The various forms of intellectual activity which together make up the culture of an age, move for the most part from different starting-points, and by unconnected roads. As products of the same generation they partake indeed of a common character, and unconsciously illustrate each other; but of the producers themselves, each group is solitary, gaining what advantage or disadvantage there may be in intellectual isolation. Art and poetry, philosophy and the religious life, and that other life of refined pleasure and action in the open places of the world, are each of them confined to its own circle of ideas, and those who prosecute either [16] of them are generally little curious of the thoughts of others. There come, however, from time to time, eras of more

---

12. This word, which is French for "rebirth," came into use in England in the mid-19th century to denote the great revival of arts and letters, under the influence of classical models, which began in Italy in the 14th century and continued through the 16th century. Pater thought of it as beginning in France at the end of the 12th century.
13. More usually, the Middle Ages.
14. French poet (1524–60), the subject of an essay in *The Renaissance*.
15. In his essay *Style*, Pater makes this Greek word equivalent with "self-restraint, a skilful economy of means."
16. If Pater were writing now, he would say "any one of them," but "either" was in his day sometimes used to refer to more than two objects or persons.

favourable conditions, in which the thoughts of men draw nearer together than is their wont, and the many interests of the intellectual world combine in one complete type of general culture. The fifteenth century in Italy is one of these happier eras; and what is sometimes said of the age of Pericles is true of that of Lorenzo: [17]—it is an age productive in personalities, many-sided, centralised, complete. Here, artists and philosophers and those whom the action of the world has elevated and made keen, do not live in isolation, but breathe a common air, and catch light and heat from each other's thoughts. There is a spirit of general elevation and enlightenment in which all alike communicate. It is the unity of this spirit which gives unity to all the various products of the Renaissance; and it is to this intimate alliance with mind, this participation in the best thoughts which that age produced, that the art of Italy in the fifteenth century owes much of its grave dignity and influence.

I have added an essay on Winckelmann,[18] as not incongruous with the studies which precede it, because Winckelmann, coming in the eighteenth century, really belongs in spirit to an earlier age. By his enthusiasm for the things of the intellect and the imagination for their own sake, by his Hellenism, his life-long struggle to attain to the Greek spirit, he is in sympathy with the humanists of an earlier century. He is the last fruit of the Renaissance, and explains in a striking way its motive and tendencies.

1873                                                                                           1873

### Conclusion

Λέγει που Ἡράκλειτος ὅτι πάντα χωρεῖ καὶ οὐδὲν μένει[1]

To regard all things and principles of things as inconstant modes or fashions has more and more become the tendency of modern thought. Let us begin with that which is without—our physical life. Fix upon it in one of its more exquisite intervals, the moment, for instance, of delicious recoil from the flood of water in summer heat.[2] What is the whole physical life in that moment but a combination of natural elements to which science gives their names? But these elements, phosphorus and lime and delicate fibres, are present not in the human body alone: we detect them in places most remote from it. Our physical life is a perpetual motion of them—the passage of the blood, the wasting and repairing of the lenses of the eye, the modification of the tissues of the brain by every ray of light and sound—processes which science reduces to simpler and more elementary forces. Like the elements of which we are

17. Pericles, the great statesman of Athens in the 5th century B.C., under whose rule the city achieved its pre-eminence in art. Lorenzo de Medici (1449–92), prince of Florence, was not only a patron of the arts but himself a poet and scholar.
18. Johann Joachim Winckelmann (1717–68), the German classical scholar who did much to establish the idea of the flawless perfection of Greek art.

1. "Heracleitus says, 'All things give way; nothing remains.'" Plato, Cratylus 402 A, Pater's translation. Heraclitus was a Greek philosopher of about 500 B.C. At the heart of his thought was the doctrine of perpetual flux; he held fire to be the basis of all material exist-ence. The sense of flux, of the impermanence of things, which Pater in his opening sentence says is characteristic of the 19th centuryy, may be thought of as a consequence of the great acceleration of historical and scientific research, both of which emphasized the idea of process and change.
2. What Pater asks us to consider is simply what it feels like to plunge into a cool stream on a hot day!

composed, the action of these forces extends beyond us; it rusts iron and ripens corn. Far out on every side of us those elements are broadcast, driven by many forces; and birth and gesture and death and the springing of violets from the grave are but a few out of ten thousand resultant combinations. That clear, perpetual outline of face and limb is but an image of ours, under which we group them—a design in a web, the actual threads of which pass out beyond it. This at least of flame-like our life has, that it is but the concurrence, renewed from moment to moment, of forces parting sooner or later on their ways.

Or if we begin with the inward world of thought and feeling, the whirlpool is still more rapid, the flame more eager and devouring. There it is no longer the gradual darkening of the eye and fading of colour from the wall,—the movement of the shore-side, where the water flows down indeed, though in apparent rest,—but the race of the mid-stream, a drift of momentary acts of sight and passion and thought. At first sight experience seems to bury us under a flood of external objects, pressing upon us with a sharp and importunate reality, calling us out of ourselves in a thousand forms of action. But when reflexion begins to act upon those objects they are dissipated under its influence; the cohesive force seems suspended like a trick of magic; each object is loosed into a group of impressions—colour, odour, texture—in the mind of the observer.[3] And if we continue to dwell in thought on this world, not of objects in the solidity with which language invests them, but of impressions unstable, flickering, inconsistent, which burn and are extinguished with our consciousness of them, it contracts still further; the whole scope of observation is dwarfed to the narrow chamber of the individual mind. Experience, already reduced to a swarm of impressions, is ringed round for each one of us by that thick wall of personality through which no real voice has ever pierced on its way to us, or from us to that which we can only conjecture to be without. Every one of those impressions is the impression of the individual in his isolation, each mind keeping as a solitary prisoner its own dream of a world.[4] Analysis goes a step farther still, and assures us that those impressions of the individual mind to which, for each one of us, experience dwindles down, are in perpetual flight; that each of them is limited by time, and that as time is infinitely divisible, each of them is infinitely divisible also; all that is actual in it being a single moment, gone while we try to apprehend it, of which it may ever be more truly said that it has ceased to be than that it is. To such a tremulous wisp constantly re-forming itself on the stream, to a single sharp impression, with a sense in it, a relic more or less fleeting, of such moments gone by, what is real in our life fines itself down. It is with this movement, with the passage and dissolution of impressions, images, sensations, that analysis leaves off—that continual vanishing away, that strange, perpetual weaving and unweaving of ourselves.[5]

3. The idea which Pater is advancing here is that it is only through habit and convention that the influx of multitudinous sense-impressions which we momently experience cohere into significance.
4. Pater here touches upon "solipsism," the idea that the self is the only thing that can be known as a reality.
5. That is, the continuity and actuality of the self is to be thought of not as something given and ineluctable but as the consequence of choice and will.

*Philosophiren*, says Novalis, *ist dephlegmatisiren, vivificiren.*[6] The service of philosophy, of speculative culture, towards the human spirit is to rouse, to startle it into sharp and eager observation. Every moment some form grows perfect in hand or face; some tone on the hills or the sea is choicer than the rest; some mood of passion or insight or intellectual excitement is irresistibly real and attractive for us,—for that moment only. Not the fruit of experience, but experience itself, is the end. A counted number of pulses only is given to us of a variegated, dramatic life. How may we see in them all that is to be seen in them by the finest senses? How shall we pass most swiftly from point to point, and be present always at the focus where the greatest number of vital forces unite in their purest energy?

To burn always with this hard, gemlike flame,[7] to maintain this ecstasy, is success in life. In a sense it might even be said that our failure is to form habits: for, after all, habit is relative to a stereotyped world, and meantime it is only the roughness of the eye that makes any two persons, things, situations, seem alike. While all melts under our feet, we may well catch at any exquisite passion, or any contribution to knowledge that seems by a lifted horizon to set the spirit free for a moment, or any stirring of the senses, strange dyes, strange colours, and curious odours, or work of the artist's hands, or the face of one's friend. Not to discriminate every moment some passionate attitude in those about us, and in the brilliancy of their gifts some tragic dividing of forces on their ways, is, on this short day of frost and sun, to sleep before evening. With this sense of the splendour of our experience and of its awful brevity, gathering all we are into one desperate effort to see and touch, we shall hardly have time to make theories about the things we see and touch. What we have to do is to be for ever curiously testing new opinions and courting new impressions, never acquiescing in a facile orthodoxy of Comte, or of Hegel,[8] or of our own. Philosophical theories or ideas, as points of view, instruments of criticism, may help us to gather up what might otherwise pass unregarded by us. 'Philosophy is the microscope of thought.'[9] The theory or idea or system which requires of us the sacrifice of any part of this experience, in consideration of some interest into which we cannot enter, or some abstract theory we have not identified with ourselves, or what is only conventional, has no real claim upon us.

One of the most beautiful passages in the writings of Rousseau is that in the sixth book of the *Confessions*, where he describes the awakening in him of the literary sense. An undefinable taint of death had always clung about him, and now in early manhood he believed himself smitten by mortal disease. He asked himself how he might make as much as possible of the interval that remained; and he was not biassed by anything in his previous life when he decided that it must be by intellectual excitement, which he found just then in the clear,

6. "To philosophize is to cast off sluggishness, to make oneself alive." Novalis is the pen-name of Friedrich Leopold von Hardenberg (1772–1801), one of the leading spirits of German Romanticism.
7. This famous phrase refers to Heraclitus' idea that the principle of life is fire.
8. Auguste Comte (1798–1857) and Georg Wilhelm Friedrich Hegel (1770–1831). Pater refers to the two philosophers, one French, one German, not to express disagreement with the substance of their thought but to oppose the static condition of the mind which follows from acquiescence in any systematic representation of life.
9. Victor Hugo, *Les Misérables* II.2.

fresh writings of Voltaire.[10] Well! we are all *condamnés,* as Victor Hugo says: we are all under sentence of death but with a sort of indefinite reprieve—*les hommes sont tous condamnés à mort avec des sursis indéfinis:* we have an interval, and then our place knows us no more. Some spend this interval in listlessness, some in high passions, the wisest, at least among 'the children of this world,' [11] in art and song. For our one chance lies in expanding that interval, in getting as many pulsations as possible into the given time. Great passions may give us this quickened sense of life, ecstasy and sorrow of love, the various forms of enthusiastic activity, disinterested or otherwise, which come naturally to many of us. Only be sure it is passion—that it does yield you this fruit of a quickened, multiplied consciousness. Of this wisdom, the poetic passion, the desire of beauty, the love of art for art's sake, has most; for art comes to you professing frankly to give nothing but the highest quality to your moments as they pass, and simply for those moments' sake.

1873

1873, 1888

# Romanticism [1]

αἴνει δὲ παλαιὸν μὲν οἶνον, ἄνθεα δ' ὕμνων νεωτέρων[2]

The words, *classical* and *romantic,* although, like many other critical expressions, sometimes abused by those who have understood them too vaguely or too absolutely, yet define two real tendencies in the history of art and literature. Used in an exaggerated sense, to express a greater opposition between those tendencies than really exists, they have at times tended to divide people of taste into opposite camps. But in that *House Beautiful,*[3] which the creative minds of all generations—the artists and those who have treated life in the spirit of art—are always building together, for the refreshment of the human spirit, these oppositions cease; and the *Interpreter* [4] of the *House Beautiful,* the true aesthetic critic,[5] uses these divisions, only so far as they enable him to enter into the peculiarities of the objects with which he has to do. The term *classical,* fixed, as it is, to a well-defined literature, and a well-defined group in art, is clear, indeed; but then it has often been used in a hard, and merely

---

10. The "just then" is important to Pater's point, for if at this moment Rousseau delighted in Voltaire's writings, at a later stage of his development he attacked them fiercely.
11. Luke 16:8, ". . . for the children of this world are in their generation wiser than the children of light."

1. This essay first appeared, under its present title, in *Macmillan's Magazine,* November 1876. In 1889, when Pater collected a group of his critical writings to make the volume *Appreciations,* he placed this essay last, although it had been composed before most of the others, and called it "Postscript," seeming by this to suggest that it formulates the principles upon which the preceding critical judgments were made. The cordiality with which it receives works in a large variety of modes, its readiness to overlook extravagances so long as the work is charged with "energy" and "curiosity," are in striking contrast with the strictness of the criteria Matthew Arnold uses in *The Study of Poetry.*
2. "When you praise the wine that is old, praise also the flowers of song that are new." Pindar, *Olympian Odes* IX.48–49.
3. In Bunyan's *Pilgrim's Progress,* the palace in which Christian rests from his journey and has sight of the Delectable Mountains.
4. At the Interpreter's House many significances are disclosed to Christian by its master.
5. See note 1 to the Preface to *The Renaissance.*

scholastic sense, by the praisers of what is old and accustomed, at the expense of what is new, by critics who would never have discovered for themselves the charm of any work, whether new or old, who value what is old, in art or literature, for its accessories, and chiefly for the conventional authority that has gathered about it—people who would never really have been made glad by any Venus fresh-risen from the sea, and who praise the Venus of old Greece and Rome, only because they fancy her grown now into something staid and tame.

And as the term, *classical*, has been used in a too absolute, and therefore in a misleading sense, so the term, *romantic*, has been used much too vaguely, in various accidental senses. The sense in which Scott is called a romantic writer is chiefly this; that, in opposition to the literary tradition of the last century, he loved strange adventure, and sought it in the Middle Age.[6] Much later,[7] in a Yorkshire village, the spirit of romanticism bore a more really characteristic fruit in the work of a young girl, Emily Brontë, the romance of *Wuthering Heights*; the figures of Hareton Earnshaw, of Catherine Linton, and of Heathcliffe—tearing open Catherine's grave, removing one side of her coffin, that he may really lie beside her in death—figures so passionate, yet woven on a background of delicately beautiful, moorland scenery, being typical examples of that spirit. In Germany, again, that spirit is shown less in Tieck,[8] its professional representative, than in Meinhold,[9] the author of *Sidonia the Sorceress* and the *Amber-Witch*. In Germany and France, within the last hundred years, the term has been used to describe a particular school of writers; [10] and, consequently, when Heine [11] criticises the *Romantic School* in Germany—that movement which culminated in Goethe's *Goetz von Berlichingen;* [12] or when Théophile Gautier [13] criticises the romantic movement in France, where, indeed, it bore its most characteristic fruits, and its play is hardly yet over where, by a certain audacity, or *bizarrerie* [14] of motive, united with faultless literary execution, it still shows itself in imaginative literature, they use the word, with an exact

6. Doubtless Pater suggests that Scott is not essentially a Romantic writer because he has in mind Scott's conservative temperament and his strong sense of fact.
7. Not so *very* much later—Scott's first novel, *Waverley*, appeared in 1814, his last in 1832; *Wuthering Heights* appeared in 1847.
8. Johann Ludwig Tieck (1773–1853) was not only a novelist in the Romantic mode but also a propagandist for it.
9. Wilhelm Meinhold (1797–1851). When *The Amber Witch* was published in 1843, it was thought to be an authentic chronicle from the 17th century.
10. Pater means that German and French literary historians and critics do not conceive of Romanticism as a tendency of art that manifests itself in various ways and degrees in various times and places but, rather, as the defining quality of a particular group of artists.
11. Heinrich Heine (1797–1856), the German poet and critic, perhaps the wittiest man of his time, was himself of the Romantic school, in the sense that Pater speaks of. His book about it appeared in 1836.
12. Goethe wrote this play in 1773. Its title is the name of its hero, an actual German knight devoted to an ideal of justice. Its form is Shakespearean, its language colloquial prose.
13. French poet, novelist, and critic (1811–72), in his early youth a passionate propagandist for Romanticism in its extreme manifestations, later devoted to the ideal of formal precision. He was one of the proponents of the doctrine of "art for art's sake" (*l'art pour l'art*), to which Pater gives expression in the Conclusion to *The Renaissance*. His unfinished *History of Romanticism* appeared in 1874.
14. Oddness, extravagance.

sense of special artistic qualities, indeed; but use it, nevertheless, with a limited application to the manifestation of those qualities at a particular period. But the romantic spirit is, in reality, an ever-present, an enduring principle, in the artistic temperament; and the qualities of thought and style which that, and other similar uses of the word *romantic* really indicate, are indeed but symptoms of a very continuous and widely working influence.

Though the words *classical* and *romantic*, then, have acquired an almost technical meaning, in application to certain developments of German and French taste, yet this is but one variation of an old opposition, which may be traced from the very beginning of the formation of European art and literature. From the first formation of anything like a standard of taste in these things, the restless curiosity of their more eager lovers necessarily made itself felt, in the craving for new motives, new subjects of interest, new modifications of style. Hence, the opposition between the classicists and the romanticists— between the adherents, in the culture of beauty, of the principles of liberty, and authority, respectively—of strength, and order or what the Greeks called κοσμιότης.[15]

Sainte-Beuve,[16] in the third volume of the *Causeries du Lundi*, has discussed the question, *What is meant by a classic?* It was a question he was well fitted to answer, having himself lived through many phases of taste, and having been in earlier life an enthusiastic member of the romantic school: he was also a great master of that sort of 'philosophy of literature,' which delights in tracing traditions in it, and the way in which various phases of thought and sentiment maintain themselves, through successive modifications, from epoch to epoch. His aim, then, is to give the word *classic* a wider and, as he says, a more generous sense than it commonly bears, to make it expressly *grandiose et flottant*; [17] and, in doing this, he develops, in a masterly manner, those qualities of measure, purity, temperance, of which it is the especial function of classical art and literature, whatever meaning, narrower or wider, we attach to the term, to take care.

The charm, therefore, of what is classical, in art or literature, is that of the well-known tale, to which we can, nevertheless, listen over and over again, because it is told so well. To the absolute beauty of its artistic form, is added the accidental, tranquil, charm of familiarity. There are times, indeed, at which these charms fail to work on our spirits at all, because they fail to excite us. 'Romanticism,' says Stendhal,[18] 'is the art of presenting to people the literary works which, in the actual state of their habits and beliefs, are capable of giving them the greatest possible pleasure; classicism, on the contrary, of pre-

15. Orderly behavior (kosmiótes).
16. Charles-Augustin Sainte-Beuve (1804–69) is generally accounted the pre-eminent French critic of the mid-19th century. His series of critical essays *Causeries du Lundi* (Monday Chats), appeared in Parisian newspapers between 1849 and 1869. Pater refers to the fact that Sainte-Beuve's later attitude to the Romantics was at least skeptical and often antagonistic.
17. Imposing and not rigid.
18. The pseudonym of Henri Beyle (1783–1842). Now accounted one of the great novelists of the 19th century, he was ignored in France until the century's end and scarcely heard of in England. Pater quotes from his *Racine and Shakespeare* (1823, 1825), originally two pamphlets in defense of Romanticism.

senting them with that which gave the greatest possible pleasure to their grandfathers.' But then, beneath all changes of habits and beliefs, our love of that mere abstract proportion—of music—which what is classical in literature possesses, still maintains itself in the best of us, and what pleased our grandparents may at least tranquillise us. The 'classic' comes to us out of the cool and quiet of other times, as the measure of what a long experience has shown will at least never displease us. And in the classical literature of Greece and Rome, as in the classics of the last century, the essentially classical element is that quality of order in beauty, which they possess, indeed, in a pre-eminent degree, and which impresses some minds to the exclusion of everything else in them.

It is the addition of strangeness to beauty, that constitutes the romantic character in art; [19] and the desire of beauty being a fixed element in every artistic organisation, it is the addition of curiosity to this desire of beauty, that constitutes the romantic temper. Curiosity and the desire of beauty, have each their place in art, as in all true criticism. When one's curiosity is deficient, when one is not eager enough for new impressions, and new pleasures, one is liable to value mere academical proprieties too highly, to be satisfied with worn-out or conventional types, with the insipid ornament of Racine,[20] or the prettiness of that later Greek sculpture, which passed so long for true Hellenic work; [21] to miss those places where the handiwork of nature, or of the artist, has been most cunning; to find the most stimulating products of art a mere irritation. And when one's curiosity is in excess, when it overbalances the desire of beauty, then one is liable to value in works of art what is inartistic in them; to be satisfied with what is exaggerated in art, with productions like some of those of the romantic school in Germany; not to distinguish, jealously enough, between what is admirably done, and what is done not quite so well, in the writings, for instance, of Jean Paul.[22] And if I had to give instances of these defects, then I should say, that Pope, in common with the age of literature to which he belonged, had too little curiosity, so that there is always a certain insipidity in the effect of his work, exquisite as it is; and, coming down to our own time, that Balzac had an excess of curiosity—curiosity not duly tempered with the desire of beauty.

But, however falsely those two tendencies may be opposed by critics, or exaggerated by artists themselves, they are tendencies really at work at all times in art, moulding it, with the balance sometimes a little on one side, sometimes a little on the other, generating, respectively, as the balance inclines on this side or that, two principles, two traditions, in art, and in literature so far as it partakes of the spirit of art. If there is a great overbalance of curiosity, then, we have the grotesque in art: if the union of strangeness and beauty, under very difficult and complex conditions, be a successful one, if the union

19. The definition has become famous, almost proverbial.
20. The prevailing 19th-century English opinion of this poet, whom the French so much admire.
21. In part through the influence of Winckelmann; see note 18 to the Preface to *The Renaissance*.
22. Jean Paul Friedrich Richter (1763–1825), German humorous novelist and aesthetic theorist, wrote under his first two Christian names.

be entire, then the resultant beauty is very exquisite, very attractive. With a passionate care for beauty, the romantic spirit refuses to have it, unless the condition of strangeness be first fulfilled. Its desire is for a beauty born of unlikely elements, by a profound alchemy, by a difficult initiation, by the charm which wrings it even out of terrible things; and a trace of distortion, of the grotesque, may perhaps linger, as an additional element of expression, about its ultimate grace. Its eager, excited spirit will have strength, the grotesque, first of all—the trees shrieking as you tear off the leaves; [23] for Jean Valjean,[24] the long years of convict life; for Redgauntlet,[25] the quicksands of Solway Moss; then, incorporate with this strangeness, and intensified by restraint, as much sweetness, as much beauty, as is compatible with that. *Énergique, frais, et dispos*—these, according to Sainte-Beuve, are the characteristics of a genuine classic—*les ouvrages anciens ne sont pas classiques parce qu'ils sont vieux, mais parce qu'ils sont énergiques, frais, et dispos.*[26] Energy, freshness, intelligent and masterly disposition:—these are characteristics of Victor Hugo when his alchemy is complete, in certain figures, like Marius and Cosette,[27] in certain scenes, like that in the opening of *Les Travailleurs de la Mer,*[28] where Déruchette writes the name of *Gilliatt* in the snow, on Christmas morning; but always there is a certain note of strangeness discernible there, as well.

The essential elements, then, of the romantic spirit are curiosity and the love of beauty; and it is only as an illustration of these qualities, that it seeks the Middle Age, because, in the over-charged atmosphere of the Middle Age, there are unworked sources of romantic effect, of a strange beauty, to be won, by strong imagination, out of things unlikely or remote.

Few, probably, now read Madame de Staël's *De l'Allemagne,*[29] though it has its interest, the interest which never quite fades out of work really touched with the enthusiasm of the spiritual adventurer, the pioneer in culture. It was published in 1810, to introduce to French readers a new school of writers— the romantic school, from beyond the Rhine; and it was followed, twenty-three years later, by Heine's *Romantische Schule,* as at once a supplement and a correction. Both these books, then, connect romanticism with Germany, with the names especially of Goethe and Tieck; and, to many English readers, the idea of romanticism is still inseparably connected with Germany—that Germany which, in its quaint old towns, under the spire of Strasburg or the towers of Heidelberg, was always listening in rapt inaction to the melodious, fascinating voices of the Middle Age, and which, now that it has got Strasburg

---

23. This happens in the *Aeneid* III.19–72.
24. The hero of Victor Hugo's *Les Misérables.*
25. A chief character of the novel by Scott that bears his name.
26. "Ancient works are classics not because they are old but because they are energetic, fresh, and well shaped."
27. Characters—young lovers—in *Les Misérables.*
28. *Toilers of the Sea.*
29. Mme de Staël (1766–1817), born Anne-Louise-Germaine Necker (her father was chief minister to Louis XVI), was famous as a liberal and an intellectual. Her book in praise of Germany and its culture, *De l'Allemagne,* was first published in Paris in 1810. All copies were confiscated and destroyed and the author was exiled. One of its chapters is devoted to a comparison of Classic and Romantic poetry.

back again,[30] has, I suppose, almost ceased to exist. But neither Germany, with its Goethe and Tieck, nor England, with its Byron and Scott, is nearly so representative of the romantic temper as France, with Murger,[31] and Gautier, and Victor Hugo. It is in French literature that its most characteristic expression is to be found; and that, as most closely derivative, historically, from such peculiar conditions, as ever reinforce it to the utmost.

For, although temperament has much to do with the generation of the romantic spirit, and although this spirit, with its curiosity, its thirst for a curious beauty, may be always traceable in excellent art (traceable even in Sophocles) yet still, in a limited sense, it may be said to be a product of special epochs. Outbreaks of this spirit, that is, come naturally with particular periods —times, when, in men's approaches towards art and poetry, curiosity may be noticed to take the lead, when men come to art and poetry, with a deep thirst for intellectual excitement, after a long ennui, or in reaction against the strain of outward, practical things: in the later Middle Age, for instance; so that medieval poetry, centering in Dante, is often opposed to Greek and Roman poetry, as romantic poetry to the classical. What the romanticism of Dante is, may be estimated, if we compare the lines in which Virgil describes the hazelwood, from whose broken twigs flows the blood of Polydorus, not without the expression of a real shudder at the ghastly incident, with the whole canto of the Inferno, into which Dante has expanded them, beautifying and softening it, meanwhile, by a sentiment of profound pity.[32] And it is especially in that period of intellectual disturbance, immediately preceding Dante, amid which the romance languages define themselves at last, that this temper is manifested. Here, in the literature of Provence, the very name of romanticism is stamped with its true signification: [33] here we have indeed a romantic world, grotesque even, in the strength of its passions, almost insane in its curious expression of them, drawing all things into its sphere, making the birds, nay! lifeless things, its voices and messengers, yet so penetrated with the desire for beauty and sweetness, that it begets a wholly new species of poetry, in which the Renaissance may be said to begin. The last century was pre-eminently a classical age, an age in which, for art and literature, the element of a comely order was in the ascendant; which, passing away, left a hard battle to be fought between the classical and the romantic school. Yet, it is in the heart of this century, of Goldsmith and Stothard, of Watteau and the Siècle de Louis XIV [34] —in one of its central, if not most characteristic figures, in Rousseau—that the modern or French romanticism really originates. But, what in the eighteenth century is but an exceptional phenomenon, breaking through its fair reserve

30. Strasbourg, the capital of Alsace-Lorraine, was annexed by the French in 1681 and won back by the Germans in the Franco-Prussian War of 1870.
31. Henri Murger (1822–51) wrote novels of a sentimental kind.
32. Canto XIII.
33. Pater refers to the love poetry composed in the 12th century by the troubadours, the poets of this southern province of France.
34. By his reference to Oliver Goldsmith (1730–74) the English writer, to Thomas Stothard (1755–1834) the English painter, to Jean-Antoine Watteau (1684–1721) the French painter, and to Voltaire's history of the age of Louis XIV, Pater does not mean to say that they represent the essence of classicism but, rather, that they point toward romanticism.

and discretion only at rare intervals, is the habitual guise of the nineteenth, breaking through it perpetually, with a feverishness, and incomprehensible straining and excitement, which all experience to some degree, but yearning also, in the genuine children of the romantic school, to be *énergique, frais, et dispos*—for those qualities of energy, freshness, comely order; and often, in Murger, in Gautier, in Victor Hugo, for instance, with singular felicity attaining them.

It is in the terrible tragedy of Rousseau, in fact, that French romanticism, with much else, begins: reading his *Confessions* we seem actually to assist at the birth of this new, strong spirit in the French mind. The wildness which has shocked so many, and the fascination which has influenced almost every one, in the squalid, yet eloquent figure, we see and hear so clearly in that book, wandering under the apple-blossoms and among the vines of Neuchâtel or Vevey [35] actually give it the quality of a very successful romantic invention. His strangeness or distortion, his profound subjectivity, his passionateness— the *cor laceratum* [36]—Rousseau makes all men in love with these. *Je ne suis fait comme aucun de ceux que j'ai sus. Mais si je ne vaux pas mieux, au moins je suis autre.*—'I am not made like any one else I have ever known: yet, if I am not better, at least I am different.' These words, from the first page of the *Confessions*, anticipate all the Werthers, Renés, Obermanns,[37] of the last hundred years. For Rousseau did but anticipate a trouble in the spirit of the whole world; and thirty years afterwards, what in him was a peculiarity, became part of the general consciousness. A storm was coming: Rousseau, with others, felt it in the air, and they helped to bring it down: they introduced a disturbing element into French literature, then so trim and formal, like our own literature of the age of Queen Anne.

In 1815 the storm had come and gone, but had left, in the spirit of 'young France,' the *ennui* of an immense disillusion. In the last chapter of Edgar Quinet's *Révolution Française*,[38] a work itself full of irony, of disillusion, he distinguishes two books, Senancour's *Obermann* and Chateaubriand's *Génie du Christianisme*,[39] as characteristic of the first decade of the present century. In those two books we detect already the disease and the cure—in *Obermann* the irony, refined into a plaintive philosophy of 'indifference'—in Chateaubriand's *Génie du Christianisme*, the refuge from a tarnished actual present, a present of disillusion, into a world of strength and beauty in the Middle Age, as at an earlier period—in *René* and *Atala* [40]—into the free play of them in savage life. It is to minds in this spiritual situation, weary of the present, but

35. Towns in Switzerland associated with Rousseau.
36. The "torn heart."
37. These are all suffering young men, the heroes of, respectively, Goethe's *The Sorrows of Young Werther* (1774), Chateaubriand's *René* (1802), and Etienne Pivert de Senancour's *Obermann* (1804). All these stories were widely read and had large influence on the mode of feeling of their time.
38. Published in 1865.
39. *The Genius of Christianity*, 1802. *René* was part of this work although later it was published separately.
40. A tale of an American-Indian girl who becomes a Christian and dies in a struggle between love and her faith. Like *René*, *Atala* is part of the *Genius of Christianity*, although it was first published separately in 1801.

yearning for the spectacle of beauty and strength, that the works of French romanticism appeal. They set a positive value on the intense, the exceptional; and a certain distortion is sometimes noticeable in them, as in conceptions like Victor Hugo's *Quasimodo,* or *Gwynplaine,*[41] something of a terrible grotesque, of the *macabre,* as the French themselves call it; though always combined with perfect literary execution, as in Gautier's *La Morte Amoureuse,*[42] or the scene of the 'maimed' burial-rites of the player, dead of the frost, in his *Capitaine Fracasse*—true 'flowers of the yew.' It becomes grim humour in Victor Hugo's combat of Gilliatt with the devil-fish,[43] or the incident, with all its ghastly comedy drawn out at length, of the great gun detached from its fastenings on shipboard, in *Quatre-Vingt-Treize* [44] (perhaps the most terrible of all the accidents that can happen by sea) and in the entire episode, in that book, of the *Convention.*[45] Not less surely does it reach a genuine pathos; for the habit of noting and distinguishing one's own most intimate passages of sentiment makes one sympathetic, begetting, as it must, the power of entering, by all sorts of finer ways, into the intimate recesses of other minds; so that pity is another quality of romanticism, both Victor Hugo and Gautier being great lovers of animals, and charming writers about them, and Murger being unrivalled in the pathos of his *Scènes de la Vie de Jeunesse.*[46] Penetrating so finely into all situations which appeal to pity, above all, into the special or exceptional phases of such feeling, the romantic humour is not afraid of the quaintness or singularity of its circumstances or expression, pity, indeed, being of the essence of humour; so that Victor Hugo does but turn his romanticism into practice, in his hunger and thirst after practical *Justice!*—a justice which shall no longer wrong children, or animals, for instance, by ignoring in a stupid, mere breadth of view, minute facts about them. Yet the romanticists are antinomian,[47] too, sometimes, because the love of energy and beauty, of distinction in passion, tended naturally to become a little *bizarre,* plunging into the Middle Age, into the secrets of old Italian story. Are we in the Inferno? —we are tempted to ask, wondering at something malign in so much beauty. For over all a care for the refreshment of the human spirit by fine art manifests itself, a predominant sense of literary charm, so that, in their search for the secret of exquisite expression, the romantic school went back to the forgotten world of early French poetry, and literature itself became the most delicate of the arts—like 'goldsmith's work,' says Sainte-Beuve, of Bertrand's *Gaspard de la Nuit* [48]—

41. The hunchback in *Notre Dame* and the facially deformed boy in *The Man Who Laughs.*
42. Théophile Gautier's *La Morte amoureuse* (1857) is a collection of stories of the supernatural.
43. In *Toilers of the Sea.*
44. Pater refers to the episode in *Ninety-three* in which a great gun, having broken its lashings, rolls on its wheeled carriage with every slightest movement of the ship, endangering the lives of the crew and the ship itself.
45. *Ninety-three* is about the year 1793, in which the Reign of Terror took place.
46. Murger's *Scènes de la vie de jeunesse* (1851) is a collection of short stories on social themes.
47. Opposed to the claims of moral law.
48. Louis Bertrand (1807–41) is known for this one work, written in 1830, published in 1842; it is a series of prose poems, touched with fantasy and in feeling not unlike some of De Quincey's work.

and that peculiarly French gift, the gift of exquisite speech, *argute loqui*,[49] attained in them a perfection which it had never seen before.

Stendhal, a writer whom I have already quoted, and of whom English readers might well know much more than they do, stands between the earlier and later growths of the romantic spirit. His novels are rich in romantic quality; and his other writings—partly criticism, partly personal reminiscences—are a very curious and interesting illustration of the needs out of which romanticism arose. In his book on *Racine and Shakespeare*, Stendhal argues that all good art was romantic in its day; and this is perhaps true in Stendhal's sense. That little treatise, full of 'dry light' [50] and fertile ideas, was published in the year 1823, and its object is to defend an entire independence and liberty in the choice and treatment of subject, both in art and literature, against those who upheld the exclusive authority of precedent. In pleading the cause of romanticism, therefore, it is the novelty, both of form and of motive, in writings like the *Hernani* of Victor Hugo (which soon followed it,[51] raising a storm of criticism) that he is chiefly concerned to justify. To be interesting and really stimulating, to keep us from yawning even, art and literature must follow the subtle movements of that nimbly-shifting *Time-Spirit*, or *Zeit-Geist*, understood by French not less than by German criticism, which is always modifying men's taste, as it modifies their manners and their pleasures. This, he contends, is what all great workmen had always understood. Dante, Shakespeare, Molière, had exercised an absolute independence in their choice of subject and treatment. To turn always with that ever-changing spirit, yet to retain the flavour of what was admirably done in past generations, in the classics, as we say—is the problem of true romanticism. 'Dante,' he observes, 'was pre-eminently the romantic poet. He adored Virgil, yet he wrote the *Divine Comedy*, with the episode of Ugolino,[52] which is as unlike the *Aeneid* as can possibly be. And those who thus obey the fundamental principle of romanticism, one by one become classical, and are joined to that ever-increasing common league, formed by men of all countries, to approach nearer and nearer to perfection.'

Romanticism, then, although it has its epochs, is in its essential characteristics rather a spirit which shows itself at all times, in various degrees, in individual workmen and their work, and the amount of which criticism has to estimate in them taken one by one, than the peculiarity of a time or a school. Depending on the varying proportion of curiosity and the desire of beauty, natural tendencies of the artistic spirit at all times, it must always be partly a matter of individual temperament. The eighteenth century in England has been regarded as almost exclusively a classical period; yet William Blake, a type of so much which breaks through what are conventionally thought the influences of that century, is still a noticeable phenomenon in it, and the reaction in favour of

49. "To speak impressively."
50. "The most perfect soul, says Heracleitus, is a dry light. . . ." Plutarch, *Romulus*.
51. In 1830. This play broke all the traditional conventions and its first two performances were riotous partisan occasions in which the applause of the romanticists triumphed over the denunciatory shouts of the traditionalists.
52. Ugolino, Count of Pisa, conspired with the Archbishop Ruggiero to betray Pisa. Ruggiero turned on him and imprisoned him with his four sons until they starved to death. In *Inferno*, Canto XXXIII, Ugolino is shown frozen in the ice of the ninth circle and gnawing on the head of Ruggiero.

naturalism in poetry begins in that century, early. There are, thus, the born romanticists and the born classicists. There are the born classicists who start with *form*, to whose minds the comeliness of the old, immemorial, well-recognised types in art and literature, have revealed themselves impressively; who will entertain no matter which will not go easily and flexibly into them; whose work aspires only to be a variation upon, or study from, the older masters. ' 'Tis art's decline, my son!' [53] they are always saying, to the progressive element in their own generation; to those who care for that which in fifty years' time every one will be caring for. On the other hand, there are the born romanticists, who start with an original, untried *matter*, still in fusion; who conceive this vividly, and hold by it as the essence of their work; who, by the very vividness and heat of their conception, purge away, sooner or later, all that is not organically appropriate to it, till the whole effect adjusts itself in clear, orderly, proportionate form; which form, after a very little time, becomes classical in its turn.

The romantic or classical character of a picture, a poem, a literary work, depends, then, on the balance of certain qualities in it; and in this sense, a very real distinction may be drawn between good classical and good romantic work. But all critical terms are relative; and there is at least a valuable suggestion in that theory of Stendhal's, that all good art was romantic in its day. In the beauties of Homer and Pheidias, quiet as they now seem, there must have been, for those who confronted them for the first time, excitement and surprise, the sudden, unforeseen satisfaction of the desire of beauty. Yet the *Odyssey*, with its marvellous adventure, is more romantic than the *Iliad*, which nevertheless contains, among many other romantic episodes, that of the immortal horses of Achilles, who weep at the death of Patroclus. Aeschylus is more romantic than Sophocles, whose *Philoctetes*, were it written now, might figure, for the strangeness of its motive and the perfectness of its execution, as typically romantic; [54] while, of Euripides, it may be said, that his method in writing his plays is to sacrifice readily almost everything else, so that he may attain the fulness of a single romantic effect. These two tendencies, indeed, might be applied as a measure or standard, all through Greek and Roman art and poetry, with very illuminating results; and for an analyst of the romantic principle in art, no exercise would be more profitable, than to walk through the collection of classical antiquities at the Louvre, or the British Museum, or to examine some representative collection of Greek coins, and note how the element of curiosity, of the love of strangeness, insinuates itself into classical design, and record the effects of the romantic spirit there, the traces of struggle, of the grotesque even, though overbalanced here by sweetness; as in the sculpture of Chartres and Rheims, [55] the real sweetness of mind in the sculptor is often overbalanced by the grotesque, by the rudeness of his strength.

53. Browning, *Fra Lippo Lippi*, l. 233.
54. Philoctetes, a Greek hero, is bitten by a serpent on his way to Troy. His wound gives off a terrible stench and his comrades abandon him on the island of Lemnos. Here he lives in pain and solitude for ten years, hating his former friends. When it is disclosed to the Greeks that they can never take Troy without the bow and arrows of Heracles, which are in the possession of Philoctetes, they seek him out and appeal for his help.
55. That is, of the cathedrals of these towns.

Classicism, then, means for Stendhal, for that younger enthusiastic band of French writers whose unconscious method he formulated into principles, the reign of what is pedantic, conventional, and narrowly academical in art; for him, all good art is romantic. To Sainte-Beuve, who understands the term in a more liberal sense, it is the characteristic of certain epochs, of certain spirits in every epoch, not given to the exercise of original imagination, but rather to the working out of refinements of manner on some authorised matter; and who bring to their perfection, in this way, the elements of sanity, of order and beauty in manner. In general criticism, again, it means the spirit of Greece and Rome, of some phases in literature and art that may seem of equal authority with Greece and Rome, the age of Louis the Fourteenth, the age of Johnson; [56] though this is at best an uncritical use of the term, because in Greek and Roman work there are typical examples of the romantic spirit. But explain the terms as we may, in application to particular epochs, there are these two elements always recognisable; united in perfect art—in Sophocles, in Dante, in the highest work of Goethe, though not always absolutely balanced there; and these two elements may be not inappropriately termed the classical and romantic tendencies.

Material for the artist, motives of inspiration, are not yet exhausted: our curious, complex, aspiring age still abounds in subjects for aesthetic manipulation by the literary as well as by other forms of art. For the literary art, at all events, the problem just now is, to induce order upon the contorted, proportionless accumulation of our knowledge and experience, our science and history, our hopes and disillusion, and, in effecting this, to do consciously what has been done hitherto for the most part too unconsciously, to write our English language as the Latins wrote theirs, as the French write, as scholars should write. Appealing, as he may, to precedent in this matter, the scholar will still remember that if 'the style is the man' it is also the age: that the nineteenth century too will be found to have had its style, justified by necessity—a style very different, alike from the baldness of an impossible 'Queen Anne' revival, and an incorrect, incondite [57] exuberance, after the mode of Elizabeth: [58] that we can only return to either at the price of an impoverishment of form or matter, or both, although, an intellectually rich age such as ours being necessarily an eclectic one, we may well cultivate some of the excellences of literary types so different as those: that in literature as in other matters it is well to unite as many diverse elements as may be: that the individual writer or artist, certainly, is to be estimated by the number of graces he combines, and his power of interpenetrating them in a given work. To discriminate schools, of art, of literature, is, of course, part of the obvious business of literary criticism: but, in the work of literary production, it is easy to be overmuch occupied concerning them. For, in truth, the legitimate contention is, not of one age or school of literary art against another, but of all successive schools alike, against the stupidity which is dead to the substance, and the vulgarity which is dead to form.

1876                                                                                                1876, 1889

56. Louis XIV of France, 1643–1715; Dr. Samuel Johnson, 1709–84.
57. Crude.
58. Pater speaks pejoratively of efforts to reconstitute the taste and style of bygone epochs.

# SAMUEL BUTLER
1835–1902

Reputation came to Samuel Butler only belatedly. Of the books published in his lifetime only *Erewhon* (1872) had any degree of success, and although in his later years he did attract a coterie of admirers, of whom Bernard Shaw was the most notable, his pertinacious assaults on the orthodoxies of the age went largely unnoticed by the public. It was not until the publication of his posthumous and only novel in 1903 that he began to be known both as a writer of formidable abilities and as a figure of decisive importance in the cultural history of the English nineteenth century.

If any one book may be thought to signalize the end of the Victorian ethos, it is surely *The Way of All Flesh*. Patently autobiographical in almost all its essential details, it is a remorseless indictment of the institution of the family and as such an assault on the palladium of English piety. No sentiment had a more tenacious hold upon the English than that family life was the crown of personal existence and the source of personal and national virtue. Butler represents the family as the condition of servitude of the individual spirit—home is jail and parents are not merely turnkeys but torturers. Through its violation of a primal sanctity *The Way of All Flesh* became the rallying point for the new generation of the early twentieth century and brought Butler's other writings into general notice and regard.

Samuel Butler was born in 1835 at Langar Rectory, near Bingham in Nottinghamshire. His father was the Reverend Thomas Butler, son of the Dr. Samuel Butler who had been headmaster of Shrewsbury School and Bishop of Lichfield and Coventry. The Butlers were well-to-do—money was a constant presence and issue in the family—and in 1843 they undertook a European tour with their young son, which, in its Italian phase, exercised a decisive effect upon his notion of the quality that life ought rightly to have, that is, quite unlike the quality of English life. In 1848 Samuel entered the school over which his grandfather had once ruled and in 1854 went up to Cambridge as a member of the college his family traditionally attended, St. John's. His father destined him for the church and for several years he acquiesced in the paternal decision, but doubts began to assail him, specifically over the question of infant baptism, and led to an angry exchange of views with his father. Having no hope that his parents would further his ambition to become a painter, Butler emigrated to New Zealand in 1859. His father provided a considerable capital sum for investment in a sheep farm. This venture prospered and yielded the competence which made Butler at least temporarily independent of his family and free to pursue his professional inclinations. It was while he was in New Zealand that he made his first start in literature with an account of his experiences as an immigrant, published in 1863 as *A First Year in Canterbury Settlement,* and with a witty speculative fantasy published in a New Zealand newspaper, *Darwin Among the Machines,* which was to figure as a memorable part of *Erewhon*.

Returning to England in 1864, Butler settled himself in chambers in Clifford's Inn, which was to be his residence for the rest of his life, and devoted himself to the study of painting. His native gifts were not great and he met with no success, but it was not until 1877 that he confronted the fact that his artistic ambitions were not to be realized and at last surrendered them. In 1870–71 he diverted some of his time and energy from painting to the composition of *Erewhon*, which was published anonymously, although a second edition revealed the identity of the author. His mother died in 1873 and his father was at pains to inform him that her death had been brought about by sorrow over the heterodox views her son had expressed. *Erewhon* is a brilliant and engaging book. The name of Swift is often invoked in praise of its satire, and the comparison is not extravagant so far as it bears upon the ingenuity of the work. But of the moral passion of *Gulliver* there is no trace. This doubtless accounts for some part of the charm of the book, which does not force our feelings beyond the cool pleasures to be found in the intelligent, condescending perception of how anomalous and absurd are the institutions of respectable life. It also accounts for the book's falling short of greatness. But this judgment must seem captious and ungrateful when we consider the force of the wit that conceived, as a way of describing the attitude of the English to their established religion, the Erewhonic institution of Musical Banks which issue a currency that everyone must possess although no one will accept it in actual trade; or the imagination that levied upon Plato for the Erewhonian myth of the unborn and the elaborate legal arrangements to which it gave rise (see below); or the brilliance of the fantasy that proposed a state of affairs in which all machines must be destroyed because in their evolution they developed the ability to take over the functions of men.

In 1873 Butler began work on *The Way of All Flesh,* which was to occupy him all his life, but he was diffident of his powers as a novelist, and put the book aside to write *Life and Habit,* the first of the works of speculative biology in which he undertook to discredit the Darwinian theory of evolution. Butler was by no means inclined to reject the fact of evolution—on the contrary—but he was dismayed by the implications of Darwin's way of explaining how it came about. To say that evolution was determined by one process only, that of natural selection, the survival of the fittest, was, in Butler's view, to settle for mere mechanism as the ruling principle of life and to ignore the part played in biological existence, especially that of humans, by mind, intention, and will.

Butler was the less likely to win agreement for his own evolutionary theories because they were all frankly speculative and dialectical, based on avowedly subjective observation and not at all on scientific research. Science might be suffering persecution at the hands of the ecclesiastical spirit, as Huxley said it was, but science had established its own strict orthodoxy and had no wish to be disturbed in it. Butler did, of course, find a redoubtable disciple in Bernard Shaw, who gave entire credence to Butler's evolutionary ideas and embodied them in his enormous play, *Back to Methuselah.* And although the tendency of scientific thought since Darwin's day does not actually confirm Butler's views, there are eminent scientists who find point in them. Butler followed *Life and Habit* with *Evolution, Old and New* (1879), *Unconscious Memory* (1880), and *Luck, or Cunning, as a Main Means of Organic Modification?* (1887), all of which were silently snubbed by the scientists.

It was about this time that he turned his ambitions to music, and in 1886 his *Narcissus: A Cantata in the Handelian Form* was performed. Shaw, who is to be relied on in his judgment of music, took but a dim view of this composition, and believed it to be, together with Butler's insistence that Handel was immeasurably greater than any other musician who ever composed, including Bach, one of the "dilettante weaknesses" that characterized the latter half of Butler's life. Shaw's crossness with Butler's later concerns is not unjustified. His translations of the *Iliad* and the *Odyssey* into colloquial English prose (1898, 1900) are pleasant; *The Authoress of the Odyssey* (1897), which argues seriously the thesis proposed by its title, carries some weight; but none of these works, let alone *Shakespeare's Sonnets Reconsidered* (1899) which, though not wholly without point, is chiefly crotchety, is of commanding interest. But in 1901 Butler published the last work of his lifetime, *Erewhon Revisited,* in which the narrator-protagonist of *Erewhon* returns to find that he has become the divine person of a new religion. It is a first-rate satire, and the deep feeling with which on occasion it is strangely touched is most moving. Butler died a year after its publication.

# *From* Erewhon [1]

### *Birth Formulae*

I heard what follows not from Arowhena,[2] but from Mr. Nosnibor [3] and some of the gentlemen who occasionally dined at the house; they told me that the Erewhonians believe in pre-existence; and not only this (of which I will write more fully in the next chapter), but they believe that it is of their own free act and deed in a previous state that they come to be born into this world at all. They hold that the unborn are perpetually plaguing and tormenting the married of both sexes, fluttering about them incessantly, and giving them no peace either of mind or body until they have consented to take them under their protection. If this were not so (this at least is what they urge), it would be a monstrous freedom for one man to take with another, to say that he should undergo the chances and changes of this mortal life without any option in the matter. No man would have any right to get married at all, inasmuch as he can never tell what frightful misery his doing so may entail forcibly upon a being who cannot be unhappy as long as he does not exist. They feel this so strongly that they are resolved to shift the blame on to other shoulders; and have fashioned a long mythology as to the world in which the unborn people live, and what they do, and the arts and machinations to which they have recourse in order to get themselves into our own world. But of this more anon; what I would relate here is their manner of dealing with those who do come.

It is a distinguishing peculiarity of the Erewhonians that when they profess themselves to be quite certain about any matter, and avow it as a base on which they are to build a system of practice, they seldom quite believe in it.[4] If they smell a rat about the precincts of a cherished institution, they will always stop their noses to it if they can.

This is what most of them did in this matter of the unborn, for I cannot (and never could) think that they seriously believed in their mythology concerning pre-existence; they did and they did not; they did not know themselves what they believed; all they did know was that it was a disease not to believe as they did. The only thing of which they were quite sure was that it was the

---

1. Anagram of "nowhere." The following selections are Chaps. 18 and 19.
2. Arowhena is the Erewhonian young woman with whom the traveler falls in love; she instructs him in the customs and beliefs of her people.
3. The father of Arowhena. His name, which is Robinson spelled backward, was chosen to suggest that he is a "typical" respectable Erewhonian.
4. Butler is commenting, of course, on the state of religious belief in 19th-century England.

pestering of the unborn which caused them to be brought into this world, and that they would not have been here if they would have only let peaceable people alone.

It would be hard to disprove this position, and they might have a good case if they would only leave it as it stands. But this they will not do; they must have assurance doubly sure; they must have the written word of the child itself as soon as it is born, giving the parents indemnity from all responsibility on the score of its birth, and asserting its own pre-existence. They have therefore devised something which they call a birth formula—a document which varies in words according to the caution of parents, but is much the same practically in all cases; for it has been the business of the Erewhonian lawyers during many ages to exercise their skill in perfecting it and providing for every contingency.

These formulae are printed on common paper at a moderate cost for the poor; but the rich have them written on parchment and handsomely bound, so that the getting up of a person's birth formula is a test of his social position. They commence by setting forth, That whereas A. B.[5] was a member of the kingdom of the unborn, where he was well provided for in every way, and had no cause of discontent, etc., etc., he did of his own wanton depravity and restlessness conceive a desire to enter into this present world; that thereon having taken the necessary steps as set forth in laws of the unborn kingdom, he did with malice aforethought set himself to plague and pester two unfortunate people who had never wronged him, and who were quite contented and happy until he conceived this base design against their peace; for which wrong he now humbly entreats their pardon.

He acknowledges that he is responsible for all physical blemishes and deficiencies which may render him answerable to the laws of his country; that his parents have nothing whatever to do with any of these things; and that they have a right to kill him at once if they be so minded, though he entreats them to show their marvellous goodness and clemency by sparing his life. If they will do this, he promises to be their most obedient and abject creature during his earlier years, and indeed all his life, unless they should see fit in their abundant generosity to remit some portion of his service hereafter. And so the formula continues, going sometimes into very minute details, according to the fancies of family lawyers, who will not make it any shorter than they can help.

The deed being thus prepared, on the third or fourth day after the birth of the child, or as they call it, the 'final importunity,' the friends gather together, and there is a feast held, where they are all very melancholy—as a general rule, I believe, quite truly so—and make presents to the father and mother of the child in order to console them for the injury which has just been done them by the unborn.

By-and-by the child himself is brought down by his nurse, and the company begin to rail upon him, upbraiding him for his impertinence, and asking him what amends he proposes to make for the wrong that he has committed, and how he can look for care and nourishment from those who have perhaps already

5. The form used in framing legal documents to indicate that an actual name is to be supplied.

been injured by the unborn on some ten or twelve occasions; for they say of people with large families, that they have suffered terrible injuries from the unborn; till at last, when this has been carried far enough, some one suggests the formula, which is brought out and solemnly read to the child by the family straightener.[6] This gentleman is always invited on these occasions, for the very fact of intrusion into a peaceful family shows a depravity on the part of the child which requires his professional services.

On being teased by the reading and tweaked by the nurse, the child will commonly begin to cry, which is reckoned a good sign, as showing a consciousness of guilt. He is thereon asked, Does he assent to the formula? on which, as he still continues crying and can obviously make no answer, some one of the friends comes forward and undertakes to sign the document on his behalf, feeling sure (so he says) that the child would do it if he only knew how, and that he will release the present signer from his engagement on arriving at maturity. The friend then inscribes the signature of the child at the foot of the parchment, which is held to bind the child as much as though he had signed it himself.

Even this, however, does not fully content them, for they feel a little uneasy until they have got the child's own signature after all. So when he is about fourteen, these good people partly bribe him by promises of greater liberty and good things, and partly intimidate him through their great power of making themselves actively unpleasant to him, so that though there is a show of freedom made, there is really none; they also use the offices of the teachers in the Colleges of Unreason,[7] till at last, in one way or another, they take very good care that he shall sign the paper by which he professes to have been a free agent in coming into the world, and to take all the responsibility of having done so on to his own shoulders. And yet, though this document is obviously the most important which anyone can sign in his whole life, they will have him do so at an age when neither they nor the law will for many a year allow anyone else to bind him to the smallest obligation, no matter how righteously he may owe it, because they hold him too young to know what he is about, and do not consider it fair that he should commit himself to anything that may prejudice him in after years.

I own that all this seemed rather hard, and not of a piece with the many admirable institutions existing among them. I once ventured to say a part of what I thought about it to one of the Professors of Unreason. I did it very tenderly, but his justification of the system was quite out of my comprehension. I remember asking him whether he did not think it would do harm to a lad's principles, by weakening his sense of the sanctity of his word and of truth generally, that he should be led into entering upon a solemn declaration as to the truth of things about which all that he can certainly know is that he knows

6. Among the Erewhonians physical illness is considered to be a crime; it brings severe punishment and disgrace. But moral lapses are dealt with as indispositions over which the "patient" has no control. The persons who are trained to cure those who suffer from immorality are called straighteners.

7. Under this name Butler represents the universities of Oxford and Cambridge and the part they play in rationalizing the customs and unexamined assumptions of respectable English society.

nothing—whether, in fact, the teachers who so led him, or who taught anything as a certainty of which they were themselves uncertain, were not earning their living by impairing the truth-sense of their pupils (a delicate organization mostly), and by vitiating one of their most sacred instincts.

The Professor, who was a delightful person, seemed greatly surprised at the view which I took, but it had no influence with him whatsoever. No one, he answered, expected that the boy either would or could know all that he said he knew; but the world was full of compromises; and there was hardly any affirmation which would bear being interpreted literally. Human language was too gross a vehicle of thought—thought being incapable of absolute translation. He added, that as there can be no translation from one language into another which shall not scant the meaning somewhat, or enlarge upon it, so there is no language which can render thought without a jarring and a harshness somewhere—and so forth; all of which seemed to come to this in the end, that it was the custom of the country, and that the Erewhonians were a conservative people; that the boy would have to begin compromising sooner or later, and this was part of his education in the art. It was perhaps to be regretted that compromise should be as necessary as it was; still it was necessary, and the sooner the boy got to understand it the better for himself. But they never tell this to the boy.

From the book of their mythology about the unborn I made the extracts which will form the following chapter.

### The World of the Unborn [8]

Having waded through many chapters . . . I came at last to the unborn themselves, and found that they were held to be souls pure and simple, having no actual bodies, but living in a sort of gaseous yet more or less anthropomorphic existence, like that of a ghost; they have thus neither flesh nor blood nor warmth. Nevertheless they are supposed to have local habitations and cities wherein they dwell, though these are as unsubstantial as their inhabitants; they are even thought to eat and drink some thin ambrosial sustenance, and generally to be capable of doing whatever mankind can do, only after a visionary ghostly fashion as in a dream. On the other hand, as long as they remain where they are they never die—the only form of death in the unborn world being the leaving it for our own. They are believed to be extremely numerous, far more so than mankind. They arrive from unknown planets, full grown, in large batches at a time; but they can only leave the unborn world by taking the steps necessary for their arrival here—which is, in fact, by suicide.

They ought to be an exceedingly happy people, for they have no extremes of good or ill fortune; never marrying, but living in a state much like that fabled by the poets as the primitive condition of mankind. In spite of this, however, they are incessantly complaining; they know that we in this world have bodies, and indeed they know everything else about us, for they move among us whithersoever they will, and can read our thoughts, as well as survey our actions at pleasure. One would think that this should be enough for them;

8. Butler's conception of the world of the unborn owes much to Plato's myth of human pre-existence as narrated in the *Republic*.

and most of them are indeed alive to the desperate risk which they will run by indulging themselves in that body with 'sensible warm motion' which they so much desire; nevertheless, there are some to whom the *ennui* of a disembodied existence is so intolerable that they will venture anything for a change; so they resolve to quit. The conditions which they must accept are so uncertain, that none but the most foolish of the unborn will consent to them; and it is from these, and these only, that our own ranks are recruited.

When they have finally made up their minds to leave, they must go before the magistrate of the nearest town, and sign an affidavit of their desire to quit their then existence. On their having done this, the magistrate reads them the conditions which they must accept, and which are so long that I can only extract some of the principal points, which are mainly the following:—

First, they must take a potion which will destroy their memory and a sense of identity; they must go into the world helpless, and without a will of their own; they must draw lots for their dispositions before they go, and take them, such as they are, for better or worse—neither are they to be allowed any choice in the matter of the body which they so much desire; they are simply allotted by chance, and without appeal, to two people whom it is their business to find and pester until they adopt them. Who these are to be, whether rich or poor, kind or unkind, healthy or diseased, there is no knowing; they have, in fact, to entrust themselves for many years to the care of those for whose good constitution and good sense they have no sort of guarantee.

It is curious to read the lectures which the wiser heads give to those who are meditating a change. They talk with them as we talk with a spendthrift, and with about as much success.

'To be born,' they say, 'is a felony—it is a capital crime, for which sentence may be executed at any moment after the commission of the offence. You may perhaps happen to live for some seventy or eighty years, but what is that, compared with the eternity you now enjoy? And even though the sentence were commuted, and you were allowed to live on for ever, you would in time become so terribly weary of life that execution would be the greatest mercy to you.

'Consider the infinite risk; to be born of wicked parents and trained in vice! to be born of silly parents, and trained to unrealities! of parents who regard you as a sort of chattel or property, belonging more to them than to yourself! Again, you may draw utterly unsympathetic parents, who will never be able to understand you, and who will do their best to thwart you (as a hen when she has hatched a duckling), and then call you ungrateful because you do not love them; or, again, you may draw parents who look upon you as a thing to be cowed while it is still young, lest it should give them trouble hereafter by having wishes and feelings of its own.

'In later life, when you have been finally allowed to pass muster as a full member of the world, you will yourself become liable to the pesterings of the unborn—and a very happy life you may be led in consequence! For we solicit so strongly that a few only—nor these the best—can refuse us; and yet not to refuse is much the same as going into partnership with half a dozen different people about whom one can know absolutely nothing beforehand—not even whether one is going into partnership with men or women, nor with how many of either. Delude not yourself with thinking that you will be wiser than your parents. You may be an age in advance of those whom you have pestered, but unless you are one of the great ones you will still be an age behind those who will in their turn pester you.

'Imagine what it must be to have an unborn quartered upon you, who is of an entirely different temperament and disposition to your own; nay, half a dozen such, who will not love you though you have stinted yourself in a thousand ways to provide for their comfort and well-being,—who will forget all your self-sacrifice, and of whom you may never be sure that they are not bearing a grudge against you for errors of judgment into which you may have fallen, though you had hoped that such had been long since atoned for. Ingratitude such as this is not uncommon, yet fancy what it must be to bear! It is hard upon the duckling to have been hatched by a hen, but is it not also hard upon the hen to have hatched the duckling?

'Consider it again, we pray you, not for our sake but for your own. Your initial character you must draw by lot; but whatever it is, it can only come to a tolerably successful development after long training; remember that over that training you will have no control. It is possible, and even probable, that whatever you may get in after life which is of real pleasure and service to you, will have to be won in spite of, rather than by the help of, those whom you are now about to pester, and that you will only win your freedom after years of a painful struggle in which it will be hard to say whether you have suffered most injury, or inflicted it.

'Remember also, that if you go into the world you will have free will; that you will be obliged to have it; that there is no escaping it; that you will be fettered to it during your whole life, and must on every occasion do that which on the whole seems best to you at any given time, no matter whether you are right or wrong in choosing it. Your mind will be a balance for considerations, and your action will go with the heavier scale. How it shall fall will depend upon the kind of scales which you may have drawn at birth, the bias which they will have obtained by use, and the weight of the immediate considerations. If the scales were good to start with, and if they have not been outrageously tampered with in childhood, and if the combinations into which you enter are average ones, you may come off well; but there are too many "ifs" in this, and with the failure of any one of them your misery is assured. Reflect on this, and remember that should the ill come upon you, you will have yourself to thank, for it is your own choice to be born, and there is no compulsion in the matter.

'Not that we deny the existence of pleasures among mankind; there is a certain show of sundry phases of contentment which may even amount to very considerable happiness; but mark how they are distributed over a man's life, belonging, all the keenest of them, to the fore part, and few indeed to the after. Can there be any pleasure worth purchasing with the miseries of a decrepit age? If you are good, strong, and handsome, you have a fine fortune indeed at twenty, but how much of it will be left at sixty? For you must live on your capital; there is no investing your powers so that you may get a small annuity of life for ever; you must eat up your principal bit by bit, and be tortured by seeing it grow continually smaller and smaller, even though you happen to escape being rudely robbed of it by crime or casualty.

'Remember, too, that there never yet was a man of forty who would not come back into the world of the unborn if he could do so with decency and honour. Being in the world he will as a general rule stay till he is forced to go; but do you think that he would consent to be born again, and re-live his life, if he had the offer of doing so? Do not think it. If he could so alter the past as that he should never have come into being at all, do you not think that he would do it very gladly?

'What was it that one of their own poets meant, if it was not this, when he cried out upon the day in which he was born, and the night in which it was said there is a man child conceived? "For now," he says, "I should have lain still and been quiet, I should have slept; then had I been at rest with kings and counsellors of the earth, which built desolate places for themselves; or which princes that had gold, who filled their houses with silver; or as an hidden untimely birth, I had not been; as infants which never saw light. There the wicked cease from troubling, and there the weary are at rest." Be very sure that the guilt of being born carries this punishment at times to all men; but how can they ask for pity, or complain of any mischief that may befall them, having entered open-eyed into the snare?

'One word more and we have done. If any faint remembrance, as of a dream, flit in some puzzled moment across your brain, and you shall feel that the potion which is to be given you shall not have done its work, and the memory of this existence which you are leaving endeavours vainly to return; we say in such a moment, when you clutch at the dream but it eludes your grasp, and you watch it, as Orpheus watched Eurydice, gliding back again into the twilight kingdom, fly—fly—if you can remember the advice—to the haven of your present and immediate duty, taking shelter incessantly in the work which you have in hand. This much you may perhaps recall; and this, if you will imprint it deeply upon your every faculty, will be most likely to bring you safely and honourably home through the trials that are before you.' [9]

This is the fashion in which they reason with those who would be for leaving them, but it is seldom that they do much good, for none but the unquiet and unreasonable ever think of being born, and those who are foolish enough to think of it are generally foolish enough to do it. Finding, therefore, that they can do no more, the friends follow weeping to the court-house of the chief magistrate, where the one who wishes to be born declares solemnly and openly that he accepts the conditions attached to his decision. On this he is presented with a potion, which immediately destroys his memory and sense of identity, and dissipates the thin gaseous tenement which he has inhabited; he becomes a bare vital principle, not to be perceived by human senses, nor to be by any chemical test appreciated. He has but one instinct, which is that he is to go to such and such a place, where he will find two persons whom he is to importune till they consent to undertake him; but whether he is to find these persons among the race of Chowbok [10] or the Erewhonians themselves is not for him to choose.

1863–65, 1870–71                                                      1872

9. "The myth above alluded to exists in Erewhon with changed names, and considerable modification. I have taken the liberty of referring to the story as familiar to ourselves." (Butler)
10. Chowbok is the New Zealand aborigine who tells the traveler of the existence of Erewhon and guides him to it.

# OSCAR WILDE
1854–1900

Oscar Wilde first came into public view as a sort of intellectual mountebank and buffoon, the brilliant publicity agent for his own charm and talent and for certain ideas about art and life calculated to affront, confound, and enthrall the respectable. Then he flamed across the literary firmament with works which no one was disposed to call great but which all the world took pleasure in. At the height of his triumph —three of his plays were running in London at the time—disaster befell him: he was indicted for homosexual practices, found guilty, and sentenced to two years at hard labor; he emerged from prison a broken man, bereft of position, hope, and talent. He died solitary and destitute in a shabby hotel in Paris.

Inevitably such a career puts difficulties in the way of judging the work of the man who pursued it. But these have diminished with the passing of the years—less and less do the extravagances of Wilde's self-dramatization and the pathos of what may fairly be called his martyrdom obscure his quite momentous significance as a writer.

Wilde was born in Dublin in 1854 of parents scarcely less flamboyant than he was to become. His father was Sir William Wilde, a successful physician specializing in ophthalmology. Of diminutive stature, almost a dwarf, Sir William was notorious for his personal untidiness, even uncleanliness—a Dublin quip explained the blackness of his fingernails by his having scratched himself—and for his many love affairs, one of which ended in lawsuit and tremendous scandal. Lady Wilde was as strikingly large for a woman as her husband was small for a man. As a young girl she had been handsome, something of a revolutionary, and, under the name of "Speranza," had published a volume of poems. In her later years she was clever, erudite, and eccentric, and her *salon* in Dublin had a kind of tatty fame.

At the age of ten Oscar—his full name was Oscar Fingal O'Flahertie Wills Wilde— entered Portora Royal School (the closest approximation in Ireland to an English public school), after which he spent three years at Trinity College, Dublin, before winning a scholarship to Magdalen College, Oxford, in 1874. In his schooldays he had discovered a talent for blithe insolence which gained him attention, some hostility, and a good deal of admiration, and this mode of wit, which was to be his characteristic style in maturity, he cultivated to good effect at Oxford. He dressed flamboyantly and collected porcelain; and when a band of hearty college mates, outraged by his affectations, undertook to break up his rooms, he threw one of their number down the stairs and invited them to a brandy party. At the university his intense admiration went to two men, John Ruskin, who was lecturing as Slade Professor of Art, and Walter Pater. So great was his reverence for Ruskin that he joined the undergraduate work-party Ruskin had organized to build a road between two villages as a way of instructing upper-class young men in the dignity of labor. It was Pater, however, who was to have both the more immediate and the more permanent effect upon Wilde, that "strange influence" on his life of which Wilde spoke near his life's end. (See above, Headnote to Walter Pater.)

In 1875 Wilde traveled in Italy with John Mahaffy, his former teacher at Trinity College, a distinguished classical scholar, and in 1877, went with the same companion on a tour of Greece which confirmed him in his growing preference for Greek as against medieval culture; the spirit of Greece, he was often to say, was essentially the modern spirit. Wilde's powers as a classicist were very considerable; despite the dandaical affectations that marked his life as an undergraduate, he took his degree in 1878 with the highest honors. In the year of his graduation he won the Newdigate Prize for his poem—it is not very good—*Ravenna*.

In 1879 Wilde went to live in London. Within two years he was so much a figure in the public eye that he was invited on a lecture tour of the United States which lasted a full year. The eminence and authority to which he attained before the age of twenty-seven were not the consequence of any literary achievement—his *Poems*, published in 1881, were not highly regarded—but rather of the nature of English upper-class society at the time and Wilde's brilliant manipulation of it. The segment of the aristocracy that lived the life of fashion made a cohesive group whose goings-on as reported in the press were of consummate interest to the general public. Through friendships formed at Oxford, Wilde had entry to this society and entranced it by his wit and insolence and also, we may suppose, by his genuine sweetness of temper. To these new friends he carried the "aesthetic" doctrine, compounded of ideas derived from the Pre-Raphaelites, William Morris, and Pater, its substance being that the justification of life was the enjoyment of beauty rather than the performance of duty, that the highest beauty was to be found in art, which ought to manifest its power in all the accoutrements of material existence. The doctrine that Wilde preached had implications of a truly serious kind which a sympathetic reading of his work makes manifest, but at the time it was likely to be received as not much more than an elevated theory of interior decoration and dress. Yet even if it was no more than that, it spoke of a new age and a new kind of sensibility to people who were beginning to be receptive to the charm of the new—the excited response to Wilde may be thought of as the inauguration of a phase of culture in which art and theories about art had great authority and in which they bestowed a kind of social-spiritual prestige. Wilde's intellectual masters had habituated the public to the premises of the "aesthetic" doctrine, and now the middle classes hearkened eagerly to the reports which reached them of a new campaign in the crusade for beauty being waged by this curious young man. The gossip columns retailed his witty paradoxes; *Punch,* the humorous magazine that delighted and reassured the middle classes, caricatured him and his creed. In 1881 Gilbert and Sullivan produced *Patience; or, Bunthorne's Bride,* counting on everyone to recognize that Bunthorne in his velvet knee-breeches was Oscar Wilde giving instruction on how to go about being aesthetic.

> Though the Philistines may jostle, you will rank as an apostle in the high aesthetic line,
> If you walk down Piccadilly with a poppy or a lily in your medieval hand.

Wilde carried the aesthetic word to the farthest reaches of America, was inevitably mocked for his affectations of manner and dress but also was rather liked, and returned in 1883 not much the richer for his labors. In that year he married a beautiful, gentle, and quite unassuming young woman and established their domestic life in a house decorated according to the right principles; their first son was born in 1885, their second in 1886. Wilde was for a time enchanted by family life but inevitably it failed to hold him; inevitably it could not stand against his homosexuality and his impulse toward the raffish and the seamy.

Wilde's first notable achievement as a writer was his novel *The Picture of Dorian*

*Gray* (1890), which is based upon the ingenious idea of a portrait upon which the passing years work their ravages while the beautiful young man who is the subject of the picture remains to all appearances gloriously young; its salient intention is to celebrate the life that is devoted to the pleasures of the senses and of art, of a hedonistic program pertinaciously carried out in disregard of all the sanctions of morality and even of sentiment. The book, in which the homosexuality of the protagonist is patent though not explicit, created a scandal. Yet the conclusion of the novel is nothing if not moral and even grim in its disclosure of the ugliness, corruption, emptiness, and despair that lie beneath the surface of the mode of existence that has been made to seem so desirable. For all its faults of tone and style, *The Picture of Dorian Gray* is a significant and memorable work and perhaps in nothing so much as its Preface, which consists of a series of epigrams intended to shock by their insolence. The Preface is brief enough to be quoted entire:

> The artist is the creator of beautiful things.
> To reveal art and conceal the artist is art's aim.
> The critic is he who can translate into another manner or a new material his impression of beautiful things.
> The highest, as the lowest, form of criticism is a mode of autobiography.
> Those who find ugly meanings in beautiful things are corrupt without being charming. This is a fault.
> Those who find beautiful meanings in beautiful things are the cultivated. For these there is hope.
> They are the elect to whom beautiful things mean only Beauty.
> There is no such thing as a moral or an immoral book. Books are well written, or badly written. That is all.
> The nineteenth century dislike of Realism is the rage of Caliban seeing his own face in a glass.
> The nineteenth century dislike of Romanticism is the rage of Caliban not seeing his own face in a glass.
> The moral life of man forms part of the subject-matter of the artist, but the morality of art consists in the perfect use of an imperfect medium. No artist desires to prove anything. Even things that are true can be proved.
> No artist has ethical sympathies. An ethical sympathy in an artist is an unpardonable mannerism of style.
> No artist is ever morbid. The artist can express everything.
> Thought and language are to the artist instruments of an art.
> Vice and virtue are to the artist materials for an art.
> From the point of view of form, the type of all the arts is the art of the musician. From the point of view of feeling, the actor's craft is the type.
> All art is at once surface and symbol.
> Those who go beneath the surface do so at their peril.
> It is the spectator, and not life, that art really mirrors.
> Diversity of opinion about a work of art shows that the work is new, complex, and vital.
> When critics disagree the artist is in accord with himself.
> We can forgive a man for making a useful thing as long as he does not admire it. The only excuse for making a useless thing is that one admires it intensely.
> All art is quite useless.

The substance of this manifesto, which Wilde was to develop in his essays of the next few years, is scarcely unique with him; it represents a dominant tendency in the artistic theory of that time and of some decades to come, derived in essence from, among other French writers, Baudelaire and Flaubert, and perhaps ultimately from William Blake, or so he leads us to think when in the last paragraph of *De Profundis,* the long terrible letter he wrote in jail to review and explain his life, he says, "Time and space, succession and extension are merely accidental conditions of Thought. The Imagination can transcend them, and move in a free sphere of ideal existences. Things, also, are in their essence what we choose to make them. A thing *is*, according to the mode in which one looks at it. 'Where others,' says Blake, 'see but the Dawn coming over the hill, I see the sons of God shouting for joy.' " (*A Vision of the Last Judgment*. Wilde quotes from memory and approximately.) If we accept that Wilde in some part of his thought is in the line of Blake, we can the better understand the impulse that led this worshiper of artifice and elegance to follow *The Picture of Dorian Gray* with *The Soul of Man Under Socialism*.

In 1892 Wilde had his first great success in the theater with *Lady Windermere's Fan*, which was followed by *A Woman of No Importance* (produced in 1893) and *An Ideal Husband* (produced in 1895). Apart from the epigrammatic wit which often marks the dialogue, these plays are quite conventional and even in their own time might have seemed old-fashioned. Yet they hold the stage tenaciously, surprising generation after generation of theater-goers by their vitality. By the vitality of Wilde's last play, *The Importance of Being Earnest* (see below), no one is ever surprised, for it is by common consent one of the masterpieces of comedy.

In 1891 Wilde had formed his association with Lord Alfred Douglas, the young man who became the chief—although not the only—object of his affections. Douglas's father, from whom he and other members of his family were estranged, was the Marquess of Queensbury, a man eccentric to the verge of insanity who conceived it to be his paternal duty to rescue his son from Wilde's influence, and to this end carried on a campaign of social threat against Wilde. Wilde, after enduring this for some time, decided on the most imprudent course possible—he sued Queensbury for criminal libel. The trial went disastrously against him. Queensbury was acquitted, and on the ground of what the trial had brought to light Wilde was arrested. At the first of two trials the jury disagreed, but at the second found him guilty. He was given a maximum sentence of two years in prison at hard labor. Upon his release in 1897 he assumed the name Sebastian Melmoth—Sebastian to recall the martyr transfixed by arrows and also to commemorate the arrows printed on a convict's garb, Melmoth after the one famous diabolical hero of the novel *Melmoth the Wanderer* by his great-uncle, Charles Maturin—and departed for the Continent, where he spent the three desolate years yet remaining to him.

# The Importance of Being Earnest

In the long debate that once went on over whether Oscar Wilde was a writer and cultural figure of high significance or nothing but a showy mediocrity, one of his works was likely to rise above the battle to be acknowledged as perfect of its kind. Likely but not certain: Bernard Shaw, in his day the wittiest of Wilde's admirers, was uncompromising in his dislike of *The Importance of Being Earnest,* giving it as his reason that the play did not "touch" him and that it lacked "reality"—it does not lead us to believe in its humanity, Shaw said, and therefore "we are thrown back on the daintiness and force of its wit."

Which of course is exactly where Wilde wanted us to be thrown. Humanity was not what he aspired to—"It is by a butterfly for butterflies," he said of the play, and presumably it is *about* butterflies too. And the prevailing opinion is that one of the best possible ways of passing a few hours is as a butterfly, concerned—if that can be the word—with the goings-on of butterflies.

*The Importance of Being Earnest* is often praised in superlative terms: the best comedy in the language. But then, because *As You Like It* and *A Midsummer Night's Dream* are also comedies, defining qualifications are introduced: the best comedy of manners, the best artificial comedy. But as soon as the category is made thus precise, two great rivals spring up to make their claim, *The Way of the World* and *The School for Scandal,* and if these are true examples of the comedy of manners or of artificial comedy, then we cannot be sure that *The Importance of Being Earnest* ought to be classed with them. And a recollection of Charles Lamb's great essay, "On the Artificial Comedy of the Last Century," strengthens that dubiety.

Some considerable part of the charm of Wilde's play is the same as that of Congreve's and Sheridan's, as Lamb defines it. Lamb's point about artificial comedy is that it provides a holiday from that particularly oppressive response to reality, moral judgment. It presents conduct which is habitually the object of moral judgment, but in such a way as to have us understand that moral judgment need not be exercised on it. It liberates us from the necessities of practicality—it invites us to *play.* Lamb makes the point that the part of Joseph Surface in *The School for Scandal* must be performed not so as to represent an evil person but so as to represent an actor playing the part of an evil person. Evil is present on the stage but our pleasure comes from seeing that it is not real evil, only histrionic evil. So in *The Way of the World* the style of the play absolves us of any need to take account of the low principles that are rampant in it. But in *The Importance of Being Earnest* there is not only no real evil but also no shadow of evil, and no principles of any kind, no more than there would be in a flotilla of butterflies. The comedies that Lamb discusses give us license to suspend the operation of moral judgment. *The Importance of Being Earnest* gives us license to believe that moral judgment has not yet been invented, and probably never will be; there is no need for it.

It is surely of significance that the most actual and intense emotions of the play are generated by cucumber sandwiches and muffins, by cake or no cake, by sugar in tea, or no sugar in tea—these persons who gobble and make such a fuss about what they gobble or do not gobble are still in the nursery. That lofty asperity which they speak to each other gives them pleasure because it mimics the lofty asperity of their nurses or governesses. When they speak of marrying and giving in marriage we know that for them there is no such thing, that they inhabit the paradise of childhood, which everyone in the audience has lost. The play is the perfect realization of innocence, of harmlessness. This is a world in which it is impossible to hurt or be hurt.

It is also, of course, the world of nonsense, that curious invention of the English of the nineteenth century, of Lewis Carroll and Edward Lear, and (though he is of a lower order) W. S. Gilbert, from whom Wilde borrowed to good effect: that baby in the suitcase is sheer Gilbert. One of the mysteries of art, perhaps as impenetrable as why tragedy gives pleasure, is why nonsense commands so fascinated an attention, and why, when it succeeds, it makes more than sense.

# The Importance of Being Earnest

CHARACTERS

JOHN WORTHING, J.P.       LADY BRACKNELL
ALGERNON MONCRIEFF       HON. GWENDOLEN FAIRFAX
REV. CANON CHASUBLE, D.D.       CECILY CARDEW
MERRIMAN, *butler*       MISS PRISM, *governess*
LANE, *manservant*

THE SCENES OF THE PLAY

ACT I    Algernon Moncrieff's Flat in Half-Moon Street, W.
ACT II    The Garden at the Manor House, Woolton.
ACT III    Drawing-Room of the Manor House, Woolton.

Time—The Present.
Place—London.

## ACT I

Scene—*Morning-room in* ALGERNON's *flat in Half-Moon Street.*[1] *The room is luxuriously and artistically furnished. The sound of a piano is heard in the adjoining room.*

LANE *is arranging afternoon tea on the table, and after the music has ceased,* ALGERNON *enters.*

ALGERNON    Did you hear what I was playing, Lane?

LANE    I didn't think it polite to listen, sir.

ALGERNON    I'm sorry for that, for your sake. I don't play accurately—anyone can play accurately—but I play with wonderful expression. As far as the piano is concerned, sentiment is my forte. I keep science for Life.

LANE    Yes, sir.

ALGERNON    And, speaking of the science of Life, have you got the cucumber sandwiches cut for Lady Bracknell?

LANE    Yes, sir.

[*Hands them on a salver*]

ALGERNON [*Inspects them, takes two, and sits down on the sofa*]    Oh! . . . by the way, Lane, I see from your book [2] that on Thursday night, when Lord Shoreman and Mr. Worthing were dining with me, eight bottles of champagne are entered as having been consumed.

LANE    Yes, sir; eight bottles and a pint.

ALGERNON    Why is it that at a bachelor's establishment the servants invariably drink the champagne? I ask merely for information.

LANE    I attribute it to the superior quality of the wine, sir. I have often

1. "Flat" is the usual word in England for what Americans call an "apartment." An "apartment house" is called a "block of flats." The degree of luxury of Algernon's flat is suggested by the fact that it has a "morning room," which implies that there is yet another and more formal general room, the drawing room. Half-Moon Street is in Mayfair, at that time the most fashionable part of London.

2. His cellar-book, in which he records the purchase and use of wine.

345

observed that in married households the champagne is rarely of a first-rate brand.

ALGERNON    Good Heavens! Is marriage so demoralizing as that?

LANE    I believe it *is* a very pleasant state, sir. I have had very little experience of it myself up to the present. I have only been married once. That was in consequence of a misunderstanding between myself and a young person.

ALGERNON    [*Languidly*]    I don't know that I am much interested in your family life, Lane.

LANE    No, sir; it is not a very interesting subject. I never think of it myself.

ALGERNON    Very natural, I am sure. That will do, Lane, thank you.

LANE    Thank you, sir. [LANE *goes out*]

ALGERNON    Lane's views on marriage seem somewhat lax. Really, if the lower orders don't set us a good example, what on earth is the use of them? They seem, as a class, to have absolutely no sense of moral responsibility.[3] [*Enter* LANE]

LANE    Mr. Ernest Worthing.

[*Enter* JACK. LANE *goes out.*]

ALGERNON    How are you, my dear Ernest? What brings you up to town?

JACK    Oh, pleasure, pleasure! What else should bring one anywhere? Eating as usual, I see, Algy!

ALGERNON    [*Stiffly*]    I believe it is customary in good society to take some slight refreshment at five o'clock. Where have you been since last Thursday?

JACK    [*Sitting down on the sofa*]    In the country.

ALGERNON    What on earth do you do there?

JACK    [*Pulling off his gloves*] [4]    When one is in town one amuses oneself. When one is in the country one amuses other people. It is excessively boring.

ALGERNON    And who are the people you amuse?

JACK    [*Airily*]    Oh, neighbours, neighbours.

ALGERNON    Got nice neighbours in your part of Shropshire?

JACK    Perfectly horrid! Never speak to one of them.

ALGERNON    How immensely you must amuse them! [*Goes over and takes sandwich*] By the way, Shropshire is your county, is it not?

JACK    Eh? Shropshire? Yes, of course. Hallo! Why all these cups? Why cucumber sandwiches? Why such reckless extravagance in one so young? Who is coming to tea?

ALGERNON    Oh! merely Aunt Augusta and Gwendolen.

JACK    How perfectly delightful!

ALGERNON    Yes, that is all very well; but I am afraid Aunt Augusta won't quite approve of your being here.

JACK    May I ask why?

ALGERNON    My dear fellow, the way you flirt with Gwendolen is perfectly disgraceful. It is almost as bad as the way Gwendolen flirts with you.

3. Wilde touches on the frequently reiterated piety about the upper classes having a responsibility to serve as an example of conduct to the "lower orders."
4. At this time a gentleman wore gloves not for warmth—the season, as we learn from the garden setting of Act II, is summer—but for elegance and as a mark of his social position. Jack doesn't pull off his gloves until he is about to tackle the cucumber sandwiches.

JACK    I am in love with Gwendolen. I have come up to town expressly to propose to her.

ALGERNON    I thought you had come up for pleasure? . . . I call that business.

JACK    How utterly unromantic you are!

ALGERNON    I really don't see anything romantic in proposing. It is very romantic to be in love. But there is nothing romantic about a definite proposal. Why, one may be accepted. One usually is, I believe. Then the excitement is all over. The very essence of romance is uncertainty. If ever I get married, I'll certainly try to forget the fact.

JACK    I have no doubt about that, dear Algy. The Divorce Court was specially invented for people whose memories are so curiously constituted.

ALGERNON    Oh! there is no use speculating on that subject. Divorces are made in Heaven——[JACK *puts out his hand to take a sandwich.* ALGERNON *at once interferes.*] Please don't touch the cucumber sandwiches. They are ordered specially for Aunt Augusta. [*Takes one and eats it*]

JACK    Well, you have been eating them all the time.

ALGERNON    That is quite a different matter. She is my aunt. [*Takes plate from below*] Have some bread and butter. The bread and butter is for Gwendolen. Gwendolen is devoted to bread and butter.

JACK    [*Advancing to table and helping himself*]    And very good bread and butter it is too.

ALGERNON    Well, my dear fellow, you need not eat as if you were going to eat it all. You behave as if you were married to her already. You are not married to her already, and I don't think you ever will be.

JACK    Why on earth do you say that?

ALGERNON    Well, in the first place girls never marry the men they flirt with. Girls don't think it right.

JACK    Oh, that is nonsense!

ALGERNON    It isn't. It is a great truth. It accounts for the extraordinary number of bachelors that one sees all over the place. In the second place, I don't give my consent.

JACK    Your consent!

ALGERNON    My dear fellow, Gwendolen is my first cousin. And before I allow you to marry her, you will have to clear up the whole question of Cecily. [*Rings bell*]

JACK    Cecily! What on earth do you mean? What do you mean, Algy, by Cecily? I don't know anyone of the name of Cecily.

[*Enter* LANE]

ALGERNON    Bring me that cigarette case Mr. Worthing left in the smoking-room the last time he dined here.

LANE    Yes, sir. [LANE *goes out*]

JACK    Do you mean to say you have had my cigarette case all this time? I wish to goodness you had let me know. I have been writing frantic letters to Scotland Yard [5] about it. I was very nearly offering a large reward.

ALGERNON    Well, I wish you would offer one. I happen to be more than usually hard up.

5. The headquarters of the London metropolitan police.

JACK    There is no good offering a large reward now that the thing is found. [*Enter* LANE *with the cigarette case on a salver.* ALGERNON *takes it at once.* LANE *goes out.*]

ALGERNON    I think that is rather mean of you, Ernest, I must say. [*Opens case and examines it*] However, it makes no matter, for, now that I look at the inscription inside, I find that the thing isn't yours after all.

JACK    Of course it's mine. [*Moving to him*] You have seen me with it a hundred times, and you have no right whatsoever to read what is written inside. It is a very ungentlemanly thing to read a private cigarette case.

ALGERNON    Oh! it is absurd to have a hard-and-fast rule about what one should read and what one shouldn't. More than half of modern culture depends on what one shouldn't read.

JACK    I am quite aware of the fact, and I don't propose to discuss modern culture. It isn't the sort of thing one should talk of in private. I simply want my cigarette case back.

ALGERNON    Yes; but this isn't your cigarette case. This cigarette case is a present from someone of the name of Cecily, and you said you didn't know anyone of that name.

JACK    Well, if you want to know, Cecily happens to be my aunt.

ALGERNON    Your aunt!

JACK    Yes. Charming old lady she is, too. Lives at Tunbridge Wells.[6] Just give it back to me, Algy.

ALGERNON    [*Retreating to back of sofa*]    But why does she call herself little Cecily if she is your aunt and lives at Tunbridge Wells? [*Reading*] 'From little Cecily with her fondest love.'

JACK    [*Moving to sofa and kneeling upon it*]    My dear fellow, what on earth is there in that? Some aunts are tall, some aunts are not tall. That is a matter that surely an aunt may be allowed to decide for herself. You seem to think that every aunt should be exactly like your aunt! That is absurd! For Heaven's sake give me back my cigarette case. [*Follows* ALGERNON *round the room*]

ALGERNON    Yes. But why does your aunt call you her uncle? 'From little Cecily, with her fondest love to her dear Uncle Jack.' There is no objection, I admit, to an aunt being a small aunt, but why an aunt, no matter what her size may be, should call her own nephew her uncle, I can't quite make out. Besides, your name isn't Jack at all; it is Ernest.

JACK    It isn't Ernest; it's Jack.

ALGERNON    You have always told me it was Ernest. I have introduced you to everyone as Ernest. You answer to the name of Ernest. You look as if your name was Ernest. You are the most earnest looking person I ever saw in my life. It is perfectly absurd your saying that your name isn't Ernest. It's on your cards. Here is one of them [*Taking it from case*) 'Mr. Ernest Worthing, B 4, The Albany.'[7] I'll keep this as a proof

6. In the 18th century a gay and fashionable resort, at this time quiet and respectable.
7. The name of this large block of flats has, since the days of the Regency, carried great social prestige by reason of the elegance of its accommodations and the social distinction of its tenants.

your name is Ernest if ever you attempt to deny it to me, or to Gwendolen, or to anyone else. [*Puts the card in his pocket*]

JACK   Well, my name is Ernest in town and Jack in the country, and the
cigarette case was given to me in the country.

ALGERNON   Yes, but that does not account for the fact that your small Aunt
Cecily, who lives at Tunbridge Wells, calls you her dear uncle. Come,
old boy, you had much better have the thing out at once.

JACK   My dear Algy, you talk exactly as if you were a dentist. It is very vulgar
to talk like a dentist when one isn't a dentist. It produces a false impression.

ALGERNON   Well, that is exactly what dentists always do. Now, go on! Tell
me the whole thing. I may mention that I have always suspected you
of being a confirmed and secret Bunburyist; and I am quite sure of it
now.

JACK   Bunburyist? What on earth do you mean by a Bunburyist?

ALGERNON   I'll reveal to you the meaning of that incomparable expression as
soon as you are kind enough to inform me why you are Ernest in town
and Jack in the country.

JACK   Well, produce my cigarette case first.

ALGERNON   Here it is. [*Hands cigarette case*] Now produce your explanation,
and pray make it improbable. [*Sits on sofa*]

JACK   My dear fellow, there is nothing improbable about my explanation at
all. In fact it's perfectly ordinary. Old Mr. Thomas Cardew, who
adopted me when I was a little boy, made me in his will guardian to
his grand-daughter, Miss Cecily Cardew. Cecily, who addresses me as
her uncle from motives of respect that you could not possibly appreciate,
lives at my place in the country under the charge of her admirable
governess, Miss Prism.

ALGERNON   Where is that place in the country, by the way?

JACK   That is nothing to you, dear boy. You are not going to be invited. . . .
I may tell you candidly that the place is not in Shropshire.

ALGERNON   I suspected that, my dear fellow! I have Bunburyed all over
Shropshire on two separate occasions. Now, go on. Why are you Ernest
in town and Jack in the country?

JACK   My dear Algy, I don't know whether you will be able to understand
my real motives. You are hardly serious enough. When one is placed in
the position of guardian, one has to adopt a very high moral tone on all
subjects. It's one's duty to do so. And as a high moral tone can hardly
be said to conduce very much to either one's health or one's happiness,
in order to get up to town I have always pretended to have a younger
brother of the name of Ernest, who lives in the Albany, and gets into
the most dreadful scrapes. That, my dear Algy, is the whole truth pure
and simple.

ALGERNON   The truth is rarely pure and never simple. Modern life would be
very tedious if it were either, and modern literature a complete impossibility!

JACK   That wouldn't be at all a bad thing.

ALGERNON   Literary criticism is not your forte, my dear fellow. Don't try it.

You should leave that to people who haven't been at a University. They do it so well in the daily papers. What you really are is a Bunburyist. I was quite right in saying you were a Bunburyist. You are one of the most advanced Bunburyists I know.

JACK    What on earth do you mean?

ALGERNON    You have invented a very useful younger brother called Ernest, in order that you may be able to come up to town as often as you like. I have invented an invaluable permanent invalid called Bunbury, in order that I may be able to go down into the country whenever I choose. Bunbury is perfectly invaluable. If it wasn't for Bunbury's extraordinary bad health, for instance, I wouldn't be able to dine with you at Willis's to-night, for I have been really engaged to Aunt Augusta for more than a week.

JACK    I haven't asked you to dine with me anywhere to-night.

ALGERNON    I know. You are absurdly careless about sending out invitations. It is very foolish of you. Nothing annoys people so much as not receiving invitations.

JACK    You had much better dine with your Aunt Augusta.

ALGERNON    I haven't the smallest intention of doing anything of the kind. To begin with, I dined there on Monday, and once a week is quite enough to dine with one's own relations. In the second place, whenever I do dine there I am always treated as a member of the family, and sent down with either no woman at all, or two. In the third place, I know perfectly well whom she will place me next to, to-night. She will place me next Mary Farquhar, who always flirts with her own husband across the dinner-table. That is not very pleasant. Indeed, it is not even decent . . . and that sort of thing is enormously on the increase. The amount of women in London who flirt with their own husbands is perfectly scandalous. It looks so bad. It is simply washing one's clean linen in public. Besides, now that I know you to be a confirmed Bunburyist I naturally want to talk to you about Bunburying. I want to tell you the rules.

JACK    I'm not a Bunburyist at all. If Gwendolen accepts me, I am going to kill my brother, indeed I think I'll kill him in any case. Cecily is a little too much interested in him. It is rather a bore. So I am going to get rid of Ernest. And I strongly advise you to do the same with Mr. . . . with your invalid friend who has the absurd name.

ALGERNON    Nothing will induce me to part with Bunbury, and if you ever get married, which seems to me extremely problematic, you will be very glad to know Bunbury. A man who marries without knowing Bunbury has a very tedious time of it.

JACK    That is nonsense. If I marry a charming girl like Gwendolen, and she is the only girl I ever saw in my life that I would marry, I certainly won't want to know Bunbury.

ALGERNON    Then your wife will. You don't seem to realize, that in married life three is company and two is none.

JACK [Sententiously]    That, my dear young friend, is the theory that the corrupt French Drama has been propounding for the last fifty years.

ALGERNON    Yes; and that the happy English home has proved in half the time.

JACK    For heaven's sake, don't try to be cynical. It's perfectly easy to be cynical.

ALGERNON    My dear fellow, it isn't easy to be anything now-a-days. There's such a lot of beastly competition about. [*The sound of an electric bell* [8] *is heard*] Ah! that must be Aunt Augusta. Only relatives, or creditors, ever ring in that Wagnerian manner. Now, if I get her out of the way for ten minutes, so that you can have an opportunity for proposing to Gwendolen, may I dine with you to-night at Willis's?

JACK    I suppose so, if you want to.

ALGERNON    Yes, but you must be serious about it. I hate people who are not serious about meals. It is so shallow of them.

[*Enter* LANE]

LANE    Lady Bracknell [9] and Miss Fairfax.

[ALGERNON *goes forward to meet them. Enter* LADY BRACKNELL *and* GWENDOLEN]

LADY BRACKNELL    Good afternoon, dear Algernon, I hope you are behaving very well.

ALGERNON    I'm feeling very well, Aunt Augusta.

LADY BRACKNELL    That's not quite the same thing. In fact the two things rarely go together. [*Sees* JACK *and bows to him with icy coldness*]

ALGERNON    [*To* GWENDOLEN]    Dear me, you are smart! [10]

GWENDOLEN    I am always smart! Aren't I, Mr. Worthing?

JACK    You're quite perfect, Miss Fairfax.

GWENDOLEN    Oh! I hope I am not that. It would leave no room for developments, and I intend to develop in many directions. [GWENDOLEN *and* JACK *sit down together in the corner*]

LADY BRACKNELL    I'm sorry if we are a little late, Algernon, but I was obliged to call on dear Lady Harbury. I hadn't been there since her poor husband's death. I never saw a woman so altered; she looks quite twenty years younger. And now I'll have a cup of tea, and one of those nice cucumber sandwiches you promised me.

ALGERNON    Certainly, Aunt Augusta. [*Goes over to tea-table*]

LADY BRACKNELL    Won't you come and sit here, Gwendolen?

GWENDOLEN    Thanks, mamma, [11] I'm quite comfortable where I am.

ALGERNON    [*Picking up empty plate in horror*]    Good heavens! Lane! Why are there no cucumber sandwiches? I ordered them specially.

LANE    [*Gravely*]    There were no cucumbers in the market this morning, sir. I went down twice.

ALGERNON    No cucumbers!

LANE    No, sir. Not even for ready money.

8. The specification of this detail suggests that Algernon's flat was nothing if not *modern!*
9. Pronounced with the accent on the first syllable.
10. In England this word is used only to denote an attractively trim appearance or a high degree of fashionableness.
11. This was the accepted way in which a young woman of the upper classes would address or refer to her mother. It is pronounced with the accent put strongly on the second syllable, the first *a* scarcely sounded.

ALGERNON   That will do, Lane, thank you.

LANE   Thank you, sir. [*Goes out*]

ALGERNON   I am greatly distressed, Aunt Augusta, about there being no cucumbers, not even for ready money.

LADY BRACKNELL   It really makes no matter, Algernon. I had some crumpets [12] with Lady Harbury, who seems to me to be living entirely for pleasure now.

ALGERNON   I hear her hair has turned quite gold from grief.

LADY BRACKNELL   It certainly has changed its colour. From what cause I, of course, cannot say. [ALGERNON *crosses and hands tea*] Thank you. I've quite a treat for you to-night, Algernon. I am going to send you down with Mary Farquhar. She is such a nice woman, and so attentive to her husband. It's delightful to watch them.

ALGERNON   I am afraid, Aunt Augusta, I shall have to give up the pleasure of dining with you to-night after all.

LADY BRACKNELL   [*Frowning*]   I hope not, Algernon. It would put my table completely out.[13] Your uncle would have to dine upstairs. Fortunately he is accustomed to that.

ALGERNON   It is a great bore, and, I need hardly say, a terrible disappointment to me, but the fact is I have just had a telegram to say that my poor friend Bunbury is very ill again. [*Exchanges glances with* JACK] They seem to think I should be with him.

LADY BRACKNELL   It is very strange. This Mr. Bunbury seems to suffer from curiously bad health.

ALGERNON   Yes; poor Bunbury is a dreadful invalid.

LADY BRACKNELL   Well, I must say, Algernon, that I think it is high time that Mr. Bunbury made up his mind whether he was going to live or to die. This shilly-shallying with the question is absurd. Nor do I in any way approve of the modern sympathy with invalids. I consider it morbid. Illness of any kind is hardly a thing to be encouraged in others. Health is the primary duty of life. I am always telling that to your poor uncle, but he never seems to take much notice . . . as far as any improvement in his ailments goes. I should be much obliged if you would ask Mr. Bunbury, from me, to be kind enough not to have a relapse on Saturday, for I rely on you to arrange my music for me.[14] It is my last reception and one wants something that will encourage conversation,[15] particularly at the end of the season when everyone has practically said whatever they had to say, which, in most cases, was probably not much.

ALGERNON   I'll speak to Bunbury, Aunt Augusta, if he is still conscious, and I think I can promise you he'll be all right by Saturday. Of course the music is a great difficulty. You see, if one plays good music, people don't listen, and if one plays bad music people don't talk. But I'll run

12. A sort of muffin, usually toasted and heavily buttered.
13. She means the proper seating arrangement of her guests.
14. That is, prepare the program of what is to be played at her musical evening.
15. This makes the established joke that the English upper classes are likely to talk while music is being played at private homes.

over the programme I've drawn out, if you will kindly come into the next room for a moment.

LADY BRACKNELL    Thank you, Algernon. It is very thoughtful of you. [*Rising, and following* ALGERNON] I'm sure the programme will be delightful, after a few expurgations. French songs I cannot possibly allow. People always seem to think that they are improper, and either look shocked, which is vulgar, or laugh, which is worse. But German sounds a thoroughly respectable language, and indeed, I believe is so. Gwendolen, you will accompany me.

GWENDOLEN    Certainly, mamma.

[LADY BRACKNELL *and* ALGERNON *go into the music room,* GWENDOLEN *remains behind*]

JACK    Charming day it has been, Miss Fairfax.

GWENDOLEN    Pray don't talk to me about the weather, Mr. Worthing. Whenever people talk to me about the weather, I always feel quite certain that they mean something else. And that makes me so nervous.

JACK    I do mean something else.

GWENDOLEN    I thought so. In fact, I am never wrong.

JACK    And I would like to be allowed to take advantage of Lady Bracknell's temporary absence . . .

GWENDOLEN    I would certainly advise you to do so. Mamma has a way of coming back suddenly into a room that I have often had to speak to her about.

JACK [*Nervously*]    Miss Fairfax, ever since I met you I have admired you more than any girl . . . I have ever met since . . . I met you.

GWENDOLEN    Yes, I am quite aware of the fact. And I often wish that in public, at any rate, you had been more demonstrative. For me you have always had an irresistible fascination. Even before I met you I was far from indifferent to you. [JACK *looks at her in amazement*] We live, as I hope you know, Mr. Worthing, in an age of ideals. The fact is constantly mentioned in the more expensive monthly magazines, and has reached the provincial pulpits I am told: and my ideal has always been to love some one of the name of Ernest. There is something in that name that inspires absolute confidence. The moment Algernon first mentioned to me that he had a friend called Ernest, I knew I was destined to love you.

JACK    You really love me, Gwendolen?

GWENDOLEN    Passionately!

JACK    Darling! You don't know how happy you've made me.

GWENDOLEN    My own Ernest!

JACK    But you don't really mean to say that you couldn't love me if my name wasn't Ernest?

GWENDOLEN    But your name is Ernest.

JACK    Yes, I know it is. But supposing it was something else? Do you mean to say you couldn't love me then?

GWENDOLEN [*Glibly*]    Ah! that is clearly a metaphysical speculation, and like most metaphysical speculations has very little reference at all to the actual facts of real life, as we know them.

JACK    Personally, darling, to speak quite candidly, I don't much care about the name of Ernest . . . I don't think the name suits me at all.

GWENDOLEN    It suits you perfectly. It is a divine name. It has a music of its own. It produces vibrations.

JACK    Well, really, Gwendolen, I must say that I think there are lots of other much nicer names. I think Jack, for instance, a charming name.

GWENDOLEN    Jack? . . . No, there is very little music in the name Jack, if any at all, indeed. It does not thrill. It produces absolutely no vibrations. . . . I have known several Jacks, and they all, without exception, were more than usually plain. Besides, Jack is a notorious domesticity for John! And I pity any woman who is married to a man called John. She would probably never be allowed to know the entrancing pleasure of a single moment's solitude. The only really safe name is Ernest.

JACK    Gwendolen, I must get christened at once—I mean we must get married at once. There is no time to be lost.

GWENDOLEN    Married, Mr. Worthing?

JACK [Astounded]    Well . . . surely. You know that I love you, and you led me to believe, Miss Fairfax, that you were not absolutely indifferent to me.

GWENDOLEN    I adore you. But you haven't proposed to me yet. Nothing has been said at all about marriage. The subject has not even been touched on.

JACK    Well . . . may I propose to you now?

GWENDOLEN    I think it would be an admirable opportunity. And to spare you any possible disappointment, Mr. Worthing, I think it only fair to tell you quite frankly beforehand that I am fully determined to accept you.

JACK    Gwendolen!

GWENDOLEN    Yes, Mr. Worthing, what have you got to say to me?

JACK    You know what I have got to say to you.

GWENDOLEN    Yes, but you don't say it.

JACK    Gwendolen, will you marry me? [Goes on his knees 16]

GWENDOLEN    Of course I will, darling. How long you have been about it! I am afraid you have had very little experience in how to propose.

JACK    My own one, I have never loved anyone in the world but you.

GWENDOLEN    Yes, but men often propose for practice. I know my brother Gerald does. All my girl-friends tell me so. What wonderfully blue eyes you have, Ernest! They are quite, quite, blue. I hope you will always look at me just like that, especially when there are other people present. [Enter LADY BRACKNELL]

LADY BRACKNELL    Mr. Worthing! Rise, sir, from this semi-recumbent posture. It is most indecorous.

GWENDOLEN    Mamma! [He tries to rise; she restrains him.] I must beg you to retire. This is no place for you. Besides, Mr. Worthing has not quite finished yet.

16. The idea that when a young man proposes marriage he kneels before his beloved was sustained by the stage and by the drawings in humorous magazines. There is little likelihood that this was an actual practice.

LADY BRACKNELL    Finished what, may I ask?

GWENDOLEN    I am engaged to Mr. Worthing, mamma. [*They rise together*]

LADY BRACKNELL    Pardon me, you are not engaged to anyone. When you do become engaged to some one, I, or your father, should his health permit him, will inform you of the fact. An engagement should come on a young girl as a surprise, pleasant or unpleasant, as the case may be. It is hardly a matter that she could be allowed to arrange for herself. . . . And now I have a few questions to put to you, Mr. Worthing. While I am making these inquiries, you, Gwendolen, will wait for me below in the carriage.

GWENDOLEN [*Reproachfully*]    Mamma!

LADY BRACKNELL    In the carriage, Gwendolen!

[GWENDOLEN *goes to the door. She and* JACK *blow kisses to each other behind* LADY BRACKNELL'S *back.* LADY BRACKNELL *looks vaguely about as if she could not understand what the noise was. Finally turns round.*] Gwendolen, the carriage!

GWENDOLEN    Yes, mamma. [*Goes out, looking back at* JACK]

LADY BRACKNELL [*Sitting down*]    You can take a seat, Mr. Worthing.
[*Looks in her pocket for note-book and pencil*]

JACK    Thank you, Lady Bracknell, I prefer standing.

LADY BRACKNELL [*Pencil and note-book in hand*]    I feel bound to tell you that you are not down on my list of eligible young men, although I have the same list as the dear Duchess of Bolton has. We work together, in fact. However, I am quite ready to enter your name, should your answers be what a really affectionate mother requires. Do you smoke?

JACK    Well, yes, I must admit I smoke.

LADY BRACKNELL    I am glad to hear it. A man should always have an occupation of some kind. There are far too many idle men in London as it is. How old are you?

JACK    Twenty-nine.

LADY BRACKNELL    A very good age to be married at. I have always been of opinion that a man who desires to get married should know either everything or nothing. Which do you know?

JACK [*After some hesitation*]    I know nothing, Lady Bracknell.

LADY BRACKNELL    I am pleased to hear it. I do not approve of anything that tampers with natural ignorance. Ignorance is like a delicate exotic fruit; touch it and the bloom is gone. The whole theory of modern education is radically unsound. Fortunately in England, at any rate, education produces no effect whatsoever. If it did, it would prove a serious danger to the upper classes, and probably lead to acts of violence in Grosvenor Square.[17] What is your income?

JACK    Between seven and eight thousand a year.

LADY BRACKNELL [*Makes a note in her book*]    In land, or in investments?

JACK    In investments, chiefly.

LADY BRACKNELL    That is satisfactory. What between the duties expected of one during one's lifetime, and the duties exacted from one after one's

17. An especially elegant residential square.

death, land has ceased to be either a profit or a pleasure. It gives one position, and prevents one from keeping it up. That's all that can be said about land.[18]

JACK    I have a country house with some land, of course, attached to it, about fifteen hundred acres, I believe; but I don't depend on that for my real income. In fact, as far as I can make out, the poachers are the only people who make anything out of it.

LADY BRACKNELL    A country house! How many bedrooms? Well, that point can be cleared up afterwards. You have a town house, I hope? A girl with a simple, unspoiled nature, like Gwendolen, could hardly be expected to reside in the country.

JACK    Well, I own a house in Belgrave Square, but it is let by the year to Lady Bloxham. Of course, I can get it back whenever I like, at six months' notice.

LADY BRACKNELL    Lady Bloxham? I don't know her.

JACK    Oh, she goes about very little. She is a lady considerably advanced in years.

LADY BRACKNELL    Ah, now-a-days that is no guarantee of respectability of character. What number in Belgrave Square?

JACK    149.

LADY BRACKNELL    [Shaking her head]    The unfashionable side. I thought there was something. However, that could easily be altered.

JACK    Do you mean the fashion, or the side?

LADY BRACKNELL    [Sternly]    Both, if necessary, I presume. What are your politics?

JACK    Well, I am afraid I really have none. I am a Liberal Unionist.[19]

LADY BRACKNELL    Oh, they count as Tories. They dine with us. Or come in the evening, at any rate. Now to minor matters. Are your parents living?

JACK    I have lost both my parents.

LADY BRACKNELL    Both? . . . That seems like carelessness. Who was your father? He was evidently a man of some wealth. Was he born in what the Radical papers call the purple of commerce, or did he rise from the ranks of the aristocracy?

JACK    I am afraid I really don't know. The fact is, Lady Bracknell, I said I had lost my parents. It would be nearer the truth to say that my parents seem to have lost me . . . I don't actually know who I am by birth. I was . . . well, I was found.

LADY BRACKNELL    Found!

JACK    The late Mr. Thomas Cardew, an old gentleman of a very charitable and kindly disposition, found me, and gave me the name of Worthing, because he happened to have a first-class ticket for Worthing in his pocket at the time. Worthing is a place in Sussex. It is a seaside resort.

---

18. Lady Bracknell outrages an important English piety. Owning land and living on it for at least part of the year was thought to confer a degree of social distinction, and it was common practice among men who had succeeded in business to buy country estates, even though they were ever less likely to yield any profit.

19. A reference to the efforts of Gladstone, the prime minister, to secure Home Rule for Wilde's native Ireland.

LADY BRACKNELL    Where did the charitable gentleman who had a first-class ticket for this seaside resort find you?

JACK [*Gravely*]    In a hand-bag.

LADY BRACKNELL    A hand-bag?

JACK [*Very seriously*]    Yes, Lady Bracknell. I was in a hand-bag—a somewhat large, black leather hand-bag, with handles to it—an ordinary hand-bag in fact.

LADY BRACKNELL    In what locality did this Mr. James, or Thomas, Cardew come across this ordinary hand-bag?

JACK    In the cloak-room at Victoria Station. It was given to him in mistake for his own.

LADY BRACKNELL    The cloak-room at Victoria Station?

JACK    Yes. The Brighton line.

LADY BRACKNELL    The line is immaterial. Mr. Worthing, I confess I feel somewhat bewildered by what you have just told me. To be born, or at any rate bred, in a hand-bag, whether it had handles or not, seems to me to display a contempt for the ordinary decencies of family life that remind one of the worst excesses of the French Revolution. And I presume you know what that unfortunate movement led to? As for the particular locality in which the hand-bag was found, a cloak-room at a railway station might serve to conceal a social indiscretion—has probably, indeed, been used for that purpose before now—but it could hardly be regarded as an assured basis for a recognized position in good society.

JACK    May I ask you then what you would advise me to do? I need hardly say I would do anything in the world to ensure Gwendolen's happiness.

LADY BRACKNELL    I would strongly advise you, Mr. Worthing, to try and acquire some relations as soon as possible, and to make a definite effort to produce at any rate one parent, of either sex, before the season is quite over.

JACK    Well, I don't see how I could possibly manage to do that. I can produce the hand-bag at any moment. It is in my dressing-room at home. I really think that should satisfy you, Lady Bracknell.

LADY BRACKNELL    Me, sir! What has it to do with me? You can hardly imagine that I and Lord Bracknell would dream of allowing our only daughter—a girl brought up with the utmost care—to marry into a cloak-room, and form an alliance with a parcel? Good morning, Mr. Worthing!

[LADY BRACKNELL *sweeps out in majestic indignation*]

JACK    Good morning! [ALGERNON, *from the other room, strikes up the Wedding March.* JACK *looks perfectly furious, and goes to the door.*] For goodness' sake don't play that ghastly tune, Algy! How idiotic you are!

[*The music stops, and* ALGERNON *enters cheerily*]

ALGERNON    Didn't it go off all right, old boy? You don't mean to say Gwendolen refused you? I know it is a way she has. She is always refusing people. I think it is most ill-natured of her.

JACK    Oh, Gwendolen is as right as a trivet.[20] As far as she is concerned, we

---

20. A proverbial expression (which sounds odd coming from Jack). A trivet is a three-legged stand used for supporting cooking vessels in a fireplace.

are engaged. Her mother is perfectly unbearable. Never met such a Gorgon . . . I don't really know what a Gorgon is like, but I am quite sure that Lady Bracknell is one.[21] In any case, she is a monster, without being a myth, which is rather unfair. . . . I beg your pardon, Algy, I suppose I shouldn't talk about your own aunt in that way before you.

ALGERNON    My dear boy, I love hearing my relations abused. It is the only thing that makes me put up with them at all. Relations are simply a tedious pack of people, who haven't got the remotest knowledge of how to live, nor the smallest instinct about when to die.

JACK    Oh, that is nonsense!

ALGERNON    It isn't!

JACK    Well, I won't argue about the matter. You always want to argue about things.

ALGERNON    That is exactly what things were originally made for.

JACK    Upon my word, if I thought that, I'd shoot myself . . . [A pause] You don't think there is any chance of Gwendolen becoming like her mother in about a hundred and fifty years, do you Algy?

ALGERNON    All women become like their mothers. That is their tragedy. No man does. That's his.

JACK    Is that clever?

ALGERNON    It is perfectly phrased! and quite as true as any observation in civilized life should be.

JACK    I am sick to death of cleverness. Everybody is clever now-a-days. You can't go anywhere without meeting clever people. The thing has become an absolute public nuisance. I wish to goodness we had a few fools left.

ALGERNON    We have.

JACK    I should extremely like to meet them. What do they talk about?

ALGERNON    The fools? Oh! about the clever people, of course.

JACK    What fools!

ALGERNON    By the way, did you tell Gwendolen the truth about your being Ernest in town, and Jack in the country?

JACK [In a very patronising manner]    My dear fellow, the truth isn't quite the sort of thing one tells to a nice, sweet, refined girl. What extraordinary ideas you have about the way to behave to a woman!

ALGERNON    The only way to behave to a woman is to make love to her, if she is pretty, and to someone else if she is plain.

JACK    Oh, that is nonsense.

ALGERNON    What about your brother? What about the profligate Ernest?

JACK    Oh, before the end of the week I shall have got rid of him. I'll say he died in Paris of apoplexy. Lots of people die of apoplexy, quite suddenly, don't they?

ALGERNON    Yes, but it's hereditary, my dear fellow. It's a sort of thing that runs in families. You had much better say a severe chill.

JACK    You are sure a severe chill isn't hereditary, or anything of that kind?

---

21. It is hard to believe that Jack could have gone to school without learning that a Gorgon was one of three sister-monsters, the chief one, Medusa, having a round, ugly face, snakes for hair, sometimes a beard, and eyes that could turn people to stone.

ALGERNON    Of course it isn't!

JACK    Very well, then. My poor brother Ernest is carried off suddenly in Paris, by a severe chill. That gets rid of him.

ALGERNON    But I thought you said that . . . Miss Cardew was a little too much interested in your poor brother Ernest? Won't she feel his loss a good deal?

JACK    Oh, that is all right. Cecily is not a silly, romantic girl, I am glad to say. She has got a capital appetite, goes long walks, and pays no attention at all to her lessons.

ALGERNON    I would rather like to see Cecily.

JACK    I will take very good care you never do. She is excessively pretty, and she is only just eighteen.

ALGERNON    Have you told Gwendolen yet that you have an excessively pretty ward who is only just eighteen?

JACK    Oh! One doesn't blurt these things out to people. Cecily and Gwendolen are perfectly certain to be extremely great friends. I'll bet you anything you like that half an hour after they have met, they will be calling each other sister.

ALGERNON    Women only do that when they have called each other a lot of other things first. Now, my dear boy, if we want to get a good table at Willis's, we really must go and dress.[22] Do you know it is nearly seven?

JACK    [Irritably]    Oh! it always is nearly seven.

ALGERNON    Well, I'm hungry.

JACK    I never knew you when you weren't. . . .

ALGERNON    What shall we do after dinner? Go to a theatre?

JACK    Oh no! I loathe listening.

ALGERNON    Well, let us go to the Club?

JACK    Oh, no! I hate talking.

ALGERNON    Well, we might trot round to the Empire [23] at ten?

JACK    Oh, no! I can't bear looking at things. It is so silly.

ALGERNON    Well, what shall we do?

JACK    Nothing!

ALGERNON    It is awfully hard work doing nothing. However, I don't mind hard work where there is no definite object of any kind.

[Enter LANE]

LANE    Miss Fairfax.

[Enter GWENDOLEN. LANE goes out.]

ALGERNON    Gwendolen, upon my word!

GWENDOLEN    Algy, kindly turn your back. I have something very particular to say to Mr. Worthing.

ALGERNON    Really, Gwendolen, I don't think I can allow this at all.

GWENDOLEN    Algy, you always adopt a strictly immoral attitude towards life. You are not quite old enough to do that. [ALGERNON retires to the fireplace]

---

22. He means in a tailcoat with white tie. The dinner jacket with black tie did not come into use until almost a quarter-century later.
23. A music hall, i.e. a vaudeville theater.

JACK    My own darling!

GWENDOLEN    Ernest, we may never be married. From the expression on mamma's face I fear we never shall. Few parents now-a-days pay any regard to what their children say to them. The old-fashioned respect for the young is fast dying out. Whatever influence I ever had over mamma, I lost at the age of three. But although she may prevent us from becoming man and wife, and I may marry someone else, and marry often, nothing that she can possibly do can alter my eternal devotion to you.

JACK    Dear Gwendolen!

GWENDOLEN    The story of your romantic origin, as related to me by mamma, with unpleasing comments, has naturally stirred the deeper fibres of my nature. Your Christian name has an irresistible fascination. The simplicity of your character makes you exquisitely incomprehensible to me. Your town address at the Albany I have. What is your address in the country?

JACK    The Manor House, Woolton, Hertfordshire.

[ALGERNON, *who has been carefully listening, smiles to himself, and writes the address on his shirt-cuff.*[24] *Then picks up the Railway Guide.*]

GWENDOLEN    There is a good postal service, I suppose? It may be necessary to do something desperate. That, of course, will require serious consideration. I will communicate with you daily.

JACK    My own one!

GWENDOLEN    How long do you remain in town?

JACK    Till Monday.

GWENDOLEN    Good! Algy, you may turn round now.

ALGERNON    Thanks, I've turned round already.

GWENDOLEN    You may also ring the bell.

JACK    You will let me see you to your carriage, my own darling?

GWENDOLEN    Certainly.

JACK [*To* LANE, *who now enters*]    I will see Miss Fairfax out.

LANE    Yes, sir. [JACK *and* GWENDOLEN *go off.* LANE *presents several letters on a salver to* ALGERNON. *It is to be surmised that they are bills, as* ALGERNON *after looking at the envelopes, tears them up.*]

ALGERNON    A glass of sherry, Lane.

LANE    Yes, sir.

ALGERNON    To-morrow, Lane, I'm going Bunburying.

LANE    Yes, sir.

ALGERNON    I shall probably not be back till Monday. You can put up my dress clothes, my smoking jacket,[25] and all the Bunbury suits . . .

LANE    Yes, sir [*Handing sherry*]

ALGERNON    I hope to-morrow will be a fine day, Lane.

LANE    It never is, sir.

24. The cuffs of gentlemen's shirts were starched stiff and were commonly used for jotting down memoranda.
25. This would be a short jacket of silk or velvet, probably quilted, which a gentleman wore in place of his dress coat when he foregathered with other male guests at a country-house weekend to smoke (in the smoking room) before going to bed.

ALGERNON    Lane, you're a perfect pessimist.

LANE    I do my best to give satisfaction, sir.

[*Enter* JACK. LANE *goes off.*]

JACK    There's a sensible, intellectual girl! the only girl I ever cared for in my life. [ALGERNON *is laughing immoderately*] What on earth are you so amused at?

ALGERNON    Oh, I'm a little anxious about poor Bunbury, that is all.

JACK    If you don't take care, your friend Bunbury will get you into a serious scrape some day.

ALGERNON    I love scrapes. They are the only things that are never serious.

JACK    Oh, that's nonsense, Algy. You never talk anything but nonsense.

ALGERNON    Nobody ever does.

[JACK *looks indignantly at him, and leaves the room.* ALGERNON *lights a cigarette, reads his shirt-cuff, and smiles.*]

ACT-DROP

## ACT II

Scene—*Garden at the Manor House. A flight of gray stone steps leads up to the house. The garden, an old-fashioned one, full of roses. Time of year, July. Basket chairs, and a table covered with books, are set under a large yew tree.*

MISS PRISM [1] *discovered seated at the table.* CECILY *is at the back watering flowers.*

MISS PRISM [*Calling*]    Cecily, Cecily! Surely such a utilitarian occupation as the watering of flowers is rather Moulton's duty than yours? Especially at a moment when intellectual pleasures await you. Your German grammar is on the table. Pray open it at page fifteen. We will repeat yesterday's lesson.

CECILY [*Coming over very slowly*]    But I don't like German. It isn't at all a becoming language. I know perfectly well that I look quite plain after my German lesson.

MISS PRISM    Child, you know how anxious your guardian is that you should improve yourself in every way. He laid particular stress on your German, as he was leaving for town yesterday. Indeed, he always lays stress on your German when he is leaving for town.

CECILY    Dear Uncle Jack is so very serious! Sometimes he is so serious that I think he cannot be quite well.

MISS PRISM [*Drawing herself up*]    Your guardian enjoys the best of health, and his gravity of demeanour is especially to be commended in one so comparatively young as he is. I know no one who has a higher sense of duty and responsibility.

CECILY    I suppose that is why he often looks a little bored when we three are together.

---

1. Miss Prism's name is chosen with reference to the phrase "prunes and prisms," in common use to denote the proprieties taught to young ladies. It derives from a famous statement of Mrs. General, the snobbish governess in Dickens's *Little Dorrit*, who explains to her charge that there are certain words that give a "pretty form" to the lips. "Papa, potatoes, poultry, prunes and prisms are all very good words for the lips; especially prunes and prisms."

MISS PRISM    Cecily! I am surprised at you. Mr. Worthing has many troubles in his life. Idle merriment and triviality would be out of place in his conversation. You must remember his constant anxiety about that unfortunate young man, his brother.

CECILY    I wish Uncle Jack would allow that unfortunate young man, his brother, to come down here sometimes. We might have a good influence over him, Miss Prism. I am sure you certainly would. You know German, and geology, and things of that kind influence a man very much. [CECILY *begins to write in her diary*]

MISS PRISM    [*Shaking her head*]    I do not think that even I could produce any effect on a character that according to his own brother's admission is irretrievably weak and vacillating. Indeed I am not sure that I would desire to reclaim him. I am not in favour of this modern mania for turning bad people into good people at a moment's notice. As a man sows so let him reap. You must put away your diary, Cecily. I really don't see why you should keep a diary at all.

CECILY    I keep a diary in order to enter the wonderful secrets of my life. If I didn't write them down I should probably forget all about them.

MISS PRISM    Memory, my dear Cecily, is the diary that we all carry about with us.

CECILY    Yes, but it usually chronicles the things that have never happened, and couldn't possibly have happened. I believe that Memory is responsible for nearly all the three-volume novels that Mudie[2] sends us.

MISS PRISM    Do not speak slightingly of the three-volume novel, Cecily. I wrote one myself in earlier days.

CECILY    Did you really, Miss Prism? How wonderfully clever you are! I hope it did not end happily? I don't like novels that end happily. They depress me so much.

MISS PRISM    The good ended happily, and the bad unhappily. That is what Fiction means.

CECILY    I suppose so. But it seems very unfair. And was your novel ever published?

MISS PRISM    Alas! no. The manuscript unfortunately was abandoned. I use the word in the sense of lost or mislaid.[3] To your work, child, these speculations are profitless.

CECILY    [*Smiling*]    But I see dear Dr. Chasuble coming up through the garden.

MISS PRISM    [*Rising and advancing*]    Dr. Chasuble! This is indeed a pleasure. [*Enter* CANON CHASUBLE[4]]

CHASUBLE    And how are we this morning? Miss Prism, you are, I trust, well? CECILY    Miss Prism has just been complaining of a slight headache. I think it

---

2. Mudie's was the great commercial lending-library in London. The name was synonymous with sentimental novels.
3. Rather than in the sense (once more common than now) of immoral and shameless.
4. He is Dr. Chasuble because he is a Doctor of Divinity. He is Canon Chasuble because he is connected with a cathedral as a member of the bishop's counsel. He is Chasuble because Wilde thought it would be convenient and amusing to suggest his character by naming him after an ecclesiastical vestment: he is what he wears.

would do her so much good to have a short stroll with you in the park,[5] Dr. Chasuble.

MISS PRISM    Cecily, I have not mentioned anything about a headache.

CECILY    No, dear Miss Prism, I know that, but I felt instinctively that you had a headache. Indeed I was thinking about that, and not about my German lesson, when the Rector came in.

CHASUBLE    I hope, Cecily, you are not inattentive.

CECILY    Oh, I am afraid I am.

CHASUBLE    That is strange. Were I fortunate enough to be Miss Prism's pupil, I would hang upon her lips. [MISS PRISM glares] I spoke metaphorically. —My metaphor was drawn from bees. Ahem! Mr. Worthing, I suppose, has not returned from town yet?

MISS PRISM    We do not expect him till Monday afternoon.

CHASUBLE    Ah yes, he usually likes to spend his Sunday in London. He is not one of those whose sole aim is enjoyment, as, by all accounts, that unfortunate young man, his brother, seems to be. But I must not disturb Egeria[6] and her pupil any longer.

MISS PRISM    Egeria? My name is Lætitia, Doctor.

CHASUBLE    [Bowing] A classical allusion merely, drawn from the Pagan authors. I shall see you both no doubt at Evensong.[7]

MISS PRISM    I think, dear Doctor, I will have a stroll with you. I find I have a headache after all, and a walk might do it good.

CHASUBLE    With pleasure, Miss Prism, with pleasure. We might go as far as the schools and back.

MISS PRISM    That would be delightful. Cecily, you will read your Political Economy in my absence. The chapter on the Fall of the Rupee[8] you may omit. It is somewhat too sensational. Even these metallic problems have their melodramatic side.

[Goes down the garden with DR. CHASUBLE]

CECILY    [Picks up books and throws them back on table] Horrid Political Economy! Horrid Geography! Horrid, horrid German!

[Enter MERRIMAN with a card on a salver]

MERRIMAN    Mr. Ernest Worthing has just driven over from the station. He has brought his luggage with him.

CECILY    [Takes the card and reads it] 'Mr. Ernest Worthing, B 4 The Albany, W.' Uncle Jack's brother! Did you tell him Mr. Worthing was in town?

MERRIMAN    Yes, Miss. He seemed very much disappointed. I mentioned that you and Miss Prism were in the garden. He said he was anxious to speak to you privately for a moment.

CECILY    Ask Mr. Ernest Worthing to come here. I suppose you had better talk to the housekeeper about a room for him.

5. The grounds of the estate.
6. A Roman goddess of fountains, birth, and prophecy. She was said to be the consort and counselor of Numa, a legendary king of Rome renowned for his wisdom.
7. Evening prayer in the Anglican Church.
8. The rupee is the basic monetary unit of India. At a time when India was an important part of the Empire, its fall on the money market—which was frequent—was of considerable consequence, especially to those retired Englishmen who had been in the civil or military services in India and who, on retirement, lived in England on a pension paid in rupees.

MERRIMAN    Yes, Miss.

[MERRIMAN *goes off*]

CECILY    I have never met any really wicked person before. I feel rather frightened. I am so afraid he will look just like everyone else.

[*Enter* ALGERNON, *very gay and debonair*]

He does!

ALGERNON    [*Raising his hat*]    You are my little cousin Cecily, I'm sure.

CECILY    You are under some strange mistake. I am not little. In fact, I believe I am more than usually tall for my age. [ALGERNON *is rather taken aback*] But I am your cousin Cecily. You, I see from your card, are Uncle Jack's brother, my cousin Ernest, my wicked cousin Ernest.

ALGERNON    Oh! I am not really wicked at all, cousin Cecily. You musn't think that I am wicked.

CECILY    If you are not, then you have certainly been deceiving us all in a very inexcusable manner. I hope you have not been leading a double life, pretending to be wicked and being really good all the time. That would be hypocrisy.

ALGERNON    [*Looks at her in amazement*]    Oh! of course I have been rather reckless.

CECILY    I am glad to hear it.

ALGERNON    In fact, now you mention the subject, I have been very bad in my own small way.

CECILY    I don't think you should be so proud of that, though I am sure it must have been very pleasant.

ALGERNON    It is much pleasanter being here with you.

CECILY    I can't understand how you are here at all. Uncle Jack won't be back till Monday afternoon.

ALGERNON    That is a great disappointment. I am obliged to go up by the first train on Monday morning. I have a business appointment that I am anxious . . . to miss.

CECILY    Couldn't you miss it anywhere but in London?

ALGERNON    No: the appointment is in London.

CECILY    Well, I know, of course, how important it is not to keep a business engagement, if one wants to retain any sense of the beauty of life, but still I think you had better wait till Uncle Jack arrives. I know he wants to speak to you about your emigrating.

ALGERNON    About my what?

CECILY    Your emigrating. He has gone up to buy your outfit.

ALGERNON    I certainly wouldn't let Jack buy my outfit. He has no taste in neckties at all.

CECILY    I don't think you will require neckties. Uncle Jack is sending you to Australia.

ALGERNON    Australia! I'd sooner die.

CECILY    Well, he said at dinner on Wednesday night, that you would have to choose between this world, the next world, and Australia.

ALGERNON    Oh, well! The accounts I have received of Australia and the next world, are not particularly encouraging. This world is good enough for me, cousin Cecily.

CECILY   Yes, but are you good enough for it?

ALGERNON   I'm afraid I'm not that. That is why I want you to reform me. You might make that your mission, if you don't mind, cousin Cecily.

CECILY   I'm afraid I've no time, this afternoon.

ALGERNON   Well, would you mind my reforming myself this afternoon?

CECILY   It is rather Quixotic of you. But I think you should try.

ALGERNON   I will. I feel better already.

CECILY   You are looking a little worse.

ALGERNON   That is because I am hungry.

CECILY   How thoughtless of me. I should have remembered that when one is going to lead an entirely new life, one requires regular and wholesome meals. Won't you come in?

ALGERNON   Thank you. Might I have a buttonhole[9] first? I never have any appetite unless I have a buttonhole first.

CECILY   A Maréchal Niel?[10] [Picks up scissors]

ALGERNON   No, I'd sooner have a pink rose.

CECILY   Why? [Cuts a flower]

ALGERNON   Because you are like a pink rose, cousin Cecily.

CECILY   I don't think it can be right for you to talk to me like that. Miss Prism never says such things to me.

ALGERNON   Then Miss Prism is a short-sighted old lady. [CECILY puts the rose in his buttonhole] You are the prettiest girl I ever saw.

CECILY   Miss Prism says that all good looks are a snare.

ALGERNON   They are a snare that every sensible man would like to be caught in.

CECILY   Oh! I don't think I would care to catch a sensible man. I shouldn't know what to talk to him about.

[They pass into the house. MISS PRISM and DR. CHASUBLE return.]

MISS PRISM   You are too much alone, dear Dr. Chasuble. You should get married. A misanthrope I can understand— a womanthrope, never!

CHASUBLE   [With a scholar's shudder[11]]   Believe me, I do not deserve so neologistic a phrase. The precept as well as the practice of the Primitive Church was distinctly against matrimony.

MISS PRISM   [Sententiously]   That is obviously the reason why the Primitive Church has not lasted up to the present day. And you do not seem to realize, dear Doctor, that by persistently remaining single, a man converts himself into a permanent public temptation. Men should be more careful; this very celibacy leads weaker vessels astray.

CHASUBLE   But is a man not equally attractive when married?

MISS PRISM   No married man is ever attractive except to his wife.

CHASUBLE   And often, I've been told, not even to her.

MISS PRISM   That depends on the intellectual sympathies of the woman. Matu-

---

9. The word used in England for a *boutonnière,* a flower or small nosegay in the buttonhole of a man's lapel. The practice of wearing them was quite common and Wilde's were famous for their flamboyance.

10. The name of a yellow rose.

11. At her not knowing that a hater of women is a misogynist and her making a new word— a neologism—by combining an English and a Greek element.

rity can always be depended on. Ripeness can be trusted. Young women are green. [DR. CHASUBLE *starts*] I spoke horticulturally. My metaphor was drawn from fruits. But where is Cecily?

CHASUBLE    Perhaps she followed us to the schools.

[*Enter* JACK *slowly from the back of the garden. He is dressed in the deepest mourning, with crape hat-band and black gloves.*[12]]

MISS PRISM    Mr. Worthing!

CHASUBLE    Mr. Worthing?

MISS PRISM    This is indeed a surprise. We did not look for you till Monday afternoon.

JACK [*Shakes* MISS PRISM'*s hand in a tragic manner*]    I have returned sooner than I expected. Dr. Chasuble, I hope you are well?

CHASUBLE    Dear Mr. Worthing, I trust this garb of woe does not betoken some terrible calamity?

JACK    My brother.

MISS PRISM    More shameful debts and extravagance?

CHASUBLE    Still leading his life of pleasure?

JACK [*Shaking his head*]    Dead!

CHASUBLE    Your brother Ernest dead?

JACK    Quite dead.

MISS PRISM    What a lesson for him! I trust he will profit by it.

CHASUBLE    Mr. Worthing, I offer you my sincere condolence. You have at least the consolation of knowing that you were always the most generous and forgiving of brothers.

JACK    Poor-Ernest! He had many faults, but it is a sad, sad blow.

CHASUBLE    Very sad indeed. Were you with him at the end?

JACK    No. He died abroad; in Paris, in fact. I had a telegram last night from the manager of the Grand Hotel.

CHASUBLE    Was the cause of death mentioned?

JACK    A severe chill, it seems.

MISS PRISM    As a man sows, so shall he reap.

CHASUBLE [*Raising his hand*]    Charity, dear Miss Prism, charity! None of us are perfect. I myself am peculiarly susceptible to draughts. Will the interment take place here?

JACK    No. He seemed to have expressed a desire to be buried in Paris.

CHASUBLE    In Paris! [*Shakes his head*] I fear that hardly points to any very serious state of mind at the last. You would no doubt wish me to make some slight allusion to this tragic domestic affliction next Sunday. [JACK *presses his hand convulsively*] My sermon on the meaning of the manna [13] in the wilderness can be adapted to almost any occasion, joyful, or, as in the present case, distressing. [*All sigh*] I have preached it at harvest celebrations, christenings, confirmations, on days of humiliation and

---

12. The wearing of black clothing in token of mourning was a custom once rigorously observed by both men and women. The hat around which Jack has bound a wide band of black crape is a "high" hat, silk and black. He wears a black frock coat, coming down almost to his knees; his trousers are black. Black also are his necktie, his gloves, his walking stick, and of course his shoes, and his handkerchief has a wide border of black.

13. The food miraculously provided for the Israelites after their flight from Egypt.

festal days. The last time I delivered it was in the Cathedral, as a charity sermon on behalf of the Society for the Prevention of Discontent among the Upper Orders. The Bishop, who was present, was much struck by some of the analogies I drew.

JACK   Ah! that reminds me, you mentioned christenings I think, Dr. Chasuble? I suppose you know how to christen all right? [DR. CHASUBLE *looks astounded*] I mean, of course, you are continually christening, aren't you?

MISS PRISM   It is, I regret to say, one of the Rector's most constant duties in this parish. I have often spoken to the poorer classes on the subject. But they don't seem to know what thrift is.

CHASUBLE   But is there any particular infant in whom you are interested, Mr. Worthing? Your brother was, I believe, unmarried, was he not?

JACK   Oh, yes.

MISS PRISM   [*Bitterly*]   People who live entirely for pleasure usually are.

JACK   But it is not for any child, dear Doctor. I am very fond of children. No! the fact is, I would like to be christened myself, this afternoon, if you have nothing better to do.

CHASUBLE   But surely, Mr. Worthing, you have been christened already?

JACK   I don't remember anything about it.

CHASUBLE   But have you any grave doubts on the subject?

JACK   I certainly intend to have. Of course, I don't know if the thing would bother you in any way, or if you think I am a little too old now.

CHASUBLE   Not at all. The sprinkling, and, indeed, the immersion of adults is a perfectly canonical practice.

JACK   Immersion!

CHASUBLE   You need have no apprehensions. Sprinkling is all that is necessary, or indeed I think advisable. Our weather is so changeable. At what hour would you wish the ceremony performed?

JACK   Oh, I might trot round about five if that would suit you.

CHASUBLE   Perfectly, perfectly! In fact I have two similar ceremonies to perform at that time. A case of twins that occurred recently in one of the outlying cottages on your own estate. Poor Jenkins the carter, a most hard-working man.

JACK   Oh! I don't see much fun in being christened along with other babies. It would be childish. Would half-past five do?

CHASUBLE   Admirably! Admirably! [*Takes out watch*] And now, dear Mr. Worthing, I will not intrude any longer into a house of sorrow. I would merely beg you not to be too much bowed down by grief. What seem to us bitter trials are often blessings in disguise.

MISS PRISM   This seems to me a blessing of an extremely obvious kind.

[*Enter* CECILY *from the house*]

CECILY   Uncle Jack! Oh, I am pleased to see you back. But what horrid clothes you have got on! Do go and change them.

MISS PRISM   Cecily!

CHASUBLE   My child! my child!

[CECILY *goes towards* JACK; *he kisses her brow in a melancholy manner.*]

CECILY   What is the matter, Uncle Jack? Do look happy! You look as if you had toothache, and I have got such a surprise for you. Who do you think is in the dining-room? Your brother!

JACK    Who?

CECILY    Your brother Ernest. He arrived about half an hour ago.

JACK    What nonsense! I haven't got a brother.

CECILY    Oh, don't say that. However badly he may have behaved to you in the past he is still your brother. You couldn't be so heartless as to disown him. I'll tell him to come out. And you will shake hands with him, won't you, Uncle Jack? [*Runs back into the house*]

CHASUBLE    These are very joyful tidings.

MISS PRISM    After we had all been resigned to his loss, his sudden return seems to me peculiarly distressing.

JACK    My brother is in the dining-room? I don't know what it all means. I think it is perfectly absurd.

[*Enter* ALGERNON *and* CECILY *hand in hand. They come slowly up to* JACK.]

JACK    Good heavens! [*Motions* ALGERNON *away*]

ALGERNON    Brother John, I have come down from town to tell you that I am very sorry for all the trouble I have given you, and that I intend to lead a better life in the future. [JACK *glares at him and does not take his hand*]

CECILY    Uncle Jack, you are not going to refuse your own brother's hand?

JACK    Nothing will induce me to take his hand. I think his coming down here disgraceful. He knows perfectly well why.

CECILY    Uncle Jack, do be nice. There is some good in everyone. Ernest has just been telling me about his poor invalid friend Mr. Bunbury, whom he goes to visit so often. And surely there must be much good in one who is kind to an invalid, and leaves the pleasures of London to sit by a bed of pain.

JACK    Oh! he has been talking about Bunbury, has he?

CECILY    Yes, he has told me all about poor Mr. Bunbury, and his terrible state of health.

JACK    Bunbury! Well, I won't have him talk to you about Bunbury or about anything else. It is enough to drive one perfectly frantic.

ALGERNON    Of course I admit that the faults were all on my side. But I must say that I think that brother John's coldness to me is peculiarly painful. I expected a more enthusiastic welcome, especially considering it is the first time I have come here.

CECILY    Uncle Jack, if you don't shake hands with Ernest I will never forgive you.

JACK    Never forgive me?

CECILY    Never, never, never!

JACK    Well, this is the last time I shall ever do it. [*Shakes hand with* ALGERNON *and glares*]

CHASUBLE    It's pleasant, is it not, to see so perfect a reconciliation? I think we might leave the two brothers together.

MISS PRISM    Cecily, you will come with us.

CECILY    Certainly, Miss Prism. My little task of reconciliation is over.

CHASUBLE   You have done a beautiful action to-day, dear child.

MISS PRISM   We must not be premature in our judgments.

CECILY   I feel very happy. [*They all go off*]

JACK   You young scoundrel, Algy, you must get out of this place as soon as possible. I don't allow any Bunburying here.

[*Enter* MERRIMAN]

MERRIMAN   I have put Mr. Ernest's things in the room next to yours, sir. I suppose that is all right?

JACK   What?

MERRIMAN   Mr. Ernest's luggage, sir. I have unpacked it and put it in the room next to your own.

JACK   His luggage?

MERRIMAN   Yes, sir. Three portmanteaus,[14] a dressing-case,[15] two hat-boxes, and a large luncheon-basket.

ALGERNON   I am afraid I can't stay more than a week this time.

JACK   Merriman, order the dog-cart [16] at once. Mr. Ernest has been suddenly called back to town.

MERRIMAN   Yes, sir. [*Goes back into the house*]

ALGERNON   What a fearful liar you are, Jack. I have not been called back to town at all.

JACK   Yes, you have.

ALGERNON   I haven't heard anyone call me.

JACK   Your duty as a gentleman calls you back.

ALGERNON   My duty as a gentleman has never interfered with my pleasures in the smallest degree.

JACK   I can quite understand that.

ALGERNON   Well, Cecily is a darling.

JACK   You are not to talk of Miss Cardew like that. I don't like it.

ALGERNON   Well, I don't like your clothes. You look perfectly ridiculous in them. Why on earth don't you go up and change? It is perfectly childish to be in deep mourning for a man who is actually staying for a whole week with you in your house as a guest. I call it grotesque.

JACK   You are certainly not staying with me for a whole week as a guest or anything else. You have got to leave . . . by the four-five train.

ALGERNON   I certainly won't leave you so long as you are in mourning. It would be most unfriendly. If I were in mourning you would stay with me, I suppose. I should think it very unkind if you didn't.

JACK   Well, will you go if I change my clothes?

ALGERNON   Yes, if you are not too long. I never saw anybody take so long to dress, and with such little result.

JACK   Well, at any rate, that is better than being always over-dressed as you are.

ALGERNON   If I am occasionally a little over-dressed, I make up for it by being always immensely over-educated.

JACK   Your vanity is ridiculous, your conduct an outrage, and your presence

14. Large leather suitcases.
15. A traveling case fitted with toilet articles.
16. A cart drawn by one horse and accommodating two persons sitting back to back.

in my garden utterly absurd. However, you have got to catch the four-five, and I hope you will have a pleasant journey back to town. This Bunburying, as you call it, has not been a great success for you. [*Goes into the house*]

ALGERNON   I think it has been a great success. I'm in love with Cecily, and that is everything.

[*Enter* CECILY *at the back of the garden. She picks up the can and begins to water the flowers.*]

But I must see her before I go, and make arrangements for another Bunbury. Ah, there she is.

CECILY   Oh, I merely came back to water the roses. I thought you were with Uncle Jack.

ALGERNON   He's gone to order the dog-cart for me.

CECILY   Oh, is he going to take you for a nice drive?

ALGERNON   He's going to send me away.

CECILY   Then have we got to part?

ALGERNON   I am afraid so. It's a very painful parting.

CECILY   It is always painful to part from people whom one has known for a very brief space of time. The absence of old friends one can endure with equanimity. But even a momentary separation from anyone to whom one has just been introduced is almost unbearable.

ALGERNON   Thank you.

[*Enter* MERRIMAN]

MERRIMAN   The dog-cart is at the door, sir. [ALGERNON *looks appealingly at* CECILY]

CECILY   It can wait, Merriman . . . for . . . five minutes.

MERRIMAN   Yes, Miss. [*Exit* MERRIMAN]

ALGERNON   I hope, Cecily, I shall not offend you if I state quite frankly and openly that you seem to me to be in every way the visible personification of absolute perfection.

CECILY   I think your frankness does you great credit, Ernest. If you will allow me I will copy your remarks into my diary. [*Goes over to table and begins writing in diary*]

ALGERNON   Do you really keep a diary? I'd give anything to look at it. May I?

CECILY   Oh, no. [*Puts her hand over it*] You see, it is simply a very young girl's record of her own thoughts and impressions, and consequently meant for publication. When it appears in volume form I hope you will order a copy. But pray, Ernest, don't stop. I delight in taking down from dictation. I have reached 'absolute perfection.' You can go on. I am quite ready for more.

ALGERNON   [*Somewhat taken aback*]   Ahem! Ahem!

CECILY   Oh, don't cough, Ernest. When one is dictating one should speak fluently and not cough. Besides, I don't know how to spell a cough. [*Writes as* ALGERNON *speaks*]

ALGERNON   [*Speaking very rapidly*]   Cecily, ever since I first looked upon your wonderful and incomparable beauty, I have dared to love you wildly, passionately, devotedly, hopelessly.

CECILY   I don't think that you should tell me that you love me wildly, passionately, devotedly, hopelessly. Hopelessly doesn't seem to make much sense, does it?

ALGERNON    Cecily!

[*Enter* MERRIMAN]

MERRIMAN    The dog-cart is waiting, sir.

ALGERNON    Tell it to come round next week, at the same hour.

MERRIMAN [*Looks at* CECILY, *who makes no sign*]    Yes, sir. [MERRIMAN *retires*]

CECILY    Uncle Jack would be very much annoyed if he knew you were staying on till next week, at the same hour.

ALGERNON    Oh, I don't care about Jack. I don't care for anybody in the whole world but you. I love you, Cecily. You will marry me, won't you?

CECILY    You silly boy! Of course. Why, we have been engaged for the last three months.

ALGERNON    For the last three months?

CECILY    Yes, it will be exactly three months on Thursday.

ALGERNON    But how did we become engaged?

CECILY    Well, ever since dear Uncle Jack first confessed to us that he had a younger brother who was very wicked and bad, you of course have formed the chief topic of conversation between myself and Miss Prism. And of course a man who is much talked about is always very attractive. One feels there must be something in him after all. I daresay it was foolish of me, but I fell in love with you, Ernest.

ALGERNON    Darling! And when was the engagement actually settled?

CECILY    On the 4th of February last. Worn out by your entire ignorance of my existence, I determined to end the matter one way or the other, and after a long struggle with myself I accepted you under this dear old tree here. The next day I bought this little ring in your name, and this is the little bangle [17] with the true lovers' knot I promised you always to wear.

ALGERNON    Did I give you this? It's very pretty, isn't it?

CECILY    Yes, you've wonderfully good taste, Ernest. It's the excuse I've always given for your leading such a bad life. And this is the box in which I keep all your dear letters. [*Kneels at table, opens box, and produces letters tied up with blue ribbon*]

ALGERNON    My letters! But my own sweet Cecily, I have never written you any letters.

CECILY    You need hardly remind me of that, Ernest. I remember only too well that I was forced to write your letters for you. I wrote always three times a week, and sometimes oftener.

ALGERNON    Oh, do let me read them, Cecily?

CECILY    Oh, I couldn't possibly. They would make you far too conceited. [*Replaces box*] The three you wrote me after I had broken off the engagement are so beautiful, and so badly spelled, that even now I can hardly read them without crying a little.

ALGERNON    But was our engagement ever broken off?

CECILY    Of course it was. On the 22nd of last March. You can see the entry

17. A rigid bracelet, usually with no clasp.

if you like. [*Shows diary*] 'To-day I broke off my engagement with Ernest. I feel it is better to do so. The weather still continues charming.'

ALGERNON    But why on earth did you break it off? What had I done? I had done nothing at all. Cecily, I am very much hurt indeed to hear you broke it off. Particularly when the weather was so charming.

CECILY    It would hardly have been a really serious engagement if it hadn't been broken off at least once. But I forgave you before the week was out.

ALGERNON    [*Crossing to her, and kneeling*]    What a perfect angel you are, Cecily.

CECILY    You dear romantic boy. [*He kisses her, she puts her fingers through his hair*] I hope your hair curls naturally, does it?

ALGERNON    Yes, darling, with a little help from others.

CECILY    I am so glad.

ALGERNON    You'll never break off our engagement again, Cecily?

CECILY    I don't think I could break it off now that I have actually met you. Besides, of course, there is the question of your name.

ALGERNON    Yes, of course. [*Nervously*]

CECILY    You must not laugh at me, darling, but it had always been a girlish dream of mine to love some one whose name was Ernest. [ALGERNON *rises*, CECILY *also*] There is something in that name that seems to inspire absolute confidence. I pity any poor married woman whose husband is not called Ernest.

ALGERNON    But, my dear child, do you mean to say you could not love me if I had some other name?

CECILY    But what name?

ALGERNON    Oh, any name you like—Algernon—for instance . . .

CECILY    But I don't like the name of Algernon.

ALGERNON    Well, my own dear, sweet, loving little darling, I really can't see why you should object to the name of Algernon. It is not at all a bad name. In fact, it is rather an aristocratic name. Half of the chaps who get into the Bankruptcy Court are called Algernon. But seriously, Cecily . . . [*Moving to her*] . . . if my name was Algy, couldn't you love me?

CECILY    [*Rising*]    I might respect you, Ernest, I might admire your character, but I fear that I should not be able to give you my undivided attention.

ALGERNON    Ahem! Cecily! [*Picking up hat*] Your Rector here is, I suppose, thoroughly experienced in the practice of all the rites and ceremonials of the Church?

CECILY    Oh yes. Dr. Chasuble is a most learned man. He has never written a single book, so you can imagine how much he knows.

ALGERNON    I must see him at once on a most important christening—I mean on most important business.

CECILY    Oh!

ALGERNON    I shan't be away more than half an hour.

CECILY    Considering that we have been engaged since February the 14th, and that I only met you to-day for the first time, I think it is rather hard that you should leave me for so long a period as half an hour. Couldn't you make it twenty minutes?

ALGERNON    I'll be back in no time.

[*Kisses her and rushes down the garden*]

CECILY    What an impetuous boy he is! I like his hair so much. I must enter his proposal in my diary.

[*Enter* MERRIMAN]

MERRIMAN    A Miss Fairfax has just called to see Mr. Worthing. On very important business Miss Fairfax states.

CECILY    Isn't Mr. Worthing in his library?

MERRIMAN    Mr. Worthing went over in the direction of the Rectory some time ago.

CECILY    Pray ask the lady to come out here; Mr. Worthing is sure to be back soon. And you can bring tea.

MERRIMAN    Yes, Miss. [*Goes out*]

CECILY    Miss Fairfax! I suppose one of the many good elderly women who are associated with Uncle Jack in some of his philanthropic work in London. I don't quite like women who are interested in philanthropic work. I think it is so forward of them.

[*Enter* MERRIMAN]

MERRIMAN    Miss Fairfax.

[*Enter* GWENDOLEN. *Exit* MERRIMAN.]

CECILY    [*Advancing to meet her*]    Pray let me introduce myself to you. My name is Cecily Cardew.

GWENDOLEN    Cecily Cardew? [*Moving to her and shaking hands*] What a very sweet name! Something tells me that we are going to be great friends. I like you already more than I can say. My first impressions of people are never wrong.

CECILY    How nice of you to like me so much after we have known each other such a comparatively short time. Pray sit down.

GWENDOLEN    [*Still standing up*]    I may call you Cecily, may I not?

CECILY    With pleasure!

GWENDOLEN    And you will always call me Gwendolen, won't you.

CECILY    If you wish.

GWENDOLEN    Then that is all quite settled, is it not?

CECILY    I hope so. [*A pause. They both sit down together.*]

GWENDOLEN    Perhaps this might be a favorable opportunity for my mentioning who I am. My father is Lord Bracknell. You have never heard of papa, I suppose?

CECILY    I don't think so.

GWENDOLEN    Outside the family circle, papa, I am glad to say, is entirely unknown. I think that is quite as it should be. The home seems to me to be the proper sphere for the man. And certainly once a man begins to neglect his domestic duties he becomes painfully effeminate, does he not? And I don't like that. It makes men so very attractive. Cecily, mamma, whose views on education are remarkably strict, has brought me up to be extremely short-sighted; it is part of her system; so do you mind my looking at you through my glasses?

CECILY    Oh! not at all, Gwendolen. I am very fond of being looked at.

GWENDOLEN [*After examining* CECILY *carefully through a lorgnette* 18] You are here on a short visit I suppose.

CECILY    Oh no! I live here.

GWENDOLEN [*Severely*]    Really? Your mother, no doubt, or some female relative of advanced years, resides here also?

CECILY    Oh no! I have no mother, nor, in fact, any relations.

GWENDOLEN    Indeed?

CECILY    My dear guardian, with the assistance of Miss Prism, has the arduous task of looking after me.

GWENDOLEN    Your guardian?

CECILY    Yes, I am Mr. Worthing's ward.

GWENDOLEN    Oh! It is strange he never mentioned to me that he had a ward. How secretive of him! He grows more interesting hourly. I am not sure, however, that the news inspires me with feelings of unmixed delight. [*Rising and going to her*] I am very fond of you, Cecily; I have liked you ever since I met you! But I am bound to state that now that I know that you are Mr. Worthing's ward, I cannot help expressing a wish you were—well just a little older than you seem to be—and not quite so very alluring in appearance. In fact, if I may speak candidly——

CECILY    Pray do! I think that whenever one has anything unpleasant to say, one should always be quite candid.

GWENDOLEN    Well, to speak with perfect candour, Cecily, I wish that you were fully forty-two, and more than usually plain for your age. Ernest has a strong upright nature. He is the very soul of truth and honour. Disloyalty would be as impossible to him as deception. But even men of the noblest possible moral character are extremely susceptible to the influence of the physical charms of others. Modern, no less than Ancient History, supplies us with many most painful examples of what I refer to. If it were not so, indeed, History would be quite unreadable.

CECILY    I beg your pardon, Gwendolen, did you say Ernest?

GWENDOLEN    Yes.

CECILY    Oh, but it is not Mr. Ernest Worthing who is my guardian. It is his brother—his elder brother.

GWENDOLEN [*Sitting down again*]    Ernest never mentioned to me that he had a brother.

CECILY    I am sorry to say they have not been on good terms for a long time.

GWENDOLEN    Ah! that accounts for it. And now that I think of it I have never heard any man mention his brother. The subject seems distasteful to most men. Cecily, you have lifted a load from my mind. I was growing almost anxious. It would have been terrible if any cloud had come across a friendship like ours, would it not? Of course you are quite, quite sure that it is not Mr. Ernest Worthing who is your guardian?

CECILY    Quite sure. [*A pause*] In fact, I am going to be his.

GWENDOLEN [*Enquiringly*]    I beg your pardon?

CECILY [*Rather shy and confidingly*]    Dearest Gwendolen, there is no reason

---

18. Eyeglasses with a short handle. They were likely to be used by older women and suggested haughty condescension, which makes Gwendolen's use of them amusing.

why I should make a secret of it to you. Our little county newspaper is sure to chronicle the fact next week. Mr. Ernest Worthing and I are engaged to be married.

GWENDOLEN [*Quite politely, rising*]   My darling Cecily, I think there must be some slight error. Mr. Ernest Worthing is engaged to me. The announcement will appear in the 'Morning Post' on Saturday at the latest.

CECILY [*Very politely, rising*]   I am afraid you must be under some misconception. Ernest proposed to me exactly ten minutes ago. [*Shows diary*]

GWENDOLEN [*Examines diary through her lorgnette carefully*]   It is certainly very curious, for he asked me to be his wife yesterday afternoon at 5.30. If you would care to verify the incident, pray do so. [*Produces diary of her own*] I never travel without my diary. One should always have something sensational to read in the train. I am so sorry, dear Cecily, if it is any disappointment to you, but I am afraid *I* have the prior claim.

CECILY   It would distress me more than I can tell you, dear Gwendolen, if it caused you any mental or physical anguish, but I feel bound to point out that since Ernest proposed to you he clearly has changed his mind.

GWENDOLEN [*Meditatively*]   If the poor fellow has been entrapped into any foolish promise I shall consider it my duty to rescue him at once, and with a firm hand.

CECILY [*Thoughtfully and sadly*]   Whatever unfortunate entanglement my dear boy may have got into, I will never reproach him with it after we are married.

GWENDOLEN   Do you allude to me, Miss Cardew, as an entanglement? You are presumptuous. On an occasion of this kind it becomes more than a moral duty to speak one's mind. It becomes a pleasure.

CECILY   Do you suggest, Miss Fairfax, that I entrapped Ernest into an engagement? How dare you? This is no time for wearing the shallow mask of manners. When I see a spade I call it a spade.

GWENDOLEN [*Satirically*]   I am glad to say that I have never seen a spade. It is obvious that our social spheres have been widely different.

[*Enter* MERRIMAN, *followed by the footman. He carries a salver, table cloth, and plate stand.* CECILY *is about to retort. The presence of the servants exercises a restraining influence, under which both girls chafe.*]

MERRIMAN   Shall I lay tea here as usual, Miss?

CECILY [*Sternly, in a calm voice*]   Yes, as usual. [MERRIMAN *begins to clear and lay cloth. A long pause.* CECILY *and* GWENDOLEN *glare at each other.*]

GWENDOLEN   Are there many interesting walks in the vicinity, Miss Cardew?

CECILY   Oh! yes! a great many. From the top of one of the hills quite close one can see five counties.

GWENDOLEN   Five counties! I don't think I should like that. I hate crowds.

CECILY [*Sweetly*]   I suppose that is why you live in town? [GWENDOLEN *bites her lip, and beats her foot nervously with her parasol*]

GWENDOLEN [*Looking round*]   Quite a well-kept garden this is, Miss Cardew.

CECILY   So glad you like it, Miss Fairfax.

GWENDOLEN   I had no idea there were any flowers in the country.

CECILY   Oh, flowers are as common here, Miss Fairfax, as people are in London.

GWENDOLEN    Personally I cannot understand how anybody manages to exist in the country, if anybody who is anybody does. The country always bores me to death.

CECILY    Ah! This is what the newspapers call agricultural depression, is it not? I believe the aristocracy are suffering very much from it just at present. It is almost an epidemic amongst them, I have been told. May I offer you some tea, Miss Fairfax?

GWENDOLEN    [*With elaborate politeness*]    Thank you. [*Aside*] Detestable girl! But I require tea!

CECILY [*Sweetly*]    Sugar?

GWENDOLEN [*Superciliously*]    No, thank you. Sugar is not fashionable any more. [CECILY *looks angrily at her, takes up the tongs and puts four lumps of sugar into the cup*]

CECILY [*Severely*]    Cake or bread and butter?

GWENDOLEN [*In a bored manner*]    Bread and butter, please. Cake is rarely seen at the best houses nowadays.

CECILY [*Cuts a very large slice of cake, and puts it on the tray*]    Hand that to Miss Fairfax.

[MERRIMAN *does so, and goes out with footman.* GWENDOLEN *drinks the tea and makes a grimace. Puts down cup at once, reaches out her hand to the bread and butter, looks at it, and finds it is cake. Rises in indignation.*]

GWENDOLEN    You have filled my tea with lumps of sugar, and though I asked most distinctly for bread and butter, you have given me cake. I am known for the gentleness of my disposition, and the extraordinary sweetness of my nature, but I warn you, Miss Cardew, you may go too far.

CECILY [*Rising*]    To save my poor, innocent, trusting boy from the machinations of any other girl there are no lengths to which I would not go.

GWENDOLEN    From the moment I saw you I distrusted you. I felt that you were false and deceitful. I am never deceived in such matters. My first impressions of people are invariably right.

CECILY    It seems to me, Miss Fairfax, that I am trespassing on your valuable time. No doubt you have many other calls of a similar character to make in the neighbourhood.

[*Enter* JACK]

GWENDOLEN [*Catching sight of him*]    Ernest! My own Ernest!

JACK    Gwendolen! Darling! [*Offers to kiss her*]

GWENDOLEN [*Drawing back*]    A moment! May I ask if you are engaged to be married to this young lady? [*Points to* CECILY]

JACK [*Laughing*]    To dear little Cecily! Of course not! What could have put such an idea into your pretty little head?

GWENDOLEN    Thank you. You may. [*Offers her cheek*]

CECILY [*Very sweetly*]    I knew there must be some misunderstanding, Miss Fairfax. The gentleman whose arm is at present around your waist is my dear guardian, Mr. John Worthing.

GWENDOLEN    I beg your pardon?

CECILY    This is Uncle Jack.

GWENDOLEN [*Receding*]    Jack! Oh!

[*Enter* ALGERNON]

CECILY    Here is Ernest.

ALGERNON [*Goes straight over to* CECILY *without noticing anyone else*]    My own love! [*Offers to kiss her*]

CECILY [*Drawing back*]    A moment, Ernest! May I ask you—are you engaged to be married to this young lady?

ALGERNON [*Looking round*]    To what young lady? Good heavens! Gwendolen!

CECILY    Yes! to good heavens, Gwendolen, I mean to Gwendolen.

ALGERNON [*Laughing*]    Of course not! What could have put such an idea into your pretty little head?

CECILY    Thank you. [*Presenting her cheek to be kissed*] You may. [ALGERNON *kisses her*]

GWENDOLEN    I felt there was some slight error, Miss Cardew. The gentleman who is now embracing you is my cousin, Mr. Algernon Moncrieff.[19]

CECILY [*Breaking away from* ALGERNON]    Algernon Moncrieff! Oh! [*The two girls move towards each other and put their arms round each other's waist as if for protection*]

CECILY    Are you called Algernon?

ALGERNON    I cannot deny it.

CECILY    Oh!

GWENDOLEN    Is your name really John?

JACK [*Standing rather proudly*]    I could deny it if I liked. I could deny anything if I liked. But my name certainly is John. It has been John for years.

CECILY [*To* GWENDOLEN]    A gross deception has been practised on both of us.

GWENDOLEN    My poor wounded Cecily!

CECILY    My sweet wronged Gwendolen!

GWENDOLEN [*Slowly and seriously*]    You will call me sister, will you not? [*They embrace.* JACK *and* ALGERNON *groan and walk up and down.*]

CECILY [*Rather brightly*]    There is just one question I would like to be allowed to ask my guardian.

GWENDOLEN    An admirable idea! Mr. Worthing, there is just one question I would like to be permitted to put to you. Where is your brother Ernest? We are both engaged to be married to your brother Ernest, so it is a matter of some importance to us to know where your brother Ernest is at present.

JACK [*Slowly and hesitatingly*]    Gwendolen—Cecily—it is very painful for me to be forced to speak the truth. It is the first time in my life that I have ever been reduced to such a painful position, and I am really quite inexperienced in doing anything of the kind. However, I will tell you quite frankly that I have no brother Ernest. I have no brother at all. I never had a brother in my life, and I certainly have not the smallest intention of ever having one in the future.

CECILY [*Surprised*]    No brother at all?

JACK [*Cheerily*]    None!

19. Pronounced Mon*creef.*

GWENDOLEN [*Severely*]   Had you never a brother of any kind?

JACK [*Pleasantly*]   Never. Not even of any kind.

GWENDOLEN   I am afraid it is quite clear, Cecily, that neither of us is engaged to be married to anyone.

CECILY   It is not a very pleasant position for a young girl suddenly to find herself in. Is it?

GWENDOLEN   Let us go into the house. They will hardly venture to come after us there.

CECILY   No, men are so cowardly, aren't they?

[*They retire into the house with scornful looks*]

JACK   This ghastly state of things is what you call Bunburying, I suppose?

ALGERNON   Yes, and a perfectly wonderful Bunbury it is. The most wonderful Bunbury I have ever had in my life.

JACK   Well, you've no right whatsoever to Bunbury here.

ALGERNON   That is absurd. One has a right to Bunbury anywhere one chooses. Every serious Bunburyist knows that.

JACK   Serious Bunburyist! Good heavens!

ALGERNON   Well, one must be serious about something, if one wants to have any amusement in life. I happen to be serious about Bunburying. What on earth you are serious about I haven't got the remotest idea. About everything, I should fancy. You have such an absolutely trivial nature.

JACK   Well, the only small satisfaction I have in the whole of this wretched business is that your friend Bunbury is quite exploded. You won't be able to run down to the country quite so often as you used to do, dear Algy. And a very good thing too.

ALGERNON   Your brother is a little off colour, isn't he, dear Jack? You won't be able to disappear to London quite so frequently as your wicked custom was. And not a bad thing either.

JACK   As for your conduct towards Miss Cardew, I must say that your taking in a sweet, simple, innocent girl like that is quite inexcusable. To say nothing of the fact that she is my ward.

ALGERNON   I can see no possible defence at all for your deceiving a brilliant, clever, thoroughly experienced young lady like Miss Fairfax. To say nothing of the fact that she is my cousin.

JACK   I wanted to be engaged to Gwendolen, that is all. I love her.

ALGERNON   Well, I simply wanted to be engaged to Cecily. I adore her.

JACK   There is certainly no chance of your marrying Miss Cardew.

ALGERNON   I don't think there is much likelihood, Jack, of you and Miss Fairfax being united.

JACK   Well, that is no business of yours.

ALGERNON   If it was my business, I wouldn't talk about it. [*Begins to eat muffins*] It is very vulgar to talk about one's business. Only people like stockbrokers do that, and then merely at dinner parties.

JACK   How can you sit there, calmly eating muffins when we are in this horrible trouble, I can't make out. You seem to me to be perfectly heartless.

ALGERNON   Well, I can't eat muffins in an agitated manner. The butter would probably get on my cuffs. One should always eat muffins quite calmly. It is the only way to eat them.

JACK     I say it's perfectly heartless your eating muffins at all, under the circumstances.

ALGERNON     When I am in trouble, eating is the only thing that consoles me. Indeed, when I am in really great trouble, as anyone who knows me intimately will tell you, I refuse everything except food and drink. At the present moment I am eating muffins because I am unhappy. Besides, I am particularly fond of muffins. [*Rising*]

JACK     [*Rising*]     Well, that is no reason why you should eat them all in that greedy way. [*Takes muffins from* ALGERNON]

ALGERNON     [*Offering tea-cake*]     I wish you would have tea-cake instead. I don't like tea-cake.

JACK     Good heavens! I suppose a man may eat his own muffins in his own garden.

ALGERNON     But you have just said it was perfectly heartless to eat muffins.

JACK     I said it was perfectly heartless of you, under the circumstances. That is a very different thing.

ALGERNON     That may be. But the muffins are the same. [*He seizes the muffin-dish from* JACK]

JACK     Algy, I wish to goodness you would go.

ALGERNON     You can't possibly ask me to go without having some dinner. It's absurd. I never go without my dinner. No one ever does, except vegetarians and people like that. Besides I have just made arrangements with Dr. Chasuble to be christened at a quarter to six under the name of Ernest.

JACK     My dear fellow, the sooner you give up that nonsense the better. I made arrangements this morning with Dr. Chasuble to be christened myself at 5.30, and I naturally will take the name of Ernest. Gwendolen would wish it. We can't both be christened Ernest. It's absurd. Besides, I have a perfect right to be christened if I like. There is no evidence at all that I ever have been christened by anybody. I should think it extremely probable I never was, and so does Dr. Chasuble. It is entirely different in your case. You have been christened already.

ALGERNON     Yes, but I have not been christened for years.

JACK     Yes, but you have been christened. That is the important thing.

ALGERNON     Quite so. So I know my constitution can stand it. If you are not quite sure about your ever having been christened, I must say I think it rather dangerous your venturing on it now. It might make you very unwell. You can hardly have forgotten that someone very closely connected with you was very nearly carried off this week in Paris by a severe chill.

JACK     Yes, but you said yourself that a severe chill was not hereditary.

ALGERNON     It usen't to be, I know—but I daresay it is now. Science is always making wonderful improvements in things.

JACK     [*Picking up the muffin-dish*]     Oh, that is nonsense; you are always talking nonsense.

ALGERNON     Jack, you are at the muffins again! I wish you wouldn't. There are only two left. [*Takes them*] I told you I was particularly fond of muffins.

JACK     But I hate tea-cake.

ALGERNON    Why on earth then do you allow tea-cake to be served up for your guests? What ideas you have of hospitality!

JACK    Algernon! I have already told you to go. I don't want you here. Why don't you go!

ALGERNON    I haven't quite finished my tea yet! and there is still one muffin left. [JACK *groans, and sinks into a chair.* ALGERNON *continues eating.*] ACT-DROP

## ACT III

Scene—*Morning-room at the Manor House.*

GWENDOLEN *and* CECILY *are at the window, looking out into the garden.*

GWENDOLEN    The fact that they did not follow us at once into the house, as anyone else would have done, seems to me to show that they have some sense of shame left.

CECILY    They have been eating muffins. That looks like repentance.

GWENDOLEN [*After a pause*]    They don't seem to notice us at all. Couldn't you cough?

CECILY    But I haven't a cough.

GWENDOLEN    They're looking at us. What effrontery!

CECILY    They're approaching. That's very forward of them.

GWENDOLEN    Let us preserve a dignified silence.

CECILY    Certainly. It's the only thing to do now.

[*Enter* JACK *followed by* ALGERNON. *They whistle some dreadful popular air from a British Opera*1]

GWENDOLEN    This dignified silence seems to produce an unpleasant effect.

CECILY    A most distasteful one.

GWENDOLEN    But we will not be the first to speak.

CECILY    Certainly not.

GWENDOLEN    Mr. Worthing, I have something very particular to ask you. Much depends on your reply.

CECILY    Gwendolen, your common sense is invaluable. Mr. Moncrieff, kindly answer me the following question. Why did you pretend to be my guardian's brother?

ALGERNON    In order that I might have an opportunity of meeting you.

CECILY [*To* GWENDOLEN]    That certainly seems a satisfactory explanation, does it not?

GWENDOLEN    Yes, dear, if you can believe him.

CECILY    I don't. But that does not affect the wonderful beauty of his answer.

GWENDOLEN    True. In matters of grave importance, style, not sincerity is the vital thing. Mr. Worthing, what explanation can you offer to me for pretending to have a brother? Was it in order that you might have an opportunity of coming up to town to see me as often as possible?

JACK    Can you doubt it, Miss Fairfax?

GWENDOLEN    I have the gravest doubts upon the subject. But I intend to crush

1. This may be a swipe at Gilbert and Sullivan, who had caricatured Wilde as Bunthorne in *Patience* (1881).

them. This is not the moment for German scepticism.[2] [*Moving to* CECILY] Their explanations appear to be quite satisfactoory, especially Mr. Worthing's. That seems to me to have the stamp of truth upon it.

CECILY    I am more than content with what Mr. Moncrieff said. His voice alone inspires one with absolute credulity.

GWENDOLEN    Then you think we should forgive them?

CECILY    Yes. I mean no.

GWENDOLEN    True! I had forgotten. There are principles at stake that one cannot surrender. Which of us should tell them? The task is not a pleasant one.

CECILY    Could we not both speak at the same time?

GWENDOLEN    An excellent idea! I nearly always speak at the same time as other people. Will you take the time from me?

CECILY    Certainly. [CWENDOLEN *beats time with uplifted finger*]

GWENDOLEN and CECILY [*Speaking together*]    Your Christian names are still an insuperable barrier. That is all!

JACK and ALGERNON [*Speaking together*]    Our Christian names! Is that all? But we are going to be christened this afternoon.

GWENDOLEN [*To* JACK]    For my sake you are prepared to do this terrible thing?

JACK    I am.

CECILY [*To* ALGERNON]    To please me you are ready to face this fearful ordeal?

ALGERNON    I am!

GWENDOLEN    How absurd to talk of the equality of the sexes! Where questions of self-sacrifice are concerned, men are infinitely beyond us.

JACK    We are. [*Clasps hands with* ALGERNON]

CECILY    They have moments of physical courage of which we women know absolutely nothing.

GWENDOLEN [*To* JACK]    Darling!

ALGERNON [*To* CECILY]    Darling! [*They fall into each other's arms*] [*Enter* MERRIMAN. *When he enters he coughs loudly, seeing the situation.*]

MERRIMAN    Ahem! Ahem! Lady Bracknell!

JACK    Good heavens!
[*Enter* LADY BRACKNELL. *The couples separate in alarm. Exit* MERRIMAN.]

LADY BRACKNELL    Gwendolen! What does this mean?

GWENDOLEN    Merely that I am engaged to be married to Mr. Worthing, mamma.

LADY BRACKNELL    Come here. Sit down. Sit down immediately. Hesitation of any kind is a sign of mental decay in the young, of physical weakness in the old. [*Turns to* JACK] Apprised, sir, of my daughter's sudden flight by her trusty maid, whose confidence I purchased by means of a small coin, I followed her at once by a luggage train. Her unhappy father is, I am glad to say, under the impression that she is attending a more than usually lengthy lecture by the University Extension Scheme [3] on

---

2. She seems to have been reading Immanuel Kant, who undertook to show that there could be no proof of the existence of God.

3. Courses given by university professors to members of the general public.

the Influence of a permanent income on Thought. I do not propose to undeceive him. Indeed I have never undeceived him on any question. I would consider it wrong. But of course, you will clearly understand that all communication between yourself and my daughter must cease immediately from this moment. On this point, as indeed on all points, I am firm.

JACK    I am engaged to be married to Gwendolen, Lady Bracknell!

LADY BRACKNELL    You are nothing of the kind, sir. And now, as regards Algernon! . . . Algernon!

ALGERNON    Yes, Aunt Augusta.

LADY BRACKNELL    May I ask if it is in this house that your invalid friend Mr. Bunbury resides?

ALGERNON    [Stammering]  Oh! No! Bunbury doesn't live here. Bunbury is somewhere else at present. In fact, Bunbury is dead.

LADY BRACKNELL    Dead! When did Mr. Bunbury die? His death must have been extremely sudden.

ALGERNON    [Airily]  Oh! I killed Bunbury this afternoon. I mean poor Bunbury died this afternoon.

LADY BRACKNELL    What did he die of?

ALGERNON    Bunbury? Oh, he was quite exploded.

LADY BRACKNELL    Exploded! Was he the victim of a revolutionary outrage? I was not aware that Mr. Bunbury was interested in social legislation. If so, he is well punished for his morbidity.

ALGERNON    My dear Aunt Augusta, I mean he was found out! The doctors found out that Bunbury could not live, that is what I mean—so Bunbury died.

LADY BRACKNELL    He seems to have had great confidence in the opinion of his physicians. I am glad, however, that he made up his mind at the last to some definite course of action, and acted under proper medical advice. And now that we have finally got rid of this Mr. Bunbury, may I ask, Mr. Worthing, who is that young person whose hand my nephew Algernon is now holding in what seems to me a peculiarly unnecessary manner?

JACK    That lady is Miss Cecily Cardew, my ward. [LADY BRACKNELL bows coldly to CECILY]

ALGERNON    I am engaged to be married to Cecily, Aunt Augusta.

LADY BRACKNELL    I beg your pardon?

CECILY    Mr. Moncrieff and I are engaged to be married, Lady Bracknell.

LADY BRACKNELL    [With a shiver, crossing to the sofa and sitting down]  I do not know whether there is anything peculiarly exciting in the air of this particular part of Hertfordshire, but the number of engagements that go on seems to me considerably above the proper average that statistics have laid down for our guidance. I think some preliminary enquiry on my part would not be out of place. Mr. Worthing, is Miss Cardew at all connected with any of the larger railway stations in London? I merely desire information. Until yesterday I had no idea that there were any families or persons whose origin was a Terminus. [JACK looks perfectly furious, but restrains himself]

JACK  [*In a clear, cold voice*]  Miss Cardew is the granddaughter of the late
Mr. Thomas Cardew of 149, Belgrave Square, S.W.; Gervase Park,
Dorking, Surrey; and the Sporran, Fifeshire, N.B.[4]

LADY BRACKNELL  That sounds not unsatisfactory. Three addresses always
inspire confidence, even in tradesmen. But what proof have I of their
authenticity?

JACK  I have carefully preserved the Court Guides of the period. They are
open to your inspection, Lady Bracknell.

LADY BRACKNELL  [*Grimly*]  I have known strange errors in that publication.

JACK  Miss Cardew's family solicitors are Messrs. Markby, Markby, and
Markby.

LADY BRACKNELL  Markby, Markby, and Markby! A firm of the very highest
position in their profession. Indeed I am told that one of the Mr. Mark-
bys is occasionally to be seen at dinner parties. So far I am satisfied.

JACK  [*Very irritably*]  How extremely kind of you, Lady Bracknell! I have also
in my possession, you will be pleased to hear, certificates of Miss Cardew's birth, baptism, whooping cough, registration, vaccination, confirmation, and the measles; both the German and the English variety.

LADY BRACKNELL  Ah! A life crowded with incident, I see; though perhaps
somewhat too exciting for a young girl. I am not myself in favour of
premature experiences. [*Rises, looks at her watch*] Gwendolen! the time
approaches for our departure. We have not a moment to lose. As a
matter of form, Mr. Worthing, I had better ask you if Miss Cardew
has any little fortune?

JACK  Oh! about a hundred and thirty thousand pounds in the Funds. That
is all. Good-bye, Lady Bracknell. So pleased to have seen you.

LADY BRACKNELL  [*Sitting down again*]  A moment, Mr. Worthing. A hundred
and thirty thousand pounds! And in the Funds! Miss Cardew seems to
me a most attractive young lady, now that I look at her. Few girls of
the present day have any really solid qualities, any of the qualities that
last, and improve with time. We live, I regret to say, in an age of surfaces. [*To* CECILY] Come over here, dear. [CECILY *goes across*] Pretty
child! your dress is sadly simple, and your hair seems almost as Nature
might have left it. But we can soon alter all that. A thoroughly experienced French maid produces a really marvellous result in a very brief
space of time. I remember recommending one to young Lady Lancing,
and after three months her own husband did not know her.

JACK  [*Aside*]  And after six months nobody knew her.[5]

LADY BRACKNELL  [*Glares at* JACK *for a few moments. Then bends, with a practised smile, to* CECILY.] Kindly turn round, sweet child. [CECILY *turns
completely round*] No, the side view is what I want. [CECILY *presents
her profile*] Yes, quite as I expected. There are distinct social possibilities in your profile. The two weak points in our age are its want of
principle and its want of profile. The chin a little higher, dear. Style

---

4. Presumably North Britain, a way of referring to Scotland not much liked by the Scots.
5. She had become so "fast" that she was not received in respectable society.

largely depends on the way the chin is worn. They are worn very high, just at present. Algernon!

ALGERNON    Yes, Aunt Augusta!

LADY BRACKNELL    There are distinct social possibilities in Miss Cardew's profile.

ALGERNON    Cecily is the sweetest, dearest, prettiest girl in the whole world. And I don't care twopence about social possibilities.

LADY BRACKNELL    Never speak disrespectfully of Society, Algernon. Only people who can't get into it do that. [*To* CECILY] Dear child, of course you know that Algernon has nothing but his debts to depend upon. But I do not approve of mercenary marriages. When I married Lord Bracknell I had no fortune of any kind. But I never dreamed for a moment of allowing that to stand in my way. Well, I suppose I must give my consent.

ALGERNON    Thank you, Aunt Augusta.

LADY BRACKNELL    Cecily, you may kiss me!

CECILY [*Kisses her*]    Thank you, Lady Bracknell.

LADY BRACKNELL    You may also address me as Aunt Augusta for the future.

CECILY    Thank you, Aunt Augusta.

LADY BRACKNELL    The marriage, I think, had better take place quite soon.

ALGERNON    Thank you, Aunt Augusta.

CECILY    Thank you, Aunt Augusta.

LADY BRACKNELL    To speak frankly, I am not in favour of long engagements. They give people the opportunity of finding out each other's character before marriage, which I think is never advisable.

JACK    I beg your pardon for interrupting you, Lady Bracknell, but this engagement is quite out of the question. I am Miss Cardew's guardian, and she cannot marry without my consent until she comes of age. That consent I absolutely decline to give.

LADY BRACKNELL    Upon what grounds, may I ask? Algernon is an extremely, I may almost say an ostentatiously, eligible young man. He has nothing, but he looks everything. What more can one desire?

JACK    It pains me very much to have to speak frankly to you, Lady Bracknell, about your nephew, but the fact is that I do not approve at all of his moral character. I suspect him of being untruthful. [ALGERNON *and* CECILY *look at him in indignant amazement*]

LADY BRACKNELL    Untruthful! My nephew Algernon? Impossible! He is an Oxonian.[6]

JACK    I fear there can be no possible doubt about the matter. This afternoon, during my temporary absence in London on an important question of romance, he obtained admission to my house by means of the false pretence of being my brother. Under an assumed name he drank, I've just been informed by my butler, an entire pint bottle of my Perrier-Jouet, Brut, '89; a wine I was specially reserving for myself. Continuing his disgraceful deception, he succeeded in the course of the afternoon in alienating the affections of my only ward. He subsequently stayed to

6. A graduate of Oxford. The line is perhaps the only failure in the play.

tea, and devoured every single muffin. And what makes his conduct all the more heartless is, that he was perfectly well aware from the first that I have no brother, that I never had a brother, and that I don't intend to have a brother, not even of any kind. I distinctly told him so myself yesterday afternoon.

LADY BRACKNELL    Ahem! Mr. Worthing, after careful consideration I have decided entirely to overlook my nephew's conduct to you.

JACK    That is very generous of you, Lady Bracknell. My own decision, however, is unalterable. I decline to give my consent.

LADY BRACKNELL    [To CECILY]    Come here, sweet child. [CECILY goes over] How old are you, dear?

CECILY    Well, I am really only eighteen, but I always admit to twenty when I go to evening parties.

LADY BRACKNELL    You are perfectly right in making some slight alteration. Indeed, no woman should ever be quite accurate about her age. It looks so calculating. . . . [In a meditative manner] Eighteen, but admitting to twenty at evening parties. Well, it will not be very long before you are of age and free from the restraints of tutelage. So I don't think your guardian's consent is, after all, a matter of any importance.

JACK    Pray excuse me, Lady Bracknell, for interrupting you again, but it is only fair to tell you that according to the terms of her grandfather's will Miss Cardew does not come legally of age till she is thirty-five.

LADY BRACKNELL    That does not seem to me to be a grave objection. Thirty-five is a very attractive age. London society is full of women of the very highest birth who have, of their own free choice, remained thirty-five for years. Lady Dumbleton is an instance in point. To my own knowledge she has been thirty-five ever since she arrived at the age of forty, which was many years ago now. I see no reason why our dear Cecily should not be even still more attractive at the age you mention than she is at present. There will be a large accumulation of property.

CECILY    Algy, could you wait for me till I was thirty-five?

ALGERNON    Of course I could, Cecily. You know I could.

CECILY    Yes, I felt it instinctively, but I couldn't wait all that time. I hate waiting even five minutes for anybody. It always makes me rather cross. I am not punctual myself, I know, but I do like punctuality in others, and waiting, even to be married, is quite out of the question.

ALGERNON    Then what is to be done, Cecily?

CECILY    I don't know, Mr. Moncrieff.

LADY BRACKNELL    My dear Mr. Worthing, as Miss Cardew states positively that she cannot wait till she is thirty-five—a remark which I am bound to says seems to me to show a somewhat impatient nature—I would beg of you to reconsider your decision.

JACK    But my dear Lady Bracknell, the matter is entirely in your own hands. The moment you consent to my marriage with Gwendolen, I will most gladly allow your nephew to form an alliance with my ward.

LADY BRACKNELL    [Rising and drawing herself up]    You must be quite aware that what you propose is out of the question.

JACK    Then a passionate celibacy is all that any of us can look forward to.

LADY BRACKNELL    That is not the destiny I propose for Gwendolen. Algernon, of course, can choose for himself. [*Pulls out her watch*] Come dear; [GWENDOLEN *rises*] we have already missed five, if not six, trains. To miss any more might expose us to comment on the platform. [*Enter* DR. CHASUBLE]

CHASUBLE    Everything is quite ready for the christenings.

LADY BRACKNELL    The christenings, sir! Is not that somewhat premature?

CHASUBLE [*Looking rather puzzled, and pointing to* JACK *and* ALGERNON]    Both these gentlemen have expressed a desire for immediate baptism.

LADY BRACKNELL    At their age? The idea is grotesque and irreligious! Algernon, I forbid you to be baptised. I will not hear of such excesses. Lord Bracknell would be highly displeased if he learned that that was the way in which you wasted your time and money.

CHASUBLE    Am I to understand then that there are to be no christenings at all this afternoon?

JACK    I don't think that, as things are now, it would be of much practical value to either of us, Dr. Chasuble.

CHASUBLE    I am grieved to hear such sentiments from you, Mr. Worthing. They savour of the heretical views of the Anabaptists,[7] views that I have completely refuted in four of my unpublished sermons. However, as your present mood seems to be one peculiarly secular, I will return to the church at once. Indeed, I have just been informed by the pew-opener that for the last hour and a half Miss Prism has been waiting for me in the vestry.

LADY BRACKNELL [*Starting*]    Miss Prism! Did I hear you mention a Miss Prism?

CHASUBLE    Yes, Lady Bracknell. I am on my way to join her.

LADY BRACKNELL    Pray allow me to detain you for a moment. This matter may prove to be one of vital importance to Lord Bracknell and myself. Is this Miss Prism a female of repellent aspect, remotely connected with education?

CHASUBLE [*Somewhat indignantly*]    She is the most cultivated of ladies, and the very picture of respectability.

LADY BRACKNELL    It is obviously the same person. May I ask what position she holds in your household?

CHASUBLE [*Severely*]    I am a celibate, madam.

JACK [*Interposing*]    Miss Prism, Lady Bracknell, has been for the last three years Miss Cardew's esteemed governess and valued companion.

LADY BRACKNELL    In spite of what I hear of her, I must see her at once. Let her be sent for.

CHASUBLE [*Looking off*]    She approaches; she is nigh.

[*Enter* MISS PRISM *hurriedly*]

MISS PRISM    I was told you expected me in the vestry, dear Canon. I have been waiting for you there for an hour and three-quarters. [*Catches sight of*

---

7. This Reformation sect held that only adult baptism was valid, which doesn't bring their view into accord with Jack's present position.

LADY BRACKNELL, *who has fixed her with a stony glare.* MISS PRISM *grows pale and quails. She looks anxiously round as if desirous to escape.*]

LADY BRACKNELL [*In a severe, judicial voice*]  Prism! [MISS PRISM *bows her head in shame*] Come here, Prism! [MISS PRISM *approaches in a humble manner*] Prism! Where is that baby? [*General consternation. The Canon starts back in horror.* ALGERNON *and* JACK *pretend to be anxious to shield* CECILY *and* GWENDOLEN *from hearing the details of a terrible public scandal.*] Twenty-eight years ago, Prism, you left Lord Bracknell's house, Number 104, Upper Grosvenor Street, in charge of a perambulator that contained a baby, of the male sex. You never returned. A few weeks later, through the elaborate investigations of the Metropolitan police, the perambulator was discover at midnight, standing by itself in a remote corner of Bayswater. It contained the manuscript of a three-volume novel of more than usually revolting sentimentality. [MISS PRISM *starts in involuntary indignation*] But the baby was not there! [*Everyone looks at* MISS PRISM] Prism: Where is that baby? [*A pause*]

MISS PRISM  Lady Bracknell, I admit with shame that I do not know. I only wish I did. The plain facts of the case are these. On the morning of the day you mention, a day that is for ever branded on my memory, I prepared as usual to take the baby out in its perambulator. I had also with me a somewhat old, but capacious hand-bag in which I had intended to place the manuscript of a work of fiction that I had written during my few unoccupied hours. In a moment of mental abstraction, for which I never can forgive myself, I deposited the mansucript in the bassinette, and placed the baby in the hand-bag.

JACK [*Who has been listening attentively*]  But where did you deposit the hand-bag?

MISS PRISM  Do not ask me, Mr. Worthing.

JACK  Miss Prism, this is a matter of no small importance to me. I insist on knowing where you deposited the hand-bag that contained that infant.

MISS PRISM  I left it in the cloak room of one of the larger railway stations in London.

JACK  What railway station?

MISS PRISM [*Quite crushed*]  Victoria. The Brighton line. [*Sinks into a chair*]

JACK  I must retire to my room for a moment. Gwendolen, wait here for me.

GWENDOLEN  If you are not too long, I will wait here for you all my life.

[*Exit* JACK *in great excitement*]

CHASUBLE  What do you think this means, Lady Bracknell?

LADY BRACKNELL  I dare not even suspect, Dr. Chasuble. I need hardly tell you that in families of high position strange coincidences are not supposed to occur. They are hardly considered the thing.

[*Noises heard overhead as if someone was throwing trunks about. Everyone looks up.*]

CECILY  Uncle Jack seems strangely agitated.

CHASUBLE  Your guardian has a very emotional nature.

LADY BRACKNELL    This noise is extremely unpleasant. It sounds as if he was having an argument. I dislike arguments of any kind. They are always vulgar, and often convincing.

CHASUBLE [*Looking up*]    It has stopped now. [*The noise is redoubled*]

LADY BRACKNELL    I wish he would arrive at some conclusion.

GWENDOLEN    This suspense is terrible. I hope it will last.

[*Enter* JACK *with a hand-bag of black leather in his hand*]

JACK [*Rushing over to* MISS PRISM]    Is this the hand-bag, Miss Prism? Examine it carefully before you speak. The happiness of more than one life depends on your answer.

MISS PRISM [*Calmly*]    It seems to be mine. Yes, here is the injury it received through the upsetting of a Gower Street omnibus in younger and happier days. Here is the stain on the lining caused by the explosion of a temperance beverage, an incident that occurred at Leamington. And here, on the lock, are my initials. I had forgotten that in an extravagant mood I had had them placed there. The bag is undoubtedly mine. I am delighted to have it so unexpectedly restored to me. It has been a great inconvenience being without it all these years.

JACK [*In a pathetic voice*]    Miss Prism, more is restored to you than this hand-bag. I was the baby you placed in it.

MISS PRISM [*Amazed*]    You?

JACK [*Embracing her*]    Yes . . . mother!

MISS PRISM [*Recoiling in indignant astonishment*]    Mr. Worthing! I am unmarried!

JACK    Unmarried! I do not deny that is a serious blow. But after all, who has the right to cast a stone against one who has suffered? Cannot repentance wipe out an act of folly? Why should there be one law for men, and another for women? Mother, I forgive you. [*Tries to embrace her again*]

MISS PRISM [*Still more indignant*]    Mr. Worthing, there is some error. [*Pointing to* LADY BRACKNELL]    There is the lady who can tell you who you really are.

JACK [*After a pause*]    Lady Bracknell, I hate to seem inquisitive, but would you kindly inform me who I am?

LADY BRACKNELL    I am afraid that the news I have to give you will not altogether please you. You are the son of my poor sister, Mrs. Moncrieff, and consequently Algernon's elder brother.

JACK    Algy's elder brother! Then I have a brother after all. I knew I had a brother! I always said I had a brother! Cecily,—how could you have ever doubted that I had a brother. [*Seizes hold of* ALGERNON]    Dr. Chasuble, my unfortunate brother. Miss Prism, my unfortunate brother. Gwendolen, my unfortunate brother. Algy, you young scoundrel, you will have to treat me with more respect in the future. You have never behaved to me like a brother in all your life.

ALGERNON    Well, not till to-day, old boy, I admit. I did my best, however, though I was out of practice. [*Shakes hands*]

GWENDOLEN [*To* JACK]    My own! But what own are you? What is your Christian name, now that you have become someone else?

JACK    Good heavens! . . . I had quite forgotten that point. Your decision on the subject of my name is irrevocable, I suppose?

GWENDOLEN    I never change, except in my affections.

CECILY    What a noble nature you have, Gwendolen!

JACK    Then the question had better be cleared up at once. Aunt Augusta, a moment. At the time when Miss Prism left me in the hand-bag, had I been christened already?

LADY BRACKNELL    Every luxury that money could buy, including christening, had been lavished on you by your fond and doting parents.

JACK    Then I was christened! That is settled. Now, what name was I given? Let me know the worst.

LADY BRACKNELL    Being the eldest son you were naturally christened after your father.

JACK    [Irritably]    Yes, but what was my father's Christian name?

LADY BRACKNELL    [Meditatively]    I cannot at the present moment recall what the General's Christian name was. But I have no doubt he had one. He was eccentric, I admit. But only in later years. And that was the result of the Indian climate, and marriage, and indigestion, and other things of that kind.

JACK    Algy! Can't you recollect what our father's Christian name was?

ALGERNON    My dear boy, we were never even on speaking terms. He died before I was a year old.

JACK    His name would appear in the Army Lists of the period, I suppose, Aunt Augusta?

LADY BRACKNELL    The General was essentially a man of peace, except in his domestic life. But I have no doubt his name would appear in any military directory.

JACK    The Army Lists of the last forty years are here. These delightful records should have been my constant study [Rushes to bookcase and tears the books out] M. Generals . . . Mallam, Maxbohm[8] Magley, what ghastly names they have—Markby, Migsby, Moss, Moncrieff! Lieutenant 1840, Captain, Lieutenant-Colonel, Colonel, General 1869, Christian names, Ernest John [Puts book very quietly down and speaks quite calmly] I always told you, Gwendolen, my name was Ernest, didn't I? Well, it is Ernest after all. I mean it naturally is Ernest.

LADY BRACKNELL    Yes, I remember that the General was called Ernest. I knew I had some particular reason for disliking the name.

GWENDOLEN    Ernest! My own Ernest! I felt from the first that you could have no other name!

JACK    Gwendolen, it is a terrible thing for a man to find out suddenly that all his life he has been speaking nothing but the truth. Can you forgive me?

GWENDOLEN    I can. For I feel that you are sure to change.

JACK    My own one!

CHASUBLE    [To MISS PRISM]    Lætitia! [Embraces her]

MISS PRISM    [Enthusiastically]    Frederick! At last!

8. Wilde contrived this name to tease Max Beerbohm (1875–1956), later to be known as essayist, parodist, dramatic critic, caricaturist.

ALGERNON   Cecily! [*Embraces her*] At last!

JACK   Gwendolen! [*Embraces her*] At last!

LADY BRACKNELL   My nephew, you seem to be displaying signs of triviality.

JACK   On the contrary, Aunt Augusta, I've now realized for the first time in my life the vital Importance of Being Earnest.

TABLEAU [9]

CURTAIN

1894

1895, 1899

9. French for "picture," designation for the stage device in which all the actors in a scene stand motionless in postures they have taken.

# Victorian Poetry

Walter Pater, the great critic whose marvelous sensibility we do a kind of violence by naming it Decadent, remarked in his essay on "Style" (in Appreciations, 1889) that imaginative prose was "the special art of the modern world." Pater had a certain self-interest here, since he had burned his early poems (supposedly for being too religious, but probably also because they were bad) and had devoted his life to writing imaginative prose. Yet Pater had strong impersonal grounds for his assertion, and gave two in particular: "the chaotic variety and complexity" of the modern world's interests, unsuitable for "the restraint proper to verse form, so that the most characteristic verse of the nineteenth century has been lawless verse," and "an all-pervading naturalism" also unsuitable for verse, since verse is more "ambitious" than prose.

Whether the nineteenth-century novel and nonfictional prose of England represent a larger achievement than its verse is highly disputable. What is increasingly certain is that nineteenth-century English poetry is one of the world's major imaginative achievements, almost comparable to the poetry of the English Renaissance. No poet of the absolute eminence of Spenser, Shakespeare, or Milton composed in England during the nineteenth century, but the six major High Romantics—Blake, Wordsworth, Coleridge, Byron, Shelley, Keats—and the somewhat less titanic six major Victorians—Tennyson, Browning, Arnold, Rossetti, Swinburne, and Hopkins—present an extraordinary variety and intensity, not matched by twentieth-century poetry in English, not even by Hardy, Yeats, Stevens. Perhaps only Blake and Wordsworth stand near Chaucer and the greater Renaissance poets, but all of these creators have survived the sorrows of literary fashion, and will go on surviving. More centrally, led by Wordsworth, these poets created "modern poetry," as becomes steadily more apparent with each year that twentieth-century literary Modernism recedes into history.

Victorian poetry, in the perspective made possible by nearly a century's passage, is essentially a continuation of Romantic poetry into the third and fourth generations. If Yeats was right in believing that he and his friends who came to their dark maturity in the 'Nineties were "the Last Romantics," then English Romanticism lasted for five generations: Blake, Wordsworth, and Coleridge (born 1757–72); Byron, Shelley, Keats (born 1788–95); Tennyson and Browning (born 1809–12); Arnold, Rossetti, Morris, Swinburne, Hardy, and Hopkins (born 1822–44), and finally Yeats (born 1865). To trace this main continuity (as broken by highly deliberate attempts at discontinuity) is to sketch also a miniature of the development of modern poetic consciousness.

What allies all the principal Victorian poets is their imaginative, stylistic, and procedural indebtedness to either Keats or Shelley. The division is, Keats: Tennyson, Arnold, Rossetti, Morris, and Hopkins; Shelley: Browning, Swinburne, Hardy, and Yeats. The same complex pattern of influence that dominated the Romantics is at work here also; Blake and Wordsworth struggled with the shadow of Milton, yet the younger Romantics had to wrestle a composite precursor, Milton and Wordsworth. The younger Victorians tended to engage a parent compounded of Keats and Tennyson, or of Shelley and Browning. Pre-Raphaelite poetry is at once a consolidation of the Keats-Tennyson tradition of sensuous naturalism, and a curiously subverting phantasmagoric rebellion against it. But this is still only part of the immense labyrinth of poetic influence in the nineteenth century. Except for Rossetti and Swinburne, who are overt Romantic ideologists, every important Victorian poet attempted, in very diverse ways, to break away from the High Romantic erotic quest. Arnold's explicit (but equivocal) classicism, his dismissal as "morbidity" of everything Romantic except for Wordsworth's most direct nature poetry, is the best known of these swerves away from the precursors, but all the others swerved more subtly (and more successfully).

Shelley and Keats owed to Wordsworth an example he himself wished to repudiate, the self-conscious quester of The Excursion, the melancholy Solitary, of whom the Byron of Childe Harold's Pilgrimage III and IV was an indeliberate parody. The Victorian poets owed to Shelley and Keats examples provided by the tragic brevity of their lives, and the contrast they (and Byron) afforded to Wordsworth, who had outlived his own imaginative energies. Even Tennyson and Browning had a deep uneasiness at finding themselves accepted, eventually, as public sages, lest they should awaken to discover they shared Wordsworth's fate. The prophetic burden of Romantic poetry was assumed by the Victorian prose seers: Carlyle, Newman, Mill, Ruskin, the later Arnold, the later Morris, and Pater, a displacement which reduced both the ambitions and the risks of Victorian verse. This may account for a curious effect created by every Victorian poet except Swinburne, a sense that they never delivered the whole of their Word. Even the outspoken Browning rightly doubted that he had given his full report to God:

> We may learn from the biography whether his spirit invariably saw and spoke from the last height to which it had attained. An absolute vision is not for this world, but we are permitted a continual approximation to it, every degree of which in the individual, provided it exceed the attainment of the masses, must procure him a clear advantage. Did the poet ever attain to a higher platform than where he rested and exhibited a result? Did he know more than he spoke of?

This is from Browning's essay on his precursor, Shelley, and is meant to be answered: "No," for Shelley, more than any other, continually was permitted an approximation to an absolute vision. As applied to himself, these crucial questions assume a positive answer, and Browning confronts his own relative failure. But Tennyson, the other great poetic imagination of the age, also knew more of a vision than he allowed himself to render. Hopkins, who had both a genius for sensuous apprehension and an immense capacity for language, each almost of Keatsian dimension, scarcely allowed himself to realize the full individuality of his own vision. The largest unanswered question about the major Victorian poets is: why could they neither sustain nor wish to sustain a High Romantic confidence in the autonomy of their own imaginations, when they were sons of Keats and of Shelley who more than any poets except Blake shared a confidence in the imagination's freedom and priority?

The simpler answers here are not adequate, and reduce finally to Pater's historical explanation; the "all-pervading naturalism," as the century advanced, negated high poetic ambitions. Yeats, a Paterian in his prose and in his ideology, agreed and fought back with an all-pervading supernaturalism, free from any orthodox associations. Yet Blake (though Yeats declined to see this) was no more a supernaturalist than he was a naturalist, nor was the skeptical Shelley, Yeats's other poetic father. Scholars rely too much on reductive versions of Pater's argument, and dwell long on Victorian advances in geology, evolutionary theory, and social analysis. Doubtless these were all factors in the Victorian refusal to see that the imagination insists upon being indulged, whatever the pressures of an age's realities. The profound religious uncertainties of the middle and later nineteenth century did constitute the largest force in the violence from without that pressed in upon the poetic mind. But the question remains: why was the answering violence from within the embattled poetic consciousness as subdued as it rapidly became? In what hope did Tennyson and Browning, let alone Arnold and Hopkins, abide when they turned aside from the full intensities of the Romantic quest?

If we glance at the programmatic Victorian Romantics of the Pre-Raphaelite grouping, we will find that there the larger vision was abandoned also, because the sense of the personal predicament of the poet-as-man had become even more acute than it was for Shelley. Swinburne, the most ambitious of these late Romantics, could write a poem like *Hertha* only by excluding himself from the poem's situation, but in spite of his artistry his personal pathology drifted back into the poem's undersong. No Victorian poet, not even Browning, showed the full range of the Romantic audacity that could allow Blake, Wordsworth, and Shelley (more skeptically and unsteadily) to believe that they represented the Divine Vision for their time, or that made possible Keats's and Byron's emphasis on the central, potentially universal significance of their own intellectual and sensuous experience.

Arnold and the principal Pre-Raphaelites, like the younger Romantics, were not Christians, and followed the logic of Romantic tradition by displacing the hopes of Protestantism into cultural (and largely poetic) contexts. Tennyson, very dubiously, remained a vague kind of Christian universalist. Browning, by temperament and belief, is one of the most vehement Protestants in the language, while Hopkins courageously but hopelessly attempted to convert his Paterian temperament to the demands of a Catholic devotional poetry. Arnold, in turning away both from Christianity and Romanticism, found he could not continue as a poet. The answer to the earlier question seems to be that the major Victorian poets modified or abandoned their early Romanticism in order to trust (however faintly) in an even larger and more traditional hope, the Christian humanism that had helped to sustain the young Milton. Whether the hope had even a minimal basis in reality we may doubt, but who can argue against hope? Where Victorian poetry still moves us most is where it exceeds us in hope.

# ALFRED, LORD TENNYSON
1809–1892

Tennyson, in some respects the most accomplished artist of all English poets since Pope, was born and raised at Somersby in Lincolnshire, where his father was rector. Two of his elder brothers, Frederick and Charles, were also poets of talent. Himself a natural poet, he began writing at five, and continued his juvenile production until he entered Trinity College, Cambridge, in 1827, where he fell in love with Arthur Henry Hallam, who became the true Muse of all Tennyson's mature work. The friendship between the two was the most important experience of Tennyson's life, and if it had a repressed sexual element, neither Tennyson nor Hallam (nor anyone else) seems ever to have been aware of this. Under Hallam's guidance (he had remarkable critical talents), Tennyson became a Keatsian poet, which despite later development he always remained.

In 1827, together with his brothers Frederick and Charles, Tennyson published the mistitled *Poems by Two Brothers,* but his first real book was *Poems, Chiefly Lyrical* in 1830, followed by *Poems* late in 1832. Both volumes received some negative reviews, and the oversensitive poet did not appear again before the British public until 1842, when he attained a just fame and financial rewards unknown since Byron, by bringing out *Poems* in two volumes. But, between 1830 and 1842, the decisive events of Tennyson's life occurred. His father died in 1831, and subsequently he left Cambridge without taking his degree. On September 15, 1833, Arthur Hallam died suddenly at twenty-two, in Vienna, of a brain seizure. Tennyson had met Emily Sellwood and reached an understanding with her as early as 1830; they became engaged in 1838, but did not marry until 1850. Biographers explain this twenty-year delay as financial in nature, but that seems mildly preposterous. Tennyson would not marry until then, and surely it is significant that his marriage took place only after the first publication (anonymous) of *In Memoriam,* his completed sequence of elegies for Hallam.

In 1850 Tennyson followed Wordsworth as Poet Laureate, and henceforth he was an English institution, whether he wrote well or badly. From 1853 on, he lived in great comfort on an estate on the Isle of Wight, cultivating his close friendships with the other luminaries of the age, cared for faithfully by Mrs. Tennyson, who also bore him two sons, Hallam and Lionel. In 1884, he accepted a barony, having declined the offer twice previously. His reputation remained high until his death in 1892, declined in the earlier twentieth century, and is rightly very high again today. In retrospect, his life had one event only, and that was the terrible experience of losing Hallam. It is hardly an overstatement to say that most of his best poetry, quite aside from *In Memoriam,* is elegiac in nature, and the subject of the sense of loss is always Hallam. "Ulysses," "Tithonus," *Morte d'Arthur,* "Tears, Idle Tears," much of *Idylls of the King,* the late *Merlin and the Gleam,* all mourn Hallam (sometimes obliquely), just as the living Hallam directly inspired the best poems of the 1830 and 1832 volumes. This matter hardly can be overemphasized in considering Tennyson's poetry. He became, in his best poetry after 1833, the perfect model of a poet who is a bereaved lover, and the largest clues we can have to the strength of his poetry lie in its relationship to Hallam. In a sense, Hallam represented Romanticism to Tennyson, and it seems clear that the later Tennyson would have been more of a High Romantic and less of a societal spokesman if Hallam had lived.

Hallam reviewed Tennyson's *Poems, Chiefly Lyrical* in 1831, and characterized his friend's poetry as belonging to the Romantic school of Keats and Shelley as opposed to that of Wordsworth. Yeats, who said that Hallam's review was crucial for his own early work, usefully summarized Hallam's distinction between the two schools: "Keats and Shelley, unlike Wordsworth, intermixed into their poetry no elements from the general thought, but wrote out of the impression made by the world upon their delicate senses." Yeats was remembering one of Hallam's most acute sentences about Keats and Shelley: "So vivid was the delight attending the simple exertions of eye and ear, that it became mingled more and more with trains of active thought, and tended to absorb their whole being into the energy of sense." This is the particular poetic strength of the young Tennyson under Hallam's influence (1828–33), who is genuinely a poet of sensation, and the necessary link between the Keats of *The Eve of St. Agnes* and the great Odes, and the Pre-Raphaelite and Aesthetic poets later in the century. While Hallam lived, and when he wrote in memory of Hallam, Tennyson did not mix into his poetry "elements from the general thought" without taking that thought up into the highly original context of his own imagination. He kept before him a crucial admonition of Hallam's, also included in the invaluable review of 1830: "That delicate sense of fitness which grows with the growth of artist feelings, and strengthens with their strength, until it acquires a celerity and weight of decision hardly inferior to the correspondent judgments of conscience, is weakened by every indulgence of heterogeneous aspirations, however pure they may be, however lofty, however suitable to human nature." Tennyson forgot this too often, particularly after 1850, and perhaps he delayed his marriage and consequent domestication and institutionalization because something in him accurately feared that he would forget it.

Tennyson, like Coleridge but very unlike Keats, always feared his own imagination, and distrusted its tendency to assert autonomy. Hallam's gift to Tennyson, his liberating virtue, was to give the poet enough confidence in the value of his own imagination to allow him to indulge it, for a time. The best early poems—"Mariana," *The Lady of Shalott, The Palace of Art, The Lotos-Eaters* (all except the magical *The Hesperides)*—manifest an uneasiness at their own Spenserian-Keatsian luxuriance, but in all of them the poetry is at work celebrating itself, so that as readers we believe the song and not the singer. What stays with us is the embowered, self-delighting consciousness in the sensuous prison-paradise, and not the societal censor that disapproves of such delight. If we follow a distinction of D. H. Lawrence's, and say that a daemon wrote what is most valuable in Tennyson's early poems, we can add that this daemon, fortunately, never vanished entirely from the later poetry, so long as Hallam continued to haunt it.

Yet this is only part of the truth, even about what is most valuable in Tennyson's poetry. He wrote in praise of Virgil and (very powerfully) in unfair dispraise of Lucretius, because he was at peace with the Virgilian strain in his own poetry, and feared the Lucretian, which he knew secretly he possessed also. This Epicurean tendency, which was to triumph in Pater, in much of Yeats, and in some of Yeats's friends of the 'Nineties, made no intellectual appeal to Tennyson, yet moved him deep within. *In Memoriam* is so troubled by the materialistic metaphysical implications of Victorian geology because Tennyson's imagination responded naturally and even buoyantly to speculations which his moral intellect could not tolerate.

If Tennyson is something of a poetic split personality, this does not make his work less interesting, nor does it affect his work where it is strongest, in style, by which more than diction and metric is meant. Tennyson's style, the most flawless in English poetry after Milton's and Pope's, is itself a sensibility, a means of apprehending both the internal and the external world. Intuitively, Tennyson understood what poetry was, argument that could not be separated from song, gesture, dance, and the rhythms of a unique but representative individual's breath-soul. Browning and Yeats, and the High Romantics before Tennyson, were all more powerful and original conceptualizers than Tennyson, and all of them mastered a great style, but none of them wrote so well so consistently as he did. A reader who knows no Latin and so cannot read Virgil has lost a great deal, but it is Tennyson's triumph that any such reader can remedy the loss by reading Tennyson, who richly sustains the comparison.


# Mariana°

Mariana in the moated grange
(*Measure for Measure*)

With blackest moss the flower-plots
    Were thickly crusted, one and all:
The rusted nails fell from the knots
    That held the pear to the gable-wall.
The broken sheds looked sad and strange:
    Unlifted was the clinking latch;
    Weeded and worn the ancient thatch
Upon the lonely moated grange.
        She only said, 'My life is dreary,
            He cometh not,' she said;
        She said, 'I am aweary, aweary,
            I would that I were dead!'

Her tears fell with the dews at even;
    Her tears fell ere the dews were dried;
She could not look on the sweet heaven,
    Either at morn or eventide.
After the flitting of the bats,
    When thickest dark did trance° the sky,
    She drew her casement-curtain by,
And glanced athwart the glooming flats.
        She only said, 'The night is dreary,
            He cometh not,' she said;
        She said, 'I am aweary, aweary,
            I would that I were dead!'

Upon the middle of the night,
    Waking she heard the night-fowl crow:
The cock sung out an hour ere light:
    From the dark fen the oxen's low

---

Mariana  In Shakespeare's *Measure for Measure*
III.i.212 ff., she waits, dejectedly, in an isolated
farmhouse or grange for her faithless lover. But
the heroine of Keats's *Isabella* is more in Tennyson's mind; see stanzas XXX to XXXIV of
Keats's poem.
trance  throw into a trance

Came to her: without hope of change,
30    In sleep she seemed to walk forlorn,
Till cold winds woke the gray-eyed morn
About the lonely moated grange.
    She only said, 'The day is dreary,
      He cometh not,' she said;
    She said, 'I am aweary, aweary,
      I would that I were dead!'

About a stone-cast from the wall
A sluice with blackened waters slept,
And o'er it many, round and small,
40    The clustered marish-mosses° crept.
Hard by a poplar shook alway,
All silver-green with gnarlèd bark:
For leagues no other tree did mark
The level waste, the rounding gray.
    She only said, 'My life is dreary,
      He cometh not,' she said;
    She said, 'I am aweary, aweary,
      I would that I were dead!'

And ever when the moon was low,
50    And the shrill winds were up and away,
In the white curtain, to and fro,
    She saw the gusty shadow sway.
But when the moon was very low,
    And wild winds bound within their cell,
The shadow of the poplar fell
Upon her bed, across her brow.
    She only said, 'The night is dreary,
      He cometh not,' she said;
    She said, 'I am aweary, aweary,
60      I would that I were dead!'

All day within the dreamy house,
    The doors upon their hinges creaked;
The blue fly sung in the pane; the mouse
    Behind the mouldering wainscot shrieked,
Or from the crevice peered about.
    Old faces glimmered through the doors,
    Old footsteps trod the upper floors,
Old voices called her from without.
    She only said, 'My life is dreary,
70      He cometh not,' she said;
    She said, 'I am aweary, aweary,
      I would that I were dead!'

**marish-mosses** marsh-moss lumps floating on the    surface of the floodgate-dammed water

The sparrow's chirrup on the roof,
   The slow clock ticking, and the sound
Which to the wooing wind aloof
   The poplar made, did all confound
Her sense; but most she loathed the hour
   When the thick-moted sunbeam lay
   Athwart the chambers, and the day
80 Was sloping toward his western bower.
      Then, said she, 'I am very dreary,
         He will not come,' she said;
      She wept, 'I am aweary, aweary,
         Oh God, that I were dead!'
                                      1830


# The Kraken

Below the thunders of the upper deep;
Far, far beneath in the abysmal sea,
His ancient, dreamless, uninvaded sleep
The Kraken° sleepeth: faintest sunlights flee
About his shadowy sides: above him swell
Huge sponges of millennial growth and height;
And far away into the sickly light,
From many a wondrous grot and secret cell
Unnumbered and enormous polypi°
10 Winnow with giant arms the slumbering green.
There hath he lain for ages and will lie
Battening upon huge seaworms in his sleep,
Until the latter fire° shall heat the deep;
Then once by man and angels to be seen,
In roaring he shall rise and on the surface die.
                                      1830


# The Lady of Shalott°

PART I
On either side the river lie
Long fields of barley and of rye,
That clothe the wold° and meet the sky;
And through the field the road runs by
   To many-towered Camelot;°
And up and down the people go,

Kraken fabulous sea-monster
polypi hydras, perhaps watersnakes
latter fire Apocalypse; see Revelation 8:8–9, and
13:1
The Lady of Shalott This poem helped form the
style of Pre-Raphaelite poetry and that of Poe.

Shalott is a variant of Astolat, which makes the
Lady "the lily maid of Astolat," Elaine, and
the poem a prefiguration of "Lancelot and
Elaine" in Tennyson's Arthurian cycle.
wold a rolling plain
Camelot mythical capital of Arthur's kingdom

Gazing where the lilies blow° ⌐
Round an island there below, ⌐
   The island of Shalott. ⌐

10 Willows whiten,° aspens quiver,
Little breezes dusk and shiver
Through the wave that runs for ever
By the island in the river
   Flowing down to Camelot.
Four gray walls, and four gray towers,
Overlook a space of flowers,
And the silent isle imbowers
   The Lady of Shalott.

By the margin, willow-veiled,
20 Slide the heavy barges trailed
By slow horses; and unhailed
The shallop° flitteth silken-sailed
   Skimming down to Camelot:
But who hath seen her wave her hand?
Or at the casement seen her stand?
Or is she known in all the land,
   The Lady of Shalott?

Only reapers, reaping early
In among the bearded barley,
30 Hear a song that echoes cheerly
From the river winding clearly,
   Down to towered Camelot:
And by the moon the reaper weary,
Piling sheaves in uplands airy,
Listening, whispers ' 'Tis the fairy
   Lady of Shalott.'

      PART II
There she weaves by night and day
A magic web with colours gay.
She has heard a whisper say,
40 A curse is on her if she stay
   To look down to Camelot.
She knows not what the curse may be,
And so she weaveth steadily,
And little other care hath she,
   The Lady of Shalott.

And moving through a mirror clear°
That hangs before her all the year,

blow blossom
Willows whiten The white undersides of willow
leaves are turned up by the wind.

shallop small, open boat
a mirror clear See Britomart's mirror in *The
Faerie Queene* III. ii.

Shadows of the world appear.
There she sees the highway near
50    Winding down to Camelot:
There the river eddy whirls,
And there the surly village-churls,
And the red cloaks of market girls,
    Pass onward from Shalott.

Sometimes a troop of damsels glad,
An abbot on an ambling pad,°
Sometimes a curly shepherd-lad,
Or long-haired page in crimson clad,
    Goes by to towered Camelot;
60  And sometimes through the mirror blue
The knights come riding two and two:
She hath no loyal knight and true,
    The Lady of Shalott.

But in her web she still delights
To weave the mirror's magic sights,
For often through the silent nights
A funeral, with plumes and lights
    And music, went to Camelot:
Or when the moon was overhead,
70  Came two young lovers lately wed;
'I am half sick of shadows,' said
    The Lady of Shalott.

     PART III
A bow-shot from her bower-eaves,
He rode between the barley-sheaves,
The sun came dazzling through the leaves,
And flamed upon the brazen greaves°
    Of bold Sir Lancelot.
A red-cross knight° for ever kneeled
To a lady in his shield,
80  That sparkled on the yellow field,
    Beside remote Shalott.

The gemmy bridle glittered free,
Like to some branch of stars we see
.Hung in the golden Galaxy.°
The bridle bells rang merrily
    As he rode down to Camelot:
And from his blazoned baldric° slung

pad gentle, easy-paced horse
greaves shin-armor
red-cross knight not usually Lancelot's emblem,
and so may refer to Spenser's St. George of *The
Faerie Queene* I

Galaxy the Milky Way
blazoned baldric heraldic shoulder belt, to hold
up a bugle

1. Tennyson in 1857; the photograph by Lewis Carroll.
*The Granger Collection.*

2. Tennyson in 1880. *The Granger Collection.*

3. Browning at forty-three, by Dante Gabriel Rossetti (1828–82). The inscription reads "October 1855." *The Granger Collection.*

4. Browning, c. 1880.
*The Granger Collection.*

5. Matthew Arnold.
*The Granger Collection.*

6. John Henry Cardinal Newman.
*The Granger Collection.*

I

II

*1. Past and Present,* by Augustus Egg, R.A. (1816–63). This sequence of three paintings, completed in 1858, deals with the highly sentimentalized Victorian theme of the fallen woman, here shown in a bourgeois version of the more dynamic and mythologically powerful Rossettian prostitute. The adulteress is an upper middle-class mother; her infidelity is discovered in picture **I**, while her daughters are only distracted from building their house of cards (such is the instability of the family when threatened by sexual passion) by their mother's collapse. The paintings on the wall are of the Expulsion from Eden and of a shipwreck. Pictures **II** and **III** (now a decade later, in the present) are supposed to be simultaneous (note the configuration of moon and cloud), showing the motherless and miserable girls and, elsewhere in London by a bridge near the Strand, the fallen mother as she clutches to her unwarming bosom a young child, another mark of her infamy. The "reading" of the narrative and emblems in pictures like this and Holman Hunt's *The Awakened Conscience* was frequently aided, in exhibitions, by descriptive catalogues and commentary, *The Tate Gallery,* London.

**III**

8. The painting by Henry Wallis (1830–1916) usually known as *The Death of Chatterton* (1856) enshrines in a typical literary canvas of its age the Romantic myth of the Dead Young Poet. Wallis painted it in the attic in which Thomas Chatterton actually poisoned himself. Incidentally, Wallis's model was his friend George Meredith, with whose wife (Thomas Love Peacock's daughter) the painter ran off two years later—an event occasioning some of the sonnets of Meredith's *Modern Love* (which are rather better than Wallis's painting). *The Tate Gallery.*

9. The young Queen Victoria
in her Coronation Robes,
by Sir George Hayter (1792–1871).
*National Portrait Gallery,* London.

10. The Albert Memorial, in Kensington Gardens, a perfect example of High Victorian neo-Gothic, designed by Sir George Gilbert Scott (1811–78) and completed in 1872, eleven years after the Prince Consort's death. Surrounding the central portrait are allegorical figures of Agriculture, Commerce, and Engineering, the four continents, and a frieze representing the greatest poets, artists, and musicians of the world. The only inscription is the word "Albert." *British Tourist Authority.*

11. *The Derby Day. The Tate Gallery.*

12. *The Railway Station. Royal Holloway College, University of London.*

## OFFICIAL VICTORIAN TASTE

These two celebrated Academy pictures by William Powell Frith, R.A. (1819–1909), represent the attitude toward narrative detail dear to the middle-class aesthetic. *The Derby Day* was exhibited in 1858, and *The Railway Station,* in 1862. Frith boasted that his painting was free of "Pre-Raphaelite taint."

13. The Houses of Parliament (1836–67), by Sir Charles Barry (1795–1860) and A. W. N. Pugin (1812–52). *BOAC.*

14. Eaton Hall, Cheshire (1867–80), brings to a private house the self-assured grossness of a High Victorian railway station. *Country Life*, London.

15. The Crystal Palace (1851), designed by Sir Joseph Paxton (1803–65). The Great Exhibition Building in Hyde Park was the largest building erected of cast iron and glass up to that time. It was thematic of the Great Exhibition of 1851. *The Museum of Modern Art, New York.*

16. The Clifton Suspension Bridge, Bristol (1836), by Isambard Kingdom Brunel (1806–59), represents the kind of Victorian industrial designing whose beauty remains bright to even the most historically intolerant modern eye. *A. F. Kersting.*

17. *Dante Gabriel Rossetti,* a portrait by William Holman Hunt (1827–1910), done around the time in 1848 when Rossetti, Hunt, John Everett Millais, and others had formed the Pre-Raphaelite Brotherhood. The movement brought to illustrative painting not so much the influence of Italian Renaissance art as the attempted transcription of the visionary light and detail in the poetry of Keats, Tennyson, and Rossetti himself. Ford Madox Brown was affiliated with the brotherhood, though never a member, and Sir Edward Coley Burne-Jones and William Morris were more closely associated with Rossetti after the 1850's, by which time the group had dissolved. *City Art Gallery,* Manchester.

18. *Mariana.*   She only said, 'My life is dreary,
                 He cometh not,' she said;
                 She said, 'I am aweary, aweary,
                 I would that I were dead.'

Sir John Everett Millais's (1829–96) painting of Tennyson's protagonist (1851) concentrates on her wasting sexuality rather than on the more complex imagery of the poem's later stanzas (see "Mariana in the Moated Grange." *Courtesy Lord Sherfield (Photo Sydney W. Newberry).*

**19.** Dante Gabriel Rossetti, *Found* (begun 1853, never completed). This painting used as models the painter Ford Madox Brown and Fanny Cornforth, a former prostitute who was Rossetti's mistress and whom he frequently depicted. The anecdote represents a young cattle drover coming to a market town and finding his youthful love literally, and figuratively, a "fallen" woman. Rossetti wrote the following sonnet to accompany the painting:

'There is a budding morrow in midnight' —
So sang our Keats, our English nightingale.
And here, as lamps across the bridge turn pale
In London's smokeless resurrection-light
Dark breaks to dawn. But o'er the deadly blight
Of love deflowered and sorrow of none avail
Which makes this man gasp and this woman quail,
Can day from darkness ever again take flight?
Ah! gave not these two hearts their mutual pledge,
Under one mantle sheltered 'neath the hedge
In gloaming courtship? And O God! today
He only knows he holds her—but what part
Can life now take? She cries in her locked heart,
'Leave me—I do not know you—go away!'

*The Samuel and Mary R. Bancroft Collection, Delaware Art Museum*, Wilmington.

20. John Ruskin, a portrait by Sir John Everett Millais, finished in 1854. *Christie, Manson, and Woods*, London.

21. *The Last of England.* Ford Madox Brown (1821–93), one of the first of the Pre-Raphaelites, painted this contrary vision of Victorian England in 1855. The couple staring at the receding shore are portraits of Brown and his wife; the subject of emigration was suggested by the departure of the sculptor Thomas Woolner to Australia three years earlier. Though forced (as in the words of Brown's sonnet accompanying the picture) to listen to

> Low ribaldry from sots, and share rough cheer
> With rudely-nurtur'd men, . . .

nevertheless

> She grips his listless hand and clasps her child,
> Through rainbow tears she sees a sunnier gleam,
> She cannot see a void where he will be.

*Birmingham* (England) *Museum and Art Gallery.*

22. *Work,* Ford Madox Brown's vision of Victorian social consciousness (1852–68), representing a view halfway up Heath Street, in Hampstead, London, where excavations force a diversion of traffic. The manual laborers in the central group are, in Brown's words, "the outward and visible type of Work"; on the right stand two of the "brain workers, who, seeming to be idle, work, and are the cause of well-ordained work and happiness in others—sages, such as in ancient Greece published their opinions in the market square." These are, in fact, portraits: of Carlyle (the hatted one), whose "Produce! Produce!" underlies many of the picture's ideas, and the Rev. Frederick Denison Maurice (1803–72), founder of a working men's college, where Ruskin and his followers taught drawing. Brown's own sonnet on the painting reflects this higher Victorian view of work as sublimated eros:

> Work, which beads the brow and tans the flesh
> Of lusty manhood, casting out its devils,
> By whose weird art transmuting poor man's evils
> Their bed seems down, their one dish ever fresh.

*City Art Gallery,* Manchester.

23. *Autumn Leaves* (dated 1856), by Sir John Everett Millais. The painting's narrative elements, such as the range of human meditative responses to natural symbols indicated in the children's various expressions, are triumphantly fulfilled in the imagery of the trees receding into the twilight, dwindling in perspective like past moments. Millais was quoted as having remarked of the odor of burning leaves, "To me nothing brings back sweeter memories of days that are gone; it is the incense offered by departing summer to the sky ...". The scene is a twilit one. *City Art Gallery*, Manchester.

24. *The Awakened Conscience,* by William Holman Hunt (1827–1910); exhibited 1854. This moment catches the response of the "kept" woman to an old song: the music on the piano is Thomas Moore's "Oft, in the Stilly Night" in which

> Fond Memory brings the light
> Of other days around me.

She is recalling her home and her own other purer days and, in the painter's own words, "breaking away from her gilded cage with a startled holy resolve, while her shallow companion still sings on, ignorantly intensifying her repentant purpose." Hunt wrote that he had been thinking of a text from Proverbs 25:20:"'As he that taketh away a garment in cold weather, so is he that singeth songs to a heavy heart." The picture is crowded with emblematic details: the cat under the table toying with its captured bird, the glove on the floor "flung aside" (like a cast-off mistress), the music on the floor (it is a setting of Tennyson's recent "Tears, Idle Tears"; as Ruskin commented, even "the very hem of the poor girl's dress . . . has a story in it, if we think how soon its pure whiteness may be soiled with dust and rain, her outcast feet failing in the street." *Birmingham Museum and Art Gallery.*

25. Rossetti's *Lady Lilith* (1864):

> And subtly of herself contemplative,
> Draws men to watch the bright web she can weave,
> Till heart and body and life are in its hold.

The text is from *The House of Life*, Sonnet LXXVIII; the model was Fanny Cornforth. *The Samuel and Mary R. Bancroft Collection, Delaware Art Museum.*

26. *Astarte Syriaca,* Rossetti's 1877 painting of Jane (Mrs. William) Morris as the primal goddess. His own sonnet expounds her identity:

Mystery: lo! between the sun and moon
Astarte of the Syrians: Venus Queen
Ere Aphrodite was. In silver sheen
Her twofold girdle clasps the infinite boon
Of bliss whereof the heaven and earth commune:
And from her neck's inclining flower-stem lean
Love-freighted lips and absolute eyes that wean
The pulse of hearts to the spheres' dominant tune.

Torch-bearing, her sweet ministers compel
All thrones of light beyond the sky and sea
The witnesses of Beauty's face to be.
That face, of Love's all-penetrating spell
Amulet, talisman, and oracle,—
Betwixt the sun and moon a mystery.

*City Art Gallery,* Manchester.

"Around her, lovers, newly met
'Mid deathless love's acclaim,
Spoke evermore among th...
Their rapturous new name...

*First Sketch for background picture "Dro..."*
1876

27. *The Blessed Damozel:* a preliminary sketch for the background of Rossetti's own illustrative painting (1876), embellishing the lines:

> Around her, lovers, newly met
> 'Mid deathless love's acclaims,
> Spoke evermore among themselves
> Their rapturous new names.

See "The Blessed Damozel," ll. 37–40, rather different in the published text. *Fogg Art Museum, Harvard University, Grenville L. Winthrop Bequest.*

28. *The Golden Stairs* (1880), by Sir Edward Coley Burne-Jones (1833–98) who, influenced by Rossetti, Morris, and Ruskin, continued Pre-Raphaelite traditions later into the century, both in strictly illustrative painting and graphics, and in invented mythologies such as are embodied in the present picture, which provides its own text. The almost spooky repetition of facial type is a convention with him, and that face itself, as well as the treatment of drapery, comes from Rossetti. *The Tate Gallery.*

29. One of his famous floral wallpapers. *A. F. Kersting.*

30. An opened spread from the so-called Kelmscott Chaucer (1896), Morris's triumph of neo-medieval book production. The woodcuts were by Burne-Jones. *Spencer Collection, New York Public Library.*

31. Thomas Carlyle, by James McNeill Whistler (1834–1903); The American expatriate painter's study, characteristically entitled *Arrangement in Grey and Black No. 2 (No. 1 was the famous portrait of the artist's mother)*, was completed in 1873. *Glasgow Art Gallery and Museum.*

32. *The Lady of Shalott.* Holman Hunt worked on this—one of two versions of his illustrative painting of Tennyson's poem—between 1890 and 1905, completing it a half-century after he had helped to found the Pre-Raphaelite Brotherhood. *City Art Gallery,* Manchester.

33. Illustration by Aubrey Beardsley (1872–92) of the climactic moment in Oscar Wilde's *Salome* (1894). Here the heroine kisses the severed head of John the Baptist.

34. Aubrey Beardsley's own bookplate.

35. Walter Pater.
*The Granger Collection.*

36. Gerard Manley Hopkins.
*The Granger Collection.*

A mighty silver bugle hung,
And as he rode his armour rung,
90      Beside remote Shalott.

All in the blue unclouded weather
Thick-jewelled shone the saddle-leather,
The helmet and the helmet-feather
Burned like one burning flame together,
      As he rode down to Camelot.
As often through the purple night,
Below the starry clusters bright,
Some bearded meteor, trailing light,
      Moves over still Shalott.

100   His broad clear brow in sunlight glowed;
On burnished hooves his war-horse trode;
From underneath his helmet flowed
His coal-black curls as on he rode,
      As he rode down to Camelot.
From the bank and from the river
He flashed into the crystal mirror,
'Tirra lirra,' by the river
      Sang Sir Lancelot.

She left the web, she left the loom,
110   She made three paces through the room,
She saw the water-lily bloom,
She saw the helmet and the plume,
      She looked down to Camelot.
Out flew the web and floated wide;
The mirror cracked from side to side;
'The curse is come upon me,' cried
      The Lady of Shalott.

      PART IV
In the stormy east-wind straining,
The pale yellow woods were waning,
120   The broad stream in his banks complaining.
Heavily the low sky raining
      Over towered Camelot;
Down she came and found a boat
Beneath a willow left afloat,
And round about the prow she wrote
      *The Lady of Shalott.*

And down the river's dim expanse
Like some bold seer in a trance,
Seeing all his own mischance—
130   With a glassy countenance
      Did she look to Camelot.

And at the closing of the day
She loosed the chain, and down she lay;
The broad stream bore her far away,
    The Lady of Shalott.

Lying, robed in snowy white
That loosely flew to left and right—
The leaves upon her falling light—
Through the noises of the night
140    She floated down to Camelot:
And as the boat-head wound along
The willowy hills and fields among,
They heard her singing her last song,
    The Lady of Shalott.

Heard a carol, mournful, holy,
Chanted loudly, chanted lowly,
Till her blood was frozen slowly,
And her eyes were darkened wholly,
    Turned to towered Camelot.
150    For ere she reached upon the tide
The first house by the water-side,
Singing in her song she died,
    The Lady of Shalott.

Under tower and balcony,
By garden-wall and gallery,
A gleaming shape she floated by,
Dead-pale between the houses high,
    Silent into Camelot.
Out upon the wharfs they came,
160    Knight and burgher, lord and dame,
And round the prow they read her name,
    *The Lady of Shalott.*

Who is this? and what is here?
And in the lighted palace near
Died the sound of royal cheer;
And they crossed themselves for fear,
    All the knights at Camelot:
But Lancelot mused a little space;
He said, 'She has a lovely face;
170    God in his mercy lend her grace,
    The Lady of Shalott.'
                1832

# The Hesperides°

Hesperus and his daughters three,
That sing about the golden tree.

*Comus* [982–83]°

The Northwind fallen, in the newstarrèd night
Zidonian Hanno,° voyaging beyond
The hoary promontory of Soloë
Past Thymiaterion, in calmèd bays,
Between the southern and the western Horn,
Heard neither warbling of the nightingale,
Nor melody o' the Lybian lotusflute
Blown seaward from the shore; but from a slope
That ran bloombright into the Atlantic blue,
10  Beneath a highland leaning down a weight
Of cliffs, and zoned below with cedarshade,
Came voices, like the voices in a dream,
Continuous, till he reached the outer sea.

SONG°

I

The golden apple, the golden apple, the hallowed fruit,
Guard it well, guard it warily,
Singing airily,
Standing about the charmèd root.
Round about all is mute,
As the snowfield on the mountain-peaks,
20  As the sandfield at the mountain-foot.
Crocodiles in briny creeks
Sleep and stir not: all is mute.
If ye sing not, if ye make false measure,
We shall lose eternal pleasure,
Worth eternal want of rest.
Laugh not loudly: watch the treasure
Of the wisdom of the west.
In a corner wisdom whispers. Five and three

**The Hesperides** This, one of Tennyson's master-pieces, was rejected by the censorious superego in the poet, who declined to reprint it after 1833. G. R. Stange points out its strong affinities to Shelley and Keats, and to the aesthetics of Hallam; on this reading the poem itself is a "Garden of Art," akin to what Tennyson sought to reject in his poem *The Palace of Art.* Some of the implications of *The Hesperides* would have delighted Blake, who wrote his own version of this myth in *Visions of the Daughters of Albion.*
**Comus** In Milton's poem, there is a marvelous description (ll. 976–91) of the gardens from which the Attendant Spirit descends, a more religious version of Spenser's Gardens of Adonis. Though his starting point is Milton's *Comus,* the young Tennyson returns to something of

Spenser's freedom in singing of the Lower Paradise.
**Hanno** Taken from a passage in the *Periplus* of Hanno, Carthaginian voyager in the 5th century B.C. The places referred to are on the west coast of Africa.
**Song** Sung by the Daughters of Hesperus, who with a dragon guard the golden fruit of the Western Isles, until Heracles kills the dragon, and bears away the fruit. Tennyson's surprising invention is that the Daughters sing continuously, so as to create an enchantment so unbroken that the fruit becomes unattainable. Perhaps this means that poetry of this pure, rapturous, incantatory kind is as much of paradise as we can know, but it may also imply that such ravishment by poetry keeps us in our fallen condition.

(Let it not be preached abroad) make an awful mystery.°
30   For the blossom unto threefold music° bloweth;
Evermore it is born anew;
And the sap to threefold music floweth,
From the root
Drawn in the dark,
Up to the fruit,
Creeping under the fragrant bark,
Liquid gold, honeysweet, through and through.
Keen-eyed Sisters, singing airily,
Looking warily
40   Every way,
Guard the apple night and day,
Lest one from the East come and take it away.


II

Father Hesper, Father Hesper, watch, watch, ever and aye,
Looking under silver hair with a silver eye.°
Father, twinkle not thy steadfast sight;
Kingdoms lapse, and climates change, and races die;
Honour comes with mystery;
Hoarded wisdom brings delight.
Number, tell them over and number
50   How many the mystic fruittree holds,
Lest the redcombed dragon slumber
Rolled together in purple folds.
Look to him, father, lest he wink, and the golden
     apple be stolen away,
For his ancient heart is drunk with overwatchings night and day,
Round about the hallowed fruittree curled—
Sing away, sing aloud evermore in the wind, without stop,
Lest his scalèd eyelid drop,
For he is older than the world.
If he waken, we waken,
60   Rapidly levelling eager eyes.
If he sleep, we sleep,
Dropping the eyelid over the eyes.
If the golden apple be taken
The world will be overwise.
Five links, a golden chain, are we,
Hesper, the dragon, and sisters three,
Bound about the golden tree.


mystery Why the number 8 should be a mystery has been explained by several scholars (Stange, Paden, Bush, Ricks) as having reference to several Romantic mythologists (G. S. Faber, Edward Davies, Jacob Bryant, the last two of whom influenced Blake's similar number symbolism); Stange's identification of the "five" as the five senses, and the "three" as a natural unity-in-multiplicity is in the spirit of these mythologists.
threefold music the highest that natural sexual song can attain, as in Blake and the mythologists
silver eye presumably Hesperus as the Western, or Evening, Star

III

Father Hesper, Father Hesper, watch, watch, night and day,
Lest the old wound of the world be healèd,°
70  The glory unsealèd,
The golden apple stolen away,
And the ancient secret revealèd.
Look from west to east along:
Father, old Himala weakens, Caucasus is bold and strong.
Wandering waters unto wandering waters call;
Let them clash together, foam and fall.
Out of watchings, out of wiles,
Comes the bliss of secret smiles.
All things are not told to all.
80  Half-round the mantling night is drawn,
Purplefringèd with even and dawn.
Hesper hateth Phosphor,° evening hateth morn.

IV

Every flower and every fruit the redolent breath
Of this warm seawind ripeneth,
Arching the billow in his sleep;
But the landwind wandereth,
Broken by the highland-steep,
Two streams upon the violet deep:
For the western sun and the western star,
90  And the low west wind, breathing afar,
The end of day and beginning of night
Make the apple holy and bright;
Holy and bright, round and full, bright and blest,
Mellowed in a land of rest;
Watch it warily day and night;
All good things are in the west.
Till midnoon the cool east light
Is shut out by the round of the tall hillbrow;
But when the fullfaced sunset yellowly
100  Stays on the flowering arch of the bough,
The luscious fruitage clustereth mellowly,
Goldenkernelled, goldencored,
Sunset-ripened above on the tree.
The world is wasted with fire and sword,
But the apple of gold hangs over the sea.
Five links, a golden chain, are we,
Hesper, the dragon, and sisters three,
Daughters three,
Bound about

**be healèd** Ricks gives the likely reference as Revelation 13:3.
**Phosphor** Lucifer, the Morning Star; i.e., the planet Venus when visible before sunrise, called Hesperus at its evening appearance

110 All round about
The gnarlèd bole of the charmèd tree.
The golden apple, the golden apple, the hallowed fruit,
Guard it well, guard it warily,
Watch it warily,
Singing airily,
Standing about the charmèd root.
1832


The Lotos-Eaters°

'Courage!' he° said, and pointed toward the land,
'This mounting wave will roll us shoreward soon.'
In the afternoon they came unto a land
In which it seemèd always afternoon.
All round the coast the languid air did swoon,
Breathing like one that hath a weary dream.
Full-faced above the valley stood the moon;
And like a downward smoke, the slender stream
Along the cliff to fall and pause and fall did seem.

10 A land of streams! some, like a downward smoke,
Slow-dropping veils of thinnest lawn,° did go;
And some through wavering lights and shadows broke,
Rolling a slumbrous sheet of foam below.
They saw the gleaming river seaward flow
From the inner land: far off, three mountain-tops,
Three silent pinnacles of agèd snow,
Stood sunset-flushed: and, dewed with showery drops,
Up-clomb the shadowy pine above the woven copse.

The charmèd sunset lingered low adown
20 In the red West: through mountain clefts the dale
Was seen far inland, and the yellow down
Bordered with palm, and many a winding vale
And meadow, set with slender galingale;°
A land where all things always seemed the same!
And round about the keel with faces pale,
Dark faces pale against that rosy flame,
The mild-eyed melancholy Lotos-eaters came.

The Lotos-Eaters In Homer's *Odyssey* IX.82 ff.,
Odysseus tells Alcìnous the story of how, after
sailing from Troy, he and his men were driven
by the winds to the coast of Africa, where the
Lotos-Eaters lived: "Now it never entered the
heads of these natives to kill my friends; what
they did was to give them some lotos to taste,
and as soon as each had eaten the honeyed
fruit of the plant, all thoughts of reporting to
us or escaping were banished from his mind."
But Tennyson's poem is more Spenserian than
Homeric, with the first five stanzas being written
in Spenserian stanzas, and the "Choric Song"
recalling the Cave of Morpheus in The Faerie
*Queene* I.i.39–41.
he Odysseus
lawn cotton fabric
galingale aromatic herb

Branches they bore of that enchanted stem,
Laden with flower and fruit, whereof they gave
30 To each, but whoso did receive of them,
And taste, to him the gushing of the wave
Far far away did seem to mourn and rave
On alien shores; and if his fellow spake,
His voice was thin, as voices from the grave;
And deep-asleep he seemed, yet all awake,
And music in his ears his beating heart did make.

They sat them down upon the yellow sand,
Between the sun and moon upon the shore;
And sweet it was to dream of Fatherland,
40 Of child, and wife, and slave; but evermore
Most weary seemed the sea, weary the oar,
Weary the wandering fields of barren foam.
Then some one said, 'We will return no more;'
And all at once they sang, 'Our island home°
Is far beyond the wave; we will no longer roam.'

CHORIC SONG
I
There is sweet music here that softer falls
Than petals from blown roses on the grass,
Or night-dews on still waters between walls
Of shadowy granite, in a gleaming pass;
50 Music that gentlier on the spirit lies,
Than tired eyelids upon tired eyes;
Music that brings sweet sleep down from the blissful skies.
Here are cool mosses deep,
And through the moss the ivies creep,
And in the stream the long-leaved flowers weep,
And from the craggy ledge the poppy hangs in sleep.

II
Why are we weighed upon with heaviness,
And utterly consumed with sharp distress,
While all things else have rest from weariness?
60 All things have rest: why should we toil alone,
We only toil, who are the first of things,
And make perpetual moan,
Still from one sorrow to another thrown:
Nor ever fold our wings,
And cease from wanderings,
Nor steep our brows in slumber's holy balm;
Nor harken what the inner spirit sings,

**island home** Ithaca

'There is no joy but calm!'
Why should we only toil, the roof and crown of things?


### III

70    Lo! in the middle of the wood,
The folded leaf is wooed from out the bud
With winds upon the branch, and there
Grows green and broad, and takes no care,
Sun-steeped at noon, and in the moon
Nightly dew-fed; and turning yellow
Falls, and floats adown the air.
Lo! sweetened with the summer light,
The full-juiced apple, waxing over-mellow,
Drops in a silent autumn night.
80    All its allotted length of days,
The flower ripens in its place,
Ripens and fades, and falls, and hath no toil,
Fast-rooted in the fruitful soil.


### IV

Hateful is the dark-blue sky,
Vaulted o'er the dark-blue sea.
Death is the end of life; ah, why
Should life all labour be?
Let us alone. Time driveth onward fast,
And in a little while our lips are dumb.
90    Let us alone. What is it that will last?
All things are taken from us, and become
Portions and parcels of the dreadful Past.
Let us alone. What pleasure can we have
To war with evil? Is there any peace
In ever climbing up the climbing wave?
All things have rest, and ripen toward the grave
In silence; ripen, fall and cease:
Give us long rest or death, dark death, or dreamful ease.


### V

How sweet it were, hearing the downward stream,
100    With half-shut eyes ever to seem
Falling asleep in a half-dream!
To dream and dream, like yonder amber light,
Which will not leave the myrrh-bush on the height;
To hear each other's whispered speech;
Eating the Lotos day by day,
To watch the crisping ripples on the beach,
And tender curving lines of creamy spray;
To lend our hearts and spirits wholly
To the influence of mild-minded melancholy;

110 To muse and brood and live again in memory,
With those old faces of our infancy
Heaped over with a mound of grass,
Two handfuls of white dust, shut in an urn of brass!

VI

Dear is the memory of our wedded lives,
And dear the last embraces of our wives
And their warm tears: but all hath suffered change:
For surely now our household hearths are cold:
Our sons inherit us: our looks are strange:
And we should come like ghosts to trouble joy.
120 Or else the island princes over-bold
Have eat our substance, and the minstrel sings
Before them of the ten years' war in Troy,
And our great deeds, as half-forgotten things.
Is there confusion in the little isle?
Let what is broken so remain.
The Gods are hard to reconcile:
'Tis hard to settle order once again.
There *is* confusion worse than death,
Trouble on trouble, pain on pain,
130 Long labour unto agèd breath,
Sore task to hearts worn out by many wars
And eyes grown dim with gazing on the pilot-stars.

VII

But, propped on beds of amaranth and moly,°
How sweet (while warm airs lull us, blowing lowly)
With half-dropped eyelid still,
Beneath a heaven dark and holy,
To watch the long bright river drawing slowly
His waters from the purple hill—
To hear the dewy echoes calling
140 From cave to cave through the thick-twinèd vine—
To watch the emerald-coloured water falling
Through many a woven acanthus°-wreath divine!
Only to hear and see the far-off sparkling brine,
Only to hear were sweet, stretched out beneath the pine.

VIII

The Lotos blooms below the barren peak:
The Lotos blows by every winding creek:
All day the wind breathes low with mellower tone:
Through every hollow cave and alley lone

amaranth mythical unfading flower; moly herb
of occult power, given by Hermes to Odysseus
in the *Odyssey* X, to protect him from the enchantress Circe
acanthus sacred herb

Round and round the spicy downs the yellow Lotos-dust is blown.
150 We have had enough of action, and of motion we,
Rolled to starboard, rolled to larboard, when the surge was seething free,
Where the wallowing monster spouted his foam-fountains in the sea.
Let us swear an oath, and keep it with an equal mind,
In the hollow Lotos-land to live and lie reclined
On the hills like Gods° together, careless of mankind.
For they lie beside their nectar, and the bolts are hurled
Far below them in the valleys, and the clouds are lightly curled
Round their golden houses, girdled with the gleaming world:
Where they smile in secret, looking over wasted lands,
Blight and famine, plague and earthquake, roaring
160   deeps and fiery sands,
Clanging fights, and flaming towns, and sinking ships,
  and praying hands.
But they smile, they find a music centred in a doleful song
Steaming up, a lamentation and an ancient tale of wrong,
Like a tale of little meaning though the words are strong;
Chanted from an ill-used race of men that cleave the soil,
Sow the seed, and reap the harvest with enduring toil,
Storing yearly little dues of wheat, and wine and oil;
Till they perish and they suffer—some, 'tis whispered—down in hell
Suffer endless anguish, others in Elysian valleys° dwell,
170 Resting weary limbs at last on beds of asphodel.
Surely, surely, slumber is more sweet than toil, the shore
Than labour in the deep mid-ocean, wind and wave and oar;
Oh rest ye, brother mariners, we will not wander more.
1830–32                                    1832


# The Eagle

FRAGMENT

He clasps the crag with crookèd hands;
Close to the sun in lonely lands,
Ringed with the azure world, he stands.

The wrinkled sea beneath him crawls;
He watches from his mountain walls,
And like a thunderbolt he falls.
1851

like Gods These are the Epicurean gods as seen
by Lucretius, in *De Rerum Natura* IV. 724 ff.,
V. 83 ff., VI. 58 ff.
Elysian valleys The Elysian Fields (one Greek
version of Paradise) were covered with asphodel, which may have been the narcissus, not the
daffodil or English asphodel.

# St. Simeon Stylites°

Although I be the basest of mankind,
From scalp to sole one slough and crust of sin,
Unfit for earth, unfit for heaven, scarce meet
For troops of devils, mad with blasphemy,
I will not cease to grasp the hope I hold
Of saintdom, and to clamour, mourn and sob,
Battering the gates of heaven with storms of prayer,
Have mercy, Lord, and take away my sin.

Let this avail, just, dreadful, mighty God,
10 This not be all in vain, that thrice ten years,
Thrice multiplied by superhuman pangs,
In hungers and in thirsts, fevers and cold,
In coughs, aches, stitches, ulcerous throes and cramps,
A sign betwixt the meadow and the cloud,
Patient on this tall pillar I have borne
Rain, wind, frost, heat, hail, damp, and sleet, and snow;
And I had hoped that ere this period closed
Thou wouldst have caught me up into thy rest,
Denying not these weather-beaten limbs
20 The meed° of saints, the white robe and the palm.

O take the meaning, Lord: I do not breathe,
Not whisper, any murmur of complaint.
Pain heaped ten-hundred-fold to this, were still
Less burthen, by ten-hundred-fold, to bear,
Then were those lead-like tons of sin that crushed
My spirit flat before thee.
                          O Lord, Lord,
Thou knowest I bore this better at the first,
For I was strong and hale of body then;
And though my teeth, which now are dropped away,
30 Would chatter with the cold, and all my beard
Was tagged with icy fringes in the moon,
I drowned the whoopings of the owl with sound
Of pious hymns and psalms, and sometimes saw
An angel stand and watch me, as I sang.
Now am I feeble grown; my end draws nigh;
I hope my end draws nigh: half deaf I am,
So that I scarce can hear the people hum

St. Simeon Stylites Stylites is from the Greek for "pillar." St. Simeon (390–459) was notorious for his ascetic severities. At the age of 30, he mounted a pillar and lived upon it for 30 years without condescending to come down at all. The pillar eventually was built up to 60 feet in height, with a railing around the top, and a ladder by which the holy man's disciples were enabled to bring him sustenance. St. Simeon preached regularly from his pillar to large and adoring audiences. Tennyson's source is partly Gibbon's Decline and Fall of the Roman Empire IV. 320, where the saint is given the treatment he merits, a treatment completed in Tennyson's dramatic monologue, which Browning admired enormously.
meed reward; the white robe and the palm are promised to the saints in heaven in Revelation 7:9

About the column's base, and almost blind,
And scarce can recognize the fields I know;
40   And both my thighs are rotted with the dew;
Yet cease I not to clamour and to cry,
While my stiff spine can hold my weary head,
Till all my limbs drop piecemeal from the stone,
Have mercy, mercy: take away my sin.

O Jesus, if thou wilt not save my soul,
Who may be saved?° who is it may be saved?
Who may be made a saint, if I fail here?
Show me the man hath suffered more than I.
For did not all thy martyrs die one death?
50   For either they were stoned, or crucified,
Or burned in fire, or boiled in oil, or sawn
In twain beneath the ribs; but I die here
Today, and whole years long, a life of death.
Bear witness, if I could have found a way
(And heedfully I sifted all my thought)
More slowly-painful to subdue this home
Of sin, my flesh, which I despise and hate,
I had not stinted practice, O my God.

For not alone this pillar-punishment;
60   Not this alone I bore: but while I lived
In the white convent down the valley there,
For many weeks about my loins I wore
The rope that haled the buckets from the well,
Twisted as tight as I could knot the noose;
And spake not of it to a single soul,
Until the ulcer, eating through my skin,
Betrayed my secret penance, so that all
My brethren marvelled greatly. More than this
I bore, whereof, O God, thou knowest all.

70   Three winters, that my soul might grow to thee,
I lived up there on yonder mountain side.
My right leg chained into the crag, I lay
Pent in a roofless close of ragged stones;
Inswathed sometimes in wandering mist, and twice
Blacked with thy branding thunder, and sometimes
Sucking the damps for drink, and eating not,
Except the spare chance-gift of those that came
To touch my body and be healed, and live:
And they say then that I worked miracles,
80   Whereof my fame is loud amongst mankind,
Cured lameness, palsies, cancers. Thou, O God,

**Who may be saved?** See Matthew 19:25.

Knowest alone whether this was or no.
Have mercy, mercy! cover all my sin.°

Then, that I might be more alone with thee,
Three years I lived upon a pillar, high
Six cubits,° and three years on one of twelve;
And twice three years I crouched on one that rose
Twenty by measure; last of all, I grew
Twice ten long weary weary years to this,
90    That numbers forty cubits from the soil.

I think that I have borne as much as this—
Or else I dream—and for so long a time,
If I may measure time by yon slow light,
And this high dial,° which my sorrow crowns—
So much—even so.
                        And yet I know not well,
For that the evil ones come here, and say,
'Fall down, O Simeon; thou hast suffered long
For ages and for ages!' then they prate
Of penances I cannot have gone through,
100    Perplexing me with lies; and oft I fall,
Maybe for months, in such blind lethargies
That Heaven, and Earth, and Time are choked.
                        But yet
Bethink thee, Lord, while thou and all the saints
Enjoy themselves in heaven, and men on earth
House in the shade of comfortable roofs,
Sit with their wives by fires, eat wholesome food,
And wear warm clothes, and even beasts have stalls,
I, 'tween the spring and downfall of the light,
Bow down one thousand and two hundred times,
110    To Christ, the Virgin Mother, and the saints;
Or in the night, after a little sleep,
I wake: the chill stars sparkle; I am wet
With drenching dews, or stiff with crackling frost.
I wear an undressed goatskin on my back;
A grazing iron collar grinds my neck;
And in my weak, lean arms I lift the cross,
And strive and wrestle with thee till I die:
O mercy, mercy! wash away my sin.

O Lord, thou knowest what a man I am;
120    A sinful man, conceived and born in sin:
'Tis their own doing; this is none of mine;
Lay it not to me. Am I to blame for this,

cover all my sin See Psalms 85:2.
six cubits Since a cubit was about 18 inches, the
saint measures the height of his piety as having

augmented from about 9 feet to its culminating 60.
high dial The pillar and saint together make a
sundial.

That here come those that worship me? Ha! ha!
They think that I am somewhat. What am I?
The silly people take me for a saint,
And bring me offerings of fruit and flowers:
And I, in truth (thou wilt bear witness here)
Have all in all endured as much, and more
Than many just and holy men, whose names
130    Are registered and calendared for saints.

Good people, you do ill to kneel to me.
What is it I can have done to merit this?
I am a sinner viler than you all.
It may be I have wrought some miracles,
And cured some halt and mained; but what of that?
It may be, no one, even among the saints,
May match his pains with mine; but what of that?
Yet do not rise; for you may look on me,
And in your looking you may kneel to God.
140    Speak! is there any of you halt or maimed?
I think you know I have some power with Heaven
From my long penance: let him speak his wish.

Yes, I can heal him. Power goes forth from me.
They say that they are healed. Ah, hark! they shout
'St. Simeon Stylites.' Why, if so,
God reaps a harvest in me. O my soul,
God reaps a harvest in thee. If this be,
Can I work miracles and not be saved?
This is not told of any. They were saints.
It cannot be but that I shall be saved;
150    Yea, crowned, a saint. They shout, 'Behold a saint!'
And lower voices saint me from above.
Courage, St. Simeon! This dull chrysalis°
Cracks into shining wings, and hope ere death
Spreads more and more and more, that God hath now
Sponged and made blank of crimeful record all
My mortal archives.
                 O my sons, my sons,
I, Simeon of the pillar, by surname
Stylites, among men; I, Simeon,
160    The watcher on the column till the end;
I, Simeon, whose brain the sunshine bakes;
I, whose bald brows in silent hours become
Unnaturally hoar with rime, do now
From my high nest of penance here proclaim
That Pontius and Iscariot° by my side

chrysalis The holy man compares himself to the
cocoon of a butterfly.
**Pontius and Iscariot** Pontius Pilate, Roman governor of Judea during the career of Jesus; Judas
Iscariot, the betrayer of Jesus

Showed like fair seraphs. On the coals I lay,
A vessel full of sin: all hell beneath
Made me boil over. Devils plucked my sleeve,
Abaddon and Asmodeus° caught at me.
170   I smote them with the cross; they swarmed again.
In bed like monstrous apes they crushed my chest:
They flapped my light out as I read: I saw
Their faces grow between me and my book;
With colt-like whinny and with hoggish whine
They burst my prayer. Yet this way was left,
And by this way I 'scaped them. Mortify
Your flesh, like me, with scourges and with thorns;
Smite, shrink not, spare not. If it may be, fast
Whole Lents, and pray. I hardly, with slow steps,
180   With slow, faint steps, and much exceeding pain,
Have scrambled past those pits of fire, that still
Sing in mine ears. But yield not me the praise:
God only through his bounty hath thought fit,
Among the powers and princes of this world,
To make me an example to mankind,
Which few can reach to. Yet I do not say
But that a time may come—yea, even now,
Now, now, his footsteps smite the threshold stairs
Of life—I say, that time is at the doors
190   When you may worship me without reproach;
For I will leave my relics in your land,
And you may carve a shrine about my dust,
And burn a fragrant lamp before my bones,
When I am gathered to the glorious saints.

    While I spake then, a sting of shrewdest pain
Ran shrivelling through me, and a cloudlike change,
In passing, with a grosser film made thick
These heavy, horny eyes. The end! the end!
Surely the end! What's here? a shape, a shade,
200   A flash of light. Is that the angel there
That holds a crown? Come, blessèd brother, come.
I know thy glittering face. I waited long;
My brows are ready. What! deny it now?
Nay, draw, draw, draw nigh. So I clutch it. Christ!
'Tis gone: 'tis here again; the crown! the crown!
So now 'tis fitted on and grows to me,
And from it melt the dews of Paradise,
Sweet! sweet! spikenard, and balm, and frankincense.
Ah! let me not be fooled, sweet saints: I trust
210   That I am whole, and clean, and meet for Heaven.

---

**Abaddon and Asmodeus** Abaddon was the Angel     is an evil spirit in Tobit 3:8.
of Destruction; see Revelation 9:11. Asmodeus

Speak, if there be a priest, a man of God,
Among you there, and let him presently
Approach, and lean a ladder on the shaft,
And climbing up into my airy home,
Deliver me the blessèd sacrament;
For by the warning of the Holy Ghost,
I prophesy that I shall die tonight,
A quarter before twelve.
                              But thou, O Lord,
Aid all this foolish people; let them take
220   Example, pattern: lead them to thy light.
1833                                    1842


# Ulysses

This subtle, equivocal dramatic monologue was written in the autumn of 1833, when Tennyson's despairing grief for Hallam was most oppressive. Retrospectively, the poet insisted that it stated his "feeling about the need of going forward, and braving the struggle of life perhaps more simply than anything in *In Memoriam*." Yet the poem is founded more upon the evil counselor Ulysses of Dante's *Inferno* XXVI (whom nevertheless Dante in some sense admired) than on the hero of the prophecy of Tiresias in the *Odyssey* (XI.100–37). Dante's Trojan sympathies stem from his nationality and from his guide Virgil, who sang the flight of Aeneas from fallen Troy, and that hero's subsequent founding of Rome. In the *Inferno*, Ulysses goes forth again on a last voyage, to "explore the world, and search the ways of life,/Man's evil and his virtue" (Cary's translation, which Tennyson probably used); when the Ithacans' ship comes to the Pillars of Hercules, "the boundaries not to be o'erstepped by man," the wily Ulysses urges his "small faithful band/That yet cleaved to me" to attempt a breakthrough into forbidden realms: "Ye were not formed to live the life of brutes,/But virtue to pursue and knowledge high." His followers obey him, and are washed down with Ulysses in the forbidden gulfs when they sight the Mount of Purgatory. Though Tennyson apparently takes, in contrast to Dante, a High Romantic view of Ulysses as an indomitable quester animated by heroic humanism and a sustained drive for knowledge, the poem persistently qualifies our admiration for its speaker. He appears to lack a capacity for loving other human beings, scorns his son's sense of responsibility, and in his closing lines echoes the defiant Satan of Milton's *Paradise Lost* I–II.


# Ulysses

It little profits that an idle king,°
By this still hearth, among these barren crags,
Matched with an agèd wife, I mete and dole

idle king In Dante, Ulysses sets out for the west
after leaving Circe. Significantly, Tennyson has
him return home first, experience boredom, and
then quest forth again.

Unequal° laws unto a savage race,
That hoard, and sleep, and feed, and know not me.

I cannot rest from travel: I will drink
Life to the lees: all times I have enjoyed
Greatly, have suffered greatly, both with those
That loved me, and alone; on shore, and when
10  Through scudding drifts the rainy Hyades°
Vexed the dim sea: I am become a name;
For always roaming with a hungry heart
Much have I seen and known; cities of men
And manners, climates, councils, governments,
Myself not least, but honoured of them all;
And drunk delight of battle with my peers,
Far on the ringing plains of windy Troy.
I am a part of all that I have met;
Yet all experience is an arch wherethrough
20  Gleams that untravelled world, whose margin fades
For ever and for ever when I move.
How dull it is to pause, to make an end,
To rust unburnished, not to shine in use!
As though to breathe were life. Life piled on life
Were all too little, and of one to me
Little remains: but every hour is saved
From that eternal silence, something more,
A bringer of new things; and vile it were
For some three suns° to store and hoard myself,
30  And this grey spirit yearning in desire
To follow knowledge like a sinking star,
Beyond the utmost bound of human thought.

This is my son, mine own Telemachus,
To whom I leave the sceptre and the isle—
Well-loved of me, discerning to fulfil
This labour, by slow prudence to make mild
A rugged people, and through soft degrees
Subdue them to the useful and the good.
Most blameless is he, centred in the sphere
40  Of common duties, decent not to fail
In offices of tenderness, and pay
Meet adoration to my household gods,
When I am gone. He works his work, I mine.

There lies the port; the vessel puffs her sail:
There gloom the dark broad seas. My mariners,

---

**Unequal** Possibly "unjust," but more likely reflecting a still "savage" society. Notice that when talking to himself, Ulysses calls his subjects "savage" (l. 4) but shifts to "rugged" (l. 37) when he speaks out loud.

**rainy Hyades** 5 stars in the head of the constellation Taurus; their name, "the rainy ones," stems from the fact that their simultaneous rise with the sun heralded the spring rains
**three suns** three years

Souls that have toiled, and wrought, and thought with me—
That ever with a frolic welcome took
The thunder and the sunshine, and opposed
Free hearts, free foreheads—you and I are old;
50    Old age hath yet his honour and his toil;
Death closes all:° but something ere the end,
Some work of noble note, may yet be done,
Not unbecoming men that strove with Gods.
The lights begin to twinkle from the rocks:
The long day wanes: the slow moon climbs: the deep
Moans round with many voices. Come, my friends,
'Tis not too late to seek a newer world.
Push off, and sitting well in order smite
The sounding furrows; for my purpose holds
60    To sail beyond the sunset, and the baths
Of all the western stars, until I die.
It may be that the gulfs will wash us down:
It may be we shall touch the Happy Isles,°
And see the great Achilles,° whom we knew.
Though much is taken, much abides; and though
We are not now that strength which in old days
Moved earth and heaven; that which we are, we are;
One equal temper of heroic hearts,
Made weak by time and fate, but strong in will
70    To strive, to seek, to find, and not to yield.°
1833                                    1842

## Tithonus°

The woods decay, the woods decay and fall,
The vapours weep their burthen to the ground,
Man comes and tills the field and lies beneath,
And after many a summer dies the swan.
Me only cruel immortality

---

**Death closes all** Unlike Tennyson, this Ulysses does not believe in immortality.
**Happy Isles** the Isles of the Blessed or the Elysian Fields, abode of heroes after death, and lying beyond the Strait of Gibraltar
**Achilles** hero of the Greeks, scourge of the Trojans, and perhaps in some sense Hallam
**not to yield** Compare Satan, in his first speech, *Paradise Lost* I.84–124, particularly: "And courage never to submit or yield: / And what is else not to be overcome?"
**Tithonus** Written originally, in shorter form, as a pendant to *Ulysses* in autumn 1833, and expressing obliquely again the poet's deep grief at continuing in life without Hallam. Tennyson took the story from the Homeric *Hymn to Aphrodite*; Tithonus, beloved of the goddess of

the dawn, Eos or Aurora, received eternal life but not perpetual youth. His withered body was at last transformed into a grasshopper. Profoundly Virgilian in tone, *Tithonus* echoes several Romantic poets in its equivocal lament for a dehumanizing immortality. Whatever Tennyson's intentions, it is notable that this dramatic monologue, like *Ulysses,* gives us a speaker evidently incapable of ever having loved anyone. Though his situation is extreme, Tithonus nevertheless shows no affection for Aurora, who continues to love him, as he can recognize. Mingled with his desire to die is a still profound capacity for aesthetic as opposed to emotional experience. Compare the song, "Tears, Idle Tears."

Consumes: I wither slowly in thine arms,°
Here at the quiet limit of the world,
A white-haired shadow roaming like a dream
The ever-silent spaces of the East,
10  Far-folded mists, and gleaming halls of morn.

Alas! for this grey shadow, once a man—
So glorious in his beauty and thy choice,
Who madest him thy chosen, that he seemed
To his great heart none other than a God!
I asked thee, 'Give me immortality.'
Then didst thou grant mine asking with a smile,
Like wealthy men who care not how they give.
But thy strong Hours° indignant worked their wills,
And beat me down and marred and wasted me,
20  And though they could not end me, left me maimed
To dwell in presence of immortal youth,°
Immortal age beside immortal youth,
And all I was, in ashes. Can thy love,
Thy beauty, make amends, though even now,
Close over us, the silver star,° thy guide,
Shines in those tremulous eyes that fill with tears
To hear me? Let me go: take back thy gift:
Why should a man desire in any way
To vary from the kindly° race of men,
30  Or pass beyond the goal of ordinance°
Where all should pause, as is most meet for all?

A soft air fans the cloud apart; there comes
A glimpse of that dark world where I was born.
Once more the old mysterious glimmer steals
From thy pure brows, and from thy shoulders pure,
And bosom beating with a heart renewed.
Thy cheek begins to redden through the gloom,
Thy sweet eyes brighten slowly close to mine,
Ere yet they blind the stars, and the wild team°
40  Which love thee, yearning for thy yoke, arise,
And shake the darkness from their loosened manes,
And beat the twilight into flakes of fire.

Lo! ever thus thou growest beautiful
In silence, then before thine answer given
Departest, and thy tears are on my cheek.

thine arms Aurora's
Hours Like the Hours in Shelley's *Prometheus*
*Unbound*, these companions of the dawn god-
dess are responsible for birth, maturation, and
decay and are indignant that they cannot destroy
Tithonus.

immortal youth Aurora, since she is a goddess
silver star the Morning Star, Venus
kindly human, one's own kind
goal of ordinance fixed limit
team Aurora's chariot and horses, which each
morning carry her from Ocean to Olympus

Why wilt thou ever scare me with thy tears,
And make me tremble lest a saying learnt,
In days far-off, on that dark earth, be true?
'The Gods themselves cannot recall their gifts.'

50    Ay me! aye me! with what another heart
In days far-off, and with what other eyes
I used to watch—if I be he that watched—
The lucid outline forming round thee; saw
The dim curls kindle into sunny rings;
Changed with thy mystic change, and felt my blood
Glow with the glow that slowly crimsoned all
Thy presence and thy portals, while I lay,
Mouth, forehead, eyelids, growing dewy-warm
With kisses balmier than half-opening buds
60    Of April, and could hear the lips that kissed
Whispering I knew not what of wild and sweet,
Like that strange song I heard Apollo sing,°
While Ilion like a mist rose into towers.

Yet hold me not for ever in thine East:
How can my nature longer mix with thine?
Coldly thy rosy shadows bathe me, cold
Are all thy lights, and cold my wrinkled feet
Upon thy glimmering thresholds, when the steam
Floats up from those dim fields about the homes
70    Of happy men that have the power to die,
And grassy barrows° of the happier dead.
Release me, and restore me to the ground;
Thou seest all things, thou wilt see my grave:
Thou wilt renew thy beauty morn by morn;
I earth in earth forget these empty courts,
And thee returning on thy silver wheels.
1833, 1859                              1860


# Morte d'Arthur°

So all day long the noise of battle° rolled
Among the mountains by the winter sea;
Until King Arthur's table, man by man,

Apollo sing Troy (Ilion) was built by Apollo's music
barrows burial mounds
Morte d'Arthur This is Tennyson's first major Arthurian poem, a direct reaction to Hallam's death, and the best poem in Idylls of the King, where it is included in full, but rather spoiled by the inadequate passages which surround it. If Tennyson closely follows Malory's Morte

Darthur XXI.3–5, his tone has little in common with Malory's. Essentially, this is a mythologizing earlier version of In Memoriam, as well as a successful attempt at a lament in the sublime mode.
battle the last, apocalyptic battle between Arthur and the traitors led by his nephew Modred

Had fallen in Lyonnesse° about their Lord,
King Arthur: then, because his wound was deep,
The bold Sir Bedivere uplifted him,
Sir Bedivere, the last of all his knights,
And bore him to a chapel nigh the field,
A broken chancel° with a broken cross,
10   That stood on a dark strait of barren land.
On one side lay the Ocean, and on one
Lay a great water, and the moon was full.

Then spake King Arthur to Sir Bedivere:
'The sequel of today unsolders all
The goodliest fellowship of famous knights
Whereof this world holds record. Such a sleep
They sleep—the men I loved. I think that we
Shall never more, at any future time,
Delight our souls with talk of knightly deeds,
20   Walking about the gardens and the halls
Of Camelot, as in the days that were.
I perish by this people which I made,—
Though Merlin sware that I should come again
To rule once more—but let what will be, be,
I am so deeply smitten through the helm
That without help I cannot last till morn.
Thou therefore take my brand Excalibur,
Which was my pride: for thou rememberest how
In those old days, one summer noon, an arm
30   Rose up from out the bosom of the lake,
Clothed in white samite,° mystic, wonderful,
Holding the sword and how I rowed across
And took it, and have worn it, like a king:
And, wheresoever I am sung or told
In aftertime, this also shall be known:
But now delay not: take Excalibur,
And fling him far into the middle mere:°
Watch what thou seest, and lightly bring me word.'

To him replied the bold Sir Bedivere:
40   'It is not meet, Sir King, to leave thee thus,
Aidless, alone, and smitten through the helm.
A little thing may harm a wounded man.
Yet I thy hest will all perform at full,
Watch what I see, and lightly° bring thee word.'

So saying, from the ruined shrine he stepped
And in the moon athwart the place of tombs,

Lyonnesse mythical country off south coast of
Cornwall and now supposedly sunk beneath the
sea
chancel sanctuary, here the entire chapel

samite heavy silk material in which gold threads
are interwoven
middle mere inland sea
lightly swiftly

Where lay the mighty bones of ancient men,
Old knights, and over them the sea-wind sang
Shrill, chill, with flakes of foam. He, stepping down
50   By zig-zag paths, and juts of pointed rock,
Came on the shining levels of the lake.

There drew he forth the brand Excalibur,
And o'er him, drawing it, the winter moon,
Brightening the skirts of a long cloud, ran forth
And sparkled keen with frost against the hilt:
For all the haft twinkled with diamond sparks,
Myriads of topaz-lights, and jacinth-work°
Of subtlest jewellery. He gazed so long
That both his eyes were dazzled, as he stood,
60   This way and that dividing the swift mind,°
In act to throw: but at the last it seemed
Better to leave Excalibur concealed
There in the many-knotted waterflags,
That whistled stiff and dry about the marge.
So strode he back slow to the wounded King.

Then spake King Arthur to Sir Bedivere:
'Hast thou performed my mission which I gave?
What is it thou hast seen? or what hast heard?'

And answer made the bold Sir Bedivere:
'I heard the ripple washing in the reeds,
And the wild water lapping on the crag.'

To whom replied King Arthur, faint and pale:
'Thou hast betrayed thy nature and thy name,
Not rendering true answer, as beseemed
Thy fealty, nor like a noble knight:
For surer sign had followed, either hand,
Or voice, or else a motion of the mere.
This is a shameful thing for men to lie.
Yet now, I charge thee, quickly go again
80   As thou art lief° and dear, and do the thing
I bad thee, watch, and lightly bring me word.'

Then went Sir Bedivere the second time
Across the ridge, and paced beside the mere,
Counting the dewy pebbles, fixed in thought;
But when he saw the wonder of the hilt,
How curiously and strangely chased,° he smote
His palms together, and he cried aloud,

'And if indeed I cast the brand away,
Surely a precious thing, one worthy note,

jacinth-work gemmed                       lief beloved
swift mind See Virgil's *Aeneid* IV.285.       chased engraved

90   Should thus be lost for ever from the earth,
Which might have pleased the eyes of many men.
What good should follow this, if this were done?
What harm, undone? deep harm to disobey,
Seeing obedience is the bond of rule.
Were it well to obey then, if a king demand
An act unprofitable, against himself?
The King is sick, and knows not what he does.
What record, or what relic of my lord
Should be to aftertime, but empty breath
100   And rumours of a doubt? but were this kept,
Stored in some treasure-house of mighty kings,
Some one might show it at a joust of arms,
Saying, "King Arthur's sword, Excalibur,
Wrought by the lonely maiden of the Lake.
Nine years she wrought it, sitting in the deeps
Upon the hidden bases of the hills."
So might some old man speak in the aftertime
To all the people, winning reverence.
But now much honour and much fame were lost.'

110   So spake he, clouded with his own conceit,°
And hid Excalibur the second time,
And so strode back slow to the wounded King.

Then spoke King Arthur, breathing heavily:
'What is it thou hast seen? or what hast heard?'

And answer made the bold Sir Bedivere:
'I heard the water lapping on the crag,
And the long ripple washing in the reeds.'

To whom replied King Arthur, much in wrath:
'Ah, miserable and unkind, untrue,
120   Unknightly, traitor-hearted! Woe is me!
Authority forgets a dying king,
Laid widowed of the power in his eye
That bowed the will. I see thee what thou art,
For thou, the latest-left of all my knights,
In whom should meet the offices of all,
Thou wouldst betray me for the precious hilt;
Either from lust of gold, or like a girl
Valuing the giddy pleasure of the eyes.
Yet, for a man may fail in duty twice,
130   And the third time may prosper, get thee hence:
But, if thou spare to fling Excalibur,
I will arise and slay thee with my hands.'

conceit notion

Then quickly rose Sir Bedivere, and ran,
And, leaping down the ridges lightly, plunged
Among the bulrush-beds, and clutched the sword,
And strongly wheeled and threw it. The great brand
Made lightnings in the splendour of the moon,
And flashing round and round, and whirled in an arch,
Shot like a streamer° of the northern morn,
140   Seen where the moving isles of winter shock
By night,° with noises of the northern sea.
So flashed and fell the brand Excalibur:
But ere he dipped the surface, rose an arm
Clothed in white samite, mystic, wonderful,
And caught him by the hilt, and brandished him
Three times, and drew him under in the mere.
And lightly went the other to the King.

Then spoke King Arthur, drawing thicker breath:
'Now see I by thine eyes that this is done.
150   Speak out: what is it thou hast heard, or seen?'

And answer made the bold Sir Bedivere:
'Sir King, I closed mine eyelids, lest the gems
Should blind my purpose, for I never saw,
Nor shall see, here or elsewhere, till I die,
Not though I live three lives of mortal men,
So great a miracle as yonder hilt.
Then with both hands I flung him, wheeling him;
But when I looked again, behold an arm,
Clothed in white samite, mystic, wonderful,
160   That caught him by the hilt, and brandished him
Three times, and drew him under in the mere.'

And answer made King Arthur, breathing hard:
'My end draws nigh; 'tis time that I were gone.
Make broad thy shoulders to receive my weight,
And bear me to the margin; yet I fear
My wound hath taken cold, and I shall die.'

So saying, from the pavement he half rose,
Slowly, with pain, reclining on his arm,
And looking wistfully with wide blue eyes
170   As in a picture. Him Sir Bedivere
Remorsefully regarded through his tears,
And would have spoken, but he found not words,
Then took with care, and kneeling on one knee,
O'er both his shoulders drew the languid hands,
And rising bore him through the place of tombs.

**streamer** aurora borealis or northern lights
**moving isles . . . night** icebergs colliding in
the darkness

But, as he walked, King Arthur panted hard,
Like one that feels a nightmare on his bed
When all the house is mute. So sighed the King,
Muttering and murmuring at his ear, 'Quick, quick!
180  I fear it is too late, and I shall die.'
But the other swiftly strode from ridge to ridge,
Clothed with his breath, and looking, as he walked,
Larger than human on the frozen hills.
He heard the deep behind him, and a cry
Before. His own thought drove him, like a goad.
Dry° clashed his harness in the icy caves
And barren chasms, and all to left and right
The bare black cliff clanged round him, as he based
His feet on juts of slippery crag that rang
190  Sharp-smitten with the dint of armèd heels—
And on a sudden, lo! the level lake,
And the long glories of the winter moon.

Then saw they how there hove a dusky barge,
Dark as a funeral scarf from stem to stern,
Beneath them; and descending they were ware
That all the decks were dense with stately forms
Black-stoled, black-hooded, like a dream—by these
Three Queens° with crowns of gold—and from them rose
A cry that shivered to the tingling stars,
200  And, as it were one voice, an agony
Of lamentation, like a wind, that shrills
All night in a waste land, where no one comes,
Or hath come, since the making of the world.

Then murmured Arthur, 'Place me in the barge,'
And to the barge they came. There those three Queens
Put forth their hands, and took the King, and wept.
But she, that rose the tallest of them all
And fairest, laid his head upon her lap,
And loosed the shattered casque, and chafed his hands,
210  And called him by his name, complaining° loud,
And dropping bitter tears against his brow
Striped with dark blood: for all his face was white
And colourless, and like the withered moon
Smote by the fresh beam of the springing east;
And all his greaves and cuisses dashed with drops°
Of onset; and the light and lustrous curls—
That made his forehead like a rising sun
High from the dais-throne—were parched with dust;

Dry harshly
Three Queens Tennyson compared them to the
Three Graces, but asserted their significance
was larger.

complaining lamenting
greaves and cuisses . . . drops his thigh- and
leg-armour, bloody from the battle

Or, clotted into points and hanging loose,
220    Mixed with the knightly growth that fringed his lips.
So like a shattered column lay the King;
Not like that Arthur who, with lance in rest,
From spur to plume a star of tournament,
Shot through the lists at Camelot, and charged
Before the eyes of ladies and of kings.

Then loudly cried the bold Sir Bedivere,
'Ah! my Lord Arthur, whither shall I go?
Where shall I hide my forehead and my eyes?
For now I see the true old times are dead,
230    When every morning brought a noble chance,
And every chance brought out a noble knight.
Such times have been not since the light that led°
The holy Elders with the gift of myrrh.
But now the whole ROUND TABLE is dissolved
Which was an image of the mighty world;
And I, the last, go forth companionless,
And the days darken round me, and the years,
Among new men, strange faces, other minds.'

And slowly answered Arthur from the barge:
240    'The old order changeth, yielding place to new,
And God fulfils Himself in many ways,
Lest one good custom should corrupt the world.
Comfort thyself: what comfort is in me?
I have lived my life, and that which I have done
May He within Himself make pure! but thou,
If thou shouldst never see my face again,
Pray for my soul. More things are wrought by prayer
Than this world dreams of. Wherefore, let thy voice
Rise like a fountain for me night and day.
250    For what are men better than sheep or goats
That nourish a blind life within the brain,
If, knowing God, they lift not hands of prayer
Both for themselves and those who call them friend?
For so the whole round earth is every way
Bound by gold chains° about the feet of God.
But now farewell. I am going a long way
With these thou seest—if indeed I go—
(For all my mind is clouded with a doubt)
To the island-valley of Avilion;°
260    Where falls not hail, or rain, or any snow,°
Nor ever wind blows loudly; but it lies

**light that led** star that guided the Three Kings
to Christ's birthplace in Bethlehem
**gold chains** See *Paradise Lost* II.1051.
**Avilion** Avalon, Celtic version of the Isles of
the Blessed

**or any snow** See Lucretius, *De Rerum Natura*
III.18, and Tennyson's poem *Lucretius*, ll. 104–
10.

Deep-meadowed, happy, fair with orchard-lawns
And bowery hollows crowned with summer sea,
Where I will heal me of my grievous wound.'

So said he, and the barge with oar and sail
Moved from the brink, like some full-breasted swan
That, fluting a wild carol ere her death,
Ruffles her pure cold plume, and takes the flood
With swarthy webs. Long stood Sir Bedivere
270 Revolving many memories, till the hull
Looked one black dot against the verge of dawn,
And on the mere the wailing died away.
1833–34                              1842

## Locksley Hall°

Comrades,° leave me here a little, while as yet 'tis early morn:
Leave me here, and when you want me, sound upon the bugle-horn.

'Tis the place, and all around it, as of old, the curlews call,
Dreary gleams° about the moorland flying over Locksley Hall;

Locksley Hall, that in the distance overlooks the sandy tracts,
And the hollow ocean-ridges roaring into cataracts.

Many a night from yonder ivied casement, ere I went to rest,
Did I look on great Orion° sloping slowly to the west.

Many a night I saw the Pleiads,° rising through the mellow shade,
10  Glitter like a swarm of fire-flies tangled in a silver braid.

Here about the beach I wandered, nourishing a youth sublime
With the fairy tales of science, and the long result of time;

When the centuries behind me like a fruitful land reposed;
When I clung to all the present for the promise that it closed:

When I dipped into the future far as human eye could see;
Saw the Vision of the world, and all the wonder that would be.—

In the spring a fuller crimson comes upon the robin's breast;
In the spring the wanton lapwing° gets himself another crest;

**Locksley Hall** This popular poem may have its origin in Tennyson's early, unhappy love for Rosa Baring, who made an arranged marriage. The 8-stress trochaic couplets effectively convey the tone of a ranting young man, who is the precursor of the morbid youth of sensibility who speaks throughout the more accomplished *Maud.*
**Comrades** There is a suggestion, here and at the poem's close, that the speaker and his friends are outward-bound soldiers.
**Dreary gleams** "the flying gleams of light across a dreary moorland" (Tennyson)
**Orion** constellation of winter sky, named for mythical hunter
**Pleiads** seven stars within constellation Taurus, named for the daughters of Atlas pursued by Orion
**lapwing** crested plover

In the spring a livelier iris° changes on the burnished dove;
20  In the spring a young man's fancy lightly turns to thoughts of love.

Then her cheek was pale and thinner than should be for one so young,
And her eyes on all my motions with a mute observance hung.

And I said, 'My cousin Amy, speak, and speak the truth to me,
Trust me, cousin, all the current of my being sets to thee.'

On her pallid cheek and forehead came a colour and a light,
As I have seen the rosy red flushing in the northern night.

And she turned—her bosom shaken with a sudden storm of sighs—
All the spirit deeply dawning in the dark of hazel eyes—

Saying, 'I have hid my feelings, fearing they should do me wrong;
30  Saying, 'Dost thou love me, cousin?' weeping, 'I have loved thee long.'

Love took up the glass of Time, and turned it in his glowing hands;
Every moment, lightly shaken, ran itself in golden sands.

Love took up the harp of Life, and smote on all the chords with might;
Smote the chord of Self, that, trembling, passed in music out of sight.

Many a morning on the moorland did we hear the copses ring,
And her whisper thronged my pulses with the fulness of the spring.

Many an evening by the waters did we watch the stately ships,
And our spirits rushed together at the touching of the lips.

O my cousin, shallow-hearted! O my Amy, mine no more!
40  O the dreary, dreary moorland! O the barren, barren shore!

Falser than all fancy fathoms,° falser than all songs have sung,
Puppet to a father's threat, and servile to a shrewish tongue!

Is it well to wish thee happy?—having known me—to decline
On a range of lower feelings and a narrower heart than mine!

Yet it shall be: thou shalt lower to his level day by day,
What is fine within thee growing coarse to sympathize with clay.

As the husband is, the wife is: thou art mated with a clown,
And the grossness of his nature will have weight to drag thee down.

He will hold thee, when his passion shall have spent its novel force,
50  Something better than his dog, a little dearer than his horse.

What is this? his eyes are heavy: think not they are glazed with wine.
Go to him: it is thy duty: kiss him: take his hand in thine.

It may be my lord is weary, that his brain is overwrought:
Soothe him with thy finer fancies, touch him with thy lighter thought.

iris  iridescent coloring on the dove's throat,          fancy fathoms  imagination realizes; i.e. Amy is
which brightens in the mating season                     falser than his imagination can realize

He will answer to the purpose, easy things to understand—
Better thou wert dead before me, though I slew thee with my hand!

Better thou and I were lying, hidden from the heart's disgrace,
Rolled in one another's arms, and silent in a last embrace.

Cursèd be the social wants that sin against the strength of youth!
60  Cursèd be the social lies that warp us from the living truth!

Cursèd be the sickly forms that err from honest Nature's rule!
Cursèd be the gold that gilds the straitened forehead of the fool!

Well—'tis well that I should bluster!—Hadst thou less unworthy proved—
Would to God—for I had loved thee more than ever wife was loved.

Am I mad, that I should cherish that which bears but bitter fruit?
I will pluck it from my bosom, though my heart be at the root.

Never, though my mortal summers to such length of years should come
As the many-wintered crow° that leads the clanging rookery home.

Where is comfort? in division of the records of the mind?
70  Can I part her from herself, and love her, as I knew her, kind?

I remember one that perished: sweetly did she speak and move:
Such a one do I remember, whom to look at was to love.

Can I think of her as dead, and love her for the love she bore?
No—she never loved me truly: love is love for evermore.

Comfort? comfort scorned of devils! this is truth the poet° sings,
That a sorrow's crown of sorrow is remembering happier things.

Drug thy memories, lest thou learn it, lest thy heart be put to proof,
In the dead unhappy night, and when the rain is on the roof.

Like a dog, he° hunts in dreams, and thou art staring at the wall,
80  Where the dying night-lamp flickers, and the shadows rise and fall.

Then a hand shall pass before thee, pointing to his drunken sleep,
To thy widowed marriage-pillows, to the tears that thou wilt weep.

Thou shalt hear the 'Never, never,' whispered by the phantom years,
And a song from out the distance in the ringing of thine ears;

And an eye shall vex thee, looking ancient kindness on thy pain.
Turn thee, turn thee on thy pillow: get thee to thy rest again.

Nay, but Nature brings thee solace; for a tender voice will cry.
'Tis a purer life than thine; a lip to drain thy trouble dry.

Baby lips will laugh me down: my latest rival brings thee rest.
90  Baby fingers, waxen touches, press me from the mother's breast.

crow the rook, reputed to live to a great age
the poet Dante; see the *Inferno* V.121, "There
is no greater grief than to remember days of
joy, when misery is at hand."
he Amy's husband

O, the child too clothes the father with a dearness not his due.
Half is thine and half is his: it will be worthy of the two.

O, I see thee old and formal, fitted to thy petty part,
With a little hoard of maxims preaching down a daughter's heart.

'They were dangerous guides the feelings—she herself was not exempt—
Truly, she herself had suffered'—Perish in thy self-contempt!

Overlive it—lower yet—be happy! wherefore should I care?
I myself must mix with action, lest I wither by despair.

What is that which I should turn to, lighting upon days like these?
100    Every door is barred with gold, and opens but to golden keys.

Every gate is thronged with suitors, all the markets overflow.
I have but an angry fancy: what is that which I should do?

I had been content to perish, falling on the foeman's ground,
When the ranks are rolled in vapour, and the winds are laid with sound.

But the jingling of the guinea helps the hurt that Honour feels,
And the nations do but murmur, snarling at each other's heels.

Can I but relive in sadness? I will turn that earlier page.
Hide me from my deep emotion, O thou wondrous Mother-Age!

Make me feel the wild pulsation that I felt before the strife,
110    When I heard my days before me, and the tumult of my life;

Yearning for the large excitement that the coming years would yield,
Eager-hearted as a boy when first he leaves his father's field,

And at night along the dusky highway near and nearer drawn,
Sees in heaven the light of London flaring like a dreary dawn;

And his spirit leaps within him to be gone before him then,
Underneath the light he looks at, in among the throngs of men:

Men, my brothers, men the workers, ever reaping something new:
That which they have done but earnest of the things that they shall do:

For I dipped into the future, far as human eye could see,
120    Saw the Vision of the world, and all the wonder that would be;

Saw the heavens fill with commerce, argosies of magic sails,°
Pilots of the purple twilight, dropping down with costly bales;

Heard the heavens fill with shouting, and there rained a ghastly dew
From the nations' airy navies grappling in the central blue;

Far along the world-wide whisper of the south-wind rushing warm,
With the standards of the peoples plunging through the thunder-storm;

Till the war-drum throbbed no longer, and the battle-flags were furled
In the Parliament of man, the Federation of the world.

**magic sails** balloons

There the common sense of most shall hold a fretful realm in awe,
130    And the kindly earth shall slumber, lapped in universal law.

So I triumphed ere my passion sweeping through me left me dry,
Left me with the palsied heart, and left me with the jaundiced eye;

Eye, to which all order festers, all things here are out of joint:
Science moves, but slowly slowly, creeping on from point to point:

Slowly comes a hungry people, as a lion creeping nigher,
Glares at one that nods and winks behind a slowly-dying fire.

Yet I doubt not through the ages one increasing purpose runs,
And the thoughts of men are widened with the process of the suns.°

What is that to him that reaps not harvest of his youthful joys,
140    Though the deep heart of existence beat for ever like a boy's?

Knowledge comes, but wisdom lingers, and I linger on the shore,
And the individual withers, and the world is more and more.

Knowledge comes, but wisdom lingers, and he bears a laden breast,
Full of sad experience, moving toward the stillness of his rest.

Hark, my merry comrades call me, sounding on the bugle-horn,
They to whom my foolish passion were a target for their scorn:

Shall it not be scorn to me to harp on such a mouldered string?
I am shamed through all my nature to have loved so slight a thing.

Weakness to be wroth with weakness! woman's pleasure, woman's pain—
150    Nature made them blinder motions° bounded in a shallower brain:

Woman is the lesser man, and all thy passions, matched with mine,
Are as moonlight unto sunlight, and as water unto wine—

Here at least, where nature sickens, nothing. Ah, for some retreat
Deep in yonder shining Orient, where my life began to beat;

Where in wild Mahratta°-battle fell my father evil-starred;—
I was left a trampled orphan, and a selfish uncle's ward.

Or to burst all links of habit—there to wander far away,
On from island unto island at the gateways of the day.

Larger constellations burning, mellow moons and happy skies,
160    Breadths of tropic shade and palms in cluster, knots of Paradise.

Never comes the trader, never floats an European flag,
Slides the bird o'er lustrous woodland, swings the trailer° from the crag;

Droops the heavy-blossomed bower, hangs the heavy-fruited tree—
Summer isles of Eden lying in dark-purple spheres of sea.

**suns** years
**motions** affective impulses
**Mahratta** tribe in central India that fought the

British repeatedly in the early 19th century
**trailer** trailing vine

There methinks would be enjoyment more than in this march of mind,°
In the steamship, in the railway, in the thoughts that shake mankind.

There the passions cramped no longer shall have scope and breathing space;
I will take some savage woman, she shall rear my dusky race.

Iron jointed, supple-sinewed, they shall dive, and they shall run,
170  Catch the wild goat by the hair, and hurl their lances in the sun;

Whistle back the parrot's call, and leap the rainbows of the brooks,
Not with blinded eyesight poring over miserable books—

Fool, again the dream, the fancy! but I *know* my words are wild,
But I count the grey barbarian lower than the Christian child.

I, to herd with narrow foreheads, vacant of our glorious gains,
Like a beast with lower pleasures, like a beast with lower pains!

Mated with a squalid savage—what to me were sun or clime?
I the heir of all the ages, in the foremost files of time—

I that rather held it better men should perish one by one,
180  Than that earth should stand at gaze like Joshua's moon° in Ajalon!

Not in vain the distance beacons.° Forward let us range,
Let the great world spin for ever down the ringing grooves° of change.

Through the shadow of the globe we sweep into the younger day:
Better fifty years of Europe than a cycle of Cathay.°

Mother-Age (for mine I knew not) help me as when life begun:
Rift the hills, and roll the waters, flash the lightnings, weigh the Sun.

O, I see the crescent promise of my spirit hath not set.
Ancient founts of inspiration well through all my fancy yet.

Howsoever these things be, a long farewell to Locksley Hall!
190  Now for me the woods may wither, now for me the roof-tree fall.

Comes a vapour from the margin, blackening over heath and holt,
Cramming all the blast before it, in its breast a thunderbolt.

Let it fall on Locksley Hall, with rain or hail, or fire or snow;
For the mighty wind arises, roaring seaward, and I go.

1842

march of mind technological progress, particularly in the 1840's
Joshua's moon Joshua 10:11–12; needing time
to complete a victory, Joshua was permitted by
God to order the sun and moon to stand still.
beacons shines like a beacon light

ringing grooves a famous mistake, made after
the poet's first ride on the steam railroad, whose
wheels he thought ran in a groove
Cathay European name for northern China, during the Middle Ages

# The Vision of Sin°

## I

I had a vision when the night was late:
A youth came riding toward a palace-gate.
He rode a horse with wings,° that would have flown,
But that his heavy rider° kept him down.
And from the palace came a child of sin,
And took him by the curls, and led him in,
Where sat a company with heated eyes,
Expecting when a fountain should arise:
As sleepy light upon their brows and lips—
10  As when the sun, a crescent of eclipse,
Dreams over lake and lawn, and isles and capes—
Suffused them, sitting, lying, languid shapes,
By heaps of gourds, and skins of wine, and piles of grapes.

## II

Then methought I heard a mellow sound,
Gathering up from all the lower ground;
Narrowing in to where they sat assembled
Low voluptuous music winding trembled,
Woven in circles: they that heard it sighed,
Panted hand-in-hand with faces pale,
20  Swung themselves, and in low tones replied;
Till the fountain spouted, showering wide
Sleet of diamond-drift and pearly hail;
Then the music touched the gates and died;
Rose again from where it seemed to fail,
Stormed in orbs of song, a growing gale;
Till thronging in and in, to where they waited,
As 'twere a hundred-throated nightingale,
The strong tempestuous treble throbbed and palpitated;
Ran into its giddiest whirl of sound,
30  Caught the sparkles, and in circles,
Purple gauzes, golden hazes, liquid mazes,
Flung the torrent rainbow round:
Then they started from their places,
Moved with violence, changed in hue,
Caught each other with wild grimaces,
Half-invisible to the view,
Wheeling with precipitate paces
To the melody, till they flew,

**The Vision of Sin** Tennyson had a special fondness for this vivid dream-vision, and summarized it: "This describes the soul of a youth who has given himself up to pleasure and Epicureanism. He at length is worn out and wrapped in the mists of satiety. Afterwards he grows into a cynical old man afflicted with the 'curse of nature,' and joining in the Feast of Death. Then we see the landscape which symbolizes God, Law and the future life." **horse with wings** Pegasus **heavy rider** the body

Hair, and eyes, and limbs, and faces,
40  Twisted hard in fierce embraces,
Like to Furies, like to Graces,°
Dashed together in blinding dew:
Till, killed with some luxurious agony,
The nerve-dissolving melody
Fluttered headlong from the sky.

### III

And then I looked up toward a mountain-tract,
That girt the region with high cliff and lawn:
I saw that every morning, far withdrawn
Beyond the darkness and the cataract,
50  God made Himself an awful rose of dawn,
Unheeded: and detaching, fold by fold,
From those still heights, and, slowly drawing near,
A vapour heavy, hueless, formless, cold,
Came floating on for many a month and year,
Unheeded: and I thought I would have spoken,
And warned that madman ere it grew too late:
But, as in dreams, I could not. Mine was broken,
When that cold vapour touched the palace gate,
And linked again. I saw within my head
60  A grey and gap-toothed man as lean as death,
Who slowly rode across a withered heath,
And lighted at a ruined inn, and said:

### IV

'Wrinkled ostler,° grim and thin!
    Here is custom come your way;
Take my brute, and lead him in,
    Stuff his ribs with mouldy hay.

'Bitter barmaid, waning fast!
    See that sheets are on my bed;
What! the flower of life is past:
70      It is long before you wed.

'Slip-shod waiter, lank and sour,
    At the Dragon° on the heath!
Let us have a quiet hour,
    Let us hob-and-nob with Death.

'I am old, but let me drink;
    Bring me spices, bring me wine;

Furies . . . Graces The three Furies (or Eu-     ostler stableman, groom
menides) were avenging goddesses, fearful to     Dragon a tavern
behold; the three Graces, in contrast, were
goddesses of beauty.

I remember, when I think,
  That my youth was half divine.

'Wine is good for shrivelled lips,
  When a blanket wraps the day,
When the rotten woodland drips,
  And the leaf is stamped in clay.

'Sit thee down, and have no shame,
  Cheek by jowl, and knee by knee:
What care I for any name?
  What for order or degree?

'Let me screw thee up a peg:
  Let me loose thy tongue with wine:
Callest thou that thing a leg?
  Which is thinnest? thine or mine?

'Thou shalt not be saved by works:
  Thou hast been a sinner too:
Ruined trunks on withered forks,
  Empty scarecrows, I and you!

'Fill the cup, and fill the can:
  Have a rouse° before the morn:
Every moment dies a man,
  Every moment one is born.

'We are men of ruined blood;
  Therefore comes it we are wise.
Fish are we that love the mud,
  Rising to no fancy-flies.

'Name and fame! to fly sublime
  Through the courts, the camps, the schools,
Is to be the ball of Time,
  Bandied by the hands of fools.

'Friendship!—to be two in one—
  Let the ranting liar pack!
Well I know, when I am gone,
  How she mouths behind my back.

'Virtue!—to be good and just—
  Every heart, when sifted well,
Is a clot of warmer dust,
  Mixed with cunning sparks of hell.

'O! we two as well can look
  Whited thought and cleanly life
As the priest, above his book
  Leering at his neighbour's wife.

**rouse** drinking bout

'Fill the cup, and fill the can:
120    Have a rouse before the morn:
Every moment dies a man,
    Every moment one is born.

'Drink, and let the parties rave:
    They are filled with idle spleen;
Rising, falling, like a wave,
    For they know not what they mean.

'He that roars for liberty
    Faster binds a tyrant's power;
And the tyrant's cruel glee
130    Forces on the freer hour.

'Fill the can, and fill the cup:
    All the windy ways of men
Are but dust that rises up,
    And is lightly laid again.

'Greet her with applausive breath,
    Freedom, gaily doth she tread;
In her right a civic wreath,
    In her left a human head.

'No, I love not what is new;
140    She is of an ancient house:
And I think we know the hue°
    Of that cap upon her brows.

'Let her go! her thirst she slakes
    Where the bloody conduit runs,
Then her sweetest meal she makes
    On the first-born of her sons.

'Drink to lofty hopes that cool°—
    Visions of a perfect State:
Drink we, last, the public fool,
150    Frantic love and frantic hate.

'Chant me now some wicked stave,°
    Till thy drooping courage rise,
And the glow-worm of the grave
    Glimmer in thy rheumy eyes.

'Fear not thou to loose thy tongue;
    Set thy hoary fancies free;
What is loathsome to the young
    Savours well to thee and me.

**hue** blood-red cap of allegorical figure of Liberty, representing the French Revolution and its ensuing terror
**hopes that cool** Tennyson may be thinking of Coleridge and Wordsworth, disillusioned partisans of the Revolution.
**stave** song

'Change, reverting to the years,
160    When thy nerves could understand
What there is in loving tears,
    And the warmth of hand in hand.

'Tell me tales of thy first love—
    April hopes, the fools of chance;
Till the graves begin to move,
    And the dead begin to dance.

'Fill the can, and fill the cup:
    All the windy ways of men
Are but dust that rises up,
170    And is lightly laid again.

'Trooping from their mouldy dens
    The chap-fallen° circle spreads:
Welcome, fellow-citizens,
    Hollow hearts and empty heads!

'You are bones, and what of that?
    Every face, however full,
Padded round with flesh and fat,
    Is but modelled on a skull.

'Death is king, and Vivat Rex!°
180    Tread a measure on the stones,
Madam—if I know your sex,
    From the fashion of your bones.

'No, I cannot praise the fire
    In your eye—nor yet your lip:
All the more do I admire
    Joints of cunning workmanship.

'Lo! God's likeness—the ground-plan—
    Neither modelled, glazed, nor framed:
Buss° me, thou rough sketch of man,
190    Far too naked to be shamed!

'Drink to Fortune, drink to Chance,
    While we keep a little breath!
Drink to heavy Ignorance!
    Hob-and-nob with brother Death!

'Thou art mazed, the night is long,
    And the longer night is near:
What! I am not all as wrong
    As a bitter jest is dear.

**chap-fallen** disconsolate          **buss** kiss
**Vivat Rex** long live the king

'Youthful hopes, by scores, to all,
200     When the locks are crisp and curled;
Unto me my maudlin gall
And my mockeries of the world.

'Fill the cup, and fill the can:
Mingle madness, mingle scorn!
Dregs of life, and lees of man:
Yet we will not die forlorn.'


v

The voice grew faint: there came a further change:
Once more uprose the mystic mountain-range:
Below were men and horses pierced with worms,
210     And slowly quickening into lower forms;
By shards and scurf of salt, and scum of dross,
Old plash of rains, and refuse patched with moss.
Then some one spake: 'Behold! it was a crime
Of sense avenged by sense that wore with time.'
Another said: 'The crime of sense became
The crime of malice, and is equal blame.'
And one: 'He had not wholly quenched his power;
A little grain of conscience made him sour.'
At last I heard a voice upon the slope
220     Cry to the summit, 'Is there any hope?'
To which an answer pealed from that high land,
But in a tongue no man could understand;
And on the glimmering limit far withdrawn
God made Himself an awful rose of dawn.°
1835–39                                    1842


## Songs from The Princess

## The Splendour Falls

The splendour falls on castle walls
And snowy summits old in story:
The long light shakes across the lakes,
And the wild cataract leaps in glory.
Blow, bugle, blow, set the wild echoes flying,
Blow, bugle; answer, echoes, dying, dying, dying.

O hark, O hear! how thin and clear,
And thinner, clearer, farther going!
O sweet and far from cliff and scar
10     The horns of Elfland° faintly blowing!
Blow, let us hear the purple glens replying:

rose of dawn See Keats's *Hyperion* I.203–12.        Elfland fairyland; the lyric's setting is Ireland

Blow, bugle; answer, echoes, dying, dying, dying.
 O love, they die in yon rich sky,
    They faint on hill or field or river:
 Our echoes roll from soul to soul,
    And grow for ever and for ever.°
Blow, bugle, blow, set the wild echoes flying,
And answer, echoes, answer, dying, dying, dying.

                                   1850


## Tears, Idle Tears°

'Tears, idle tears, I know not what they mean,
Tears from the depth of some divine despair
Rise in the heart, and gather to the eyes,
In looking on the happy Autumn-fields,
And thinking of the days that are no more.

'Fresh as the first beam glittering on a sail,
That brings our friends up from the underworld,
Sad as the last which reddens over one
That sinks with all we love below the verge;
So sad, so fresh, the days that are no more.

'Ah, sad and strange as in dark summer dawns
The earliest pipe of half-awakened birds°
To dying ears, when unto dying eyes
The casement slowly grows a glimmering square;
So sad, so strange, the days that are no more.

'Dear as remembered kisses after death,
And sweet as those by hopeless fancy feigned
On lips that are for others; deep as love,
Deep as first love, and wild with all regret;
O Death in Life, the days that are no more.

                                   1847


## Come Down, O Maid°

'Come down, O maid, from yonder mountain height:
What pleasure lives in height (the shepherd sang)
In height and cold, the splendour of the hills?
But cease to move so near the Heavens, and cease
To glide a sunbeam by the blasted Pine,

**Our echoes . . . for ever** our echoes of one
another are not illusive, but all others are
**Tears, Idle Tears** This Virgilian lyric is another lament for Hallam, written at Tintern
Abbey, and echoing the *Intimations* Ode as well
as *Tintern Abbey.*

**half-awakened birds** Compare Wallace Stevens's
*Sunday Morning* IV.1–5.
**Come Down, O Maid** title taken from Theoc-
ritus, *Idylls* XI

To sit a star upon the sparkling spire;
And come, for Love is of the valley, come,
For Love is of the valley, come thou down
And find him; by the happy threshold, he,
10    Or hand in hand with Plenty in the maize,
Or red with spirted purple of the vats,
Or foxlike in the vine°; nor cares to walk
With Death and Morning on the silver horns,°
Nor wilt thou snare him in the white ravine,
Nor find him dropped upon the firths of ice,
That huddling slant in furrow-cloven falls
To roll the torrent out of dusky doors:
But follow; let the torrent dance thee down
To find him in the valley; let the wild
20    Lean-headed Eagles yelp alone, and leave
The monstrous ledges there to slope, and spill
Their thousand wreaths of dangling water-smoke,
That like a broken purpose waste in air:
So waste not thou; but come; for all the vales
Await thee; azure pillars° of the hearth
Arise to thee; the children call, and I
Thy shepherd pipe, and sweet is every sound,
Sweeter thy voice, but every sound is sweet;
Myriads of rivulets hurrying through the lawn,
30    The moan of doves in immemorial elms,
And murmuring of innumerable bees.'°

1847

## In Memoriam A. H. H.

This is Tennyson's central poem, and as much the characteristic poem of its time as
Eliot's The Waste Land was of the 'twenties and 'thirties of this century. "It happens
now and then that a poet by some strange accident expresses the mood of his generation, at the same time that he is expressing a mood of his own which is quite remote
from that of his generation." Eliot shrewdly links In Memoriam with The Waste Land
in this remark. Both—despite all critical blindness—seem to this editor to be poems
of repressed passions, presumably of a man for a man. Eliot notes again, in Tennyson,
"emotion so deeply suppressed, even from himself, as to tend rather towards the
blackest melancholia." Neo-orthodox critics of both ages have made both poems
celebrations of the necessity for Christianity, but neither of these poems (discontinuous
sequences both), is very convincing when it argues, implicitly or explicitly, against
modern doubt and materialism. Both poems are violently personal, eccentric, High
Romantic at the core, and the quest in each is yet another version of what Yeats
called "the antithetical" and accurately traced back to Shelley's Alastor.

foxlike in the vine See Song of Solomon 2:15.          the moan . . . innumerable bees These lines
silver horns The Silberhorn is a peak in the Alps.     echo Virgil, Eclogues V.59 and IX.39–43.
azure pillars smoke going up

A. C. Bradley has given the best account of the structure of *In Memoriam.* Following Tennyson's own statement that the poem's divisions are made by the Christmas sections (XXVIII, LXXVIII, CIV), Bradley sees the poem as a three-year cycle (though written, of course, over many other years). The turning-point, in Bradley's view, is the second Christmas poem, LXXVIII, after which deeper sorrow has passed. This editor would urge attention to sections XCV and CIII, as being not only the best poems in the sequence, but as establishing the deeper enterprise of Tennyson's imagination In the poem. Section XCV is Tennyson's extreme version of Wordsworth's "Intimations" Ode, while section CIII is a variation upon the concluding love voyage of Shelley's *Epipsychidion.* Also remarkable is the apotheosis of Hallam in sections CXXVI to CXXX, a version of the transfiguration of Keats in the closing stanzas of *Adonais,* and about as Christian in its vision as Shelley's poem was.

## From In Memoriam A. H. H.

### Obiit MDCCCXXXIII

[PROLOGUE]°
Strong Son of God, immortal Love,°
　　Whom we, that have not seen thy face,
　　By faith, and faith alone, embrace,
Believing where we cannot prove;

Thine are these orbs of light and shade;°
　　Thou madest Life in man and brute;
　　Thou madest Death; and lo, thy foot
Is on the skull which thou hast made.

Thou wilt not leave us in the dust:
10　　Thou madest man, he knows not why,
　　He thinks he was not made to die;
And thou hast made him: thou art just.°

Thou seemest human and divine,
　　The highest, holiest manhood, thou:
　　Our wills are ours, we know not how;
Our wills are ours, to make them thine.

Our little systems° have their day;
　　They have their day and cease to be:
　　They are but broken lights of thee,
20　And thou, O Lord, art more than they.

**[Prologue]** written last (1849) and far more orthodox in its religious statement than anything else in the poem; thus, where Wordsworth, Shelley, and Keats are the strongest influences upon the rest of the poem, George Herbert is an overwhelming influence upon the "Prologue"
**immortal Love** See the opening stanza of George

Herbert's "Love"; Tennyson gave I John 4 as a reference.
**light and shade** earth and the planets, always half in light and half in shadow, half in life and half in death
**Thou wilt . . . thou art just** See George Herbert's "The Discharge."
**systems** of thought

We have but faith: we cannot know;
    For knowledge is of things we see;
    And yet we trust it comes from thee,
A beam in darkness: let it grow.

Let knowledge grow from more to more,
    But more of reverence in us dwell;
    That mind and soul, according well,
May make one music as before,°

But vaster. We are fools and slight;
30    We mock thee when we do not fear:
    But help thy foolish ones to bear;
Help thy vain worlds to bear thy light.°

Forgive what seemed my sin in me;
    What seemed my worth since I began;
    For merit lives from man to man,
And not from man, O Lord, to thee.

Forgive my grief for one removed,
    Thy creature, whom I found so fair.
    I trust he lives in thee, and there
40    I find him worthier to be loved.

Forgive these wild and wandering cries,
    Confusions of a wasted° youth;
    Forgive them where they fail in truth,
And in thy wisdom make me wise.

                    1849
            I

I held it truth, with him who sings°
    To one clear harp in divers tones,
    That men may rise on stepping-stones
Of their dead selves to higher things.

But who shall so forecast the years
    And find in loss a gain to match?
    Or reach a hand through time to catch
The far-off interest° of tears?

Let Love clasp Grief lest both be drowned,
10    Let darkness keep her raven gloss:
    Ah, sweeter to be drunk with loss,
To dance with death, to beat the ground,

Than that the victor Hours should scorn
    The long result of love, and boast,

---

as before before supposed increases in knowledge destroyed their harmony
thy light the light that is the knowledge of God
wasted desolated, not thrown away

him who sings Goethe, probably as interpreted
by Carlyle
interest as on a loan, the recompense for use

'Behold the man that loved and lost,
But all he was is overworn.'

## II

Old Yew, which graspest at the stones
That name the under-lying dead,
Thy fibres net the dreamless head,
Thy roots are wrapped about the bones.°

The seasons bring the flower again,
And bring the firstling to the flock;
And in the dusk of thee, the clock
Beats out the little lives of men.

O not for thee the glow, the bloom,
10Who changest not in any gale,
Nor branding summer suns avail
To touch thy thousand years of gloom:

And gazing on thee, sullen tree,
Sick for thy stubborn hardihood,
I seem to fail from out my blood
And grow incorporate into thee.

## III

O Sorrow, cruel fellowship,
O Priestess in the vaults of Death,
O sweet and bitter in a breath,
What whispers from thy lying lip?

'The stars,' she whispers, 'blindly run;
A web is woven across the sky;
From out waste places comes a cry,
And murmurs from the dying sun:°

'And all the phantom, Nature, stands—
10With all the music in her tone,
A hollow echo of my own,—
A hollow form with empty hands.'

And shall I take a thing so blind,
Embrace her as my natural good;
Or crush her, like a vice of blood,
Upon the threshold of the mind?

.   .   .

## V

I sometimes hold it half a sin
To put in words the grief I feel;

Thy roots . . . bones See Job 8:17.
dying sun Tennyson's doubt here is due to the
now long-discredited nebular hypothesis, which
asserted that the earth was a fiery discharge
from the sun (CXVIII.9).

For words, like Nature, half reveal
And half conceal the Soul within.

But, for the unquiet heart and brain,
A use in measured language lies;
The sad mechanic exercise,
Like dull narcotics, numbing pain.

In words, like weeds,° I'll wrap me o'er,
Like coarsest clothes against the cold:
But that large grief which these enfold
Is given in outline and no more.

.   .   .

VII

Dark house,° by which once more I stand
Here in the long unlovely street,
Doors, where my heart was used to beat
So quickly, waiting for a hand,

A hand that can be clasped no more—
Behold me, for I cannot sleep,
And like a guilty thing° I creep
At earliest morning to the door.

He is not here; but far away
The noise of life begins again,
And ghastly through the drizzling rain
On the bald street breaks the blank day.

.   .   .

IX

Fair ship,° that from the Italian shore
Sailest the placid ocean-plains
With my lost Arthur's loved remains,
Spread thy full wings, and waft him o'er.

So draw him home to those that mourn
In vain; a favourable speed
Ruffle thy mirrored mast, and lead
Through prosperous floods his holy urn.

All night no ruder air perplex
Thy sliding keel, till Phosphor,° bright
As our pure love, through early light
Shall glimmer on the dewy decks.

**weeds** garments
**Dark house** the Hallam house, 67 Wimpole Street, London
**guilty thing** See Wordsworth's *Intimations*

Ode IX.19 and *Hamlet* I.i.148.
**Fair ship** bringing home Hallam's corpse
**Phosphor** "star of dawn" (Tennyson)

Sphere all your lights around, above;
　　Sleep, gentle heavens, before the prow;
　　Sleep, gentle winds, as he sleeps now,
My friend, the brother of my love;

My Arthur, whom I shall not see
　　Till all my widowed race be run;
　　Dear as the mother to the son,
20　More than my brothers are to me.

　　　　　.　.　.


　　　xv
Tonight the winds begin to rise
　　And roar from yonder dropping day:
　　The last red leaf° is whirled away,
The rooks are blown about the skies;

The forest cracked, the waters curled,
　　The cattle huddled on the lea;
　　And wildly dashed on tower and tree
The sunbeam strikes along the world:

And but for fancies, which aver
10　　That all thy motions° gently pass
　　Athwart a plane of molten glass,°
I scarce could brook the strain and stir

That makes the barren branches loud;
　　And but for fear it is not so,
　　The wild unrest that lives in woe
Would dote and pore on yonder cloud

That rises upward always higher,
　　And onward drags a labouring breast,
　　And topples round the dreary west,
20　A looming bastion fringed with fire.

　　　　　.　.　.


　　　xxi
I sing to him that rests below,°
　　And, since the grasses round me wave,
　　I take the grasses of the grave,
And make them pipes whereon to blow.

The traveller hears me now and then,
　　And sometimes harshly will he speak:
　　'This fellow would make weakness weak,
And melt the waxen hearts of men.'

last red leaf See Coleridge's *Christabel*, ll. 49–
50.
motions of the ship

molton glass See Job 37:18 and Revelation 15:2.
rests below set at Clevedon, Hallam's burial
place

Another answers, 'Let him be,
10      He loves to make parade of pain,
        That with his piping he may gain
        The praise that comes to constancy.'

A third is wroth: 'Is this an hour
        For private sorrow's barren song,
        When more and more the people throng
        The chairs and thrones of civil power?°

'A time to sicken and to swoon,
        When Science reaches forth her arms
        To feel from world to world, and charms
20      Her secret from the latest moon?'°

Behold, ye speak an idle thing:
        Ye never knew the sacred dust:
        I do but sing because I must,
        And pipe but as the linnets sing:°

And one is glad; her note is gay,
        For now her little ones have ranged;
        And one is sad: her note is changed,
        Because her brood is stolen away.

                    .    .    .


              XXIV
And was the day of my delight
        As pure and perfect as I say?
        The very source and fount of Day
Is dashed with wandering isles of night.°

If all was good and fair we met,
        This earth had been the Paradise
        It never looked to human eyes
Since our first Sun arose and set.

And is it that the haze of grief
10      Makes former gladness loom so great?
        The lowness of the present state,
That sets the past in this relief?

Or that the past will always win
        A glory from its being far;
        And orb into the perfect star
We saw not, when we moved therein?°

                    .    .    .

the people . . . civil power the Chartist Movement and, ultimately, the French Revolution
latest moon perhaps the discovery of Neptune
and its moon in 1846
linnets sing See the "Harper's Song" in Goethe's

*Wilhelm Meister's Travels* II, XI.
isles of night sun-spots
Or that the past . . . moved therein the imperfections seen up close vanish in the distance

**XXVII**

I envy not in any moods
  The captive void of noble rage,
  The linnet born within the cage,
That never knew the summer woods:

I envy not the beast that takes
  His license in the field of time,
  Unfettered by the sense of crime,
To whom a conscience never wakes;

Nor, what may count itself as blest,
10    The heart that never plighted troth
  But stagnates in the weeds of sloth;
Nor any want-begotten rest.

I hold it true, whate'er befall;
  I feel it, when I sorrow most;
  'Tis better to have loved and lost
Than never to have loved at all.

**XXVIII°**

The time draws near the birth of Christ:
  The moon is hid; the night is still;
  The Christmas bells from hill to hill
Answer each other in the mist.

Four voices of four hamlets round,
  From far and near, on mead and moor,
  Swell out and fail, as if a door
Were shut between me and the sound:

Each voice four° changes on the wind,
10    That now dilate, and now decrease,
  Peace and goodwill, goodwill and peace,
Peace and goodwill, to all mankind.

This year I slept and woke with pain,
  I almost wished no more to wake,
  And that my hold on life would break
Before I heard those bells again:

But they my troubled spirit rule,
  For they controlled me when a boy;
  They bring me sorrow touched with joy,
20    The merry merry bells of Yule.

·   ·   ·

XXVIII This begins the poem's second move-    Each voice four Each church has four bells.
ment, and was one of the first sections written.

### xxx

With trembling fingers did we weave
  The holly round the Christmas hearth;
  A rainy cloud possessed the earth,
And sadly fell our Christmas-eve.

At our old pastimes in the hall
  We gambolled, making vain pretence
  Of gladness, with an awful sense
Of one mute Shadow° watching all.

We paused: the winds were in the beech:
10  We heard them sweep the winter land;
  And in a circle hand-in-hand
Sat silent, looking each at each.

Then echo-like our voices rang;
  We sung, though every eye was dim,
  A merry song we sang with him
Last year: impetuously we sang:

We ceased: a gentler feeling crept
  Upon us: surely rest is meet:
  'They rest,' we said, 'their sleep is sweet,'
20  And silence followed, and we wept.

Our voices took a higher range;
  Once more we sang: 'They do not die
  Nor lose their mortal sympathy,
Nor change to us, although they change;

'Rapt from the fickle and the frail
  With gathered power, yet the same,°
  Pierces the keen seraphic flame
From orb to orb, from veil to veil.'

Rise, happy morn, rise, holy morn,
30  Draw forth the cheerful day from night:
  O Father, touch the east, and light
The light that shone when Hope was born.°

### xxxi

When Lazarus left his charnel-cave,°
  And home to Mary's house returned,
  Was this demanded—if he yearned
To hear her weeping by his grave?

'Where wert thou, brother, those four days?'
  There lives no record of reply,

mute **Shadow** Hallam
**yet the same** the soul survives unchanged
**Hope was born** overtly a reference to the birth

of Christ, but the stanza derives from *Adonais*,
particularly its final lines
**charnel-cave** See John 11:32–44.

Which telling what it is to die
Had surely added praise to praise.

From every house the neighbours met,
10    The streets were filled with joyful sound,
A solemn gladness even crowned
The purple brows of Olivet.°

Behold a man raised up by Christ!
The rest remaineth unrevealed;
He told it not; or something sealed
The lips of that Evangelist.°

. . .

#### XXXIV

My own dim life should teach me this,
That life shall live for evermore,
Else earth is darkness at the core,
And dust and ashes all that is;

This round of green, this orb of flame,
Fantastic beauty; such as lurks
In some wild Poet, when he works
Without a conscience or an aim.°

What then were God to such as I?
10    'Twere hardly worth my while to choose
Of things all mortal, or to use
A little patience ere I die;

'Twere best at once to sink to peace,
Like birds the charming serpent draws,
To drop head-foremost in the jaws
Of vacant darkness and to cease.

#### XXXV

Yet if some voice that man could trust
Should murmur from the narrow house,
'The cheeks drop in; the body bows;
Man dies: nor is there hope in dust:'

Might I not say? 'Yet even here,
But for one hour, O Love, I strive
To keep so sweet a thing alive:'
But I should turn mine ears and hear

The moanings of the homeless sea,
10    The sound of streams that swift or slow

Olivet high hill near Jerusalem
Evangelist St. John, who alone tells the story
(John 11:1–45)
when he works . . . or an aim Yet Hallam had
countenanced this, almost urged it, and certainly
the poet in Tennyson had felt the temptation;
the reference may be to Thomas Lovell Beddoes.

Draw down Aeonian hills,° and sow
The dust of continents to be;

And Love would answer with a sigh,
'The sound of that forgetful shore°
Will change my sweetness more and more,
Half-dead to know that I shall die.'

O me, what profits it to put
An idle case? If Death were seen
At first as Death, Love had not been,
20    Or been in narrowest working shut,

Mere fellowship of sluggish moods,
Or in his coarsest Satyr-shape
Had bruised the herb and crushed the grape,
And basked and battened° in the woods.


XXXVI

Though truths in manhood darkly join,
Deep-seated in our mystic frame,
We yield all blessing to the name
Of Him that made them current coin;

For Wisdom dealt with mortal powers,
Where truth in closest words shall fail,
When truth embodied in a tale
Shall enter in at lowly doors.

And so the Word° had breath, and wrought
10    With human hands the creed of creeds
In loveliness of perfect deeds,
More strong than all poetic thought;

Which he may read that binds the sheaf,
Or builds the house, or digs the grave,
And those wild eyes° that watch the wave
In roarings round the coral reef.


XXXVII

Urania° speaks with darkened brow:
'Thou pratest here where thou art least;
This faith has many a purer priest,
And many an abler voice than thou.

'Go down beside thy native rill,
On thy Parnassus set thy feet,

**Aeonian hills** hills that have lasted whole eons or geological ages
**forgetful shore** shore of the river Lethe
**basked and battened** fed grossly like a beast
**the Word** Tennyson said that he meant the Logos (Christ, the divine Word) of St. John.

**wild eyes** According to Tennyson, this meant the Pacific Islanders, then undergoing the unhappy process of being introduced to Christian civilization.
**Urania** Muse of heavenly poetry, in Milton's invocation to Book VII, *Paradise Lost*

And hear thy laurel whisper sweet
About the ledges of the hill.'

And my Melpomene° replies,
10    A touch of shame upon her cheek:
'I am not worthy even to speak
Of thy prevailing mysteries;

'For I am but an earthly Muse,
And owning but a little art
To lull with song an aching heart,
And render human love his dues;

'But brooding on the dear one dead,
And all he said of things divine,
(And dear to me as sacred wine
20    To dying lips is all he said),

'I murmured, as I came along,
Of comfort clasped in truth revealed;
And loitered in the master's field,
And darkened sanctities with song.'

.    .    .

XLIX
From art, from nature, from the schools,°
Let random influences glance,
Like light in many a shivered lance
That breaks about the dappled pools:

The lightest wave of thought shall lisp,
The fancy's tenderest eddy wreathe,
The slightest air of song shall breathe
To make the sullen surface crisp.°

And look thy look, and go thy way,
10    But blame not thou the winds that make
The seeming-wanton ripple break,
The tender-pencilled shadow play.

Beneath all fancied hopes and fears
Ay me, the sorrow deepens down,
Whose muffled motions blindly drown
The bases of my life in tears.

L
Be near me when my light is low,
When the blood creeps, and the nerves prick
And tingle; and the heart is sick,
And all the wheels of Being slow.

Melpomene  ordinarily  Muse  of  tragedy,  here     the schools of philosophy
evidently of elegy                                  crisp ripple

Be near me when the sensuous frame
  Is racked with pangs that conquer trust;
    And Time, a maniac scattering dust,
And Life, a Fury slinging flame.

Be near me when my faith is dry,
10    And men the flies of latter spring,
      That lay their eggs, and sting and sing°
And weave their petty cells and die.

Be near me when I fade away,
  To point the term of human strife,
    And on the low dark verge of life
The twilight of eternal day.

LI

Do we indeed desire the dead
  Should still be near us at our side?
    Is there no baseness we would hide?
No inner vileness that we dread?

Shall he for whose applause I strove,
  I had such reverence for his blame,
    See with clear eye some hidden shame
And I be lessened in his love?

I wrong the grave with fears untrue:
10    Shall love be blamed for want of faith?
      There must be wisdom with great Death:
The dead shall look me through and through.

Be near us when we climb or fall:
  Ye watch, like God, the rolling hours
    With larger other eyes than ours,
To make allowance for us all.

. . .

LIV

Oh yet we trust that somehow good
  Will be the final goal of ill,
    To pangs of nature, sins of will,
Defects of doubt, and taints of blood;

That nothing walks with aimless feet;
  That not one life shall be destroyed,
    Or cast as rubbish to the void,
When God hath made the pile complete;

That not a worm is cloven in vain;
10    That not a moth with vain desire

sting and sing See Pope's *Epistle to Dr. Arbuthnot*, ll. 309–10.

Is shrivelled in a fruitless fire,
Or but subserves another's gain.

Behold, we know not anything;
  I can but trust that good shall fall
  At last—far off°—at last, to all,
And every winter change to spring.

So runs my dream: but what am I?
  An infant crying in the night:
  An infant crying for the light:
20 And with no language but a cry.

LV

The wish, that of the living whole
  No life may fail beyond the grave,
  Derives it not from what we have
The likest God within the soul?

Are God and Nature then at strife,
  That Nature lends such evil dreams?
  So careful of the type she seems,
So careless of the single life;°

That I, considering everywhere
10  Her secret meaning in her deeds,
  And finding that of fifty seeds
She often brings but one to bear,

I falter where I firmly trod,
  And falling with my weight of cares
  Upon the great world's altar-stairs
That slope through darkness up to God,

I stretch lame hands of faith, and grope,
  And gather dust and chaff, and call
  To what I feel is Lord of all,
20 And faintly trust the larger hope.°

LVI

'So careful of the type?' but no.
  From scarpèd° cliff and quarried stone
  She cries, 'A thousand types are gone:
I care for nothing, all shall go.

---

**far off** See the next to the last line of the poem.
**single life** nature is not interested in any kind
of individual immortality. This and the next
section precede Darwin's *Origin of Species* by
nine years, and probably derive from Charles
Lyell's books on geology of the 1830's.
**larger hope** the hope "that the whole human

race would through, perhaps, ages of suffering,
be at length purified and saved" (Tennyson)
**scarpèd** cut away vertically, exposing strata,
which revealed fossils of extinct species, thus
demonstrating the so-called "supersession of
types"

'Thou makest thine appeal to me:
    I bring to life, I bring to death:
    The spirit does but mean the breath:
I know no more.' And he, shall he,

Man, her last work, who seemed so fair,
10      Such splendid purpose in his eyes,
    Who rolled the psalm to wintry skies,
Who built him fanes° of fruitless prayer,

Who trusted God was love indeed
    And love Creation's final law—
    Though Nature, red in tooth and claw
With ravine, shrieked against his creed—

Who loved, who suffered countless ills,
    Who battled for the True, the Just,
    Be blown about the desert dust,
20  Or sealed within the iron hills?°

No more? A monster then, a dream,
    A discord. Dragons of the prime,°
    That tare° each other in their slime,
Were mellow music matched with him.

O life as futile, then, as frail!
    O for thy voice to soothe and bless!
    What hope of answer, or redress?
Behind the veil, behind the veil.

·   ·   ·


          LXVII
When on my bed the moonlight falls,
    I know that in thy place of rest°
    By that broad water of the west,
There comes a glory on the walls;

Thy marble bright in dark appears,
    As slowly steals a silver flame
    Along the letters of thy name,
And o'er the number of thy years.

The mystic glory swims away;
10      From off my bed the moonlight dies;
    And closing eaves of wearied eyes
I sleep till dusk is dipped in grey:

And then I know the mist is drawn
    A lucid veil from coast to coast,

fanes temples                                    tare tore
iron hills like fossils                          place of rest Hallam's grave
Dragons of the prime prehistoric monsters

And in the dark church like a ghost
Thy tablet glimmers to the dawn.

. . .

LXXVII

What hope is here for modern rhyme
    To him, who turns a musing eye
    On songs, and deeds, and lives, that lie
Foreshortened in the tract of time?

These mortal lullabies of pain
    May bind a book, may line a box,
    May serve to curl a maiden's locks;
Or when a thousand moons shall wane

A man upon a stall may find,
10    And, passing, turn the page that tells
    A grief, then changed to something else,
Sung by a long-forgotten mind.

But what of that? My darkened ways
    Shall ring with music all the same;
    To breathe my loss is more than fame,
To utter love more sweet than praise.

LXXVIII

Again at Christmas° did we weave
    The holly round the Christmas hearth;
    The silent snow possessed the earth,
And calmly fell our Christmas eve:

The yule-clog° sparkled keen with frost,
    No wing of wind the region swept,
    But over all things brooding slept
The quiet sense of something lost.

As in the winters left behind,
10    Again our ancient games had place,
    The mimic picture's breathing grace,°
And dance and song and hoodman-blind.°

Who showed a token of distress?
    No single tear, no mark of pain:
    O sorrow, then can sorrow wane?
O grief, can grief be changed to less?

O last regret, regret can die!
    No—mixed with all this mystic frame,

Her deep relations are the same,
20    But with long use her tears are dry.

### LXXIX

'More than my brothers are to me,'—
Let this not vex thee, noble heart!°
I know thee of what force thou art
To hold the costliest love in fee.°

But thou and I are one in kind,
As moulded like in Nature's mint;
And hill and wood and field did print
The same sweet forms in either mind.

For us the same cold streamlet curled
10    Through all his eddying coves; the same
All winds that roam the twilight came
In whispers of the beauteous world.

At one dear knee we proffered vows,
One lesson from one book we learned,
Ere childhood's flaxen ringlet turned
To black and brown on kindred brows.

And so my wealth resembles thine,
But he was rich where I was poor,
And he supplied my want the more
20    As his unlikeness fitted mine.

.    .    .

### XCV°

By night we lingered on the lawn,
For underfoot the herb was dry;
And genial warmth; and o'er the sky
The silvery haze of summer drawn;

And calm that let the tapers burn
Unwavering: not a cricket chirred:
The brook alone far-off was heard,
And on the board the fluttering urn:°

And bats went round in fragrant skies,
10    And wheeled or lit the filmy shapes°
That haunt the dusk, with ermine capes
And woolly breasts and beaded eyes;

**noble heart** Tennyson's brother Charles, also a poet
**in fee** absolute possession
**XCV** This and CIII are surely the two greatest sections of the poem, but although that is a Shelleyan and Promethean dream-vision, this section of epiphany and near-trance is deeply Wordsworthian, the renewal of "a spot of time."
**urn** tea-urn, fluttering because of the flame under it
**filmy shapes** ermine moths

While now we sang old songs that pealed
   From knoll to knoll, where, couched at ease,
   The white kine glimmered, and the trees
Laid their dark arms about the field.

But when those others, one by one,
   Withdrew themselves from me and night,
   And in the house light after light
20  Went out, and I was all alone,

A hunger seized my heart; I read
   Of that glad year° which once had been,
   In those fallen leaves which kept their green,
The noble letters of the dead:

And strangely on the silence broke
   The silent-speaking words, and strange
   Was love's dumb cry defying change
To test his worth; and strangely spoke

The faith, the vigour, bold to dwell
30   On doubts that drive the coward back,
   And keen through wordy snares to track
Suggestion to her inmost cell.

So word by word, and line by line,°
   The dead man touched me from the past,
   And all at once it seemed at last
The living soul was flashed on mine,

And mine in this was wound, and whirled
   About empyreal heights of thought,
   And came on that which is, and caught
40  The deep pulsations of the world,

Aeonian music° measuring out
   The steps of Time—the shocks of Chance—
   The blows of Death. At length my trance
Was cancelled, stricken through with doubt.

Vague words! but ah, how hard to frame
   In matter-moulded forms of speech,
   Or even for intellect to reach
Through memory that which I became:

Till now the doubtful dusk revealed
50   The knolls once more where, couched at ease,
   The white kine glimmered, and the trees
Laid their dark arms about the field:

---

**glad year** probably a particular year of their love, but unidentified
**line by line** See Isaiah 28: 13.

**Aeonian music** music transcending space and time, by returning to a deeper space, and eternal time

And sucked from out the distant gloom
  A breeze began to tremble o'er
  The large leaves of the sycamore,
And fluctuate all the still perfume,

And gathering freshlier overhead,
  Rocked the full-foliaged elms, and swung
  The heavy-folded rose, and flung
60  The lilies to and fro, and said

'The dawn, the dawn,' and died away;
  And East and West, without a breath,
  Mixed their dim lights, like life and death,
To broaden into boundless day.°

. . .

CIII

On that last night before we went
  From out the doors where I was bred,
  I dreamed a vision of the dead,°
Which left my after-morn content.

Methought I dwelt within a hall,
  And maidens° with me: distant hills
  From hidden summits° fed with rills
A river sliding by the wall.

The hall with harp and carol rang.
10  They sang of what is wise and good
  And graceful. In the centre stood
A statue veiled,° to which they sang;

And which, though veiled, was known to me,
  The shape of him I loved, and love
  For ever: then flew in a dove
And brought a summons from the sea:

And when they learnt that I must go
  They wept and wailed, but led the way
  To where a little shallop° lay
20  At anchor in the flood below;

And on by many a level mead,
  And shadowing bluff that made the banks,

---

**The dawn . . . boundless day** the wind of inspiration rises, announcing the dawn, and then dies away; in that moment of stillness, gazing at the West, the direction of death, Tennyson sees the reflection of the sunrise in the East **vision of the dead** the other climax of the poem, wholly visionary and with no moral sanction, the ultimate (and wholly revealing) wish-fulfillment in the poem **maidens** the Muses

**summits** the divine **statue veiled** Hallam, about to be resurrected, like Hermione in Shakespeare's *The Winter's Tale* **shallop** boat. The symbolism of the boat of death and resurrection goes back to Shelley's *Alastor*, and figures in *The Lady of Shalott, Monte d'Arthur*, and "Crossing the Bar"; a modern parallel is Lawrence's "Ship of Death."

We glided winding under ranks
Of iris, and the golden reed;

And still as vaster grew the shore
And rolled the floods in grander space,
The maidens gathered strength and grace
And presence, lordlier than before;

And I myself, who sat apart
30    And watched them, waxed in every limb;
I felt the thews of Anakim,°
The pulses of a Titan's heart;°

As one would sing the death of war,
And one would chant the history
Of that great race, which is to be,°
And one the shaping of a star;

Until the forward-creeping tides
Began to foam, and we to draw
From deep to deep, to where we saw
40    A great ship lift her shining sides.

The man we loved was there on deck,
But thrice as large as man he bent
To greet us. Up the side I went,
And fell in silence on his neck:

Whereat those maidens with one mind
Bewailed their lot; I did them wrong:
'We served thee here,' they said, 'so long,
And wilt thou leave us now behind?'°

So rapt I was, they could not win
50    An answer from my lips, but he
Replying, 'Enter likewise ye
And go with us': they entered in.

And while the wind began to sweep
A music out of sheet and shroud,
We steered her toward a crimson cloud
That landlike slept along the deep.

CIV

The time draws near the birth of Christ;°
The moon is hid, the night is still;
A single church below the hill
Is pealing, folded in the mist.

Anakim the giants of Deuteronomy 2:10 and Numbers 13:33; "thews" are sinews or muscles
Titan's heart Prometheus, whose heart was tortured, but then redeemed
is to be in another evolutionary turn

And wilt . . . behind the Muses' fear of being abandoned, as Hallam so clearly is Tennyson's Muse
birth of Christ third Christmas since the death, and start of the poem's last movement

A single peal of bells below,
    That wakens at this hour of rest
    A single murmur in the breast,
That these are not the bells I know.

Like strangers' voices here they sound,
10      In lands where not a memory strays,
    Nor landmark breathes of other days,
But all is new unhallowed ground.

CV

Tonight ungathered let us leave
    This laurel, let this holly stand:
    We live within the stranger's land,
And strangely falls our Christmas-eve.

Our father's dust is left alone
    And silent under other snows:°
    There in due time the woodbine blows,
The violet comes, but we are gone.

No more shall wayward grief abuse
10      The genial hour with mask and mime;
    For change of place, like growth of time,
Has broke the bond of dying use.

Let cares that petty shadows cast,
    By which our lives are chiefly proved,
    A little spare the night I loved,
And hold it solemn to the past.

But let no footstep beat the floor,
    Nor bowl of wassail° mantle warm;
    For who would keep an ancient form
20  Through which the spirit breathes no more?

Be neither song, nor game, nor feast;
    Nor harp be touched, nor flute be blown;
    No dance, no motion, save alone
What lightens in the lucid east

Of rising worlds° by yonder wood.
    Long sleeps the summer in the seed;
    Run out your measured arcs, and lead
The closing cycle rich in good.

CVI

Ring out, wild bells, to the wild sky,
    The flying cloud, the frosty light:

other snows The poet moved to Epping Forest in 1837; his father was buried in Somersby, their former home, in 1831.

wassail spiced wine causing the face to glow
rising worlds rising planets

The year is dying in the night;
Ring out, wild bells, and let him die.

Ring out the old, ring in the new,
Ring, happy bells, across the snow:
The year is going, let him go;
Ring out the false, ring in the true.

Ring out the grief that saps the mind,
10      For those that here we see no more;
Ring out the feud of rich and poor,
Ring in redress to all mankind.

Ring out a slowly dying cause,
And ancient forms of party strife;
Ring in the nobler modes of life,
With sweeter manners, purer laws.

Ring out the want, the care, the sin,
The faithless coldness of the times;
Ring out, ring out my mournful rhymes,
20      But ring the fuller minstrel in.

Ring out false pride in place and blood,
The civic slander and the spite;
Ring in the love of truth and right,
Ring in the common love of good.

Ring out old shapes of foul disease;
Ring out the narrowing lust of gold;
Ring out the thousand wars of old,
Ring in the thousand years of peace.°

Ring in the valiant man and free,
30      The larger heart, the kindlier hand;
Ring out the darkness of the land,
Ring in the Christ that is to be.°

.   .   .

CXVIII
Contemplate all this work of Time,°
The giant labouring in his youth;
Nor dream of human love and truth,
As dying Nature's earth and lime;°

But trust that those we call the dead
Are breathers of an ampler day°

thousand years of peace (ll. 27–28) See Revelation 20:2–4.
Christ that is to be a vision of a broader, future
Christianity, free of sects and creeds
work of Time influenced by Lyell again

Nor dream . . . earth and lime what is valuable in us is not perishable
ampler day See Virgil, Aeneid VI.640, where
the phrase is "largior aether."

For ever nobler ends. They say,°
The solid earth whereon we tread

In tracts of fluent heat° began,
10    And grew to seeming-random forms,
The seeming prey of cyclic storms,°
Till at the last arose the man;

Who throve and branched from clime to clime,
The herald of a higher race,
And of himself in higher place,
If so he type° this work of time

Within himself, from more to more;
Or, crowned with attributes of woe
Like glories, move his course, and show
20    That life is not as idle ore,

But iron dug from central gloom,
And heated hot with burning fears,
And dipped in baths of hissing tears,
And battered with the shocks of doom

To shape and use. Arise and fly
The reeling Faun,° the sensual feast;
Move upward, working out the beast,
And let the ape and tiger die.°

.    .    .

CXX

I trust I have not wasted breath:
I think we are not wholly brain,
Magnetic mockeries;° not in vain,
Like Paul with beasts, I fought with Death;°

Not only cunning casts in clay:
Let Science prove we are, and then
What matters Science unto men,°
At least to me? I would not stay.

Let him, the wiser man who springs
10    Hereafter, up from childhood shape
His action like the greater ape,
But I was *born* to other things.

.    .    .

They say Lyell and other geologists
fluent heat the nebular hypothesis of Laplace
that the earth is a fiery discharge from the sun
cyclic storms disasters that will come again, as
they came before
type emulate; thus man's growth shows all
growth in time
reeling Faun half-man, half-goat, drunken and
lustful
ape and tiger die This does not deny our evolutionary heritage, but insists that we must
transcend it.
Magnetic mockeries as though our brains were
electromagnetic mechanisms
fought with Death See I Corinthians 15:32,
where St. Paul says: "If after the manner of
men I have fought with beasts at Ephesus, what
advantageth it me, if the dead rise not?"
What . . . unto men if we are mechanisms

CXXIII
There rolls the deep where grew the tree.
　O earth, what changes° hast thou seen!
　There where the long street roars, hath been
The stillness of the central sea.

The hills are shadows, and they flow
　From form to form, and nothing stands;
　They melt like mist, the solid lands,
Like clouds they shape themselves and go.

But in my spirit will I dwell,
10　And dream my dream, and hold it true;
　For though my lips may breathe adieu,
I cannot think the thing farewell.

CXXIV
That which we dare invoke to bless;
　Our dearest faith; our ghastliest doubt;
　He, They, One, All; within, without;
The Power in darkness whom we guess;°

I found Him not in world or sun,°
　Or eagle's wing, or insect's eye;
　Nor through the questions men may try,
The petty cobwebs we have spun:

If e'er when faith had fallen asleep,
10　I heard a voice 'believe no more'
　And heard an ever-breaking shore
That tumbled in the Godless deep;

A warmth within the breast would melt
　The freezing reason's colder part,
　And like a man in wrath the heart
Stood up and answered 'I have felt.'

No, like a child in doubt and fear:
　But that blind clamour made me wise;
　Then was I as a child that cries,
20　But, crying, knows his father near;

And what I am beheld again
　What is, and no man understands;
　And out of darkness came the hands
That reach through nature, moulding men.

． ． ．

---

**changes** Geology demonstrates that oceans replace continents and continents oceans, or so
Tennyson thought.
**Our dearest faith . . . whom we guess** God,
however expressed, is found equally by our faith
or our doubt.
**world or sun** God may be present in nature, but
Tennyson did not find him there.

CXXVII

And all is well, though faith and form
  Be sundered in the night of fear;
  Well roars the storm to those that hear
A deeper voice across the storm,

Proclaiming social truth shall spread,
  And justice, even though thrice again°
  The red fool-fury of the Seine
Should pile her barricades with dead.

But ill for him that wears a crown,
10  And him, the lazar, in his rags:
  They tremble, the sustaining crags;
The spires of ice are toppled down,

And molten up, and roar in flood;
  The fortress crashes from on high,
  The brute earth lightens to the sky,
And the great Aeon° sinks in blood,

And compassed by the fires of Hell;
  While thou, dear spirit, happy star,
  O'erlook'st the tumult from afar,
20  And smilest, knowing all is well.

                . . .


CXXIX

Dear friend, far off, my lost desire,
  So far, so near in woe and weal;
  O loved the most, when most I feel
There is a lower and a higher;

Known and unknown; human, divine;
  Sweet human hand and lips and eye;
  Dear heavenly friend that canst not die,
Mine, mine, for ever, ever mine;

Strange friend, past, present, and to be;
10  Loved deeplier, darklier understood;
  Behold, I dream a dream of good,
And mingle all the world with thee.


CXXX

Thy voice is on the rolling air;
  I hear thee where the waters run;
  Thou standest in the rising sun,
And in the setting thou art fair.

---

thrice again probably a reference to the three-
day revolution of July 1830 which overthrew

Charles X, last of the French Bourbon monarchs
Aeon huge period of time

What art thou then? I cannot guess;
But though I seem in star and flower
To feel thee some diffusive power,
I do not therefore love thee less:

My love involves the love before;
10   My love is vaster passion now;
Though mixed with God and Nature thou,
I seem to love thee more and more.

Far off thou art, but ever nigh;
I have thee still, and I rejoice;
I prosper, circled with thy voice;
I shall not lose thee though I die.

CXXXI

O living will° that shalt endure
When all that seems shall suffer shock,
Rise in the spiritual rock,°
Flow through our deeds and make them pure,

That we may lift from out of dust
A voice as unto him that hears,
A cry above the conquered years
To one that with us works, and trust,

With faith that comes of self-control,
10   The truths that never can be proved
Until we close with all we loved,
And all we flow from, soul in soul.

[EPILOGUE]°
O true and tried, so well and long,
Demand not thou a marriage lay;
In that it is thy marriage day
Is music more than any song.

.  .  .
And touch with shade the bridal doors,
With tender gloom the roof, the wall;
And breaking let the splendour fall
120   To spangle all the happy shores

By which they rest, and ocean sounds,
And, star and system rolling past,
A soul shall draw from out the vast
And strike his being into bounds,

**will** Tennyson said he meant free will.
**spiritual rock** See I Corinthians 10:4.

[**Epilogue**] This is a marriage song for one of
the poet's sisters.

And, moved through life of lower phase,
　　Result in man, be born and think,
　　And act and love, a closer link
　　Betwixt us and the crowning race

Of those that, eye to eye, shall look
130　　On knowledge; under whose command
　　Is Earth and Earth's, and in their hand
　　Is Nature like an open book;

No longer half-akin to brute,
　　For all we thought and loved and did,
　　And hoped, and suffered, is but seed
　　Of what in them is flower and fruit;

Whereof the man,° that with me trod
　　This planet, was a noble type
　　Appearing ere the times were ripe,
140　　That friend of mine who lives in God,

That God, which ever lives and loves,
　　One God, one law, one element,
　　And one far-off divine event,
　　To which the whole creation moves.
1833–50　　　　　　　　　　1850

# Maud

*Maud*, published during the Crimean war against Russia, which its final section (printed here) absurdly glorifies, was subtitled "A Monodrama" because all of it is acted out by only one speaker, a young man of intensely morbid, indeed paranoid, sensibility. The nameless young man is a kind of parody of Tennyson himself, and so compensates for his monomania by the fascination of his perceptions and the continuous eloquence of his language. He is a stunted Byronic figure, and the poem is more a *Manfred*-in-little than the "little *Hamlet*" Tennyson liked to think it.

　　The direct stimulus for *Maud* seems to have been the challenge (illusory) of the "Spasmodic" poets, Byronic revivalists of the 1850's, particularly Alexander Smith's *A Life Drama* and Sydney Dobell's *Balder*. There is not enough genuine story in *Maud* to bear lengthy summary. The four selections given below convey, in turn: the height of the young man's passion for Maud, his grief at having lost her, his consequent madness, and his return to sanity and proportion as he goes off virtuously to slaughter Russians.

**the man** Hallam raised to the Divine, as a
Newer Adam than Christ

# Maud: A Monodrama
## From *Part I*

### XXII

#### I

<sup></sup>

850 Come into the garden, Maud,
　　For the black bat, night, has flown,
Come into the garden, Maud,
　　I am here at the gate alone;
And the woodbine spices are wafted abroad,
　　And the musk of the rose is blown.

#### II

For a breeze of morning moves,
　　And the planet of Love° is on high,
Beginning to faint in the light that she loves
　　On a bed of daffodil sky,
860 To faint in the light of the sun she loves,
　　To faint in his light, and to die.

#### III

All night have the roses heard
　　The flute, violin, bassoon;
All night has the casement jessamine stirred
　　To the dancers dancing in tune;
Till a silence fell with the waking bird,
　　And a hush with the setting moon.

#### IV

I said to the lily, 'There is but one
　　With whom she has heart to be gay.
870 When will the dancers leave her alone?
　　She is weary of dance and play.'
Now half to the setting moon are gone,
　　And half to the rising day;
Low on the sand and loud on the stone
　　The last wheel echoes away.

#### V

I said to the rose, 'The brief night goes
　　In babble and revel and wine.
O young lord-lover, what sighs are those,
　　For one that will never be thine?
880 But mine, but mine,' so I swore to the rose,
　　'For ever and ever, mine.'

**planet of Love** Venus, the Morning Star

VI

And the soul of the rose went into my blood,
    As the music clashed in the hall;
And long by the garden lake I stood,
    For I heard your rivulet fall
From the lake to the meadow and on to the wood,
    Our wood, that is dearer than all;

VII

From the meadow your walks have left so sweet
    That whenever a March-wind sighs
890    He sets the jewel-print of your feet
    In violets blue as your eyes,
To the woody hollows in which we meet
    And the valleys of Paradise.

VIII

The slender acacia would not shake
    One long milk-bloom on the tree;
The white lake-blossom fell into the lake
    As the pimpernel° dozed on the lea;
But the rose was awake all night for your sake,
    Knowing your promise to me;
900    The lilies and roses were all awake,
    They sighed for the dawn and thee.

IX

Queen rose of the rosebud garden of girls,
    Come hither, the dances are done,
In gloss of satin and glimmer of pearls,
    Queen lily and rose in one;
Shine out, little head, sunning over with curls,
    To the flowers, and be their sun.

X

There has fallen a splendid tear
    From the passion-flower at the gate.
910    She is coming, my dove, my dear;
    She is coming, my life, my fate;
The red rose cries, 'She is near, she is near;'
    And the white rose weeps, 'She is late;'
The larkspur listens, 'I hear, I hear;'
    And the lily whispers, 'I wait.'

pimpernel a flower that seems to go to sleep in
wet weather

XI

She is coming, my own, my sweet;
    Were it ever so airy a tread,
My heart would hear her and beat,
    Were it earth in an earthy bed;
920 My dust would hear her and beat,
    Had I lain for a century dead;
Would start and tremble under her feet,
    And blossom in purple and red.

        .   .   .

From *Part II*

IV

I

O that 'twere possible
After long grief and pain
To find the arms of my true love
Round me once again!°

II

When I was wont to meet her
In the silent woody places
By the home that gave me birth,
We stood tranced in long embraces
Mixed with kisses sweeter sweeter
150 Than anything on earth.

III

A shadow flits before me,
Not thou, but like to thee:
Ah Christ, that it were possible
For one short hour to see
The souls we loved, that they might tell us
What and where they be.

        .   .   .

V

I

Dead, long dead,°
240 Long dead!
And my heart is a handful of dust,°
And the wheels go over my head,°
And my bones are shaken with pain,
For into a shallow grave they are thrust,

O that . . . once again Compare this stanza to
the little medieval lyric, "Western Wind."
long dead The young man is now insane and

confined, and has the fantasy that he is dead.
a handful of dust See Eliot's *Waste Land* I.30.
over my head a fantasy of burial

Only a yard beneath the street,
And the hoofs of the horses beat, beat,
The hoofs of the horses beat,
Beat into my scalp and my brain,
With never an end to the stream of passing feet,
250    Driving, hurrying, marrying, burying,
Clamour and rumble, and ringing and clatter,
And here beneath it is all as bad,
For I thought the dead had peace, but it is not so;
To have no peace in the grave, is that not sad?
But up and down and to and fro,
Ever about me the dead men go;°
And then to hear a dead man chatter
Is enough to drive one mad.

II
Wretchedest age, since Time began,
260    They cannot even bury a man;
And though we paid our tithes in the days that are gone,
Not a bell was rung, not a prayer was read;
It is that which makes us loud in the world of the dead;
There is none that does his work, not one;
A touch of their office might have sufficed,
But the churchmen fain would kill their church,
As the churches have killed their Christ.°

.   .   .

From *Part III*

VI°

I
My life has crept so long on a broken wing°
Through cells of madness, haunts of horror and fear,
That I come to be grateful at last for a little thing:
My mood is changed, for it fell at a time of year
When the face of night is fair on the dewy downs,
And the shining daffodil dies, and the Charioteer°
And starry Gemini hang like glorious crowns
Over Orion's grave low down in the west,°
That like a silent lightning under the stars
10   She seemed to divide in a dream from a band of the blest,
And spoke of a hope for the world in the coming wars°

---

**the dead men go** the other inmates of the mad-house
**killed their Christ** with formalism and commerce
**VI** Section numbering for Part III carries on from Part II.
**on a broken wing** He is sane again.
**Charioteer** constellation Auriga

**And starry . . . in the west** The Gemini (Castor and Pollux) are in the southern hemisphere; the season is spring, so Orion is low in the west because it is a winter constellation.
**She seemed . . . coming wars** Maud, as a phantasm, appears to him and champions the war against Russia.

'And in that hope, dear soul, let trouble have rest,
Knowing I tarry for thee,' and pointed to Mars
As he glowed like a ruddy shield on the Lion's breast.°

II

And it was but a dream, yet it yielded a dear delight
To have looked, though but in a dream, upon eyes so fair,
That had been in a weary world my one thing bright;
And it was but a dream, yet it lightened my despair
When I thought that a war would arise in defense of the right,
20    That an iron tyranny° now should bend or cease,
The glory of manhood stand on his ancient height,
Nor Britain's one sole God be the millionaire:
No more shall commerce be all in all, and Peace
Pipe on her pastoral hillock a languid note,
And watch her harvest ripen, her herd increase,
Nor the cannon-bullet rust on a slothful shore,
And the cobweb woven across the cannon's throat
Shall shake its threaded tears in the wind no more.

III

And as months ran on and rumour of battle grew,
30    'It is time, it is time, O passionate heart,' said I
(For I cleaved to a cause that I felt to be pure and true),
'It is time, O passionate heart and morbid eye,
That old hysterical mock-disease should die.'
And I stood on a giant deck° and mixed my breath
With a loyal people shouting a battle cry,
Till I saw the dreary phantom arise and fly
Far into the North, and battle, and seas of death.°

IV

Let it go or stay, so I wake to the higher aims
Of a land that has lost for a little her lust of gold,
40    And love of a peace that was full of wrongs and shames,
Horrible, hateful, monstrous, not to be told;
And hail once more to the banner of battle unrolled!
Though many a light shall darken, and many shall weep
For those that are crushed in the clash of jarring claims,
Yet God's just wrath shall be wreaked on a giant liar;°
And many a darkness into the light shall leap,
And shine in the sudden making of splendid names,
And noble thought be freer under the sun,

Lion's breast northern hemisphere constellation,
symbolizing England; Mars, then in the constellation of the Lion, signifies war
iron tyranny Czarist Russia
giant deck On a troop transport going to the
Crimea he finds solidarity with other soldiers.

Till I saw . . . seas of death He rids himself
at last of Maud's haunting presence, thanks to
his war fever.
giant liar the Czar of Russia, Nicholas I, no
more or less a liar than the English rulers and
statesmen

And the heart of a people beat with one desire;
50  For the peace, that I deemed no peace, is over and done,
And now by the side of the Black and the Baltic deep,
And deathful-grinning mouths of the fortress, flames
The blood-red blossom of war with a heart of fire.


V

Let it flame or fade, and the war roll down like a wind,
We have proved we have hearts in a cause, we are noble still,
And myself have awaked, as it seems, to the better mind;
It is better to fight for the good than to rail at the ill;
I have felt with my native land, I am one with my kind,
I embrace the purpose of God, and the doom assigned.
1854–55                                                    1855


## From Idylls of the King
### [VIVIEN'S SONG]°

But now the wholesome music of the wood
Was dumbed by one from out the hall of Mark,
A damsel-errant, warbling, as she rode
The woodland alleys, Vivien, with her Squire.

'The fire of Heaven has killed the barren cold,
And kindled all the plain and all the wold.
The new leaf ever pushes off the old.
The fire of Heaven is not the flame of Hell.

'Old priest, who mumbled worship in your quire—
10  Old monk and nun, ye scorn the world's desire,
Yet in your frosty cells ye feel the fire!
The fire of Heaven is not the flame of Hell.

'The fire of Heaven is on the dusty ways.
The wayside blossoms open to the blaze.
The whole wood-world is one full peal of praise.
The fire of Heaven is not the flame of Hell.

'The fire of Heaven is lord of all things good,
And starve not thou this fire within thy blood,
But follow Vivien through the fiery flood!
20  The fire of Heaven is not the flame of Hell!'


[Vivien's Song] from Balin and Balan (ll. 430–53). This savage and splendid hymn to Eros by Vivien, the evil King Mark's creature who will destroy Merlin, is one of the last outbursts of Tennyson's daemon. It is given here for its excellence and its contrast to Percivale's quest from The Holy Grail. Whereas Percivale is meant to illustrate the subtler force that overthrows Arthurian civilization, an over-spiritualized ascetic impulse, Vivien embodies the other, more primal force, the body's lust.

Then turning to her Squire 'This fire of Heaven,
This old sun-worship, boy, will rise again,
And beat the cross to earth, and break the King
And all his Table.'. . .

1873                                1885


## [Percivale's Quest]

This is the most powerful sustained passage in *Idylls of the King*, though Tennyson himself did not think so, and clearly rated it below the Protestant speech of Arthur at the close of *The Holy Grail*. But, though he made Percivale, Tennyson would not wholly understand him. In Percivale's phantasmagoric quest that wastes the land he traverses, we are given a rival to Browning's *Childe Roland to the Dark Tower Came*, another parable of a dangerous thwarted poetic consciousness burning its way through nature and through other selves. Like Childe Roland, Percivale is a direct descendant of Wordsworth's *Solitary* and the remorseless "Poet" of Shelley's *Alastor*. Percivale, as Tennyson uneasily did not acknowledge, represents not so much an ascetic Catholic consciousness (Tennyson's intention) as he does the antithetical, dangerous element in Tennyson's poetic mind, a desire to put aside everything that is not purely the solipsistic celebration of the self's own sublimity. Percivale seeks to re-beget himself in questing after the Holy Grail, for him (though not for Galahad) only another version of Childe Roland's Dark Tower.


[PERCIVALE'S QUEST]°


'But when the next day brake from under ground —
O brother, had you known our Camelot,
340    Built by old kings, age after age, so old
The King himself had fears that it would fall,
So strange, and rich, and dim; for where the roofs
Tottered toward each other in the sky,
Met foreheads all along the street of those
Who watched us pass; and lower, and where the long
Rich galleries, lady-laden, weighed the necks
Of dragons clinging to the crazy walls,
Thicker than drops from thunder, showers of flowers
Fell as we past; and men and boys astride
350    On wyvern,° lion, dragon, griffin,° swan,

[Percivale's Quest] from *The Holy Grail* (ll. 338–565). Percivale, called "the Pure," has given up his knighthood and become a monk. Soon before his death, he tells the story of the Holy Grail to a kindly, practical-minded fellow monk, Ambrosius. In medieval English legend, the Holy Grail was believed to be the dish in which Joseph of Arimathea preserved the blood of the crucified Christ. Alternately, it was held to be the cup used for sacramental wine at the Passover service that was the Last Supper. In Percivale's narration, we have reached the moment after miracle; the Holy Grail has manifested itself in a vision to the Round Table, when Arthur was absent. To the King's sensible horror, his knights vow to quest after it.
**wyvern** two-legged dragon
**griffin** half-eagle, half-lion

At all the corners, named us each by name,
Calling "God speed!" but in the ways below
The knights and ladies wept, and rich and poor
Wept, and the King himself could hardly speak
For grief, and all in middle street the Queen,
Who rode by Lancelot, wailed and shrieked aloud,
"This madness has come on us for our sins."
So to the Gate of the three Queens° we came,
Where Arthur's wars are rendered mystically,
360    And thence departed every one his way.

'And I was lifted up in heart, and thought
Of all my late-shown prowess in the lists,°
How my strong lance had beaten down the knights,
So many and famous names; and never yet
Had heaven appeared so blue, nor earth so green,
For all my blood danced in me, and I knew
That I should light upon the Holy Grail.

'Thereafter, the dark warning of our King,
That most of us would follow wandering fires,
370    Came like a driving gloom across my mind.
Then every evil word I had spoken once,
And every evil thought I had thought of old,
And every evil deed I ever did,
Awoke and cried, "This Quest is not for thee."
And lifting up mine eyes, I found myself
Alone, and in a land of sand and thorns,
And I was thirsty even unto death;
And I, too, cried, "This Quest is not for thee."

'And on I rode, and when I thought my thirst
380    Would slay me, saw deep lawns, and then a brook,
With one sharp rapid, where the crisping white
Played ever back upon the sloping wave,
And took both ear and eye; and o'er the brook
Were apple-trees, and apples by the brook
Fallen, and on the lawns. "I will rest here,"
I said, "I am not worthy of the Quest;"
But even while I drank the brook, and ate
The goodly apples, all these things at once
Fell into dust, and I was left alone,
390    And thirsting, in a land of sand and thorns.

'And then behold a woman at a door
Spinning; and fair the house whereby she sat,
And kind the woman's eyes and innocent,
And all her bearing gracious; and she rose
Opening her arms to meet me, as who should say,

the three Queens who take the dead Arthur to      lists i.e. in combat
Avalon in *Morte d'Arthur*

"Rest here;" but when I touched her, lo! she, too,
Fell into dust and nothing, and the house
Became no better than a broken shed,
And in it a dead babe; and also this
400   Fell into dust, and I was left alone.

'And on I rode, and greater was my thirst.
Then flashed a yellow gleam across the world,
And where it smote the plowshare in the field,
The plowman left his plowing, and fell down
Before it; where it glittered on her pail,
The milkmaid left her milking, and fell down
Before it, and I know not why, but thought
"The sun is rising," though the sun had risen.
Then was I ware of one that on me moved
410   In golden armour with a crown of gold
About a casque all jewels; and his horse
In golden armour jewelled everywhere:
And on the splendour came, flashing me blind;
And seemed to me the Lord of all the world,
Being so huge. But when I thought he meant
To crush me, moving on me, lo! he, too,
Opened his arms to embrace me as he came,
And up I went and touched him, and he, too,
Fell into dust, and I was left alone
420   And wearying in a land of sand and thorns.

'And I rode on and found a mighty hill,
And on the top, a city walled: the spires
Pricked with incredible pinnacles into heaven.
And by the gateway stirred a crowd; and these
Cried to me climbing, "Welcome, Percivale!
Thou mightiest and thou purest among men!"
And glad was I and clomb, but found at top
No man, nor any voice. And thence I past
Far through a ruinous city, and I saw
430   That man had once dwelt there; but there I found
Only one man of an exceeding age.
"Where is that goodly company," said I,
"That so cried out upon me?" and he had
Scarce any voice to answer, and yet gasped,
"Whence and what art thou?" and even as he spoke
Fell into dust, and disappeared, and I
Was left alone once more, and cried in grief,
"Lo, if I find the Holy Grail itself
And touch it, it will crumble into dust."

440       'And thence I dropped into a lowly vale,
Low as the hill was high, and where the vale
Was lowest, found a chapel, and thereby

A holy hermit in a hermitage,
To whom I told my phantoms, and he said:

  '"O son, thou hast not true humility,
The highest virtue, mother of them all;
For when the Lord of all things made Himself
Naked of glory for His mortal change,
'Take thou my robe,' she° said, 'for all is thine,'
<sup>450</sup> And all her form shone forth with sudden light
So that the angels were amazed, and she
Followed Him down, and like a flying star°
Led on the grey-haired wisdom of the east;
But her thou hast not known: for what is this
Thou thoughtest of thy prowess and thy sins?
Thou hast not lost thyself to save thyself
As Galahad." When the hermit made an end,
In silver armour suddenly Galahad shone
Before us, and against the chapel door
<sup>460</sup> Laid lance, and entered, and we knelt in prayer.
And there the hermit slaked my burning thirst,
And at the sacring° of the mass I saw
The holy elements alone; but he,
"Saw ye no more? I, Galahad, saw the Grail,
The Holy Grail, descend upon the shrine:
I saw the fiery face as of a child
That smote itself into the bread, and went;
And hither am I come; and never yet
Hath what thy sister taught me first to see,
<sup>470</sup> This Holy Thing, failed from my side, nor come
Covered, but moving with me night and day,
Fainter by day, but always in the night
Blood-red, and sliding down the blackened marsh
Blood-red, and on the naked mountain top
Blood-red, and in the sleeping mere below
Blood-red. And in the strength of this I rode,
Shattering all evil customs everywhere,
And past through Pagan realms, and made them mine,
And clashed with Pagan hordes, and bore them down,
<sup>480</sup> And broke through all, and in the strength of this
Come victor. But my time is hard at hand,
And hence I go; and one will crown me king
Far in the spiritual city; and come thou, too,
For thou shalt see the vision when I go."

  'While thus he spake, his eye, dwelling on mine,
Drew me, with power upon me, till I grew

---

**she** Humility                             **sacring** consecration that transforms bread and
**flying star** of Bethlehem                 wine into Christ's flesh and blood

One with him, to believe as he believed.
Then, when the day began to wane, we went.

'There rose a hill that none but man could climb,
490   Scarred with a hundred wintry water-courses—
Storm at the top, and when we gained it, storm
Round us and death; for every moment glanced
His silver arms and gloomed: so quick and thick
The lightnings here and there to left and right
Struck, till the dry old trunks about us, dead,
Yea, rotten with a hundred years of death,
Sprang into fire: and at the base we found
On either hand, as far as eye could see,
A great black swamp and of an evil smell,
500   Part black, part whitened with the bones of men,
Not to be crossed, save that some ancient king
Had built a way, where, linked with many a bridge,
A thousand piers ran into the great Sea.
And Galahad fled along them bridge by bridge,
And every bridge as quickly as he crossed
Sprang into fire and vanished, though I yearned
To follow; and thrice above him all the heavens
Opened and blazed with thunder such as seemed
Shoutings of all the sons of God:° and first
510   At once I saw him far on the great Sea,
In silver-shining armour starry-clear;
And o'er his head the Holy Vessel hung
Clothed in white samite° or a luminous cloud.
And with exceeding swiftness ran the boat,
If boat it were—I saw not whence it came.
And when the heavens opened and blazed again
Roaring, I saw him like a silver star—
And had he set the sail, or had the boat
Become a living creature clad with wings?
520   And o'er his head the Holy Vessel hung
Redder than any rose, a joy to me,
For now I knew the veil had been withdrawn.
Then in a moment when they blazed again
Opening, I saw the least of little stars
Down on the waste, and straight beyond the star
I saw the spiritual city and all her spires°
And gateways in a glory like one pearl—
No larger, though the goal of all the saints—
Strike from the sea; and from the star there shot
530   A rose-red sparkle to the city, and there
Dwelt, and I knew it was the Holy Grail,

Opened . . . sons of God See Job 38:7.          spiritual city . . . spires See Revelation 21:2.
samite silk shot with gold

Which never eyes on earth again shall see.
Then fell the floods of heaven drowning the deep.
And how my feet recrossed the deathful ridge
No memory in me lives; but that I touched
The chapel-doors at dawn I know; and thence
Taking my war-horse from the holy man,
Glad that no phantom vexed me more, returned
To whence I came, the gate of Arthur's wars.'

540    'O brother,' asked Ambrosius,—'for in sooth
These ancient books—and they would win thee—teem,
Only I find not there this Holy Grail,
With miracles and marvels like to these,
Not all unlike; which oftentime I read,
Who read but on my breviary° with ease,
Till my head swims; and then go forth and pass
Down to the little thorpe° that lies so close,
And almost plastered like a martin's nest
To these old walls—and mingle with our folk;
550    And knowing every honest face of theirs
As well as ever shepherd knew his sheep,
And every homely secret in their hearts,
Delight myself with gossip and old wives,
And ills and aches, and teethings, lyings-in,
And mirthful sayings, children of the place,
That have no meaning half a league away:
Or lulling random squabbles when they rise,
Chafferings and chatterings at the market-cross,°
Rejoice, small man, in this small world of mine,
560    Yea, even in their hens and in their eggs—
O brother, saving this Sir Galahad,
Came ye on none but phantoms in your quest,
No man, no woman?'

Then Sir Percivale:
'All men, to one so bound by such a vow,
And women were as phantoms. . . .'
1868                              1869

breviary book of Scripture readings recited daily     thorpe small town
by priests and monks                                  market-cross cross in the marketplace

# Lucretius°

Lucilia, wedded to Lucretius, found
Her master cold; for when the morning flush
Of passion and the first embrace had died
Between them, though he loved her none the less,
Yet often when the woman heard his foot
Return from pacings in the field, and ran
To greet him with a kiss, the master took
Small notice, or austerely, for—his mind
Half buried in some weightier argument,
10  Or fancy-borne perhaps upon the rise
And long roll of the Hexameter° he passed
To turn and ponder those three hundred scrolls
Left by the Teacher,° whom he held divine.
She brooked it not; but wrathful, petulant,
Dreaming some rival, sought and found a witch
Who brewed the philtre which had power, they said,
To lead an errant passion home again.
And this, at times, she mingled with his drink,
And this destroyed him; for the wicked broth
20  Confused the chemic labour of the blood,
And tickling the brute brain within the man's
Made havoc among those tender cells, and checked
His power to shape: he loathed himself; and once
After a tempest woke upon a morn
That mocked him with returning calm, and cried:

'Storm in the night! for thrice I heard the rain
Rushing; and once the flash of a thunderbolt—
Methought I never saw so fierce a fork—
Struck out the streaming mountain-side, and showed
30  A riotous confluence of watercourses
Blanching and billowing in a hollow of it,
Where all but yester-eve was dusty-dry.

'Storm, and what dreams, ye holy Gods, what dreams!
For thrice I wakened after dreams. Perchance

We do but recollect the dreams that come
Just ere the waking: terrible! for it seemed
A void was made in Nature; all her bonds
Cracked; and I saw the flaring atom-streams°
And torrents of her myriad universe,
40    Ruining along the illimitable inane,
Fly on to clash together again, and make
Another and another frame of things
For ever: that was mine, my dream, I knew it—
Of and belonging to me, as the dog
With inward yelp and restless forefoot plies
His function of the woodland: but the next!
I thought that all the blood by Sylla° shed
Came driving rainlike down again on earth,
And where it dashed the reddening meadow, sprang
50    No dragon warriors from Cadmean teeth,°
For these I thought my dream would show to me,
But girls, Hetairai,° curious in their art,
Hired animalisms, vile as those that made
The mulberry-faced Dictator's° orgies worse
Than aught they fable of the quiet Gods.
And hands they mixed, and yelled and round me drove
In narrowing circles till I yelled again
Half-suffocated, and sprang up, and saw—
Was it the first beam of my latest day?

60        'Then, then, from utter gloom stood out the breasts,
The breasts of Helen,° and hoveringly a sword
Now over and now under, now direct,
Pointed itself to pierce, but sank down shamed
At all that beauty; and as I stared, a fire,
The fire that left a roofless Ilion,
Shot out of them, and scorched me that I woke.

        'Is this thy vengeance, holy Venus, thine,
Because I would not one of thine own doves,
Not even a rose, were offered to thee? thine,
70    Forgetful how my rich prooemion° makes
Thy glory fly along the Italian field,
In lays that will outlast thy Deity?

---

**flaring atom-streams** Closely following *De Rerum Natura*, here as elsewhere in the poem, Tennyson gives an epitome of the Lucretian vision of atomic creation and subsequent reduction to chaos.
**Sylla** Sulla, dictator of Rome, 82–79 B.C.
**Cadmean teeth** Cadmus, founder of Thebes, is reputed to have sown dragon's teeth in the earth, after which armed men were harvested from it.

**Hetairai** whores
**mulberry-faced Dictator's** that of Sulla, notorious for his sexual excesses
**Helen** of Troy, whose allurements caused the Trojan war
**prooemion** proem, introduction. In the introduction to his poem, Lucretius had celebrated Venus rationally, as the principle of life.

'Deity? nay, thy worshippers. My tongue
Trips, or I speak profanely. Which of these
Angers thee most, or angers thee at all?
Not if thou be'st of those who, far aloof
From envy, hate and pity, and spite and scorn,
Live the great life which all our greatest fain
Would follow, centred in eternal calm.

80  'Nay, if thou canst, O Goddess, like ourselves
Touch, and be touched, then would I cry to thee
To kiss thy Mavors,° roll thy tender arms
Round him, and keep him from the lust of blood
That makes a steaming slaughter-house of Rome.

'Ay, but I meant not thee; I meant not her,
Whom all the pines of Ida° shook to see
Slide from that quiet heaven of hers, and tempt
The Trojan,° while his neat-herds were abroad;
Nor her that o'er her wounded hunter° wept
90  Her Deity false in human-amorous tears;
Nor whom her beardless apple-arbiter°
Decided fairest. Rather, O ye Gods,
Poet-like, as the great Sicilian° called
Calliope° to grace his golden verse—
Ay, and this Kypris° also—did I take
That popular name of thine to shadow forth
The all-generating powers and genial heat
Of Nature, when she strikes through the thick blood
Of cattle, and light is large, and lambs are glad
100  Nosing the mother's udder, and the bird
Makes his heart voice amid the blaze of flowers:
Which things appear the work of mighty Gods.

'The Gods! and if I go my work is left
Unfinished—if I go. The Gods, who haunt
The lucid interspace of world and world,
Where never creeps a cloud, or moves a wind,
Nor ever falls the least white star of snow,
Nor ever lowest roll of thunder moans,
Nor sound of human sorrow mounts to mar
110  Their sacred everlasting calm! and such,
Not all so fine, nor so divine a calm,
Not such, nor all unlike it, man may gain
Letting his own life go. The Gods, the Gods!

**Mavors** Mars
**Ida** mountain near Troy
**The Trojan** Anchises, who begot Aeneas upon
Venus
**wounded hunter** Adonis, beautiful youth be-

loved of Venus; he died of a boar-wound
**apple-arbiter** Paris
**great Sicilian** Empedocles the poet-philosopher
**Calliope** Muse of epic poetry
**Kypris** Cyprus, sacred to Venus

If all be atoms, how then should the Gods
Being atomic not be dissoluble,
Not follow the great law? My master° held
That Gods there are, for all men so believe.
I pressed my footsteps into his, and meant
Surely to lead my Memmius° in a train
120  Of flowery clauses onward to the proof
That Gods there are, and deathless. Meant? I meant?
I have forgotten what I meant: my mind
Stumbles, and all my faculties are lamed.

   'Look where another of our Gods, the Sun,
Apollo, Delius, or of older use
All-seeing Hyperion°—what you will—
Has mounted yonder; since he never sware,
Except his wrath were wreaked on wretched man,
That he would only shine among the dead
130  Hereafter; tales! for never yet on earth
Could dead flesh creep, or bits of roasting ox
Moan round the spit—nor knows he what he sees;
King of the East although he seem, and girt
With song and flame and fragrance, slowly lifts
His golden feet on those empurpled stairs
That climb into the windy halls of heaven:
And here he glances on an eye new-born,
And gets for greeting but a wail of pain;
And here he stays upon a freezing orb
140  That fain would gaze upon him to the last;
And here upon a yellow eyelid fallen
And closed by those who mourn a friend in vain,
Not thankful that his troubles are no more.
And me, although his fire is on my face
Blinding, he sees not, nor at all can tell
Whether I mean this day to end myself,
Or lend an ear to Plato° where he says,
That men like soldiers may not quit the post
Allotted by the Gods: but he that holds
150  The Gods are careless, wherefore need he care
Greatly for them, nor rather plunge at once,
Being troubled, wholly out of sight, and sink
Past earthquake—ay, and gout and stone, that break
Body toward death, and palsy, death-in-life,
And wretched age—and worst disease of all,
These prodigies of myriad nakednesses,
And twisted shapes of lust, unspeakable,
Abominable, strangers at my hearth

master Epicurus
Memmius C. Memmius Gemellus, man of letters to whom Lucretius dedicated his poem

Hyperion like Apollo and Delius, a name for
the sun god
Plato See *Phaedo* VI.

160    Not welcome, harpies miring every dish,
       The phantom husks of something foully done,
       And fleeting through the boundless universe,
       And blasting the long quiet of my breast
       With animal heat and dire insanity?

       'How should the mind, except it loved them, clasp
       These idols to herself? or do they fly
       Now thinner, and now thicker, like the flakes
       In a fall of snow, and so press in, perforce
       Of multitude, as crowds that in an hour
       Of civic tumult jam the doors, and bear
170    The keepers down, and throng, their rags and they
       The basest, far into that council-hall
       Where sit the best and stateliest of the land?

       'Can I not fling this horror off me again,
       Seeing with how great ease Nature can smile,
       Balmier and nobler from her bath of storm,
       At random ravage? and how easily
       The mountain there has cast his cloudy slough,
       Now towering o'er him in serenest air,
       A mountain o'er a mountain,—ay, and within
180    All hollow as the hopes and fears of men?

       'But who was he, that in the garden snared
       Picus and Faunus,° rustic Gods? a tale
       To laugh at—more to laugh at in myself—
       For look! what is it? there? yon arbutus
       Totters; a noiseless riot underneath
       Strikes through the wood, sets all the tops quivering—
       The mountain quickens into Nymph and Faun;
       And here an Oread°—how the sun delights
       To glance and shift about her slippery sides,
190    And rosy knees and supple roundedness,
       And budded bosom-peaks—who this way runs
       Before the rest—A satyr,° a satyr, see,
       Follows; but him I proved impossible;°
       Twy-natured° is no nature: yet he draws
       Nearer and nearer, and I scan him now
       Beastlier than any phantom of his kind
       That ever butted his rough brother-brute
       For lust or lusty blood or provender:
       I hate, abhor, spit, sicken at him; and she
200    Loathes him as well; such a precipitate heel,

Picus and Faunus rural gods of early Rome;
trapped by King Numa, and compelled to give
up their secrets
Oread mountain nymph

satyr half-goat, half-man; an emblem of sexual
lust
impossible Lucretius had argued that rational
nature could not create such creatures.
Twy-natured two-natured

Fledged as it were with Mercury's ankle-wing,
Whirls her to me: but will she fling herself,
Shameless upon me? Catch her, goat-foot: nay,
Hide, hide them, million-myrtled wilderness,
And cavern-shadowing laurels, hide! do I wish—
What?—that the bush were leafless? or to whelm
All of them in one massacre? O ye Gods,
I know you careless, yet, behold, to you
From childly wont and ancient use I call—
210  I thought I lived securely as yourselves—
No lewdness, narrowing envy, monkey-spite,
No madness of ambition, avarice, none:
No larger feast than under plane or pine
With neighbours laid along the grass, to take
Only such cups as left us friendly-warm,
Affirming each his own philosophy—
Nothing to mar the sober majesties
Of settled, sweet, Epicurean life.
But now it seems some unseen monster lays
220  His vast and filthy hands upon my will,
Wrenching it backward into his; and spoils
My bliss in being; and it was not great;
For save when shutting reasons up in rhythm,
Or Heliconian° honey in living words,
To make a truth less harsh, I often grew
Tired of so much within our little life,
Or of so little in our little life—
Poor little life that toddles half an hour
Crowned with a flower or two, and there an end—
230  And since the nobler pleasure seems to fade,
Why should I, beastlike as I find myself,
Not manlike end myself?—our privilege—
What beast has heart to do it? And what man,
What Roman would be dragged in triumph thus?
Not I; not he, who bears one name with her°
Whose death-blow struck the dateless doom of kings,
When, brooking not the Tarquin in her veins,
She made her blood in sight of Collatine
And all his peers, flushing the guiltless air,
240  Spout from the maiden fountain in her heart.
And from it sprang the Commonwealth, which breaks
As I am breaking now!

          'And therefore now
Let her, that is the womb and tomb of all,°
Great Nature, take, and forcing far apart

---

Heliconian pertaining to Helicon, sacred mountain of the Muses
her Lucretia, raped by Sextus, son of King

Tarquin; see Shakespeare's *Rape of Lucrece*
*womb and tomb of all* Nature: see *Paradise Lost*
II.911

Those blind beginnings that have made me man,
Dash them anew together at her will
Through all her cycles—into man once more,
Or beast or bird or fish, or opulent flower:
But till this cosmic order everywhere
250  Shattered into one earthquake in one day
Cracks all to pieces,—and that hour perhaps
Is not so far when momentary man
Shall seem no more a something to himself,
But he, his hopes and hates, his homes and fanes,°
And even his bones long laid within the grave,
The very sides of the grave itself shall pass,
Vanishing, atom and void, atom and void,
Into the unseen for ever,—till that hour,
My golden work in which I told a truth
260  That stays the rolling Ixionian wheel,°
And numbs the Fury's ringlet-snake, and plucks
The mortal soul from out immortal hell,
Shall stand: ay, surely: then it fails at last
And perishes as I must; for O Thou,
Passionless bride, divine Tranquillity,
Yearned after by the wisest of the wise,
Who fail to find thee, being as thou art
Without one pleasure and without one pain,
Howbeit I know thou surely must be mine
270  Or soon or late, yet out of season, thus
I woo thee roughly, for thou carest not
How roughly men may woo thee so they win—
Thus—thus: the soul flies out and dies in the air.'

    With that he drove the knife into his side:
She° heard him raging, heard him fall; ran in,
Beat breast, tore hair, cried out upon herself
As having failed in duty to him, shrieked
That she but meant to win him back, fell on him,
Clasped, kissed him, wailed: he answered, 'Care not thou!
280  Thy duty? What is duty? Fare thee well!'
1865–68                              1868

fanes temples
Ixionian wheel Ixion, as punishment for his
sexual attempt at Hera, was bound by Zeus to
an eternally revolving wheel in the nether-
world.

She Lucilia, Lucretius' wife, who in dubious
Christian chronicles was said to have driven
him insane by a love potion, thus causing his
suicide

# To Virgil°

*Written at the Request of the Mantuans for
the Nineteenth Centenary of Virgil's Death*°

I

Roman Virgil, thou that singest
    Ilion's lofty temples robed in fire,
Ilion falling, Rome arising,
    wars, and filial faith, and Dido's pyre;°

II

Landscape-lover, lord of language
    more than he that sang the Works and Days,°
All the chosen coin of fancy
    flashing out from many a golden phrase;

III

Thou that singest wheat and woodland,
10          tilth and vineyard, hive and horse and herd;°
All the charm of all the Muses
    often flowering in a lonely word;

IV

Poet of the happy Tityrus°
    piping underneath his beechen bowers;
Poet of the poet-satyr
    whom the laughing shepherd bound with flowers;°

V

Chanter of the Pollio, glorying
    in the blissful years again to be,
Summers of the snakeless meadow,
20          unlaborious earth and oarless sea;°

VI

Thou that seest Universal
    Nature moved by Universal Mind;°

**Virgil** Born on a farm near Mantua in 70 B.C., died in 19 B.C. Tennyson knew himself to be the most Virgilian of English poets, so that in describing his precursor here, he also described himself.
**Virgil's Death** The sub-title is inaccurate, as the occasion for the poem, a request from the Virgilian Academy of Mantua, came in 1882.
**Dido's pyre.** The first stanza celebrates the principal incidents and themes of the *Aeneid*. Ilion is Troy, and poor Dido, Queen of Carthage, immolated herself upon a pyre when the prig Aeneas abandoned her.
**Works and Days** didactic epic by Hesiod, 8th

century B.C. Greek poet, who influenced Virgil's *Georgics* even as Homer influenced the *Aeneid*
**Thou . . . herd** This stanza refers to the *Georgics*, Virgil's best poem.
**Tityrus** See Virgil's *Eclogue* I.
**poet-satyr . . . flowers** in *Eclogue* VI
**Chanter . . . oarless sea** description of *Eclogue* IV, called the Pollio because it mentions C. Asinius Pollio, Virgil's patron. The poem, Virgil's most famous, celebrates Augustus as a kind of Messiah, and by later Christian readers (Dante included) was read as a vision of Christ's birth.
**Universal Mind** See *Aeneid* VI.727.

Thou majestic in thy sadness
    at the doubtful doom of human kind;°

### VII

Light among the vanished ages;
    star that gildest yet this phantom shore;
Golden branch amid the shadows,°
    kings and realms that pass to rise no more;

### VIII

Now thy Forum° roars no longer,
30      fallen every purple Cæsar's dome—
Though thine ocean-roll of rhythm
    sound for ever of Imperial Rome—

### IX

Now the Rome of slaves hath perished,
    and the Rome of freemen holds her place,°
I, from out the Northern Island
    sundered once from all the human race,°

### X

I salute thee, Mantovano,°
    I that loved thee since my day began,
Wielder of the stateliest measure°
40      ever moulded by the lips of man.
    1882                    1882

# Merlin and The Gleam°

### I

O young Mariner,°
You from the haven
Under the sea-cliff,
You that are watching
The grey Magician
With eyes of wonder,
*I* am Merlin,

human kind See *Aeneid* I.462.
Golden . . . shadows See *Aeneid* VI.208; here
Virgil himself becomes, in Tennyson's praise, the
golden bough that keeps us safe in the underworld.
Forum assembly place of Rome
holds her place Rome joined the Republic of
Italy in 1870.
human race See *Eclogue* I.66.
Mantovano Mantuan; Dante so addresses Virgil
in *Purgatorio* VI.74

measure the Latin hexameter, the effect of
which this poem vainly tries to give by a
trochaic meter
Merlin and The Gleam A much better poem
than the famous but stale "Crossing the Bar,"
this is Tennyson's true farewell to his art. Like
Emerson in his "Merlin," Tennyson identifies
himself with the prophetic bard. For the
"gleam" see Wordsworth's *Intimations* Ode.
young Mariner a young poet setting out

And *I* am dying,
*I* am Merlin
10    Who follow The Gleam.

II

Mighty the Wizard°
Who found me at sunrise
Sleeping, and woke me
And learned me Magic!
Great the Master,
And sweet the Magic,
When over the valley,
In early summers,
Over the mountain,
20    On human faces,
And all around me,
Moving to melody,
Floated The Gleam.°

III

Once at the croak of a Raven° who crossed it,
A barbarous people,
Blind to the magic,
And deaf to the melody,
Snarled at and cursed me.
A demon vexed me,°
30    The light retreated,
The landskip darkened,
The melody deadened,°
The Master whispered
'Follow The Gleam.'

IV

Then to the melody,
Over a wilderness
Gliding, and glancing at
Elf of the woodland,
Gnome of the cavern,
40    Griffin and Giant,
And dancing of Fairies
In desolate hollows,
And wraiths of the mountain,
And rolling of dragons

Wizard Tennyson's precursor, a composite figure made up of his poetic father, Keats, and
poetic grandfather, Wordsworth; hardly Scott,
as some critics have said
Floated The Gleam Tennyson's early poetry,
the volumes of 1830 and 1832

Raven John Wilson ("Christopher North"), who
reviewed Tennyson savagely in 1833
demon vexed me John Lockhart, who also reviewed Tennyson harshly in 1833
melody deadened Tennyson's poetic "silence"
from 1833 to 1842

By warble of water,
Or cataract music
Of falling torrents,
Flitted The Gleam.°

V

Down from the mountain
50   And over the level,
And streaming and shining on
Silent river,
Silvery willow,
Pasture and plowland,
Innocent maidens,
Garrulous children,
Homestead and harvest,
Reaper and gleaner,
And rough-ruddy faces
60   Of lowly labour,
Slided The Gleam°—

VI

Then, with a melody
Stronger and statelier,
Led me at length
To the city and palace
Of Arthur the king;
Touched at the golden
Cross of the churches,
Flashed on the Tournament,
70   Flickered and bickered
From helmet to helmet,
And last on the forehead
Of Arthur the blameless
Rested The Gleam.°

VII

Clouds and darkness
Closed upon Camelot;
Arthur had vanished
I knew not whither,
The king who loved me,
80   And cannot die;°
For out of the darkness
Silent and slowly

**Flitted The Gleam** Stanza refers to the volumes
he published in 1842.
**Slided The Gleam** the English idylls, also
printed in 1842

**Rested The Gleam** the first group of Arthurian
idylls, published in 1859
**cannot die** a break in chronology, going back
to Hallam's death in 1833

The Gleam, that had waned to a wintry glimmer
On icy fallow
And faded forest,
Drew to the valley
Named of the shadow,
And slowly brightening
Out of the glimmer,
⁹⁰ And slowly moving again to a melody
Yearningly tender,
Fell on the shadow,
No longer a shadow,
But clothed with The Gleam.°

VIII
And broader and brighter
The Gleam flying onward,
Wed to the melody,
Sang through the world;°
And slower and fainter,
¹⁰⁰ Old and weary,
But eager to follow,
I saw, whenever
In passing it glanced upon
Hamlet or city,
That under the Crosses
The dead man's garden,
The mortal hillock,
Would break into blossom;
And so to the land's
¹¹⁰ Last limit I came—
And can no longer,
But die rejoicing,
For through the Magic
Of Him the Mighty,
Who taught me in childhood,
There on the border
Of boundless Ocean,
And all but in Heaven
Hovers The Gleam.°

IX
¹²⁰ Not of the sunlight,
Not of the moonlight,

clothed with The Gleam *In Memoriam*
Sang through the world his later poetry, in-
cluding *Maud*
Hovers The Gleam Not only the gleam but the

association of childhood with "the border / Of
boundless Ocean" suggests Wordsworth's *Intimations* Ode.

Not of the starlight!°
O young Mariner,
Down to the haven,
Call your companions,
Launch your vessel,
And crowd your canvas,
And, ere it vanishes
Over the margin,
130    After it, follow it,
Follow The Gleam.
1889                  1889

## Crossing the Bar°

Sunset and evening star,
    And one clear call for me!
And may there be no moaning of the bar,
    When I put out to sea,

But such a tide as moving seems asleep,
    Too full for sound and foam,
When that which drew from out the boundless deep
    Turns again home.

Twilight and evening bell,
10        And after that the dark!
And may there be no sadness of farewell,
    When I embark;

For though from out our bourne° of Time and Place
    The flood may bear me far,
I hope to see my Pilot face to face°
    When I have crossed the bar.
1889                  1889

**the starlight** Tennyson may be distinguishing his more supernatural and mystical Gleam from the natural "sunlight" of Wordsworth, "moonlight" of Keats, and "starlight" of Shelley. **Crossing the Bar** A few days before his death, Tennyson directed that this lyric conclude all editions of his work; the "bar" is a sand-bar at the harbor's mouth, but also the barrier between different realms of being. This is an immensely popular poem, but some critics find it simplistic and confused. **bourne** boundary or limit **The flood . . . face to face** Tennyson rather lamely said that the Pilot "has been on board all the while, but in the dark I have not seen him." (Actually, pilots leave the boats they guide once the harbor-bar is passed.) More tiresomely, he added that the Pilot was that "Divine and Unseen Who is always guiding us," not the most imaginative of his notions.

# ROBERT BROWNING
1812–1889

Browning was born on May 7, 1812, in Camberwell, an outlying district of London, the first-born child of his well-to-do parents. Though the senior Robert Browning worked for the Bank of England, his interests were strongly scholarly and artistic, and his son grew up among the six thousand volumes of a carefully selected and thoroughly used library. Browning's mother, of Scottish and German descent, was an evangelical Protestant, and her dissenting religious views, though in altered form, were always to remain vital in Browning's consciousness.

Educated largely at home after fourteen, Browning set his heart early on being a poet, and prevailed, for against the strong wills of his parents he relied stubbornly upon the preternatural power of his own will. Unusually attached to his mother, Browning partly overcame his own Oedipal anxieties in regard to her, but the intense struggle was probably responsible for some of the stranger patterns in his life and his poetry. In 1826, when he was fourteen, he was given a small, pirated edition of Shelley's lyrics, and the major influence upon his poetry began, quite violently. Under the first impact of Shelley's spirit, Browning renounced his mother's religion. In a veiled form, Browning's first important poem, *Pauline,* based on Shelley's *Alastor,* told the story of the ensuing conflict, and the lasting shame of the boy's defeat. His attachment for his mother proved immediately more compelling than his need for his own integrity, and he yielded. Something fundamental in him was never to forget.

*Pauline* sold no copies, but the young John Stuart Mill read a review copy, and Mill's written comments reached and affected Browning. Mill, an authority on self-consciousness, saw clearly that *Pauline* only pretended to purge the young poet of that state, and that Browning was free neither of Shelleyanism nor of the psychological consequences of having yielded up his rebellion against society, religion, and parents. Attempting to work out of his conflicts, Browning wrote two more verse romances in the Shelleyan mode, *Paracelsus* (1835) and *Sordello* (1840). Neither is wholly successful, yet each is a remarkable work, but difficult, particularly *Sordello,* which baffled whoever read it. The subjective quest had led Browning into a puzzle of history mixed with personal reflections that is repeated by his poetic disciple, Ezra Pound, in the *Cantos.* Between 1840 and 1842, when *Dramatic Lyrics* appeared, by a process still concealed from his critics Browning accomplished a remarkable transfiguration of his Shelleyan heritage, and emerged with his characteristic and triumphant form, the dramatic monologue.

In 1844 Browning revisited Italy, and for the first time seems to have decided it was the proper context for his vision. He returned to England more lonely and intense than ever, and began in January 1845 a correspondence with the invalid poetess Elizabeth Barrett. This famous and complex courtship continued for almost two years, as the thirty-three-year-old Browning attempted to win over the thirty-nine-year-old poetess. The lovers did not meet until May 1845, and a close reading of the correspondence is both fascinating and troubling, as Browning wavered continually, desiring the lady, but wishing her to be the stronger and make the final decision. On September 19, 1846, by some small miracle, these two immense selfhoods somehow managed to elope together to Italy.

The Brownings' life together was reasonably happy, though it had its hidden difficulties, and some open conflicts. Unfortunately, it lasted only fifteen years, until Mrs. Browning suddenly died on June 29, 1861, in Florence, where they had lived for many years. Browning was left with a son, born in 1849, the year also of his mother's death, which affected him almost as deeply as his wife's, twelve years later. For many reasons, including his wariness at yielding up his new freedom but also because in a way he had become the prisoner of his own myth of perfect married love, Browning never remarried, but he became a social lion both in London and in Italy, and experienced some passionate involvements. His wariness fell away once, in 1869, when he proposed marriage to Lady Ashburton, but he was rejected (rather painfully, for him).

When Browning had fallen in love with Elizabeth Barrett, she had enjoyed a more considerable poetical reputation than he did, despite the *Dramatic Lyrics* of 1842 and the *Dramatic Romances* of 1845. Indeed, throughout even the 1850's, Browning was better known as a husband than as a poet. But in 1855 Browning published his first masterpiece, the fifty magnificent monologues of the two-volume *Men and Women*, and though only a few discerning poets and critics at first realized his achievement, the book's fame grew steadily over a decade. In 1864, *Dramatis Personae,* a collection almost as powerful, appeared, to be followed by his culminating work and second masterpiece, the long poem *The Ring and the Book,* in 1868. After that, and until his death, Browning at last achieved an audience and critical reputation almost equal to Tennyson's. Though he published copiously for the next twenty years, he never again equalled his greatest imaginings. There are, however, some remarkable lyrics in his last volume, *Asolando: Fancies and Facts,* published in London on December 12, 1889, the day that Browning died in Venice, at the house of his son.

Browning, in this editor's judgment, is the most considerable poet in English since the major Romantics, surpassing his great contemporary rival Tennyson, and the principal twentieth-century poets, including even Yeats, Hardy, and Wallace Stevens, let alone the various fashionable modernists whose reputations are now rightly in rapid decline. But Browning is a very difficult poet, notoriously badly served by criticism, and rather badly served also by his own accounts of what he was doing as a poet. His public statements and letters, his conversational asides, and the implicit polemic of his one important essay (inevitably on Shelley) all work together to emphasize the dramatic and objective elements in his poetry. Thus, his essay on Shelley implicitly claims kinship for himself with Shakespeare, classified as the supreme objective poet, as against Shelley, who is judged (with reverence) the outstanding example of the subjective poet. In the advertisement to the original *Dramatic Lyrics* of 1842, Browning insisted that the poems were, "though for the most part Lyric in expression, always Dramatic in principle, and so many utterances of so many imaginary persons, not mine." This insistence he maintained until the end.

Clearly, Browning himself could not *be* the varied group that included Johannes Agricola, the tomb-ordering Bishop, Fra Lippo Lippi, Childe Roland, Andrea del Sarto, Cleon, Abt Vogler, Caliban, the Pope of *The Ring and the Book,* and dozens more, but just as clearly his relation to them is *not* that of Shakespeare to Antony, Lear, Hamlet, Falstaff, Prospero, and the rest, or of Chaucer to his fellow pilgrims. Browning's form is dramatic, but his imaginative procedure is not. His company of ruined questers, imperfect poets, self-sabotaged artists, failed lovers, inspired fanatics, charlatans, monomaniacs, and self-deceiving confidence men all have a certain family resemblance, and they outweigh finally the other groups among his creations. We harm Browning by comparing his work to Shakespeare's or Chaucer's, not only because his range and depth of characterization are narrow and shallow compared with theirs, but because his poems are neither dramatic nor monologues, but something else. They are not dramatic, but lyrical and subjective, despite their coverings and gestures, and they are not monologues, but antiphons in which many voices speak, including several that belong to Browning himself. Browning, in his uncanny greatness, was a kind of psychological atomist, like Blake, Balzac, Proust, Kafka, Lawrence, Yeats, and some other modern innovators. In his work, older conceptions of personality disappear, and a more incoherent individual continuity is allowed to express the truths of actual existence. Whether Browning ever understood how wide the chasm between his own inner and outer selves had become, his art constantly explores the multiplicity of selves that inhabit apparently single, unitary personalities, some of them not at all unlike some of his own. Each of his men and women is at least several men and women, and his lovers learn that we can never embrace any one person at a time, but only the whole of an incoherence, the cluster of voices and beings that jostles in any separate self.

Browning had swerved away from the remorseless, questing, lyrical art of Shelley, where the poet seeks to fulfill desire by associating desire with the Intellectual Beauty that manifests itself just beyond the range of the senses. In Browning's vision the family resemblance to Shelley remains very strong, for all of his beings suffer from a quester's temperament, are self-deceived, and seek a sensuous fulfillment, yet manage all too frequently to turn aside from any fulfillment as being inadequate to the contradictory desires of their own crowded selves.

The uniqueness of Browning's art might have dismayed him, if he could see it in the perspective of a hundred years after, for he meant his speakers to give us their involuntary self-revelations, and just as strongly he did *not* mean them to give us his. Yet when you read your way into his world, precisely his largest gift to you is his involuntary unfolding of one of the largest, most enigmatic, and most multi-personed literary and human selves you can hope to encounter. In a brilliant monologue by the contemporary poet Richard Howard, "November, 1889," Browning is made to observe: "I am not interested in art, but in the obstacles to art." His poems, obsessed with those obstacles, do more to remove them than any others of the last century.

## *From* Pauline°

### A Fragment of a Confession

Thou wilt remember. Thou art not more dear
Than song was once to me; and I ne'er sung
But as one entering bright halls where all

**Pauline** Browning's first published poem, printed at his own expense in March 1833. The young poet making the confession is himself; "Pauline" probably was Eliza Flower, nine years older than Browning; it is unlikely that he was in love with her, as his heart, at this stage, was pretty well taken up by a triad of his mother, Shelley, and, as John Stuart Mill observed, mostly himself.

Will rise and shout for him: sure I must own
80  That I am fallen, having chosen gifts
Distinct from theirs—that I am sad and fain
Would give up all to be but where I was,
Not high as I had been if faithful found,
But low and weak yet full of hope, and sure
Of goodness as of life—that I would lose
All this gay mastery of mind, to sit
Once more with them, trusting in truth and love
And with an aim—not being what I am.

Oh Pauline, I am ruined who believed
90  That though my soul had floated from its sphere
Of wild dominion into the dim orb
Of self—that it was strong and free as ever!
It has conformed itself to that dim orb,
Reflecting all its shades and shapes, and now
Must stay where it alone can be adored.
I have felt this in dreams—in dreams in which
I seemed the fate from which I fled; I felt
A strange delight in causing my decay.
I was a fiend in darkness chained for ever
100  Within some ocean-cave; and ages rolled,
Till through the cleft rock, like a moonbeam, came
A white swan° to remain with me; and ages
Rolled, yet I tired not of my first free joy
In gazing on the peace of its pure wings:
And then I said 'It is most fair to me,
Yet its soft wings must sure have suffered change
From the thick darkness, sure its eyes are dim,
Its silver pinions must be cramped and numbed
With sleeping ages here; it cannot leave me,
110  For it would seem, in light beside its kind,
Withered, though here to me most beautiful.'
And then I was a young witch whose blue eyes,
As she stood naked by the river springs,
Drew down a god: I watched his radiant form
Growing less radiant, and it gladdened me;
Till one morn, as he sat in the sunshine
Upon my knees, singing to me of heaven,
He turned to look at me, ere I could lose
The grin with which I viewed his perishing:
120  And he shrieked and departed and sat long
By his deserted throne, but sunk at last
Murmuring, as I kissed his lips and curled
Around him, 'I am still a god—to thee.'

**white swan** See Shelley's *Alastor*, ll. 275–90.

Still I can lay my soul bare in its fall,
Since all the wandering and all the weakness
Will be a saddest comment on the song:
And if, that done, I can be young again,
I will give up all gained, as willingly
As one gives up a charm which shuts him out
130    From hope or part or care in human kind.
As life wanes, all its care and strife and toil
Seem strangely valueless, while the old trees
Which grew by our youth's home, the waving mass
Of climbing plants heavy with bloom and dew,
The morning swallows with their songs like words,
All these seem clear and only worth our thoughts:
So, aught connected with my early life,
My rude songs or my wild imaginings,
How I look on them—most distinct amid
140    The fever and the stir of after years!

I ne'er had ventured e'en to hope for this,
Had not the glow I felt at HIS award,°
Assured me all was not extinct within:
HIS whom all honour, whose renown springs up
Like sunlight which will visit all the world,
So that e'en they who sneered at him at first,
Come out to it, as some dark spider crawls
From his foul nest which some lit torch invades,
Yet spinning still new films for his retreat.
150    Thou didst smile, poet, but can we forgive?

Sun-treader, life and light be thine for ever!
Thou art gone from us; years go by and spring
Gladdens and the young earth is beautiful,
Yet thy songs come not, other bards arise,
But none like thee: they stand, thy majesties,
Like mighty works which tell some spirit there
Hath sat regardless of neglect and scorn,
Till, its long task completed, it hath risen
And left us, never to return, and all
160    Rush in to peer and praise when all in vain.
The air seems bright with thy past presence yet,
But thou art still for me as thou hast been
When I have stood with thee as on a throne
With all thy dim creations gathered round
Like mountains, and I felt of mould like them,
And with them creatures of my own were mixed,
Like things half-lived, catching and giving life.
But thou art still for me who have adored

HIS award Shelley's

Though single, panting but to hear thy name
170 Which I believed a spell to me alone,
Scarce deeming thou wast as a star to men!
As one should worship long a sacred spring
Scarce worth a moth's flitting, which long grasses cross,
And one small tree embowers droopingly—
Joying to see some wandering insect won
To live in its few rushes, or some locust
To pasture on its boughs, or some wild bird
Stoop for its freshness from the trackless air:
And then should find it but the fountain-head
180 Long lost, of some great river washing towns
And towers, and seeing old woods which will live
But by its banks untrod of human foot,
Which, when the great sun sinks, lie quivering
In light as some thing lieth half of life
Before God's foot, waiting a wondrous change;
Then girt with rocks which seek to turn or stay
Its course in vain, for it does ever spread
Like a sea's arm as it goes rolling on,
Being the pulse of some great country—so
190 Wast thou to me, and art thou to the world!
And I, perchance, half feel a strange regret
That I am not what I have been to thee:
Like a girl one has silently loved long
In her first loneliness in some retreat,
When, late emerged, all gaze and glow to view
Her fresh eyes and soft hair and lips which bloom
Like a mountain berry: doubtless it is sweet
To see her thus adored, but there have been
Moments when all the world was in our praise,
200 Sweeter than any pride of after hours.
Yet, sun-treader, all hail! From my heart's heart
I bid thee hail! E'en in my wildest dreams,
I proudly feel I would have thrown to dust
The wreaths of fame which seemed o'erhanging me,
To see thee for a moment as thou art.

And if thou livest, if thou lovest, spirit!
Remember me who set this final seal
To wandering thought—that one so pure as thou
Could never die. Remember me who flung
210 All honour from my soul,° yet paused and said
'There is one spark of love remaining yet,
For I have nought in common with him, shapes
Which followed him avoid me, and foul forms

flung . . . my soul when he renounced Shelley
and re-embraced religion, so as to be reconciled with his mother

Seek me, which ne'er could fasten on his mind;
And though I feel how low I am to him,
Yet I aim not even to catch a tone
Of harmonies he called profusely up;
So, one gleam still remains, although the last.'
Remember me who praise thee e'en with tears,
220   For never more shall I walk calm with thee;
Thy sweet imaginings are as an air,
A melody some wondrous singer sings,
Which, though it haunt men oft in the still eve,
They dream not to essay; yet it no less
But more is honoured. I was thine in shame,
And now when all thy proud renown is out,
I am a watcher whose eyes have grown dim
With looking for some star which breaks on him
Altered and worn and weak and full of tears.

1832–33                              1833


## Johannes Agricola in Meditation°

There's heaven above, and night by night
    I look right through its gorgeous roof;
No suns and moons though e'er so bright
    Avail to stop me; splendour-proof
    I keep the broods of stars aloof:
For I intend to get to God,
    For 'tis to God I speed so fast,
For in God's breast, my own abode,°
    Those shoals of dazzling glory, passed,
10    I lay my spirit down at last.
I lie where I have always lain,
    God smiles as he has always smiled;
Ere suns and moons could wax and wane,
    Ere stars were thundergirt, or piled
    The heavens, God thought on me his child;
Ordained a life for me, arrayed
    Its circumstances every one
To the minutest; ay, God said
    This head this hand should rest upon

---

**Johannes Agricola in Meditation** This vehement poem, one of the earliest of Browning's dramatic monologues, first appeared together with *Porphyria's Lover* under the common title *Madhouse Cells*. Johannes Agricola (1492–1566) broke away from Luther to found the sect of Antinomians. Browning quoted this description of the Antinomians: "they say that good works do not further, nor evil works hinder salvation; that the child of God cannot sin, that God never chastiseth him, that murder, drunkenness, etc. are sins in the wicked but not in him, that child of grace, being once assured of salvation, afterwards never doubteth. . . ." Whether Agricola is mad, or merely very dangerous, his zest and vigor manifest a genuine imaginative energy, though twisted askew.
**abode** because he is persuaded of his election

20       Thus, ere he fashioned star or sun.
        And having thus created me,
        Thus rooted me, he bade me grow,
        Guiltless for ever, like a tree
        That buds and blooms, nor seeks to know
        The law by which it prospers so:
        But sure that thought and word and deed
        All go to swell his love for me,
        Me, made because that love had need
        Of something irreversibly
30       Pledged solely its content to be.
        Yes, yes, a tree which must ascend,
        No poison-gourd° foredoomed to stoop!
        I have God's warrant, could I blend
        All hideous sin, as in a cup,
        To drink the mingled venoms up;
        Secure my nature will convert
        The draught to blossoming gladness fast:
        While sweet dews turn to the gourd's hurt,
        And bloat, and while they bloat it, blast,
40       As from the first its lot was cast.
        For as I lie, smiled on, full-fed
        By unexhausted° power to bless,
        I gaze below on hell's fierce bed,
        And those its waves of flame oppress,
        Swarming in ghastly wretchedness;
        Whose life on earth aspired to be
        One altar-smoke, so pure!—to win
        If not love like God's love for me,
        At least to keep his anger in;
50       And all their striving turned to sin.
        Priest, doctor, hermit, monk grown white
        With prayer, the broken-hearted nun,
        The martyr, the wan acolyte,°
        The incense-swinging child,—undone
        Before God fashioned star or sun!
        God, whom I praise; how could I praise,
        If such as I might understand,
        Make out and reckon on his ways,
        And bargain for his love, and stand,
60       Paying a price, at his right hand?
        1834                1836

**poison-gourd** a figure for the damned        **acolyte** priest's attendant in celebrating Mass
**unexhausted** inexhaustible

# Soliloquy of the Spanish Cloister°

## I

Gr-rr—there go, my heart's abhorrence!
Water your damned flower-pots, do!
If hate killed men, Brother Lawrence,
God's blood,° would not mine kill you!
What? your myrtle-bush wants trimming?
Oh, that rose has prior claims—
Needs its leaden vase filled brimming?
Hell dry you up with its flames!

## II

At the meal we sit together:
10   *Salve tibi!°* I must hear
Wise talk of the kind of weather,
Sort of season, time of year:
*Not a plenteous cork-crop: scarcely
Dare we hope oak-galls,° I doubt:
What's the Latin name for 'parsley'?*
What's the Greek name for Swine's Snout?

## III

Whew! We'll have our platter burnished,
Laid with care on our own shelf!
With a fire-new spoon we're furnished,
20   And a goblet for ourself,
Rinsed like something sacrificial
Ere 'tis fit to touch our chaps°—
Marked with L. for our initial!
(He-he! There his lily snaps!)

## IV

*Saint,* forsooth! While brown Dolores
Squats outside the Convent bank
With Sanchicha, telling stories,
Steeping tresses in the tank,
Blue-black, lustrous, thick like horsehairs,
30   —Can't I see his dead eye glow,
Bright as 'twere a Barbary corsair's?°
(That is, if he'd let it show!)

Soliloquy of the Spanish Cloister In one sense,
this madly humorous monologue resembles
Tennyson's *St. Simeon Stylites,* and simply reflects Browning's extreme Protestant prejudices.
But, in a finer sense, the zestful hatred felt by
the unnamed speaker for the sincerely pious and
good-natured Brother Lawrence is curiously in-
fectious, because of its shocking exuberance.
Not that we share the hatred as hatred, or come
to like the oddly hypocritical yet still credulous
Spanish monk, but we enjoy his daemonic inten-

sity, his remorseless verve.
**God's blood** oath based on the doctrine of
transubstantiation (in the Mass the wine is
transformed into the blood of Jesus Christ)
**Salve tibi!** hail to thee; here and in ll. 13–15,
the speaker bitterly quotes Lawrence's good-
natured salutation and conversation
**oak-galls** disease of oak-leaves, valuable as
source of tannic acid for ink-making
**chaps** lips
**Barbary corsair's** northern African pirate's

V

When he finishes refection,
  Knife and fork he never lays
Cross-wise, to my recollection,
  As do I, in Jesu's praise.
I the Trinity illustrate,°
  Drinking watered orange-pulp—
In three sips the Arian° frustrate;
40  While he drains his at one gulp.

VI

Oh, those melons? If he's able
  We're to have a feast! so nice!
One goes to the Abbot's table,
  All of us get each a slice.
How go on your flowers? None double?
  Not one fruit-sort can you spy?
Strange!—And I, too, at such trouble,
  Keep them close-nipped on the sly!

VII

There's a great text in Galatians,°
50  Once you trip on it, entails
Twenty-nine distinct damnations,
  One sure, if another fails:
If I trip him just a-dying,
  Sure of heaven as sure can be,
Spin him round and send him flying
  Off to hell, a Manichee?°

VIII

Or, my scrofulous° French novel
  On grey paper with blunt type!
Simply glance at it, you grovel
60  Hand and foot in Belial's gripe:°
If I double down its pages
  At the woeful° sixteenth print,
When he gathers his greengages,
  Ope a sieve and slip it in't?

illustrate by my crossing of eating utensils
Arian follower of 4th-century heresy that
denied the Trinity
Galatians The text must be Galatians 5:19–21,
which confines itself, however, to a mere 17
damnations, not all of them quite distinct; the
Monk adds 12 in the pardonable enthusiasm of
his faith.
Manichee follower of radically dualistic heresy,
of the 4th century and later. The joke is that
the speaker himself has an inverted Manichean
temperament.
scrofulous morally corrupt, from scrofula, an
enlarging and degenerating disease of the
lymphatic glands
Belial's gripe grip of Belial, a name for the
Devil
woeful deplorable

IX

Or, there's Satan!—one might venture
    Pledge one's soul to him, yet leave
Such a flaw in the indenture
    As he'd miss till, past retrieve,
Blasted lay that rose-acacia
70    We're so proud of! *Hy, Zy, Hine* . . .°
'St, there's Vespers!° *Plena gratiâ*
    *Ave, Virgo!°* Gr-r-r—you swine!
1839                    1842


# My Last Duchess

FERRARA°

That's my last Duchess° painted on the wall,
Looking as if she were alive. I call
That piece a wonder, now: Frà Pandolf's hands
Worked busily a day, and there she stands.
Will't please you sit and look at her? I said
'Fra Pandolf' by design, for never read
Strangers like you that pictured countenance,
The depth and passion of its earnest glance,
But to myself they turned (since none puts by
10    The curtain I have drawn for you, but I)
And seemed as they would ask me, if they durst,    *dared*
How such a glance came there; so, not the first
Are you to turn and ask thus. Sir, 'twas not
Her husband's presence only, called that spot
Of joy into the Duchess' cheek: perhaps
Frà Pandolf chanced to say 'Her mantle laps
Over my lady's wrist too much,' or 'Paint
Must never hope to reproduce the faint
Half-flush that dies along her throat:' such stuff
20    Was courtesy, she thought, and cause enough
For calling up that spot of joy. She had
A heart—how shall I say?—too soon made glad,
Too easily impressed; she liked whate'er
She looked on, and her looks went everywhere.
Sir, 'twas all one! My favour at her breast,
The dropping of the daylight in the West,
The bough of cherries some officious fool
Broke in the orchard for her, the white mule

**Hy, Zy, Hine** personal curse directed against Lawrence, possibly based on popular Satanism
**there's Vespers** bell signaling evening prayers
**Plena . . . Virgo!** Hail Virgin, full of grace
**Ferrara** Alfonso II of the House of Este, Duke of Ferrara, was negotiating (in 1564) for the niece of the Count of Tyrol.
**last Duchess** The unfortunate lady died in 1561, at the age of 17 and was believed to have been poisoned.

She rode with round the terrace—all and each
30  Would draw from her alike the approving speech,
Or blush, at least. She thanked men,—good! but thanked
Somehow—I know not how—as if she ranked
My gift of a nine-hundred-years-old name
With anybody's gift. Who'd stoop to blame
This sort of trifling? Even had you skill
In speech—(which I have not)—to make your will
Quite clear to such an one, and say, 'Just this
Or that in you disgusts me; here you miss,
Or there exceed the mark'—and if she let
40  Herself be lessoned so, nor plainly set
Her wits to yours, forsooth, and made excuse,
—E'en then would be some stooping; and I choose
Never to stoop. Oh sir, she smiled, no doubt,
Whene'er I passed her; but who passed without
Much the same smile? This grew; I gave commands;
Then all smiles stopped together. There she stands
As if alive. Will't please you rise? We'll meet
The company below, then. I repeat,
The Count your master's known munificence
50  Is ample warrant that no just pretence
Of mine for dowry will be disallowed;
Though his fair daughter's self, as I avowed
At starting, is my object. Nay, we'll go
Together down, sir. Notice Neptune, though,      *Duke taming Duchesses*
Taming a sea-horse, thought a rarity,
Which Claus of Innsbruck° cast in bronze for me!
1842                                    1842


# The Bishop Orders His Tomb°
## at Saint Praxed's Church°

Rome, 15—
Vanity, saith° the preacher, vanity!
Draw round my bed: is Anselm° keeping back?
Nephews—sons mine°. . . ah, God, I know not! Well—

**Claus of Innsbruck** an imaginary sculptor
**The Bishop Orders His Tomb . . .** This brilliant poem may be regarded as Browning's response to the challenge of Tennyson's *St. Simeon Stylites*, a dramatic monologue Browning acknowledged as "perfect." The Bishop, Gandolf, and everything else central to the poem are all entirely Browning's own creations, yet Ruskin (in *Modern Painters* IV.380) in 1856 was justified in saying: "I know of no other piece of modern English, prose or poetry, in which there is so much told, as in these lines, of the Renaissance spirit,—its worldliness, inconsistency, pride, hypocrisy, ignorance of itself, love of art, of luxury, and of good Latin. It is nearly all that I have said of the central Renaissance in thirty pages of *The Stones of Venice*, put into as many lines," Browning's also being the antecedent work."
**St. Praxed's Church** Roman church of St. Praxedes, 2nd-century martyred virgin
**Vanity saith** in Ecclesiastes 1:2 (*Koheleth*, or the preacher)
**Anselm** probably the bishop's first-born natural son
**sons mine** At the moment of death, the bishop can acknowledge that his "nephews" are actually his sons.

She, men would have to be your mother once,
Old Gandolf envied me, so fair she was!
What's done is done, and she is dead beside,
Dead long ago, and I am Bishop since,
And as she died so must we die ourselves,
And thence ye may perceive the world's a dream.
10    Life, how and what is it? As here I lie
In this state-chamber, dying by degrees,
Hours and long hours in the dead night, I ask
'Do I live, am I dead?' Peace, peace seems all.
Saint Praxed's ever was the church for peace;
And so, about this tomb of mine. I fought
With tooth and nail to save my niche, ye know:
—Old Gandolf cozened me, despite my care;
Shrewd was that snatch from out the corner South
He graced his carrion with, God curse the same!
20    Yet still my niche is not so cramped but thence
One sees the pulpit o' the epistle-side,°
And somewhat of the choir, those silent seats,
And up into the aery dome where live
The angels, and a sunbeam's sure to lurk:
And I shall fill my slab of basalt there,
And 'neath my tabernacle° take my rest,
With those nine columns round me, two and two,
The odd one at my feet where Anselm stands:
Peach-blossom marble all, the rare, the ripe
30    As fresh-poured red wine of a mighty pulse.°
—Old Gandolf with his paltry onion-stone,°
Put me where I may look at him! True peach,
Rosy and flawless: how I earned the prize!
Draw close: that conflagration of my church
—What then? So much was saved if aught were missed!
My sons, ye would not be my death? Go dig
The white-grape vineyard where the oil-press stood,
Drop water gently till the surface sink,
And if ye find . . . Ah God, I know not, I! . . .
40    Bedded in store of rotten fig-leaves soft,
And corded up in a tight olive-frail,
Some lump, ah God, of *lapis lazuli,*°
Big as a Jew's head° cut off at the nape,
Blue as a vein o'er the Madonna's breast . . .
Sons, all have I bequeathed you, villas, all,
That brave Frascati° villa with its bath,
So, let the blue lump poise between my knees,

---

**epistle-side** right side as one faces the altar;
**gospel-side** on the left
**tabernacle** canopy above the tomb
**pulse** grape's pulp

**onion-stone** poor marble, colored like an onion
and peeling like it
**lapis lazuli** blue stone, semi-precious
**head** John the Baptist's
**Frascati** elegant Roman suburb

Like God the Father's globe on both his hands
Ye worship in the Jesu Church° so gay,
50  For Gandolf shall not choose but see and burst!
Swift as a weaver's shuttle° fleet our years:
Man goeth to the grave, and where is he?
Did I say basalt for my slab, sons? Black—
'Twas ever antique-black° I meant! How else
Shall ye contrast my frieze to come beneath?
The bas-relief in bronze ye promised me,
Those Pans and Nymphs ye wot of, and perchance
Some tripod,° thyrsus,°, with a vase or so
The Saviour at his sermon on the mount,
60  Saint Praxed in a glory, and one Pan
Ready to twitch the Nymph's last garment off,
And Moses with the tables°. . . but I know
Ye mark me not! What do they whisper thee,
Child of my bowels, Anselm? Ah, ye hope
To revel down my villas while I gasp
Bricked o'er with beggar's mouldy travertine°
Which Gandolf from his tomb-top chuckles at!
Nay, boys, ye love me—all of jasper,° then!
'Tis jasper ye stand pledged to, lest I grieve
70  My bath must needs be left behind, alas!
One block, pure green as a pistachio-nut,
There's plenty jasper somewhere in the world—
And have I not Saint Praxed's ear to pray
Horses for ye, and brown Greek manuscripts,
And mistresses with great smooth marbly limbs?
—That's if ye carve my epitaph aright,
Choice Latin, picked phrase, Tully's° every word,
No gaudy ware like Gandolf's second line—
Tully, my masters? Ulpian° serves his need!
80  And then how I shall lie through centuries,
And hear the blessed mutter of the mass,
And see God made and eaten° all day long,
And feel the steady candle-flame, and taste
Good strong thick stupefying incense-smoke!
For as I lie here, hours of the dead night,
Dying in state and by such slow degrees,
I fold my arms as if they clasped a crook,°
And stretch my feet forth straight as stone can point,

Jesu Church *Il Gesù*, a Jesuit church in Rome
shuttle Job 7:6: "My days are swifter than a weaver's shuttle, and are spent without hope."
antique-black "neroantico," beautiful black stone
tripod three-legged stool used by oracle of Apollo at Delphi
thyrsus staff decorated with ivy or wine branches, carried by Dionysus and his Votaries
tables tablets of the Law, carried down from

Sinai by Moses; see Exodus 32:15
travertine light yellow limestone
jasper quartz
Tully Marcus Tullius Cicero (106–43 B.C.), the orator whose style set the standard for good Latin prose
Ulpian Domitius Ulpianus (170–228 A.D.), late Roman jurist notorious for his bad prose
God . . . eaten in the ceremony of the Mass
crook bishop's crozier or staff

And let the bedclothes, for a mortcloth°, drop
90   Into great laps and folds of sculptor's-work:
And as yon tapers dwindle, and strange thoughts
Grow, with a certain humming in my ears,
About the life before I lived this life,
And this life too, popes, cardinals and priests,
Saint Praxed° at his sermon on the mount,
Your tall pale mother with her talking eyes,
And new-found agate urns as fresh as day,
And marble's language, Latin pure, discreet,
—Aha, ELUCESCEBAT° quoth our friend?
100  No Tully, said I, Ulpian at the best!
Evil and brief hath been my pilgrimage.°
All *lapis*, all, sons! Else I give the Pope
My villas! Will ye ever eat my heart?
Ever your eyes were as a lizard's quick,
They glitter like your mother's for my soul,
Or ye would heighten my impoverished frieze,
Piece out its starved design, and fill my vase
With grapes, and add a vizor° and a Term,°
And to the tripod ye would tie a lynx°
110  That in his struggle throws the thyrsus down,
To comfort me on my entablature
Whereon I am to lie till I must ask
'Do I live, am I dead?' There, leave me, there!
For ye have stabbed me with ingratitude
To death—ye wish it—God, ye wish it! Stone—
Gritstone,° a-crumble! Clammy squares which sweat
As if the corpse they keep were oozing through—
And no more *lapis* to delight the world!
Well go! I bless ye. Fewer tapers there,
120  But in a row: and, going, turn your backs
—Ay, like departing altar-ministrants,
And leave me in my church, the church for peace,
That I may watch at leisure if he leers—
Old Gandolf, at me, from his onion-stone,
As still he envied me, so fair she was!
1844                              1845

mortcloth funeral pall
Saint Praxed The bishop is close to death, and
mistakenly attributes the Sermon on the Mount
to her instead of Christ.
ELUCESCEBAT "he was illustrious," an example
of bad, decadent Latin, whereas Cicero would
have written: "elucebat"
pilgrimage Jacob to Pharaoh, in Genesis 47:9:
". . . few and evil have the days of the years
of my life been, and have not attained unto

the days of the years of the life of my fathers
in the days of their pilgrimage." Jacob, as the
Bishop knew, was gracefully boasting, being
130 at the time.
vizor . . . Term a mask and a bust terminat-
ing in a pillar or pedestal (like representations
of the Roman god Terminus)
lynx Dionysus was accompanied by lynxes.
Gritstone poor sandstone

# Love Among the Ruins°

## I

Where the quiet-coloured end of evening smiles,
     Miles and miles
On the solitary pastures where our sheep
     Half-asleep
Tinkle homeward through the twilight, stray or stop
     As they crop—
Was the site once of a city great and gay,
     (So they say)
Of our country's very capital, its prince
     Ages since
Held his court in, gathered councils, wielding far
     Peace or war.

## II

Now,—the country does not even boast a tree,
     As you see,
To distinguish slopes of verdure, certain rills
     From the hills
Intersect and give a name to, (else they run
     Into one)
Where the domed and daring palace shot its spires
     Up like fires
O'er the hundred-gated circuit of a wall
     Bounding all,
Made of marble, men might march on nor be pressed,
     Twelve abreast.

## III

And such plenty and perfection, see, of grass
     Never was!
Such a carpet as, this summer time, o'erspreads
     And embeds
Every vestige of the city, guessed alone,
     Stock or stone—
Where a multitude of men breathed joy and woe
     Long ago;
Lust of glory pricked their hearts up, dread of shame
     Struck them tame;
And that glory and that shame alike, the gold
     Bought and sold.

Love . . . Ruins evidently more of an ancient
Near Eastern city, like Babylon or Nineveh,
than an Italian city, though the poem's setting
presumably is Italian. The poem was written
the day after *Childe Roland*, and one can see
similarities in the poems' landscapes.

IV

Now,—the single little turret that remains
        On the plains,
By the caper° overrooted, by the gourd°
40        Overscored,
While the patching houseleek's° head of blossom winks
        Through the chinks—
Marks the basement whence a tower in ancient time
        Sprang sublime,
And a burning ring, all round, the chariots traced
        As they raced,
And the monarch and his minions and his dames
        Viewed the games.

V

And I know, while thus the quiet-coloured eve
50        Smiles to leave
To their folding, all our many-tinkling fleece
        In such peace,
And the slopes and rills in undistinguished grey
        Melt away—
That a girl with eager eyes and yellow hair
        Waits me there
In the turret whence the charioteers caught soul
        For the goal,
When the king looked, where she looks now, breathless, dumb
60        Till I come.

VI

But he looked upon the city, every side,
        Far and wide,
All the mountains topped with temples, all the glades'
        Colonnades,
All the causeys,° bridges, aqueducts,—and then,
        All the men!
When I do come, she will speak not, she will stand,
        Either hand
On my shoulder, give her eyes the first embrace
70        Of my face,
Ere we rush, ere we extinguish sight and speech
        Each on each.

VII

In one year they sent a million fighters forth
        South and North,

caper a prickly bush
gourd the fruit of a climbing plant

houseleek's small plant, with petals giving
clustered effect
causeys raised roads

And they built their gods a brazen pillar high
    As the sky,
Yet reserved a thousand chariots in full force—
    Gold, of course.
Oh heart! oh blood that freezes, blood that burns!
80      Earth's returns
For whole centuries of folly, noise and sin!
    Shut them in,
With their triumphs and their glories and the rest!
    Love is best!
1852                    1855

# Fra Lippo Lippi°

I am poor brother Lippo, by your leave!
You need not clap your torches to my face.
Zooks,° what's to blame? you think you see a monk!
What, 'tis past midnight, and you go the rounds,
And here you catch me at an alley's end
Where sportive ladies leave their doors ajar?
The Carmine's my cloister: hunt it up,
Do,—harry out, if you must show your zeal,
Whatever rat, there, haps on his wrong hole,
10  And nip each softling of a wee white mouse,
*Weke, weke,* that's crept to keep him company!
Aha, you know your betters? Then, you'll take
Your hand away that's fiddling on my throat,
And please to know me likewise. Who am I?
Why, one, sir, who is lodging with a friend
Three streets off—he's a certain . . . how d'ye call?
Master—a . . . Cosimo of the Medici,°
In the house that caps the corner. Boh! you were best!
Remember and tell me, the day you're hanged,
20  How you affected such a gullet's-gripe!
But you, sir, it concerns you that your knaves
Pick up a manner nor discredit you:
Zooks, are we pilchards,° that they sweep the streets
And count fair prize what comes into their net?
He's Judas to a tittle, that man is!
Just such a face! Why, sir, you make amends.
Lord, I'm not angry! Bid your hangdogs go

**Fra Lippo Lippi** (1406–69), Florentine painter and libertine Carmelite friar, was a superb (though not innovative, contrary to Browning's judgment) naturalistic artist, in the manner of his teacher, Masaccio. Browning was anxious to portray Lippi as an artist of originality, since the poem totally identifies his own art with Lippi's.

**Zooks** the oath "Gadzooks," the meaning of which is obscure
**Cosimo of the Medici** (1389–1464), renowned as art patron, politician, financier, ruler of Florence
**pilchards** small fish

Drink out this quarter-florin° to the health
Of the munificent House that harbours me
30    (And many more beside, lads! more beside!)
And all's come square again. I'd like his face—
His, elbowing on his comrade in the door
With the pike and lantern,—for the slave that holds
John Baptist's head° a-dangle by the hair
With one hand ('Look you, now,' as who should say)
And his weapon in the other, yet unwiped!
It's not your chance to have a bit of chalk,
A wood-coal or the like? or you should see!
Yes, I'm the painter, since you style me so.
40    What, brother Lippo's doings, up and down,
You know them and they take you? like enough!
I saw the proper twinkle in your eye—
'Tell you, I liked your looks at very first.
Let's sit and set things straight now, hip to haunch.
Here's spring come, and the nights one makes up bands
To roam the town and sing out carnival,
And I've been three weeks shut within my mew,
A-painting for the great man, saints and saints
And saints again. I could not paint all night—
50    Ouf! I leaned out of window for fresh air.
There came a hurry of feet and little feet,
A sweep of lute-strings, laughs, and whifts of song,—
*Flower o' the broom,*°
*Take away love, and our earth is a tomb!*
*Flower o' the quince,*
*I let Lisa go, and what good in life since?*
*Flower o' the thyme*—and so on. Round they went.
Scarce had they turned the corner when a titter
Like the skipping of rabbits by moonlight,—three slim shapes,
60    And a face that looked up . . . zooks, sir, flesh and blood,
That's all I'm made of! Into shreds it went,
Curtain and counterpane and coverlet,
All the bed furniture—a dozen knots,
There was a ladder! Down I let myself,
Hands and feet, scrambling somehow, and so dropped,
And after them. I came up with the fun
Hard by St. Laurence,° hail fellow, well met.—
*Flower o' the rose,*
*If I've been merry, what matter who knows?*
70    And so as I was stealing back again
To get to bed and have a bit of sleep

quarter-florin coin of Florence
for the slave . . . head Matthew 14:1–12
Flower o' the broom This and the other flower-
songs that the cheerful Lippi keeps humming
to himself are meant to suggest the *Stornelli,*
a popular kind of folk song in Italy.
Laurence church of San Lorenzo

Ere I rise up to-morrow and go work
On Jerome° knocking at his poor old breast
With his great round stone to subdue the flesh,
You snap me of the sudden. Ah, I see!
Though your eye twinkles still, you shake your head—
Mine's shaved,—a monk, you say—the sting's in that!
If Master Cosimo announced himself,
Mum's the word naturally; but a monk!
80    Come, what am I a beast for? tell us, now!
I was a baby when my mother died
And father died and left me in the street.
I starved there, God knows how, a year or two
On fig-skins, melon-parings, rinds and shucks,
Refuse and rubbish. One fine frosty day,
My stomach being empty as your hat,
The wind doubled me up and down I went.
Old Aunt Lapaccia° trussed me with one hand,
(Its fellow was a stinger as I knew)
90    And so along the wall, over the bridge,
By the straight cut to the convent. Six words there,
While I stood munching my first bread that month:
'So, boy, you're minded,' quoth the good fat father
Wiping his own mouth, 'twas refection-time,°—
To quit this very miserable world?
Will you renounce' . . . 'the mouthful of bread?' thought I;
By no means! Brief, they made a monk of me;
I did renounce the world, its pride and greed,
Palace, farm, villa, shop and banking-house,
100   Trash, such as these poor devils of Medici
Have given their hearts to—all at eight years old.
Well, sir, I found in time, you may be sure,
'Twas not for nothing—the good bellyful,
The warm serge and the rope that goes all round,
And day-long blessed idleness beside!
'Let's see what the urchin's fit for'—that came next.
Not overmuch their way, I must confess.
Such a to-do! they tried me with their books:
Lord, they'd have taught me Latin in pure waste!
110   *Flower o' the clove,*
*All the Latin I construe is, 'amo' I love!*
But, mind you, when a boy starves in the streets
Eight years together, as my fortune was,
Watching folk's faces to know who will fling
The bit of half-stripped grape-bunch he desires,
And who will curse or kick him for his pains,—

Jerome saint (340–420), renowned for learning and ascetic zeal; never painted by Lippi,
for splendidly obvious reasons

Lapaccia Lippi's foster mother until he joined
the Carmelites
refection-time mealtime

Which gentleman processional° and fine,
Holding a candle to the Sacrament,
Will wink and let him lift a plate and catch
120    The droppings of the wax to sell again,
Or holla for the Eight° and have him whipped,—
How say I?—nay, which dog bites, which lets drop
His bone from the heap of offal in the street,—
Why, soul and sense of him grow sharp alike,
He learns the look of things, and none the less
For admonition from the hunger-pinch.
I had a store of such remarks, be sure,
Which, after I found leisure, turned to use.
I drew men's faces on my copy-books,
130    Scrawled them within the antiphonary's marge,°
Joined legs and arms to the long music-notes,
Found eyes and nose and chin for A's and B's,
And made a string of pictures of the world
Betwixt the ins and outs of verb and noun,
On the wall, the bench, the door. The monks looked black.
'Nay,' quoth the Prior, 'turn him out, d'ye say?
In no wise. Lose a crow and catch a lark.
What if at last we get our man of parts,
We Carmelites,° like those Camaldolese°
140    And Preaching Friars,° to do our church up fine
And put the front on it that ought to be!'
And hereupon he bade me daub away.
Thank you! my head being crammed, the walls a blank,
Never was such prompt disemburdening.
First, every sort of monk, the black and white,
I drew them, fat and lean: then, folk at church,
From good old gossips waiting to confess
Their cribs° of barrel-droppings, candle-ends,—
To the breathless fellow at the altar-foot,
150    Fresh from his murder, safe and sitting there
With the little children round him in a row
Of admiration, half for his beard and half
For that white anger of his victim's son
Shaking a fist at him with one fierce arm,
Signing himself with the other because of Christ
(Whose sad face on the cross sees only this
After the passion of a thousand years)
Till some poor girl, her apron o'er her head,
(Which the intense eyes looked through) came at eve
160    On tiptoe, said a word, dropped in a loaf,

---

**processional** garbed for marching in religious parade
**Eight** magistrates governing Florence
**marge** margins of books used by choir boys

**Carmelites** monks of order of Mount Carmel
**Camaldolese** rival Florentine religious order
**Preaching Friars** Dominicans
**cribs** small thefts

Her pair of earrings and a bunch of flowers
(The brute took growling), prayed, and so was gone.
I painted all, then cried, ' 'Tis ask and have;
Choose, for more's ready!—laid the ladder flat,
And showed my covered bit of cloister-wall.
The monks closed in a circle and praised loud
Till checked, taught what to see and not to see,
Being simple bodies,—'That's the very man!
Look at the boy who stoops to pat the dog!
170   That woman's like the Prior's niece° who comes
To care about his asthma: it's the life!'
But there my triumph's straw-fire flared and funked;°
Their betters took their turn to see and say:
The Prior and the learnèd pull a face
And stopped all that in no time. 'How? what's here?
Quite from the mark of painting, bless us all!
Faces, arms, legs and bodies like the true
As much as pea and pea! it's devil's-game!
Your business is not to catch men with show,
180   With homage to the perishable clay,
But lift them over it, ignore it all,
Make them forget there's such a thing as flesh.
Your business is to paint the souls of men—
Man's soul, and it's a fire, smoke . . . no, it's not . . .
It's vapour done up like a new-born babe—
(In that shape when you die it leaves your mouth)
It's . . . well, what matters talking, it's the soul!
Give us no more of body than shows soul!
Here's Giotto,° with his Saint a-praising God,
190   That sets up praising,—why not stop with him?
Why put all thoughts of praise out of our head
With wonder at lines, colours, and what not?
Paint the soul, never mind the legs and arms!
Rub all out, try at it a second time.
Oh, that white smallish female with the breasts,
She's just my niece . . . Herodias,° I would say,—
Who went and danced and got men's heads cut off!
Have it all out!' Now, is this sense, I ask?
A fine way to paint soul, by painting body
200   So ill, the eye can't stop there, must go further
And can't fare worse! Thus, yellow does for white
When what you put for yellow's simply black,
And any sort of meaning looks intense

Prior's niece probably the Prior's natural daughter
funked gone up in smoke
Giotto   Giotto   di   Bondone   (1276–1337),
founder of school of painting against which

Masaccio (and Lippi) rebelled as being over-
spiritualized
Herodias Herod's sister-in-law; mother of
Salome who demanded and got John the Bap-
tist's head as payment for her dance before
Herod

When all beside itself means and looks nought.
Why can't a painter lift each foot in turn,
Left foot and right foot, go a double step,
Make his flesh liker and his soul more like,
Both in their order? Take the prettiest face,
The Prior's niece . . . patron-saint—is it so pretty
210    You can't discover if it means hope, fear,
Sorrow or joy? won't beauty go with these?
Suppose I've made her eyes all right and blue,
Can't I take breath and try to add life's flash,
And then add soul and heighten them threefold?
Or say there's beauty with no soul at all—
(I never saw it—put the case the same—)
If you get simple beauty and nought else,
You get about the best thing God invents:
That's somewhat: and you'll find the soul you have missed,
220    Within yourself, when you return him thanks.
'Rub all out!' Well, well, there's my life, in short,
And so the thing has gone on ever since.
I'm grown a man no doubt, I've broken bounds:
You should not take a fellow eight years old
And make him swear to never kiss the girls.
I'm my own master, paint now as I please—
Having a friend, you see, in the Corner-house!°
Lord, it's fast holding by the rings in front—
Those great rings serve more purposes than just
230    To plant a flag in, or tie up a horse!
And yet the old schooling sticks, the old grave eyes
Are peeping o'er my shoulder as I work,
The heads shake still—'It's art's decline, my son!
You're not of the true painters, great and old;
Brother Angelico's° the man, you'll find;
Brother Lorenzo° stands his single peer:
Fag on at flesh, you'll never make the third!'
*Flower o' the pine,*
*You keep your mistr . . . manners, and I'll stick to mine!*
240    I'm not the third, then: bless us, they must know!
Don't you think they're the likeliest to know,
They with their Latin? So, I swallow my rage,
Clench my teeth, suck my lips in tight, and paint
To please them—sometimes do and sometimes don't;
For, doing most, there's pretty sure to come
A turn, some warm eve finds me at my saints—
A laugh, a cry, the business of the world—

---

**Corner-house** palace of the Medici
**Angelico** Fra Angelico (1387–1455), major painter of the school of Giotto; renowned for his piety

**Lorenzo** Lorenzo Monaco (1370–1425), school of Giotto

*(Flower o' the peach,*
*Death for us all, and his own life for each!)*
250 And my whole soul revolves, the cup runs over,
The world and life's too big to pass for a dream,
And I do these wild things in sheer despite,
And play the fooleries you catch me at,
In pure rage! The old mill-horse, out at grass
After hard years, throws up his stiff heels so,
Although the miller does not preach to him
The only good of grass is to make chaff.
What would men have? Do they like grass or no—
May they or mayn't they? all I want's the thing
260 Settled for ever one way. As it is,
You tell too many lies and hurt yourself:
You don't like what you only like too much,
You do like what, if given you at your word,
You find abundantly detestable.
For me, I think I speak as I was taught;
I always see the garden and God there
A-making man's wife: and, my lesson learned,
The value and significance of flesh,
I can't unlearn ten minutes afterwards.

270    You understand me: I'm a beast, I know.
But see, now—why, I see as certainly
As that the morning-star's about to shine,
What will hap some day. We've a youngster here
Comes to our convent, studies what I do,
Slouches and stares and lets no atom drop:
His name is Guidi°—he'll not mind the monks—
They call him Hulking Tom, he lets them talk—
He picks my practice up—he'll paint apace,
I hope so—though I never live so long,
280 I know what's sure to follow. You be judge!
You speak no Latin more than I, belike,
However, you're my man, you've seen the world
—The beauty and the wonder and the power,
The shapes of things, their colours, lights and shades,
Changes, surprises,—and God made it all!
—For what? Do you feel thankful, ay or no,
For this fair town's face, yonder river's line,
The mountain round it and the sky above,
Much more the figures of man, woman, child,
290 These are the frame to? What's it all about?
To be passed over, despised? or dwelt upon,
Wondered at? oh, this last of course!—you say.

**Guidi** Tommaso Guidi (1401–28), known as
Masaccio, translatable as "Hulking Tom" or
"Big Tom"

But why not do as well as say,—paint these
Just as they are, careless what comes of it?
God's works—paint anyone, and count it crime
To let a truth slip. Don't object, 'His works
Are here already; nature is complete:
Suppose you reproduce her—(which you can't)
There's no advantage! you must beat her, then.'
300    For, don't you mark? we're made so that we love
First when we see them painted, things we have passed
Perhaps a hundred times nor cared to see;
And so they are better, painted—better to us,
Which is the same thing. Art was given for that;
God uses us to help each other so,
Lending our minds out. Have you noticed, now,
Your cullion's° hanging face? A bit of chalk,
And trust me but you should, though! How much more,
If I drew higher things with the same truth!
310    That were to take the Prior's pulpit-place,
Interpret God to all of you! Oh, oh,
It makes me mad to see what men shall do
And we in our graves! This world's no blot for us,
Nor blank; it means intensely, and means good:
To find its meaning is my meat and drink.
'Ay, but you don't so instigate to prayer!'
Strikes in the Prior: 'when your meaning's plain
It does not say to folk—remember matins,
Or, mind you fast next Friday!' Why, for this
320    What need of art at all? A skull and bones,
Two bits of stick nailed crosswise, or, what's best,
A bell to chime the hour with, does as well.
I painted a Saint Laurence° six months since
At Prato,° splashed the fresco in fine style:
'How looks my painting, now the scaffold's down?'
I ask a brother: 'Hugely,' he returns—
'Already not one phiz of your three slaves
Who turn the Deacon off his toasted side,
But's scratched and prodded to our heart's content,
330    The pious people have so eased their own
With coming to say prayers there in a rage:
We get on fast to see the bricks beneath.
Expect another job this time next year,
For piety and religion grow in the crowd—
Your painting serves its purpose!' Hang the fools!
—That is—you'll not mistake an idle word
Spoke in a huff by a poor monk, God wot,

cullion's base or vile man                    Prato near Florence
Laurence martyr-saint roasted on a grid-iron
in 258

Tasting the air this spicy night which turns
The unaccustomed head like Chianti° wine!
340 Oh, the church knows! don't misreport me, now!
It's natural a poor monk out of bounds
Should have his apt word to excuse himself:
And hearken how I plot to make amends.
I have bethought me: I shall paint a piece
. . . There's for you! Give me six months, then go, see
Something in Sant' Ambrogio's!° Bless the nuns!
They want a cast o' my office° I shall paint
God in the midst, Madonna and her babe,
Ringed by a bowery flowery angel-brood,
350 Lilies and vestments and white faces, sweet
As puff on puff of grated orris-root°
When ladies crowd to Church at midsummer.
And then in the front, of course a saint or two—
Saint John, because he saves the Florentines,
Saint Ambrose, who puts down in black and white
The convent's friends and gives them a long day,
And Job, I must have him there past mistake,
The man of Uz° (and Us without the z,
Painters who need his patience). Well, all these
360 Secured at their devotion, up shall come
Out of a corner when you least expect,
As one by a dark stair into a great light,
Music and talking, who but Lippo! I!—
Mazed, motionless and moonstruck—I'm the man!
Back I shrink—what is this I see and hear?
I, caught up with my monk's things by mistake,
My old serge gown and rope that goes all round,
I, in this presence, this pure company!
Where's a hole, where's a corner for escape?
370 Then steps a sweet angelic slip of a thing
Forward, puts out a soft palm—'Not so fast!'
—Addresses the celestial presence, 'nay—
He made you and devised you, after all,
Though he's none of you! Could Saint John° there draw—
His camel-hair make up a painting-brush?
We come to brother Lippo for all that,
*Iste perfecit opus!*° So, all smile—
I shuffle sideways with my blushing face
Under the cover of a hundred wings
380 Thrown like a spread of kirtles° when you're gay

Chianti region south of Florence, still famous for its wine
Sant' Ambrogio's nuns' convent
cast o' my office sample of my work
orris-root iris-root made into perfume
Uz Job's birthplace
John Mark 1:6: "And John was clothed with camel's hair"
Iste . . . opus This man made the work
kirtles dresses

And play hot cockles,° all the doors being shut,
Till, wholly unexpected, in there pops
The hothead husband! Thus I scuttle off
To some safe bench behind, not letting go
The palm of her, the little lily thing
That spoke the good word for me in the nick,
Like the Prior's niece . . . Saint Lucy°, I would say.
And so all's saved for me, and for the church
A pretty picture gained. Go, six months hence!
390  Your hand, sir, and good-bye: no lights, no lights!
The street's hushed, and I know my own way back,
Don't fear me! There's the grey beginning. Zooks!
1853                                        1855


# A Toccata of Galuppi's°

### I

Oh Galuppi, Baldassaro, this is very sad to find!
I can hardly misconceive you; it would prove me deaf and blind;
But although I take your meaning, 'tis with such a heavy mind!

### II

Here you come with your old music, and here's all the good it brings.
What, they lived once thus at Venice where the merchants were the kings,
Where Saint Mark's° is, where the Doges° used to wed the sea with rings?°

### III

Ay, because the sea's the street there; and 'tis arched by . . . what you call
. . . Shylock's bridge° with houses on it, where they kept the carnival:
I was never out of England°—it's as if I saw it all.

### IV

10  Did young people take their pleasure when the sea was warm in May?
Balls and masks begun at midnight, burning ever to mid-day,
When they made up fresh adventures for the morrow, do you say?

hot cockles sexual variant on game of blind-
man's buff
Saint Lucy Prior's "niece" who served as model
A Toccata of Galuppi's Baldassare Galuppi
(1706–85), Venetian composer, organist at St.
Mark's, and renowned in his own day for his
light operas. A *toccata* or "touch piece" resembles improvisation in its spirit and movement, and is meant to show off the performer's
technique, even as this poem demonstrates
Browning's uncanny skill at mingling several
voices with their rival tones.

St. Mark's cathedral of Venice
Doges Venice's chief magistrate was called
the Doge
rings From Ascension Day, 1000 A.D. on, for
several centuries, the Doge annually officiated
at the marriage of the Adriatic (as bride) to
Venice, by ceremonially tossing a ring into the
sea, thus symbolizing Venice's domination of
the waters.
bridge the Rialto, spanning the Grand Canal
England Browning's way of making clear that
he is not this monologue's speaker

V

Was a lady such a lady, cheeks so round and lips so red,—
On her neck the small face buoyant, like a bell-flower on its bed,
O'er the breast's superb abundance where a man might base his head?

VI

Well, and it was graceful of them—they'd break talk off and afford
—She, to bite her mask's black velvet—he, to finger on his sword,
While you sat and played Toccatas, stately at the clavichord?°

VII

What? Those lesser thirds so plaintive, sixths diminished, sigh on sigh,
20    Told them something? Those suspensions, those solutions—'Must we die?'
Those commiserating sevenths°—'Life might last! we can but try!'

VIII

'Were you happy?'—'Yes.'—'And are you still as happy?'—'Yes. And you?'
—'Then, more kisses!'—'Did I stop them, when a million seemed so few?'
Hark, the dominant's persistence till it must be answered to!

IX

So, an octave struck the answer. Oh, they praised you, I dare say!
'Brave Galuppi! that was music! good alike at grave and gay!
I can always leave off talking when I hear a master play!'

X

Then they left you for their pleasure: till in due time, one by one,
Some with lives that came to nothing, some with deeds as well undone,
30    Death stepped tacitly and took them where they never see the sun.

XI

But when I sit down to reason, think to take my stand nor swerve,
While I triumph o'er a secret wrung from nature's close reserve,°
In you come with your cold music till I creep through every nerve.

XII

Yes, you, like a ghostly cricket, creaking where a house was burned:
'Dust and ashes, dead and done with, Venice spent what Venice earned.
The soul, doubtless, is immortal—where a soul can be discerned.

XIII

'Yours for instance: you know physics, something of geology,
Mathematics are your pastime; souls shall rise in their degree;
Butterflies may dread extinction,—you'll not die, it cannot be!

clavichord stringed keyboard instrument; pre-cursor of the piano
sevenths The intervals, and the other musical terms employed, are brilliantly explained by Browning's own implicit comments.
But when . . . reserve The speaker may be a scientist or metaphysician, or simply a culti-vated man actively interested in the advances of 19th-century science; either way he tries to abide in an intellectual compromise that seeks natural evidences for immortality, but Galuppi and his public knew better in one way, and Browning (whose faith transcends mere nature) in another.

### XIV

40 'As for Venice and her people, merely born to bloom and drop,
Here on earth they bore their fruitage, mirth and folly were the crop:
What of soul was left, I wonder, when the kissing had to stop?

### XV

'Dust and ashes!' So you creak it, and I want the heart to scold.
Dear dead women, with such hair, too—what's become of all the gold
Used to hang and brush their bosoms? I feel chilly and grown old.
1847                                                           1855

# By the Fire-side

### I

How well I know what I mean to do
    When the long dark autumn-evenings come
And where, my soul, is thy pleasant hue?
    With the music of all thy voices, dumb
In life's November too!

### II

I shall be found by the fire, suppose,
    O'er a great wise book as beseemeth age,
While the shutters flap as the cross-wind blows
    And I turn the page, and I turn the page,
10 Not verse now, only prose!

### III

Till the young ones whisper, finger on lip,
    'There he is at it, deep in Greek:
Now then, or never, out we slip
    To cut from the hazels by the creek
A mainmast for our ship!'

### IV

I shall be at it indeed, my friends:
    Greek puts already on either side
Such a branch-work forth as soon extends
    To a vista opening far and wide,
20 And I pass out where it ends.

### V

The outside-frame like your hazel-trees:
    But the inside-archway widens fast,
And a rarer sort succeeds to these,
    And we slope to Italy at last
And youth, by green degrees.

### VI

I follow wherever I am led,
 Knowing so well the leader's hand:
Oh woman-country, wooed not wed,
 Loved all the more by earth's male-lands,
30    Laid to their hearts instead!

### VII

Look at the ruined chapel again
 Half-way up in the Alpine gorge!
Is that a tower, I point you plain,
 Or is it a mill, or an iron-forge
Breaks solitude in vain?

### VIII

A turn, and we stand in the heart of things;
 The woods are round us, heaped and dim;
From slab to slab how it slips and springs,
 The thread of water single and slim,
40    Through the ravage some torrent brings!

### IX

Does it feed the little lake below?
 That speck of white just on its marge
Is Pella;° see, in the evening glow,
 How sharp the silver spear-heads charge
When Alp meets heaven in snow!

### X

On our other side is the straight-up rock;
 And a path is kept 'twixt the gorge and it
By boulder-stones where lichens mock
 The marks on a moth, and small ferns fit
50    Their teeth to the polished block.

### XI

Oh the sense of the yellow mountain flowers,
 And thorny balls, each three in one,
The chestnuts throw on our path in showers!
 For the drop of the woodland fruit's begun,
These early November hours,

### XII

That crimson the creeper's leaf across
 Like a splash of blood, intense, abrupt,

**Pella** a high peak

O'er a shield else gold from rim to boss,
   And lay it for show on the fairy-cupped
60    Elf-needled mat of moss,

### XIII

By the rose-flesh mushrooms, undivulged
   Last evening—nay, in today's first dew
Yon sudden coral nipple bulged,
   Where a freaked fawn-coloured flaky crew
Of toadstools peep indulged.

### XIV

And yonder, at foot of the fronting ridge
   That takes the turn to a range beyond,
Is the chapel reached by the one-arched bridge
   Where the water is stopped in a stagnant pond
70    Danced over by the midge.

### XV

The chapel and bridge are of stone alike,
   Blackish-grey and mostly wet;
Cut hemp-stalks steep in the narrow dyke.
   See here again, how the lichens fret
And the roots of the ivy strike!

### XVI

Poor little place, where its one priest comes
   On a festa-day, if he comes at all,
To the dozen folk from their scattered homes,
   Gathered within that precinct small
80    By the dozen ways one roams—

### XVII

To drop from the charcoal-burners' huts,
   Or climb from the hemp-dressers' low shed,
Leave the grange where the woodman stores his nuts,
   Or the wattled cote where the fowlers spread
Their gear on the rock's bare juts.

### XVIII

It has some pretension too, this front,
   With its bit of fresco half-moon-wise
Set over the porch, Art's early wont:
   'Tis John in the Desert,° I surmise,
90    But has borne the weather's brunt—

**John . . . Desert** Saint John the Evangelist died religious poem, *A Death in the Desert.*
in the desert; see Browning's harsh but strong

### XIX

Not from the fault of the builder, though,
    For a pent-house properly projects
Where three carved beams make a certain show,
    Dating—good thought of our architect's—
'Five, six, nine, he lets you know.

### XX

And all day long a bird sings there,
    And a stray sheep drinks at the pond at times;
The place is silent and aware;
    It has had its scenes, its joys and crimes,
But that is its own affair.

### XXI

My perfect wife, my Leonor,°
    Oh heart, my own, oh eyes, mine too,
Whom else could I dare look backward for,
    With whom beside should I dare pursue
The path grey heads abhor?

### XXII

For it leads to a crag's sheer edge with them;
    Youth, flowery all the way, there stops—
Not they; age threatens and they contemn,
    Till they reach the gulf wherein youth drops,
One inch from life's safe hem!

### XXIII

With me, youth led . . . I will speak now,
    No longer watch you as you sit
Reading by fire-light, that great brow
    And the spirit-small hand propping it,
Mutely, my heart knows how—

### XXIV

When, if I think but deep enough,
    You are wont to answer, prompt as rhyme;
And you, too, find without rebuff
    Response your soul seeks many a time
Piercing its fine flesh-stuff.

### XXV

My own, confirm me! If I tread
    This path back, is it not in pride

100

110

120

Leonor affectionate name for Mrs. Browning,
based on Leonora of *Fidelio*, Beethoven's opera

To think how little I dreamed it led
    To an age so blest that, by its side,
Youth seems the waste instead?

### XXVI

My own, see where the years conduct!
    At first, 'twas something our two souls
Should mix as mists do; each is sucked
    Into each now: on, the new stream rolls,
130    Whatever rocks obstruct.

### XXVII

Think, when our one soul understands
    The great Word° which makes all things new,
When earth breaks up and heaven expands,
    How will the change strike me and you
In the house not made with hands?

### XXVIII

Oh I must feel your brain prompt mine,
    Your heart anticipate my heart,
You must be just before, in fine,
    See and make me see, for your part,
140    New depths of the divine!

### XXIX

But who could have expected this
    When we two drew together first
Just for the obvious human bliss,
    To satisfy life's daily thirst
With a thing men seldom miss?

### XXX

Come back with me to the first of all,
    Let us lean and love it over again,
Let us now forget and now recall,
    Break the rosary in a pearly rain,
150    And gather what we let fall!

### XXXI

What did I say?—that a small bird sings
    All day long, save when a brown pair
Of hawks from the wood float with wide wings
    Strained to a bell: 'gainst noon-day glare
You count the streaks and rings.

great Word . . . new Revelation 21:5: "Behold, I make all things new"

XXXII

But at afternoon or almost eve
    'Tis better; then the silence grows
To that degree, you half believe
    It must get rid of what it knows,
160 Its bosom does so heave.

XXXIII

Hither we walked then, side by side,
    Arm in arm and cheek to cheek,
And still I questioned or replied,
    While my heart, convulsed to really speak,
Lay choking in its pride.

XXXIV

Silent the crumbling bridge we cross,
    And pity and praise the chapel sweet,
And care about the fresco's loss,
    And wish for our souls a like retreat,
170 And wonder at the moss.

XXXV

Stoop and kneel on the settle under,
    Look through the window's grated square:
Nothing to see! For fear of plunder,
    The cross is down and the altar bare,
As if thieves don't fear thunder.

XXXVI

We stoop and look in through the grate,
    See the little porch and rustic door,
Read duly the dead builder's date;
    Then cross the bridge that we crossed before,
180 Take the path again—but wait!

XXXVII

Oh moment, one and infinite!
    The water slips o'er stock and stone;
The West is tender, hardly bright:
    How grey at once is the evening grown—
One star, its chrysolite!°

XXXVIII

We two stood there with never a third,
    But each by each, as each knew well:
The sights we saw and the sounds we heard,
    The lights and the shades made up a spell
190 Till the trouble grew and stirred.

**chrysolite**  green semi-precious stone

XXXIX

Oh, the little more, and how much it is!
And the little less, and what worlds away!
How a sound shall quicken content to bliss,
    Or a breath suspend the blood's best play,
And life be a proof of this!

XL

Had she willed it, still had stood the screen
    So light, so sure, 'twixt my love and her:
I could fix her face with a guard between,
    And find her soul as when friends confer,
200    Friends—lovers that might have been.

XLI

For my heart had a touch of the woodland-time,
    Wanting to sleep now over its best.
Shake the whole tree in the summer-prime,
    But bring to the last leaf no such test!
'Hold the last fast!' runs the rhyme.

XLII

For a chance to make your little much,
    To gain a lover and lose a friend,
Venture the tree and a myriad such,
    When nothing you mar but the year can mend:
210    But a last leaf—fear to touch!

XLIII

Yet should it unfasten itself and fall
    Eddying down till it find your face
At some slight wind—best chance of all!
    Be your heart henceforth its dwelling-place
You trembled to forestall!

XLIV

Worth how well, those dark grey eyes,
    That hair so dark and dear, how worth
That a man should strive and agonize,
    And taste a veriest hell on earth
220    For the hope of such a prize!

XLV

You might have turned and tried a man,
    Set him a space to weary and wear,
And prove which suited more your plan,
    His best of hope or his worst despair,
Yet end as he began.

#### XLVI

But you spared me this, like the heart you are,
 And filled my empty heart at a word.
If two lives join, there is oft a scar,
 They are one and one, with a shadowy third;
230 One near one is too far.

#### XLVII

A moment after, and hands unseen
 Were hanging the night around us fast;
But we knew that a bar was broken between
 Life and life: we were mixed at last
In spite of the mortal screen.

#### XLVIII

The forests had done it; there they stood;
 We caught for a moment the powers at play:
They had mingled us so, for once and good,
 Their work was done—we might go or stay,
240 They relapsed to their ancient mood.

#### XLIX

How the world is made for each of us!
 How all we perceive and know in it
Tends to some moment's product thus,
 When a soul declares itself—to wit,
By its fruit, the thing it does!

#### L

Be hate that fruit or love that fruit,
 It forwards the general deed of man,
And each of the Many helps to recruit
 The life of the race by a general plan;
250 Each living his own, to boot.

#### LI

I am named and known by that moment's feat;
 There took my station and degree;
So grew my own small life complete,
 As nature obtained her best of me—
One born to love you, sweet!

#### LII

And to watch you sink by the fire-side now
 Back again, as you mutely sit
Musing by fire-light, that great brow
 And the spirit-small hand propping it,
260 Yonder, my heart knows how!

LIII
So, earth has gained by one man the more,
    And the gain of earth must be heaven's gain too;
And the whole is well worth thinking o'er
    When autumn comes: which I mean to do
One day, as I said before.
1853                1855


# 'Childe Roland to the Dark Tower Came'

This nightmare poem, according to Browning, had no overt allegorical purpose, but the phantasmagoria is so powerful as to invite many allegorizings. W.C. DeVane traced much of the landscape to one chapter of a book Browning had memorized as a boy, Gerard de Lairesse's *The Art of Painting in All Its Branches*. The chapter's title, "Of Things Deformed and Broken," might be a motto to the poem. However the poem is interpreted, its universal appeal seems to center upon its vision of a willfully ruined quester, whose own strength of imagination has become a deform- ing and breaking agent, and who calls into question the meaningfulness of all premeditated human action. The relation of Childe Roland to his band of brothers, the questers who failed one by one before him, may suggest the relation of Browning to his own poetic precursors, and prefigures the relation between the hero and the cowards in Yeats's death poem, *Cuchulain Comforted*.

The title is taken from Shakespeare's *King Lear* (III.iv.173). A "childe" is a well- born youth who is still a candidate for knighthood.


# 'Childe Roland to the Dark Tower Came'
### (See Edgar's Song in *Lear*)

I
My first thought was, he lied in every word,
    That hoary cripple, with malicious eye
    Askance to watch the working of his lie
On mine, and mouth scarce able to afford
Suppression of the glee, that pursed and scored
    Its edge, at one more victim gained thereby.


II
What else should he be set for, with his staff?
    What, save to waylay with his lies, ensnare
    All travellers who might find him posted there,
10    And ask the road? I guessed what skull-like laugh
Would break, what crutch 'gin° write my epitaph
    For pastime in the dusty thoroughfare,

'gin begin to

### III

If at his counsel I should turn aside
  Into that ominous tract which, all agree,
  Hides the Dark Tower. Yet acquiescingly
I did turn as he pointed: neither pride
Nor hope rekindling at the end descried,
  So much as gladness that some end might be.

### IV

For, what with my whole world wide wandering,
20    What with my search drawn out through years, my hope
  Dwindled into a ghost not fit to cope
With that obstreperous joy success would bring,—
I hardly tried now to rebuke the spring
  My heart made, finding failure in its scope.

### V

As when a sick man very near to death
  Seems dead indeed, and feels begin and end
  The tears and takes the farewell of each friend,
And hears one bid the other go, draw breath
Freelier outside, ('since all is o'er,' he saith,
30    'And the blow fallen no grieving can amend');

### VI

While some discuss if near the other graves
  Be room enough for this, and when a day
  Suits best for carrying the corpse away,
With care about the banners, scarves and staves:
And still the man hears all, and only craves
  He may not shame such tender love and stay.

### VII

Thus, I had so long suffered in this quest,
  Heard failure prophesied so oft, been writ
  So many times among 'The Band'—to wit,
40    The knights who to the Dark Tower's search addressed
Their steps—that just to fail as they, seemed best,
  And all the doubt was now—should I be fit?

### VIII

So, quiet as despair, I turned from him,
  That hateful cripple, out of his highway
  Into the path he pointed. All the day
Had been a dreary one at best, and dim
Was settling to its close, yet shot one grim
  Red leer to see the plain catch its estray.°

**estray** potential victim who has strayed

### IX

For mark! no sooner was I fairly found
50    Pledged to the plain, after a pace or two,
    Than, pausing to throw backward a last view
    O'er the safe road, 'twas gone; grey plain all round:
    Nothing but plain to the horizon's bound.
    I might go on; nought else remained to do.

### X

So, on I went. I think I never saw
    Such starved ignoble nature; nothing throve:
    For flowers—as well expect a cedar grove!
    But cockle, spurge,° according to their law
    Might propagate their kind, with none to awe,
60    You'd think; a burr had been a treasure-trove.

### XI

No! penury, inertness and grimace,
    In some strange sort, were the land's portion. 'See
    Or shut your eyes,' said Nature peevishly,
    'It nothing skills: I cannot help my case:
    'Tis the Last Judgment's fire must cure this place,
    Calcine° its clods and set my prisoners free.'

### XII

If there pushed any ragged thistle-stalk
    Above its mates, the head was chopped; the bents°
    Were jealous else. What made those holes and rents
70    In the dock's harsh swarth leaves, bruised as to baulk
    All hope of greenness? 'tis a brute must walk
    Pashing° their life out, with a brute's intents.

### XIII

As for the grass, it grew as scant as hair
    In leprosy; thin dry blades pricked the mud
    Which underneath looked kneaded up with blood.
    One stiff blind horse, his every bone a-stare,
    Stood stupefied, however he came there:
    Thrust out past service from the devil's stud!

### XIV

Alive? he might be dead for aught I know,
80    With that red gaunt and colloped° neck a-strain,
    And shut eyes underneath the rusty mane;
    Seldom went such grotesqueness with such woe;

cockle, spurge weeds
Calcine melt to a powder
bents very coarse grasses

Pashing trampling down
colloped ridged

I never saw a brute I hated so;
He must be wicked to deserve such pain.

### XV

I shut my eyes and turned them on my heart.
As a man calls for wine before he fights,
I asked one draught of earlier, happier sights,
Ere fitly I could hope to play my part.
Think first, fight afterwards—the soldier's art:
One taste of the old time sets all to rights.

### XVI

Not it! I fancied Cuthbert's reddening face
Beneath its garniture of curly gold,
Dear fellow, till I almost felt him fold
An arm in mine to fix me to the place,
That way he used. Alas, one night's disgrace!
Out went my heart's new fire and left it cold.

### XVII

Giles then, the soul of honour—there he stands
Frank as ten years ago when knighted first.
What honest men should dare (he said) he durst.
Good—but the scene shifts—faugh! what hangman-hands
Pin to his breast a parchment? his own bands
Read it. Poor traitor, spit upon and curst!

### XVIII

Better this present than a past like that;
Back therefore to my darkening path again!
No sound, no sight as far as eye could strain.
Will the night send a howlet or a bat?
I asked: when something on the dismal flat
Came to arrest my thoughts and change their train.

### XIX

A sudden little river crossed my path
As unexpected as a serpent comes.
No sluggish tide congenial to the glooms;
This, as it frothed by, might have been a bath
For the fiend's glowing hoof—to see the wrath
Of its black eddy bespate° with flakes and spumes.

### XX

So petty yet so spiteful! All along,
Low scrubby alders kneeled down over it;
Drenched willows flung them headlong in a fit

**bespate** bespattered

Of mute despair, a suicidal throng:
The river which had done them all the wrong,
120    Whate'er that was, rolled by, deterred no whit.

### XXI

Which, while I forded,—good saints, how I feared
To set my foot upon a dead man's cheek,
Each step, or feel the spear I thrust to seek
For hollows, tangled in his hair or beard!
—It may have been a water-rat I speared,
But, ugh! it sounded like a baby's shriek.

### XXII

Glad was I when I reached the other bank.
Now for a better country. Vain presage!
Who were the strugglers, what war did they wage,
130    Whose savage trample thus could pad the dank
Soil to a plash? Toads in a poisoned tank,
Or wild cats in a red-hot iron cage—

### XXIII

The fight must so have seemed in that fell cirque.
What penned them there, with all the plain to choose?
No foot-print leading to the horrid mews,
None out of it. Mad brewage set to work
Their brains, no doubt, like galley-slaves the Turk
Pits for his pastime, Christians against Jews.

### XXIV

And more than that—a furlong on—why, there!
140    What bad use was that engine for, that wheel,
Or brake, not wheel—that harrow fit to reel
Men's bodies out like silk? with all the air
Of Tophet's° tool, on earth left unaware,
Or brought to sharpen its rusty teeth of steel.

### XXV

Then came a bit of stubbed ground, once a wood,
Next a marsh, it would seem, and now mere earth
Desperate and done with; (so a fool finds mirth,
Makes a thing and then mars it, till his mood
Changes and off he goes!) within a rood°—
150    Bog, clay and rubble, sand and stark black dearth.

### XXVI

Now blotches rankling, coloured gay and grim,
Now patches where some leanness of the soil's

**Tophet's** Hebrew for Hell                    **rood** quarter-acre

Broke into moss or substances like boils;
Then came some palsied oak, a cleft in him
Like a distorted mouth that splits its rim
Gaping at death, and dies while it recoils.

#### XXVII

And just as far as ever from the end!
　Nought in the distance but the evening, nought
　To point my footstep further! At the thought,
A great black bird, Apollyon's° bosom-friend,
Sailed past, nor beat his wide wing dragon-penned°
　That brushed my cap—perchance the guide I sought.

#### XXVIII

For, looking up, aware I somehow grew,
　'Spite of the dusk, the plain had given place
　All round to mountains—with such name to grace
Mere ugly heights and heaps now stolen in view.
How thus they had surprised me,—solve it, you!
　How to get from them was no clearer case.

#### XXIX

Yet half I seemed to recognize some trick
　Of mischief happened to me, God knows when—
　In a bad dream perhaps. Here ended, then,
Progress this way. When, in the very nick
Of giving up, one time more, came a click
　As when a trap shuts—you're inside the den!

#### XXX

Burningly it came on me all at once,
　This was the place! those two hills on the right,
　Crouched like two bulls locked horn in horn in fight;
While to the left, a tall scalped mountain . . . Dunce,
Dotard, a-dozing at the very nonce,
　After a life spent training for the sight!

#### XXXI

What in the midst lay but the Tower itself?
　The round squat turret, blind as the fool's heart,
　Built of brown stone, without a counterpart
In the whole world. The tempest's mocking elf
Points to the shipman thus the unseen shelf
　He strikes on, only when the timbers start.

**Apollyon** Revelation 9:11: "an angel of the **dragon-penned** dragon-winged
bottomless pit, . . . . Apollyon"

XXXII

Not see? because of night perhaps?—why, day
Came back again for that! before it left,
The dying sunset kindled through a cleft:
190    The hills, like giants at a hunting, lay,
Chin upon hand, to see the game at bay,—
'Now stab and end the creature—to the heft!'

XXXIII

Not hear? when noise was everywhere! it tolled
Increasing like a bell. Names in my ears
Of all the lost adventurers my peers,—
How such a one was strong, and such was bold,
And such was fortunate, yet each of old
Lost, lost! one moment knelled the woe of years.

XXXIV

There they stood, ranged along the hill-sides, met
200    To view the last of me, a living frame
For one more picture! in a sheet of flame
I saw them and I knew them all. And yet
Dauntless the slug-horn° to my lips I set,
And blew. 'Childe Roland to the Dark Tower came.'
1852                                        1855

## How It Strikes a Contemporary°

I only knew one poet in my life:
And this, or something like it, was his way.

You saw go up and down Valladolid,°
A man of mark, to know next time you saw.
His very serviceable suit of black
Was courtly once and conscientious still,
And many might have worn it, though none did:
The cloak, that somewhat shone and showed the threads,
Had purpose, and the ruff, significance.
10    He walked and tapped the pavement with his cane,

slug-horn a word appearing only in the 18th-century poet Chatterton; his mistake of an archaic spelling of "slogan" to mean a "trumpet" How It Strikes a Contemporary This poem's imaginary "poet of Valladolid" represents Browning himself, primarily in his imaginative stance, but Browning increasingly (after his wife's death) was to become a fiercely socializing man-about-town. When Browning wrote this poem, he was preparing his essay on Shelley, and rereading both Shelley and Shakespeare. Behind "How It Strikes . . ." are Shelley's suggestion that "poets are the un-

acknowledged legislators of the world" and King Lear's "As if we were God's spies." A few years after writing this poem, Browning wrote to Ruskin, "A poet's affair is with God, to whom he is accountable, and of whom is his reward. . . ." Like Browning, the apparently lighthearted "poet of Valladolid" beholds the world and mankind "in their actual state of perfection in imperfection" ("Essay on Shelley") and understands that (as Wallace Stevens liked to observe) the imperfect is our paradise.
Valladolid city in north-central Spain, where presumably Browning had never been

Scenting the world, looking it full in face,
An old dog, bald and blindish, at his heels.
They turned up, now, the alley by the church,
That leads nowhither; now, they breathed themselves°
On the main promenade just at the wrong time:
You'd come upon his scrutinizing hat,
Making a peaked shade blacker than itself
Against the single window spared some house
Intact yet with its mouldered Moorish work,—
20 Or else surprise the ferrel° of his stick
Trying the mortar's temper 'tween the chinks
Of some new shop a-building, French and fine.
He stood and watched the cobbler at his trade,
The man who slices lemons into drink,
The coffee-roaster's brazier, and the boys
That volunteer to help him turn its winch.
He glanced o'er books on stalls with half an eye,
And fly-leaf ballads on the vendor's string,
And broad-edge bold-print posters by the wall.
30 He took such cognizance of men and things,
If any beat a horse, you felt he saw;
If any cursed a woman, he took note;
Yet stared at nobody,—you stared at him,
And found, less to your pleasure than surprise,
He seemed to know you and expect as much.
So, next time that a neighbour's tongue was loosed,
It marked the shameful and notorious fact,
We had among us, not so much a spy,
As a recording chief-inquisitor,
40 The town's true master if the town but knew!
We merely kept a governor for form,
While this man walked about and took account
Of all thought, said and acted, then went home,
And wrote it fully to our Lord the King°
Who has an itch to know things, he knows why,
And reads them in his bedroom of a night.
Oh, you might smile! there wanted not a touch,
A tang of . . . well, it was not wholly ease
As back into your mind the man's look came.
50 Stricken in years a little,—such a brow
His eyes had to live under!—clear as flint
On either side the formidable nose
Curved, cut and coloured like an eagle's claw.
Had he to do with A.'s surprising fate?
When altogether old B. disappeared
And young C. got his mistress,—was't our friend,

breathed themselves walked to take the air        King ultimately, God
ferrel metal point

His letter to the King, that did it all?
What paid the bloodless man for so much pains?
Our Lord the King has favourites manifold,
60    And shifts his ministry some once a month;
Our city gets new governors at whiles,—
But never word or sign, that I could hear,
Notified to this man about the streets
The King's approval of those letters conned
The last thing duly at the dead of night.
Did the man love his office? Frowned our Lord,
Exhorting when none heard—'Beseech me not!
Too far above my people,—beneath me!
I set the watch,—how should the people know?
70    Forget them, keep me all the more in mind!'
Was some such understanding 'twixt the two?

I found no truth in one report at least—
That if you tracked him to his home, down lanes
Beyond the Jewry,° and as clean to pace,
You found he ate his supper in a room
Blazing with lights, four Titians° on the wall,
And twenty naked girls to change his plate!
Poor man, he lived another kind of life
In that new stuccoed third house by the bridge,
80    Fresh-painted, rather smart than otherwise!
The whole street might o'erlook him as he sat,
Leg crossing leg, one foot on the dog's back,
Playing a decent cribbage with his maid
(Jacynth, you're sure her name was) o'er the cheese
And fruit, three red halves of starved winter-pears,
Or treat of radishes in April. Nine,
Ten, struck the church clock, straight to bed went he.

My father, like the man of sense he was,
Would point him out to me a dozen times;
90    ' 'St—'St,' he'd whisper, 'the Corregidor!'°
I had been used to think that personage
Was one with lacquered breeches, lustrous belt,
And feathers like a forest in his hat,
Who blew a trumpet and proclaimed the news,
Announced the bull-fights, gave each church its turn,
And memorized the miracle in vogue!
He had a great observance from us boys;
We were in error; that was not the man.

I'd like now, yet had haply been afraid,
100    To have just looked, when this man came to die,

Jewry Jewish quarter of the city          Corregidor chief magistrate
Titians paintings by Titian, Venetian (1477–
1576)

And seen who lined the clean gay garret-sides
And stood about the neat low truckle-bed,°
With the heavenly manner of relieving guard.
Here had been, mark, the general-in-chief,
Through a whole campaign of the world's life and death,
Doing the King's work all the dim day long,
In his old coat and up to knees in mud,
Smoked like a herring, dining on a crust,—
And, now the day was won, relieved at once!
110    No further show or need for that old coat,
You are sure, for one thing! Bless us, all the while
How sprucely we are dressed out, you and I!
A second, and the angels alter that.
Well, I could never write a verse,—could you?
Let's to the Prado° and make the most of time.
1851–52                                              1855


# Master Hugues of Saxe-Gotha°

### I

Hist, but a word, fair and soft!
    Forth and be judged, Master Hugues!
Answer the question I've put you so oft:—
    What do you mean by your mountainous fugues?°
See, we're alone in the loft,—

### II

I, the poor organist here,
    Hugues, the composer of note,
Dead though, and done with, this many a year:
    Let's have a colloquy, something to quote,
10    Make the world prick up its ear!

### III

See, the church empties apace:
    Fast they extinguish the lights.
Hallo there, sacristan!° Five minutes' grace!
    Here's a crank pedal wants setting to rights,
Baulks one of holding the base.

truckle-bed trundle-bed
Prado the principal street of the city
Master Hugues of Saxe-Gotha Master Hugues
is an imaginary composer, a cumbersome imi-
tator of Bach, who came from Saxe-Gotha. But
the poem is scarcely interested in him. What
it reveals, unforgettably, is the questing imagination of the "poor organist" who indeed does
"carry the moon" in his pocket.

fugues The root meaning is "flight"; a musical
form in which successive voices take up a
melody, each voice entering before its predecessor has completed the melody; frequently
intricate development ensues, concluded by a
return to the original key.
sacristan church custodian

#### IV

See, our huge house of the sounds,
  Hushing its hundreds at once,
Bids the last loiterer back to his bounds!
  —O you may challenge them, not a response
20  Get the church-saints on their rounds!

#### V

(Saints go their rounds, who shall doubt?
  —March, with the moon to admire,
Up nave, down chancel, turn transept about,
  Supervise all betwixt pavement and spire,
Put rats and mice to the rout—

#### VI

Aloys and Jurien and Just°—
  Order things back to their place,
Have a sharp eye lest the candlesticks rust,
  Rub the church-plate, darn the sacrament-lace,
30  Clear the desk-velvet of dust.)

#### VII

Here's your book, younger folks shelve!
  Played I not off-hand and runningly,
Just now, your masterpiece, hard number twelve?
  Here's what should strike, could one handle it cunningly:
Help the axe, give it a helve!°

#### VIII

Page after page as I played,
  Every bar's rest, where one wipes
Sweat from one's brow, I looked up and surveyed,
  O'er my three claviers,° yon forest of pipes
40  Whence you still peeped in the shade.

#### IX

Sure you were wishful to speak?
  You, with brow ruled like a score,
Yes, and eyes buried in pits on each cheek,
  Like two great breves,° as they wrote them of yore,
Each side that bar, your straight beak!

#### X

Sure you said—'Good, the mere notes!
  Still, couldst thou take my intent,

Aloys . . . Just patron saints
helve handle
claviers here, banked keyboards

breves longest notes in the score, indicated by
square marks

Know what procured me our Company's votes—
  A master were lauded and sciolists shent,°
50 Parted the sheep from the goats!'


### XI

Well then, speak up, never flinch!
  Quick, ere my candle's a snuff
—Burnt, do you see? to its uttermost inch—
  I believe in you, but that's not enough:
Give my conviction a clinch!


### XII

First you deliver your phrase
  —Nothing propound, that I see,
Fit in itself for much blame or much praise—
  Answered no less, where no answer needs be:
60 Off start the Two on their ways.


### XIII

Straight must a Third interpose,
  Volunteer needlessly help;
In strikes a Fourth, a Fifth thrusts in his nose,
  So the cry's open, the kennel's a-yelp,
Argument's hot to the close.


### XIV

One dissertates, he is candid;
  Two must discept,°—has distinguished;
Three helps the couple, if ever yet man did;
  Four protests; Five makes a dart at the thing wished:
70 Back to One, goes the case bandied.


### XV

One says his say with a difference;
  More of expounding, explaining!
All now is wrangle, abuse, and vociferance;
  Now there's a truce, all's subdued, self-restraining;
Five, though, stands out all the stiffer hence.


### XVI

One is incisive, corrosive;
  Two retorts, nettled, curt, crepitant;
Three makes rejoinder, expansive, explosive;
  Four overbears them all, strident and strepitant:
80 Five . . . O Danaides, O Sieve!°

---

**sciolists shent** scholarly pretenders shamed
**discept** differ
**Sieve** The Danaides, daughters of Danaus, slew

their bridegrooms on their wedding night, and
were condemned eternally to Tartarus, where
they pour water through a sieve.

XVII

Now, they ply axes and crowbars;
    Now, they prick pins at a tissue
Fine as a skein of the casuist Escobar's°
    Worked on the bone of a lie. To what issue?
Where is our gain at the Two-bars?

XVIII

Est fuga, volvitur rota.°
    On we drift: where looms the dim port?
One, Two, Three, Four, Five, contribute their quota;
    Something is gained, if one caught but the import—
90  Show it us, Hugues of Saxe-Gotha!

XIX

What with affirming, denying,
    Holding, risposting,° subjoining,
All's like . . . it's like . . . for an instance I'm trying . . .
    There! See our roof, its gilt moulding and groining
Under those spider-webs lying!

XX

So your fugue broadens and thickens,
    Greatens and deepens and lengthens,
Till we exclaim—'But where's music, the dickens?
    Blot ye the gold, while your spider-web strengthens
100 —Blacked to the stoutest of tickens?'°

XXI

I for man's effort am zealous:
    Prove me such censure unfounded!
Seems it surprising a lover grows jealous—
    Hopes 'twas for something, his organ-pipes sounded,
Tiring three boys at the bellows?

XXII

Is it your moral of Life?
    Such a web, simple and subtle,
Weave we on earth here in impotent strife,
    Backward and forward each throwing his shuttle,
110 Death ending all with a knife?

XXIII

Over our heads truth and nature—
    Still our life's zigzags and dodges,

Escobar's Escobar y Mendoza (1589–1669),
Jesuit writer
Est fuga, volvitur rota It is a flight, the wheel
revolves.

risposting delivering a counter-stroke
tickens mattress ticking

Ins and outs, weaving a new legislature—
God's gold just shining its last where that lodges,
Palled beneath man's usurpature.

### XXIV

So we o'ershroud stars and roses,
  Cherub and trophy and garland;
Nothings grow something which quietly closes
  Heaven's earnest eye: not a glimpse of the far land
120 Gets through our comments and glozes.

### XXV

Ah but traditions, inventions,
  (Say we and make up a visage)
So many men with such various intentions,
  Down the past ages, must know more than this age!
Leave we the web its dimensions!

### XXVI

Who thinks Hugues wrote for the deaf,
  Proved a mere mountain in labour?
Better submit; try again; what's the clef?°
  'Faith, 'tis no trifle for pipe and for tabor°—
130 Four flats, the minor in F.

### XXVII

Friend, your fugue taxes the finger:
  Learning it once, who would lose it?
Yet all the while a misgiving will linger,
  Truth's golden o'er us although we refuse it—
Nature, through cobwebs we string her.

### XXVIII

Hugues! I advise meâ pœnâ°
  (Counterpoint glares like a Gorgon°)
Bid One, Two, Three, Four, Five, clear the arena!
  Say the word, straight I unstop the full-organ,
140 Blare out the mode Palestrina.°

### XXIX

While in the roof, if I'm right there,
  . . . Lo you, the wick in the socket!
Hallo, you sacristan, show us a light there!
  Down it dips, gone like a rocket.

**clef** pitch indication
**tabor** small drum
**meâ pœnâ** at my risk
**Gorgon** one of three snaky-locked ladies whose
glance turned men to stone

**mode Palestrina** the manner of the great Italian
composer Palestrina (1524–94), who rebelled
against the decadence of compositional artifices
and intricacies, and restored a gracious simplicity to contrapuntal music

What, you want, do you, to come unawares,
Sweeping the church up for first morning-prayers,
And find a poor devil has ended his cares
At the foot of your rotten-runged rat-riddled stairs?
  Do I carry the moon in my pocket?
  1852–53                          1855


# Memorabilia°

### I

Ah, did you once see Shelley plain,
  And did he stop and speak to you,
And did you speak to him again?
  How strange it seems and new!

### II

But you were living before that,
  And also you are living after;
And the memory I started at—
  My starting moves your laughter.

### III

I crossed a moor, with a name of its own
  And a certain use in the world no doubt,
Yet a hand's-breadth of it shines alone
  'Mid the blank miles round about:

### IV

For there I picked up on the heather
  And there I put inside my breast
A moulted feather, an eagle-feather!
  Well, I forget the rest.
  1851                          1855


# Andrea del Sarto

Andrea, the son of a Florentine tailor (hence "del Sarto"), lived from 1486 until 1531, when he died of the plague, deserted by his wife and by everyone else. Vasari, who was Browning's major source for Andrea's life (see *The Lives of the Most Eminent Painters, Sculptors and Architects*), and who had been Andrea's pupil, sums up the mingled glory and sorrow of this painter:

**Memorabilia** The title, which means "things worth remembering," hardly conveys the importance of this little poem for the understanding of Browning's relation to Shelley, his prime precursor. A friend recorded Browning as saying "with characteristic vehemence: 'I was one day in the shop of Hodgson, the well-known London bookseller, when a stranger . . . spoke of something that Shelley had once said to him. Suddenly the stranger paused, and burst into laughter as he observed me staring at him with blanched face; and,' the poet continued, 'I still vividly remember how strangely the presence of a man who had seen and spoken with Shelley affected me'."

. . . that truly excellent Andrea del Sarto, in whom art and nature combined to show all that may be done in painting, when design, colouring and invention unite in one and the same person. Had this master possessed a somewhat bolder and more elevated mind; had he been as much distinguished for higher qualifications as he was for genius and depth of judgment in the art he practiced, he would beyond all doubt, have been without an equal. But there was a certain timidity of mind, a sort of diffidence and want of force in his nature, which rendered it impossible that those evidences of ardour and animation, which are proper to the more exalted character, should ever appear in him; nor did he at any time display one particle of that elevation which, could it have been added to the advantages wherewith he was endowed, would have rendered him a truly divine painter: wherefore the works of Andrea are wanting in those ornaments of grandeur, richness, and force, which appear so conspicuously in those of many other masters.

In this deep study of a deliberate artistic self-crippling, Browning gives us a dramatic speaker who has arranged cunningly his own ruin. Andrea has chosen a wife who he knows will betray him, and an existence which must compromise his own vision as a painter. Fearing to fail by attempting greatness, Andrea is content to have been his own knowing parody of what he might have been.

# Andrea del Sarto
### (Called 'The Faultless Painter')

But do not let us quarrel any more,
No, my Lucrezia; bear with me for once:
Sit down and all shall happen as you wish.
You turn your face, but does it bring your heart?
I'll work then for your friend's friend, never fear,
Treat his own subject after his own way,
Fix his own time, accept too his own price,
And shut the money into this small hand
When next it takes mine. Will it? tenderly?
10    Oh, I'll content him,—but tomorrow, Love!
I often am much wearier than you think,
This evening more than usual, and it seems
As if—forgive now—should you let me sit
Here by the window with your hand in mine
And look a half-hour forth on Fiesole,°
Both of one mind, as married people use,
Quietly, quietly the evening through,
I might get up tomorrow to my work
Cheerful and fresh as ever. Let us try.
20    Tomorrow, how you shall be glad for this!
Your soft hand is a woman of itself,
And mine the man's bared breast she curls inside.
Don't count the time lost, neither; you must serve
For each of the five pictures we require:

Fiesole town on hill outside Florence

It saves a model. So! keep looking so—
My serpentining beauty, rounds on rounds!
—How could you ever prick those perfect ears,
Even to put the pearl there! oh, so sweet—
My face, my moon, my everybody's moon,
30   Which everybody looks on and calls his,
And, I suppose, is looked on by in turn,
While she looks—no one's: very dear, no less.
You smile? why, there's my picture ready made,
There's what we painters call our harmony!
A common greyness silvers everything,—
All in a twilight, you and I alike
—You, at the point of your first pride in me
(That's gone you know),—but I, at every point;
My youth, my hope, my art, being all toned down
40   To yonder sober pleasant Fiesole.
There's the bell clinking from the chapel-top;
That length of convent-wall across the way
Holds the trees safer, huddled more inside;
The last monk leaves the garden; days decrease,
And autumn grows, autumn in everything.
Eh? the whole seems to fall into a shape
As if I saw alike my work and self
And all that I was born to be and do,
A twilight-piece. Love, we are in God's hand.
50   How strange now, looks the life he makes us lead;
So free we seem, so fettered fast we are!
I feel he laid the fetter: let it lie!
This chamber for example—turn your head—
All that's behind us! You don't understand
Nor care to understand about my art,
But you can hear at least when people speak:
And that cartoon,° the second from the door
—It is the thing, Love! so such things should be—
Behold Madonna!—I am bold to say.
60   I can do with my pencil what I know,
What I see, what at bottom of my heart
I wish for, if I ever wish so deep—
Do easily, too—when I say, perfectly,
I do not boast, perhaps: yourself are judge,
Who listened to the Legate's° talk last week,
And just as much they used to say in France.
At any rate 'tis easy, all of it!
No sketches first, no studies, that's long past:
I do what many dream of, all their lives,
70   —Dream? strive to do, and agonize to do,

**cartoon** drawing preliminary to a fresco     **Legate's** papal representative

And fail in doing. I could count twenty such
On twice your fingers, and not leave this town,
Who strive—you don't know how the others strive
To paint a little thing like that you smeared
Carelessly passing with your robes afloat,—
Yet do much less, so much less, Someone° says,
(I know his name, no matter)—so much less!
Well, less is more, Lucrezia. I am judged.
There burns a truer light of God in them.
In their vexed beating stuffed and stopped-up brain,
Heart, or whate'er else, than goes on to prompt
This low-pulsed forthright craftsman's hand of mine.
Their works drop groundward, but themselves, I know,
Reach many a time a heaven that's shut to me,
Enter and take their place there sure enough,
Though they come back and cannot tell the world.
My works are nearer heaven, but I sit here.
The sudden blood of these men! at a word—
Praise them, it boils, or blame them, it boils too.
I, painting from myself and to myself,
Know what I do, am unmoved by men's blame
Or their praise either. Somebody remarks
Morello's outline° there is wrongly traced,
His hue mistaken; what of that? or else,
Rightly traced and well ordered; what of that?
Speak as they please, what does the mountain care?
Ah, but a man's reach should exceed his grasp,
Or what's a heaven for? All is silver-grey
Placid and perfect with my art: the worse!
I know both what I want and what might gain,
And yet how profitless to know, to sigh
'Had I been two, another and myself,
Our head would have o'erlooked the world!' No doubt.
Yonder's a work now, of that famous youth
The Urbinate° who died five years ago.
('Tis copied, George Vasari sent it me.)
Well, I can fancy how he did it all,
Pouring his soul, with kings and popes to see,
Reaching, that heaven might so replenish him,
Above and through his art—for it gives way;
That arm is wrongly put—and there again—
A fault to pardon in the drawing's lines,
Its body, so to speak; its soul is right,
He means right—that, a child may understand.
Still, what an arm! and I could alter it:

80

90

100

110

---

**Someone**  Michelangelo  Buonarotti  (1475–1564)

**Morello's outline** a mountain in the Apennines, north of Florence

**Urbinate** Raphael (1483–1520), born in Urbino

But all the play, the insight and the stretch—
Out of me, out of me! And wherefore out?
Had you enjoined them on me, given me soul,
We might have risen to Rafael, I and you!
120    Nay, Love, you did give all I asked, I think—
More than I merit, yes, by many times.
But had you—oh, with the same perfect brow,
And perfect eyes, and more than perfect mouth,
And the low voice my soul hears, as a bird
The fowler's pipe, and follows to the snare—
Had you, with these the same, but brought a mind!
Some women do so. Had the mouth there urged
'God and the glory! never care for gain.
The present by the future, what is that?
130    Live for fame, side by side with Agnolo!°
Rafael is waiting: up to God, all three!'
I might have done it for you. So it seems:
Perhaps not. All is as God over-rules.
Besides, incentives come from the soul's self;
The rest avail not. Why do I need you?
What wife had Rafael, or has Agnolo?
In this world, who can do a thing, will not;
And who would do it, cannot, I perceive:
Yet the will's somewhat—somewhat, too, the power—
140    And thus we half-men struggle. At the end,
God, I conclude, compensates, punishes.
'Tis safer for me, if the award be strict,
That I am something underrated here,
Poor this long while, despised, to speak the truth.
I dared not, do you know, leave home all day,
For fear of chancing on the Paris lords.
The best is when they pass and look aside;
But they speak sometimes; I must bear it all.
Well may they speak! That Francis,° that first time,
150    And that long festal year at Fontainebleau!
I surely then could sometimes leave the ground,
Put on the glory, Rafael's daily wear,
In that humane great monarch's golden look,—
One finger in his beard or twisted curl
Over his mouth's good mark that made the smile,
One arm about my shoulder, round my neck,
The jingle of his gold chain in my ear,
I painting proudly with his breath on me,
All his court round him, seeing with his eyes,
160    Such frank French eyes, and such a fire of souls
Profuse, my hand kept plying by those hearts,—

**Agnolo** Michelangelo                 **Francis** King Francis I of France (1494–1547),
whose money Andrea had embezzled

And, best of all, this, this, this face beyond,
This in the background, waiting on my work,
To crown the issue with a last reward!
A good time, was it not, my kingly days?
And had you not grown restless . . . but I know—
'Tis done and past; 'twas right, my instinct said;
Too live the life grew, golden and not grey,
And I'm the weak-eyed bat no sun should tempt
170 Out of the grange° whose four walls make his world.
How could it end in any other way?
You called me, and I came home to your heart.
The triumph was—to reach and stay there; since
I reached it ere the triumph, what is lost?
Let my hands frame your face in your hair's gold,
You beautiful Lucrezia that are mine!
'Rafael did this, Andrea painted that;
The Roman's° is the better when you pray,
But still the other's Virgin was his wife—'
180 Men will excuse me. I am glad to judge
Both pictures in your presence; clearer grows
My better fortune, I resolve to think.
For, do you know, Lucrezia, as God lives,
Said one day Agnolo, his very self,
To Rafael . . . I have known it all these years . . .
(When the young man was flaming out his thoughts
Upon a palace-wall for Rome to see,
Too lifted up in heart because of it)
'Friend, there's a certain sorry little scrub
190 Goes up and down our Florence, none cares how,
Who, were he set to plan and execute
As you are, pricked on by your popes and kings,
Would bring the sweat into that brow of yours!'
To Rafael's!—And indeed the arm is wrong.
I hardly dare . . . yet, only you to see,
Give the chalk here—quick, thus the line should go!
Ay, but the soul! he's Rafael! rub it out!
Still, all I care for, if he spoke the truth,
(What he? why, who but Michel Agnolo?
200 Do you forget already words like those?)
If really there was such a chance, so lost,—
Is, whether you're—not grateful—but more pleased.
Well, let me think so. And you smile indeed!
This hour has been an hour! Another smile?
If you would sit thus by me every night
I should work better, do you comprehend?
I mean that I should earn more, give you more.

**grange** barn                    **Roman's** Raphael's

See, it is settled dusk now; there's a star;
Morello's gone, the watch-lights show the wall,
210    The cue-owls° speak the name we call them by.
Come from the window, love,—come in, at last,
Inside the melancholy little house
We built to be so gay with. God is just.
King Francis may forgive me: oft at nights
When I look up from painting, eyes tired out,
The walls become illumined, brick from brick
Distinct, instead of mortar, fierce bright gold,
That gold of his I did cement them with!
Let us but love each other. Must you go?
220    That Cousin° here again? he waits outside?
Must see you—you, and not with me? Those loans?
More gaming debts to pay? you smiled for that?
Well, let smiles buy me! have you more to spend?
While hand and eye and something of a heart
Are left me, work's my ware, and what's it worth?
I'll pay my fancy. Only let me sit
The grey remainder of the evening out,
Idle, you call it, and muse perfectly
How I could paint, were I but back in France,
230    One picture, just one more—the Virgin's face,
Not yours this time! I want you at my side
To hear them—that is, Michel Agnolo—
Judge all I do and tell you of its worth.
Will you? Tomorrow, satisfy your friend.
I take the subjects for his corridor,
Finish the portrait out of hand—there, there,
And throw him in another thing or two
If he demurs; the whole should prove enough
To pay for this same Cousin's freak. Beside,
240    What's better and what's all I care about,
Get you the thirteen scudi° for the ruff!
Love, does that please you? Ah, but what does he,
The Cousin! what does he to please you more?

    I am grown peaceful as old age tonight.
I regret little, I would change still less.
Since there my past life lies, why alter it?
The very wrong to Francis!—it is true
I took his coin, was tempted and complied,
And built this house and sinned, and all is said.
250    My father and my mother died of want.°
Well, had I riches of my own? you see
How one gets rich! Let each one bear his lot.

cue-owls little owls
Cousin an evasive term for Lucretia's lover
scudi Italian coins

father . . . want Vasari charges Andrea with
neglecting his parents

They were born poor, lived poor, and poor they died:
And I have laboured somewhat in my time
And not been paid profusely. Some good son
Paint my two hundred pictures—let him try!
No doubt, there's something strikes a balance. Yes,
You loved me quite enough, it seems tonight.
This must suffice me here. What would one have?
260 In heaven, perhaps, new chances, one more chance—
Four great walls in the New Jerusalem,°
Meted on each side by the angel's reed,
For Leonard,° Rafael, Agnolo and me
To cover—the three first without a wife,
While I have mine! So—still they overcome
Because there's still Lucrezia,—as I choose.

Again the Cousin's whistle! Go, my Love.
1853       1855

# Cleon°

   'As certain also of your own poets have said'°—

Cleon the poet (from the sprinkled isles,°
Lily on lily, that o'erlace the sea,
And laugh their pride when the light wave lisps
 'Greece')—
To Protus in his Tyranny:° much health!

 They give thy letter to me, even now:
I read and seem as if I heard thee speak.
The master of thy galley still unlades
Gift after gift; they block my court at last
And pile themselves along its portico
10 Royal with sunset,° like a thought of thee:
And one white she-slave from the group dispersed
Of black and white slaves (like the chequer-work
Pavement, at once my nation's work and gift,

---

**New Jerusalem** as in Revelation 21:10–21
**Leonard** Leonardo da Vinci (1452–1519)
**Cleon** This dramatic monologue of an imaginary Greek poet contemporary with St. Paul's ministry (50 A.D. or so) combines two characteristic kinds of Browning's poems, since it both expresses his own very personal religious synthesis (though only by indirection) and takes its place also in the great sequence of involuntary total self-revelations of failed questers, sometimes relatively inadequate artists and musicians, sometimes charlatans. Cleon, though no charlatan, betrays a deep inner doubt as to his own artistic eminence, for he is more an absorber of culture than a maker of it, and clearly a more considerable critic of

the arts than an artist. Created by Browning in response to Arnold's *Empedocles on Etna*, in some sense he is a kind of Hellenic Matthew Arnold.
**As certain . . . have said** St. Paul to the Athenian philosophers, Acts 17:28: "For in him [God] we live, and move, and have our being; as certain also of your own poets have said, for we are also his offspring"
**sprinkled isles** the Sporades, near Crete
**Tyranny** Protus, an imaginary king or tyrant; "tyranny" simply means a small kingdom, and has no pejorative overtone here
**sunset** sunset gives a purple (thus royal) tinge to the marble

Now covered with this settle-down of doves),
One lyric woman, in her crocus vest
Woven of sea-wools, with her two white hands
Commends to me the strainer and the cup
Thy lip hath bettered ere it blesses mine.

Well-counselled, king, in thy munificence!
20  For so shall men remark, in such an act
Of love for him whose song gives life its joy,
Thy recognition of the use of life;
Nor call thy spirit barely adequate
To help on life in straight ways, broad enough
For vulgar souls, by ruling and the rest.
Thou, in the daily building of thy tower,°—
Whether in fierce and sudden spasms of toil,
Or through dim lulls of unapparent growth,
Or when the general work 'mid good acclaim
30  Climbed with the eye to cheer the architect,—
Didst ne'er engage in work for mere work's sake—
Hadst ever in thy heart the luring hope
Of some eventual rest a-top of it,
Whence, all the tumult of the building hushed,
Thou first of men mightst look out to the East:°
The vulgar saw thy tower, thou sawest the sun.
For this, I promise on thy festival
To pour libation,° looking o'er the sea,
Making this slave narrate thy fortunes, speak
Thy great words, and describe thy royal face—
40  Wishing thee wholly where Zeus lives the most,
Within the eventual element of calm.

Thy letter's first requirement meets me here.
It is as thou hast heard: in one short life
I, Cleon, have effected all those things
Thou wonderingly dost enumerate.
That epos on thy hundred plates of gold°
Is mine,—and also mine the little chant,
So sure to rise from every fishing-bark
50  When, lights at prow, the seamen haul their net.
The image of the sun-god on the phare,°
Men turn from the sun's self to see, is mine;
The Pœcile,° o'er-storied its whole length,
As thou didst hear, with painting, is mine too.

**tower** the monument Protus is building as a symbol of his reign; Cleon uses it as a symbol of poetic achievement, reflecting Shelley's influence upon Browning
**East** symbolizing the devotion of Protus to Phoebus Apollo, the sun god, but the land of Christ lies to the east also
**libation** wine poured to the gods

**gold** Protus has honored Cleon by donating 100 golden tablets upon which Cleon's epic poem has been engraved
**phare** lighthouse
**Pœcile** name of portico (Painted Porch) in marketplace of ancient Athens, adorned with frescoes of the battle of Marathon

I know the true proportions of a man
And woman also, not observed before;
And I have written three books on the soul,
Proving absurd all written hitherto,
And putting us to ignorance again.
60    For music,—why, I have combined the moods,°
Inventing one. In brief, all arts are mine;
Thus much the people know and recognize,
Throughout our seventeen islands. Marvel not.
We of these latter days, with greater mind
Then our forerunners, since more composite,
Look not so great, beside their simple way,
To a judge who only sees one way at once,
One mind-point and no other at a time,—
Compares the small part of a man of us
70    With some whole man of the heroic age,
Great in his way—not ours, nor meant for ours.
And ours is greater, had we skill to know:
For, what we call this life of men on earth,
This sequence of the soul's achievements here
Being, as I find much reason to conceive,
Intended to be viewed eventually
As a great whole, not analyzed to parts,
But each part having reference to all,—
How shall a certain part, pronounced complete,
80    Endure effacement by another part?
Was the thing done?—then, what's to do again?
See, in the chequered pavement opposite,
Suppose the artist made a perfect rhomb,
And next a lozenge, then a trapezoid°—
He did not overlay them, superimpose
The new upon the old and blot it out,
But laid them on a level in his work,
Making at last a picture; there it lies.
So, first the perfect separate forms were made,
90    The portions of mankind; and after, so,
Occurred the combination of the same.
For where had been a progress, otherwise?
Mankind, made up of all the single men,—
In such a synthesis the labour ends.
Now mark me! those divine men of old time
Have reached, thou sayest well, each at one point
The outside verge that rounds our faculty;
And where they reached, who can do more than reach?
It takes but little water just to touch

**moods** musical modes or scales
**rhomb trapezoid** A rhomb is a non-right-angled
semi-square; a lozenge is a figure shaped like a
diamond; a trapezoid is a figure with four sides,
none parallel to another.

100  At some one point the inside of a sphere,
And, as we turn the sphere, touch all the rest
In due succession: but the finer air
Which not so palpably nor obviously,
Though no less universally, can touch
The whole circumference of that emptied sphere,
Fills it more fully than the water did;
Holds thrice the weight of water in itself
Resolved into a subtler element.
And yet the vulgar call the sphere first full
110  Up to the visible height—and after, void;
Not knowing air's more hidden properties.
And thus our soul, misknown, cries out to Zeus
To vindicate his purpose in our life:
Why stay we on the earth unless to grow?
Long since, I imaged, wrote the fiction out,
That he or other god descended here
And, once for all, showed simultaneously
What, in its nature, never can be shown,
Piecemeal or in succession;—showed, I say,
120  The worth both absolute and relative
Of all his children from the birth of time,
His instruments for all appointed work.
I now go on to image,—might we hear
The judgment which should give the due to each,
Show where the labour lay and where the ease,
And prove Zeus' self, the latent everywhere!
This is a dream:—but no dream, let us hope,
That years and days, the summers and the springs,
Follow each other with unwaning powers.
130  The grapes which dye thy wine are richer far,
Through culture, than the wild wealth of the rock;
The suave plum than the savage-tasted drupe;°
The pastured honey-bee drops choicer sweet;
The flowers turn double, and the leaves turn flowers;
That young and tender crescent-moon, thy slave,
Sleeping above her robe as buoyed by clouds,
Refines upon the women of my youth.
What, and the soul alone deteriorates?
I have not chanted verse like Homer, no—
140  Nor swept string like Terpander,° no—nor carved
And painted men like Phidias° and his friend:
I am not great as they are, point by point.
But I have entered into sympathy

drupe wild plum
Terpander active about 650 B.C., poet and
musician who worked in Sparta, reputed to
have set Homer to lyre music

Phidias 500–432 B.C., sculpted the Parthenon
statues; his "friend" was probably Polygnotus,
who helped to decorate the Painted Porch

With these four, running these into one soul,
Who, separate, ignored each other's art.
Say, is it nothing that I know them all?
The wild flower was the larger; I have dashed
Rose-blood upon its petals, pricked its cup's
Honey with wine, and driven its seed to fruit,
150  And show a better flower if not so large:
I stand myself. Refer this to the gods
Whose gift alone it is! which, shall I dare
(All pride apart) upon the absurd pretext
That such a gift by chance lay in my hand,
Discourse of lightly or depreciate?
It might have fallen to another's hand: what then?
I pass too surely: let at least truth stay!

And next, of what thou followest on to ask.
This being with me as I declare, O king,
160  My works, in all these varicoloured kinds,
So done by me, accepted so by men—
Thou askest, if (my soul thus in men's hearts)
I must not be accounted to attain
The very crown and proper end of life?
Inquiring thence how, now life closeth up,
I face death with success in my right hand:
Whether I fear death less than dost thyself
The fortunate of men? 'For' (writest thou)
'Thou leavest much behind, while I leave nought.
170  Thy life stays in the poems men shall sing,
The pictures men shall study; while my life,
Complete and whole now in its power and joy,
Dies altogether with my brain and arm,
Is lost indeed; since, what survives myself?
The brazen statue to o'erlook my grave,
Set on the promontory which I named.
And that—some supple courtier of my heir
Shall use its robed and sceptred arm, perhaps,
To fix the rope to, which best drags it down.
180  I go then: triumph thou, who dost not go!'

Nay, thou art worthy of hearing my whole mind.
Is this apparent, when thou turn'st to muse
Upon the scheme of earth and man in chief,
That admiration grows as knowledge grows?
That imperfection means perfection hid,
Reserved in part, to grace the after-time?
If, in the morning of philosophy,
Ere aught had been recorded, nay perceived,
Thou, with the light now in thee, couldst have looked
190  On all earth's tenantry, from worm to bird,

Ere man, her last, appeared upon the stage—
Thou wouldst have seen them perfect, and deduced
The perfectness of others yet unseen.
Conceding which,—had Zeus then questioned thee
'Shall I go on a step, improve on this,
Do more for visible creatures than is done?'
Thou wouldst have answered, 'Ay, by making each
Grow conscious in himself—by that alone.
All's perfect else: the shell sucks fast the rock,
200   The fish strikes through the sea, the snake both swims
And slides, forth range the beasts, the birds take flight,
Till life's mechanics can no further go—
And all this joy in natural life is put
Like fire from off thy finger into each,
So exquisitely perfect is the same.
But 'tis pure fire, and they mere matter are;
It has them, not they it: and so I choose
For man, thy last premeditated work
(If I might add a glory to the scheme)
210   That a third thing should stand apart from both,
A quality arise within his soul,
Which, intro-active, made to supervise
And feel the force it has, may view itself,
And so be happy.' Man might live at first
The animal life: but is there nothing more?
In due time, let him critically learn
How he lives; and, the more he gets to know
Of his own life's adaptabilities,
The more joy-giving will his life become.
220   Thus man, who hath this quality, is best.

But thou, king, hadst more reasonably said:
'Let progress end at once,—man make no step
Beyond the natural man, the better beast,
Using his senses, not the sense of sense.'°
In man there's failure, only since he left
The lower and inconscious forms of life.
We called it an advance, the rendering plain
Man's spirit might grow conscious of man's life,
And, by new lore so added to the old,
230   Take each step higher over the brute's head.
This grew the only life, the pleasure-house,
Watch-tower° and treasure-fortress of the soul,
Which whole surrounding flats of natural life
Seemed only fit to yield subsistence to;
A tower that crowns a country. But alas,

---

**sense of sense** consciousness of consciousness
**Watch-tower** point of survey of the higher

consciousness, an image going back to Isaiah,
and prevalent in Coleridge and Shelley

The soul now climbs it just to perish there!
For thence we have discovered ('tis no dream—
We know this, which we had not else perceived)
That there's a world of capability
240   For joy, spread round about us, meant for us,
Inviting us; and still the soul craves all,
And still the flesh replies, 'Take no jot more
Than ere thou clombst the tower to look abroad!
Nay, so much less as that fatigue has brought
Deduction to it.' We struggle, fain to enlarge
Our bounded physical recipiency,
Increase our power, supply fresh oil to life,
Repair the waste of age and sickness: no,
It skills not!° life's inadequate to joy,
250   As the soul sees joy, tempting life to take.
They praise a fountain in my garden here
Wherein a Naiad° sends the water-bow
Thin from her tube; she smiles to see it rise.
What if I told her, it is just a thread
From that great river which the hills shut up,
And mock her with my leave to take the same?
The artificer has given her one small tube
Past power to widen or exchange—what boots
To know she might spout oceans if she could?
260   She cannot lift beyond her first thin thread:
And so a man can use but a man's joy
While he sees God's. Is it for Zeus to boast,
'See, man, how happy I live, and despair—
That I may be still happier—for thy use!'
If this were so, we could not thank our lord,
As hearts beat on to doing: 'tis not so—
Malice it is not. Is it carelessness?
Still, no. If care—where is the sign? I ask,
And get no answer, and agree in sum,
270   O king, with thy profound discouragement,
Who seest the wider but to sigh the more.
Most progress is most failure: thou sayest well.

    The last point now:—thou dost except a case—
Holding joy not impossible to one
With artist-gifts—to such a man as I
Who leave behind me living works indeed;
For, such a poem, such a painting lives.
What? dost thou verily trip upon a word,
Confound the accurate view of what joy is
280   (Caught somewhat clearer by my eyes than thine)
With feeling joy? confound the knowing how

**skills not** does not suffice           **Naiad** nymph

And showing how to live (my faculty)
With actually living?—Otherwise
Where is the artist's vantage o'er the king?
Because in my great epos I display
How divers men young, strong, fair, wise, can act—
Is this as though I acted? if I paint,
Carve the young Phœbus,° am I therefore young?
Methinks I'm older that I bowed myself
290    The many years of pain that taught me art!
Indeed, to know is something, and to prove
How all this beauty might be enjoyed, is more:
But, knowing nought, to enjoy is something too.
Yon rower, with the moulded muscles there,
Lowering the sail, is nearer it than I.
I can write love-odes: thy fair slave's an ode.
I get to sing of love, when grown too grey
For being beloved: she turns to that young man
The muscles all a-ripple on his back.
300    I know the joy of kingship: well, thou art king!

'But,' sayest thou—(and I marvel, I repeat,
To find thee trip on such a mere word) 'what
Thou writest, paintest, stays; that does not die:
Sappho° survives, because we sing her songs,
And Æschylus,° because we read his plays!'
Why, if they live still, let them come and take
Thy slave in my despite, drink from thy cup,
Speak in my place. Thou diest while I survive?
Say rather that my fate is deadlier still,
310    In this, that every day my sense of joy
Grows more acute, my soul (intensified
In power and insight) more enlarged, more keen;
While every day my hairs fall more and more,
My hand shakes, and the heavy years increase—
The horror quickening still from year to year,
The consummation coming past escape
When I shall know most, and yet least enjoy—
When all my works wherein I prove my worth,
Being present still to mock me in men's mouths,
320    Alive still, in the praise of such as thou,
I, I the feeling, thinking, acting man,
The man who loved his life so over-much,
Sleep in my urn. It is so horrible,
I dare at times imagine to my need
Some future state revealed to us by Zeus,

---

**Phœbus** The young Apollo traditionally symbolizes the perpetual youth of poetry, as in
Keats's *Hyperion*.
**Sappho** (born *c.* 610 B.C.) greatest lyric poet
of Greece, whose work survives only in fragments
**Æschylus** (525–456 B.C.) greatest of the Greek
tragic dramatists

Unlimited in capability
For joy, as this is in desire for joy,
—To seek which, the joy-hunger forces us:
That, stung by straitness of our life, made strait
330  On purpose to make prized the life at large—
Freed by the throbbing impulse we call death,
We burst there as the worm into the fly,
Who, while a worm still, wants° his wings. But no!
Zeus has not yet revealed it;° and alas,
He must have done so, were it possible!

Live long and happy, and in that thought die:
Glad for what was! Farewell. And for the rest,
I cannot tell thy messenger aright
Where to deliver what he bears of thine
340  To one called Paulus;° we have heard his fame
Indeed, if Christus be not one with him—
I know not, nor am troubled much to know.
Thou canst not think a mere barbarian Jew
As Paulus proves to be, one circumcised,°
Hath access to a secret shut from us?
Thou wrongest our philosophy, O king,
In stooping to inquire of such an one,
As if his answer could impose at all!
He writeth, doth he? well, and he may write.
350  Oh, the Jew findeth scholars! certain slaves
Who touched on this same isle, preached him and Christ;
And (as I gathered from a bystander)
Their doctrine could be held by no sane man.
1854                      1855

# Popularity

### I

Stand still, true poet that you are!
    I know you; let me try and draw you.
Some night you'll fail us: when afar
    You rise, remember one man saw you,
Knew you, and named a star!

### II

My star, God's glow-worm! Why extend
    That loving hand of his which leads you,
Yet locks you safe from end to end
    Of this dark world, unless he needs you,
10  Just saves your light to spend?

**wants** lacks
**revealed it** Immortality, in the Olympian faith,
was granted only by special dispensation.

**Paulus** Saint Paul, Saul of Tarsus
**circumcised** Jewish mark of the Covenant

III

His clenched hand shall unclose at last,
    I know, and let out all the beauty:
My poet holds the future fast,
    Accepts the coming ages' duty,
    Their present for this past.


IV

That day, the earth's feast-master's brow
    Shall clear, to God the chalice raising;
'Others give best at first, but thou
    Forever set'st our table praising,
20  Keep'st the good wine till now!'°


V

Meantime, I'll draw you as you stand,
    With few or none to watch and wonder:
I'll say—a fisher, on the sand
    By Tyre° the old, his ocean-plunder,
A netful, brought to land.


VI

Who has not heard how Tyrian shells
    Enclosed the blue, that dye of dyes
Whereof one drop worked miracles,
    And coloured like Astarte's° eyes
30  Raw silk the merchant sells?


VII

And each bystander of them all
    Could criticize, and quote tradition
How depths of blue sublimed some pall
    —To get which, pricked a king's ambition;
Worth sceptre, crown and ball.


VIII

Yet there's the dye, in that rough mesh,
    The sea has only just o'erwhispered!
Live whelks, each lip's beard dripping fresh,
    As if they still the water's lisp heard
40  Through foam the rock-weeds thresh.


IX

Enough to furnish Solomon°
    Such hangings for his cedar-house,

Keep'st . . . now See John 2:1–10.
Tyre great Phoenician trading port; the purple
or blue Tyrian-dyed cloths became the European emblems of royalty

Astarte's goddess of the Gentile Semites; wor-
shiped in Tyre, and associated with the Morning Star (Venus)
Solomon See I Kings 6–7.

That, when gold-robed he took the throne
   In that abyss of blue, the Spouse
Might swear his presence shone

X

Most like the centre-spike of gold
   Which burns deep in the blue-bell's womb,
What time, with ardours manifold,
   The bee goes singing to her groom,
50 Drunken and overbold.

XI

Mere conchs! not fit for warp or woof!
   Till cunning come to pound and squeeze
And clarify,—refine to proof
   The liquor filtered by degrees,
While the world stands aloof.

XII

And there's the extract, flasked and fine,
   And priced and saleable at last!
And Hobbs, Nobbs, Stokes and Nokes° combine
   To paint the future from the past,
60 Put blue into their line.

XIII

Hobbs hints blue,—straight he turtle eats:
   Nobbs prints blue,—claret crowns his cup:
Nokes outdares Stokes in azure feats,—
   Both gorge. Who fished the murex° up?
What porridge had John Keats?
1854                    1855

# The Heretic's Tragedy°

A Middle-Age Interlude°

Rosa mundi; seu, fulcite me floribus.° A conceit° of Master Gysbrecht,
canon-regular of Saint Jodocus-by-the-bar, Ypres city. Cantuque, *Vir-*

---

**Hobbs . . . and Nokes** this may refer to Rossetti, Morris, and Keats's other Pre-Raphaelite followers
**murex** the mussel that is the source of Tyrian purple dye
**The Heretic's Tragedy** Jacques du Bourg-Molay (called "John" in this poem) was the last Grand Master of the Knights Templars, originally a crusading order, but later essentially a supranational political and financial organization. Philip IV of France repressed the order, con-

fiscated its funds, and burned Molay at the stake in 1314, on the evidently false charges of heresy, simony, and sodomy. Dante, in his *Purgatorio*, maintains the innocence of the Templars.
**Interlude** short play, here a farce
**Rosa mundi . . . floribus** "Rose of the world support me with flowers" (Song of Solomon 2:5)
**conceit** invention

*gilius.*° And hath often been sung at hock-tide° and Festivals. Gavisus eram, *Jessides.*°

(It would seem to be a glimpse from the burning of Jacques du Bourg-Molay, at Paris, A.D. 1314; as distorted by the refraction from Flemish brain to brain, during the course of a couple of centuries.)

I

PREADMONISHETH THE ABBOT DEODÆT

The Lord, we look to once for all,
    Is the Lord we should look at, all at once:
He knows not to vary, saith Saint Paul,
    Nor the shadow of turning, for the nonce.
See him no other than as he is!
    Give both the infinitudes their due—
Infinite mercy, but, I wis,
    As infinite a justice too.
        [*Organ: plagal-cadence.*°
As infinite a justice too.

II

ONE SINGETH

10   John, Master of the Temple of God,
    Falling to sin the Unknown Sin,
What he bought of Emperor Aldabrod,
    He sold it to Sultan Saladin:°
Till, caught by Pope Clement,° a-buzzing there,
    Hornet-prince of the mad wasps' hive,
And clipped of his wings in Paris square,
    They bring him now to be burned alive.

[*And wanteth there grace of lute or clavicithern,*°
*ye shall say to confirm him who singeth*—

We bring John now to be burned alive.

III

In the midst is a goodly gallows built;
20   'Twixt fork and fork, a stake is stuck;
But first they set divers tumbrils° a-tilt,
    Make a trench all round with the city muck;

Cantuque, Virgilius The music is by one Virgilius.
hock-tide the second Monday and Tuesday after
Easter
Gavisus . . . Jessides "I, a son of Jesse, rejoice
in it"; this is Browning's irony; the interlude's
supposed author, full of hatred, dares to put
himself in the line of David, son of Jesse, and
the traditional author of the Book of Psalms.
plagal-cadence closing progression of chords

Saladin One charge against Molay was that he
had committed the "Unknown Sin" of simony,
here the selling of holy treasures to the Saracen
Sultan. Actually Saladin lived almost two centuries before Molay. There never was an
Emperor Aldabrod.
Clement Clement I who suppressed the Templars in 1312
clavicithern stringed keyboard instrument
tumbrils carts

Inside they pile log upon log, good store;
Faggots no few, blocks great and small,
Reach a man's mid-thigh, no less, no more,—
For they mean he should roast in the sight of all.

CHORUS

We mean he should roast in the sight of all.

IV

Good sappy bavins° that kindle forthwith;
Billets that blaze substantial and slow;
30    Pine-stump split deftly, dry as pith;
Larch-heart that chars to a chalk-white glow:
Then up they hoist me John in a chafe,
Sling him fast like a hog to scorch,
Spit in his face, then leap back safe,
Sing 'Laudes'° and bid clap-to the torch.

CHORUS

Laus Deo° —who bids clap-to the torch.

V

John of the Temple, whose fame so bragged,
Is burning alive in Paris square!
How can he curse, if his mouth is gagged?
40    Or wriggle his neck, with a collar there?
Or heave his chest, which a band goes round?
Or threat with his fist, since his arms are spliced?
Or kick with his feet, now his legs are bound?
—Thinks John, I will call upon Jesus Christ.
[Here one crosseth himself.

VI

Jesus Christ—John had bought and sold,
Jesus Christ—John had eaten and drunk;
To him, the Flesh meant silver and gold.
(Salvâ reverentiâ.)°
Now it was, 'Saviour, bountiful lamb,
50    I have roasted thee Turks, though men roast me!
See thy servant, the plight wherein I am!
Art thou a saviour? Save thou me!'

CHORUS

'Tis John the mocker cries, 'Save thou me!'

VII

Who maketh God's menace an idle word?
—Saith, it no more means what it proclaims,

bavins bundles of brushwood for kindling
Laudes the seven Psalms of praise
Laus Deo Praise be to God

Salvâ reverentiâ (literally "a saving reverence")
direction to genuflect to the body of Christ
("Flesh") in the Eucharist

Than a damsel's threat to her wanton bird?—
For she too prattles of ugly names.
—Saith, he knoweth but one thing,—what he knows?
That God is good and the rest is breath;
60    Why else is the same styled Sharon's rose?°
Once a rose, ever a rose, he saith.

CHORUS
O, John shall yet find a rose, he saith!


VIII
Alack, there be roses and roses, John!
Some, honied of taste like your leman's° tongue:
Some, bitter; for why? (roast gaily on!)
Their tree struck root in devil's dung.
When Paul once reasoned of righteousness
And of temperance and of judgment to come,
Good Felix° trembled, he could no less:
70    John, snickering, crooked his wicked thumb.

CHORUS
What cometh to John of the wicked thumb?


IX
Ha ha, John plucketh now at his rose
To rid himself of a sorrow at heart!
Lo,—petal on petal, fierce rays unclose;
Anther° on anther, sharp spikes outstart;
And with blood for dew, the bosom boils;
And a gust of sulphur is all its smell;
And lo, he is horribly in the toils
Of a coal-black giant flower of hell!

CHORUS
80    What maketh heaven, That maketh hell.


X
So, as John called now, through the fire amain,°
On the Name, he had cursed with, all his life—
To the Person, he bought and sold again—
For the Face, with his daily buffets rife—
Feature by feature It took its place:
And his voice, like a mad dog's choking bark,
At the steady whole of the Judge's face—
Died. Forth John's soul flared into the dark.

---

Sharon's rose "I am the rose of Sharon, and
the lily of the valleys" (Song of Solomon 2:1)
leman mistress

Felix Felix Antonius, Roman governor of Judea
(51–60 A.D.); see Acts 24:25
Anther part of the flower containing the pollen
amain vehemently

SUBJOINETH THE ABBOT DEODAET
God help all poor souls lost in the dark!
1852                    1855


# Two in the Campagna°

### I
I wonder do you feel to-day
   As I have felt since, hand in hand,
We sat down on the grass, to stray
   In spirit better through the land,
This morn of Rome and May?

### II
For me, I touched a thought, I know,
   Has tantalized me many times,
(Like turns of thread the spiders throw
   Mocking across our path) for rhymes
10   To catch at and let go.

### III
Help me to hold it! First it left
   The yellowing fennel, run to seed
There, branching from the brickwork's cleft,
   Some old tomb's ruin: yonder weed
Took up the floating weft,°

### IV
Where one small orange cup amassed
   Five beetles, —blind and green they grope
Among the honey-meal: and last,
   Everywhere on the grassy slope
20   I traced it. Hold it fast!

### V
The champaign° with its endless fleece
   Of feathery grasses everywhere!
Silence and passion, joy and peace,
   An everlasting wash of air—
Rome's ghost° since her decease.

### VI
Such life here, through such lengths of hours,
   Such miracles performed in play,

Campagna the *Campagna di Roma*, large, open countryside around the city; contains many ruins    champaign open field
weft weaver's cross-threads    ghost ruins of old cities

Such primal naked forms of flowers,
    Such letting nature have her way
30  While heaven looks from its towers!

### VII

How say you? Let us, O my dove,
    Let us be unashamed of soul,
As earth lies bare to heaven above!
    How is it under our control
To love or not to love?

### VIII

I would that you were all to me,
    You that are just so much, no more.
Nor yours nor mine, nor slave nor free!
    Where does the fault lie? What the core
40  O' the wound, since wound must be?

### IX

I would I could adopt your will,
    See with your eyes, and set my heart
Beating by yours, and drink my fill
    At your soul's springs,—your part my part
In life, for good and ill.

### X

No. I yearn upward, touch you close,
    Then stand away. I kiss your cheek,
Catch your soul's warmth,—I pluck the rose
    And love it more than tongue can speak—
50  Then the good minute° goes.

### XI

Already how am I so far
    Out of that minute? Must I go
Still like the thistle-ball°, no bar,
    Onward, whenever light winds blow,
Fixed° by no friendly star?

### XII

Just when I seemed about to learn!
    Where is the thread now? Off again!
The old trick! Only I discern—
    Infinite passion, and the pain
60  Of finite hearts that yearn.
1854            1855

**good minute** one of Browning's central phrases; his version of the Romantic epiphany or privileged moment, here of complete communion between lovers       **thistle-ball** driven, as it is, by the wind    **fixed** guided

# Abt Vogler

Georg Joseph Vogler (1749–1814), whose title of "Abt" (Abbé, Father) was honorary, is remembered today as the teacher of the composers Weber and Meyerbeer, and as the speaker of this poem. Vogler, known as an extraordinary extemporizer, particularly upon the organ, was also reputed to be a charlatan, a pious fraud, and perhaps he belongs in Browning's company of failed artists, self-ruined questers, and grand mountebanks. The poem *seems* to celebrate his spirituality, but there are profound demoniac elements revealed by it as well. What the poem's parenthetical subtitle calls the "instrument of his own invention," an "orchestrion" or small portable organ, had the charming knack of sounding superb only when he played upon it but, like the other organs he built, sounding inadequate when played upon by others.

## Abt Vogler

(after he has been extemporizing upon
the musical instrument of his invention)

### I

Would that the structure brave, the manifold music I build,
  Bidding my organ obey, calling its keys to their work,
Claiming each slave of the sound, at a touch, as when Solomon° willed
  Armies of angels that soar, legions of demons that lurk,
Man, brute, reptile, fly,—alien of end and of aim,
  Adverse, each from the other heaven-high, hell-deep removed,
Should rush into sight at once as he named the ineffable Name,
  And pile him a palace straight, to pleasure the princess he loved!

### II

Would it might tarry like his, the beautiful building of mine,
  This which my keys in a crowd pressed and importuned to raise!
Ah, one and all, how they helped, would dispart° now and now combine,
  Zealous to hasten the work, heighten their master his praise!
And one would bury his brow with a blind plunge down to hell,
  Burrow awhile and build, broad on the roots of things,
Then up again swim into sight, having based me my palace well,
  Founded it, fearless of flame, flat on the nether springs.

### III

And another would mount and march, like the excellent minion he was,
  Ay, another and yet another, one crowd but with many a crest,
Raising my rampired walls of gold as transparent as glass,

Solomon There is a tradition that Solomon had    God, by means of which he could command
a magical seal bearing the "ineffable Name" of    angels and demons.
                                                                            dispart separate

20    Eager to do and die, yield each his place to the rest:
For higher still and higher (as a runner tips with fire,
    When a great illumination surprises a festal night—
Outlining round and round Rome's dome from space to spire)
    Up, the pinnacled glory reached, and the pride of my soul was in sight.

IV

In sight? Not half! for it seemed, it was certain, to match man's birth,
    Nature in turn conceived, obeying an impulse as I;
And the emulous heaven yearned down, made effort to reach the earth,
    As the earth had done her best, in my passion, to scale the sky:
Novel splendours burst forth, grew familiar and dwelt with mine,
30    Not a point nor peak but found and fixed its wandering star;
Meteor-moons, balls of blaze: and they did not pale nor pine,
    For earth had attained to heaven, there was no more near nor far.

V

Nay more; for there wanted not who walked in the glare and glow,
    Presences plain in the place; or, fresh from the Protoplast,°
Furnished for ages to come, when a kindlier wind should blow,
    Lured now to begin and live, in a house to their liking at last;
Or else the wonderful Dead who have passed through the body and gone,
    But were back once more to breathe in an old world worth their new:
What never had been, was now; what was, as it shall be anon;
40    And what is,—shall I say, matched both? for I was made perfect too.

VI

All through my keys that gave their sounds to a wish of my soul,
    All through my soul that praised as its wish flowed visibly forth,
All through music and me! For think, had I painted the whole,
    Why, there it had stood, to see, nor the process so wonder-worth:
Had I written the same, made verse—still, effect proceeds from cause,
    Ye know why the forms are fair, ye hear how the tale is told;
It is all triumphant art, but art in obedience to laws,
    Painter and poet are proud in the artist-list enrolled:—

VII

But here is the finger of God, a flash of the will that can,
50    Existent behind all laws, that made them and, lo, they are!
And I know not if, save in this, such gift be allowed to man,
    That out of three sounds he frame, not a fourth sound, but a star.
Consider it well: each tone of our scale in itself is nought;
    It is everywhere in the world—loud, soft, and all is said:
Give it to me to use! I mix it with two in my thought:
    And, there! Ye have heard and seen: consider and bow the head!

**Protoplast** basic protoplasm, or substance of
life (rather like the beings of Phase 1 in Yeats's
*A Vision*)

VIII

Well, it is gone at last, the palace of music I reared;
Gone! and the good tears start, the praises that come too slow;
For one is assured at first, one scarce can say that he feared,
60    That he even gave it a thought, the gone thing was to go.
Never to be again! But many more of the kind
    As good, nay, better perchance: is this your comfort to me?
To me, who must be saved because I cling with my mind
    To the same, same self, same love, same God: ay, what was, shall be.

IX

Therefore to whom turn I but to thee, the ineffable Name?
    Builder and maker, thou, of houses not made with hands!°
What, have fear of change from thee who art ever the same?
    Doubt that thy power can fill the heart that thy power expands?
There shall never be one lost good! What was, shall live as before;
70    The evil is null, is nought, is silence implying sound;
What was good shall be good, with, for evil, so much good more;
    On the earth the broken arcs; in the heaven, a perfect round.

X

All we have willed or hoped or dreamed of good shall exist;
    Not its semblance, but itself; no beauty, nor good, nor power
Whose voice has gone forth, but each survives for the melodist
    When eternity affirms the conception of an hour.
The high that proved too high, the heroic for earth too hard,
    The passion that left the ground to lose itself in the sky,
Are music sent up to God by the lover and the bard,
80    Enough that he heard it once: we shall hear it by-and-by.

XI

And what is our failure here but a triumph's evidence
    For the fulness of the days? Have we withered or agonized?
Why else was the pause prolonged but that singing might issue thence?
    Why rushed the discords in but that harmony should be prized?
Sorrow is hard to bear, and doubt is slow to clear,
    Each sufferer says his say, his scheme of the weal and woe:
But God has a few of us whom he whispers in the ear;
    The rest may reason and welcome: 'tis we musicians know.

XII

Well, it is earth with me; silence resumes her reign:
90    I will be patient and proud, and soberly acquiesce.
Give me the keys. I feel for the common chord° again,
    Sliding by semitones, till I sink to the minor,—yes,

houses . . . hands See II Corinthians 5:1.    C Major, where there are no sharps or flats,
chord Vogler descends to the common chord,    "The C Major of this life" in l. 96.
that is, our earth, to end in the "natural" key,

And I blunt it into a ninth, and I stand on alien ground,
 Surveying awhile the heights I rolled from into the deep;
Which, hark, I have dared and done,° for my resting-place is found,
 The C Major of this life: so, now I will try to sleep.
                                                              1864

# Caliban upon Setebos

This masterpiece of grotesque imagination can be read as being primarily an intellectual satire upon anthropomorphic theology, but the correctness of such a reading is
uncertain. The poem may reflect the influence upon Browning's own theology of
the American Transcendentalist Theodore Parker, who with Emerson had led a spiritual revolt against Boston Unitarianism. Parker, before meeting Browning in December 1859, was reading Darwin's *Origin of Species,* which had only just been published.
Parker's deliberate humanizing of God, mingled with new notions of evolution, evidently caused Browning to remember Shakespeare's Caliban in *The Tempest,* and
led to the writing of this poem. C. R. Tracy suggests that Caliban's evolving theology,
in Browning's poem, is a much less sophisticated version of Browning's humanization
of Jesus, rather than just a satire upon natural theology or, as some have said, upon the
Calvinist doctrine of predestination.

# Caliban upon Setebos;°
# or Natural Theology° in the Island

> 'Thou thoughtest that I was altogether such a one as thyself.'°

['Will° sprawl, now that the heat of day is best,
Flat on his belly in the pit's much mire,
With elbows wide, fists clenched to prop his chin.
And, while he kicks both feet in the cool slush,
And feels about his spine small eft-things° course,
Run in and out each arm, and make him laugh:
And while above his head a pompion-plant,°
Coating the cave-top as a brow its eye,
Creeps down to touch and tickle hair and beard,
10  And now a flower drops with a bee inside,
And now a fruit to snap at, catch and crunch,—

---

**dared and done** an echo of the closing line of
Christopher Smart's *A Song to David:* "Determined, dared and done"
**Setebos** In *The Tempest,* Caliban's mother, the
witch Sycorax, worships Setebos as her god.
**Natural Theology** the attempt to demonstrate
God's existence and his nature by arguing back
to Him from his creation, as opposed to revealed
theology, handed down by God

**Thou thoughtest . . . thyself** so God says to
the wicked in Psalms 50:21
**'Will** he will, that is, Caliban will. In the
bracketed passages that begin and end the
poem, Caliban is meditating; he does not speak
out till l. 24; his shifts between third and first
person have not been shown to follow any in-
controvertible pattern.
**eft-things** perhaps lizards
**pompion-plant** a sort of pumpkin vine

He looks out o'er yon sea which sunbeams cross
And recross till they weave a spider-web
(Meshes of fire, some great fish breaks at times)
And talks to his own self, howe'er he please,
Touching that other, whom his dam° called God.
Because to talk about Him,° vexes—ha,
Could He but know! and time to vex is now,
When talk is safer than in winter-time.
20   Moreover Prosper and Miranda sleep
In confidence he drudges at their task,
And it is good to cheat the pair, and gibe,
Letting the rank tongue blossom into speech.]

Setebos, Setebos, and Setebos!
'Thinketh, He dwelleth in the cold o' the moon.

'Thinketh, He made it, with the sun to match,
But not the stars; the stars came otherwise;
Only made clouds, winds, meteors, such as that:
Also this isle, what lives and grows thereon,
30   And snaky sea which rounds and ends the same.

'Thinketh, it came of being ill at ease:
He hated that He cannot change His cold,
Nor cure its ache. 'Hath spied an icy fish
That longed to 'scape the rock-stream where she lived,
And thaw herself within the lukewarm brine
O' the lazy sea her stream thrusts far amid,
A crystal spike 'twixt two warm walls of wave;
Only, she ever sickened, found repulse
At the other kind of water, not her life,
40   (Green-dense and dim-delicious, bred o' the sun)
Flounced back from bliss she was not born to breathe,
And in her old bounds buried her despair,
Hating and loving warmth alike: so He.

'Thinketh, He made thereat the sun, this isle,
Trees and the fowls here, beast and creeping thing.
Yon otter, sleek-wet, black, lithe as a leech;
Yon auk, one fire-eye in a ball of foam,
That floats and feeds; a certain badger brown
He hath watched hunt with that slant white-wedge eye
50   By moonlight; and the pie° with the long tongue
That pricks deep into oakwarts for a worm,
And says a plain word when she finds her prize,
But will not eat the ants; the ants themselves
That build a wall of seeds and settled stalks
About their hole—He made all these and more,

dam his mother, Sycorax                    pie magpie
Him refers throughout to Setebos

Made all we see, and us, in spite: how else?
He could not, Himself, make a second self
To be His mate; as well have made Himself:
He would not make what he mislikes or slights,
60    An eyesore to Him, or not worth His pains:
But did, in envy, listlessness or sport,
Make what Himself would fain, in a manner, be—
Weaker in most points, stronger in a few,
Worthy, and yet mere playthings all the while,
Things He admires and mocks too,—that is it.
Because, so brave, so better though they be,
It nothing skills if He begin to plague.
Look now, I melt a gourd-fruit into mash,
Add honeycomb and pods, I have perceived,
70    Which bite like finches when they bill and kiss,—
Then, when froth rises bladdery,° drink up all,
Quick, quick, till maggots scamper through my brain;
Last, throw me on my back in the seeded thyme,
And wanton, wishing I were born a bird.
Put case, unable to be what I wish,
I yet could make a live bird out of clay:
Would not I take clay, pinch my Caliban
Able to fly?—for, there, see, he hath wings,
And great comb like the hoopoe's° to admire,
80    And there, a sting to do his foes offence,
There, and I will that he begin to live,
Fly to yon rock-top, nip me off the horns
Of grigs° high up that make the merry din,
Saucy through their veined wings, and mind me not.
In which feat, if his leg snapped, brittle clay,
And he lay stupid-like,—why, I should laugh;
And if he, spying me, should fall to weep,
Beseech me to be good, repair his wrong,
Bid his poor leg smart less or grow again,—
90    Well, as the chance were, this might take or else
Not take my fancy: I might hear his cry,
And give the mankin three sound legs for one,
Or pluck the other off, leave him like an egg,
And lessoned he was mine and merely clay.
Were this no pleasure, lying in the thyme,
Drinking the mash, with brain become alive,
Making and marring clay at will? So He.
'Thinketh, such shows nor right nor wrong in Him,
Nor kind, nor cruel: He is strong and Lord.
100   'Am strong myself compared to yonder crabs
That march now from the mountain to the sea,

---

**bladdery** the bubbles of his fermenting mash rise like bladders

**hoopoe's** brightly colored, great crested bird

**grigs** grasshoppers

'Let twenty pass, and stone the twenty-first,
Loving not, hating not, just choosing so.
'Say, the first straggler that boasts purple spots
Shall join the file, one pincer twisted off;
'Say, this bruised fellow shall receive a worm,
And two worms he whose nippers end in red;
As it likes me each time, I do: so He.

Well then, 'supposeth He is good in the main,
110    Placable if His mind and ways were guessed,
But rougher than His handiwork, be sure!
Oh, He hath made things worthier than Himself,
And envieth that, so helped, such things do more
Than He who made them! What consoles but this?
That they, unless through Him, do nought at all,
And must submit: what other use in things?
'Hath cut a pipe of pithless elder-joint
That, blown through, gives exact the scream o' the jay
When from her wing you twitch the feathers blue:
120    Sound this, and little birds that hate the jay
Flock within stone's throw, glad their foe is hurt:
Put case such pipe could prattle and boast forsooth
'I catch the birds, I am the crafty thing,
I make the cry my maker cannot make
With his great round mouth; he must blow through mine!'
Would not I smash it with my foot? So He.

But wherefore rough, why cold and ill at ease?
Aha, that is a question! Ask, for that,
What knows,—the something over Setebos
130    That made Him, or He, may be, found and fought,
Worsted, drove off and did to nothing, perchance.
There may be something quiet o'er His head,
Out of His reach, that feels nor joy nor grief,
Since both derive from weakness in some way.
I joy because the quails come; would not joy
Could I bring quails here when I have a mind:
This Quiet,° all it hath a mind to, doth.
'Esteemeth stars the outposts of its couch,
But never spends much thought nor care that way.
140    It may look up, work up,—the worse for those
It works on! 'Careth but for Setebos
The many-handed as a cuttle-fish,
Who, making Himself feared through what He does,
Looks up, first, and perceives he cannot soar
To what is quiet and hath happy life;
Next looks down here, and out of very spite

**Quiet** the Deity beyond Setebos, a kind of
Transcendental Oversoul

Makes this a bauble-world to ape yon real,
These good things to match those as hips° do grapes.
'Tis solace making baubles, ay, and sport.
150   Himself peeped late, eyed Prosper at his books
Careless and lofty, lord now of the isle:
Vexed, 'stiched a book of broad leaves, arrow-shaped,
Wrote thereon, he knows what, prodigious words;
Has peeled a wand and called it by a name;
Weareth at whiles for an enchanter's robe
The eyed skin of a supple oncelot;°
And hath an ounce° sleeker than youngling mole,
A four-legged serpent he makes cower and couch,
Now snarl, now hold its breath and mind his eye,
160   And saith she is Miranda and my wife:
'Keeps for his Ariel a tall pouch-bill crane
He bids go wade for fish and straight disgorge;
Also a sea-beast, lumpish, which he snared,
Blinded the eyes of, and brought somewhat tame,
And split its toe-webs, and now pens the drudge
In a hole o' the rock and calls him Caliban;
A bitter heart that bides its time and bites.
'Plays thus at being Prosper in a way,
Taketh his mirth with make-believes: so He.

170   His dam held that the Quiet made all things
Which Setebos vexed only: 'holds not so.
Who made them weak, meant weakness He might vex.
Had He meant other, while His hand was in,
Why not make horny eyes no thorn could prick,
Or plate my scalp with bone against the snow,
Or overscale my flesh 'neath joint and joint,
Like an orc's° armour? Ay,—so spoil His sport!
He is the One now: only He doth all.

'Saith, He may like, perchance, what profits Him.
180   Ay, himself loves what does him good; but why?
'Gets good no otherwise. This blinded beast
Loves whoso places flesh-meat on his nose,
But, had he eyes, would want no help, but hate
Or love, just as it liked him: He hath eyes.
Also it pleaseth Setebos to work,
Use all His hands, and exercise much craft,
By no means for the love of what is worked.
'Tasteth, himself, no finer good in the world
When all goes right, in this safe summer-time,
190   And he wants little, hungers, aches not much,
Than trying what to do with wit and strength.

**hips** berries                                        **ounce** another kind of leopard
**oncelot** ocelot or leopard                    **orc** sea monster

'Falls to make something: 'piled yon pile of turfs,
And squared and stuck there squares of soft white chalk,
And, with a fish-tooth, scratched a moon on each,
And set up endwise certain spikes of tree,
And crowned the whole with a sloth's skull a-top,
Found dead in the woods, too hard for one to kill.
No use at all in the work, for work's sole sake;
'Shall some day knock it down again: so He.

200   'Saith He is terrible: watch His feats in proof!
One hurricane will spoil six good months' hope.
He hath a spite against me, that I know,
Just as He favours Prosper, who knows why?
So it is, all the same, as well I find.
'Wove wattles° half the winter, fenced them firm
With stone and stake to stop she-tortoises
Crawling to lay their eggs here: well, one wave,
Feeling the foot of Him upon its neck,
Gaped as a snake does, lolled out its large tongue,
210   And licked the whole labour flat: so much for spite.
'Saw a ball flame down late (yonder it lies)
Where, half an hour before, I slept in the shade:
Often they scatter sparkles: there is force!
'Dug up a newt He may have envied once
And turned to stone, shut up inside a stone.
Please Him and hinder this?—What Prosper does?
Aha, if He would tell me how! Not He!
There is the sport: discover how or die!
All need not die, for of the things o' the isle
220   Some flee afar, some dive, some run up trees;
Those at His mercy,—why, they please Him most
When . . . when . . . well, never try the same way twice!
Repeat what act has pleased, He may grow wroth.
You must not know His ways, and play Him off,
Sure of the issue. 'Doth the like himself:
'Spareth a squirrel that it nothing fears
But steals the nut from underneath my thumb,
And when I threat, bites stoutly in defence:
'Spareth an urchin° that contrariwise,
230   Curls up into a ball, pretending death
For fright at my approach: the two ways please.
But what would move my choler more than this,
That either creature counted on its life
Tomorrow and next day and all days to come,
Saying, forsooth, in the inmost of its heart,
'Because he did so yesterday with me,
And otherwise with such another brute,

**wattles** twigs                              **urchin** hedgehog

So must he do henceforth and always.'—Ay?
Would teach the reasoning couple what 'must' means!
240  'Doth as he likes, or wherefore Lord? So He.

'Conceiveth all things will continue thus,
And we shall have to live in fear of Him
So long as He lives, keeps His strength: no change,
If He have done His best, make no new world
To please Him more, so leave off watching this,—
If He surprise not even the Quiet's self
Some strange day,—or, suppose, grow into it
As grubs grow butterflies: else, here are we,
And there is He, and nowhere help at all.
250  'Believeth with the life, the pain shall stop.
His dam held different, that after death
He both plagued enemies and feasted friends:
Idly! He doth His worst in this our life,
Giving just respite lest we die through pain,
Saving last pain for worst,—with which, an end.
Meanwhile, the best way to escape His ire
Is, not to seem too happy. 'Sees, himself,
Yonder two flies, with purple films and pink,
Bask on the pompion-bell above: kills both.
260  'Sees two black painful beetles roll their ball
On head and tail as if to save their lives:
Moves them the stick away they strive to clear.

Even so, 'would have Him misconceive, suppose
This Caliban strives hard and ails no less,
And always, above all else, envies Him;
Wherefore he mainly dances on dark nights,
Moans in the sun, gets under holes to laugh,
And never speaks his mind save housed as now:
Outside, 'groans, curses. If He caught me here,
270  O'erheard this speech, and asked 'What chucklest at?'
'Would, to appease Him, cut a finger off,
Or of my three kid yearlings burn the best,
Or let the toothsome apples rot on tree,
Or push my tame beast for the orc to taste:
While myself lit a fire, and made a song
And sung it, 'What I hate, be consecrate
To celebrate Thee and Thy state, no mate
For Thee; what see for envy in poor me?'
Hoping the while, since evils sometimes mend,
280  Warts rub away and sores are cured with slime,
That some strange day, will either the Quiet catch
And conquer Setebos, or likelier He
Decrepit may doze, doze, as good as die.

[What, what? A curtain o'er the world at once!

Crickets stop hissing; not a bird—or, yes,
There scuds His raven that has told Him all!
It was fool's play, this prattling! Ha! The wind
Shoulders the pillared dust, death's house o' the move,
And fast invading fires begin! White blaze—
290   A tree's head snaps—and there, there, there, there, there,
His thunder follows! Fool to gibe at Him!
Lo! 'Lieth flat and loveth Setebos!
'Maketh his teeth meet through his upper lip,
Will let those quails fly, will not eat this month
One little mess of whelks, so he may 'scape!]
1859–60                                     1864

## Thamuris Marching°

Thamuris marching—lyre and song of Thrace—
(Perpend the first, the worst of woes that were
Allotted lyre and song, ye poet-race!)

Thamuris from Oichalia,° feasted there
By kingly Eurutos of late, now bound
For Dorion at the uprise broad and bare

Of Mount Pangaios (ore with earth enwound
Glittered beneath his footstep)—marching gay
And glad, Thessalia through, came, robed and crowned,

10   From triumph on to triumph, mid a ray
Of early morn—came, saw and knew the spot
Assigned him for his worst of woes, that day.

Balura°—happier while its name was not—
Met him, but nowise menaced; slipped aside,
Obsequious river to pursue its lot

Of solacing the valley—say, some wide
Thick busy human cluster, house and home,
Embanked for peace, or thrift that thanks the tide.

Thamuris, marching, laughed 'Each flake of foam'
20   (As sparklingly the ripple raced him by)
'Mocks slower clouds adrift in the blue dome!'

**Thamuris Marching** This song, excerpted from a late long poem, *Aristophanes' Apology* (ll. 104–80), was one of Browning's favorite pieces for reading aloud. It is perhaps the most direct expression of High Romanticism in the Victorian period, and a demonstration of how abiding the Shelleyan influence was in Browning. Homer (*Iliad* 2.594 ff.) told the story of Thamyris, a Thracian bard, who in his pride boasted that he would win a poetic contest even if the Muses themselves opposed him. The Muses defeated him, punished him by blindness, and then made him forget his poetic skill. In Browning's song, Thamyris is shown in his human glory, marching courageously toward his doomed contest with the Muses.
**Oichalia** This and the other Greek place names are merely here for local color.
**Balura** The river Balyra (from the Greek for "cast away") received its name because Thamyris, after he was blinded, threw his lyre into it.

For Autumn was the season; red the sky
Held morn's conclusive signet of the sun
To break the mists up, bid them blaze and die.

Morn had the mastery as, one by one
All pomps produced themselves along the tract
From earth's far ending to near Heaven begun.

Was there a ravaged tree? it laughed compact
With gold, a leaf-ball crisp, high-brandished now,
30    Tempting to onset frost which late attacked.

Was there a wizened shrub, a starveling bough,
A fleecy thistle filched from by the wind,
A weed, Pan's trampling hoof would disallow?

Each, with a glory and a rapture twined
About it, joined the rush of air and light
And force: the world was of one joyous mind.

Say not the birds flew! they forebore their right—
Swam, reveling onward in the roll of things.
Say not the beasts' mirth bounded! that was flight—

40    How could the creatures leap, no lift of wings?
Such earth's community of purpose, such
The ease of earth's fulfilled imaginings—

So did the near and far appear to touch
In the moment's transport—that an interchange
Of function, far with near, seemed scarce too much;

And had the rooted plant aspired to range
With the snake's license, while the insect yearned
To glow fixed as the flower, it were not strange—

No more than if the fluttery treetop turned
50    To actual music, sang itself aloft;
Or if the wind, impassioned chantress, earned

The right to soar embodied in some soft
Fine form all fit for cloud-companionship,
And, blissful, once touched beauty chased so oft.

Thamuris, marching, let no fancy slip
Born of the fiery transport; lyre and song
Were his, to smite with hand and launch from lip—

Peerless recorded, since the list grew long
Of poets (saith Homeros) free to stand
60    Pedestaled mid the Muses' temple-throng,

A statued service, laureled, lyre in hand,
(Ay, for we see them)—Thamuris of Thrace
Predominating foremost of the band.

Therefore the morn-ray that enriched his face,
If it gave lambent chill, took flame again
From flush of pride; he saw, he knew the place.

What wind arrived with all the rhythms from plain,
Hill, dale, and that rough wildwood interspersed?
Compounding these to one consummate strain,

70    It reached him, music; but his own outburst
Of victory concluded the account,
And that grew song which was mere music erst.

'Be my Parnassos, thou Pangaian mount!
And turn thee, river, nameless hitherto!
Famed shalt thou vie with famed Pieria's fount!°

'Here I await the end of this ado:
Which wins—Earth's poet or the Heavenly Muse.'

1874                    1875

# Prologue
## *From* Asolando°

PROLOGUE

'The Poet's age is sad: for why?
   In youth, the natural world could show
No common object but his eye
    At once involved with alien glow—
His own soul's iris-bow.ᵛ

'And now a flower is just a flower:
   Man, bird, beast are but beast, bird, man—
Simply themselves, uncinct° by dower
    Of dyes which, when life's day began,
10   Round each in glory ran.'°

Friend, did you need an optic glass,
   Which were your choice? A lens to drape
In ruby, emerald, chrysopras,°
    Each object—or reveal its shape
Clear outlined, past escape,

The naked very thing?—so clear
   That, when you had the chance to gaze,

**fount** place of the Muses
**Asolando** Browning's last volume, which was published in London on the same day that he died in Venice. The title refers to Asolo, a village near Venice that was a sacred place for the poet. The "Prologue," a powerful variation upon Wordsworth's "Intimations" Ode, goes back 50 years to the first time Browning saw Asolo. But where Wordsworth somberly weighs gain against loss, the fierce spirit of Browning

burns through all loss into a last transcendence.
**iris-bow** rainbow
**uncinct** not surrounded
**The Poet's . . . glory ran** The first two stanzas are spoken by what Blake would have called Browning's "Idiot Questioner," either an aspect of Browning himself, or a well-meaning but obtuse interlocutor.
**chrysopras** apple-green chalcedony, a precious stone

You found its inmost self appear
Through outer seeming—truth ablaze,
20   Not falsehood's fancy-haze?

How many a year, my Asolo,
Since—one step just from sea to land—
I found you, loved yet feared you so—
For natural objects seemed to stand
Palpably fire-clothed! No—

No mastery of mine o'er these!
Terror with beauty, like the Bush°
Burning but unconsumed. Bend knees,
Drop eyes to earthward! Language? Tush!
30   Silence 'tis awe decrees.

And now? The lambent flame is—where?
Lost from the naked world: earth, sky,
Hill, vale, tree, flower,—Italia's rare
O'er-running beauty crowds the eye—
But flame? The Bush is bare.

Hill, vale, tree, flower—they stand distinct,
Nature to know and name. What then?
A Voice spoke thence which straight unlinked
Fancy from fact: see, all's in ken:°
40   Has once my eyelid winked?

No, for the purged ear apprehends
Earth's import, not the eye late dazed:
The Voice said 'Call my works thy friends!
At Nature dost thou shrink amazed?
God is it who transcends.'°
1889                    1889


## Bad Dreams   III°

This was my dream! I saw a Forest
Old as the earth, no track nor trace
Of unmade man. Thou, Soul, explorest—
Though in a trembling rapture—space
Immeasurable! Shrubs, turned trees,
Trees that touch heaven, support its frieze
Studded with sun and moon and star:

Bush See Exodus 3:2, the manifestation of
Jehovah to Moses in the burning bush.
ken knowledge, apprehension, perhaps here sight
transcends goes beyond, but the word is charged
here with extraordinary meaning, for this is
God's ultimate relation to nature
Bad Dreams III This is the third of a sequence
of four nightmare poems depicting the break-up
of a marriage (something like Meredith's Mod-

ern Love), developed here as phantasmagoria.
In this poem the man dreams, seeing first a vision of wild nature; then of a city of art, and
then a horror of nature and art devouring one
another. In some way he identifies himself with
the forest of nature, his wife with the city of
art, and their marriage with the mutual destruction.

While—oh, the enormous growths that bar
Mine eye from penetrating past
10    Their tangled twine where lurks—nay, lives
Royally lone, some brute-type cast
In the rough, time cancels, man forgives.

On, Soul! I saw a lucid City°
Of architectural device
Every way perfect. Pause for pity,
Lightning! Nor leave a cicatrice°
On those bright marbles, dome and spire,
Structures palatial,—streets which mire
Dares not defile, paved all too fine
20    For human footstep's smirch, not thine—
Proud solitary traverser,
My Soul, of silent lengths of way—
With what ecstatic dread, aver,
Lest life start sanctioned by thy stay!

Ah, but the last sight was the hideous!
A City, yes,—a Forest, true,—
But each devouring each. Perfidious
Snake-plants had strangled what I knew
Was a pavilion once: each oak
30    Held on his horns some spoil he broke
By surreptitiously beneath
Upthrusting: pavements, as with teeth,
Griped huge weed widening crack and split
In squares and circles stone-work erst.
Oh, Nature—good! Oh, Art— no whit
Less worthy! Both in one—accurst!
1888                              1889

# MATTHEW ARNOLD
1822–1888

Arnold is a Romantic poet who did not wish to be one, an impossible conflict which maimed his poetic talent, and caused him finally to abandon poetry for literary criticism and prose prophecy. From the middle 1850's on, Arnold was primarily a prose writer, and so this introductory note will take him only up to that time.

Arnold was born on December 24, 1822, the eldest son of the formidable Dr. Thomas Arnold, who from 1828 on was to be Headmaster of Rugby School. Dr. Arnold, a historian of some limited distinction, was a Protestant moralist of the rationalizing kind. His son did well at Rugby, but alarmed Dr. Arnold with a defensive

**On, Soul . . . City** Compare this stanza with Yeats's "Byzantium," which also excludes the fury and the mire of human veins.

**cicatrice** the scar of a healed wound

posture of continuous gaiety, which became a mock-dandyism at Balliol College, Oxford, where his closest friend was the poet Arthur Hugh Clough. After a fellowship at Oriel College, Oxford, Arnold went to London in 1847, as private secretary to a high official. In September 1848, holidaying in Switzerland, he fell in love with the "Marguerite" of his early poems, which were published in 1849 as *The Strayed Reveller, and Other Poems*. By 1850, at the latest, he had given up "Marguerite" (evidently because of his own prudery) and fell more properly in love with a judge's daughter, whom he married in 1851, after being appointed an Inspector of Schools.

In 1852 Arnold published his principal poem, the ambitious and uneasy *Empedocles on Etna*. When he brought his *Poems* together in 1853, he excluded *Empedocles*, explaining in the volume's famous anti-Romantic "Preface" that passive suffering was not a fit theme for poetry. When in 1857, he was elected Professor of Poetry at Oxford, almost all his best poetry had been written. Thus, his next poem, *Merope. A Tragedy*, published in 1858, is rather bad, and the outstanding poems of his last volume, *New Poems* (1867), were composed many years before. Whatever his achievement as a critic of literature, society, religion, his work as a poet may not merit the reputation it has continued to hold in the twentieth century. Arnold is, at his best, a very good but highly derivative poet, unlike Tennyson, Browning, Hopkins, Swinburne, and Rossetti, all of whom individualized their voices. As with Tennyson, Hopkins, and Rossetti, Arnold's dominant precursor was Keats, but this is an unhappy puzzle, since Arnold (unlike the others) professed not to admire Keats, while writing his own elegiac poems in a diction, meter, imagistic procedure, that are embarrassingly close to Keats (any reader who believes that this judgment is too harsh ought to experiment immediately by reading side-by-side the odes of Keats and Arnold's "The Scholar-Gypsy" or "Thyrsis"). Tennyson, Hopkins, and D. G. Rossetti retain distinctive Keatsian elements in their mature styles, but these elements are subdued to larger effects. But Arnold in "The Scholar-Gypsy," his best poem of some length, uses the language and movement of Keats even though the effect is irrelevant to his poem's theme. With few exceptions, Arnold's poems are seriously flawed, and yet few critics have been bothered by this; some even have argued that Arnold's faults make him more direct.

Still, it is not a mean distinction to have written lyrics as strong as the famous "To Marguerite—Continued" and "Dover Beach" or a meditative poem as insightful as "The Buried Life." Arnold got into his poetry what Tennyson and Browning scarcely needed (but absorbed anyway), the main march of mind in his time. His frequently dry tone and flatness of statement may not have been, as he happily believed, evidences of classicism, but of a lack of poetic exuberance, a failure in the vitality of his language. But much abides in his work, and he is usefully prophetic also of the anti-Romantic "Modernism" of our time, so much of which, like Arnold, has turned out to be Romantic in spite of itself.

# The Strayed Reveller

Used as the title poem in Arnold's first book, this is his poetic manifesto, comparable to Keats's "Sleep and Poetry," but attempting to rebel against Keats's, Shelley's, and Byron's imaginative stances. Arnold himself is the strayed reveller, the youth who

carries himself as a Regency dandy but who bides his time, sojourning only provisionally with Circe. The bards of Romanticism, the reveller's precursors, purchase their
intense power through the loss of objective knowledge, and what little knowledge
they have through the loss of moral power. To avoid their fate, the reveller or new
poet goes to Circe, goddess of forgetfulness, and is able to observe "without pain,
without labour." When he is strong enough, he will go forth to make his own, hopefully different kind of poetry out of "the bright procession / Of eddying forms."
Though Arnold (like all young poets) partly deceived himself, "The Strayed Reveller"
is a classic statement of the dilemma of young poets seeking to evade the many (and
crippling) anxieties of influence that are endemic in Romantic tradition.

# The Strayed Reveller

*The portico of Circe's palace.° Evening*

A YOUTH    CIRCE

THE YOUTH
Faster, faster,
O Circe, Goddess,
Let the wild, thronging train,
The bright procession
Of eddying forms,
Sweep through my soul!

Thou standest, smiling
Down on me! thy right arm,
Leaned up against the column there,
10   Props thy soft cheek;
Thy left holds, hanging loosely,
The deep cup, ivy-cinctured,°
I held but now.

Is it, then, evening
So soon? I see, the night-dews,
Clustered in thick beads, dim
The agate brooch-stones
On thy white shoulder;
The cool night-wind, too,
20   Blows through the portico,
Stirs thy hair, Goddess,
Waves thy white robe!

CIRCE
Whence art thou, sleeper?

Circe's palace  The setting is from Homer's    ivy-cinctured circled by ivy
*Odyssey* X.210–13.

THE YOUTH

When the white dawn first
Through the rough fir-planks
Of my hut, by the chestnuts,
Up at the valley-head,
Came breaking, Goddess!
I sprang up, I threw round me
30 My dappled fawn-skin;°
Passing out, from the wet turf,
Where they° lay, by the hut door,
I snatched up my vine-crown, my fir-staff,
All drenched in dew—
Came swift down to join
The rout° early gathered
In the town, round the temple,
Iacchus' white fane°
On yonder hill.
40 Quick I passed, following
The wood-cutters' cart-track
Down the dark valley;—I saw
On my left, through the beeches,
Thy palace, Goddess,
Smokeless, empty!
Trembling, I entered; beheld
The court all silent,
The lions sleeping,
On the altar this bowl.
50 I drank, Goddess!
And sank down here, sleeping,
On the steps of thy portico.

CIRCE

Foolish boy! Why tremblest thou?
Thou lovest it, then, my wine?
Wouldst more of it? See, how glows,
Through the delicate, flushed marble,
The red, creaming liquor,
Strown with dark seeds!
Drink, then! I chide thee not,
60 Deny thee not my bowl.
Come, stretch forth thy hand, then—so!
Drink—drink again!

THE YOUTH

Thanks, gracious one!
Ah, the sweet fumes again!

**fawn-skin** costume of a Dionysiac reveller
**they** the followers of Ulysses
**rout** Dionysiac or Bacchic orgiastic procession

**Iacchus' white fane** temple of Iacchus, a god of the Eleusinian mysteries, but Arnold confuses him with Bacchus

More soft, ah me,
More subtle-winding
Than Pan's flute-music!°
Faint—faint! Ah me,
Again the sweet sleep!

CIRCE
70  Hist! Thou—within there!
Come forth, Ulysses!
Art tired with hunting?
While we range the woodland,
See what the day brings.

ULYSSES
Ever new magic!
Hast thou then lured hither,
Wonderful Goddess, by thy art,
The young, languid-eyed Ampelus,°
Iacchus' darling—
80  Or some youth beloved of Pan,
Of Pan and the Nymphs?
That he sits, bending downward
His white, delicate neck
To the ivy-wreathed marge°
Of thy cup; the bright, glancing vine-leaves
That crown his hair,
Falling forward, mingling
With the dark ivy-plants—
His fawn-skin, half untied,
90  Smeared with red wine-stains? Who is he,
That he sits, overweighed
By fumes of wine and sleep,
So late, in thy portico?
What youth, Goddess,—what guest
Of Gods or mortals?

CIRCE
Hist! he wakes!
I lured him not hither, Ulysses.
Nay, ask him!

THE YOUTH
Who speaks? Ah, who comes forth
100  To thy side, Goddess, from within?
How shall I name him?
This spare, dark-featured,

Pan's flute music here the pastoral verse of the
younger Romantics, particularly Keats's *Endymion* and his "Ode on a Grecian Urn"

Ampelus a satyr whom Dionysus loved
marge brim

Quick-eyed stranger?
Ah, and I see too
His sailor's bonnet,
His short coat, travel-tarnished
With one arm bare!—
Art thou not he, whom fame
This long time rumours
110    The favoured guest of Circe, brought by the waves?
Art thou he, stranger?
The wise Ulysses,
Laertes' son?

ULYSSES

I am Ulysses.
And thou, too, sleeper?
Thy voice is sweet.
It may be thou hast followed
Through the islands some divine bard,°
By age taught many things,
120    Age and the Muses;
And heard him delighting
The chiefs and people
In the banquet, and learned his songs,
Of Gods and Heroes,
Of war and arts,
And peopled cities,
Inland, or built
By the grey sea.—If so, then hail!
I honour and welcome thee.

THE YOUTH

130    The Gods are happy.
They turn on all sides
Their shining eyes,
And see below them
The earth and men.

They see Tiresias°
Sitting, staff in hand,
On the warm, grassy
Asopus bank,
His robe drawn over

some divine bard a precursor poet
Tiresias Seer of Thebes, possessor of the Oedipal truth. He experienced sexual love both as a woman and a man, but he made his usual mistake of scrupulously telling the truth when Zeus and Hera insisted he judge whether women or men received more pleasure from copulation. After he confirmed the argument of Zeus, that women were more gratified, Hera blinded him, on the outrageous grounds that he was telling secrets. Zeus made what amends he could, granting Tiresias the powers of a seer, and stretching out his life to seven times the normal span. Tennyson wrote a powerful late poem on Tiresias, who also helps define the hidden homosexual theme of Eliot's Waste Land. Arnold brings him in because of his confrontation with Ulysses in Hades.

140    His old, sightless head,
       Revolving inly
       The doom of Thebes.

       They see the Centaurs°
       In the upper glens
       Of Pelion, in the streams,
       Where red-berried ashes fringe
       The clear-brown shallow pools,
       With streaming flanks, and heads
       Reared proudly, snuffing
150    The mountain wind.

       They see the Indian°
       Drifting, knife in hand,
       His frail boat moored to
       A floating isle thick-matted
       With large-leaved, low-creeping melon-plants,
       And the dark cucumber.
       He reaps, and stows them,
       Drifting—drifting;—round him,
       Round his green harvest-plot,
160    Flow the cool lake-waves,
       The mountains ring them.

       They see the Scythian°
       On the wide steppe, unharnessing
       His wheeled house at noon.
       He tethers his beast down, and makes his meal—
       Mares' milk, and bread
       Baked on the embers;—all around
       The boundless, waving grass-plains stretch, thick-starred
       With saffron and the yellow hollyhock
170    And flag-leaved iris-flowers.
       Sitting in his cart
       He makes his meal; before him, for long miles,
       Alive with bright green lizards,
       And the springing bustard-fowl,
       The track, a straight black line,
       Furrows the rich soil; here and there
       Clusters of lonely mounds
       Topped with rough-hewn,
       Grey, rain-bleared statues, overpeer
180    The sunny waste.

Centaurs savages—half-man, half-horse—who
live on Mt. Pelion in Thessaly
Indian Lines 151–61 and 181–200 take their
details from *Travels into Bokhara* (1834) by
Sir Alexander Burnes, one of Arnold's favorite
substitutes for actual experience.

Scythian barbarian people who came down into
Greece from what is now southern Russia; their
shamanism deeply affected pre-Socratic poet-
philosophers like Empedocles

They see the ferry
On the broad, clay-laden
Lone Chorasmian° stream;—thereon,
With snort and strain,
Two horses, strongly swimming, tow
The ferry-boat, with woven ropes
To either bow
Firm harnessed by the mane; a chief,
With shout and shaken spear,
190    Stands at the prow, and guides them; but astern
The cowering merchants, in long robes,
Sit pale beside their wealth
Of silk-bales and of balsam-drops,
Of gold and ivory,
Of turquoise-earth and amethyst,
Jasper and chalcedony,°
And milk-barred onyx-stones.
The loaded boat swings groaning
In the yellow eddies;
200    The Gods behold them.
They see the Heroes
Sitting in the dark ship
On the foamless, long-heaving
Violet sea,
At sunset nearing
The Happy Islands.°

     These things, Ulysses,
The wise bards also
Behold and sing.
210    But oh, what labour!
O prince, what pain!

They too can see
Tiresias;—but the Gods,
Who give them vision,
Added this law:
That they should bear too
His groping blindness,
His dark foreboding,
His scorned white hairs;
220    Bear Hera's anger
Through a life lengthened
To seven ages.

They see the Centaurs
On Pelion;—then they feel,

Chorasmian Oxus River, south of Aral Sea; the
locale is crucial in Shelley's *Alastor*, one of the
hidden influences on "The Strayed Reveller"
chalcedony transparent precious stone

Happy Islands Isles of the Blessed, where
Achilles went after death, beyond Gibraltar,
where Ulysses was at last to be destroyed

They too, the maddening wine
Swell their large veins to bursting; in wild pain
They feel the biting spears
Of the grim Lapithæ,° and Theseus, drive,
Drive crashing through their bones; they feel
230  High on a jutting rock in the red stream
Alcmena's dreadful son°
Ply his bow;—such a price
The Gods exact for songs:
To become what we sing.°

They see the Indian
On his mountain lake; but squalls
Make their skiff reel, and worms
In the unkind spring have gnawn
Their melon-harvest to the heart.—They see
240  The Scythian; but long frosts
Parch them in winter-time on the bare steppe,
Till they too fade like grass; they crawl
Like shadows forth in spring.

They see the merchants
On the Oxus stream;—but care
Must visit first them too, and make them pale.
Whether, through whirling sand,
A cloud of desert robber-horse have burst
Upon their caravan; or greedy kings,
250  In the walled cities the way passes through,
Crushed them with tolls; or fever-airs,
On some great river's marge,
Mown them down, far from home.

They see the Heroes
Near harbour;—but they share
Their lives, and former violent toil in Thebes,
Seven-gated Thebes, or Troy;
Or where the echoing oars
Of Argo° first
260  Startled the unknown sea.

The old Silenus°
Came, lolling in the sunshine,
From the dewy forest-coverts,
This way, at noon.

Lapithæ neighbors of the Centaurs, whom they
invited to a wedding feast, but the lustful Centaurs tried to carry off the King's bride; in a
subsequent battle, King Theseus of Athens
fought for the Lapithae
Alcmena's dreadful son Heracles, another opponent of the Centaurs
become what we sing See Rousseau in Shelley's
The Triumph of Life, ll. 279–80: "I/Have suffered what I wrote, or viler pain!"; and Byron-
as-Maddalo in Shelley's Julian and Maddalo,
ll. 544–46: "Most wretched men/Are cradled
into poetry by wrong,/They learn in suffering
what they teach in song"
Argo Jason's ship in the quest for the Golden
Fleece
Silenus wisest and deepest-drinking of the
satyrs, teacher of the boy Dionysus

Sitting by me, while his Fauns
Down at the water-side
Sprinkled and smoothed
His drooping garland,
He told me these things.

270    But I, Ulysses,
Sitting on the warm steps,
Looking over the valley,
All day long, have seen,
Without pain, without labour,
Sometimes a wild-haired Mænad°—
Sometimes a Faun with torches—
And sometimes, for a moment,
Passing through the dark stems
Flowing-robed, the beloved,
280    The desired, the divine,
Beloved Iacchus.

Ah, cool night-wind, tremulous stars!
Ah, glimmering water,
Fitful earth-murmur,
Dreaming woods!
Ah, golden-haired, strangely smiling Goddess,
And thou, proved, much enduring,
Wave-tossed Wanderer!
Who can stand still?
290    Ye fade, ye swim, ye waver before me—
The cup again!

Faster, faster,
O Circe, Goddess,
Let the wild, thronging train,
The bright procession
Of eddying forms,
Sweep through my soul!
1847–48            1849

# To Marguerite—Continued°

Yes! in the sea of life enisled,°
With echoing straits between us thrown,
Dotting the shoreless watery wild,
We mortal millions live *alone*.

---

**Mænad** frenzied female follower of Dionysus
**To Marguerite** . . . This is not so much a
tragic love poem, as it is Arnold's self-justifica-
tion for having denied love, and a moving but
lame attempt to assign the cause of his own
erotic failure to Necessity, the "God" of l. 22.
**enisled** cut off as though on an island

The islands feel the enclasping flow,
And then their endless bounds they know.

But when the moon their hollows lights,
And they are swept by balms of spring,
And in their glens, on starry nights,
10  The nightingales divinely sing;
And lovely notes, from shore to shore,
Across the sounds and channels pour—

Oh! then a longing like despair
Is to their farthest caverns sent;
For surely once, they feel, we were
Parts of a single continent!
Now round us spreads the watery plain—
Oh might our marges meet again!

Who ordered, that their longing's fire
20  Should be, as soon as kindled, cooled?
Who renders vain their deep desire?—
A God, a God their severance ruled!
And bade betwixt their shores to be
The unplumbed, salt, estranging sea.
1849                              1852

## Courage°

True, we must tame our rebel will:
True, we must bow to Nature's law:
Must bear in silence many an ill;
Must learn to wait, renounce, withdraw.°

Yet now, when boldest wills give place,
When Fate and Circumstance are strong,
And in their rush the human race
Are swept, like huddling sheep, along;

Those sterner spirits let me prize,
10  Who, though the tendence of the whole
They less than us might recognize,
Kept, more than us, their strength of soul.

Yes, be the second Cato° praised!
Not that he took the course to die—
But that, when 'gainst himself he raised
His arm, he raised it dauntlessly.

**Courage** This is Arnold's own comment on the
irresolution of his conduct in his love affair with
Marguerite; the longing for Byronic strength is
extraordinarily revealing.
**Must learn . . . withdraw** reflecting the probable moral influence of Carlyle and (through
him) of Goethe
**Cato** Stoic descendant of the first Cato; he
committed suicide (46 B.C.) to spite Caesar's
desire to take him captive

And, Byron! let us dare admire,
If not thy fierce and turbid song,
Yet that, in anguish, doubt, desire,
20    Thy fiery courage still was strong.°

The sun that on thy tossing pain
Did with such cold derision shine,
He crushed thee not with his disdain—
He had his glow; and thou hadst thine.

Our bane, disguise it as we may,
Is weakness, is a faltering course.
Oh that past times could give our day,
Joined to its clearness, of their force!
1849                          1852

## From Empedocles on Etna

[SONG OF CALLICLES]°

CALLICLES *from below*
Through the black, rushing smoke-bursts,
Thick breaks the red flame;
All Etna heaves fiercely
420    Her forest-clothed frame.

Not here, O Apollo!
Are haunts meet for thee.
But, where Helicon° breaks down
In cliff to the sea,

Where the moon-silvered inlets
Send far their light voice
Up the still vale of Thisbe,°
O speed, and rejoice!

On the sward at the cliff-top
430    Lie strewn the white flocks,
On the cliff-side the pigeons
Roost deep in the rocks.

In the moonlight the shepherds,
Soft lulled by the rills,

**And, Byron . . . strong** See the description of
Byron in Arnold's "Memorial Verses."
[**Song of Callicles**] This lyric concludes the dramatic poem *Empedocles on Etna*, whose theme
is the inadequacy of the modern world to sustain the classical poetic imagination. Empedocles, Greek poet-philosopher who lived in
Sicily about 440 B.C., is Arnold's Byronic hero,
who dies because of excessive self-consciousness,
and who is afflicted by his acute sense of being
a spiritual latecomer, alive after the proper context for his work has vanished. The strangely
exultant but still despairing Empedocles has
just destroyed himself by plunging into the volcano's crater. His harp player, Callicles (whose
name is derived from a Greek word for beauty),
survives him to sing this triumphal Keatsian
song of the Muses, which derives many of its
details from Hesiod's *Theogony*, ll. 1–39.
**Helicon** Boetian mountain of the Muses
**Thisbe** town between Helicon and Gulf of
Corinth

Lie wrapped in their blankets
Asleep on the hills.

—What forms are these coming
So white through the gloom?
What garments out-glistening
440   The gold-flowered broom?

What sweet-breathing presence
Out-perfumes the thyme?
What voices enrapture
The night's balmy prime?—

'Tis Apollo comes leading
His choir, the Nine.
—The leader is fairest,
But all are divine.

They are lost in the hollows!
450   They stream up again!
What seeks on this mountain
The glorified train?—

They bathe on this mountain,
In the spring by their road;
Then on to Olympus,
Their endless abode.

—Whose praise do they mention?
Of what is it told?—
What will be for ever;
460   What was from of old.

First hymn they the Father
Of all things; and then,
The rest of immortals,
The action of men.

The day in his hotness,
The strife with the palm;
The night in her silence,
The stars in their calm.
1849–52         1852

# Memorial Verses

### April, 1850°

Goethe in Weimar sleeps, and Greece,
Long since, saw Byron's struggle cease.°

**April, 1850** Wordsworth died on April 23, 1850.
**Goethe . . . cease** Byron died in Greece in 1824; notice that Arnold could not conceive of Byron as "sleeping," like the dead sage Goethe, but only as having ceased in his intense struggle.

But one such death remained to come;
The last poetic voice is dumb°—
We stand today by Wordsworth's tomb.

When Byron's eyes were shut in death,
We bowed our head and held our breath.
He taught us little; but our soul
Had *felt* him like the thunder's roll.
10    With shivering heart the strife we saw
Of passion with eternal law;
And yet with reverential awe
We watched the fount of fiery life
Which served for that Titanic strife.°
    When Goethe's death was told, we said:
Sunk, then, is Europe's sagest head.
Physician of the iron age,°
Goethe has done his pilgrimage.
He took the suffering human race,
20    He read each wound, each weakness clear;
And struck his finger on the place,
And said: *Thou ailest here, and here!*
He looked on Europe's dying hour°
Of fitful dream and feverish power;
His eye plunged down the weltering strife,
The turmoil of expiring life—
He said: *The end is everywhere,
Art still has truth, take refuge there!*
And he was happy, if to know
30    Causes of things, and far below
His feet to see the lurid flow
Of terror, and insane distress,
And headlong fate, be happiness.°

And Wordsworth!—Ah, pale ghosts, rejoice!
For never has such soothing voice
Been to your shadowy world conveyed,°
Since erst, at morn, some wandering shade
Heard the clear song of Orpheus come
Through Hades,° and the mournful gloom.
40    Wordsworth has gone from us—and ye,°
Ah, may ye feel his voice as we!
He too upon a wintry clime
Had fallen—on this iron time

is dumb hardly a compliment to Tennyson and Browning, among others
Titanic strife the battle between the Promethean Byron and the moral law; an internalized battle, and so the more impressive
iron age classical way of describing an age in acute decline
dying hour the end of the European Enlightenment, and the advent of revolution and Romanticism
happiness Lines 29–33 are a fairly close trans-
lation of Virgil (*Georgics* II. 480–82), where Virgil is brooding about Lucretius. Arnold is therefore casting himself as Virgil in relation to Wordsworth or Goethe as Lucretius.
conveyed Wordsworth has gone to Hades, rather than any version of a Christian heaven; an impressive touch on Arnold's part.
Orpheus . . . Hades when Orpheus descended in the vain attempt to bring back his wife, Eurydice
ye inhabitants of Hades

Of doubts, disputes, distractions, fears.
He found us when the age had bound
Our souls in its benumbing round;
He spoke, and loosed our heart in tears.
He laid us as we lay at birth
On the cool flowery lap of earth,
50 Smiles broke from us and we had ease;
The hills were round us, and the breeze
Went o'er the sun-lit fields again;
Our foreheads felt the wind and rain.
Our youth returned; for there was shed
On spirits that had long been dead,
Spirits dried up and closely furled,
The freshness of the early world.

Ah! since dark days still bring to light
Man's prudence and man's fiery might,
60 Time may restore us in his course
Goethe's sage mind and Byron's force;
But where will Europe's latter hour
Again find Wordsworth's healing power?
Others will teach us how to dare,
And against fear our breast to steel;
Others will strengthen us to bear—
But who, ah! who, will make us feel?
The cloud of mortal destiny,
Others will front it fearlessly—
70 But who, like him, will put it by?

Keep fresh the grass upon his grave
O Rotha,° with thy living wave!
Sing him thy best! for few or none
Hears thy voice right, now he is gone.
1850                           1850


## Dover Beach°

The sea is calm tonight.
The tide is full, the moon lies fair
Upon the straits;—on the French coast the light
Gleams and is gone; the cliffs of England stand, *white cliffs of Dover*

put it by a subtle tribute to Wordsworth's
"Intimations" Ode
Rotha the river that flows close to Grasmere
churchyard, where Wordsworth was buried
Dover Beach Arnold's most famous poem, presumably because it is believed to convey a universal sorrow of his time, this nevertheless has
some flaws. Though it cannot be dated with any
certainty, it may go back as far as 1848, and
reflect not only the European revolutions of
that year, but Arnold's anguish about Mar-

guerite. Whatever its date, a troubled reader,
however justly admiring, can wonder whether
the poem earns the transition between its last
two stanzas. As in the great lyric to Marguerite,
Arnold is rather too ready to ascribe his own
failure of nerve, erotically speaking, to a larger
crisis in the history of culture. For a wry contemporary comment on this fascinating poem,
see Anthony Hecht's poem, "The Dover Bitch,"
which rewrites Arnold from the young lady's
point of view.

*light / dark*
*enlightenment / ignorance*

Glimmering and vast, out in the tranquil bay.
Come to the window, sweet is the night-air!

*pebbles to beach*
*man to life*

Only, from the long line of spray
Where the sea meets the moon-blanched land,
Listen! you hear the grating roar
10  Of pebbles which the waves draw back, and fling,
At their return, up the high strand,
Begin, and cease, and then again begin,
With tremulous cadence slow, and bring
The eternal note of sadness in.

*ebb + flow*
*happiness -> darkness*
*line length*

Sophocles long ago°
Heard it on the Ægæan, and it brought
Into his mind the turbid ebb and flow
Of human misery; we
Find also in the sound a thought,
20  Hearing it by this distant northern sea.

*Fate*

The Sea of Faith
Was once, too, at the full, and round earth's shore
Lay like the folds of a bright girdle furled.°    *sash men wear to war -> belongs to woman*
But now I only hear
Its melancholy, long, withdrawing roar,
Retreating, to the breath
Of the night-wind, down the vast edges drear
And naked shingles of the world.

*Faith*

Ah, love, let us be true
30  To one another! for the world, which seems
To lie before us like a land of dreams,
So various, so beautiful, so new,
Hath really neither joy, nor love, nor light,
Nor certitude, nor peace, nor help for pain;
And we are here as on a darkling plain      *Fate vs Faith*
Swept with confused alarms of struggle and flight,   *Faith loses.*
Where ignorant armies clash by night.°
?1848                          1867

**Sophocles long ago** Though Arnold preferred Sophocles to the other Greek dramatists, one can suspect that "Sophocles" here is a mask for the palpable indebtedness to Wordsworth, rather like the pseudo-reference to Otway in Coleridge's "Dejection: An Ode." Every passage scholars have cited from Sophocles is absurdly far from Arnold's lines, but the Wordsworth of "Tintern Abbey," the "Intimations" Ode, and the sonnets of 1802 is very close. Arnold, like Wordsworth, is hearing "the still, sad music of humanity,/Nor harsh nor grating, though of ample power/To chasten and subdue."
**bright girdle furled** a difficult line; to be construed only by excessive ingenuity
**clash by night** Possibly an echo of a passage in a poem by his friend Clough, but the ultimate source, as all scholars have said, is almost certainly the account by the Athenian historian Thucydides of the battle of Epipolae, between the Syracusans and the Athenians. In the translation of Thucydides by Arnold's father, the soldiers "see before them the form of the object but . . . mistrust their knowing who was friend and who was foe." The Loeb translation, with greater clarity, gives: "seeing before them the vision of a person but mistrusting their recognition of their own friends. . . ." If the poem was written in 1848 or 1849, then Arnold is manifesting a very ambiguous attitude toward the third wave of the European revolution, but tradition has solved this problem by deciding that the passage is a characterization of the entire Victorian Age, or even of the modern world in general.

# The Buried Life°

Light flows our war° of mocking words, and yet,
Behold, with tears mine eyes are wet!°
I feel a nameless sadness o'er me roll.°
Yes, yes, we know that we can jest,
We know, we know that we can smile!
But there's a something in this breast,
To which thy light words bring no rest,
And thy gay smiles no anodyne.°
Give me thy hand, and hush awhile,°
10 And turn those limpid eyes on mine,
And let me read there, love! thy inmost soul.

Alas! is even love too weak
To unlock the heart, and let it speak?
Are even lovers powerless to reveal
To one another what indeed they feel?
I knew the mass of men concealed
Their thoughts, for fear that if revealed
They would by other men be met
With blank indifference, or with blame reproved;
20 I knew they lived and moved
Tricked in disguises, alien to the rest
Of men, and alien to themselves—and yet
The same heart beats in every human breast!

But we, my love!—doth a like spell benumb
Our hearts, our voices?—must we too be dumb?
Ah! well for us, if even we,
Even for a moment, can get free
Our heart, and have our lips unchained;
For that which seals them hath been deep-ordained!
30 Fate, which foresaw
How frivolous a baby man would be—
By what distractions he would be possessed,
How he would pour himself in every strife,
And well-nigh change his own identity—
That it might keep from his capricious play

**The Buried Life** Again difficult to date, this most profound of Arnold's poems belongs to the 1848–52 period, and is closely related to the Marguerite poems and to "Dover Beach" (particularly if that is a Marguerite poem also). The parent poem is Keats's "Ode on Melancholy," but there are clear debts also to Wordsworth, and perhaps even to Tennyson. Of all Arnold's poems, this is the most authentic attempt to exorcise the demons of self-consciousness, and not merely to exploit them.
**our war** Evidently refers to banter between Marguerite and the poet, and yet suddenly he finds himself in tears.

**are wet** perhaps a reference to Tennyson's "Tears, Idle Tears" (from *The Princess*, 1847), but the resemblance may exist because Keats and Wordsworth inform both poems
**I feel . . . roll** See Wordsworth's "Resolution and Independence," l. 28.
**anodyne** pain-killing drug
**hush awhile** Marguerite was much more vivacious than Arnold, whose lightness of spirit was always a mask; ll. 9–11 clearly stem from Keats's "Ode on Melancholy," ll. 19–20, but Keats's peculiar sense of "melancholy" as a heightened, oxymoronic, creative sense of consciousness pervades Arnold's entire poem.

His genuine self, and force him to obey
Even in his own despite his being's law,
Bade through the deep recesses of our breast
The unregarded river of our life
40   Pursue with indiscernible flow its way;
And that we should not see
The buried stream, and seem to be
Eddying at large in blind uncertainty,
Though driving on with it eternally.

But often, in the world's most crowded streets,
But often, in the din of strife,°
There rises an unspeakable desire°
After the knowledge of our buried life;
A thirst to spend our fire and restless force
50   In tracking out our true, original course;
A longing to inquire
Into the mystery of this heart which beats
So wild, so deep in us—to know
Whence our lives come and where they go.
And many a man in his own breast then delves,
But deep enough, alas! none ever mines.
And we have been on many thousand lines,
And we have shown, on each, spirit and power;
But hardly have we, for one little hour,
60   Been on our own line, have we been ourselves—
Hardly had skill to utter one of all
The nameless feelings that course through our breast,
But they course on for ever unexpressed.

And long we try in vain to speak and act
Our hidden self, and what we say and do
Is eloquent, is well—but 'tis not true!
And then we will no more be racked
With inward striving, and demand
Of all the thousand nothings of the hour
70   Their stupefying° power;
Ah yes, and they benumb us at our call!°
Yet still, from time to time, vague and forlorn,
From the soul's subterranean depth upborne
As from an infinitely distant land,
Come airs, and floating echoes, and convey
A melancholy° into all our day.

Only—but this is rare—
When a belovéd hand is laid in ours,
When, jaded with the rush and glare

din of strife See "Tintern Abbey," ll. 25–26.        at our call when we call them
unspeakable desire See *Paradise Lost* III.662–63.    melancholy but in the Keatsian, rich sense; not
stupefying to deaden our sense of being lost        the ordinary one

80 Of the interminable hours,
Our eyes can in another's eyes read clear,
When our world-deafened ear
Is by the tones of a loved voice caressed—
A bolt is shot back somewhere in our breast,
And a lost pulse of feeling stirs again.
The eye sinks inward, and the heart lies plain,
And what we mean, we say, and what we would, we know.
A man becomes aware of his life's flow,
And hears its winding murmur; and he sees
90 The meadows where it glides, the sun, the breeze.

And there arrives a lull in the hot race
Wherein he doth for ever chase
That flying and elusive shadow, rest.
An air of coolness plays upon his face,
And an unwonted calm pervades his breast.
And then he thinks he knows
The hills where his life rose,
And the sea where it goes.°
1848–52                1852

# Stanzas from the Grande Chartreuse

This rugged and impressive poem triumphs over its own confusions, and by any standards is one of Arnold's finest. The central confusion is that the monastery which is his ostensible subject has not much to do with Arnold's theme, and indeed he cares so little for the Grande Chartreuse in itself that he cannot be bothered to get the procedures of the Carthusians right. They are so irrelevant to the modern world's problems, in his view, that he cannot be interested in them. As Tinker and Lowry note in their *Commentary*, in his mind's eye Arnold sees not the Chartreuse, but St. Mary's at Oxford, the church of Newman. The rejection, in the poem, is of the Oxford Movement, but also of the Protestantism in which Arnold was reared, and (most powerfully, because most ambivalently) of High Romanticism, particularly of the Prometheans Byron and Shelley. What is most moving and disarming about the poem is Arnold's candor in telling us he has nothing to install in the place of the ideologies he is compelled to reject. This distinguishes the poem's argument from the aggressiveness of Carlyle, with whom nevertheless it shares many attitudes. Though Arnold speaks of a more fortunate age that may come, his heart, in this poem, remains a handful of dust.

**where it goes** The general imagery of the "Intimations" Ode is at work here.

# Stanzas from the Grande Chartreuse

Through Alpine meadows soft-suffused
With rain, where thick the crocus blows,°
Past the dark forges long disused,
The mule-track from Saint Laurent° goes.
The bridge is crossed, and slow we ride,
Through forest, up the mountainside.

The autumnal evening darkens round,
The wind is up, and drives the rain;
While, hark! far down, with strangled sound
10  Doth the Dead Guier's stream° complain,
Where that wet smoke, among the woods,
Over his boiling cauldron broods.

Swift rush the spectral vapours white
Past limestone scars° with ragged pines,
Showing—then blotting from our sight!—
Halt—through the cloud-drift something shines!
High in the valley, wet and drear,
The huts of Courrerie° appear.

*Strike leftward!* cries our guide; and higher
20  Mounts up the stony forest-way.
At last the encircling trees retire;
Look! through the showery twilight grey
What pointed roofs are these advance?—
A palace of the Kings of France?

Approach, for what we seek is here!
Alight, and sparely sup, and wait
For rest in this outbuilding near;°
Then cross the sward and reach that gate.
Knock; pass the wicket! Thou art come
30  To the Carthusians' world-famed home.°

The silent courts, where night and day
Into their stone-carved basins cold
The splashing icy fountains play—
The humid corridors behold!
Where, ghostlike in the deepening night,
Cowled forms brush by in gleaming white.

The chapel, where no organ's peal
Invests the stern and naked prayer—

blows blossoms
Saint Laurent a village near the monastery
stream Guier's Mort River
scars cliffs
Courrerie a village near by
outbuilding near guesthouse
Carthusians' world-famed home On September

7, 1851, soon after they married, Arnold and
his wife visited La Grande Chartreuse, the
Carthusian monastery near Grenoble, France.
The Carthusians were renowned for their strict
discipline, and the superb liqueur that they
produced, for commercial purposes.

With penitential cries they kneel
40 And wrestle; rising then, with bare°
And white uplifted faces stand,
Passing the Host from hand to hand;°

Each takes, and then his visage wan
Is buried in his cowl once more.
The cells!—the suffering Son of Man
Upon the wall—the knee-worn floor—
And where they sleep, that wooden bed,
Which shall their coffin be, when dead!°

The library, where tract and tome
50 Not to feed priestly pride are there,
To hymn the conquering march of Rome,°
Nor yet to amuse, as ours are!
They paint of souls the inner strife,
Their drops of blood, their death in life.

The garden, overgrown—yet mild,
See, fragrant herbs are flowering there!
Strong children of the Alpine wild
Whose culture is the brethren's care;
Of human tasks their only one,
60 And cheerful works beneath the sun.°

Those halls, too, destined to contain
Each its own pilgrim-host of old,
From England, Germany, or Spain—
All are before me! I behold
The House, the Brotherhood austere!
—And what am I, that I am here?

For rigorous teachers seized my youth,°
And purged its faith,° and trimmed its fire,
Showed me the high, white star of Truth,
70 There bade me gaze, and there aspire.
Even now their whispers pierce the gloom:
*What dost thou in this living tomb?*

Forgive me, masters of the mind!
At whose behest I long ago
So much unlearnt, so much resigned—
I come not here to be your foe!

I seek these anchorites,° not in ruth,°
To curse and to deny your truth:

Not as their friend, or child, I speak!
80  But as, on some far northern strand,
Thinking of his own Gods, a Greek
In pity and mournful awe might stand
Before some fallen Runic stone°—
For both were faiths, and both are gone.

Wandering between two worlds, one dead,
The other powerless to be born,
With nowhere yet to rest my head,°
Like these, on earth I wait forlorn.
Their faith, my tears, the world deride—
90  I come to shed them at their side.

Oh, hide me in your gloom profound,
Ye solemn seats of holy pain!
Take me, cowled forms, and fence me round,
Till I possess my soul again;
Till free my thoughts before me roll,
Not chafed by hourly false control!

For the world cries your faith is now
But a dead time's exploded dream;
My melancholy, sciolists° say,
100  Is a passed mode, an outworn theme—
As if the world had ever had
A faith, or sciolists been sad!

Ah, if it *be* passed, take away,
At least, the restlessness, the pain;
Be man henceforth no more a prey
To these out-dated stings again!
The nobleness of grief is gone—
Ah, leave us not the fret alone!

But—if you cannot give us ease—
110  Last of the race of them who grieve
Here leave us to die out with these
Last of the people who believe!

anchorites monks
ruth penitence
Runic stone northern stone inscribed with letters
of earliest Teutonic alphabet. As an emancipated Greek might feel a vain regret both for
his own dead faith and the dead northern religion, so Arnold studies the nostalgias of his
father's Protestantism and the Carthusians'
Catholicism, knowing them both to be gone
forever.

rest my head Notice the "yet," in which there
is some wan hope, and perhaps a touch of the
outcast prophet, with its possibly unconscious
echo of Matthew 8:20: "The foxes have holes,
and the birds of the air have nests; but the
Son of man hath not where to lay his head."
sciolists superficial pretenders to knowledge;
academic impostors

Silent, while years engrave° the brow;
Silent—the best are silent now.°

Achilles ponders in his tent,°
The kings of modern thought are dumb;°
Silent they are, though not content,
And wait to see the future come.
They have the grief men had of yore,
120    But they contend and cry no more.

Our fathers° watered with their tears
This sea of time whereon we sail,
Their voices were in all men's ears
Who passed within their puissant hail.
Still the same ocean round us raves,
But we stand mute, and watch the waves.

For what availed it, all the noise
And outcry of the former men?—
Say, have their sons achieved more joys,
130    Say, is life lighter now than then?
The sufferers died, they left their pain—
The pangs which tortured them remain.

What helps it now, that Byron bore,
With haughty scorn which mocked the smart,
Through Europe to the Ætolian shore°
The pageant of his bleeding heart?
That thousands counted every groan,
And Europe made his woe her own?°

What boots it, Shelley! that the breeze
140    Carried thy lovely wail away,
Musical through Italian trees
Which fringe thy soft blue Spezzian bay?
Inheritors of thy distress
Have restless hearts one throb the less?°

engrave make the brow furrowed
silent now a puzzling line, since the early
1850's hardly was a time when the best were
silent (see Yeats's "The Second Coming," ll.
7–8, where this combines with a passage from
Shelley's *Prometheus Unbound*)
in his tent Scholars generally say this is Newman, but Dwight Culler pungently remarks that
"Newman would not have been called 'Achilles'
in 1851–52 when he was in process of being
sued for libel by a defrocked priest named
Achilli." Culler plausibly suggests Carlyle as
Achilles.
are dumb Probably the "kings of modern
thought" are poets, since Arnold is indebted to
Shelley's *Adonais*, ll. 430–31, where the "kings

of thought/Who waged contention with their
time's decay" are the poets to whom Keats is
gathered after his death.
Ætolian shore region in Greece where Byron
died a hero's death
woe her own probably a reference to *Childe
Harold's Pilgrimage*
throb the less Shelley drowned in the Bay of
Spezzia; his poetry is not recognizable from
this stanza, or from anything else that Arnold
ever said about it; whatever Shelley wished
to do for his readers, he was not trying to
make their hearts less restless, since he was
always a dedicated revolutionary agitator.

Or are we easier, to have read,
O Obermann!° the sad, stern page,
Which tells us how thou hidd'st thy head
From the fierce tempest of thine age
In the lone brakes of Fontainebleau,°
150    Or chalets near the Alpine snow?

Ye slumber in your silent grave!—
The world, which for an idle day
Grace to your mood of sadness gave,
Long since hath flung her weeds° away.
The eternal trifler breaks your spell;
But we—we learnt your lore too well!

Years hence, perhaps, may dawn an age,
More fortunate, alas! than we,
Which without hardness will be sage,
160    And gay without frivolity.
Sons of the world, oh, speed those years;
But, while we wait, allow our tears!

Allow them! We admire with awe
The exulting thunder of your race;
You give the universe your law,
Your triumph over time and space!
Your pride of life, your tireless powers,
We laud them, but they are not ours.

We are like children reared in shade
170    Beneath some old-world abbey wall,
Forgotten in a forest-glade,
And secret from the eyes of all.
Deep, deep the greenwood round them waves,
Their abbey, and its close° of graves!

But, where the road runs near the stream,
Oft through the trees they catch a glance
Of passing troops in the sun's beam—
Pennon, and plume, and flashing lance!
Forth to the world those soldiers fare,
180    To life, to cities, and to war!

And through the wood, another way,
Faint bugle-notes from far are borne,
Where hunters gather, staghounds bay,
Round some fair forest-lodge at morn.

**Obermann** Etienne Pivert de Senancour (1770–1846), French moralist, wrote *Obermann*, a series of letters reflecting on nature and the soul. One of Arnold's favorite books (he wrote an essay and two poems about it), *Obermann* is a severe, melancholy (and rather boring) work, and tempted Arnold with a *persona* he fortunately did not adopt. **Fontainebleau** where Senancour died, near Paris **weeds** mourning clothes **close** enclosure

Gay dames are there, in sylvan green;
Laughter and cries—those notes between!

The banners flashing through the trees
Make their blood dance and chain their eyes;
That bugle-music on the breeze
190    Arrests them with a charmed surprise.
Banner by turns and bugle woo:
*Ye shy recluses, follow too!*

O children, what do ye reply?—
'Action and pleasure, will ye roam
Through these secluded dells to cry
And call us?—but too late ye come!
Too late for us your call ye blow,
Whose bent was taken long ago.

'Long since we pace this shadowed nave;
200    We watch those yellow tapers shine,
Emblems of hope over the grave,
In the high altar's depth divine;
The organ carries to our ear
Its accents of another sphere.°

'Fenced early in this cloistral round
Of reverie, of shade, of prayer,
How should we grow in other ground?
How can we flower in foreign air?
—Pass, banners, pass, and bugles, cease;
210    And leave our desert° to its peace!'
1851–55                    1855


# The Scholar-Gipsy

Arnold based this pastoral on a passage from Joseph Glanvil's *Vanity of Dogmatizing* (1661), which he condensed so as to make it an introduction to the poem:

> There was very lately a lad in the University of Oxford, who was by his poverty forced to leave his studies there; and at last to join himself to a company of vagabond gypsies. Among these extravagant people, by the insinuating subtilty of his carriage, he quickly got so much of their love and esteem as that they discovered to him their mystery. After he had been a pretty while exercised in the trade, there chanced to ride by a couple of scholars, who had formerly been of his acquaintance. They quickly spied out their old friend among the gypsies; and he gave them an account of the necessity which drove him to that kind of life, and told them that the people he went with were not such impostors as they were taken for, but that they had a traditional kind of learning among them, and could do wonders by the power of imagination, their fancy binding that of others: that himself had

---

sphere As Carthusians did not have organs,    desert in the voice-in-the-wilderness sense
Arnold clearly is thinking of the Oxford Move-
ment and other ritualists.

learned much of their art, and when he had compassed the whole secret, he intended, he said, to leave their company, and give the world an account of what he had learned.

## The Scholar-Gipsy

Go, for they call you, shepherd,° from the hill;
   Go, shepherd, and untie the wattled cotes!°
   No longer leave thy wistful flock unfed,
   Nor let thy bawling fellows° rack their throats,
   Nor the cropped herbage shoot another head.
      But when the fields are still,°
   And the tired men and dogs all gone to rest,
   And only the white sheep are sometimes seen
   Cross and recross the strips of moon-blanched green,
10   Come, shepherd, and again begin the quest!°

Here, where the reaper was at work of late—
   In this high field's dark corner, where he leaves
   His coat, his basket, and his earthen cruse,°
   And in the sun all morning binds the sheaves,
   Then here, at noon, comes back his stores to use—
      Here will I sit and wait,
   While to my ear from uplands far away
   The bleating of the folded° flocks is borne,
   With distant cries of reapers in the corn°—
20   All the live murmur of a summer's day.

Screened is this nook o'er the high, half-reaped field,
   And here till sun-down, shepherd! will I be.
   Through the thick corn the scarlet poppies peep,
   And round green roots and yellowing stalks I see
   Pale pink convolvulus° in tendrils creep;
      And air-swept lindens yield
   Their scent, and rustle down their perfumed showers
   Of bloom on the bent grass where I am laid,
   And bower me from the August sun with shade;
30   And the eye travels down to Oxford's towers.

**shepherd** probably his friend, the poet Clough **wattled cotes** sheepfolds constructed of twigs **bawling fellows** the bleating sheep he tends. Arnold's irony is savage, as it will be later in this poem in the barely hidden attack upon Tennyson's *In Memoriam*, for which see ll. 182–91. **fields are still** when revolutionary social agitation is momentarily over, freeing Clough for the more Arnoldian activities of contemplation and writing reflective verse

**the quest** presumably for the Scholar-Gipsy and his art, but that is a rather inadequate emblem for what Arnold means, which is nothing less than the whole of his enterprise, personal and cultural **cruse** water jar **folded** properly enclosed **corn** wheat or other grain, in England **convolvulus** morning-glory

And near me on the grass lies Glanvil's book—
Come, let me read the oft-read tale again!
The story of the Oxford scholar poor,
Of pregnant parts° and quick inventive brain,
Who, tired of knocking at preferment's door,
One summermorn forsook
His friends, and went to learn the gipsy-lore,
And roamed the world with that wild brotherhood,
And came, as most men deemed, to little good,
40    But came to Oxford and his friends no more.

But once, years after, in the country-lanes,
Two scholars, whom at college erst he knew,
Met him, and of his way of life enquired;
Whereat he answered that the gipsy-crew,
His mates, had arts to rule as they desired
The workings of men's brains.
And they can bind them to what thoughts they will.
'And I,' he said, 'the secret of their art,
When fully learned, will to the world impart;
50    But it needs heaven-sent moments for this skill.'

This said, he left them, and returned no more.—
But rumours hung about the countryside,
That the lost Scholar long was seen to stray,
Seen by rare glimpses, pensive and tongue-tied,
In hat of antique shape, and cloak of grey,
The same the gipsies wore.
Shepherds had met him on the Hurst° in spring;
At some lone alehouse in the Berkshire moors,°
On the warm ingle-bench,° the smock-frocked boors°
60    Had found him seated at their entering,

But, 'mid their drink and clatter, he would fly.
And I myself seem half to know thy looks,
And put the shepherds, wanderer! on thy trace;
And boys who in lone wheatfields scare the rooks
I ask if thou hast passed their quiet place;
Or in my boat I lie
Moored to the cool bank in the summer-heats,
'Mid wide grass meadows which the sunshine fills,
And watch the warm, green-muffled Cumner hills,
70    And wonder if thou haunt'st their shy retreats.

For most, I know, thou lov'st retired ground!
Thee at the ferry Oxford riders blithe,

**pregnant parts** promising intellectual gifts
**Hurst** hill near Oxford
**Berkshire moors** south of Oxford

**ingle-bench** chimney nook bench
**smock-frocked boors** smock-attired farm workers

Returning home on summer-nights, have met
Crossing the stripling Thames° at Bab-lock-hithe,°
Trailing in the cool stream thy fingers wet,
   As the punt's rope chops round;
   And leaning backward in a pensive dream,
   And fostering in thy lap a heap of flowers
      Plucked in shy fields and distant Wychwood° bowers,
80 And thine eyes resting on the moonlit stream.

And then they land, and thou art seen no more!—
Maidens, who from the distant hamlets come
To dance around the Fyfield elm° in May,
   Oft through the darkening fields have seen thee roam,
   Or cross a stile into the public way.
      Oft thou hast given them store
Of flowers—the frail-leafed, white anemony,
   Dark bluebells drenched with dews of summer eves,
   And purple orchises with spotted leaves—
90 But none hath words she can report of thee.

And, above Godstow Bridge,° when hay-time's here
In June, and many a scythe in sunshine flames,
   Men who through those wide fields of breezy grass
   Where black-winged swallows haunt the glittering Thames,
      To bathe in the abandoned lasher° pass,
      Have often passed thee near
Sitting upon the river bank o'ergrown;
   Marked thine outlandish garb, thy figure spare,
   Thy dark vague eyes, and soft abstracted air—
100 But, when they came from bathing, thou wast gone!

At some lone homestead in the Cumner hills,
Where at her open door the housewife darns,
   Thou hast been seen, or hanging on a gate
   To watch the threshers in the mossy barns.
      Children, who early range these slopes and late
      For cresses from the rills,
Have known thee eying, all an April-day,
   The springing pastures and the feeding kine;
   And marked thee, when the stars come out and shine,
110 Through the long dewy grass move slow away.

In autumn, on the skirts of Bagley Wood°—
Where most the gipsies by the turf-edged way
   Pitch their smoked tents, and every bush you see
   With scarlet patches tagged and shreds of grey,

**stripling Thames** Thames near Oxford is just a stream.
**Bab-lock-hithe** Thames ferry near village of Cumner
**Wychwood** wood ten miles north of Oxford

**Fyfield elm** At Fyfield, near Oxford, an elm tree served as a Maypole for festivities on May 1.
**Godstow Bridge** near Oxford, over Thames
**lasher** pool formed below dam
**Bagley Wood** three miles south of Oxford

Above the forest-ground called Thessaly°—
  The blackbird, picking food,
Sees thee, nor stops his meal, nor fears at all;
  So often has he known thee past him stray,
  Rapt, twirling in thy hand a withered spray,
120  And waiting for the spark from heaven to fall.

And once, in winter, on the causeway chill
  Where home through flooded fields foot-travellers go,
Have I not passed thee on the wooden bridge,
  Wrapped in thy cloak and battling with the snow,
  Thy face toward Hinksey° and its wintry ridge?
  And thou hast climbed the hill,
  And gained the white brow of the Cumner range;
Turned once to watch, while thick the snowflakes fall,
  The line of festal light in Christ-Church hall°—
130  Then sought thy straw in some sequestered grange.

But what—I dream! Two hundred years are flown
  Since first thy story ran through Oxford halls,
And the grave Glanvil did the tale inscribe
  That thou wert wandered from the studious walls
  To learn strange arts, and join a gipsy-tribe;
  And thou from earth art gone
Long since, and in some quiet churchyard laid—
  Some country-nook, where o'er thy unknown grave
  Tall grasses and white flowering nettles wave,
140  Under a dark, red-fruited yew-tree's shade.

—No, no, thou hast not felt the lapse of hours!
  For what wears out the life of mortal men?
'Tis that from change to change their being rolls;
  'Tis that repeated shocks, again, again,
  Exhaust the energy of strongest souls
  And numb the elastic powers.
Till having used our nerves with bliss and teen,°
  And tired upon a thousand schemes our wit,
  To the just-pausing Genius° we remit
150  Our worn-out life, and are—what we have been.

Thou hast not lived, why should'st thou perish, so?
  Thou hadst *one* aim, *one* business, *one* desire;
Else wert thou long since numbered with the dead!
  Else hadst thou spent, like other men, thy fire!
  The generations of thy peers are fled,
  And we ourselves shall go;

Thessaly Oxford men called a spot near Bagley
Wood by this name
Hinksey village south of Oxford
Christ-Church hall dining hall of an Oxford
college

teen sorrow
just-pausing Genius a transcendental entity
which pauses only momentarily for our individual demises

But thou possessest an immortal lot,
And we imagine thee exempt from age
And living as thou livest on Glanvil's page,
160   Because thou hadst—what we, alas! have not.

For early didst thou leave the world, with powers
Fresh, undiverted to the world without,
Firm to their mark, not spent on other things;
Free from the sick fatigue, the languid doubt,
Which much to have tried, in much been baffled, brings.
O life unlike to ours!
Who fluctuate idly without term or scope,
Of whom each strives, nor knows for what he strives,
And each half lives a hundred different lives;
170   Who wait like thee, but not, like thee, in hope.

Thou waitest for the spark from heaven! and we,
Light half-believers of our casual creeds,
Who never deeply felt, not clearly willed,
Whose insight never has borne fruit in deeds,
Whose vague resolves never have been fulfilled;
For whom each year we see
Breeds new beginnings, disappointments new;
Who hesitate and falter life away,
And lose tomorrow the ground won today—
180   Ah! do not we, wanderer! await it too?

Yes, we await it!—but it still delays,
And then we suffer! and amongst us one,°
Who most has suffered, takes dejectedly
His seat upon the intellectual throne;
And all his store of sad experience he
Lays bare of wretched days;
Tells us his misery's birth and growth and signs,
And how the dying spark of hope was fed,
And how the breast was soothed, and how the head,
190   And all his hourly varied anodynes.

This for our wisest!° and we others pine,
And wish the long unhappy dream would end,
And waive all claim to bliss, and try to bear;
With close-lipped patience for our only friend,
Sad patience, too near neighbour to despair—
But none has hope like thine!
Thou through the fields and through the woods dost stray,
Roaming the countryside, a truant boy,

one a barely disguised ironic portrait of Tennyson's performance in the elegies for Hallam,
*In Memoriam*. To cover his savagery, Arnold

insisted he meant Goethe, but it is Tennyson
nevertheless.
wisest an irony: Arnold did not find much wisdom in Tennyson's poetry

Nursing thy project in unclouded joy,
200    And every doubt long blown by time away.

O born in days when wits were fresh and clear,
    And life ran gaily as the sparkling Thames;
        Before this strange disease of modern life,
    With its sick hurry, its divided aims,
          Its heads o'ertaxed, its palsied hearts, was rife—
            Fly hence, our contact fear!
    Still fly, plunge deeper in the bowering wood!
        Averse, as Dido did with gesture stern
        From her false friend's approach in Hades turn,°
210    Wave us away, and keep thy solitude!

Still nursing the unconquerable hope,
    Still clutching the inviolable shade,
        With a free, onward impulse brushing through,
    By night, the silvered branches of the glade—
          Far on the forest-skirts, where none pursue.
            On some mild pastoral slope
    Emerge, and resting on the moonlit pales°
        Freshen thy flowers as in former years
        With dew, or listen with enchanted ears,
220    From the dark dingles,° to the nightingales!

But fly our paths, our feverish contact fly!
    For strong the infection of our mental strife,
        Which, though it gives no bliss, yet spoils for rest;
    And we should win thee from thy own fair life,
          Like us distracted, and like us unblest.
            Soon, soon thy cheer would die,
    Thy hopes grow timorous, and unfixed thy powers,
        And thy clear aims be cross and shifting made;
        And then thy glad perennial youth would fade,
230    Fade, and grow old at last, and die like ours.

Then fly our greetings, fly our speech and smiles!
    —As some grave Tyrian trader, from the sea,
        Descried at sunrise an emerging prow
    Lifting the cool-haired creepers stealthily,
          The fringes of a southward-facing brow
            Among the Ægæan isles;
    And saw the merry Grecian coaster come,
        Freighted with amber grapes, and Chian° wine,
        Green, bursting figs, and tunnies steeped in brine—
240    And knew the intruders on his ancient home,

**Hades turn** See Virgil's *Aeneid* VI.450–71,    **pales** fences
where Dido will not speak to Aeneas when   **dingles** valleys
they encounter each other, during his descent   **Chian** from Greek island of Chios
to Avernus.

The young light-hearted masters of the waves—
And snatched his rudder, and shook out more sail;
And day and night held on indignantly
O'er the blue Midland waters with the gale,
　Betwixt the Syrtes° and soft Sicily,
　　To where the Atlantic raves
　Outside the western straits; and unbent sails
　　There, where down cloudy cliffs, through sheets of foam,
　　Shy traffickers, the dark Iberians come;
250　And on the beach undid his corded bales.
1852–53　　　　　　　　　　　　1853


# Philomela°

Hark! ah, the nightingale—
The tawny-throated!
Hark, from that moonlit cedar what a burst!
What triumph! hark!—what pain!
O wanderer from a Grecian shore,
Still, after many years, in distant lands,
Still nourishing in thy bewildered brain
That wild, unquenched, deep-sunken, old-world pain—
Say, will it never heal?
10　And can this fragrant lawn
With its cool trees, and night,
And the sweet, tranquil Thames,
And moonshine, and the dew,
To thy racked heart and brain
Afford no balm?
Dost thou tonight behold,
Here, through the moonlight on this English grass,
The unfriendly palace in the Thracian wild?
Dost thou again peruse
20　With hot cheeks and seared eyes
The too clear web,° and thy dumb sister's shame?°

---

**Syrtes** Gulf of Sidra, on north coast of Africa
**Philomela** In Greek myth, she was the sister
of Procne, wife of King Tereus of Thrace,
who raped her and tore out her tongue to conceal his outrage. Philomela revealed the horror to her sister by weaving the story into a
tapestry; in revenge, Procne killed her son
Itys and served his cooked flesh to his father.
Tereus, this crime made known, attempted to
kill both sisters, but all were transformed into
birds, Procne into the nightingale (to become
the unusual bird mourning her lost son), Philomela into the swallow, and Tereus into the
crested hoopoe. Ovid's Latin version of the
story, followed by most Renaissance and later
writers, makes Philomela the nightingale, dra-
matically restoring song to the mute raped
sister. Arnold seems to have got mixed up in
this poem: up through line 19 he is consistently
following the Ovidian version, but in lines 20–
21 he is clearly referring to Procne. Had he
entitled the poem "Procne" or "The Nightingale" Arnold might have simply been using
the Greek version. (Swinburne wrote a powerful poem "Itylus," and the story is also used in
Eliot's *Waste Land.*)
**web** the tapestry
**shame** In some sense, Philomela's humiliation
is greater in the inability to protest her ravishment itself, for Arnold's poem has as its hidden
theme the fear of not being able to go on
writing poetry.

Dost thou once more assay
Thy flight, and feel come over thee,
Poor fugitive, the feathery change
Once more, and once more seem to make resound
With love and hate, triumph and agony,
Lone Daulis,° and the high Cephissian vale?°
Listen, Eugenia°—
How thick the bursts come crowding through the leaves!
30    —Again—thou hearest?
Eternal passion!
Eternal pain!

1852–53                                          1853


# Palladium°

Set where the upper streams of Simois° flow
Was the Palladium, high 'mid rock and wood;
And Hector was in Ilium, far below,
And fought, and saw it not—but there it stood!

It stood, and sun and moonshine rained their light
On the pure columns of its glen-built hall.
Backward and forward rolled the waves of fight
Round Troy—but while this stood, Troy could not fall.

So, in its lovely moonlight, lives the soul.
10   Mountains surround it, and sweet virgin air;
Cold plashing, past it, crystal waters roll;
We visit it by moments, ah, too rare!

We shall renew the battle in the plain
Tomorrow;—red with blood will Xanthus° be;
Hector and Ajax will be there again,
Helen will come upon the wall to see.

Then we shall rust in shade, or shine in strife,
And fluctuate 'twixt blind hopes and blind despairs,
And fancy that we put forth all our life,
20   And never know how with the soul it fares.

---

Daulis town in Phocis, the region occupied by
the kingdom of Thrace
Cephissian vale valley of the River Cephisus,
running through Phocis
Eugenia Arnold's companion is not identified;
her name means "well born."
Palladium This genuinely classical lyric is the
one perfect exemplification by Arnold of the
kind of poetry he called for in his "Preface" of
1853, and is his one successful poem that
stands outside the main traditions of English
Romanticism; Gray and Landor have something of this stoic quality and this cool splendor.
The Palladium was a wooden image of Pallas
Athena, kept in Troy as a magic talisman for
the city's survival.
Simois river running near Troy (Ilium)
Xanthus a river near the battlefield outside
Troy

Still doth the soul, from its lone fastness high,
Upon our life a ruling effluence send.
And when it fails, fight as we will, we die;
And while it lasts, we cannot wholly end.
?1864                              1867


## Growing Old°

What is it to grow old?
Is it to lose the glory of the form,
The lustre of the eye?
Is it for beauty to forego her wreath?
—Yes, but not this alone.

Is it to feel our strength—
Not our bloom only, but our strength—decay?
Is it to feel each limb
Grow stiffer, every function less exact,
10   Each nerve more loosely strung?

Yes, this, and more; but not
Ah, 'tis not what in youth we dreamed 'twould be!
'Tis not to have our life
Mellowed and softened as with sunset-glow,
A golden day's decline.

'Tis not to see the world
As from a height, with rapt prophetic eyes,
And heart profoundly stirred;
And weep, and feel the fulness of the past,
20   The years that are no more.°

It is to spend long days
And not once feel that we were ever young;
It is to add, immured
In the hot prison of the present, month
To month with weary pain.

It is to suffer this,
And feel but half, and feebly, what we feel.
Deep in our hidden heart
Festers the dull remembrance of a change,
30   But no emotion—none.

It is—last stage of all—

Growing Old   This seems an ironic reply both
to Browning ("Rabbi Ben Ezra") and to
Wordsworth's consoling reflections upon old age.

no more   an echo, without irony, of Tennyson's
"Tears, Idle Tears"

When we are frozen up within, and quite
The phantom of ourselves,
To hear the world applaud the hollow ghost
Which blamed the living man.

                    1867


# The Last Word°

Creep into thy narrow bed,°
Creep, and let no more be said!
Vain thy onset! all stands fast.
Thou thyself must break at last.

Let the long contention cease!
Geese are swans, and swans are geese.
Let them have it how they will!
Thou art tired; best be still.

They out-talked thee, hissed thee, tore thee?
10   Better men fared thus before thee;
Fired their ringing shot and passed,
Hotly charged—and sank at last.

Charge once more, then, and be dumb!
Let the victors, when they come,
When the forts of folly fall,
Find thy body by the wall!

                    1867


# From Bacchanalia; or, The New Age

II

The epoch ends, the world is still.
The age has talked and worked its fill—
The famous orators have shone,
The famous poets sung and gone,
The famous men of war have fought,
The famous speculators thought,
The famous players, sculptors, wrought,
The famous painters filled their wall,
The famous critics judged it all.
10   The combatants are parted now—
Uphung the spear, unbent the bow,

**The Last Word** a bitter reaction to the cam-    **narrow bed** the tomb
paign for the Reform Bill of 1867, widely ex-
tending the vote

The puissant crowned, the weak laid low.
And in the after-silence sweet,
Now strifes are hushed, our ears doth meet,
Ascending pure, the bell-like fame
Of this or that down-trodden name,
Delicate spirits, pushed away
In the hot press of the noon-day.
And o'er the plain, where the dead age
20    Did its now silent warfare wage—
O'er that wide plain, now wrapt in gloom,
Where many a splendour finds its tomb,
Many spent fames and fallen mights—
The one or two immortal lights
Rise slowly up into the sky
To shine there everlastingly,
Like stars over the bounding hill.
The epoch ends, the world is still.

    Thundering and bursting
30        In torrents, in waves—
    Carolling and shouting
    Over tombs, amid graves—
    See! on the cumbered plain
    Clearing a stage,
    Scattering the past about,
    Comes the new age.
    Bards make new poems,
    Thinkers new schools,
    Statesmen new systems,
40        Critics new rules.
    New things begin again;
    Life is their prize;
    Earth with their deeds they fill,
    Fill with their cries.

    Poet, what ails thee, then?
    Say, why so mute?
    Forth with thy praising voice!
    Forth with thy flute!
    Loiterer! why sittest thou
50        Sunk in thy dream?
    Tempts not the bright new age?
    Shines not its stream?
    Look, ah, what genius,
    Art, science, wit!
    Soldiers like Cæsar,
    Statesmen like Pitt!
    Sculptors like Phidias,
    Raphaels in shoals,

60      Poets like Shakespeare—
        Beautiful souls!
        See, on their glowing cheeks
        Heavenly the flush!
        *—Ah, so the silence was!*
        *So was the hush!*

        The world but feels the present's spell,
        The poet feels the past as well;
        Whatever men have done, might do,
        Whatever thought, might think it too.

                1867

# THE PRE-RAPHAELITE POETS

As a literary term, "Pre-Raphaelite" is almost meaningless, yet it survives because we need some name for the cluster of poets who are the overt Romantics among the Victorians. Most accurately, Pre-Raphaelite poetry was written by Dante Gabriel Rossetti and his circle, to which we can add other figures for convenience, such as FitzGerald because Rossetti "discovered" and popularized his version of The Rubáiyát, Patmore because he published in the Pre-Raphaelite magazine, The Germ, and Meredith because his poetry has deep affinities with Rossetti's. Christina Rossetti is here for obvious reasons, though her devotional verse has not much in common with her brother's poetry. Rossetti himself and Morris are the Pre-Raphaelite poets proper; Swinburne is Shelleyan where they are Keatsian, and their characteristic mode of hard-edged phantasmagoria has little to do with his high rhetoric and polemical zeal. Still, insofar as Swinburne had a home in any poetic school of his age, it was here.

Pre-Raphaelitism started as a Brotherhood of young painters, in September 1848, the founders being William Holman Hunt, John Everett Millais (later to elope with Ruskin's neglected wife), and Rossetti. Unhappy (with reason) at mid-century, they sought to change the nature of English painting. Not so much Raphael, but his imitators, had to be rejected, in favor of the example of Pre-Raphaelite artists, the freshness of Gozzoli (c. 1421–97) and other Pisan painters. Like many schools of art, their watchword was the ambiguous "Back to nature!"—which always turns out to mean something rather different. Painters, sculptors, and critics rallied to the three young founders, and a highly confused nonmovement had begun. About the only common characteristic of English Pre-Raphaelite painting was its obsession with naturalistic detail, rendered so artificially as to make it not natural but phantasmagoric. Essentially, Pre-Raphaelite painting failed (with a few brilliant exceptions) but the poetry associated with it did not, because the poetry was the legitimate continuation of a central Romantic current, the daemonic element in Coleridge's poetry and the main achievement of Keats (to some extent, as it had been modified in early Tennyson).

In the mid-'fifties, at Oxford, William Morris and the painter Edward Burne-Jones became Rossetti's disciples, and moved to London to join him. Also at Oxford, in 1857, Swinburne met Rossetti through Morris and Burne-Jones and began a close, long friendship with the group. Through Swinburne's critical writings (rather than his High Romantic verse) the ideas of the movement, greatly altered, helped produce

Pater and the characteristic theory of English Aestheticism, resulting in Oscar Wilde, Aubrey Beardsley, the poetry of the 'Nineties, and the early work of Yeats.

**Dante Gabriel Rossetti** (1828–82), though out of favor in our time, seems to this editor the best poet of the Victorian period, after Browning and Tennyson, surpassing Arnold and even Hopkins and Swinburne (greatly undervalued as Swinburne now is). Space does not permit including his lyrical masterpiece, *The Stream's Secret*, but the selection given does include a fair representation of his lyrics, and ten sonnets from his other major work, *The House of Life*.

Rossetti was born in London on May 12, 1828, the son of a Neapolitan refugee scholar and a half-English mother. Educated as an artist, and thinking of himself primarily as a painter, his literary culture was narrow but intense, owing most to Keats for English style, and to Dante and other early Italian poets for thematic procedures. His translations from Dante and allied poets are the finest of their kind in English, particularly the sestina given here. His own poetry suffered from the turbulence and irregularity of his life. He could not bear criticism, personal or artistic, and could be described, not unfairly, as a monomaniac, frequently drugged on his characteristic mixture of chloral and whiskey.

Rossetti married his model, the beautiful Elizabeth Siddal, in 1860, after an affair lasting nearly a decade. The marriage was unhappy, and Mrs. Rossetti killed herself after less than two years. Her contrite husband buried his manuscripts with her, and had to exhume them in 1869, when he was preparing his first volume of *Poems* (1870).

In 1857, three years before marrying Elizabeth Siddal, Rossetti had met the other two women in his life, Fanny Cornforth, with whom he lived after the death of Elizabeth, and Jane Burden, who married William Morris in April 1859. The difficult relation between Mrs. Morris and Rossetti was long-lasting, and helped to derange his already overwrought sensibility. Rossetti, when attacked in 1871 by Robert Buchanan (with Swinburne and Morris as fellow victims) as leader of "The Fleshly School of Poetry," reacted with the beginnings of a ghastly persecution mania, which continued until his death on April 14, 1882.

Rossetti is a difficult poet, not only because his art is deliberately committed to sustaining an intensity that precludes mere action, but because the intensity almost invariably is one of baffled passion. Though Rossetti's master was Keats, he was rightly associated with Shelley by Yeats, who observed that the genius of both poets "can hardly stir but to the rejection of Nature." Shelley, though skeptically accepting a pragmatic dualism of heart and head, quested for a monistic Absolute, but one of his own curious invention, neither Platonic nor Christian. Rossetti, a convinced sensualist, writes a naturalistic poetry that yet rejects natural forms, which is almost an impossibility. His lyrics and sonnets are set in a world that is at once phantasmagoria and nature, giving the effect of an artificial nature. His Blessed Damozel leans down to him from a Heaven where a woman's hair glistens "along her back . . . yellow like ripe corn." It is impossible, amid the forests and fountains in *The House of Life*, to decide whether we stand in the remembered natural world, or in some purgatorial realm heavier and more naturally luxurious than nature could ever have been. Rossetti's symbolic world is oppressive to the spirit, but this oppressiveness is his poetry's unique strength. He gives us neither a vision of nature, as Keats did, nor of a second nature, as Shelley rendered, but a surrealistic or fantastic blend of both, and since all are damned in his mixed realm, he gives us also a wholly oblique, and finally nihilistic, vision of judgment in which we cannot be saved through sensual fulfillment, and yet achieve no lasting release without it.

**George Meredith** (1828–1909), though deeply affected by Rossetti, is by contrast a more refreshing, more simply naturalistic poet, though of lesser achievement. Never a popular novelist, and still not a poet who has attracted critics, let alone a public, Meredith nevertheless was a master in both mediums. At least three of his novels are still vital—*The Ordeal of Richard Feverel* (1859), *The Egoist* (1879), *Diana of the Crossways* (1885), as are two of his major poetic works—"Love in the Valley" (1851) and the sequence *Modern Love* (1862).

Meredith was born on February 12, 1828, in Portsmouth, to a family of naval tailors. He had little formal education, gave up an early attempt to study law, and earned his living as a literary journalist and publisher's reader. His early poetry (*Poems,* 1851) had no success, and his marriage to Thomas Love Peacock's daughter Mary ended in 1858 after nine bad years, to be commemorated in *Modern Love.* He then attempted to share a house in London with Rossetti and Swinburne, a quixotic adventure from which he was rescued by his happy second marriage, in 1864. In his later years, as his literary reputation slowly grew, he worked out his own difficult version of a Wordsworthian natural religion. He died on May 18, 1909, still resolute and independent despite years of ill health.

Meredith's poetry is rugged going, because of his Rossetti-like clusters of detail, but he is rhythmically persuasive, open, and passionate compared with Rossetti. He lacks Rossetti's convincing originality, and can sound too much like Rossetti, like Wordsworth, like Keats, but his stature as poet deserves more from criticism than he has as yet received.

**Christina Georgina Rossetti** (1830–94), two years younger than her brother, was born in London on December 5, 1830. Educated at home, she composed poetry from an early age, but did not publish her first book until the appearance of *Goblin Market and Other Poems* in 1862. Primarily a devotional poet (except for the powerful *Goblin Market,* too long to include here), she does not sustain comparison with Emily Dickinson, her American contemporary, but can be judged superior to any other woman who wrote poetry in English before the twentieth century.

Having twice declined marriage because of Anglican religious scruples (in 1850 and in 1866), and suffering ill health from middle age on, she gave herself over to a life of seclusion, emphasizing good works and religious meditation. Her poems are as intense as her brother's, but much simpler, being wholly orthodox in their sharp dualism of nature and spirit. Though she lacks dramatic juxtaposition, in which Hopkins abounds, her curious literal-mindedness produces a wholly original kind of devotional poetry, astonishing historically because it gives the effect of being free from self-consciousness—and this in the later 19th century.

**William Morris** (1834–96), though he wrote a more diffuse poetry than the other Pre-Raphaelites, is a much better poet than his current reputation would suggest. Morris is remembered today more for his personality, energies, Socialist politics, and vision of the arts (in which he followed Ruskin) than for either his verse or prose romances, which is a pity.

Morris was born March 24, 1834, into the family of a wealthy discount broker. After private study, he entered Exeter College, Oxford, where he met Burne-Jones the painter, and the two together became disciples and friends of Rossetti. In 1855, Morris began to write romances in both poetry and prose, which he continued doing, but on and off, throughout the next forty, heroically busy, years of his life. After graduating from Oxford, in 1855, he studied both architecture and painting, and published a superb volume of Pre-Raphaelite poems in *The Defence of Guenevere* (1858). The next year he married Rossetti's beloved Jane Burden, and abandoned poetry for seven years, during which he founded a company whose intent was to reform all the decorative arts of England: furniture, wallpaper, windows, glassware, tapestries, carpets, tiles, and nearly everything else. Morris himself did much of the work, both in designing and manufacturing, and later he triumphantly extended his craftsmanship to the art of bookmaking.

He returned to poetry with the looser, less Pre-Raphaelite than quasi-Chaucerian, narratives of *The Life and Death of Jason* (1867) and *The Earthly Paradise* (1868–70). A further phase of his poetry, probably his strongest as narrative alone, came with interest in Icelandic literature, resulting in his translation of the *Volsunga Saga* and his original *Sigurd the Volsung* (1876).

In the 1880's, Morris's Socialism became very active, in organizing, lecturing, and agitating, and resulted in the Socialistic prose romances *The Dream of John Ball* (1888) and *News from Nowhere* (1890). In his last literary phase, until his death in 1896, Morris wrote a series of visionary prose romances, which profoundly influenced Yeats, particularly *The Well at the World's End,* which inspired Yeats's fine play *At the Hawk's Well.*

The first four poems by Morris below are from *The Defence of Guenevere,* followed by one lyric from *The Life and Death of Jason* and a defining "Apology" from *The Earthly Paradise.* They show Morris at his best, except for the powerful *Sigurd the Volsung,* which is hard to represent by excerpts. Morris derives from a whole series of major 19th-century poets—Keats, Tennyson, Browning, and Rossetti—but his directness, detachment in depicting savagery, and ability to convey swiftly the effect of violent action are entirely his own, and still unique in the language (a comparison with Robinson Jeffers is not to the American poet's advantage). Medieval poems by Morris are utterly unlike Tennyson's; the blood shed in them is not word painting, and the freedom from intrusive moral judgments is absolute. Morris is one of the very few poets ever who can be criticized for not being ambitious enough. His poems demonstrate more genius than he was willing to concentrate. If his interests had been fewer, his poetry would have sprawled less, and meant more, but he valued his other enterprises at least as much as he cared for his poetry.

**Algernon Charles Swinburne** (1837–1909), a major lyrical poet now almost totally neglected, was born in London on April 6, 1837, son of an admiral and an earl's daughter. Raised on the Isle of Wight, Swinburne grew up obsessed with the sea (as Whitman did, and for much the same psychic reasons). After attending Eton and Balliol College, Oxford, Swinburne moved to London without taking a degree. A sado-masochist, at times a semi-alcoholic, and his health always uncertain, Swinburne cannot be said to have lived a happy life. But his genius was prodigal, from his best earlier poetry, *Atalanta in Calydon* (1865) and *Poems and Ballads, First Series* (1866), through his critical studies of Blake (1868), Shakespeare (1880), Victor Hugo

(1886), and Ben Jonson (1889), on to the superb late lyrics of *Poems and Ballads, Third Series* (1889), and *A Channel Passage* (1904). Politically, religiously, and critically, Swinburne followed in the path of Shelley, supporting Mazzini and Italian liberation, prophesying against institutional and historical Christianity, and celebrating the main Romantic tradition of nineteenth-century literature. Unfortunately, Swinburne's psycho-sexual nature was arrested in development, and his devotion to the Marquis de Sade cannot be accounted one of his prime imaginative virtues. Worn out by the time he was forty-two, he spent his last thirty years at a villa in Putney, nursed by Theodore Watts-Dunton, a solicitor with literary ambitions. Swinburne died at Putney, on April 10, 1909, and was buried on the Isle of Wight.

Though he never wholly swerved away from Shelley's influence, Swinburne is an astonishingly original stylist, absurdly deprecated in a critical age that remains afraid of high rhetoric. His faults are too obvious to be interesting; his splendors are not so obvious as they at first may seem. His deliberate self-parodies, like "Poeta Loquitur," leave his negative critics no work to do, but they have gone on anyway, parodying Swinburne's parodies of himself. Swinburne was very nearly a great critic, though usually a touch too enthusiastic and overwrought; and his best poems, like *Hertha* and the elegy for Baudelaire, are intellectually more powerful than any Victorian poetry except Browning's. Yet the case for Swinburne is finally not to be based upon the power of the philosophical materialism of his poetic mind, authentic as that is, for here he compares poorly with his master, Shelley. The prime virtue of Swinburne's poetry, in the context that matters, of 19th-century verse, is the element of significant variety that it introduces. Faced by the problem of every new poet in the Romantic, that is to say, Modern tradition, Swinburne radically made it new, and wrote a poetry that does extend the circumference of literary experience.

**Coventry Patmore** (1823–96), remembered today mostly because of his friendships with Hopkins, Tennyson, and the Pre-Raphaelites, is one of the most neglected of good poets in the Victorian period, and would be more fully represented here if space permitted. Born in 1823, he was a spoiled child, and never entirely grew up. He married in 1847, and celebrated his connubial bliss in the dreadful but very popular long poem, *The Angel in the House* (1854–62). Mrs. Patmore died in 1862, and under the influence of his second wife, whom he married in 1864, he converted to Roman Catholicism. His good poems are the odes of *The Unknown Eros* (1877), of which one is given here. His complex, distasteful but compelling blend of sexuality and mystical religion is also manifested in the posthumously published prose aphorisms and essays. He died in 1896, largely forgotten, yet he has attracted a small but steady audience since.

# DANTE GABRIEL ROSSETTI

## The Blessed Damozel°

The blessed damozel leaned out
  From the gold bar of heaven;
Her eyes were deeper than the depth
  Of waters stilled at even;°
She had three lilies° in her hand,
  And the stars in her hair were seven.°

Her robe, ungirt from clasp to hem,
  No wrought flowers did adorn,
But a white rose° of Mary's gift,
10    For service meetly° worn;
Her hair that lay along her back
  Was yellow like ripe corn.°

Herseemed she scarce had been a day
  One of God's choristers;
The wonder was not yet quite gone
  From that still look of hers;
Albeit, to them she left, her day
  Had counted as ten years.

(To one, it is ten years of years.
20    . . . Yet now, and in this place,
Surely she leaned o'er me—her hair
  Fell all about my face. . . .
Nothing: the autumn-fall of leaves.
  The whole year sets apace.)

It was the rampart of God's house
  That she was standing on;
By God built over the sheer depth
  The which is Space begun;
So high, that looking downward thence
30    She scarce could see the sun.

It lies in Heaven, across the flood
  Of ether, as a bridge.
Beneath, the tides of day and night
  With flame and darkness ridge
The void, as low as where this earth
  Spins like a fretful midge.

---

**Damozel** form of "damsel," a young virgin. Rossetti related his poem to Poe's bad poem, "The Raven," but with little reason. The Book of Revelation and Dante are likelier sources and analogues, though Rossetti's tone has little in common with either.
**even** evening
**three lilies** possibly an allusion to the Trinity

**seven** See Revelation 1:16, where Jesus "had in his right hand seven stars," and Revelation 12:1, where a woman wears a crown of stars, though they number twelve.
**white rose** for purity
**meetly** suitably
**corn** wheat

Around her, lovers, newly met
    'Mid deathless love's acclaims,
Spoke evermore among themselves
40      Their heart-remembered names;
And the souls mounting up to God
    Went by her like thin flames.

And still she bowed herself and stooped
    Out of the circling charm;
Until her bosom must have made
    The bar she leaned on warm,
And the lilies lay as if asleep
    Along her bended arm.

From the fixed place of Heaven she saw
50      Time like a pulse shake fierce
Through all the worlds. Her gaze still strove
    Within the gulf to pierce
Its path; and now she spoke as when
    The stars sang in their spheres.

The sun was gone now; the curled moon
    Was like a little feather
Fluttering far down the gulf; and now
    She spoke through the still weather.
Her voice was like the voice the stars
60      Had when they sang together.

(Ah sweet! Even now, in that bird's song,
    Strove not her accents there,
Fain to be hearkened? When those bells
    Possessed the mid-day air,
Strove not her steps to reach my side
    Down all the echoing stair?) °

'I wish that he were come to me,
    For he will come,' she said.
'Have I not prayed in Heaven?—on earth,
70      Lord, Lord, has he not prayed?
Are not two prayers a perfect strength?
    And shall I feel afraid?

'When round his head the aureole clings,
    And he is clothed in white,
I'll take his hand and go with him
    To the deep wells of light;
As unto a stream we will step down,
    And bathe there in God's sight.

**echoing stair** the sounds from a purgatorial
stair

'We two will stand beside that shrine,
80    Occult, withheld, untrod,
Whose lamps are stirred continually
    With prayer sent up to God;
And see our old prayers, granted, melt
    Each like a little cloud.

'We two will lie in the shadow of
    That living mystic tree°
Within whose secret growth the Dove°
    Is sometimes felt to be,
While every leaf that His plumes touch
90    Saith His Name audibly.

'And I myself will teach to him,
    I myself, lying so,
The songs I sing here; which his voice
    Shall pause in, hushed and slow,
And find some knowledge at each pause,
    Or some new thing to know.'

(Alas! We two, we two, thou say'st!
    Yea, one wast thou with me
That once of old. But shall God lift
100    To endless unity
The soul whose likeness with thy soul
    Was but its love for thee?)

'We two,' she said, 'will seek the groves
    Where the lady Mary is,
With her five handmaidens, whose names
    Are five sweet symphonies,
Cecily, Gertrude, Magdalen,
    Margaret and Rosalys.

'Circlewise sit they, with bound locks
110    And foreheads garlanded;
Into the fine cloth white like flame
    Weaving the golden thread,
To fashion the birth-robes for them
    Who are just born, being dead.

'He shall fear, haply, and be dumb:
    Then will I lay my cheek
To his, and tell about our love,
    Not once abashed or weak:
And the dear Mother will approve
120    My pride, and let me speak.

mystic tree See Revelation 22:2 for "the tree    Dove the Holy Spirit
of life."

'Herself shall bring us, hand in hand,
　　To Him round whom all souls
Kneel, the clear-ranged unnumbered heads
　　Bowed with their aureoles:
And angels meeting us shall sing
　　To their citherns and citoles.°

'There will I ask of Christ the Lord
　　Thus much for him and me:—
Only to live as once on earth
130　　With Love,—only to be,
As then awhile, for ever now
　　Together, I and he.'

She gazed and listened and then said,
　　Less sad of speech than mild,—
'All this is when he comes.' She ceased.
　　The light thrilled towards her, filled
With angels in strong level flight.
　　Her eyes prayed, and she smiled.

(I saw her smile.) But soon their path
140　　Was vague in distant spheres:
And then she cast her arms along
　　The golden barriers,
And laid her face between her hands,
　　And wept. (I heard her tears.)
　　1847　　　　　　　1850

## The Woodspurge

The wind flapped loose, the wind was still,
Shaken out dead from tree and hill:
I had walked on at the wind's will,—
I sat now, for the wind was still.

Between my knees my forehead was,—
My lips, drawn in, said not Alas!
My hair was over in the grass,
My naked ears heard the day pass.

My eyes, wide open, had the run
10　Of some ten weeds to fix upon;
Among those few, out of the sun,
The woodspurge flowered, three cups in one.

From perfect grief there need not be
Wisdom or even memory:

citherns and citoles medieval stringed instruments

One thing then learnt remains to me,—
That woodspurge has a cup of three.°

1856                          1870


## Sestina (after Dante)

### Of the Lady Pietra degli Scrovigni°

To the dim light and the large circle of shade
I have clomb, and to the whitening of the hills,
There where we see no colour in the grass.
Natheless my longing loses not its green,
It has so taken root in the hard stone
Which talks and hears as though it were a lady.

Utterly frozen is this youthful lady,
Even as the snow that lies within the shade;
For she is no more moved than is the stone
By the sweet season which makes warm the hills
And alters them afresh from white to green,
Covering their sides again with flowers and grass.

When on her hair she sets a crown of grass
The thought has no more room for other lady,
Because she weaves the yellow with the green
So well that Love sits down there in the shade,—
Love who has shut me in among low hills
Faster than between walls of granite-stone.

She is more bright than is a precious stone;
The wound she gives may not be healed with grass:
I therefore have fled far o'er plains and hills
For refuge from so dangerous a lady;
But from her sunshine nothing can give shade,—
Not any hill, nor wall, nor summer-green.

A while ago, I saw her dressed in green,—
So fair, she might have wakened in a stone
This love which I do feel even for her shade;
And therefore, as one woos a graceful lady,
I wooed her in a field that was all grass
Girdled about with very lofty hills.

10

20

30

a cup of three The best comment on this subtle poem is Jerome McGann's: "When the three-in-one detail is completely freed of its possible religious connotations we suddenly realize the enormous relevance of the flower's unsymbolic fact. At that time and in that place this poet gained a measure of relief from a simple act of observation. . . ." There is no better instance of Rossetti's polemical naturalism, which is at the center of the Pre-Raphaelite vision. Pietra degli Scrovigni The hard-hearted lady addressed by Dante in this, the most powerful of his "stony rimes" (the root meaning of "Pietra" is stone). No more successful version of anything by Dante exists in English, and here, more than anywhere else, Rossetti achieves his individual version of the Grand Style.

Yet shall the streams turn back and climb the hills
Before Love's flame in this damp wood and green
Burn, as it burns within a youthful lady,
For my sake, who would sleep away in stone
My life, or feed like beasts upon the grass,
Only to see her garments cast a shade.

How dark soe'er the hills throw out their shade,
Under her summer-green the beautiful lady
Covers it, like a stone covered in grass.
1861

## Sudden Light

I have been here before,
But when or how I cannot tell:
I know the grass beyond the door,
The sweet keen smell,
The sighing sound, the lights around the shore.

You have been mine before,—
How long ago I may not know:
But just when at that swallow's soar
Your neck turned so,
10   Some veil did fall,—I knew it all of yore.

Then, now,—perchance again! . . .
O round mine eyes your tresses shake!
Shall we not lie as we have lain
Thus for Love's sake,
And sleep, and wake, yet never break the chain?
1870

## The Sea-Limits

Consider the sea's listless chime:
Time's self it is, made audible,—
The murmur of the earth's own shell.
Secret continuance sublime
Is the sea's end: our sight may pass
No furlong further. Since time was,
This sound hath told the lapse of time.

No quiet, which is death's,—it hath
The mournfulness of ancient life,
10   Enduring always at dull strife.
As the world's heart of rest and wrath,

Its painful pulse is in the sands.
Last utterly, the whole sky stands,
Grey and not known, along its path.

Listen alone beside the sea,
    Listen alone among the woods;
    Those voices of twin solitudes
Shall have one sound alike to thee:
    Hark where the murmurs of thronged men
20      Surge and sink back and surge again,—
Still the one voice of wave and tree.

Gather a shell from the strown beach
    And listen at its lips: they sigh
    The same desire and mystery,
The echo of the whole sea's speech.
    And all mankind is thus at heart
    Not anything but what thou art:
And Earth, Sea, Man, are all in each.
1849                                1850


## From The House of Life: A Sonnet Sequence

The title may be taken from astrology, the first of whose twelve "houses" is called
"the house of Life," but more likely only the architectural sense of "house" is intended. Whether there is actually a sequence here, despite Rossetti's subtitle, is
disputable. Three women are involved or are addressed throughout the sonnets. The
first is the poet's wife, Elizabeth Siddal, who killed herself in 1862, and in whose
grave he buried his manuscripts as an act of penance (but dug them out in 1869).
She appears as Beata Beatrix, a version of Dante's Blessed Beatrice. The wife of William
Morris, the beautiful Jane, appears as a composite goddess, Proserpine-Pandora,
while Rossetti's housekeeper, Fanny Cornforth, enters as Lilith. But, though the major
loves and sorrows of Rossetti's life are always in view, the sonnets are scarcely bio-
graphical, and have in common only their verse form and their author.


SONNETS XLIX, L, LI, LII

## Willowwood°

XLIX

I sat with Love upon a woodside well,
    Leaning across the water, I and he;
    Nor ever did he speak nor looked at me,
But touched his lute wherein was audible
The certain secret thing he had to tell:

**Willowwood** willows symbolize grief; Willowwood is a forest of grief enclosing a fountain
of lost love

Only our mirrored eyes met silently
In the low wave; and that sound came to be
The passionate voice I knew; and my tears fell.

And at their fall, his eyes beneath grew° hers;
10   And with his foot and with his wing-feathers
He swept the spring that watered my heart's drouth.
Then the dark ripples spread to waving hair,
And as I stooped, her own lips rising there
Bubbled with brimming kisses at my mouth.°

### L

And now Love sang: but his was such a song,
So meshed with half-remembrance hard to free,
As souls disused in death's sterility°
May sing when the new birthday tarries long.°
And I was made aware of a dumb throng°
That stood aloof, one form by every tree,
All mournful forms, for each was I or she,
The shades of those our days that had no tongue.°

They looked on us, and knew us and were known;
10   While fast together, alive from the abyss,
Clung the soul-wrung implacable close kiss;
And pity of self through all made broken moan
Which said, 'For once, for once, for once alone!'
And still Love sang, and what he sang was this:—

### LI

'O ye, all ye that walk in Willowwood,
That walk with hollow faces burning white;
What fathom-depth of soul-struck widowhood,°
What long, what longer hours, one lifelong night,
Ere ye again, who so in vain have wooed
Your last hope lost, who so in vain invite
Your lips to that their unforgotten food,
Ere ye, ere ye again shall see the light!

'Alas! the bitter banks in Willowwood,
10   With tear-spurge° wan, with blood-wort° burning red:
Alas! if ever such a pillow could
Steep deep the soul in sleep till she were dead,—

**grew** transformed into
**at my mouth** Rossetti's own reading: "The sonnet describes a dream or trance of divided love momentarily re-united by the longing fancy; and in the imagery of the dream, the face of the beloved rises through deep waters to kiss the lover."
**death's sterility** the souls will be reincarnated, but still abide in death
**tarries long** yet still is expected

**dumb throng** the wasted days when love went undeclared
**no tongue** in contrast to the reflected kiss in l. 11
**widowhood** not actually widowhood, but a state like it
**tear-spurge** See "The Woodspurge"; here Rossetti's coinage combines anguish and the forlorn weed.
**blood-wort** red-veined dock; here the plant is emblematic of suffering

Better all life forget her than this thing,
That Willowwood should hold her wandering!'

LII

So sang he: and as meeting rose and rose
   Together cling through the wind's wellaway°
   Nor change at once, yet near the end of day
The leaves drop loosened where the heart-stain glows,—
So when the song died did the kiss unclose;
   And her face fell back drowned, and was as grey
   As its grey eyes; and if it ever may
Meet mine again I know not if Love knows.

Only I know that I leaned low and drank
A long draught from the water where she sank,
   Her breath and all her tears and all her soul:
And as I leaned, I know I felt Love's face
Pressed on my neck with moan of pity and grace,
   Till both our heads were in his aureole.°
1868                       1869

SONNET LXIV

## Ardour and Memory

The cuckoo-throb, the heartbeat of the Spring;
   The rosebud's blush that leaves it as it grows
   Into the full-eyed fair unblushing rose;
The summer clouds that visit every wing
With fires of sunrise and of sunsetting;
   The furtive flickering streams to light re-born
   'Mid airs new-fledged and valorous lusts of morn,
While all the daughters of the daybreak sing:—

These ardour loves, and memory: and when flown
   All joys, and through dark forest-boughs in flight
   The wind swoops onward brandishing the light,
Even yet the rose-tree's verdure left alone
Will flush all ruddy though the rose be gone;
   With ditties and with dirges infinite.
1879                       1881

**wellaway** lamentation                      **aureole** nimbus or halo

## Autumn Idleness

This sunlight shames November where he grieves
In dead red leaves, and will not let him shun
The day, though bough with bough be over-run.
But with a blessing every glade receives
High salutation; while from hillock-caves
The deer gaze calling, dappled white and dun,
As if, being foresters of old, the sun
Had marked them with the shade of forest-leaves.

Here dawn today unveiled her magic glass;°
10  Here noon now gives the thirst and takes the dew;
Till eve bring rest when other good things pass.
And here the lost hours the lost hours renew
While I still lead my shadow o'er the grass,
Nor know, for longing, that which I should do.
1850                                    1870

## Body's Beauty°

Of Adam's first wife, Lilith, it is told
( The witch he loved before the gift of Eve, )
That, ere the snake's, her sweet tongue could deceive,
And her enchanted hair was the first gold.
And still she sits, young while the earth is old,
And, subtly of herself contemplative,
Draws men to watch the bright web° she can weave,
Till heart and body and life are in its hold.

The rose and poppy are her flowers;° for where
10  Is he not found, O Lilith, whom shed scent
And soft-shed kisses and soft sleep shall snare?
Lo! as that youth's eyes burned at thine, so went
Thy spell through him, and left his straight neck bent
And round his heart one strangling golden hair.
1867                                    1868

magic glass frost as a reflector of light
Body's Beauty first entitled "Lilith," and is a
description of Rossetti's painting of her (Fanny
Cornforth); by Hebrew oral tradition, Lilith
was Adam's wicked first wife

bright web her yellow hair
her flowers The rose is emblematic of sexual
passion; the poppy of a swooning away to
death.

# Barren Spring

Once more the changed year's turning wheel returns:
  And as a girl sails balanced in the wind,°
  And now before and now again behind
Stoops as it swoops, with cheek that laughs and burns,—
So Spring comes merry towards me here, but earns
  No answering smile from me, whose life is twined
  With the dead boughs that winter still must bind,
And whom today the Spring no more concerns.

Behold, this crocus is a withering flame;
10    This snowdrop, snow; this apple-blossom's part
    To breed the fruit that breeds the serpent's art.°
Nay, for these Spring-flowers, turn thy face from them,
Now stay till on the year's last lily-stem
    The white cup shrivels round the golden heart.
  1870                                    1870

# A Superscription°

Look in my face; my name is Might-have-been;
  I am also called No-more, Too-late, Farewell;
  Unto thine ear I hold the dead-sea shell
Cast up thy Life's foam-fretted feet between;°
Unto thine eyes the glass° where that is seen
  Which had Life's form and Love's, but by my spell
  Is now a shaken shadow intolerable,
Of ultimate things unuttered the frail screen.

Mark me, how still I am! But should there dart
10    One moment through thy soul the soft surprise
    Of that winged Peace which lulls the breath of sighs,—
Then shalt thou see me smile, and turn apart
Thy visage to mine ambush at thy heart
    Sleepless with cold commemorative eyes.
  1869                                    1869

---

**in the wind** probably on a swing
**serpent's art** as in Genesis 3
**Superscription** one message written on top of another; here one love engraved atop another

**between** He stands in the sea, just beyond the water's edge.
**glass** a demonic mirror

# The One Hope

When vain desire at last and vain regret
　　Go hand in hand to death, and all is vain,
　　What shall assuage the unforgotten pain
And teach the unforgetful to forget?
Shall Peace be still a sunk stream long unmet,—
　　Or may the soul at once in a green plain
　　Stoop through the spray of some sweet life fountain
And cull the dew-drenched flowering amulet?°

Ah! When the wan soul in that golden air
10　　Between the scriptured petals° softly blown
　　Peers breathless for the gift of grace unknown,—
Ah! let none other alien spell soe'er
But only the one Hope's one name be there,—
　　Not less nor more, but even that word alone.
　　1870?　　　　　　　　　　　　　　　1870

# The Orchard-Pit

### A FRAGMENT

Piled deep below the screening apple branch
　　They lie with bitter° apples in their hands:
And some are only ancient bones that blanch,
And some had ships that last year's wind did launch,
　　And some were yesterday the lords of lands.

In the soft dell, among the apple trees,
　　High up above the hidden pit she stands,°
And there forever sings, who gave to these,
That lie below, her magic hour of ease,
10　　And those her apples holden in their hands.

This in my dreams is shown me; and her hair
　　Crosses my lips and draws my burning breath;
Her song spreads golden wings upon the air,
Life's eyes are gleaming from her forehead fair,
　　And from her breasts the ravishing eyes of Death.°

Men say to me that sleep hath many dreams,
　　Yet I knew never but this dream alone:

amulet a charm worn against danger; here it is a flower
scriptured petals of the amulet-flower; as in the story of Hyacinthus, the petals carry the letters of lamentation αιαι (alas, alas)
bitter Printed text has "bitter" but Rossetti may have used "bitten," which makes better sense.

she stands This sinister Belle Dame or sorceress appears to be Proserpina, Queen of Hell, and probably was identified by Rossetti with Jane Morris.
eyes of Death By popular superstition, vampire women had eyes in their breasts.

There, from a dried-up channel, once the stream's,
The glen slopes up; even such in sleep it seems
20      As to my waking sight the place well known.

My love I call her, and she loves me well:
   But I love her as in the maelstrom's cup
The whirled stone loves the leaf inseparable
That clings to it round all the circling swell,
   And that the same last eddy swallows up.
1869                                        1886


# GEORGE MEREDITH

## Love in the Valley

Under yonder beech-tree single on the green-sward,
   Couched with her arms behind her golden head,
Knees and tresses folded to slip and ripple idly,
   Lies my young love sleeping in the shade.
Had I the heart to slide an arm beneath her,
   Press her parting lips as her waist I gather slow,
Waking in amazement she could not but embrace me:
   Then would she hold me and never let me go?

Shy as the squirrel and wayward as the swallow,
10      Swift as the swallow along the river's light
Circleting the surface to meet his mirrored winglets,
   Fleeter she seems in her stay than in her flight.
Shy as the squirrel that leaps among the pine-tops,
   Wayward as the swallow overhead at set of sun,
She whom I love is hard to catch and conquer,
   Hard, but O the glory of the winning were she won!

When her mother tends her before the laughing mirror,
   Tying up her laces,° looping up her hair,
Often she thinks, were this wild thing wedded,
20      More love should I have, and much less care.
When her mother tends her before the lighted mirror,
   Loosening her laces, combing down her curls,
Often she thinks, were this wild thing wedded,
   I should miss but one for many boys and girls.

Heartless she is as the shadow in the meadows
   Flying to the hills on a blue and breezy noon.
No, she is athirst and drinking up her wonder:

laces presumably of her bodice

Earth to her is young as the slip of the new moon.
Deals she an unkindness, 'tis but her rapid measure,
30    Even as in a dance; and her smile can heal no less:
Like the swinging May-cloud that pelts the flowers with hailstones
Off a sunny border, she was made to bruise and bless.

Lovely are the curves of the white owl sweeping
    Wavy in the dusk lit by one large star.
Lone on the fir-branch, his rattle-note unvaried,
    Brooding o'er the gloom, spins the brown eve-jar.°
Darker grows the valley, more and more forgetting:
    So were it with me if forgetting could be willed.
Tell the grassy hollow that holds the bubbling well-spring,
40    Tell it to forget the source that keeps it filled.

Stepping down the hill with her fair companions,
    Arm in arm, all against the raying West,°
Boldly she sings, to the merry tune she marches,
    Brave in her shape, and sweeter unpossessed.
Sweeter, for she is what my heart first awaking
    Whispered the world was; morning light is she.
Love that so desires would fain keep her changeless;
    Fain would fling the net, and fain have her free.

Happy happy time, when the white star hovers
50    Low over dim fields fresh with bloomy dew,
Near the face of dawn, that draws athwart the darkness,
    Threading it with colour, like yewberries the yew.
Thicker crowd the shades as the grave East deepens
    Glowing, and with crimson a long cloud swells
Maiden still the morn is; and strange she is, and secret;
    Strange her eyes; her cheeks are cold as cold sea-shells.

Sunrays, leaning on our southern hills and lighting
    Wild cloud-mountains that drag the hills along,
Oft ends the day of your shifting brilliant laughter
60    Chill as a dull face frowning on a song.
Ay, but shows the South-West a ripple-feathered bosom
    Blown to silver while the clouds are shaken and ascend
Scaling the mid-heavens as they stream, there comes a sunset
    Rich, deep like love in beauty without end.

When at dawn she sighs, and like an infant to the window
    Turns grave eyes craving light, released from dreams,
Beautiful she looks, like a white water-lily
    Bursting out of bud in havens of the streams.
When from bed she rises clothed from neck to ankle
70    In her long nightgown sweet as boughs of May,

eve-jar whippoorwill                        raying West sunset

Beautiful she looks, like a tall garden lily
Pure from the night, and splendid for the day.

Mother of the dews, dark eye-lashed twilight,
Low-lidded twilight, o'er the valley's brim,
Rounding on thy breast sings the dew-delighted skylark,
Clear as though the dewdrops had their voice in him.
Hidden where the rose-flush drinks the rayless planet,°
Fountain-full he pours the spraying fountain-showers.
Let me hear her laughter, I would have her ever
80    Cool as dew in twilight, the lark above the flowers.

All the girls are out with their baskets for the primrose;
Up lanes, woods through, they troop in joyful bands.
My sweet leads: she knows not why, but now she loiters,
Eyes the bent anemones, and hangs her hands.
Such a look will tell that the violets are peeping,
Coming the rose: and unaware a cry
Springs in her bosom for odours and for colour,
Covert and the nightingale; she knows not why.

Kerchiefed head and chin she darts between her tulips,
90    Streaming like a willow grey in arrowy rain:
Some bend beaten cheek to gravel, and their angel
She will be; she lifts them, and on she speeds again.
Black the driving raincloud breasts the iron gateway:
She is forth to cheer a neighbour lacking mirth.
So when sky and grass met rolling dumb for thunder
Saw I once a white dove, sole light of earth.

Prim little scholars are the flowers of her garden,
Trained to stand in rows, and asking if they please.
I might love them well but for loving more the wild ones:
100    O my wild ones! they tell me more than these.
You, my wild one, you tell of honied field-rose,
Violet, blushing eglantine in life; and even as they,
They by the wayside are earnest of your goodness,
You are of life's, on the banks that line the way.

Peering at her chamber the white crowns the red rose,
Jasmine winds the porch with stars two and three.
Parted is the window; she sleeps; the starry jasmine
Breathes a falling breath that carries thoughts of me,
Sweeter unpossessed, have I said of her my sweetest?
110    Not while she sleeps: while she sleeps the jasmine breathes,
Luring her to love; she sleeps; the starry jasmine
Bears me to her pillow under white rose-wreaths.

Yellow with birdfoot-trefoil° are the grass-glades;
Yellow with cinquefoil° of the dew-grey leaf;

---

**rayless planet** Evening Star                    **cinquefoil** plant with five-lobed leaves
**birdfoot-trefoil** three-lobed flower

Yellow with stonecrop; the moss-mounds are yellow;
    Blue-necked the wheat sways, yellowing to the sheaf.
Green-yellow burst from the copse the laughing yaffle;°
    Sharp as a sickle is the edge of shade and shine:
Earth in her heart laughs looking at the heavens,
120     Thinking of the harvest: I look and think of mine.

This I may know: her dressing and undressing
    Such a change of light shows as when the skies in sport
Shift from cloud to moonlight; or edging over thunder
    Slips a ray of sun; or sweeping into port
White sails furl; or on the ocean borders
    White sails lean along the waves leaping green.
Visions of her shower before me, but from eyesight
    Guarded she would be like the sun were she seen.

Front door and back of the mossed old farmhouse
130     Open with the morn, and in a breezy link°
Freshly sparkles garden to stripe-shadowed orchard,
    Green across a rill where on sand the minnows wink.
Busy in the grass the early sun of summer
    Swarms, and the blackbird's mellow fluting notes
Call my darling up with round and roguish challenge:
    Quaintest, richest carol of all the singing throats!

Cool was the woodside; cool as her white dairy
    Keeping sweet the cream pan; and there the boys from school,
Cricketing below, rushed brown and red with sunshine;
140     O the dark translucence of the deep-eyed cool!
Spying from the farm, herself she fetched a pitcher
    Full of milk, and tilted for each in turn the beak.
Then a little fellow, mouth up and on tiptoe,
    Said, 'I will kiss you'; she laughed and leaned her cheek.

Doves of the fir-wood walling high our red roof
    Through the long noon coo, crooning through the coo.
Loose droop the leaves, and down the sleepy roadway
    Sometimes pipes a chaffinch; loose droops the blue.
Cows flap a slow tail knee-deep in the river,
150     Breathless, given up to sun and gnat and fly.
Nowhere is she seen; and if I see her nowhere,
    Lightning may come, straight rains and tiger sky.

O the golden sheaf, the rustling treasure-armful!
    O the nutbrown tresses nodding interlaced!
O the treasure-tresses one another over
    Nodding! O the girdle slack about the waist!
Slain are the poppies that shot their random scarlet
    Quick amid the wheatears: wound about the waist,

yaffle green woodpecker                 link river ground, near a bend

Gathered, see the brides of Earth one blush of ripeness!
160    O the nutbrown tresses nodding interlaced!

Large and smoky red the sun's cold disk drops,
    Clipped by naked hills, on violet shaded snow:
Eastward large and still lights up a bower of moonrise,
    Whence at her leisure steps the moon aglow.
Nightlong on black print-branches our beech-tree
    Gazes in this whiteness; nightlong could I.
Here may life on death or death on life be painted.
    Let me clasp her soul to know she cannot die!

Gossips count her faults: they scour a narrow chamber
170    Where there is no window, read not heaven or her.
'When she was a tiny,' one aged woman quavers,
    Plucks at my heart and leads me by the ear.
Faults she had once as she learnt to run and tumbled:
    Faults of feature some see, beauty not complete.
Yet, good gossips, beauty that makes holy
    Earth and air, may have faults from head to feet.

Hither she comes; she comes to me; she lingers,
    Deepens her brown eyebrows, while in new surprise
High rise the lashes in wonder of a stranger;
180    Yet am I the light and living of her eyes.
Something friends have told her fills her heart to brimming,
    Nets her in her blushes, and wounds her, and tames.—
Sure of her haven, O like a dove alighting,
    Arms up, she dropped: our souls were in our names.

Soon will she lie like a white frost sunrise.
    Yellow oats and brown wheat, barley pale as rye,
Long since your sheaves have yielded to the thresher,
    Felt the girdle loosened, seen the tresses fly.
Soon will she lie like a blood-red sunset.
190    Swift with the tomorrow, green-winged Spring!
Sing from the South-West, bring her back the truants,
    Nightingale and swallow, song and dipping wing.

Soft new beech-leaves, up to beamy April
    Spreading bough on bough a primrose mountain, you
Lucid in the moon, raise lilies to the skyfields,
    Youngest green transfused in silver shining through:
Fairer than the lily, than the wild white cherry:
    Fair as in image my seraph love appears
Borne to me by dreams when dawn is at my eyelids:
200    Fair as in the flesh she swims to me on tears.

Could I find a place to be alone with heaven,
    I would speak my heart out: heaven is my need.
Every woodland tree is flushing like the dogwood,

Flashing like the whitebeam,° swaying like the reed.
Flushing like the dogwood crimson in October;
Streaming like the flag-reed South-West blown;
Flashing as in gusts the sudden-lighted whitebeam:
All seem to know what is for heaven alone.
1851                                    1878


*From* Modern Love°

I

By this he knew she wept with waking eyes:
That, at his hand's light quiver by her head,
The strange low sobs that shook their common bed,
Were called into her with a sharp surprise,
And strangled mute, like little gaping snakes,
Dreadfully venomous to him. She lay
Stone-still, and the long darkness flowed away
With muffled pulses. Then, as midnight makes
Her giant heart of Memory and Tears
10    Drink the pale drug of silence, and so beat
Sleep's heavy measure, they from head to feet
Were moveless, looking through their dead black years,
By vain regret scrawled over the blank wall.
Like sculptured effigies° they might be seen
Upon their marriage-tomb, the sword between;°
Each wishing for the sword that severs all.°


XLVII

We saw the swallows gathering in the sky,
And in the osier-isle° we heard them noise.
We had not to look back on summer joys,
Or forward to a summer of bright dye:
But in the largeness of the evening earth
Our spirits grew as we went side by side.
The hour became her husband and my bride.
Love that had robbed us so, thus blessed our dearth!
The pilgrims of the year°waxed very loud
10    In multitudinous chatterings, as the flood
Full brown came from the West, and like pale blood
Expanded to the upper crimson cloud.

whitebeam leaves white on nether-side
Modern Love This is a tight sequence of fifty
16-line sonnet-like poems presenting a highly
fictionalized account of Meredith's first marriage, which ended badly enough, but not with
his wife's suicide, as happens here. (From 1849
until 1858, when she eloped with an indifferent
artist, Meredith was married to the daughter of
Thomas Love Peacock.) Given here are the

first poem and the last four of the sequence.
sculptured effigies as on medieval tombs
sword between image of their sexual failure;
based on the romance tradition of lovers sleeping with a sword between them, to symbolize
continued chastity
severs all this sword is death
osier-isle group of willow trees
pilgrims of the year the swallows migrating

Love, that had robbed us of immortal things,
This little moment mercifully gave,
Where I have seen across the twilight wave
The swan sail with her young beneath her wings.

### XLVIII

Their sense is with their senses all mixed in,
Destroyed by subtleties these women are!
More brain, O Lord, more brain! or we shall mar
Utterly this fair garden we might win.
Behold! I looked for peace, and thought it near.
Our inmost hearts had opened, each to each.
We drank the pure daylight of honest speech.
Alas! that was the fatal draught, I fear.
For when of my lost Lady came the word,
This woman, O this agony of flesh!
Jealous devotion bade her break the mesh,
That I might seek that other like a bird.
I do adore the nobleness! despise
The act! She has gone forth, I know not where.
Will the hard world my sentience° of her share?
I feel the truth; so let the world surmise.

### XLIX

He found her by the ocean's moaning verge,
Nor any wicked change in her discerned;
And she believed his old love had returned,
Which was her exultation, and her scourge.
She took his hand, and walked with him, and seemed
The wife he sought, though shadow-like and dry.
She had one terror, lest her heart should sigh,
And tell her loudly she no longer dreamed.
She dared not say, 'This is my breast: look in.'
But there's a strength to help the desperate weak.
That night he learned how silence best can speak
The awful things when Pity pleads for Sin.
About the middle of the night her call
Was heard, and he came wondering to the bed.
'Now kiss me, dear! it may be, now!' she said.
Lethe° had passed those lips, and he knew all.

### L

Thus piteously Love closed what he begat:
The union of this ever-diverse pair!
These two were rapid falcons in a snare,
Condemned to do the flitting of the bat.

sentience consciousness                    Lethe river in Hades whose water caused forget-
                                           fulness

Lovers beneath the singing sky of May,
They wandered once; clear as the dew on flowers:
But they fed not on the advancing hours:
Their hearts held cravings for the buried day.
Then each applied to each that fatal knife,
10   Deep questioning, which probes to endless dole.°
Ah, what a dusty answer gets the soul
When hot for certainties in this our life!—
In tragic hints here see what evermore
Moves dark as yonder midnight ocean's force,
Thundering like ramping hosts of warrior horse,
To throw that faint thin line upon the shore!
1862                                    1892


# A Ballad of Past Meridian°

Last night returning from my twilight walk
I met the grey mist Death, whose eyeless brow
Was bent on me, and from his hand of chalk
He reached me flowers as from a withered bough.
O Death, what bitter nosegays givest thou!

Death said, 'I gather,' and pursued his way.
Another stood by me, a shape in stone,
Sword-hacked and iron-stained, with breasts of clay,
And metal veins that sometimes fiery shone.
10   O Life, how naked and how hard when known!

Life said, 'As thou hast carved me, such am I.'
Then Memory, like the nightjar on the pine,
And sightless Hope, a woodlark in night sky,
Joined notes of Death and Life till night's decline.
Of Death, of Life, those inwound notes are mine.
1876


# Lucifer in Starlight

On a starred night Prince Lucifer uprose.
Tired of his dark dominion swung the fiend
Above the rolling ball in cloud part screened,
Where sinners hugged their spectre of repose.
Poor prey to his hot fit of pride were those.
And now upon his western wing he leaned,
Now his huge bulk o'er Afric's sands careened,

---

dole anguish
Past Meridian past the period of a person's
greatest elevation (see Wallace Stevens's "Le

Monocle de Mon Oncle" II.9: "No spring can
follow past meridian," where "meridian" is
forty)

Now the black planet° shadowed Arctic snows.
Soaring through wider zones that pricked his scars°
10   With memory of the old revolt from Awe,
He reached a middle height, and at the stars,
Which are the brain of heaven, he looked, and sank.
Around the ancient track marched, rank on rank,
The army of unalterable law.

1883

# CHRISTINA ROSSETTI

## Song

When I am dead, my dearest,
    Sing no sad songs for me;
Plant thou no roses at my head,
    Nor shady cypress tree:°
Be the green grass above me
    With showers and dewdrops wet:
And if thou wilt, remember,
    And if thou wilt, forget.

I shall not see the shadows,
10       I shall not feel the rain;
I shall not hear the nightingale
    Sing on as if in pain:
And dreaming through the twilight
    That doth not rise nor set,
Haply° I may remember,
    And haply may forget.

1848                    1862

## Rest

O Earth, lie heavily upon her eyes;
    Seal her sweet eyes weary of watching, Earth;
    Lie close around her; leave no room for mirth
With its harsh laughter, nor for sound of sighs.
She hath no questions, she hath no replies,
    Hushed in and curtained with a blessed dearth
    Of all that irked her from the hour of birth;
With stillness that is almost Paradise.
Darkness more clear than noonday holdeth her,

---

black planet Though "Lucifer," the Morning       cypress tree emblematic of mourning
Star, means "light bearer," this is fallen Lucifer.    Haply perhaps
scars See *Paradise Lost* I.601.

10    Silence more musical than any song;
Even her very heart has ceased to stir:
Until the morning of Eternity
Her rest shall not begin nor end, but be;
And when she wakes she will not think it long.
1844                                    1862

## Remember

Remember me when I am gone away,
Gone far away into the silent land;
When you can no more hold me by the hand,
Nor I half turn to go yet turning stay.
Remember me when no more day by day
You tell me of our future that you planned:
Only remember me; you understand
It will be late to counsel then or pray.
Yet if you should forget me for a while
10    And afterwards remember, do not grieve:
For if the darkness and corruption leave
A vestige of the thoughts that once I had,
Better by far you should forget and smile
Than that you should remember and be sad.
1849                                    1862

## Echo

Come to me in the silence of the night;
Come in the speaking silence of a dream;
Come with soft rounded cheeks and eyes as bright
As sunlight on a stream;
Come back in tears,
O memory, hope, love of finished years.

O dream how sweet, too sweet, too bitter sweet,
Whose wakening should have been in Paradise,
Where souls brimfull of love abide and meet;
10    Where thirsting longing eyes
Watch the slow door
That opening, letting in, lets out no more.

Yet come to me in dreams, that I may live
My very life again though cold in death:
Come back to me in dreams, that I may give
Pulse for pulse, breath for breath:
Speak low, lean low,
As long ago, my love, how long ago.
1854                                    1862

# A Birthday

My heart is like a singing bird
  Whose nest is in a watered shoot:°
My heart is like an apple-tree
  Whose boughs are bent with thickset fruit;
My heart is like a rainbow shell
  That paddles in a halcyon° sea;
My heart is gladder than all these
  Because my love is come to me.

Raise me a dais of silk and down;
  Hang it with vair° and purple dyes;
Carve it in doves and pomegranates,
  And peacocks with a hundred eyes;
Work it in gold and silver grapes,
  In leaves and silver fleurs-de-lys;°
Because the birthday of my life
  Is come, my love is come to me.
1857                              1862

# Up-Hill

Does the road wind up-hill all the way?
  Yes, to the very end.
Will the day's journey take the whole long day?
  From morn to night, my friend.

But is there for the night a resting-place?
  A roof for when the silow dark hours begin.
May not the darkness hide it from my face?
  You cannot miss that inn.

Shall I meet other wayfarers at night?
  Those who have gone before.
Then must I knock, or call when just in sight?
  They will not keep you standing at that door.

Shall I find comfort, travel-sore and weak?
  Of labour you shall find the sum.
Will there be beds for me and all who seek?
  Yea, beds for all who come.
1858                              1862

shoot fresh growth               vair heraldic gray squirrel fur
halcyon placid                   fleurs-de-lys heraldic lilies

642

## Passing Away°

Passing away, saith the World, passing away:
Chances, beauty, and youth, sapped day by day:
Thy life never continueth in one stay.
Is the eye waxen dim, is the dark hair changing to grey
That hath won neither laurel nor bay?°
I shall clothe myself in Spring and bud in May:
Thou, root-stricken, shalt not rebuild thy decay
On my bosom for aye.
Then I answered: Yea.

10 Passing away, saith my Soul, passing away:
With its burden of fear and hope, of labour and play,
Hearken what the past doth witness and say:
Rust in thy gold, a moth is in thine array,
A canker is in thy bud, thy leaf must decay.
A midnight, at cockcrow, at morning, one certain day
Lo the Bridegroom shall come and shall not delay;°
Watch thou and pray.
Then I answered: Yea.

Passing away, saith my God, passing away:
20 Winter passeth° after the long delay:
New grapes on the vine, new figs on the tender spray,
Turtle calleth turtle in Heaven's May.
Though I tarry, wait for Me, trust Me, watch and pray:
Arise, come away, night is past and lo it is day,
My love, My sister, My spouse, thou shalt hear Me say.
Then I answered: Yea.
1860            1862

# WILLIAM MORRIS

## The Haystack in the Floods°

Had she come all the way for this,
To part at last without a kiss?

Passing Away This virtuoso lyric on one rhyme is a farewell to the poetess's twenties, being written on the last day of a decade, and a study toward a farewell to all worldiness.
neither laurel nor bay At this time she was scarcely recognized as a poet.
shall not delay a beautiful use of Christ's parable of the wise and foolish virgins; see Matthew 25:1–13.
Winter passeth This and most of the stanza closely echo Song of Solomon 2:11–13.
The Haystack in the Floods The story here is Morris's own invention, but the circumstances are strictly historical. Morris sets the poem in the late autumn of 1356 in southern France after the battle of Poictiers, fought in Septem-

ber, in which the English badly defeated the French. Sir Robert de Marny, an English commander, with his mistress, a French woman Jehane, and a small band of men are ambushed by Godmar and a group of French partisans. In the tangled treacheries of this direct, brutal, and wonderfully detached poem, Godmar earlier had served the English, and then betrayed them, and Jehane may have been Godmar's mistress and then left him for Robert. In the action of the poem, Robert's band proceeds to betray him and joins Godmar, leaving Jehane the only decision of honor, when she, at the highest price, refuses a last betrayal.

Yea, had she borne the dirt and rain
That her own eyes might see him slain
Beside the haystack in the floods?

Along the dripping leafless woods,
The stirrup touching either shoe,
She rode astride as troopers do;
With kirtle kilted to her knee,°
10  To which the mud splashed wretchedly;
And the wet dripped from every tree
Upon her head and heavy hair,
And on her eyelids broad and fair;
The tears and rain ran down her face.
By fits and starts they rode apace,
And very often was his place
Far off from her; he had to ride
Ahead, to see what might betide
When the roads crossed; and sometimes, when
20  There rose a murmuring from his men,
Had to turn back with promises;
Ah me! she had but little ease;
And often for pure doubt and dread
She sobbed, made giddy in the head
By the swift riding; while, for cold,
Her slender fingers scarce could hold
The wet reins; yea, and scarcely, too,
She felt the foot within her shoe
Against the stirrup: all for this,
30  To part at last without a kiss
Beside the haystack in the floods.

For when they neared that old soaked hay,
They saw across the only way
That Judas, Godmar, and the three
Red running lions dismally
Grinned from his pennon,° under which
In one straight line along the ditch,
They counted thirty heads.
                                So then,
While Robert turned round to his men,
40  She saw at once the wretched end,
And, stooping down, tried hard to rend
Her coif° the wrong way from her head,
And hid her eyes; while Robert said:
'Nay, love, 'tis scarcely two to one,
At Poictiers° where we made them run

kirtle . . . her knee skirts tucked up to the
knee
from his pennon The lions are the emblem on
Godmar's banner.

coif head covering; she reverses it to cover
her eyes
Poictiers 6500 English mauled 16,000 French
at Poictiers.

So fast—why, sweet my love, good cheer.
The Gascon frontier° is so near,
Nought after this.'

           But, 'O,' she said,
'My God! my God! I have to tread
50    The long way back without you; then
The court at Paris; those six men;°
The gratings of the Chatelet;°
The swift Seine on some rainy day
Like this, and people standing by,
And laughing, while my weak hands try
To recollect how strong men swim.°
All this, or else a life with him,
For which I should be damned at last.
Would God that this next hour were past!'

60    He answered not, but cried his cry,
'St. George for Marny!'° cheerily;
And laid his hand upon her rein.
Alas! no man of all his train
Gave back that cheery cry again;
And, while for rage his thumb beat fast
Upon his sword-hilts, some one cast
About his neck a kerchief long,
And bound him.

           Then they went along
70    To Godmar; who said: 'Now, Jehane,
Your lover's life is on the wane
So fast, that, if this very hour
You yield not as my paramour,
He will not see the rain leave off—
Nay, keep your tongue from gibe and scoff,
Sir Robert, or I slay you now.'

She laid her hand upon her brow,
Then gazed upon the palm, as though
She thought her forehead bled, and—'No!'
She said, and turned her head away,
80    As there were nothing else to say,
And everything were settled: red
Grew Godmar's face from chin to head:
'Jehane, on yonder hill there stands

Gascon frontier Gascony was English territory
(now part of southwestern France).
six men judges in Paris who will put Jehane
on trial
Chatelet prison bars of Parisian dungeon
men swim As a traitress, she will be condemned
to the "trial" of a witch. She will be tossed
into the River Seine; if she drowns, then she
is innocent, but if she survives by swimming,
she will be burned alive as having received the
Devil's aid. The only other possibility, as she
says, is Godmar, but (to her) he is a fate
worse than drowning or burning.
St. George for Marny! St. George is the patron
saint of England.

My castle, guarding well my lands:
What hinders me from taking you,
And doing that I list to do
To your fair wilful body, while
Your knight lies dead?'
                          A wicked smile
Wrinkled her face, her lips grew thin,
90    A long way out she thrust her chin:
'You know that I should strangle you
While you were sleeping; or bite through
Your throat, by God's help—ah!' she said,
'Lord Jesus, pity your poor maid!
For in such wise they hem me in,
I cannot choose but sin and sin,
Whatever happens: yet I think
They could not make me eat or drink,
And so should I just reach my rest.'
100   'Nay, if you do not my behest,
O Jehane! though I love you well,'
Said Godmar, 'would I fail to tell
All that I know?' 'Foul lies,' she said.
'Eh? lies my Jehane? by God's head,
At Paris folks would deem them true!
Do you know, Jehane, they cry for you:
"Jehane the brown! Jehane the brown!
Give us Jehane to burn or drown!"—
Eh—gag me Robert!°—sweet my friend,
110   This were indeed a piteous end
For those long fingers, and long feet,
And long neck, and smooth shoulders sweet,
An end that few men would forget
That saw it—So, an hour yet:
Consider, Jehane, which to take
Of life or death!'
                    So, scarce awake,
Dismounting, did she leave that place,
And totter some yards: with her face
Turned upward to the sky she lay,
120   Her head on a wet heap of hay,
And fell asleep: and while she slept,
And did not dream, the minutes crept
Round to the twelve again; but she,
Being waked at last, sighed quietly,
And strangely childlike came, and said:
'I will not.' Straightway Godmar's head,

gag me Robert! Godmar orders Robert's own
men to gag him, so as to prepare him for execution.

As though it hung on strong wires, turned
Most sharply round, and his face burned.

For Robert—both his eyes were dry,
130   He could not weep, but gloomily
He seemed to watch the rain; yea, too,
His lips were firm; he tried once more
To touch her lips; she reached out, sore
And vain desire so tortured them,
The poor grey lips and now the hem
Of his sleeve brushed them.
                              With a start
Up Godmar rose, thrust them apart;
From Robert's throat he loosed the bands
Of silk and mail; with empty hands
140   Held out, she stood and gazed, and saw
The long bright blade without a flaw
Glide out from Godmar's sheath, his hand
From Robert's throat he loosed the bands
Back Robert's head; she saw him send
The thin steel down; the blow told well,
Right backward the knight Robert fell,
And moaned as dogs do, being half dead,
Unwitting, as I deem: so then
Godmar turned grinning to his men,
150   Who ran, some five or six, and beat
His head to pieces at their feet.

Then Godmar turned again and said:
'So, Jehane, the first fitte° is read!
Take note, my lady, that your way
Lies backward to the Chatelet!'
She shook her head and gazed awhile
At her cold hands with a rueful smile,
As though this thing had made her mad.

This was the parting that they had
Beside the haystack in the floods.
                                    1858


# Near Avalon°

A ship with shields before the sun,
Six maidens round the mast,
A red-gold crown on every one,
A green gown on the last.

first fitte first part of a story
Avalon the Celtic version of the Isles of the
Blessed, where Arthur sojourned in his apparent death, and from which he will return

The fluttering green banners there
Are wrought with ladies' heads most fair,
And a portraiture of Guenevere
The middle of each sail doth bear.

A ship with sails before the wind,
10   And round the helm six knights,
Their heaumes° are on, whereby, half blind,
They pass by many sights.

The tattered scarlet banners there,
Right soon will leave the spear-heads bare,
Those six knights sorrowfully bear
In all their heaumes some yellow hair.°
                            1858


# Summer Dawn

Pray but one prayer for me 'twixt thy closed lips,
    Think but one thought of me up in the stars.
The summer night waneth, the morning light slips,
    Faint and grey 'twixt the leaves of the aspen, betwixt the cloud-bars,
That are patiently waiting there for the dawn:
    Patient and colourless, though Heaven's gold
Waits to float through them along with the sun.
Far out in the meadows, above the young corn,°
    The heavy elms wait, and restless and cold
10   The uneasy wind rises; the roses are dun;°
Through the long twilight they pray for the dawn.
Round the lone house in the midst of the corn.
    Speak but one word to me over the corn,
    Over the tender, bowed locks° of the corn.
1856                              1858


# Riding Together

For many, many days together
    The wind blew steady from the East;
For many days hot grew the weather,
    About the time of our Lady's Feast.°

For many days we rode together,
    Yet met we neither friend nor foe;

heaumes helmets
yellow hair pledges of their ladies; the heroines
of romance are generally blondes, the tempt-
resses brunettes
corn wheat

dun brownish gray in color
bowed locks because of the wind, like a person
kneeling
our Lady's Feast Feast of the Annunciation,
March 25

Hotter and clearer grew the weather,
    Steadily did the East wind blow.

We saw the trees in the hot, bright weather,
10  Clear-cut, with shadows very black,
As freely we rode on together
    With helms unlaced and bridles slack.

And often as we rode together,
    We, looking down the green-banked stream,
Saw flowers in the sunny weather,
    And saw the bubble-making bream.°

And in the night lay down together,
    And hung above our heads the rood,°
Or watched night-long in the dewy weather,
20    The while the moon did watch the wood.

Our spears stood bright and thick together,
    Straight out the banners streamed behind,
As we galloped on in the sunny weather,
    With faces turned towards the wind.

Down sank our threescore spears together,°
    As thick we saw the pagans ride;
His eager face in the clear fresh weather,
    Shone out that last time by my side.

Up the sweep of the bridge we dashed together,
30    It rocked to the crash of the meeting spears,
Down rained the buds of the dear spring weather,
    The elm-tree flowers fell like tears.

There, as we rolled and writhed together,
    I threw my arms above my head,
For close by my side in the lovely weather,
    I saw him reel and fall back dead.

I and the slayer met together,
    He wanted the death-stroke there in his place,
With thoughts of death, in the lovely weather,
40    Gapingly mazed° at my maddened face.

Madly I fought as we fought together;
    In vain: the little Christian band
The pagans drowned, as in stormy weather
    The river drowns low-lying land.

They bound my blood-stained hands together,
    They bound his corpse to nod by my side:

---

**bream** a fish
**rood** cross
**together** The sixty Crusaders prepare for battle.

**Gapingly mazed** His antagonist, astonished at the knight's ferocity, lets his mouth hang open.

Then on we rode, in the bright March weather,
    With clash of cymbals did we ride.

We ride no more, no more together;
50      My prison-bars are thick and strong,
I take no heed of any weather,
    The sweet Saints grant I live not long.
1856                               1858


## A Garden by the Sea

I know a little garden-close,°
Set thick with lily and red rose,
Where I would wander if I might
From dewy dawn to dewy night,
And have one with me wandering.

And though within it no birds sing,
And though no pillared house is there,
And though the apple-boughs are bare
Of fruit and blossom, would to God
10  Her feet upon the green grass trod,
And I beheld them as before.

There comes a murmur from the shore,
And in the place two fair streams are,
Drawn from the purple hills afar,
Drawn down unto the restless sea:
Dark hills whose heath-bloom feeds no bee,
Dark shore no ship has ever seen,
Tormented by the billows green
Whose murmur comes unceasingly
20  Unto the place for which I cry.

For which I cry both day and night,
For which I let slip all delight,
Whereby I grow both deaf and blind,
Careless to win, unskilled to find,
And quick to loose what all men seek.
Yet tottering as I am and weak,
Still have I left a little breath
To seek within the jaws of death
An entrance to that happy place,
30  To seek the unforgotten face,
Once seen, once kissed, once reft° from me
Anigh the murmuring of the sea.
1867                               1891

garden-close an enclosed garden                    reft robbed

# *From* The Earthly Paradise

Of Heaven or Hell I have no power to sing,°
I cannot ease the burden of your fears,
Or make quick-coming death a little thing,
Or bring again the pleasure of past years,
Nor for my words shall ye forget your tears,
Or hope again for aught that I can say,
The idle° singer of an empty day.

But rather, when aweary of your mirth,
From full hearts still unsatisfied ye sigh,
10 And, feeling kindly unto all the earth,
Grudge every minute as it passes by,
Made the more mindful that the sweet days die—
Remember me a little then I pray,
The idle singer of an empty day.

The heavy trouble, the bewildering care
That weighs us down who live and earn our bread,
These idle verses have no power to bear;
So let me sing of names rememberèd,°
Because they, living not, can ne'er be dead,
20 Or long time take their memory quite away
From us poor singers of an empty day.

Dreamer of dreams, born out of my due time,
Why should I strive to set the crooked straight?
Let it suffice me that my murmuring rhyme
Beats with light wing against the ivory gate,°
Telling a tale not too importunate°
To those who in the sleepy region stay,
Lulled by the singer of an empty day.

Folk say, a wizard to a northern king°
30 At Christmas-tide such wondrous things did show,
That through one window men beheld the spring,
And through another saw the summer glow,
And through a third the fruited vines a-row,
While still, unheard, but in its wonted way,
Piped the drear wind of that December day.

So with this Earthly Paradise it is,
If ye will read aright, and pardon me,

---

**Apology** a defense of Morris's poetic stance, of art for the sake of art, despite Morris's convinced and active Socialism
**no power to sing** unlike Dante or Milton
**idle** in the sense of pleasantly idle
**names rememberèd** in mythology or familiar literature

**ivory gate** In Homer and Virgil, true dreams emerge through the gates of horn, and false ones through the gates of ivory.
**importunate** pressing
**northern king** possibly a reference to a legend of Dr. Faustus

Who strive to build a shadowy isle of bliss
Midmost the beating of the steely sea,
40    Where tossed about all hearts of men must be;
Whose ravening monsters mighty men shall slay,
Not the poor singer of an empty day.

1868

# ALGERNON CHARLES SWINBURNE

## Atalanta in Calydon

This dramatic poem, Swinburne's finest work, follows closely a number of Greek models for its form, but takes its story mostly from Ovid (*Metamorphoses* VIII. 260 ff.). The choruses are the great strength of the poem, and the two most important are given below.

Althaea, queen of Calydon, pregnant with Meleager, dreams that she gives birth to a burning brand. When the child is born, the Fates prophesy he will die when the brand already in the fire is consumed. Althaea snatches the brand from the fire, puts it out, and then conceals it. After Meleager grows up to be a heroic warrior, the goddess Artemis, patroness of the hunt and of chastity, becomes angry with his father, for not sacrificing to her. She sends a boar, which makes the land of Calydon desolate. Among the Greek heroes who assemble to hunt the boar is the maiden Atalanta of Arcadia, whose life is consecrated to Artemis. The goddess therefore allows her follower the honor of slaying the boar. Althaea's two brothers, shamed by a woman's triumph, intervene against Atalanta, but are killed by their nephew Meleager, who has fallen in love with the maiden. Althaea, in revenge, throws the hidden brand into the fire, thus destroying her son.

The first chorus given here is the first of the play, and is sung by maidens as an invocation to Artemis, before the hunt. The second, Swinburne's most audacious antireligious work, sums up the poem's dark theme, which is the utter hopelessness of human existence since all human desire is, by its nature, self-destructive, a condition for which the chorus holds the divine world responsible.

## *From* Atalanta in Calydon

CHORUS

When the hounds of spring are on winter's traces,
    The mother of months° in meadow or plain
Fills the shadows and windy places
    With lisp of leaves and ripple of rain;
And the brown bright nightingale amorous
70    Is half assuaged for Itylus,°

mother of months Artemis is also goddess of the moon, and so presides over the monthly cycle.

Itylus the diminutive of Itys, the son of Procne, the nightingale (see notes to Matthew Arnold's "Philomela")

For the Thracian° ships and the foreign faces,
The tongueless vigil, and all the pain.

Come with bows bent° and with emptying of quivers,
Maiden most perfect, lady of light,
With a noise of winds and many rivers,
With a clamour of waters, and with might;
Bind on thy sandals, O thou most fleet,°
Over the splendour and speed of thy feet;
For the faint east quickens, the wan west shivers,
80    Round the feet of the day and the feet of the night.

Where shall we find her, how shall we sing to her,
Fold our hands round her knees, and cling?
O that man's heart were as fire and could spring to her,
Fire, or the strength of the streams that spring!
For the stars and the winds are unto her
As raiment, as songs of the harp-player;
For the risen stars and the fallen cling to her,
And the southwest-wind and the west-wind sing.

For winter's rains and ruins are over,
90    And all the season of snows and sins;
The days dividing lover and lover,
The light that loses,° the night that wins;
And time remembered is grief forgotten,
And frosts are slain and flowers begotten,
And in green underwood and cover
Blossom by blossom the spring begins.

The full streams feed on flower of rushes,
Ripe grasses trammel a travelling foot,
The faint fresh flame of the young year flushes
100    From leaf to flower and flower to fruit;
And fruit and leaf are as gold and fire,
And the oat° is heard above the lyre,
And the hoofèd heel of a satyr crushes
The chestnut-husk at the chestnut-root.

And Pan by noon and Bacchus by night,
Fleeter of foot than the fleet-foot kid,
Follows with dancing and fills with delight
The Maenad and the Bassarid;°
And soft as lips that laugh and hide
110    The laughing leaves of the trees divide,
And screen from seeing and leave in sight
The god pursuing, the maiden hid.

Thracian the locus of horror in the Procne-Philomela story; the "tongueless vigil" is that of Procne's sister, Philomela
bows bent Artemis as huntress
most fleet Artemis was swiftest of the gods.

that loses short days of winter
oat shepherd's pipe made of oat straws
Bassarid Maenad and Bassarid are alternative names for female followers of Dionysus.

The ivy falls with the Bacchanal's° hair
   Over her eyebrows hiding her eyes;
The wild vine slipping down leaves bare
   Her bright breast shortening into sighs;
The wild vine slips with the weight of its leaves,
But the berried ivy catches and cleaves
To the limbs that glitter, the feet that scare
120     The wolf that follows, the fawn that flies.

. . .

CHORUS
Who hath given man speech? or who hath set therein
A thorn for peril and a snare for sin?
1040  For in the word his life is and his breath,
   And in the word his death,
That madness and the infatuate heart may breed
   From the word's womb the deed
And life bring one thing forth ere all pass by,
Even one thing which is ours yet cannot die—
Death. Hast thou seen him ever anywhere,
Time's twin-born brother, imperishable as he
Is perishable and plaintive, clothed with care
   And mutable as sand,
1050  But death is strong and full of blood and fair
And perdurable and like a lord of land?
Nay, time thou seest not, death thou wilt not see
Till life's right hand be loosened from thine hand
   And thy life-days from thee.

For the gods very subtly fashion
   Madness with sadness upon earth:
Not knowing in any wise compassion,
   Nor holding pity on any worth;
And many things they have given and taken,
1060    And wrought and ruined many things;
The firm land have they loosed and shaken,
   And sealed the sea with all her springs;
They have wearied time with heavy burdens
   And vexed the lips of life with breath:
Set men to labour and given them guerdons,°
   Death, and great darkness after death:
Put moans into the bridal measure
   And on the bridal wools a stain;
And circled pain about with pleasure,
1070    And girdled pleasure about with pain;

Bacchanal's another name for Maenad or Bas-    guerdons rewards
sarid, based on Bacchus, alternate name of
Dionysus

And strewed one marriage-bed with tears and fire
For extreme loathing and supreme desire.

What shall be done with all these tears of ours?
   Shall they make watersprings in the fair heaven
To bathe the brows of morning? or like flowers
Be shed and shine before the starriest hours,
   Or made the raiment of the weeping Seven?°
Or rather, O our masters, shall they be
Food for the famine of the grievous sea,
1080    A great well-head of lamentation
Satiating the sad gods? or fall and flow
Among the years and seasons to and fro,
   And wash their feet with tribulation
And fill them full with grieving ere they go?
   Alas, our lords, and yet alas again,
Seeing all your iron heaven is gilt as gold
   But all we smite thereat in vain;
Smite the gates barred with groanings manifold,
   But all the floors are paven with our pain.
1090 Yea, and with weariness of lips and eyes,
With breaking of the bosom, and with sighs,
   We labour, and are clad and fed with grief
And filled with days we would not fain behold
And nights we would not hear of; we wax old,
   All we wax old and wither like a leaf.
We are outcast, strayed between bright sun and moon;
   Our light and darkness are as leaves of flowers,
Black flowers and white, that perish; and the noon
   As midnight, and the night as daylight hours.
1100    A little fruit a little while is ours,
      And the worm finds it soon.

But up in heaven the high gods one by one
   Lay hands upon the draught that quickeneth,
Fulfilled with all tears shed and all things done,
   And stir with soft imperishable breath
   The bubbling bitterness of life and death,
And hold it to our lips and laugh; but they
   Preserve their lips from tasting night or day,
Lest they too change and sleep, the fates that spun,
1110 The lips that made us and the hands that slay;
   Lest all these change, and heaven bow down to none,
Change and be subject to the secular sway
And terrene° revolution of the sun.

---

weeping Seven The Pleiades, group of seven stars in constellation Taurus, though only six are usually visible; in Greek mythology the Pleiades were the seven daughters of Atlas and Pleione. The eldest is the lost Pleiad, or star that cannot be seen. The sisters weep for being separated.
terrene earthly

Therefore they thrust it from them, putting time away.
I would the wine of time, made sharp and sweet
  With multitudinous days and nights and tears
  And many mixing savours of strange years,
Were no more trodden of them under feet,
  Cast out and spilt about their holy places:
1120 That life were given them as a fruit to eat
And death to drink as water; that the light
Might ebb, drawn backward from their eyes, and night
  Hide for one hour the imperishable faces.
That they might rise up sad in heaven, and know
Sorrow and sleep, one paler than young snow,
  One cold as blight of dew and ruinous rain;
Rise up and rest and suffer a little, and be
Awhile as all things born with us and we,
  And grieve as men, and like slain men be slain.

1130 For now we know not of them; but one saith
  The gods are gracious, praising God; and one,
When hast thou seen? or hast thou felt his breath
  Touch, nor consume thine eyelids as the sun,
Nor fill thee to the lips with fiery death?
  None hath beheld him, none
Seen above other gods and shapes of things,
Swift without feet and flying without wings,
  Intolerable, not clad with death or life,
  Insatiable, not known of night or day,
1140 The lord of love and loathing and of strife
  Who gives a star and takes a sun away;
Who shapes the soul, and makes her a barren wife
  To the earthly body and grievous growth of clay;
Who turns the large limbs to a little flame
  And binds the great sea with a little sand;
Who makes desire, and slays desire with shame;
  Who shakes the heaven as ashes in his hand;
Who, seeing the light and shadow for the same,
  Bids day waste night as fire devours a brand,
1150 Smites without sword, and scourges without rod;
  The supreme evil, God.°
Yea, with thine hate, O God, thou hast covered us,
  One saith, and hidden our eyes away from sight,
And made us transitory and hazardous,
  Light things and slight;
Yet have men praised thee, saying, He hath made man thus,
  And he doeth right.
Thou hast kissed us, and hast smitten; thou hast laid

**The supreme evil, God** Swinburne's most notorious line

Upon us with thy left hand life, and said,
<sup></sup>1160 Live: and again thou hast said, Yield up your breath,
And with thy right hand laid upon us death.
Thou hast sent us sleep, and stricken sleep with dreams,
    Saying, Joy is not, but love of joy shall be;
Thou hast made sweet springs for all the pleasant streams,
    In the end thou hast made them bitter with the sea.
Thou hast fed one rose with dust of many men;
    Thou hast marred one face with fire of many tears;
Thou hast taken love, and given us sorrow again;
    With pain thou hast filled us full to the eyes and ears.
1170 Therefore because thou art strong, our father, and we
    Feeble; and thou art against us, and thine hand
Constrains us in the shallows of the sea
    And breaks us at the limits of the land;
Because thou hast bent thy lightnings as a bow,
    And loosed the hours like arrows; and let fall
Sins and wild words and many a wingèd woe
    And wars among us, and one end of all;
Because thou hast made the thunder, and thy feet
    Are as a rushing water when the skies
1180 Break, but thy face as an exceeding heat
    And flames of fire the eyelids of thine eyes;
Because thou art over all who are over us;
    Because thy name is life and our name death;
Because thou art cruel and men are piteous,
    And our hands labour and thine hand scattereth;
Lo, with hearts rent and knees made tremulous,
    Lo, with ephemeral lips and casual breath,
    At least we witness of thee ere we die
That these things are not otherwise, but thus;
1190    That each man in his heart sigheth, and saith,
        That all men even as I,
All we are against thee, against thee, O God most high.

But ye, keep ye on earth
    Your lips from over-speech,
Loud words and longing are so little worth;
    And the end is hard to reach.
For silence after grievous things is good,
    And reverence, and the fear that makes men whole,
And shame, and righteous governance of blood,
1200    And lordship of the soul.
But from sharp words and wits men pluck no fruit,
And gathering thorns they shake the tree at rest;
    For words divide and rend;
But silence is most noble till the end.

1865

# Hymn to Proserpine°

*After the Proclamation in Rome of the Christian Faith*

Vicisti, Galilaee°

I have lived long enough, having seen one thing, that love hath an end;
Goddess and maiden and queen, be near me now and befriend.
Thou art more than the day or the morrow, the seasons that laugh or that weep;
For these give joy and sorrow; but thou, Prosperpina, sleep.
Sweet is the treading of wine,° and sweet the feet of the dove;°
But a goodlier gift is thine than foam of the grapes or love.
Yea, is not even Apollo, with hair and harpstring of gold,
A bitter God to follow, a beautiful God to behold?
I am sick of singing: the bays° burn deep and chafe: I am fain
10   To rest a little from praise and grievous pleasure and pain.
For the Gods we know not of, who give us our daily breath,
We know they are cruel as love or life, and lovely as death.
O Gods dethroned and deceased, cast forth, wiped out in a day!
From your wrath is the world released, redeemed from your chains, men say.
New Gods are crowned in the city; their flowers have broken your rods;
They are merciful, clothed with pity, the young compassionate Gods.
But for me their new device is barren, the days are bare;
Things long past over suffice, and men forgotten that were.
Time and the Gods are at strife; ye dwell in the midst thereof,
20   Draining a little life from the barren breasts of love.
I say to you, cease, take rest; yea, I say to you all, be at peace,
Till the bitter milk of her breast and the barren bosom shall cease.
Wilt thou yet take all, Galilean? but these thou shalt not take,
The laurel, the palms and the paean, the breasts of the nymphs in the brake;
Breasts more soft than a dove's, that tremble with tenderer breath;
And all the wings of the Loves, and all the joy before death;
All the feet of the hours that sound as a single lyre,
Dropped and deep in the flowers, with strings that flicker like fire.
More than these wilt thou give, things fairer than all these things?
30   Nay, for a little we live, and life hath mutable wings.
A little while and we die; shall life not thrive as it may?
For no man under the sky lives twice, outliving his day.
And grief is a grievous thing, and a man hath enough of his tears:

**Hymn to Proserpine** The chanter of this hymn is a 4th-century Roman poet, a follower of the ancient pagan faith, who foresees the rapid disappearance of the old religion after the Edict of Milan (313) has granted Christianity equal status in the Empire. Though there is deep spiritual defeat throughout the poem, it does not yield to Christianity so much as to the Heraclitean flux, i.e., the necessity for endless change, and to the speaker's overwhelming desire for oblivion, of which he makes Proserpine the goddess. Proserpine was the Queen of the dead; she was stolen from her mother, Ceres, by Pluto, the ruler of Hades, to be his bride.

**Vicisti, Galilaee** "You have conquered, Galilean"; supposedly said by the philosophic emperor Julian (331–63 A.D., called "the Apostate" by Christian chroniclers), after he received his death wound from a Christian. Julian, raised as a Christian, renounced Christianity for the old religion upon assuming the throne.

**treading of wine** worship of Bacchus
**dove** sacred to Venus
**bays** laurels, emblems of poetic achievement

Why should he labour, and bring fresh grief to blacken his years?
Thou hast conquered, O pale Galilean; the world has grown grey from thy breath;
We have drunken of things Lethean, and fed on the fullness of death.
Laurel is green for a season, and love is sweet for a day;
But love grows bitter with treason, and laurel outlives not May.
Sleep, shall we sleep after all? for the world is not sweet in the end;
40  For the old faiths loosen and fall, the new years ruin and rend.
Fate is a sea without shore, and the soul is a rock that abides;
But her ears are vexed with the roar and her face with the foam of the tides.
O lips that the live blood faints in, the leavings of racks and rods!
O ghastly glories of saints, dead limbs of gibbeted Gods!
Though all men abase them before you in spirit, and all knees bend,
I kneel not neither adore you, but standing, look to the end.
All delicate days and pleasant, all spirits and sorrows are cast
Far out with the foam of the present that sweeps to the surf of the past:
Waste water washes, and tall ships founder, and deep death waits:
50  Where beyond the extreme sea-wall, and between the remote sea-gates
Where, mighty with deepening sides, clad about with the seas as with wings,
And impelled of invisible tides, and fulfilled of unspeakable things,
White-eyed and poisonous-finned, shark-toothed and serpentine-curled
Rolls, under the whitening wind of the future, the wave of the world.
The depths stand naked in sunder behind it, the storms flee away;
In the hollow before it the thunder is taken and snared as a prey;
In its sides is the north-wind bound; and its salt is of all men's tears;
With light of ruin, and sound of changes, and pulse of years:
With travail of day after day, and with trouble of hour upon hour;
60  And bitter as blood is the spray; and the crests are as fangs that devour:
And its vapour and storm of its steam as the sighing of spirits to be;
And its noise as the noise in a dream; and its depth as the roots of the sea;
And the height of its heads as the height of the utmost stars of the air:
And the ends of the earth at the might thereof tremble, and time is made bare.
Will ye bridle the deep sea with reins, will ye chasten the high sea with rods?
Will ye take her to chain her with chains, who is older than all ye Gods?
All ye as a wind shall go by, as a fire shall ye pass and be past;
Ye are Gods, and behold, ye shall die, and the waves be upon you at last.
In the darkness of time, in the deeps of the years, in the changes of things,
70  Ye shall sleep as a slain man sleeps, and the world shall forget you for kings.
Though the feet of thine high priests tread where thy lords and our forefathers
    trod,
Though these that were Gods are dead, and thou being dead art a God,
Though before thee the throned Cytherean° be fallen, and hidden her head,
Yet thy kingdom shall pass, Galilean, thy dead shall go down to thee dead.
Of the maiden thy mother° men sing as a goddess with grace clad around;
Thou art crowned where another was king; where another was queen she is
    crowned.
Yea, once we had sight of another; but now she is queen, say these.

**Cytherean** Venus                    **maiden thy mother** the Virgin Mary

Not as thine, not as thine was our mother,° a blossom of flowering seas,
Clothed round with the world's desire as with raiment, and fair as the foam.
80 And fleeter than kindled fire, and a goddess, and mother of Rome.°
For thine came pale and a maiden, and sister to sorrow; but ours,
Her deep hair heavily laden with odour and colour of flowers,
White rose of the rose-white water, a silver splendour, a flame,
Bent down unto us that besought her, and earth grew sweet with her name.
For thine came weeping, a slave among slaves, and rejected; but she
Came flushed from the full-flushed wave, and imperial, her foot on the sea.
And the wonderful waters knew her, the winds and the viewless ways,
And the roses grew rosier, and bluer the sea-blue stream of the bays.
Ye are fallen, our lords, by what token? we wist° that ye should not fall.
90 Ye were all so fair that are broken; and one more fair than ye all.
But I turn to her still, having seen she shall surely abide in the end;
Goddess and maiden and queen, be near me now and befriend.
O daughter of earth, of my mother, her crown and blossom of birth,
I am also, I also, thy brother; I go as I came unto earth.°
In the night where thine eyes are as moons are in heaven, the night where thou
    art,
Where the silence is more than all tunes, where sleep overflows from the heart,
Where the poppies° are sweet as the rose in our world, and the red rose is white,°
And the wind falls faint as it blows with the fume of the flowers of the night,
And the murmur of spirits that sleep in the shadow of Gods from afar
100 Grows dim in thine ears and deep as the deep dim soul of a star,
In the sweet low light of thy face, under heavens untrod by the sun.
Let my soul with their souls find place, and forget what is done and undone.
Thou art more than the Gods who number the days of our temporal breath;
For these give labour and slumber; but thou, Proserpina, death.
Therefore now at thy feet I abide for a season in silence. I know
I shall die as my fathers died, and sleep as they sleep; even so.
For the glass of the years is brittle wherein we gaze for a span;
A little soul for a little bears up this corpse which is man.°
So long I endure, no longer; and laugh not again, neither weep.
110 For there is no God found stronger than death; and death is a sleep.
1862                                                           1866

# Hertha°

I am° that which began;
Out of me the years roll;
Out of me God and man;
I am equal and whole;
God changes, and man, and the form of them bodily; I am the soul.

Before ever land was,
Before ever the sea,
Or soft hair of the grass,
Or fair limbs of the tree,
10 Or the flesh-coloured fruits of my branches, I was, and thy soul was in me.

First life on my sources
First drifted and swam;
Out of me are the forces
That save it or damn;
Out of me man and woman, and wild-beast and bird; before God was, I am.

Beside or above me
Nought is there to go;
Love or unlove me,
Unknow me or know,
20 I am that which unloves me and loves; I am stricken, and I am the blow.°

I the mark that is missed
And the arrows that miss,
I the mouth that is kissed
And the breath in the kiss,
The search, and the sought, and the seeker, the soul and the body that is.

I am that thing which blesses
My spirit elate;
That which caresses
With hands uncreate
30 My limbs unbegotten that measure the length of the measure of fate.

But what thing dost thou now,
Looking Godward, to cry

**Hertha** This is Swinburne's central, doctrinal poem, in which the ancient northern earth goddess, patroness of fertility and growth, attempts to define her own nature. Highly eclectic in its sources (the principal ones are Blake, Emerson, Whitman, Victor Hugo, and even—alas—Sade), *Hertha* is a genuinely mythopoeic poem, and perhaps one in which Swinburne created something surprising even to himself. His working ideas in the poem are typical of a late 19th-century naturalistic world view, positivistic and evolutionary, but the emergent mythology is darker in its implications as to what lies beyond the pleasure principle, which Hertha nevertheless urges upon mankind. One critic, Cecil Lang, usefully describes *Hertha* as a deliberately static poem about growth, and Swinburne himself rated it first among his poems, "finding in it the most of lyric force and music combined with the most of condensed and clarified thought."
**I am** See the statement of Jesus in John 8:58: "Before Abraham was, I am" with its backward reference to Exodus 3:14: "And God said unto Moses, 'I AM THAT I AM'."
**I am the blow** l.l. 20–40 are very close to Emerson's *Brahma*.

'I am I, thou art thou,
I am low, thou art high'?
I am thou, whom thou seekest to find him; find thou but thyself, thou art I.

I the grain and the furrow,
The plough-cloven clod
And the ploughshare drawn thorough,
The germ and the sod,
⁴⁰   The deed and the doer, the seed and the sower, the dust which is God.

Hast thou known° how I fashioned thee,
Child, underground?
Fire that impassioned thee,
Iron that bound,
Dim changes of water, what thing of all these hast thou known of or found?

Canst thou say in thine heart
Thou hast seen with thine eyes
With what cunning of art
Thou wast wrought in what wise,
⁵⁰   By what force of what stuff thou wast shapen, and shown on my breast to the
skies?

Who hath given, who hath sold it thee,
Knowledge of me?
Hath the wilderness told it thee?
Hast thou learnt of the sea?
Hast thou communed in spirit with night? have the winds taken counsel with
thee?

Have I set such a star
To show light on thy brow
That thou sawest from afar
What I show to thee now?
⁶⁰   Have ye spoken as brethren together, the sun and the mountains and thou?

What is here, dost thou know it?
What was, hast thou known?
Prophet nor poet
Nor tripod° nor throne
Nor spirit nor flesh can make answer, but only thy mother alone.

Mother, not maker,
Born, and not made;°
Though her children forsake her,
Allured or afraid,

---

Hast thou known . . . Ll. 41–62 echo God's
Voice out of the whirlwind with its unanswer-
able questions, in Job 38–39.
tripod three-legged stool sat upon by the
priestess of the oracle at Delphi; hence priesthood in general
not made Nature evolves, and so there was no
single act of creation, as Judaism and Christianity insisted.

70 Praying prayers to the God of their fashion,° she stirs not for all that have
prayed.

A creed is a rod,°
And a crown is of night;°
But this thing is God,°
To be man with thy might,
To grow straight in the strength of thy spirit, and live out thy life as the light.

I am in thee to save thee,°
As my soul in thee saith;
Give thou as I gave thee,
Thy life-blood and breath,
80 Green leaves of thy labour, white flowers of thy thought, and red fruit° of thy
death.

Be the ways of thy giving
As mine were to thee;
The free life of thy living,
Be the gift of it free;
Not as servant to lord, nor as master to slave, shalt thou give thee to me.

O children of banishment,
Souls overcast,
Were the lights° ye see vanish meant
Always to last,
90 Ye would know not the sun overshining the shadows and stars overpast.

I that saw where ye trod
The dim paths of the night
Set the shadow called God
In your skies to give light;
But the morning of manhood is risen, and the shadowless soul is in sight.

The tree many-rooted°
That swells to the sky
With frondage red-fruited,
The life-tree am I;
100 In the buds of your lives is the sap of my leaves: ye shall live and not die.

But the Gods of your fashion
That take and that give,
In their pity and passion
That scourge and forgive,
They are worms that are bred in the back that falls off; they shall die and not
live.

fashion made by men's fears
rod instrument of chastisement
And a crown is of night ignorance begets kingship
God a humanist Godhead
save thee from religions and patriotisms
Green leaves . . . red fruit The green, white,
and red colors are a salute to the Italian flag,
and to Swinburne's hero Mazzini.
lights religions, particularly the varieties of
Christianity
many-rooted Yggdrasil, the ash world-tree of
northern myth

My own blood is what stanches
The wounds in my bark;
Stars° caught in my branches
Make day of the dark,
110    And are worshipped as suns till the sunrise shall tread out their fires as a spark.

Where dead ages hide under
The live roots of the tree,
In my darkness the thunder
Makes utterance of me;
In the clash of my boughs with each other ye hear the waves sound of the sea.

That noise is of Time,
As his feathers are spread
And his feet set to climb
Through the boughs overhead,
120    And my foliage rings round him and rustles, and branches are bent with his
tread.

The storm-winds of ages
Blow through me and cease,
The war-wind that rages,
The spring-wind of peace,
Ere the breath of them roughen my tresses, ere one of my blossoms increase.

All sounds of all changes,
All shadows and lights
On the world's mountain-ranges
And stream-riven heights,
130    Whose tongue is the wind's tongue and language of storm-clouds on earth-
shaking mights;

All forms of all faces,
All works of all hands
In unsearchable places
Of time-stricken lands,
All death and all life, and all reigns and all ruins, drop through me as sands.

Though sore be my burden
And more than ye know,
And my growth have no guerdon°
But only to grow,
140    Yet I fail not of growing for lightnings above me or death-worms below.

These too have their part in me,
As I too in these;
Such fire is at heart in me,
Such sap is this tree's,
Which hath in it all sounds and all secrets of infinite lands and of seas.

Stars false religions again                    guerdon reward

In the spring-coloured hours
    When my mind was as May's,
    There brake forth of me flowers
    By centuries of days,
150 Strong blossoms with perfume of manhood, shot out from my spirit as rays.

And the sound of them springing
    And smell of their shoots
    Were as warmth and sweet singing
    And strength to my roots;
And the lives of my children made perfect with freedom of soul were my fruits.

I bid you but be;
    I have need not of prayer;
    I have need of you free°
    As your mouths of mine air;
160 That my heart may be greater within me, beholding the fruits of me fair.

More fair than strange fruit is
    Of faiths ye espouse;
    In me only the root is
    That blooms in your boughs;
Behold now your God that ye made you, to feed him with faith of your vows.

In the darkening and whitening
    Abysses adored,
    With dayspring and lightning
    For lamp and for sword,
170 God thunders in heaven, and his angels are red with the wrath of the Lord.

O my sons, O too dutiful
    Toward Gods not of me,
    Was not I enough beautiful?
    Was it hard to be free?
For behold, I am with you, am in you and of you; look forth now and see.

Lo, winged with world's wonders,
    With miracles shod,
    With the fires of his thunders
    For raiment and rod,
180 God trembles in heaven, and his angels are white with the terror of God.

For his twilight° is come on him,
    His anguish is here;
    And his spirits gaze dumb on him,
    Grown grey from his fear;
And his hour taketh hold on him stricken, the last of his infinite year.

Thought made him and breaks him,
    Truth slays and forgives;

free but only of superstitions, not of Necessity    prophecy of the twilght of the gods by passing
twilight Christianity will fulfill the northern    away.

But to you, as time takes him,
This new thing it gives,
190 Even love, the beloved Republic, that feeds upon freedom and lives.

For truth only is living,
Truth only is whole,
And the love of his giving
Man's polestar and pole;
Man, pulse of my centre, and fruit of my body, and seed of my soul.

One birth of my bosom;
One beam of mine eye;
One topmost blossom
That scales the sky;
200 Man, equal and one with me, man that is made of me, man that is I.

1871

## Ave Atque Vale°

### In Memory of Charles Baudelaire

Nous devrions pourtant lui porter quelques fleurs;
Les morts, les pauvres morts, ont de grandes douleurs,
Et quand Octobre souffle, émondeur des vieux arbres,
Son vent mélancolique à l'entour de leurs marbres,
Certe, ils doivent trouver les vivants bien ingrats.°
Les Fleurs du Mal.

I

Shall I strew on thee rose or rue or laurel,°
Brother, on this that was the veil° of thee?
Or quiet sea-flower moulded by the sea,
Or simplest growth of meadow-sweet or sorrel,
Such as the summer-sleepy Dryads° weave,
Waked up by snow-soft sudden rains at eve?
Or wilt thou rather, as on earth before,
Half-faded fiery blossoms, pale with heat
And full of bitter summer, but more sweet

**Ave Atque Vale** Swinburne never met Charles Baudelaire, the poet of Les Fleurs du mal (Flowers of Evil) who died, aged 46, in 1867, but he admired him most among modern French poets, after his demi-god, Victor Hugo. Ave Atque Vale, though it deliberately echoes Baudelaire, is very much a poem in the tradition of English pastoral elegies, from Spenser's Astrophel on through Milton's Lycidas and their Romantic descendants in Shelley's Adonais and Arnold's Thyrsis. Swinburne is necessarily closest to Shelley's agnostic lament, but tries to go beyond Shelley by offering even less consolation, as in the immensely noble and stoic final stanza.

The title, Ave Atque Vale, is taken from the last line of Catullus' lament for his brother (Carmen 101): Atque in perpetuum, frater, ave atque vale (and now forever, brother, hail and farewell).

**Nous . . . ingrats** "Still, we ought to bring him some flowers. The dead, the unhappy dead, are very sorrowful, and when October blows its melancholy breath, pruning the old trees, around their tombs, surely they must discover that the living are truly ungrateful."

**rose . . . laurel** the rose is emblematic of love, rue of memory, the laurel of poetry
**veil** the body as covering, as in Shelley's poetry
**Dryads** wood nymphs

10  To thee than gleanings of a northern shore
      Trod by no tropic feet?


                II
      For always thee the fervid languid glories
        Allured of heavier suns in mightier skies;
        Thine ears knew all the wandering watery sighs
      Where the sea sobs round Lesbian promontories,
        The barren kiss of piteous wave to wave
        That knows not where is that Leucadian grave
      Which hides too deep the supreme head of song.°
        Ah, salt and sterile as her kisses were,
20      The wild sea winds her and the green gulfs bear
      Hither and thither, and vex and work her wrong,
        Blind gods that cannot spare.


                III
      Thou sawest, in thine old singing season, brother,
        Secrets and sorrows unbeheld of us:
        Fierce loves, and lovely leaf-buds poisonous,
      Bare to thy subtler eye, but for none other
        Blowing by night in some unbreathed-in clime;
        The hidden harvest of luxurious time,
      Sin without shape, and pleasure without speech;
30      And where strange dreams in a tumultuous sleep
        Make the shut eyes of stricken spirits weep;
      And with each face thou sawest the shadow on each,
        Seeing as men sow men reap.°


                IV
      O sleepless heart and sombre soul unsleeping,
        That were athirst for sleep and no more life
        And no more love, for peace and no more strife!
      Now the dim gods of death have in their keeping
        Spirit and body and all the springs of song,
        Is it well now where love can do no wrong,
40      Where stingless pleasure has no foam or fang
        Behind the unopening closure of her lips?
        Is it not well where soul from body slips
      And flesh from bone divides without a pang
        As dew from flower-bell drips?


                V
      It is enough; the end and the beginning
        Are one thing to thee, who art past the end.

**supreme head of song** the great poetess Sappho
of Lesbos, 7th century B.C., who according to
one tradition drowned herself by leaping from
the heights of the Ionian island Leucas
**as men . . . reap** Galatians 6:7

O hand unclasped of unbeholden friend,
For thee no fruits to pluck, no palms for willing,
  No triumph and no labour and no lust,
50    Only dead yew-leaves and a little dust.
O quiet eyes wherein the light saith nought,
  Whereto the day is dumb, nor any night
  With obscure finger silences your sight,
Nor in your speech the sudden soul speaks thought,
  Sleep, and have sleep for light.

VI

Now all strange hours and all strange loves are over,
  Dreams and desires and sombre songs and sweet,
  Hast thou found place at the great knees and feet
Of some pale Titan-woman° like a lover,
60    Such as thy vision here solicited,
  Under the shadow of her fair vast head,
The deep division of prodigious breasts,
  The solemn slope of mighty limbs asleep,
  The weight of awful tresses that still keep
The savour and shade of old-world pine-forests
  Where the wet hill-winds weep?

VII

Hast thou found any likeness for thy vision?
  O gardener of strange flowers, what bud, what bloom,
  Hast thou found sown, what gathered in the gloom?
70 What of despair, of rapture, of derision.
  What of life is there, what of ill or good?
  Are the fruits grey like dust or bright like blood?
Does the dim ground grow any seed of ours,
  The faint fields quicken any terrene° root,
  In low lands where the sun and moon are mute
And all the stars keep silence? Are there flowers
  At all, or any fruit?

VIII

Alas, but though my flying song flies after,
  O sweet strange elder singer, thy more fleet
80    Singing, and footprints of thy fleeter feet,
Some dim derision of mysterious laughter
  From the blind tongueless warders of the dead,
  Some gainless glimpse of Proserpine's veiled head,
Some little sound of unregarded tears
  Wept by effaced unprofitable eyes,
  And from pale mouths some cadence of dead sighs—

Titan-woman See Baudelaire's poem *La Géante*
(The Giantess).
terrene of the earth

These only, these the hearkening spirit hears,
  Sees only such things rise.

### IX

Thou art far too far for wings of words to follow,
90    Far too far off for thought or any prayer.
What ails us with thee, who art wind and air?
What ails us gazing where all seen is hollow?
  Yet with some fancy, yet with some desire,
  Dreams pursue death as winds a flying fire,
Our dreams pursue our dead and do not find.
  Still, and more swift than they, the thin flame flies,
  The low light fails us in elusive skies,
Still the foiled earnest ear is deaf, and blind
  Are still the eluded eyes.

### X

100  Not thee, O never thee, in all time's changes,
    Not thee, but this the sound of thy sad soul,
    The shadow of thy swift spirit, this shut scroll
I lay my hand on, and not death estranges
  My spirit from communion of thy song—
  These memories and these melodies that throng
Veiled porches of a Muse funereal—
  These I salute, these touch, these clasp and fold
  As though a hand were in my hand to hold,
Or through mine ears a mourning musical
110    Of many mourners rolled.

### XI

I among these, I also, in such station
  As when the pyre was charred, and piled the sods,
  And offering to the dead made, and their gods,
The old mourners had, standing to make libation,
  I stand, and to the gods and to the dead
  Do reverence without prayer or praise, and shed
Offering to these unknown, the gods of gloom,
  And what of honey and spice my seedlands bear,
  And what I may of fruits in this chilled air,
120  And lay, Orestes-like,° across the tomb
  A curl of severed hair.

### XII

But by no hand nor any treason stricken,
  Not like the low-lying head of Him, the King,°

**Orestes-like** Orestes, Agamemnon's son, gives
a tress of his hair in sacrifice to his dead father
in the first scene of *The Choëphoroe* (The Liba-
tion-Bearers) of Aeschylus.
**King** Agamemnon

The flame that made of Troy a ruinous thing,
Thou liest, and on this dust no tears could quicken
There fall no tears like theirs that all men hear
Fall tear by sweet imperishable tear
Down the opening leaves of holy poets' pages.
Thee not Orestes, not Electra° mourns;
130    But bending us-ward with memorial urns
The most high Muses that fulfil all ages
Weep, and our God's heart yearns.

XIII

For, sparing of his sacred strength, not often
Among us darkling here the lord of light°
Makes manifest his music and his might
In hearts that open and in lips that soften
With the soft flame and heat of songs that shine.
Thy lips indeed he touched with bitter wine,
And nourished them indeed with bitter bread;
140    Yet surely from his hand thy soul's food came,
The fire that scarred thy spirit at his flame
Was lighted, and thine hungering heart he fed
Who feeds our hearts with fame.

XIV

Therefore be too now at thy soul's sunsetting,
God of all suns and songs, he too bends down
To mix his laurel with the cypress° crown,
And save thy dust from blame and from forgetting.
Therefore he too, seeing all thou wert and art,
Compassionate, with sad and sacred heart,
150    Mourns thee of many his children the last dead,
And hallows with strange tears and alien sighs
Thine unmelodious mouth and sunless eyes,
And over thine irrevocable head
Sheds light from the under skies.

XV

And one weeps with him in the ways Lethean,°
And stains with tears her changing bosom chill:
That obscure Venus of the hollow hill,°
That thing transformed which was the Cytherean,°
With lips that lost their Grecian laugh divine
160    Long since, and face no more called Erycine;°
A ghost, a bitter and luxurious god.

Electra sister of Orestes, daughter of Agamemnon
lord of light Apollo
cypress tree of mourning
Lethean Lethe was the river of forgetfulness
in the underworld.
hollow hill the mountain of Venus where as an
enchantress she collects her victims in the
medieval story of the knight Tannhäuser
Cytherean Venus, who rose from the foam near
the island Cythera
Erycine another title of Venus, from Mt. Eryx
in Sicily, one of her several places of worship

Thee also with fair flesh and singing spell
Did she, a sad and second prey, compel
Into the footless places once more trod,
And shadows hot from hell.

### XVI

And now no sacred staff shall break in blossom,°
No choral salutation lure to light
A spirit sick with perfume and sweet night
And love's tired eyes and hands and barren bosom.
170 There is no help for these things; none to mend
And none to mar; not all our songs, O friend,
Will make death clear or make life durable.
Howbeit with rose and ivy and wild vine
And with wild notes about this dust of thine
At least I fill the place where white dreams dwell
And wreathe an unseen shrine.

### XVII

Sleep; and if life was bitter to thee, pardon,
If sweet, give thanks; thou hast no more to live;
And to give thanks is good, and to forgive.
180 Out of the mystic and the mournful garden
Where all day through thine hands in barren braid
Wove the sick flowers of secrecy and shade,
Green buds of sorrow and sin, and remnants grey,
Sweet-smelling, pale with poison, sanguine-hearted,
Passions that sprang from sleep and thoughts that started,
Shall death not bring us all as thee one day
Among the days departed?

### XVIII

For thee, O now a silent soul, my brother,
Take at my hands this garland, and farewell.
190 Thin is the leaf, and chill and wintry smell,
And chill the solemn earth, a fatal mother,
With sadder than the Niobean° womb,
And in the hollow of her breasts a tomb.
Content thee, howsoe'er, whose days are done;
There lies not any troublous thing before,
Nor sight nor sound to war against thee more,
For whom all winds are quiet as the sun,
All waters as the shore.
1868          1878

And now . . . blossom The miracle which almost saved Tannhäuser is not available for
Baudelaire; Tannhäuser, after a year as the
lover of Venus, quested for penance to Rome,
but absolution was refused by the pope until
the papal staff should burst into bloom. Soon

after Tannhäuser returned to Venus, the staff
began to flower.
Niobean All Niobe's children were slain by
Artemis and Apollo, to satisfy their jealous
mother, Leto, who resented Niobe's boast of
having had more children than Leto.

# A Forsaken Garden°

In a coign° of the cliff between lowland and highland,
　　At the sea-down's° edge between windward and lee,
Walled round with rocks as an inland island,
　　The ghost of a garden fronts the sea.
A girdle of brushwood and thorn encloses
　　The steep square slope of the blossomless bed
Where the weeds that grew green from the graves of its roses°
　　　　Now lie dead.

The fields fall southward, abrupt and broken,
10　　To the low last edge of the long lone land.
If a step should sound or a word be spoken,
　　Would a ghost not rise at the strange guest's hand?
So long have the grey bare walks lain guestless,
　　Through branches and briars if a man make way,
He shall find no life but the sea-wind's, restless
　　　　Night and day.

The dense hard passage is blind and stifled
　　That crawls by a track none turn to climb
To the strait waste place that the years have rifled
20　　Of all but the thorns that are touched not of time.
The thorns he° spares when the rose is taken;
　　The rocks are left when he wastes the plain.
The wind that wanders, the weeds wind-shaken,
　　　　These remain.

Not a flower to be pressed of the foot that falls not;
　　As the heart of a dead man the seed-plots are dry;
From the thicket of thorns whence the nightingale calls not,
　　Could she call, there were never a rose to reply.
Over the meadows that blossom and wither
30　　Rings but the note of a sea-bird's song;
Only the sun and the rain come hither
　　　　All year long.

The sun burns sere and the rain dishevels
　　One gaunt bleak blossom of scentless breath.
Only the wind here hovers and revels
　　In a round where life seems barren as death.
Here there was laughing of old, there was weeping,
　　Haply, of lovers none ever will know,
Whose eyes went seaward a hundred sleeping
40　　　　Years ago.

**A Forsaken Garden** a memory of a garden on
the Isle of Wight, where Swinburne lived as a
boy; the coast is sinking into the sea, which
now makes the garden a desolation; the vision
of absolute entropy and hopelessness here is
central to Swinburne

**coign** corner
**sea-down's** seashore dune of sand
**roses** sea-flowers
**he** presumably time

Heart handfast in heart as they stood, 'Look thither,'
  Did he whisper? 'look forth from the flowers to the sea;
For the foam-flowers endure when the rose-blossoms wither,
  And men that love lightly may die—but we?'
And the same wind sang and the same waves whitened,
  And or ever the garden's last petals were shed,
In the lips that had whispered, the eyes that had lightened,
  Love was dead.

Or they loved their life through, and then went whither?
50    And were one to the end—but what end who knows?
Love deep as the sea as a rose must wither,
  As the rose-red seaweed that mocks the rose.
Shall the dead take thought for the dead to love them?
  What love was ever as deep as a grave?
They are loveless now as the grass above them
  Or the wave.

All are at one now, roses and lovers,
  Not known of the cliffs and the fields and the sea.
Not a breath of the time that has been hovers
60    In the air now soft with a summer to be.
Not a breath shall there sweeten the seasons hereafter
  Of the flowers or the lovers that laugh now or weep,
When as they that are free now of weeping and laughter
  We shall sleep.

Here death may deal not again for ever;
  Here change may come not till all change end.
From the graves they have made they shall rise up never,
  Who have left nought living to ravage and rend.
Earth, stones, and thorns of the wild ground growing,
70    While the sun and the rain live, these shall be;
Till a last wind's breath upon all these blowing
  Roll the sea.

Till the slow sea rise and the sheer cliff crumble,
  Till terrace and meadow the deep gulfs drink,
Till the strength of the waves of the high tides humble
  The fields that lessen, the rocks that shrink,
Here now in his triumph where all things falter,
  Stretched out on the spoils that his own hand spread,
As a god self-slain on his own strange altar,
80    Death lies dead.
    1876      1878

# Sonnet for a Picture°

That nose is out of drawing. With a gasp,
  She pants upon the passionate lips that ache
  With the red drain of her own mouth, and make
A monochord of colour. Like an asp,
One lithe lock wriggles in his rutilant° grasp.
  Her bosom is an oven of myrrh,° to bake
  Love's white warm shewbread° to a browner cake.
The lock his fingers clench has burst its hasp.
The legs are absolutely abominable.
10   Ah! what keen overgust of wild-eyed woes
  Flags in that bosom, flushes in that nose?
Nay! Death sets riddles for desire to spell,
  Responsive. What red hem earth's passion sews,
But may be ravenously unripped in hell?

1880

# Poeta Loquitur°

If a person conceives an opinion
  That my verses are stuff that will wash,
Or my Muse has one plume on her pinion,
  That person's opinion is bosh.
My philosophy, politics, free-thought!
  Are worth not three skips of a flea,
And the emptiest of thoughts that can be thought
  Are mine on the sea.

In a maze of monotonous murmur
10   Where reason roves ruined by rhyme,
In a voice neither graver nor firmer
  Than the bells on a fool's cap chime,
A party pretentiously pensive,
  With a Muse that deserves to be skinned,
Makes language and metre offensive
  With rhymes on the wind.

A perennial procession of phrases
  Pranked primly, though pruriently prime,
Precipitates preachings on praises
20   In a ruffianly riot of rhyme

Sonnet for a Picture from Swinburne's anonymous volume *The Heptalogia, or the Seven Against Sense* . . . (1880). This is an unsparing parody of D. G. Rossetti's sonnets for pictures in *The House of Life*.
**rutilant** glowing or shining, with reddish or golden light
**myrrh** gum resin used in perfume and incense

**shewbread** 12 loaves placed every Sabbath before Jehovah, to be eaten by the priests alone at the end of the week
**Poeta Loquitur** "The Poet Speaks"; the greatest *deliberate* self-parody in the language, not published until after Swinburne's death. The last two (extra) stanzas were transcribed by Cecil Lang.

Through the pressure of print on my pages:
    But reckless the reader must be
Who imagines me one of the sages
    That steer through Time's sea.

Mad mixtures of Frenchified offal
    With insults to Christendom's creed,
Blind blasphemy, schoolboylike scoff, all
    These blazon me blockhead indeed.
I conceive myself obviously some one
30     Whose audience will never be thinned,
But the pupil must needs be a ruin one
    Whose teacher is wind.

In my poems, with ravishing rapture
    Storm strikes me and strokes me and stings:
But I'm scarcely the bird you might capture
    Out of doors in the thick of such things.
I prefer to be well out of harm's way
    When tempest makes tremble the tree,
And the wind with omnipotent arm-sway
40     Makes soap of the sea.

Hanging hard on the rent rags of others,
    Who before me did better, I try
To believe them my sisters and brothers,
    Though I know what a low lot am I.
The mere sight of a church sets me yelping
    Like a boy that at football is shinned!
But the cause must indeed be past helping
    Whose gospel is wind!

All the pale past's red record of history
50     Is dusty with damnable deeds;
But the future's mild motherly mystery
    Peers pure of all crowns and all creeds.
Truth dawns on time's resonant ruin,
    Frank, fulminant,° fragrant, and free:
And apparently this is the doing
    Of wind on the sea.

Fame flutters in front of pretension
    Whose flagstaff is flagrantly fine:
And it cannot be needful to mention
60     That such beyond question is mine.
Some singers indulging in curses,
    Though sinful, have splendidly sinned:
But my would-be maleficent verses
    Are nothing but wind.

**fulminant** explosive, thundering

[For freedom to swagger and scribble,
    In a style that's too silly for school,
At the heels of his betters to nibble,
    While flaunting the flag of a fool,
May to me seem the part of a poet,
70      But where out of Bedlam is he
Who can think that in struggling to show it
    I am not at sea?]

[I may think to get honour and glory at
    The rate of a comet of star,
By maligning the Muse of a Laureate,
    Or denouncing the deeds of a Czar.
But such rollicking rhymsters get duly
    (As schoolboys at football say) shinned,
When their Muse, as such trollops will truly,
80      Sails too near the wind.]
                1918


# The Lake of Gaube°

The sun is lord and god, sublime, serene,
    And sovereign on the mountains: earth and air
Lie prone in passion, blind with bliss unseen
    By force of sight and might of rapture, fair
    As dreams that die and know not what they were.
The lawns,° the gorges, and the peaks, are one
Glad glory, thrilled with sense of unison
In strong compulsive silence of the sun.

Flowers dense and keen as midnight stars aflame
10      And living things° of light like flames in flower
That glance and flash as though no hand might tame
    Lightnings whose life outshone their stormlit hour
    And played and laughed on earth, with all their power
Gone, and with all their joy of life made long
And harmless as the lightning life of song,
Shine sweet like stars when darkness feels them strong.

The deep mild purple flaked with moonbright gold
    That makes the scales seem flowers of hardened light,
The flamelike tongue, the feet that noon leaves cold,
20      The kindly trust in man, when once the sight
    Grew less than strange, and faith bade fear take flight,

**The Lake of Gaube** This end-of-the-century
poem recalls Swinburne's experience of the
*Lac de Gaube*, in the Pyrenees, near Cauterets,
nearly 40 years before. In his *Notes of Travel*
(1894), Swinburne vividly described the experience: ". . . the deliciously keen and exquisite

shock of a first plunge under its tempting and
threatening surface . . .", the temptation being
that of the ultimate masochism of suicide.
**lawns** opens spaces
**living things** salamanders, which in alchemical
tradition could live in fire

Outlive the little harmless life that shone
And gladdened eyes that loved it, and was gone
Ere love might fear that fear had looked thereon.

Fear held the bright thing hateful, even as fear,
    Whose name is one with hate and horror, saith
That heaven, the dark deep heaven of water near,
    Is deadly deep as hell and dark as death.°
    The rapturous plunge that quickens blood and breath
30  With pause more sweet than passion, ere they strive
To raise again the limbs that yet would dive
Deeper, should there have slain the soul alive.

As the bright salamander in fire of the noonshine exults and is glad his day,
The spirit that quickens my body rejoices to pass from the sunlight away,
To pass from the glow of the mountainous flowerage, the high multitudinous
    bloom,
Far down through the fathomless night of the water, the gladness of silence
    and gloom.
Death-dark and delicious as death in the dream of a lover and dreamer may be,
It clasps and encompasses body and soul with delight to be living and free:
Free utterly now, though the freedom endure but the space of a perilous breath,
40  And living, though girdled about with the darkness and coldness and strangeness
    of death:
Each limb and each pulse of the body rejoicing, each nerve of the spirit at rest,
All sense of the soul's life rapture, a passionate peace in its blindness blest.
So plunges the downward swimmer, embraced of the water unfathomed of man,
The darkness unplummeted, icier than seas in midwinter, for blessing or ban;
And swiftly and sweetly, when strength and breath fall short, and the dive is
    done,
Shoots up as a shaft from the dark depth shot, sped straight into sight of the sun;
And sheer through the snow-soft water, more dark than the roof of the pines
    above,
Strikes forth, and is glad as a bird whose flight is impelled and sustained of love.
As a sea-mew's love of the sea-wind breasted and ridden for rapture's sake
50  Is the love of his body and soul for the darkling delight of the soundless lake:
As the silent speed of a dream too living to live for a thought's space more
Is the flight of his limbs through the still strong chill of the darkness from shore
    to shore.
Might life be as this is and death be as life that casts off time as a robe,
The likeness of infinite heaven were a symbol revealed of the lake of Gaube.

            Whose thought has fathomed and measured
                The darkness of life and of death,
            The secret within them treasured,
                The spirit that is not breath?
            Whose vision has yet beholden
60              The splendour of death and of life?

death There was a local tradition that to bathe
in the lake of Gaube was certain to bring death.

Though sunset as dawn be golden,
Is the word of them peace, not strife?
Deep silence answers: the glory
We dream of may be but a dream,
And the sun of the soul wax hoary
As ashes that show not a gleam.
But well shall it be with us ever
Who drive through the darkness here,
If the soul that we live by never,
For aught that a lie saith, fear.

1899                    1904


# COVENTRY PATMORE

## To the Body°

Creation's and Creator's crowning good;
Wall of infinitude;
Foundation of the sky,
In Heaven forecast
And longed for from eternity,
Though laid the last;
Reverberating dome,
Of music cunningly built home
Against the void and indolent disgrace
10  Of unresponsive space;
Little, sequestered pleasure-house
For God and for His Spouse;
Elaborately, yea, past conceiving, fair,
Since, from the graced decorum of the hair,
Even to the tingling, sweet
Soles of the simple, earth-confiding feet,
And from the inmost heart
Outwards unto the thin
Silk curtains of the skin,
20  Every least part
Astonished hears
And sweet replies to some like region of the spheres;
Formed for a dignity prophets but darkly name,
Lest shameless men cry 'Shame!'
So rich with wealth concealed
That Heaven and Hell fight chiefly for this field;
Clinging to everything that pleases thee
With indefectible fidelity;

To the Body is an ode from Patmore's *The Unknown Eros.*

Alas, so true
30  To all thy friendships that no grace
Thee from thy sin can wholly disembrace;
Which thus 'bides with thee as the Jebusite,°
That, maugre° all God's promises could do,
The chosen People never conquered quite,
Who therefore lived with them,
And that by formal truce and as of right,
In metropolitan Jerusalem.
For which false fealty
Thou needs must, for a season, lie
40  In the grave's arms, foul and unshriven,
Albeit, in Heaven,
Thy crimson-throbbing Glow
Into its old abode aye pants to go,
And does with envy see
Enoch, Elijah, and the Lady,° she
Who left the lilies in her body's lieu.
Or, if the pleasure I have known in thee
But my poor faith's poor first-fruits be,
What quintessential, keen, ethereal bliss
50  Then shall be his
Who has thy birth-time's consecrating dew
For death's sweet chrism° retained,
Quick, tender, virginal, and unprofaned!
                                1877

# GERARD MANLEY HOPKINS

1844–1889

Of all Victorian poets, Hopkins has been the most misrepresented and overpraised by modern critics. He has been discussed as though his closest affinities were with Donne on the one side, and T. S. Eliot on the other. Yet his poetry stems directly from Keats and the Pre-Raphaelites, and the dominant influences upon his literary thought came from Ruskin and Pater. A disciple of Newman, he is as High Romantic as his master, and his best poetry, with all its peculiarities of diction and metric, is less of a departure from the Victorian norm than Browning's, or Swinburne's, or even Patmore's. His case is analogous to Emily Dickinson's. Published out of their own century, they became for a time pseudo-contemporaries of twentieth-century poets,

---

**Jebusite** See Joshua 15:63.
**maugre** in spite of
**the Lady** Like Enoch and Elijah, Mary the Mother was translated (carried over) soul and

body into Heaven; as the next line says, her tomb held lilies instead of her body.
**chrism** oil mixed with balm to anoint the dead

but perspectives later became corrected, and we learned to read both poets as very much involved in the literature and thought of their own generation. Hopkins was, in many of his attitudes, a representative Victorian gentleman; indeed he was as much a nationalistic jingo as Tennyson or Kipling, and his religious anguish is clearly related to a characteristic sorrow of his age. His more properly poetic anguish is wholly Romantic, like Arnold's, for it derives both from baffled or repressed sexual passion (possibly homosexual, in Hopkins) and from an incurably Romantic sensibility desperately striving not to be Romantic, but to make a return to a lost tradition. Hopkins quested for ideas of order that were not available to his poetic mind, and as a poet he ended in bitterness, convinced that he had failed his genius.

Hopkins was born on July 28, 1844, at Stratford in Essex, the eldest of nine children, into a very religious High Anglican family, of comfortable means. He did not enjoy his early school years, but flowered at Balliol College, Oxford, where he studied Classics from 1863 to 1867, and became a student of Walter Pater, who corrected his essays. In the atmosphere of the continuing Oxford Movement, Hopkins underwent a crisis, which came in March 1865 and resulted from meeting an enthusiastic, very young, and beautiful religious poet, Digby Dolben, who was to drown in June 1867 at the age of nineteen.

In 1866, under Newman's sponsorship, Hopkins was received into the Roman Catholic Church. Two years later, he began his Jesuit novitiate, and continued faithful to the Order until he died. Ordained a priest in 1877, he preached in Liverpool, taught at Stonyhurst, a Jesuit seminary, and from 1884 until his death in 1889 served as Professor of Greek at the Catholic University in Dublin. Though perfectly free to write poems and paint pictures, so far as his superiors in the Society of Jesus were concerned, Hopkins was a congenital self-torturer, and so much a Romantic that he found the professions of priest and poet to be mutually exclusive.

Much fuss has been made over Hopkins's poetic ideas, but in fact they were commonplaces of his century, and are surprising only in vocabulary, just as his poems are original only in diction and rhythm, but never in imagery or vision, or indeed in any observations upon the human condition. Austin Warren, one of Hopkins' best and most sympathetic critics, justly remarked that in Hopkins's most ambitious poems there is "a discrepancy between texture and structure: the copious, violent detail is matched by no corresponding intellectual or mythic vigor." Following Keats's advice to Shelley, that an artist must serve Mammon by loading every rift of his poem with ore, Hopkins sometimes went too far, and even a sympathetic reader can decide that the poems are overloaded. Some of the accusations made by modern criticism against Swinburne might be directed more accurately against Hopkins.

What then is Hopkins's achievement as poet? It remains considerable, for all the reservations that this editor has expressed, which are not so much directed at Hopkins as they are at an absurd critical tradition that has fastened to him. The original, almost incredible, accomplishment of Hopkins is to have made Keatsian poetry into a devotional mode, however strained. In the "Subtle Doctor," the Scottish Franciscan philosopher Duns Scotus (1265–1308), also an Oxonian, Hopkins found doctrine to reconcile a concern for individual form, for the "thisness" of people and natural things, with the universal truths of the church. Following his own understanding of Scotus, Hopkins coined the word "inscape" for every natural pattern he apprehended. "Instress," another coinage, meant for him the effect of each pattern upon his own imagination. Taken together, the terms are an attempt at scholasticizing Keats's fundamental approach to perception: detachment, the poet's recourse to nonidentity, Negative Capability.

Hopkins's accomplishment as an innovator is almost entirely technical, and no longer excites poets as it did some decades ago. Hopkins remained unpublished until his friend, the poet Robert Bridges, brought out a first edition of the poems in 1918, nearly thirty years after Hopkins's death. By chance, this first publication almost coincided with the start of the aggressive literary modernism that dominated British and American poetry until the 1950's, and Hopkins was acclaimed by poets and critics as the true continuator of English poetry in the otherwise benighted 19th century, and as a precursor who could help justify modern experiments in diction, metrics, and imagistic procedure. This produced some quaint interpretations of English literary history, and exaggerated the nature and importance of Hopkins's technical innovations.

Hopkins's diction adds to its Keatsian and Pre-Raphaelite base a large stock of language derived from his study of Welsh and Old English, and from an amorphous group of Victorian philologists who sought a "pure English," less contaminated by the Latin and French elements that are incurably part of the language. Hopkins's metric is best left to the specialists who delight in such matters, but simply it was based, as he said, upon nursery rhymes, the choruses of Milton's *Samson Agonistes,* and Welsh poetry. Against what he called the "running" or "common" rhythm of 19th-century poetry, Hopkins espoused "sprung rhythm," which he insisted was inherent in the English language, the older, purely accentual meter of Anglo-Saxon verse. Evidently, Hopkins read Keats's odes as having this rhythm, despite Keats's Spenserian smoothness.

Though Hopkins came to the study of Old English late, his essential metrical achievement was to revive the schemes of Old English poetry. But the main traditions of English poetic rhythm go from Chaucer to Spenser and Milton and on to the major Romantics, and Hopkins's archaizing return to Cynewulf and Langland, though influential for a time, now seems an honorable eccentricity. Nevertheless, its expressive effectiveness is undeniable. The metrical basis of many of Hopkins's poems is a fixed number of primary-stressed syllables, surrounded by a variable number of unstressed ones, or "outrides" as he called them. The alliterations of early Germanic poetry also work powerfully to recast the poetic line into a chain of rhythmic bursts. Thus, in "The Windhover," the first two lines each have five of Hopkins's beats (as opposed to five regularized, alternating, accentual-syllabic ones):

> I caught this mórning mórning's minión, kíng-
> dom of dáylight's daúphin, dapple-dáwn-drawn Fálcon, in his ríding . . .

But the first line has ten syllables, and might be mistaken for an iambic pentameter, while the second has sixteen; and we realize as we read through the poem that what is common to them, their *meter* rather than their individual rhythms, is the sequence of five major stresses. Moreover, the phrase "dapple-*dawn*-drawn" is so accented as to preserve the meaning "drawn by dappled dawn" through its interior rhyme and alliterative clusters. Hopkins's own invented metrical terminology is, like his other philosophical vocabulary, highly figurative: "hangers" or "outrides," "sprung rhythm," "counterpointing" (or superposition of rhythmic schemes), even the blended emotive-linguistic meanings of "stress" itself, all invoke the imagery of his poems, and are as subjective, in their interpretation of what was, after all, a fairly obvious neo-accentual technique, as are his metaphysical concepts.

# God's Grandeur

The world is charged with the grandeur of God.°
It will flame out, like shining from shook foil;°
It gathers to a greatness, like the ooze of oil°
Crushed. Why do men then now not reck his rod?°
Generations have trod, have trod, have trod;
And all is seared with trade; bleared, smeared with toil;
And wears man's smudge and shares man's smell: the soil
Is bare now, nor can foot feel, being shod.

And for all this, nature is never spent;
There lives the dearest freshness deep down things;
And though the last lights off the black West went
Oh, morning, at the brown brink eastward, springs—
Because the Holy Ghost over the bent
World broods with warm breast and with ah! bright wings.°

1877                                                          1918

# Spring

Nothing is so beautiful as Spring—
When weeds, in wheels, shoot long and lovely and lush;
Thrush's eggs look little low heavens, and thrush
Through the echoing timber does so rinse and wring
The ear, it strikes like lightnings to hear him sing;
The glassy peartree leaves and blooms, they brush
The descending blue; that blue is all in a rush
With richness; the racing lambs too have fair their fling.

What is all this juice and all this joy?
A strain of the earth's sweet being in the beginning
In Eden garden.—Have, get,° before it cloy,
Before it cloud, Christ, lord, and sour with sinning,
Innocent mind and Mayday in girl and boy,
Most, O maid's child,° thy choice and worthy the winning.

1877                                                          1918

grandeur of God "All things therefore are charged with love, are charged with God and if we know how to touch them give off sparks and take fire, yield drops and flow, ring and tell of him." Hopkins, *Sermons and Devotional Writings*, ed. Devlin, p. 195.
shook foil In a letter to Bridges, January 4, 1883, Hopkins explained: "I mean foil in its sense of leaf or tinsel . . . Shaken goldfoil gives off broad glares like sheet lightning . . .".
ooze of oil as in the process of crushing olives
Why do . . . rod Why do men now not recognize God's discipline?
bright wings See Luke 3:22, Genesis 1:2, and Milton, *Paradise Lost* I.19–22.
Have, get a plea to Christ to secure young minds before they "sour with sinning"
O maid's child Christ, as son of Mary

# The Windhover:°

### To Christ our Lord°

I caught° this morning morning's minion,° king-
dom of daylight's dauphin,° dapple-dawn-drawn°Falcon, in his riding
Of the rolling level underneath him steady air, and striding
High there, how he rung upon the rein° of a wimpling° wing
In his ecstasy! then off, off forth on swing,
    As a skate's heel sweeps smooth on a bow-bend: the hurl and gliding
Rebuffed the big wind. My heart in hiding
Stirred for a bird,—the achieve of, the mastery of the thing!

Brute beauty and valour and act, oh, air, pride, plume, here
10    Buckle!° AND° the fire that breaks from thee° then, a billion
Times told lovelier, more dangerous, O my chevalier!

No wonder of it: shéer plód makes plough down sillion°
Shine, and blue-bleak embers, ah my dear,°
Fall, gall themselves, and gash gold-vermilion.
1877                                   1918

# Pied Beauty°

Glory be to God for dappled things—
    For skies of couple-colour as a brinded° cow;
       For rose-moles all in stipple° upon trout that swim;
Fresh-firecoal chestnut-falls; finches' wings;
    Landscape plotted and pieced—fold, fallow, and plough;
       And áll trádes, their gear and tackle and trim.
All things counter, original, spare, strange;
    Whatever is fickle, freckled (who knows how?)
       With swift, slow; sweet, sour; adazzle, dim;
10 He fathers-forth whose beauty is past change:
                    Praise him.
1877                                   1918

**The Windhover** Hopkins thought this his best poem. The sparrow-hawk or kestrel can hover in the wind, even head-on.
**To Christ our Lord** a unique dedication in Hopkins; see "my chevalier" in line 11; there as here we are given a suggestion of chivalric, medieval service
**I caught** as in falconry
**minion** beloved
**dauphin** heir to the throne
**dapple-dawn-drawn** drawn out by the dappled dawns
**rung upon the rein** to check at rein's end, as in horse training
**wimpling** rippling
**Buckle!** a much-disputed word here; it may mean "to give way as if under stress," or it may mean "buckle on! fasten!," or even "get ready to fight!," or it may be some combination of these
**AND** Presumably the capitals here indicate an epiphany, or moment of breakthrough.
**thee** Christ our Lord
**sillion** furrow
**ah my dear** See George Herbert's "Love," II: "I the unkinde, ungratefull? Ah my deare, / I cannot look on thee," where "my dear" is Christ, as it is here.
**Pied Beauty** particolored or variegated beauty
**brinded** streaked
**stipple** colored dots

# Inversnaid°

This darksome burn,° horseback brown,
His rollrock highroad roaring down,
In coop° and in comb° the fleece of his foam
Flutes and low to the lake falls home.

A windpuff-bonnet of fáwn-fróth
Turns and twindles° over the broth
Of a pool so pitchblack, féll-frówning,
It rounds and rounds Despair to drowning.

Degged° with dew, dappled with dew
10  Are the groins of the braes° that the brook treads through,
Wiry heathpacks,° flitches° of fern,
And the beadbonny ash° that sits over the burn.

What would the world be, once bereft
Of wet and of wildness? Let them be left,
O let them be left, wildness and wet;
Long live the weeds and the wilderness yet.
1881                                    1918


# Spelt from Sibyl's Leaves°

Earnest, earthless, equal, attuneable,° | vaulty, voluminous, . . . stupendous
Evening strains° to be tíme's vást, | womb-of-all, home-of-all, hearse-of-all night.
Her fond yellow hornlight° wound° to the west, | her wild hollow hoarlight°
    hung to the height
Waste;° her earliest stars, earlstars, | stárs principal, overbend us,
Fíre-féaturing heaven. For earth | her being has unbound; her dapple° is at an
    end, as-
tray or aswarm, all throughther,° in throngs; | self ín self steepèd and páshed°—
    qúite
Disremembering,° dísmémbering | áll now. Heart, you round° me right

<br>

Inversnaid town in Scottish Highlands
burn Scots for stream
coop a hollow, an enclosed spot
comb crest of the water
twindles W. H. Gardner reads this as a portmanteau coinage combining "twists," "twitches,"
and "dwindles"; but it may mean "dwindling
into twins," dividing exactly in half.
Degged sprinkled
braes Scots for deep banks of river valley
heathpacks heather clumps
flitches bunches
beadbonny ash ash trees clustered like lovely
beads
Spelt from Sibyl's Leaves One of Hopkins's
darkest poems, this is technically a vision of
Apocalypse; the title tells us that the poet is
spelling out our condition by reading the leaves
scattered in the wind by the seeress or Sibyl at
Cumae, leaves upon which she has written her
prophecies. Gardner suggests, as hints Hopkins

took up, the *Aeneid* VI.11–12, 268–72, 539–
43, and the medieval Latin hymn by Thomas
of Celano, *Dies irae* ("Day of wrath, that
fearful day, / When all the earth shall pass
away, / as David and the Sibyl say").
attuneable harmonious, unlike more various daylight
strains seeks to become
hornlight either moonlight, or the light of the
setting sun
wound either "is wound up" or else "blown"
as in the "winding" or blowing of a horn
hoarlight bleak light, like hoar-frost
Waste wasteland of sky at night
dapple here a noun, evidently meaning a variety
of colors
throughther through-other
pashed fallen apart into formlessness
Disremembering forgetting
round whisper to, warn against

With:° Óur évening is over us; óur night | whélms, whélms, ánd will end us.
Only the beakleaved boughs dragonish | damask° the tool-smooth bleak light;
    black,°
10  Ever so black on it. Óur tale,° O óur oracle!° | Lét life, wáned, ah lét life wind
Off hér once skéined stained véined varíety | upon, áll on twó spools; párt, pen,
    páck°
Now her áll in twó flocks, twó folds—black, white; | right, wrong; reckon but,
    reck but, mind
But thése two: wáre° of a wórld where bút these | twó tell,° each off the óther;
    of a rack°
Where, selfwrung, selfstrung,° sheathe- and shelterless, | thóughts agaínst
    thoughts ín groans grínd.
1885                                                                                    1918


## (Carrion Comfort)°

Not, I'll not, carrion comfort, Despair, not feast on thee;
Not untwist—slack they may be—these last strands of man
In me ór, most weary, cry I can no more, I can;°
Can something, hope, wish day come, not choose not to be.

But ah, but O thou terrible,° why wouldst thou rude° on me
Thy wring-world° right foot rock?° lay a lionlimb against me? scan
With darksome devouring eyes my bruisèd bones? and fan,
O in turns of tempest, me heaped there; me frantic to avoid thee and flee?

Why? That my chaff might fly; my grain lie, sheer and clear.
10  Nay in all that toil, that coil, since (seems) I kissed the rod,
Hand rather,° my heart lo! lapped strength, stole joy, would laugh, chéer.
Cheer whom though? The hero° whose heaven-handling flung me, fóot tród
Me? or me° that fought him? O which one? is it each one? That night, that year
Of now done darkness I wretch lay wrestling° with (my God!)° my God.
1885                                                                                    1918

---

With the heart speaks, and gives the warning that follows
damask to make a complex pattern
black this may be a verb, to blacken
tale story, but it may be "tally," our sins numbered up
oracle presumably the Cumaen Sibyl
pack the parable of sheep and goats; let life part us into two groups, pen us down as one or the other, and then pack us into one of the two folds
ware be wary of, be aware of, beware of both this world and the one to come
tell add up
rack our world, but also perhaps a Hell to come, both seen as a rack or instrument of torture
selfstrung we string ourselves upon the rack, here and hereafter
(Carrion Comfort) Bridges gave the poem this title; the phrase defines religious despair, or feeding upon the corpse of one's own soul; Bridges thought this to be the sonnet of which Hopkins said: "If ever anything was written in blood, one of these was."
I can I can do more
O thou terrible not despair but Christ the Wrestler
rude violently
wring-world powerful enough to wring all the world
rock wouldst rock
Hand rather God's hand chastising Hopkins
hero Christ
Me? or me the first "me" passively accepts; the second wrestles
wrestling The great original is certainly Jacob wrestling with the Angel of God, Genesis 32: 24–30, in order to secure the blessing of the name "Israel."
(my God!) a horrified whisper at his own daring

## No Worst, There Is None

No worst, there is none.° Pitched past pitch° of grief,
More pangs will, schooled at forepangs,° wilder wring.
Comforter,° where, where is your comforting?
Mary, mother of us, where is your relief?
My cries heave, herds-long;° huddle in a main,° a chief-
woe, world-sorrow; on an age-old anvil wince and sing°—
Then lull, then leave off. Fury had shrieked 'No ling-
ering! Let me be fell:° force I must be brief.'
O the mind, mind has mountains; cliffs of fall
10 Frightful, sheer, no-man-fathomed. Hold them cheap
May who ne'er hung there. Nor does long our small
Durance° deal with that steep or deep. Here! creep,
Wretch, under a comfort serves in a whirlwind:° all
Life death does end and each day dies with sleep.
1885                                                      1918


## I Wake and Feel the Fell of Dark

I wake and feel the fell° of dark, not day.
What hours, O what black hoürs we have spent
This night! what sights you, heart, saw; ways you went!
And more must, in yet longer light's delay.

With witness I speak this. But where I say
Hours I mean years, mean life. And my lament
Is cries countless, cries like dead letters sent
To dearest him that lives alas! away.

I am gall, I am heartburn. God's most deep decree
10 Bitter would have me taste: my taste was me;
Bones built in me, flesh filled, blood brimmed the curse.

Selfyeast of spirit a dull dough sours.° I see
The lost are like this, and their scourge to be
As I am mine, their sweating selves; but worse.°
1885                                                      1918

---

**there is none** no greater agony than religious despair, like Satan on Mt. Niphates, at the opening of *Paradise Lost* IV
**Pitched past pitch** Made blacker than black? Thrown farther than grief can throw? Pitched as high in consciousness of self as to be beyond measurable pitch? Or perhaps all of these at once?
**schooled at forepangs** educated by earlier pangs
**Comforter** the Paraclete, the Holy Spirit
**herds-long** like a procession of abandoned sheep; the forsaken pastoral image is crucial in this context
**huddle in a main** bunch themselves together like terrified sheep
**wince and sing** like the keening of metal beaten out upon an anvil

**fell** savage, even malevolent
**Durance** strength, our capacity to endure
**whirlwind** the comfort that serves here as the sin of suicidal despair. It cannot hope to serve in this whirlwind (the poem's final terrible irony) for out of the whirlwind, as in the Book of Job, will come the voice of God demanding that Hopkins (Job) confront him.
**fell** evidently both adjective and noun; as adjective it means "evil," as non "hairy skin"
**sours** The subject of "sours" is "selfyeast" rather than "dough."
**but worse** He believes that the lost in Hell are in a worse condition than he is, but he just barely believes it.

686

# That Nature Is a Heraclitean Fire and of the Comfort of the Resurrection°

Cloud-puffball,° torn tufts, tossed pillows° | flaunt forth, then chevy° on an air-
built thoroughfare: heaven-roysterers, in gay-gangs° | they throng; they glitter
in marches.
Down roughcast, down dazzling whitewash,° | wherever an elm arches.
Shivelights° and shadowtackle° in long | lashes lace, lance, and pair.
Delightfully the bright wind boisterous | ropes, wrestles, beats° earth bare
Of yestertempest's creases; | in pool and rutpeel parches
Squandering ooze to squeezed | dough, crust, dust; stanches, starches
Squadroned masks° and manmarks | treadmire toil there
Footfretted in it. Million-fuelèd, | nature's bonfire° burns on.
10 But quench her bonniest, dearest | to her, her clearest-selvèd spark
Man, how fast his firedint,° | his mark on mind, is gone!
Both are in an unfathomable, all is in an enormous dark
Drowned. O pity and indig | nation! Manshape, that shone
Sheer off, disseveral,° a star, | death blots black out; nor mark
Is any of him at all so stark
But vastness blurs and time | beats level. Enough! the Resurrection,
A heart's-clarion! Away grief's gasping, | joyless days, dejection.
Across my foundering deck shone
A beacon, an eternal beam. | Flesh fade, and mortal trash
20 Fall to the residuary worm; | world's wildfire, leave but ash:
In a flash, at a trumpet crash,
I am all at once what Christ is, | since he was what I am, and
This Jack,° joke, poor potsherd,° | patch,° matchwood, immortal diamond,
Is immortal diamond.°

1888                    1918

---

**That nature . . . the Resurrection** The poem's
title contrasts an ancient but still prevalent
metaphysical materialism with the most spiritual
of events, Christ's Resurrection and the promised resurrection of mankind. Heraclitus (535–
475 B.C.) made fire the first element, and proclaimed that no single thing abides, but all
things flow, since all things are distinguished
from fire only through incessant strife which
divides them out of the fire.
**Cloud-puffball** reminding us of air and water,
and the instability of those elements
**tossed pillows** clouds
**chevy** scamper
**gay-gangs** See Whitman's "The Sleepers," 3:
"Onward we move! a gay gang of blackguards";
the influence of Walt Whitman was conceded
by Hopkins himself. Hopkins admired but
dreaded Whitman's poetry.
**whitewash** rain falling on leaves of the arching
elms

**Shivelights** splinters of light
**shadowtackle** trees outlined against the sky's
light, throwing a shadow like a ship's tackle
**beats** the wind's power striking the earth into
changes
**masks** impressions, as in plaster casts
**bonfire** original meaning: funeral pyre, or fire
of bones
**firedint** a coinage: fire-mark, the stamp of the
fire on man
**disseveral** another coinage: both disseveral and
several
**Jack** Everyman
**potsherd** broken pot, shard; see Isaiah 64:8:
". . . we are the clay, and thou our potter;
and we are all the work of thy hand."
**patch** fool
**diamond** the hardest substance made by the
Heraclitean fire that is Nature

# Thou Art Indeed Just, Lord°

Justus quidem tu es, Domine, si disputem tecum; verumtamen
justa loquar ad te: Quare via impiorum prosperatur? &c.°

Thou art indeed just, Lord, if I contend
With thee; but, sir, so what I plead is just.
Why do sinners' ways prosper? and why must
Disappointment all I endeavour end?

Wert thou my enemy, O thou my friend,
How wouldst thou worse, I wonder, than thou dost
Defeat, thwart me? Oh, the sots and thralls of lust
Do in spare hours more thrive than I that spend,

Sir, life upon thy cause. See, banks and brakes°
10  Now, leavèd how thick! lacèd they are again
With fretty chervil,° look, and fresh wind shakes

Them; birds build—but not I build; no, but strain,
Time's eunuch, and not breed one work that wakes.
Mine, O thou lord of life, send my roots rain.
1889                                    1918


# To R.B.°

The fine delight that fathers° thought; the strong
Spur, live and lancing like the blowpipe flame,
Breathes once and, quenchèd faster than it came,
Leaves yet the mind a mother of immortal song.

Nine months she then, nay years, nine years she long
Within her wears, bears, cares and combs° the same:
The widow of an insight lost she lives,° with aim
Now known and hand at work now never wrong.

Sweet fire the sire of muse, my soul needs this;
10  I want the one rapture of an inspiration
O then if in my lagging lines you miss

**Thou Art Indeed Just, Lord** a poem of creative despair, written in the last year of the poet's life
**Justus quidem . . . prosperatur? &c.** the Vulgate or Latin translation of Jeremiah 12:1. As the "&c" indicates, later parts of chap. 12 are employed in the rest of the sonnet; the poem's first three lines translate this epigraph.
**brakes** thickets
**fretty chervil** wild parsley with fringed (fretted) leaves

**R.B.** Robert Bridges, his close friend, later Poet Laureate, and first editor of Hopkins's poems. More than the other poems, this is Hopkins's lament for the waste and loss of his poetic gift.
**fathers** begets
**combs** the mind is a mother caring for the child
**she lives** close to Shelley's "the mind in creation is like a fading coal"; the inspiration goes, but the mind brings forth what the insight fathered

The roll, the rise, the carol, the creation,
My winter world, that scarcely breathes that bliss
Now, yields you, with some sighs, our explanation.
1889                              1918


# OTHER VICTORIAN POETS

These half-dozen poets are united only in being Victorian, having no Pre-Raphaelite connections, and in being significant without achieving major status, at least for their poetry alone. Mrs. Browning had an enormous contemporary reputation, and now survives only in her husband's work and in a handful of lyrics, of which "A Musical Instrument" is the best. Edward Lear is the greatest master of nonsense verse in the language, and Lewis Carroll and Emily Brontë are remembered for their very different prose fictions. Clough, a fine satirical poet and moving skeptical consciousness still receives little recognition for his talents. Finally, the second James Thomson (not to be confused with his 18th-century namesake) carries the poetic passion for affirmation of what might be called Christian unbelief rather farther even than Swinburne could manage.


**Elizabeth Barrett Browning** (1806–61) was born in Durham. Her unfortunate father, who has been immortalized as the villain in the most famous literary love affair of the 19th century, carries the stigma in addition of having derived his income from West Indian slave plantations. Educated at home, Miss Barrett became an invalid (for still mysterious reasons) from 1838 to 1846 when, Andromeda to Browning's Perseus, she eloped with the best poet of the age. Her long poem *Aurora Leigh* (1856) was much admired, even by Ruskin, but is very bad. Quite bad too are the famous *Sonnets from the Portuguese*, dedicated to Browning (who thought she looked Portuguese). Though the Brownings' married life was reasonably happy, Mrs. Browning's enthusiasms for Napoleon III, spiritualism, and dressing her only child, a son, as though he were a toy, all gave her husband much pain. She died in Florence, June 29, 1861, to her husband's great grief.


**Edward Lear** (1812–88), a delightful personality, was primarily a landscape painter who traveled to exotic climes (Sinai, Albania) to find subjects for his work. His first *A Book of Nonsense* (1864) was his best, featuring his marvelous limericks and his curious visionary nonsense lyrics which combine Shelley and Tennyson to produce mysterious, uneasy quest-poems of lost love that can be read as utterly cheerful madness. He died happy at San Remo in Italy, while at work illustrating the poems of his good friend Tennyson.

**Emily Brontë** (1818–48), born and raised at Haworth in Yorkshire, wrote only one novel, but that was *Wuthering Heights* (1847). She published her poems in a joint volume in 1846 with her novelist sisters, as *Poems by Currer, Ellis and Acton Bell* (Emily was Ellis). Many of those poems, as well as some published posthumously, were written for the Gondal Saga, a childlike vision of Byronic passion, that Emily Brontë never quite gave up. She died in 1848 of tuberculosis, aged only thirty.

**Arthur Hugh Clough** (1819–61) was born January 1, 1819, into a family of cotton merchants and bankers, in Liverpool. He spent five years of his childhood in South Carolina, and then attended Rugby and Balliol College, Oxford, becoming Matthew Arnold's close friend. In 1848, Clough resigned his Fellowship at Oriel College, Oxford, because he refused to subscribe to the Thirty-Nine Articles of the Church of England. He went to Paris to observe the 1848 revolution, with which he sympathized, and began to write his longer poems, of which the best are *Dipsychus* (finished in 1850, but not published in his lifetime) and *Amours de Voyage* (1858). A man of enormous talents, even larger doubts, and engaging personality, he was the close friend not only of Arnold and Thackeray, but of the Boston and Concord literary men of America— Emerson, Charles Eliot Norton, Longfellow, and Lowell—all of whom burdened him with excessive expectations (he had been Dr. Thomas Arnold's prize pupil). Clough's sardonic temper rebelled against these expectations, against the Arnoldian High Seriousness, and against all the pieties of the age. But the effort was too great for Clough; a broken man, and a self-accused failure, he subsided (in 1854) into a marriage with a cousin of the formidable Florence Nightingale, for whom he became a kind of glorified errand-boy. He died on November 13, 1861, in Florence, where he had gone for his health, and was mourned by Arnold in the pastoral elegy *Thyrsis*.

**Lewis Carroll** (1832–98) (pen-name of the mathematician Charles Lutwidge Dodgson), spent his life lecturing at Oxford. As a solitary eccentric, he was much given to the company of little girls, and to these Muses he wrote *Alice's Adventures in Wonderland* (1865), *Through the Looking-Glass* (1871), *The Hunting of the Snark* (1876), and *Silvie and Bruno* (1889–93), all of which have survived his *Symbolic Logic* (1896).

**James Thomson** (1834–82), who led the most miserable life of any Victorian poet, wrote his poems under the dark initials of "B.V.," for "Bysshe Vanolis," to signify his allegiance to two great Romantic poets, Shelley and Novalis, the pen-name of the German Romantic poet Friedrich Leopold von Hardenberg (1772–1801). Orphaned at eight, and desperately poor throughout his youth, Thomson was enrolled by his guardians as an army schoolmaster. Serving in Ireland, he fell in love with a Miss Matilda Weller, but her early death augmented his already intense melancholia. A sad but pungent atheist, suffering from alcoholism and depression mania, he kept himself going by courage and will. In 1874, he wrote his best but bleakest poem, *The City of Dreadful Night*, which was published in 1880. Despite George Meredith's kind encouragement, Thomson could restrain neither his depressions nor his drinking, and he died a street vagrant in London, in 1882, when he was forty-eight. Despite its unrelieved gloom, *The City of Dreadful Night* maintains a fine negative exuberance, and is a superb period-piece.

# ELIZABETH BARRETT BROWNING

## A Musical Instrument

What was he doing, the great god Pan,°
   Down in the reeds by the river?
Spreading ruin and scattering ban,°
Splashing and paddling with hoofs of a goat,
And breaking the golden lilies afloat
   With the dragon-fly on the river.

He tore out a reed, the great god Pan,
   From the deep cool bed of the river;
The limpid water turbidly ran,
And the broken lilies a-dying lay,
And the dragon-fly had fled away,
   Ere he brought it out of the river.

High on the shore sat the great god Pan
   While turbidly flowed the river;
And hacked and hewed as a great god can,
With his hard bleak steel at the patient reed,
Till there was not a sign of the leaf indeed
   To prove it fresh from the river.

He cut it short, did the great god Pan
   (How tall it stood in the river!),
Then drew the pith, like the heart of a man.
Steadily from the outside ring,
And notched the poor dry empty thing
   In holes, as he sat by the river.

'This is the way,' laughed the great god Pan
   (Laughed while he sat by the river),
'The only way, since gods began
To make a sweet music, they could succeed.'
Then, dropping his mouth to a hole in the reed,
   He blew in power by the river.

Sweet, sweet, sweet, O Pan!
   Piercing sweet by the river!
Blinding sweet, O great god Pan!
The sun on the hill forgot to die,
And the lilies revived, and the dragon-fly
   Came back to dream on the river.

Yet half a beast is the great god Pan,
   To laugh as he sits by the river,

---

the great god Pan Pan was the god of forest
life and pastoral life; a man from the waist up,
but a goat in his lower half; his name means
"all" and essentially he represented everything
that is vital.
ban ruin, destruction

Making a poet out of a man;
40    The true gods sigh for the cost and pain
For the reed which grows nevermore again
As a reed with the reeds in the river.
                                        1860


# EDWARD LEAR

## Incidents in the Life
## of My Uncle Arly°

I

O my agèd Uncle Arly!
Sitting on a heap of Barley
    Through the silent hours of night,—
Close beside a leafy thicket:—
On his nose there was a Cricket,—
In his hat a Railway-Ticket;—
    (But his shoes were far too tight.)


II

Long ago, in youth, he squandered
All his goods away, and wandered
    To the Tiniskoop-hills afar.
There on golden sunsets blazing,
Every evening found him gazing,—
Singing,—'Orb! you're quite amazing!
    How I wonder what you are!'


III

Like the ancient Medes and Persians,
Always by his own exertions
    He subsisted on those hills;—
Whiles,—by teaching children spelling,—
Or at times by merely yelling,—
Or at intervals by selling
    'Propter's Nicodemus Pills.'


IV

Later in his morning rambles
He perceived the moving brambles—
    Something square and white disclose;—
'Twas a First-Class Railway-Ticket;

Incidents . . . Uncle Arly a parody of Wordsworth's "Resolution and Independence"; cf.
below Lewis Carroll's "The White Knight's
Song" for a rival parody of the same indomitable leech-gatherer and his poetic questioner
who does not listen to any replies

But, on stooping down to pick it
Off the ground,—a pea-green Cricket
   Settled on my uncle's Nose.


     v
Never—never more,—oh! never,
Did that Cricket leave him ever,—
   Dawn or evening, day or night;—
Clinging as a constant treasure,—
Chirping with a cheerious measure,—
Wholly to my uncle's pleasure,—
    (Though his shoes were far too tight.)


     vi
So for three-and-forty winters,
Till his shoes were worn to splinters,
   All those hills he wandered o'er,—
Sometimes silent;—sometimes yelling;—
Till he came to Borley-Melling,
Near his old ancestral dwelling;—
    (But his shoes were far too tight.)


     vii
On a little heap of Barley
Died my agèd uncle Arly,
   And they buried him one night;—
Close beside the leafy thicket;—
There,—his hat and Railway-Ticket;—
There,—his ever-faithful Cricket;—
    (But his shoes were far too tight.)
         1895


# The Courtship of
# the Yonghy-Bonghy-Bò

     i
On the Coast of Coromandel
Where the early pumpkins blow,
In the middle of the woods
   Lived the Yonghy-Bonghy-Bò.
Two old chairs, and half a candle,—
One old jug without a handle,—
   These were all the worldly goods,
   In the middle of the woods,
   These were all the worldly goods,
Of the Yonghy-Bonghy-Bò,
Of the Yonghy-Bonghy-Bò.

II

Once, among the Bong-trees walking
    Where the early pumpkins blow,
        To a little heap of stones
    Came the Yonghy-Bonghy-Bò.
There he heard a Lady talking,
To some milk-white Hens of Dorking,—
    ' 'Tis the Lady Jingly Jones!
        On that little heap of stones
    Sits the Lady Jingly Jones!'
Said the Yonghy-Bonghy-Bò,
Said the Yonghy-Bonghy-Bò.

III

'Lady Jingly! Lady Jingly!
    Sitting where the pumpkins blow,
        Will you come and be my wife?'
    Said the Yonghy-Bonghy-Bò.
'I am tired of living singly,—
On this coast so wild and shingly,—
    I'm a-weary of my life:
        If you'll come and be my wife,
    Quite serene would be my life!'—
Said the Yonghy-Bonghy-Bò,
Said the Yonghy-Bonghy-Bò.

IV

'On this Coast of Coromandel,
    Shrimps and watercresses grow,
        Prawns are plentiful and cheap,'
    Said the Yonghy-Bonghy-Bò.
'You shall have my chairs and candle,
And my jug without a handle!—
    Gaze upon the rolling deep
        (Fish is plentiful and cheap)
    As the sea, my love is deep!'
Said the Yonghy-Bonghy-Bò,
Said the Yonghy-Bonghy-Bò.

V

Lady Jingly answered sadly,
    And her tears began to flow,—
        'Your proposal comes too late,
    Mr. Yonghy-Bonghy-Bò!
I would be your wife most gladly!'
(Here she twirled her fingers madly,)
    'But in England I've a mate!
        Yes! you've asked me far too late,
    For in England I've a mate,

Mr. Yonghy-Bonghy-Bò!
Mr. Yonghy-Bonghy-Bò!'

VI

'Mr. Jones—(his name is Handel,—
Handel Jones, Esquire, & Co.)
    Dorking fowls delights to send,
    Mr. Yonghy-Bonghy-Bò!
Keep, oh! keep your chairs and candle,
And your jug without a handle,—
        I can merely be your friend!
        —Should my Jones more Dorkings send,
        I will give you three, my friend!
    Mr. Yonghy-Bonghy-Bò!
    Mr. Yonghy-Bonghy-Bò!'

VII

'Though you've such a tiny body,
    And your head so large doth grow,—
    Though your hat may blow away,
    Mr. Yonghy-Bonghy-Bò!
Though you're such a Hoddy Doddy—
Yet I wish that I could modi-
        fy the words I needs must say!
        Will you please to go away?
        That is all I have to say—
    Mr. Yonghy-Bonghy-Bò!
    Mr. Yonghy-Bonghy-Bò!'

VIII

Down the slippery slopes of Myrtle,
    Where the early pumpkins blow,
    To the calm and silent sea
    Fled the Yonghy-Bonghy-Bò.
There, beyond the Bay of Gurtle,
Lay a large and lively Turtle;—
        'You're the Cove,' he said, 'for me
        On your back beyond the sea,
        Turtle, you shall carry me!'
    Said the Yonghy-Bonghy-Bò,
    Said the Yonghy-Bonghy-Bò.

IX

Through the silent-roaring ocean
    Did the Turtle swiftly go;
    Holding fast upon his shell
    Rode the Yonghy-Bonghy-Bò.
With a sad primæval motion
Towards the sunset isles of Boshen

Still the Turtle bore him well.
Holding fast upon his shell,
'Lady Jingly Jones, farewell!'
Sang the Yonghy-Bonghy-Bò,
Sang the Yonghy-Bonghy-Bò.

x

From the Coast of Coromandel,
Did that Lady never go;
On that heap of stones she mourns
For the Yonghy-Bonghy-Bò.
On that Coast of Coromandel,
In his jug without a handle
Still she weeps, and daily moans;
On that little heap of stones
To her Dorking Hens she moans,
For the Yonghy-Bonghy-Bò,
For the Yonghy-Bonghy-Bò.
1877

# EMILY BRONTË

## Stanzas

Often rebuked, yet always back returning
    To those first feelings that were born with me,
And leaving busy chase of wealth and learning
    For idle dreams of things which cannot be:

Today, I will seek not the shadowy region;
    Its unsustaining vastness waxes drear;
And visions rising, legion after legion,
    Bring the unreal world too strangely near.

I'll walk, but not in old heroic traces,
10    And not in paths of high morality,
And not among the half-distinguished faces,
    The clouded forms of long-past history.

I'll walk where my own nature would be leading—
    It ve es me to choose another guide—
Where t. e grey flocks in ferny glens are feeding,
    Where the wild wind blows on the mountainside.

What have those lonely mountains worth revealing?
    More glory and more grief than I can tell:
The earth that wakes one human heart to feeling
20    Can centre both the worlds of Heaven and Hell.
1850

# Last Lines

No coward soul is mine,
No trembler in the world's storm-troubled sphere;
I see Heaven's glories shine,
And faith shines equal, arming me from fear.

O God within my breast,
Almighty, ever-present Deity!
Life—that in me has rest,
As I—undying Life—have power in Thee!

Vain are the thousand creeds
10  That move men's hearts—unutterably vain;
Worthless as withered weeds,
Or idlest froth amid the boundless main,

To waken doubt in one
Holding so fast by Thine infinity;
So surely anchored on
The steadfast rock of immortality.

With wide-embracing love
Thy spirit animates eternal years,
Pervades and broods above,
20  Changes, sustains, dissolves, creates, and rears.

Though earth and man were gone,
And suns and universes ceased to be,
And Thou were left alone,
Every existence would exist in Thee.

There is not room for Death,
Nor atom that his might could render void;
Thou—Thou art Being and Breath,
And what that Thou art may never be destroyed.
1846                          1850

# ARTHUR HUGH CLOUGH
## The Latest Decalogue°

Thou shalt have one God only; who
Would be at the expense of two?
No graven images may be
Worshipped, except the currency:
Swear not at all; for for thy curse
Thine enemy is none the worse:

**The Latest Decalogue** the Ten Commandments
as Clough saw them lived by his contemporaries

At church on Sunday to attend
Will serve to keep the world thy friend:
Honour thy parents; that is, all
10    From whom advancement may befall:

Thou shalt not kill; but needst not strive
Officiously to keep alive:
Do not adultery commit;
Advantage rarely comes of it:
Thou shalt not steal; an empty feat,
When it's so lucrative to cheat:
Bear not false witness; let the lie
Have time on its own wings to fly:
Thou shalt not covet; but tradition
20    Approves all forms of competition.

The sum of all is, thou shalt love,
If any body, God above:
At any rate shall never labour
*More* than thyself to love thy neighbour.
1847                                    1862


# Say Not the Struggle Nought Availeth

Say not the struggle° nought availeth,
    The labour and the wounds are vain,
The enemy faints not, nor faileth,
    And as things have been, things remain.

If hopes were dupes, fears may be liars;
    It may be, in yon smoke concealed,
Your comrades chase e'en now the fliers,
    And, but for you, possess the field.

For while the tired waves, vainly breaking,
10    Seem here no painful inch to gain,
Far back through creeks and inlets making
    Came, silent, flooding in, the main,

And not by eastern windows only,
    When daylight comes, comes in the light,
In front the sun climbs slow, how slowly,
    But westward, look, the land is bright.
1849                                    1862

**struggle** Clough had supported the European
revolutions of 1848; he wrote this poem after
they had been defeated.

# From Dipsychus°

[SPIRIT'S SONG]

130   As I sat at the café, I said to myself,
They may talk as they please about what they call pelf,°
They may sneer as they like about eating and drinking,
But help it I cannot, I cannot help thinking
    How pleasant it is to have money, heigh ho!
    How pleasant it is to have money.

I sit at my table *en grand seigneur,*°
And when I have done, throw a crust to the poor;
Not only the pleasure, one's self, of good living,
But also the pleasure of now and then giving.
140     So pleasant it is to have money, heigh ho!
    So pleasant it is to have money.

It was but last winter I came up to Town,
But already I'm getting a little renown;
I make new acquaintance where'er I appear;
I am not too shy, and have nothing to fear.
    So pleasant it is to have money, heigh ho!
    So pleasant it is to have money.

I drive through the streets, and I care not a d—mn;
The people they stare, and they ask who I am;
150 And if I should chance to run over a cad,
I can pay for the damage if ever so bad.
    So pleasant it is to have money, heigh ho!
    So pleasant it is to have money.

We stroll to our box and look down on the pit,
And if it weren't low should be tempted to spit;
We loll and we talk until people look up,
And when it's half over we go out and sup.
    So pleasant it is to have money, heigh ho!
    So pleasant it is to have money.

160 The best of the tables and best of the fare—
And as for the others, the devil may care;
It isn't our fault if they dare not afford
To sup like a prince and be drunk as a lord.
    So pleasant it is to have money, heigh ho!
    So pleasant it is to have money.

**Dipsychus** This is Clough's sardonic version of *Faust* and consists of dialogues between "Dipsychus" (his Faust), whose name means "double-minded" or "of two minds," and a Spirit like Mephistopheles. The poem's high point is the following Spirit's song, which expresses a universal truth, and hits hard at Ruskin's *The Stones of Venice.*
**pelf** derogatory term for wealth
**en grand seigneur** as a noble lord

We sit at our tables and tipple champagne;
Ere one bottle goes, comes another again;
The waiters they skip and they scuttle about,
And the landlord attends us so civilly out.
170    So pleasant it is to have money, heigh ho!
So pleasant it is to have money.

It was but last winter I came up to town,
But already I'm getting a little renown;
I get to good houses without much ado,
Am beginning to see the nobility too.
So pleasant it is to have money, heigh ho!
So pleasant it is to have money.

O dear! what a pity they ever should lose it!
For they are the gentry that know how to use it;
180    So grand and so graceful, such manners, such dinners,
But yet, after all, it is we are the winners.
So pleasant it is to have money, heigh ho!
So pleasant it is to have money.

Thus I sat at my table *en grand seigneur,*
And when I had done threw a crust to the poor;
Not only the pleasure, one's self, of good eating,
But also the pleasure of now and then treating.
So pleasant it is to have money, heigh ho!
So pleasant it is to have money.

190    They may talk as they please about what they call pelf,
And how one ought never to think of one's self,
And how pleasures of thought surpass eating and drinking—
My pleasure of thought is the pleasure of thinking
How pleasant it is to have money, heigh ho!
How pleasant it is to have money.

(Written in Venice, but for all parts true,
'Twas not a crust I gave him, but a sou.°)

A gondola here, and a gondola there,
'Tis the pleasantest fashion of taking the air.
200    To right and to left; stop, turn, and go yonder,
And let us repeat, o'er the tide as we wander,
How pleasant it is to have money, heigh ho!
How pleasant it is to have money.

   Come, leave your Gothic, worn-out story,
   San Giorgio and the Redemptore;°
   I from no building, gay or solemn,

sou French penny
San Giorgio and the Redemptore Against Ruskin, the Spirit denounces not only Gothic architecture, but the Italian classic or Palladian style,
as exemplified by two great Renaissance Venetian churches, San Giorgio Maggiore and Red-
entore.

Can spare the shapely Grecian column.
'Tis not, these centuries four,° for nought
Our European world of thought
210   Hath made familiar to its home
The classic mind of Greece and Rome;
In all new work that would look forth
To more than antiquarian worth,
Palladio's° pediments and bases,
Or something such, will find their places:
Maturer optics don't delight,
In childish dim religious light,°
In evanescent vague effects
That shirk, not face, one's intellects;
220   They love not fancies fast betrayed,
And artful tricks of light and shade,
But pure form nakedly displayed,
And all things absolutely made.
The Doge's palace° though, from hence,
In spite of Ruskin's d——d pretence,
The tide now level with the quay,
Is certainly a thing to see.
We'll turn to the Rialto° soon;
One's told to see it by the moon.

230   A gondola here, and a gondola there,
'Tis the pleasantest fashion of taking the air.
To right and to left; stop, turn, and go yonder,
And let us repeat, o'er the flood as we wander,
    How pleasant it is to have money, heigh ho!
    How pleasant it is to have money.
    1850–51                    1865

centuries four since the Renaissance began
Palladio's Andrea Palladio, greatest architect
of the Italian 16th century

dim religious light a smack at Milton's *Il Penseroso*, l. 160
Doge's palace where Venice's rulers governed
Rialto bridge over Venice's Grand Canal

# LEWIS CARROLL
## (Charles Lutwidge Dodgson)

### Songs from Through the Looking-Glass

### Jabberwocky°

'Twas brillig,° and the slithy° toves°
Did gyre° and gimble° in the wabe;°
All mimsy° were the borogoves,°
And the mome° raths° outgrabe.°

'Beware the Jabberwock, my son!
The jaws that bite, the claws that catch!
Beware the Jubjub bird, and shun
The frumious° Bandersnatch!'

He took his vorpal sword in hand;
Long time the manxome foe he sought—
So rested he by the Tumtum tree,
And stood awhile in thought.

And, as in uffish thought he stood,
The Jabberwock, with eyes of flame,
Came whiffling through the tulgey wood,
And burbled as it came!

One, two! One, two! And through and through
The vorpal blade went snicker-snack!
He left it dead, and with its head
He went galumphing back.

'And hast thou slain the Jabberwock?
Come to my arms, my beamish boy
O frabjous day! Callooh! Callay!'
He chortled in his joy.

'Twas brillig, and the slithy toves
Did gyre and gimble in the wabe;

---

**Jabberwocky** The definitions following are those given by Humpty Dumpty in *Through the Looking-Glass,* except for the last, which comes from the "Preface" to *The Hunting of the Snark.*
**brillig** ". . . four o'clock in the afternoon . . . when you begin *broiling* things for dinner"
**slithy** ". . . 'Lithe and slimy.' 'Lithe' is the same as 'active'. . . like a portmanteau . . . two meanings packed up into one word"
**toves** ". . . something like badgers—they're something like lizards—and they're something like corkscrews . . . they make their nests under sundials—also they live on cheese."
**gyre** ". . . to go round and round like a gyroscope. . . ."
**gimble** ". . . to make holes like a gimlet."
**wabe** "the grass plot round a sundial . . . be-

cause it goes a long way before it, and a long way behind it——" "And a long way beyond it on each side. . . ."
**mimsy** ". . .'flimsy and miserable'. . . ."
**borogove** ". . . a thin, shabby-looking bird with its feathers sticking out all round—something like a live mop."
**mome** Here Humpty Dumpty said: " 'mome' I'm not certain about. I think it's short for 'from home'—meaning that they'd lost their way. . . ."
**raths** ". . . a sort of green pig. . . ."
**outgrabe** (past tense of "outgribe") ". . . 'outgribing' is something between bellowing and whistling, with a kind of sneeze in the middle. . . ."
**frumious** ". . . fuming" and "furious'. . . ."

All mimsy were the borogoves,
And the mome raths outgrabe.
1872

## The White Knight's Song°

*Haddock's Eyes* or *The Aged Aged Man*
or *Ways and Means* or *A-Sitting On A Gate*

I'll tell thee everything I can;
There's little to relate.
I saw an aged, aged man,
A-sitting on a gate.
'Who are you, aged man?' I said.
'And how is it you live?'
And his answer trickled through my head
Like water through a sieve.

He said 'I look for butterflies
10    That sleep among the wheat;
I make them into mutton-pies,
And sell them in the street.
I sell them unto men,' he said,
'Who sail on stormy seas;
And that's the way I get my bread—
A trifle, if you please.'

But I was thinking of a plan
To dye one's whiskers green,
And always use so large a fan
20    That it could not be seen.
So, having no reply to give
To what the old man said,
I cried, 'Come, tell me how you live!'
And thumped him on the head.

His accents mild took up the tale;
He said, 'I go my ways,
And when I find a mountain-rill,
I set it in a blaze;
And thence they make a stuff they call
30    Rowland's Macassar Oil—
Yet twopence-halfpenny is all
They give me for my toil.'

But I was thinking of a way
To feed oneself on batter,

**The White Knight's Son** Like Edward Lear's
"Incidents in the Life of My Uncle Arly," this
is a parody of Wordsworth's "Resolution and
Independence."

And so go on from day to day
    Getting a little fatter.
I shook him well from side to side,
    Until his face was blue;
'Come, tell me how you live,' I cried
40    'And what it is you do!'

He said, 'I hunt for haddocks' eyes
    Among the heather bright,
And work them into waistcoat-buttons
    In the silent night.
And these I do not sell for gold
    Or coin of silvery shine,
But for a copper halfpenny,
    And that will purchase nine.

'I sometimes dig for buttered rolls,
50    Or set limed twigs for crabs;
I sometimes search the grassy knolls
    For wheels of hansom-cabs.
And that's the way' (he gave a wink)
    'By which I get my wealth—
And very gladly will I drink
    Your Honour's noble health.'

I heard him then, for I had just
    Completed my design
To keep the Menai bridge from rust
60    By boiling it in wine.
I thanked him much for telling me
    The way he got his wealth,
But chiefly for his wish that he
    Might drink my noble health.

And now, if e'er by chance I put
    My fingers into glue,
Or madly squeeze a right-hand foot
    Into a left-hand shoe,
Or if I drop upon my toe
70    A very heavy weight,
I weep, for it reminds me so
    Of that old man I used to know—
Whose look was mild, whose speech was slow,
Whose hair was whiter than the snow,
Whose face was very like a crow,
With eyes, like cinders, all aglow,
Who seemed distracted with his woe,
Who rocked his body to and fro,

And mutttered mumblingly and low,
80   As if his mouth were full of dough,
Who snorted like a buffalo—
That summer evening long ago
A-sitting on a gate.
1872


# JAMES THOMSON

## *From* The City of Dreadful Night

### XIV

Large glooms were gathered in the mighty fane,°
   With tinted moongleams slanting here and there;
And all was hush—no swelling organ-strain,
   No chant, no voice or murmuring of prayer;
690   No priests came forth, no tinkling censers fumed,
And the high altar space was unillumed.

Around the pillars and against the walls
   Leaned men and shadows; others seemed to brood,
Bent or recumbent, in secluded stalls.
   Perchance they were not a great multitude
Save in that city of so lonely streets
Where one may count up every face he meets.

All patiently awaited the event
   Without a stir or sound, as if no less
700   Self-occupied, doomstricken, while attent.
   And then we heard a voice of solemn stress
From the dark pulpit, and our gaze there met
Two eyes which burned as never eyes burned yet—

Two steadfast and intolerable eyes
   Burning beneath a broad and rugged brow;
The head behind it of enormous size.
   And as black fir-groves in a large wind bow,
Our rooted congregation, gloom-arrayed,
By that great sad voice deep and full were swayed:

710   'O melancholy Brothers, dark, dark, dark!°
O battling in black floods without an ark!

---

fane temple, here a cathedral, but given over     dark, dark, dark See Milton's *Samson Agonistes*,
to a very different kind of sermon than is        l. 80.
customary

O spectral wanderers of unholy Night!
My soul hath bled for you these sunless years,
With bitter blood-drops running down like tears;
 Oh, dark, dark, dark, withdrawn from joy and light!

'My heart is sick with anguish for your bale;°
Your woe hath been my anguish; yea, I quail
 And perish in your perishing unblest.
And I have searched the heights and depths, the scope
720 Of all our universe, with desperate hope
 To find some solace for your wild unrest.

'And now at last authentic word I bring,
Witnessed by every dead and living thing;
 Good tidings of great joy for you, for all;
There is no God; no Fiend with names divine
Made us and tortures us; if we must pine,
 It is to satiate no Being's gall.

'It was the dark delusion of a dream,
That living Person conscious and surpreme,
730 Whom we must curse for cursing us with life;
Whom we must curse because the life He gave
Could not be buried in the quiet grave,
 Could not be killed by poison or by knife.

'This little life is all we must endure,
The grave's most holy peace is ever sure,
 We fall asleep and never wake again;
Nothing is of us but the moldering flesh,
Whose elements dissolve and merge afresh
 In earth, air, water, plants, and other men.

740 'We finish thus; and all our wretched race
Shall finish with its cycle, and give place
 To other beings, with their own time-doom;
Infinite æons ere our kind began;
Infinite æons after the last man
 Has joined the mammoth° in earth's tomb and womb.

'We bow down to the universal laws,
Which never had for man a special clause
 Of cruelty or kindness, love or hate;
If toads and vultures are obscene to sight,
750 If tigers burn with beauty and with might,°
 Is it by favour or by wrath of fate?

bale torment      If tigers . . . with might an allusion to Blake's
mammoth prehistoric beast   "The Tyger"

'All substance lives and struggles evermore
Through countless shapes continually at war,
    By countless interactions interknit;
If one is born a certain day on earth,
All times and forces tended to that birth,
    Not all the world could change or hinder it.

'I find no hint throughout the Universe
Of good or ill, of blessing or of curse;
760     I find alone Necessity Supreme;
With infinite Mystery, abysmal, dark,
Unlighted ever by the faintest spark
    For us the flitting shadows of a dream.

'O Brothers of sad lives; they are so brief;
A few short years must bring us all relief—
    Can we not bear these years of labouring breath?
But if you would not this poor life fulfill,
Lo, you are free to end it when you will,
    Without the fear of waking after death.'

770    The organ-like vibrations of his voice
    Thrilled through the vaulted aisles and died away;
    The yearning of the tones which bade rejoice
    Was sad and tender as a requiem lay;
Our shadowy congregation rested still
As brooding on that 'End it when you will.'
1870–74                            1874


# POETRY OF THE 'NINETIES

Yeats named the poets of the 'Nineties, who were the friends of his youth, the "Tragic Generation." In his cosmological book, *A Vision*, Yeats said of the phase of the moon which, he claimed, characterized the poet Ernest Dowson and the artist Aubrey Beardsley that in it self-hatred reached a height, and through this hatred there came the slow liberation of intellectual love. In his beautiful *Autobiographies*, Yeats gave the best account of the 'Nineties, as an apocalyptic time when the young aesthetes lived as though time must have a stop. The decade ended with Yeats's fine volume of lyrics *The Wind Among the Reeds*, which catches the irrational intensity of the moment at the end of a turbulent century.

This intensity is the particular mark of the doomed poets of the 'Nineties. The Aesthetic Movement in England began with Swinburne and Pater and the American expatriate painter James Whistler, and reached its height in the 'Nineties with the work of the novelist George Moore, with Oscar Wilde as playwright, critic, and conversationalist, with Beardsley the illustrator in such periodicals as *The Savoy* and *The*

*Yellow Book,* and with the work of what seemed a hopeful school of new poets that met as the Rhymers' Club. They included Dowson, Yeats, Arthur Symons, whose translations from the French Symbolists were influential, and Lionel Johnson, who was to write the best poem of the 'Nineties in his tragic "The Dark Angel." John Davidson, a Nietzschean Scots poet, hovered at the edges of this group. Except for one great ballad by Davidson, the powerfully proletarian "Thirty Bob a Week," and a few fine lyrics by Dowson and Johnson, only Yeats's early poetry seems today to have survived, of all the intensities of the 'Nineties. Wilde was a poor poet, though a superb critic and dazzling dramatist, and the other men of talent wasted themselves in dissipation, self-hatred, or sudden conversions to a Catholicism they could not hope to sustain. But this tragic decade retains a peculiar fascination, and is now inseparable from Yeats's heightening vision of it.

This section begins with **W. S. Gilbert's** (1836–1911) parody of Wilde as the Aesthetic poetaster Bunthorne in the comic opera *Patience* (1881). Gilbert, besides his light operas with Sir Arthur Sullivan, wrote the *Bab Ballads* (1869), a rather nasty volume of light verse. Though his parodic portrait of Wilde in his glory precedes the 'Nineties by a decade, it sets the scene.

A short biography of **Oscar Wilde** (1856–1900) is given elsewhere in this volume. His first volume, *Poems* (1881), was worthy of Gilbert's parody. As a writer of verse, Wilde was overwhelmed by influences of very nearly the whole Romantic tradition. Even *The Ballad of Reading Gaol,* given here in curtailed (and thus improved) form, his best poem, is altogether too haunted by Coleridge's *Ancient Mariner.* The prose poem "The Disciple," bitterly charming in itself, is given as one of the rare instances of a successful English domestication of a French literary form.

**John Davidson** (1857–1909), the son of a Scottish minister, came to London in 1889, where he led a life of fierce dreams and terrible poverty. His best volume was *Ballads and Songs,* from which "Thirty Bob a Week" is taken. He killed himself before completing a series of "Testaments," hortatory works proclaiming a new gospel of evolutionary selfishness.

**Ernest Dowson** (1867–1900), largely remembered now, like Lionel Johnson, because of Yeats's descriptions of him, was raised mostly in France. He left Oxford without a degree in 1887, and lived poorly as a translator, frequently drunk or drugged. He died in Paris, aged thirty-three, as the century ended. His best work is in *Verses* (1896), but there are excellent Horatian lyrics scattered throughout his books.

**Lionel Johnson** (1867–1902), the epitome of his generation, associated himself with the Irish literary movement though he was an Englishman. He came from a family with a long military tradition, and he could not come to terms with his own homosexuality, though he sought solace in the Roman Catholic Church in 1891. Although he was an excellent critic, whose book on Thomas Hardy (1894) is still useful, his overwhelming ambitions were poetic, but only "The Dark Angel" fully realizes his gifts.

# WILLIAM SCHWENK GILBERT

## Bunthorne's Song: The Aesthete°

If you're anxious for to shine in the high aesthetic line as a man of culture rare,
You must get up all the germs of the transcendental terms, and plant them everywhere.
You must lie upon the daisies, and discourse in novel phrases of your complicated state of mind
(The meaning doesn't matter if it's only idle chatter of a transcendental kind).
      And everyone will say,
      As you walk your mystic way,
'If this young man expresses himself in terms too deep for *me*,
Why, what a very singularly deep young man this deep young man must be!'

Be eloquent in praise of the very dull old days which have long since passed away.
10 And convince 'em, if you can, that the reign of good Queen Anne° was Culture's palmiest day.
Of course you will pooh-pooh whatever's fresh and new, and declare it's crude and mean.
For Art stopped short in the cultivated court of the Empress Josephine.°
      And everyone will say,
      As you walk your mystic way,
'If that's not good enough for him which is good enough for *me*,
Why, what a very cultivated kind of youth this kind of youth must be!'

Then a sentimental passion of a vegetable fashion must excite your languid spleen,
An attachment *à la* Plato for a bashful young potato, or a not-too-French French bean!
Though the Philistines° may jostle, you will rank as an apostle in the high aesthetic band,
20 If you walk down Piccadilly with a poppy or a lily in your medieval hand.
      And everyone will say,
      As you walk your flowery way,
'If he's content with a vegetable love, which would certainly not suit *me*,
Why, what a most particularly pure young man this pure young man must be!'
1881                         1881

---

**Bunthorne's . . . Aesthete** from *Patience*
**good Queen Anne** daughter of James II; born 1665, Queen of Great Britain 1702–14, patroness of the Tory writers
**Empress Josephine** Empress of the French

(1804–9) as wife of Napoleon
**Philistines** Biblical enemies of the Hebrews; popularized by Arnold as a term for middle-class hostility to high culture

# OSCAR WILDE

## The Disciple

When Narcissus° died the pool of his pleasure changed from a cup of sweet waters into a cup of salt tears, and the Oreads° came weeping through the woodland that they might sing to the pool and give it comfort.

And when they saw that the pool had changed from a cup of sweet waters into a cup of salt tears, they loosened the green tresses of their hair and cried to the pool and said, 'We do not wonder that you should mourn in this manner for Narcissus, so beautiful was he.'

'But was Narcissus beautiful?' said the pool.

'Who should know better than you?' answered the Oreads. 'Us did he ever pass by, but you he sought for, and would lie on your banks and look down at you, and in the mirror of your waters he would mirror his own beauty.'

And the pool answered, 'But I loved Narcissus because, as he lay on my banks and looked down at me, in the mirror of his eyes I saw ever my own beauty mirrored.'

1893

## From The Ballad of Reading Gaol°

I

He did not wear his scarlet coat,
   For blood and wine are red,
And blood and wine were on his hands
   When they found him with the dead,
The poor dead woman whom he loved,
   And murdered in her bed.

He walked amongst the Trial Men°
   In a suit of shabby grey;
A cricket cap was on his head,
   And his step seemed light and gay;
But I never saw a man who looked
   So wistfully at the day.

I never saw a man who looked
   With such a wistful eye
Upon that little tent of blue
   Which prisoners call the sky,
And at every drifting cloud that went
   With sails of silver by.

10

Narcissus beautiful youth who spurned the nymph Echo and fell in love with the reflection of his own face in a forest pool; as he could not satisfy this love, he pined away and changed into the flower named for him
Oreads mountain nymphs

Reading Gaol where Wilde was imprisoned in 1896–97. A soldier was executed there, for murder, on July 7, 1896; Wilde wrote the poem in France after his release.
Trial Men men who had been sentenced but whose verdict still might be appealed

I walked, with other souls in pain,
20    Within another ring,
And was wondering if the man had done
    A great or little thing,
When a voice behind me whispered low,
    'That fellow's got to swing.'

                .    .    .

                II
For oak and elm have pleasant leaves
    That in the spring-time shoot:
But grim to see is the gallows-tree,
    With its adder-bitten root,
And, green or dry, a man must die
    Before it bears its fruit!

The loftiest place is that seat of grace
    For which all worldlings try:
140    But who would stand in hempen band
    Upon a scaffold high,
And through a murderer's collar take
    His last look at the sky?

It is sweet to dance to violins
    When Love and Life are fair:
To dance to flutes, to dance to lutes
    Is delicate and rare:
But it is not sweet with nimble feet
    To dance upon the air!

150    So with curious eyes and sick surmise
    We watched him day by day,
And wondered if each one of us
    Would end the self-same way,
For none can tell to what red Hell
    His sightless soul may stray.

At last the dead man walked no more
    Amongst the Trial Men,
And I knew that he was standing up
    In the black dock's dreadful pen,
160    And that never would I see his face
    In God's sweet world again.

Like two doomed ships that pass in storm
    We had crossed each other's way:
But we made no sign, we said no word,
    We had no word to say;
For we did not meet in the holy night,
    But in the shameful day.

A prison wall was round us both,
  Two outcast men we were:
170 The world had thrust us from its heart,
  And God from out His care:
And the iron gin° that waits for Sin
  Had caught us in its snare.

    III

In Debtors' Yard° the stones are hard,
  And the dripping wall is high,
So it was there he took the air
  Beneath the leaden sky,
And by each side a Warder walked,
  For fear the man might die.

180 Or else he sat with those who watched
  His anguish night and day;
Who watched him when he rose to weep,
  And when he crouched to pray;
Who watched him lest himself should rob
  Their scaffold of its prey.

    .  .  .

And twice a day he smoked his pipe,
  And drank his quart of beer:
His soul was resolute, and held
  No hiding-place for fear;
He often said that he was glad
  The hangman's hands were near.

But why he said so strange a thing
  No Warder dared to ask:
200 For he to whom a watcher's doom
  Is given as his task,
Must set a lock upon his lips,
  And make his face a mask.

Or else he might be moved, and try
  To comfort or console:
And what should Human Pity do
  Pent up in Murderers' Hole?
What word of grace in such a place
  Could help a brother's soul?

    .  .  .

We tore the tarry rope to shreds°
  With blunt and bleeding nails;

gin trap
Debtors' Yard part of the exercise ground in
Reading Gaol, once used for debtors

rope to shreds Wilde was condemned to hard
labor; he tore ropes to shreds to produce oakum
used in calking vessels.

We rubbed the doors, and scrubbed the floors,
   And cleaned the shining rails:
220  And, rank by rank, we soaped the plank,
   And clattered with the pails.

We sewed the sacks, we broke the stones,
   We turned the dusty drill:
We banged the tins, and bawled the hymns,
   And sweated on the mill:
But in the heart of every man
   Terror was lying still.

So still it lay that every day
   Crawled like a weed-clogged wave:
230  And we forgot the bitter lot
   That waits for fool and knave,
Till once, as we tramped in from work,
   We passed an open grave.

With yawning mouth the yellow hole
   Gaped for a living thing;
The very mud cried out for blood
   To the thirsty asphalte ring:
And we knew that ere one dawn grew fair
   Some prisoner had to swing.

240  Right in we went, with soul intent
   On Death and Dread and Doom:
The hangman, with his little bag,
   Went shuffling through the gloom:
And each man trembled as he crept
   Into his numbered tomb.

That night the empty corridors
   Were full of forms of Fear,
And up and down the iron town
   Stole feet we could not hear,
250  And through the bars that hide the stars
   White faces seemed to peer.

He lay as one who lies and dreams
   In a pleasant meadow-land,
The watchers watched him as he slept,
   And could not understand
How one could sleep so sweet a sleep
   With a hangman close at hand.

But there is no sleep when men must weep
   Who never yet have wept:
260  So we—the fool, the fraud, the knave—
   That endless vigil kept,

And through each brain on hands of pain
  Another's terror crept.

.  .  .

    IV

There is no chapel on the day
  On which they hang a man:
The Chaplain's heart is far too sick,
  Or his face is far too wan,
280  Or there is that written in his eyes
  Which none should look upon.

So they kept us close till nigh on noon,
  And then they rang the bell,
And the Warders with their jingling keys
  Opened each listening cell,
And down the iron stair we tramped,
  Each from his separate Hell.

Out into God's sweet air we went,
  But not in wonted way,
290  For this man's face was white with fear,
  And that man's face was gray,
And I never saw sad men who looked
  So wistfully at the day.

I never saw sad men who looked
  With such a wistful eye
Upon that little tent of blue
  We prisoners called the sky,
And at every careless cloud that passed
  In happy freedom by.

.  .  .

The Warders strutted up and down,
  And kept their herd of brutes,
Their uniforms were spick and span,
  And they wore their Sunday suits,
But we knew the work they had been at,
  By the quicklime on their boots.

330  For where a grave had opened wide,
  There was no grave at all:
Only a stretch of mud and sand
  By the hideous prison-wall,
And a little heap of burning lime,
  That the man should have his pall.

.  .  .

For three long years they will not sow
  Or root or seedling there:

350 For three long years the unblessed spot
    Will sterile be and bare,
And look upon the wondering sky
    With unreproachful stare.

They think a murderer's heart would taint
    Each simple seed they sow.
It is not true! God's kindly earth
    Is kindlier than men know,
And the red rose would but blow more red,
    The white rose whiter blow.
1897                    1898


# JOHN DAVIDSON

## Thirty Bob° a Week

I couldn't touch a stop and turn a screw,
    And set the blooming world a-work for me
Like such as cut their teeth—I hope, like you—
    On the handle of a skeleton gold key;
I cut mine on a leek, which I eat it every week:
    I'm a clerk at thirty bob as you can see.

But I don't allow it's luck and all a toss;
    There's no such thing as being starred and crossed;
It's just the power of some to be a boss,
10      And the bally° power of others to be bossed:
I face the music, sir; you bet I ain't a cur;
    Strike me lucky if I don't believe I'm lost!

For like a mole I journey in the dark,
    A-travelling along the underground
From my Pillared Halls and broad Suburbean Park,
    To come the daily dull official round;
And home again at night with my pipe all alight,
    A-scheming how to count° ten bob a pound.

And it's often very cold and very wet,
20      And my missis stitches towels for a hunks;°
And the Pillared Halls is half of it to let—
    Three rooms about the size of travelling trunks.
And we cough, my wife and I, to dislocate a sigh,
    When the noisy little kids are in their bunks.

But you never hear her do a growl or whine,
    For she's made of flint and roses, very odd;
And I've got to cut my meaning rather fine,

**Bob** shilling
**bally** euphemism for "bloody"

**count** make it count for
**hunks** stingy old fellow

Or I'd blubber, for I'm made of greens and sod:
So p'r'aps we are in Hell for all that I can tell,
30    And lost and damn'd and served up hot to God.

I ain't blaspheming, Mr. Silver-tongue;
I'm saying things a bit beyond your art:
Of all the rummy starts you ever sprung,
Thirty bob a week's the rummiest start!
With your science and your books and your the'ries about spooks,
Did you ever hear of looking in your heart?

I didn't mean your pocket, Mr., no:
I mean that having children and a wife,
With thirty bob on which to come and go,
40    Isn't dancing to the tabor and the fife:
When it doesn't make you drink, by Heaven! it makes you think,
And notice curious items about life.

I step into my heart and there I meet
A god-almighty devil singing small,
Who would like to shout and whistle in the street,
And squelch the passers flat against the wall;
If the whole world was a cake he had the power to take,
He would take it, ask for more, and eat it all.

And I meet a sort of simpleton beside,
50    The kind that life is always giving beans;
With thirty bob a week to keep a bride
He fell in love and married in his teens:
At thirty bob he stuck; but he knows it isn't luck:
He knows the seas are deeper than tureens.

And the god-almighty devil and the fool
That meet me in the High Street on the strike,
When I walk about my heart a-gathering wool,
Are my good and evil angels if you like.
And both of them together in every kind of weather
60    Ride me like a double-seated bike.

That's rough a bit and needs its meaning curled.
But I have a high old hot un in my mind—
A most engrugious° notion of the world,
That leaves your lightning 'rithmetic behind—
I give it a glance when I say 'There ain't no chance,
Nor nothing of the lucky-lottery kind.'

And it's this way that I make it out to be:
No fathers, mothers, countries, climates—none;
Not Adam was responsible for me,
70    Nor society, not systems, nary one:

**engrugious** egregious, shocking

A little sleeping seed, I woke—I did, indeed—
A million years before the blooming sun.

I woke because I thought the time had come;
Beyond my will there was no other cause;
And everywhere I found myself at home,
Because I chose to be the thing I was;
And in whatever shape of mollusc or of ape
I always went according to the laws.

I was the love that chose my mother out;
80     I joined two lives and from the union burst;
My weakness and my strength without a doubt
Are mine alone for ever from the first:
It's just the very same with a difference in the name
As 'Thy will be done.' You say it if you durst!

They say it daily up and down the land
As easy as you take a drink, it's true;
But the difficultest go to understand,
And the difficultest job a man can do,
Is to come it brave and meek with thirty bob a week,
90     And feel that that's the proper thing for you.

It's a naked child against a hungry wolf;
It's playing bowls upon a splitting wreck;
It's walking on a string across a gulf
With millstones fore-and-aft about your neck;
But the thing is daily done by many and many a one;
And we fall, face forward, fighting, on the deck.

1894

# ERNEST DOWSON

## Non sum qualis eram bonae sub regno Cynarae°

Last night, ah, yesternight, betwixt her lips and mine
There fell thy shadow, Cynara! thy breath was shed
Upon my soul between the kisses and the wine;
And I was desolate and sick of an old passion,
    Yea, I was desolate and bowed my head:
I have been faithful to thee, Cynara! in my fashion.

All night upon mine heart I felt her warm heart beat,
Night-long within mine arms in love and sleep she lay;
Surely the kisses of her bought red mouth were sweet;
10     But I was desolate and sick of an old passion,

Non sum. . . Cynarae "I am not what once
I was under the reign of the kind Cynara"    Horace, Odes IV.i.3–4. Dowson's use of this as
title is a bitter irony.

When I awoke and found the dawn was gray:
I have been faithful to thee, Cynara! in my fashion.

I have forgot much, Cynara! gone with the wind,
Flung roses, roses riotously with the throng,
Dancing, to put thy pale, lost lilies out of mind;
But I was desolate and sick of an old passion,
    Yea, all the time, because the dance was long:
I have been faithful to thee, Cynara! in my fashion.

I cried for madder music and for stronger wine,
20    But when the feast is finished and the lamps expire,
Then falls thy shadow, Cynara! the night is thine;
And I am desolate and sick of an old passion,
    Yea, hungry for the lips of my desire:
I have been faithful to thee, Cynara! in my fashion.

                                          1896


## Extreme Unction°

Upon the eyes, the lips, the feet,
    On all the passages of sense,
The atoning oil is spread with sweet
    Renewal of lost innocence.

The feet, that lately ran so fast
    To meet desire, are soothly sealed;
The eyes, that were so often cast
    On vanity, are touched and healed.

From troublous sights and sounds set free;
10    In such a twilight hour of breath,
Shall one retrace his life, or see,
    Through shadows, the true face of death?

Vials of mercy! Sacring° oils!
    I know not where nor when I come,
Nor through what wanderings and toils,
    To crave of you Viaticum.°

Yet, when the walls of flesh grow weak,
    In such an hour, it well may be,
Through mist and darkness, light will break,
20    And each anointed sense will see.

                                          1899

# LIONEL JOHNSON°

## The Church of a Dream

Sadly the dead leaves rustle in the whistling wind,
Around the weather-worn, grey church, low down the vale:
The Saints in golden vesture shake before the gale;
The glorious windows shake, where still they dwell enshrined;
Old Saints by long-dead, shrivelled hands, long since designed:
There still, although the world autumnal be, and pale,
Still in their golden vesture the old Saints prevail;
Alone with Christ, desolate else, left by mankind.
Only one ancient Priest offers the Sacrifice,
10   Murmuring holy Latin immemorial:
Swaying with tremulous hands the old censer full of spice,
In grey, sweet incense clouds; blue, sweet clouds mystical:
To him, in place of men, for he is old, suffice
   Melancholy remembrances and vesperal.°

1890

## To Morfydd°

A voice on the winds,
A voice by the waters,
   Wanders and cries:
*Oh! what are the winds?*
*And what are the waters?*
   *Mine are your eyes!*

Western the winds are,
And western the waters,
   Where the light lies:
10   *Oh! what are the winds?*
*And what are the waters?*
   *Mine are your eyes!*

Cold, cold, grow the winds,
And wild grow the waters,
   Where the sun dies:
*Oh! what are the winds?*
*And what are the waters?*
   *Mine are your eyes!*

**The Church of a Dream** Another of Yeats's favorites, this is echoed in "Sailing to Byzantium" and more crucially in Yeats's last poem, "The Black Tower."
**vesperal** a little book or antiphonary containing the chants used at vespers (evening prayers)

**To Morfydd** Yeats thought this almost disembodied love lyric, to a probably imaginary Welsh girl, an "incomparable" poem. It is a deliberately knowing narcist's self-confrontation (see the refrain) and might have been written by Beddoes, like Johnson a homosexual struggling against his condition.

719

And down the night winds,
20    And down the night waters,
　　　The music flies:
　　　*Oh! what are the winds?*
　　　*And what are the waters?*
　　　*Cold be the winds,*
　　　*And wild be the waters,*
　　　　*So mine be your eyes!*
　　　　　1891

## The Dark Angel°

Dark Angel, with thine aching lust
To rid the world of penitence:°
Malicious Angel, who still dost
My soul such subtile violence!

Because of thee, no thought, no thing
Abides for me undesecrate:
Dark Angel, ever on the wing,
Who never reachest me too late!

When music sounds, then changest thou
10    Its silvery to a sultry fire:
Nor will thine envious heart allow
Delight untortured by desire.

Through thee, the gracious Muses turn
To Furies, O mine Enemy!
And all the things of beauty burn
With flames of evil ecstasy.°

Because of thee, the land of dreams
Becomes a gathering-place of fears:
Until tormented slumber seems
20    One vehemence of useless tears.

When sunlight glows upon the flowers,
Or ripples down the dancing sea:
Thou, with thy troop of passionate powers,
Beleaguerest, bewilderest me.

Within the breath of autumn woods,
Within the winter silences:

**The Dark Angel** Johnson's masterpiece, both
the most representative and the best poem of
the 'Nineties; the Dark Angel is a composite of
Satan, Johnson's shadow self, his homosexuality,
his idol Shelley, who had so passionately argued
against remorse, and also his other idol, Pater,
who had urged an intensity of aesthetic experience that Johnson could not sustain.

**To rid . . . penitence** Johnson's Shelleyan heritage; see Shelley's *The Revolt of Islam,* where
remorse is denounced repeatedly, as being only
"the dark idolatry of self"
**flames of evil ecstasy** Pater's "gem-like flame,"
but here found morally unacceptable

Thy venomous spirit stirs and broods,
O master of impieties!

The ardour of red flame is thine,
30  And thine the steely soul of ice:
Thou poisonest the fair design
Of nature, with unfair device.

Apples of ashes, golden bright;
Waters of bitterness, how sweet!
O banquet of a foul delight,
Prepared by thee, dark Paraclete.°

Thou art the whisper in the gloom,
The hinting tone, the haunting laugh:
Thou art the adorner of my tomb,
40  The minstrel of mine epitaph.

I fight thee, in the Holy Name!
Yet, what thou dost, is what God saith:°
Tempter! should I escape thy flame,
Thou wilt have helped my soul from Death:

The second Death, that never dies,°
That cannot die, when time is dead:
Live Death, wherein the lost soul cries,
Eternally uncomforted.

Dark Angel, with thine aching lust!
50  Of two defeats, of two despairs:°
Less dread, a change to drifting dust,
Than thine eternity of cares.

Do what thou wilt, thou shalt not so,
Dark Angel! triumph over me:
*Lonely, unto the Lone I go;*
*Divine, to the Divinity.*°
1893

**dark Paraclete** a parody of the Holy Spirit as comforter
**God saith** Like the Satan of Job, the Dark Angel is sanctioned by God to try Johnson.
**never dies** spiritual death, damnation
**two despairs** the first defeat and despair is the death-in-life of giving up homosexual love; the second is the Dark Angel's

**Lonely . . . Divinity** Ian Fletcher notes the source in Plotinus, *Enneads* VI. ix: "This, therefore, is the life of the Gods, and of divine and happy men, a liberation from all terrene concerns, a life unaccompanied with human pleasures, and a flight of the alone to the alone."

# Glossary

## A Commentary on Selected Literary and Historical Terms

**Allegory**   Literally, "other reading"; originally a way of interpreting a narrative or other text in order to extract a more general, or a less literal, meaning from it, e.g. reading Homer's *Odyssey* as the universal voyage of human life—with Odysseus standing for all men—which must be made toward a final goal. In the Middle Ages allegory came to be associated with ways of reading the Bible, particularly the Old Testament in relation to the New. In addition, stories came to be written with the intention of being interpreted symbolically; thus e.g. the *Psychomachia* or "battle for the soul" of Prudentius (b. 348 A.D.) figured the virtues and vices as contending soldiers in a battle (see *Personification*). There is allegorical lyric poetry and allegorical drama as well as allegorical narrative. In works such as Spenser's *The Faerie Queene* and Bunyan's *Pilgrim's Progress* allegory becomes a dominant literary form. See also *Figure*, under *Rhetoric; Type, Typology*.

**Alliteration**   A repeated initial consonant in successive words. In Old English verse, any vowel alliterates with any other, and alliteration is not an unusual or expressive phenomenon but a regularly recurring structural feature of the verse, occurring on the first and third, and often on the first, second, and third, primary-stressed syllables of the four-stressed line. Thus, from "The Seafarer":

> hréran mid hóndum hrimcælde sǽ
> ("to stir with his hand the rime-cold sea")

In later English verse tradition, alliteration becomes expressive in a variety of ways. Spenser uses it decoratively, or to link adjective and noun, verb and object, as in the line: "Much daunted with that dint, her sense was dazed." In the 18th and 19th centuries it becomes even less systematic and more "musical."

**Assonance**   A repeated vowel sound, a part-rhyme, which has great expressive effect when used internally (within lines), e.g. "An old, mad, blind, despised and dying king,—" (Shelley, "Sonnet: England in 1819").

**Baroque**   (1) Originally (and still), an oddly shaped rather than a spherical pearl, and hence something twisted, contorted, involuted. (2) By a complicated analogy, a term designating stylistic periods in art, music, and literature during the 16th and 17th centuries in Europe. The analogies among the arts are frequently strained, and the stylistic periods by no means completely coincide. But the relation between the poetry of Richard Crashaw in English and Latin, and the sculpture and architecture of Gianlorenzo Bernini (1598–1680), is frequently taken to typify the spirit of the baroque. (See Wylie Sypher, *Four Stages of Renaissance Style*, 1955.)

**Balade, Ballade**    The dominant lyric form in French poetry of the 14th and 15th centuries; a strict form consisting of three stanzas of eight lines each, with an *envoi* (*q.v.*), or four-line conclusion, addressing either a person of importance or a personification. Each stanza, including the *envoi*, ends in a refrain.

**Ballad Meter**    Or *common meter;* four-lined stanzas, rhyming *abab*, the first and third lines in iambic tetrameter (four beats), and the second and fourth lines in iambic trimeter (three beats). See *Meter*.

**Courtly Love**    Modern scholarship has coined this name for a set of conventions around which medieval love-poetry was written. It was essentially chivalric and a product of 12th-century France, especially of the troubadours. This poetry involves an idealization of the beloved woman, whose love, like all love, refines and ennobles the lover so that the union of their minds and/or bodies—a union that ought not to be apparent to others—allows them to attain excellence of character.

**Dada**    A satirical, anti-literary movement in European art and literature, 1916–21, its name having been selected to connote *nothing* (the movement's founders are in dispute over its method of selection). Dadaists engaged in a systematic nullification of reason, religion, and art itself, producing pictures and poems out of the random and the absurd, sculpture out of ordinary objects, and entertainments out of elaborately staged exhibitions that must have been alternately hilarious and tedious. Founded in Zurich by Tristan Tzara, Hans Arp, Hugo Ball, and Richard Huelsenbeck, Dada moved to Paris in 1919, took on a more international character, and was embraced by many young writers who would thereafter become attached to Surrealism (*q.v.*).

**Decorum**    Propriety of discourse; what is becoming in action, character, and style; the avoidance of impossibilities and incongruities in action, style, and character: "the good grace of everything after his kind" and the "great masterpiece to observe." More formally, a neoclassical doctrine maintaining that literary style—grand, or high, middle, and low—be appropriate to the subject, occasion, and genre. Thus Milton, in *Paradise Lost* (I.13–14), invokes his "adventurous song, / That with no middle flight intends to soar. . . ." See also *Rhetoric*.

**Dissenters**    In England, members of Protestant churches and sects that do not conform to the doctrines of the established Church of England; from the 16th century on, this would include Baptists, Puritans of various sorts within the Anglican Church, Presbyterians, Congregationalists, and (in the 18th century) Methodists. Another term, more current in the 19th century, is *Nonconformist*.

**Elegy**    Originally, in Greek and Latin poetry, a poem composed not in the hexameter lines of epic (*q.v.*) and, later, of pastoral, but in the elegiac couplets consisting of one hexameter line followed by a pentameter. Elegiac poetry was amatory, epigrammatic. By the end of the 16th century, English poets were using heroic couplets (*q.v.*), to stand for both hexameters and elegiacs; and an elegiac poem was any serious meditative piece. Perhaps because of the tradition of the pastoral elegy (*q.v.*), the general term "elegy" came to be reserved, in modern terminology, for an elaborate and formal lament, longer than a *dirge* or *threnody*, for a dead person. By extension, "elegiac" has come to mean, in general speech, broodingly sad.

**Enjambment**    The "straddling" of a clause or sentence across two lines of verse, as opposed to closed, or end-stopped, lines. Thus, in the opening lines of Shakespeare's *Twelfth Night:*

> If music be the food of love, play on!
> Give me excess of it, that, surfeiting
> The appetite may sicken and so die . . .

the first line is stopped, the second enjambed. When enjambment becomes strong or violent, it may have an ironic or comic effect.

**The Enlightenment**    A term used very generally, to refer to the late 17th and the 18th century in Europe, a period characterized by a programmatic rationalism—i.e. a belief in the ability of human reason to understand the world and thereby to transform whatever in it needed transforming; an age in which ideas of science and progress accompanied the rise of new philosophies of the relation of man to the state, an age which saw many of its hopes for human betterment fulfilled in the French Revolution.

**Envoi, Envoy**    Short concluding stanza found in certain French poetic forms and their English imitations, e.g. the *ballade* (*q.v.*). It serves as a dedicatory postscript, and a summing up of the poem of which it repeats the refrain.

**Epic**    Or, *heroic poetry;* originally, oral narrative delivered in a style different from that of normal discourse by reason of verse, music, and heightened diction, and concerning the great deeds of a central heroic figure, or group of figures, usually having to do with a crisis in the history of a race or culture. Its setting lies in this earlier "heroic" period, and it will often have been written down only after a long period of oral transmission. The Greek *Iliad* and *Odyssey* and the Old English *Beowulf* are examples of this, in their narration mixing details from both the heroic period described and the actual time of their own composition and narration. What is called *secondary* or *literary* epic is a long, ambitious poem, composed by a single poet on the model of the older, primary forms, and of necessity being more allusive and figurative than its predecessors. Homer's poems lead to Virgil's *Aeneid,* which leads to Milton's *Paradise Lost,* in a chain of literary dependency. Spenser's *Faerie Queene* might be called *romantic epic* of the secondary sort, and Dante's *Divine Comedy* might also be assimilated to post-Virgilian epic tradition.

**Epic Simile**    An extended comparison, in Homeric and subsequently in Virgilian and later epic poetry, between an event in the story (the *fable*) and something in the experience of the epic audience, to the effect of making the fabulous comprehensible in terms of the familiar. From the Renaissance on, additional complications have emerged from the fact that what is the familiar for the classical audience becomes, because of historical change, itself fabled (usually, pastoral) for the modern audience. Epic similes compare the fabled with the familiar usually with respect to one property or element; thus, in the *Odyssey*, when the stalwart forward motion of a ship in high winds is described, the simile goes:

> And as amids a fair field four brave horse
> Before a chariot, stung into their course
> With fervent lashes of the smarting scourge
> That all their fire blows high, and makes them rise
> To utmost speed the measure of their ground:
> So bore the ship aloft her fiery bound
> About whom rushed the billows, black and vast
> In which the sea-roars burst . . .
> *( Chapman translation )*

Notice the formal order of presentation: "even as . . .": *the familiar event, often described in detail;* "just so . . .": *the fabled one.*

**Epicureanism**    A system of philosophy founded by the Greek Epicurus (342–270 B.C.), who taught that the five senses are the sole source of ideas and sole criterion of truth, and that the goal of human life is pleasure (i.e. hedonism), though this can be achieved only by practicing moderation. Later the term came to connote bestial self-indulgence, which Epicurus had clearly rejected.

**Figurative Language**    In a general sense, any shift away from a literal meaning of words, brought about by the use of tropes (*q.v.*) or other rhetorical devices. See *Rhetoric*.

**Free Verse, Vers Libre**    Generally, any English verse form whose lines are measured neither by the number of 1) stressed syllables (see *Meter* §3, accentual verse), 2) alternations of stressed and unstressed syllables (§4, accentual-syllabic verse), nor syllables alone (§2, syllabic verse). The earliest English free verse —that of Christopher Smart in *Jubilate Agno* (18th century)—imitates the prosody of Hebrew poetry (reflected also in the translation of the English Bible), in maintaining unmeasured units marked by syntactic parallelism. While many free-verse traditions (e.g. that of Walt Whitman) remain close to the impulses of this biblical poetry, yet others, in the 20th century, have developed new *ad hoc* patternings of their own. *Vers libre* usually refers to the experimental, frequently very short unmeasured lines favored by poets of the World War I period, although the term, rather than the form, was adopted from French poetry of the 19th century.

**Gothic**    Term (originally pejorative, as alluding to the Teutonic barbarians) designating the architectural style of the Middle Ages. The revival of interest in medieval architecture in the later 18th century produced not only pseudo-Gothic castles like Horace Walpole's "Strawberry Hill", and more modest artificial ruins on modern estates, but also a vogue for atmospheric prose romances set in medieval surroundings and involving improbable terrors, and known as Gothic novels. The taste for the Gothic, arising during the Age of Sensibility (*q.v.*), is another reflection of a reaction against earlier 18th-century neoclassicism (*q.v*).

**Heroic Couplet**    In English prosody, a pair of rhyming, iambic pentameter lines, used at first for closure—as at the end of the Shakespearean sonnet (*q.v.*)— or to terminate a scene in blank-verse drama; later adapted to correspond in English poetry to the elegiac couplet of classical verse as well as to the heroic, unrhymed, Greek and Latin hexameter. Octosyllabic couplets, with four stresses (eight syllables) to the line, are a minor, shorter, jumpier form, used satirically unless in implicit allusion to the form of Milton's "Il Penseroso," in which they develop great lyrical power. (See *Meter.*)

**Irony**    Generally, a mode of saying one thing to mean another. *Sarcasm*, in which one means exactly the opposite of what one says, is the easiest and cheapest form; thus, e.g. "Yeah, it's a *nice day—*" when one means that it's a miserable one. But serious literature produces ironies of a much more complex and revealing sort. *Dramatic irony* occurs when a character in a play or story asserts something whose meaning the audience or reader knows will change in time. Thus, in Genesis when Abraham assures his son Isaac (whom he is about to sacrifice) that "God will provide his own lamb," the statement is lighted with dramatic irony when a sacrificial ram is actually provided at the last minute to save Isaac. Or, in the case of Sophocles' *Oedipus*, when almost everything the protagonist says about the predicament of his city is hideously ironic in view of the fact (which he does not know) that he is responsible therefor. The ironies generated by the acknowledged use of non-literal language (see *Rhetoric*) and fictions in drama, song, and narrative are at the core of imaginative literature.

**Kenning**    An Old Norse form designating, strictly, a condensed simile or metaphor of the kind frequently used in Old Germanic poetry; a figurative circumlocution for a thing not actually named—e.g. "swan's path" for sea; "world candle" or "sky-candle" for sun. More loosely, often used to mean also a metaphorical compound word or phrase such as "ring-necked" or "foamy-necked" for a ship, these being descriptive rather than figurative in character.

**Macaronic**    Verse in which two languages are mingled, usually for burlesque purposes.

**Meter**    Verse may be made to differ from prose and from ordinary speech in a number of ways, and in various languages these ways may be very different. Broadly speaking, lines of verse may be marked out by the following regularities of pattern:

1. *Quantitative Verse*, used in ancient Greek poetry and adopted by the Romans, used a fixed number of what were almost musical measures, called *feet;* they were built up of long and short syllables (like half- and quarter-notes in music), which depended on the vowel and consonants in them. *Stress accent* (the *word* stress which, when accompanied by vowel reduction, distinguishes the English noun "*content*" from the adjective "*content*") did not exist in ancient Greek, and played no part in the rhythm of the poetic line. Thus, the first line of the *Odyssey: Andra moi ennepe mousa, polytropon hos mala polla* ("Sing me, O muse, of that man of many resources who, after great hardship . . .") is composed in *dactyls* of one long syllable followed by two shorts (but, as in musical rhythm, replaceable by two longs, a *spondee*).

With six dactyls to a line, the resulting meter is called *dactylic hexameter* (*hexameter,* for short), the standard form for epic poetry. Other kinds of foot or measure were: the *anapest* ($\cup \cup -$); the *iamb* ($\cup -$); the *trochee* ($- \cup$); and a host of complex patterns used in lyric poetry. Because of substitutions, however, the number of syllables in a classical line was not fixed, only the number of measures.

2. *Syllabic Verse,* used in French, Japanese, and many other languages, and in English poetry of the mid-20th century, measures only the *number* of syllables per line with no regard to considerations of *quantity* or *stress.* Because of the prominence of stress in the English language, two lines of the same purely syllabic length may not necessarily sound at all as though they were in the same meter, e.g.:

> These two incommensurably sounding
> Lines are both written with ten syllables.

3. *Accentual Verse,* used in early Germanic poetry, and thus in Old English poetry, depended upon the number of strong *stress accents* per line. These accents were four in number, with no fixed number of unstressed. Folk poetry and nursery rhymes often preserve this accentual verse, e.g.:

> Sing, sing, what shall I sing?
> The cat's run away with the pudding-bag string

The first line has six syllables, the second, eleven, but they sound more alike (and not merely by reason of their rhyme) than the two syllabic lines quoted above.

4. *Accentual-Syllabic Verse,* the traditional meter of English poetry from Chaucer on, depends upon both numbered *stresses* and numbered *syllables,* a standard form consisting of ten syllables alternately stressed and un-stressed, and having five stresses; thus it may be said to consist of five syllable pairs.

For complex historical reasons, accentual-syllabic groups of stressed and unstressed syllables came to be known by the names used for Greek and Latin feet—which can be very confusing. The analogy was made between *long* syllables in the classical languages, and *stressed* syllables in English. Thus, the pair of syllables in the adjective "*content*" is called an *iamb,* and in the noun "*content,*" a *trochee;* the word "classical" is a *dactyll,* and the phrase "of the best," an *anapest.* When English poetry is being discussed, these terms are always used in their adapted, accentual-syllabic meanings, and hence the ten-syllable line mentioned earlier is called "iambic pentameter" in English. The phrase "high-tide" would be a *spondee* (as would, in general, two monosyllables comprising a proper name, e.g. "John Smith"); whereas compound nouns like "highway" would be *trochaic.* In this adaptation of classical nomenclature, the terms *dimeter, trimeter, tetrameter, pentameter, hexameter* refer not to the number of quantitative feet but to the number of syllable-groups (pairs or triplets, from one to six) composing the line. Iambic pentameter and tetrameter lines are frequently also called *decasyllabic* and *octosyllabic* respectively.

5. *Versification.* In verse, lines may be arranged in patterns called *stichic*

or *strophic*, that is, the same linear form (say, iambic pentameter) repeated without grouping by rhyme or interlarded lines of another form, or varied in just such a way into *stanzas* or *strophes* ("turns"). Unrhymed iambic pentameter, called *blank verse*, is the English stichic form that Milton thought most similar to classic hexameter or *heroic* verse. But in the Augustan period iambic pentameter rhymed pairs, called heroic couplets (*q.v.*), came to stand for this ancient form as well as for the classical elegiac verse (*q.v.*). Taking couplets as the simplest strophic unit, we may proceed to *tercets* (groups of three lines) and to *quatrains* (groups of four), rhymed *abab* or *abcb*, and with equal or unequal line lengths. Other stanzaic forms: *ottava rima*, an eight-line, iambic pentameter stanza, rhyming *abababcc; Spenserian stanza*, rhyming *ababbcbcc*, all pentameter save for the last line, an iambic hexameter, or *alexandrine*. There have been adaptations in English (by Shelley, notably, and without rhyme by T. S. Eliot) of the Italian *terza rima* used by Dante in *The Divine Comedy*, interlocking tercets rhyming *aba bcb cdc ded*, etc. More elaborate stanza forms developed in the texts of some Elizabethan songs and in connection with the ode (*q.v.*).

**Myth**    A primitive story explaining the origins of certain phenomena in the world and in human life, and usually embodying gods or other supernatural forces, heroes (men who are either part human and part divine, or are placed between an ordinary mortal and a divine being), men, and animals. Literature continues to incorporate myths long after the mythology (the system of stories containing them) ceases to be a matter of actual belief. Moreover, discarded beliefs of all sorts tend to become myths when they are remembered but no longer literally clung to, and are used in literature in a similar way. The classical mythology of the Greeks and Romans was apprehended in this literary, or interpreted, way, even in ancient times. The gods and heroes and their deeds came to be read as allegory (*q.v.*). During the Renaissance, *mythography*—the interpretation of myths in order to make them reveal a moral or historical significance (rather than merely remaining entertaining but insignificant stories)—was extremely important, both for literature and for painting and sculpture. In modern criticism, mythical or *archetypal* situations and personages have been interpreted as being central objects of the work of the imagination.

**Neoclassicism**    (1) In general the term refers to Renaissance and post-Renaissance attempts to model enterprises in the various arts on Roman and Greek originals—or as much as was known of them. Thus, in the late Renaissance, the architectural innovations of Andrea Palladio may be called "neoclassic," as may Ben Jonson's relation, and Alexander Pope's as well, to the Roman poet Horace. The whole Augustan period in English literary history (1660–1740) was a deliberately neoclassical one.

(2) More specifically, neoclassicism refers to that period in the history of all European art spanning the very late 18th and early 19th century, which period may be seen as accompanying the fulfillment, and the termination, of the Enlightenment (*q.v.*). In England such neoclassic artists as Henry Fuseli, John Flaxman, George Romney, and even, in some measure, William Blake, are close to the origins of pictorial and literary Romanticism itself.

**Neoplatonism**    See *Platonism*.
**Nonconformist**    See *Dissenters*.

**Octosyllabic Couplet**    See *Heroic Couplet; Meter*.
**Ode**    A basic poetic form, originating in Greek antiquity. The *choral ode* was a public event, sung and danced, at a large ceremony, or as part of the tragic and comic drama. Often called *Pindaric ode*, after a great Greek poet, the form consisted of *triads* (groups of three sections each). These were units of song and dance, and had the form *aab*—that is, a *strophe* (or "turn"), an *antistrophe* (or "counter-turn"), and an *epode* (or "stand"), the first two being identical musically and metrically, the third different. In English poetry, the Pindaric ode form, only in its metrical aspects, became in the 17th century a mode for almost essayistic poetic comment, and was often used also as a kind of cantata libretto, in praise of music and poetry (the so-called *musical ode*). By the 18th century the ode became the form for a certain kind of personal, visionary poem, and it is this form that Wordsworth and Coleridge transmitted to Romantic tradition. A second English form, known as *Horatian ode*, was based on the lyric (not choral) poems of Horace, and is written in *aabb* quatrains, with the last two lines shorter than the first two by a pair of syllables or more.

**Paradox**    In logic, a self-contradictory statement, hence meaningless (or a situation producing one), with an indication that something is wrong with the language in which such a situation can occur, e.g. the famous paradox of Epimenedes the Cretan, who held that all Cretans are liars (and thus could be lying if— and only if—he wasn't), or that of Zeno, of the arrow in flight: since at any instant of time the point of the arrow can always be said to be at one precise point, therefore it is continually at rest at a continuous sequence of such points, and therefore never moves. In literature, however, particularly in the language of lyric poetry, paradox plays another role. From the beginnings of lyric poetry, paradox has been deemed necessary to express feelings and other aspects of human inner states, e.g. Sappho's invention of the Greek word *glykypikron* ("bittersweet") to describe love, or her assertion that she was freezing and burning at the same time. So too the Latin poet Catullus, in his famous couplet

> I'm in hate and I'm in love; why do I? you may ask.
> Well, I don't know, but I feel it, and I'm in agony.

may be declaring thereby that true love poetry must be illogical.

In Elizabethan poetry, paradoxes were frequently baldly laid out in the rhetorical form called *oxymoron* (see *Rhetoric*), as in "the victor-victim," or across a fairly mechanical sentence structure, as in "My feast of joy is but a dish of pain." In the highest poetic art, however, the seeming self-contradiction is removed when one realizes that either, or both, of the conflicting terms is to be taken figuratively, rather than literally. The apparent absurdity, or strangeness, thus gives rhetorical power to the utterance. Elaborate and sophisticated paradoxes, insisting on their own absurdity, typify the poetic idiom of the tradition of John Donne.

**Pastoral**    A literary mode in which the lives of simple country people are celebrated, described, and used allegorically by sophisticated urban poets and writers. The *idylls* of Sicilian poet Theocritus (3rd century B.C.) were imitated and made more symbolic in Virgil's *eclogues;* shepherds in an Arcadian landscape stood for literary and political personages, and the Renaissance adapted these narrative and lyric pieces for moral and aesthetic discussion. Spenser's *Shepheardes Calendar* is an experimental collection of eclogues involving an array of forms and subjects. In subsequent literary tradition, the pastoral imagery of both Old and New Testaments (Psalms, Song of Songs, priest as *pastor* or shepherd of his flock, and so on) joins with the classical mode. Modern critics, William Empson in particular, have seen the continuation of pastoral tradition in other versions of the country-city confrontation, such as child-adult and criminal-businessman. See *Pastoral Elegy.*

**Pastoral Elegy**    A form of lament for the death of a poet, originating in Greek bucolic tradition (Bion's lament for Adonis, a lament for Bion by a fellow poet, Theocritus' first idyll, Virgil's tenth eclogue) and continued in use by Renaissance poets as a public mode for the presentation of private, inner, and even coterie matters affecting poets and their lives, while conventionally treating questions of general human importance. At a death one is moved to ask, "Why this death? Why now?" and funeral elegy must always confront these questions, avoiding easy resignation as an answer. Pastoral elegy handled these questions with formal mythological apparatus, such as the Muses, who should have protected their dead poet, local spirits, and other presences appropriate to the circumstances of the life and death, and perhaps figures of more general mythological power. The end of such poems is the eternalization of the dead poet in a monument of myth, stronger than stone or bronze: Spenser's *Astrophel,* a lament for Sir Philip Sidney, concludes with an Ovidian change—the dead poet's harp, like Orpheus' lyre, becomes the constellation Lyra. Milton's *Lycidas* both exemplifies and transforms the convention. Later examples include Shelley's *Adonais* (for Keats), Arnold's *Thyrsis* (for Clough), and Swinburne's *Ave Atque Vale* (for Baudelaire).

**Pathetic Fallacy**    John Ruskin's term (used in *Modern Painters,* 1856) for the projection of human emotions onto the world in such a way as to personify inanimate things ineptly or falsely.

**Personification**    Treating a thing or, more properly, an abstract quality, as though it were a person. Thus, "Surely *goodness* and *mercy* shall follow me all the days of my life" tends to personify the italicized terms by reason of the metaphoric use of "follow me." On the other hand, a conventional, complete personification, like *Justice* (whom we recognize by her *attributes*—she is blindfolded, she has scales and a sword) might also be called an *allegorical figure* in her own right, and her attributes *symbols* (blindness = impartiality; scales = justly deciding; sword = power to mete out what is deserved). Often the term "personification" applies to momentary, or *ad hoc,* humanizations.

**Platonism**    The legacy of Plato (429–347 B.C.) is virtually the history of philosophy. His *Timaeus* was an important source of later cosmology; his doctrine of ideas is central to Platonic tradition. His doctrine of love (especially in the *Symposium*) had enormous influence in the Renaissance, at which time its applicability was shifted to heterosexual love specifically. The *Republic* and the *Laws* underlie a vast amount of political thought, and the *Republic* contains also a philosophical attack on poetry (fiction) which defenders of the arts have always had to answer. Neoplatonism—a synthesis of Platonism, Pythagoreanism, and Aristotelianism—was dominant in the 3rd century A.D.; and the whole tradition was revived in the 15th and 16th centuries. The medieval Plato was Latinized, largely at second-hand; the revival of Greek learning in the 15th century led to another Neoplatonism: a synthesis of Platonism, the medieval Christian Aristotle, and Christian doctrine. Out of this came the doctrines of love we associate with some Renaissance poetry; a sophisticated version of older systems of allegory and symbol; and notions of the relation of spirit and matter reflected in Marvell and many other poets.

**Rhetoric**  In classical times, rhetoric was the art of persuading through the use of language. The major treatises on style and structure of discourse—Aristotle's *Rhetoric,* Quintilian's *Institutes of Oratory,* the *Rhetorica ad Herrenium* ascribed for centuries to Cicero—were concerned with the "arts" of language in the older sense of "skills." In the Middle Ages the *trivium* (*q.v.*), or program that led to the degree of Bachelor of Arts, consisted of grammar, logic, and rhetoric, but it was an abstract study, based on the Roman tradition. In the Renaissance, classical rhetorical study became a matter of the first importance, and it led to the study of literary stylistics and the application of principles and concepts of the production and structure of eloquence to the higher eloquence of poetry.

Rhetoricians distinguished three stages in the production of discourse: *inventio* (finding or discovery), *dispositio* (arranging), and *elocutio* (style). Since the classical discipline aimed always at practical oratory (e.g. winning a case in court, or making a point effectively in council), *memoria* (memory) and *pronuntiatio* (delivery) were added. For the Renaissance, however, rhetoric became the art of writing. Under the heading of *elocutio,* style became stratified into three levels, *elevated* or high, *elegant* or middle, and *plain* or low. The proper fitting of these styles to the subject of discourse comprised the subject of decorum (*q.v.*).

Another area of rhetorical theory was concerned with classification of devices of language into *schemes, tropes,* and *figures.* A basic but somewhat confused distinction between figures of speech and figures of thought need not concern us here, but we may roughly distinguish between schemes (or patterns) of words, and tropes as manipulations of meanings, and of making words non-literal.

### Common Schemes

**anadiplosis**  repeating the terminal word in a clause as the start of the next one: "Pleasure might cause her read; reading might cause her know; / Knowledge might pity win, and pity grace obtain" (Sidney, *Astrophel and Stella*).

**anaphora**  the repetition of a word or phrase at the openings of successive clauses, e.g. "The Lord sitteth above the water floods. The Lord remaineth King forever. The Lord shall give strength unto his people. The Lord shall give his people the blessing of peace."

**chiasmus**  a pattern of criss-crossing a syntactic structure, whether of noun and adjective, e.g. "Empty his bottle, and his girlfriend gone," or of a reversal of normal syntax with similar effect, e.g. "A fop her passion, and her prize, a sot," reinforced by assonance (q.v.). Chiasmus may even extend to assonance, as in Coleridge's line "In Xanadu did Kubla Khan."

### Common Tropes

**metaphor and simile**   both involve comparison of one thing to another, the difference being that the *simile* will actually compare, using the words "like" or "as," while the metaphor identifies one with the other, thus producing a non-literal use of a word or attribution. Thus, Robert Burns's "O, my love is like a red, red rose / That's newly sprung in June" is a simile; had Burns written, "My love, thou art a red, red rose . . .", it would have been a metaphor—and indeed, it would not mean that the lady had acquired petals. In modern critical theory, *metaphor* has come to stand for various non-expository kinds of evocative signification. I. A. Richards, the modern critic most interested in a general theory of metaphor in this sense, has contributed the terms *tenor* (as in the case above, the girl) and *vehicle* (the rose) to designate the components. See also *Epic Simile*.

**metonymy**   a trope in which the vehicle is closely and conventionally associated with the tenor, e.g. "crown" and "king," "pen" and "writing," "pencil" and "drawing," "sword" and "warfare."

**synecdoche**   a trope in which the part stands for the whole, e.g. "sail" for "ship."

**hyperbole**   intensifying exaggeration, e.g. the combined synecdoche and hyperbole in which Christopher Marlowe's Faustus asks of Helen of Troy "Is this the face that launched a thousand ships / And burned the topless towers of Ilium?"

**oxymoron**   literally, sharp-dull; a figure of speech involving a witty paradox, e.g. "sweet harm"; "darkness visible" (Milton, *Paradise Lost* I.63).

**Satire**   A literary mode painting a distorted verbal picture of part of the world in order to show its true moral, as opposed merely to its physical, nature. In this sense, Circe, the enchantress in Homer's *Odyssey* who changed Odysseus' men into pigs (because they made pigs of themselves while eating) and would have changed Odysseus into a fox (for he was indeed foxy), was the first satirist. Originally the Latin word *satura* meant a kind of literary grab bag, or medley, and a satire was a fanciful kind of tale in mixed prose and verse; but later a false etymology connected the word with *satyr* and thus with the grotesque. Satire may be in verse or in prose; in the 16th and 17th centuries, the Roman poets Horace and Juvenal were imitated and expanded upon by writers of satiric moral verse, the tone of the verse being wise, smooth, skeptical, and urbane, that of the prose, sharp, harsh, and sometimes nasty. A tradition of English verse satire runs through Donne, Jonson, Dryden, Pope, and Samuel Johnson; of prose satire, Addison, Swift, and Fielding.

**Seneca**   Lucius Annaeus Seneca (4 B.C.–65 A.D.) was an important source of Renaissance stoicism (q.v.), a model for the "closet" drama of the period, and an exemplar for the kind of prose that shunned the Ciceronian loquacity of early humanism and cultivated terseness. He was Nero's tutor; in 62 A.D. he retired from public life, and in 65 was compelled to commit suicide for taking part in a political conspiracy. He produced writings on ethics and physics, as well as ten tragedies often imitated in the Renaissance.

**Sensibility**   (1) In the mid-18th century, the term came to be used in a literary context to refer to a susceptibility to fine or tender feelings, particularly involving the feelings and sorrows of others. This became a quality to be cultivated in despite of stoical rejections of unreasonable emotion which the neoclassicism (*q.v.*) of the earlier Augustan age had prized. The meaning of the word blended easily into "sentimentality"; but the literary period in England characterized by the work of writers such as Sterne, Goldsmith, Gray, Collins, and Cowper is often called the Age of Sensibility.

(2) A meaning more important for modern literature is that of a special kind of total awareness, an ability to make the finest discriminations in its perception of the world, and yet at the same time not lacking in a kind of force by the very virtue of its own receptive power. The varieties of awareness celebrated in French literature from Baudelaire through Marcel Proust have been adapted by modernist English critics, notably T. S. Eliot, for a fuller extension of the meaning of *sensibility*. By the term "dissociation of sensibility," Eliot implied the split between the sensuous and the intellectual faculties which he thought characterized English poetry after the Restoration (1660).

**Sententia**   A wise, fruitful saying, functioning as a guide to morally correct thought or action.

**Sestina**   Originally a Provençal lyric form supposedly invented by Arnaut Daniel in the 12th century, and one of the most complex of those structures. It has six stanzas of six lines each, folllowed by an *envoi* (*q.v.*) or *tornada* of three lines. Instead of rhyming, the end-words of the lines of the first stanza are all repeated in the following stanzas, but in a constant set of permutations. The *envoi* contains all six words, three in the middle of each line. D. G. Rossetti, Swinburne, Pound, Auden, and other modern poets have used the form, and Sir Philip Sidney composed a magnificent double-sestina, "Ye Goat-herd Gods."

**Skepticism**   A philosophy that denies the possibility of certain knowledge, and, although opposed to Stoicism and Epicureanism (*q.v.*), advocated *ataraxy*, imperturbability of mind. Skepticism originated with Pyrrhon (*c.* 360–270 B.C.), and its chief transmitter was Sextus Empiricus (*c.* 200 B.C.). In the Renaissance, skepticism had importance as questioning the power of the human mind to know truly (for a classic exposition see Donne's *Second Anniversary*, ll. 254–300), and became a powerful influence in morals and religion through the advocacy of Montaigne.

**Sonnet**   A basic lyric form, consisting of fourteen lines of iambic pentameter rhymed in various patterns. The *Italian* or *Petrarchan* sonnet is divided clearly into *octave* and *sestet*, the first rhyming *abba abba* and the second in a pattern such as *cdc dcd*. The *Shakespearean* sonnet consists of three quatrains followed by a couplet: *abab cdcd efef gg*. In the late 16th century in England, sonnets were written either independently as short epigrammatic forms, or grouped in sonnet sequences, i.e. collections of upwards of a hundred poems, in imitation of Petrarch, purportedly addressed to one central figure or muse—a lady usually with a symbolic name like "Stella" or "Idea." Milton made a new kind of use of the Petrarchan form, and the Romantic poets continued in the Miltonic tradition. Several variations have been devised, including the addition of "tails" or extra lines, or the recasting into sixteen lines, instead of fourteen.

**Stoicism, Stoics**  Philosophy founded by Zeno (335–263 B.C.), and opposing the hedonistic tendencies of Epicureanism (q.v.). The Stoics' world-view was pantheistic: God was the energy that formed and maintained the world, and wisdom lay in obedience to this law of nature as revealed by the conscience. Moreover, every man is free because the life according to nature and conscience is available to all; so too is suicide—a natural right. Certain Stoics saw the end of the world as caused by fire. In the Renaissance, Latin Stoicism, especially that of Seneca (q.v.), had a revival of influence and was Christianized in various ways.

**Stream of Consciousness**  A literary technique of modern fiction which attempts to imitate or duplicate, in patterns other than those of discourse, the flow of thoughts, impressions, memories, meditations, musings, and other products of an individual character's consciousness. It can result either in the fragmentation of sentence structure, or the overwhelming of it in long strings of eloquence. In James Joyce's *Ulysses*, where it is called "interior monologue," it operates in different styles to represent the thoughts of different characters, but its most celebrated use is in Molly Bloom's forty-two page soliloquy that concludes the book.

**Style**  See *Decorum*.

**Sublime**  "Lofty"; as a literary idea, originally the basic concept of a Greek treatise (by the so-called "Longinus") on style. In the 18th century, however, the *sublime* came to mean a loftiness perceivable in nature, and sometimes in art—a loftiness different from the composed vision of landscape known as the *picturesque*, because of the element of wildness, power, and even terror. The *beautiful*, the picturesque, and the sublime became three modes for the perception of nature.

**Surrealism**  (1) A literary and artistic movement, predominantly French but with vast international influence; initiated after World War I by André Breton and others, and enshrining the irrational as the best mode of perceiving and representing reality. Pathological forms of vision, hallucination, psychotic utterance, automatic writing, free association, and other means of nullifying even the structures of Symbolist poetic tradition were celebrated. Poetic form was abandoned as though it were as inauthentic as bookkeeping or scientific language, and the surrealistic "texts" are neither prose nor verse. The unconscious, the impulsive, and particularly the erotic are the domains of the surrealistic imagination, which occupied many European painters including Pablo Picasso at a phase in his career, and particularly and with greatest success, René Magritte. Among French writers associated with the movement were Paul Eluard, Louis Aragon, Philippe Soupault, Antonin Artaud, René Char, and Raymond Queneau.

(2) In a looser sense, "surrealist" has been commonly (and misleadingly) used to describe representations in modern literature of the visionary, the dreamlike, the fantastic in any of its forms.

**Symbolism**  (1) Broadly, the process by which one phenomenon, in literature, stands for another, or group of others, and usually of a different sort. Clearcut cases of this in medieval and Renaissance literature are *emblems* or *attributes* (see *Personification; Allegory*). Sometimes conventional symbols may be used in more than one way, e.g. a mirror betokening both truth and vanity. See also *Figure*, under *Rhetoric*.

(2) In a specific sense (and often given in its French form, *symbolisme*), an important esthetic concept for modern literature, formulated by French poets and critics of the later 19th century following Baudelaire. In this view, the literary symbol becomes something closer to a kind of commanding, central metaphor, taking precedence over any more discursive linguistic mode for poetic communication. The effects of this concept on literature in English have been immense; and some version of the concept survives in modern notions of the poetic *image,* or *fiction.*

**Trope**    (1) See *Rhetoric.* (2) In the liturgy of the Catholic Church, a phrase, sentence, or verse with its musical setting, introduced to amplify or embellish some part of the text of the mass or the office (i.e. the prayers and Scripture readings recited daily by priests, religious, and even laymen) when chanted in choir. Tropes of this second kind were discontinued in 1570 by the authority of Pope Pius V. Troping new material into older or conventional patterns seems to have been, in a general way, a basic device of medieval literature, and was the genesis of modern drama.

**Type, Typology**    (1) Strictly, in medieval biblical interpretation, the prefiguration of the persons and events of the New Testament by persons and events of the Old, the Old Testament being fulfilled in, but not entirely superseded by, the New. Thus, the Temptation and Fall of Man were held to prefigure the first Temptation of Christ, pride in each case being the root of the temptation, and a warning against gluttony the moral lesson to be drawn from both. The Brazen Serpent raised up by Moses was held to prefigure the crucifixion of Christ; Isaac, as a sacrificial victim ("God will provide his own Lamb," says Abraham to him) is a *type* of Christ. The forty days and nights of the Deluge, the forty years of Israel's wandering in the desert, Moses' forty days in the desert are all typologically related.

(2) In a looser sense, a person or event seen as a model or paradigm. See also *Figure,* under *Rhetoric.*

**Villanelle**    A lyric form originally used in French Renaissance poetry for pastoral subjects, adopted by 19th-century English writers of light verse, and eventually taken up again by poets such as James Joyce, William Empson, and Dylan Thomas for more than trivial effects. The form consists of five (see *Meter* §5) tercets rhyming *aba,* followed by a quatrain rhyming *abaa.* The first and last line of the first tercet are alternately repeated as refrains at the end of each following tercet. Thus, in Edward Arlington Robinson's famous villanelle beginning

> They are all gone away,
> The house is shut and still,
> There is nothing more to say.

the first and third line are alternated, finally to follow each other in the last tercet. Modern use of the form depends upon subtle variations of the meaning of the refrain lines at each repetition.

# Suggestions for Further Reading

## The Period in General

**Political and Social Backgrounds**   Asa Briggs, *The Making of Modern England: The Age of Improvement, 1783–1867*, 1959; *Victorian Cities*, 1965; and *Victorian People*, 1954 (rev. 1965). Friedrich Engels, *The Condition of the Working Class in England*, 1844. The W. O. Henderson and W. H. Chaloner translation (1958) is the best and most complete. Despite Engels's errors of detail, which the translators are at pains to remark, this work is still of great authority and importance. Norman Gash, *Politics in the Age of Peel*, 1953. Elie Halévy, *History of the English People in the Nineteenth Century*, Vols. III–IV, 1949–52. This classic work by an eminent French scholar has had a decisive influence on all later historians of 19th-century England. E. P. Thompson's *The Making of the English Working Class*, 1963, is the authoritative account of that subject. R. K. Webb's *Modern England: From the Eighteenth Century to the Present*, 1968, is an excellent summary account. Ernest L. Woodward, *The Age of Reform, 1815–1870*, 1939. G. M. Young's *Victorian England: Portrait of an Age*, 1936, is a classic work but often difficult by reason of its brilliant allusiveness. Young also edited two useful collections of essays: *Victorian Essays*, 1962, and *Early Victorian England, 1830–1865*, 1934.

**Cultural and Literary History**   Crane Brinton, *English Political Thought in the Nineteenth Century*, 1933. Jerome H. Buckley's *The Victorian Temper*, 1951, is an excellent summary introduction to the culture of the period. W. L. Burn, *The Age of Equipoise*, 1964. Owen Chadwick, *The Victorian Church*, Vol. I, 1966. G. K. Chesterton's *The Victorian Age in Literature*, 1913, is a classic work, brilliant and willful in its judgments. A useful survey is S. C. Chew's *The Nineteenth Century and After* (Vol. IV of *A Literary History of England*, ed. A. C. Baugh), 1948. John W. Dodds, *The Age of Paradox: A Biography of England, 1841–1851*, 1952, provides an engaging summary account. L. E. Elliott-Binns, *Religion in the Victorian Era*, 1936. Oliver Elton, *A Survey of English Literature*, Vol. II, 1928, is basic. An excellent summary introduction to Victorian thought and culture is Walter Houghton's *The Victorian Frame of Mind*, 1957. J. Hillis Miller, *The Disappearance of God: Five Nineteenth-Century Writers*, 1963. Raymond Williams, *Culture and Society, 1780–1950*, 1958. Basil Willey's *Nineteenth Century Studies*, 1949, and *More Nineteenth Century Studies*, 1956, bring together notable essays on the influential writers of the period.

**Bibliography**    "Victorian Bibliography for 1970," ed. R. E. Freeman, in *Victorian Studies,* XIV, 4 (June 1971). E. C. Batho and B. Dobrée, *The Victorians and After,* 1938.

# Prose

## MATTHEW ARNOLD

**Editions**    *Complete Prose Works,* ed. R. H. Super, seven vols. to date, 1960–70, is the authoritative edition. *The Prose Works,* 1903 (incomplete). *The Portable Matthew Arnold,* ed. Lionel Trilling, 1949, is a selection of the poetry and the prose. *Letters of Matthew Arnold, 1848–1888,* ed. G. W. E. Russell, 1895. *Letters of Matthew Arnold to Arthur Hugh Clough,* ed. H. F. Lowry, 1932, is an excellent edition of the young Arnold's vivacious and revealing letters to his closest friend. *The Notebooks of Matthew Arnold,* ed. H. F. Lowry, Karl Young, and W. H. Dunn, 1952.

**Critical Studies**    Edward Alexander, *Arnold and John Stuart Mill,* 1965. Warren D. Anderson, *Matthew Arnold and the Classical Tradition,* 1965. R. Bromwich, *Arnold and Celtic Literature: A Retrospect 1865–1965,* 1965. Edward K. Brown, *Matthew Arnold: A Study in Conflict,* 1948. Dwight Culler, *Imaginative Reason,* 1966. T. S. Eliot, "Arnold and Pater," *Selected Essays,* 1932, a famous essay, and his "Matthew Arnold," *The Use of Poetry and the Use of Criticism,* 1932. Leon Gottfried, *Matthew Arnold and the Romantics,* 1963. W. Stacey Johnson, *The Voices of Matthew Arnold,* 1961. F. R. Leavis, "Arnold as Critic," *The Importance of Scrutiny,* ed. Eric Bentley, 1948, an essay by one of the most notable modern critics defining Arnold's continuing importance. P. J. McCarthy's *Arnold and the Three Classes,* 1964, is a cogent discussion of Arnold's social and political thought. William Robbins, *The Ethical Idealism of Matthew Arnold,* 1959. G. Robert Stange, *Matthew Arnold: The Poet as Humanist,* 1967. C. D. Wright, *Arnold's Response to German Culture,* 1965.

**Biography**    Arnold expressed the wish that no biography of him be written, and as as yet none has been. The most recent approach is Lionel Trilling, *Matthew Arnold* (1939, 1949, 1955), of which its author observes that "it may be thought of as a biography of Arnold's mind."

## SAMUEL BUTLER

**Editions**    *The Shrewsbury Edition,* ed. Henry Festing Jones and A. T. Bartholomew, 1923–26. *The Note-books . . . Selections* arr. and ed. H. F. Jones, 1915. *Further Extracts from the Note-Books,* ed. A. T. Bartholomew, 1934. *Samuel Butler's Note Books,* ed. Geoffrey Keynes and Brian Hill, 1951. *Butleriana,* ed. A. T. Bartholomew, 1932. *The Family Letters of Samuel Butler,* ed. Arnold Silver, 1962. *The Correspondence of Samuel Butler and His Sister May,* ed. Daniel F. Howard, 1962.

**Critical Studies**    Walter Allen, *The English Novel, A Short Critical History,* 1954. Clyde T. Bissell, "A Study in *The Way of All Flesh,*" *Nineteenth-Century Studies,* ed. Herbert J. Davis, 1940. G. D. H. Cole, *Samuel Butler and "The Way of All Flesh,"* 1947. P. N. Furbank, *Samuel Butler, 1835–1902,* 1948. Arnold Kettle, *An Introduction to the English Novel,* 1953. Basil Willey's *Darwin and Butler—Two Versions* *of Evolution*, 1960, is a useful study of Butler's views on evolution. Edmund Wilson, *The Triple Thinkers: Ten Essays in Literature*, 1945. M. D. Zabel, "Butler, the Victorian Insolvency," *Craft and Character*, 1957.

**Biography**
Philip Henderson's *Samuel Butler, the Incarnate Bachelor*, 1953 is an adequate account of Butler's life, although it takes but little notice of his ideas. Lee E. Holt's *Samuel Butler*, 1964, is an excellent biography and quite the best introduction to Butler's ideas.

**Bibliography**    Stanley B. Harkness, *The Career of Samuel Butler, 1835–1902: A Bibliography*, 1956, is the definitive bibliography.


## THOMAS CARLYLE

**Editions**    *The Works of Thomas Carlyle*, Centenary Edition, in 34 volumes, ed. H. D. Traill, 1896–1901. Carlyle was an indefatigable correspondent; several volumes of his letters have been published, among the most important being Charles Eliot Norton's edition of *Correspondence of Carlyle and Emerson*, two vols., 1883; of *Correspondence between Goethe and Carlyle*, two vols., 1886; *Letters of Thomas Carlyle: 1826–1836*, two vols., 1888; and the following collections edited by Alexander Carlyle: *New Letters of Thomas Carlyle*, two vols., 1904; *Love Letters of Thomas Carlyle and Jane Welsh Carlyle*, two vols., 1909; *Letters of Thomas Carlyle to John Stuart Mill, John Sterling, and Robert Browning*, 1923; *Letters of Thomas Carlyle to His Brother Alexander*, 1968. There is also a *Selected Works, Reminiscences and Letters*, ed. Julian Symons, 1957. The Duke-Edinburgh edition of the letters of Thomas and Jane Welsh Carlyle, under the general editorship of C. R. Sanders, will be definitive upon completion. The first four volumes were published in 1970.

**Critical Studies**    Eric Bentley, *A Century of Hero-Worship*, 1944. Louis Cazamian, *Carlyle*, trans. E. K. Brown, 1932. C. F. Harrold, *Carlyle and German Thought, 1819–1834*, 1934. John Holloway, *The Victorian Sage*, 1953. Albert J. La Valley, *Carlyle and the Idea of the Modern*, 1968. Emery Neff, *Carlyle and Mill: Mystic and Utilitarian*, 1924. G. B. Tennyson, *Sartor Called Resartus*, 1965.

**Biography**    There is as yet no satisfactory modern biography of Carlyle, although J. H. Froude's *Thomas Carlyle: A History of the First Forty Years of His Life*, two vols., 1882, and *Thomas Carlyle: A History of His Life in London*, two vols., 1884, are interesting and valuable. Even more compendious is D. A. Wilson's *Life of Thomas Carlyle*, six vols., 1923–34. Emery Neff's *Carlyle*, 1934, based on these works, is a useful short account emphasizing Carlyle's intellectual rather than his emotional life.


## THOMAS HENRY HUXLEY

**Editions**    *Collected Essays*, nine vols., 1893–94. *The Scientific Memoirs of Thomas Henry Huxley*, ed. Michael Foster and E. Roy Lankester, four vols., 1898–1902; suppl. vol., 1903. *Religion Without Revelation*, ed. Julian Huxley (his grandson), 1957. Huxley's *Diary of the Voyage of HMS Rattlesnake*, ed. Julian Huxley, 1935.

**Critical Studies**   C. E. Ayres, *Huxley*, 1932. Aldous Huxley, *Huxley as a Man of Letters*, 1932. H. Peterson, *Huxley: A Prophet of Science*, 1932. J. S. Huxley and D. Cleverdon, *Julian Huxley on T. H. Huxley: A New Judgment*, 1945. Walter Houghton, "The Rhetoric of Huxley," *University of Toronto Quarterly*, XVIII (1949). William Irvine, "Carlyle and T. H. Huxley," *Booker Memorial Studies*, ed. H. Shine, 1950. William Irvine, *Apes, Angels, and the Victorians: The Story of Darwin, Huxley, and Evolution*, 1955; and *Huxley*, 1960. C. Bibby, *Huxley: Scientist, Humanist, and Educator*, 1959. A. O. J. Cockshut, "Huxley: The Scientific Sage," *Unbelievers: English Agnostic Thought, 1840–90*, 1964. Philip Appleman, W. A. Madden, and M. Wolff, eds., *1859: Entering an Age of Crisis*; 1959.

**Biography**   The biography by Huxley's son Leonard Huxley, *The Life and Letters of Thomas Henry Huxley*, two vols., 1900, is still standard.


## JOHN STUART MILL

**Editions**   *Collected Works of John Stuart Mill*, gen. ed., F. E. L. Priestley; assoc. ed., J. M. Robson, 1963, six vols. to date; when completed this will be the definitive edition. *The Earlier Letters of John Stuart Mill, 1812–1848*, ed. Francis E. Mineka (Vols. XII and XIII of the *Collected Works*), 1963. *The Early Draft of John Stuart Mill's Autobiography*, ed. Jack Stillinger, 1961. *John Stuart Mill: Literary Essays*, ed. Edward Alexander, 1967. *Mill's Essays on Literature and Society*, 1965, and *Mill: A Collection of Critical Essays*, 1968, both ed. Jerome Schneewind. *Essays on Politics and Culture*, ed. Gertrude Himmelfarb, 1962. *The Spirit of the Age*, ed. Frederick A. von Hayek, 1942, is a series of articles published by Mill in the *Examiner* in 1831.

**Critical Studies**   Edward Alexander, *Matthew Arnold and John Stuart Mill*, 1965. R. P. Anschutz, *The Philosophy of John Stuart Mill*, 1953. Karl Britton, *John Stuart Mill*, 1953. Joseph Hamburger, *Intellectuals in Politics: John Stuart Mill and the Philosophical Radicals*, 1965. Emery Neff, *Carlyle and Mill: Mystic and Utilitarian*, 1926. Dorothea Krook, *Three Traditions of Moral Thought*, 1959. F. R. Leavis, Introduction to *Mill on Bentham and Coleridge*, 1950. John M. Robson, *The Improvement of Mankind: The Social and Political Thought of John Stuart Mill*, 1968. Basil Willey, *Nineteenth Century Studies*, 1949. Raymond Williams, *Culture and Society, 1780–1950*, 1958.

**Biography**   Michael St. John Packe, *The Life of John Stuart Mill* (1954), is the best biography.


## WILLIAM MORRIS

**Editions**   *Collected Works*, edited in 24 volumes by his daughter May Morris, 1910–15 (repr. 1966); two suppl. vols., *William Morris, Artist, Writer, Socialist*, published in 1936 (repr. 1966). *The Letters of William Morris*, ed. Philip Henderson, 1950. *William Morris, Selected Writings and Designs*, ed. Asa Briggs, 1962.

**Critical Studies**   E. P. Thompson, *William Morris, Romantic to Revolutionary*, 1955. George Bernard Shaw, *William Morris As I Knew Him*, 1936. Graham Hough, *The Last Romantics*, 1949. W. B. Yeats, "Happiest of the Poets," in *Essays and Introductions*, 1961.

**Biography**    Philip Henderson's *William Morris, His Life, Work, and Friends*, 1967, is the best biography. R. P. Arnot, *Morris: The Man and the Myth*, 1964. J. W. Mackail, *The Life of William Morris*, 1899 (repr. 1950), still excellent, although its treatment of Morris's personal life is limited by piety and convention.

## JOHN HENRY CARDINAL NEWMAN

**Editions**    [*Works*] 41 vols., 1874–1921: "Uniform Edition of Dr. Newman's Works." *Letters and Diaries of John Henry Newman*, ed. C. Stephen Dessain, 1961. *Letters and Correspondence of John Henry Newman During His Life in the English Church*, ed. Anne Mozley, 1891. *John Henry Newman: Autobiographical Writings*, ed. Henry Tristram, 1957.

**Critical Studies**    R. W. Church, *The Oxford Movement 1833–1845*, 1891. A. Dwight Culler, *The Imperial Intellect: A Study of Cardinal Newman's Educational Ideal*, 1955. C. F. Harrold, *John Henry Newman: An Expository and Critical Study of Ilis Mind, Thought, and Art*. 1945. John Holloway, *The Victorian Sage*, 1953. Walter Houghton, *The Art of Newman's Apologia*, 1945. Meriol Trevor, *Newman;* Vol. I: *The Pillar of Cloud*, 1962; Vol. II: *Light in Winter*, 1963. Thomas Vargish, *Newman: The Contemplation of Mind*, 1970. J. H. Walgrave, *Newman the Theologian*, 1960.

**Biography**    The best introduction to Newman's life and thought is the brief and lucid work of C. Stephen Dessain, *John Henry Newman*, 1966. Louis Bouyer, *Newman: His Life and Spirituality*, 1958. Wilfrid Ward, *Life of John Henry Cardinal Newman*, two vols., 1912.

## WALTER PATER

**Editions**    *Works*, ten vols., 1910 (reissued 1971). *Letters of Walter Pater*, ed. Lawrence Evans, 1970. *Selected Writings*, ed. H. Bloom, 1973.

**Critical Studies**    P. Appleman, "Darwin, Pater and a Crisis in Classicism," *1859: Entering a Year of Crisis*, ed. P. Appleman and others, 1959. C. M. Bowra, "Walter Pater," *Inspiration and Poetry*, 1957. David Cecil, *Pater: The Scholar-Artist*, 1955. B. Charlesworth, *Dark Passages: The Decadent Consciousness in Victorian Literature*, 1965. T. S. Eliot, "Arnold and Pater," *Selected Essays*, 1932. Graham Hough, *The Last Romantics*, 1949. R. V. Johnson, *Pater as Critic: His Critical Practices Considered in Relation to His Theories of Life and Art*, 1962. U. C. Knoepflmacher, *Religious Humanism and the Victorian Novel*, 1965. Mario Praz, *The Romantic Agony*, 1933. Ruth Z. Temple, "The Ivory Tower as Lighthouse," *Edwardians and Late Victorians*, ed. Richard Ellmann, 1960. Geoffrey Tillotson, "Arnold and Pater," *Criticism of the Nineteenth Century*, 1951. René Wellek, "Pater's Literary Theory and Criticism," in *History of Modern Criticism, 1750–1950*, Vol. III, 1958. The most comprehensive study is the monograph *Walter Pater*, by Ian Fletcher, rev. ed., 1972.

**Biography**    The only extensive biography is that by Thomas Wright, *The Life of Walter Pater*, two vols., 1907.

JOHN RUSKIN

**Editions**   The Works of John Ruskin, ed. E. T. Cook and Alexander Wedderburn, 1903–12. Diaries of John Ruskin, ed. Joan Evans and J. H. Whitehouse, 1956. Brantwood Diary (1878), ed. Helen Wilhuen, 1971.

**Critical Studies**   George Landow, Aesthetic and Cultural Theories of Ruskin, 1971. Frederick W. Roe, Social Philosophy of Carlyle and Ruskin, 1921. John Rosenberg's The Darkening Glass: A Portrait of John Ruskin's Genius, 1961, is the fullest account of Ruskin's intellectual life. George Bernard Shaw, Ruskin's Politics, 1921. R. H. Wilenski, John Ruskin, 1933.

**Biography**   Joan Evans, John Ruskin, 1952. John Holloway, The Victorian Sage, 1953. Graham Hough, The Last Romantics, 1949.


OSCAR WILDE

**Editions**   Complete Works, ed. G. F. Maine, first collected ed., 1948 (rev. ed., P. Drake, 1966). The Artist as Critic: Critical Writings of Oscar Wilde, ed. Richard Ellmann, 1969, The Letters of Oscar Wilde, ed. Rupert Hart-Davis, 1962, contains the full text of the famous letter from prison, previously published in various curtailed versions under the title De Profundis.

**Critical Studies**   Oscar Wilde: The Critical Heritage, ed. Karl Beckson, 1970, a collection of early critical responses to Wilde. St. John Ervine, Oscar Wilde: A Present Time Appraisal, 1951. André Gide, Oscar Wilde: A Study, 1905. Holbrook Jackson, The Eighteen-Nineties, 1913 (revised 1922). G. Wilson Knight, Christian Renaissance, 1962. Edouard Roditi, Oscar Wilde, 1947. Arthur Symons, A Study of Oscar Wilde, 1930. Frances Winwar, Oscar Wilde and the Yellow Nineties, 1940.

**Biography**   There is to date no satisfactory biography of Wilde and presumably there will be none until Richard Ellmann completes the one he is engaged on. The following works are useful in one way or another: Rupert Croft-Cooke, The Unrecorded Life of Oscar Wilde, 1972. André Gide, Oscar Wilde: In Memoriam, 1949. Frank Harris's The Life and Confessions of Oscar Wilde, 1918 (repr. 1960), is notoriously unreliable but of some interest. Vyvyan Holland's Oscar Wilde, a Pictorial Biography, 1960, is an attractive and engaging book; the pictorial method is most appropriate to Wilde. H. Montgomery Hyde has edited The Trials of Oscar Wilde, 1950, 1960, and also written Oscar Wilde in Prison, 1956, and The Three Trials of Oscar Wilde, 1956. Hesketh Pearson's Oscar Wilde, His Life and Wit, 1946, is the fullest account. Robert H. Sherard, Bernard Shaw, Frank Harris, and Oscar Wilde, 1937.


# Poetry

In addition to the general references to Victorian Literature cited in the Prose section above, the reader may consult the following works having more specifically to do with Victorian Poetry.

**Bibliography**   F. E. Faverty, ed., The Victorian Poets: A Guide to Research, 1968.

Critical Studies    J. W. Beach, *The Concept of Nature in Nineteenth-Century English Poetry*, 1936. G. H. Ford, *Keats and the Victorians*, 1944. E. D. H. Johnson, *The Alien Vision of Victorian Poetry*, 1952. Robert Langbaum, *The Poetry of Experience*, 1957, and *The Modern Spirit*, 1970. F. L. Lucas, *Ten Victorian Poets*, 1940. Collections of Essays    *The Major Victorian Poets: Reconsiderations*, ed. I. Armstrong, 1969. *Victorian Literature*, ed. R. O. Preyer, 1966. *The Victorian Age*, ed. R. Langbaum, 1967. *Victorian Literature*, ed. Austin Wright, 1961.

### ALFRED, LORD TENNYSON

Editions    *The Poems of Tennyson*, ed. C. Ricks, 1969.

Critical Studies    *Critical Essays*, ed. J. Killham, 1960. J. H. Buckley, *Tennyson*, 1961. *Tennyson*, ed. A. D. Culler, 1973. On *In Memoriam:* the *Commentary* by A. C. Bradley, 1901.

Biography    Hallam Tennyson, *Alfred Lord Tennyson: A Memoir*, 1897. Sir Charles Tennyson, *Alfred Tennyson*, 1949. C. Ricks, *Tennyson*, 1972.

### ROBERT BROWNING

Editions    A modern edition, by R. A. King and others, is in progress; to date the *Complete Poetical Works*, ed. Augustine Birrell, 1915, remains the best edition. The *Letters* of Browning and Elizabeth Barrett, ed. E. Kintner, two vols., 1969. *Essay on Shelley*, ed. H. F. B. Brett-Smith, 1921.

Critical Studies    The best critical work by a single hand remains G. K. Chesterton, *Robert Browning*, 1903. Collections of Essays    *The Browning Critics*, ed. B. Litzinger and K. L. Knickerbocker, 1967. *Robert Browning*, ed. Philip Drew, 1966. *Browning*, ed. Harold Bloom, 1973. W. C. DeVane, *A Browning Handbook*, 1955, is crucial.

Biography    W. Hall Griffin and H. C. Minchin, *Life*, 1938. Betty Miller, *Portrait*, 1952.

### MATTHEW ARNOLD

Editions    *Poetical Works*, ed. C. B. Tinker and H. F. Lowry, 1950. *Poems of Arnold*, ed. K. Allott, 1965. See also Arnold references in Victorian Prose bibliography above.

### THE PRE-RAPHAELITES

Bibliography    W. E. Fredeman, *Pre-Raphaelitism; A Bibliocritical Study*, 1965.

Critical Studies    (Benjamin) Ifor Evans, *English Poetry in the Later Nineteenth Century*, 2nd ed. rev., 1966. *Pre-Raphaelite Painters*, ed. Robin Ironside, 1948. *The Pre-Raphaelites and Their Circle*, ed. C. Y. Lang, 1968.

Dante Gabriel Rossetti    *Works*, ed. W. M. Rossetti, 1911. Oswald Doughty, *A Victorian Romantic*, 1960.

George Meredith    *Poetical Works*, ed. G. M. Trevelyan, 1928. Norman Kelvin, *A Troubled Eden*, 1961.

Christina Rossetti    *Poetical Works*, ed. W. M. Rossetti, 1904. L. M. Packer, *Christina Rossetti*, 1963.

**William Morris**   See Morris references in Victorian Prose bibliography above, and the following: Paul Thompson, *The Work of William Morris*, 1967.

**Algernon Charles Swinburne**   *Collected Poetical Works*, two vols., 1924. *The Swinburne Letters*, ed. C. Y. Lang, six vols., 1959–62. Georges Lafourcade, *Swinburne: A Literary Biography*, 1932. J. J. McGann, *Swinburne*, 1972.

**Coventry Patmore**   *Poems*, ed. F. Page, 1949. D. Patmore, *Life and Times of Coventry Patmore*, 1950.


GERARD MANLEY HOPKINS

*Poems*, ed. W. H. Gardner and N. H. MacKenzie, 1970. *Hopkins*, ed. G. Hartman, 1966. W. H. Gardner, *Hopkins*, two vols., 1949. J. Pick, *Hopkins*, 1966.


OTHER VICTORIAN POETS

**Elizabeth Barrett Browning**   *Poetical Works*, 1951. G. B. Taplin, *Life*, 1957.

**Edward Lear**   *Complete Nonsense*, ed. H. Jackson, 1947. Angus Davidson, *Edward Lear*, 1938.

**Emily Brontë**   *Complete Poems*, ed. C. W. Hatfield, 1941. *Gondal's Queen*, arranged by F. E. Ratchford, 1955.

**Arthur Hugh Clough**   *Poems*, ed. A. L. Norrington, 1968. Walter Houghton, *The Poetry of Clough*, 1963.

**Lewis Carroll**   *Complete Works*, 1949. Derek Hudson, *Lewis Carroll*, 1954.

**James Thomson**   *Poetical Works*. two vols., ed. Bertram Dobell, 1895. Arthur Symons, *Studies in Two Literatures*, 1924.


THE 'NINETIES

**General Backgrounds**   O. Burdett, *The Beardsley Period*, 1925. R. Le Gallienne, *The Romantic '90s*, 1926. H. Jackson, *The Eighteen Nineties*, 1913. W. B. Yeats, *Autobiographies*, 1926. Relevant also are some of the essays in *Romantic Mythologies*, ed. Ian Fletcher, 1967.

**Editions**   The best anthology of 'Nineties verse is still Donald Davidson, ed., *British Poetry of the Eighteen-nineties*, 1937.

**William Schwenk Gilbert**, *Bab Ballads*, 1924. *The Savoy Operas*, 1926. H. Pearson, *Gilbert and Sullivan*, 1935.

**Oscar Wilde**   See Wilde references in Victorian Prose bibliography above. The definitive study, by Richard Ellmann, is in progress. Criticism is gathered in *Oscar Wilde: Collection of Critical Essays*, ed. R. Ellmann, 1969.

**John Davidson**   *Poems and Ballads*, ed. R. D. MacLeod, 1959.

**Ernest Dowson**   *Poetical Works*, ed. D. Flower, 1967.

**Lionel Johnson**   *Complete Poems*, ed. Ian Fletcher, 1953.

# Author and Title Index

# First-Line Index